BEGINNER'S SPANISH DICTIONARY

SECOND EDITION

Collins
An Imprint of HarperCollinsPublishers

Second Edition 2005

HarperCollins Publishers
10 East 53rd Street, New York, NY 10022

ISBN-10: 0-06-074916-4
ISBN-13: 978-0-06-074916-3

www.harpercollins.com

First HarperCollins edition published 2001

HarperCollins books may be purchased for educational, business, or sales promotional use. For information please write: Special Markets Department, HarperCollins Publishers, 10 East 53rd Street, New York, NY 10022.

Printed in the United States of America

06 07 08 09 10 9 8 7 6 5 4 3 2

Acknowledgements
We would like to thank those authors and publishers who kindly gave permission for copyright material to be used in the Collins Word Web. We would also like to thank Times Newspapers Ltd for providing valuable data.

GENERAL EDITORS/DIRECCIÓN
Jeremy Butterfield, Catherine Love

CONTRIBUTORS/COLABORADORES
Emma Aeppli, Teresa Álvarez, Elspeth Anderson, Gerry Breslin, Helen Newstead, Cordelia Lilly, Joyce Littlejohn, Val McNulty

LANGUAGE CONSULTANTS/
CONSULTORES LINGUÍSTICOS
John Bollard, Rima McKinzey, Borney Restrepo, Carol Styles

COMPUTING/INFORMÁTICA
Robert Scovell

ILLUSTRATIONS/ILUSTRACIONES
Richard Anderson

SERIES EDITOR/DIRECCIÓN DE LA SERIE
Lorna Knight

CONTENTS

INTRODUCTION

HarperCollins Beginner's Spanish Dictionary is an innovative dictionary designed specifically for anyone starting to learn Spanish.

ICE

INTRODUCCIÓN

HarperCollins Beginner's Spanish Dictionary es un diccionario innovador, especialmente concebido para cualquier persona que empiece a aprender inglés.

SPANISH PRONUNCIATION

▶ SPANISH VOWELS

Spanish vowels are always clearly pronounced and not relaxed in unstressed syllables as happens in English.

a – Similar to ***a*** in ***palm***
e – Similar to English ***e*** in ***end***
i – Similar to English ***i*** in ***machine***
o – Similar to English ***o*** in ***for***
u – Similar to English ***oo*** in ***pool***

▶ SPANISH CONSONANTS

Note the pronunciation of the following letters.

b,v – These letters have the same value. At the start of a word, and after written **m** and **n**, the sound is similar to English ***b***oy
– In all other positions the sound is softer, the lips do not touch
c – Before **a**, **o**, **u** or a consonant, like English ***k***eep
– Before **e** or **i** it is pronounced like English ***s***ame
ch – Like English ***ch***ur***ch***
d – At the start of the word and after **l** or **n**, it is pronounced similarly to English ***d***eep
– Between vowels and after consonants (except **l** or **n**), it is pronounced very like English ***th***ough
– At the end of words it is often not pronounced
g – Before **e** or **i**, the sound is similar to English ***h***ouse
– At the start of a word and after **n**, it is pronounced like English ***g***et
– In other positions it is softer than in **g**et
– Note that in the group **gue**, **gui**, the **u** is silent, as in English g**u**itar unless it is marked **güe**, **güi**, when it is pronounced like English **w**alk
h – This is always silent
j – Like the sound in English lo***ch***
ll – Similar to English *-ll-* in mi***ll***ion, but often like English ***y***et
ñ – As in English o***ni***on
q – Always followed by silent letter **u**, and pronounced as in English ***k***eep, but softer
r – Single trill, in a way that does not exist in English
– Pronounced like **rr** below at the start of a word and after **l**, **n** or **s**
rr – Strongly trilled, in a way that does not exist in English
s – Except where mentioned below, like English **s**ing
– When followed by **b**, **d**, **g**, **l**, **m**, **n** like English ro**s**e
w – Usually pronounced as English ***v***, but sometimes kept as English ***w***
y – Similar to English ***y***es
z – Like English **s**end

f, **k**, **l**, **m**, **n**, **p**, **t**, **x** are pronounced as in English.

DICTIONARY SKILLS

Using a dictionary is a skill you can improve with practice and by following some basic guidelines. This section gives you a detailed explanation of how to use this dictionary to ensure you get the most out of it.

The answers to all the questions in this section are on page 14.

▶ MAKE SURE YOU LOOK ON THE RIGHT SIDE OF THE DICTIONARY

The Spanish-English side comes first, followed by the English-Spanish. At the top of the page, you will see either **Spanish ~ English** or **English ~ Spanish**, so you know immediately if you're looking up the side you want. The middle pages of the book have a blue border so that you can see where one side finishes and the other starts.

> 1 Which side of the dictionary would you look up to translate "*la bicicleta*"?

▶ FINDING THE WORD YOU WANT

When looking for a word, for example **feliz**, look at the first letter - **f** - and find the **F** section in the Spanish-English side. At the top of each page, you'll find the first and last words on that page. When you find the page with the words starting with **fe**, scan down the page until you find the word you want. Remember that even if a word has an accent on it, for example *fórmula*, it makes no difference to the alphabetical order. The exception to this rule is **ñ** (*n tilde*), which is treated as a separate letter in Spanish, so that *leña* follows *lento*.

> 2 On which page will you find the word "*hermana*"?
> 3 Which comes first – "*francesa*" or "*francés*"?

▶ MAKE SURE YOU LOOK AT THE RIGHT ENTRY

An entry is made up of a **word**, its <u>translations</u>, and, often, example phrases to show you how to use the translations. If there is more than one entry for the same word, then there is a warning box to tell you so. Look at the following example entries:

cold [kould] ADJECTIVE

see also **cold** NOUN

frío ◇ *The water is cold.* El agua está fría. ◇ *It's cold.* Hace frío. ◇ *Are you cold?* ¿Tienes frío?

cold [kould] NOUN

see also **cold** ADJECTIVE

1 el frío ◇ *I can't stand the cold.* No soporto el frío.

2 el resfriado (*illness*)

◆ **to catch a cold** resfriarse*

◆ **to have a cold** estar* resfriado

4 Which entry should you look at if you want to translate the phrase *"The water's cold"*?

Always pay attention to information boxes – they tell you if there is more than one entry for the same word, give you guidance on grammatical points, or tell you about differences between Latin American and North American life.

▶ CHOOSING THE RIGHT TRANSLATION

The main translation of a word is shown on a new line and is underlined to make it stand out from the rest of the entry. If there is more than one main translation for a word, each one is numbered. If an entry continues over the page there is a signpost to indicate this ☞.

Often you will see phrases in *italics*, preceded by a white diamond ◇. These help you to choose the translation you want because they show how the translation they follow can be used.

5 Use the phrases given at the entry *"hard"* to help you translate: *"This bread is hard"*.

Words often have more than one meaning and more than one translation. For example, a **pool** can be a puddle, a pond or a swimming pool; **pool** can also be a game. When you are translating from English into Spanish, be careful to choose the Spanish word that has the particular meaning you want. The dictionary offers you a lot of help with this. Look at the following entry:

pool [pu:l] NOUN

1 el estanque (*pond*)

2 la piscina

la alberca *Mexico*

(*swimming pool*)

3 el billar (*game*)

◆ **a pool table** una mesa de billar

◆ **typing pool** el servicio de mecanografía

The underlining highlights all the main translations, the numbers tell you that there is more than one possible translation and the words in parentheses in *italics* after the translations help you choose which translation you want.

6 How would you translate "*I like playing pool*"?

Never take the first translation you see without looking at the others. Always look to see if there is more than one underlined translation.

Phrases in **bold type** preceded by a black diamond ◆ are phrases which are particularly common or important. Sometimes these phrases have a completely different translation from the main translation; sometimes the translation is the same. For example:

el **acuerdo** SUSTANTIVO
agreement ◇ *llegar a un acuerdo* to reach an agreement
◆ **estar* de acuerdo con alguien** to agree with somebody
◆ **ponerse* de acuerdo** to agree ◇ *Al final no nos pusimos de acuerdo.* In the end we couldn't agree. ◇ *Nos pusimos de acuerdo para prepararle una bienvenida.* We agreed to organize a welcome for him.
◆ **¡De acuerdo!** All right!

packet [ˈpækɪt] NOUN
el paquete
◆ **a packet of chips** un paquete de papas fritas

When you look up a word, make sure you look beyond the main translations to see if the entry includes any **bold phrases.**

7 Look up "ir" to help you translate the sentence "Voy a casa manana"?

▶ MAKING USE OF THE PHRASES IN THE DICTIONARY

Sometimes when you look up a word you will find not only the word, but the exact phrase you want. For example, you might want to say *"What's the date today"*? Look up date and you will find that exact phrase and its translation.

Sometimes you have to adapt what you find in the dictionary. If you want to say *"I ate a sandwich"* and look up eat you will find:

to **eat** [iːt] VERB **(ate, eaten)**
comer ◇ *Would you like something to eat?* ¿Quieres comer algo?

You have to substitute *comí* for the infinitive form *comer*. You will often have to adapt the infinitive in this way, adding the correct ending and choosing the present, future or past form. For help with this, look at the verb tables, **comer** is a regular verb and it is set out on page 327.

8 How would you say "*I don't eat meat*"?

Phrases containing nouns and adjectives also need to be adapted. You may need to make the noun plural, or the adjective feminine or plural. Remember that some Spanish nouns and adjectives change their spelling in the feminine or plural and that this is shown in the entry.

9 How would you say "*The boys are French*"?

▶ DON'T OVERUSE THE DICTIONARY

It takes time to look up words so try to avoid using the dictionary unnecessarily, especially during tests. Think carefully about what you want to say and see if you can put it another way, using words you already know. To rephrase things you can:

- Use a word with a similar meaning. This is particularly easy with adjectives, as there are a lot of words which mean *good*, *bad*, *big* etc and you're sure to know at least one.
- Use negatives: if the cake you made was a total disaster, you could just say it wasn't very good.
- Use particular examples instead of general terms. If you are asked to describe the sports facilities in your area, and time is short, you could say something like "In our town there is a swimming pool and a football ground."

10 How could you say "*Argentina is huge*" without looking up the word "*huge*"?

You can also often guess the meaning of a Spanish word by using others to give you a clue. If you see the sentence *"María lee un buen libro"*, you may not know the meaning of the word **lee**, but you know it's a verb because it's preceded by **María**. Therefore it must be something you can do to a book: **read**. So the translation is: *María is reading a good book.*

11 Try NOT to use your dictionary to work out the meaning of the sentence "*La chica escribe una carta a su amiga en español*".

PARTS OF SPEECH

If you look up the word **cold**, you will see that there are two entries for this word as it can be a noun or an adjective. It helps to choose correctly between entries if you know how to recognize these different types of words.

▶ NOUNS AND PRONOUNS

Nouns often appear with words like *a, the, this, that, my, your* and *his.* They can be singular (abbreviated to SING in the dictionary):

his **dog** her **cat** a **street**

or plural (abbreviated to PL in the dictionary):

the **facts** those **people** his **shoes** *our* **vacations**

They can be the subject of a verb:

Vegetables are good for you

or the object of a verb:

I play **tennis**

Words like *I, me, you, he, she, him, her* and *they* are pronouns. They can be used instead of nouns. You can refer to a person as *he* or *she* or to a thing as *it.*

I bought my mother a box of chocolates.

12 Which three words in this sentence are nouns?
13 Which of the nouns is plural?
14 Which word is a pronoun in this sentence?

Spanish nouns are either masculine or feminine (abbreviated to MASC or FEM in the dictionary). Masculine nouns are shown by **el**:

el hombre **el** gato **el** fútbol

feminine nouns are shown by **la**:

la *mujer* **la** *economía* **la** *fábrica*

The plural forms of **el** and **la** are **los** and **las**. The plural of most Spanish nouns is made by adding **s** if the word ends in a vowel, or **es** if it ends in a consonant:

*los gato**s*** *las mujer**es***

▶ ADJECTIVES

Cold can be an adjective as well as a noun. Adjectives describe nouns: the water can be **cold**, you can have a bad **cold**.

I'm afraid of the dark.
The girl has dark hair.

15 In which sentence is "*dark*" an adjective?

Nearly all Spanish adjectives have separate masculine and feminine, and singular and plural forms, depending on the gender of the noun they are describing:

*un chico **guapo*** (MASCULINE SINGULAR)
*una chica **guapa*** (FEMININE SINGULAR: replace *-o* of masculine with *-a*)
*unos chicos **guapos*** (MASCULINE PLURAL = masculine singular + *s*)
*unas chicas **guapas*** (FEMININE PLURAL = feminine singular + *s*)

"guapo" is a regular adjective, and in the dictionary only the masculine singular form of these adjectives is shown. So if you want to find out what kind of girls **unas chicas guapas** are, look under **guapo**. Adjectives which do not end in "o" in the masculine singular follow the patterns shown below.

There are separate masculine and feminine, singular and plural forms for irregular adjectives of nationality not ending in "o", for adjectives ending in **-án**, **-ín**, **-ón**, eg **español** MASCULINE SINGULAR, **español<u>a</u>**, FEMININE SINGULAR, **español<u>es</u>** MASCULINE PLURAL, **español<u>as</u>** FEMININE PLURAL.

Adjectives ending in **-or** also follow the above pattern unless they are comparatives. The feminine is shown in the dictionary for adjectives of this type.

hablador ADJETIVO (FEM **habladora**)
1 chatty (*parlanchín*)
2 gossipy (*chismoso*)
3 lying (*mentiroso*) *Mexico*

talkative ['tɑːkətɪv] ADJECTIVE
hablador (FEM habladora)

Other adjectives ending in a consonant do not have a separate feminine form, but do change in the plural, eg **azul** MASCULINE and FEMININE SINGULAR, **azul<u>es</u>** MASCULINE and FEMININE PLURAL.

feliz ADJETIVO (PL **felices**)
happy ◇ *Se la ve muy feliz.* She looks very happy.
◆ **¡Feliz cumpleaños!** Happy birthday!
◆ **¡Feliz Año Nuevo!** Happy New Year!
◆ **¡Feliz Navidad!** Happy Christmas!

happy ['hæpi] ADJECTIVE
feliz (PL felices) ◇ *Janet looks happy.* Janet se ve feliz.
◆ **to be happy with something** estar* contento con algo ◇ *I'm very happy with your work.* Estoy muy contento con tu trabajo.
◆ **Happy birthday!** ¡Feliz cumpleaños!
◆ **a happy ending** un final feliz

If the masculine form of an adjective ends in **-e** or **-a**, the feminine form is the same, and both the masculine and feminine plurals are formed by adding **-s** to the masculine, eg **verde** MASCULINE and FEMININE SINGULAR, **verdes** MASCULINE and FEMININE PLURAL. Some adjectives, particularly those referring to color, remain the same whether they're masculine, feminine or plural. This is also shown in the dictionary:

el **rosa** ADJETIVO, SUSTANTIVO
pink ◇ *Va vestida de rosa.* She's wearing pink.
◆ **Llevaba unos calcetines rosa.** He was wearing pink socks.

16 What is the feminine singular form of "*rojo*"?
17 What is the basic form of the adjective in the sentence "*Las flores son hermosas*"?

▶ VERBS

She's going to record the program for me.
His time in the race was a new world record.

Record is a verb in the first sentence, and a noun in the second.

One way to recognize a verb is that it frequently comes with a pronoun such as **I**, **you** or **she**, or with somebody's name. Verbs can relate to the present, the past or the future. They have a number of different forms to show this: **I'm going** (present), **he will go** (future), and **Nicola went by herself** (past). Often verbs appear with **to: they promised to go**. This basic form of the verb is called the infinitive.

In this dictionary, verbs are preceded by "to", so you can identify them at a glance. No matter which of the four previous examples you want to translate, you should look up **to go**, not **going** or **went**. If you want to translate **I thought**, look up **to think**.

18 What would you look up to translate the verbs in these phrases?

I ***came*** she'***s crying*** they'***ve done*** it he'***s*** out

Verbs have different endings in Spanish, depending on whether you are talking about **yo, tú, nosotros** etc: **yo hablo, tú hablas, nosotros hablamos** etc. They also have different forms for the present, future, past etc. **Hablamos** (*we speak* = present), **hablamos** (*we spoke* = past), **hablaremos** (*we will speak* = future). **Hablar** is the infinitive and is the form that appears in the dictionary.

Sometimes the verb changes completely between the infinitive form and the **yo, tú, él** etc form. For example, *to give* is **dar**, but *I give* is **doy**, and **digo** comes from **decir** (*to say*).

On pages 326-329 of the dictionary, you will find tables of regular Spanish verbs. On pages 330-341 you will find tables of the most important irregular verbs, followed by a list of other irregular verbs with the number of the model verb they are like. Irregular Spanish verbs are marked in the dictionary with an asterisk.

to **fulfill** [ful'fıl] VERB
realizar* ◇ *He fulfilled his dream to visit China.* Realizó su sueño de viajar a China.
◆ **to fulfill a promise** cumplir una promesa

ir* VERBO
to go ◇ *Anoche fuimos al cine.* We went to the movies last night. ◇ *¿A qué colegio vas?* What school do you go to?
◆ **ir de vacaciones** to go on vacation

19 Look up the dictionary to find the imperfect and perfect tenses of "comer."

▶ ADVERBS

An adverb is a word that describes a verb or an adjective:

Write ***soon.*** Check your work ***carefully.***
The movie was ***very*** good.

In the sentence *"The swimming pool is open daily"*, **daily** is an adverb describing the adjective **open**. In the phrase *"my daily routine"*, **daily** is an adjective describing the noun **routine**. We use the same word in English for both adjective and adverb forms, but to get the right Spanish translation, it is important to know if it's being used as an adjective or an adverb. When you look up **daily** you find:

daily ['deɪli] ADJECTIVE, ADVERB

1 diario ◇ *daily life* la vida diaria ◇ *It's part of my daily routine.* Forma parte de mi rutina diaria.

◆ **a daily paper** un periódico

2 todos los días ◇ *The library is open daily.* La biblioteca abre todos los días.

The examples show you **daily** being used as an adjective and as an adverb and will help you choose the right Spanish translation.

Take the sentence "The menu changes daily".

20 Is "*daily*" an adverb or an adjective here?

▶ PREPOSITIONS

Prepositions are words like **for**, **with** and **across**, which are followed by nouns or pronouns:

I've got a present ***for*** David. Come ***with*** me. He ran ***across*** the road.

The party's over.
The ball went over the wall.

21 Which sentence shows a preposition followed by a noun?

▶ ANSWERS

1 the Spanish-English side
2 on page 158
3 **francés** comes first
4 the first (ADJECTIVE) entry
5 **Este pan está duro.**
6 **Me gusta jugar billar.**
7 **I'm going home tomorrow.**
8 **No como carne.**
9 **Los niños son franceses.**
10 **Argentina es muy grande.**
11 **The girl is writing a letter to her friend in Spanish.**
12 **mother**, **box** and **chocolates** are nouns
13 **chocolates** is plural
14 **I** is a pronoun
15 in the second sentence
16 **roja**
17 **hermoso**
18 to **come**, to **cry**, to **do**, to **be**
19 the imperfect tense is **comía**, the perfect tense is **he comido**
20 daily is an **adverb**
21 the second sentence

LA PRONUNCIACIÓN INGLESA

► VOCALES

calm, part, rot	[ɑː]
hat	[æ]
egg, set, parent	[ɛ]
above	[ə]
earn, girl	[ɜː]
hit, give	[ɪ]
fairly, city	[i]
green, peace	[iː]
born	[ɔː]
hut	[ʌ]
full	[u]
pool	[uː]

► DIPTONGOS

buy, die, my	[aɪ]
house, now	[au]
pay, mate	[eɪ]
pair, mare	[ɛə]
no, boat	[ou]
here, near	[ɪə]
boy, coin	[ɔɪ]
tour, poor	[uə]

► SEMIVOCALES

yet, million	[j]
wet, why	[w]

► CONSONANTES

ball	[b]
child	[tʃ]
field	[f]
good	[g]
hand	[h]
just	[dʒ]
kind, catch	[k]
left, little	[l]
mat	[m]
nest	[n]
long	[ŋ]
put	[p]
run	[r]
sit	[s]
shallow	[ʃ]
tag	[t]
thing	[θ]
this	[ð]
very	[v]
loch	[x]
ours, zipper	[z]
measure	[ʒ]

► OTROS SÍMBOLOS

Acento	[ˈ]
Accento secundario	[ˌ]

Como guía para pronunciar el inglés correctamente, en la parte de inglés-español aparece la transcripción fonética tras el lema en todas las entradas.

CÓMO USAR ESTE DICCIONARIO

La utilización de un diccionario es una habilidad que consigue mejorarse con un poco de práctica y siguiendo algunas reglas básicas. En las páginas siguientes puedes encontrar la información necesaria para sacar el máximo provecho de este diccionario.

Las soluciones a las preguntas de esta sección se encuentran en la página 25.

▶ CÓMO ASEGURARSE DE QUE ESTAMOS EN LA PARTE CORRECTA DEL DICCIONARIO

La parte de español-inglés viene en primer lugar, seguida de la parte de inglés-español. En la esquina superior de cada página puede verse la inscripción **español ~ inglés** o **inglés ~ español**, lo que nos ayuda a identificar de forma inmediata en qué parte del diccionario nos encontramos. Las páginas centrales están bordeadas en azul para que podamos ver dónde acaba una parte y dónde empieza la siguiente.

1 Si queremos encontrar "*la bicicleta*" ¿miraremos en la parte de español-inglés o de inglés-español?

▶ CÓMO ENCONTRAR LA PALABRA QUE BUSCAMOS

Si estamos buscando una palabra, por ejemplo **temprano**, tendremos que ver por qué letra empieza. En este caso, **t-** y por ello nos vamos a la letra T de la parte de español-inglés. En la esquina de cada página pueden leerse la primera y la última palabra de cada página. Cuando encontremos la página con las palabras que empiezan por **tem**, tendremos que seguir mirando más abajo hasta que encontremos la palabra que buscamos.

2 ¿En qué página encontraremos la palabra "*ayer*"?
3 ¿Qué viene antes – "*cáscara*" o "*centro*"?

▶ CÓMO ASEGURARSE DE QUE ESTAMOS EN LA ENTRADA CORRECTA

Una entrada léxica consta de una **palabra**, sus traducciones y, con frecuencia, de algunos ejemplos que nos sirven de guía en el uso de las traducciones. Si hay más de una entrada para la misma palabra en la parte de inglés-español, entonces aparece un recuadro que nos remite a la otra entrada. Observa el siguiente ejemplo:

cold [kould] ADJECTIVE
see also **cold** NOUN
frío ◇ *The water is cold.* El agua ◇ *It's cold.* Hace frío. ◇ *Are you* ¿Tienes frío?

cold [kould] NOUN
see also **cold** ADJECTIVE
1 el frío ◇ *I can't stand the cold.* No el frío.
2 el resfriado (*illness*)
◆ **to catch a cold** resfriarse*
◆ **to have a cold** estar* resfriado

4 ¿Qué entrada de las dos anteriores habría que consultar para traducir la frase "*The water's cold*"?

En numerosas ocasiones aparecen también recuadros con información adicional sobre algún punto de interés gramatical o sobre las diferencias culturales entre Latinoamérica y los Estados Unidos.

▶ CÓMO ELEGIR LA TRADUCCIÓN CORRECTA

La traducción principal de una palabra aparece subrayada y en una línea aparte a fin de distinguirla del resto de la entrada. Si existe más de una traducción principal para una misma palabra, cada una de ellas aparece numerada y si una entrada continúa en la página siguiente aparece una señal indicándolo .

Con frecuencia aparecen algunos ejemplos en cursiva, precedidos de un rombo blanco ◇, que nos servirán de ayuda a la hora de elegir la traducción que queremos, pues muestran el uso que hay que dar a la traducción que estamos buscando.

5 Emplea los ejemplos que aparecen en la entrada "*intención*" para traducir: "*Tenía intención de irme a vivir al extranjero*".

Las palabras suelen tener más de un significado y más de una traducción y cuando estamos traduciendo del español al inglés hay que tener cuidado de usar la palabra que tiene el significado específico que queremos. Este diccionario te facilita toda la ayuda que necesitas para hacerlo.

El siguiente ejemplo muestra la división de una de estas entradas. Las traducciones principales van subrayadas, la numeración advierte que hay más de una traducción y las palabras escritas en cursiva entre paréntesis nos ayudan a elegir el ejemplo correcto.

la **cinta** SUSTANTIVO
1 ribbon (*de adorno, para el pelo*)
2 tape (*para grabar*)
- ◆ **una cinta de video** a videotape
- ◆ **cinta aislante** electrical tape
- ◆ **cinta Dúrex®** Scotch tape®
- ◆ **una cinta transportadora** a conveyor belt

6 ¿Cómo podríamos traducir: "*Tenía una cinta en el pelo*"?

Es importante recordar que nunca hay que tomar la primera traducción que nos encontramos sin antes mirar las demás. Siempre hay que echar un vistazo a toda la entrada para comprobar si hay más de una traducción subrayada.

Los ejemplos que aparecen **en negrita** precedidos de un rombo negro ◆ son construcciones de uso bastante frecuente, que a veces tienen una traducción completamente distinta de la traducción principal; otras veces la traducción puede ser la misma. Por ejemplo:

packet ['pækɪt] NOUN
el paquete
- ◆ **a packet of chips** un paquete de papas fritas

el **acuerdo** SUSTANTIVO
agreement ◇ *llegar a un acuerdo* to reach an agreement
- ◆ **estar* de acuerdo con alguien** to agree with somebody
- ◆ **ponerse* de acuerdo** to agree ◇ *Al final no nos pusimos de acuerdo.* In the end we couldn't agree. ◇ *Nos pusimos de acuerdo para prepararle una bienvenida.* We agreed to organize a welcome for him.
- ◆ **¡De acuerdo!** All right!

Cuando consultamos una palabra conviene mirar siempre más allá de las traducciones principales para comprobar si la entrada contiene algunas frases en negrita.

7 Consulta la entrada "*out*" y traduce al español "*We're out of gas*".

▶ CÓMO UTILIZAR LOS EJEMPLOS DEL DICCIONARIO

Cuando consultamos una palabra, encontramos con frecuencia no sólo la palabra sino la frase exacta que estamos buscando. Por ejemplo, si queremos decir "*¿qué hora es?*" consultamos la palabra **hora** y encontraremos el ejemplo completo con su traducción.

En otras ocasiones tenemos que adaptar la información que encontramos en el diccionario. Si queremos decir *"nunca viajo en tren"* y miramos la palabra **tren** encontraremos:

el **tren** SUSTANTIVO
train
- **viajar en tren** to travel by train
- **Tomé un tren directo.** I took an express train.
- **con este tren de vida** with such a hectic life

Hay que sustituir la forma de infinitivo *to travel* por la forma conjugada *I travel*. Esto ocurrirá con frecuencia, especialmente en el caso de los verbos, en que tendremos que utilizar el pronombre y la forma correspondientes. Conviene consultar la sección dedicada a la tablas de verbos, que nos ayudará en el uso de los mismos.

8 ¿Cómo dirías "*Estamos jugando tenis*"?

Los ejemplos que contienen sustantivos también hay que adaptarlos, especialmente si el sustantivo que buscamos tiene un plural irregular, que viene indicado en la entrada.

9 ¿Cómo dirías "*Las flores rojas son muy bonitas*"?

▶ CÓMO HACER UN MEJOR USO DEL DICCIONARIO

Consultar una palabra requiere su tiempo, por lo que aconsejamos reducir el uso del diccionario cuando no sea realmente necesario. Por eso hay también formas de evitar su uso: primero hay que pensar detenidamente en lo que queremos decir y después ver si podemos expresarlo de otra manera, utilizando las palabras que ya conocemos o cambiando la estructura de la frase, para lo que podremos recurrir a los siguientes trucos:

- Utilizar una palabra con un significado parecido. Esto es más fácil con los adjetivos, ya que existen muchas palabras que significan *bueno*, *malo*, *grande*, etc y seguramente conoceremos más de una.
- Emplear frases negativas: si el pastel que hemos hecho nos ha salido muy malo, siempre podremos decir que no ha salido muy bueno.
- Usar ejemplos concretos en lugar de palabras generales e innecesarias. En lugar de decir: "En nuestra ciudad hay varias instalaciones deportivas" si no conocemos alguna de las palabras del ejemplo, podemos decir en cambio: "En nuestra ciudad hay una piscina y una cancha de tenis".

10 ¿Cómo podrías decir "*Bogotá es una ciudad enorme*", sin necesidad de mirar la palabra "*enorme*"?

También podemos tratar de adivinar el significado de una palabra inglesa mediante el uso de otras que nos sirvan de pista. Si vemos la frase "*My father drives a red car*", a lo mejor no conocemos el significado de la palabra **drives**, pero sabemos que es un verbo, porque va precedida de un sustantivo y sabemos que tiene algo que ver con un carro. Por tanto debe tratarse de algo que podemos hacer con un carro, o sea, ... **manejar**. Así que la traducción sería: *mi padre maneja un carro rojo.*

11 Sin usar el diccionario, intenta averiguar el significado de la palabra "*essay*" en la frase "*We have to write an essay before the exam*".

LAS CATEGORÍAS GRAMATICALES

Si consultamos la palabra **plano**, veremos que hay dos entradas para esta palabra, ya que puede tratarse de un sustantivo o de un adjetivo.

Por ello es importante aprender a distinguir unos tipos de palabras de otros para reconocer la entrada correcta.

A continuación vamos a dar información sobre las distintas categorías gramaticales y algunos consejos que nos ayudarán a traducir correctamente los sustantivos, preposiciones, etc. al inglés y a descifrar la función de algunas palabras inglesas que desconocemos cuando las encontramos en un determinado contexto.

▶ SUSTANTIVOS

Los sustantivos son las palabras que sirven para nombrar a personas, animales y cosas. En inglés suelen venir acompañados de palabras como *a*, *the*, *this*, *that*, *your* o *his*:

his **dog** her **cat** a **street**

En la parte de inglés-español aparecen marcados como NOUN.

Si queremos traducir un sustantivo en plural al inglés, lo primero que hay hacer es encontrar en la parte español-inglés la forma en singular. Así, si queremos decir "los cuadros" en inglés, tendremos que buscar "el cuadro".

12 ¿En qué entrada del diccionario podremos encontrar "*camiones*"?

El plural se construye en inglés, por regla general, añadiendo una "**s**" a la forma del singular:

many book**s** two house**s**

Los sustantivos acabados en **-s**, **-sh** o **-x** construyen el plural añadiendo "**es**":

many kiss**es** three brush**es** some box**es**

Algunos sustantivos que acaban en **-y** forman el plural cambiando a "**ies**":

several bab**ies** two pupp**ies**

Algunos sustantivos tienen una forma irregular en plural:

two **children** many **mice** six **loaves** of bread

one child

two children

Si el plural no se construye añadiendo una "**s**" a la forma del singular, la forma del plural aparece en el diccionario. Los plurales irregulares de los sustantivos ingleses tienen además su propia entrada en la parte de inglés-español con una remisión a la forma en singular.

children ['tʃɪldrən] PL NOUN *see* **child**

Normalmente, los sustantivos vienen en singular. Sin embargo, algunos no tienen esta forma, por lo que aparecen en plural, seguidos por la abreviatura PL NOUN.

french fries ['frɛntʃ,fraɪz] PL NOUN
las papas fritas

The children gave their teacher a box of chocolates.

13 ¿Cuántos sustantivos contiene esta frase?
14 ¿Cuántos sustantivos en plural hay en esta frase?
15 ¿Cuál es el singular de "*children*"?
16 Busca en el diccionario el plural de la palabra inglesa "*calf*".

▶ ADJETIVOS

Los adjetivos son palabras que describen las cualidades del sustantivo. En la parte de inglés-español aparecen marcadas como ADJECTIVE. Los adjetivos en español pueden cambiar de género o número, según el sustantivo al que acompañen, pero el adjetivo en inglés no varía:

a **black** cat | **black** dogs | the cat is **black**

¿Qué entrada habría que consultar para traducir las siguientes oraciones: single ADJECTIVE o single NOUN?

17 She hadn't said a single word.
18 He bought the latest U2 single.
19 Not a single thing!

▶ PRONOMBRES

Los pronombres son palabras como *yo, tú, él, me*, que pueden ocupar el lugar de un sustantivo en una oración. En la parte de inglés-español aparecen marcadas como PRONOUN.

A diferencia del español, en inglés siempre hay que colocar el pronombre personal (I, you, he, etc) cuando el sujeto de la frase no es un sustantivo.

▶ VERBOS

Los verbos se utilizan para expresar acciones o estados y, como ya hemos dicho, en inglés van precedidos de pronombres personales, o bien de sustantivos. En este diccionario los verbos se distinguen también porque aparecen precedidos de la partícula **to** y además están marcados por la palabra VERB.

¿Qué entrada habría que consultar para traducir las siguientes frases: fight NOUN o fight VERB?

20 He is always fighting with his brothers.
21 Tyson won most of his fights.

Los verbos pueden ir en distintos tiempos, por ejemplo, en presente (**leo un libro**) o en pasado (**leí un libro** o **he leído un libro**). Además, pueden estar en voz activa (**leo un libro**) o pasiva (**el libro es leído**). Todas estas formas verbales se deducen a partir de la forma base o forma de infinitivo, que es la que aparece en el diccionario. Por eso, si tenemos que traducir **ella lee un libro** tendremos que buscar en la entrada correspondiente a **leer**.

¿En qué forma de infinitivo encontraremos las siguientes formas verbales conjugadas?

22 Canté una canción.
23 Es ingeniero.

Al igual que en español, en inglés existen también verbos irregulares. Para facilitar la localización de la forma de infinitivo, las formas de pasado y participio de los verbos irregulares más importantes aparecen como entradas independientes en la parte de inglés-español, con una remisión a la forma de infinitivo.

found [faund] VERB *see* **find**

En la parte de inglés-español aparecen indicadas después del verbo inglés en infinitivo la forma irregular de pasado y de participio de perfecto.

to **sew** [sou] VERB **(sewed, sewn)**

En las páginas 350-361 se puede encontrar más información sobre las formas más importantes de los verbos ingleses.

Traduce las siguientes frases al inglés:

24 Ella va al colegio.
25 Él fue al cine.
26 Ya se han ido.

▶ ADVERBIOS

Los adverbios se utilizan para modificar el sentido de los adjetivos o de los verbos. En la parte de inglés-español del diccionario aparecen marcados como ADVERB y en inglés se reconocen a menudo por terminar en "**ly**".

Tanto en inglés como en español hay algunos adjetivos que presentan la misma forma que los adverbios, por lo que es importante aprender a distinguirlos para encontrar la traducción correcta.

rápido (1) ADJETIVO
1 fast (*veloz*) ◇ *un carro muy rápido* a very fast car
2 quick (*de poca duración*) ◇ *Fue una visita muy rápida.* It was a very quick visit.
rápido (2) ADVERBIO
fast ◇ *Manejas demasiado rápido.* You drive too fast.
◆ **Lo hice tan rápido como pude.** I did it as quickly as I could.
◆ **¡Rápido!** Hurry up!

¿Qué entrada habría que consultar para traducir las siguientes oraciones: rápido ADJETIVO o rápido ADVERBIO?

27 Un tren muy rápido.
28 Ha sido un cambio muy rápido.
29 Se fue muy rápido.

▶ PREPOSICIONES

Las preposiciones son palabras como *sobre*, *por*, *de* en español y *on*, *for*, *of* en inglés y aparecen habitualmente delante de los sustantivos y pronombres. Es importante reconocerlas, ya que a veces pueden tener la misma forma que un adverbio. En la parte de inglés-español aparecen seguidas de la marca PREPOSITION.

> *The party's over.*
> *The ball went over the wall.*
>
> 30 ¿En qué oración es "*over*" una preposición?
> 31 Traduce al inglés: "*Una película sobre África*".

▶ SOLUCIONES

1 en la parte de **español-inglés**
2 59
3 **cáscara**
4 Front **ADJECTIVE**
5 **I intended to go and live abroad.**
6 **She had a ribbon in her hair.**
7 **Se nos acabó la gasolina.**
8 **We're playing tennis.**
9 **The red flowers are very pretty.**
10 **Bogotá is a very big city.**
11 **redacción: Tenemos que hacer una redacción antes del examen.**
12 **camión**
13 **4**: children, teacher, box, chocolates
14 **2**: children, chocolates
15 **child**
16 **calves**
17 **ADJECTIVE**
18 **NOUN**
19 **ADJECTIVE**
20 **VERB**
21 **NOUN**
22 **cantar**
23 **ser**
24 **She goes to school.**
25 **He went to the movies.**
26 **They've already left.**
27 **ADJETIVO**
28 **ADJETIVO**
29 **ADVERBIO**
30 **The ball went over the wall.**
31 **A movie about Africa.**

A

a (*a + el = al*) PREPOSICIÓN

[1] to

*Se usa **to** hablando de movimiento, dirección.*

◇ *Fueron a Bogotá.* They went to Bogotá.

Pero a menudo depende de cómo se entienda la dirección: dentro, encima de..., así como del verbo que la preceda.

- **Me caí al río.** I fell into the river.
- **Se subieron al tejado.** They climbed onto the roof.
- **Marta llegó a la oficina.** Marta arrived at the office.
- **Está a 15 millas de aquí.** It's 15 miles from here.

[2] at

*Se usa **at** hablando de la hora, la fecha, la edad, la velocidad.*

◇ *a las 10* at 10 o'clock ◇ *a medianoche* at midnight ◇ *a los 24 años* at the age of 24 ◇ *Íbamos a más de 90 km por hora.* We were going over 90 km an hour.

- **Estamos a 9 de julio.** It's July 9th.
- **Los huevos están a 10 pesos la docena.** Eggs are 10 pesos a dozen.
- **una vez a la semana** once a week

*También se usa normalmente **to** delante de un infinitivo.*

◇ *Voy a verlo.* I'm going to see him. ◇ *Vine a decírtelo.* I came to tell you. ◇ *Me obligaban a comer.* They forced me to eat.

- **Al verlo, lo reconocí inmediatamente.** When I saw him, I recognized him immediately.
- **Nos cruzamos al salir.** We bumped into each other as we were going out.

*Cuando **a** forma parte del complemento indirecto también se traduce por **to**, a menos que siga directamente al verbo.*

◇ *Se lo di a Ana.* I gave it to Ana. ◇ *Le mostré a Pablo el libro que me dejaste.* I showed Pablo the book you lent me.

- **Se lo compré a él.** I bought it from him.

En muchas otras ocasiones, como por ejemplo en complementos directos de persona, no se traduce.

- **Vi a Juan.** I saw Juan.
- **Llamé al médico.** I called the doctor.
- **Voltea a la derecha.** Turn right.
- **Me voy a la casa.** I'm going home.
- **¡A comer!** Lunch is ready!

la **abadía** SUSTANTIVO

abbey (PL abbeys)

abajo ADVERBIO

[1] below ◇ *Los platos y las tazas están abajo.* The plates and cups are below. ◇ *La montaña no parece tan alta desde abajo.* The mountain doesn't seem so high from below.

- **Mete las cervezas abajo de todo.** Put the beers at the bottom.
- **El estante de abajo.** The bottom shelf.
- **La parte de abajo del contenedor.** The bottom of the container.

[2] downstairs

*Se usa **downstairs** hablando de los distintos pisos de un edificio.*

◇ *Abajo están la cocina y el salón.* The kitchen and lounge are downstairs. ◇ *Hay una fiesta en el departamento de abajo.* There's a party in the apartment downstairs.

- **más abajo** further down
- **ir* calle abajo** to go down the street
- **Todos las carteras son de 100 pesos para abajo.** All the bags are 100 pesos or under.
- **abajo de** under

abandonado ADJETIVO

- **un pueblo abandonado** a deserted village

abandonar VERBO

[1] to leave (*lugar, zona, edificio*)

◇ *Decidieron abandonar el país.* They decided to leave the country.

- **Abandonó a su familia.** He deserted his family.
- **Mucha gente abandona a sus perros.** A lot of people abandon their dogs.

[2] to give up (*planes, proyecto*) ◇ *Tuve que abandonar la idea de comprarme otro carro.* I had to give up the idea of buying another car.

el **abanico** SUSTANTIVO

fan

abarrotado ADJETIVO

packed ◇ *abarrotado de gente* packed with people

la **abarrotería** SUSTANTIVO *Mexico*

grocery store

los **abarrotes** SUSTANTIVO *Mexico*

groceries

- **tienda de abarrotes** grocery store

abastecer* VERBO

- **abastecer de algo a alguien** to supply somebody with something
- **Nos abastecimos bien de comida para el viaje.** We stocked up with food for the trip.

el **abdomen** SUSTANTIVO

stomach

los **abdominales** SUSTANTIVO

sit-ups ◇ *hacer abdominales* to do sit-ups

el **abecedario** SUSTANTIVO

alphabet

la **abeja** SUSTANTIVO

bee

el **abeto** SUSTANTIVO

fir

abierto (1) VERBO *ver* **abrir**

abierto (2) ADJETIVO

[1] open ◇ *¿Están abiertas las tiendas?* Are the stores open?

[2] on ◇ *No dejes el gas abierto.* Don't leave the gas on.

el **abogado,** la **abogada** SUSTANTIVO
lawyer

abolir* VERBO
to abolish

abollar VERBO
to dent ◇ *Me abollaron el carro.* Someone has dented my car.
◆ **abollarse** to get dented

abombarse VERBO
to go bad

abonar VERBO
1 to pay ◇ *abonar dinero en una cuenta* to pay money into an account
2 to fertilize ◇ *Hay que abonar el terreno antes de sembrar.* The land has to be fertilized before sowing.
◆ **abonarse a** (*canal de televisión*) to take out a subscription to

el **abono** SUSTANTIVO
1 fertilizer (*para las plantas*)
2 season ticket (*de transporte, fútbol*)
3 installment (*pago parcial*) Mexico

abortar VERBO
1 to have an abortion (*cuando es provocado*)
2 to miscarry (*espontáneamente*)

el **aborto** SUSTANTIVO
1 abortion (*provocado*)
2 miscarriage (*espontáneo*)

abrasar VERBO
to burn ◇ *El fuego le abrasó las manos.* The fire burned his hands.
◆ **abrasarse** to be burned ◇ *Mucha gente se abrasó viva en el incendio.* A lot of people were burned alive in the fire.

abrazar* VERBO
to hug ◇ *Al verme me abrazó.* He hugged me when he saw me.
◆ **¡Abrázame fuerte!** Give me a big hug!
◆ **abrazarse** to hug ◇ *Se abrazaron y se besaron.* They hugged and kissed.

el **abrazo** SUSTANTIVO
hug ◇ *¡Dame un abrazo!* Give me a hug!
◆ **Siempre están dándose besos y abrazos.** They're always hugging and kissing.
◆ **"un abrazo"** (*en cartas*) "with best wishes"

el **abrebotellas** SUSTANTIVO (PL los **abrebotellas**)
bottle opener

el **abrelatas** SUSTANTIVO (PL los **abrelatas**)
can opener

la **abreviatura** SUSTANTIVO
abbreviation

el **abridor** SUSTANTIVO
1 bottle opener (*de botellas*)
2 can opener (*de latas*)

abrigar* VERBO
◆ **Esta chaqueta abriga mucho.** This jacket's great for keeping warm.
◆ **Ponte algo que te abrigue.** Put something warm on.
◆ **Abriga bien al niño, que hace frío.** Wrap the baby up well – it's cold.
◆ **abrigarse** to wrap up well

el **abrigo** SUSTANTIVO
coat ◇ *un abrigo de pieles* a fur coat
◆ **ropa de abrigo** warm clothing

abril SUSTANTIVO MASC
En inglés, los meses se escriben con mayúscula.
April ◇ *en abril* in April ◇ *Nació el 20 de abril.* He was born on April 20.

abrir* VERBO
1 to open ◇ *La tienda abre a las diez.* The store opens at ten o'clock. ◇ *Abre la ventana.* Open the window.
◆ **¡Abre, soy yo!** Open the door, it's me!
2 to turn on ◇ *¿Abriste el gas?* Have you turned the gas on?
◆ **abrirse** to open ◇ *De repente se abrió la puerta.* Suddenly the door opened.

abrocharse VERBO
to do up ◇ *Abróchate la camisa.* Do your shirt up.
◆ **Abróchense los cinturones.** Please fasten your seatbelts.

absoluto ADJETIVO
absolute ◇ *Nos dio garantía absoluta.* He gave us an absolute guarantee.
◆ **La operación fue un éxito absoluto.** The operation was a complete success.
◆ **en absoluto** at all ◇ *¿Te molesta que fume? – En absoluto.* Do you mind if I smoke? – Not at all. ◇ *nada en absoluto* nothing at all

absorber VERBO
to absorb

abstemio ADJETIVO
teetotal ◇ *Soy abstemio.* I'm teetotal.

la **abstención** SUSTANTIVO (PL las **abstenciones**)
abstention

abstenerse* VERBO
to abstain (*en una votación*) ◇ *Yo me abstengo.* I'm abstaining.
◆ **abstenerse de hacer algo** to refrain from doing something

abstracto ADJETIVO
abstract

absurdo ADJETIVO
absurd
◆ **lo absurdo es que...** the absurd thing is that...

la **abuela** SUSTANTIVO
grandmother ◇ *mi abuela* my grandmother
◆ **¿Dónde está la abuela?** Where's Grandma?

el **abuelo** SUSTANTIVO
grandfather ◇ *mi abuelo* my grandfather
◆ **¿Dónde está el abuelo?** Where's Grandad?
◆ **mis abuelos** my grandparents

abultado ADJETIVO
bulky

abultar VERBO

* Verbs marked with this symbol are irregular. See pages 346–348 for further details.

to be bulky ◇ *No abulta mucho.* It isn't very bulky.

◆ **Tus cosas apenas abultan.** Your things hardly take up any space at all.

abundante ADJETIVO

1 plenty of ◇ *Habrá abundante comida y bebida.* There'll be plenty of food and drink.

2 enormous ◇ *El año pasado tuvimos abundantes pérdidas.* We had enormous losses last year.

aburrido ADJETIVO

1 bored ◇ *Estaba aburrida y me marché.* I was bored so I left.

2 boring ◇ *una película muy aburrida* a very boring movie ◇ *No seas aburrida y vente al cine, mujer.* Don't be boring and come to the movies.

3 tired (*harto*) ◇ *Estaba aburrido de esperarte, así que me fui.* I was tired of waiting for you, so I left.

el **aburrimiento** SUSTANTIVO

◆ **¡Qué aburrimiento!** What a bore this is!

◆ **Estoy muerto de aburrimiento.** I'm bored stiff.

aburrirse VERBO

to get bored ◇ *Me aburro viendo la tele.* I get bored watching television.

abusar VERBO

◆ **abusar de alguien (1)** (*de su confianza, hospitalidad*) to take advantage of somebody

◆ **abusar de alguien (2)** (*sexualmente*) to abuse somebody

◆ **Está bien beber de vez en cuando pero sin abusar.** Drinking every so often is fine as long as you don't overdo it.

◆ **No conviene abusar del aceite en las comidas.** You shouldn't use too much oil in food.

◆ **Abusó de nuestra hospitalidad.** He abused our hospitality.

el **abuso** SUSTANTIVO

abuse ◇ *el abuso de las drogas* drug abuse

◆ **los abusos sexuales** sexual abuse SING

◆ **Lo que han hecho me parece un abuso.** I think what they've done is outrageous.

acá ADVERBIO

here ◇ *¡Vente para acá!* Come over here!

◆ **Hay que ponerlo más acá.** You'll have to bring it closer.

acabar VERBO

to finish ◇ *Cuando acabe esta cerveza me voy.* When I've finished this beer I'm going. ◇ *Ayer acabé de pintar la valla.* Yesterday I finished painting the fence.

◆ **acabar con (1)** to put an end to ◇ *Hay que acabar con tanto desorden.* We must put an end to all this confusion.

◆ **acabar con (2)** (*agotar*) to finish ◇ *Hemos acabado con todas las provisiones.* We've finished all our provisions.

◆ **Acabo de ver a tu padre.** I've just seen your father. ◇ *Acababa de entrar cuando sonó el teléfono.* I had just come in when the phone rang.

◆ **acabarse** to run out ◇ *La impresora te avisa cuando se acaba el papel.* The printer tells you when the paper runs out. ◇ *Se me acabaron los cigarrillos.* I ran out of cigarettes.

la **academia** SUSTANTIVO

school ◇ *una academia de idiomas* a language school

◆ **una academia militar** a military academy

académico ADJETIVO

academic ◇ *el curso académico* the academic year

la **acampada** SUSTANTIVO

◆ **ir* de acampada** to go camping

acampar VERBO

to camp

el **acantilado** SUSTANTIVO

cliff

acariciar VERBO

1 to stroke (*pelo, animal*)

2 to caress (*mejilla, niño, amante*)

acaso ADVERBIO

◆ **¿Acaso tengo yo la culpa?** Is it MY fault?

◆ **por si acaso** just in case

◆ **No necesito nada; si acaso, un poco de leche.** I don't need anything; well maybe a little milk.

◆ **Si acaso lo ves, dile que me llame.** If you should see him, tell him to call me.

acatarrarse VERBO

to catch cold

acceder VERBO

◆ **acceder a (1)** to agree to ◇ *Al final accedió a venir.* In the end he agreed to come.

◆ **acceder a (2)** (*un lugar*) to gain access to

accesible ADJETIVO

1 accessible ◇ *Es un lugar sólo accesible por barco.* The place is only accessible by boat.

2 approachable ◇ *Es una persona muy accesible.* He's very approachable.

el **acceso** SUSTANTIVO

access ◇ *La casa tiene acceso por delante y por detrás.* Access to the house is from the front and from the rear. ◇ *Tiene acceso a información confidencial.* He has access to confidential information.

◆ **Quieren mejorar los accesos al aeropuerto.** They want to improve access to the airport.

◆ **los exámenes para entrar a la universidad** university entrance exams

el **accesorio** SUSTANTIVO

accessories ◇ *accesorios para el automóvil* car accessories

accidentado ADJETIVO

1 rough (*terreno*)

2 eventful (*viaje*)

el **accidente** SUSTANTIVO

accident ◇ *los accidentes de trabajo* accidents in the workplace

☞

- **Han tenido un accidente.** They've had a car accident.

la **acción** SUSTANTIVO (PL las **acciones**)
[1] action ◇ *una película llena de acción* an action-packed movie
- **entrar en acción** to go into action

[2] share ◇ *comprar acciones de una empresa* to buy shares in a company

el/la **accionista** SUSTANTIVO
shareholder

el **aceite** SUSTANTIVO
oil
- **el aceite de girasol** sunflower oil
- **el aceite de oliva** olive oil

aceitoso ADJETIVO
oily

la **aceituna** SUSTANTIVO
olive ◇ *aceitunas rellenas* stuffed olives

el **acelerador** SUSTANTIVO
accelerator

acelerar VERBO
to accelerate ◇ *Aceleré para adelantarlos.* I accelerated to pass them.
- **¡Acelera, que no llegamos!** Speed up or we'll never get there!
- **acelerar el paso** to walk faster

las **acelgas** SUSTANTIVO
Swiss chard SING

el **acento** SUSTANTIVO
[1] accent (*tilde, pronunciación*) ◇ *"Té" lleva acento cuando significa "bebida".* "Té" has an accent when it means "drink". ◇ *Tiene mucho acento sureño.* He has a strong southern accent.
[2] stress (*en sílaba sin tilde*) ◇ *¿Qué sílaba lleva el acento en "microphone"?* Which syllable is the stress on in "microphone"?

acentuarse* VERBO
to have an accent ◇ *No se acentúa.* It doesn't have an accent.

aceptable ADJETIVO
acceptable

aceptar VERBO
to accept ◇ *Acepté su invitación.* I accepted his invitation. ◇ *Aquí aceptan cheques de viaje.* Traveler's checks are accepted here. ◇ *Cuesta aceptar la derrota.* It's hard to accept defeat.
- **aceptar hacer algo** to agree to do something

la **acequia** SUSTANTIVO
irrigation channel

la **acera** SUSTANTIVO
sidewalk

acerca ADVERBIO
- **acerca de** about ◇ *un documental acerca de la fauna africana* a documentary about African wildlife

acercar* VERBO
[1] to pass ◇ *¿Me acercas los alicates?* Could you pass me the pliers?
[2] to bring over ◇ *Acerca la silla.* Bring your chair over here.
- **¿Acerco más la cama a la ventana?** Shall I put the bed nearer the window?
- **Nos acercaron al aeropuerto.** They gave us a lift to the airport.
- **acercarse (1)** to come closer ◇ *Acércate, que te vea.* Come closer so that I can see you.
- **acercarse (2)** to go over ◇ *Me acerqué a la ventana.* I went over to the window. ◇ *Acércate a la tienda y trae una botella de agua.* Go to the store and get a bottle of water.
- **Ya se acerca la Navidad.** Christmas is getting near.

el **acero** SUSTANTIVO
steel ◇ *acero inoxidable* stainless steel

acertar* VERBO
[1] to get...right (*pregunta, respuesta, solución*) ◇ *Acerté todas las respuestas.* I got all the answers right.
- **No acerté.** I got it wrong.
- **Creo que hemos acertado con estas cortinas.** I think these curtains were a good choice.

[2] to guess ◇ *Si aciertas cuántos caramelos hay, te los regalo todos.* If you guess how many candies there are, I'll give you all of them.
- **Acerté en el blanco.** I hit the target.

ácido ADJETIVO
acid

el **ácido** SUSTANTIVO
acid

acierto VERBO *ver* **acertar**

el **acierto** SUSTANTIVO
[1] right answer ◇ *Tuve más aciertos que errores en el examen.* I got more right answers than wrong ones in the exam.
[2] good idea ◇ *Fue un acierto ir de vacaciones a la montaña.* Going to the mountains on vacation was a good idea.

aclarar VERBO
to clear up ◇ *Necesito que me aclares unas dudas.* I need you to clear up some doubts for me. ◇ *No me iré hasta que no se aclare este asunto.* I won't go until this business is cleared up.
- **Con tantos números no me aclaro.** There are so many numbers that I can't get it straight.

el **acné** SUSTANTIVO
acne

acobardarse VERBO
- **No se acobarda por nada.** He isn't frightened by anything.

acogedor ADJETIVO (FEM **acogedora**)
cozy ◇ *un cuarto muy acogedor* a very cozy room

acoger* VERBO
to receive ◇ *La ciudad acoge todos los años a miles de visitantes.* The city receives

* Verbs marked with this symbol are irregular. See pages 346–348 for further details.

thousands of visitors every year.

◆ **Me acogieron muy bien en Estados Unidos.** I was made very welcome in the United States.

acomodado ADJETIVO
well-off

el **acomodador** SUSTANTIVO
usher

la **acomodadora** SUSTANTIVO
usherette

acompañar VERBO
[1] to come with ◇ *Si vas al centro te acompaño.* If you're going to the center of town I'll come with you.
[2] to go with ◇ *Me pidió que la acompañara a la estación.* She asked me to go to the station with her.

◆ **¿Quieres que te acompañe a casa?** Would you like me to see you home?
[3] to stay with ◇ *Me acompañó hasta que llegó el autobús.* He stayed with me until the bus arrived.

aconsejar VERBO
[1] to advise

◆ **aconsejar a alguien que haga algo** to advise somebody to do something

◆ **Te aconsejo que lo hagas.** I'd advise you to do it.
[2] to recommend ◇ *Debe de ser bueno cuando lo aconseja el médico.* It must be good if the doctor recommends it.

el **acontecimiento** SUSTANTIVO
event

acordar* VERBO
to agree on ◇ *Acordamos un precio y unas condiciones.* We agreed on a price and terms.

◆ **acordar hacer algo** to agree to do something

acordarse* VERBO
to remember ◇ *Ahora mismo no me acuerdo.* Right now I can't remember.

◆ **acordarse de** to remember ◇ *¿Te acuerdas de mí?* Do you remember me? ◇ *Acuérdate de cerrar la puerta con llave.* Remember to lock the door.

◆ **acordarse de haber hecho algo** to remember doing something

el **acordeón** SUSTANTIVO (PL los **acordeones**)
accordion

acostado ADJETIVO

◆ **estar* acostado** to be in bed

acostarse* VERBO
[1] to lie down (*para descansar*)
[2] to go to bed (*para dormir*)

◆ **acostarse con alguien** to go to bed with somebody

acostumbrarse VERBO

◆ **acostumbrarse a** to get used to ◇ *No me acostumbro a la vida en la ciudad.* I can't get used to city life.

◆ **acostumbrarse a hacer algo** to get used to doing something ◇ *Ya me he acostumbrado a trabajar de noche.* I've gotten used to working at night now.

el **acotamiento** SUSTANTIVO [Mexico]
shoulder (*en carretera*)

el/la **acróbata** SUSTANTIVO
acrobat

la **actitud** SUSTANTIVO
attitude

la **actividad** SUSTANTIVO
activity (PL activities)

activo ADJETIVO
active ◇ *Es una mujer muy activa.* She's a very active woman.

el **acto** SUSTANTIVO
[1] act ◇ *Romper el carnet fue un acto de rebeldía.* Tearing his ID card up was an act of rebellion.
[2] ceremony (PL ceremonies) ◇ *Grandes personalidades acudieron al acto.* There were some important people at the ceremony.

◆ **acto seguido** immediately afterwards ◇ *Acto seguido la gente echó a correr.* Immediately afterwards people began running.

◆ **en el acto** instantly

◆ **Te arreglan tus zapatos en el acto.** They will repair your shoes while you wait.

el **actor** SUSTANTIVO
actor

la **actriz** SUSTANTIVO (PL las **actrices**)
actress (PL actresses)

la **actuación** SUSTANTIVO (PL las **actuaciones**)
[1] performance ◇ *Fue una actuación muy buena.* It was a very good performance.
[2] gig ◇ *Esta noche tenemos una actuación en el Café del Mar.* Tonight we're doing a gig at the Café del Mar.

actual ADJETIVO
present ◇ *la situación actual del país* the country's present situation

◆ **uno de los mejores pintores del arte actual** one of the greatest painters of today

*No confundir con el inglés **actual**, que significa "de verdad".*

la **actualidad** SUSTANTIVO

◆ **un repaso a la actualidad nacional** a round-up of the national news

◆ **un tema de gran actualidad** a very topical issue

◆ **en la actualidad (1)** (*ahora*) currently ◇ *Hay en la actualidad más de dos millones de desempleados.* There are currently over two million unemployed.

◆ **en la actualidad (2)** (*hoy en día*) nowadays ◇ *Eso ya no ocurre en la actualidad.* That doesn't happen nowadays.

actualmente ADVERBIO
[1] nowadays (*hoy día*) ◇ *Actualmente apenas se utilizan las máquinas de escribir.* Typewriters are hardly used nowadays.
[2] currently (*ahora*) ◇ *Soy geólogo, pero*

☞

actualmente estoy sin trabajo. I'm a geologist, but I'm currently out of work.

*No confundir con el inglés **actually**, que significa "verdaderamente".*

actuar* VERBO

[1] to act ◇ *Es difícil actuar con naturalidad delante de las cámaras.* It's hard to act naturally in front of the cameras.

- **Hay que actuar con cautela.** We'll have to be cautious.
- **No comprendo tu forma de actuar.** I can't understand your behavior.
- **No actuó en esa película.** He wasn't in that movie.

[2] to perform (*grupo musical, teatral, humorista*) ◇ *Hoy actúan en el Café del Jazz.* Today they'll be performing at the Café del Jazz.

la **acuarela** SUSTANTIVO

watercolor

el **acuario** SUSTANTIVO

aquarium

Acuario SUSTANTIVO MASC

Aquarius ◇ *Soy acuario.* I'm an Aquarius.

acuático ADJETIVO

- **esquí acuático** water skiing
- **aves acuáticas** waterfowl PL

acudir VERBO

[1] to go ◇ *Acudieron en su ayuda.* They went to her aid. ◇ *Acudió a un amigo en busca de consejo.* He went to a friend for advice.

- **No tengo a quien acudir.** I have no one to turn to.
- **acudir a una cita** to keep an appointment

[2] to come ◇ *El perro acude cuando lo llamo.* The dog comes when I call.

acuerdo VERBO *ver* **acordar**

el **acuerdo** SUSTANTIVO

agreement ◇ *llegar a un acuerdo* to reach an agreement

- **estar* de acuerdo con alguien** to agree with somebody
- **ponerse* de acuerdo** to agree ◇ *Al final no nos pusimos de acuerdo.* In the end we couldn't agree. ◇ *Nos pusimos de acuerdo para prepararle una bienvenida.* We agreed to organize a welcome for him.
- **¡De acuerdo!** All right!

la **acupuntura** SUSTANTIVO

acupuncture

acurrucarse* VERBO

to curl up

acusar VERBO

[1] to accuse ◇ *Su novia lo acusaba de mentiroso.* His girlfriend accused him of being a liar.

- **Los otros te acusan a ti de haber roto el jarrón.** The others say it was you who broke the vase.

[2] to charge ◇ *Me acusan de homicidio.* They're charging me with homicide.

acústico ADJETIVO

acoustic ◇ *una guitarra acústica* an acoustic guitar

adaptar VERBO

to adapt ◇ *Es la misma receta pero adaptada.* It's the same recipe, but I've adapted it.

- **adaptarse** to adapt ◇ *No consigo adaptarme a la vida en el campo.* I can't seem to adapt to country life.

adecuado ADJETIVO

[1] suitable ◇ *No es la ropa más adecuada para ir de boda.* They aren't the most suitable clothes to wear to a wedding.

[2] right ◇ *Has entrado en el momento adecuado.* You've arrived at just the right moment. ◇ *el hombre adecuado para el puesto* the right man for the job

a. de J.C. ABREVIATURA (= *antes de Jesucristo*)

B.C. (= before Christ)

adelantado ADJETIVO

[1] advanced ◇ *Suecia es un país muy adelantado.* Sweden is a very advanced country.

- **los niños más adelantados de la clase** the children who are doing best in the class

[2] fast ◇ *Este reloj está adelantado.* This watch is fast.

- **pagar* por adelantado** to pay in advance

adelantar VERBO

[1] to bring...forward ◇ *Tuvimos que adelantar la boda.* We had to bring the wedding forward.

[2] to pass ◇ *Adelanta a ese camión cuando puedas.* Pass that truck when you can.

[3] to put...forward ◇ *El domingo hay que adelantar los relojes una hora.* On Sunday we'll have to put the clocks forward an hour.

- **Así no adelantas nada.** You won't get anywhere that way.
- **Tu reloj adelanta.** Your watch gains time.

adelantarse VERBO

to go on ahead ◇ *Me adelanté para agarrar asiento.* I went on ahead to get a seat.

- **adelantarse a alguien** to get ahead of somebody ◇ *Se nos adelantaron los de la competencia.* The competition got ahead of us.

adelante (1) ADVERBIO

forward ◇ *Se inclinó hacia adelante.* He leaned forward.

- **¿Nos vamos adelante para ver mejor?** Shall we sit near the front to get a better view?
- **más adelante (1)** (*más allá*) further on ◇ *El pueblo está más adelante.* The village is further on.
- **más adelante (2)** (*después*) later ◇ *Más adelante hablaremos de los resultados.* Later we'll discuss the results.

◆ **adelante de** in front of
◆ **Hay que seguir adelante.** We must go on.
◆ **de ahora en adelante** from now on

adelante (2) EXCLAMACIÓN
[1] come on! (*para animar*)
[2] come in! (*autorizando a entrar*)

el **adelanto** SUSTANTIVO
advance ◇ *los adelantos de la ciencia* the advances in science ◇ *Le pidió un adelanto a su jefe.* He asked his boss for an advance.

adelgazar* VERBO
to lose weight ◇ *¡Cómo has adelgazado!* What a lot of weight you've lost!
◆ **He adelgazado cinco kilos.** I've lost five kilos.

además ADVERBIO
[1] as well ◇ *Es profesor y además carpintero.* He's a teacher and a carpenter as well.
[2] what's more ◇ *El baño es demasiado pequeño y, además, no tiene ventana.* The bathroom's too small and, what's more, it hasn't got a window.
[3] besides ◇ *Además, no tienes nada que perder.* Besides, you've got nothing to lose.
◆ **además de** as well as ◇ *La computadora es, además de rápido, eficaz.* The computer is efficient as well as fast.

adentro ADVERBIO
inside ◇ *Empezó a llover y se metieron adentro.* It began to rain so they went inside.
◆ **tierra adentro** inland
◆ **adentro de** inside ◇ *desde adentro de la casa* from inside the house

adhesivo ADJETIVO
sticky ◇ *cinta adhesiva* sticky tape

el **adhesivo** SUSTANTIVO
sticker

la **adicción** SUSTANTIVO (PL las **adicciones**)
addiction

adicto ADJETIVO
addicted ◇ *Es adicto a la cafeína.* He is addicted to caffeine.

el **adicto**, la **adicta** SUSTANTIVO
addict ◇ *un adicto a las drogas* a drug addict

adinerado ADJETIVO
wealthy

adiós EXCLAMACIÓN
[1] goodbye! (*para despedirse*)
◆ **decir* adiós a alguien** to say goodbye to somebody
[2] hello! (*al pasar*)

el **aditivo** SUSTANTIVO
additive

la **adivinanza** SUSTANTIVO
guess (PL guesses)

adivinar VERBO
to guess ◇ *Adivina quién viene.* Guess who's coming.
◆ **adivinar el pensamiento a alguien** to read somebody's mind
◆ **adivinar el futuro** to see into the future

el **adjetivo** SUSTANTIVO
adjective

adjunto ADJETIVO
[1] enclosed (*en el mismo sobre*)
[2] attached (*con grapas, clips*)
[3] deputy ◇ *el director adjunto* the deputy head

la **administración** SUSTANTIVO (PL las **administraciones**)
[1] administration ◇ *Master de Administración de Empresas* Master of Business Administration
[2] civil service ◇ *Carmen trabaja en la administración.* Carmen works for the civil service.

el **administrador de Web**, la **administradora de Web** SUSTANTIVO
webmaster

administrativo ADJETIVO
administrative ◇ *gastos administrativos* administrative expenses
◆ **trabajo administrativo** clerical work

el **administrativo**, la **administrativa** SUSTANTIVO
clerk

la **admiración** SUSTANTIVO
[1] admiration ◇ *Siento profunda admiración por él.* I have great admiration for him.
[2] amazement ◇ *para admiración de todos* to everyone's amazement
◆ **Su franqueza causó admiración entre los presentes.** His frankness amazed everyone there.
◆ **signo de admiración** exclamation mark

admirar VERBO
to admire ◇ *Todos la admiran.* Everyone admires her.
◆ **Me admira lo poco que gastas en ropa.** I'm amazed at how little you spend on clothes.

admitir VERBO
[1] to admit ◇ *Admite que estabas equivocado.* Admit you were wrong.
[2] to accept ◇ *La máquina no admite monedas de 5 pesos.* The machine doesn't accept 5-peso coins.
◆ **Espero que me admitan en la universidad.** I hope I'll get into college.
[3] to allow in ◇ *Aquí no admiten perros.* Dogs aren't allowed in here.

el/la **adolescente** SUSTANTIVO
teenager

adonde CONJUNCIÓN
where
◆ **la ciudad adonde nos dirigimos** the city we're going to

adónde ADVERBIO
where ◇ *¿Adónde ibas?* Where were you going?

la **adopción** SUSTANTIVO (PL las **adopciones**)

☞

adoption

adoptar VERBO
to adopt

adoptivo ADJETIVO
- **un hijo adoptivo** an adopted child
- **mis padres adoptivos** my adoptive parents

adorar VERBO
1 to adore ◇ *Adora a sus hijos.* He adores his children.
2 to worship ◇ *adorar a Dios* to worship God

adornar VERBO
to decorate

el **adorno** SUSTANTIVO
1 ornament ◇ *Quitó los adornos de la estantería para limpiarla.* He took the ornaments off the shelf to clean it.
2 decoration ◇ *Habían puesto adornos en las calles.* Decorations had been put up in the streets. ◇ *Es sólo de adorno.* It's only for decoration.

adquirir* VERBO
to acquire ◇ *adquirir conocimientos de algo* to acquire a knowledge of something
- **adquirir velocidad** to gain speed
- **adquirir fama** to achieve fame
- **adquirir una vivienda** to purchase a property
- **adquirir importancia** to become important
- **Lo podrá adquirir en tiendas especializadas.** You'll be able to get it from specialist stores.

adrede ADVERBIO
on purpose

la **aduana** SUSTANTIVO
customs SING

el **aduanero,** la **aduanera** SUSTANTIVO
customs officer

el **adulto** SUSTANTIVO
adult
- **educación de adultos** adult education

el **adverbio** SUSTANTIVO
adverb

el **adversario,** la **adversaria** SUSTANTIVO
opponent

la **advertencia** SUSTANTIVO
warning

advertir* VERBO
1 to warn ◇ *Ya te advertí que no intervinieras.* I warned you not to get involved.
- **advertir a alguien de algo** to warn somebody about something
- **Te advierto que no va a ser nada fácil.** I must warn you that it won't be at all easy.

2 to notice ◇ *No advertí nada extraño en su comportamiento.* I didn't notice anything strange about his behavior.

aéreo ADJETIVO
air

***air** en este caso va siempre delante del sustantivo.*

◇ *un ataque aéreo* an air raid
- **por vía aérea** by air mail
- **una fotografía aérea** an aerial photograph

el **aerobic** SUSTANTIVO
aerobics SING

el **aerobics** SUSTANTIVO Mexico
aerobics SING

el **aeromozo,** la **aeromoza** SUSTANTIVO
flight attendant

el **aeropuerto** SUSTANTIVO
airport

el **aerosol** SUSTANTIVO
aerosol

el **afán** SUSTANTIVO (PL los **afanes**)
1 ambition (*deseo*) ◇ *Todo su afán era ser pintora.* Her great ambition was to be a painter.
2 effort (*empeño*)
- **Trabajan con mucho afán.** They put a lot of effort into their work.

afectado ADJETIVO
upset ◇ *Está muy afectado por la noticia.* He's very upset at the news.

afectar VERBO
to affect ◇ *Esto a ti no te afecta.* This doesn't affect you.
- **Me afectó mucho la noticia.** The news upset me terribly.

afectivo ADJETIVO
emotional ◇ *problemas afectivos* emotional problems

el **afecto** SUSTANTIVO
affection ◇ *Me cuesta demostrar* afecto.* I find it difficult to show affection.
- **tener* afecto a alguien** to be fond of somebody

afectuoso ADJETIVO
affectionate ◇ *Es un chico muy afectuoso.* He's a very affectionate boy.
- **"Un saludo afectuoso"** (*en cartas*) "With best wishes"

afeitar VERBO
to shave
- **afeitarse** to shave ◇ *Voy a afeitarme.* I'm going to shave.
- **Me afeité la barba.** I shaved off my beard.

Afganistán SUSTANTIVO MASC
Afghanistan

el **afiche** SUSTANTIVO
poster

la **afición** SUSTANTIVO (PL las **aficiones**)
1 hobby (PL hobbies) ◇ *Mi afición es la filatelia.* My hobby is stamp collecting. ◇ *por afición* as a hobby
- **Tengo mucha afición por el ciclismo.** I'm very keen on cycling.
- **En este país hay poca afición al teatro.** In this country people aren't very interested in the theater.

2 fans PL ◇ *la afición del River* fans of

* Verbs marked with this symbol are irregular. See pages 346–348 for further details.

River

aficionado ADJETIVO
1 keen ◇ *Es muy aficionada a la pintura.* She's very keen on painting.
2 amateur ◇ *un equipo de fútbol aficionado* an amateur soccer team

el **aficionado,** la **aficionada** SUSTANTIVO
1 enthusiast ◇ *un libro para los aficionados al bricolaje* a book for do-it-yourself enthusiasts
2 lover ◇ *los aficionados al teatro* theater lovers
3 amateur ◇ *un partido para aficionados* a game for amateurs

aficionarse VERBO
◆ **aficionarse a algo (1)** (*como participante*) to take up something ◇ *Raúl se aficionó al golf.* Raúl took up golf.
◆ **aficionarse a algo (2)** (*como espectador*) to become interested in something ◇ *Me he aficionado al teatro.* I've become interested in the theater.
◆ **Me he aficionado al chocolate suizo.** I've developed a taste for Swiss chocolate.

afilado ADJETIVO
sharp

afilar VERBO
to sharpen

afiliarse VERBO
◆ **afiliarse a algo** to join something

afinar VERBO
to tune ◇ *afinar un violín* to tune a violin

afirmar VERBO
◆ **afirmar que...** to say that... ◇ *Afirmaba que no la conocía.* He said that he didn't know her.
◆ **Afirma haberla visto aquella noche.** He says that he saw her that night.

afirmativo ADJETIVO
affirmative

aflojar VERBO
to loosen (*cuerda, corbata, tornillo*)
◆ **Tengo que aflojarme la corbata.** I must loosen my tie.
◆ **aflojarse** to come loose ◇ *Se aflojó un tornillo.* A screw has come loose.

el **afluente** SUSTANTIVO
tributary (PL tributaries)

afónico ADJETIVO
◆ **Estoy afónico.** I've lost my voice.

el **aforo** SUSTANTIVO
capacity (PL capacities) (*de teatro, cine*) ◇ *El teatro tiene un aforo de 2.000 personas.* The theater has a capacity of 2,000 people.

afortunadamente ADVERBIO
fortunately

afortunado ADJETIVO
lucky ◇ *Es un tipo afortunado.* He's a lucky guy.

África SUSTANTIVO FEM
Africa

el **africano,** la **africana** ADJETIVO, SUSTANTIVO
African

afrontar VERBO
to face up to ◇ *afrontar un problema* to face up to a problem

afuera ADVERBIO
outside ◇ *Vámonos afuera.* Let's go outside.
◆ **afuera de** outside

las **afueras** SUSTANTIVO
outskirts ◇ *En las afueras de Lima.* On the outskirts of Lima.
◆ **un barrio a las afueras de Los Ángeles** a Los Angeles suburb

agacharse VERBO
1 to crouch down (*en cuclillas*)
2 to bend down (*hacia delante*)

la **agarradera** SUSTANTIVO
handle

agarrado ADJETIVO
stingy (*coloquial*)

agarrar VERBO
1 to grab ◇ *Agarró al niño por el hombro.* He grabbed the child by the shoulder.
2 to hold ◇ *Agarra bien la sartén.* Hold the frying pan firmly.
3 to catch ◇ *Ya han agarrado al ladrón.* They've already caught the thief. ◇ *Agarré un buen resfriado.* I've caught an awful cold.
4 to take ◇ *Agarré otro pedazo de pastel.* I took another piece of cake.
◆ **agarrarse** to hold on ◇ *Agárrate a la barandilla.* Hold on to the rail.

la **agencia** SUSTANTIVO
agency (PL agencies) ◇ *una agencia de noticias* a news agency ◇ *una agencia de publicidad* an advertising agency
◆ **una agencia inmobiliaria** a real estate agency
◆ **una agencia de viajes** a travel agency

la **agenda** SUSTANTIVO
1 diary (PL diaries) (*de notas, trabajo*)
2 address book (*de direcciones, teléfonos*)
No confundir ***agenda*** *con la palabra inglesa* ***agenda.***

el/la **agente** SUSTANTIVO
agent (*secreto, de artistas*)
◆ **un agente de bolsa** a stockbroker
◆ **un agente de seguros** an insurance broker
◆ **un agente de policía** a police officer
◆ **un agente de tránsito** Mexico traffic cop

ágil ADJETIVO
agile

agitado ADJETIVO
hectic

agitar VERBO
1 to shake ◇ *Agítese antes de usar.* Shake before use.
2 to wave ◇ *Los bailarines agitaban los pañuelos.* The dancers were waving their handkerchiefs.

aglomerarse VERBO

◆ **La gente se aglomeraba a la entrada.** People were crowding around the entrance.

agobiante ADJETIVO
[1] stifling (*calor*)
[2] overwhelming (*situación*)
[3] exhausting (*trabajo*)

agobiar VERBO
◆ **Lo agobian sus problemas.** His problems are getting on top of him.

agosto SUSTANTIVO MASC
En inglés, los meses se escriben con mayúscula.
August ◇ *en agosto* in August ◇ *Nació el 8 de agosto.* He was born on August 8th.

agotado ADJETIVO
[1] exhausted ◇ *Estoy agotado.* I'm exhausted.
[2] sold out ◇ *Ese modelo en concreto está agotado.* That particular model is sold out.

agotador ADJETIVO (FEM **agotadora**)
exhausting

agotar VERBO
[1] to use up ◇ *Agotamos todas nuestras reservas.* We used up all our supplies.
[2] to tire out ◇ *Me agota tanto ejercicio.* All this exercise is tiring me out.
◆ **agotarse** to run out ◇ *Se está agotando la leña.* The firewood's running out.
◆ **Se agotaron todas las entradas.** The tickets sold out.

agradable ADJETIVO
nice

agradar VERBO
◆ **Esto no me agrada.** I don't like this.

agradecer* VERBO
◆ **agradecer algo a alguien** to thank somebody for something
◆ **Te agradezco tu interés.** Thank you for your interest.
◆ **Le agradecería me enviara...** I would be grateful if you would send me...

agradecido ADJETIVO
◆ **estar agradecido a alguien por algo** to be grateful to somebody for something

el **agrado** SUSTANTIVO
◆ **Lo haré con mucho agrado.** I'll gladly do it.

agrario ADJETIVO
agricultural

agredir VERBO
to attack

la **agresión** SUSTANTIVO (PL las **agresiones**)
[1] attack ◇ *una brutal agresión de dos jóvenes* a brutal attack on two young people
[2] aggression ◇ *un acto de agresión* an act of aggression

agresivo ADJETIVO
aggressive

agrícola ADJETIVO
agricultural

el **agricultor,** la **agricultora** SUSTANTIVO
farmer

la **agricultura** SUSTANTIVO
farming

agridulce ADJETIVO
sweet-and-sour

agrio ADJETIVO
[1] sour (*leche*)
[2] tart (*limón, vino*)

la **agrupación** SUSTANTIVO (PL las **agrupaciones**)
group

agrupar VERBO
[1] to group ◇ *agrupados en distintas categorías* grouped into different categories ◇ *Los insectos se agrupan en varias categorías.* Insects can be grouped into several categories.
[2] to bring together ◇ *una organización que agrupa a varios países* an organization which brings several countries together
◆ **Los ecologistas se han agrupado en varios partidos.** The ecologists have formed several parties.
◆ **Se agruparon en torno a su jefe.** They gathered round their boss.

el **agua** SUSTANTIVO FEM
water
◆ **agua corriente** running water
◆ **agua potable** drinking water
◆ **agua dulce** fresh water
◆ **agua salada** salt water
◆ **agua de colonia** cologne
◆ **agua oxigenada** peroxide

el **aguacate** SUSTANTIVO
avocado (PL avocados)

el/la **aguafiestas** SUSTANTIVO (PL los/las **aguafiestas**)
spoilsport

el **aguanieve** SUSTANTIVO FEM
sleet

aguantar VERBO
[1] to stand ◇ *No aguanto la ópera.* I can't stand opera. ◇ *Su vecina no la aguanta.* Her neighbor can't stand her.
[2] to take ◇ *La estantería no va a aguantar el peso.* The shelf won't take the weight. ◇ *¡No aguanto más!* I can't take any more!
[3] to hold ◇ *Aguántame el martillo un momento.* Can you hold the hammer for me for a moment? ◇ *Aguanta la respiración.* Hold your breath.
[4] to last ◇ *Este abrigo ya no aguanta otro invierno.* This coat won't last another winter.
◆ **No pude aguantar la risa.** I couldn't help laughing.
◆ **Últimamente estás que no hay quien te aguante.** You've been unbearable lately.
◆ **¿Puedes aguantarte hasta que lleguemos a casa?** Can you hold out until we get home?
◆ **Si no puede venir, que se aguante.** If he can't come, he'll just have to put up with it.

el **aguante** SUSTANTIVO
- **tener* aguante (1)** (*paciencia*) to be patient
- **tener* aguante (2)** (*resistencia*) to have stamina

agudo ADJETIVO
1 sharp (*oído, dolor*)
2 high-pitched (*sonido, voz*)
3 acute (*enfermedad*)
4 witty (*comentario*)

el **aguijón** SUSTANTIVO (PL los **aguijones**)
sting (*de avispa, escorpión*)

el **águila** SUSTANTIVO FEM
eagle

la **aguja** SUSTANTIVO
needle (*de coser, tocadiscos*)
- **las agujas del reloj** the hands of the clock

el **agujero** SUSTANTIVO
1 hole
- **hacer* un agujero** to make a hole

2 pocket (*en billar*)

la **agujeta** SUSTANTIVO *Mexico*
shoe lace

las **agujetas** SUSTANTIVO
- **tener* agujetas** to be stiff

ahí ADVERBIO
there ◇ *¡Ahí están!* There they are! ◇ *Ahí llega el tren.* There's the train.
- **Ahí está el problema.** That's the problem.
- **ahí arriba** up there
- **Están ahí dentro.** They're in there.
- **Lo tienes ahí mismo.** You've got it right there.
- **de ahí que** that's why
- **por ahí (1)** (*en ese lugar*) over there ◇ *Tú busca por ahí.* You look over there.
- **por ahí (2)** (*en algún lugar*) somewhere ◇ *Nos iremos por ahí a celebrarlo.* We'll go out somewhere to celebrate.
- **¿Las tijeras? Andarán por ahí.** The scissors? They must be somewhere around.
- **por ahí (3)** (*aproximadamente*) thereabouts ◇ *200 o por ahí* 200 or thereabouts

ahogarse* VERBO
1 to drown ◇ *Se ahogó en el río.* He drowned in the river.
2 to suffocate ◇ *Se ahogaron por falta de aire.* They suffocated for lack of air.
3 to get breathless ◇ *Me ahogo subiendo las cuestas.* I get breathless going uphill.

ahora ADVERBIO
now ◇ *¿Dónde vamos ahora?* Where are we going now?
- **Ahora te lo digo.** I'll tell you in a moment.
- **ahora mismo** right now ◇ *Ahora mismo está de viaje.* He's away on a trip right now.
- **Ahora mismo voy.** I'm just coming.
- **de ahora en adelante** from now on
- **hasta ahora (1)** so far ◇ *Hasta ahora nadie se ha quejado.* Nobody has complained so far.
- **hasta ahora (2)** till now ◇ *Hasta ahora nadie se había quejado.* Nobody had complained till now.
- **¡Hasta ahora!** See you shortly!
- **ahora bien** however ◇ *Aceptó las condiciones. Ahora bien, hace falta que las cumpla.* He accepted the conditions. However, he now needs to comply with them.
- **por ahora** for the moment ◇ *Por ahora no cambies nada.* Don't change anything for the moment.

ahorcar* VERBO
to hang
- **ahorcarse** to hang oneself

ahorita ADVERBIO
now

ahorrar VERBO
to save

los **ahorros** SUSTANTIVO
savings

ahumado ADJETIVO
smoked

el **aire** SUSTANTIVO
1 air ◇ *Necesitamos aire para respirar.* We need air to breathe.
- **aire acondicionado** air conditioning
- **tomar el aire** to get some fresh air

2 wind ◇ *El aire se le llevó el sombrero.* The wind blew his hat off.
- **Hace mucho aire.** It's very windy.
- **al aire libre (1)** outdoors ◇ *Comimos al aire libre.* We had lunch outdoors.
- **al aire libre (2)** outdoor ◇ *una fiesta al aire libre* an outdoor party

aislado ADJETIVO
isolated ◇ *Es un caso aislado.* It's an isolated case.
- **El pueblo estaba aislado por la nieve.** The village was cut off by the snow.

el **ajedrez** (PL los **ajedreces**) SUSTANTIVO
1 chess ◇ *jugar al ajedrez* to play chess
2 chess set ◇ *Tráete el ajedrez y echamos una partida.* Get the chess set and we'll have a game.

ajeno ADJETIVO
- **No respeta la opinión ajena.** He doesn't respect other people's opinions.
- **por razones ajenas a nuestra voluntad** for reasons beyond our control

ajetreado ADJETIVO
busy ◇ *Ha sido un día muy ajetreado.* It has been a very busy day.

el **ají** SUSTANTIVO
chili sauce

el **ajo** SUSTANTIVO
garlic

ajustado ADJETIVO
tight ◇ *Lleva ropa muy ajustada.* He wears very tight clothes. ◇ *La falda me queda un poco ajustada.* The skirt's a bit tight on me.

ajustar VERBO
1 to adjust ◇ *Hay que ajustar los frenos.* The brakes need adjusting.

☞

2 to tighten ◇ *Ajusté bien todas las tuercas.* I tightened up all the nuts.
3 to fit ◇ *Esta puerta no ajusta bien.* This door doesn't fit very well.
◆ **ajustarse a (1)** to fit in with ◇ *Tendremos que ajustarnos al horario previsto.* We'll have to fit in with the program. ◇ *Tu versión no se ajusta a la realidad.* Your version doesn't fit in with the facts.
◆ **ajustarse a (2)** to keep to ◇ *Nos ajustaremos al presupuesto.* We'll keep to the budget.

al PREPOSICIÓN
(*= a + el*) *ver* **a**

el **ala** SUSTANTIVO FEM
1 wing (*de ave, avión*)
2 brim (*de sombrero*)

alabar VERBO
to praise

la **alambrada** SUSTANTIVO
fence ◇ *una alambrada eléctrica* an electric fence

el **alambre** SUSTANTIVO
wire

el **álamo** SUSTANTIVO
poplar

alardear VERBO
◆ **alardear de algo** to boast about something

el **alargador** SUSTANTIVO
extension cord

alargar* VERBO
1 to lengthen ◇ *Hay que alargar un poco las mangas.* We'll need to lengthen the sleeves a little.
2 to extend ◇ *Van a alargar esta línea de metro.* This subway line is going to be extended. ◇ *Decidieron alargar las vacaciones.* They decided to extend their vacation.
3 to stretch out ◇ *Alargué el brazo para apagar la luz.* I stretched out my arm to put out the light.
4 to pass ◇ *¿Me alargas la llave inglesa?* Will you pass me the wrench?
◆ **alargarse (1)** to get longer ◇ *Ya van alargándose los días.* The days are getting longer.
◆ **alargarse (2)** to go on ◇ *La fiesta se alargó hasta el amanecer.* The party went on into the early hours.

la **alarma** SUSTANTIVO
alarm ◇ *Sonó la alarma.* The alarm went off.
◆ **dar* la voz de alarma** to raise the alarm
◆ **alarma de incendios** fire alarm

el **alba** SUSTANTIVO FEM
dawn
◆ **al alba** at dawn

el/la **albañil** SUSTANTIVO
1 builder (*más cualificado*)
2 bricklayer (*que sólo pone ladrillos*)

el **albaricoque** SUSTANTIVO
apricot

la **alberca** SUSTANTIVO Mexico
swimming pool

el **albergue** SUSTANTIVO
1 mountain refuge (*de montaña*)
2 hostel (*para gente sin hogar*)
◆ **un albergue juvenil** a youth hostel

las **albóndigas** SUSTANTIVO
meatballs

el **alboroto** SUSTANTIVO
racket ◇ *¡Vaya alboroto que estaban montando los niños!* What a racket the kids were making!

el **álbum** SUSTANTIVO (PL los **álbumes**)
album

la **alcachofa** SUSTANTIVO
1 artichoke (*verdura*)
2 shower head (*de ducha*)
3 rose (*de regadera*)

el **alcalde,** la **alcaldesa** SUSTANTIVO
mayor

el **alcance** SUSTANTIVO
1 range (*de arma, cohete*) ◇ *misiles de largo alcance* long-range missiles
2 scale (*de problema*) ◇ *Se desconoce el alcance de la catástrofe.* The scale of the disaster isn't yet known.
◆ **Está al alcance de todos.** It's within everybody's reach.

la **alcantarilla** SUSTANTIVO
1 sewer (*para residuos*)
2 drain (*para la lluvia*)
◆ **una boca de alcantarilla** a manhole

alcanzar* VERBO
1 to catch up with ◇ *La alcancé cuando salía por la puerta.* I caught up with her just as she was going out the door.
2 to reach ◇ *alcanzar la cima de la montaña* to reach the top of the mountain
3 to find ◇ *alcanzar la fama* to find fame
4 to pass ◇ *¿Me alcanzas las tijeras?* Could you pass me the scissors?
◆ **Con dos botellas alcanzará para todos.** Two bottles will be enough for all of us.

la **alcoba** SUSTANTIVO
bedroom
*No confundir con el inglés **alcove**, que significa "hueco en la pared".*

el **alcohol** SUSTANTIVO
alcohol
◆ **cerveza sin alcohol** non-alcoholic beer

alcohólico ADJETIVO
alcoholic

la **aldea** SUSTANTIVO
village

el **aldeano,** la **aldeana** SUSTANTIVO
villager

alegrar VERBO
to cheer up ◇ *Intenté alegrarlos con unos*

chistes. I tried to cheer them up with a few jokes.
- **Me alegra que hayas venido.** I'm glad you've come.
- **alegrarse** to be glad ◇ *¿Te gusta? Me alegro.* You like it? I'm glad.
- **alegrarse de algo** to be glad about something ◇ *Me alegro de tu ascenso.* I'm glad about your promotion.
- **Me alegro de oír que estás bien.** I'm glad to hear that you're well.
- **alegrarse por alguien** to be happy for somebody ◇ *Me alegro por ti.* I'm happy for you.

alegre ADJETIVO
cheerful (*tela, música, carácter*)
- **Estoy muy alegre.** I'm feeling very happy.

la **alegría** SUSTANTIVO
- **Sentí una gran alegría.** I was really happy.
- **¡Qué alegría!** How lovely!

alejarse VERBO
to move away ◇ *Aléjate un poco del fuego.* Move a bit further away from the fire.
- **El barco se iba alejando de la costa.** The boat was getting further and further away from the coast.

el **alemán,** la **alemana** ADJETIVO, SUSTANTIVO
(MASC PL los **alemanes**)
German

el **alemán** SUSTANTIVO
German (*idioma*)

Alemania SUSTANTIVO FEM
Germany

alentador ADJETIVO (FEM **alentadora**)
encouraging

la **alergia** SUSTANTIVO
allergy (PL allergies)
- **la alergia al polen** hay fever

la **alerta** ADJETIVO, SUSTANTIVO, ADVERBIO
alert
- **dar* la alerta** to give the alert
- **estar* alerta** to be alert

la **aleta** SUSTANTIVO
1 fin (*de pez*)
2 flipper (*para bucear*)
3 wing (*de automóvil*)

el **alfabeto** SUSTANTIVO
alphabet

la **alfarería** SUSTANTIVO
pottery (PL potteries)

el **alfarero,** la **alfarera** SUSTANTIVO
potter

el **alféizar** SUSTANTIVO
windowsill

el **alfil** SUSTANTIVO
bishop

el **alfiler** SUSTANTIVO
pin

la **alfombra** SUSTANTIVO
1 rug (*pequeña*)
2 carpet (*más grande*)

la **alfombrilla** SUSTANTIVO
mat

las **algas** SUSTANTIVO
seaweed SING

algo (1) PRONOMBRE
1 something
En oraciones afirmativas y en preguntas si se espera una respuesta afirmativa.
◇ *Algo se está quemando.* Something is burning. ◇ *¿Quieres algo de comer?* Would you like something to eat? ◇ *¿Te pasa algo?* Is something the matter?
- **Aún queda algo de café.** There's still some coffee left.

2 anything
En preguntas en general.
◇ *¿Algo más?* Anything else? ◇ *¿Has visto algo que te guste?* Have you seen anything you like?
- **algo así como** a bit like ◇ *Es algo así como una nave espacial.* It's a bit like a spaceship.
- **o algo así** or something of the sort
- **Por algo será.** There must be a reason for it.

algo (2) ADVERBIO
rather ◇ *La falda te queda algo corta, pero puede servir.* The skirt's rather short on you, but it may be all right.

el **algodón** SUSTANTIVO (PL los **algodones**)
cotton ◇ *ropa de algodón* cotton clothes
- **Me puse algodones en los oídos.** I put some cotton in my ears.

alguien PRONOMBRE
1 somebody
En oraciones afirmativas y en preguntas si se espera una respuesta afirmativa.
◇ *Alguien llama a la puerta.* There's somebody knocking at the door.
◇ *¿Necesitas que te ayude alguien?* Do you need somebody to help you?

2 anybody
En preguntas en general.
◇ *¿Conoces a alguien aquí?* Do you know anybody here?

algún ADJETIVO (FEM **alguna**, MASC PL **algunos**)
1 some
En oraciones afirmativas.
◇ *Algún día iré.* I'll go there some day.

2 any
*Se usa **any** en preguntas, con un sustantivo en plural.*
◇ *¿Compraste algún cuadro?* Did you buy any pictures?
- **¿Quieres alguna cosa más?** Was there anything else?
- **algún que otro...** the odd... ◇ *He leído algún que otro libro sobre el tema.* I've read the odd book on the subject.

alguno PRONOMBRE (FEM **alguna**)
1 somebody ◇ *Siempre hay alguno que se queja.* There's always somebody who complains.
- **Algunos piensan que no ocurrió así.** Some ☞

people think that it didn't happen like that.
2 one ◇ *Tiene que haber sido alguno de ellos.* It must have been one of them.
◇ *Tiene que estar en alguna de estas cajas.* It must be in one of these boxes.
3 some ◇ *Son tantas maletas que alguna siempre se pierde.* There are so many suitcases that some inevitably get lost.
◆ **Sólo conozco a algunos de los vecinos.** I only know some of the neighbors.
4 any ◇ *Necesito una aspirina. ¿Te queda alguna?* I need an aspirin. Do you have any left? ◇ *Si alguno quiere irse que se vaya.* If any of them want to leave, fine. ◇ *¿Lo sabe alguno de ustedes?* Do any of you know?

el **aliado,** la **aliada** SUSTANTIVO
ally (PL allies)

la **alianza** SUSTANTIVO
1 alliance ◇ *formar una alianza* to form an alliance
2 wedding ring (*anillo*)

aliarse* VERBO
◆ **aliarse con alguien** to form an alliance with somebody

los **alicates** SUSTANTIVO
pliers

el **aliento** SUSTANTIVO
breath ◇ *Tengo mal aliento.* I've got bad breath.
◆ **Llegué sin aliento.** I arrived out of breath.

aligerar VERBO
to make...lighter ◇ *aligerar la carga del barco* to make the cargo lighter
◆ **¡Aligera o llegaremos tarde!** Hurry up or we'll be late!

la **alimentación** SUSTANTIVO
diet ◇ *Hay que cuidar la alimentación.* You need to be sensible about your diet.
◆ **una tienda de alimentación** a grocer's shop

alimentar VERBO
to feed ◇ *alimentar a un niño* to feed a child
◆ **Esto no alimenta.** That's not very nutritious.
◆ **alimentarse de algo** to live on something

el **alimento** SUSTANTIVO
food
◆ **alimentos congelados** frozen food SING
◆ **Las legumbres tienen mucho alimento.** Pulses are very nutritious.

la **alineación** SUSTANTIVO (PL las **alineaciones**)
line-up

aliñar VERBO
to season

el **aliño** SUSTANTIVO
dressing

aliviar VERBO
to make...better ◇ *El jarabe te aliviará la tos.* The syrup will make your cough better.
◇ *Estas pastillas te aliviarán.* These pills will make you better.

el **alivio** SUSTANTIVO
relief
◆ **¡Qué alivio!** What a relief!

allá ADVERBIO
there ◇ *allá arriba* up there
◆ **más allá** further on
◆ **Échate un poco más allá.** Move over that way a bit.
◆ **más allá de** beyond
◆ **¡Allá tú!** That's up to you!
◆ **el más allá** the next world

allanar VERBO
to level

allí ADVERBIO
there ◇ *Allí está.* There it is.
◆ **Allí viene tu hermana.** Here comes your sister.
◆ **allí abajo** down there
◆ **allí mismo** right there
◆ **Marta es de por allí.** Marta comes from somewhere around there.

el **alma** SUSTANTIVO FEM
soul
◆ **Lo siento en el alma.** I'm really sorry.

el **almacén** SUSTANTIVO (PL los **almacenes**)
store
◆ **unos grandes almacenes** a department store

almacenar VERBO
to store

la **almeja** SUSTANTIVO
clam

la **almendra** SUSTANTIVO
almond

el **almíbar** SUSTANTIVO
syrup
◆ **en almíbar** in syrup

el **almirante** SUSTANTIVO
admiral

la **almohada** SUSTANTIVO
pillow

la **almohadilla** SUSTANTIVO
cushion

almorzar* VERBO
to have lunch ◇ *No he almorzado todavía.* I haven't had lunch yet.
◆ **¿Qué almorzaste?** What did you have for lunch?

almuerzo VERBO *ver* **almorzar**

el **almuerzo** SUSTANTIVO
lunch (PL lunches)

aló EXCLAMACIÓN
hello!

alocado ADJETIVO
crazy ◇ *una decisión alocada* a crazy decision
◆ **una chica un poco alocada** a rather silly girl

el **alojamiento** SUSTANTIVO
accommodations

alojarse VERBO
to stay ◇ *¿Dónde se alojan?* Where are you staying?

la **alpargata** SUSTANTIVO
a type of sandal

los **Alpes** SUSTANTIVO
the Alps

el **alpinismo** SUSTANTIVO
mountaineering

el/la **alpinista** SUSTANTIVO
mountaineer

alquilar VERBO
1 to rent (1) (*el inquilino*) ◇ *Alquilaremos un apartamento en la playa.* We'll rent an apartment near the beach.
2 to rent (2) (*carro, bicicleta, traje*) ◇ *Alquilamos un carro.* We rented a car.
◆ **"se alquila"** "for rent"
3 to let (*el dueño*) ◇ *Alquilan habitaciones a estudiantes.* They let rooms to students.

el **alquiler** SUSTANTIVO
rent ◇ *pagar el alquiler* to pay the rent
◆ **un departamento de alquiler** a rented apartment
◆ **un carro de alquiler** a rental car
◆ **alquiler de automóviles** car rental

alrededor ADVERBIO
◆ **alrededor de (1)** around ◇ *El satélite gira alrededor de la Tierra.* The satellite goes around the Earth. ◇ *A su alrededor todos gritaban.* Everybody around him was shouting.
◆ **alrededor de (2)** about ◇ *Deben de ser alrededor de las dos.* It must be about two o'clock.

los **alrededores** SUSTANTIVO
◆ **Ocurrió en los alrededores de Caracas.** It happened near Caracas.
◆ **Hay muchas tiendas en los alrededores del museo.** There are a lot of stores in the area around the museum.

el **alta** SUSTANTIVO FEM
◆ **dar* de alta a alguien** (*en hospital*) to discharge somebody
◆ **darse* de alta** (*en club, asociación*) to join

el **altar** SUSTANTIVO
altar

el **altavoz** SUSTANTIVO (PL los **altavoces**)
loudspeaker

alterar VERBO
to change ◇ *Alteraron el orden.* They changed the order.
◆ **alterar el orden público** to cause a breach of the peace
◆ **alterarse** to get upset ◇ *¡No te alteres!* Don't get upset!

alternar VERBO
◆ **alternar algo con algo** to alternate something with something
◆ **Alterna con gente del teatro.** He mixes with people from the theater.

la **alternativa** SUSTANTIVO
alternative
◆ **No tenemos otra alternativa.** We have no alternative.

alterno ADJETIVO
alternate ◇ *en días alternos* on alternate days
◆ **corriente alterna** alternating current

los **altibajos** SUSTANTIVO
ups and downs ◇ *tener altibajos* to have ups and downs

la **altitud** SUSTANTIVO
altitude

alto (1) ADJETIVO
1 tall ◇ *Es un chico muy alto.* He's a very tall boy. ◇ *un edificio muy alto* a very tall building
2 high ◇ *Sacó notas altas en todos los exámenes.* He got high grades in all his exams.
◆ **El Everest es la montaña más alta del mundo.** Everest is the highest mountain in the world.
3 loud ◇ *La música está demasiado alta.* The music's too loud.
◆ **a altas horas de la noche** in the middle of the night
◆ **Celebraron la victoria por todo lo alto.** They celebrated the victory in style.
◆ **alta fidelidad** high fidelity
◆ **una familia de clase alta** an upper-class family

alto (2) ADVERBIO
high ◇ *subir muy alto* to go up very high
◆ **Pepe habla muy alto.** Pepe has got a very loud voice.
◆ **¡Más alto, por favor!** Speak up, please!
◆ **Pon el volumen más alto.** Turn the volume up.

el **alto** SUSTANTIVO
◆ **La pared tiene dos metros de alto.** The wall is two meters high.
◆ **en lo alto de** at the top of
◆ **hacer* un alto** to stop ◇ *A las dos haremos un alto para comer.* We'll stop to have lunch at two o'clock.
◆ **pasar algo por alto** to overlook something
◆ **el alto el fuego** ceasefire

alto (4) EXCLAMACIÓN
stop!

el **altoparlante** SUSTANTIVO
loudspeaker

la **altura** SUSTANTIVO
height ◇ *Volamos a una altura de 15.000 pies.* We're flying at a height of 15,000 feet.
◆ **La pared tiene dos metros de altura.** The wall's two meters high.
◆ **cuando llegues a la altura del hospital** when you reach the hospital
◆ **a estas alturas** at this stage ◇ *A estas alturas no podemos hacer nada.* There's nothing we can do at this stage.

el **alud** SUSTANTIVO
avalanche

aludir VERBO

to refer ◇ *No aludió a lo del otro día.* He didn't refer to that business the other day.
◆ **No se dio por aludida.** She didn't take the hint.

el **aluminio** SUSTANTIVO
aluminum

el **alumno,** la **alumna** SUSTANTIVO
pupil

la **alusión** SUSTANTIVO (PL las **alusiones**)
◆ **hacer* alusión a** to refer to

el **alza** SUSTANTIVO FEM
rise ◇ *un alza de los precios* a rise in prices
◆ **El balonmano es un deporte en alza.** Handball is becoming increasingly popular.

alzar* VERBO
to raise ◇ *alzar la voz* to raise one's voice
◆ **alzarse** to rise ◇ *Se alzó el telón.* The curtain rose.
◆ **alzarse en armas** to take up arms

el **ama** SUSTANTIVO FEM
owner
◆ **ama de casa** housewife
◆ **ama de llaves** housekeeper

amable ADJETIVO
kind
◆ **Es usted muy amable.** You're very kind.

amamantar VERBO
1 to breast-feed (*niño*)
2 to suckle (*animal*)

amanecer* VERBO
1 to get light ◇ *Amanece a las siete.* It gets light at seven.
2 to wake up ◇ *El niño amaneció con fiebre.* The boy woke up with a temperature.

el **amanecer** SUSTANTIVO
dawn

el/la **amante** SUSTANTIVO
lover
◆ **amantes del cine** movie lovers

la **amapola** SUSTANTIVO
poppy (PL poppies)

amar VERBO
to love

amargado ADJETIVO
bitter
◆ **estar* amargado por algo** to be bitter about something

amargar* VERBO
to spoil ◇ *Ya me amargaron la tarde.* You've spoiled my evening.
◆ **amargar la vida a alguien** to make somebody's life a misery
◆ **amargarse** to get upset ◇ *No te amargues por tan poca cosa.* It's not worth getting upset about such a little thing.

amargo ADJETIVO
bitter

el **amarillo** ADJETIVO, SUSTANTIVO
yellow
◆ **la prensa amarilla** the gutter press

amarrar VERBO
1 to moor (*barco*)
2 to tie up (*animal, persona*)
3 to do up ◇ *Se amarró los zapatos.* He did up his shoes.

el/la **amateur** ADJETIVO, SUSTANTIVO (PL los/las **amateurs**)
amateur

el **Amazonas** SUSTANTIVO
the Amazon

el **ámbar** SUSTANTIVO
amber

la **ambición** SUSTANTIVO (PL las **ambiciones**)
ambition

ambicioso ADJETIVO
ambitious

el **ambientador** SUSTANTIVO
air freshener

el **ambiente** SUSTANTIVO
atmosphere ◇ *Se respira un ambiente tenso.* There's a tense atmosphere.
◆ **Había un ambiente muy cargado en la habitación.** It was very stuffy in the room.
◆ **Necesito cambiar de ambiente.** I need a change of scene.
◆ **el medio ambiente** the environment

ambiguo ADJETIVO
ambiguous

el **ámbito** SUSTANTIVO
scope

ambos PRONOMBRE (FEM **ambas**)
both ◇ *Vinieron ambos.* They both came. ◇ *Ambos tienen los ojos azules.* You've both got blue eyes.

la **ambulancia** SUSTANTIVO
ambulance

el **ambulatorio** SUSTANTIVO *Spain*
out-patient department

amén EXCLAMACIÓN
amen

amenace VERBO *ver* **amenazar**

la **amenaza** SUSTANTIVO
threat

amenazar* VERBO
to threaten
◆ **amenazar a alguien con hacer algo** to threaten to do something ◇ *Lo amenazó con decírselo al profesor.* He threatened to tell the teacher.

ameno ADJETIVO
enjoyable

América SUSTANTIVO FEM
the Americas (*continente*)
◆ **América Central** Central America
◆ **América Latina** Latin America
◆ **América del Sur** South America
◆ **el español de América** Latin American Spanish

la **americana** SUSTANTIVO
1 American (*persona*)

[2] jacket (*chaqueta*) [Spain]

el **americano** ADJETIVO, SUSTANTIVO
American

la **ametralladora** SUSTANTIVO
machine gun

las **amígdalas** SUSTANTIVO
tonsils

el **amigo,** la **amiga** SUSTANTIVO
friend
- **hacerse* amigos** to become friends
- **ser* muy amigos** to be good friends

la **amistad** SUSTANTIVO
friendship
- **hacer* amistad con alguien** to make friends with somebody
- **las amistades** friends

amistoso ADJETIVO
friendly

el **amo** SUSTANTIVO
owner ◇ *el amo del perro* the dog's owner

amontonar VERBO
to pile up
- **Se me amontona el trabajo.** My work's piling up.

el **amor** SUSTANTIVO
love
- **hacer* el amor** to make love
- **amor propio** self-esteem

amoratado ADJETIVO
[1] blue (*por el frío*)
[2] black and blue (*por los golpes*)

amortiguar* VERBO
[1] to cushion (*golpe*)
[2] to muffle (*ruido*)

ampliar* VERBO
[1] to expand (*negocio*)
[2] to enlarge (*fotografía*)
[3] to extend (*plazo, local*)

el **amplificador** SUSTANTIVO
amplifier

amplio ADJETIVO
[1] wide ◇ *una calle muy amplia* a very wide street
[2] spacious ◇ *una habitación amplia* a spacious room
[3] loose ◇ *ropa amplia* loose clothing

la **ampolla** SUSTANTIVO
blister

amputar VERBO
to amputate

amueblar VERBO
to furnish ◇ *un departamento amueblado* a furnished apartment ◇ *un departamento sin amueblar* an unfurnished apartment

analfabeto ADJETIVO
illiterate

el **analgésico** SUSTANTIVO
painkiller

el **análisis** SUSTANTIVO (PL los **análisis**)
[1] analysis (*estudio*) (PL analyses) ◇ *un análisis de la situación* an analysis of the situation
[2] test (*prueba*) ◇ *un análisis de sangre* a blood test

analizar* VERBO
to analyze

la **anarquía** SUSTANTIVO
anarchy

la **anatomía** SUSTANTIVO
anatomy

ancho ADJETIVO
[1] wide ◇ *una calle ancha* a wide street
[2] loose ◇ *Le gusta llevar ropa ancha.* He likes to wear loose clothing.
- **Me queda ancho el vestido.** The dress is too big for me.
- **Es ancho de espaldas.** He's broad-shouldered.

el **ancho** SUSTANTIVO
width ◇ *el ancho de la tela* the width of the cloth
- **¿Cuánto mide de ancho?** How wide is it?
- **Mide tres metros de ancho.** It's three meters wide.
- **Le hice un corte a lo ancho.** I cut it crossways.

la **anchoa** SUSTANTIVO
anchovy

la **anchura** SUSTANTIVO
width ◇ *Midió la anchura de la mesa.* He measured the width of the table.
- **¿Qué anchura tiene?** How wide is it?
- **Tiene tres metros de anchura.** It's three meters wide.

la **anciana** SUSTANTIVO
elderly woman

anciano ADJETIVO
elderly

el **anciano** SUSTANTIVO
elderly man
- **los ancianos** the elderly

el **ancla** SUSTANTIVO FEM
anchor

anda EXCLAMACIÓN
[1] hey! ◇ *¡Anda, un billete de $10!* Hey, a $10 bill!
[2] come on (*para animar*) ◇ *¡Anda, ponte el abrigo y vámonos!* Come on, put your coat on and let's go!
- **¡Anda ya!** You're not serious!

el **andamio** SUSTANTIVO
scaffolding ◇ *Ya quitaron los andamios.* They've taken the scaffolding down now.

andar* VERBO
[1] to walk (*caminar*) ◇ *Anduvimos varios millas.* We walked several miles.
- **Iremos andando a la estación.** We'll walk to the station.

[2] to be ◇ *Últimamente ando muy ocupado.* I've been very busy lately. ◇ *No sé por dónde anda.* I don't know where he is. ◇ *¿Qué tal andas?* How are you? ◇ *Ando buscando un socio.* I'm looking for a partner. ☞

- **andar mal de dinero** to be short of money
- **Anda por los cuarenta.** He's about forty.
- **Siempre andan a gritos.** They're always shouting.

[3] to go (*funcionar*) ◇ *Este reloj anda muy bien.* This watch goes very well.

- **¡No andes ahí!** Keep away from there!
- **Ándate con cuidado.** Take care.

el **andén** SUSTANTIVO (PL los **andenes**)
platform

los **Andes** SUSTANTIVO
the Andes

el **andinismo** SUSTANTIVO
mountaineering

el/la **andinista** SUSTANTIVO
mountaineer

anduve VERBO *ver* **andar**

la **anécdota** SUSTANTIVO
anecdote

la **anemia** SUSTANTIVO
anemia

la **anestesia** SUSTANTIVO
anesthetic

- **poner* anestesia a alguien** to give somebody an anesthetic

el **anfiteatro** SUSTANTIVO
[1] amphitheater (*romano*)
[2] lecture hall (*para clases*)

el **ángel** SUSTANTIVO
angel

las **anginas** SUSTANTIVO

- **tener* anginas** to have tonsillitis

el **anglosajón,** la **anglosajona** ADJETIVO, SUSTANTIVO (MASC PL los **anglosajones**)
Anglo-Saxon

el **ángulo** SUSTANTIVO
angle

- **en ángulo recto** at right angles

el **anillo** SUSTANTIVO
ring ◇ *un anillo de boda* a wedding ring

animado ADJETIVO
[1] cheerful ◇ *Últimamente parece que está más animada.* She has seemed more cheerful lately.
[2] lively ◇ *una fiesta animada* a lively party

- **dibujos animados** cartoons

el **animador,** la **animadora** SUSTANTIVO
[1] entertainment officer (*en centro turístico*)
[2] animator (*gráfico*)

el **animal** SUSTANTIVO
animal

- **los animales domésticos** pets

animar VERBO
[1] to cheer up ◇ *Lo ha pasado muy mal y necesita que la animen.* She has had a rough time and needs cheering up.
[2] to cheer on ◇ *Estuvimos animando al equipo.* We were cheering the team on.
[3] to liven up ◇ *Sus chistes animaron la fiesta.* His jokes livened up the party.

- **animar a alguien a que haga algo** to encourage somebody to do something
- **animarse** to cheer up ◇ *¡Vamos, anímate!* Come on, cheer up!
- **animarse a hacer algo** to make up one's mind to do something

el **ánimo** SUSTANTIVO

- **Está muy mal de ánimo.** He's in very low spirits.
- **dar* ánimos a alguien (1)** (*si está triste*) to cheer somebody up
- **dar* ánimos a alguien (2)** (*si necesita apoyo*) to give somebody moral support
- **tener* ánimos para hacer algo** to feel like doing something

ánimo EXCLAMACIÓN
cheer up! ◇ *¡Ánimo, que no es el fin del mundo!* Cheer up, it's not the end of the world!

el **anís** SUSTANTIVO (PL los **anises**)
anisette (*licor*)

el **aniversario** SUSTANTIVO
anniversary (PL anniversaries) ◇ *su aniversario de boda* their wedding anniversary

anoche ADVERBIO
last night

- **antes de anoche** the night before last

anochecer* VERBO
to get dark ◇ *En invierno anochece muy temprano.* It gets dark very early in winter.

anónimo ADJETIVO
anonymous

el **anónimo** SUSTANTIVO
anonymous threat

el **anorak** SUSTANTIVO (PL los **anoraks**)
anorak

anormal ADJETIVO
odd ◇ *Yo no noté nada anormal en su comportamiento.* I didn't notice anything odd about his behavior.

anotar VERBO
[1] to take a note of ◇ *Anota mi dirección.* Take a note of my address.
[2] to score ◇ *Jones anotó 34 puntos.* Jones scored 34 points.

la **ansiedad** SUSTANTIVO
anxiety

ansioso ADJETIVO

- **estar* ansioso por hacer algo** to be eager to do something

el **Antártico** SUSTANTIVO
the Antarctic

ante PREPOSICIÓN
[1] before ◇ *Le da vergüenza aparecer ante tanta gente.* She's shy about appearing before so many people.
[2] in the face of ◇ *Mantuvo la calma ante el peligro.* He remained calm in the face of danger.

el **ante** SUSTANTIVO
suede

anteanoche ADVERBIO
the night before last

anteayer ADVERBIO
the day before yesterday

los **antecedentes** SUSTANTIVO
◆ **antecedentes penales** criminal record SING

la **antelación** SUSTANTIVO
◆ **hacer* una reserva con antelación** to make an advance booking
◆ **Deben avisarte con un mes de antelación.** They must give you a month's notice.

antemano ADVERBIO
◆ **de antemano** in advance ◇ *Yo lo sabía de antemano.* I knew in advance.

la **antena** SUSTANTIVO
aerial (*de radio, televisión*)
◆ **una antena parabólica** a satellite dish

los **anteojos** SUSTANTIVO
glasses
◆ **los anteojos de sol** sunglasses

los **antepasados** SUSTANTIVO
ancestors

anterior ADJETIVO (FEM **anterior**)
1 before ◇ *La semana anterior llovió mucho.* It rained a lot the week before. ◇ *Su boda fue anterior a la nuestra.* Their wedding was before ours.
2 front ◇ *las extremidades anteriores* the front limbs

anteriormente ADVERBIO
previously

antes ADVERBIO
1 before ◇ *Esta película ya la he visto antes.* I've seen this movie before. ◇ *Él estaba aquí antes que yo.* He was here before me. ◇ *la noche antes* the night before
◆ **El supermercado está justo antes del semáforo.** The supermarket is just before the lights.
◆ **antes de** before ◇ *antes de la cena* before dinner ◇ *antes de ir al teatro* before going to the theater ◇ *antes de que te vayas* before you go
2 first ◇ *Nosotros llegamos antes.* We arrived first.
◆ **Antes no había tanto desempleo.** There didn't use to be so much unemployment.
◆ **cuanto antes mejor** sooner, the better
◆ **lo antes posible** as soon as possible
◆ **antes de nada** first and foremost
◆ **Antes que verlo prefiero esperar aquí.** I'd rather wait here than see him.

el **antibiótico** SUSTANTIVO
antibiotic

anticipado ADJETIVO
early ◇ *la jubilación anticipada* early retirement
◆ **por anticipado** in advance ◇ *pagar por anticipado* to pay in advance

anticipar VERBO
1 to foresee ◇ *Es imposible anticiparlo que va a ocurrir.* It's impossible to foresee what will happen.
2 to bring...forward ◇ *Habrá que anticipar la reunión.* We'll have to bring the meeting forward.
3 to pay...in advance ◇ *Tuvimos que anticipar el alquiler de dos meses.* We had to pay two months' rent in advance.
◆ **anticiparse a alguien** to get in before somebody ◇ *Se me anticipó y pagó la cuenta.* He got in before me and paid the check.
◆ **Se anticipó a su tiempo.** He was ahead of his time.

el **anticipo** SUSTANTIVO
advance ◇ *pedir un anticipo* to ask for an advance
◆ **ser* un anticipo de algo** to be a foretaste of something

el **anticonceptivo** ADJETIVO, SUSTANTIVO
contraceptive

anticuado ADJETIVO
outdated
◆ **quedarse anticuado** to become outdated

la **anticuaria** SUSTANTIVO
antique dealer

el **anticuario** SUSTANTIVO
1 antique shop (*tienda*)
2 antique dealer (*persona*)

el **antifaz** SUSTANTIVO (PL los **antifaces**)
mask

antiguamente ADVERBIO
1 in the past ◇ *Antiguamente no se gastaba tanto.* In the past people didn't spend so much money.
2 formerly ◇ *Antiguamente tenía el nombre de Sociedad de Naciones.* Formerly it was called the Society of Nations.

la **antigüedad** SUSTANTIVO
◆ **Es un monumento de gran antigüedad.** It's a very old monument.
◆ **en la antigüedad** in ancient times
◆ **las antigüedades** antiques
◆ **una tienda de antigüedades** an antique shop

antiguo ADJETIVO
1 old ◇ *Este reloj es muy antiguo.* This clock is very old.
2 ancient ◇ *Estudia historia antigua.* He studies ancient history.
3 former ◇ *el antiguo secretario general del partido* the former general secretary of the party

las **Antillas** SUSTANTIVO
the West Indies

antipático ADJETIVO
unfriendly

antirrobo ADJETIVO (PL **antirrobo**)
anti-theft ◇ *un sistema antirrobo* an anti-theft system

el **antiséptico** ADJETIVO, SUSTANTIVO
antiseptic

antojarse VERBO
to feel like (*querer*) ◇ *Se me antojó un helado.* I felt like having an ice cream.
◇ *Siempre hace lo que se le antoja.* He always does what he feels like.

la **antorcha** SUSTANTIVO
torch (PL torches)

la **antropología** SUSTANTIVO
anthropology

anual ADJETIVO
annual

anular VERBO
1 to call off ◇ *Anularon el partido por la lluvia.* The game was called off because of the rain.
2 to disallow ◇ *El árbitro anuló el gol.* The referee disallowed the goal.
3 to overturn ◇ *El Tribunal Supremo anuló la sentencia.* The Supreme Court overturned the sentence.

el **anular** SUSTANTIVO
ring finger

anunciar VERBO
1 to advertise ◇ *anunciar detergente* to advertise soap powder
2 to announce ◇ *anunciar una decisión* to announce a decision

el **anuncio** SUSTANTIVO
1 advertisement ◇ *Pusieron un anuncio en el periódico.* They put an advertisement in the paper.
◆ **anuncios por palabras** small ads
2 announcement ◇ *Tengo que hacer un anuncio importante.* I have an important announcement to make.

el **anzuelo** SUSTANTIVO
hook

la **añadidura** SUSTANTIVO
◆ **por añadidura** in addition

añadir VERBO
to add

los **añicos** SUSTANTIVO
◆ **hacer* algo añicos** to smash something to pieces
◆ **hacerse* añicos** to smash to pieces

el **año** SUSTANTIVO
year ◇ *Estuve allí el año pasado.* I was there last year.
◆ **el año que viene** next year
◆ **el año escolar** the school year
◆ **¡Feliz Año Nuevo!** Happy New Year!
◆ **los años 80** the 80s
◆ **¿Cuántos años tiene?** How old is he?
◆ **Tiene 15 años.** He's 15.

apagado ADJETIVO
switched off ◇ *La tele estaba apagada.* The TV was switched off.

apagar* VERBO
1 to switch off ◇ *Apaga la tele.* Switch the TV off. ◇ *No apagues la luz.* Don't switch the light off.
2 to put out ◇ *Por favor, apaguen sus cigarrillos.* Please put your cigarettes out.
◆ **apagar* el fuego** to put the fire out

el **apagón** SUSTANTIVO (PL los **apagones**)
power outage

apañado ADJETIVO
resourceful ◇ *¡Qué apañada eres!* How resourceful you are!

apañarse VERBO
to manage ◇ *¿Podrás hacerlo solo? – Ya me apañaré.* Can you do it on your own? – I'll manage.
◆ **apañarse con algo** to make do with something ◇ *Nos apañaremos con la comida que sobró.* We can make do with the leftovers.

el **aparador** SUSTANTIVO
1 sideboard (*mueble*)
2 store window (*en tienda*) *Mexico*

el **aparato** SUSTANTIVO
◆ **No sé manejar este aparato.** I don't know how to operate this.
◆ **un aparato de televisión** a television set
◆ **los aparatos de gimnasia** the apparatus
◆ **Fabrican aparatos electrónicos.** They make electronic equipment.
◆ **un aparato electrodoméstico** an electrical appliance

el **aparcamiento** SUSTANTIVO *Spain*
parking lot

aparecer* VERBO
1 to appear ◇ *De repente apareció la policía.* Suddenly the police appeared.
2 to turn up ◇ *Aparecieron casi una hora tarde.* They turned up nearly an hour late.
◇ *¿Han aparecido ya las tijeras?* Have the scissors turned up yet?
3 to come out ◇ *Su nueva novela aparecerá el mes próximo.* His latest novel will come out next month.

aparentar VERBO
to appear ◇ *Aparentaba no enterarse.* He appeared not to understand.
◆ **Aparenta más edad de la que tiene.** He looks older than he is.

aparente ADJETIVO
apparent

aparentemente ADVERBIO
apparently

la **apariencia** SUSTANTIVO
◆ **Tiene la apariencia de un profesor de universidad.** He looks like a university professor.
◆ **En apariencia nada ha cambiado.** On the surface, nothing had changed.
◆ **guardar las apariencias** to keep up appearances

* Verbs marked with this symbol are irregular. See pages 346–348 for further details.

apartado ADJETIVO
isolated ◇ *un lugar apartado* an isolated place
◆ **Vive apartado de todos.** He lives a secluded life.

el **apartado** SUSTANTIVO
section ◇ *en el siguiente apartado* in the following section
◆ **apartado postal** post office box

el **apartamento** SUSTANTIVO
apartment

apartar VERBO
1 to remove ◇ *Lo apartaron del equipo.* They removed him from the team.
2 to move out of the way ◇ *Aparta todas las sillas.* Move all the chairs out of the way.
◆ **¡Aparta!** Stand back!
3 to set aside ◇ *Hay que apartar algo del sueldo para las vacaciones.* You'll have to set aside some of your pay for the vacations.
◆ **apartarse** to stand back ◇ *Apártense de la puerta.* Stand back from the door.

aparte (1) ADVERBIO
separately ◇ *Cada caso será tratado aparte.* Each case will be dealt with separately.
◆ **La ropa que no valga ponla aparte.** Put the clothes that aren't any use on one side.
◆ **aparte de (1)** (*excepto*) apart from ◇ *Nadie protestó aparte de ella.* Nobody complained apart from her.
◆ **aparte de (2)** (*además de*) as well as ◇ *Aparte de los patines, también quería una bici.* I'd like a bike as well as the skates.
◆ **punto y aparte** period, new paragraph

aparte (2) ADJETIVO
separate ◇ *El tuyo es un caso aparte.* You're a separate case.

apasionante ADJETIVO
exciting

apasionar VERBO
◆ **Le apasiona el fútbol.** He's crazy about soccer.

apdo. ABREVIATURA (= *apartado de correos*)
PO box (= post office box)

apearse VERBO
◆ **apearse de** to get off

apellidarse VERBO
◆ **Se apellida Pérez.** His surname is Pérez.

el **apellido** SUSTANTIVO
surname

apenado ADJETIVO
1 sad (*triste*)
2 embarrassed (*avergonzado*)

apenas ADVERBIO, CONJUNCIÓN
1 hardly ◇ *Apenas tenemos que comer.* We have hardly anything to eat. ◇ *Apenas podía levantarse.* He could hardly stand up.
2 hardly ever
Se usa ***hardly ever*** *cuando se refiere a la frecuencia de una acción.*
◇ *Apenas voy al cine.* I hardly ever go to the movies.
3 barely
Se usa ***barely*** *cuando precede a un número.*
◇ *Hace apenas 10 minutos que hablé con ella.* I spoke to her barely 10 minutes ago.
◆ **Terminé en apenas dos horas.** It only took me two hours to finish.
4 as soon as ◇ *Apenas me vio, se puso a llorar.* As soon as he saw me he began to cry.

la **apendicitis** SUSTANTIVO
appendicitis

el **aperitivo** SUSTANTIVO
aperitif

la **apertura** SUSTANTIVO
opening ◇ *el acto de apertura* the opening ceremony

apestar VERBO
to stink ◇ *Te apestan los pies.* Your feet stink.
◆ **apestar a** to stink of

apetecer* VERBO
◆ **¿Te apetece un café?** Do you feel like a coffee?
◆ **No, gracias, ahora no me apetece.** No, thanks, I don't feel like it just now.

el **apetito** SUSTANTIVO
appetite ◇ *Eso te va a quitar el apetito.* You won't have any appetite left.
◆ **No tengo apetito.** I'm not hungry.

apetitoso ADJETIVO
1 tasty (*sabroso*)
2 tempting (*tentador*)

el **apio** SUSTANTIVO
celery

aplastante ADJETIVO
overwhelming

aplastar VERBO
to squash

aplaudir VERBO
to clap ◇ *Todos aplaudían.* Everyone clapped.

el **aplauso** SUSTANTIVO
applause
◆ **Los aplausos duraron varios minutos.** The applause lasted for several minutes.

aplazar* VERBO
to postpone

la **aplicación** SUSTANTIVO (PL las **aplicaciones**)
application ◇ *un producto con muchas aplicaciones* a product with a lot of applications

aplicado ADJETIVO
hard-working ◇ *un alumno aplicado* a hard-working student

aplicar* VERBO
1 to apply ◇ *Aplíquese sobre la zona afectada.* Apply to the affected area.
2 to enforce ◇ *No se aplicaron las normas.* The rules weren't enforced.

apoderarse VERBO
◆ **apoderarse de un lugar** to take over a place ☞

◆ **Se apoderaron de las joyas.** They went off with the jewels.

el **apodo** SUSTANTIVO
nickname

el **apogeo** SUSTANTIVO
height ◇ *en el apogeo de su poder* at the height of his power
◆ **La fiesta estaba en su apogeo.** The party was in full swing.

aportar VERBO
to provide

aposta ADVERBIO
on purpose

apostar* VERBO
to bet
◆ **apostar* por algo** to bet on something
◆ **¿Qué te apuestas a que...?** What's the betting that...?

el **apóstrofo** SUSTANTIVO
apostrophe

apoyar VERBO
1 to lean ◇ *Apoya el espejo contra la pared.* Lean the mirror against the wall.
2 to rest ◇ *Apoya la espalda en este cojín.* Rest your back against this cushion.
3 to support ◇ *Todos mis compañeros me apoyan.* All my colleagues support me.
◆ **apoyarse** to lean ◇ *No te apoyes en la mesa.* Don't lean on the table.

el **apoyo** SUSTANTIVO
support

apreciar VERBO
◆ **apreciar a alguien** to be fond of somebody ◇ *Lo apreciábamos mucho.* We were very fond of him.
◆ **Aprecio mucho mi tiempo libre.** I really value my free time.

el **aprecio** SUSTANTIVO
◆ **tener* aprecio a alguien** to be fond of somebody

aprender VERBO
to learn ◇ *Ya me aprendí los verbos irregulares.* I've already learned the irregular verbs.
◆ **aprender a hacer algo** to learn to do something
◆ **aprender algo de memoria** to learn something by heart

el **aprendiz,** la **aprendiza** SUSTANTIVO (MASC PL los **aprendices**)
trainee ◇ *Es aprendiz de mecánico.* He's a trainee mechanic.
◆ **estar* de aprendiz** to be doing an apprenticeship

aprensivo ADJETIVO
overanxious

apresurado ADJETIVO
hasty (*decisión*)

apresurarse VERBO
◆ **No nos apresuremos.** Let's not be hasty.
◆ **Me apresuré a sugerir que...** I hastily suggested that...

apretado ADJETIVO
1 tight ◇ *Estos pantalones me quedan muy apretados.* These pants are very tight on me. ◇ *Tenemos un programa muy apretado.* We've got a very tight program.
2 cramped ◇ *Íbamos muy apretados en el tren.* We were very cramped on the train.

apretar* VERBO
1 to tighten ◇ *Aprieta bien los tornillos.* Tighten up the screws.
2 to press ◇ *Aprieta este botón.* Press this button.
◆ **apretar* el gatillo** to press the trigger
◆ **Me aprietan los zapatos.** My shoes are too tight.
◆ **La apretó contra su pecho.** He clasped her to his bosom.
◆ **Apriétense un poco para que me siente yo también.** Move up a bit so I can sit down, too.
◆ **apretarse el cinturón** to tighten one's belt

el **aprieto** SUSTANTIVO
◆ **estar* en un aprieto** to be in a tight spot

aprisa ADVERBIO
fast ◇ *No vayas tan aprisa.* Don't go so fast.
◆ **¡Aprisa!** Hurry up!

aprobar* VERBO
1 to pass ◇ *aprobar un examen* to pass an exam
◆ **Han aprobado una ley antitabaco.** They've passed an anti-smoking law.
◆ **aprobar por los pelos** to scrape through
2 to approve ◇ *La decisión fue aprobada por mayoría.* The decision was approved by a majority.
3 to approve of ◇ *No apruebo esa conducta.* I don't approve of that sort of behavior.

apropiado ADJETIVO
suitable

aprovechar VERBO
1 to make good use of ◇ *No aprovecha el tiempo.* He doesn't make good use of his time. ◇ *Mi madre aprovecha toda la comida que sobra.* My mother makes good use of any leftovers.
2 to use ◇ *Aprovecharé los ratos libres para estudiar.* I'll use the free time to study.
◆ **aprovecho la ocasión para decirles...** I'd like to take this opportunity to tell you...
◆ **Aprovecharé ahora que estoy solo para llamarlo.** I'll call him now while I'm on my own.
◆ **¡Que aproveche!** Enjoy your meal!
◆ **aprovecharse de** to take advantage of ◇ *Me aproveché de la situación.* I took advantage of the situation. ◇ *Todos se aprovechan del pobre chico.* Everyone takes advantage of the poor boy.

aproximadamente ADVERBIO

about

aproximado ADJETIVO
approximate

aproximarse VERBO
to approach

apruebo VERBO *ver* **aprobar**

la **aptitud** SUSTANTIVO
1 suitability (*conveniencia*)
2 aptitude (*capacidad*)

apto ADJETIVO
- **ser* apto para algo** to be suitable for something ◇ *No es apta para el puesto.* She isn't suitable for the job.
- **una película no apta para niños** an unsuitable movie for children

la **apuesta** SUSTANTIVO
bet ◇ *Hicimos una apuesta.* We had a bet.

apuesto VERBO *ver* **apostar**

apuntar VERBO
1 to write down ◇ *Apúntalo o se te olvidará.* Write it down or you'll forget.
- **Apunta mis datos.** Can you take a note of my details?

2 to point ◇ *Apuntó el arma hacia nosotros.* He pointed the gun at us.
- **Me apuntó con el dedo.** He pointed at me.
- **apuntarse** to put one's name down ◇ *Nos apuntamos para el viaje a Brasil.* We've put our names down for the trip to Brazil.
- **apuntarse a un curso** to enroll in a course
- **¡Yo me apunto!** Count me in!

No confundir ***apuntar*** *con* ***to appoint.***

los **apuntes** SUSTANTIVO
notes
- **tomar apuntes** to take notes

apuñalar VERBO
to stab

apurado ADJETIVO
1 difficult (*difícil*)
2 in a hurry (*con prisa*)
- **Si estás apurado de dinero, dímelo.** If you're short of money, tell me.
- **estar* apurado** (*avergonzado*) to feel embarrassed

apurar VERBO
to finish up ◇ *Apura la cerveza que nos vamos.* Finish up your beer and let's go.
- **apurarse (1)** to hurry up ◇ *¡Apúrate!* Hurry up!
- **apurarse (2)** to worry ◇ *Yo me encargo; no te apures por nada.* I'll deal with it – don't you worry about anything.

el **apuro** SUSTANTIVO
fix ◇ *El dinero de la herencia los sacó del apuro.* The money they inherited got them out of the fix.
- **Pasé muchos apuros para salir del agua.** I had a lot of trouble getting out of the water.
- **Me da mucho apuro no llevar ningún regalo.** I feel very embarrassed about not taking a present.
- **estar* en apuros** to be in trouble

aquel ADJETIVO (FEM **aquella**)
that ◇ *Me gusta más aquella mesa.* I prefer that table.

aquél PRONOMBRE (FEM **aquélla**)
that one ◇ *Éste no, aquél.* Not this one, that one.
- **Aquél no era el que yo quería.** That wasn't the one I wanted.

aquello PRONOMBRE
- **aquello que hay allí** that thing over there
- **Me fui; aquello era insoportable.** I left. It was just unbearable.
- **¿Qué fue de aquello del viaje alrededor del mundo?** What ever happened to that round-the-world trip idea?

aquellos ADJETIVO PL (FEM **aquellas**)
those ◇ *¿Ves aquellas montañas?* Can you see those mountains?

aquéllos PRONOMBRE PL (FEM **aquéllas**)
those ones ◇ *Aquéllos de allí son mejores.* Those ones over there are better.
- **Aquéllos no eran los que vimos ayer.** Those aren't the ones we saw yesterday.

aquí ADVERBIO
1 here (*en este lugar*) ◇ *Aquí está el informe que me pediste.* Here's the report you asked me for.
- **aquí abajo** down here
- **aquí arriba** up here
- **aquí mismo** right here
- **por aquí (1)** around here ◇ *Lo tenía por aquí en alguna parte.* I had it around here somewhere.
- **por aquí (2)** this way ◇ *Pasen por aquí, si son tan amables.* Please come this way.

2 now (*ahora*)
- **de aquí en adelante** from now on
- **de aquí a siete días** a week from now
- **hasta aquí (1)** up to here ◇ *Hasta aquí el camino es cuesta abajo.* Up to here the path goes downhill.
- **hasta aquí (2)** up to now ◇ *Hasta aquí todos han ido pagando.* Up to now everyone has paid.

el/la **árabe** ADJETIVO, SUSTANTIVO
Arab

el **árabe** SUSTANTIVO
Arabic (*idioma*)

Arabia SUSTANTIVO FEM
- **Arabia Saudí** Saudi Arabia

el **arado** SUSTANTIVO
plough

la **araña** SUSTANTIVO
spider

arañar VERBO
to scratch ◇ *Me arañó el gato.* The cat scratched me. ◇ *Me arañé la cara con las zarzas.* I scratched my face on the brambles.
- **Pedro se arañó las rodillas al caer.** Pedro grazed his knees when he fell over.

el **arañazo** SUSTANTIVO
scratch (PL scratches)

arar VERBO
to plough

el **árbitro,** la **árbitra** SUSTANTIVO
referee

el **árbol** SUSTANTIVO
tree ◇ *un árbol frutal* a fruit tree
◆ **el árbol de Navidad** the Christmas tree
◆ **un árbol genealógico** a family tree

el **arbusto** SUSTANTIVO
1 bush (*salvaje*) (PL bushes)
2 shrub (*plantado*)

el **arca** SUSTANTIVO FEM
chest
◆ **el Arca de Noé** Noah's Ark

las **arcadas** SUSTANTIVO
◆ **Me dieron arcadas con el olor.** The smell made me retch.

el **arcén** SUSTANTIVO (PL los **arcenes**)
shoulder (*de carretera*)

el **archivador** SUSTANTIVO
1 filing cabinet (*mueble*)
2 file (*carpeta*)

archivar VERBO
to file

el **archivo** SUSTANTIVO
1 archive (*lugar*)
2 file (*documento*)
◆ **los archivos policiales** police files

la **arcilla** SUSTANTIVO
clay

el **arco** SUSTANTIVO
1 bow (*de flechas*)
2 arch (*en edificio, monumento*) (PL arches)
◆ **el arco iris** the rainbow

arder VERBO
to burn ◇ *Ese tronco no va a arder.* That log won't burn.
◆ **¡La sopa está ardiendo!** The soup's boiling hot!
◆ **El jefe está que arde.** The boss is seething.

la **ardilla** SUSTANTIVO
squirrel

el **ardor** SUSTANTIVO
passion
◆ **Defiende sus ideas con ardor.** He defends his ideas passionately.
◆ **tener* ardor de estómago** to have heartburn

el **área** SUSTANTIVO FEM
1 area ◇ *el área del triángulo* the area of the triangle ◇ *en áreas muy pobladas* in heavily populated areas
◆ **en distintas áreas del país** in different parts of the country
◆ **un área de descanso** a rest area
◆ **un área de servicios** (*en autopista*) a service area
2 penalty area ◇ *una falta al borde del área* a foul on the edge of the penalty area

la **arena** SUSTANTIVO
sand
◆ **arenas movedizas** quicksand SING

el **arenque** SUSTANTIVO
herring
◆ **arenques ahumados** kippers

Argelia SUSTANTIVO FEM
Algeria

el **argelino,** la **argelina** ADJETIVO, SUSTANTIVO
Algerian

Argentina SUSTANTIVO FEM
Argentina

el **argentino,** la **argentina** ADJETIVO, SUSTANTIVO
Argentinian

la **argolla** SUSTANTIVO
ring

el **argot** SUSTANTIVO (PL los **argots**)
1 slang (*de la calle*)
2 jargon (*de una profesión*)

el **argumento** SUSTANTIVO
1 argument ◇ *los argumentos a favor del desarme* the arguments in favor of disarmament
2 plot ◇ *el argumento de la película* the plot of the movie

árido ADJETIVO
arid

Aries SUSTANTIVO MASC
Aries ◇ *Soy aries.* I'm an Aries.

el/la **aristócrata** SUSTANTIVO
aristocrat

el **arma** SUSTANTIVO FEM
1 weapon ◇ *Los guerrilleros entregaron las armas.* The guerrillas handed over their weapons. ◇ *Se prohibió el uso de armas químicas.* The use of chemical weapons was banned.
◆ **un fabricante de armas** an arms manufacturer
2 gun ◇ *Nos apuntaba con un arma.* He pointed a gun at us.
◆ **un arma de fuego** a firearm

la **armada** SUSTANTIVO
navy (PL navies)

la **armadura** SUSTANTIVO
armor
◆ **una armadura medieval** a medieval suit of armor

el **armamento** SUSTANTIVO
arms PL ◇ *negociaciones para la limitación de armamento* talks on arms control

armar VERBO
1 to arm ◇ *No iban armados.* They weren't armed.
2 to assemble ◇ *El armario viene desmontado y luego tú lo armas.* The cupboard comes in pieces and you assemble it.
3 to make ◇ *Los vecinos de arriba arman mucho jaleo.* Our upstairs neighbors make a

lot of noise.

◆ **Si no aceptan voy a armar un escándalo.** If they don't agree I'm going to make a fuss.

◆ **armarse un lío** to get in a muddle

◆ **armarse de paciencia** to be patient

◆ **armarse de valor** to summon up one's courage

el **armario** SUSTANTIVO

[1] cupboard

◆ **un armario de cocina** a kitchen cupboard

[2] closet (*de ropa*)

◆ **un armario empotrado** a built-in closet

el **armazón** SUSTANTIVO (PL los **armazones**)

frame

la **armonía** SUSTANTIVO

harmony

la **armónica** SUSTANTIVO

mouth organ

el **aro** SUSTANTIVO

[1] ring ◇ *los aros olímpicos* the Olympic rings

[2] hoop (*para gimnasia, juegos*)

el **aroma** SUSTANTIVO

aroma

la **aromaterapia** SUSTANTIVO

aromatherapy

el **arpa** SUSTANTIVO FEM

harp

la **arqueóloga** SUSTANTIVO

archaeologist

la **arqueología** SUSTANTIVO

archaeology

el **arqueólogo** SUSTANTIVO

archaeologist

el **arquero,** la **arquera** SUSTANTIVO

goalkeeper

el **arquitecto,** la **arquitecta** SUSTANTIVO

architect

la **arquitectura** SUSTANTIVO

architecture

arrancar* VERBO

[1] to pull up (*planta*) ◇ *Estaba arrancando malas hierbas.* I was pulling up weeds.

◆ **El viento arrancó varios árboles.** Several trees were uprooted by the wind.

◆ **arrancar algo de raíz** to pull something up by the roots

[2] to pull out (*clavo, espina*) ◇ *Le arranqué una espina del dedo.* I pulled a thorn out of his finger.

[3] to tear out (*hoja, página*) ◇ *Arrancó una hoja del cuaderno.* He tore a page out of the notebook.

[4] to pull off (*cartel, esparadrapo*) ◇ *Arranqué la etiqueta.* I pulled off the label.

[5] to snatch ◇ *Me lo arrancaron de las manos.* They snatched it from me.

◆ **Arranca y vámonos.** Start the engine and let's get going.

◆ **arrancarle información a alguien** to drag information out of somebody

arrasar VERBO

[1] to sweep away ◇ *El pueblo fue arrasado por las inundaciones.* The village was swept away by the floods.

[2] to destroy ◇ *El fuego arrasó la cosecha.* The harvest was destroyed by fire.

◆ **Los socialistas arrasaron en las elecciones.** The socialists swept the board in the elections.

arrastrar VERBO

[1] to drag ◇ *Arrastraba una enorme maleta.* He was dragging an enormous suitcase.

[2] to sweep along ◇ *El aire nos arrastraba.* The wind swept us along.

[3] to trail on the ground ◇ *Las cortinas arrastran un poco.* The drapes trail on the ground slightly. ◇ *Llevas la falda arrastrando.* Your skirt's trailing on the ground.

◆ **arrastrarse** to crawl ◇ *Llegaron hasta la valla arrastrándose.* They crawled up to the fence.

arrebatar VERBO

snatch ◇ *Me lo arrebató de las manos.* He snatched it from me.

el **arrecife** SUSTANTIVO

reef

◆ **los arrecifes de coral** coral reefs

arreglar VERBO

[1] to fix (*aparato, mecanismo*) ◇ *¿Sabrás arreglarme la llave?* Could you fix the faucet for me?

◆ **Está arreglando la acera.** The sidewalk is being repaired.

[2] to do up (*casa, habitación*) ◇ *Este verano hemos arreglado la cocina.* This summer we did up the kitchen.

[3] to sort out ◇ *Si tienes algún problema, él te lo arregla.* If you have any problems, he'll sort them out for you.

◆ **Deja tu cuarto arreglado antes de salir.** Leave your room neat before going out.

◆ **arreglarse (1)** to get ready ◇ *Se arregló para salir.* She got ready to go out.

◆ **arreglarse (2)** to work out ◇ *Ya verás como todo se arregla.* It'll all work out, you'll see.

◆ **arreglarse (3)** to manage ◇ *¿Qué tal te arreglas sin carro?* How are you managing without a car?

◆ **arreglarse el pelo** to do one's hair

◆ **arreglárselas para hacer algo** to manage to do something

el **arreglo** SUSTANTIVO

[1] repair ◇ *El tostador sólo necesita un pequeño arreglo.* The toaster only needs a minor repair.

◆ **Esta tele no tiene arreglo.** This TV is unrepairable.

◆ **Este problema no tiene arreglo.** There's no solution to this problem.

[2] compromise ◇ *Llegamos a un arreglo.* ☞

We reached a compromise.
◆ **con arreglo a** in accordance with

arrepentirse* VERBO
◆ **arrepentirse de algo** to regret something
◆ **arrepentirse de haber hecho algo** to regret doing something

arrestar VERBO
to arrest

el **arresto** SUSTANTIVO
arrest ◇ *un arresto domiciliario* a house arrest

arriba ADVERBIO
above ◇ *Los platos y las tazas están arriba.* The plates and mugs are above. ◇ *Visto desde arriba parece más pequeño.* Seen from above it looks smaller.
◆ **Pon esos libros arriba del todo.** Put those books on top.
◆ **la parte de arriba del biquini** the bikini top

*Se usa **upstairs** hablando de los distintos pisos de un edificio.*

◇ *Arriba están los dormitorios.* The bedrooms are upstairs. ◇ *los vecinos de arriba* our upstairs neighbors
◆ **allí arriba** up there
◆ **más arriba** further up
◆ **ir* calle arriba** to go up the street
◆ **Tenemos carteras de 200 pesos para arriba.** We've got bags from 200 pesos upwards.
◆ **arriba de (1)** on top of ◇ *Lo dejé arriba del refrigerador.* I left it on top of the fridge.
◆ **arriba de (2)** above ◇ *Viven en el departamento arriba del mío.* They live in the apartment above mine.
◆ **mirar a alguien de arriba abajo** to look somebody up and down

arriesgado ADJETIVO
risky

arriesgar* VERBO
to risk ◇ *Carlos arriesgó su vida para salvar a su perro.* Carlos risked his life to save his dog.
◆ **arriesgarse** to take a risk ◇ *Se arriesgó pero salió ganando.* He took a risk but he came out on top.
◆ **arriesgarse a hacer algo** to risk doing something ◇ *Me arriesgo a perderlo todo.* I risk losing everything.

arrimar VERBO
to bring...closer ◇ *Arrima tu silla a la mía.* Bring your chair closer to mine.
◆ **Vamos a arrimar la mesa a la pared.** Let's put the table by the wall.
◆ **arrimarse** to get close ◇ *Al estacionar procura arrimarte al borde de la acera.* Try to get close to the curb when parking.
◆ **Arrímate a mí.** Come closer.

arrodillarse VERBO
to kneel down

arrogante ADJETIVO
arrogant

arrojar VERBO
[1] to throw ◇ *Arrojaban piedras y palos.* They were throwing sticks and stones.
◆ **arrojar a alguien de un sitio** to throw somebody out of a place
[2] to dump ◇ *"Prohibido arrojar basuras"* "No dumping"
◆ **arrojarse** to throw oneself ◇ *Un hincha se arrojó al campo.* A fan threw himself onto the field.

arropar VERBO
[1] to tuck in (*en la cama*) ◇ *Voy a arropar al niño.* I'll go and tuck the baby in.
[2] to wrap up ◇ *Arrópala bien.* Wrap her up well.
◆ **arrópate bien (1)** (*en la cama*) tuck yourself up warmly
◆ **arrópate bien (2)** (*antes de salir*) wrap up well

el **arroyo** SUSTANTIVO
stream

el **arroz** SUSTANTIVO (PL los **arroces**)
rice
◆ **arroz blanco** white rice
◆ **arroz con leche** rice pudding

la **arruga** SUSTANTIVO
[1] wrinkle (*en la piel*)
[2] crease (*en la ropa, el papel*)

arrugarse* VERBO
[1] to get wrinkled ◇ *La piel se va arrugando.* Skin gets increasingly wrinkled.
[2] to get creased ◇ *Se me arrugaron los pantalones.* My pants have gotten creased. ◇ *Procura que no se arrugue el sobre.* Try not to let the envelope get creased.

arruinar VERBO
to ruin ◇ *Esto arruinó mis planes.* That ruined my plans.
◆ **arruinarse** to be ruined ◇ *Con aquel negocio se arruinó.* He was ruined thanks to that deal.

el **arte** SUSTANTIVO (PL las **artes**)
[1] art ◇ *el arte del Renacimiento* Renaissance art
◆ **el arte abstracto** abstract art
◆ **el arte dramático** drama
◆ **las artes plásticas** plastic arts
[2] flair (*maña*) ◇ *Tiene arte para la cocina.* She has a flair for cooking.
◆ **por arte de magia** by magic

el **artefacto** SUSTANTIVO
device ◇ *un artefacto explosivo* an explosive device

la **arteria** SUSTANTIVO
artery (PL arteries)

la **artesana** SUSTANTIVO
craftswoman (PL craftswomen)

la **artesanía** SUSTANTIVO
◆ **la artesanía local** local crafts
◆ **objetos de artesanía** hand-crafted goods

el **artesano** SUSTANTIVO
craftsman (PL craftsmen)

ártico ADJETIVO
arctic

la **articulación** SUSTANTIVO (PL las **articulaciones**)
joint

el **artículo** SUSTANTIVO
article (*en periódico, de ley*) ◇ *el artículo determinado* the definite article ◇ *el artículo indeterminado* the indefinite article
◆ **artículos de lujo** luxury goods
◆ **artículos de escritorio** stationery
◆ **artículos de tocador** toiletries

artificial ADJETIVO
artificial

el/la **artista** SUSTANTIVO
artist (*pintor, escultor*)
◆ **un artista** (*de cine, teatro*) actor
◆ **una artista** (*de cine, teatro*) actress

la **arveja** SUSTANTIVO
pea

el **arzobispo** SUSTANTIVO
archbishop

el **as** SUSTANTIVO
ace ◇ *el as de picas* the ace of spades
◆ **ser* un as de la cocina** to be a wizard at cooking

el **asa** SUSTANTIVO FEM
handle

asado ADJETIVO
roast ◇ *pollo asado* roast chicken

el **asado** SUSTANTIVO
[1] roast (*en horno*)
[2] barbecue (*a la parrilla*)

asaltar VERBO
[1] to storm ◇ *Los rebeldes asaltaron la embajada.* The rebels stormed the embassy.
[2] to raid ◇ *Asaltaron un banco.* They raided a bank.
[3] to mug ◇ *Me asaltaron a la salida del banco.* I was mugged coming out of the bank.

el **asalto** SUSTANTIVO
[1] raid ◇ *un asalto a un campo militar* a raid on a military camp
◆ **durante el asalto a la embajada** during the storming of the embassy
[2] round (*en boxeo*)

la **asamblea** SUSTANTIVO
[1] meeting (*reunión*) ◇ *organizar* una asamblea* to organize a meeting
[2] assembly (*corporación*) ◇ *una asamblea legislativa* a legislative assembly

asar VERBO
to roast (*al horno*)
◆ **asar algo a la parrilla** to grill something
◆ **Me aso de calor.** I'm boiling.
◆ **Aquí se asa uno.** It's boiling in here.

ascender* VERBO
[1] to rise ◇ *El globo comenzó a ascender.* The balloon began to rise.
[2] to be promoted ◇ *Ascendió a teniente.* He was promoted to lieutenant.
◆ **ascender a primera división** to go up to the first division

el **ascenso** SUSTANTIVO
promotion (*de empleado, militar*)

el **ascensor** SUSTANTIVO
elevator

asciendo VERBO *ver* **ascender**

el **asco** SUSTANTIVO
◆ **El ajo me da asco.** I think garlic's revolting.
◆ **¡Puaj! ¡Qué asco!** Yuck! How revolting!
◆ **La casa está hecha un asco.** The house is filthy.

asegurar VERBO
[1] to insure ◇ *Hemos asegurado la casa.* We've insured the house.
[2] to assure ◇ *Te aseguro que es verdad.* I assure you it's true.
◆ **No he sido yo. Te lo aseguro.** It wasn't me, I assure you.
◆ **Ella asegura que no lo conoce.** She says that she doesn't know him.
[3] to fasten securely ◇ *Asegura bien la cuerda.* Fasten the rope securely.
◆ **asegurarse de** to make sure ◇ *Asegúrate de que las llaves están cerradas.* Make sure the faucets are turned off.

el **aseo** SUSTANTIVO
◆ **el cuarto de aseo** the bathroom
◆ **el aseo personal** personal hygiene
◆ **los aseos** [*Spain*] the restroom SING

asequible ADJETIVO
[1] affordable ◇ *un precio asequible* an affordable price
[2] achievable ◇ *una meta asequible* an achievable goal

la **asesina** SUSTANTIVO
murderer

asesinar VERBO
to murder

el **asesinato** SUSTANTIVO
murder

el **asesino** SUSTANTIVO
murderer

el **asesor**, la **asesora** SUSTANTIVO
consultant
◆ **asesor fiscal** tax consultant
◆ **asesor de imagen** public relations consultant

el **asfalto** SUSTANTIVO
asphalt

la **asfixia** SUSTANTIVO
suffocation

asfixiarse VERBO
to suffocate ◇ *Me asfixio de calor.* I'm suffocating in this heat.

así ADVERBIO
[1] like this ◇ *Se hace así.* You do it like this.
[2] like that ◇ *Es así: como lo hace Jorge.* It's like that: the way Jorge is doing it. ◇ *¿Ves* ☞

aquel abrigo? Quiero algo así. Do you see that coat? I'd like something like that.
- **un tomate así de grande** a tomato this big
- **Así es la vida.** That's life.
- **así, así** so-so ◇ *¿Te gusta? – Así, así.* Do you like it? – So-so.
- **así es** that's right ◇ *¿Y ocurrió todo en un día? – Así es.* And it all happened the same day? – That's right.
- **¿No es así?** Isn't that so?
- **así que...** so... ◇ *No me gusta, así que lo tiraré.* I don't like it, so I'll throw it away.
- **...o así** ...or thereabouts ◇ *mil pesos o así* a thousand pesos or thereabouts
- **y así sucesivamente** and so on

Asia SUSTANTIVO FEM
Asia

el **asiático,** la **asiática** ADJETIVO, SUSTANTIVO
Asian

el **asiento** SUSTANTIVO
seat
- **el asiento delantero** the front seat
- **el asiento trasero** the back seat

la **asignatura** SUSTANTIVO
subject
- **Tiene dos asignaturas pendientes.** He's got two subjects to take over.

el **asilo** SUSTANTIVO
1 home
- **un asilo de ancianos** an old people's home
- **un asilo de pobres** a shelter for the poor

2 asylum ◇ *asilo político* political asylum

asimilar VERBO
to assimilate ◇ *Hay que asimilar lo aprendido.* You have to assimilate what you've learned.
- **El cambio es grande y cuesta asimilarlo.** It's a big change and it takes getting used to.

la **asistencia** SUSTANTIVO
- **asistencia médica (1)** medical attention ◇ *Tuvieron que recibir asistencia médica.* They needed medical attention.
- **asistencia médica (2)** medical care ◇ *El seguro cubre la asistencia médica.* The insurance covers medical care.
- **asistencia técnica** technical support

la **asistenta** SUSTANTIVO
maid

el/la **asistente** SUSTANTIVO
assistant
- **asistente social** social worker
- **los asistentes al acto** those present at the ceremony

asistir VERBO
1 to go ◇ *No asistieron a la ceremonia.* They didn't go to the ceremony.
2 to treat ◇ *Lo asistió un médico que había de guardia.* He was treated by a doctor on duty.

el **asma** SUSTANTIVO FEM
asthma

la **asociación** SUSTANTIVO (PL las **asociaciones**)
association ◇ *por asociación de ideas* by an association of ideas

asociar VERBO
to associate ◇ *Asocio la lluvia con Escocia.* I associate rain with Scotland.
- **asociarse** to go into partnership ◇ *Los dos empresarios decidieron asociarse.* The two businessmen decided to go into partnership.

asolearse VERBO
to sunbathe

asomar VERBO
- **Te asoma el pañuelo por el bolsillo.** Your handkerchief's sticking out of your pocket.
- **No asomes la cabeza por la ventanilla.** Don't lean out of the window.
- **Me asomé a la terraza a ver quién gritaba.** I went out onto the balcony to see who was shouting.
- **Asómate a la ventana.** Look out of the window.

asombrar VERBO
to amaze ◇ *Me asombra que no lo sepas.* I'm amazed you don't know.
- **Intentaba asombrarnos con sus conocimientos.** He was trying to stun us with his knowledge.
- **asombrarse** to be amazed ◇ *Se asombró de lo tarde que era.* He was amazed at how late it was.

el **asombro** SUSTANTIVO
amazement ◇ *La gente la observaba con asombro.* People were looking at her in amazement.

asombroso ADJETIVO
amazing

el **aspecto** SUSTANTIVO
1 appearance ◇ *A ver si cuidas más tu aspecto.* Try taking a bit more trouble with your appearance.
2 aspect ◇ *Nos interesa mucho el aspecto económico.* We are very interested in the financial aspect.
- **tener* buen aspecto (1)** (*persona*) to look well
- **tener* buen aspecto (2)** (*comida*) to look good

áspero ADJETIVO
1 rough (*mano, toalla*)
2 harsh (*voz*)

la **aspiradora** SUSTANTIVO
vacuum cleaner
- **pasar la aspiradora** to vacuum

aspirar VERBO
1 to breathe in
- **Aspire profundamente.** Take a deep breath.
- **aspirar a hacer algo** to hope to do something

2 to vacuum ◇ *Tengo que aspirar mi cuarto.* I have to vacuum my bedroom.

la **aspirina** SUSTANTIVO
aspirin

asqueroso ADJETIVO
1 disgusting (*comida, olor*)
2 filthy (*cocina, manos*) ◇ *Esta cocina está asquerosa.* This kitchen is filthy.
3 horrible ◇ *Esta gente es asquerosa.* They're horrible people.

la **astilla** SUSTANTIVO
splinter

el **astro** SUSTANTIVO
star

la **astrología** SUSTANTIVO
astrology

el/la **astronauta** SUSTANTIVO
astronaut

la **astronomía** SUSTANTIVO
astronomy

astuto ADJETIVO
clever

asumir VERBO
to accept ◇ *Ya he asumido que no voy a ganar.* I've already accepted that I'm not going to win.
- **Asumo toda la responsabilidad.** I take full responsibility.

el **asunto** SUSTANTIVO
matter ◇ *Es un asunto muy delicado.* It's a very delicate matter.
- **el ministro de asuntos exteriores** the secretary for foreign affairs
- **No me gusta que se metan en mis asuntos.** I don't like anyone meddling in my affairs.
- **¡Eso no es asunto tuyo!** That's none of your business!

asustar VERBO
1 to frighten ◇ *Trata de no asustar a los niños.* Try not to frighten the children.
2 to startle ◇ *¡Huy! Me asustaste.* Goodness! You startled me.
- **asustarse** to get frightened ◇ *Se asusta por nada.* He gets frightened over nothing.
- **No te asustes.** Don't be frightened.

atacar* VERBO
to attack

el **atajo** SUSTANTIVO
short cut ◇ *Tomaremos un atajo.* We'll take a short cut.

el **ataque** SUSTANTIVO
attack ◇ *un ataque contra alguien* an attack on somebody
- **un ataque cardíaco** a heart attack
- **Le dio un ataque de risa.** He burst out laughing.
- **un ataque de nervios** a fit of panic

atar VERBO
to tie ◇ *Ata al perro a la farola.* Tie the dog to the lamppost.
- **Átate los cordones.** Tie your shoelaces.

atardecer* VERBO
to get dark

el **atardecer** SUSTANTIVO
dusk ◇ *al atardecer* at dusk

atareado ADJETIVO
busy

el **atasco** SUSTANTIVO
traffic jam

el **ataúd** SUSTANTIVO
coffin

Atenas SUSTANTIVO FEM
Athens

la **atención** SUSTANTIVO (PL las **atenciones**)
- **Hay que poner más atención.** You should pay more attention.
- **Escucha con atención.** He listens attentively.
- **Me llamó la atención lo grande que era la casa.** I was struck by how big the house was.
- **El director del colegio le llamó la atención.** The principal gave him a talking-to.
- **Estás llamando la atención con ese sombrero.** You're attracting attention in that hat.

atención EXCLAMACIÓN
Attention! (*a los soldados*)
- **¡Atención, por favor!** May I have your attention please?
- **"¡Atención!"** (*como aviso*) "Danger!"

atender* VERBO
1 to serve (*en un bar, tienda*) ◇ *¿La atienden?* Are you being served?
2 to attend to (*en un banco, oficina*) ◇ *Tengo que atender a un par de clientes.* I've got a couple of clients to attend to.
3 to look after ◇ *atender a los enfermos* to look after the sick
4 to pay attention to ◇ *Todos en clase atendían al profesor.* Everyone in the class was paying attention to the teacher.
- **atender los consejos de alguien** to listen to somebody's advice
- **La recepcionista atiende al teléfono.** The receptionist answers the telephone.
- **No atendieron nuestra petición.** They didn't take any notice of our petition.

el **atentado** SUSTANTIVO
- **un atentado terrorista** a terrorist attack
- **un atentado suicida** a suicide attack

el **atentado** SUSTANTIVO
- **un atentado terrorista** a terrorist attack
- **un atentado suicida** a suicide attack

atentamente ADVERBIO
Sincerely yours

atento ADJETIVO
thoughtful ◇ *Es un chico muy atento.* He's a very thoughtful boy.
- **Estaban atentos a las explicaciones del instructor.** They were listening attentively to the instructor's explanations.

el **aterrizaje** SUSTANTIVO
landing
- **un aterrizaje forzoso** an emergency landing

aterrizar* VERBO

☞

to land

atestado ADJETIVO

packed ◇ *El local estaba atestado de gente.* The place was packed with people.

atiborrarse VERBO

to stuff oneself ◇ *Se atiborró de pasteles.* He stuffed himself with cakes.

el **ático** SUSTANTIVO

top-floor attic

◆ **un ático de lujo** a luxurious penthouse

atiendo VERBO *ver* **atender**

atlántico ADJETIVO

Atlantic ◇ *el Océano Atlántico* the Atlantic Ocean

el **atlas** SUSTANTIVO (PL los **atlas**)

atlas (PL atlases)

el/la **atleta** SUSTANTIVO

athlete

el **atletismo** SUSTANTIVO

athletics

la **atmósfera** SUSTANTIVO

atmosphere

atolondrado ADJETIVO

scatterbrained

atómico ADJETIVO

atomic

atónito ADJETIVO

amazed

◆ **quedarse atónito** to be amazed

el **atracador**, la **atracadora** SUSTANTIVO

1 robber ◇ *un atracador de bancos* a bank robber

2 mugger ◇ *Unos atracadores le robaron el bolso.* She had her bag stolen by muggers.

atracar* VERBO

1 to hold up ◇ *atracar un banco* to hold up a bank

2 to mug ◇ *La atracaron en la plaza.* She was mugged in the square.

la **atracción** SUSTANTIVO (PL las **atracciones**)

attraction ◇ *una atracción turística* a tourist attraction

◆ **sentir* atracción por algo** to be attracted to something ◇ *Sentía atracción por él.* I was attracted to him.

el **atraco** SUSTANTIVO

1 hold-up ◇ *un atraco a un banco* a hold-up at a bank

2 mugging ◇ *un atraco en plena calle* a mugging in broad daylight

atractivo ADJETIVO

attractive

el **atractivo** SUSTANTIVO

attraction

◆ **Es una chica con un atractivo especial.** She's a really charming girl.

atraer* VERBO

to attract ◇ *Si bajamos los precios atraeremos a más clientes.* If we put our prices down we'll attract more customers.

◆ **Esa chica me atrae mucho.** I find that girl very attractive.

◆ **No me atrae mucho lo del viaje a Cancún.** That Cancún trip doesn't appeal to me much.

atrapar VERBO

to catch

atrás ADVERBIO

*Se usa **the back**, como sustantivo, cuando nos referimos a la parte posterior de algo.*

◇ *Los niños viajan siempre atrás.* The children always travel in the back.

◆ **la parte de atrás** the back

◆ **el asiento de atrás** the back seat

*Se usa **back**, como adverbio, cuando se habla de la dirección o de una posición posterior en general.*

◇ *Mirar hacia atrás.* to look back ◇ *Está más atrás.* It's further back.

◆ **ir* para atrás** to go backward

*Se usa **behind** cuando se habla de una posición posterior en relación a otra delantera.*

◇ *El carro de atrás va a adelantarnos.* The car behind is going to pass us. ◇ *Yo me quedé atrás.* I stayed behind.

◆ **años atrás** years ago

atrasado ADJETIVO

1 backward ◇ *Es un país muy atrasado.* It's a very backward country.

2 back ◇ *números atrasados de una revista* back numbers of a magazine ◇ *pagos atrasados* back payments

3 behind ◇ *Va bastante atrasado en la escuela.* He's rather behind at school.

◆ **Tengo mucho trabajo atrasado.** I'm very behind with my work.

◆ **El reloj está atrasado.** The clock's slow.

4 late ◇ *Siempre llega atrasada al trabajo.* She's always late for work.

atrasar VERBO

1 to delay ◇ *Tuvimos que atrasar nuestra salida.* We had to delay our departure.

2 to put back ◇ *Acuérdense de atrasar una hora los relojes.* Remember to put the time on your watches back by one hour.

◆ **atrasarse** to be late

atravesar* VERBO

1 to cross ◇ *Atravesamos el río.* We crossed the river.

2 to go through ◇ *La navaja le atravesó el hígado.* The blade went through his liver. ◇ *Atravesamos un mal momento.* We're going through a bad patch.

atravieso VERBO *ver* **atravesar**

atreverse VERBO

to dare ◇ *No me atreví a decírselo.* I didn't dare tell him.

◆ **No me atrevo.** I don't dare.

◆ **La gente no se atreve a salir de noche.** People are afraid of going out at night.

atrevido ADJETIVO

1 daring ◇ *El periodista le hizo preguntas muy atrevidas.* The reporter asked him some very daring questions. ◇ *un escote muy atrevido* a very daring neckline
2 impudent ◇ *No seas tan atrevido con el jefe.* Don't be so impudent to the boss.

atropellar VERBO
to run over ◇ *Un carro atropelló al perro.* The dog was run over by a car.

el **atún** SUSTANTIVO (PL los **atunes**)
tuna (PL tuna *o* tunas)

audaz ADJETIVO (PL **audaces**)
daring

la **audiencia** SUSTANTIVO
audience ◇ *Su programa tiene mucha audiencia.* His program has a large audience.

los **audífonos** SUSTANTIVO
headphones

audiovisual ADJETIVO
audiovisual

el **auditorio** SUSTANTIVO
1 auditorium ◇ *El auditorio estaba lleno.* The auditorium was full.
2 audience ◇ *Todo el auditorio aplaudió a la orquesta.* The whole audience applauded the orchestra.

el **aula** SUSTANTIVO FEM
classroom

aumentar VERBO
to increase ◇ *El gobierno ha aumentado el presupuesto de educación.* The government has increased the education budget.
◆ **aumentar de peso** to put on weight

el **aumento** SUSTANTIVO
increase ◇ *Se ha producido un aumento de la productividad.* There has been an increase in productivity.
◆ **Los precios van en aumento.** Prices are going up.

aun ADVERBIO
even ◇ *Aun sentado me duele la pierna.* Even when I'm sitting down, my leg hurts.
◆ **aun así** even so
◆ **aun cuando** even if

aún ADVERBIO
1 still
En oraciones afirmativas o preguntas.
◇ *Aún me queda un poco para terminar.* I've still got a little bit left to finish. ◇ *¿Aún te duele?* Is it still hurting?
2 yet
En oraciones o preguntas negativas.
◇ *Aún no han llegado los periódicos de hoy.* Today's papers haven't arrived yet. ◇ *¿No ha venido aún?* Hasn't he got here yet?
Cuando se usa de forma enfática en una oración o pregunta negativa se puede usar ***still.***
◇ *Y aún no me has devuelto el libro.* You still haven't given me the book back.
3 even
Cuando ***aún*** *es parte de una comparación.*
◇ *La película es aún más aburrida de lo que creía.* The movie is even more boring than I thought it would be. ◇ *Aquello nos unió aún más.* That brought us even closer together.

aunque CONJUNCIÓN
1 although ◇ *Me gusta el francés, aunque prefiero el alemán.* I like French, although I prefer German.
Lo mismo puede expresarse de una forma más coloquial con ***though.***
◇ *Estoy pensando en ir, aunque no sé cuándo.* I'm thinking of going, though I don't know when.
2 even though ◇ *Seguí andando, aunque me dolía mucho la pierna.* I went on walking, even though my leg was hurting badly.
◆ **No te lo daré, aunque protestes.** I won't give it to you however much you complain.
3 even if ◇ *Pienso irme, aunque tenga que salir por la ventana.* I'll leave, even if I have to climb out the window.

el **auricular** SUSTANTIVO
receiver (*del teléfono*)
◆ **los auriculares** (*de radio, aparato de música*) headphones

la **ausencia** SUSTANTIVO
absence

ausente ADJETIVO
absent

Australia SUSTANTIVO FEM
Australia

el **australiano**, la **australiana** ADJETIVO, SUSTANTIVO
Australian

Austria SUSTANTIVO FEM
Austria

el **austriaco**, la **austriaca** ADJETIVO, SUSTANTIVO
Austrian

auténtico ADJETIVO
1 real (*no sintético*) ◇ *Es de cuero auténtico.* It's real leather.
2 genuine (*no falso*) ◇ *El cuadro era auténtico.* The painting was genuine.
◆ **Es un auténtico campeón.** He's a real champion.

el **auto** SUSTANTIVO
car

la **autobiografía** SUSTANTIVO
autobiography (PL autobiographies)

el **autobús** SUSTANTIVO (PL los **autobuses**)
bus (PL buses)
◆ **en autobús** by bus

el **autocar** *Spain* SUSTANTIVO
bus (PL buses)

la **autoedición** SUSTANTIVO
desktop publishing

la **autoescuela** SUSTANTIVO
driving school

el **autoestop** SUSTANTIVO
hitchhiking

☞

◆ **hacer* autoestop** to hitchhike

el **autógrafo** SUSTANTIVO
autograph

automático ADJETIVO
automatic

el **automóvil** SUSTANTIVO
car

el/la **automovilista** SUSTANTIVO
motorist

la **autonomía** SUSTANTIVO
1 autonomy ◇ *un estatuto de autonomía* a statute of autonomy ◇ *Tengo mucha autonomía en mi trabajo.* I have a lot of autonomy in my work.
2 autonomous region Spain ◇ *Andalucía es una de las autonomías más extensas.* Andalusia is one of the biggest autonomous regions.

autonómico ADJETIVO
regional

autónomo ADJETIVO
1 autonomous ◇ *las comunidades autónomas* the autonomous regions
2 self-employed ◇ *Ser autónomo tiene sus ventajas.* Being self-employed has its advantages.

la **autopista** SUSTANTIVO
freeway
◆ **autopista de peaje** turnpike

el **autor,** la **autora** SUSTANTIVO
author ◇ *el autor de la novela* the author of the novel
◆ **el autor del cuadro** the painter
◆ **los presuntos autores del crimen** the suspected killers

la **autoridad** SUSTANTIVO
authority (PL authorities)

autorizado ADJETIVO
authorized

autorizar* VERBO
to authorize ◇ *No le han autorizado la entrada al país.* His entry into the country hasn't been authorized.
◆ **Eso no te autoriza a tratarlo así.** That doesn't give you the right to treat him this way.

el **autoservicio** SUSTANTIVO
1 supermarket ◇ *Sale más económico comprar en el autoservicio.* It's cheaper to shop at the supermarket.
2 self-service restaurant ◇ *Comimos en un autoservicio.* We ate at a self-service restaurant.

el **autostop** SUSTANTIVO
hitchhiking
◆ **hacer* autostop** to hitchhike

el/la **autostopista** SUSTANTIVO
hitchhiker

la **autovía** SUSTANTIVO
divided highway

el **auxilio** SUSTANTIVO
help ◇ *una llamada de auxilio* a call for help
◆ **los primeros auxilios** first aid

auxilio EXCLAMACIÓN
help!

avanzar* VERBO
to make progress ◇ *Isabel avanzó mucho el pasado trimestre.* Isabel made a lot of progress last term.
◆ **¿Qué tal avanza el proyecto?** How's the project coming on?

avaro ADJETIVO
miserly

Avda. ABREVIATURA (= *Avenida*)
Ave. (= Avenue)

el **ave** SUSTANTIVO FEM
bird ◇ *un ave de rapiña* a bird of prey
◆ **aves de corral** poultry SING

la **avellana** SUSTANTIVO
hazelnut

la **avena** SUSTANTIVO
oats PL

la **avenida** SUSTANTIVO
avenue

aventajar VERBO
◆ **Juan aventaja a Pablo por cuatro puntos.** Juan leads Pablo by four points.

aventar* VERBO Mexico
to throw

el **aventón** SUSTANTIVO (PL los **aventones**)
Mexico
ride ◇ *Le di aventón.* I gave him a ride.

la **aventura** SUSTANTIVO
1 adventure ◇ *nuestras aventuras en África* our adventures in Africa
2 affair ◇ *Tuvo una aventura con su vecino.* She had an affair with her neighbor.

avergonzar* VERBO
to embarrass ◇ *Me avergonzaste delante de todos.* You embarrassed me in front of everyone.
◆ **Me avergüenzan estas situaciones.** I find this sort of situation embarrassing.
◆ **No me avergüenza nuestra relación.** I'm not ashamed of our relationship.
◆ **avergonzarse de algo** to be ashamed of something ◇ *No hay de qué avergonzarse.* There's nothing to be ashamed of.
◆ **Me avergüenzo de haberme portado tan mal.** I'm ashamed of myself for behaving so badly.

la **avería** SUSTANTIVO
◆ **El carro tiene una avería.** The car has broken down.

averiarse* VERBO
to break down

averiguar* VERBO
to find out ◇ *La policía no ha conseguido averiguar dónde se escondió el arma.* The police haven't managed to find out where the weapon was hidden.

el **avestruz** SUSTANTIVO (PL los **avestruces**)
ostrich (PL ostriches)

la **aviación** SUSTANTIVO (PL las **aviaciones**)
1 aviation ◇ *aviación civil* civil aviation
2 air force ◇ *Es oficial de aviación.* He's an officer in the air force.

aviento VERBO *ver* **aventar**

el **avión** SUSTANTIVO (PL los **aviones**)
plane
◆ **ir* en avión** to fly

la **avioneta** SUSTANTIVO
light aircraft

avisar VERBO
1 to warn ◇ *Ya nos avisaron de que había nieve en la carretera.* They had warned us that there was snow on the roads.
2 to let...know ◇ *Avísanos si hay alguna novedad.* Let us know if there's any news.
3 to call ◇ *avisar al médico* to call the doctor ◇ *Avisaron a una ambulancia.* They called an ambulance.

el **aviso** SUSTANTIVO
1 warning ◇ *El árbitro le dio un aviso.* The referee gave him a warning.
2 notice ◇ *Había un aviso en la puerta.* There was a notice on the door.
◆ **hasta nuevo aviso** until further notice

la **avispa** SUSTANTIVO
wasp

ay EXCLAMACIÓN
1 ow! ◇ *¡Ay! ¡Me pisaste!* Ow! You've stepped on my toe!
2 oh no! ◇ *¡Ay! ¡Creo que nos han engañado!* Oh no! I think they've cheated us!

ayer ADVERBIO
yesterday
◆ **antes de ayer** the day before yesterday
◆ **ayer por la mañana** yesterday morning
◆ **ayer por la tarde (1)** (*si es de día*) yesterday afternoon
◆ **ayer por la tarde (2)** (*si no es de día*) yesterday evening
◆ **ayer por la noche** last night

la **ayuda** SUSTANTIVO
help
◆ **la ayuda humanitaria** humanitarian aid

el/la **ayudante** SUSTANTIVO
assistant

ayudar VERBO
to help ◇ *¿Me ayudas con los ejercicios?* Could you help me with these exercises?
◆ **ayudar a alguien a hacer algo** to help somebody do something

el **ayuntamiento** SUSTANTIVO
1 council ◇ *El ayuntamiento recauda sus propios impuestos.* The council collects its own taxes.
2 town hall (*en pueblo*) ◇ *¿Dónde está el ayuntamiento?* Where's the town hall?
3 city hall (*en ciudad grande*) ◇ *¿Dónde está el ayuntamiento?* Where's the city hall?

la **azafata** SUSTANTIVO
female flight attendant (*de avión*)
◆ **una azafata de congresos** a conference hostess

el **azar** SUSTANTIVO
chance ◇ *Nos encontramos por azar.* We met by chance.
◆ **al azar** at random ◇ *Escoge uno al azar.* Pick one at random.

azotar VERBO
to whip

la **azotea** SUSTANTIVO
roof

el/la **azteca** ADJETIVO, SUSTANTIVO
Aztec

el **azúcar** SUSTANTIVO
sugar
◆ **azúcar moreno** brown sugar
◆ **un caramelo sin azúcar** a sugar-free candy

el **azul** ADJETIVO, SUSTANTIVO
blue ◇ *una puerta azul* a blue door ◇ *Yo iba de azul.* I was dressed in blue.
◆ **azul celeste** sky blue
◆ **azul marino** navy blue

el **azulejo** SUSTANTIVO
tile

B

el **babero** SUSTANTIVO
bib

el **bacalao** SUSTANTIVO
cod

el **bache** SUSTANTIVO
pothole (*en camino*)
◆ **pasar por un mal bache** to go through a bad patch

el **Bachillerato** SUSTANTIVO

> ℹ *The **Bachillerato** is a higher secondary school course leading to university.*

la **bacteria** SUSTANTIVO
bacterium (PL bacteria)

el **bafle** SUSTANTIVO
loudspeaker

la **bahía** SUSTANTIVO
bay (PL bays)

bailar VERBO
to dance
◆ **sacar* a bailar a alguien** to ask someone to dance

el **bailarín**, la **bailarina** SUSTANTIVO (MASC PL los **bailarines**)
dancer

el **baile** SUSTANTIVO
dance ◇ *Me invitaron a un baile.* I have been invited to a dance.

la **baja** SUSTANTIVO
◆ **dar* de baja** to discharge ◇ *Lo dieron de baja en el ejército.* He was discharged from the army.
◆ **darse* de baja** to leave ◇ *Se dieron de baja en el club.* They left the club.

la **bajada** SUSTANTIVO
drop ◇ *Anuciaron una bajada de las temperaturas.* They forecast a drop in temperatures.
◆ **Me caí en la bajada de la montaña.** I fell going down the mountain.
◆ **La bajada hasta la playa es muy pronunciada.** The road down to the beach is very steep.

bajar VERBO
[1] to go down
Cuando el hablante está arriba.
◇ *Bajó la escalera muy despacio.* He went down the stairs very slowly.
[2] to come down
Cuando el hablante está abajo.
◇ *Baja y ayúdame.* Come down and help me.
◇ *Han bajado los precios.* Prices have come down.
◆ **Los carros han bajado de precio.** Cars have come down in price.
[3] to take down
Cuando el hablante está arriba.
◇ *¿Bajaste la basura?* Have you taken the trash down?
[4] to bring down
Cuando el hablante está abajo.
◇ *¿Me bajas el abrigo? Hace frío aquí afuera.* Could you bring my coat down? It's cold out here.
[5] to get down
Cuando no se alcanza algo.
◇ *¿Me bajas la maleta del closet?* Could you get me the suitcase down from the closet?
[6] to put down ◇ *¿Bajo la persiana?* Shall I put the blind down? ◇ *El comercio ha bajado los precios.* Businesses have put their prices down.
◆ **¡Baja la voz, que no estoy sordo!** Keep your voice down, I'm not deaf!
[7] to turn down ◇ *Baja la radio que no oigo nada.* Turn the radio down, I can't hear a thing.
[8] to download (*Internet*)
◆ **bajarse de (1)** to get off (*de un bus, tren, avión*) ◇ *Se bajó del tren antes que yo.* He got off the train before me.
◆ **bajarse de (2)** to get out of (*de un carro*) ◇ *¡Bájate del carro!* Get out of the car!
◆ **bajarse de (3)** (*de un árbol, escalera, silla*) to get down from ◇ *¡Bájate de ahí!* Get down from there!

bajo (1) ADJETIVO
[1] low (*notas, temperaturas, nivel*) ◇ *una silla muy baja* a very low chair
◆ **la temporada baja** the off season
[2] short ◇ *Mi hermano es muy bajo.* My brother is very short.
◆ **Viven en la planta baja.** They live on the first floor.
◆ **Hablaban en voz baja.** They spoke quietly.

bajo (2) PREPOSICIÓN
under ◇ *bajo el título de...* under the title of... ◇ *Juan llevaba un libro bajo el brazo.* Juan was carrying a book under his arm.
◆ **bajo tierra** underground

bajo (3) ADVERBIO
[1] low ◇ *El avión volaba muy bajo.* The plane was flying very low.
[2] quietly ◇ *¡Habla bajo!* Speak quietly!

el **bajo** SUSTANTIVO
[1] bass (*instrumento*) (PL basses) ◇ *Elena toca el bajo en un grupo.* Elena plays bass in a group.
[2] first floor (*de un edificio*) ◇ *Vivo en un bajo.* I live on the first floor.

la **bala** SUSTANTIVO
bullet

el **balcón** SUSTANTIVO (PL los **balcones**)
balcony (PL balconies)

el **balde** SUSTANTIVO
bucket

* Verbs marked with this symbol are irregular. See pages 346–348 for further details.

- **en balde** in vain ◇ *El viaje no ha sido en balde.* The journey wasn't in vain.

la **baldosa** SUSTANTIVO
tile

el **baldosín** SUSTANTIVO (PL los **baldosines**)
tile

balear ADJETIVO
Balearic

la **ballena** SUSTANTIVO
whale

el **ballet** SUSTANTIVO (PL los **ballets**)
ballet

el **balneario** SUSTANTIVO
1 spa (*de aguas medicinales*)
2 seaside resort (*en la costa*)

el **balón** SUSTANTIVO (PL los **balones**)
ball

el **baloncesto** SUSTANTIVO
basketball

el **balonmano** SUSTANTIVO
handball

el **balonvolea** SUSTANTIVO
volleyball

la **balsa** SUSTANTIVO
raft

el **banano** SUSTANTIVO
banana tree (*árbol*)

el **banco** SUSTANTIVO
1 bank (*para el dinero*)
2 bench (PL benches) (*de un parque*)
3 pew (*de iglesia*)

la **banda** SUSTANTIVO
1 band ◇ *Toca la trompeta en la banda del colegio.* He plays the trumpet in the school band.
2 gang ◇ *La policía capturó a toda la banda.* The police caught the whole gang.
3 sash (PL sashes) ◇ *Las autoridades llevaban una banda azul.* The dignitaries were wearing a blue sash.
4 hair band [Mexico]

- **la banda ancha** broadband
- **la banda sonora** the soundtrack

la **bandeja** SUSTANTIVO
tray (PL trays)

la **bandera** SUSTANTIVO
flag

- **la bandera blanca** the white flag

el **bandido** SUSTANTIVO
bandit

el **bando** SUSTANTIVO
side ◇ *Un bando está a favor y el otro en contra.* One side is in favor and the other is against.

la **banqueta** SUSTANTIVO
1 stool (*asiento*)
2 sidewalk [Mexico]

- **estacionarse en banqueta** [Mexico] to park at an angle to the curb

el **banquete** SUSTANTIVO
banquet

- **el banquete de bodas** the wedding reception

el **banquillo** SUSTANTIVO
bench (PL benches) ◇ *El entrenador siempre se sienta en el banquillo.* The trainer always sits on the bench.

- **el banquillo de los acusados** the dock

bañarse VERBO
1 to have a bath ◇ *Me gusta más bañarme que ducharme.* I prefer having a bath to having a shower.
2 to go for a swim ◇ *Estuve en la playa pero no me bañé.* I was on the beach but I didn't go for a swim.

la **bañera** SUSTANTIVO
1 bootblack [Mexico]
2 bathtub (*para bañarse*)

el **baño** SUSTANTIVO
bathroom ◇ *¿Podría decirme dónde está el baño?* Could you tell me where the bathroom is?

- **darse* un baño (1)** (*en la bañera*) to have a bath
- **darse* un baño (2)** (*en el mar*) to go for a swim

el **bar** SUSTANTIVO
bar

la **baraja** SUSTANTIVO
deck of cards

la **barandilla** SUSTANTIVO
1 banisters PL (*de una escalera*)
2 railing (*de un balcón*)

la **barata** SUSTANTIVO [Mexico]
sale

barato (1) ADJETIVO
cheap ◇ *Esta marca es más barata que aquélla.* This brand is cheaper than that one.

barato (2) ADVERBIO
cheaply ◇ *Aquí se come muy barato.* You can eat really cheaply here.

la **barba** SUSTANTIVO
beard

- **dejarse barba** to grow a beard

la **barbacoa** SUSTANTIVO
barbecue (*parrillada*)

> ℹ *In Mexico,* ***barbacoa*** *is meat cooked in an oven dug in the ground.*

la **barbaridad** SUSTANTIVO
atrocity (PL atrocities) ◇ *Cometieron barbaridades en la guerra.* They committed atrocities during the war.

- **Pablo come una barbaridad.** Pablo eats an awful lot.
- **decir* barbaridades** to talk nonsense
- **¡Qué barbaridad!** Good grief!

la **barbilla** SUSTANTIVO
chin

la **barca** SUSTANTIVO
boat

el **barco** SUSTANTIVO ☞

[1] ship (*más grande*)
◆ **un barco de guerra** a warship
[2] boat (*más pequeño*)
◆ **un barco de vela** sailboat

la **barda** SUSTANTIVO [*Mexico*]
[1] fence (*de madera*)
[2] wall (*de cemento*)

el **barniz** SUSTANTIVO (PL los **barnices**)
varnish (PL varnishes)

barnizar* VERBO
to varnish

la **barra** SUSTANTIVO
bar ◇ *una barra de chocolate* a bar of chocolate ◇ *una barra metálica* a metal bar ◇ *Me tomé un café en la barra.* I had a coffee at the bar.
◆ **una barra de pan** a French loaf
◆ **las barras paralelas** the parallel bars

la **barraca** SUSTANTIVO
[1] warehouse (*depósito*)
[2] shack [*Mexico*]
[3] small farmhouse (*en Murcia y Valencia*)

el **barranco** SUSTANTIVO
ravine

barrer VERBO
to sweep
◆ **barrerse** [*Mexico*] to skid ◇ *Se me barrió la bicicleta.* My bicycle skidded.

la **barrera** SUSTANTIVO
barrier
◆ **una barrera de seguridad** a safety barrier

la **barriga** SUSTANTIVO
belly (*coloquial*) (PL bellies) ◇ *Estás echando barriga.* You're getting a bit of a belly.
◆ **Me duele la barriga.** I have a sore stomach.

el **barril** SUSTANTIVO
barrel

el **barrio** SUSTANTIVO
area ◇ *Ese chico no es del barrio.* That boy's not from this area.
◆ **la pescadería del barrio** the local fish market
◆ **el barrio chino** Chinatown

el **barro** SUSTANTIVO
[1] mud ◇ *Metí el pie en un charco y me llené de barro.* I stood in a puddle and got covered in mud.
[2] clay ◇ *una vasija de barro* a clay pot

el **barrote** SUSTANTIVO
bar ◇ *los barrotes de la ventana* the bars on the window

el **barullo** SUSTANTIVO
[1] racket
◆ **armar barullo** to make a racket
[2] mess ◇ *Esta habitación está hecha un barullo.* This room is a mess.

basarse VERBO
◆ **Mi conclusión se basa en los datos.** My conclusion is based on the facts.
◆ **¿En qué te basas para decir eso?** What grounds do you have for saying that?
◆ **Para la novela me basé en la vida de mi abuela.** I based the novel on the life of my grandmother.

la **báscula** SUSTANTIVO
scales PL

la **base** SUSTANTIVO
[1] base ◇ *la base de la columna* the base of the column
[2] basis (PL bases) ◇ *El esfuerzo es la base del éxito.* Effort is the basis for success.
◆ **las bases del concurso** the rules of the competition
◆ **Lo consiguió a base de mucho trabajo.** She managed it through hard work.
◆ **una base militar** a military base
◆ **una base de datos** a database

básico ADJETIVO
basic

el **basquetbol** SUSTANTIVO [*Mexico*]
basketball

el **básquetbol** SUSTANTIVO
basketball

bastante (1) ADJETIVO, PRONOMBRE
[1] enough
Cuando significa suficiente.
◇ *No tengo bastante dinero.* I don't have enough money. ◇ *Ya hay bastantes libros en casa.* There are enough books in the house. ◇ *¿Hay bastante?* Is there enough?
[2] quite a lot of
Cuando significa una cantidad considerable.
◇ *Vino bastante gente.* Quite a lot of people came.
◆ **Se tarda bastante tiempo en llegar.** It takes quite a while to get there.
◆ **Voy a tardar bastante.** I'm going to take quite a while.

bastante (2) ADVERBIO
[1] quite ◇ *Son bastante ricos.* They are quite rich. ◇ *Juegas bastante bien.* You play quite well.
[2] quite a lot ◇ *Sus padres ganan bastante.* Their parents earn quite a lot.

bastar VERBO
to be enough ◇ *Con esto basta.* That's enough. ◇ *¡Basta ya de tonterías!* That's enough of your nonsense!
◆ **¡Basta!** That's enough!
◆ **bastarse** to manage ◇ *Yo me basto solo.* I can manage on my own.

basto ADJETIVO
coarse ◇ *Esta tela es muy basta.* It's a very coarse material.
◆ **¡Qué basto eres!** You have no manners!

el **bastón** SUSTANTIVO (PL los **bastones**)
walking stick
◆ **un bastón de esquí** a ski pole

la **basura** SUSTANTIVO
[1] trash ◇ *Eso es basura.* That's trash.

* Verbs marked with this symbol are irregular. See pages 346–348 for further details.

- **tirar algo a la basura** to put something in the trash

[2] litter ◇ *Hay mucha basura en la calle.* There's a lot of litter in the street.

el **basurero** SUSTANTIVO
[1] garbage collector
[2] garbage dump (*vertedero*)
[3] trash can *Mexico*

la **bata** SUSTANTIVO
[1] bathrobe (*de casa*)
[2] lab coat (*de laboratorio*)

la **batalla** SUSTANTIVO
battle

la **batata** SUSTANTIVO
sweet potato

la **batería** SUSTANTIVO
[1] battery (PL batteries) ◇ *Se agotó la batería.* The battery is dead.
[2] drums PL ◇ *¿Tocas la batería?* Do you play the drums?

- **una batería de cocina** a set of kitchen equipment

[3] drummer (*en grupo*) ◇ *La batería del grupo se llama Pilar.* The group's drummer is called Pilar.

el **batería** SUSTANTIVO
drummer ◇ *El batería del grupo se llama Juan.* The group's drummer is called Juan.

el **batido** SUSTANTIVO
milkshake ◇ *un batido de fresa* a strawberry milkshake

la **batidora** SUSTANTIVO
mixer

batir VERBO
[1] to beat (*un huevo*)
[2] to whip (*crema*)
[3] to break (*un récord*)

- **batirse** (*ensuciarse*) *Mexico* to get dirty
- **La niña se batió de helado el vestido.** The little girl got her dress dirty with ice cream.

el **baúl** SUSTANTIVO
[1] chest (*para ropa*)
[2] trunk (*para viajar*)

el **bautizo** SUSTANTIVO
christening

la **bayeta** SUSTANTIVO
cloth

- **¿Has pasado la bayeta por la mesa?** Have you wiped the table?

el **bebé** SUSTANTIVO (PL los **bebés**)
baby (PL babies)

el **bebedero** SUSTANTIVO *Mexico*
drinking fountain

beber VERBO
to drink

- **Se bebió la leche de un trago.** He drank the milk in one gulp.

la **bebida** SUSTANTIVO
drink

- **bebidas alcohólicas** alcoholic drinks

bebido ADJETIVO
drunk

- **estar* bebido** to be drunk

la **beca** SUSTANTIVO
[1] grant (*ayuda económica general*)
[2] scholarship (*dada por méritos o en concurso*)

el **beisbol** SUSTANTIVO *Mexico*
baseball

el **béisbol** SUSTANTIVO
baseball

el/la **belga** ADJETIVO, SUSTANTIVO
Belgian

Bélgica SUSTANTIVO FEM
Belgium

la **belleza** SUSTANTIVO
beauty (PL beauties)

bendecir* VERBO
to bless

la **bendición** SUSTANTIVO (PL las **bendiciones**)
blessing

beneficiar VERBO
to benefit

- **beneficiarse de algo** to benefit from something

el **beneficio** SUSTANTIVO
profit ◇ *Obtuvieron un beneficio de dos millones de pesos.* They made a profit of two million pesos.

- **No han tenido beneficios este año.** They didn't make any profit this year.
- **sacar* beneficio de algo** to benefit from something ◇ *Seguro que espera sacar algún beneficio.* He definitely expects to benefit from it.
- **a beneficio de** in aid of ◇ *Un concierto a beneficio de las víctimas del terremoto.* A concert in aid of the earthquake victims.

benéfico ADJETIVO
benefit

***benefit** en este caso va siempre delante del sustantivo.*

◇ *un concierto benéfico* a benefit concert

el **berberecho** SUSTANTIVO
cockle

la **berenjena** SUSTANTIVO
eggplant

la **berma** SUSTANTIVO
[1] berm (*de asfalto*)
[2] soft shoulder (*de tierra*)

las **bermudas** SUSTANTIVO
Bermuda shorts

- **unas bermudas** a pair of Bermuda shorts

besar VERBO
to kiss

- **Ana y Pepe se besaron.** Ana and Pepe kissed each other.

el **beso** SUSTANTIVO
kiss (PL kisses)

- **dar* un beso a alguien** to give somebody a kiss

la **bestia** SUSTANTIVO

☞

B

beast

bestia ADJETIVO
- **¡Qué bestia eres!** You're so rough! (*coloquial*)
- **Tiró de él a lo bestia.** He pulled him roughly.

el **besugo** SUSTANTIVO
sea bream

el **betabel** SUSTANTIVO [Mexico]
beet

la **betarraga** SUSTANTIVO
beet

el **betún** SUSTANTIVO
shoe polish

el **biberón** SUSTANTIVO (PL los **biberones**)
baby's bottle
- **Voy a dar el biberón al niño.** I'm going to give the baby his bottle.

la **Biblia** SUSTANTIVO
Bible

la **biblioteca** SUSTANTIVO
library (PL libraries)

el **bicarbonato** SUSTANTIVO
bicarbonate

el **bicho** SUSTANTIVO
insect ◇ *Me picó un bicho.* I've been bitten by an insect.
- **un bicho raro** an oddball (*coloquial*)

la **bici** SUSTANTIVO
bike

la **bicicleta** SUSTANTIVO
bicycle
- **una bicicleta de montaña** a mountain bike

el **bidé** SUSTANTIVO (PL los **bidés**)
bidet

el **bidón** SUSTANTIVO (PL los **bidones**)
drum

el **bien** SUSTANTIVO
good ◇ *Lo digo por tu bien.* I'm telling you for your own good.
- **los bienes** possessions ◇ *todos los bienes de la familia* all the family's possessions

bien ADVERBIO
1 well ◇ *Habla bien el castellano.* He speaks Spanish well. ◇ *El traje me queda bien.* The suit fits me well.
2 good
Con verbos que expresan una sensación física.
◇ *Huele bien.* It smells good. ◇ *Sabe bien.* It tastes good.
- **Has contestado bien.** You gave the right answer.
- **Lo pasamos muy bien.** We had a very good time.

3 very
Cuando acompaña a un adjetivo.
◇ *un café bien caliente* a very hot coffee
- **¿Estás bien?** Are you OK?
- **¡Está bien! Lo haré.** OK! I'll do it.
- **Ese libro está muy bien.** That's a very good book.
- **Está muy bien que ahorres dinero.** It's good that you're saving.
- **¡Eso no está bien!** That's not very nice!
- **Hiciste bien en decírselo.** You were right to tell him.
- **¡Ya está bien!** That's enough!
- **¡Qué bien!** Excellent!

el **bienestar** SUSTANTIVO
well-being

la **bienvenida** SUSTANTIVO
- **dar* la bienvenida a alguien** to welcome somebody
- **una fiesta de bienvenida** a welcome party

bienvenido ADJETIVO
welcome ◇ *Siempre serás bienvenido aquí.* You will always be welcome here.
◇ *¡Bienvenidos a mi casa!* Welcome to my home!

la **bifurcación** SUSTANTIVO (PL las **bifurcaciones**)
fork

el **bigote** SUSTANTIVO
mustache

el **bikini** SUSTANTIVO
bikini

bilingüe ADJETIVO
bilingual

el **billar** SUSTANTIVO
billiards SING
- **el billar americano** pool

el **billete** SUSTANTIVO
1 bill ◇ *un billete de veinte pesos* a twenty peso bill
2 ticket [Spain]

el **billón** SUSTANTIVO (PL los **billones**)
- **un billón** a thousand million

el **bingo** SUSTANTIVO
1 bingo ◇ *jugar al bingo* to play bingo
2 bingo hall ◇ *Van a abrir un bingo aquí.* They're opening a bingo hall here.

biodegradable ADJETIVO
biodegradable

la **biografía** SUSTANTIVO
biography (PL biographies)

la **biología** SUSTANTIVO
biology

biológico ADJETIVO
1 organic (*alimento*)
2 biological (*ciclo, padre, guerra*)

el **biombo** SUSTANTIVO
folding screen

el **biquini** SUSTANTIVO
bikini (PL bikinis)

la **bisabuela** SUSTANTIVO
great-grandmother

el **bisabuelo** SUSTANTIVO
great-grandfather
- **mis bisabuelos** my great-grandparents

la **bisagra** SUSTANTIVO
hinge

bisiesto ADJETIVO
- **un año bisiesto** a leap year

la **bisnieta** SUSTANTIVO
great-granddaughter

el **bisnieto** SUSTANTIVO
great-grandson
- **tus bisnietos** your great-grandchildren

el **bistec** SUSTANTIVO (PL los **bistecs**)
steak

la **bisutería** SUSTANTIVO
costume jewellery
- **Son de bisutería.** They're costume jewellery.

bizco ADJETIVO
cross-eyed

el **bizcocho** SUSTANTIVO
sponge cake

blanco ADJETIVO
white ◇ *un vestido blanco* a white dress

el **blanco** SUSTANTIVO
white ◇ *Me gusta el blanco.* I like white.
- **dar* en el blanco** to hit the target
- **dejar algo en blanco** to leave something blank
- **Cuando iba a responder me quedé en blanco.** Just as I was about to reply my mind went blank.

blando ADJETIVO
1 soft ◇ *Este colchón es muy blando.* This mattress is very soft.
2 easy ◇ *Es muy blando con sus alumnos.* He's very easy on his students.

el **bloc** SUSTANTIVO (PL los **blocs**)
writing pad
- **un bloc de dibujo** a drawing pad

el **bloque** SUSTANTIVO
block
- **un bloque de departamentos** an apartment block

bloquear VERBO
to block ◇ *La nieve bloqueó las carreteras.* The snow blocked the roads.

la **blusa** SUSTANTIVO
blouse

la **bobada** SUSTANTIVO
- **hacer* bobadas** to do stupid things
- **Este programa es una bobada.** This program is stupid.
- **decir* bobadas** to talk nonsense

la **bobina** SUSTANTIVO
reel

bobo ADJETIVO
silly

la **boca** SUSTANTIVO
mouth ◇ *No debes hablar con la boca llena.* You shouldn't talk with your mouth full. ◇ *No abrió la boca en toda la tarde.* He didn't open his mouth all afternoon.
- **boca abajo** face down
- **boca arriba** face up
- **Me quedé con la boca abierta.** I was dumbfounded.
- **la boca del metro** the entrance to the subway

la **bocacalle** SUSTANTIVO
- **Es una bocacalle del Paseo Central.** It's a side street off the Paseo Central.
- **La primera bocacalle a la derecha.** The first road on the right.

el **bocadillo** SUSTANTIVO *Spain*
sandwich

el **bocado** SUSTANTIVO
1 bite ◇ *Se comió el trozo de un bocado.* He ate the piece in one bite.
- **No he probado bocado desde ayer.** I haven't had a bite to eat since yesterday.

2 mouthful ◇ *Trataba de hablar entre bocado y bocado.* I was trying to talk between mouthfuls.

el **bochorno** SUSTANTIVO
- **Hace bochorno.** It's muggy.

la **bocina** SUSTANTIVO
1 horn (*del carro*)
2 receiver (*del teléfono*) *Mexico*

la **boda** SUSTANTIVO
wedding
- **las bodas de oro** golden wedding SING
- **las bodas de plata** silver wedding SING

la **bodega** SUSTANTIVO
1 cellar (*de una casa*)
2 wine cellar (*para guardar el vino*)
3 wine store (*para vender vino*)
4 storehouse (*depósito*) *Mexico*
5 storeroom (*en una tienda, un edificio*) *Mexico*
6 hold (*de un avión*)

la **bofetada** SUSTANTIVO
slap ◇ *dar una bofetada a alguien* to give somebody a slap

el **boicot** SUSTANTIVO (PL los **boicots**)
boycott
- **hacer* el boicot a algo** to boycott something

la **boina** SUSTANTIVO
beret

el **bol** SUSTANTIVO
bowl

la **bola** SUSTANTIVO
ball
- **una bola de nieve** a snowball

la **bolera** SUSTANTIVO
bowling alley

el **bolero**, la **bolera** SUSTANTIVO *Mexico*
bootblack

la **boleta** SUSTANTIVO
ticket (*de rifa*)
- **una boleta de calificaciones** *Mexico* a report card

la **boletería** SUSTANTIVO
ticket office

el **boletín** SUSTANTIVO (PL los **boletines**)
bulletin
- **un boletín informativo** a news bulletin

el **boleto** SUSTANTIVO
ticket ◇ *un boleto de rifa* a raffle ticket ◇ *un* ☞

boleto de metro a subway ticket
- **comprar un boleto** to buy a ticket
- **un boleto de ida y vuelta** a round-trip ticket
- **un boleto redondo** (*Mexico*) a round-trip ticket
- **un boleto electrónico** an e-ticket

el **boli** SUSTANTIVO
pen (*coloquial*)

el **bolígrafo** SUSTANTIVO
pen

el **bolillo** SUSTANTIVO *Mexico*
bun

Bolivia SUSTANTIVO FEM
Bolivia

el **boliviano,** la **boliviana** ADJETIVO, SUSTANTIVO
Bolivian

el **bollo** SUSTANTIVO
bun ◇ *Me comí un bollo para el desayuno.* I had a bun for breakfast.

los **bolos** SUSTANTIVO
1 bowls SING (*juego al aire libre*)
2 tenpin bowling SING (*juego en bolera*)

la **bolsa** SUSTANTIVO
1 bag ◇ *una bolsa de plástico* a plastic bag
- **una bolsa de deportes** a sports bag

2 purse (*para mujer*) *Mexico*
3 pocket (*bolsillo*) *Mexico*
- **la Bolsa** the Stock Exchange

el **bolsillo** SUSTANTIVO
pocket ◇ *Sacó las llaves del bolsillo.* He took the keys out of his pocket.
- **un libro de bolsillo** a paperback

el **bolso** SUSTANTIVO
bag
- **un bolso de mano** a traveling bag

la **bomba** SUSTANTIVO
1 bomb ◇ *la bomba atómica* the atomic bomb
2 pump ◇ *una bomba de agua* a water pump
- **pasarlo bomba** to have a ball (*coloquial*)

bombardear VERBO
to bombard
- **bombardear a alguien a preguntas** to bombard somebody with questions

el **bombero** SUSTANTIVO
fireman (PL firemen)
- **llamar a los bomberos** to call the fire department

la **bombilla** SUSTANTIVO
lightbulb

el **bombo** SUSTANTIVO
bass drum

el **bombón** SUSTANTIVO (PL los **bombones**)
chocolate

la **bombona** SUSTANTIVO
gas cylinder

la **bondad** SUSTANTIVO
kindness ◇ *un acto de bondad* an act of kindness
- **¿Tendría la bondad de...?** Would you be so kind as to...?

el **boniato** SUSTANTIVO
sweet potato (PL sweet potatoes)

bonito (1) ADJETIVO
pretty ◇ *una casa muy bonita* a very pretty house

bonito (2) ADVERBIO
well ◇ *Canta muy bonito.* She sings very well.

el **bonito** SUSTANTIVO
tuna (PL tuna *o* tunas)

el **boquerón** SUSTANTIVO (PL los **boquerones**)
anchovy (PL anchovies)

el **boquete** SUSTANTIVO
hole ◇ *Abrieron un boquete en el muro.* They made a hole in the wall.

la **borda** SUSTANTIVO
- **echar algo por la borda** to throw something overboard

bordar VERBO
to embroider

el **borde** SUSTANTIVO
edge ◇ *al borde de la mesa* at the edge of the table
- **estar* al borde de algo** to be on the verge of something
- **el borde de la banqueta** *Mexico* the curb

el **bordillo** SUSTANTIVO
curb ◇ *Los carros no pueden subirse al bordillo.* Cars are not allowed onto the curb.

bordo SUSTANTIVO MASC
- **subir a bordo** to get on board

la **borrachera** SUSTANTIVO
- **pegarse* una borrachera** to get drunk

borracho ADJETIVO
drunk ◇ *Estás borracho.* You're drunk.

el **borrador** SUSTANTIVO
1 rough draft ◇ *Escribe primero un borrador.* First write a rough draft.
2 dustcloth ◇ *Usó un trapo como borrador.* He used a rag as a dustcloth.

borrar VERBO
1 to erase ◇ *Borra toda la palabra.* Erase the whole word.
2 to clean ◇ *Borra la pizarra.* Clean the blackboard.
3 to wipe ◇ *No borres esa cinta.* Don't wipe that tape.
- **borrarse de** to take one's name off ◇ *Voy a borrarme de la lista.* I'm going to take my name off the list.

la **borrasca** SUSTANTIVO
- **Viene una borrasca por el Atlántico.** There's low pressure over the Atlantic.

el **borrón** SUSTANTIVO (PL los **borrones**)
smudge ◇ *Presentó la tarea llena de borrones.* He handed in his homework covered in smudges.
- **un borrón de tinta** an inkblot

borroso ADJETIVO
blurred ◇ *Lo veo muy borroso.* It looks very blurred.

Bosnia SUSTANTIVO FEM
Bosnia

el **bosnio,** la **bosnia** ADJETIVO, SUSTANTIVO
Bosnian

el **bosque** SUSTANTIVO
1 wood (*pequeño*)
2 forest (*más grande*)

bostezar* VERBO
to yawn

la **bota** SUSTANTIVO
boot
◆ **unas botas de agua** a pair of waterproof boots
◆ **una bota de vino** a wineskin

la **botana** SUSTANTIVO *Mexico*
snack

> ℹ *In Mexico,* ***botanas*** *are small portions of food like peanuts, olives, etc, which are served with drinks, in bars and on social occasions.*

la **botánica** SUSTANTIVO
botany

botánico ADJETIVO
botanical

botar VERBO
1 to throw out (*desechar*) ◇ *Bota eso a la basura.* Throw that out.
2 to knock down (*derribar*) ◇ *Vamos a botar esta pared.* We are going to knock this wall down.

el **bote** SUSTANTIVO
1 boat (*barco*)
◆ **un bote salvavidas** a lifeboat
2 bounce
◆ **Esta pelota no da bote.** This ball doesn't bounce.
◆ **el bote de la basura** *Mexico* the garbage can

la **botella** SUSTANTIVO
bottle

el **botijo** SUSTANTIVO

> ℹ *A* ***botijo*** *is an earthenware water container with spouts.*

el **botín** SUSTANTIVO (PL los **botines**)
1 ankle boot (*bota*)
2 haul (*de un robo*)

el **botiquín** SUSTANTIVO (PL los **botiquines**)
1 medicine cabinet (*armario*)
2 first-aid kit (*conjunto de medicinas*)
3 infirmary (*enfermería*)

el **botón** SUSTANTIVO (PL los **botones**)
button ◇ *Perdí un botón de la camisa.* I've lost a button off my shirt.
◆ **pulsar un botón** to press a button

la **bóveda** SUSTANTIVO
vault

el **boxeador,** la **boxeadora** SUSTANTIVO
boxer

boxear VERBO
to box

el **boxeo** SUSTANTIVO
boxing

el **bozal** SUSTANTIVO
muzzle

las **bragas** SUSTANTIVO *Spain*
panties
◆ **unas bragas** a pair of panties

la **bragueta** SUSTANTIVO
fly (PL flies) (*de pantalones*)

la **brasa** SUSTANTIVO
◆ **carne a la brasa** barbecued meat
◆ **las brasas** the embers

el **brasier** SUSTANTIVO *Mexico*
bra

Brasil SUSTANTIVO MASC
Brazil

el **brasileño,** la **brasileña** ADJETIVO, SUSTANTIVO
Brazilian

el **brasilero,** la **brasilera** ADJETIVO, SUSTANTIVO = **brasileño**

bravo (1) ADJETIVO
◆ **un toro bravo** a fighting bull
◆ **un perro bravo** a fierce dog

bravo (2) EXCLAMACIÓN
well done!

el **brazalete** SUSTANTIVO
bracelet

el **brazo** SUSTANTIVO
arm ◇ *Me duele el brazo.* My arm hurts.
◇ *Estaba sentada con los brazos cruzados.* She was sitting with her arms folded.
◆ **ir* del brazo** to walk arm-in-arm

la **brecha** SUSTANTIVO
opening (*en un muro*)

breve ADJETIVO
1 brief ◇ *por breves momentos* for a few brief moments ◇ *Para no aburrirlos seré breve.* To avoid boring you I will be brief.
2 short ◇ *un relato breve* a short story
◆ **en breve** shortly

el **bricolaje** SUSTANTIVO
do-it-yourself ◇ *una tienda de bricolaje* a do-it-yourself store

brillante ADJETIVO
1 shiny ◇ *Tenía el pelo brillante.* Her hair was shiny.
◆ **El carro estaba brillante.** The car was shining.
◆ **blanco brillante** brilliant white
2 outstanding ◇ *un alumno brillante* an outstanding student

el **brillante** SUSTANTIVO
diamond

brillar VERBO
1 to shine (*muebles, metal*) ◇ *Hoy brilla el* ☞

sol. The sun is shining today.
[2] to sparkle (*diamantes, agua*)

el **brillo** SUSTANTIVO
[1] shine (*de muebles, metal*)
[2] sparkle (*de joyas*)
◆ **La pantalla tiene mucho brillo.** The screen is too bright.
◆ **sacar* brillo a algo** to polish something

brincar* VERBO
to jump up and down ◇ *¡Deja de brincar!* Stop jumping up and down!
◆ **brincar de alegría** to jump for joy

el **brinco** SUSTANTIVO
◆ **pegar* un brinco** to jump
◆ **Bajé tres escalones de un brinco.** I jumped down three steps.

brindar VERBO
◆ **brindar por** to drink a toast to
◆ **brindarse a hacer algo** to offer to do something ◇ *Se brindó a ayudarme.* He offered to help me.

el **brindis** SUSTANTIVO (PL los **brindis**)
toast
◆ **hacer* un brindis** to make a toast

la **brisa** SUSTANTIVO
breeze

británico ADJETIVO
British

el **británico**, la **británica** SUSTANTIVO
British person
◆ **los británicos** the British

la **brocha** SUSTANTIVO
[1] paintbrush (*para pintar*) (PL paintbrushes)
[2] shaving brush (*para afeitarse*) (PL shaving brushes)

el **broche** SUSTANTIVO
[1] brooch (*joya*) (PL brooches)
[2] clasp (*de un collar, pulsera*)
[3] barrette (*para el pelo*) [*Mexico*]

la **broma** SUSTANTIVO
joke
◆ **gastar una broma a alguien** to play a joke on someone
◆ **decir* algo en broma** to say something as a joke
◆ **una broma pesada** a practical joke

bromear VERBO
to joke

el/la **bromista** SUSTANTIVO
joker

la **bronca** SUSTANTIVO
[1] quarrel (*pelea*) ◇ *Tuvieron una bronca muy gorda.* They had a huge quarrel.
◆ **echar una bronca a alguien** to tell somebody off
[2] fuss (*escándalo*)
◆ **armar una bronca** to kick up a fuss

el **bronce** SUSTANTIVO
bronze

bronceado ADJETIVO
tanned
◆ **ponerse* bronceado** to get a tan

el **bronceado** SUSTANTIVO
suntan

el **bronceador** SUSTANTIVO
suntan lotion

la **bronquitis** SUSTANTIVO
bronchitis

brotar VERBO
to sprout

bruces ADVERBIO
◆ **Me caí de bruces.** I fell flat on my face.

la **bruja** SUSTANTIVO
witch (PL witches)

el **brujo** SUSTANTIVO
wizard

la **brújula** SUSTANTIVO
compass (PL compasses)

la **bruma** SUSTANTIVO
mist

brusco ADJETIVO
[1] sudden ◇ *un movimiento brusco* a sudden movement
[2] abrupt ◇ *una persona brusca* an abrupt person

bruto ADJETIVO
gross ◇ *el salario bruto* gross salary
◆ **¡No seas bruto!** Don't be so rough!
◆ **un diamante en bruto** a diamond in the rough

bucear VERBO
to dive

buen ADJETIVO = **bueno**

buenmozo ADJETIVO
handsome ◇ *Su padre es muy buenmozo.* Her father is very handsome.

bueno ADJETIVO
good ◇ *Es un buen libro.* It's a good book. ◇ *Hace buen tiempo.* The weather's good. ◇ *Tiene buena voz.* She has a good voice. ◇ *Es buena persona.* He's a good person. ◇ *un buen trozo* a good slice ◇ *Le eché un buen regaño.* I gave him a good telling-off.
◆ **ser* bueno para** to be good for ◇ *Esta bebida es buena para la salud.* This drink is good for your health.
◆ **Está muy bueno este bizcocho.** This sponge cake is delicious.
◆ **Lo bueno fue que ni siquiera quiso venir.** The best thing was that he didn't even want to come.
◆ **¡Bueno! (1)** (*para aceptar una sugerencia*) OK!
◆ **¡Bueno! (2)** (*al teléfono*) [*Mexico*] Hello!
◆ **Bueno. ¿Y qué?** Well?
◆ **¡Buenas!** Hello!
◆ **Irás por las buenas o por las malas.** You'll go whether you like it or not.

el **buey** SUSTANTIVO
ox (PL oxen)

la **bufanda** SUSTANTIVO
scarf (PL scarves)

el **bufete** SUSTANTIVO
◆ **un bufete de abogados** a legal practice

el **buffet** SUSTANTIVO (PL los **buffets**)
buffet
◆ **buffet libre** free buffet

la **buhardilla** SUSTANTIVO
attic

el **búho** SUSTANTIVO
owl

el **buitre** SUSTANTIVO
vulture

la **bujía** SUSTANTIVO
spark plug (*de un motor*)

Bulgaria SUSTANTIVO FEM
Bulgaria

el **búlgaro,** la **búlgara** ADJETIVO, SUSTANTIVO
Bulgarian

el **búlgaro** SUSTANTIVO
Bulgarian (*idioma*)

el **bulto** SUSTANTIVO
[1] lump ◇ *Tengo un bulto en la frente.* I have a lump on my forehead.
[2] figure ◇ *Sólo vi un bulto.* I only saw a figure.
◆ **Llevábamos muchos bultos.** We were carrying a lot of bags.

el **buñuelo** SUSTANTIVO
doughnut

el **buque** SUSTANTIVO
ship
◆ **un buque de guerra** a warship

la **burbuja** SUSTANTIVO
bubble ◇ *Este jabón hace muchas burbujas.* This soap makes lots of bubbles.
◆ **un refresco sin burbujas** a still drink
◆ **un refresco con burbujas** a carbonated drink

la **burla** SUSTANTIVO
◆ **hacer* burla de alguien** to make fun of someone

burlarse VERBO
◆ **burlarse de alguien** to make fun of someone

el **buró** SUSTANTIVO [Mexico] (PL los **burós**)
bedside table

la **burocracia** SUSTANTIVO
bureaucracy (PL bureaucracies)

la **burrada** SUSTANTIVO
(*coloquial*)
◆ **hacer* burradas** to do stupid things ◇ *No hagas burradas con el carro.* Don't do anything stupid with the car.

el **burro** SUSTANTIVO
[1] donkey (*animal*) (PL donkeys)
[2] idiot (*persona*) ◇ *Eres un burro.* You're an idiot.
[3] ironing board (*para planchar*) [Mexico]
[4] stepladder (*escalera*) [Mexico]

burro ADJETIVO
[1] thick (*estúpido*)
[2] rough (*bruto*)

el **bus** SUSTANTIVO (PL los **buses**)
bus (PL buses) ◇ *en bus* by bus
◆ **el bus escolar** the school bus

la **busca** SUSTANTIVO
◆ **en busca de** in search of

el **busca** SUSTANTIVO
bleeper

el **buscador** SUSTANTIVO
search engine (*en Internet*)

buscar* VERBO
to look for ◇ *Estoy buscando los lentes.* I'm looking for my glasses. ◇ *Ana busca trabajo.* Ana's looking for work.
◆ **Te voy a buscar a la estación.** I'll come and get you at the station.
◆ **Mi madre siempre me viene a buscar al colegio en el carro.** My mother always picks me up from school in the car.
◆ **buscar una palabra en el diccionario** to look up a word in the dictionary
◆ **Él se lo ha buscado.** He was asking for it.

la **búsqueda** SUSTANTIVO
search (PL searches)

la **butaca** SUSTANTIVO
[1] armchair (*sillón*)
[2] seat (*en el cine*)

el **butano** SUSTANTIVO
bottled gas

el **buzo** SUSTANTIVO
diver (*persona*)

el **buzón** SUSTANTIVO (PL los **buzones**)
mailbox (PL mailboxes)
◆ **echar una carta al buzón** to mail a letter
◆ **buzón de voz** voice mail

C

C/ ABREVIATURA (= *calle*)
St (= Street)

el **caballero** SUSTANTIVO
gentleman (PL gentlemen) ◇ *damas y caballeros* ladies and gentlemen

◆ **¿Dónde está la sección de caballeros?** Where is the men's department?

◆ **"Caballeros"** (*en baños*) "Men"

el **caballo** SUSTANTIVO
1 horse

◆ **¿Te gusta andar a caballo?** Do you like riding?

◆ **un caballo de carreras** a racehorse

2 knight (*en ajedrez*)

la **cabaña** SUSTANTIVO
hut

el **cabello** SUSTANTIVO
hair

caber* VERBO
to fit ◇ *Tu guitarra no cabe en mi armario.* Your guitar won't fit in my closet.

◆ **En mi carro caben dos maletas más.** There's room for two more suitcases in my car.

◆ **No cabe nadie más.** There's no room for anyone else.

la **cabeza** SUSTANTIVO
head ◇ *Se rascó la cabeza.* He scratched his head.

◆ **Al oírlos volví la cabeza.** When I heard them I looked round.

◆ **Se tiró al agua de cabeza.** He dove headfirst into the water.

◆ **estar* a la cabeza de la clasificación** to be at the top of the league

la **cabina** SUSTANTIVO
1 phone booth (*de teléfonos*)
2 booth (*de disc-jockey, intérprete*)
3 cockpit (*del piloto*)
4 cubicle (*en vestuarios*)

el **cable** SUSTANTIVO
cable

el **cabo** SUSTANTIVO
1 cape

◆ **Cabo Cañaveral** Cape Canaveral

2 corporal (*en el ejército*)

◆ **al cabo de dos días** after two days

◆ **llevar algo a cabo** to carry something out

la **cabra** SUSTANTIVO
goat

◆ **¡Estás como una cabra!** You're crazy! (*coloquial*)

cabrá VERBO *ver* **caber**

cabreado ADJETIVO
annoyed

cabrear VERBO

◆ **Lo que más me cabrea es que me mientas.** What really annoys me is when you lie to me.

◆ **cabrearse** to get annoyed

la **caca** SUSTANTIVO

◆ **hacer* caca** (*en lenguaje infantil*) to poop

el **cacahuate** SUSTANTIVO *Mexico*
peanut

el **cacao** SUSTANTIVO
1 cocoa (*polvo*)
2 lipsalve (*para los labios*)

la **cacerola** SUSTANTIVO
saucepan

el **cacharro** SUSTANTIVO

◆ **los cacharros** the pots and pans

el **cachorro**, la **cachorra** SUSTANTIVO
1 puppy (PL puppies) (*de perro*)
2 cub (*de león, lobo*)

el **cactus** SUSTANTIVO (PL los **cactus**)
cactus (PL cacti)

cada ADJETIVO
1 each ◇ *Cada libro es de un color distinto.* Each book is a different color.

◆ **cada uno** each one

2 every (*con tiempo, números*) ◇ *cada año* every year ◇ *cada vez que la veo* every time I see her ◇ *uno de cada diez* one out of every ten

◆ **Viene cada vez más gente.** More and more people are coming.

◆ **Viene cada vez menos.** He comes less and less often.

◆ **Cada vez hace más frío.** It's getting colder and colder.

◆ **¿Cada cuánto vas al dentista?** How often do you go to the dentist?

el **cadáver** SUSTANTIVO
corpse

la **cadena** SUSTANTIVO
1 chain ◇ *una cadena de oro* a gold chain

◆ **una reacción en cadena** a chain reaction

◆ **tirar de la cadena** to pull the chain

◆ **la cadena de montaje** the assembly line

2 channel ◇ *Por la cadena 3 dan una película.* There's a movie on channel 3.

◆ **cadena perpetua** life imprisonment

la **cadera** SUSTANTIVO
hip

caducar* VERBO
to expire (*pasaporte, carnet*)

◆ **Esta leche está caducada.** This milk is past its expiration date.

caer* VERBO
to fall ◇ *Me lastimé al caer.* I fell and hurt myself.

◆ **El avión cayó al mar.** The plane came down in the sea.

◆ **Su cumpleaños cae en viernes.** Her birthday falls on a Friday.

◆ **caerse** to fall ◇ *Tropecé y me caí.* I tripped and fell.

◆ **El niño se cayó de la cama.** The child fell out of bed.

- **No te vayas a caer del caballo.** Be careful not to fall off the horse.
- **Se cayó por la ventana.** He fell out of the window.
- **Se me cayeron las monedas.** I dropped the coins.
- **¡No caigo!** I don't get it!
- **Su hermano me cae muy bien.** I really like his brother.

el **café** SUSTANTIVO (PL los **cafés**)
1 coffee
- **un café con leche** a coffee with milk
- **un café solo** a black coffee

2 café (*establecimiento*)

la **cafetera** SUSTANTIVO
coffee pot

la **cafetería** SUSTANTIVO
café

caigo VERBO *ver* **caer**

el **caimán** SUSTANTIVO (PL los **caimanes**)
alligator

la **caja** SUSTANTIVO
1 box (PL boxes) ◇ *una caja de zapatos* a shoe box
2 case (*de vino, champán*)
3 crate (*de cervezas, refrescos*)
4 checkout (*en supermercado*)
5 cash register (*en tienda, restaurante*)
6 cashier's window (*en banco*)
- **la caja de ahorros** the savings bank
- **la caja de cambios** the gearbox
- **la caja fuerte** the safe

el **cajero** SUSTANTIVO
- **un cajero automático** an ATM

el **cajero,** la **cajera** SUSTANTIVO
- **Trabajo de cajera en un supermercado.** I work at the checkout in a supermarket.

el **cajón** SUSTANTIVO (PL los **cajones**)
1 drawer (*de mueble*)
2 crate (*para embalaje*)
3 coffin (*ataúd*)

la **cajuela** SUSTANTIVO *Mexico*
trunk (*de carro*)

la **cala** SUSTANTIVO
cove

el **calabacín** SUSTANTIVO (PL los **calabacines**)
zucchini

la **calabacita** SUSTANTIVO *Mexico*
zucchini

la **calabaza** SUSTANTIVO
pumpkin

calado ADJETIVO
soaked ◇ *Estaba calado hasta los huesos.* He was soaked to the skin.

el **calamar** SUSTANTIVO
squid
- **calamares a la romana** squid fried in batter

el **calambre** SUSTANTIVO
1 cramp ◇ *Tengo un calambre en la pierna.* I have a cramp in my leg.
2 electric shock ◇ *Si tocas el cable te dará calambre.* If you touch the cable you'll get an electric shock.

calar VERBO
to soak ◇ *La lluvia me caló hasta los huesos.* I got soaked to the skin in the rain.

la **calavera** SUSTANTIVO
skull

calcar* VERBO
to trace
- **Es calcado a su abuelo.** He's the spitting image of his grandfather.

el **calcetín** SUSTANTIVO (PL los **calcetines**)
sock

el **calcio** SUSTANTIVO
calcium

la **calculadora** SUSTANTIVO
calculator

calcular VERBO
to calculate ◇ *Calculé lo que nos costaría.* I calculated what it would cost us.
- **Calculo que nos llevará unos tres días.** I reckon that it will take us around three days.

el **cálculo** SUSTANTIVO
calculation ◇ *según mis cálculos* according to my calculations

el **caldo** SUSTANTIVO
broth ◇ *Yo tomaré el caldo de verduras.* I'll take the vegetable broth.
- **un cubito de caldo** a bouillon cube

la **calefacción** SUSTANTIVO
heating ◇ *calefacción central* central heating

el **calendario** SUSTANTIVO
calendar

el **calentador** SUSTANTIVO
heater

el **calentamiento** SUSTANTIVO
- **el calentamiento del planeta** global warming
- **ejercicios de calentamiento** warm-up exercises

calentar* VERBO
1 to heat up (*comida, agua*) ◇ *¿Quieres que te caliente la leche?* Do you want me to heat up the milk for you?
2 to warm up (*habitación*)
- **calentarse (1)** (*comida, agua*) to heat up ◇ *Espera a que se caliente el agua.* Wait for the water to heat up.
- **calentarse (2)** (*habitación, persona*) to warm up ◇ *Deja que se caliente el motor.* Let the engine warm up.

la **calentura** SUSTANTIVO
1 temperature ◇ *Tiene un poco de calentura.* He has a bit of a temperature.
2 cold sore (*en los labios*)

la **calidad** SUSTANTIVO
quality (PL qualities) ◇ *Lo que importa es la calidad.* What matters is quality.

caliente (1) VERBO *ver* **calentar**

caliente (2) ADJETIVO
1 hot

☞

Cuando nos referimos a una temperatura que puede quemar.
◇ *Esta sopa está muy caliente.* This soup is very hot.
[2] warm
Cuando nos referimos a algo que está templado, que no quema o que no está suficientemente frío.
◇ *¡Esta cerveza está caliente!* This beer is warm!

la **calificación** SUSTANTIVO (PL las **calificaciones**)
grade (*nota escolar*) ◇ *Siempre saca buenas calificaciones.* He always gets good grades.
◆ **boletín de calificaciones** report card

calificar* VERBO
to mark ◇ *El profesor califica los ejercicios.* The teacher marks the exercises.
◆ **Me calificó con sobresaliente.** He gave me an A.

callado ADJETIVO
quiet ◇ *Estuvo callado bastante rato.* He was quiet for quite a while. ◇ *una persona muy callada* a very quiet person

callar VERBO
to be quiet ◇ *Calla, que no me dejas concentrarme.* Be quiet, I can't concentrate.
◆ **callarse (1)** to keep quiet ◇ *Prefirió callarse.* He preferred to keep quiet.
◆ **callarse (2)** to stop talking ◇ *Al entrar el profesor todos se callaron.* When the teacher came in, everyone stopped talking.
◆ **¡Cállate!** Shut up! (*coloquial*)

la **calle** SUSTANTIVO
[1] street ◇ *Viven en la calle Peñalver, 13.* They live at number 13, Peñalver Street.
◆ **Hoy no he salido a la calle.** I haven't been out today.
◆ **una calle peatonal** a pedestrian mall
[2] lane (*en circuito, piscina*)

el **callejón** SUSTANTIVO (PL los **callejones**)
alley

el **callo** SUSTANTIVO
[1] corn (*en los pies*)
[2] callus (PL calluses) (*en las manos*)
◆ **callos** (*comida*) tripe SING

la **calma** SUSTANTIVO
calm
◆ **Todo estaba en calma.** Everything was calm.
◆ **Logró mantener la calma.** He managed to keep calm.
◆ **Piénsalo con calma.** Think about it calmly.
◆ **Tómalo con calma.** Take it easy.

el **calmante** SUSTANTIVO
[1] painkiller (*para el dolor*)
[2] tranquilizer (*para los nervios*)

calmar VERBO
[1] to calm down ◇ *Intenté calmarla un poco.* I tried to calm her down a little.
◇ *¡Cálmate!* Calm down!
[2] to relieve (*dolor*)

el **calor** SUSTANTIVO
heat ◇ *No se puede trabajar con este calor.* It's impossible to work in this heat.
◆ **Hace calor.** It's hot.
◆ **Tengo calor.** I'm hot.
◆ **entrar en calor** to get warm

la **caloría** SUSTANTIVO
calorie

caluroso ADJETIVO
hot (*día, tiempo*)

calvo ADJETIVO
bald
◆ **Se está quedando calvo.** He's going bald.

los **calzoncillos** SUSTANTIVO
underpants
◆ **unos calzoncillos** a pair of underpants

la **cama** SUSTANTIVO
bed
◆ **hacer* la cama** to make the bed
◆ **Está en la cama.** He's in bed.
◆ **meterse en la cama** to get into bed

la **cámara** SUSTANTIVO
[1] camera (*de cine, fotos*)
◆ **una cámara digital** a digital camera
◆ **a cámara lenta** in slow motion
[2] inner tube (*de neumático*)
◆ **la cámara de comercio** the Chamber of Commerce

la **camarera** SUSTANTIVO
[1] waitress (PL waitresses) (*de restaurante*)
[2] maid (*de hotel*)

el **camarero** SUSTANTIVO Spain
[1] waiter (*de restaurante*)
[2] bellhop (*de hotel*)

el **camarón** SUSTANTIVO (PL los **camarones**)
shrimp

el **camarote** SUSTANTIVO
cabin

cambiar VERBO
[1] to change ◇ *No has cambiado nada.* You haven't changed a bit.
◆ **Quiero cambiar este abrigo por uno más grande.** I want to change this coat for a larger size.
◆ **Tenemos que cambiar de tren en Kansas.** We have to change trains in Kansas.
◆ **He cambiado de idea.** I've changed my mind.
[2] to swap ◇ *Te cambio mi lápiz por tu goma.* I'll swap my pencil for your eraser.
◆ **Me gusta el tuyo, te lo cambio.** I like yours; let's swap.
◆ **cambiarse** to get changed ◇ *Voy a cambiarme.* I'm going to get changed.
◆ **Cambiaron de carro.** They have changed cars.
◆ **cambiarse de sitio** to move
◆ **cambiarse de casa** to move house

el **cambio** SUSTANTIVO
[1] change ◇ *un cambio brusco de*

temperatura a sudden change in temperature ◇ *¿Tiene cambio de cien?* Do you have change for a hundred? ◇ *¿Te han dado bien el cambio?* Have they given you the right change?
2 small change ◇ *Necesito cambio.* I need small change.
3 exchange rate ◇ *¿A cómo está el cambio?* What's the exchange rate?
◆ **Me lo regaló a cambio del favor que le hice.** He gave it to me in return for the favor I did him.
◆ **en cambio** on the other hand

el **camello** SUSTANTIVO
1 camel (*animal*)
2 dealer (*coloquial: traficante*)

la **camilla** SUSTANTIVO
1 stretcher (*de ambulancia*)
2 couch (PL couches) (*en consultorio médico*)

caminar VERBO
to walk

la **caminata** SUSTANTIVO
long walk

el **camino** SUSTANTIVO
1 path (*sendero*)
◆ **un camino de montaña** a mountain track
2 way ◇ *¿Sabes el camino a su casa?* Do you know the way to his house?
◆ **A medio camino paramos a comer.** Halfway there, we stopped to eat.
◆ **La farmacia me queda de camino.** The pharmacy is on my way.

el **camión** SUSTANTIVO (PL los **camiones**)
1 truck
◆ **un camión cisterna** a tanker
◆ **el camión de la basura** the garbage truck
2 bus (PL buses) *Mexico*

el **camionero**, la **camionera** SUSTANTIVO
1 truck driver
2 bus driver *Mexico*

la **camioneta** SUSTANTIVO
van

la **camisa** SUSTANTIVO
shirt

la **camiseta** SUSTANTIVO
1 T-shirt (*de manga corta*)
2 undershirt (*ropa interior*)
3 jersey (*de deportes*)

el **camisón** SUSTANTIVO (PL los **camisones**)
nightdress (PL nightdresses)

el **camote** SUSTANTIVO *Mexico*
sweet potato (PL sweet potatoes)

el **campamento** SUSTANTIVO
camp ◇ *un campamento de verano* a summer camp

la **campana** SUSTANTIVO
bell

la **campaña** SUSTANTIVO
campaign
◆ **la campaña electoral** the election campaign

el **campeón**, la **campeona** SUSTANTIVO (MASC PL los **campeones**)
champion

el **campeonato** SUSTANTIVO
championship

el **campesino**, la **campesina** SUSTANTIVO
1 country person (PL country people) (*persona del campo*)
2 peasant (*labrador pobre*)

el **camping** SUSTANTIVO (PL los **campings**)
1 camping ◇ *ir de camping* to go camping
2 campsite ◇ *Estamos en un camping.* We're at a campsite.

el **campo** SUSTANTIVO
1 country ◇ *Prefiero vivir en el campo.* I prefer living in the country.
2 countryside (*paisaje*) ◇ *El campo se pone verde en primavera.* The countryside turns green in springtime.
◆ **Corrían a campo traviesa.** They were running cross-country.
◆ **el trabajo del campo** farm work
◆ **Ya no se ven bueyes en el campo.** You don't see oxen in the fields any more.
3 field (*de fútbol*)
◆ **un campo de golf** a golf course
◆ **un campo de concentración** a concentration camp

la **cana** SUSTANTIVO
gray hair
◆ **Tiene canas.** He has gray hair.
◆ **Le están saliendo canas.** He's going gray.

Canadá SUSTANTIVO MASC
Canada

el/la **canadiense** ADJETIVO, SUSTANTIVO
Canadian

el **canal** SUSTANTIVO
1 channel ◇ *Por el canal 2 dan una película.* They're showing a movie on channel 2.
◆ **el Canal de la Mancha** the English Channel
2 canal (*artificial*) ◇ *un canal de riego* an irrigation canal
◆ **el Canal de Panamá** the Panama Canal

el **canapé** SUSTANTIVO (PL los **canapés**)
canapé

Canarias SUSTANTIVO FEM PL
the Canaries
◆ **las Islas Canarias** the Canary Islands

el **canario** SUSTANTIVO
canary (PL canaries)

la **canasta** SUSTANTIVO
basket

cancelar VERBO
to cancel

el **cáncer** SUSTANTIVO
cancer ◇ *cáncer de mama* breast cancer

Cáncer SUSTANTIVO MASC
Cancer ◇ *Soy cáncer.* I'm a Cancer.

la **cancha** SUSTANTIVO
1 court (*de baloncesto, tenis*)

☞

[2] field (*de fútbol, rugby*)

la **canción** SUSTANTIVO (PL las **canciones**)
song
◆ **una canción de cuna** a lullaby

el **candado** SUSTANTIVO
padlock
◆ **Estaba cerrado con candado.** It was padlocked.

el **candidato,** la **candidata** SUSTANTIVO
candidate
◆ **presentarse como candidato a la presidencia** to run for president

la **canela** SUSTANTIVO
cinnamon

los **canelones** SUSTANTIVO
cannelloni SING

el **cangrejo** SUSTANTIVO
[1] crab (*de mar*)
[2] crawfish (PL crawfish) (*de río*)

el **canguro** SUSTANTIVO
kangaroo

la **canica** SUSTANTIVO
marble
◆ **jugar* a las canicas** to play marbles

la **canoa** SUSTANTIVO
canoe

cansado ADJETIVO
[1] tired ◇ *Estoy muy cansado.* I'm very tired.
◆ **Estoy cansado de hacer lo mismo todos los días.** I'm tired of doing the same thing every day.
[2] tiring ◇ *Es un trabajo muy cansado.* It's a very tiring job.

el **cansancio** SUSTANTIVO
◆ **¡Qué cansancio!** I'm so tired!

cansar VERBO
◆ **Es un viaje que cansa.** It's a tiring journey.
◆ **cansarse** to get tired
◆ **Me cansé de esperarlo y me marché.** I got tired of waiting for him and I left.

el/la **cantante** SUSTANTIVO
singer

cantar VERBO
to sing

la **cantidad** SUSTANTIVO
[1] amount ◇ *una cierta cantidad de dinero* a certain amount of money
[2] quantity (PL quantities) ◇ *La calidad es más importante que la cantidad.* Quality is more important than quantity.
◆ **¡Qué cantidad de gente!** What a lot of people!
◆ **Había cantidad de turistas.** There were loads of tourists.

la **cantimplora** SUSTANTIVO
water bottle

el **canto** SUSTANTIVO
[1] edge (*de mesa, moneda*)
[2] singing (*arte*) ◇ *Mi hermana estudia canto.* My sister is studying singing.
[3] song (*de pájaro*)

la **caña** SUSTANTIVO
cane
◆ **caña de azúcar** sugar cane
◆ **una caña de pescar** a fishing rod

la **cañería** SUSTANTIVO
pipe

el **caos** SUSTANTIVO
chaos ◇ *Aquello fue un verdadero caos.* That was absolute chaos.

la **capa** SUSTANTIVO
[1] layer (*de nieve, polvo*)
◆ **la capa de ozono** the ozone layer
[2] cloak (*prenda*)

la **capacidad** SUSTANTIVO
[1] ability (PL abilities) (*aptitud*) ◇ *Nadie duda de tu capacidad.* No one doubts your ability.
[2] capacity (PL capacities) (*de recipiente, lugar*) ◇ *El teatro tiene capacidad para mil espectadores.* The theater has a seating capacity of a thousand.

capaz ADJETIVO (PL **capaces**)
capable ◇ *Es capaz de olvidarse el pasaporte.* He's quite capable of forgetting his passport.
◆ **Por ella sería capaz de cualquier cosa.** He would do anything for her.

la **capilla** SUSTANTIVO
chapel

la **capital** SUSTANTIVO
capital

el **capitán,** la **capitana** SUSTANTIVO (MASC PL los **capitanes**)
captain

el **capítulo** SUSTANTIVO
[1] chapter (*de un libro*)
[2] episode (*de una serie*)

el **capote** SUSTANTIVO Mexico
hood (*de carro*)

el **capricho** SUSTANTIVO
whim ◇ *Hacer un crucero fue un puro capricho.* Going on a cruise was just a whim.
◆ **Lo compré por capricho.** I bought it on a whim.
◆ **Decidí viajar en primera para darme un capricho.** I decided to travel first class to give myself a treat.

Capricornio SUSTANTIVO MASC
Capricorn ◇ *Soy capricornio.* I'm a Capricorn.

capturar VERBO
to capture

la **capucha** SUSTANTIVO
hood (*de ropa*)

caqui ADJETIVO (PL **caqui**)
khaki

la **cara** SUSTANTIVO
[1] face ◇ *Tiene la cara alargada.* He has a

long face.
- **Tienes mala cara.** You don't look well.
- **Tenía cara de pocos amigos.** He looked very unfriendly.
- **No pongas esa cara.** Don't look like that.

[2] cheek (*coloquial: descaro*) ◇ *¡Qué cara!* What cheek!
[3] side (*de disco, papel*) ◇ *un folio escrito por las dos caras* a sheet written on both sides
- **¿Cara o cruz?** Heads or tails?
- **Lo echamos a cara o cruz.** We tossed for it.

el **caracol** SUSTANTIVO
[1] snail (*de tierra*)
[2] periwinkle (*de mar*)

el **carácter** SUSTANTIVO (PL los **caracteres**)
nature ◇ *Tiene el carácter de su padre.* He has his father's nature.
- **tener* buen carácter** to be good-natured
- **tener* mal carácter** to be bad-tempered
- **La chica tiene mucho carácter.** The girl has a strong personality.

la **característica** SUSTANTIVO
characteristic

caramba EXCLAMACIÓN
my goodness!

el **caramelo** SUSTANTIVO
piece of candy

la **caravana** SUSTANTIVO
trailer (*remolque*)
- **Había una caravana de dos kilómetros.** There was a two kilometer traffic jam.

el **carbón** SUSTANTIVO
coal
- **carbón de leña** charcoal

la **carcajada** SUSTANTIVO
- **soltar* una carcajada** to burst out laughing
- **reírse* a carcajadas** to roar with laughter

la **cárcel** SUSTANTIVO
prison ◇ *Está en la cárcel.* He's in prison.

el **cardenal** SUSTANTIVO
[1] bruise (*moretón*)
[2] cardinal (*prelado*)

cardiaco ADJETIVO
cardiac ◇ *ataque cardiaco* heart attack

la **careta** SUSTANTIVO
mask

la **carga** SUSTANTIVO
[1] load ◇ *carga máxima* maximum load
[2] burden ◇ *No quiero ser una carga para ellos.* I don't want to be a burden to them.
[3] refill (*de bolígrafo, pluma*)

cargado ADJETIVO
[1] loaded (*arma, cámara*)
[2] stuffy (*ambiente, habitación*)
[3] strong (*café*)
- **Venía cargada de paquetes.** She was laden with parcels.

el **cargamento** SUSTANTIVO
[1] cargo (PL cargoes) (*de avión, barco*)
[2] load (*de camión*)

cargar* VERBO
[1] to load ◇ *Cargaron el carro de maletas.* They loaded the car with suitcases.
[2] to fill (*pluma, encendedor*)
[3] to charge (*batería, pilas*)
- **Tuve que cargar con todo.** I had to take responsibility for everything.

C

el **cargo** SUSTANTIVO
position ◇ *un cargo de mucha responsabilidad* a very responsible position
- **Está a cargo de la contabilidad.** He's in charge of keeping the books.

el **Caribe** SUSTANTIVO
the Caribbean

el **caribeño**, la **caribeña** ADJETIVO, SUSTANTIVO
Caribbean

la **caricatura** SUSTANTIVO
caricature

la **caricia** SUSTANTIVO
caress (PL caresses)
- **Le hacía caricias al bebé.** She was caressing the baby.

la **caridad** SUSTANTIVO
charity (PL charities)

la **caries** SUSTANTIVO (PL las **caries**)
[1] tooth decay ◇ *Es importante prevenir la caries dental.* It's important to prevent tooth decay.
[2] cavity (PL cavities) (*agujero*)

el **cariño** SUSTANTIVO
affection ◇ *Lo recuerdo con cariño.* I remember him with affection.
- **Les tengo mucho cariño.** I'm very fond of them.
- **Le ha tomado cariño al gato.** He has become fond of the cat.
- **Ven aquí, cariño.** Come here, darling.

cariñoso ADJETIVO
affectionate

el **carnaval** SUSTANTIVO
carnival

> ℹ *The **carnaval** is the traditional period of celebrating prior to the start of Lent.*

la **carne** SUSTANTIVO
meat ◇ *No como carne.* I don't eat meat.
- **carne de cerdo** pork
- **carne de puerco** [Mexico] pork
- **carne de cordero** lamb
- **carne molida** ground beef
- **carne de ternera** veal
- **carne de vaca** beef
- **carne de res** [Mexico] beef

el **carnet** SUSTANTIVO (PL los **carnets**)
card
- **el carnet de identidad** identity card
- **un carnet de manejar** a driver's license

la **carnicería** SUSTANTIVO
butcher's ◇ *Lo compré en la carnicería.* I bought it at the butcher's.

el **carnicero,** la **carnicera** SUSTANTIVO
butcher

caro ADJETIVO, ADVERBIO
expensive ◇ *Las entradas me costaron muy caras.* The tickets were very expensive.
◇ *Aquí todo lo venden tan caro.* Everything is so expensive here.

la **carpeta** SUSTANTIVO
folder

la **carpintería** SUSTANTIVO
1 carpenter's shop (*taller*)
2 carpentry (*actividad*)

el **carpintero,** la **carpintera** SUSTANTIVO
carpenter

la **carrera** SUSTANTIVO
1 race ◇ *una carrera de caballos* a horse race
◆ **Me di una carrera para alcanzar el autobús.** I had to run to catch the bus.
2 degree ◇ *Está haciendo la carrera de derecho.* He's doing a law degree.
3 career ◇ *Estaba en el mejor momento de su carrera.* He was at the height of his career.
4 run ◇ *Tienes una carrera en las medias.* You have a run in your pantyhose.

el **carrete** SUSTANTIVO
1 film (*de fotos*)
2 reel (*de hilo*)

la **carretera** SUSTANTIVO
road
◆ **una carretera nacional** a US state road
◆ **una carretera de circunvalación** a beltway

la **carretilla** SUSTANTIVO
wheelbarrow

el **carril** SUSTANTIVO
1 lane (*de carretera, autopista*)
2 rail (*de vía de tren*)

el **carrito** SUSTANTIVO
cart

el **carro** SUSTANTIVO
1 car (*automóvil*) ◇ *Fuimos a Lima en carro.* We went to Lima by car.
2 cart (*en aeropuerto*)
◆ **un carro de bomberos** a fire truck
◆ **un carro de carreras** a race car
◆ **un carro de combate** a tank
◆ **un carro de la compra** a shopping cart

la **carroza** SUSTANTIVO
1 coach (PL coaches) (*de caballos*)
2 float (*de carnaval*)

el **carrusel** SUSTANTIVO
merry-go-round

la **carta** SUSTANTIVO
1 letter ◇ *Le escribí una carta a Juan.* I've written Juan a letter.
◆ **echar una carta** to mail a letter
2 card ◇ *jugar a las cartas* to play cards
3 menu ◇ *El mesero nos trajo la carta.* The waiter brought us the menu.
◆ **la carta de vinos** the wine list

el **cartel** SUSTANTIVO
1 poster (*de propaganda*)
2 sign ◇ *Un cartel que dice "prohibida la entrada".* A sign which says "no entry".

la **cartelera** SUSTANTIVO
1 billboard (*en un teatro, cine*)
2 listings PL (*en un periódico*)
◆ **Estuvo tres años en la cartelera.** It ran for three years.

la **cartera** SUSTANTIVO
1 wallet (*para el dinero*)
2 briefcase (*para documentos*)
3 satchel (*de colegial*)
4 purse (*bolso de mujer*)
5 female letter carrier (*empleada de Correos*)

el **cartero** SUSTANTIVO
mailman (PL mailmen)

el **cartón** SUSTANTIVO (PL los **cartones**)
1 cardboard ◇ *una caja de cartón* a cardboard box
2 carton (*de tabaco, leche*)

el **cartucho** SUSTANTIVO
cartridge

la **cartulina** SUSTANTIVO
card

la **casa** SUSTANTIVO
1 house
Cuando nos referimos al edificio.
◇ *una casa de dos plantas* a two-story house
2 home
Cuando nos referimos al hogar.
◇ *Estábamos en casa.* We were at home.
◇ *Le dolía la cabeza y se fue a casa.* She had a headache so she went home.
◆ **Estábamos en casa de Juan.** We were at Juan's place.
◆ **una casa de discos** a record company

casado ADJETIVO
married ◇ *una mujer casada* a married woman
◆ **Está casado con una francesa.** He's married to a French woman.

casarse VERBO
to get married ◇ *Quieren casarse.* They want to get married.
◆ **Se casó con una periodista.** He married a journalist.

el **cascabel** SUSTANTIVO
small bell

la **cascada** SUSTANTIVO
waterfall

cascar* VERBO
to crack (*nuez, huevo*)

la **cáscara** SUSTANTIVO
1 shell (*de huevo, nuez*)
2 skin (*de plátano, papa*)

el **casco** SUSTANTIVO
helmet ◇ *El ciclista llevaba casco.* The

* Verbs marked with this symbol are irregular. See pages 346–348 for further details.

cyclist was wearing a helmet.
◆ **el casco antiguo de la ciudad** the old part of the town

casero ADJETIVO
homemade ◇ *mermelada casera* homemade jelly

la **caseta** SUSTANTIVO
1 doghouse (*de perro*)
2 cabana (*en la playa*)
3 stall (*de feria*)

el **casete** SUSTANTIVO
1 cassette player (*magnetófono*)
2 cassette (*cinta*)

la **casete** SUSTANTIVO
cassette

casi ADVERBIO
almost ◇ *Casi me ahogo.* I almost drowned. ◇ *Son casi las cinco.* It's almost five o'clock.
En oraciones afirmativas se pueden usar tanto ***almost*** *como* ***nearly***.
◇ *Casi me ahogo.* I nearly drowned.
En oraciones negativas se suele usar ***hardly***.
◇ *Casi no comí.* I hardly ate. ◇ *No queda casi nada en la nevera.* There's hardly anything left in the refrigerator. ◇ *Casi nunca se equivoca.* He hardly ever makes a mistake.

la **casilla** SUSTANTIVO
1 box (PL boxes) (*en formulario*)
2 square (*en crucigrama, tablero de ajedrez*)

el **casino** SUSTANTIVO
casino

el **caso** SUSTANTIVO
case ◇ *En casos así es preferible callarse.* In such cases it's better to keep quiet.
◆ **en ese caso** in that case
◆ **En caso de que llueva, iremos en autobús.** If it rains, we'll go by bus.
◆ **El caso es que no me queda dinero.** The thing is, I don't have any money left.
◆ **No le hagas caso.** Don't take any notice of him.
◆ **Hazle caso que ella tiene más experiencia.** Listen to her; she has more experience.

la **caspa** SUSTANTIVO
dandruff

la **cassette** = **casete**

el **cassette** = **casete**

la **castaña** SUSTANTIVO
chestnut

castaño ADJETIVO
chestnut ◇ *Mi hermana tiene el pelo castaño.* My sister has chestnut hair.

las **castañuelas** SUSTANTIVO
castanets

el **castellano**, la **castellana** ADJETIVO, SUSTANTIVO
Castilian

el **castellano** SUSTANTIVO
Spanish (*idioma*)

castigar* VERBO
to punish ◇ *Mi padre me castigó por contestarle.* My father punished me for answering him back.

el **castigo** SUSTANTIVO
punishment ◇ *Tuve que escribirlo diez veces, como castigo.* I had to write it out ten times, as punishment.

C

Castilla SUSTANTIVO FEM
Castile

el **castillo** SUSTANTIVO
castle

la **casualidad** SUSTANTIVO
coincidence ◇ *¡Qué casualidad!* What a coincidence!
◆ **Nos encontramos por casualidad.** We met by chance.
◆ **Da la casualidad que nacimos el mismo día.** It so happens that we were born on the same day.

el **catalán**, la **catalana** ADJETIVO, SUSTANTIVO (MASC PL los **catalanes**)
Catalan

el **catalán** SUSTANTIVO
Catalan (*idioma*)

el **catálogo** SUSTANTIVO
catalog

Cataluña SUSTANTIVO FEM
Catalonia

la **catarata** SUSTANTIVO
waterfall
◆ **las cataratas del Niágara** Niagara Falls

el **catarro** SUSTANTIVO
cold ◇ *Vas a pillar un catarro.* You're going to catch a cold.

la **catástrofe** SUSTANTIVO
catastrophe

la **catedral** SUSTANTIVO
cathedral

el **catedrático**, la **catedrática** SUSTANTIVO
1 professor (*de universidad*)
2 principal teacher (*de instituto*)

la **categoría** SUSTANTIVO
category (PL categories) ◇ *Cada grupo está dividido en tres categorías.* Each group is divided into three categories.
◆ **un hotel de primera categoría** a first-class hotel
◆ **un puesto de poca categoría** a low-ranking position

el **católico**, la **católica** ADJETIVO, SUSTANTIVO
Catholic ◇ *Soy católico.* I am a Catholic.

catorce ADJETIVO, PRONOMBRE
fourteen
◆ **el catorce de enero** January fourteenth

el **caucho** SUSTANTIVO
rubber

la **causa** SUSTANTIVO
cause ◇ *No se sabe la causa del accidente.* The cause of the accident is unknown.
◆ **a causa de** because of

causar VERBO
to cause ◇ *La lluvia causó muchos daños.* ☞

The rain caused a lot of damage.

- **Su visita me causó mucha alegría.** His visit made me very happy.
- **Rosa me causó buena impresión.** Rosa made a good impression on me.

cavar VERBO
to dig ◇ *cavar un hoyo* to dig a hole

cayendo VERBO *ver* **caer**

la **caza** SUSTANTIVO
1 hunting (*de animales grandes*)
2 shooting (*de aves*)

el **cazador** SUSTANTIVO
hunter

la **cazadora** SUSTANTIVO
1 jacket (*chaqueta*)
2 hunter (*mujer*)

cazar* VERBO
1 to hunt (*animales grandes*) ◇ *Salieron a cazar ciervos.* They went deer hunting.
2 to shoot (*aves*) ◇ *Cazaron muchas codornices.* They shot a lot of quail.

el **cazo** SUSTANTIVO
1 saucepan (*cacerola*)
2 ladle (*cucharón*)

la **cazuela** SUSTANTIVO
pot

el **CD** SUSTANTIVO (PL los **CDs**)
CD

el **CD-ROM** SUSTANTIVO (PL los **CD-ROMs**)
CD-ROM

la **CE** ABREVIATURA (= *Comunidad Europea*)
EC (= European Community)

el **cebo** SUSTANTIVO
bait

la **cebolla** SUSTANTIVO
onion

la **cebolleta** SUSTANTIVO
1 scallion
2 pickled onion (*en vinagre*)

la **cebra** SUSTANTIVO
zebra

- **un paso de cebra** a crosswalk

ceder VERBO
1 to give in ◇ *Al final tuve que ceder.* Finally I had to give in.
2 to give way ◇ *La estantería cedió por el peso de los libros.* The shelves gave way under the weight of the books.

- **"Ceda el paso"** "Yield"

la **ceguera** SUSTANTIVO
blindness

la **ceja** SUSTANTIVO
eyebrow

la **celda** SUSTANTIVO
cell

la **celebración** SUSTANTIVO (PL las **celebraciones**)
celebration (*fiesta*)

celebrar VERBO
1 to celebrate (*cumpleaños, Navidad*)

- **En octubre se celebra el día de la Raza.** Columbus Day is in October.

2 to hold (*reunión, elecciones*)

célebre ADJETIVO
famous

el **celofán** SUSTANTIVO
cellophane

los **celos** SUSTANTIVO
jealousy SING ◇ *Lo hizo por celos.* He did it out of jealousy.

- **Tiene celos de su mejor amiga.** She's jealous of her best friend.
- **Lo hace para darle celos.** He does it to make her jealous.

celoso ADJETIVO
jealous ◇ *Está celoso de su hermano.* He's jealous of his brother.

la **célula** SUSTANTIVO
cell

el **celular** SUSTANTIVO
cellular phone

la **celulitis** SUSTANTIVO
cellulite

el **cementerio** SUSTANTIVO
cemetery (PL cemeteries) (*para difuntos*)

- **un cementerio de carros** a junkyard

el **cemento** SUSTANTIVO
1 cement (*material de construcción*)

- **el cemento armado** reinforced concrete

2 glue (*pegamento*)

la **cena** SUSTANTIVO
dinner ◇ *La cena es a las nueve.* Dinner is at nine o'clock.

cenar VERBO
to have dinner ◇ *No he cenado.* I haven't had dinner.

- **¿Qué quieres cenar?** What do you want for dinner?

el **cenicero** SUSTANTIVO
ashtray

la **ceniza** SUSTANTIVO
ash (PL ashes)

la **censura** SUSTANTIVO
censorship

el **centavo** SUSTANTIVO
cent

la **centésima** SUSTANTIVO

- **una centésima de segundo** a hundredth of a second

centígrado ADJETIVO
centigrade ◇ *veinte grados centígrados* twenty degrees centigrade

el **centímetro** SUSTANTIVO
centimeter

el **céntimo** SUSTANTIVO
cent

central ADJETIVO
central

la **central** SUSTANTIVO
head office (*oficina principal*)

- **una central eléctrica** a power station

* Verbs marked with this symbol are irregular. See pages 346–348 for further details.

◆ **una central nuclear** a nuclear power station

la **centralita** SUSTANTIVO *Spain*
switchboard

céntrico ADJETIVO
central ◇ *Está en un barrio céntrico.* It's in a central area.
◆ **Es un departamento céntrico.** The apartment is in the center of town.

el **centro** SUSTANTIVO
center ◇ *en pleno centro de la ciudad* right in the town center
◆ **Fui al centro a hacer unas compras.** I went into town to do some shopping.
◆ **un centro comercial** a shopping center
◆ **un centro de deportes** a sports center
◆ **un centro médico** a hospital

el **centroamericano,** la **centroamericana** ADJETIVO, SUSTANTIVO
Central American

ceñido ADJETIVO
tight ◇ *Esta falda me queda muy ceñida.* This skirt's too tight for me.

cepillar VERBO
to brush (*chaqueta, pelo*)
◆ **Se está cepillando los dientes.** He's brushing his teeth.

el **cepillo** SUSTANTIVO
brush (PL brushes)
◆ **un cepillo de dientes** a toothbrush

la **cera** SUSTANTIVO
wax

la **cerámica** SUSTANTIVO
pottery ◇ *Me gusta la cerámica.* I like pottery.
◆ **una cerámica** a piece of pottery

cerca ADVERBIO
near ◇ *El colegio está muy cerca.* The school is very near.
◆ **¿Hay algún banco por aquí cerca?** Is there a bank nearby?
◆ **cerca de la iglesia** near the church
◆ **cerca de dos horas** nearly two hours
◆ **Quería verlo de cerca.** I wanted to see it close up.

cercano ADJETIVO
nearby ◇ *Viven en un pueblo cercano.* They live in a nearby village.
◆ **una de las calles cercanas a la catedral** one of the streets close to the cathedral
◆ **el Cercano Oriente** the Near East

el **cerdo** SUSTANTIVO
1 pig ◇ *Tienen cerdos.* They keep pigs.
2 pork ◇ *No comemos cerdo.* We don't eat pork.

el **cereal** SUSTANTIVO
cereal
◆ **Los niños desayunan con cereales.** The children have cereal for breakfast.

el **cerebro** SUSTANTIVO
brain

la **ceremonia** SUSTANTIVO
ceremony (PL ceremonies)

la **cereza** SUSTANTIVO
cherry (PL cherries)

la **cerilla** SUSTANTIVO
match (PL matches) ◇ *una caja de cerillas* a box of matches

el **cerillo** SUSTANTIVO *Mexico*
match (PL matches)

el **cero** SUSTANTIVO
zero (PL zeros *o* zeroes)
◆ **Estamos a cinco grados bajo cero.** It's five degrees below zero.
◆ **cero coma tres** zero point three
◆ **Van dos a cero.** The score is two to nothing.
◆ **Empataron a cero.** It was a scoreless tie.
◆ **quince a cero** (*en tenis*) fifteen-love
◆ **Tuve que empezar desde cero.** I had to start from scratch.

el **cerquillo** SUSTANTIVO
bangs PL

cerrado ADJETIVO
closed ◇ *Las tiendas están cerradas.* The stores are closed.
◆ **una curva muy cerrada** a very sharp bend

la **cerradura** SUSTANTIVO
lock

cerrar* VERBO
1 to close ◇ *No cierran al mediodía.* They don't close at noon. ◇ *Cerró el libro.* He closed the book.
En la mayoría de los casos se puede usar tanto ***shut*** *como* ***close.***
◇ *No puedo cerrar la maleta.* I can't shut this suitcase.
2 to turn off (*llave*) ◇ *Cierra la llave.* Turn off the faucet.
◆ **Cerré la puerta con llave.** I locked the door.
◆ **La puerta se cerró de golpe.** The door slammed shut.
◆ **Se me cierran los ojos.** I can't keep my eyes open.

el **cerrojo** SUSTANTIVO
bolt
◆ **echar el cerrojo** to bolt the door

certificado ADJETIVO
certified (*carta*)
◆ **Mandé el paquete certificado.** I sent the parcel by certified mail.

el **certificado** SUSTANTIVO
certificate

la **cerveza** SUSTANTIVO
beer ◇ *Fuimos a tomar unas cervezas.* We went to have a few beers.
◆ **la cerveza de barril** draft beer

cesar VERBO
to stop
◆ **No cesa de hablar.** He never stops talking.
◆ **No cesaba de repetirlo.** He kept repeating it.

el **césped** SUSTANTIVO
grass ◇ *"no pisar el césped"* "keep off the grass"

C

la **cesta** SUSTANTIVO
basket
◆ **una cesta de Navidad** a Christmas basket
el **cesto** SUSTANTIVO
basket
el **chabacano** SUSTANTIVO *Mexico*
apricot
el **chaleco** SUSTANTIVO
waistcoat
◆ **un chaleco salvavidas** a life jacket
el **chalet** SUSTANTIVO (PL los **chalets**)
1 cottage (*en el campo*)
2 villa (*en centro turístico*)
3 house (*adosado*)
el **champán** SUSTANTIVO (PL los **champanes**)
champagne
el **champiñón** SUSTANTIVO (PL los **champiñones**)
mushroom
el **champú** SUSTANTIVO (PL los **champús**)
shampoo
la **chancleta** SUSTANTIVO
thong
◆ **unas chancletas** a pair of thongs
el **chantaje** SUSTANTIVO
blackmail
◆ **hacer* chantaje a alguien** to blackmail somebody
la **chapa** SUSTANTIVO
1 badge (*insignia*)
2 top (*de botella*)
3 sheet (*de metal*)
4 lock (*cerradura*)
5 panel (*de madera*)
chapado ADJETIVO
◆ **chapado en oro** gold-plated
el **chaparrón** SUSTANTIVO (PL los **chaparrones**)
◆ **Anoche cayó un buen chaparrón.** There was a real downpour last night.
◆ **Es sólo un chaparrón.** It's just a shower.
chapopote SUSTANTIVO *Mexico*
asphalt (*asfalto*)
chapotear VERBO
to splash around
la **chapuza** SUSTANTIVO
botched job
el **chapuzón** SUSTANTIVO (PL los **chapuzones**)
◆ **darse* un chapuzón** to go for a dip
la **chaqueta** SUSTANTIVO
1 jacket
2 cardigan (*de punto*)
la **charca** SUSTANTIVO
pond
el **charco** SUSTANTIVO
puddle
la **charcutería** SUSTANTIVO
delicatessen
la **charla** SUSTANTIVO
1 chat ◇ *Estuvimos de charla.* We had a chat.
2 talk ◇ *Dio una charla sobre teatro clásico.* He gave a talk on classical theater.
charlar VERBO
to chat
la **charola** SUSTANTIVO *Mexico*
tray
el **chasco** SUSTANTIVO
◆ **llevarse un chasco** to be disappointed
el **chat** SUSTANTIVO
chatroom
la **chatarra** SUSTANTIVO
scrap metal
la **chava** SUSTANTIVO *Mexico*
girl
el **chavo** SUSTANTIVO *Mexico*
boy
checar* VERBO *Mexico*
to check
el **checo**, la **checa** ADJETIVO, SUSTANTIVO
Czech
◆ **la República Checa** the Czech Republic
el **checo** SUSTANTIVO
Czech (*idioma*)
el **chef** SUSTANTIVO (PL los **chefs**)
chef
el **cheque** SUSTANTIVO
check
◆ **los cheques de viaje** traveler's checks
el **chequeo** SUSTANTIVO
checkup ◇ *hacerse un chequeo* to have a checkup
chévere ADJETIVO, ADVERBIO
great (*coloquial*)
la **chica** SUSTANTIVO
girl
el **chícharo** SUSTANTIVO *Mexico*
pea
el **chichón** SUSTANTIVO (PL los **chichones**)
bump ◇ *Me salió un chichón en la frente.* I have a bump on my forehead.
el **chicle** SUSTANTIVO
chewing gum
chico ADJETIVO
small
el **chico** SUSTANTIVO
1 boy ◇ *los chicos de la clase* the boys in the class
2 guy ◇ *Me parece un chico muy simpático.* He seems like a nice guy.
el **chile** SUSTANTIVO
chili
Chile SUSTANTIVO MASC
Chile
el **chileno**, la **chilena** ADJETIVO, SUSTANTIVO
Chilean
chillar VERBO
1 to scream (*persona*)
2 to squeak (*ratón*)
3 to squeal (*cerdo*)
4 to screech (*gaviotas*)

la **chimenea** SUSTANTIVO
1 chimney ◇ *Salía humo de la chimenea.* There was smoke coming out of the chimney.
2 fireplace ◇ *sentado frente a la chimenea* sitting in front of the fireplace
◆ **Enciende la chimenea.** Light the fire.

el **chimpancé** SUSTANTIVO (PL los **chimpancés**)
chimpanzee

la **china** SUSTANTIVO
Chinese woman (PL Chinese women)

China SUSTANTIVO FEM
China

la **chinche** SUSTANTIVO Mexico
thumbtack

chino ADJETIVO
Chinese

el **chino** SUSTANTIVO
1 Chinese man (PL Chinese men) (*persona*)
◆ **los chinos** the Chinese
2 Chinese (*idioma*)

Chipre SUSTANTIVO MASC
Cyprus

la **chirimoya** SUSTANTIVO
custard apple

chirriar* VERBO
to squeak

el **chisme** SUSTANTIVO
1 thing (*coloquial: cosa*)
2 piece of gossip (*cuento*) ◇ *un chisme muy sabroso* a juicy piece of gossip
◆ **Siempre está contando chismes.** He's always gossiping.

chismorrear VERBO
to gossip

el **chismorreo** SUSTANTIVO
gossip

chismoso ADJETIVO
◆ **¡No seas chismoso!** Don't be such a gossip!

el **chiste** SUSTANTIVO
1 joke ◇ *contar un chiste* to tell a joke
◆ **un chiste verde** a dirty joke
2 cartoon ◇ *el chiste del periódico* the newspaper cartoon

chocar* VERBO
◆ **chocar contra (1)** to hit ◇ *El carro chocó contra un árbol.* The car hit a tree.
◆ **chocar contra (2)** (*andando*) to bump into ◇ *Choqué contra una farol.* I bumped into a lamppost.
◆ **chocar con algo** to crash into something
◆ **Los trenes chocaron de frente.** The trains crashed head-on.
◆ **Me choca que no sepas nada.** I'm shocked that you don't know anything about it.

el **chocolate** SUSTANTIVO
chocolate ◇ *chocolate con leche* milk chocolate
◆ **¿Quieres un chocolate?** Would you like a chocolate?
◆ **Nos tomamos un chocolate.** We had a cup of hot chocolate.

la **chocolatina** SUSTANTIVO
chocolate bar

el **chofer**, la **chofer** SUSTANTIVO
1 driver (*de carro, camión*)
2 chauffeur (*empleado*)

el **chopo** SUSTANTIVO
black poplar

el **choque** SUSTANTIVO
1 crash (PL crashes) (*de vehículos*)
2 clash (PL clashes) (*entre personas, culturas*)

el **chorizo** SUSTANTIVO
spicy sausage

el **chorrito** SUSTANTIVO
dash ◇ *Échame un chorrito de leche.* Just a dash of milk, please.

el **chorro** SUSTANTIVO
◆ **salir* a chorros** to gush out

la **choza** SUSTANTIVO
hut

el **chubasco** SUSTANTIVO
heavy shower

el **chubasquero** SUSTANTIVO
waterproof jacket with a hood

la **chuleta** SUSTANTIVO
chop ◇ *una chuleta de cerdo* a pork chop

chulo ADJETIVO
1 cocky (*coloquial*)
2 neat (*coloquial*) ◇ *¡Qué mochila más chula!* What a neat backpack!

chupar VERBO
to suck ◇ *Se chupaba el dedo.* He was sucking his thumb.

el **chupete** SUSTANTIVO
pacifier

el **cibercafé** SUSTANTIVO (PL los **cibercafés**)
Internet café

la **cicatriz** SUSTANTIVO (PL las **cicatrices**)
scar

el **ciclismo** SUSTANTIVO
cycling
◆ **Mi hermano hace ciclismo.** My brother is a cyclist.

el/la **ciclista** SUSTANTIVO
cyclist

el **ciclo** SUSTANTIVO
cycle

la **ciega** SUSTANTIVO
blind woman (PL blind women)
◆ **Avanzábamos a ciegas.** We couldn't see where we were going.
◆ **Tomaron la decisión a ciegas.** They took the decision blindly.

ciego ADJETIVO
blind ◇ *quedarse ciego* to go blind

el **ciego** SUSTANTIVO
blind man
◆ **los ciegos** the blind

el **cielo** SUSTANTIVO
1 sky (PL skies) ◇ *No había ni una nube en* ☞

C

el cielo. There wasn't a single cloud in the sky.
[2] heaven ◇ *ir al cielo* to go to heaven

cien ADJETIVO, PRONOMBRE
a hundred ◇ *Había unos cien invitados a la boda.* There were about a hundred guests at the wedding. ◇ *cien mil* a hundred thousand
◆ **cien por cien** a hundred percent ◇ *Es cien por cien algodón.* It's a hundred percent cotton.

la **ciencia** SUSTANTIVO
science ◇ *Me gustan mucho las ciencias.* I really enjoy science. ◇ *ciencias sociales* social sciences
◆ **ciencias empresariales** business studies

la **ciencia-ficción** SUSTANTIVO
science fiction

la **científica** SUSTANTIVO
scientist

científico ADJETIVO
scientific

el **científico** SUSTANTIVO
scientist

ciento ADJETIVO, PRONOMBRE
a hundred ◇ *ciento cuarenta y dos dólares* a hundred and forty two dollars ◇ *Recibimos cientos de cartas.* We received hundreds of letters.
◆ **el diez por ciento de la población** ten percent of the population

el **cierre** SUSTANTIVO
[1] clasp (*de pulsera, bolso*)
[2] closing-down (*de empresa, hospital*)

cierro VERBO *ver* **cerrar**

cierto ADJETIVO
[1] true (*verdadero*) ◇ *No, eso no es cierto.* No, that's not true.
[2] certain ◇ *Viene ciertos días a la semana.* He comes certain days of the week.
◆ **por cierto** by the way

el **ciervo** SUSTANTIVO
deer (PL deer)

la **cifra** SUSTANTIVO
figure ◇ *un número de cuatro cifras* a four-figure number

el **cigarrillo** SUSTANTIVO
cigarette

el **cigarro** SUSTANTIVO
cigarette

la **cigüeña** SUSTANTIVO
stork

la **cima** SUSTANTIVO
top ◇ *Quiere llegar a la cima.* He wants to get to the top.

los **cimientos** SUSTANTIVO
foundations

cinco ADJETIVO, PRONOMBRE
five
◆ **Son las cinco.** It's five o'clock.
◆ **el cinco de enero** January fifth

cincuenta ADJETIVO, PRONOMBRE
fifty ◇ *Tiene cincuenta años.* He's fifty.
◆ **el cincuenta aniversario** the fiftieth anniversary

el **cine** SUSTANTIVO
[1] cinema (*arte*)
[2] movie theater (*local*)
◆ **ir* al cine** to go to the movies
◆ **una actriz de cine** a movie actress

cínico ADJETIVO
cynical

la **cinta** SUSTANTIVO
[1] ribbon (*de adorno, para el pelo*)
[2] tape (*para grabar*)
◆ **una cinta de video** a videotape
◆ **cinta aislante** electrical tape
◆ **cinta Dúrex ®** Scotch tape ®
◆ **una cinta transportadora** a conveyor belt

la **cintura** SUSTANTIVO
waist ◇ *¿Cuánto mides de cintura?* What's your waist size?

el **cinturón** SUSTANTIVO (PL los **cinturones**)
belt
◆ **el cinturón de seguridad** the safety belt

el **ciprés** SUSTANTIVO (PL los **cipreses**)
cypress

el **circo** SUSTANTIVO
circus (PL circuses)

el **circuito** SUSTANTIVO
[1] track (*deportivo*) ◇ *El corredor dio cuatro vueltas al circuito.* The runner ran four laps around the track.
[2] circuit (*eléctrico*)
◆ **circuito cerrado de televisión** closed-circuit television

la **circulación** SUSTANTIVO
[1] traffic (*de vehículos*) ◇ *un accidente de circulación* a traffic accident
[2] circulation (*de la sangre*)

circular VERBO
[1] to drive (*en carro*) ◇ *En Australia se circula por la izquierda.* In Australia they drive on the left.
◆ **¡Circulen!** Move along please!
[2] to circulate (*sangre*)
[3] to go round (*rumor*) ◇ *Circula el rumor de que se van casar.* There's a rumor going round that they're getting married.

el **círculo** SUSTANTIVO
circle ◇ *Las sillas estaban puestas en círculo.* The chairs were set out in a circle.

la **circunferencia** SUSTANTIVO
circumference

la **circunstancia** SUSTANTIVO
circumstance

la **ciruela** SUSTANTIVO
plum
◆ **una ciruela pasa** a prune

la **cirugía** SUSTANTIVO
surgery ◇ *hacerse* la cirugía plástica* to

have plastic surgery

el **cirujano,** la **cirujana** SUSTANTIVO
surgeon

el **cisne** SUSTANTIVO
swan

la **cisterna** SUSTANTIVO
cistern (*del wáter*)

la **cita** SUSTANTIVO
1 appointment (*profesional*) ◇ *Tengo cita con el Sr. Pérez.* I have an appointment with Mr. Pérez.
2 date (*romántica*) ◇ *No llegues tarde a la cita.* Don't be late for your date.
3 quotation (*textual*) ◇ *una cita de Quevedo* a quotation from Quevedo

citar VERBO
1 to quote (*frase, texto*) ◇ *Siempre está citando a los clásicos.* He's always quoting the classics.
2 to mention ◇ *Citó el caso que ocurrió el otro día.* He mentioned as an example what happened the other day.
◆ **Nos han citado a las diez.** We've been given an appointment for ten o'clock.
◆ **Me he citado con Elena.** I've arranged to meet Elena.

la **ciudad** SUSTANTIVO
1 city (PL cities) ◇ *una ciudad como Salamanca* a city like Salamanca
2 town ◇ *una pequeña ciudad al norte de Houston* a small town north of Houston
◆ **la ciudad universitaria** the university campus

el **ciudadano,** la **ciudadana** SUSTANTIVO
citizen ◇ *ser ciudadano mexicano* to be a Mexican citizen

civil ADJETIVO
civil ◇ *la guerra civil* the Civil War

la **civilización** SUSTANTIVO (PL las **civilizaciones**)
civilization

civilizado ADJETIVO
civilized

la **clara** SUSTANTIVO
white (*de huevo*)

el **clarinete** SUSTANTIVO
clarinet

claro (1) ADJETIVO
1 clear (*explicación, idea*) ◇ *Lo quiero mañana. ¿Está claro?* I want it tomorrow. Is that clear?
◆ **Está claro que esconden algo.** It's obvious that they are hiding something.
◆ **No tengo muy claro lo que quiero hacer.** I'm not very sure about what I want to do.
2 light (*color*) ◇ *una camisa azul claro* a light blue shirt

claro (2) ADVERBIO
clearly ◇ *Lo oí muy claro.* I heard it very clearly.
◆ **Quiero que me hables claro.** I want you to be frank with me.
◆ **No he sacado nada en claro de la reunión.** I'm none the wiser after that meeting.
◆ **¡Claro! (1)** Sure! ◇ *¿Te gusta el fútbol? – ¡Claro!* Do you like soccer? – Sure!
◆ **¡Claro! (2)** Of course! ◇ *¿Te oyó? – ¡Claro que me oyó!* Did he hear you? – Of course he heard me!

C

la **clase** SUSTANTIVO
1 class (PL classes) ◇ *A las diez tengo clase de física.* At ten o'clock I have a physics class.
◆ **Mi hermana da clases de inglés.** My sister teaches English.
◆ **Hoy no hay clase.** There's no school today.
◆ **clases de conducir** driving lessons
◆ **clases particulares** private classes
2 classroom (*aula*)
3 kind (*tipo*) ◇ *Había juguetes de todas clases.* There were all kinds of toys.
◆ **la clase media** the middle class

clásico ADJETIVO
1 classical ◇ *Me gusta la música clásica.* I like classical music.
2 classic (*típico*) ◇ *Es el clásico ejemplo de malnutrición.* It's a classic case of malnutrition.

la **clasificación** SUSTANTIVO (PL las **clasificaciones**)
classification (*de libros, plantas*)
◆ **estar* a la cabeza de la clasificación** to lead the table

clasificar* VERBO
to classify (*libros, plantas*)
◆ **Esperan clasificarse para la final.** They hope to qualify for the final.
◆ **Se clasificaron en tercer lugar.** They came in third.

clavar VERBO
◆ **clavar una tachuela en algo** to hammer a tack into something
◆ **Las tablas están mal clavadas.** The boards aren't properly nailed down.
◆ **Me clavé una espina en el dedo.** I got a thorn in my finger.
◆ **Aquí te clavan.** You get ripped off in this place. (*coloquial*)

la **clave** SUSTANTIVO
1 code (*de caja fuerte, secreta*)
◆ **un mensaje en clave** a coded message
◆ **la clave de acceso** the password
2 key ◇ *la clave del éxito* the key to success

el **clavel** SUSTANTIVO
carnation

la **clavícula** SUSTANTIVO
collar bone

el **clavo** SUSTANTIVO
nail

el **clic** SUSTANTIVO
click
◆ **hacer* clic en** to click on
◆ **hacer* doble clic en** to double-click on

el **cliente,** la **clienta** SUSTANTIVO

☞

[1] customer (*de tienda, restaurante*)
[2] client (*de empresa, banco*)
[3] guest (*de hotel*)

el **clima** SUSTANTIVO
climate ◇ *Es un país de clima tropical.* It's a country with a tropical climate.

climatizado ADJETIVO
[1] air-conditioned (*lugar*)
[2] heated (*piscina*)

la **clínica** SUSTANTIVO
hospital

clínico ADJETIVO
clinical

el **clip** SUSTANTIVO (PL los **clips**)
[1] paper clip (*para papeles*)
[2] clip (*para el pelo*)

cliquear VERBO
to click

la **cloaca** SUSTANTIVO
sewer

el **cloro** SUSTANTIVO
chlorine

el **club** SUSTANTIVO (PL los **clubs**)
club ◇ *el club de tenis* the tennis club

cobarde ADJETIVO
cowardly ◇ *una actitud cobarde* a cowardly attitude
◆ **¡No seas cobarde!** Don't be such a coward!

el/la **cobarde** SUSTANTIVO
coward

la **cobaya** SUSTANTIVO
guinea pig

la **cobija** SUSTANTIVO
blanket

el **cobrador,** la **cobradora** SUSTANTIVO
[1] collector (*de impuestos*)
[2] guard (*en tren*)

cobrar VERBO
to charge ◇ *Me cobró quinientos pesos por la reparación.* He charged me five hundred pesos for the repair.
◆ **cuando cobre el sueldo de este mes** when I get my wages this month
◆ **¿Me cobra los cafés?** How much do I owe for the coffees?
◆ **¡Cóbrese, por favor!** Can I pay, please?
◆ **cobrar un cheque** to cash a check

el **cobre** SUSTANTIVO
copper

el **cobro** SUSTANTIVO
◆ **llamar a cobro revertido** to call collect

la **Coca-Cola** ® SUSTANTIVO (PL las **Coca-Colas**)
Coke ®

la **cocaína** SUSTANTIVO
cocaine

cocer* VERBO
[1] to boil (*hervir*) ◇ *Cocer las verduras durante tres minutos.* Boil the vegetables for three minutes.
[2] to cook (*cocinar*) ◇ *Las zanahorias no están cocidas todavía.* The carrots aren't properly cooked yet.
◆ **Tarda diez minutos en cocerse.** It takes ten minutes to cook.

el **coche** SUSTANTIVO
[1] car (1) (*automóvil*)
[2] car (2) (*de tren*)
◆ **Fuimos en coche cama.** We took the sleeping car.
[3] baby carriage (*para el bebé*)

cochino ADJETIVO
filthy

el **cochino** SUSTANTIVO
pig

la **cocina** SUSTANTIVO
[1] kitchen ◇ *Comemos en la cocina.* We eat in the kitchen.
[2] cooker ◇ *una cocina de gas* a gas cooker
◆ **la cocina italiana** Italian cuisine
◆ **un libro de cocina** a cookbook

cocinar VERBO
to cook ◇ *No sabe cocinar.* He can't cook.
◆ **Cocinas muy bien.** You're a very good cook.

el **cocinero,** la **cocinera** SUSTANTIVO
cook ◇ *Soy cocinero.* I'm a cook.

el **coco** SUSTANTIVO
coconut (*fruto*)

el **cocodrilo** SUSTANTIVO
crocodile

el **código** SUSTANTIVO
code ◇ *el código postal* the zip code

el **codo** SUSTANTIVO
elbow

la **codorniz** SUSTANTIVO (PL las **codornices**)
quail

coger* VERBO
[1] to take (*tomar*) ◇ *Coge el que más te guste.* Take the one which you like best. ◇ *Coja la primera calle a la derecha.* Take the first street on the right.
[2] to catch (*pillar*) ◇ *¡Coge la pelota!* Catch the ball! ◇ *La cogieron robando.* They caught her stealing.
◆ **coger un resfriado** to catch a cold
[3] to pick up (*levantar*) ◇ *Coge al niño, que está llorando.* Pick up the baby; he's crying.
[4] to get (*obtener*) ◇ *¿Nos coges dos entradas?* Would you get us two tickets?
[5] to borrow (*tomar prestado*) ◇ *¿Te puedo coger el bolígrafo?* Can I borrow your pen?
◆ **Le cogió cariño al gato.** He took a liking to the cat.
◆ **Iban cogidos de la mano.** They were walking hand in hand.

el **cohete** SUSTANTIVO
rocket
◆ **un cohete espacial** a rocket

cohibido ADJETIVO
inhibited
◆ **sentirse* cohibido** to feel inhibited

la **coincidencia** SUSTANTIVO
coincidence
◆ **¡Qué coincidencia!** What a coincidence!

coincidir VERBO
to match ◇ *Las huellas dactilares coinciden.* The fingerprints match.
◆ **Coincidimos en el tren.** We happened to meet on the train.
◆ **Es que esas fechas coinciden con mi viaje.** The problem is, those dates clash with my trip.

cojear VERBO
1 to limp ◇ *Todavía cojea un poco.* He's still limping a little.
2 to be lame (*ser cojo*) ◇ *Cojea del pie izquierdo.* He's lame in his left leg.
3 to wobble (*silla, mesa*)

el **cojín** SUSTANTIVO (PL los **cojines**)
cushion

cojo (1) VERBO *ver* **coger**

cojo (2) ADJETIVO
1 lame ◇ *Está cojo.* He's lame.
◆ **Vas un poco cojo.** You're limping a bit.
2 wobbly (*mueble*)

la **col** SUSTANTIVO
cabbage
◆ **las coles de Bruselas** Brussels sprouts

la **cola** SUSTANTIVO
1 tail (*de animal*)
2 line (*de gente*) ◇ *Había mucha cola para los baños.* There was a long line for the toilets.
◆ **hacer* cola** to stand in line
3 glue (*pegamento*)

colaborar VERBO
◆ **Todo el pueblo colaboró.** Everyone in the village joined in.
◆ **Se negó a colaborar con nosotros.** He refused to cooperate with us.

el **colador** SUSTANTIVO
1 strainer (*para líquidos*)
2 sieve (*para arroz, verduras*)

colar VERBO
to strain (*verduras, té*)
◆ **colarse** to butt in (*coloquial*) ◇ *No te cueles.* Don't butt in.
◆ **Nos colamos en el cine.** We sneaked into the movies without paying.

la **colcha** SUSTANTIVO
bedspread

el **colchón** SUSTANTIVO (PL los **colchones**)
mattress (PL mattresses)
◆ **un colchón de aire** an air bed

la **colchoneta** SUSTANTIVO
1 mat (*gimnasia*)
2 air mattress (PL air mattresses) (*de aire*)

la **colección** SUSTANTIVO (PL las **colecciones**)
collection

coleccionar VERBO
to collect

la **colecta** SUSTANTIVO
collection ◇ *Hicieron una colecta para comprarle el pasaje.* They took a collection to buy him the ticket.

el/la **colega** SUSTANTIVO
1 colleague (*de profesión*)
2 buddy (PL buddies) (*coloquial: amigo*)

el **colegio** SUSTANTIVO
school ◇ *Voy al colegio en bicicleta.* I bike to school. ◇ *¿Todavía vas al colegio?* Are you still in school? ◇ *Mi hermano estaba en el colegio.* My brother was at school.
◆ **un colegio de curas** a Catholic boys' school
◆ **un colegio secundario** high school
◆ **un colegio de monjas** a convent school
◆ **un colegio público** a public school
◆ **un colegio mayor** Spain residence hall

el **colesterol** SUSTANTIVO
cholesterol

la **coleta** SUSTANTIVO
ponytail

colgado ADJETIVO
hanging ◇ *Había varios cuadros colgados en la pared.* There were several pictures hanging on the wall.
◆ **Debe de tener el teléfono mal colgado.** He must have the telephone off the hook.

el **colgante** SUSTANTIVO
pendant

colgar* VERBO
to hang ◇ *Colgamos un cuadro en la pared.* We hung a picture on the wall.
◆ **¡No dejes la chaqueta en la silla, cuélgala!** Don't leave your jacket on the chair; hang it up!
◆ **Me colgó el teléfono.** He hung up on me.
◆ **¡Cuelga, por favor, que quiero hacer una llamada!** Hang up, please. I want to use the phone!
◆ **No cuelgue, por favor.** Please hold.

la **coliflor** SUSTANTIVO
cauliflower

la **colilla** SUSTANTIVO
cigarette butt

la **colina** SUSTANTIVO
hill

el **collar** SUSTANTIVO
1 necklace (*joya*)
2 collar (*de perro, gato*)

la **colmena** SUSTANTIVO
beehive

el **colmillo** SUSTANTIVO
1 canine tooth (PL canine teeth) (*de persona, perro*)
2 fang (*de vampiro, cobra*)
3 tusk (*de elefante*)

el **colmo** SUSTANTIVO
◆ **¡Esto ya es el colmo!** This really is the last straw!
◆ **Para colmo de males, empezó a llover.** To make matters worse, it started to rain.

colocar* VERBO

☞

1 to put (*poner*) ◇ *Colocamos la mesa en medio del comedor.* We put the table in the middle of the dining room.
2 to arrange (*ordenar*)
◆ **colocarse (1)** to get a job ◇ *Se colocó de aprendiz en un taller mecánico.* He got a job as an apprentice in a garage.
◆ **colocarse (2)** (*coloquial: con alcohol*) to get plastered
◆ **colocarse (3)** (*coloquial: con drogas*) to get high
◆ **¡Colocaos en fila!** Get into line!
◆ **El equipo americano se ha colocado en quinto lugar.** The American team is now in fifth place.

Colombia SUSTANTIVO FEM
Colombia

el **colombiano,** la **colombiana** ADJETIVO, SUSTANTIVO
Colombian

la **colonia** SUSTANTIVO
1 perfume (*de buen olor*)
2 colony (PL colonies) (*de otro país*)
3 district *Mexico*
◆ **una colonia de verano** a summer camp

colonizar* VERBO
to colonize

coloquial ADJETIVO
colloquial

el **color** SUSTANTIVO
color ◇ *¿De qué color son?* What color are they?
◆ **un vestido de color azul** a blue dress
◆ **una televisión en color** a color television

colorado ADJETIVO
red
◆ **ponerse* colorado** to blush

la **columna** SUSTANTIVO
column
◆ **la columna vertebral** the spine

el **columpio** SUSTANTIVO
swing

la **coma** SUSTANTIVO
comma ◇ *palabras separadas por comas* words separated by commas
◆ **cero coma ocho** zero point eight

el **coma** SUSTANTIVO
coma
◆ **estar* en coma** to be in a coma
◆ **entrar en coma** to go into a coma

la **comadrona** SUSTANTIVO
midwife (PL midwives)

el/la **comandante** SUSTANTIVO
major
◆ **el comandante en jefe** the commander in chief

el **combate** SUSTANTIVO
battle ◇ *entrar en combate* to go into battle
◆ **un piloto de combate** a fighter pilot
◆ **un combate de boxeo** a boxing match

combinar VERBO
1 to combine ◇ *Combina los estudios con el trabajo.* He combines his studies with work.
2 to match (*ropa, colores*) ◇ *colores que combinan con el azul* colors which match with blue

el **combustible** SUSTANTIVO
fuel

la **comedia** SUSTANTIVO
comedy (PL comedies)

> ℹ *A **comedia** is a type of soap opera on television in Latin America which usually attracts huge audiences.*

el **comedor** SUSTANTIVO
1 dining room (*en casa, hotel*)
2 dining hall (*en colegio*)
3 canteen (*en lugar de trabajo*)

comentar VERBO
1 to say ◇ *Comentó que le había parecido muy joven.* He said that she had seemed very young.
2 to discuss ◇ *Comentamos el tema en clase.* We discussed the subject in class.
◆ **Me han comentado que es una película muy buena.** I've been told that is a very good movie.

el **comentario** SUSTANTIVO
comment (*observación*) ◇ *No hizo ningún comentario.* He made no comment.
◆ **Fue un comentario desagradable.** It was an unpleasant remark.

el/la **comentarista** SUSTANTIVO
commentator

comenzar* VERBO
to begin
◆ **Comenzó a llover.** It began to rain.

comer VERBO
1 to eat ◇ *¿Quieres comer algo?* Do you want something to eat?
◆ **Me comí una manzana.** I had an apple.
2 to have lunch (*al mediodía*) ◇ *Comimos en el hotel.* We had lunch in the hotel.
◆ **Comimos paella.** We had paella.
◆ **¿Qué hay para comer?** What is there for lunch?
3 to have dinner
◆ **Le estaba dando de comer a su hijo.** She was feeding her son.

comercial ADJETIVO
1 business (*relación, zona, estructura*)
***business** en este caso va siempre delante del sustantivo.*
2 trade (*déficit, guerra*)
***trade** en este caso va siempre delante del sustantivo.*
3 commercial ◇ *una película muy comercial* a very commercial movie

* Verbs marked with this symbol are irregular. See pages 346–348 for further details.

el/la **comerciante** SUSTANTIVO
storekeeper

el **comercio** SUSTANTIVO
1 trade ◇ *el comercio exterior* foreign trade
◆ **el comercio electrónico** e-commerce
2 stores PL ◇ *¿A qué hora cierra el comercio?* What time do the stores close?

el **cometa** SUSTANTIVO
comet

la **cometa** SUSTANTIVO
kite

cometer VERBO
1 to commit (*un delito*)
2 to make (*un error*)

el **cómic** SUSTANTIVO (PL los **cómics**) Spain
comic ◇ *un cómic nuevo* a new comic
◆ **un personaje de cómic** a comic-book character

cómico ADJETIVO
1 comical ◇ *Fue muy cómico.* It was very comical.
2 comic ◇ *un actor cómico* a comic actor

la **comida** SUSTANTIVO
1 food ◇ *La comida es muy buena en el hotel.* The food in the hotel is very good.
◆ **la comida basura** junk food
2 lunch (PL lunches) (*al mediodía*) ◇ *La comida es a la una y media.* Lunch is at half past one.
3 supper (*por la noche*)
4 meal ◇ *Es la comida más importante del día.* It's the most important meal of the day.

comienzo VERBO *ver* **comenzar**

las **comillas** SUSTANTIVO
quotation marks
◆ **entre comillas** in quotation marks

la **comisaría** SUSTANTIVO
police station

la **comisión** SUSTANTIVO (PL las **comisiones**)
1 commission ◇ *una comisión del 20%* a 20% commission
2 committee ◇ *La comisión organizadora del festival.* The festival organizing committee.

el **comité** SUSTANTIVO (PL los **comités**)
committee

como ADVERBIO, CONJUNCIÓN
1 like ◇ *Tienen un perro como el nuestro.* They have a dog like ours. ◇ *Se portó como un imbécil.* He behaved like an idiot.
◆ **Sabe como a cebolla.** It tastes a bit like onion.
2 as ◇ *Lo hice como me habían enseñado.* I did it as I had been taught. ◇ *Lo usé como cuchara.* I used it as a spoon. ◇ *blanco como la nieve* as white as snow ◇ *Como ella no llegaba, me fui.* As she didn't arrive, I left.
◆ **Hazlo como te dijo ella.** Do it the way she told you.
◆ **Es tan alto como tú.** He is as tall as you.
◆ **tal como lo había planeado** just as I had planned it
◆ **como si** as if ◇ *Siguió leyendo, como si no hubiera oído nada.* He kept on reading, as if he had heard nothing.
3 if ◇ *Como lo vuelvas a hacer se lo digo a tu mamá.* If you do it again I'll tell your mother.
4 about ◇ *Vinieron como unas diez personas.* About ten people came. ◇ *Llegó como a las cuatro.* He arrived about four o'clock.

cómo ADVERBIO
how ◇ *¿Cómo se dice en inglés?* How do you say it in English? ◇ *¿Cómo están tus padres?* How are your parents? ◇ *No sé cómo voy a explicárselo.* I don't know how I'm going to explain it to him.
◆ **¿A cómo están las manzanas?** How much are the apples?
◆ **¿Cómo es de grande?** How big is it?
◆ **¿Cómo es su novio? (1)** (*de personalidad*) What's her boyfriend like?
◆ **¿Cómo es su novio? (2)** (*de físico*) What does her boyfriend look like?
◆ **Perdón, ¿cómo dijiste?** Sorry, what did you say?
◆ **¡Cómo! ¿Mañana?** What? Tomorrow?
◆ **¡Cómo corría!** Boy, was he running!

la **cómoda** SUSTANTIVO
chest of drawers (PL chests of drawers)

la **comodidad** SUSTANTIVO
1 comfort ◇ *Sólo le interesa su propia comodidad.* He's only interested in his own comfort.
2 convenience ◇ *la comodidad de vivir en el centro* the convenience of living in the center of town

cómodo ADJETIVO
1 comfortable ◇ *un sillón cómodo* a comfortable chair ◇ *Me siento cómodo en tu casa.* I feel comfortable in your house.
2 convenient ◇ *Tener un carro es muy cómodo.* Having a car is very convenient.

el **compact disc** SUSTANTIVO (PL los **compact discs**)
1 compact disc (*disco*)
2 compact disc player (*aparato*)

compadecer* VERBO
to feel sorry for ◇ *Te compadezco.* I feel sorry for you.

el **compañero,** la **compañera** SUSTANTIVO
1 classmate (*de clase*)
2 workmate (*de trabajo*)
3 partner (*pareja*)
◆ **un compañero de cuarto** a roommate

la **compañía** SUSTANTIVO
company (PL companies) ◇ *una compañía de seguros* an insurance company
◆ **El chico andaba en malas compañías.** The boy was keeping bad company.
◆ **Ana vino a hacerme compañía.** Ana came to keep me company.

C

◆ **una compañía aérea** an airline

la **comparación** SUSTANTIVO (PL las **comparaciones**)
comparison ◇ *Mi carro no tiene comparación con el tuyo.* There's no comparison between my car and yours.
◆ **Mi cuarto es pequeñísimo en comparación con el tuyo.** My room is tiny compared to yours.

comparar VERBO
to compare ◇ *Siempre me comparan con mi hermana.* I'm always being compared to my sister.

compartir VERBO
to share

el **compás** SUSTANTIVO (PL los **compases**)
compass (PL compasses) (*para dibujo*)
◆ **bailar al compás de la música** to dance in time to the music

compatible ADJETIVO
compatible

compensar VERBO
1 to make up for ◇ *Intentan compensar la falta de medios con imaginación.* What they lack in resources they try to make up for in imagination.
2 to compensate (*económicamente*) ◇ *El gobierno compensará a los agricultores por la mala cosecha.* The government will compensate farmers for the bad harvest.
◆ **No me compensa con el sueldo que pagan.** It's not worth my while for the salary they pay.
◆ **No compensa viajar tan lejos por tan poco tiempo.** It's not worth traveling that far for such a short time.
◆ **No sé si compensa.** I don't know if it's worth it.

la **competencia** SUSTANTIVO
1 rivalry ◇ *la competencia entre dos hermanos* the rivalry between two brothers
2 competition ◇ *una campaña para desacreditar a la competencia* a campaign to discredit the competition ◇ *una competencia deportiva* a sports competition
◆ **No quiere hacerle la competencia a su mejor amigo.** He doesn't want to compete with his best friend.

competente ADJETIVO
competent

la **competición** SUSTANTIVO (PL las **competiciones**) Spain
competition

competir* VERBO
to compete ◇ *Van a competir contra los mejores del mundo.* They're going to compete against the best in the world.
◇ *competir por un título* to compete for a title

complacer* VERBO
to please

el **complejo** SUSTANTIVO
complex (PL complexes)
◆ **Tiene complejo porque es gordo.** He has a complex about being fat.
◆ **un complejo deportivo** a sports complex

completar VERBO
to complete

completo ADJETIVO
1 complete ◇ *las obras completas de Lorca* the complete works of Lorca
2 full (*lleno*) ◇ *Los hoteles estaban completos.* The hotels were full.
◆ **Me olvidé por completo.** I completely forgot.

complicado ADJETIVO
complicated

complicar* VERBO
to complicate
◆ **complicarse** to get complicated ◇ *La situación se fue complicando cada día más.* The situation was getting more complicated by the day.
◆ **No quiero complicarme la vida.** I don't want to make life more difficult for myself.

el/la **cómplice** SUSTANTIVO
accomplice

componer* VERBO
to compose ◇ *Él compuso la música.* He composed the music.
◆ **El comité se compone de seis miembros.** The committee is made up of six members.

el **comportamiento** SUSTANTIVO
behavior

comportarse VERBO
to behave

la **compra** SUSTANTIVO
shopping
◆ **hacer* la compra** to do the shopping
◆ **Hice unas compras en el centro.** I did some shopping in the center of town.
◆ **ir* de compras** to go shopping

comprar VERBO
to buy ◇ *Les compré helados a los niños.* I bought some ice cream for the children.
◆ **Le compré el carro a mi amigo.** I bought my friend's car.
◆ **Quiero comprarme unos zapatos.** I want to buy a pair of shoes.

comprender VERBO
to understand ◇ *¡No lo comprendo!* I don't understand it!

comprensivo ADJETIVO
understanding

la **compresa** SUSTANTIVO
sanitary napkin

el **comprimido** SUSTANTIVO
pill

el **comprobante** SUSTANTIVO
receipt

comprobar* VERBO

to check

comprometerse VERBO

- **Me he comprometido a ayudarlos.** I have promised to help them.
- **No quiero comprometerme por si después no puedo ir.** I don't want to commit myself in case I can't go.

el **compromiso** SUSTANTIVO

engagement ◇ *El ministro canceló sus compromisos.* The minister canceled his engagements. ◇ *Se iban a casar pero rompieron el compromiso.* They were going to get married but they broke off their engagement.

- **Puede probarlo sin ningún compromiso.** You can try it with no obligation.
- **Iba a ir pero sólo por compromiso.** I was going to go but only out of duty.
- **poner* a alguien en un compromiso** to put someone in a difficult situation

compruebo VERBO *ver* **comprobar**

compuesto (1) VERBO *ver* **componer**

compuesto (2) ADJETIVO

- **un jurado compuesto de seis miembros** a jury made up of six members

el **computador,** la **computadora** SUSTANTIVO

computer

- **un computador portátil** a laptop

común ADJETIVO

common (*frontera, característica, objetivo*) ◇ *un apellido muy común* a very common surname

- **No tenemos nada en común.** We have nothing in common.
- **Hicimos el trabajo en común.** We did the work between us.
- **las zonas de uso común** the communal areas

la **comunicación** SUSTANTIVO (PL las **comunicaciones**)

communication

- **Se cortó la comunicación.** We've been cut off.

comunicar* VERBO

to be busy (*teléfono*) [Spain] ◇ *Siempre está comunicando.* The line is always busy.

- **comunicarse** to communicate ◇ *Le cuesta comunicarse con los demás.* He finds it hard to communicate with others.
- **Los dos despachos se comunican.** The two offices are connected.

la **comunidad** SUSTANTIVO

community (PL communities)

- **la Comunidad Europea** the European Community

la **comunión** SUSTANTIVO (PL las **comuniones**)

communion

- **Voy a hacer la primera comunión.** I'm going to make my first communion.

el/la **comunista** ADJETIVO, SUSTANTIVO

communist

con PREPOSICIÓN

with ◇ *Vivo con mis padres.* I live with my parents. ◇ *¿Con quién vas a ir?* Who are you going with?

- **Lo escribí con pluma.** I wrote it in pen.
- **Voy a hablar con Luis.** I'll talk to Luis.
- **café con leche** coffee with milk
- **Ábrelo con cuidado.** Open it carefully.
- **Con estudiar un poco apruebas.** With a bit of studying you should pass.
- **Con que me digas tu teléfono basta.** If you just give me your phone number that'll be enough.
- **con tal de que no llegues tarde** as long as you don't arrive late

el **concejal,** la **concejala** SUSTANTIVO

town councilor

concentrarse VERBO

[1] to concentrate ◇ *Me cuesta concentrarme.* I find it hard to concentrate.

- **Concéntrate en lo que estás haciendo.** Concentrate on what you're doing.

[2] to gather ◇ *Los manifestantes se concentraron en la plaza.* The demonstrators gathered in the square.

concertar* VERBO

to arrange (*entrevista*)

la **concha** SUSTANTIVO

shell (*de molusco*)

la **conciencia** SUSTANTIVO

conscience ◇ *Tengo la conciencia tranquila.* My conscience is clear. ◇ *Le remuerde la conciencia.* His conscience is bothering him.

- **Lo han estudiado a conciencia.** They've studied it thoroughly.

el **concierto** SUSTANTIVO

[1] concert ◇ *Van a dar varios conciertos.* They're going to give several concerts.

[2] concerto (PL concerti) ◇ *un concierto para violín* a violin concerto

la **conclusión** SUSTANTIVO (PL las **conclusiones**)

conclusion ◇ *Llegamos a la conclusión de que no valía la pena.* We reached the conclusion that it wasn't worthwhile.

concreto ADJETIVO

[1] specific ◇ *por poner un ejemplo concreto...* to take a specific example...

- **No hablo de personas concretas.** I don't mean anyone in particular.

[2] definite ◇ *Todavía no hay fechas concretas.* There are no definite dates yet.

- **este modelo en concreto** this particular model
- **No me refiero a nadie en concreto.** I don't mean anyone in particular.
- **Todavía no hemos decidido nada en concreto.** We still haven't decided anything definite.

concurrido ADJETIVO

busy (*calle, local*)

el/la **concursante** SUSTANTIVO

competitor

el **concurso** SUSTANTIVO

☞

1 game show (*de televisión*)
2 competition ◇ *un concurso de poesía* a poetry competition
◆ **un concurso de belleza** a beauty contest

el **conde** SUSTANTIVO
count

la **condecoración** SUSTANTIVO (PL las **condecoraciones**)
decoration

la **condena** SUSTANTIVO
sentence
◆ **cumplir una condena** to serve a sentence

condenar VERBO
to sentence ◇ *Lo condenaron a tres años de prisión.* He was sentenced to three years in prison.

la **condesa** SUSTANTIVO
countess

la **condición** SUSTANTIVO (PL las **condiciones**)
condition
◆ **a condición de que apruebes** on condition that you pass
◆ **El departamento está en muy malas condiciones.** The apartment is in a very bad state.
◆ **No está en condiciones de viajar.** He's not fit to travel.

el **condón** SUSTANTIVO (PL los **condones**)
condom

conducir* VERBO
1 to drive (*coche*)
◆ **No sé conducir.** I can't drive.
2 to ride (*moto*)
◆ **Enfadarse no conduce a nada.** Getting angry won't get you anywhere.

la **conducta** SUSTANTIVO
behavior

el **conductor,** la **conductora** SUSTANTIVO
driver

conduzco VERBO *ver* **conducir**

conectar VERBO
to connect ◇ *conectar dos cables* to connect two cables
◆ **Vamos a conectar ahora con el estadio.** Now we go over to the stadium.
◆ **Le cuesta conectar con la gente.** He has trouble relating to people.

el **conejillo** SUSTANTIVO
◆ **un conejillo de Indias** a guinea pig

el **conejo** SUSTANTIVO
rabbit

la **conexión** SUSTANTIVO (PL las **conexiones**)
connection

la **conferencia** SUSTANTIVO
1 lecture (*de un experto*)
2 conference (*congreso*)

confesar* VERBO
1 to confess to ◇ *confesar un crimen* to confess to a crime
2 to admit ◇ *Confesó que había sido él.* He admitted that it had been him.
◆ **confesarse** to go to confession ◇ *Se confiesa todos los sábados.* He goes to confession every Saturday.

el **confeti** SUSTANTIVO
confetti

la **confianza** SUSTANTIVO
trust ◇ *Han puesto toda su confianza en él.* They have put all their trust in him.
◆ **Tengo confianza en ti.** I trust you.
◆ **No tiene confianza en sí mismo.** He has no self-confidence.
◆ **un empleado de confianza** a trusted employee
◆ **Se lo dije porque tenemos mucha confianza.** I told her about it because we're very close.
◆ **Los alumnos se toman muchas confianzas con él.** The pupils take too many liberties with him.

confiar* VERBO
to trust ◇ *No confío en ella.* I don't trust her.
◆ **Confiaba en que su familia le ayudaría.** He was confident that his family would help him.
◆ **No hay que confiarse demasiado.** You mustn't be over-confident.

confidencial ADJETIVO
confidential

confieso VERBO *ver* **confesar**

confirmar VERBO
to confirm

la **confitería** SUSTANTIVO
cake shop

el **conflicto** SUSTANTIVO
conflict

conformarse VERBO
◆ **conformarse con** to be satisfied with ◇ *Tengo que conformarme con lo que tengo.* I have to be satisfied with what I have.
◆ **Se conforman con poco.** They're easily satisfied.
◆ **Tendrás que conformarte con uno más barato.** You'll have to make do with a cheaper one.

conforme ADJETIVO
satisfied ◇ *No se quedó muy conforme con esa explicación.* He wasn't very satisfied with that explanation.
◆ **estar* conforme** to agree ◇ *¿Estáis todos conformes?* Do you all agree?

confundir VERBO
1 to mistake ◇ *confundir la sal con el azúcar* to mistake the salt for the sugar ◇ *La gente me confunde con mi hermana.* People mistake me for my sister.
2 to confuse ◇ *Su explicación me confundió todavía más.* His explanation confused me even more.
◆ **Confundí las fechas.** I got the dates mixed up.
◆ **¡Vaya! ¡Me he confundido!** Oh! I've made a mistake!

◆ **Me confundí de departamento.** I got the wrong apartment.

la **confusión** SUSTANTIVO (PL las **confusiones**)
confusion

confuso ADJETIVO
confused

congelado ADJETIVO
frozen

el **congelador** SUSTANTIVO
freezer

congelar VERBO
to freeze

◆ **Me estoy congelando.** I'm freezing.

congestionado ADJETIVO
1 blocked (*nariz*)
2 congested (*carretera*)

el **congreso** SUSTANTIVO
conference ◇ *un congreso médico* a medical conference

la **conjunción** SUSTANTIVO (PL las **conjunciones**)
conjunction

el **conjunto** SUSTANTIVO
1 collection ◇ *El libro es un conjunto de poemas de amor.* The book is a collection of love poems.
2 group ◇ *un conjunto de música pop* a pop group

◆ **un conjunto de falda y blusa** a matching skirt and blouse

◆ **Hay que estudiar esos países en conjunto.** You have to study these countries as a whole.

conmemorar VERBO
to commemorate

conmigo PRONOMBRE
with me ◇ *¿Por qué no vienes conmigo?* Why don't you come with me?

◆ **Rosa quiere hablar conmigo.** Rosa wants to talk to me.

◆ **No estoy satisfecho conmigo mismo.** I'm not proud of myself.

conmovedor ADJETIVO (FEM **conmovedora**)
moving

conmover* VERBO
to move

conmutador SUSTANTIVO
switchboard

el **cono** SUSTANTIVO
cone

◆ **el Cono Sur** the Southern Cone

conocer* VERBO
1 to know ◇ *Conozco a todos sus hermanos.* I know all his brothers. ◇ *Conozco un restaurante donde se come bien.* I know a restaurant where the food is very good. ◇ *Nos conocemos desde el colegio.* We know each other from school.

◆ **Me encantaría conocer China.** I would love to visit China.

2 to meet (*por primera vez*) ◇ *La conocí en una fiesta.* I met her at a party. ◇ *¿Dónde se conocieron?* Where did you first meet?

la **conocida** SUSTANTIVO
acquaintance ◇ *Es una conocida mía.* She's an acquaintance of mine.

conocido ADJETIVO
well-known ◇ *un actor muy conocido* a well-known actor

el **conocido** SUSTANTIVO
acquaintance ◇ *Son conocidos nuestros.* They are acquaintances of ours.

el **conocimiento** SUSTANTIVO
consciousness

◆ **perder* el conocimiento** to lose consciousness

◆ **Tengo algunos conocimientos de francés.** I have some knowledge of French.

conozco VERBO *ver* **conocer**

conque CONJUNCIÓN
so ◇ *Hemos terminado, conque se pueden ir.* We've finished, so you may leave now.

conquistar VERBO
1 to conquer ◇ *los países conquistados por los romanos* the countries conquered by the Romans
2 to win...over ◇ *La conquistó con su sonrisa.* He won her over with his smile.

consciente ADJETIVO
conscious ◇ *El enfermo no estaba consciente.* The patient wasn't conscious.

◆ **Es plenamente consciente de sus limitaciones.** He's fully aware of his shortcomings.

la **consecuencia** SUSTANTIVO
consequence ◇ *Todo es una consecuencia de su falta de disciplina.* Everything is a consequence of his lack of discipline.

◆ **Perdió el conocimiento a consecuencia del golpe.** He lost consciousness as a result of the blow.

consecutivo ADJETIVO
consecutive ◇ *tres semanas consecutivas* three consecutive weeks

conseguir* VERBO
1 to get (*trabajo, boleto*) ◇ *Él me consiguió el trabajo.* He got me the job.
2 to achieve (*objetivo*) ◇ *Consiguió las mejores calificaciones de la clase.* He achieved the best results in the class.

◆ **Nuestro equipo consiguió el triunfo.** Our team won.

◆ **Después de muchos intentos, al final lo consiguió.** After many attempts, he finally succeeded.

◆ **Finalmente conseguí convencerla.** I finally managed to convince her.

◆ **No conseguí que se lo comiera.** I couldn't get him to eat it.

el **consejo** SUSTANTIVO
advice ◇ *Fui a pedirle consejo.* I went to ask him for advice.

◆ **¿Quieres que te dé un consejo?** Would you like me to give you some advice?

consentir* VERBO

☞

1 to allow ◇ *No consiento que me faltes al respeto.* I won't allow you to be disrespectful to me.
2 to spoil ◇ *Su abuela lo consiente demasiado.* His grandmother spoils him too much.

el/la **conserje** SUSTANTIVO
1 caretaker (*de edificio*)
2 janitor (*de colegio*)
3 porter (*de hotel*)

la **conserva** SUSTANTIVO
◆ **No comemos muchas conservas.** We don't eat much canned food.
◆ **atún en conserva** canned tuna

conservador ADJETIVO (FEM **conservadora**)
conservative

el **conservante** SUSTANTIVO
preservative

conservar VERBO
1 to keep ◇ *Debe conservarse en la nevera.* It should be kept in the fridge. ◇ *conservar las amistades* to keep friends
2 to preserve ◇ *El frío conserva mejor los alimentos.* The cold preserves food better.
◆ **Enrique se conserva joven.** Enrique looks good for his age.

el **conservatorio** SUSTANTIVO
music school

considerable ADJETIVO
considerable

considerado ADJETIVO
considerate ◇ *Es muy considerado con su madre.* He's very considerate towards his mother.
◆ **Está muy bien considerada entre los profesores.** She's very highly regarded among the teachers.

considerar VERBO
to consider ◇ *Lo considero una pérdida de tiempo.* I consider it a waste of time.

consiento VERBO *ver* **consentir**

la **consigna** SUSTANTIVO
checkroom

consigo (1) VERBO *ver* **conseguir**

consigo (2) PRONOMBRE
1 with him (*con él*)
2 with her (*con ella*)
3 with you (*con usted, ustedes*)
◆ **No está satisfecho consigo mismo.** He is not proud of himself.

consiguiendo VERBO *ver* **conseguir**

consiguiente ADJETIVO
consequent
◆ **por consiguiente** therefore

consintiendo VERBO *ver* **consentir**

consistir VERBO
◆ **El menú consiste en tres platos.** The menu consists of three courses.
◆ **¿En qué consiste el trabajo?** What does the job involve?
◆ **En eso consiste el secreto.** That's the secret.

la **consola** SUSTANTIVO
console
◆ **consola de videojuegos** games console

consolar* VERBO
to console ◇ *No conseguíamos consolarla.* We were unable to console her.
◆ **Para consolarme me compré un helado.** I bought an ice cream to cheer myself up.

la **consonante** SUSTANTIVO
consonant

constante ADJETIVO
constant ◇ *el ruido constante de los carros* the constant noise of the cars
◆ **Tienes que ser más constante.** You should keep working at it.

constantemente ADVERBIO
constantly

constar VERBO
◆ **La obra consta de siete relatos.** The work consists of seven stories.
◆ **¡Que conste que yo pagué mi parte!** Don't forget that I paid my share!

constipado ADJETIVO
◆ **estar* constipado** to have a cold

No confundir con el inglés ***constipated****, que significa "estreñido".*

el **constipado** SUSTANTIVO
cold ◇ *coger un constipado* to catch a cold

la **constitución** SUSTANTIVO (PL las **constituciones**)
constitution

la **construcción** SUSTANTIVO (PL las **construcciones**)
construction ◇ *un edificio en construcción* a building under construction
◆ **Trabajan en la construcción.** They work in the construction industry.

construir* VERBO
to build

consuelo VERBO *ver* **consolar**

el **consuelo** SUSTANTIVO
consolation

el/la **cónsul** SUSTANTIVO
consul

el **consulado** SUSTANTIVO
consulate

la **consulta** SUSTANTIVO
doctor's office ◇ *La consulta está en el centro de la ciudad.* The doctor's office is in the center of town.
◆ **La doctora no tiene consulta los martes.** The doctor doesn't hold office hours on Tuesdays.
◆ **horas de consulta** office hours
◆ **un libro de consulta** a reference book

consultar VERBO
to consult ◇ *consultar a un médico* to consult a doctor
◆ **Tengo que consultarlo con mi familia.** I must discuss it with my family.

consumir VERBO
[1] to use (*energía, gasolina, drogas*)
[2] to drink (*alcohol*)
◆ **No podemos estar en el bar sin consumir.** We can't stay in the bar without buying a drink.
◆ **Sólo piensan en consumir.** Spending money is all they think about.

el **consumo** SUSTANTIVO
consumption ◇ *el consumo de bebidas alcohólicas* alcohol consumption
◆ **una charla sobre el consumo de drogas** a talk on drug use
◆ **la sociedad de consumo** the consumer society

la **contabilidad** SUSTANTIVO
accounting ◇ *Estudia contabilidad.* He's studying accounting.
◆ **Mi madre lleva la contabilidad.** My mother keeps the books.

el **contacto** SUSTANTIVO
[1] contact ◇ *el contacto físico* physical contact
[2] touch ◇ *Nos mantenemos en contacto por teléfono.* We keep in touch by phone. ◇ *Me puse en contacto con su familia.* I got in touch with her family.

contado ADVERBIO
◆ **al contado** cash down
◆ **Lo pagué al contado.** I paid cash for it.

el **contador** SUSTANTIVO
meter ◇ *el contador de la luz* the electricity meter

el **contador**, la **contadora** SUSTANTIVO
accountant

contagiar VERBO
◆ **No quiero contagiarte.** (*enfermedad*) I don't want to give it to you.
◆ **Tiene la gripe y no quiere que los niños se contagien.** He has the flu and doesn't want the children to catch it.

contagioso ADJETIVO
infectious

la **contaminación** SUSTANTIVO
pollution ◇ *la contaminación del aire* air pollution

contaminar VERBO
to pollute ◇ *El humo contamina la atmósfera.* Smoke pollutes the atmosphere.

contar* VERBO
[1] to count (*dinero*) ◇ *Sabe contar hasta diez.* He can count to ten.
[2] to tell (*historia*) ◇ *Les conté un cuento a los niños.* I told the children a story. ◇ *Cuéntame lo que pasó.* Tell me what happened.
◆ **Cuento contigo.** I'm counting on you.
◆ **¿Qué te cuentas?** How are things? (*coloquial*)

contendrá VERBO *ver* **contener**

contener* VERBO
to contain
◆ **contenerse** to control oneself

el **contenido** SUSTANTIVO
contents PL ◇ *el contenido de la maleta* the contents of the suitcase

contentarse VERBO
◆ **Se contenta con cualquier juguete.** She is happy with any toy.
◆ **Tuve que contentarme con el segundo premio.** I had to be satisfied with second prize.

contento ADJETIVO
happy ◇ *Estaba contento porque era su cumpleaños.* He was happy because it was his birthday.
◆ **estar* contento con algo** to be pleased with something

la **contestación** SUSTANTIVO (PL las **contestaciones**)
reply (PL replies)
◆ **No me des esas contestaciones.** Don't answer back.

el **contestador** SUSTANTIVO
◆ **el contestador automático** the answering machine

contestar VERBO
to answer ◇ *Contesté a todas las preguntas.* I answered all the questions.
◆ **Les he llamado varias veces y no contestan.** I've called them several times and there's no answer.
◆ **Me escribieron y tengo que contestarles.** They wrote to me and I have to reply to them.

contigo PRONOMBRE
with you ◇ *Quiero ir contigo.* I want to go with you.
◆ **Necesito hablar contigo.** I need to talk to you.

el **continente** SUSTANTIVO
continent

continuamente ADVERBIO
constantly

continuar* VERBO
to continue ◇ *Continuaremos la reunión por la tarde.* We will continue the meeting in the afternoon. ◇ *Si continúa así habrá que llevarlo al hospital.* If he continues like this, he'll have to be taken to the hospital.
◆ **Continuó estudiando toda la noche.** He carried on studying right through the night.

continuo ADJETIVO
[1] constant (*viajes, quejas*)
[2] continuous (*línea*)

contra PREPOSICIÓN
against ◇ *Eran dos contra uno.* They were two against one. ◇ *El domingo jugamos contra el Costa Rica.* We play against Costa Rica on Sunday.
◆ **Me choqué contra una farola.** I bumped into a lamppost.
◆ **Estoy en contra de la pena de muerte.** I'm against the death penalty.

C

el **contrabajo** SUSTANTIVO
double bass (PL double basses)

el **contrabando** SUSTANTIVO
smuggling ◇ *el contrabando de drogas* drug smuggling
◆ **Lo trajeron al país de contrabando.** They smuggled it into the country.

contradecir* VERBO
to contradict

la **contradicción** SUSTANTIVO (PL las **contradicciones**)
contradiction

contradicho VERBO *ver* **contradecir**

contradigo VERBO *ver* **contradecir**

contradije VERBO *ver* **contradecir**

contradiré VERBO *ver* **contradecir**

contraer* VERBO
1 to tense (*músculo*)
2 to contract (*enfermedad*)
◆ **contraerse** (*material, metal*) to contract

la **contraria** SUSTANTIVO
◆ **llevar la contraria a alguien (1)** (*en discusión*) to contradict somebody
◆ **llevar la contraria a alguien (2)** (*en comportamiento*) to do the opposite of what somebody wants

contrario ADJETIVO
1 opposing (*equipo, argumento*)
2 opposite (*dirección, lado*) ◇ *Los dos carros viajaban en dirección contraria.* The two cars were traveling in opposite directions.
◆ **Ella opina lo contrario.** She thinks the opposite.
◆ **Al contrario, me gusta mucho.** On the contrary, I like it a lot.
◆ **De lo contrario, tendré que castigarte.** Otherwise, I will have to punish you.

la **contraseña** SUSTANTIVO
password

contrastar VERBO
to contrast ◇ *El rojo contrasta con el negro.* Red contrasts with black.

el **contraste** SUSTANTIVO
contrast

contratar VERBO
1 to hire (*empleado*)
2 to sign up (*deportista, artista*)

el **contrato** SUSTANTIVO
contract

la **contribución** SUSTANTIVO (PL las **contribuciones**)
1 contribution ◇ *Le agradecemos su contribución.* Thank you for your contribution.
2 tax (PL taxes) ◇ *la contribución municipal* local tax

contribuir* VERBO
to contribute ◇ *Todos contribuyeron al éxito de la fiesta.* Everyone contributed to the success of the party. ◇ *Cada uno contribuyó con veinte pesos para el regalo.* Each person contributed twenty pesos towards the present.

el/la **contribuyente** SUSTANTIVO
taxpayer

el/la **contrincante** SUSTANTIVO
opponent

el **control** SUSTANTIVO
1 control ◇ *Nunca pierde el control.* He never loses control.
2 road-block ◇ *Hay un control a 3 kilómetros.* There's a road-block 3 kilometers further on.
◆ **el control de pasaportes** immigration control

controlar VERBO
to control (*situación, personas, impulsos*)
◆ **Tuve que controlarme para no pegarle.** I had to control myself, otherwise I would have hit him.
◆ **No te preocupes, todo está controlado.** Don't worry, everything is under control.

convencer* VERBO
1 to convince ◇ *Su argumento me convenció.* His argument convinced me. ◇ *La convencí de que era necesario.* I convinced her that it was necessary.
◆ **No me convence nada la idea.** I'm not convinced by the idea.
2 to persuade ◇ *La convencimos para que nos acompañara.* We persuaded her to go with us.

convencional ADJETIVO
conventional

conveniente ADJETIVO
convenient (*hora, lugar*) ◇ *Cuando te sea más conveniente.* Whenever is more convenient for you.
◆ **Sería conveniente que se lo dijeras.** It would be advisable to tell him.

convenir* VERBO
1 to suit ◇ *el método que más le convenga* the method that suits you best
2 to be good for ◇ *Te conviene descansar un poco.* It would be good for you to get some rest.
◆ **Quizá convenga recordar que...** It might be appropriate to recall that...

la **conversación** SUSTANTIVO (PL las **conversaciones**)
conversation ◇ *Necesito clases de conversación.* I need conversation classes.
◆ **las conversaciones de paz** peace talks

convertir* VERBO
to turn ◇ *Convirtieron la casa en colegio.* They turned the house into a school.
◆ **convertirse** to convert ◇ *Se convirtió al cristianismo.* He converted to Christianity.
◆ **convertirse en (1)** to become ◇ *Se convirtió*

en un hombre rico. He became a rich man. ◇ *El convento se convirtió en hotel.* The convent became a hotel.

◆ **convertirse en (2)** to turn into ◇ *Se convirtió en una pesadilla.* It turned into a nightmare. ◇ *La oruga se convierte en mariposa.* The caterpillar turns into a butterfly.

convocar* VERBO
to call (*reunión, huelga*) ◇ *Nos convocaron a una reunión.* They called us to a meeting.

el **coñac** SUSTANTIVO (PL los **coñacs**)
brandy (PL brandies)

la **cooperación** SUSTANTIVO
cooperation

cooperar VERBO
to cooperate

la **copa** SUSTANTIVO
1 glass (PL glasses) (*vaso*) ◇ *Sólo tomé una copa de champán.* I only had one glass of champagne.
2 drink (*bebida*)
◆ **Fuimos a tomar unas copas.** We went for a few drinks.
3 top (*de árbol*)

la **copia** SUSTANTIVO
copy (PL copies) ◇ *hacer una copia* to make a copy
◆ **una copia impresa** (*informática*) a printout

copiar VERBO
to copy
◆ **copiar y pegar** (*informática*) to copy and paste

el **copo** SUSTANTIVO
◆ **un copo de nieve** a snowflake
◆ **copos de avena** rolled oats

el **corazón** SUSTANTIVO (PL los **corazones**)
heart ◇ *Está mal del corazón.* He has heart trouble.
◆ **Tiene muy buen corazón.** He is very kindhearted.

la **corbata** SUSTANTIVO
necktie
◆ **corbata de moño** bow tie

el **corcho** SUSTANTIVO
cork
◆ **un tapón de corcho** a cork

el **cordel** SUSTANTIVO
cord

el **cordero** SUSTANTIVO
lamb ◇ *Comimos chuletas de cordero.* We had lamb chops.

el **cordón** SUSTANTIVO (PL los **cordones**)
1 shoelace (*para los zapatos*)
2 cable (*eléctrico*)

la **corneta** SUSTANTIVO
cornet

el **coro** SUSTANTIVO
1 choir (*de iglesia, colegio*)
2 chorus (*en obra musical*)

la **corona** SUSTANTIVO
crown (*de rey*)
◆ **una corona de flores** a garland

el **coronel** SUSTANTIVO
colonel

corporal ADJETIVO
1 body (*temperatura, olor, fluidos*)
***body** en este caso va siempre delante del sustantivo.*
2 corporal (*castigo*)
3 personal (*higiene*)

el **corral** SUSTANTIVO
1 farmyard (*para gallinas*)
2 playpen (*para niños*)

la **correa** SUSTANTIVO
1 belt (*cinturón*)
2 leash (*de perro*)
3 strap (*de reloj*)

correcto ADJETIVO
correct ◇ *Las respuestas eran correctas.* The answers were correct.

el **corredor,** la **corredora** SUSTANTIVO
runner

corregir* VERBO
1 to correct (*error, postura*) ◇ *Corrígeme si me equivoco.* Correct me if I get it wrong.
2 to mark ◇ *Tengo que corregir los exámenes.* I have to mark the tests.

el **correo** SUSTANTIVO
1 mail ◇ *Me lo mandó por correo.* He sent it to me by mail.
2 post office ◇ *Fui al correo a echar una carta.* I went to the post office to mail a letter.
◆ **Correos** *Spain* post office
◆ **el correo basura** spam
◆ **el correo electrónico** email
◆ **el correo web** webmail

correr VERBO
1 to run ◇ *Tuve que correr para alcanzar el tren.* I had to run to catch the train.
◆ **El ladrón echó a correr.** The thief started to run.
2 to hurry ◇ *Corre que llegamos tarde.* Hurry or we'll be late.
◆ **No corras que te equivocarás.** Don't rush or you'll make a mistake.
3 to go fast ◇ *No corras tanto, que hay hielo en la carretera.* Don't go so fast; the road's icy.
4 to move ◇ *Corre un poco la silla para allá.* Move the chair that way a little. ◇ *Córrete un poco hacia la izquierda.* Move a bit to the left.
◆ **¿Quieres que corra la cortina?** Do you want me to draw the curtains?

la **correspondencia** SUSTANTIVO
◆ **un curso por correspondencia** a correspondence course

corresponder VERBO
◆ **Me pagó lo que me correspondía.** He paid me my share.
◆ **Estas fotos corresponden a otro álbum.** These photos belong to another album.
◆ **No me corresponde a mí hacerlo.** It's not up ☞

C

to me to do it.

correspondiente ADJETIVO
relevant (*apropiado*) ◇ *toda la documentación correspondiente* all the relevant documentation
◆ **los datos correspondientes al año pasado** the figures for last year

el/la **corresponsal** SUSTANTIVO
correspondent

la **corrida** SUSTANTIVO
bullfight

corriente ADJETIVO
common ◇ *Pérez es un apellido muy corriente.* Pérez is a very common surname.
◆ **Es un caso poco corriente.** It's an unusual case.
◆ **Tengo que ponerlo al corriente de lo que ha pasado.** I have to let him know what has happened.

la **corriente** SUSTANTIVO
1 current (*de agua, electricidad*)
◆ **Te va a dar corriente.** You'll get an electric shock.
2 draft (*de aire*)
◆ **Si está de mal humor es mejor seguirle la corriente.** If he's in a bad mood it's best just to humor him.

corrijo VERBO *ver* **corregir**

el **corro** SUSTANTIVO
ring ◇ *Los niños hicieron un corro.* The children formed a ring.

la **corrupción** SUSTANTIVO
corruption

cortado ADJETIVO
1 sour (*leche*)
2 closed (*calle, carretera*)

el **cortado** SUSTANTIVO

> ℹ *A* ***cortado*** *is a small cup of coffee with only a little milk.*

cortar VERBO
1 to cut (*carne, pastel*) ◇ *Corta la manzana por la mitad.* Cut the apple in half. ◇ *Me corté el dedo con un vidrio.* I cut my finger on a piece of broken glass.
◆ **Te vas a cortar.** You're going to cut yourself.
◆ **Estas tijeras no cortan.** These scissors are blunt.
2 to cut off (*agua, luz*) ◇ *Cortaron el gas.* The gas has been cut off.
3 to close (*calle, carretera*)
◆ **Fui a cortarme el pelo.** I went to get my hair cut.
◆ **De repente se cortó la comunicación.** Suddenly we were cut off.

el **cortaúñas** SUSTANTIVO (PL los **cortaúñas**)
nail clippers PL

el **corte** SUSTANTIVO
cut ◇ *Tenía un corte en la frente.* He had a cut on his forehead.
◆ **un corte de pelo** a haircut

cortés (PL **corteses**) ADJETIVO
polite

la **cortesía** SUSTANTIVO
courtesy
◆ **por cortesía** as a courtesy

la **corteza** SUSTANTIVO
1 crust (*del pan*)
2 rind (*del queso*)
3 bark (*de árbol*)

la **cortina** SUSTANTIVO
curtain

corto ADJETIVO
short ◇ *Susana tiene el pelo corto.* Susana has short hair.
◆ **Las mangas me quedan cortas.** The sleeves are too short for me.
◆ **ser* corto de vista** to be nearsighted

el **cortocircuito** SUSTANTIVO
short circuit

la **cosa** SUSTANTIVO
thing ◇ *¿Qué es esa cosa redonda?* What's that round thing? ◇ *Agarré mis cosas y me fui.* I picked up my things and left.
◆ **cualquier cosa** anything
◆ **¿Me puedes decir una cosa?** Can you tell me something?
◆ **¡Qué cosa más rara!** How strange!
◆ **Son cosas de la edad.** It's just old age.

la **cosecha** SUSTANTIVO
harvest

cosechar VERBO
to harvest

coser VERBO
to sew ◇ *Me estaba cosiendo un botón.* I was sewing on a button.

el **cosmético** SUSTANTIVO
cosmetic

las **cosquillas** SUSTANTIVO
◆ **hacer* cosquillas a alguien** to tickle someone
◆ **Tiene muchas cosquillas.** He's very ticklish.

la **costa** SUSTANTIVO
coast ◇ *Pasamos el verano en la costa.* We spend the summer on the coast.
◆ **Vive a costa de los demás.** He lives at the expense of others.

el **costado** SUSTANTIVO
side ◇ *Estaba tumbado de costado.* He was lying on his side.

costar* VERBO
to cost ◇ *Cuesta mucho dinero.* It costs a lot of money. ◇ *¿Cuánto cuesta?* How much does it cost? ◇ *Me costó diez pesos.* It cost me ten pesos.
◆ **Las matemáticas le cuestan mucho.** He finds math very difficult.
◆ **Me cuesta hablarle.** I find it hard to talk to him.

Costa Rica SUSTANTIVO FEM

Costa Rica

el/la **costarricense** ADJETIVO, SUSTANTIVO
Costa Rican

el **costarriqueño,** la **costarriqueña** ADJETIVO, SUSTANTIVO
Costa Rican

el **coste** SUSTANTIVO Spain
cost

la **costilla** SUSTANTIVO
rib

el **costo** SUSTANTIVO
cost ◇ *el costo de la vida* the cost of living

costoso ADJETIVO
expensive

la **costra** SUSTANTIVO
1 scab (*de herida*)
2 crust (*del pan*)

la **costumbre** SUSTANTIVO
1 habit (*de persona*) ◇ *Tiene la mala costumbre de morderse las uñas.* He has the bad habit of biting his nails.
2 custom (*de país, pueblo*) ◇ *una costumbre chilena* a Chilean custom
◆ **Se le olvidó, como de costumbre.** He forgot, as usual.
◆ **Nos sentamos en el sitio de costumbre.** We sat in our usual place.

la **costura** SUSTANTIVO
1 seam ◇ *Se te descosió la costura de la falda.* Your skirt has come apart at the seam.
2 sewing ◇ *No me gusta la costura.* I don't like sewing.

el **cráneo** SUSTANTIVO
skull

la **creación** SUSTANTIVO (PL las **creaciones**)
creation

crear VERBO
to create
◆ **No quiero crearme problemas.** I don't want to create problems for myself.
◆ **crearse enemigos** to make enemies

creativo ADJETIVO
creative

crecer* VERBO
1 to grow ◇ *Me crece mucho el pelo.* My hair grows very fast. ◇ *¡Cómo has crecido!* How you have grown!
2 to grow up ◇ *Crecí en Sevilla.* I grew up in Seville.

el **crecimiento** SUSTANTIVO
growth

el **crédito** SUSTANTIVO
1 loan ◇ *Pedí un crédito al banco.* I asked the bank for a loan.
2 credit ◇ *comprar algo a crédito* to buy something on credit

la **creencia** SUSTANTIVO
belief

creer* VERBO
1 to believe ◇ *¿Crees en los fantasmas?* Do you believe in ghosts? ◇ *Nadie me cree.* Nobody believes me.
◆ **Eso no se lo cree nadie.** No one will believe that.
2 to think ◇ *No creo que pueda ir.* I don't think I'll be able to go.
◆ **Se cree muy lista.** She thinks she's pretty clever.
◆ **Creo que sí.** I think so.
◆ **Creo que no.** I don't think so.

creído ADJETIVO
◆ **Es muy creído.** He's so full of himself.

la **crema** SUSTANTIVO
cream ◇ *Me pongo crema en las manos.* I put cream on my hands.
◆ **la crema de afeitar** shaving cream
◆ **crema de champiñones** cream of mushroom soup
◆ **la crema de leche** cream
◆ **una blusa de color crema** a cream-colored blouse

la **cremallera** SUSTANTIVO
zipper ◇ *Súbete la cremallera.* Pull up your zipper.

el **crematorio** SUSTANTIVO
crematorium (PL crematoria)

creyendo VERBO *ver* **creer**

el/la **creyente** SUSTANTIVO
believer

crezco VERBO *ver* **crecer**

la **cría** SUSTANTIVO
◆ **una cría de cebra** a baby zebra
◆ **La leona tuvo dos crías.** The lioness had two cubs.
◆ **La hembra es muy protectora de sus crías.** The female is very protective of her young.

la **criada** SUSTANTIVO
maid

el **criado** SUSTANTIVO
servant

criar* VERBO
1 to raise (*ganado*)
2 to breed (*conejos, perros*)
3 to bring up ◇ *Me criaron mis abuelos.* My grandparents brought me up.
◆ **Me crié en Sevilla.** I grew up in Seville.

el **crimen** SUSTANTIVO (PL los **crímenes**)
1 murder ◇ *cometer un crimen* to commit murder
2 crime ◇ *los crímenes de guerra* war crimes

el/la **criminal** SUSTANTIVO
criminal

la **crisis** SUSTANTIVO (PL las **crisis**)
crisis (PL crises) ◇ *una crisis política* a political crisis
◆ **una crisis nerviosa** a nervous breakdown

el **cristal** SUSTANTIVO
1 crystal (*vidrio fino, mineral*) ◇ *una estatuilla de cristal* a crystal statuette
2 glass (PL glasses) (*vidrio normal*) Spain ◇ *una botella de cristal* a glass bottle

C

el **cristiano,** la **cristiana** ADJETIVO, SUSTANTIVO
Christian

Cristo SUSTANTIVO MASC
Christ

la **crítica** SUSTANTIVO
1 criticism
◆ **No hagas caso de sus críticas.** Pay no attention to his criticism.
2 review ◇ *La película ha tenido muy buenas críticas.* The movie got very good reviews.
3 critic ◇ *Es crítica de cine.* She's a movie critic.

criticar* VERBO
to criticize

crítico ADJETIVO
critical ◇ *Llegó en un momento crítico.* He arrived at a critical moment.

el **crítico** SUSTANTIVO
critic ◇ *Es crítico de cine.* He's a movie critic.

el **croissant** SUSTANTIVO (PL los **croissants**)
croissant

el **cromo** SUSTANTIVO
picture card

crónico ADJETIVO
chronic

cronometrar VERBO
to time

el **cronómetro** SUSTANTIVO
stopwatch (PL stopwatches)

la **croqueta** SUSTANTIVO
croquette ◇ *croquetas de pollo* chicken croquettes

el **cruce** SUSTANTIVO
intersection ◇ *En el cruce hay un semáforo.* There are traffic lights at the intersection.
◆ **un cruce de peatones** a crosswalk

crucial ADJETIVO
crucial

el **crucifijo** SUSTANTIVO
crucifix (PL crucifixes)

el **crucigrama** SUSTANTIVO
crossword puzzle

crudo ADJETIVO
1 raw (*sin cocinar*) ◇ *las zanahorias crudas* raw carrots
2 underdone (*poco hecho*) ◇ *El filete estaba crudo.* The filet was underdone.

cruel ADJETIVO
cruel

la **crueldad** SUSTANTIVO
cruelty

crujiente ADJETIVO
1 crunchy (*galletas, zanahoria*)
2 crusty (*pan*)

crujir VERBO
1 to rustle (*hojas secas*)
2 to creak (*ramas, tablas*)
3 to crunch (*nieve, galletas*)

la **cruz** SUSTANTIVO (PL las **cruces**)
cross (PL crosses)
◆ **la Cruz Roja** the Red Cross

cruzado ADJETIVO
◆ **Había un tronco cruzado en la carretera.** There was a tree trunk lying across the road.

cruzar* VERBO
1 to cross (*calle, desierto, río*)
2 to fold (*brazos*)
◆ **Nos cruzamos en la calle.** We passed each other on the street.

el **cuaderno** SUSTANTIVO
notebook
◆ **un cuaderno de ejercicios** an exercise book

la **cuadra** SUSTANTIVO
1 stable
2 block ◇ *Está a dos cuadras de aquí.* It's two blocks from here.

el **cuadrado** ADJETIVO, SUSTANTIVO
square
◆ **dos metros cuadrados** two square meters

cuadrar VERBO
to tally ◇ *Las cuentas no cuadran.* The accounts don't tally.
◆ **Eso no cuadra con lo que ella nos contó.** That doesn't fit in with what she told us.

cuadriculado ADJETIVO
◆ **papel cuadriculado** squared paper

el **cuadro** SUSTANTIVO
1 painting (*pintura*) ◇ *un cuadro de Picasso* a painting by Picasso ◇ *¿Quién pintó ese cuadro?* Who did that painting?
2 picture (*reproducción*) ◇ *Hay varios cuadros en la pared.* There are several pictures on the wall.
◆ **un mantel a cuadros** a checkered tablecloth

cuajar VERBO
1 to set (*flan, yogur*)
2 to lie (*nieve*)
◆ **cuajarse** (*leche*) to curdle

cual PRONOMBRE
1 who
*Se usa **who** cuando nos referimos a una persona.*
◇ *el primo del cual te estuve hablando* the cousin who I was speaking to you about
2 which
*Se usa **which** cuando nos referimos a una cosa.*
◇ *la ventana desde la cual nos observaban* the window from which they were watching us
◆ **lo cual** which ◇ *Se ofendió, lo cual es comprensible.* He took offense, which is understandable.
◆ **con lo cual** with the result that
◆ **sea cual sea la razón** whatever the reason may be

cuál PRONOMBRE
1 what ◇ *¿Cuál es la solución?* What is the

solution? ◇ *No sé cuál es la solución.* I don't know what the solution is.

2 which one (*entre varios*) ◇ *¿Cuál te gusta más?* Which one do you like best?

la **cualidad** SUSTANTIVO
quality (PL qualities)

cualquier ADJETIVO *ver* **cualquiera**

cualquiera (1) ADJETIVO
any ◇ *en cualquier ciudad mexicana* in any Mexican town ◇ *Puedes usar un bolígrafo cualquiera.* You can use any pen.
- **No es un empleo cualquiera.** It's not just any job.
- **cualquier cosa** anything
- **cualquier persona** anyone
- **en cualquier sitio** anywhere

cualquiera (2) PRONOMBRE
1 anyone (*personas*) ◇ *Cualquiera puede hacer eso.* Anyone can do that.
- **cualquiera que lo conozca** anyone who knows him

2 any one (*de varias cosas*) ◇ *Me da igual, cualquiera está bien.* It doesn't matter, any one will do.
- **en cualquiera de las habitaciones** in any one of the rooms
- **cualquiera que elijas** whichever one you choose

3 either (*entre dos personas o cosas*) ◇ *¿Cuál de los dos prefieres? – Cualquiera.* Which of the two do you prefer? – Either.

cuando CONJUNCIÓN
when ◇ *cuando vienen a vernos* when they come to see us ◇ *Lo haré cuando tenga tiempo.* I'll do it when I have time.
- **Puedes venir cuando quieras.** You can come whenever you like.

cuándo ADVERBIO
when ◇ *¿Cuándo te viene mejor?* When does it suit you? ◇ *No sabe cuándo ocurrió.* He doesn't know when it happened.
- **¿Desde cuándo trabajas aquí?** How long have you worked here?

cuanto ADJETIVO, PRONOMBRE (FEM **cuanta**)
- **Termínalo cuanto antes.** Finish it as soon as possible.
- **Cuanto más lo pienso menos lo entiendo.** The more I think about it, the less I understand it.
- **Cuantas menos personas haya mejor.** The fewer people, the better.
- **En cuanto oí su voz me eché a llorar.** As soon as I heard his voice, I began to cry.
- **Había sólo unos cuantos invitados.** There were only a few guests.

cuánto ADJETIVO, PRONOMBRE (FEM **cuánta**)
1 how much ◇ *¿Cuánto dinero?* How much money? ◇ *¿Cuánto le debo?* How much do I owe you? ◇ *Me dijo cuánto costaba.* He told me how much it was.

2 how many ◇ *¿Cuántas sillas?* How many chairs? ◇ *No sé cuántos necesito.* I don't know how many I need.
- **¿A cuántos estamos?** What's the date?
- **¡Cuánta gente!** What a lot of people!
- **¿Cuánto hay de aquí a Cuzco?** How far is it from here to Cuzco?
- **¿Cuánto tiempo llevas estudiando inglés?** How long have you been studying English?

C

cuarenta ADJETIVO, PRONOMBRE
forty ◇ *Tiene cuarenta años.* He's forty.
- **el cuarenta aniversario** the fortieth anniversary

el **cuartel** SUSTANTIVO
barracks (PL barracks)
- **el cuartel general** the headquarters

cuarto ADJETIVO, PRONOMBRE (FEM **cuarta**)
fourth ◇ *Vivo en el cuarto piso.* I live on the fifth floor.

el **cuarto** SUSTANTIVO
1 room ◇ *Los niños jugaban en su cuarto.* The children were playing in their room.
- **el cuarto de estar** the living room
- **el cuarto de baño** the bathroom

2 quarter ◇ *un cuarto de hora* a quarter of an hour
- **Son las once y cuarto.** It's a quarter past eleven.
- **A las diez menos cuarto.** (*Spain*) At a quarter to ten.
- **Es un cuarto para las diez.** It's a quarter to ten.

el **cuate** SUSTANTIVO *Mexico*
1 twin brother (*hermano*)
2 guy (*coloquial: tipo*)
3 buddy (*coloquial: amigo*)

cuatro ADJETIVO, PRONOMBRE
four
- **Son las cuatro.** It's four o'clock.
- **el cuatro de abril** April fourth

cuatrocientos ADJETIVO, PRONOMBRE (FEM **cuatrocientas**)
four hundred

Cuba SUSTANTIVO FEM
Cuba

el **cubano**, la **cubana** ADJETIVO, SUSTANTIVO
Cuban

la **cubertería** SUSTANTIVO
cutlery

la **cubeta** SUSTANTIVO *Mexico*
bucket

cúbico ADJETIVO
cubic ◇ *tres metros cúbicos* three cubic meters

la **cubierta** SUSTANTIVO
1 cover (*de libro*)
2 tire (*de neumático*)
3 deck (*de barco*)

cubierto (1) VERBO *ver* **cubrir**

cubierto (2) ADJETIVO
covered ◇ *Estaba todo cubierto de nieve.* Everything was covered in snow.
- **una piscina cubierta** an indoor swimming

☞

pool

los **cubiertos** SUSTANTIVO PL
cutlery SING

el **cubito** SUSTANTIVO
- **cubito de caldo** bouillon cube
- **cubito de hielo** ice cube

el **cubo** SUSTANTIVO
bucket
- **el cubo de la basura** the garbage can
- **tres elevado al cubo** three cubed

cubrir* VERBO
to cover ◇ *Son capaces de cubrir grandes distancias.* They can cover great distances.
- **Las mujeres se cubren la cara con un velo.** The women cover their face with a veil.
- **El agua casi me cubría.** I was almost out of my depth.

la **cucaracha** SUSTANTIVO
cockroach

la **cuchara** SUSTANTIVO
spoon

la **cucharada** SUSTANTIVO
spoonful

la **cucharilla** SUSTANTIVO
teaspoon

el **cucharón** SUSTANTIVO (PL los **cucharones**)
ladle

cuchichear VERBO
to whisper

la **cuchilla** SUSTANTIVO
blade
- **una cuchilla de afeitar** a razor blade

el **cuchillo** SUSTANTIVO
knife (PL knives)

cuclillas ADVERBIO
- **en cuclillas** squatting
- **ponerse* en cuclillas** to squat down

el **cucurucho** SUSTANTIVO
cone (*helado*)

cuelgo VERBO *ver* **colgar**

el **cuello** SUSTANTIVO
1 neck (*de persona, botella*)
2 collar (*de camisa, chaqueta*)

la **cuenta** SUSTANTIVO
1 bill (*factura*) ◇ *la cuenta de teléfono* the telephone bill
2 check (*en restaurante*) ◇ *El camarero nos trajo la cuenta.* The waiter brought us the check.
3 account (*de banco*)
- **una cuenta corriente** a checking account
- **Ahora trabaja por su cuenta.** He's self-employed now.
- **una cuenta de correo** an email account
- **darse* cuenta (1)** (*enterarse*) to realize ◇ *Perdona, no me di cuenta de que eras vegetariano.* Sorry, I didn't realize you were a vegetarian.
- **darse* cuenta (2)** (*ver*) to notice ◇ *¿Te has diste cuenta de que cortaron el árbol?* Did you notice they've cut down that tree?
- **tener* algo en cuenta** to bear something in mind ◇ *También hay que tener en cuenta su edad.* You must also bear in mind her age.

cuento VERBO *ver* **contar**

el **cuento** SUSTANTIVO
story (PL stories) ◇ *La abuela nos contaba cuentos.* Grandma used to tell us stories.
- **un cuento de hadas** a fairy tale

la **cuerda** SUSTANTIVO
1 rope (*gruesa*) ◇ *Le ataron las manos con una cuerda.* They tied his hands together with a rope.
2 string (*fina*) ◇ *Necesito una cuerda para atar este paquete.* I need some string to tie up this parcel. ◇ *La guitarra tiene seis cuerdas.* The guitar has six strings.
- **la cuerda floja** the tightrope
- **dar* cuerda a un reloj** to wind up a watch

el **cuerno** SUSTANTIVO
horn

el **cuero** SUSTANTIVO
leather ◇ *una chaqueta de cuero* a leather jacket

el **cuerpo** SUSTANTIVO
body (PL bodies) ◇ *el cuerpo humano* the human body
- **el cuerpo de bomberos** the fire department

el **cuervo** SUSTANTIVO
raven

cuesta VERBO *ver* **costar**

la **cuesta** SUSTANTIVO
slope ◇ *una cuesta muy empinada* a very steep slope
- **ir* cuesta abajo** to go downhill
- **ir* cuesta arriba** to go uphill
- **Llevaba la caja a cuestas.** He was carrying the box on his back.

la **cuestión** SUSTANTIVO (PL las **cuestiones**)
matter ◇ *Eso es otra cuestión.* That's another matter.
- **Llegaron en cuestión de minutos.** They arrived in a matter of minutes.

la **cueva** SUSTANTIVO
cave

cuezo VERBO *ver* **cocer**

el **cuidado** SUSTANTIVO
care ◇ *Pone mucho cuidado en su trabajo.* He takes great care over his work.
- **Conducía con cuidado.** He was driving carefully.
- **Debes tener mucho cuidado al cruzar la calle.** You must be very careful crossing the street.
- **¡Cuidado!** Careful!
- **Carlos está al cuidado de los niños.** Carlos looks after the children.

cuidadoso ADJETIVO
careful

cuidar VERBO
to look after (*libros, plantas, niño*) ◇ *Ella*

cuida de los niños. She looks after the children.
◆ **cuidarse** to take care of oneself ◇ *Tienes que cuidarte.* Make sure you take care of yourself.
◆ **¡Cuídate!** Take care!

la **culebra** SUSTANTIVO
snake

el **culebrón** (PL los **culebrones**) SUSTANTIVO
soap (*coloquial*)

el **culo** SUSTANTIVO
butt (*coloquial*)

la **culpa** SUSTANTIVO
fault ◇ *La culpa es mía.* It's my fault.
◆ **Tú tienes la culpa de todo.** It's all your fault.
◆ **Siempre me echan la culpa a mí.** They're always blaming me.
◆ **por culpa del mal tiempo** because of the bad weather

culpable ADJETIVO
guilty ◇ *Yo no soy culpable.* I'm not guilty. ◇ *Se siente culpable de lo que ha pasado.* He feels guilty about what has happened.

el/la **culpable** SUSTANTIVO
culprit (*de delito*)
◆ **Ella es la culpable de todo.** She is to blame for everything.

cultivar VERBO
1 to grow (*cereales, hortalizas*)
2 to farm (*la tierra*)

culto ADJETIVO
1 cultured (*persona*)
2 formal (*lenguaje*)

la **cultura** SUSTANTIVO
culture

el **culturismo** SUSTANTIVO
bodybuilding

la **cumbre** SUSTANTIVO
summit (*de montaña*)

el **cumpleaños** SUSTANTIVO (PL los **cumpleaños**)
birthday ◇ *Mañana es mi cumpleaños.* It's my birthday tomorrow.
◆ **¡Feliz cumpleaños!** Happy birthday!

cumplir VERBO
1 to carry out (*orden, objetivo*)
2 to keep (*promesa*)
3 to observe (*ley*)
4 to serve (*condena*)
◆ **Sólo he cumplido con mi deber.** I have only done my duty.
◆ **Mañana cumplo dieciséis años.** I'll be sixteen tomorrow.
◆ **El viernes se cumple el plazo para entregar las solicitudes.** Friday is the deadline for handing in applications.

la **cuna** SUSTANTIVO
cradle

la **cuneta** SUSTANTIVO
ditch (PL ditches)

la **cuñada** SUSTANTIVO
sister-in-law (PL sisters-in-law)

el **cuñado** SUSTANTIVO
brother-in-law (PL brothers-in-law)

la **cuota** SUSTANTIVO
fee ◇ *La cuota de socio son 100 pesos anuales.* The membership fee is 100 pesos per year.

cupo VERBO *ver* **caber**

el **cupón** SUSTANTIVO (PL los **cupones**)
coupon (*vale*)

la **cura** SUSTANTIVO
1 cure ◇ *No tiene cura.* There is no cure for it.
2 therapy (PL therapies) ◇ *una cura de reposo* rest therapy

el **cura** SUSTANTIVO
priest

curar VERBO
1 to cure (*enfermo, enfermedad*)
2 to treat (*herida*)
◆ **Espero que te cures pronto.** I hope that you get better soon.
◆ **Ya se le ha curado la herida.** His wound has already healed.

la **curiosidad** SUSTANTIVO
curiosity ◇ *Lo pregunté por curiosidad.* I asked out of curiosity.
◆ **Tengo curiosidad por saber cuánto gana.** I'm curious to know how much he earns.

curioso ADJETIVO
1 curious ◇ *Tiene una forma muy curiosa.* It's a very curious shape.
◆ **¡Qué curioso!** How odd!
2 nosy ◇ *No seas curioso.* Don't be nosy.

la **curita** SUSTANTIVO
Band-Aid®

cursi ADJETIVO
1 affected (*persona*)
2 cutesy (*objeto*)

el **cursillo** SUSTANTIVO
course ◇ *un cursillo de cocina* a cooking course
◆ **hacer* un cursillo de natación** to have swimming lessons

el **curso** SUSTANTIVO
1 class ◇ *un chico de mi curso* a boy in my class
◆ **el curso académico** the academic year
2 course ◇ *Hice un curso de alemán.* I took a German course.

la **curva** SUSTANTIVO
1 bend (*en carretera*)
2 curve (*línea*) ◇ *dibujar una curva* to draw a curve

cuyo ADJETIVO
whose ◇ *El marido, cuyo nombre era Ricardo, estaba jubilado.* The husband, whose name was Ricardo, was retired. ◇ *La señora en cuya casa me hospedé.* The lady whose house I stayed in.

D

el **dado** SUSTANTIVO
dice (PL dice)
- **jugar* a los dados** to play dice

la **dama** SUSTANTIVO
lady (PL ladies) ◇ *Damas y caballeros...* Ladies and gentlemen...
- **las damas** checkers ◇ *jugar a las damas* to play checkers

el **damasco** SUSTANTIVO
apricot

danés ADJETIVO (FEM **danesa**, MASC PL **daneses**)
Danish

el **danés,** la **danesa** SUSTANTIVO (MASC PL los **daneses**)
Dane

el **danés** SUSTANTIVO
Danish (*idioma*)

dañar VERBO
1 to damage (*objeto*)
2 to hurt (*persona*)
- **Se dañó la pierna.** She hurt her leg.

el **daño** SUSTANTIVO
damage ◇ *El daño producido no es muy grave.* The damage isn't very serious.
- **ocasionar daños** to cause damage ◇ *La sequía ha ocasionado grandes daños.* The drought has caused a lot of damage.
- **hacer* daño a alguien** to hurt somebody
- **hacerse* daño** to hurt oneself

dar* VERBO
1 to give ◇ *Le dio una manzana a su hijo.* He gave his son an apple. ◇ *Se lo di a Teresa.* I gave it to Teresa.
- **Me dio mucha alegría verla.** I was very pleased to see her.
- **Deme dos kilos.** Two kilos please.

2 to strike ◇ *El reloj dio las seis.* The clock struck six.
- **dar a** to look out onto ◇ *Mi ventana da al jardín.* My window looks out onto the garden.
- **dar con** to find ◇ *Dimos con él dos horas más tarde.* We found him two hours later.
- **Al final di con la solución.** I finally came up with the answer.
- **El sol me da en la cara.** The sun is shining in my face.
- **¿Qué más te da?** What does it matter to you?
- **Se han dado muchos casos.** There have been a lot of cases.
- **Se me dan bien las ciencias.** I'm good at science.
- **darse un baño** to take a bath
- **darse por vencido** to give up

el **dátil** SUSTANTIVO
date (*fruta*)

el **dato** SUSTANTIVO
- **Ése es un dato importante.** That's an important piece of information.
- **Necesito más datos para poder juzgar.** I need more information to be able to judge.
- **reunir* datos para un proyecto de investigación** to gather data for a research project
- **los datos personales** personal details

de (*de + el = del*) PREPOSICIÓN
1 of ◇ *un paquete de caramelos* a packet of candy
- **una copa de vino (1)** (*llena*) a glass of wine
- **una copa de vino (2)** (*vacía*) a wine glass
- **la casa de Isabel** Isabel's house
- **las clases de inglés** English classes
- **un anillo de oro** a gold ring
- **una máquina de coser** a sewing machine
- **es de ellos** it's theirs
- **a las ocho de la mañana** at eight o'clock in the morning

2 from ◇ *Soy de León.* I'm from León.
- **salir* del cine** to leave the movie theater

3 than ◇ *Es más difícil de lo que creía.* It's more difficult than I thought it would be.
- **más de 500 personas** over 500 people
- **De haberlo sabido...** If I'd known...

dé VERBO *ver* **dar**

debajo ADVERBIO
underneath ◇ *Levanta la maceta, la llave está debajo.* Lift up the flowerpot, the key is underneath.
- **debajo de** under ◇ *debajo de la mesa* under the table

el **debate** SUSTANTIVO
debate

debatir VERBO
to debate

el **deber** SUSTANTIVO
duty (PL duties) ◇ *Sólo cumplí con mi deber.* I simply did my duty.
- **los deberes** homework SING (*escolares*)

deber VERBO
1 must ◇ *Debo intentar verla.* I must try to see her.
- **No debes preocuparte.** Don't worry.
- **Debería dejar de fumar.** I should stop smoking.
- **No deberías haberla dejado sola.** You shouldn't have left her alone.
- **como debe ser** as it should be
- **deber de** must ◇ *Debe de ser canadiense.* He must be Canadian.
- **No debe de tener mucho dinero.** He can't have much money.

2 to owe ◇ *¿Cuánto le debo?* How much do I owe you?
- **deberse a** to be due to ◇ *El retraso se debió a una huelga.* The delay was due to a strike.

debido ADJETIVO
- **debido a** owing to ◇ *Debido al mal tiempo,*

el vuelo se suspendió. Owing to the bad weather, the flight was canceled.
- **Habla como es debido.** Speak properly.

débil ADJETIVO
weak

la **debilidad** SUSTANTIVO
weakness (PL weaknesses)
- **tener* debilidad por algo** to have a weakness for something
- **tener* debilidad por alguien** to have a soft spot for somebody

debilitar VERBO
to weaken

la **década** SUSTANTIVO
decade

la **decena** SUSTANTIVO
ten ◇ *decenas de miles de* tens of thousands of
- **Habrá una decena de libros.** There must be about ten books.

decente ADJETIVO
decent ◇ *Exigen un sueldo decente.* They are demanding a decent wage.

la **decepción** SUSTANTIVO (PL las **decepciones**)
disappointment

*No confundir **decepción** con **deception**.*

decepcionar VERBO
to disappoint ◇ *Me has decepcionado de nuevo.* You've disappointed me again.
- **La película me decepcionó.** The movie was disappointing.

decidido ADJETIVO
determined ◇ *Estoy decidido a hacerlo.* I'm determined to do it. ◇ *Julia es una mujer muy decidida.* Julia is a very determined woman.

decidir VERBO
to decide ◇ *Tú decides.* You decide.
- **decidirse a hacer algo** to decide to do something
- **decidirse por algo** to decide on something
- **¡Decídete!** Make up your mind!

el **decimal** ADJETIVO, SUSTANTIVO
decimal

décimo ADJETIVO, PRONOMBRE (FEM **décima**)
tenth
- **Vivo en el décimo.** I live on the eleventh floor.

el **décimo** SUSTANTIVO
- **un décimo de lotería** a tenth part of a lottery ticket

decir* VERBO
[1] to say ◇ *¿Qué dijo?* What did he say? ◇ *¿Cómo se dice "casa" en inglés?* How do you say "casa" in English?
- **es decir** that's to say
- **es un decir** it's a manner of speaking

[2] to tell ◇ *Me dijo que no vendría.* He told me that he wouldn't come.
- **decirle a alguien que haga algo** to tell somebody to do something ◇ *Me dijo que esperara fuera.* He told me to wait outside.
- **¡No me digas!** Really?
- **querer* decir** to mean ◇ *No sé lo que quiere decir.* I don't know what it means.

la **decisión** SUSTANTIVO (PL las **decisiones**)
decision ◇ *tomar una decisión* to make a decision

decisivo ADJETIVO
decisive

la **declaración** SUSTANTIVO (PL las **declaraciones**)
[1] statement ◇ *El ministro no quiso hacer ninguna declaración.* The minister didn't want to make a statement.
[2] evidence ◇ *Prestó declaración ante el juez.* He gave evidence before the judge.
- **una declaración de amor** a declaration of love
- **la declaración del impuesto sobre la renta** the income tax return

declarar VERBO
[1] to declare ◇ *¿Algo que declarar?* Anything to declare? ◇ *El presidente declaró que apoyaría el proyecto.* The president declared his support for the project.
[2] to give evidence ◇ *declarar en un juicio* to give evidence at a trial
- **declarar culpable a alguien** to find somebody guilty
- **declararse (1)** to declare oneself ◇ *Se declaró partidario de hacerlo.* He declared himself in favor of doing it.
- **declararse (2)** to break out ◇ *Se declaró un incendio en el bosque.* A fire broke out in the forest.
- **declararse a alguien** to propose to somebody

el **decorador**, la **decoradora** SUSTANTIVO
interior decorator

decorar VERBO
to decorate

el **decreto** SUSTANTIVO
decree

el **dedal** SUSTANTIVO
thimble

dedicar* VERBO
[1] to devote ◇ *Dedicó su vida a los demás.* He devoted his life to others.
[2] to dedicate ◇ *Dedicó el poema a su padre.* He dedicated the poem to his father.
- **¿A qué se dedica?** What does he do for a living?
- **Ayer me dediqué a arreglar los cajones.** I spent yesterday straightening out the drawers.

la **dedicatoria** SUSTANTIVO
dedication

el **dedo** SUSTANTIVO
[1] finger (*de la mano*) ◇ *Lleva un anillo en el dedo meñique.* She wears a ring on her little finger.
- **hacer* dedo** to hitch a ride
- **no mover* un dedo** not to lift a finger

☞

2 toe (*del pie*)
- **el dedo gordo (1)** (*de la mano*) the thumb
- **el dedo gordo (2)** (*del pie*) the big toe

deducir* VERBO
to deduce ◇ *Deduje que había mentido.* I deduced that he'd lied.

el **defecto** SUSTANTIVO
1 defect ◇ *El jarrón tiene un pequeño defecto.* The vase has a small defect.
2 fault ◇ *Le encuentra defectos a todo.* He finds fault with everything.

defender* VERBO
to defend ◇ *Defendió a su amigo de las críticas.* He defended his friend against criticisms.
- **defenderse** to defend oneself ◇ *Tenemos que defendernos del enemigo.* We have to defend ourselves against the enemy.
- **Me defiendo en inglés.** I can get by in English.

la **defensa** SUSTANTIVO
defense
- **salir* en defensa de alguien** to come to somebody's defense
- **en defensa propia** in self-defense

el **defensor,** la **defensora** SUSTANTIVO
defender

deficiente ADJETIVO
poor ◇ *Su trabajo es muy deficiente.* His work is very poor.

la **definición** SUSTANTIVO (PL las **definiciones**)
definition

definir VERBO
to define

definitivo ADJETIVO
definitive ◇ *Esta solución no es definitiva.* This is not a definitive solution.
- **en definitiva** in short

deformar VERBO
1 to deform (*pie, mano*)
- **No cuelgues el suéter así que lo deformarás.** Don't hang the sweater up like that or you'll pull it out of shape.

2 to distort (*imagen, metal*)
- **deformarse** (*pie, mano*) to become deformed
- **Si lo lavas en la lavadora, se deformará.** If you wash it in the washing machine, it'll lose its shape.

defraudar VERBO
1 to disappoint ◇ *Su comportamiento la defraudó.* His behavior disappointed her.
2 to defraud ◇ *Defraudar dinero a Hacienda es delito.* It's an offense to defraud the Treasury Department of money.

dejar VERBO
1 to leave ◇ *Dejé las llaves en la mesa.* I left the keys on the table. ◇ *Su novio la dejó.* Her fiancé left her. ◇ *Déjame tranquilo.* Leave me alone. ◇ *Dejó todo su dinero a sus hijos.* He left all his money to his children.
- **¡Déjalo ya!** Don't worry about it!
- **Deja mucho que desear.** It leaves a lot to be desired.

2 to let ◇ *Mis padres no me dejan salir de noche.* My parents won't let me go out at night.
- **dejar caer** (*objeto*) to drop ◇ *Dejó caer la bandeja.* She dropped the tray.

3 to lend ◇ *Le dejé mi libro de matemáticas.* I lent him my math book.
4 to give up ◇ *Dejó el esquí después del accidente.* He gave up skiing after the accident.
- **dejar de** to stop ◇ *dejar de fumar* to stop smoking

del PREPOSICIÓN
(= *de* + *el*) *ver* **de**

el **delantal** SUSTANTIVO
apron

delante ADVERBIO
in front ◇ *Siéntate delante.* You sit in front.
- **de delante** front ◇ *la rueda de delante* the front wheel
- **la parte de delante** the front
- **delante de (1)** in front of ◇ *No digas nada delante de los niños.* Don't say anything in front of the children.
- **delante de (2)** opposite ◇ *Mi casa está delante de la escuela.* My house is opposite the school.
- **pasar por delante de** to go past ◇ *Ayer pasé por delante de tu casa.* I went past your house yesterday.
- **hacia delante** forward ◇ *Se inclinó hacia delante.* He leaned forward.

delantero ADJETIVO
front ◇ *los asientos delanteros* the front seats
- **la parte delantera del carro** the front of the car

delatar VERBO
1 to inform on ◇ *el hombre que delató a los dos secuestradores* the man who informed on the two kidnappers
- **Los delató a la policía.** He tipped the police off about them.

2 to give away ◇ *Tu sonrisa te delata.* Your smile gives you away.

la **delegación** SUSTANTIVO (PL las **delegaciones**)
Mexico
police station

el **delegado,** la **delegada** SUSTANTIVO
delegate
- **el delegado de clase** the class representative

deletrear VERBO
to spell out

el **delfín** SUSTANTIVO (PL los **delfines**)
dolphin

delgado ADJETIVO
1 slim ◇ *Todas las modelos son delgadas.*

* Verbs marked with this symbol are irregular. See pages 346–348 for further details.

All the models are slim.
[2] thin ◇ *Esta tela es demasiado delgada.* This material is too thin.

delicado ADJETIVO
[1] delicate ◇ *Estas copas son muy delicadas.* These glasses are very delicate. ◇ *Se trata de un asunto muy delicado.* It's a very delicate subject.
[2] thoughtful ◇ *Enviarte flores ha sido un gesto muy delicado.* Sending flowers was a very thoughtful gesture.

la **delicia** SUSTANTIVO
delight ◇ *¡Qué delicia!* What a delight!
◆ **Este guiso es una delicia.** This stew is delicious.

delicioso ADJETIVO
delicious

el/la **delincuente** SUSTANTIVO
criminal ◇ *Es uno de los delincuentes más buscados.* He's one of the most wanted criminals.
◆ **un delincuente juvenil** a juvenile delinquent

el **delito** SUSTANTIVO
crime

la **demanda** SUSTANTIVO
demand ◇ *la oferta y la demanda* supply and demand
◆ **Se manifestaron en demanda de un aumento salarial.** They demonstrated for a wage increase.
◆ **presentar una demanda contra alguien** to sue somebody

demás (1) ADJETIVO
other ◇ *los demás niños* the other children

demás (2) PRONOMBRE
◆ **los demás** the others
◆ **lo demás** the rest ◇ *Yo limpio las ventanas y lo demás lo limpias tú.* I'll clean the windows and you clean the rest.
◆ **todo lo demás** everything else

demasiado (1) ADJETIVO
too much (PL too many) ◇ *demasiado vino* too much wine ◇ *demasiados libros* too many books

demasiado (2) ADVERBIO
[1] too ◇ *Es demasiado pesado para levantarlo.* It's too heavy to lift. ◇ *Caminas demasiado rápido.* You walk too quickly.
[2] too much ◇ *Hablas demasiado.* You talk too much.

la **democracia** SUSTANTIVO
democracy (PL democracies)

democrático ADJETIVO
democratic

el **demonio** SUSTANTIVO
devil
◆ **¡Jaime es un auténtico demonio!** Jaime's a real devil! (*coloquial*)
◆ **¡Demonios!** Hell! (*coloquial*)
◆ **¿Qué demonios será?** What the devil can it be? (*coloquial*)

la **demostración** SUSTANTIVO (PL las **demostraciones**)
[1] demonstration (*de funcionamiento, método*)
[2] proof (*de teoría*)

demostrar* VERBO
[1] to demonstrate (*funcionamiento, método*)
[2] to prove (*teoría*) ◇ *Tendrá que demostrar su inocencia.* He will have to prove his innocence.
◆ **Así sólo demuestras tu ignorancia.** That way you only show how ignorant you are.

la **densidad** SUSTANTIVO
density ◇ *la densidad de población* population density

denso ADJETIVO
[1] thick (*humo, niebla*)
[2] heavy (*novela, discurso*)

la **dentadura** SUSTANTIVO
teeth PL
◆ **la dentadura postiza** false teeth PL

el **dentífrico** SUSTANTIVO
toothpaste

el/la **dentista** SUSTANTIVO
dentist

dentro ADVERBIO
inside ◇ *¿Qué hay dentro?* What's inside?
◆ **por dentro** inside ◇ *Mira bien por dentro.* Have a good look inside.
◆ **Está aquí dentro.** It's in here.
◆ **dentro de** in ◇ *Mételo dentro del sobre.* Put it in the envelope. ◇ *dentro de tres meses* in three months
◆ **dentro de poco** soon
◆ **dentro de lo que cabe** as far as it goes

la **denuncia** SUSTANTIVO
◆ **Voy a ponerle una denuncia por hacer tanto ruido.** I'm going to report him for making so much noise.
◆ **Le pusieron una denuncia por verter residuos en el río.** He was reported to the authorities for dumping waste into the river.

denunciar VERBO
to report (*un delito*)

el **departamento** SUSTANTIVO
[1] apartment (*apartamento*)
[2] department (*de grandes almacenes, empresa*)
[3] compartment (*de tren*)

depender VERBO
◆ **depender de** to depend on ◇ *El precio depende de la calidad.* The price depends on the quality.
◆ **Depende.** It depends.
◆ **No depende de mí.** It's not up to me.

el **dependiente,** la **dependienta** SUSTANTIVO
sales clerk

el **deporte** SUSTANTIVO
sport ◇ *No hago mucho deporte.* I don't play sports much. ◇ *los deportes de invierno* ☞

D

winter sports

deportista ADJETIVO
sporty ◇ *Alicia es poco deportista.* Alicia is not very sporty.

el **deportista** SUSTANTIVO
sportsman (PL sportsmen)

la **deportista** SUSTANTIVO
sportswoman (PL sportswomen)

deportivo ADJETIVO
[1] sports (*ropa, carro*)
***sports** en este caso va siempre delante del sustantivo.*
◇ *un club deportivo* a sports club
[2] sporting (*actitud, espíritu*)

el **depósito** SUSTANTIVO
[1] tank (*de agua, gasolina*)
[2] deposit (*de dinero*)

la **depresión** SUSTANTIVO (PL las **depresiones**)
[1] depression (*enfermedad*)
◆ **tener* una depresión** to be suffering from depression
[2] hollow (*de terreno*)

deprimir VERBO
to depress
◆ **deprimirse por algo** to get depressed about something

deprisa ADVERBIO
quickly ◇ *Acabaron muy deprisa.* They finished very quickly.
◆ **¡Deprisa!** Hurry up!
◆ **Lo hacen todo deprisa y corriendo.** They do everything in a rush.

la **derecha** SUSTANTIVO
[1] right hand (*mano*) ◇ *Escribo con la derecha.* I write with my right hand.
[2] right (*dirección, grupo político*) ◇ *doblar a la derecha* to turn right ◇ *La derecha ganó las elecciones.* The elections were won by the right.
◆ **ser* de derecha** to be right-wing ◇ *un partido de derecha* a right-wing party
◆ **a la derecha** on the right ◇ *la segunda calle a la derecha* the second turning on the right
◆ **a la derecha del castillo** to the right of the castle
◆ **manejar por la derecha** to drive on the right

derecho (1) ADJETIVO
[1] right ◇ *Me duele el ojo derecho.* I have a pain in my right eye. ◇ *Escribo con la mano derecha.* I write with my right hand.
◆ **a mano derecha** on the right-hand side
[2] straight ◇ *¡Ponte derecho!* Stand up straight!

derecho (2) ADVERBIO
straight ◇ *Vino derecho hacia mí.* He came straight towards me.
◆ **Siga derecho.** Continue straight on.

el **derecho** SUSTANTIVO
[1] right ◇ *tener derecho a hacer algo* to have the right to do something ◇ *No tienes derecho a decir eso.* You have no right to say that. ◇ *los derechos humanos* human rights
◆ **¡No hay derecho!** It's not fair!
[2] law ◇ *Estudio derecho.* I'm studying law.
◆ **Ponte la camiseta al derecho.** Put your T-shirt on right side out.

derramar VERBO
to spill ◇ *Derramó vino sobre el mantel.* He spilled wine on the tablecloth.

derretir* VERBO
to melt
◆ **derretirse** to melt ◇ *El queso se ha derretido.* The cheese has melted. ◇ *El hielo se está derritiendo.* The ice is melting.
◆ **derretirse de calor** to be melting

derribar VERBO
[1] to demolish (*construcción*)
[2] to shoot down (*avión*)
[3] to overthrow (*persona, gobierno*)

la **derrota** SUSTANTIVO
defeat ◇ *sufrir una derrota* to be defeated

derrotar VERBO
to defeat

derrumbar VERBO
to pull down ◇ *Derrumbaron el cine.* The movie theater has been pulled down.
◆ **derrumbarse** to collapse ◇ *El edificio se derrumbó.* The building collapsed.

desabrochar VERBO
to undo
◆ **desabrocharse (1)** to undo ◇ *Me desabroché la blusa.* I undid my blouse.
◆ **desabrocharse (2)** to come undone ◇ *Se te ha desabrochado el vestido.* Your dress has come undone.

el **desacuerdo** SUSTANTIVO
disagreement

desafiar* VERBO
to challenge ◇ *Mi hermano me desafió a una carrera.* My brother challenged me to a race.

desafinar VERBO
to go out of tune

el **desafío** SUSTANTIVO
challenge

desafortunado ADJETIVO
unfortunate

desagradable ADJETIVO
unpleasant ◇ *un olor muy desagradable* a very unpleasant smell
◆ **ser* desagradable con alguien** to be unpleasant to somebody

desagradecido ADJETIVO
ungrateful

el **desagüe** SUSTANTIVO
[1] drainpipe (*de lavabo*)
[2] drain (*de patio, terraza*)

desahogarse* VERBO
◆ **Se desahogó conmigo.** He poured out his

heart to me.
- **Lloraba para desahogarse.** He was crying to let off steam.

desalojar VERBO
to clear ◇ *La policía desalojó a los manifestantes.* The police cleared the demonstrators. ◇ *Los bomberos desalojaron el edificio.* The firemen cleared the building.

desanimado ADJETIVO
1 downhearted (*persona*)
2 dull (*espectáculo, fiesta*)

desanimar VERBO
to discourage ◇ *Me desanimó su falta de interés.* His lack of interest discouraged me.
- **desanimarse** to lose heart

desaparecer* VERBO
to disappear ◇ *La mancha desapareció.* The stain has disappeared.
- **¡Desaparece de mi vista!** Get out of my sight!
- **desaparecerse** to disappear ◇ *Se me desapareció el reloj.* My watch has disappeared.

la **desaparición** SUSTANTIVO (PL las **desapariciones**)
disappearance

desapercibido ADJETIVO
- **pasar desapercibido** to go unnoticed

desaprovechar VERBO
to waste ◇ *Han desaprovechado una gran oportunidad.* They've wasted a great opportunity.

desarmador SUSTANTIVO *Mexico*
screwdriver

desarmar VERBO
1 to take apart (*mueble*)
2 to take down (*tienda de campaña*)
3 to strip down (*motor*)

el **desarme** SUSTANTIVO
disarmament ◇ *el desarme nuclear* nuclear disarmament

desarrollar VERBO
to develop ◇ *El estudio desarrolla la mente.* Study develops the mind.
- **La UNICEF desarrolla una labor importante.** UNICEF carries out important work.
- **desarrollarse (1)** to develop ◇ *La empresa se está desarrollando rápidamente.* The business is developing rapidly.
- **desarrollarse (2)** to take place ◇ *La reunión se desarrolló sin incidentes.* The meeting took place without incident.

el **desarrollo** SUSTANTIVO
development ◇ *La alimentación es importante para el desarrollo del niño.* Diet is important for a child's development.
- **La industria está en pleno desarrollo.** The industry is expanding steadily.
- **un país en vías de desarrollo** a developing country

el **desastre** SUSTANTIVO
disaster ◇ *un gran desastre económico* a major economic disaster ◇ *La función fue un desastre.* The show was a disaster.
- **Soy un desastre para la gimnasia.** I'm hopeless at gymnastics.
- **Siempre va hecho un desastre.** He always looks a mess.

desastroso ADJETIVO
disastrous

desatar VERBO
1 to undo (*nudo, lazo*)
2 to untie (*cordones, cuerda*)
- **desatarse (1)** (*nudo, cordones*) to come undone
- **desatarse (2)** (*perro*) to get loose
- **desatarse (3)** (*tormenta*) to break

desayunar VERBO
1 to have breakfast ◇ *Nunca desayuno.* I never have breakfast.
2 to have...for breakfast ◇ *Desayuné café y pan tostado.* I had coffee and toast for breakfast.
- **desayunarse** to have breakfast

el **desayuno** SUSTANTIVO
breakfast

descalzarse* VERBO
to take one's shoes off

descalzo ADJETIVO
barefoot ◇ *Paseaban descalzos por la playa.* They walked barefoot along the beach.
- **No entres en la cocina descalzo.** Don't come into the kitchen in bare feet.

el **descampado** SUSTANTIVO
open space

descansar VERBO
1 to rest ◇ *Tienes que descansar.* You must rest.
- **descanse en paz** may he rest in peace

2 to sleep ◇ *¡Que descanses!* Sleep well!

el **descansillo** SUSTANTIVO
landing (*en escalera*)

el **descanso** SUSTANTIVO
1 rest ◇ *He caminado mucho, necesito un descanso.* I've done a lot of walking; I need a rest.
2 break ◇ *Cada dos horas me tomo un descanso.* I have a break every two hours.
3 relief (*alivio*) ◇ *¡Qué descanso!* What a relief!
4 interval (*en el teatro*)
5 half time (*en un partido*)
- **tomarse unos días de descanso** to take a few days off

el **descapotable** SUSTANTIVO
convertible

descarado ADJETIVO
impudent ◇ *¡No seas descarado!* Don't be impudent!

la **descarga** SUSTANTIVO
1 unloading (*de mercancías*)

☞

[2] discharge (*de electricidad*)

descargar* VERBO

[1] to unload ◇ *Me ayudó a descargar los muebles de la camioneta.* He helped me unload the furniture from the van.

[2] to take out ◇ *Descarga su mal humor sobre mí.* He takes his bad moods out on me.

[3] to download (*informática*)

◆ **descargarse** (*batería, pila*) to go dead

el **descaro** SUSTANTIVO

nerve ◇ *¡Qué descaro!* What a nerve!

descender* VERBO

to go down ◇ *Descendieron por la escalinata.* They went down the staircase. ◇ *Ha descendido el nivel del embalse.* The level of the reservoir has gone down.

◆ **descender de** to be descended from ◇ *Desciende de una familia noble.* He is descended from a noble family.

◆ **Mi equipo ha descendido de categoría.** My team has been relegated to a lower division.

el/la **descendiente** SUSTANTIVO

descendant

el **descenso** SUSTANTIVO

[1] drop ◇ *El descenso de la temperatura ha causado heladas.* The drop in temperature has brought frost.

[2] descent ◇ *Los ciclistas iniciaron el descenso del puerto.* The cyclists began the descent from the mountain pass.

[3] relegation ◇ *el descenso a segunda división* relegation to the second division

descolgar* VERBO

[1] to take down ◇ *Descolgó las cortinas para lavarlas.* He took down the curtains to wash them.

[2] to pick up the phone ◇ *Descolgó y marcó el número.* He picked up the phone and dialed the number.

◆ **descolgar el teléfono** (*para contestar*) to pick up the phone

◆ **descolgarse por una pared** to climb down a wall

descomponerse* VERBO

to break down (*máquina, carro*)

desconcertar* VERBO

to disconcert

◆ **desconcertarse** to be disconcerted ◇ *Se desconcertó al verla allí.* He was disconcerted to see her there.

desconectar VERBO

[1] to unplug (*aparato*)

[2] to disconnect (*línea*)

desconfiado ADJETIVO

distrustful

la **desconfianza** SUSTANTIVO

distrust

desconfiar* VERBO

◆ **Desconfío de él.** I don't trust him.

◆ **Desconfía siempre de los desconocidos.** Always beware of strangers.

descongelar VERBO

to defrost (*comida, refrigerador*)

◆ **descongelarse** to defrost (*comida, refrigerador*)

el **desconocido**, la **desconocida** SUSTANTIVO

stranger

desconocido ADJETIVO

unknown ◇ *un actor desconocido* an unknown actor

descontar* VERBO

to deduct ◇ *Me descuentan un porcentaje del sueldo por impuestos.* A percentage of my salary is deducted for taxes.

◆ **Descuentan el 5% si se paga en metálico.** They give a 5% discount if you pay cash.

◆ **Descontaron diez pesos del precio marcado.** They took ten pesos off the marked price.

descontento ADJETIVO

unhappy ◇ *Están descontentos con mis notas.* They're unhappy with my grades.

descoser VERBO

to unpick

◆ **descoserse** to come apart at the seams

descremado ADJETIVO

skimmed

describir* VERBO

to describe

la **descripción** SUSTANTIVO (PL las **descripciones**)

description

el **descubrimiento** SUSTANTIVO

discovery (PL discoveries)

descubrir* VERBO

[1] to discover ◇ *Fleming descubrió la penicilina.* Fleming discovered penicillin.

[2] to find out ◇ *¡Me descubriste!* You've found me out!

el **descuento** SUSTANTIVO

discount ◇ *Me hicieron un descuento del 3%.* They gave me a 3% discount.

◆ **con descuento** at a discount

descuidado ADJETIVO

[1] careless ◇ *Es muy descuidada con sus juguetes.* She's very careless with her toys.

[2] neglected ◇ *El jardín estaba descuidado.* The garden was neglected.

descuidar VERBO

to neglect ◇ *Descuidó su negocio.* He neglected his business.

◆ **Descuida, que yo lo haré.** Don't worry, I'll do it.

◆ **descuidarse** to let one's attention wander ◇ *Se descuidó un segundo y el niño cruzó la calle.* He let his attention wander for a second and the child crossed the road.

el **descuido** SUSTANTIVO

oversight ◇ *Me olvidé de invitarla, fue un descuido.* I forgot to invite her; it was an oversight.

desde PREPOSICIÓN

1 from ◇ *Desde Cuernavaca hasta mi casa hay 20 millas.* It's 20 miles from Cuernavaca to my house. ◇ *Lo llamaré desde la oficina.* I'll ring him from the office.
2 since ◇ *Desde que llegó no ha salido.* He hasn't been out since he arrived. ◇ *La conozco desde niño.* I've known her since I was a child. ◇ *desde entonces* since then

- **¿Desde cuándo vives aquí?** How long have you been living here?
- **desde hace tres años** for three years
- **desde ahora en adelante** from now on
- **desde luego** of course

desdichado ADJETIVO
1 ill-fated (*suceso*)
2 unlucky (*persona*)

desdoblar VERBO
to unfold ◇ *Desdobló el mapa.* He unfolded the map.

desear VERBO
to wish ◇ *Te deseo mucha suerte.* I wish you lots of luck.
- **Estoy deseando que esto termine.** I'm longing for this to finish.
- **¿Qué desea?** What can I do for you?
- **dejar mucho que desear** to leave a lot to be desired

desechable ADJETIVO
disposable

los **desechos** SUSTANTIVO
waste SING ◇ *los materiales de desecho* waste material ◇ *los desechos nucleares* nuclear waste

desembarcar* VERBO
1 to disembark ◇ *Fue el primero en desembarcar.* He was the first to disembark.
2 to unload ◇ *Desembarcaron la mercancía.* They've unloaded the goods.

el **desembarco** SUSTANTIVO
disembarkation (*de pasajeros*)

desembocar* VERBO
- **desembocar en (1)** (*río*) to flow into ◇ *El Orinoco desemboca en el Atlántico.* The Orinoco flows into the Atlantic.
- **desembocar en (2)** (*calle*) to lead into ◇ *Este callejón desemboca en la Avenida Pablo Casals.* This alley leads into Avenida Pablo Casals.

desempacar* VERBO
to unpack

el **desempate** SUSTANTIVO
play-off
- **el partido de desempate** the deciding game
- **En el minuto veinte llegó el gol del desempate.** The goal which broke the deadlock came in the twentieth minute.

el **desempleado**, la **desempleada** SUSTANTIVO
unemployed person
- **los desempleados** the unemployed

el **desempleo** SUSTANTIVO
unemployment

desenchufar VERBO
to unplug

desengañar VERBO
- **Su traición la desengañó.** His betrayal opened her eyes.
- **¡Desengáñate! No está interesada en ti.** Stop fooling yourself! She isn't interested in you.

el **desengaño** SUSTANTIVO
disappointment ◇ *¡Qué desengaño!* What a disappointment!
- **llevarse un desengaño** to be disappointed
- **sufrir un desengaño amoroso** to be disappointed in love

desenredar VERBO
1 to untangle (*pelo*)
2 to resolve (*asunto*)

desenrollar VERBO
1 to unwind (*hilo, cinta*)
2 to unroll (*papel*)

desenroscar* VERBO
to unscrew

desenvolver* VERBO
to unwrap ◇ *Desenvolvió todos los regalos.* He unwrapped all the presents.
- **desenvolverse** to cope ◇ *No sabe desenvolverse en este tipo de situaciones.* He can't cope in this sort of situation.
- **desenvolverse bien** to do well

el **deseo** SUSTANTIVO
wish (PL wishes) ◇ *Pide un deseo.* Make a wish.

desequilibrado ADJETIVO
unbalanced

desértico ADJETIVO
desert

***desert** en este caso va siempre delante del sustantivo.*

◇ *una región desértica* a desert region

desesperado ADJETIVO
desperate

el **desesperado**, la **desesperada** SUSTANTIVO
- **Corría como un desesperado.** He was running like mad. (*coloquial*)

desesperante ADJETIVO
infuriating

desesperar VERBO
1 to drive...mad ◇ *Los atascos me desesperan.* Traffic jams drive me mad.
2 to despair ◇ *No desesperes y sigue intentándolo.* Don't despair, just keep trying.
- **desesperarse** to get exasperated

desfavorable ADJETIVO
unfavorable

el **desfiladero** SUSTANTIVO
gorge

desfilar VERBO
to parade

el **desfile** SUSTANTIVO
parade (*de soldados*)
- **un desfile de modas** a fashion show

D

desganado ADJETIVO
- **estar* desganado (1)** (*sin ánimos*) to be lethargic
- **estar* desganado (2)** (*sin apetito*) to have little appetite

el **desgano** SUSTANTIVO
1 loss of appetite (*falta de apetito*)
2 reluctance (*falta de entusiasmo*)
- **hacer* algo con desgano** to do something reluctantly

desgarrar VERBO
to tear up ◇ *Desgarró la sábana para hacer trapos.* He tore up the sheet to make rags.
- **desgarrarse** to rip ◇ *La cortina se desgarró.* The curtain ripped.

el **desgarrón** SUSTANTIVO (PL los **desgarrones**)
rip

desgastar VERBO
1 to wear out (*ropa, zapatos*)
2 to wear away (*roca*)
- **desgastarse** to get worn out

el **desgaste** SUSTANTIVO
1 wear and tear (*de ropa, zapatos*)
2 erosion (*de roca*)

la **desgracia** SUSTANTIVO
tragedy (PL tragedies) ◇ *La muerte de su marido fue una auténtica desgracia.* Her husband's death was an absolute tragedy.
- **Ha tenido una vida llena de desgracias.** He's had a lot of misfortune in his life.
- **por desgracia (1)** sadly ◇ *Por desgracia no se salvó nadie.* Sadly, there were no survivors.
- **por desgracia (2)** unfortunately ◇ *Por desgracia no aprobé el examen.* Unfortunately, I didn't pass the exam.
- **tener* la desgracia de** to be unfortunate enough to ◇ *Tuvo la desgracia de perder un brazo en la guerra.* He was unfortunate enough to lose an arm in the war.
- **No hubo desgracias personales.** There were no casualties.

desgraciado ADJETIVO
1 unhappy ◇ *Desde que Ana lo dejó ha sido muy desgraciado.* He has been very unhappy since Ana left him.
2 tragic ◇ *Murió en un desgraciado accidente.* He died in a tragic accident.

deshabitado ADJETIVO
1 uninhabited (*edificio*)
2 unoccupied (*zona*)

deshacer* VERBO
1 to untie (*nudo*)
2 to unpack (*maleta*)
3 to melt (*helado, mantequilla*)
4 to unpick (*labor*)
- **deshacerse (1)** (*nudo, labor*) to come undone
- **deshacerse (2)** (*helado, mantequilla*) to melt
- **deshacerse de algo** to get rid of something

deshecho ADJETIVO
1 undone (*nudo, costura*)
2 unmade (*cama*)
3 broken (*matrimonio*)
4 melted (*helado, mantequilla*)
- **Estoy deshecho. (1)** (*cansado*) I'm shattered.
- **Estoy deshecho. (2)** (*apenado*) I'm devastated.

deshidratarse VERBO
to become dehydrated

el **deshielo** SUSTANTIVO
thaw

desierto ADJETIVO
deserted ◇ *El pueblo parecía desierto.* The village seemed deserted.

el **desierto** SUSTANTIVO
desert

desigual ADJETIVO
1 different (*tamaño*)
2 uneven (*escritura, terreno*)
3 unequal (*lucha*)

la **desilusión** SUSTANTIVO (PL las **desilusiones**)
disappointment ◇ *¡Qué desilusión!* What a disappointment!
- **llevarse una desilusión** to be disappointed

desilusionar VERBO
to disappoint ◇ *No quiero desilusionarte, pero...* I don't want to disappoint you, but...
- **Su conferencia me desilusionó.** His lecture was disappointing.
- **desilusionarse** to be disappointed

el **desinfectante** SUSTANTIVO
disinfectant

desinfectar VERBO
to disinfect

desinflar VERBO
to let the air out of ◇ *Alguien me desinfló los neumáticos.* Somebody let the air out of my tires.

el **desinterés** SUSTANTIVO
lack of interest ◇ *Muestra un total desinterés por sus estudios.* He shows a total lack of interest in his studies.

deslizarse* VERBO
to slide ◇ *El trineo se deslizaba por la nieve.* The sled slid over the snow.

deslumbrar VERBO
to dazzle ◇ *Las luces del carro me deslumbraron.* The car headlights dazzled me. ◇ *Tanta riqueza la deslumbró.* She was dazzled by so much wealth.

desmayarse VERBO
to faint

el **desmayo** SUSTANTIVO
faint
- **sufrir un desmayo** to faint

desmemoriado ADJETIVO
forgetful

desmontar VERBO
1 to take apart (*mueble*)
2 to take down (*tienda de campaña*)

[3] to strip down (*motor*)
[4] to dismount (*jinete*)

desnudar VERBO
to undress
◆ **desnudarse** to get undressed

desnudo ADJETIVO
[1] naked ◇ *una escultura de un hombre desnudo* a sculpture of a naked man
◆ **Duerme desnudo.** He sleeps in the nude.
[2] bare ◇ *Sin los cuadros la pared se ve desnuda.* The wall looks bare without the paintings.

desobedecer* VERBO
to disobey

desobediente ADJETIVO
disobedient

el **desodorante** SUSTANTIVO
deodorant

el **desorden** SUSTANTIVO (PL los **desórdenes**)
mess ◇ *Toda la casa estaba en desorden.* The whole house was in a mess.
◆ **los desórdenes callejeros** street disturbances

desordenado ADJETIVO
untidy

desordenar VERBO
to mess up ◇ *Los niños desordenaron la pieza.* The children have messed up the room.

la **desorganización** SUSTANTIVO
disorganization

desorientar VERBO
to confuse ◇ *Sus consejos la desorientaron todavía más.* His advice confused her even more.
◆ **desorientarse** to lose one's way ◇ *Se desorientó al salir del metro.* He lost his way when he came out of the subway.

despachar VERBO
[1] to sell ◇ *También despachamos pan.* We also sell bread.
[2] to serve ◇ *Me despachó un dependiente muy educado.* I was served by a very polite sales assistant.
[3] to dismiss ◇ *Me despachó sin ninguna explicación.* He dismissed me without any explanation.

el **despacho** SUSTANTIVO
[1] office
◆ **los muebles de despacho** office furniture
◆ **una mesa de despacho** a desk
[2] study (PL studies) ◇ *Cuando llega a casa se encierra en el despacho.* When he gets home he shuts himself away in the study.
◆ **un despacho de boletos** a ticket office

despacio ADVERBIO
slowly ◇ *Maneja despacio.* Drive slowly.
◆ **¡Despacio!** Take it easy!

despectivo ADJETIVO
[1] contemptuous ◇ *Habla a sus alumnos en un tono muy despectivo.* He speaks to his pupils in a very contemptuous tone.
[2] pejorative ◇ *"Mujerzuela" es una palabra despectiva.* "Mujerzuela" is a pejorative term.

la **despedida** SUSTANTIVO
◆ **Le hicimos una buena despedida a Marta.** We gave Marta a good send-off.
◆ **una fiesta de despedida** a farewell party
◆ **una despedida de soltero** a bachelor party
◆ **una despedida de soltera** a bachelorette party

D

despedir* VERBO
[1] to say goodbye to ◇ *Salí a la calle a despedirla.* I went out into the street to say goodbye to her.
◆ **Fueron a despedirlo al aeropuerto.** They went to the airport to see him off.
[2] to dismiss ◇ *Lo despidieron por llegar tarde.* He was dismissed for being late.
◆ **despedirse** to say goodbye ◇ *Se despidieron en la estación.* They said goodbye at the station. ◇ *despedirse de alguien* to say goodbye to somebody

despegar* VERBO
to take off ◇ *Despegó la etiqueta del precio.* He took the price tag off. ◇ *El avión despegó con retraso.* The plane took off late.
◆ **despegarse** to come unstuck

el **despegue** SUSTANTIVO
takeoff

despeinar VERBO
◆ **despeinar a alguien** to mess somebody's hair up
◆ **No me toques el pelo, que me despeinas.** Don't touch my hair, you'll mess it up.
◆ **Se despeinó al vestirse.** She messed up her hair getting dressed.

despejado ADJETIVO
clear ◇ *El cielo estaba despejado.* The sky was clear. ◇ *Por las mañanas tengo la mente más despejada.* My head's clearer in the mornings.

despejar VERBO
to clear ◇ *La policía ha despejado la zona.* The police have cleared the area. ◇ *El aire fresco te despejará.* The fresh air will clear your head.
◆ **¡Despejen!** Move along!
◆ **Tomaré un café para despejarme.** I'll have a coffee to wake myself up.

despellejar VERBO
to skin

la **despensa** SUSTANTIVO
pantry (PL pantries)

desperdiciar VERBO
[1] to waste ◇ *Está mal desperdiciar la comida.* It's wrong to waste food.
[2] to throw away ◇ *Desperdició la oportunidad de hacerse rico.* He threw away the chance to get rich.

el **desperdicio** SUSTANTIVO
waste ◇ *Tirar toda esta comida es un*

☞

desperdicio. It's a waste to throw away all this food.

◆ **los desperdicios** scraps ◇ *Le dimos los desperdicios al perro.* We gave the dog the scraps.

◆ **El libro no tiene desperdicio.** It's an excellent book from beginning to end.

desperezarse* VERBO
to stretch

el **desperfecto** SUSTANTIVO
flaw

◆ **El pantalón tenía un pequeño desperfecto.** There was a slight flaw in the pants.

◆ **sufrir desperfectos** to get damaged

el **despertador** SUSTANTIVO
alarm clock

despertar* VERBO
1 to wake up ◇ *No me despiertes hasta las once.* Don't wake me up until eleven o'clock.
2 to arouse ◇ *El debate despertó un gran interés.* The debate aroused a lot of interest.

◆ **despertarse** to wake up

el **despido** SUSTANTIVO
dismissal

despierto ADJETIVO
1 awake ◇ *A las siete ya estaba despierto.* He was already awake by seven o'clock.
2 bright ◇ *Es un niño muy despierto.* He's a very bright boy.

el **despistado,** la **despistada** SUSTANTIVO
scatterbrain ◇ *Eres un despistado.* You're a scatterbrain.

despistado ADJETIVO
absent-minded ◇ *Es tan despistado que siempre se olvida las llaves.* He's so absent-minded that he's always forgetting his keys.

despistar VERBO
1 to shake off ◇ *Despistaron al carro que los seguía.* They managed to shake off the car that was following them.
2 to be misleading ◇ *Estas instrucciones más que ayudar despistan.* These instructions are more misleading than helpful.

◆ **Me despisté y salí de la autopista demasiado tarde.** I wasn't concentrating and I turned off the freeway too late.

el **despiste** SUSTANTIVO
absent-mindedness ◇ *Su despiste es conocido por todos.* His absent-mindedness is notorious.

desplegar* VERBO
1 to unfold ◇ *Desplegó el mapa.* He unfolded the map.
2 to spread ◇ *El águila desplegó las alas.* The eagle spread its wings.

◆ **desplegarse** to be deployed ◇ *El ejército se desplegó por la ciudad.* The army was deployed throughout the city.

desplomarse VERBO
to collapse ◇ *Se desplomó el techo.* The roof collapsed.

despreciar VERBO
to despise

el **desprecio** SUSTANTIVO
contempt

◆ **Habló de ellos con desprecio.** He spoke of them contemptuously.

◆ **Le hicieron el desprecio de no acudir.** They snubbed him by not turning up.

desprender VERBO
to give off (*olor, calor*)

◆ **desprenderse** to fall off ◇ *Se desprendió una baldosa.* A tile fell off.

◆ **desprenderse de algo** to give something up ◇ *No quería desprenderse de la casa.* He didn't want to give the house up.

despreocuparse VERBO
to stop worrying ◇ *Despreocúpate porque ya no tiene remedio.* Stop worrying because there's nothing we can do about it now.

◆ **despreocuparse de todo** to show no concern for anything

desprevenido ADJETIVO

◆ **pillar a alguien desprevenido** to catch somebody unawares

después ADVERBIO
1 afterward ◇ *Después todos estábamos muy cansados.* Afterward we were all very tired.

◆ **Primero cenaré y después saldré.** I'll have dinner first and go out after that.
2 later ◇ *Ellos llegaron después.* They arrived later. ◇ *un año después* a year later
3 next ◇ *¿Qué viene después?* What comes next?

◆ **después de** after ◇ *Tu nombre está después del mío.* Your name comes after mine. ◇ *Después de comer fuimos de paseo.* After lunch we went for a walk.

◆ **después de todo** after all

◆ **después de que** after ◇ *después de que hayas terminado* after you have finished

destacar* VERBO
1 to stress ◇ *Me gustaría destacar la importancia de esto.* I'd like to stress the importance of this.
2 to stand out ◇ *Isabel destacaba por su generosidad.* Isabel's generosity made her stand out.

◆ **destacarse** to stand out ◇ *Ana se destacaba por su inteligencia.* Ana stood out because of her intelligence.

el **destapador** SUSTANTIVO
bottle opener

destapar VERBO
1 to open (*botella*)
2 to take the lid off (*cacerola*)

◆ **destaparse** to get uncovered ◇ *El niño se*

destapa por las noches. The child gets uncovered during the night.

desteñir* VERBO

[1] to run ◇ *Estos colores destiñen.* These colors run in the wash. ◇ *La camisa se destiñó al lavarla.* The shirt ran in the wash.

[2] to fade ◇ *El sol ha desteñido las cortinas.* The sun has faded the curtains.

◆ **desteñirse** to fade ◇ *Se destiñó el suéter.* This sweater has faded.

desternillarse VERBO

◆ **desternillarse de risa** to split one's sides laughing (*coloquial*)

destinar VERBO

[1] to assign ◇ *Lo destinaron a Lima.* He has been assigned to Lima.

[2] to earmark ◇ *Destinaron los fondos a la compra de maquinaria.* The funds were earmarked for purchasing machinery.

◆ **El libro está destinado al público infantil.** The book is aimed at children.

el **destinatario,** la **destinataria** SUSTANTIVO

addressee

el **destino** SUSTANTIVO

[1] destination ◇ *Por fin llegamos a nuestro destino.* We finally arrived at our destination.

◆ **el tren con destino a Guadalajara** the train to Guadalajara

◆ **salir* con destino a** to leave for

[2] assignment ◇ *Cada dos años me cambian de destino.* They give me a new assignment every two years.

[3] use ◇ *Quiero saber qué destino tendrá este dinero.* I want to know what use will be made of this money.

el **destornillador** SUSTANTIVO

screwdriver

destornillar VERBO

to unscrew

la **destreza** SUSTANTIVO

skill

destrozar* VERBO

to wreck ◇ *Tu perro ha destrozado las zapatillas.* Your dog has wrecked the slippers.

◆ **La noticia le destrozó el corazón.** The news broke his heart.

los **destrozos** SUSTANTIVO

damage SING ◇ *La lluvia ocasionó grandes destrozos.* The rain caused a lot of damage.

la **destrucción** SUSTANTIVO

destruction

destruir* VERBO

[1] to destroy ◇ *Los huracanes destruyen edificios enteros.* Hurricanes can destroy whole buildings.

[2] to ruin ◇ *Aquello destruyó su carrera.* That business ruined his career.

[3] to demolish ◇ *Con cuatro palabras destruyó todos mis argumentos.* He demolished all my arguments with a few words.

desvalijar VERBO

[1] to ransack (*casa*)

[2] to rob (*persona*)

el **desván** SUSTANTIVO (PL los **desvanes**)

attic

desvelar VERBO

[1] to keep...awake ◇ *El café me desvela.* Coffee keeps me awake.

[2] to reveal ◇ *Nos desveló todos sus secretos.* He revealed all his secrets to us.

◆ **Se desvelan por sus hijos.** They're devoted to their children.

la **desventaja** SUSTANTIVO

disadvantage

◆ **estar* en desventaja** to be at a disadvantage

la **desviación** SUSTANTIVO (PL las **desviaciones**)

detour ◇ *una desviación de la circulación* a traffic detour ◇ *Hicimos una desviación para evitar el tráfico del centro.* We made a detour to avoid the traffic in the center of town.

desviar* VERBO

to detour ◇ *Desviaron la circulación.* Traffic was detoured.

◆ **Quería desviar mi atención.** He wanted to divert my attention.

◆ **desviar la mirada** to look away

◆ **desviarse** to turn off ◇ *No debes desviarte de la carretera principal.* You must not turn off the main road. ◇ *Nos estamos desviando del tema.* We're getting off the point.

el **desvío** SUSTANTIVO

[1] turning ◇ *Toma el primer desvío a la derecha.* Take the first turning on the right.

[2] detour ◇ *Hay un desvío por obras.* There's a detour due to construction.

el **detalle** SUSTANTIVO

detail ◇ *No recuerdo todos los detalles.* I don't remember all the details.

◆ **No pierde detalle.** He doesn't miss a trick.

◆ **Quiero comprarte un detalle.** I want to buy you a little something.

◆ **tener* un detalle con alguien** to be considerate towards somebody

◆ **¡Qué detalle!** How thoughtful!

◆ **vender al detalle** to sell retail

detectar VERBO

to detect

el/la **detective** SUSTANTIVO

detective ◇ *un detective privado* a private detective

detener* VERBO

[1] to stop ◇ *¡Detenlos!* Stop them!

[2] to arrest ◇ *Detuvieron a los ladrones.* They've arrested the thieves.

◆ **detenerse** to stop ◇ *Nos detuvimos en el semáforo.* We stopped at the lights.

◆ **¡Deténgase!** Stop!

el **detergente** SUSTANTIVO

detergent

deteriorar VERBO

to damage ◇ *La contaminación ha deteriorado el medioambiente.* Pollution ☞

has damaged the environment.
◆ **deteriorarse** to deteriorate ◇ *Su salud se ha deteriorado.* His health has deteriorated.

la **determinación** SUSTANTIVO
determination ◇ *Luchó contra su enfermedad con gran determinación.* He fought his illness with great determination.
◆ **tomar una determinación** to make a decision

determinado ADJETIVO
1 certain ◇ *En determinadas ocasiones es mejor callarse.* There are certain occasions when it's better to say nothing.
◆ **No quedamos a una hora determinada.** We haven't fixed a definite time.
2 particular ◇ *¿Buscas algún libro determinado?* Are you looking for a particular book?

determinar VERBO
1 to determine ◇ *Trataron de determinar la causa del accidente.* They tried to determine the cause of the accident.
2 to fix ◇ *determinar la fecha de una reunión* to fix the date of a meeting
3 to bring about ◇ *Aquello determinó la caída del gobierno.* That brought about the fall of the government.
4 to state ◇ *El reglamento determina que...* The rules state that...

detestar VERBO
to detest

detrás ADVERBIO
behind ◇ *El resto de los niños vienen detrás.* The rest of the children are coming on behind.
◆ **detrás de** behind ◇ *Se escondió detrás de un árbol.* He hid behind a tree.
◆ **uno detrás de otro** one after another
◆ **La critican por detrás.** They criticize her behind her back.

la **deuda** SUSTANTIVO
debt
◆ **contraer deudas** to get into debt
◆ **estar* en deuda con alguien** to be in somebody's debt

la **devolución** SUSTANTIVO (PL las **devoluciones**)
1 return (*de carta, libro*)
2 refund (*de dinero*)
◆ **No se admiten devoluciones.** Goods cannot be returned.

devolver* VERBO
1 to give back ◇ *¿Me puedes devolver la cinta que te presté?* Could you give me back the tape I lent you?
◆ **Me devolvieron mal el cambio.** They gave me the wrong change.
◆ **Me devolvieron el dinero.** They gave me a refund.
◆ **Te devolveré el favor cuando pueda.** I'll return the favor when I can.
2 to take back ◇ *Devolví la falda porque me quedaba chica.* I took the skirt back, as it was too small for me.
3 to throw up (*coloquial*) ◇ *Devolvió toda la cena.* He threw up his dinner.
◆ **devolverse (1)** (*a donde se estaba*) to go back
◆ **devolverse (2)** (*a donde se está*) to come back

devorar VERBO
to devour ◇ *Los leones devoraron una cebra.* The lions devoured a zebra.
◆ **devorar la comida** to wolf down food

di VERBO *ver* **dar, decir**

el **día** SUSTANTIVO
day ◇ *Pasaré dos días en la playa.* I'll spend a couple of days at the beach. ◇ *Duerme de día y trabaja de noche.* He sleeps during the day and works at night.
◆ **Es de día.** It's daylight.
◆ **el día de mañana** tomorrow
◆ **al día siguiente** the following day
◆ **todos los días** every day
◆ **un día de estos** one of these days
◆ **un día sí y otro no** every other day
◆ **¡Buenos días!** Good morning!
◆ **un día feriado** a public holiday
◆ **un día laborable** a working day
◆ **pan del día** fresh bread
◆ **el Día de los Muertos**

> ℹ ***El Día de los Muertos*** *is traditionally the day on which many Latin Americans honor their dead. In Mexico, a week-long festival begins on November 1st.*

el **diablo** SUSTANTIVO
devil ◇ *No creo en el diablo.* I don't believe in the devil. ◇ *Juanito es un verdadero diablo.* Juanito's a real little devil.
◆ **¿Cómo diablos lo hiciste?** How the devil did you do it? (*coloquial*)
◆ **¡Diablos!** Hell! (*coloquial*)
◆ **Hace un frío de mil diablos.** It's hellishly cold. (*coloquial*)

el **diagnóstico** SUSTANTIVO
diagnosis (PL diagnoses)

la **diagonal** ADJETIVO, SUSTANTIVO
diagonal
◆ **en diagonal** diagonally

el **dialecto** SUSTANTIVO
dialect

dialogar* VERBO
◆ **dialogar con alguien** to hold talks with somebody ◇ *El jefe dialogará con los sindicatos.* The boss will hold talks with the unions.

el **diálogo** SUSTANTIVO
conversation ◇ *Fue un diálogo interesante.* It was an interesting conversation.
◆ **No hay diálogo entre los dos bandos.** There's no dialogue between the two sides.

el **diamante** SUSTANTIVO
diamond

◆ **diamantes** (*en naipes*) diamonds

el **diámetro** SUSTANTIVO
diameter

la **diapositiva** SUSTANTIVO
slide

diario ADJETIVO
daily ◇ *la rutina diaria* the daily routine
◆ **la ropa de diario** everyday clothes
◆ **a diario** every day ◇ *Va al gimnasio a diario.* He goes to the gym every day.

el **diario** SUSTANTIVO
1 newspaper (*periódico*)
2 diary (PL diaries) (*libro diario*)

la **diarrea** SUSTANTIVO
diarrhea

el/la **dibujante** SUSTANTIVO
1 artist (*en general*)
2 cartoonist (*de dibujos animados*)
3 draftsman (PL draftsmen) (*de dibujo técnico*)

dibujar VERBO
to draw ◇ *No sé dibujar.* I can't draw. ◇ *Dibujó un árbol en el pizarrón.* He drew a tree on the chalkboard.

el **dibujo** SUSTANTIVO
drawing ◇ *el dibujo técnico* technical drawing
◆ **los dibujos animados** cartoons

el **diccionario** SUSTANTIVO
dictionary (PL dictionaries)

dicho (1) VERBO *ver* **decir**

dicho (2) ADJETIVO
◆ **en dichos países** in the countries mentioned above
◆ **mejor dicho** or rather ◇ *Vendré el lunes, mejor dicho, el martes.* I'll come on Monday, or rather, on Tuesday.
◆ **dicho y hecho** no sooner said than done

el **dicho** SUSTANTIVO
saying

dichoso ADJETIVO
1 happy (*feliz*)
2 lucky (*afortunado*)
◆ **¡Dichoso ruido!** Damned noise! (*coloquial*)

diciembre SUSTANTIVO MASC
En inglés, los meses se escriben con mayúscula.
December ◇ *en diciembre* in December ◇ *Llegaron el 6 de diciembre.* They arrived on December 6th.

diciendo VERBO *ver* **decir**

el **dictado** SUSTANTIVO
dictation ◇ *La maestra nos hizo un dictado.* The teacher gave us a dictation.

el **dictador**, la **dictadora** SUSTANTIVO
dictator

la **dictadura** SUSTANTIVO
dictatorship

dictar VERBO
to dictate ◇ *El maestro nos dictó un párrafo del libro.* The teacher dictated a paragraph of the book to us.
◆ **dictar sentencia** to pass sentence

diecinueve ADJETIVO, PRONOMBRE
nineteen ◇ *Tengo diecinueve años.* I'm nineteen.
◆ **el diecinueve de julio** July nineteenth
◆ **en el siglo diecinueve** in the nineteenth century

dieciocho ADJETIVO, PRONOMBRE
eighteen ◇ *Tengo dieciocho años.* I'm eighteen.
◆ **el dieciocho de abril** April eighteenth
◆ **en el siglo dieciocho** in the eighteenth century

dieciséis ADJETIVO, PRONOMBRE
sixteen ◇ *Tengo dieciséis años.* I'm sixteen.
◆ **el dieciséis de febrero** February sixteenth
◆ **en el siglo dieciséis** in the sixteenth century

diecisiete ADJETIVO, PRONOMBRE
seventeen ◇ *Tengo diecisiete años.* I'm seventeen.
◆ **el diecisiete de enero** January seventeenth
◆ **en el siglo diecisiete** in the seventeenth century

el **diente** SUSTANTIVO
tooth (PL teeth) (*de persona, sierra*) ◇ *lavarse los dientes* to clean one's teeth
◆ **un diente de leche** a milk tooth
◆ **un diente de ajo** a clove of garlic

la **dieta** SUSTANTIVO
diet ◇ *una dieta vegetariana* a vegetarian diet
◆ **estar* a dieta** to be on a diet
◆ **ponerse* a dieta** to go on a diet
◆ **dietas** (*de viaje, hotel*) expenses

diez ADJETIVO, PRONOMBRE
ten ◇ *Tengo diez años.* I'm ten.
◆ **Son las diez.** It's ten o'clock.
◆ **el diez de agosto** August tenth
◆ **el siglo diez** the tenth century

la **diferencia** SUSTANTIVO
difference
◆ **a diferencia de** unlike ◇ *A diferencia de su hermana, a ella le encanta viajar.* Unlike her sister, she loves traveling.

diferenciar VERBO
◆ **¿En qué se diferencian?** What's the difference between them?
◆ **Sólo se diferencian en el tamaño.** The only difference between them is their size.
◆ **Se diferencia de los demás por su bondad.** His kindness sets him apart from the rest.
◆ **No diferencia el color rojo del verde.** He can't tell the difference between red and green.

diferente ADJETIVO
different

difícil ADJETIVO
difficult ◇ *Es un problema difícil de entender.* It's a difficult problem to understand. ◇ *Resulta difícil concentrarse.* It's difficult to concentrate. ◇ *Es un hombre difícil.* He's a difficult man.

D

la **dificultad** SUSTANTIVO
difficulty (PL difficulties) ◇ *con dificultad* with difficulty
◆ **tener* dificultades para hacer algo** to have difficulty doing something
◆ **Nos pusieron muchas dificultades para obtener el visado.** They made it very difficult for us to get a visa.

dificultar VERBO
to make...difficult ◇ *La niebla dificultaba la visibilidad.* The fog made visibility difficult.

digerir* VERBO
to digest

la **digestión** SUSTANTIVO
digestion
◆ **hacer* la digestión** to digest

digestivo ADJETIVO
digestive

digital ADJETIVO
digital ◇ *un reloj digital* a digital watch
◆ **una huella digital** a fingerprint

la **dignidad** SUSTANTIVO
dignity

digno ADJETIVO
1 decent (*sueldo, vivienda*)
2 honorable (*comportamiento*)
◆ **digno de mención** worth mentioning
◆ **digno de verse** worth seeing

digo VERBO *ver* **decir**

dije VERBO *ver* **decir**

diluir* VERBO
to dilute

diluviar VERBO
◆ **Está diluviando.** It's pouring rain.

el **diluvio** SUSTANTIVO
downpour ◇ *Cayó un diluvio.* There was a downpour.
◆ **un diluvio de cartas** a flood of letters

la **dimensión** SUSTANTIVO (PL las **dimensiones**)
dimension ◇ *en tres dimensiones* in three dimensions
◆ **un cine de grandes dimensiones** a huge movie theater

el **diminutivo** SUSTANTIVO
diminutive

diminuto ADJETIVO
tiny

la **dimisión** SUSTANTIVO (PL las **dimisiones**)
resignation ◇ *presentar la dimisión* to hand in one's resignation

dimitir VERBO
to resign ◇ *Ha dimitido de su cargo.* He has resigned from his post.

Dinamarca SUSTANTIVO FEM
Denmark

dinámico ADJETIVO
dynamic

el **dinero** SUSTANTIVO
money ◇ *No tengo más dinero.* I don't have any more money.
◆ **una familia de dinero** a wealthy family
◆ **andar* mal de dinero** to be short of money
◆ **dinero suelto** loose change

el **dinosaurio** SUSTANTIVO
dinosaur

dio VERBO *ver* **dar**

Dios SUSTANTIVO MASC
God ◇ *¡Gracias a Dios!* Thank God! ◇ *¡Dios mío!* My God!
◆ **¡Por Dios!** For God's sake!
◆ **¡Si Dios quiere!** God willing!

el **dios** SUSTANTIVO (PL los **dioses**)
god

la **diosa** SUSTANTIVO
goddess (PL goddesses)

el **diploma** SUSTANTIVO
diploma

la **diplomacia** SUSTANTIVO
diplomacy

diplomático ADJETIVO
diplomatic

el **diplomático**, la **diplomática** SUSTANTIVO
diplomat

el **diptongo** SUSTANTIVO
diphthong

el **diputado**, la **diputada** SUSTANTIVO
representative

dirá VERBO *ver* **decir**

la **dirección** SUSTANTIVO (PL las **direcciones**)
1 direction ◇ *Íbamos en dirección equivocada.* We were going in the wrong direction.
◆ **Tienes que ir en esta dirección.** You have to go this way.
◆ **una calle de dirección única** a one-way street
◆ **"dirección prohibida"** "no entry"
◆ **"todas direcciones"** "all routes"
2 address (PL addresses) ◇ *Apúntame tu dirección aquí.* Can you write your address down here for me?
3 management ◇ *la dirección de la empresa* the management of the company ◇ *Ha tomado la dirección del proyecto.* He's taken over the management of the project.

la **direccional** SUSTANTIVO *Mexico*
turn signal

directo ADJETIVO
1 direct ◇ *Hay un tren directo a Monterrey.* There's a direct train to Monterrey. ◇ *una pregunta directa* a direct question
2 straight ◇ *Se fue directa a casa.* She went straight home.
◆ **transmitir en directo** to broadcast live

el **director**, la **directora** SUSTANTIVO
1 manager (*de empresa*)
2 principal (*de colegio*)
3 director (*de cine*)
4 conductor (*de orquesta*)
5 editor (*de periódico*)

el **directorio** SUSTANTIVO
1 directory (PL directories) (*también informática*)
2 phone book (*de teléfono*)

el/la **dirigente** SUSTANTIVO
1 leader (*de partido político*)
2 manager (*de empresa*)

dirigir* VERBO
1 to manage ◇ *Dirige la empresa desde hace diez años.* He has been managing the company for ten years.
2 to lead ◇ *Dirigirá la expedición.* He'll be leading the expedition.
3 to aim at ◇ *Este anuncio va dirigido a los niños.* This advertisement is aimed at children.
- **no dirigir la palabra a alguien** not to speak to somebody

4 to direct (*película*)
5 to conduct (*orquesta*)
- **dirigirse a (1)** to address ◇ *El presidente se dirigió a la nación.* The President addressed the nation.
- **dirigirse a (2)** to write to ◇ *Me dirijo a ustedes para pedirles información sobre sus cursos de idiomas.* I am writing to you to ask you for information about language courses.
- **dirigirse a (3)** to make one's way to ◇ *Se dirigió a la terminal del aeropuerto.* He made his way to the airport terminal.

discapacitado ADJETIVO
disabled

discar* VERBO
to dial

la **disciplina** SUSTANTIVO
discipline

el **disco** SUSTANTIVO
1 record (*de música*)
2 light (*de semáforo*)
3 discus (*en deporte*)
- **un disco compacto** a compact disc
- **el disco duro** the hard disk

la **discoteca** SUSTANTIVO
discotheque

la **discreción** SUSTANTIVO
discretion
- **Ha actuado con mucha discreción.** He was very discreet.

discreto ADJETIVO
discreet ◇ *No dirá nada porque es muy discreto.* He won't say anything because he's very discreet.
- **un color discreto** a sober color
- **un sueldo discreto** a modest salary

la **discriminación** SUSTANTIVO
- **la discriminación racial** racial discrimination

la **disculpa** SUSTANTIVO
- **pedir* disculpas a alguien por algo** to apologize to somebody for something

disculpar VERBO
to excuse ◇ *Disculpa ¿me dejas pasar?* Excuse me, can I go past?
- **disculparse** to apologize ◇ *Se disculpó por llegar tarde.* He apologized for being late.

el **discurso** SUSTANTIVO
speech (PL speeches) ◇ *pronunciar un discurso* to make a speech

la **discusión** SUSTANTIVO (PL las **discusiones**)
discussion ◇ *El tema fue sometido a discusión.* The subject came up for discussion.
- **tener* una discusión con alguien** to have an argument with somebody

discutir VERBO
1 to quarrel ◇ *Siempre discuten por dinero.* They're always quarreling about money. ◇ *Siempre estaba discutiendo con mi hermana.* He was always quarreling with my sister.
- **Discutió con su madre.** He had an argument with his mother.

2 to discuss ◇ *Tenemos que discutir el nuevo proyecto.* We have to discuss the new project.

diseñar VERBO
to design

el **diseño** SUSTANTIVO
1 design (*de modas, con ordenadores*)
2 drawing (*arte*)

el **disfraz** SUSTANTIVO (PL los **disfraces**)
1 disguise ◇ *Llevaba un disfraz para que no lo reconocieran.* He wore a disguise so as not to be recognized.
2 costume ◇ *un disfraz de vaquero* a cowboy outfit
- **una fiesta de disfraces** a fancy-dress party

disfrazarse* VERBO
- **disfrazarse de (1)** to disguise oneself as ◇ *Se disfrazó de mujer para escapar.* He disguised himself as a woman in order to escape.
- **disfrazarse de (2)** to dress up as ◇ *Se disfrazó de hada.* She dressed up as a fairy.

disfrutar VERBO
to enjoy oneself ◇ *Disfruté mucho en la fiesta.* I really enjoyed myself at the party.
- **Disfruto leyendo.** I enjoy reading.
- **disfrutar de buena salud** to enjoy good health

disgustar VERBO
to upset ◇ *Me disgustó su tono.* His tone upset me.
- **disgustarse** to get upset ◇ *Me disgusté cuando descubrí que mentía.* I got upset when I found out he was lying.
- **disgustarse con alguien** to fall out with somebody

el **disgusto** SUSTANTIVO
- **dar* un disgusto a alguien** to upset somebody
- **llevarse un disgusto** to get upset
- **hacer* algo a disgusto** to do something unwillingly
- **estar* a disgusto** to be ill at ease

disimular VERBO
to hide ◇ *Intentó disimular su enfado.* He tried to hide his annoyance.
◆ **No disimules, sé que has sido tú.** Don't bother pretending; I know it was you.

la **disminución** SUSTANTIVO (PL las **disminuciones**)
fall ◇ *una disminución del número de robos* a fall in the number of thefts

el **disminuido**, la **disminuida** SUSTANTIVO
◆ **un disminuido mental** a mentally handicapped person
◆ **un disminuido físico** a physically handicapped person

disminuir* VERBO
to fall ◇ *Ha disminuido el número de accidentes.* The number of accidents has fallen.

disolver* VERBO
1 to dissolve (*azúcar*)
2 to break up (*manifestación*)
◆ **disolverse** (*manifestantes, reunión*) to break up

disparar VERBO
to shoot ◇ *Le dispararon en la pierna.* They shot him in the leg.
◆ **disparar a alguien** to shoot at somebody
◆ **Disparó dos tiros.** He fired two shots.
◆ **dispararse (1)** (*pistola*) to go off
◆ **dispararse (2)** (*precios*) to shoot up

el **disparate** SUSTANTIVO
silly thing ◇ *He hecho muchos disparates en mi vida.* I've done a lot of silly things in my life.
◆ **decir* disparates** to talk nonsense
◆ **¡Qué disparate!** How absurd!

el **disparo** SUSTANTIVO
shot (*tiro*)

disponer* VERBO
to arrange ◇ *Dispusieron las sillas en un círculo.* They arranged the chairs in a circle.
◆ **disponer de** to have ◇ *Disponen de diez minutos para leer las preguntas.* You have ten minutes to read the questions.
◆ **disponerse a hacer algo** to get ready to do something

disponible ADJETIVO
available ◇ *El director no estará disponible hasta las cuatro.* The manager won't be available until four o'clock.

dispuesto ADJETIVO
1 prepared ◇ *estar dispuesto a hacer algo* to be prepared to do something
2 ready ◇ *Todo está dispuesto para la fiesta.* Everything's ready for the party.

el **disquete** SUSTANTIVO
diskette

la **distancia** SUSTANTIVO
distance
◆ **mantenerse* a distancia** to keep at a distance
◆ **¿Qué distancia hay entre Chihauhau y Guadalajara?** How far is Chihauhau from Guadalajara?
◆ **¿A qué distancia está la estación?** How far's the station?
◆ **a 20 millas de distancia** 20 miles away

la **distinción** SUSTANTIVO (PL las **distinciones**)
distinction ◇ *hacer una distinción entre...* to make a distinction between...
◆ **No hace distinciones entre sus alumnos.** He treats all his pupils the same.

distinguido ADJETIVO
distinguished

distinguir* VERBO
1 to distinguish ◇ *Resulta difícil distinguir el macho de la hembra.* It's difficult to distinguish the male from the female.
◆ **No distingue entre el rojo y el verde.** He can't tell the difference between red and green.
◆ **No sé distinguir entre un carro u otro.** I can't tell one car from another.
◆ **Se parecen tanto que no los distingo.** They're so alike that I can't tell them apart.
2 to make...out ◇ *No pude distinguirla entre tanta gente.* I couldn't make her out among so many people.
◆ **distinguirse** to stand out ◇ *No le gusta distinguirse de los demás.* He doesn't like to stand out.

distinto ADJETIVO
different ◇ *Carlos es distinto a los demás.* Carlos is different from other people.
◆ **distintos** several ◇ *distintas clases de carros* several types of car

la **distracción** SUSTANTIVO (PL las **distracciones**)
pastime ◇ *Coser es mi distracción favorita.* My favorite pastime is sewing.
◆ **En el pueblo hay pocas distracciones.** There isn't much to do in the village.

distraer* VERBO
1 to keep...entertained ◇ *Les pondré un video para distraerlos.* I'll put a video on to keep them entertained.
2 to distract ◇ *No me distraigas, que tengo trabajo.* Don't distract me. I have work to do.
◆ **Me distrae mucho escuchar música.** I really enjoy listening to music.
◆ **Me distraje un momento y me pasé de parada.** I let my mind wander for a minute and missed my stop.

distraído ADJETIVO
absent-minded ◇ *Mi padre es muy distraído.* My father is very absent-minded.
◆ **Perdona, estaba distraído.** Sorry, I wasn't concentrating.

la **distribución** SUSTANTIVO (PL las **distribuciones**)
1 layout ◇ *la distribución de las habitaciones* the layout of the rooms

[2] distribution ◇ *la distribución de la riqueza* the distribution of wealth

distribuir* VERBO

[1] to distribute ◇ *Esta empresa distribuye nuestros productos en el extranjero.* This company distributes our products abroad. [2] to hand out ◇ *La profesora distribuyó las hojas del examen.* The teacher handed out the exam papers.

distribuyendo VERBO *ver* **distribuir**

el **distrito** SUSTANTIVO

district ◇ *un distrito postal* a postal district

◆ **un distrito electoral** a constituency

◆ **Distrito Federal** *Mexico* Federal District

> ℹ ***Distrito Federal*** *covers Mexico City and its suburbs, and is the seat of the federal government of Mexico.*

la **diversión** SUSTANTIVO (PL las **diversiones**)

entertainment

No confundir ***diversión*** *con* ***diversion***.

diverso ADJETIVO

different ◇ *Colombia y Chile dieron explicaciones muy diversas del incidente.* Colombia and Chile gave very different explanations for the incident.

◆ **diversos** various ◇ *diversos libros* various books

divertido ADJETIVO

[1] funny (*película, cómic*)
[2] enjoyable (*fiesta*)

◆ **Fue muy divertido.** It was great fun.

divertir* VERBO

to entertain ◇ *Nos divirtió con sus anécdotas.* He entertained us with his stories.

◆ **divertirse** to have a good time

dividir VERBO

to divide ◇ *El libro está dividido en dos partes.* The book is divided into two parts. ◇ *Dividió sus tierras entre sus tres hijas.* He divided his land among his three daughters. ◇ *Divide cuatro entre dos.* Divide four by two.

◆ **dividirse (1)** to divide ◇ *Nos dividimos el trabajo entre los tres.* We divided the work between the three of us.

◆ **dividirse (2)** to share ◇ *Se dividieron el dinero de la lotería.* They shared the lottery money.

divierto VERBO *ver* **divertir**

divino ADJETIVO

divine

la **división** SUSTANTIVO (PL las **divisiones**)

division ◇ *en primera división* in the first division ◇ *Ya sabe hacer divisiones.* He already knows how to do division.

divorciarse VERBO

to get divorced

◆ **Se divorció de su mujer.** He divorced his wife.

el **divorcio** SUSTANTIVO

divorce

divulgar* VERBO

to spread ◇ *divulgar rumores* to spread rumors

el **DNI** ABREVIATURA (= *Documento Nacional de Identidad*)

ID card

D

doblar VERBO

[1] to double ◇ *Le doblaron el sueldo.* They've doubled his salary. [2] to fold ◇ *Dobla los pañuelos y guárdalos.* Fold the handkerchiefs and put them away. [3] to turn ◇ *Cuando llegues al cruce, dobla a la derecha.* When you reach the junction, turn right. [4] to dub ◇ *Doblan todas las películas extranjeras.* All foreign movies are dubbed. [5] to toll ◇ *Las campanas de la iglesia doblan cuando hay un funeral.* The church bells toll when there's a funeral.

doble ADJETIVO

double ◇ *una frase con doble sentido* an expression with a double meaning ◇ *una habitación doble* a double room

el **doble** SUSTANTIVO

twice as much ◇ *Su sueldo es el doble del mío.* His salary is twice as much as mine. ◇ *Comes el doble que yo.* You eat twice as much as I do.

◆ **Trabaja el doble que tú.** He works twice as hard as you do.

◆ **jugar* un partido de dobles** to play doubles

doce ADJETIVO, PRONOMBRE

twelve ◇ *Tengo doce años.* I'm twelve.

◆ **Son las doce.** It's twelve o'clock.

◆ **el doce de mayo** May twelfth

◆ **el siglo doce** the twelfth century

la **docena** SUSTANTIVO

dozen

el **doctor,** la **doctora** SUSTANTIVO

doctor

la **doctrina** SUSTANTIVO

doctrine

el **documental** SUSTANTIVO

documentary (PL documentaries)

el **documento** SUSTANTIVO

document ◇ *un documento oficial* an official document

◆ **un documento adjunto** an attachment

el **dólar** SUSTANTIVO

dollar

doler* VERBO

to hurt ◇ *Me duele el brazo.* My arm hurts. ◇ *Esta inyección no duele.* This injection won't hurt. ◇ *Me dolió que me mintiera.* I was hurt that he lied to me.

◆ **Me duele la cabeza.** I have a headache.

◆ **Me duele el pecho.** I have a pain in my chest.

◆ **Me duele la garganta.** I have a sore throat.

el **dolor** SUSTANTIVO (PL los **dolores**)
pain ◇ *Gritó de dolor.* He cried out in pain.
◆ **Tengo dolor de cabeza.** I have a headache.
◆ **Tengo dolor de estómago.** I have a stomachache.
◆ **Tengo dolor de muelas.** I have a toothache.
◆ **Tengo dolor de oídos.** I have an earache.
◆ **Tengo dolor de garganta.** I have a sore throat.

doméstico ADJETIVO
domestic ◇ *para uso doméstico* for domestic use
◆ **las tareas domésticas** the housework SING
◆ **un animal doméstico** a pet

el **domicilio** SUSTANTIVO
residence ◇ *su domicilio particular* their private residence
◆ **servicio a domicilio** home delivery

dominar VERBO
1 to dominate ◇ *El padre dominaba totalmente a los hijos.* The father totally dominated his children.
◆ **tener* dominado a alguien** to have somebody at one's mercy
2 to control ◇ *No pudo dominar su mal genio.* He couldn't control his temper.
3 to be fluent in ◇ *Mi hermana domina el inglés.* My sister is fluent in English.
4 to bring under control ◇ *Los bomberos tardaron en dominar el incendio.* The fire department took a long time to bring the fire under control.
◆ **dominarse** to control oneself

el **domingo** SUSTANTIVO
En inglés, los días de la semana se escriben con mayúscula.
Sunday ◇ *La vi el domingo.* I saw her on Sunday. ◇ *todos los domingos* every Sunday ◇ *el domingo pasado* last Sunday ◇ *el domingo que viene* next Sunday ◇ *Jugamos los domingos.* We play on Sundays.

el **dominicano**, la **dominicana** ADJETIVO, SUSTANTIVO
Dominican

el **dominio** SUSTANTIVO
1 command ◇ *Tiene un gran dominio del inglés.* He has a good command of English.
2 rule ◇ *Francia estuvo bajo el dominio romano.* France was under Roman rule.
3 control ◇ *Ejerció un dominio absoluto sobre sus seguidores.* He exercised absolute control over his followers.
◆ **dominio de sí mismo** self-control
◆ **ser* del dominio público** to be public knowledge

el **dominó** SUSTANTIVO
1 domino (*pieza*)
2 dominoes SING (*juego*) ◇ *jugar* al dominó* to play dominoes

el **don** SUSTANTIVO
gift ◇ *Tiene un don para la música.* He has a gift for music.
◆ **tener* don de gentes** to be good with people
◆ **don Juan Gómez** Mr. Juan Gómez

> ℹ *Cuando* ***don*** *va seguido sólo del nombre de pila, se traduce por* ***Mr.*** *más el apellido.*

◆ **Es un don nadie.** He's a nobody.

la **dona** SUSTANTIVO Mexico
doughnut

el/la **donante** SUSTANTIVO
donor ◇ *un donante de órganos* an organ donor

el **donativo** SUSTANTIVO
donation

donde ADVERBIO
where ◇ *La nota está donde la dejaste.* The note is where you left it.

dónde ADVERBIO
where ◇ *¿Dónde vas?* Where are you going? ◇ *Le pregunté dónde estaba la catedral.* I asked him where the cathedral was. ◇ *¿Sabes dónde está?* Do you know where he is?
◆ **¿De dónde eres?** Where are you from?
◆ **¿Por dónde se va al cine?** How do you get to the movie theater?

la **doña** SUSTANTIVO
◆ **doña Marta García** Mrs. Marta García

> ℹ *Cuando* ***doña*** *va seguido sólo del nombre de pila, se traduce por* ***Mrs.*** *más el apellido.*

dorado ADJETIVO
golden

dormir* VERBO
to sleep ◇ *Antonio durmió 10 horas.* Antonio slept for 10 hours.
◆ **Se me durmió el brazo.** My arm has gone to sleep.
◆ **dormir la siesta** to have a nap
◆ **dormir como un tronco** to sleep like a log
◆ **estar medio dormido** to be half asleep
◆ **dormirse** to fall asleep

el **dormitorio** SUSTANTIVO
1 bedroom (*de una casa*)
2 dormitory (PL dormitories) (*de un internado*)

el **dorso** SUSTANTIVO
back ◇ *Se apuntó el teléfono en el dorso de la mano.* He wrote the telephone number on the back of his hand.
◆ **"véase al dorso"** "see over"

dos ADJETIVO, PRONOMBRE
1 two ◇ *¿Tienes los dos libros que te dejé?* Do you have the two books I lent you? ◇ *Tiene dos años.* He's two.
◆ **Son las dos.** It's two o'clock.
◆ **de dos en dos** in twos

- **el dos de enero** January second
- **cada dos por tres** every five minutes

[2] both (*ambos*) ◇ *Al final vinieron los dos.* In the end they both came. ◇ *Nos suspendieron a los dos.* We have both been suspended. ◇ *Mis dos hijos emigraron.* Both of my sons have emigrated. ◇ *Los invitamos a los dos.* We've invited both of them.

doscientos ADJETIVO, PRONOMBRE (FEM **doscientas**)
two hundred ◇ *dos cientos cincuenta* two hundred and fifty

la **dosis** SUSTANTIVO (PL las **dosis**)
dose

doy VERBO *ver* **dar**

el **dragón** SUSTANTIVO (PL los **dragones**)
dragon

el **drama** SUSTANTIVO
drama

dramático ADJETIVO
dramatic

la **droga** SUSTANTIVO
drug ◇ *las drogas blandas* soft drugs ◇ *las drogas duras* hard drugs ◇ *el problema de la droga* the drug problem

el **drogadicto,** la **drogadicta** SUSTANTIVO
drug addict

drogar* VERBO
to drug
- **drogarse** to take drugs

la **droguería** SUSTANTIVO

> ℹ *A store selling cleaning materials, paint and toiletries.*

la **ducha** SUSTANTIVO
shower ◇ *darse* una ducha* to have a shower

ducharse VERBO
to have a shower

la **duda** SUSTANTIVO
doubt
- **Tengo mis dudas.** I have my doubts.
- **sin duda** no doubt
- **sin duda alguna** without a doubt
- **no cabe duda** there's no doubt about it
- **Tengo una duda.** I have a query.
- **poner* algo en duda** to call something into question
- **¿Alguna duda?** Any questions?

dudar VERBO
to doubt ◇ *Lo dudo.* I doubt it. ◇ *Dudo que sea cierto.* I doubt if it's true.
- **Dudó si comprarlo o no.** He wasn't sure whether to buy it or not.

dudoso ADJETIVO
[1] doubtful ◇ *Es dudoso que vengan.* It's doubtful whether they'll come.
[2] dubious ◇ *un chiste de dudoso gusto* a joke in dubious taste

duelo VERBO *ver* **doler**

el **dueño,** la **dueña** SUSTANTIVO
owner
- **ser* dueño de sí mismo** to have self-control

duermo VERBO *ver* **dormir**

dulce ADJETIVO
[1] sweet (*pastel*)
[2] gentle (*persona*)

el **dulce** SUSTANTIVO
candy

el **dúo** SUSTANTIVO
duet
- **cantar a dúo** to sing a duet

la **duración** SUSTANTIVO
length ◇ *Depende de la duración de la película.* It depends on the length of the movie.
- **una pila de larga duración** a long-life battery

duradero ADJETIVO
[1] lasting (*fe, paz*)
[2] durable (*material*)

durante ADVERBIO
during ◇ *Laura tuvo que trabajar durante las vacaciones.* Laura had to work during the vacation.
- **durante toda la noche** all night long
- **Habló durante una hora.** He spoke for an hour.

durar VERBO
to last ◇ *La película duraba dos horas.* The movie lasted two hours. ◇ *Sólo duró dos meses como director.* He only lasted two months as manager. ◇ *Todavía le dura el enfado.* He's still angry.

el **durazno** SUSTANTIVO
peach (PL peaches)

la **dureza** SUSTANTIVO
[1] hardness ◇ *la dureza del acero* the hardness of steel
[2] harshness ◇ *la dureza de sus palabras* the harshness of his words
[3] callus (PL calluses) ◇ *Tiene una dureza en la planta del pie.* He has a callus on the sole of his foot.

durmiendo VERBO *ver* **dormir**

duro (1) ADJETIVO
[1] hard ◇ *Los diamantes son muy duros.* Diamonds are very hard.
[2] tough ◇ *Esta carne está dura.* This meat is tough.
[3] harsh ◇ *El clima es muy duro.* The climate is very harsh.
- **a duras penas** with great difficulty
- **ser* duro con alguien** to be hard on somebody
- **ser* duro de oído** to be hard of hearing

duro (2) ADVERBIO
hard ◇ *trabajar duro* to work hard

el **DVD** ABREVIATURA (= *Disco de Video Digital*)
DVD

D

E

e CONJUNCIÓN
***e** is used instead of **y** in front of words beginning with "i". and "hi", but not "hie".*
and ◇ *Pablo e Inés.* Pablo and Inés.

echar VERBO
1 to throw (*lanzar*)
◆ **Eché la carta al buzón.** I mailed the letter.
2 to put (*poner*) ◇ *Tengo que echar gasolina.* I need to put gas in the car.
◆ **¿Te echo más whisky?** Shall I pour you some more whiskey?
3 to throw out (*expulsar*) ◇ *Me echó de su casa.* He threw me out of the house.
4 to expel ◇ *Lo echaron del colegio.* He's been expelled from school.
◆ **La echaron del trabajo.** They fired her.
◆ **La chimenea echa humo.** Smoke is coming out of the chimney.
◆ **echar de menos a alguien** to miss somebody ◇ *Echo de menos a mi familia.* I miss my family.
◆ **¿Cuántos años me echas?** How old do you think I am?
◆ **echarse (1)** (*tumbarse*) to lie down ◇ *Me eché en el sofá y me quedé dormido.* I lay down on the sofa and fell asleep.
◆ **echarse (2)** (*lanzarse*) to jump ◇ *Los niños se echaron al agua.* The children jumped into the water.

el **eco** SUSTANTIVO
echo (PL echoes)

la **ecología** SUSTANTIVO
ecology

ecológico ADJETIVO
ecological ◇ *un desastre ecológico* an ecological disaster
◆ **un producto ecológico** an environmentally friendly product

ecologista ADJETIVO
environmental ◇ *un grupo ecologista* an environmental group

el/la **ecologista** SUSTANTIVO
environmentalist

la **economía** SUSTANTIVO
1 economy (PL economies) ◇ *Un país de economía capitalista.* A country with a capitalist economy.
2 economics SING ◇ *Quiero estudiar economía.* I want to study economics.

económico ADJETIVO
1 economic (*financiero*) ◇ *una profunda crisis económica* a deep economic crisis
2 economical (*de poco gasto*) ◇ *un motor económico* an economical engine
3 inexpensive ◇ *Comimos en un restaurante económico.* We ate in an inexpensive restaurant.

el/la **economista** SUSTANTIVO
economist

economizar* VERBO
to economize ◇ *Economiza en la comida para comprarse joyas.* She economizes on food to buy herself jewelry.

Ecuador SUSTANTIVO MASC
Ecuador

el **ecuatoriano,** la **ecuatoriana** ADJETIVO, SUSTANTIVO
Ecuadorean

la **edad** SUSTANTIVO
age ◇ *Tenemos la misma edad.* We're the same age.
◆ **¿Qué edad tienen?** How old are they?
◆ **No tiene edad para votar.** She isn't old enough to vote.
◆ **Está en la edad del pavo.** She's at that difficult age.
◆ **Está en la edad de la punzada.** *Mexico* She's at that difficult age.

la **edición** SUSTANTIVO (PL las **ediciones**)
edition ◇ *una edición de bolsillo* a pocket edition

edificar* VERBO
to build ◇ *Están edificando un centro deportivo.* They're building a sports center.

el **edificio** SUSTANTIVO
building

Edimburgo SUSTANTIVO MASC
Edinburgh

editar VERBO
to publish (*publicar*)

el **editor,** la **editora** SUSTANTIVO
publisher

la **editorial** SUSTANTIVO
publisher

el **edredón** SUSTANTIVO (PL los **edredones**)
1 eiderdown (*cubrecama*)
2 comforter (*nórdico*)

la **educación** SUSTANTIVO
1 education ◇ *Han aumentado el presupuesto de educación.* They've increased the education budget.
◆ **educación física** PE
2 upbringing ◇ *Rosa recibió una educación muy estricta.* Rosa had a very strict upbringing.
◆ **Señalar es de mala educación.** It's rude to point.
◆ **Se lo pedí con educación.** I asked her politely.
◆ **Es una falta de educación hablar con la boca llena.** It's bad manners to speak with your mouth full.

educado ADJETIVO
polite
◆ **Me contestó de forma educada.** He answered me politely.
◆ **Es un chico bien educado.** He's a

well-mannered boy.

educar* VERBO
[1] to educate ◇ *Se educó en un colegio alemán.* He was educated in a German school.
[2] to bring up ◇ *Educaron a sus hijos de una manera muy estricta.* They brought their children up very strictly.

educativo ADJETIVO
educational

EE.UU. ABREVIATURA (= *Estados Unidos*)
USA

efectivamente ADVERBIO
◆ **Efectivamente, estaba donde tú decías.** You were right; he was where you said.
◆ **Entonces, ¿Es usted su padre? – Efectivamente.** So, are you his father? – That's right.

efectivo ADJETIVO
effective (*eficaz*) ◇ *un medicamento muy efectivo* a very effective medicine
◆ **pagar* en efectivo** to pay in cash

el **efecto** SUSTANTIVO
effect
◆ **efectos especiales** special effects
◆ **hacer* efecto** to take effect ◇ *La aspirina enseguida me hizo efecto.* The aspirin took effect on me immediately.
◆ **Devolvió la pelota con efecto.** He put some spin on the ball.

efectuar* VERBO
to carry out (*operación, maniobra*)

eficaz ADJETIVO
[1] effective ◇ *un remedio eficaz* an effective remedy
[2] efficient (*persona*) ◇ *un funcionario eficaz* an efficient civil servant

eficiente ADJETIVO
efficient

el **egipcio,** la **egipcia** ADJETIVO, SUSTANTIVO
Egyptian

Egipto SUSTANTIVO MASC
Egypt

el **egoísmo** SUSTANTIVO
selfishness

egoísta ADJETIVO
selfish

el/la **egoísta** SUSTANTIVO
◆ **María es una egoísta.** Maria is very selfish.

Eire SUSTANTIVO MASC
Eire

el **eje** SUSTANTIVO
[1] axle (*de ruedas*)
[2] axis (*de la Tierra*)

la **ejecución** SUSTANTIVO (PL las **ejecuciones**)
execution (*de condenado*)

ejecutar VERBO
[1] to carry out ◇ *Ejecutaron el proyecto según lo previsto.* They carried out the project according to plan.
[2] to execute ◇ *La ejecutaron al amanecer.* They executed her at dawn.

el **ejecutivo,** la **ejecutiva** SUSTANTIVO
executive

el **ejemplar** SUSTANTIVO
copy (PL copies) (*de libro, periódico*)

el **ejemplo** SUSTANTIVO
example ◇ *¿Puedes darme un ejemplo?* Can you give me an example?
◆ **por ejemplo** for example
◆ **Debes dar ejemplo a tu hermano pequeño.** You must set an example for your younger brother.

ejercer* VERBO
◆ **Ejerce de abogado.** He's a practicing lawyer.
◆ **Ejerce mucha influencia sobre sus hermanos.** He has a lot of influence on his brothers.

el **ejercicio** SUSTANTIVO
exercise ◇ *La maestra nos puso varios ejercicios.* The teacher gave us several exercises to do.
◆ **hacer* ejercicio** to exercise

el **ejército** SUSTANTIVO
army (PL armies)

el **ejote** SUSTANTIVO Mexico
string bean

el ARTÍCULO (FEM SING **la**, PL **los**)
the ◇ *Perdí el tren.* I missed the train.
◆ **el del sombrero rojo** the one with the red hat
◆ **Yo fui el que lo encontró.** I was the one who found it.

El artículo se traduce por el posesivo en inglés cuando se refiere a una parte del cuerpo, una prenda que se lleva puesta o algo que nos pertenece.

◇ *Ayer me lavé la cabeza.* I washed my hair yesterday. ◇ *Me puse el abrigo.* I put my coat on. ◇ *Tiene un carro bonito, pero prefiero el de Juan.* He has a nice car, but I prefer Juan's.

El artículo a veces no se traduce en inglés; por ejemplo cuando se refiere a algo en general, con algunas expresiones de tiempo, o con apellidos.

◇ *No me gusta el pescado.* I don't like fish. ◇ *Vendrá el lunes que viene.* He's coming next Monday. ◇ *Llamó el Sr. Sendra.* Mr. Sendra called.

él PRONOMBRE
[1] he (*como sujeto*) ◇ *Me lo dijo él.* He told me.
[2] him (*con preposición, en comparaciones*) ◇ *Se lo di a él.* I gave it to him. ◇ *Su mujer es más alta que él.* His wife is taller than him.
◆ **él mismo** himself ◇ *No lo sabe ni él mismo.* He doesn't even know himself.
◆ **de él** his ◇ *El carro es de él.* The car is his.

elaborar VERBO
to produce (*producto*)

elástico ADJETIVO
◆ **un tejido elástico** a stretchy material
◆ **una goma elástica** a rubber band

E

la **elección** SUSTANTIVO (PL las **elecciones**)
[1] election (*votación*) ◇ *Han convocado elecciones generales.* General elections have been called.
[2] choice (*selección*) ◇ *Ésa es una buena elección.* That's a good choice. ◇ *No tuve elección.* I had no choice.

electoral ADJETIVO
◆ **la campaña electoral** the election campaign

la **electricidad** SUSTANTIVO
electricity

el/la **electricista** SUSTANTIVO
electrician ◇ *Mi primo es electricista.* My cousin is an electrician.

eléctrico ADJETIVO
[1] electric ◇ *una guitarra eléctrica* an electric guitar
[2] electrical ◇ *a causa de un falla eléctrico* due to an electrical fault
***electric** se usa para referirnos a objetos que funcionan con electricidad, mientras que **electrical** es menos frecuente y se emplea en términos de física y mecánica.*

el **electrodoméstico** SUSTANTIVO
domestic appliance

la **electrónica** SUSTANTIVO
electronics SING

electrónico ADJETIVO
electronic
◆ **el correo electrónico** email

el **elefante** SUSTANTIVO
elephant

elegante ADJETIVO
smart

elegir* VERBO
[1] to choose ◇ *No sabía qué color elegir.* I didn't know what color to choose.
◆ **Te dan a elegir entre dos modelos.** You're given a choice of two models.
[2] to elect ◇ *Me eligieron delegado de curso.* I was elected class representative.

el **elemento** SUSTANTIVO
element

elevado ADJETIVO
high (*terreno, precio, temperatura*)

elevar VERBO
to raise (*nivel, precio, voz*)

eligiendo VERBO *ver* **elegir**

elijo VERBO *ver* **elegir**

eliminar VERBO
[1] to remove ◇ *un detergente que elimina las manchas* a detergent that removes stains
[2] to eliminate ◇ *Fueron eliminados de la competencia.* They were eliminated from the competition.

ella PRONOMBRE
[1] she (*como sujeto*) ◇ *Ella no estaba en casa.* She was not at home.
[2] her (*con preposición, en comparaciones*) ◇ *El regalo es para ella.* The present is for her. ◇ *Él estaba más nervioso que ella.* He was more nervous than her.
◆ **ella misma** herself ◇ *Me lo dijo ella misma.* She told me herself.
◆ **de ella** hers ◇ *Este abrigo es de ella.* This coat is hers.

ellos PRONOMBRE PL (FEM **ellas**)
[1] they ◇ *Ellos todavía no lo saben.* They don't know yet.
[2] them (*con preposición, en comparaciones*) ◇ *Yo me iré con ellas.* I'll leave with them. ◇ *Somos mejores que ellos.* We're better than them.
◆ **ellos mismos** themselves ◇ *Me lo dijeron ellos mismos.* They told me themselves.
◆ **de ellos** theirs ◇ *El carro era de ellos.* The car was theirs.

elogiar VERBO
to praise

el **elote** SUSTANTIVO [Mexico]
[1] corncob (*mazorca*)
[2] corn (*granos*)

el **e-mail** SUSTANTIVO (PL los **e-mails**)
[1] email (*mensaje, sistema*)
[2] email address (PL email addresses) (*dirección*)

la **embajada** SUSTANTIVO
embassy (PL embassies)

el **embajador,** la **embajadora** SUSTANTIVO
ambassador

embalar VERBO
to pack

el **embalse** SUSTANTIVO
reservoir

embarazada ADJETIVO
pregnant ◇ *Estaba embarazada de cuatro meses.* She was four months pregnant.
◆ **quedar embarazada** to get pregnant
*No confundir **embarazada** con **embarrassed**.*

embarazoso ADJETIVO
embarrassing

embarcar* VERBO
to board ◇ *Los pasajeros ya estaban embarcando.* The passengers were already boarding.

el **embargo** SUSTANTIVO
embargo (PL embargoes) (*a un país*)
◆ **sin embargo** nevertheless

embobado ADJETIVO
◆ **Se quedaron mirándola embobados.** They watched her in fascination.
◆ **Está embobado con su novia.** His girlfriend has him under her spell.

emborracharse VERBO
to get drunk

embotellado ADJETIVO
bottled (*agua, vino*)

el **embotellamiento** SUSTANTIVO
traffic jam

el **embrague** SUSTANTIVO

clutch

embrollarse VERBO
[1] to get tangled up ◇ *Las cuerdas se embrollaron.* The ropes got tangled up.
[2] to get confused ◇ *Me embrollé con tanta información.* With so much information, I got confused.

el **embrollo** SUSTANTIVO
tangle (*de hilos, cuerdas*)

embrujado ADJETIVO
haunted ◇ *una casa embrujada* a haunted house

el **embudo** SUSTANTIVO
funnel

el **embustero,** la **embustera** SUSTANTIVO
liar

el **embutido** SUSTANTIVO
cold cuts PL ◇ *No comemos muchos embutidos.* We don't eat a lot of cold cuts.

la **emergencia** SUSTANTIVO
emergency (PL emergencies)
◆ **la salida de emergencia** the emergency exit
◆ **en caso de emergencia** in case of emergency

emigrar VERBO
[1] to emigrate (*personas*)
[2] to migrate (*pájaros*)

la **emisión** SUSTANTIVO (PL las **emisiones**)
[1] broadcast (*de programa*)
[2] emission (*de gases*)

emitir VERBO
[1] to broadcast (*programa*)
[2] to give off (*gases, olores*)

la **emoción** SUSTANTIVO (PL las **emociones**)
emotion ◇ *Me temblaba la voz de emoción.* My voice was trembling with emotion.
◆ **Su carta me produjo gran emoción.** I was very moved by his letter.
◆ **¡Qué emoción!** How exciting!

emocionado ADJETIVO
[1] moved (*conmovido*)
[2] excited (*entusiasmado*)

emocionante ADJETIVO
[1] moving (*conmovedor*) ◇ *La despedida fue muy emocionante.* The farewell was very moving.
[2] exciting (*apasionante*) ◇ *El final del partido fue muy emocionante.* The end of the game was very exciting.

emocionarse VERBO
to be moved ◇ *Me emocioné mucho con la película.* I was very moved by the movie.
◆ **Se emocionó al volver a ver a su padre.** She got emotional when she saw her father again.

emotivo ADJETIVO
[1] moving (*acto, discurso*)
[2] emotional ◇ *La vuelta a casa fue muy emotiva.* It was a very emotional homecoming.

empacar* VERBO
to pack

empacharse VERBO
to get a stomachache ◇ *Me empaché por comer tanto chocolate.* I got a stomachache through eating so much chocolate.

empalagoso ADJETIVO
sickly (*pastel, dulce*)

empalmar VERBO
[1] to connect ◇ *Empalma los dos cables para hacer la conexión.* Connect the two wires to make the connection.
[2] to join ◇ *Esta carretera empalma con la autopista.* This road joins the freeway.

la **empanada** SUSTANTIVO
[1] meat pie (*grande*)
[2] pastry (PL pastries) (*pequeña*)

empañarse VERBO
to get steamed up ◇ *Se me empañaron los anteojos al entrar en el museo.* My glasses got steamed up when I went into the museum.
◆ **Los vidrios del dormitorio estaban empañados.** There was condensation on the bedroom windows.

empapar VERBO
to soak ◇ *Cierra la ducha que me estás empapando.* Can you turn the shower off? You're soaking me.
◆ **Se me empaparon los calcetines.** My socks got soaked.
◆ **estar* empapado hasta los huesos** to be soaked to the skin

empapelar VERBO
to paper

empaquetar VERBO
to pack ◇ *Empaqueta todos tus libros.* Pack all your books.

emparejar VERBO
[1] to pair up (*objetos, personas*)
[2] to level (*terreno, pared*)

empastar VERBO
◆ **Me han empastado dos muelas.** I've had two teeth filled.

el **empaste** SUSTANTIVO
filling

empatar VERBO
to tie ◇ *Empatamos a uno y tuvimos que jugar tiempo suplementario.* We tied one-all and had to play extra time. ◇ *Los dos candidatos empataron en la votación.* The two candidates were tied in the voting.

el **empate** SUSTANTIVO
tie (*en partido, votación, concurso*) ◇ *un empate a cero* a scoreless tie

empedernido ADJETIVO
◆ **un fumador empedernido** a chronic smoker
◆ **Es un lector empedernido.** He's a compulsive reader.

empeñado ADJETIVO
determined ◇ *Está empeñado en aprobar el curso.* He's determined to get through the course.

☞

◆ **Está empeñada en que yo soy mayor que ella.** She insists that I'm older than she is.

empeñarse VERBO

◆ **empeñarse en hacer algo (1)** to be determined to do something ◇ *Se había empeñado en irse con él.* She was determined to go with him.

◆ **empeñarse en hacer algo (2)** to insist on doing something ◇ *Se empeñó en que nos quedáramos a cenar.* He insisted that we should stay for dinner.

empeorar VERBO

1 to get worse (*enfermo, situación*) ◇ *Mi padre empeoró con aquel medicamento.* My father got worse with that medicine.

2 to make...worse ◇ *Tu comentario sólo empeorará las cosas.* Your comment will only make matters worse.

empezar* VERBO

to start ◇ *Nuestras vacaciones empiezan el 20.* Our vacation starts on the 20th.

◆ **empezar a hacer algo** to start doing something ◇ *Ha empezado a nevar.* It has started snowing.

◆ **volver* a empezar** to start again

empinado ADJETIVO

steep (*calle, pendiente*)

el **empleado,** la **empleada** SUSTANTIVO

1 employee

2 sales clerk (*de tienda*)

emplear VERBO

1 to use ◇ *Puedes emplear cualquier jabón.* You can use any soap.

2 to employ ◇ *La fábrica emplea a veinte trabajadores.* The factory employs twenty workers.

el **empleo** SUSTANTIVO

job ◇ *Ha encontrado empleo en un restaurante.* He has found a job in a restaurant.

◆ **estar* sin empleo** to be unemployed

◆ **"modo de empleo"** "how to use"

la **empresa** SUSTANTIVO

firm ◇ *Trabaja en una empresa de informática.* He works in a computer firm.

la **empresaria** SUSTANTIVO

businesswoman (PL businesswomen)

el **empresario** SUSTANTIVO

businessman (PL businessmen)

empujar VERBO

to push ◇ *Tuvimos que empujar al carro.* We had to push the car.

el **empujón** SUSTANTIVO (PL los **empujones**)

◆ **Me dieron un empujón y caí a la piscina.** They pushed me and I fell into the pool.

◆ **abrirse* paso a empujones** to shove one's way through

en PREPOSICIÓN

1 in ◇ *en el armario* in the closet ◇ *Viven en Cuenca.* They live in Cuenca. ◇ *Nació en invierno.* He was born in winter. ◇ *Lo hice en dos días.* I did it in two days. ◇ *Hablamos en inglés.* We speak in English. ◇ *Está en el hospital.* She's in the hospital.

2 into (*con verbos que indican movimiento*) ◇ *Entré al banco.* I went into the bank. ◇ *Me metí en la cama a las diez.* I got into bed at ten o'clock.

3 on ◇ *Las llaves están en la mesa.* The keys are on the table. ◇ *Lo encontré tirado en el suelo.* I found it lying on the floor. ◇ *La librería está en la calle Pelayo.* The bookstore is on Pelayo Street. ◇ *La oficina está en el quinto piso.* The office is on the sixth floor.

◆ **Mi cumpleaños cae en viernes.** My birthday falls on a Friday.

4 at ◇ *Yo estaba en la casa.* I was at home. ◇ *Te veo en el cine.* See you at the movies. ◇ *Vivía en el número 17.* I was living at number 17. ◇ *en ese momento* at that moment ◇ *en Navidad* at Christmas

5 by ◇ *Vinimos en avión.* We came by plane.

◆ **ser* el primero en llegar** to be the first to arrive

enamorado ADJETIVO

◆ **estar* enamorado de alguien** to be in love with somebody

enamorarse VERBO

to fall in love ◇ *Se ha enamorado de Yolanda.* He's fallen in love with Yolanda. ◇ *Se enamoraron nada más verse.* They fell in love at first sight.

el **enano,** la **enana** SUSTANTIVO

dwarf (PL dwarves *o* dwarfs)

encabezar* VERBO

to lead ◇ *Puebla encabeza la Liga.* Puebla are leading the League.

◆ **la cita que encabeza el artículo** the quotation heading the article

encajar VERBO

to fit ◇ *Las piezas no encajan.* The pieces don't fit.

encaminarse VERBO

◆ **Nos encaminamos hacia el pueblo.** We headed towards the village.

encantado ADJETIVO

1 delighted (*muy contento*) ◇ *Está encantada con su nuevo carro.* She's delighted with her new car.

2 enchanted (*hechizado*) ◇ *un castillo encantado* an enchanted castle

◆ **¡Encantado de conocerla!** Pleased to meet you!

encantador ADJETIVO (FEM **encantadora**)

charming

encantar VERBO

◆ **Me encantan los animales.** I love animals.

◆ **Les encanta esquiar.** They love skiing.

◆ **Me encantaría que vinieras.** I'd love you to

come.

el **encanto** SUSTANTIVO
charm
◆ **Eugenia es un encanto.** Eugenia is charming.

encarcelar VERBO
to imprison

el **encargado,** la **encargada** SUSTANTIVO
manager ◇ *Quiero hablar con el encargado.* I'd like to talk to the manager.

encargar* VERBO
1 to order ◇ *Encargamos dos pizzas.* We ordered two pizzas.
2 to ask ◇ *Le encargó que le recogiera los documentos.* She asked him to fetch the documents for her.
◆ **Yo me encargaré de avisar a los demás.** I'll take care of letting the others know.
◆ **Estoy encargada de vender las entradas.** I'm in charge of selling the tickets.

encariñarse VERBO
◆ **encariñarse con** to grow fond of

el **encendedor** SUSTANTIVO
lighter

encender* VERBO
1 to light (*vela, hoguera, cigarro*)
2 to switch on (*luz, calefacción*)

encendido ADJETIVO
1 on (*luz, calefacción*) ◇ *La tele estaba encendida.* The TV was on.
2 lit (*fuego, hoguera*) ◇ *El cigarro no está bien encendido.* Your cigarette isn't properly lit.

encerrar* VERBO
1 to confine ◇ *Encerré el gato en la cocina.* I confined the cat in the kitchen. ◇ *Me encerré en mi cuarto para estudiar.* I confined myself in my room to study.
2 to lock up ◇ *Lo encerraron en un calabozo.* They locked him up in a cell.
◆ **Los manifestantes se encerraron en el ayuntamiento.** The demonstrators held a sit-in in the town hall.

la **enchilada** SUSTANTIVO

> ℹ *An **enchilada** is a stuffed tortilla covered in tomato and chili sauce.*

el **enchufado,** la **enchufada** SUSTANTIVO
◆ **Amelia es la enchufada del profesor.** Amelia is the teacher's pet. (*coloquial*)

enchufar VERBO
to plug in ◇ *Enchufa la tele.* Plug the TV in.

el **enchufe** SUSTANTIVO
1 plug (*macho*)
2 outlet (*hembra*)
◆ **Consiguió ese puesto por enchufe.** He got that job through pulling strings.

la **encía** SUSTANTIVO
gum

la **enciclopedia** SUSTANTIVO
encyclopedia

enciendo VERBO *ver* **encender**

encierro VERBO *ver* **encerrar**

encima ADVERBIO
on ◇ *Pon el cenicero aquí encima.* Put the ashtray on there. ◇ *No llevo dinero encima.* I don't have any money on me.
◆ **encima de (1)** on ◇ *Ponlo encima de la mesa.* Put it on the table.
◆ **encima de (2)** on top of ◇ *Mi maleta está encima del armario.* My case is on top of the closet.
◆ **Lo leí por encima.** I glanced at it.
◆ **por encima de (1)** above ◇ *Los helicópteros volaban por encima de nuestras cabezas.* The helicopters were flying above our heads. ◇ *Las temperaturas han subido por encima de lo normal.* Temperatures have been above average.
◆ **por encima de (2)** over ◇ *Tuve que saltar por encima de la mesa.* I had to jump over the table.
◆ **¡Y encima no te da ni las gracias!** And on top of it, he doesn't even thank you!

la **encina** SUSTANTIVO
oak tree

encoger* VERBO
to shrink ◇ *Este suéter ha encogido.* This sweater has shrunk.
◆ **Antonio se encogió de hombros.** Antonio shrugged his shoulders.

encontrar* VERBO
to find ◇ *Mi hermano encontró trabajo.* My brother has found a job. ◇ *Lo encuentro un poco arrogante.* I find him a bit arrogant.
◆ **No encuentro las llaves.** I can't find the keys.
◆ **encontrarse (1)** (*sentirse*) to feel ◇ *Ahora se encuentra mejor.* She's feeling better now.
◆ **encontrarse (2)** (*verse*) to meet ◇ *Nos encontramos en el cine.* We met at the movies.
◆ **Me encontré con Manolo en la calle.** I bumped into Manolo in the street.

el **encuentro** SUSTANTIVO
1 meeting (*reunión*)
◆ **punto de encuentro** meeting point
2 match (PL matches) (*partido*)

la **encuesta** SUSTANTIVO
survey

enderezar* VERBO
to straigthen

endulzar* VERBO
to sweeten

endurecer* VERBO
to tone up (*músculos*)

el **enemigo,** la **enemiga** ADJETIVO, SUSTANTIVO
enemy (PL enemies) ◇ *el ejército enemigo* the enemy army

enemistarse VERBO
to fall out ◇ *Se enemistó con la familia de su mujer.* He fell out with his wife's family.

E

la **energía** SUSTANTIVO
energy ◇ *ahorrar energía* to save energy
◆ **la energía solar** solar power
◆ **la energía eléctrica** electricity

enérgico ADJETIVO
energetic ◇ *Es una persona muy enérgica.* She's very energetic.

enero SUSTANTIVO MASC
En inglés, los meses se escriben con mayúscula.
January ◇ *en enero* in January ◇ *Nació el 6 de enero.* He was born on January 6th.

enfadado ADJETIVO
angry ◇ *Mi padre estaba muy enfadado conmigo.* My father was very angry with me.
◆ **Ana y su novio están enfadados.** Ana and her boyfriend have fallen out.

enfadarse VERBO
to be angry ◇ *Papá se va a enfadar mucho contigo.* Dad will be very angry with you.
◆ **Mi hermana y su novio se enfadaron.** My brother and his girlfriend have fallen out.

el **enfado** SUSTANTIVO
◆ **Ya se le pasó el enfado.** He isn't angry any more.

enfermarse VERBO
to fall ill
◆ **¡Me enfermas!** You make me sick!

la **enfermedad** SUSTANTIVO
1 illness (PL illnesses) ◇ *Adelgazó mucho durante su enfermedad.* He lost a lot of weight during his illness.
2 disease ◇ *Tiene una enfermedad contagiosa.* He has an infectious disease.

la **enfermería** SUSTANTIVO
infirmary (PL infirmaries)

el **enfermero,** la **enfermera** SUSTANTIVO
nurse ◇ *Mi madre es enfermera.* My mother is a nurse.

enfermo ADJETIVO
ill ◇ *He estado enferma toda la semana.* I've been ill all week.

el **enfermo,** la **enferma** SUSTANTIVO
patient (*en hospital*)
◆ **Los enfermos deben tomar precauciones especiales.** Sick people need to take special precautions.

enfocar* VERBO
1 to focus on ◇ *El fotógrafo enfocó el ciervo.* The photographer focused on the deer.
2 to approach ◇ *Depende de cómo enfoques el problema.* It depends on how you approach the problem.

enfrentarse VERBO
◆ **enfrentarse a algo** to face something ◇ *Tienes que enfrentarte al problema.* You have to face the problem.

enfrente ADVERBIO
opposite ◇ *Luisa estaba sentada enfrente.* Luisa was sitting opposite.
◆ **La panadería está enfrente.** The bakery is across the street.
◆ **de enfrente** opposite ◇ *la casa de enfrente* the house opposite
◆ **enfrente de** opposite ◇ *Mi casa está enfrente del colegio.* My house is opposite the school.

enfriarse* VERBO
1 to get cold ◇ *La sopa se enfrió.* The soup has gotten cold.
2 to cool down ◇ *Hay que dejar que se enfríe el motor.* We must let the engine cool down.
3 to catch cold ◇ *Ponte el abrigo que te vas a enfriar.* Put your coat on or you'll catch cold.

enganchar VERBO
to hook ◇ *Enganché la correa al collar del perro.* I hooked the leash onto the dog's collar.
◆ **engancharse** to get caught ◇ *Se me enganchó el suéter en el rosal.* My sweater got caught on a rosebush.

el **enganche** SUSTANTIVO *Mexico*
deposit (*depósito*)

engañar VERBO
1 to cheat ◇ *Te engañaron; no es de oro.* You've been cheated. It's not gold.
2 to lie ◇ *No me engañes y dime quién lo hizo.* Don't lie to me and tell me who did it.
3 to cheat on ◇ *Su novio la engaña.* Her boyfriend is cheating on her.
◆ **Las apariencias engañan.** Appearances can be deceptive.

el **engaño** SUSTANTIVO
1 con (*coloquial*) ◇ *Fue un engaño.* It was a con.
2 deceit ◇ *Odio la mentira y el engaño.* I hate lies and deceit.

engordar VERBO
1 to put on weight ◇ *No quiero engordar.* I don't want to put on weight.
◆ **He engordado dos kilos.** I've put on two kilos.
2 to be fattening ◇ *Los dulces engordan mucho.* Candy is very fattening.

la **engrapadora** SUSTANTIVO
stapler

engrapar VERBO
to staple

engreído ADJETIVO
conceited

la **enhorabuena** SUSTANTIVO
◆ **¡Enhorabuena!** Congratulations!
◆ **Me dieron la enhorabuena por el premio.** They congratulated me on winning the prize.

el **enlace** SUSTANTIVO
1 connection (*de trenes, autobuses*)
◆ **Perdí el enlace con Buenos Aires.** I missed

the connecting flight to Buenos Aires.
[2] link (*informática*)

enlatado ADJETIVO
canned (*verduras, carne*)

enlazar* VERBO
to connect ◇ *Este vuelo enlaza con el de Moscú.* This flight connects with the Moscow flight.

enloquecer* VERBO
to be crazy about ◇ *Lo enloquecen las motos.* He's crazy about motorbikes.

enmarcar* VERBO
to frame

enojado ADJETIVO
angry ◇ *Mi papá estaba muy enojado conmigo.* My father was very angry with me.
◆ **Ana y su novio están enojados.** Ana and her boyfriend have fallen out.

enojarse VERBO
to be angry ◇ *Mi mamá se va a enojar.* My mother will be angry. ◇ *Manolo y su novio se han enojado.* Manolo and his boyfriend have fallen out.

enorme ADJETIVO
enormous ◇ *Tienen una casa enorme.* They have an enormous house.

la **enredadera** SUSTANTIVO
vine

enredarse VERBO
[1] to get tangled up (*hilos, cuerda*) ◇ *Se me enredó el pelo.* My hair got all tangled up.
[2] to get into a tangle ◇ *Me enredé haciendo las cuentas.* I got into a tangle with the accounts. (*coloquial*)

enrevesado ADJETIVO
difficult (*problema*)

enriquecerse* VERBO
to get rich ◇ *Se enriquecieron tratando con armas.* They got rich dealing in arms.

enrollar VERBO
[1] to roll up ◇ *No dobles el póster, enróllalo.* Don't fold the poster, roll it up.
[2] to wind ◇ *Enrolla la cuerda en este palo.* Wind the rope round this stick.

enroscar* VERBO
[1] to screw in (*tornillo, tuerca*)
◆ **Enrosca bien la tapa.** Screw the top on tight.
[2] to coil (*cable, manguera*) ◇ *La manguera se le enroscó en la pierna.* The hose coiled round his leg.

la **ensalada** SUSTANTIVO
salad

ensanchar VERBO
to widen ◇ *Están ensanchando la carretera.* They're widening the road.
◆ **ensancharse** to stretch ◇ *Mi suéter se ha ensanchado.* My sweater has stretched.

ensayar VERBO
to rehearse (*obra de teatro, canción*)

el **ensayo** SUSTANTIVO
rehearsal ◇ *Esta tarde tenemos ensayo.* We have a rehearsal this afternoon.

enseguida ADVERBIO
right away ◇ *La ambulancia llegó enseguida.* The ambulance arrived right away.
◆ **Enseguida te atiendo.** I'll be with you in a minute.

la **enseñanza** SUSTANTIVO
[1] teaching ◇ *la enseñanza de lenguas extranjeras* the teaching of foreign languages
[2] education ◇ *Debería invertirse más dinero en la enseñanza.* More money should be invested in education.
◆ **la enseñanza primaria** elementary education

enseñar VERBO
[1] to teach ◇ *Ricardo enseña inglés en una academia de idiomas.* Ricardo teaches English at a language school. ◇ *Mi padre me enseñó a nadar.* My father taught me to swim.
[2] to show ◇ *Ana me enseñó todos sus videojuegos.* Ana showed me all her video games.
◆ **Les enseñé el colegio.** I showed them round the school.

ensuciar VERBO
to get...dirty ◇ *Vas a ensuciar el sofá.* You'll get the sofa dirty.
◆ **ensuciarse** to get dirty ◇ *No toques la pintura que te vas a ensuciar.* Don't touch the paint or you'll get dirty. ◇ *Me ensucié las manos.* I've got my hands dirty.
◆ **Te ensuciaste de barro los pantalones.** You have mud on your pants.

entender* VERBO
to understand ◇ *No entiendo el francés.* I don't understand French. ◇ *¿Lo entiendes?* Do you understand?
◆ **¿Entiendes lo que quiero decir?** Do you know what I mean?
◆ **Creo que lo he entendido mal.** I think I've misunderstood.
◆ **Mi primo entiende mucho de carros.** My cousin knows a lot about cars.
◆ **entenderse (1)** (*llevarse bien*) to get on ◇ *Mi hermana y yo no nos entendemos.* My sister and I don't get on.
◆ **entenderse (2)** (*comunicarse*) to communicate ◇ *Se entienden por gestos.* They communicate through sign language.
◆ **Dio a entender que no le gustaba.** He implied that he didn't like it.

el **entendido**, la **entendida** SUSTANTIVO
expert ◇ *No soy un entendido en el tema.* I'm not an expert on the subject.

enterarse VERBO
to find out (*averiguar*) ◇ *Me enteré por Manolo.* I found out from Manolo. ◇ *Entérate bien de todos los detalles.* Make sure you find out about all the details.
◆ **Se enteraron del accidente por la tele.** They ☞

heard about the accident on TV.
◆ **Me sacaron una muela y ni me enteré.** They took out a tooth and I didn't notice a thing.

entero ADJETIVO
whole ◇ *Se comió el paquete de galletas entero.* He ate the whole packet of cookies. ◇ *Se pasó la noche entera estudiando.* He spent the whole night studying.
◆ **la leche entera** whole milk

enterrar* VERBO
to bury

entiendo VERBO *ver* **entender**

entierro VERBO *ver* **enterrar**

el **entierro** SUSTANTIVO
funeral (*ceremonia*)

entonces ADVERBIO
1 then ◇ *Si no es tu padre, ¿entonces quién es?* If he isn't your father, then who is he? ◇ *Me recogió y entonces fuimos al cine.* He picked me up and then we went to the movies. ◇ *Iban andando porque entonces no tenían carro.* They used to walk because they didn't have a car then.
2 so ◇ *¿Entonces, vienes o te quedas?* So, are you coming or staying?
◆ **desde entonces** since then
◆ **para entonces** by then

el **entorno** SUSTANTIVO
surroundings PL

la **entrada** SUSTANTIVO
1 entrance ◇ *Nos vemos a la entrada.* I'll see you at the entrance.
◆ **"entrada libre"** "free admission"
2 ticket ◇ *Tengo entradas para el teatro.* I have tickets for the theater.
3 entry (PL entries) ◇ *La entrada de Chile al Mercosur.* Chile's entry into Mercosur.
◆ **"prohibida la entrada"** "no entry"
4 appetizer ◇ *¿Qué quieren de entrada?* What would you like as an appetizer?

entrar VERBO
1 to go in
Se traduce por ***go*** *cuando indica dirección diferente a donde está el hablante.*
◇ *Abrí la puerta y entré.* I opened the door and went in. ◇ *Mi amiga entró al banco.* My friend went into the bank.
◆ **Pedro entra a trabajar a las ocho.** Pedro starts work at eight o'clock.
◆ **No me dejaron entrar por ser menor de 16 años.** They wouldn't let me in because I was under 16.
2 to come in
Se traduce por ***come*** *cuando indica dirección hacia el hablante.*
◇ *¿Se puede? – Sí, entra.* May I? – Yes, come in. ◇ *Entraron a mi cuarto mientras yo dormía.* They came into my room while I was asleep.
3 to fit ◇ *Estos zapatos no me entran.* These shoes don't fit me. ◇ *La maleta no entra en el maletero.* The suitcase won't fit in the trunk.
◆ **El vino no entra en el precio.** The wine is not included in the price.
◆ **Le entraron ganas de reír.** She wanted to laugh.
◆ **De repente le entró sueño.** He suddenly felt sleepy.
◆ **Me ha entrado hambre al verte comer.** Watching you eat made me hungry.

entre PREPOSICIÓN
1 between (*dos personas o cosas*) ◇ *Lo terminamos entre los dos.* Between the two of us we finished it. ◇ *Vendrá entre las diez y las once.* He'll be coming between ten and eleven.
2 among (*más de dos personas o cosas*) ◇ *Había un baúl entre las maletas.* There was a trunk in among the suitcases. ◇ *Las mujeres hablaban entre sí.* The women were talking among themselves.
◆ **Le compraremos un regalo entre todos.** We'll buy her a present among all of us.
3 by ◇ *15 dividido entre 3 es 5.* 15 divided by 3 is 5.

entreabierto ADJETIVO
ajar (*puerta*)

entregar* VERBO
1 to hand in (*deberes, trabajo*) ◇ *Marta entregó el examen.* Marta handed her exam paper in.
2 to deliver (*carta, pedido*) ◇ *El cartero entregó el paquete.* The mailman delivered the package.
3 to present with (*premio, condecoración*) ◇ *El sargento le entregó la medalla.* The sergeant presented him with the medal.
◆ **El ladrón se entregó a la policía.** The thief gave himself up.

los **entremeses** SUSTANTIVO
appetizers

el **entrenador,** la **entrenadora** SUSTANTIVO
coach (PL coaches)

el **entrenamiento** SUSTANTIVO
training

entrenar VERBO
to train

la **entretención** SUSTANTIVO (PL las **entretenciones**)
entertainment ◇ *Lo hace por entretención.* He does it for entertainment.
◆ **Su única entretención es leer.** Her only hobby is reading.
◆ **Hay muchas entretenciones para los jóvenes.** There are many distractions for teenagers.

entretener* VERBO
1 to entertain (*divertirse*)
◆ **La tele entretiene mucho.** TV is very

entertaining.

[2] to keep (*retener*) ◇ *Una vecina me entretuvo hablando en las escaleras.* A neighbor kept me talking on the stairs.

◆ **entretenerse** (*divertirse*) to amuse oneself ◇ *Se entretienen viendo los dibujos animados.* They amuse themselves by watching cartoons.

◆ **No se entretengan jugando.** Don't hang about playing.

entretenido ADJETIVO
entertaining ◇ *La película es muy entretenida.* The movie is very entertaining.

la **entrevista** SUSTANTIVO
interview

◆ **hacer* una entrevista a alguien** to interview somebody ◇ *Le hicieron una entrevista por la radio.* They interviewed her on the radio.

el **entrevistador**, la **entrevistadora** SUSTANTIVO
interviewer

entrevistar VERBO
to interview

entrometerse VERBO
to meddle ◇ *No te entrometas en mis asuntos.* Don't meddle in my affairs.

entusiasmado ADJETIVO
excited ◇ *Estaba entusiasmado con su fiesta de cumpleaños.* He was excited about his birthday party.

entusiasmarse VERBO
to get excited ◇ *Se entusiasmó con la idea de hacer una fiesta.* He got very excited about the idea of having a party.

el **entusiasmo** SUSTANTIVO
enthusiasm

◆ **con entusiasmo** enthusiastically

enumerar VERBO
to list

el **envase** SUSTANTIVO
container ◇ *Viene en un envase de plástico.* It comes in a plastic container.

◆ **"envase no retornable"** "non-returnable bottle"

envejecer* VERBO
to age ◇ *Sus padres han envejecido mucho.* His parents have aged a lot.

enviar* VERBO
to send ◇ *Envíame las fotos.* Send me the photos.

◆ **Juan me envió el regalo por correo.** Juan mailed me the present.

la **envidia** SUSTANTIVO
envy

◆ **¡Qué envidia!** I'm so jealous!

◆ **Le tiene envidia a Ana.** She's jealous of Ana.

◆ **Le da envidia que mi carro sea mejor.** He's jealous that my car is better.

envidiar VERBO
to envy ◇ *¡No te envidio!* I don't envy you!

envidioso ADJETIVO
envious

envolver* VERBO
to wrap up ◇ *Llevaba al niño envuelto en una manta.* She carried the baby wrapped up in a blanket.

◆ **¿Desea que se lo envuelva para regalo?** Would you like it gift-wrapped?

envuelto VERBO *ver* **envolver**

la **epidemia** SUSTANTIVO
epidemic

el **episodio** SUSTANTIVO
episode

la **época** SUSTANTIVO
time ◇ *En aquella época vivíamos en Santiago.* At that time we were living in Santiago. ◇ *en esta época del año* at this time of year

◆ **la época de las lluvias** the rainy season

equilibrado ADJETIVO
balanced (*persona, dieta*)

el **equilibrio** SUSTANTIVO
balance ◇ *Perdí el equilibrio y me caí.* I lost my balance and fell over. ◇ *Luis podía mantener el equilibrio en la cuerda floja.* Luis managed to keep his balance on the tightrope.

el **equipaje** SUSTANTIVO
luggage

◆ **equipaje de mano** hand luggage

el **equipo** SUSTANTIVO
[1] team ◇ *un equipo de baloncesto* a basketball team

[2] equipment ◇ *Me robaron todo el equipo de esquí.* They stole all my skiing equipment.

◆ **el equipo de música** the stereo

◆ **un equipo de deportes** a sweat suit

la **equitación** SUSTANTIVO
riding

equivaler* VERBO

◆ **equivaler a algo** to be equivalent to something

la **equivocación** SUSTANTIVO (PL las **equivocaciones**)
mistake

◆ **Marqué otro número por equivocación.** I dialed another number by mistake.

equivocado ADJETIVO
wrong ◇ *Estás equivocada.* You're wrong. ◇ *Elena me dio el número equivocado.* Elena gave me the wrong number.

equivocarse* VERBO
[1] to make a mistake ◇ *Me equivoqué muchas veces en el examen.* I made a lot of mistakes on the test.

[2] to be wrong ◇ *Si crees que voy a dejarte ir, te equivocas.* If you think I'm going to let you go, you're wrong.

◆ **Perdone, me equivoqué de número.** Sorry, wrong number.

◆ **Se equivocaron de tren.** They caught the wrong train.

E

era VERBO *ver* **ser**
eres VERBO *ver* **ser**
el **erizo** SUSTANTIVO
hedgehog
◆ **un erizo de mar** a sea urchin
el **error** SUSTANTIVO
mistake ◇ *Fue un error contárselo a Luisa.* Telling Luisa about it was a mistake. ◇ *Cometí muchos errores en el examen.* I made a lot of mistakes on the exam.
eructar VERBO
to burp
el **eructo** SUSTANTIVO
burp
es VERBO *ver* **ser**
esa ADJETIVO *ver* **ese**
ésa PRONOMBRE *ver* **ése**
esbelto ADJETIVO
slender
escabullirse* VERBO
[1] to slip away ◇ *Se escabulló de la fiesta.* He managed to slip away from the party.
[2] to wriggle out of ◇ *No debes escabullirte de tus deberes.* You mustn't try to wriggle out of your responsibilities.
la **escala** SUSTANTIVO
[1] scale ◇ *a escala nacional* on a national scale
[2] stopover ◇ *Tenemos una escala de tres horas en Recife.* We've got a three-hour stopover in Recife.
◆ **Hicimos escala en Lima.** We stopped over in Lima.
escalar VERBO
to climb
la **escalera** SUSTANTIVO
stairs PL ◇ *bajar las escaleras* to go down the stairs
◆ **una escalera de mármol** a marble staircase
◆ **una escalera de mano** a ladder
◆ **la escalera de incendios** the fire escape
◆ **una escalera mecánica** an escalator
el **escalofrío** SUSTANTIVO
◆ **Tengo escalofríos.** I'm shivering.
◆ **La escena te produce escalofríos.** The scene makes you shudder.
el **escalón** SUSTANTIVO (PL los **escalones**)
step
la **escama** SUSTANTIVO
scale (*de pez*)
escandalizarse* VERBO
to be shocked ◇ *Mi abuela se escandalizó.* My grandmother was shocked.
el **escándalo** SUSTANTIVO
[1] scandal
◆ **La boda produjo un gran escándalo.** The wedding caused a huge scandal.
[2] racket ◇ *¿Qué escándalo es éste?* What's all this racket?
escandaloso ADJETIVO
noisy
el **escandinavo,** la **escandinava** ADJETIVO, SUSTANTIVO
Scandinavian
◆ **un escandinavo** a Scandinavian
◆ **una escandinava** a Scandinavian
◆ **los escandinavos** the Scandinavians
el **escáner** SUSTANTIVO (PL los **escáners**)
[1] scanner (*aparato*)
[2] scan (*imagen*) ◇ *hacerse un escáner* to have a scan
escapar VERBO
to escape ◇ *Conseguí escapar de la fiesta.* I managed to escape from the party.
◆ **No quiero dejar escapar esta oportunidad.** I don't want to let this opportunity slip.
◆ **escaparse** to escape ◇ *El ladrón se escapó de la cárcel.* The thief escaped from prison. ◇ *El calor se escapa por esta rendija.* The heat escapes through this grill.
◆ **Se me escapó un eructo.** I let out a burp.
el **escaparate** SUSTANTIVO
store window (*de tienda*)
el **escape** SUSTANTIVO
leak ◇ *Había un escape de gas.* There was a gas leak.
el **escarabajo** SUSTANTIVO
beetle
escarbar VERBO
to dig ◇ *Los niños escarbaban en la arena.* The children were digging in the sand.
la **escarcha** SUSTANTIVO
frost
la **escasez** SUSTANTIVO
shortage ◇ *Hay escasez de medicamentos.* There is a shortage of medicine.
escaso ADJETIVO
scarce ◇ *Los alimentos están muy escasos.* Food is scarce.
◆ **Habrá escasa visibilidad en las carreteras.** Visibility on the roads will be poor.
◆ **Duró una hora escasa.** It lasted barely an hour.
la **escena** SUSTANTIVO
scene
el **escenario** SUSTANTIVO
stage
escéptico ADJETIVO
sceptical
el **esclavo,** la **esclava** SUSTANTIVO
slave
la **escoba** SUSTANTIVO
broom
escocer* VERBO
to sting ◇ *Me escuecen los ojos.* My eyes are stinging.
escocés ADJETIVO (FEM **escocesa,** MASC PL **escoceses**)
Scottish
◆ **el whisky escocés** Scotch whisky

* Verbs marked with this symbol are irregular. See pages 346–348 for further details.

◆ **una falda escocesa** a kilt

el **escocés** SUSTANTIVO (MASC PL los **escoceses**)
Scotsman (PL Scotsmen) ◇ *los escoceses* Scottish people

la **escocesa** SUSTANTIVO
Scotswoman (PL Scotswomen)

Escocia SUSTANTIVO FEM
Scotland

escoger* VERBO
to choose ◇ *Yo escogí el azul.* I chose the blue one.

escolar ADJETIVO
school
***school** en este caso va siempre delante del sustantivo.*
◇ *el uniforme escolar* school uniform

los **escombros** SUSTANTIVO
rubble SING

esconder VERBO
to hide ◇ *Lo escondí en el cajón.* I hid it in the box.
◆ **Me escondí debajo de la cama.** I hid under the bed.

las **escondidas** SUSTANTIVO
◆ **jugar* a las escondidas** to play hide-and-seek
◆ **a escondidas** in secret ◇ *Toman alcohol a escondidas.* They drink in secret.

la **escopeta** SUSTANTIVO
shotgun

Escorpio SUSTANTIVO MASC
Scorpio
◆ **Soy escorpio.** I'm a Scorpio.

el **escorpión** SUSTANTIVO (PL los **escorpiones**)
scorpion

escribir* VERBO
to write ◇ *Les escribí una carta.* I wrote them a letter. ◇ *Escribe pronto.* Write soon.
◆ **Nos escribimos de vez en cuando.** We write to each other from time to time.
◆ **¿Cómo se escribe tu nombre?** How do you spell your name?
◆ **escribir a máquina** to type

escrito ADJETIVO
written ◇ *un examen escrito* a written exam

el **escritor**, la **escritora** SUSTANTIVO
writer ◇ *Pablo es escritor.* Pablo is a writer.

el **escritorio** SUSTANTIVO
[1] desk (*mueble*)
[2] office (*oficina*)
[3] study (PL studies) (*en una casa*)

la **escritura** SUSTANTIVO
writing

escuchar VERBO
to listen ◇ *Juan escuchaba con atención.* Juan was listening attentively. ◇ *Escucha el consejo de tus padres.* Listen to your parents' advice. ◇ *Me gusta escuchar música.* I like listening to music.

el **escudo** SUSTANTIVO
[1] shield (*de soldado*)
[2] badge (*en la solapa*)

la **escuela** SUSTANTIVO
school ◇ *Hoy no tengo que ir a la escuela.* I don't have to go to school today.
◆ **la escuela primaria** elementary school
◆ **la escuela de manejo** [Mexico] driving school

esculcar* VERBO
[1] to search (*persona, casa*)
[2] to go through (*cajón, papeles*)
◇ *Siempre está esculcando mis cosas.* He's always going through my things.

E

la **escultura** SUSTANTIVO
sculpture

escupir VERBO
to spit

escurridizo ADJETIVO
slippery (*jabón, piel*)

el **escurridor** SUSTANTIVO
[1] colander (*para pasta, verduras*)
[2] dish rack (*para los platos*)

escurrir VERBO
[1] to wring (*ropa*)
[2] to drain (*verdura, pasta*)

ese ADJETIVO (FEM **esa**)
that ◇ *Dame ese libro.* Give me that book.
◆ **A partir de ese momento empezó a mejorar.** From then on it began to get better.

ése PRONOMBRE (FEM **ésa**)
that one ◇ *Prefiero ésa.* I prefer that one.
◆ **¿Quién es ése?** Who's that?

esencial ADJETIVO
essential
◆ **He entendido lo esencial de la conversación.** I understood the main points of the conversation.

esforzarse* VERBO
to make an effort ◇ *Tienes que esforzarte si quieres ganar.* You have to make an effort if you want to win.
◆ **Se esforzó todo lo que pudo para aprobar el examen.** He did all he could to pass the exam.

el **esfuerzo** SUSTANTIVO
effort ◇ *Tuve que hacer un esfuerzo para comer.* I had to make an effort to eat.

esfumarse VERBO
to vanish (*persona, dinero*)

la **esgrima** SUSTANTIVO
fencing (*deporte*)

el **esguince** SUSTANTIVO
sprain
◆ **Me hice un esguince en el tobillo.** I've sprained my ankle.

el **esmalte** SUSTANTIVO
◆ **el esmalte de uñas** nail polish

esmerarse VERBO
◆ **Se esmeró para que todo saliera bien.** He did his best so that everything came out right.
◆ **No necesitas esmerarte tanto en la presentación.** You don't need to make such

☞

an effort with the presentation.

esnob ADJETIVO (PL **esnobs**)
snobbish

eso PRONOMBRE
that ◇ *Eso es mentira.* That's a lie. ◇ *¡Eso es!* That's it!
◆ **a eso de las cinco** at about five
◆ **En eso llamaron a la puerta.** Just then there was a ring at the door.
◆ **Por eso te lo dije.** That's why I told you.
◆ **¡Y eso que estaba lloviendo!** And it was raining and everything!

esos ADJETIVO PL (FEM **esas**)
those ◇ *Trae esas sillas aquí.* Bring those chairs over here.

ésos PRONOMBRE PL (FEM **ésas**)
those ones ◇ *Ésos de ahí son mejores.* Those ones over there are better.
◆ **Ésos no son los que vimos ayer.** Those aren't the ones we saw yesterday.

espabilar VERBO = **despabilar**

el **espacio** SUSTANTIVO
1 room (*sitio*) ◇ *No hay espacio para tantas sillas.* There isn't room for so many chairs. ◇ *El piano ocupa mucho espacio.* The piano takes up a lot of room.
2 space (*entre dos cosas, palabras*) ◇ *Deja más espacio entre las líneas.* Leave more space between the lines.
◆ **un espacio en blanco** a gap
◆ **viajar por el espacio** to travel in space

la **espada** SUSTANTIVO
sword
No confundir ***espada*** *con* ***spade.***

los **espaguetis** SUSTANTIVO
spaghetti SING

la **espalda** SUSTANTIVO
back ◇ *Me duele la espalda.* My back aches.
◆ **Estaba tumbada de espaldas.** She was lying on her back.
◆ **Ana estaba de espaldas a mí.** Ana had her back to me.
◆ **Le dispararon por la espalda.** They shot him from behind.
◆ **Me encanta nadar de espalda.** I love swimming backstroke.

el **espantapájaros** SUSTANTIVO (PL los **espantapájaros**)
scarecrow

espantoso ADJETIVO
awful ◇ *un monstruo espantoso* an awful monster ◇ *Los niños hicieron un ruido espantoso.* The children made an awful noise.
◆ **Hacía un frío espantoso.** It was awfully cold.

España SUSTANTIVO FEM
Spain

español ADJETIVO (FEM **española**)
Spanish

el **español,** la **española** SUSTANTIVO
Spaniard
◆ **los españoles** the Spanish

el **español** SUSTANTIVO
Spanish (*idioma*)

el **esparadrapo** SUSTANTIVO
bandage ◇ *Me puse un esparadrapo en el dedo.* I put a bandage on my finger.

el **espárrago** SUSTANTIVO
asparagus ◇ *¿Te gustan los espárragos?* Do you like asparagus?
◆ **La mandé a freír espárragos.** I told her to buzz off. (*coloquial*)

la **especia** SUSTANTIVO
spice

especial ADJETIVO
special ◇ *Fue un día muy especial.* It was a very special day.
◆ **en especial** particularly ◇ *¿Desea ver a alguien en especial?* Is there anybody you particularly want to see?

la **especialidad** SUSTANTIVO
specialty (PL specialties) ◇ *la especialidad de la casa* the specialty of the house

el/la **especialista** SUSTANTIVO
specialist

especializarse* VERBO
◆ **Rosario se especializó en pediatría.** Rosario specialized in pediatrics.

especialmente ADVERBIO
1 especially (*sobre todo*) ◇ *Me gusta mucho el pan, especialmente el integral.* I love bread, especially whole wheat bread.
2 specially (*expresamente*) ◇ *un vestido diseñado especialmente para ella* a dress designed specially for her

la **especie** SUSTANTIVO
species (PL species) (*animal, planta*)

específico ADJETIVO
specific

espectacular ADJETIVO
spectacular

el **espectáculo** SUSTANTIVO
performance (*función*) ◇ *El espectáculo empieza a las ocho.* The performance starts at eight.
◆ **Dio el espectáculo delante de todo el mundo.** He made a spectacle of himself in front of everyone.

el **espectador,** la **espectadora** SUSTANTIVO
spectator (*en estadio, cancha de tenis*)
◆ **los espectadores** (*en teatro, concierto*) the audience

el **espejo** SUSTANTIVO
mirror ◇ *Me miré en el espejo.* I looked at myself in the mirror.
◆ **el espejo retrovisor** rearview mirror

espeluznante ADJETIVO
hair-raising

la **espera** SUSTANTIVO
wait ◇ *tras una espera de tres horas* after a

three-hour wait
◆ **estar* a la espera de algo** to be expecting something

la **esperanza** SUSTANTIVO
hope
◆ **No tengo esperanzas de aprobar.** I have no hope of passing.
◆ **No pierdas las esperanzas.** Don't give up hope.

esperar VERBO
1 to wait ◇ *Espera en la puerta. Ahora mismo voy.* Wait at the door. I'm coming right now.
◆ **Espera un momento, por favor.** Hang on a moment, please.
2 to wait for ◇ *No me esperen.* Don't wait for me.
◆ **Me hizo esperar una hora.** He kept me waiting for an hour.
3 to expect ◇ *Llegaron antes de lo que yo esperaba.* They arrived sooner than I expected. ◇ *Esperaban que Juan les pidiera perdón.* They were expecting Juan to apologize. ◇ *Llamará cuando menos lo esperes.* He'll call when you're least expecting it. ◇ *No esperes que venga a ayudarte.* Don't expect him to come and help you.
◆ **esperar un bebé** to be expecting a baby
◆ **Me espera un largo día de trabajo.** I have a long day of work ahead of me.
◆ **Era de esperar que no viniera.** He was bound not to come.
4 to hope ◇ *Espero que no sea nada grave.* I hope it isn't anything serious.
◆ **¿Vendrás a la fiesta? – Espero que sí.** Are you coming to the party? – I hope so.
◆ **¿Crees que Carmen se enojará? – Espero que no.** Do you think Carmen will be angry? – I hope not.
◆ **Fuimos a esperarla a la estación.** We went to the station to meet her.

espeso ADJETIVO
thick (*salsa, chocolate*)

el/la **espía** SUSTANTIVO
spy (PL spies)

espiar* VERBO
to spy on ◇ *Los vecinos nos estaban espiando.* The neighbors were spying on us.

la **espina** SUSTANTIVO
1 thorn (*de rosal*)
2 bone (*de pez*)
◆ **espina dorsal** backbone

la **espinaca** SUSTANTIVO
spinach ◇ *No me gustan las espinacas.* I don't like spinach.

la **espinilla** SUSTANTIVO
1 shin (*de la pierna*)
2 pimple (*grano*)

el **espionaje** SUSTANTIVO
spying
◆ **una novela de espionaje** a spy story

espirar VERBO
to breathe out

el **espíritu** SUSTANTIVO
spirit

espiritual ADJETIVO
spiritual

espléndido ADJETIVO
splendid (*día, comida*)

la **esponja** SUSTANTIVO
sponge

esponjoso ADJETIVO
spongy

espontáneo ADJETIVO
spontaneous ◇ *Fue una reacción espontánea.* It was a spontaneous reaction.
◆ **de manera espontánea** spontaneously

la **esposa** SUSTANTIVO
wife (PL wives)
◆ **las esposas** (*para detenidos*) handcuffs

el **esposo** SUSTANTIVO
husband

la **espuma** SUSTANTIVO
1 foam (*de jabón, champú*)
2 head (*de cerveza*)
◆ **la espuma de afeitar** shaving cream

espumoso ADJETIVO
◆ **vino espumoso** sparkling wine

el **esqueleto** SUSTANTIVO
skeleton

el **esquema** SUSTANTIVO
1 outline (*resumen*)
2 diagram (*croquis*)

el **esquí** SUSTANTIVO (PL los **esquís**)
1 skiing (*deporte*) ◇ *Me gusta mucho el esquí.* I enjoy skiing a lot.
◆ **el esquí acuático** water skiing
◆ **una pista de esquí** a ski slope
2 ski (*tabla*)

esquiar* VERBO
to ski ◇ *¿Sabes esquiar?* Can you ski?

el/la **esquimal** ADJETIVO, SUSTANTIVO
Eskimo

la **esquina** SUSTANTIVO
corner
◆ **doblar la esquina** to turn the corner

los **esquites** SUSTANTIVO *Mexico*
popcorn

esquivar VERBO
to dodge (*carro, golpe*)

esta ADJETIVO *ver* **este**

ésta PRONOMBRE *ver* **éste**

está VERBO *ver* **estar**

estable ADJETIVO
stable

establecer* VERBO
to establish (*relación*) ◇ *Se ha establecido una buena relación entre los dos países.* A good relationship has been established between the two countries.
◆ **Han logrado establecer contacto con el barco.** They've managed to make contact

☞

with the boat.
◆ **La familia se estableció en Quito.** The family settled in Quito.

el **establo** SUSTANTIVO
stable

la **estación** SUSTANTIVO (PL las **estaciones**)
[1] station ◇ *la estación de autobuses* the bus station ◇ *la estación de trenes* the train station
[2] season ◇ *las cuatro estaciones del año* the four seasons of the year
◆ **una estación de esquí** a ski resort
◆ **una estación de servicio** a service station

estacionar VERBO
to park (*carro*)

estacionarse VERBO
to park

la **estadía** SUSTANTIVO
stay

el **estadio** SUSTANTIVO
stadium (PL stadiums *o* stadia)

el **estado** SUSTANTIVO
state ◇ *La carretera está en mal estado.* The road is in a bad state.
◆ **estado civil** marital status
◆ **María está en estado.** María is expecting.

los **Estados Unidos** SUSTANTIVO PL
the United States ◇ *en Estados Unidos* in the United States
*A menudo se les llama simplemente **The States**.*

el/la **estadounidense** ADJETIVO, SUSTANTIVO
American

estafar VERBO
to swindle ◇ *Les estafaron 2 millones de pesos.* They swindled 2 million pesos out of them.

estallar VERBO
[1] to explode (*bomba*)
[2] to burst (*neumático, globo*)
[3] to break out (*guerra, revolución*)

la **estampilla** SUSTANTIVO
stamp

estancado ADJETIVO
stagnant (*agua*)

la **estancia** SUSTANTIVO *Mexico*
[1] stay (*permanencia*)
[2] ranch (PL ranches) (*rancho*)

estándar ADJETIVO
standard ◇ *Éstos son los modelos estándar.* These are the standard models.

el **estanque** SUSTANTIVO
pond

el **estante** SUSTANTIVO
shelf (PL shelves) ◇ *Puse los libros en el estante.* I put the books on the shelf.

la **estantería** SUSTANTIVO
[1] shelves PL ◇ *la estantería de la cocina* the kitchen shelves
[2] bookshelves PL (*para libros*)
[3] shelf unit (*mueble*)

el **estaño** SUSTANTIVO
tin

estar* VERBO
Indicando una posición.
[1] to be
*El verbo **to be** en presente suele usarse en las formas contraídas, particularmente al hablar.*
◇ *En la cama se está muy bien.* It's nice being in bed. ◇ *¿Dónde estabas?* Where were you? ◇ *El museo está en el centro de la ciudad.* The museum is in the center of the town.
◆ **¿Está Mónica?** Is Mónica there?
Indicando una situación o estado.
◇ *¿Cómo estás?* How are you? ◇ *Estoy muy cansada.* I'm very tired. ◇ *Estamos de vacaciones.* We're on vacation.
◆ **Hoy no estoy para bromas.** I'm not in the mood for jokes today.
Indicando el aspecto de algo.
[2] to look ◇ *¡Qué linda estás esta noche!* You look really pretty tonight!
Indicando el precio de algo.
◇ *¿A cuánto está el kilo de naranjas?* What price are oranges per kilo?
Con fechas y temperaturas.
◇ *Estamos a 30 de enero.* It's January 30th.
◇ *Estábamos a 40°C.* The temperature was 40°C.
*Cuando **estar** va seguido de un gerundio o un participio también se traduce por **to be**.*
◇ *Estamos esperando a Manolo.* We're waiting for Manolo. ◇ *María estaba sentada en la arena.* María was sitting on the sand.
◇ *La radio está descompuesta.* The radio is broken.
◆ **¡Ya está! Ya sé lo que podemos hacer.** That's it! I know what we can do.
◆ **estarse** to be
◆ **¡Estáte quieto!** Keep still!

estas ADJETIVO *ver* **estos**

éstas PRONOMBRE *ver* **éstos**

estatal ADJETIVO
state
***state** en este caso va siempre delante del sustantivo.*
◆ **un colegio estatal** a public school

la **estatua** SUSTANTIVO
statue

la **estatura** SUSTANTIVO
height ◇ *¿Cuál es tu estatura?* What height are you? ◇ *Mide casi dos metros de estatura.* He's over six and half feet tall.

el **este** SUSTANTIVO, ADJETIVO
east ◇ *el este del país* the east of the country ◇ *en la costa este* on the east coast ◇ *en el este de Chile* in the east of Chile
◆ **vientos del este** easterly winds

este ADJETIVO (FEM **esta**)

this ◇ *este libro* this book

éste PRONOMBRE (FEM **ésta**)

this one ◇ *Ésta me gusta más.* I prefer this one.

◆ **Éste no es el que vi ayer.** This is not the one I saw yesterday.

esté VERBO *ver* **estar**

la **estera** SUSTANTIVO

mat

el **estéreo** SUSTANTIVO

stereo

esterlina ADJETIVO

◆ **diez libras esterlinas** ten pounds sterling

estético ADJETIVO

◆ **Se hizo la cirugía estética.** He's had plastic surgery.

el **estiércol** SUSTANTIVO

manure (*abono*)

el **estilo** SUSTANTIVO

style ◇ *Ése no es mi estilo.* That's not my style.

◆ **un estilo de vida similar al nuestro** a similar lifestyle to ours

◆ **Se viste con mucho estilo.** He dresses very stylishly.

la **estima** SUSTANTIVO

◆ **Lo tengo en gran estima.** I think very highly of him.

estimado ADJETIVO

◆ **Estimado señor Pérez** Dear Mr Pérez

estimulante ADJETIVO

stimulating (*trabajo*)

estimular VERBO

1 to encourage (*persona*) ◇ *Es una forma de estimular a los jugadores para que se esfuercen más.* It's a way of encouraging the players to try harder.

2 to stimulate (*economía*)

estirar VERBO

to stretch ◇ *Voy a salir a estirar las piernas.* I'm going to go out and stretch my legs.

esto PRONOMBRE

this ◇ *¿Para qué es esto?* What's this for?

◆ **En esto llegó Juan.** Just then Juan arrived.

el **estofado** SUSTANTIVO

stew

el **estómago** SUSTANTIVO

stomach ◇ *Me dolía el estómago.* I had stomachache.

estorbar VERBO

to be in the way ◇ *Estas maletas estorban aquí.* These suitcases are in the way here.

estornudar VERBO

to sneeze

estos ADJETIVO PL (FEM **estas**)

these ◇ *estas maletas* these suitcases

éstos PRONOMBRE PL (FEM **éstas**)

these ones ◇ *Éstos son los míos.* These ones are mine.

◆ **Éstos no son los que vimos ayer.** These are not the ones we saw yesterday.

◆ **un día de éstos** one of these days

estoy VERBO *ver* **estar**

estrafalario ADJETIVO

1 eccentric (*persona, ideas*)

2 outlandish (*ropa*)

estrangular VERBO

to strangle

estratégico ADJETIVO

strategic

estrechar VERBO

to take in ◇ *¿Me puedes estrechar esta falda?* Can you take in this skirt for me?

◆ **La carretera se estrecha en el puente.** The road gets narrower over the bridge.

◆ **Se estrecharon la mano.** They shook hands.

estrecho ADJETIVO

1 narrow (*calle, pasillo*)

2 tight ◇ *La falda me queda muy estrecha.* The skirt is very tight on me.

el **estrecho** SUSTANTIVO

strait

◆ **el Estrecho de Gibraltar** the Strait of Gibraltar

la **estrella** SUSTANTIVO

star

◆ **una estrella de cine** a movie star

◆ **una estrella de mar** a starfish

estrellarse VERBO

to smash ◇ *El camión se estrelló contra un árbol.* The truck smashed into a tree.

estrenar VERBO

to premiere ◇ *La película se estrenó en junio.* The movie was premiered in June.

◆ **Mañana estrenaré el vestido.** I'll wear the dress for the first time tomorrow.

el **estreno** SUSTANTIVO

premiere (*de película*)

estreñido ADJETIVO

constipated

el **estrés** SUSTANTIVO

stress

estricto ADJETIVO

strict

estridente ADJETIVO

loud

el **estropajo** SUSTANTIVO

scouring pad

estropeado ADJETIVO

1 broken (*lavadora, tele, radio*)

2 broken down (*carro, motor*)

estropear VERBO

1 to break (*juguete, lavadora*)

2 to ruin ◇ *Ese detergente me estropeó la ropa.* That detergent ruined my clothes. ◇ *La lluvia nos estropeó las vacaciones.* The rain ruined our vacation.

◆ **estropearse** to break ◇ *Se nos ha estropeado la tele.* The TV is broken.

◆ **Se me estropeó el carro en la autopista.** My car broke down on the freeway.

◆ **La fruta se está estropeando con este calor.** ☞

E

The fruit is going off in this heat.

la **estructura** SUSTANTIVO
structure

estrujar VERBO
to wring (*ropa, trapo*)

el **estuche** SUSTANTIVO
case (*de anteojos, lápices*)

el/la **estudiante** SUSTANTIVO
student

estudiar VERBO
to study ◇ *Quiere estudiar medicina.* She wants to study medicine.

el **estudio** SUSTANTIVO
1 studio (*de televisión*)
2 studio apartment (*departamento*)
◆ **Ha dejado los estudios.** He's given up his studies.

estudioso ADJETIVO
studious

la **estufa** SUSTANTIVO
1 heater ◇ *una estufa de gas* a gas heater ◇ *una estufa eléctrica* an electric heater
2 stove Mexico

estupendamente ADVERBIO
◆ **Me encuentro estupendamente.** I feel great. (*coloquial*)
◆ **Lo pasamos estupendamente.** We had a great time.

estupendo ADJETIVO
great ◇ *Pasamos una Navidad estupenda.* We had a great Christmas.
◆ **¡Estupendo!** Great!

la **estupidez** SUSTANTIVO (PL las **estupideces**)
◆ **No dice más que estupideces.** He just talks nonsense.
◆ **Lo que hizo fue una estupidez.** What he did was stupid.

estúpido ADJETIVO
stupid

el **estúpido,** la **estúpida** SUSTANTIVO
idiot ◇ *Ese tipo es un estúpido.* That guy's an idiot.

estuve VERBO *ver* **estar**

la **etapa** SUSTANTIVO
stage ◇ *Lo hicimos por etapas.* We did it in stages.

etc ABREVIATURA (= *etcétera*)
etc.

eterno ADJETIVO
eternal

la **ética** SUSTANTIVO
1 ethics (*asignatura*)
2 ethics PL (*principios morales*)

ético ADJETIVO
ethical

Etiopía SUSTANTIVO FEM
Ethiopia

la **etiqueta** SUSTANTIVO
label
◆ **traje de etiqueta** formal dress

étnico ADJETIVO
ethnic

eufórico ADJETIVO
ecstatic

el **euro** SUSTANTIVO
euro

Europa SUSTANTIVO FEM
Europe

el **europeo,** la **europea** ADJETIVO, SUSTANTIVO
European

evacuar* VERBO
to evacuate

evadir VERBO
1 to avoid (*peligro, pregunta*)
2 to evade (*impuestos*)

la **evaluación** SUSTANTIVO (PL las **evaluaciones**)
assessment ◇ *evaluación continua* continuous assessment

evaluar* VERBO
to assess (*pérdidas, daños, estudiante*)

el **evangelio** SUSTANTIVO
gospel

evaporarse VERBO
to evaporate

evasivo ADJETIVO
evasive

la **evidencia** SUSTANTIVO
evidence
◆ **Ante la evidencia de las hechos, se confesó culpable.** Faced with the evidence, he pleaded guilty.
◆ **Carlos la puso en evidencia delante de todos.** Carlos showed her up in front of everyone.

evidente ADJETIVO
obvious
◆ **Era evidente que estaba agotada.** She was obviously exhausted.

evidentemente ADVERBIO
obviously

evitar VERBO
1 to avoid (*eludir*) ◇ *Quiero evitar ese riesgo.* I want to avoid that risk. ◇ *Trato de evitar a Luisa.* I'm trying to avoid Luisa.
◆ **No pude evitarlo.** I couldn't help it.
2 to save (*ahorrar*) ◇ *Esto nos evitará muchos problemas.* This will save us a lot of problems.

la **evolución** SUSTANTIVO (PL las **evoluciones**)
progress ◇ *Seguimos de cerca la evolución del paciente.* We are keeping a close watch on the patient's progress.
◆ **la teoría de la evolución** the theory of evolution

evolucionar VERBO
1 to develop ◇ *Este país no ha evolucionado en la última década.* This country hasn't developed in the last decade.
◆ **El enfermo evoluciona favorablemente.** The patient is making good progress.
2 to evolve (*especie*)

ex PREFIJO
ex
◆ **su ex marido** her ex-husband

exactamente ADVERBIO
exactly

la **exactitud** SUSTANTIVO
◆ **No lo sabemos con exactitud.** We don't know exactly.

exacto ADJETIVO
1 exact ◇ *el precio exacto* the exact price
◆ **El tren salió a la hora exacta.** The train left right on time.
2 accurate ◇ *Tus conclusiones no son muy exactas.* Your conclusions aren't very accurate.
◆ **Tenemos que defender nuestros derechos. – ¡Exacto!** We have to stand up for our rights. – Exactly!

la **exageración** SUSTANTIVO (PL las **exageraciones**)
exaggeration

exagerado ADJETIVO
exaggerated (*descripción*)
◆ **¡No seas exagerada, no era tan alto!** Don't exaggerate! He wasn't that tall.
◆ **El precio me parece exagerado.** I think the price is excessive.

exagerar VERBO
to exaggerate

el **examen** SUSTANTIVO (PL los **exámenes**)
exam
◆ **el examen de manejar** driving test

examinar VERBO
to examine ◇ *El médico la examinó.* The doctor examined her.
◆ **Nos examinaron dos profesores.** We were tested by two teachers.

la **excavadora** SUSTANTIVO
excavator

excavar VERBO
to dig ◇ *Los niños excavaban en la arena.* The children were digging in the sand. ◇ *Están excavando un túnel.* They're digging a tunnel.

excelente ADJETIVO
excellent

excéntrico ADJETIVO
eccentric

la **excepción** SUSTANTIVO (PL las **excepciones**)
exception
◆ **a excepción de** except for

excepcional ADJETIVO
exceptional

excepto PREPOSICIÓN
except for ◇ *todos, excepto Juan* everyone, except for Juan

excesivo ADJETIVO
excessive

el **exceso** SUSTANTIVO
◆ **Anoche bebí en exceso.** Last night I drank to excess.
◆ **exceso de equipaje** excess luggage
◆ **Me multaron por exceso de velocidad.** They fined me for speeding.

excitarse VERBO
◆ **Se excitó mucho en la discusión.** He got very worked up in the argument.

exclamar VERBO
to exclaim

excluir* VERBO
to exclude ◇ *Me excluyeron de la lista.* They excluded me from the list.

exclusivo ADJETIVO
exclusive (*club, diseño*)

excluyendo VERBO *ver* **excluir**

la **excursión** SUSTANTIVO (PL las **excursiones**)
trip ◇ *Mañana vamos de excursión con el colegio.* Tomorrow we're going on a school trip.

la **excusa** SUSTANTIVO
excuse

la **exhibición** SUSTANTIVO (PL las **exhibiciones**)
display ◇ *hay varias esculturas en exhibición* there are various sculptures on display

exhibir VERBO
to exhibit (*obras de arte*)
◆ **Le gusta mucho exhibirse.** He likes drawing attention to himself.

exigente ADJETIVO
demanding ◇ *El jefe es muy exigente con nosotros.* The boss is very demanding with us.

exigir* VERBO
1 to demand ◇ *Exigió hablar con el encargado.* He demanded to speak to the manager.
◆ **La maestra nos exige demasiado.** Our teacher is too demanding.
2 to require ◇ *Ese puesto exige mucha paciencia.* This job requires a lot of patience.
◆ **Exigen tres años de experiencia para el puesto.** They're asking for three years' experience for the job.

el **exiliado**, la **exiliada** SUSTANTIVO
exile

existir VERBO
to exist ◇ *¿Existen los fantasmas?* Do ghosts exist?
◆ **Existen dos maneras de hacerlo.** There are two ways of doing it.

el **éxito** SUSTANTIVO
success (PL successes) ◇ *Esa novela será un gran éxito.* That novel will be a great success.
◆ **Su película tuvo mucho éxito.** His movie was very successful.
◆ **Acabaron con éxito el proyecto.** They completed the project successfully.
*No confundir **éxito** con **exit**.*

exitoso ADJETIVO
successful

exótico ADJETIVO

☞

exotic

la **expansión** SUSTANTIVO (PL las **expansiones**)
expansion

la **expedición** SUSTANTIVO (PL las **expediciones**)
expedition

el **expediente** SUSTANTIVO
file (*documentación*)
- **expediente académico** student record
- **Le han abierto expediente por mala conducta.** He has been disciplined for bad behavior.

el **expendio** SUSTANTIVO
store (*tienda*)

las **expensas** SUSTANTIVO
- **a expensas de su salud** at the cost of her health
- **vivir a expensas de alguien** to live at somebody's expense

la **experiencia** SUSTANTIVO
experience ◇ *"Se requiere experiencia laboral"* "Work experience required"
- **con experiencia** experienced
- **sin experiencia** inexperienced

experimental ADJETIVO
experimental

experimentar VERBO
1 to experiment ◇ *experimentar con animales* to experiment on animals
2 to experience (*dolor, alegría*)

el **experimento** SUSTANTIVO
experiment

el **experto,** la **experta** SUSTANTIVO
expert
- **Es un experto en computación.** He's a computer expert.

la **explanada** SUSTANTIVO
esplanade

la **explicación** SUSTANTIVO (PL las **explicaciones**)
explanation

explicar* VERBO
to explain
La preposición **to** *debe aparecer delante del objeto indirecto.*
◇ *Le expliqué cómo se hacía una paella.* I explained to her how to make a paella.
- **Antonio se explica muy bien.** Antonio is very good at expressing himself.
- **¿Me explico?** Do I make myself clear?
- **No me lo explico.** I can't understand it.

el **explorador,** la **exploradora** SUSTANTIVO
explorer

explorar VERBO
to explore

la **explosión** SUSTANTIVO (PL las **explosiones**)
explosion
- **El artefacto hizo explosión.** The device exploded.

el **explosivo** SUSTANTIVO
explosive

la **explotación** SUSTANTIVO (PL las **explotaciones**)
exploitation

explotar VERBO
1 to exploit (*tierra, trabajador*) ◇ *Sabe cómo explotar sus posibilidades.* He knows how to exploit his potential.
2 to explode ◇ *La caldera explotó.* The boiler exploded.

exponer* VERBO
1 to display (*cuadro, productos*)
2 to present (*idea*)

la **exportación** SUSTANTIVO (PL las **exportaciones**)
export

exportar VERBO
to export

la **exposición** SUSTANTIVO (PL las **exposiciones**)
exhibition ◇ *hacer una exposición* to put on an exhibition

expresamente ADVERBIO
1 specifically ◇ *Mencioné expresamente tu nombre.* I specifically mentioned your name.
2 specially ◇ *Fui expresamente a devolvérselo.* I went specially to give it back to him.

expresar VERBO
to express ◇ *No sabe expresarse.* He doesn't know how to express himself.

la **expresión** SUSTANTIVO (PL las **expresiones**)
expression

expresivo ADJETIVO
expressive

el **expreso** SUSTANTIVO
1 express (*tren*)
2 espresso (*café*)

exprimir VERBO
to squeeze (*limón, naranja*)

expuesto VERBO *ver* **exponer**

expulsar VERBO
1 to expel ◇ *La expulsaron del colegio.* They expelled her from school.
2 to send off ◇ *El árbitro lo expulsó del terreno de juego.* The referee sent him off the field.

la **expulsión** SUSTANTIVO (PL las **expulsiones**)
expulsion (*de colegio, territorio*)
- **La expulsión del jugador fue injusta.** Sending the player off was unfair.

exquisito ADJETIVO
delicious ◇ *El postre estaba exquisito.* The dessert was delicious.

el **éxtasis** SUSTANTIVO
ecstasy

extender* VERBO
to spread (*mantequilla, pintura*) ◇ *Extendí la toalla sobre la arena.* I spread the towel out on the sand. ◇ *El fuego se extendió rápidamente.* The fire spread quickly.
- **extender los brazos** to stretch one's arms out

extendido ADJETIVO

1 outstretched (*brazos, alas*)
2 widespread (*costumbre, opinión*)

la **extensión** SUSTANTIVO (PL las **extensiones**)
area ◇ *una enorme extensión de tierra* an enormous area of land
◆ **¿Me comunica con la extensión 212, por favor?** Can you put me through to extension 212, please?

extenso ADJETIVO
extensive (*superficie, conocimientos*)

exterior ADJETIVO (FEM **exterior**)
1 outside (*pared, superficie*)
2 foreign (*política, comercio*)

el **exterior** SUSTANTIVO
outside
◆ **Salimos al exterior para ver qué pasaba.** We went outside to see what was going on.

externo ADJETIVO
1 outside (*influencia*)
2 outer (*superficie*)

extiendo VERBO *ver* **extender**

la **extinción** SUSTANTIVO
putting out (*de incendio*)
◆ **una especie en vías de extinción** an endangered species

el **extinguidor** SUSTANTIVO
fire extinguisher

extinguir* VERBO
to put out (*fuego*)
◆ **extinguirse** (*volcán*) to become extinct
◆ **El fuego se fue extinguiendo lentamente.** The fire was slowly going out.

extinto ADJETIVO
extinct

extra ADJETIVO
extra ◇ *una manta extra* an extra blanket
◆ **chocolate de calidad extra** top quality chocolate

el/la **extra** SUSTANTIVO
extra (*de cine*)

el **extractor** SUSTANTIVO
extractor fan
◆ **un extractor de humos** a smoke extractor

extraer* VERBO
1 to extract ◇ *El dentista me extrajo la muela.* The dentist has extracted my tooth.
2 to draw (*conclusiones*)

extraescolar ADJETIVO
◆ **actividades extraescolares** extracurricular activities

extraigo VERBO *ver* **extraer**

extranjero ADJETIVO
foreign

el **extranjero,** la **extranjera** SUSTANTIVO
foreigner (*persona*)
◆ **vivir en el extranjero** to live abroad
◆ **viajar al extranjero** to travel abroad

extrañar VERBO
to miss ◇ *Extraña mucho a sus padres.* He misses his parents a lot.
◆ **Me extraña que no haya llegado.** I'm surprised he hasn't arrived.
◆ **¡Ya me extrañaba a mí!** I thought it was strange!
◆ **extrañarse de algo** to be surprised at something ◇ *Se extrañó de vernos juntos.* He was surprised to see us together.

la **extrañeza** SUSTANTIVO
◆ **Nos miró con extrañeza.** He looked at us in surprise.

extraño ADJETIVO
strange
◆ **¡Qué extraño!** How strange!

extraordinario ADJETIVO
extraordinary

extravagante ADJETIVO
extravagant

extraviado ADJETIVO
1 lost (*objeto*)
2 missing (*persona, animal*)

extraviar* VERBO
to mislay ◇ *Me extraviaron el equipaje en el aeropuerto.* They mislaid my luggage at the airport.

el/la **extremista** ADJETIVO, SUSTANTIVO
extremist

extremo ADJETIVO
extreme ◇ *Ése es un caso extremo.* That's an extreme case.
◆ **la extrema derecha** the far Right
◆ **extremo derecho** (*jugador*) right winger
◆ **el Extremo Oriente** the Far East

el **extremo** SUSTANTIVO
end (*punta*) ◇ *Agarré la cuerda por un extremo.* I took hold of one end of the rope.
◆ **pasar de un extremo a otro** to go from one extreme to the other
◆ **en último extremo** as a last resort

extrovertido ADJETIVO
outgoing ◇ *José es muy extrovertido.* José is very outgoing.

exuberante ADJETIVO
lush (*vegetación*)

E

F

la **fábrica** SUSTANTIVO
factory (PL factories)
- **una fábrica de conservas** a canning plant
*No confundir **fábrica** con **fabric**.*

el/la **fabricante** SUSTANTIVO
manufacturer

fabricar* VERBO
to make
- **"fabricado en China"** "made in China"

la **fachada** SUSTANTIVO
- **la fachada del edificio** the front of the building

fácil ADJETIVO
easy ◇ *El examen fue muy fácil.* The exam was very easy.
- **Es fácil de entender.** It's easy to understand.
- **Es fácil que se le haya perdido.** He may have lost it.

la **facilidad** SUSTANTIVO
- **Se me rompen las uñas con facilidad.** My nails break easily.
- **Pepe tiene facilidad para los idiomas.** Pepe has a gift for languages.
- **Dan facilidades de pago.** They offer credit facilities.

facilitar VERBO
to make...easier ◇ *Una computadora facilita mucho el trabajo.* A computer makes work much easier.
- **El banco me facilitó la información.** The bank provided me with the information.

el **factor** SUSTANTIVO
factor ◇ *La edad del paciente es un factor importante.* The age of the patient is an important factor.

la **factura** SUSTANTIVO
bill ◇ *la factura del gas* the gas bill

la **facultad** SUSTANTIVO
[1] faculty (PL faculties) ◇ *Mi abuela está perdiendo sus facultades.* My grandmother is losing her faculties.
- **la Facultad de Derecho** the Law Faculty

[2] university
- **ir a la facultad** to go to university

la **faena** SUSTANTIVO
work ◇ *Tengo mucha faena.* I've got a lot of work.
- **las faenas domésticas** the housework

la **falda** SUSTANTIVO
skirt

la **falla** SUSTANTIVO
[1] fault (*defecto leve*) ◇ *una pequeña falla eléctrica* a small electrical fault
[2] failure (*defecto grave*) ◇ *debido a una falla del motor* due to engine failure
[3] mistake (*error*) ◇ *una falla en los cálculos* a mistake in the calculations
- **Fue una falla humana.** It was human error.

fallar VERBO
to fail (*frenos, motor, vista*) ◇ *Le falla la memoria.* His memory is failing.
- **Fallé el tiro.** I missed.

fallecer* VERBO
to die

falsificar* VERBO
to forge (*firma, documento*)

falso ADJETIVO
[1] false (*nombre, pasaporte*)
[2] forged (*billete*)
- **Los diamantes eran falsos.** The diamonds were fakes.
- **Eso es falso.** That's not true.

la **falta** SUSTANTIVO
[1] lack (*carencia*) ◇ *la falta de dinero* lack of money
[2] foul (*en fútbol, básquetbol*) ◇ *Ha sido falta.* It was a foul.
- **Tiene cinco faltas de asistencia.** He has been absent five times.
- **Eso es una falta de educación.** That's bad manners.
- **una falta de ortografía** a spelling mistake
- **Me hace falta una computadora.** I need a computer.
- **No hace falta que vengan.** You don't need to come.

faltar VERBO
to be missing ◇ *Me falta un calcetín.* One of my socks is missing.
- **Faltan varios libros del estante.** There are several books missing from the shelf.
- **No podemos irnos. Falta Manolo.** We can't go. Manolo isn't here yet.
- **A la sopa le falta sal.** There isn't enough salt in the soup.
- **Falta media hora para comer.** There's half an hour to go before lunch.
- **¿Te falta mucho?** Will you be long?
- **faltar al colegio** to miss school

la **fama** SUSTANTIVO
fame
- **alcanzar* la fama** to become famous
- **tener* mala fama** to have a bad reputation
- **Tiene fama de mujeriego.** He has a reputation for being a womanizer.

la **familia** SUSTANTIVO
family (PL families)
- **una familia numerosa** a large family

familiar ADJETIVO
[1] family
***family** en este caso va siempre delante del sustantivo.*
◇ *la vida familiar* family life
[2] familiar ◇ *Su cara me es familiar.* Your face is familiar.

el/la **familiar** SUSTANTIVO

* Verbs marked with this symbol are irregular. See pages 346–348 for further details.

relative ◇ *un familiar mío* a relative of mine

famoso ADJETIVO
famous

el/la **fan** SUSTANTIVO (PL los **fans**)
fan

la **fantasía** SUSTANTIVO
fantasy (PL fantasies) ◇ *un mundo de fantasía* a fantasy world ◇ *Son fantasías infantiles.* They're just children's fantasies.
◆ **las joyas de fantasía** costume jewelry SING

el **fantasma** SUSTANTIVO
ghost

fantástico ADJETIVO
fantastic

el **farmacéutico**, la **farmacéutica** SUSTANTIVO
pharmacist

la **farmacia** SUSTANTIVO
pharmacy (PL pharmacies) ◇ *Lo compré en la farmacia.* I bought it at the pharmacy.

el **faro** SUSTANTIVO
1 lighthouse (*en la costa*)
2 headlight (*de carro, moto*)
3 light (*de bicicleta*)
◆ **los faros antiniebla** fog lights

el **farol** SUSTANTIVO
1 streetlight (*en la calle*)
2 lantern (*en el jardín*)
3 headlight (*de carro, moto*) *Mexico*

la **farra** SUSTANTIVO
◆ **irse* de farra** to go out on the town

el **fascículo** SUSTANTIVO
part ◇ *el primer fascículo del libro* the first part of the book

fascinante ADJETIVO
fascinating

el/la **fascista** ADJETIVO, SUSTANTIVO
fascist

la **fase** SUSTANTIVO
phase

fastidiar VERBO
1 to annoy ◇ *Lo que más me molesta es tener que decírselo.* What annoys me most is having to tell him.
◆ **Esa actitud me molesta mucho.** I find this attitude very annoying.
2 to pester ◇ *¡Deja ya de molestarme!* Will you stop pestering me!

el **fastidio** SUSTANTIVO
◆ **¡Qué fastidio!** What a nuisance!

fatal ADJETIVO
awful ◇ *Nos hizo un tiempo fatal.* We had awful weather. ◇ *Me siento fatal.* I feel awful. ◇ *La obra estuvo fatal.* The play was awful.

el **favor** SUSTANTIVO
favor ◇ *¿Puedes hacerme un favor?* Can you do me a favor?
◆ **por favor** please
◆ **¡Hagan el favor de callarse!** Will you please be quiet!
◆ **estar* a favor de algo** to be in favor of something

favorecer* VERBO
to suit (*vestido, peinado*) ◇ *Ese color te favorece mucho.* That color really suits you.

favorito ADJETIVO
favorite ◇ *¿Cuál es tu color favorito?* What's your favorite color?

el **fax** SUSTANTIVO (PL los **fax**)
fax (PL faxes)
◆ **mandar algo por fax** to fax something

la **fe** SUSTANTIVO
faith
◆ **tener* fe en algo** to have faith in something

febrero SUSTANTIVO MASC
En inglés, los meses se escriben con mayúscula.
February ◇ *en febrero* in February ◇ *Ella nació el 28 de febrero.* She was born on February 28th.

la **fecha** SUSTANTIVO
date ◇ *¿A qué fecha estamos?* What's the date today?
◆ **La carta tiene fecha del 21 de enero.** The letter is dated January 21st.
◆ **la fecha de caducidad** (*de alimentos*) the expiration date
◆ **la fecha límite** (*para solicitud*) the closing date
◆ **la fecha tope** the deadline
◆ **su fecha de nacimiento** his date of birth

la **felicidad** SUSTANTIVO
happiness ◇ *Carmen lloraba de felicidad.* Carmen was crying with happiness.
◆ **¡Felicidades!** (*por cumpleaños*) Happy birthday!

las **felicitaciones** SUSTANTIVO
congratulations ◇ *Mis felicitaciones al ganador.* My congratulations to the winner.
◆ **He recibido muchas felicitaciones.** Lots of people have congratulated me.
◆ **¡Felicitaciones!** Congratulations!

felicitar VERBO
to congratulate ◇ *La felicité por sus notas.* I congratulated her on her exam results.
◆ **¡Te felicito!** Congratulations!
◆ **felicitar a alguien por su cumpleaños** to wish somebody a happy birthday

feliz ADJETIVO (PL **felices**)
happy ◇ *Se la ve muy feliz.* She looks very happy.
◆ **¡Feliz cumpleaños!** Happy birthday!
◆ **¡Feliz Año Nuevo!** Happy New Year!
◆ **¡Feliz Navidad!** Happy Christmas!

el **felpudo** SUSTANTIVO
doormat

femenino ADJETIVO
1 feminine (*modales, vestido*) ◇ *una chica muy femenina* a very feminine girl
2 female (*cuerpo, órganos*) ◇ *el sexo femenino* the female sex
3 women's (*equipo, deporte*) ◇ *el tenis femenino* women's tennis

el **femenino** SUSTANTIVO
feminine ◇ *El femenino de "lobo" es "loba".* The feminine of "lobo" is "loba".

fenomenal ADJETIVO, ADVERBIO
great (*coloquial*) ◇ *Nos hizo un tiempo fenomenal.* We had great weather.
◆ **Lo pasé fenomenal.** I had a great time.

feo (1) ADJETIVO
1 ugly ◇ *un edificio muy feo* a very ugly building
2 unpleasant (*desagradable*) ◇ *un sabor feo* an unpleasant taste

feo (2) ADVERBIO
bad ◇ *Esta leche sabe feo.* This milk tastes bad.
◆ **mirar feo a alguien** to give someone a dirty look

el **féretro** SUSTANTIVO
coffin

la **feria** SUSTANTIVO
1 fair
◆ **una feria de muestras** a trade fair
2 small change (*cambio*) Mexico

el **feriado** SUSTANTIVO
holiday ◇ *El próximo lunes es feriado.* Next Monday's a holiday.

la **ferretería** SUSTANTIVO
hardware store ◇ *Lo compré en la ferretería.* I bought it at the hardware store.

el **ferrocarril** SUSTANTIVO
railroad

fértil ADJETIVO
fertile

el **fertilizante** SUSTANTIVO
fertilizer

festejar VERBO
to celebrate

el **festival** SUSTANTIVO
festival

festivo ADJETIVO
festive (*ambiente*)
◆ **un día festivo** a holiday

el **feto** SUSTANTIVO
fetus (PL fetuses)

fiable ADJETIVO
reliable

los **fiambres** SUSTANTIVO
cold cuts

la **fianza** SUSTANTIVO
deposit ◇ *Dejé una fianza de 2.000 pesos.* I left a 2000 peso deposit.

fiar* VERBO
◆ **Es un hombre de fiar.** He's completely trustworthy.
◆ **fiarse de alguien** to trust somebody ◇ *No me fío de él.* I don't trust him.

la **fibra** SUSTANTIVO
fiber ◇ *fibras artificiales* man-made fibers

la **ficha** SUSTANTIVO
1 index card (*tarjeta*)
2 counter (*en juegos de mesa*)
◆ **una ficha de dominó** a domino (PL dominoes)

el **fichero** SUSTANTIVO
1 filing cabinet (*archivador*)
2 card index (*caja con fichas*)
3 file (*informática*)

los **fideos** SUSTANTIVO
noodles (*para sopa*)

la **fiebre** SUSTANTIVO
1 temperature (*síntoma*) ◇ *Le bajó la fiebre.* His temperature came down.
◆ **tener* fiebre** to have a temperature
2 fever (*enfermedad*) ◇ *la fiebre amarilla* yellow fever

fiel ADJETIVO
faithful
◆ **ser* fiel a alguien** to be faithful to somebody

la **fiera** SUSTANTIVO
wild animal

el **fierro** SUSTANTIVO
iron ◇ *una reja de fierro* iron railings
◆ **Le pegó con un fierro.** He hit him with a metal bar.

la **fiesta** SUSTANTIVO
1 party (PL parties) ◇ *Voy a dar una fiesta para celebrarlo.* I'm going to have a party to celebrate.
◆ **una fiesta de cumpleaños** a birthday party
2 holiday ◇ *El lunes es fiesta.* Monday is a holiday.
◆ **Toda la nación está de fiesta.** The whole country is celebrating.
◆ **El pueblo está en fiestas.** There's a fiesta on in the town.
◆ **Fiestas Patrias**

> ℹ ***Fiestas Patrias** are the days on which each Latin American country celebrates its independence with ceremonies and entertainment.*

la **figura** SUSTANTIVO
figure ◇ *una figura de porcelana* a porcelain figure

figurar VERBO
to appear ◇ *Su nombre no figura en la lista.* His name doesn't appear on the list.
◆ **figurarse** to imagine ◇ *Figúrate lo que debió sufrir.* Just imagine how he must have suffered.
◆ **¡Ya me lo figuraba!** I thought as much!

fijar VERBO
to fix ◇ *Tienes que fijar la fecha.* You must fix the date.
◆ **fijarse (1)** (*prestar atención*) to pay attention ◇ *Tienes que fijarte más en lo que haces.* You must pay more attention to what you're doing.
◆ **fijarse (2)** to notice ◇ *No me fijé en la ropa que llevaba.* I didn't notice what she was

* Verbs marked with this symbol are irregular. See pages 346–348 for further details.

wearing.
◆ **¡Fíjate en esos dos!** Just look at those two!

fijo ADJETIVO
1 fixed ◇ *Gano un sueldo fijo.* I earn a fixed salary.
2 permanent (*empleado, contrato*)

la **fila** SUSTANTIVO
1 row (*de asientos*) ◇ *Estábamos sentados en segunda fila.* We were sitting in the second row.
2 line (*de personas*) ◇ *Los niños se pusieron en fila.* The children got into line.

el **filete** SUSTANTIVO
1 steak ◇ *un filete con papas fritas* a steak and french fries
2 fillet ◇ *un filete de merluza* a filet of haddock

Filipinas SUSTANTIVO FEM PL
the Philippines

filmar VERBO
to film ◇ *Mi hermano filmó nuestra boda.* My brother filmed our wedding.
◆ **filmar una película** to shoot a movie

el **filo** SUSTANTIVO
◆ **Tiene poco filo.** It isn't very sharp.

filoso ADJETIVO
sharp

la **filosofía** SUSTANTIVO
philosophy (PL philosophies)

filtrar VERBO
to filter ◇ *Hay que filtrar el agua.* The water needs filtering.
◆ **filtrarse (1)** (*agua*) to seep ◇ *El agua se filtraba por las paredes.* Water was seeping in through the walls.
◆ **filtrarse (2)** (*luz*) to filter ◇ *La luz se filtraba por las rendijas.* Light was filtering in through the cracks.

el **filtro** SUSTANTIVO
filter

el **fin** SUSTANTIVO
end ◇ *el fin de una era* the end of an era
◆ **a fines de** at the end of ◇ *a fines de abril* at the end of April
◆ **al fin** finally ◇ *Al fin llegaron a un acuerdo.* They finally reached an agreement.
◆ **al fin y al cabo** after all
◆ **En fin, ¡qué le vamos a hacer!** Oh well, what can we do about it!
◆ **por fin** at last ◇ *¡Por fin hemos llegado!* We're here at last!
◆ **el fin de año** New Year's Eve
◆ **el fin de semana** the weekend

final ADJETIVO
final ◇ *el resultado final* the final result

el **final** SUSTANTIVO
end (*de pasillo, película*) ◇ *Al final de la calle hay un semáforo.* At the end of the street there's a set of traffic lights.
◆ **a finales de mayo** at the end of May
◆ **al final** in the end ◇ *Al final tuve que darle la razón.* In the end I had to admit that he was right.
◆ **un final feliz** a happy ending

la **final** SUSTANTIVO
final ◇ *Consiguieron pasar a la final.* They managed to get through to the final.

la **finca** SUSTANTIVO
country house (*casa de campo*)

fingir* VERBO
to pretend ◇ *Fingió no haberme oído.* He pretended not to have heard me.

finlandés ADJETIVO (FEM **finlandesa**, MASC PL **finlandeses**)
Finnish

el **finlandés**, la **finlandesa** SUSTANTIVO (MASC PL los **finlandeses**)
Finn

el **finlandés** SUSTANTIVO
Finnish (*idioma*)

Finlandia SUSTANTIVO FEM
Finland

fino ADJETIVO
1 thin (*papel, capa*)
2 fine (*arena, punta, pelo*)
3 slender (*dedos, cuello*)

la **firma** SUSTANTIVO
signature

firmar VERBO
to sign

firme ADJETIVO
1 steady (*mesa, andamio*) ◇ *Mantén la escalera firme.* Can you hold the ladder steady?
2 firm (*persona*) ◇ *Se mostró muy firme con ella.* He was very firm with her.

el/la **fiscal** SUSTANTIVO
district attorney

fisgar* VERBO
to snoop (*coloquial*) ◇ *La encontré fisgando en mi bolso.* I found her snooping in my purse.

la **física** SUSTANTIVO
1 physics SING (*asignatura, ciencia*)
2 physicist (*científica*)

físico ADJETIVO
physical

el **físico** SUSTANTIVO
physicist (*científico*)

flaco ADJETIVO
thin

la **flama** SUSTANTIVO *Mexico*
flame

el **flamenco** SUSTANTIVO
flamenco

el **flan** SUSTANTIVO
creme caramel

el **flash** SUSTANTIVO (PL los **flashes**)
flash (PL flashes)

la **flauta** SUSTANTIVO
1 recorder (*dulce*)
2 flute (*travesera*)

la **flecha** SUSTANTIVO
arrow
el **flechazo** SUSTANTIVO
◆ **Fue un flechazo.** It was love at first sight.
el **fleco** SUSTANTIVO *Mexico*
bangs PL
los **flecos** SUSTANTIVO
fringe SING ◇ *un mantel con flecos* a fringed tablecloth
el **flequillo** SUSTANTIVO
bangs PL
flexible ADJETIVO
flexible
flojo ADJETIVO
1 loose (*nudo, tornillo*)
2 slack (*elástico*)
3 weak (*té, café*)
4 lazy (*persona*)
◆ **Todavía tengo las piernas muy flojas.** My legs are still very weak.
◆ **Está flojo en matemáticas.** He's weak at math.
la **flor** SUSTANTIVO
flower ◇ *un ramo de flores* a bunch of flowers
la **florería** SUSTANTIVO
florist's (PL florists') ◇ *Las compré en la florería.* I bought them at the florist's.
el **florero** SUSTANTIVO
vase
el **flotador** SUSTANTIVO
float (*para la cintura*)
◆ **flotadores** (*para el brazo*) water wings
flotar VERBO
to float
flote ADVERBIO
◆ **a flote** afloat ◇ *La barca se mantuvo a flote.* The boat stayed afloat.
fluir* VERBO
to flow
fluorescente ADJETIVO
fluorescent
fluyendo VERBO *ver* **fluir**
la **foca** SUSTANTIVO
seal (*animal*)
el **foco** SUSTANTIVO
1 spotlight (*de teatro*)
2 floodlight (*de estadio, monumento*)
3 headlight (*de carro, camión*)
4 light bulb (*de lámpara*) *Mexico*
◆ **el foco de atención** the focus of attention
el **folio** SUSTANTIVO
sheet of paper (PL sheets of paper)
◆ **un documento de 20 folios** a 20-page document
◆ **un sobre de tamaño folio** a legal-size envelope
el **folklore** SUSTANTIVO
folklore
el **folleto** SUSTANTIVO
1 brochure (*libro*)
2 leaflet (*hoja*)
fomentar VERBO
to promote (*turismo, industria*)
la **fonda** SUSTANTIVO
restaurant (*restaurante*)
el **fondo** SUSTANTIVO
1 bottom (*parte más honda*) ◇ *el fondo de la cazuela* the bottom of the pan
◆ **en el fondo del mar** at the bottom of the sea
2 end (*parte trasera*) ◇ *Mi pieza está al fondo del pasillo.* My room's at the end of the corridor.
◆ **estudiar una materia a fondo** to study a subject in depth
◆ **un corredor de fondo** a long-distance runner
◆ **en el fondo** deep down
◆ **recaudar fondos** to raise funds
el **footing** SUSTANTIVO
jogging ◇ *Hago footing todas las mañanas.* I go jogging every morning.
forestal ADJETIVO
forest
***forest** en este caso va siempre delante del sustantivo.*
◇ *un incendio forestal* a forest fire
la **forma** SUSTANTIVO
1 shape (*contorno*) ◇ *Me gusta la forma de esa mesa.* I like the shape of that table.
◆ **en forma de pera** pear-shaped
2 way (*manera*) ◇ *Me miraba de una forma extraña.* She was looking at me in a strange way.
3 form (*formulario*) *Mexico* ◇ *Hay que llenar una forma.* You have to fill out a form.
◆ **de todas formas** anyway
◆ **estar* en forma** to be fit
la **formación** SUSTANTIVO (PL las **formaciones**)
training (*educación*)
◆ **formación profesional** vocational training
formal ADJETIVO
1 responsible ◇ *un chico muy formal* a very responsible boy
◆ **Sé formal y pórtate bien.** Be good and behave yourself.
2 formal (*estilo, lenguage*)
formar VERBO
to start ◇ *Quieren formar una orquesta.* They want to start an orchestra.
◆ **Se formó una cola enorme en la puerta.** An enormous line formed at the door.
◆ **estar* formado por** to be made up of
◆ **formar parte de algo** to be part of something
formidable ADJETIVO
fantastic (*coloquial*) ◇ *Pedro tiene un carro formidable.* Pedro has a fantastic car.
◇ *Desde la oficina hay una vista formidable.* There's a fantastic view from the office.
la **fórmula** SUSTANTIVO
formula (PL formulas *o* formulae) ◇ *una*

fórmula mágica a magic formula
◆ **carros de Fórmula 1** Formula 1 cars
el **formulario** SUSTANTIVO
form ◇ *Hay que llenar un formulario.* You have to fill out a form.
forrar VERBO
1 to line (*chaqueta*)
2 to cover (*libro, sofá*)
el **forro** SUSTANTIVO
1 lining (*de chaqueta*)
2 cover (*de libro, sillón*)
la **fortuna** SUSTANTIVO
fortune ◇ *Vale una fortuna.* It's worth a fortune.
◆ **por fortuna** luckily
forzar* VERBO
to force (*puerta, sonrisa*)
◆ **Estás forzando la vista.** You're straining your eyes.
la **fosa** SUSTANTIVO
1 ditch (PL ditches) (*zanja*)
2 grave (*tumba*)
el **fósforo** SUSTANTIVO
match (PL matches) ◇ *una caja de fósforos* a box of matches
la **foto** SUSTANTIVO
photo ◇ *Les saqué una foto a los niños.* I took a photo of the children.
la **fotocopia** SUSTANTIVO
photocopy (PL photocopies) ◇ *Hice dos fotocopias del recibo.* I made two photocopies of the receipt.
la **fotocopiadora** SUSTANTIVO
photocopier
fotocopiar VERBO
to photocopy
la **fotógrafa** SUSTANTIVO
photographer
la **fotografía** SUSTANTIVO
1 photograph (*retrato*) ◇ *una fotografía de mis padres* a photograph of my parents
2 photography (*arte*) ◇ *un curso de fotografía* a photography course
el **fotógrafo** SUSTANTIVO
photographer
fracasar VERBO
to fail
el **fracaso** SUSTANTIVO
failure
la **fracción** SUSTANTIVO (PL las **fracciones**)
fraction
la **fractura** SUSTANTIVO
fracture
frágil ADJETIVO
fragile
el **fraile** SUSTANTIVO
friar
la **frambuesa** SUSTANTIVO
raspberry (PL raspberries)
francés ADJETIVO (FEM **francesa**, MASC PL **franceses**)
French
el **francés** SUSTANTIVO (MASC PL los **franceses**)
1 Frenchman (PL Frenchmen) (*persona*)
◆ **los franceses** the French
2 French (*idioma*)
la **francesa** SUSTANTIVO
Frenchwoman (PL Frenchwomen)
Francia SUSTANTIVO FEM
France
franco ADJETIVO
1 frank (*persona*)
◆ **para serte franco...** to be frank with you...
2 off (*día, hora*) *Mexico* ◇ *Tengo la mañana franca.* I have the morning off.
el **franco** SUSTANTIVO
franc (*moneda*)
el **franqueo** SUSTANTIVO
postage
el **frasco** SUSTANTIVO
1 bottle ◇ *un frasco de perfume* a bottle of perfume
2 jar ◇ *un frasco de encurtidos* a jar of pickles
la **frase** SUSTANTIVO
sentence (*oración*)
◆ **una frase hecha** a set phrase
el **fraude** SUSTANTIVO
fraud
la **frazada** SUSTANTIVO
blanket
la **frecuencia** SUSTANTIVO
frequency (PL frequencies) ◇ *¿En qué frecuencia está?* What frequency is it on?
◆ **Nos vemos con frecuencia.** We often see each other.
◆ **¿Con qué frecuencia tienen estos síntomas?** How often do they get these symptoms?
frecuente ADJETIVO
1 common (*común*) ◇ *un error bastante frecuente* a fairly common mistake
2 frequent (*reiterado*) ◇ *los frecuentes viajes del presidente al extranjero* the president's frequent trips abroad
el **fregadero** SUSTANTIVO
1 kitchen sink (*de la cocina*)
2 sink (*para lavar ropa*) *Mexico*
fregar* VERBO
to scrub ◇ *Tengo que fregar la cacerola.* I have to scrub the pan.
freír* VERBO
to fry ◇ *No sabe ni freír un huevo.* He can't even fry an egg.
frenar VERBO
to brake
el **frenazo** SUSTANTIVO
◆ **Tuve que dar un frenazo.** I had to brake suddenly.
el **freno** SUSTANTIVO
brake ◇ *Me quedé sin frenos.* My brakes failed.
◆ **el freno de mano** the handbrake
☞

◆ **frenos** (*en los dientes*) Mexico braces

la **frente** SUSTANTIVO
forehead ◇ *Tiene una cicatriz en la frente.* He has a scar on his forehead.

el **frente** SUSTANTIVO
front ◇ *un frente frío* a cold front ◇ *un frente común* a united front
◆ **frente a** opposite ◇ *Frente al hotel hay un banco.* There's a bank opposite the hotel.
◆ **Los trenes chocaron de frente.** The trains collided head on.
◆ **Viene un carro de frente.** There's a car coming straight for us.
◆ **hacer* frente a algo** to face up to something

la **fresa** SUSTANTIVO
strawberry (PL strawberries)

fresco ADJETIVO
1 cool (*lugar, tela, bebida*)
2 fresh (*pescado, verdura*)

el **fresco** SUSTANTIVO
◆ **tomar el fresco** to get some fresh air
◆ **Hace fresco. (1)** (*desagradable*) It's chilly.
◆ **Hace fresco. (2)** (*agradable*) It's cool.

friego VERBO *ver* **fregar**

el **frijol** SUSTANTIVO
bean

frío (1) VERBO *ver* **freír**

frío (2) ADJETIVO
cold ◇ *Tengo las manos frías.* My hands are cold.
◆ **Estuvo muy frío conmigo.** He was very cold towards me.

el **frío** SUSTANTIVO
◆ **Hace frío.** It's cold.
◆ **Tengo mucho frío.** I'm very cold.

frito (1) VERBO *ver* **freír**

frito (2) ADJETIVO
fried ◇ *huevos fritos* fried eggs

la **frontera** SUSTANTIVO
border ◇ *Nos pararon en la frontera.* We were stopped at the border.

el **frontón** SUSTANTIVO (PL los **frontones**)
1 fronton (*pared*)
2 jai alai court (*cancha*)
3 jai alai (*juego*)

frotar VERBO
to rub ◇ *¿Te froto la espalda?* Shall I rub your back for you?
◆ **El niño se frotaba las manos para calentarse.** The child was rubbing his hands to get warm.

fruncir* VERBO
◆ **fruncir el ceño** to frown

frustrado ADJETIVO
frustrated ◇ *Se siente frustrado.* He feels frustrated.

la **fruta** SUSTANTIVO
fruit ◇ *La fruta está muy cara.* Fruit is very expensive.

la **frutería** SUSTANTIVO
grocery store ◇ *Lo compré en la frutería.* I bought it at the grocery store.

el **fruto** SUSTANTIVO
fruit ◇ *el fruto de nuestro trabajo* the fruit of our labors
◆ **los frutos secos** nuts and dried fruits

fue VERBO *ver* **ir, ser**

el **fuego** SUSTANTIVO
fire ◇ *encender* el fuego* to light the fire
◆ **prender fuego a algo** to set fire to something
◆ **Puse la cacerola al fuego.** I put the pot on to heat.
◆ **cocinar algo a fuego lento** to cook something on a low heat
◆ **¿Tiene fuego, por favor?** Do you have a light, please?
◆ **fuegos artificiales** fireworks

la **fuente** SUSTANTIVO
1 fountain (*en la calle*)
2 dish (PL dishes) (*plato*)

fuera (1) VERBO *ver* **ir, ser**

fuera (2) ADVERBIO
1 outside ◇ *Los niños estaban jugando fuera.* The children were playing outside. ◇ *Por fuera es blanco.* It is white on the outside.
◆ **¡Estamos aquí fuera!** We are out here!
◆ **Hoy vamos a cenar fuera.** We're going out for dinner tonight.
2 away ◇ *Mis padres van a estar varios días fuera.* My parents will be away for several days.
◆ **El enfermo está fuera de peligro.** The patient is out of danger.
◆ **fuera de mi casa** outside my house

fuerte (1) ADJETIVO
1 strong (*material, olor, carácter*)
2 loud (*ruido, voz*)
3 hard (*golpe*)
4 bad (*dolor, resfriado*)
◆ **"un fuerte abrazo"** "lots of love"

fuerte (2) ADVERBIO
loudly ◇ *Hablaba fuerte.* He was talking loudly.
◆ **Agárrate fuerte.** Hold on tight.
◆ **No le pegues tan fuerte.** Don't hit him so hard.

la **fuerza** SUSTANTIVO
strength ◇ *No le quedaban fuerzas.* He had no strength left.
◆ **tener* mucha fuerza** to be very strong
◆ **Sólo lo conseguirás a fuerza de practicar.** You'll only manage it by practicing.
◆ **No te lo comas a la fuerza.** Don't force yourself to eat it.
◆ **la fuerza de gravedad** the force of gravity
◆ **la fuerza de voluntad** willpower

fuerzo VERBO *ver* **forzar**

fugarse* VERBO
to escape

fui VERBO *ver* **ir, ser**

el **fumador,** la **fumadora** SUSTANTIVO
smoker
- **sección para no fumadores** non-smoking section

fumar VERBO
to smoke ◊ *Quiero dejar de fumar.* I want to give up smoking.

la **función** SUSTANTIVO (PL las **funciones**)
1 function (*de máquina, organismo*) ◊ *Los insectos desempeñan una función muy importante.* Insects perform a very useful function.
2 role (*de persona, institución*) ◊ *la función de la policía en la sociedad* the role of the police in society
3 show (*espectáculo*) ◊ *Los niños van a presentar una función en el colegio.* The children are going to put on a show at school.

funcionar VERBO
to work ◊ *El teléfono no funciona.* The telephone isn't working.
- **"No funciona."** "Out of order."
- **Funciona con pilas.** It runs on batteries.

el **funcionario,** la **funcionaria** SUSTANTIVO
civil servant

la **funda** SUSTANTIVO
cover (*de raqueta, cojín*)
- **una funda de almohada** a pillowcase

fundamental ADJETIVO
basic ◊ *Hay dos tipos fundamentales de personas.* There are two basic types of people.
- **Es fundamental que entendamos el problema.** It is essential that we understand the problem.

fundar VERBO
to found (*hospital, colegio*)

fundirse VERBO
to melt ◊ *La nieve se está fundiendo.* The snow is melting.
- **Se fundieron los fusibles.** The fuses have blown.

el **funeral** SUSTANTIVO
funeral

la **funeraria** SUSTANTIVO
undertaker's

la **furgoneta** SUSTANTIVO
van

la **furia** SUSTANTIVO
fury

furioso ADJETIVO
furious ◊ *Mi padre estaba furioso conmigo.* My father was furious with me.

furtivo ADJETIVO
- **la pesca furtiva** poaching
- **un cazador furtivo** a poacher

el **fusible** SUSTANTIVO
fuse ◊ *Se quemaron los fusibles.* The fuses have blown.

el **fusil** SUSTANTIVO
rifle

el **futbol** SUSTANTIVO *Mexico*
football ◊ *jugar futbol* to play soccer

el **fútbol** SUSTANTIVO
soccer ◊ *jugar fútbol* to play soccer

el **futbolín** SUSTANTIVO (PL los **futbolines**)
table soccer

el/la **futbolista** SUSTANTIVO
soccer player ◊ *Quiere ser futbolista.* He wants to be a soccer player.

el **futuro** ADJETIVO, SUSTANTIVO
future ◊ *su futuro marido* your future husband
- **El futuro de "comer" es "comerás".** The future of "comer" is "comerás".
- **la futura madre** the mother-to-be

F

G

la **gabardina** SUSTANTIVO
raincoat

el **gabinete** SUSTANTIVO
1 office (*profesional*)
◆ **el gabinete de prensa** press office
2 cabinet (*de ministros*)
3 kitchen cabinet Mexico

las **gafas** SUSTANTIVO
1 glasses ◇ *Tengo que llevar gafas.* I have to wear glasses.
◆ **Había unas gafas encima de la mesa.** There was a pair of glasses on the table.
◆ **las gafas de sol** sunglasses
2 goggles (*de nadador, esquiador*)

la **gaita** SUSTANTIVO
bagpipes PL ◇ *tocar la gaita* to play the bagpipes

los **gajes** SUSTANTIVO
◆ **Son gajes del oficio.** They're occupational hazards.

el **gajo** SUSTANTIVO
segment

la **galaxia** SUSTANTIVO
galaxy (PL galaxies)

la **galería** SUSTANTIVO
gallery (PL galleries) (*en edificio, teatro, mina*)
◇ *una galería de arte* an art gallery
◆ **una galería comercial** a shopping mall

Gales SUSTANTIVO MASC
Wales
◆ **el País de Gales** Wales

galés ADJETIVO (FEM **galesa**, MASC PL **galeses**)
Welsh

el **galés** SUSTANTIVO (PL los **galeses**)
1 Welshman (PL Welshmen) (*persona*)
◆ **los galeses** the Welsh
2 Welsh (*idioma*)

la **galesa** SUSTANTIVO
Welshwoman (PL Welshwomen)

el **galgo** SUSTANTIVO
greyhound ◇ *una carrera de galgos* a greyhound race

Galicia SUSTANTIVO FEM
Galicia

el **gallego**, la **gallega** ADJETIVO, SUSTANTIVO
Galician

el **gallego** SUSTANTIVO
Galician (*idioma*)

la **galleta** SUSTANTIVO
cookie
◆ **una galleta salada** a cracker

la **gallina** SUSTANTIVO
hen
◆ **Sólo pensarlo me pone la carne de gallina.** It gives me goose bumps just thinking about it.
◆ **jugar* a la gallinita ciega** to play blind man's buff

el/la **gallina** SUSTANTIVO
◆ **¡Eres un gallina!** You're chicken! (*coloquial*)

el **gallinero** SUSTANTIVO
1 henhouse (*para las gallinas*)
2 madhouse (*coloquial*) ◇ *La clase era un gallinero.* The class was a madhouse.

el **gallo** SUSTANTIVO
rooster (*ave*)
◆ **en menos que canta un gallo** in an instant

galopar VERBO
to gallop

la **gama** SUSTANTIVO
range ◇ *una amplia gama de computadoras* a wide range of computers

la **gamba** SUSTANTIVO
large shrimp

la **gana** SUSTANTIVO
◆ **Me visto como me da la gana.** I dress the way I want to.
◆ **¡No me da la gana!** I don't want to!
◆ **Hazlo como te dé la gana.** Do it however you like.
◆ **hacer* algo de mala gana** to do something reluctantly
◆ **tener* ganas de hacer algo** to feel like doing something
◆ **Tengo ganas de que llegue el sábado.** I'm looking forward to Saturday.

la **ganadería** SUSTANTIVO
◆ **Se dedican a la ganadería.** They raise cattle.

el **ganado** SUSTANTIVO
livestock ◇ *alimento para el ganado* livestock feed
◆ **el ganado vacuno** cattle

ganador ADJETIVO (FEM **ganadora**)
winning ◇ *el equipo ganador* the winning team

el **ganador**, la **ganadora** SUSTANTIVO
winner

la **ganancia** SUSTANTIVO
profit ◇ *las pérdidas y las ganancias* profits and losses

ganar VERBO
1 to earn (*en un trabajo*) ◇ *Gana un buen sueldo.* He earns a good wage.
◆ **ganarse la vida** to earn a living
2 to win (*premio, competencia, guerra*)
◇ *¿Quién ganó la carrera?* Who won the race? ◇ *Lo importante no es ganar.* Winning isn't the most important thing.
3 to beat (*contrincante*) ◇ *Ganamos al Monterrey tres a cero.* We beat Monterrey three to nothing.
◆ **Con eso no ganas nada.** You won't achieve anything by doing that.
◆ **ganar tiempo** to save time
◆ **¡Te lo has ganado!** You deserve it!
◆ **salir* ganando** to do well ◇ *Salí ganando con la venta del carro.* I did well from the sale

of the car.

el **ganchillo** SUSTANTIVO
crochet ◇ *una aguja de ganchillo* a crochet hook
◆ **hacer* ganchillo** to crochet

el **gancho** SUSTANTIVO
[1] hook ◇ *Colgué el cuadro de un gancho.* I hung the picture on a hook.
◆ **Maradona tiene gancho.** Maradona is a crowd-puller.
[2] hanger (*para la ropa*)

gandul ADJETIVO (FEM **gandula**)
lazy

el **gandul,** la **gandula** SUSTANTIVO
good-for-nothing ◇ *Su marido es un gandul.* Her husband is a good-for-nothing.

la **ganga** SUSTANTIVO
bargain ◇ *A ese precio es una ganga.* It's a real bargain at that price.

el **gángster** SUSTANTIVO (PL los **gángsters**)
gangster

el **ganso,** la **gansa** SUSTANTIVO
goose (PL geese)

el **garabato** SUSTANTIVO
[1] doodle (*dibujo*) ◇ *una página llena de garabatos* a page full of doodles
◆ **Me pasé la clase haciendo garabatos.** I spent the whole class doodling.
[2] scribble (*escritura*) ◇ *una hoja cubierta de garabatos ininteligibles* a page full of unintelligible scribbles
◆ **Mientras pensaba iba haciendo garabatos en una libreta.** As I was thinking I scribbled away in my notebook.

el **garaje** SUSTANTIVO
garage ◇ *Metí el carro en el garaje.* I put the car in the garage.
◆ **una plaza de garaje** a parking space

la **garantía** SUSTANTIVO
guarantee ◇ *La lavadora está todavía bajo garantía.* The washing machine is still under guarantee.

garantizar* VERBO
to guarantee ◇ *No te lo puedo garantizar.* I can't guarantee it. ◇ *La lavadora está garantizada por dos años.* The washing machine is guaranteed for two years.

el **garbanzo** SUSTANTIVO
chickpea

la **garganta** SUSTANTIVO
throat ◇ *Me duele la garganta.* I have a sore throat.

la **gargantilla** SUSTANTIVO
necklace

las **gárgaras** SUSTANTIVO
◆ **hacer* gárgaras** to gargle

la **garita** SUSTANTIVO
sentry box (PL sentry boxes)

la **garra** SUSTANTIVO
[1] claw (*de tigre, gato*)
[2] talon (*de águila*)

la **garrafa** SUSTANTIVO
carafe (*pequeña*)

> ℹ *A **garrafa** is also a large bottle with handles.*

la **garúa** SUSTANTIVO
drizzle

el **gas** SUSTANTIVO (PL los **gases**)
gas ◇ *¿No hueles gas?* Can you smell gas?
◆ **agua mineral sin gas** uncarbonated mineral water
◆ **una bebida sin gas** an uncarbonated drink
◆ **agua mineral con gas** sparkling mineral water
◆ **los gases del tubo de escape** exhaust fumes
◆ **El niño tiene muchos gases.** The baby has a lot of gas.
◆ **Pasó una moto a todo gas.** A motorbike shot past at full speed.

la **gasa** SUSTANTIVO
gauze

la **gaseosa** SUSTANTIVO

> ℹ *A **gaseosa** is a soda or soft drink.*

el **gasoil** SUSTANTIVO
diesel oil

el **gasóleo** SUSTANTIVO
diesel oil

la **gasolina** SUSTANTIVO
gas ◇ *Tengo que echar gasolina.* I have to fill up with gas.
◆ **gasolina de alto octano** high-test gas
◆ **gasolina sin plomo** unleaded gas

la **gasolinera** SUSTANTIVO
gas station

gastado ADJETIVO
worn ◇ *La alfombra está muy gastada.* The carpet is very worn.

gastar VERBO
[1] to spend
◆ **Javier gasta mucho en ropa.** Javier spends a lot of money on clothes.
[2] to use (*gasolina, electricidad*)
◇ *Gastamos mucha agua.* We use a lot of water.
◆ **Gasté toda la pintura.** I used up all the paint.
◆ **Le gastamos una broma a Juan.** We played a joke on Juan.
◆ **Se gastaron las pilas.** The batteries have run out.
◆ **Se me gastaron las suelas.** The soles of my shoes have worn out.

el **gasto** SUSTANTIVO
expense ◇ *Es un gasto tremendo.* It's a horrendous expense. ◇ *Este año hemos tenido muchos gastos.* We've had a lot of expenses this year.
◆ **gastos de envío** postage and handling SING
◆ **el gasto público** public spending

la **gata** SUSTANTIVO

☞

cat
- **andar* a gatas** to crawl ◇ *El niño todavía anda a gatas.* The baby is still crawling.
- **Tienes que subir las escaleras a gatas.** You have to go up the stairs on all fours.

gatear VERBO
to crawl

el **gato** SUSTANTIVO
1 cat (*animal*)
2 jack (*para carro*)

la **gaviota** SUSTANTIVO
seagull

el **gay** ADJETIVO, SUSTANTIVO (PL los **gays**)
gay

el **gazpacho** SUSTANTIVO
cold vegetable soup

el **gel** SUSTANTIVO
gel ◇ *gel de baño* bath gel

la **gelatería** SUSTANTIVO Mexico
ice cream parlor

la **gelatina** SUSTANTIVO
gelatin

el **gemelo,** la **gemela** ADJETIVO, SUSTANTIVO
identical twin ◇ *Son gemelos.* They're identical twins. ◇ *mi hermana gemela* my identical twin sister

los **gemelos** SUSTANTIVO
1 binoculars (*prismáticos*)
2 cufflinks (*de camisa*)

Géminis SUSTANTIVO MASC
Gemini
- **Soy géminis.** I'm a Gemini.

el **gen** SUSTANTIVO
gene

la **generación** SUSTANTIVO (PL las **generaciones**)
generation

general ADJETIVO
general ◇ *medicina general* general medicine
- **en general** in general
- **por lo general** generally ◇ *Por lo general me acuesto temprano.* I generally go to bed early.

el/la **general** SUSTANTIVO
general

generalizar* VERBO
to generalize ◇ *No se puede generalizar.* You can't generalize.

generalmente ADVERBIO
generally

generar VERBO
to generate

el **género** SUSTANTIVO
1 gender (*de sustantivo, adjetivo*)
2 kind ◇ *¿Qué género de música prefieres?* What kind of music do you prefer?
3 material ◇ *Para las cortinas necesitamos un género más grueso.* We need a thicker material for the drapes.
- **el género humano** the human race

la **generosidad** SUSTANTIVO
generosity

generoso ADJETIVO
generous

genial ADJETIVO
brilliant ◇ *Antonio tuvo una idea genial.* Antonio had a brilliant idea. ◇ *El concierto estuvo genial.* It was a brilliant concert.

el **genio** SUSTANTIVO
1 temper ◇ *¡Qué genio tiene tu padre!* Your father has such a temper!
- **tener* mal genio** to have a bad temper

2 genius (PL geniuses) ◇ *¡Eres un genio!* You're a genius!
3 genie (*de la botella*)

los **genitales** SUSTANTIVO
genitals

el **genoma** SUSTANTIVO
genome

la **gente** SUSTANTIVO
1 people
El verbo va siempre en plural.
◇ *Había poca gente en la sala.* There were few people in the room. ◇ *La gente está cansada de promesas.* People are tired of promises.
- **Son buena gente.** They're good people.
- **Óscar es buena gente.** Oscar's a good sort.
- **la gente de la calle** the people in the street

2 family ◇ *Hace tiempo que no veo a mi gente.* I haven't seen my family for a while.

la **geografía** SUSTANTIVO
geography

la **geología** SUSTANTIVO
geology

la **geometría** SUSTANTIVO
geometry

el **geranio** SUSTANTIVO
geranium

el/la **gerente** SUSTANTIVO
manager ◇ *Isabel es gerente de ventas.* Isabel is a sales manager.

el **germen** SUSTANTIVO (PL los **gérmenes**)
germ

germinar VERBO
to germinate

el **gesto** SUSTANTIVO
- **Hizo un gesto de alivio.** He looked relieved.
- **Me hizo un gesto para que me sentara.** He made a gesture for me to sit down.

el/la **gigante** SUSTANTIVO
giant

gigantesco ADJETIVO
gigantic

la **gimnasia** SUSTANTIVO
gymnastics SING ◇ *Después del recreo tenemos gimnasia.* After recess, we have gymnastics.
- **Mi madre hace gimnasia todas las mañanas.** My mother does exercises every morning.

el **gimnasio** SUSTANTIVO
gym

el/la **gimnasta** SUSTANTIVO
gymnast

la **ginebra** SUSTANTIVO
gin

el **ginecólogo,** la **ginecóloga** SUSTANTIVO
gynecologist ◇ *Soy ginecóloga.* I'm a gynecologist.

la **gira** SUSTANTIVO
tour ◇ *Hicimos una gira por toda Europa.* We did a tour all around Europe.
◆ **estar* de gira** to be on tour

girar VERBO
1 to turn ◇ *Al llegar al semáforo gira a la derecha.* When you get to the lights turn right. ◇ *Giré la cabeza para ver quién era.* I turned my head to see who it was.
2 to rotate ◇ *La Tierra gira alrededor de su eje.* The Earth rotates on its axis.
◆ **La Luna gira alrededor de la Tierra.** The moon orbits the Earth.

el **girasol** SUSTANTIVO
sunflower

el **giro** SUSTANTIVO
1 turn ◇ *El avión dio un giro de 90 grados.* The plane did a 90 degree turn.
2 money order ◇ *Voy a mandarte un giro de 500 pesos.* I'll send you a 500 peso money order.

el **gitano,** la **gitana** SUSTANTIVO
gypsy (PL gypsies)

la **glándula** SUSTANTIVO
gland

global ADJETIVO
global ◇ *una solución global* a global solution

el **globo** SUSTANTIVO
balloon (*de juguete, para volar*)
◆ **un globo terráqueo** a globe

la **glorieta** SUSTANTIVO
traffic circle

glotón ADJETIVO (FEM SING **glotona,** MASC PL **glotones**)
greedy

gobernar* VERBO
to govern

el **gobierno** SUSTANTIVO
government

el **gol** SUSTANTIVO
goal
◆ **meter un gol** to score a goal

el **golf** SUSTANTIVO
golf
◆ **jugar* golf** to play golf

el **golfo** SUSTANTIVO
gulf ◇ *el Golfo pérsico* the Persian Gulf

la **golondrina** SUSTANTIVO
swallow

la **golosina** SUSTANTIVO
piece of candy

goloso ADJETIVO
◆ **ser* goloso** to have a sweet tooth ◇ *Soy muy golosa.* I have a very sweet tooth.

el **golpe** SUSTANTIVO
knock ◇ *Oímos un golpe a la puerta.* We heard a knock at the door.
◆ **Me di un golpe en el codo.** I banged my elbow.
◆ **Se dio un golpe contra la pared.** He hit the wall.
◆ **El carro de atrás nos dio un golpe.** The car behind ran into us.
◆ **Di unos golpecitos a la puerta antes de entrar.** I tapped on the door before going in.
◆ **de golpe** suddenly ◇ *De golpe decidió dejar el trabajo.* He suddenly decided to give up work.
◆ **La puerta se cerró de golpe.** The door slammed shut.

golpear VERBO
1 to hit (*pegar*) ◇ *Me golpeó en la cara con su raqueta.* He hit me in the face with his racket.
2 to bang (*objeto*) ◇ *El maestro golpeó el pupitre con la mano.* The teacher banged the desk with his hand.
◆ **Me golpeé la cabeza contra el armario.** I banged my head on the cupboard.

la **goma** SUSTANTIVO
1 eraser ◇ *¿Me prestas la goma?* Can you lend me your eraser?
◆ **una goma de borrar** an eraser
2 rubber band ◇ *Necesito una gomita para el pelo.* I need a rubber band for my hair.
◆ **unos guantes de goma** a pair of rubber gloves

gordo ADJETIVO
1 fat ◇ *Estoy muy gordo.* I'm very fat.
2 thick (*libro, suéter*)
3 big (*problema*) ◇ *Debe de ser algo bastante gordo.* It must be something pretty big.
◆ **Su mujer me cae gorda.** I can't stand his wife.

el **gorila** SUSTANTIVO
gorilla

la **gorra** SUSTANTIVO
cap
◆ **de gorra** for free ◇ *Entramos de gorra.* We got in for free.

el **gorrión** SUSTANTIVO (PL los **gorriones**)
sparrow

el **gorro** SUSTANTIVO
hat ◇ *Llevaba un gorro de lana.* He wore a woolen hat.
◆ **un gorro de baño** a bathing cap
◆ **Ya estoy hasta el gorro.** I'm absolutely fed up.

la **gota** SUSTANTIVO
drop ◇ *Sólo bebí una gota de vino.* I only had a drop of wine.
◆ **Están cayendo cuatro gotas.** It's drizzling.

gotear VERBO

☞

G

1 to drip (*llave*)
2 to leak (*cañería*)

la **gotera** SUSTANTIVO
leak ◇ *Tenemos goteras en la cocina.* We have some leaks in the kitchen.

gozar* VERBO
◆ **gozar de algo** to enjoy something ◇ *Quiere gozar de la vida.* He wants to enjoy life. ◇ *Mis abuelos gozan de buena salud.* My grandparents enjoy good health.

la **grabación** SUSTANTIVO (PL las **grabaciones**)
recording

la **grabadora** SUSTANTIVO
recorder

grabar VERBO
1 to tape ◇ *Quiero grabar esta película.* I want to tape this movie.
2 to record ◇ *Lo grabaron en vivo.* It was recorded live.
3 to engrave (*en madera, metal*) ◇ *Grabó sus iniciales en la medalla.* He engraved his initials on the medal.
◆ **Lo tengo grabado en la memoria.** It's etched on my memory.

la **gracia** SUSTANTIVO
◆ **tener* gracia** to be funny ◇ *Sus chistes tienen mucha gracia.* His jokes are very funny.
◆ **Yo no le veo la gracia.** I don't see what's so funny.
◆ **Me hizo mucha gracia.** It was very funny.
◆ **No me hace gracia tener que salir con este tiempo.** I'm not too pleased about having to go out in this weather.
◆ **¡Muchas gracias!** Thanks very much!
◆ **dar* las gracias a alguien por algo** to thank somebody for something ◇ *Vino a darme las gracias por las flores.* He came to thank me for the flowers.
◆ **Ni siquiera me dio las gracias.** He didn't even say thank you.
◆ **gracias a** thanks to ◇ *Gracias a él me encuentro con vida.* Thanks to him I'm still alive.

gracioso ADJETIVO
funny ◇ *¡Qué gracioso!* How funny!

las **gradas** SUSTANTIVO
bleachers

el **grado** SUSTANTIVO
degree ◇ *Estaban a diez grados bajo cero.* It was ten degrees below zero. ◇ *quemaduras de primer grado* first-degree burns

graduado ADJETIVO
◆ **lentes graduadas** prescription lenses

gradual ADJETIVO
gradual

graduar* VERBO
to adjust (*volumen, temperatura*)
◆ **Se graduó en Medicina hace dos años.** He graduated in medicine two years ago.

la **gráfica** SUSTANTIVO
graph

gráfico ADJETIVO
graphic

el **gráfico** SUSTANTIVO
table

la **gramática** SUSTANTIVO
grammar ◇ *un libro de gramática inglesa* a book on English grammar

el **gramo** SUSTANTIVO
gram

> ℹ *En los Estados Unidos el peso a menudo se expresa en onzas,* ***ounces****. Una onza equivale a 28,35 gramos.*

gran ADJETIVO *ver* **grande**

la **granada** SUSTANTIVO
pomegranate (*fruta*)
◆ **una granada de mano** a hand grenade

granate ADJETIVO
maroon ◇ *una bufanda granate* a maroon scarf

Gran Bretaña SUSTANTIVO FEM
Great Britain

grande ADJETIVO
1 big (*de tamaño*) ◇ *Viven en una casa muy grande.* They live in a very big house.
◆ **¿Cómo es de grande?** How big is it?
◆ **La camisa me queda grande.** The shirt is too big for me.
2 large (*de cantidad*) ◇ *un gran número de visitantes* a large number of visitors ◇ *grandes sumas de dinero* large sums of money
3 great (*en importancia, grado*) ◇ *un gran pintor* a great painter ◇ *Es una ventaja muy grande.* It's a great advantage.
◆ **Me llevé una alegría muy grande.** I felt very happy.
◆ **Lo pasamos en grande.** We had a great time.
◆ **unos grandes almacenes** a department store

granel ADVERBIO
◆ **a granel** in bulk ◇ *Venden las aceitunas a granel.* They sell olives in bulk.

el **granero** SUSTANTIVO
barn

el **granizado** SUSTANTIVO

> ℹ *A* ***granizado*** *is a crushed ice drink.*

granizar* VERBO
to hail ◇ *Está granizando.* It's hailing.

el **granizo** SUSTANTIVO
hail

la **granja** SUSTANTIVO
farm
◆ **una granja avícola** a poultry farm

el **granjero**, la **granjera** SUSTANTIVO
farmer

el **grano** SUSTANTIVO
1 grain (*de arena, arroz, azúcar*)
2 bean (*de café*)
3 spot ◇ *Me ha salido un grano en la frente.* I have a pimple on my forehead.
◆ **ir* al grano** to get to the point

la **grapa** SUSTANTIVO
staple

la **grapadora** SUSTANTIVO
stapler

la **grasa** SUSTANTIVO
1 fat ◇ *Me hace mal tanta grasa.* So much fat isn't good for me.
2 grease (*suciedad*)
◆ **La cocina está llena de grasa.** The stove is really greasy.

grasiento ADJETIVO
greasy

graso ADJETIVO
greasy ◇ *Tengo el cutis graso.* I have greasy skin.

gratis ADJETIVO, ADVERBIO (PL **gratis**)
1 free ◇ *La entrada es gratis.* Entry is free.
2 for free ◇ *Te lo arreglarán gratis.* They'll fix it for free.

gratuito ADJETIVO
free

la **grava** SUSTANTIVO
gravel

grave ADJETIVO
1 serious (*enfermedad, herida*) ◇ *Tenemos un problema grave.* We have a serious problem.
◆ **Su padre está grave.** His father is seriously ill.
2 low (*nota, sonido*)

la **gravedad** SUSTANTIVO
gravity ◇ *la ley de la gravedad* the law of gravity
◆ **estar* herido de gravedad** to be seriously injured

gravemente ADVERBIO
seriously
◆ **estar* gravemente enfermo** to be seriously ill

Grecia SUSTANTIVO FEM
Greece

el **griego**, la **griega** ADJETIVO, SUSTANTIVO
Greek

el **griego** SUSTANTIVO
Greek (*idioma*)

la **grieta** SUSTANTIVO
crack

el **grillo** SUSTANTIVO
cricket (*insecto*)

la **gripa** SUSTANTIVO Mexico
flu

la **gripe** SUSTANTIVO
flu ◇ *tener la gripe* to have the flu

el **gris** ADJETIVO, SUSTANTIVO
gray ◇ *una puerta gris* a gray door

gritar VERBO
1 to shout (*dar voces*)
◆ **El público le gritaba al árbitro.** The crowd was shouting at the referee.
◆ **Niños, no griten tanto.** Children, stop shouting so much.
2 to scream (*dar un chillido*) ◇ *El enfermo no podía dejar de gritar.* The patient couldn't stop screaming.

el **grito** SUSTANTIVO
1 shout ◇ *gritos de protesta* shouts of protest
◆ **¡No des esos gritos!** Stop shouting like that!
2 scream (*chillido*) ◇ *Oímos un grito en la calle.* We heard a scream outside.
◆ **Dando gritos a viva voz.** Screaming at the top of his voice.
◆ **Es el último grito.** It's all the rage.

la **grosella** SUSTANTIVO
currant

grosero ADJETIVO
rude

el **grosor** SUSTANTIVO
thickness
◆ **La pared tiene 30cm de grosor.** The wall is 30cm thick.

la **grúa** SUSTANTIVO
crane (*para construcción*)
◆ **La grúa se llevó el carro.** My car was towed away.

grueso ADJETIVO
1 thick (*suéter, pared, libro*)
2 stout (*persona*)

el **grumo** SUSTANTIVO
lump

gruñir* VERBO
1 to grumble (*persona*) ◇ *El abuelo siempre está gruñendo.* Grandpa is always grumbling.
2 to growl (*animal*)

el **grupo** SUSTANTIVO
1 group ◇ *Se dividieron en grupos.* They divided into groups.
◆ **el grupo sanguíneo** blood group
◆ **Los alumnos trabajan en grupo.** The students work in groups.
2 band ◇ *uno de los mejores grupos de rock* one of the best rock bands

el **guajolote** SUSTANTIVO Mexico
turkey

el **guante** SUSTANTIVO
glove ◇ *Uso guantes de goma.* I use rubber gloves.
◆ **unos guantes** a pair of gloves

la **guantera** SUSTANTIVO
glove compartment

guapo ADJETIVO
1 handsome (*hombre*)
2 pretty (*mujer*)

el/la **guarda** SUSTANTIVO
keeper (*de parque, zoo*)

☞

◆ **guarda jurado** armed security guard

el **guardabarros** SUSTANTIVO (PL los **guardabarros**)
fender

el/la **guardaespaldas** SUSTANTIVO (PL los/las **guardaespaldas**)
bodyguard

guardar VERBO
[1] to put away (*recoger*) ◇ *Los niños guardaron los juguetes.* The children put away their toys. ◇ *Guardé los documentos en el cajón.* I put the documents away in the drawer.
◆ **Raúl se guardó el pañuelo en el bolsillo.** Raúl put the handkerchief in his pocket.
[2] to keep ◇ *Guarda el recibo.* Keep the receipt. ◇ *No sabe guardar un secreto.* He can't keep a secret.
◆ **No les guardo rencor.** I don't bear them a grudge.
◆ **guardar las apariencias** to keep up appearances
◆ **guardar un fichero** (*informática*) to save a file

el **guardarropa** SUSTANTIVO
cloakroom

la **guardería** SUSTANTIVO
nursery (PL nurseries)

la **guardia** SUSTANTIVO
◆ **de guardia** on duty ◇ *Me atendió el médico de guardia.* I was seen by the doctor on duty. ◇ *Estoy de guardia.* I'm on duty.

el/la **guardia** SUSTANTIVO
police officer

güero ADJETIVO [Mexico]
blond(e)

la **guerra** SUSTANTIVO
war ◇ *la Segunda Guerra Mundial* the Second World War
◆ **declarar la guerra a un país** to declare war on a country
◆ **estar* en guerra** to be at war

el/la **guía** SUSTANTIVO
guide ◇ *El guía vino a recogernos al aeropuerto.* The guide came to pick us up at the airport.

la **guía** SUSTANTIVO
guidebook (*libro*) ◇ *Compré una guía turística de Miami.* I bought a tourist guidebook of Miami.
◆ **una guía de hoteles** a hotel guide
◆ **una guía telefónica** a telephone directory

guiar* VERBO
to guide ◇ *Mi amigo nos guió a la estación.* My friend guided us to the station.
◆ **Nos guiamos por un mapa que teníamos.** We found our way using a map that we had.

el **guijarro** SUSTANTIVO
pebble

la **guinda** SUSTANTIVO
sour cherry (PL sour cherries)

guiñar VERBO
to wink
◆ **Me guiñó el ojo.** He winked at me.

el **guión** SUSTANTIVO (PL los **guiones**)
[1] hyphen (*en palabras compuestas*)
◆ **La palabra "self-defense" lleva guión.** The word "self-defense" is hyphenated.
[2] dash (*para indicar un diálogo*)
[3] script (*de una película*)

el **guisado** SUSTANTIVO
stew

guisar VERBO
to cook

la **guitarra** SUSTANTIVO
guitar

el **gusano** SUSTANTIVO
[1] worm
◆ **un gusano de seda** a silk worm
[2] maggot (*de mosca*)
[3] caterpillar (*de mariposa*)

gustar VERBO
◆ **Me gustan las uvas.** I like grapes.
◆ **¿Te gusta viajar?** Do you like traveling?
◆ **Me gustó como hablaba.** I liked the way he spoke.
◆ **Me gustaría conocerla.** I would like to meet her.
◆ **Me gusta su hermana.** I am attracted to his sister.
◆ **Le gusta más llevar pantalones.** She prefers to wear pants.

el **gusto** SUSTANTIVO
taste ◇ *No tiene gusto para vestirse.* He has no taste in clothes. ◇ *Decoré la habitación a mi gusto.* I've decorated the room to my taste.
◆ **un comentario de mal gusto** a tasteless remark
◆ **Le noto un gusto a almendras.** It tastes of almonds.
◆ **¡Con mucho gusto!** With pleasure!
◆ **¡Mucho gusto en conocerlo!** I'm very pleased to meet you!
◆ **sentirse* a gusto** to feel at ease

H

ha VERBO *ver* **haber**

el **haba** SUSTANTIVO
fava bean

Habana SUSTANTIVO
◆ **La Habana** Havana

haber* VERBO
to have
*El verbo **to have** suele usarse en las formas contraídas, particularmente al hablar.*
◇ *He comido.* I've eaten. ◇ *Hemos comido.* We've eaten. ◇ *Había comido.* I'd eaten. (*= had*) ◇ *Se ha sentado.* She's sat down. (*= has*)
◆ **De haberlo sabido, habría ido.** If I'd known, I would have gone.
◆ **¡Haberlo dicho antes!** You should have said so before!
◆ **hay**
***Hay** seguido de complemento singular se traduce por **there is**.*
◇ *Hay una iglesia en la esquina.* There's a church on the corner. ◇ *Hubo una guerra.* There was a war.
***Hay** seguido de complemento plural se traduce por **there are**.*
◇ *Hay treinta alumnos en mi clase.* There are thirty students in my class. ◇ *¿Hay entradas?* Are there any tickets?
◆ **¡No hay de qué!** Don't mention it!
◆ **¿Qué hay?** (*¿Qué tal?*) How are things? (*coloquial*)
◆ **¿Qué hubo?** *Mexico* How are things? (*coloquial*)
◆ **hay que...**
*La expresión impersonal **hay que** se traduce normalmente utilizando el pronombre **you**, a menos que esté claro quien realiza la acción.*
◆ **Hay que ser respetuoso.** You must be respectful.
◆ **¡Habrá que decírselo!** We'll have to tell him!

hábil ADJETIVO
skillful (*diestro*) ◇ *Es un jugador muy hábil.* He's a very skillful player.
◆ **Es muy hábil con las manos.** He's very good with his hands.
◆ **Es muy hábil para los negocios.** He's a very able businessman.

la **habilidad** SUSTANTIVO
skill ◇ *Ha demostrado una gran habilidad para los negocios.* He's shown great business skill.
◆ **Tiene mucha habilidad para los idiomas.** She's very good at languages.

la **habitación** SUSTANTIVO (PL las **habitaciones**)
1 bedroom (*dormitorio*)
2 room (*en hotel*)
◆ **una habitación doble** a double room
◆ **una habitación individual** a single room

el/la **habitante** SUSTANTIVO
inhabitant
◆ **los habitantes de la zona** people living in the area

habitar VERBO
to live in ◇ *los que habitaban en la zona* those who lived in the area
◆ **La casa está todavía sin habitar.** The house is still unoccupied.

el **hábito** SUSTANTIVO
habit ◇ *Fumar es un mal hábito.* Smoking is a bad habit.

habitual ADJETIVO
usual ◇ *No es habitual verlos juntos.* It's not usual to see them together.
◆ **un cliente habitual** a regular customer

el **habla** SUSTANTIVO
speech
◆ **Perdió el habla.** He's lost the power of speech.
◆ **países de habla inglesa** English-speaking countries
◆ **¿Señor López? – Al habla.** Señor López? – Speaking.

hablador ADJETIVO (FEM **habladora**)
1 chatty (*parlanchín*)
2 gossipy (*chismoso*)
3 lying (*mentiroso*) *Mexico*

las **habladurías** SUSTANTIVO
gossip SING

el/la **hablante** SUSTANTIVO
speaker

hablar VERBO
1 to speak ◇ *¿Hablas castellano?* Do you speak Spanish?
◆ **¿Quién habla?** (*al teléfono*) Who's calling?
2 to talk ◇ *Estuvimos hablando toda la tarde.* We were talking all afternoon.
3 to call *Mexico* ◇ *Te habló Lupe.* Lupe called you.
◆ **hablar con alguien (1)** to speak to someone ◇ *¿Has hablado ya con el profesor?* Have you spoken to the teacher yet?
◆ **hablar con alguien (2)** to talk to someone ◇ *Necesito hablar contigo.* I need to talk to you.
◆ **hablar de algo** to talk about something
◆ **¿Vas a ayudarle en la mudanza? – ¡Ni hablar!** Are you going to help him with the move? – No way!

habré VERBO *ver* **haber**

hacer* VERBO
1 to make ◇ *Tengo que hacer la cama.* I have to make the bed. ◇ *Voy a hacer una ensalada.* I'm going to make a salad. ◇ *Están haciendo mucho ruido.* They're making a lot of noise.
2 to do ◇ *¿Qué haces?* What are you doing? ◇ *Estoy haciendo las tareas.* I'm doing my homework. ◇ *¿Qué hace tu padre?* What does your father do?
3 to be (*hablando del tiempo atmosférico*) ☞

◇ *Hace calor.* It's hot. ◇ *Ojalá haga buen tiempo.* I hope the weather's nice. ◇ *Hizo dos grados bajo cero.* It was two degrees below zero.
- **hace... (1)** ago ◇ *Terminé hace una hora.* I finished an hour ago. ◇ *Estaba aquí hace unos minutos.* He was here a few minutes ago.
- **hace... (2)** for ◇ *Hace un mes que voy.* I've been going for a month.
- **¿Hace mucho que esperas?** Have you been waiting long?
- **Hago mucho deporte.** I play a lot of sports.
- **hacer hacer algo** to have something done ◇ *Hicieron pintar la fachada del colegio.* They had the front of the school painted.
- **hacer a alguien hacer algo** to make someone do something ◇ *Hace estudiar a los alumnos.* He makes the pupils study.
- **hacer clic (en)** (*informática*) to click (on)
- **hacerse** to become ◇ *Quiere hacerse famoso.* He wants to become famous. ◇ *Se hicieron amigos.* They became friends.
- **Ya se está haciendo viejo.** He's getting old now.

el **hacha** SUSTANTIVO
ax (PL axes)

hacia PREPOSICIÓN
[1] towards ◇ *Venía hacia mí.* He was coming towards me. ◇ *su actitud hacia sus padres* his attitude towards his parents
[2] at about ◇ *Volveremos hacia las tres.* We'll be back at about three.
- **hacia adelante** forward
- **hacia atrás** backward
- **hacia adentro** inside
- **hacia afuera** outside
- **hacia abajo** down
- **hacia arriba** up

el **hada** SUSTANTIVO
fairy (PL fairies)
- **un hada madrina** a fairy godmother
- **un cuento de hadas** a fairy tale

hago VERBO *ver* **hacer**

halagar* VERBO
to flatter

hallar VERBO
to find
- **hallarse** to be ◇ *Se halla fuera del país.* He's out of the country.

la **hamaca** SUSTANTIVO
[1] hammock (*cama*)
[2] deck chair (*asiento plegable*)

el **hambre** SUSTANTIVO
hunger
- **tener* hambre** to be hungry ◇ *Tengo mucha hambre.* I'm very hungry.

la **hamburguesa** SUSTANTIVO
hamburger

el **hámster** SUSTANTIVO (PL los **hámsters**)
hamster

el **hardware** SUSTANTIVO
hardware

haré VERBO *ver* **hacer**

la **harina** SUSTANTIVO
flour
- **harina de trigo** wheat flour

hartar VERBO
- **hartarse** to get fed up ◇ *Me harté de estudiar.* I got fed up with studying.
- **Me harté de pasteles.** I stuffed myself with cakes. (*coloquial*)
- **¡Me estás hartando!** You're getting on my nerves!

harto (1) ADJETIVO
[1] fed up
- **estar* harto de algo** to be fed up with something ◇ *Estábamos hartos de repetirlo.* We were fed up with repeating it. ◇ *¡Me tienes harto!* I'm fed up with you!

[2] a lot of ◇ *Había harta comida.* There was a lot of food.

harto (2) ADVERBIO
[1] very ◇ *Es un idioma harto difícil.* It's a very difficult language.
[2] a lot ◇ *Tenemos harto que estudiar.* We have a lot to study.

hasta (1) ADVERBIO
even ◇ *Estudia hasta cuando está de vacaciones.* He even studies when he's on vacation.

hasta (2) PREPOSICIÓN, CONJUNCIÓN
[1] till ◇ *Está abierto hasta las cuatro.* It's open till four o'clock.
- **¿Hasta cuándo?** How long? ◇ *¿Hasta cuándo te quedas? – Hasta la semana que viene.* How long are you staying? – Till next week.
- **Hasta ahora no ha llamado nadie.** No one has called up to now.
- **hasta que** until ◇ *Espera aquí hasta que te llamen.* Wait here until you're called.

__Till__ sustituye a "until" en la lengua hablada e informal.

[2] up to ◇ *Caminamos hasta la puerta.* We walked up to the door.
[3] as far as ◇ *Desde aquí se ve hasta el pueblo vecino.* From here you can see as far as the next town.
- **¡Hasta luego!** See you!
- **¡Hasta el sábado!** See you on Saturday!

hay VERBO *ver* **haber**

haz VERBO *ver* **hacer**

he VERBO *ver* **haber**

la **hebilla** SUSTANTIVO
buckle

el **hebreo,** la **hebrea** ADJETIVO, SUSTANTIVO
Hebrew

el **hebreo** SUSTANTIVO
Hebrew (*idioma*)

el **hechizo** SUSTANTIVO
spell

hecho (1) VERBO *ver* **hacer**

hecho (2) ADJETIVO
made ◇ *¿De qué está hecho?* What's it made of?
◆ **hecho a mano** handmade
◆ **hecho a máquina** machine-made

el **hecho** SUSTANTIVO
1 fact ◇ *el hecho de que...* the fact that... ◇ *el hecho es que...* the fact is that... ◇ *de hecho* in fact
2 event (*acontecimiento*) ◇ *un hecho histórico* an historic event

la **helada** SUSTANTIVO
frost

la **heladería** SUSTANTIVO
ice-cream parlor

helado ADJETIVO
1 frozen ◇ *El lago está helado.* The lake is frozen over.
2 freezing ◇ *Este cuarto está helado.* This room is freezing. ◇ *¡Estoy helado!* I'm freezing!

el **helado** SUSTANTIVO
ice cream ◇ *helado de chocolate* chocolate ice cream

helar* VERBO
to freeze ◇ *El frío ha helado las tuberías.* The cold has frozen the pipes. ◇ *Esta noche va a helar.* It's going to freeze tonight.
◆ **helarse** to freeze ◇ *Me estoy helando.* I'm freezing.
◆ **Anoche heló.** There was a frost last night.

el **helecho** SUSTANTIVO
fern

el **helicóptero** SUSTANTIVO
helicopter

la **hembra** ADJETIVO, SUSTANTIVO
female ◇ *un elefante hembra* a female elephant

hemos VERBO *ver* **haber**

heredar VERBO
to inherit

la **heredera** SUSTANTIVO
heiress (PL heiresses)

el **heredero** SUSTANTIVO
heir

la **herencia** SUSTANTIVO
inheritance

la **herida** SUSTANTIVO
1 wound ◇ *una herida de bala* a bullet wound ◇ *una herida de cuchillo* a stab wound
2 injury (PL injuries) ◇ *Murió a causa de las heridas del accidente.* He died from injuries received in the accident.

herido ADJETIVO
1 wounded (*por un arma*)
2 injured (*en un accidente*)

herir* VERBO
1 to wound ◇ *Lo hirieron en el pecho.* He was wounded in the chest.
2 to injure ◇ *Resultó gravemente herido en la caída.* He was seriously injured in the fall.

la **hermana** SUSTANTIVO
sister

la **hermanastra** SUSTANTIVO
stepsister

el **hermanastro** SUSTANTIVO
stepbrother
◆ **mis hermanastros (1)** (*varones*) my stepbrothers
◆ **mis hermanastros (2)** (*varones y mujeres*) my stepbrothers and sisters

el **hermano** SUSTANTIVO
brother
◆ **mis hermanos (1)** (*varones*) my brothers
◆ **mis hermanos (2)** (*varones y mujeres*) my brothers and sisters

hermético ADJETIVO
airtight

hermoso ADJETIVO
beautiful

la **hermosura** SUSTANTIVO
beauty ◇ *el secreto de su hermosura* the secret of her beauty
◆ **¡Qué hermosura de paisaje!** What a beautiful landscape!

el **héroe** SUSTANTIVO
hero (PL heroes)

la **heroína** SUSTANTIVO
heroine

el **heroinómano**, la **heroinómana** SUSTANTIVO
heroin addict

la **herradura** SUSTANTIVO
horseshoe

la **herramienta** SUSTANTIVO
tool

el **herrero** SUSTANTIVO
blacksmith

hervir* VERBO
to boil ◇ *El agua está hirviendo.* The water is boiling.
◆ **hervir agua** to boil water

el/la **heterosexual** ADJETIVO, SUSTANTIVO
heterosexual

hice VERBO *ver* **hacer**

hielo VERBO *ver* **helar**

el **hielo** SUSTANTIVO
ice

la **hierba** SUSTANTIVO
1 grass (*césped*)
2 herb (*para infusión*)
◆ **una mala hierba** a weed

la **hierbabuena** SUSTANTIVO
mint

el **hierro** SUSTANTIVO
iron ◇ *una caja de hierro* an iron box

el **hígado** SUSTANTIVO
liver

H

la **higiene** SUSTANTIVO
hygiene

higiénico ADJETIVO
hygienic
- **poco higiénico** unhygienic

el **higo** SUSTANTIVO
fig

la **higuera** SUSTANTIVO
fig tree

la **hija** SUSTANTIVO
daughter
- **Soy hija única.** I'm an only child.
- **Sí, hija mía, tienes razón.** Yes, my dear, you're right.

la **hijastra** SUSTANTIVO
stepdaughter

el **hijastro** SUSTANTIVO
stepson
- **mis hijastros (1)** (*varones*) my stepsons
- **mis hijastros (2)** (*varones y mujeres*) my stepsons and daughters

el **hijo** SUSTANTIVO
son ◇ *Su hijo mayor.* His oldest son.
- **mis hijos (1)** (*varones*) my sons
- **mis hijos (2)** (*varones y mujeres*) my children
- **Soy hijo único.** I'm an only child.

la **hilera** SUSTANTIVO
1 row ◇ *una hilera de casas* a row of houses
2 line ◇ *ponerse en hilera* to get into a line

el **hilo** SUSTANTIVO
1 thread ◇ *hilo de coser* sewing thread
2 linen ◇ *un traje de hilo* a linen suit
- **los hilos del teléfono** the telephone wires

el **himno** SUSTANTIVO
hymn
- **el himno nacional** the national anthem

el/la **hincha** SUSTANTIVO
fan ◇ *los hinchas del fútbol* soccer fans

hinchado ADJETIVO
swollen

el **hipo** SUSTANTIVO
hiccups PL ◇ *Tengo hipo.* I have the hiccups. ◇ *Me dio hipo.* It's given me the hiccups.

hipócrita ADJETIVO
hypocritical
- **¡No seas hipócrita!** Don't be such a hypocrite!

el/la **hipócrita** SUSTANTIVO
hypocrite

el **hipódromo** SUSTANTIVO
racecourse

el **hipopótamo** SUSTANTIVO
hippo

la **hipoteca** SUSTANTIVO
mortgage

hiriendo VERBO *ver* **herir**

hirviendo VERBO *ver* **hervir**

hispanohablante ADJETIVO
Spanish-speaking ◇ *los países hispanohablantes* Spanish-speaking countries

el/la **hispanohablante** SUSTANTIVO
Spanish speaker

la **historia** SUSTANTIVO
1 history ◇ *la historia de México* Mexican history
2 story (PL stories) ◇ *El libro cuenta la historia de dos niños.* The book tells the story of two children.
- **la misma historia de siempre** the same old story

el **historial** SUSTANTIVO
record (*en archivo*)

histórico ADJETIVO
1 historic ◇ *una ciudad histórica* a historic city
2 historical ◇ *un personaje histórico* a historical character

la **historieta** SUSTANTIVO
comic strip

hizo VERBO *ver* **hacer**

el **hobby** SUSTANTIVO (PL los **hobbies**)
hobby (PL hobbies)
- **Lo hago por hobby.** I do it as a hobby.

*The "h" in **hobby** is pronounced like Spanish "j".*

el **hockey** SUSTANTIVO
hockey
- **el hockey sobre hielo** ice hockey

*The "h" in **hockey** is pronounced like Spanish "j".*

el **hogar** SUSTANTIVO
home ◇ *en todos los hogares mexicanos* in every Mexican home
- **productos para el hogar** household products

la **hoguera** SUSTANTIVO
bonfire

la **hoja** SUSTANTIVO
1 leaf (PL leaves) (*de árbol*)
2 sheet ◇ *una hoja de papel* a sheet of paper
- **una hoja de cálculo** a spreadsheet
- **una hoja de solicitud** an application form

3 page ◇ *las hojas de un libro* the pages of a book
- **una hoja de afeitar** a razor blade

el **hojaldre** SUSTANTIVO
puff pastry

hojear VERBO
to leaf through

hola EXCLAMACIÓN
hello!

Holanda SUSTANTIVO FEM
Holland

holandés ADJETIVO (FEM **holandesa**, MASC PL **holandeses**)
Dutch

el **holandés** SUSTANTIVO (PL los **holandeses**)
1 Dutchman (PL Dutchmen) (*persona*)

◆ **los holandeses** the Dutch
[2] Dutch (*idioma*)

la **holandesa** SUSTANTIVO
Dutchwoman (PL Dutchwomen)

holgazán ADJETIVO (FEM **holgazana**, MASC PL **holgazanes**)
lazy

el **hollín** SUSTANTIVO
soot

el **hombre** SUSTANTIVO
man (PL men)
◆ **un hombre de negocios** a businessman
◆ **la historia del hombre sobre la tierra** the history of mankind on earth

el **hombro** SUSTANTIVO
shoulder
◆ **encogerse* de hombros** to shrug one's shoulders

el **homenaje** SUSTANTIVO
tribute
◆ **en homenaje a** in honor of

el/la **homosexual** ADJETIVO, SUSTANTIVO
homosexual

hondo ADJETIVO
deep ◇ *un pozo muy hondo* a very deep well ◇ *Se tiró en la parte honda de la piscina.* He dove into the deep end of the pool.

Honduras SUSTANTIVO FEM
Honduras

el **hondureño**, la **hondureña** ADJETIVO, SUSTANTIVO
Honduran

la **honestidad** SUSTANTIVO
[1] honesty (*honradez*)
[2] decency (*decoro*)

honesto ADJETIVO
honest (*honrado*) ◇ *un vendedor honesto* an honest salesman

el **hongo** SUSTANTIVO
[1] fungus (*bacteria*)
[2] mushroom (*seta*)

el **honor** SUSTANTIVO
honor

la **honradez** SUSTANTIVO
honesty

honrado ADJETIVO
honest ◇ *Es una persona muy honrada.* He's a very honest person.

la **hora** SUSTANTIVO
[1] hour ◇ *El viaje dura una hora.* The journey lasts an hour.
[2] time ◇ *¿Qué hora es?* What's the time? ◇ *¿Tienes hora?* Do you have the time?
◆ **¿A qué hora llega?** What time is he arriving?
◆ **llegar* a la hora** to arrive on time
◆ **la hora de cenar** dinner time
◆ **a última hora** at the last minute
[3] period
◆ **Después de inglés tenemos una hora libre.** After English we have a free period.
[4] appointment ◇ *Tengo hora para el dentista.* I have an appointment at the dentist's.
◆ **horas extras** overtime SING
◆ **en mis horas libres** in my spare time

el **horario** SUSTANTIVO
timetable
◆ **el horario de trenes** the train timetable
◆ **horario de visitas** visiting hours PL

la **horchata** SUSTANTIVO

> ℹ *Horchata is a milky looking drink made with nuts and served with ice.*

horizontal ADJETIVO
horizontal

el **horizonte** SUSTANTIVO
horizon ◇ *en el horizonte* on the horizon

la **hormiga** SUSTANTIVO
ant

el **hormigón** SUSTANTIVO
concrete

el **hormigueo** SUSTANTIVO
pins and needles ◇ *Tengo un hormigueo en la pierna.* I have pins and needles in my leg.

el **horno** SUSTANTIVO
oven ◇ *¡Este lugar es un horno!* This place is like an oven!
◆ **pescado al horno** baked fish
◆ **pollo al horno** roast chicken
◆ **un horno microondas** a microwave oven

el **horóscopo** SUSTANTIVO
horoscope

la **horquilla** SUSTANTIVO
bobby pin (*para el pelo*)

horrible ADJETIVO
awful ◇ *El tiempo ha estado horrible.* The weather has been awful.

el **horror** SUSTANTIVO
horror ◇ *los horrores de la guerra* the horrors of war
◆ **tener* horror a algo** to be terrified of something ◇ *Les tengo horror a las arañas.* I'm terrified of spiders.
◆ **¡Qué horror!** How awful!

horroroso ADJETIVO
[1] horrific ◇ *un accidente horroroso* a horrific accident
[2] hideous ◇ *¡Qué camisa mas horrorosa!* What a hideous shirt!

la **hortaliza** SUSTANTIVO
vegetable

hospedarse VERBO
to stay ◇ *Se hospedaron en un hotel.* They stayed in a hotel.

el **hospital** SUSTANTIVO
hospital ◇ *La tuvieron que llevar al hospital.* She had to be taken to the hospital.

la **hospitalidad** SUSTANTIVO
hospitality

el **hostal** SUSTANTIVO
small hotel

H

la **hostia** SUSTANTIVO
host

el **hotel** SUSTANTIVO
hotel

hoy ADVERBIO
today ◇ *Hoy no tenemos clases.* We don't have any classes today. ◇ *el periódico de hoy* today's paper ◇ *los jóvenes de hoy* young people today
- **desde hoy en adelante** from now on
- **hoy en día** nowadays
- **hoy por la mañana** this morning

el **hoyo** SUSTANTIVO
hole

hube VERBO *ver* **haber**

hueco ADJETIVO
hollow

el **hueco** SUSTANTIVO
1 space ◇ *Deja un hueco para el postre.* Leave a space for the dessert.
- **Hazme un hueco para sentarme.** Make a bit of room so that I can sit down.

2 free period ◇ *Los lunes tengo un hueco entre clase y clase.* I have a free period between classes on Mondays.
- **Entró por un hueco que había en la valla.** He got in through a gap in the fence.

la **huelga** SUSTANTIVO
strike ◇ *una huelga general* a general strike
- **estar* en huelga** to be on strike
- **declararse en huelga** to go on strike

el/la **huelguista** SUSTANTIVO
striker

la **huella** SUSTANTIVO
footprint (*pisada*)
- **huellas** (*de animal, vehículo*) tracks
- **Desapareció sin dejar huella.** He disappeared without trace.
- **huella digital** fingerprint

huelo VERBO *ver* **oler**

huérfano ADJETIVO
- **un niño huérfano** an orphan
- **ser* huérfano** to be an orphan
- **es huérfano de padre** he has lost his father
- **quedarse huérfano** to be orphaned

el **huérfano**, la **huérfana** SUSTANTIVO
orphan

la **huerta** SUSTANTIVO
1 vegetable garden (*de hortalizas*)
2 orchard (*de árboles frutales*)

el **huerto** SUSTANTIVO
1 kitchen garden (*de hortalizas*)
2 orchard (*de árboles frutales*)

el **hueso** SUSTANTIVO
1 bone (*de humano, animal*)
2 pit (*de fruta*)
- **aceitunas sin hueso** pitted olives

el/la **huésped** SUSTANTIVO
guest

el **huevo** SUSTANTIVO
egg
- **un huevo duro** a hard-boiled egg
- **un huevo escalfado** a poached egg
- **un huevo estrellado** a fried egg
- **un huevo frito** a fried egg
- **huevos revueltos** scrambled eggs
- **un huevo pasado por agua** a soft-boiled egg
- **un huevo tibio** [*Mexico*] a soft-boiled egg

huir* VERBO
to escape ◇ *Huyó de la cárcel.* He escaped from prison.
- **Huyeron del país.** They fled the country.
- **salir* huyendo** to run away

el **hule** SUSTANTIVO
1 oilcloth (*mantel*)
2 rubber (*goma*) [*Mexico*] ◇ *una liga de hule* a rubber band

la **humanidad** SUSTANTIVO
humanity

humano ADJETIVO ◇ *el cuerpo humano* the human body
- **los seres humanos** human beings

el **humano** SUSTANTIVO
human being

la **humareda** SUSTANTIVO
cloud of smoke

la **humedad** SUSTANTIVO
1 dampness (*de la ropa, las paredes*)
2 humidity (*del aire*)

húmedo ADJETIVO
1 damp (*ropa, pared*) ◇ *La ropa está todavía húmeda.* The clothes are still damp.
2 humid (*clima*) ◇ *El día estaba muy húmedo.* It was a very humid day.

humilde ADJETIVO
humble ◇ *Era de familia humilde.* She was from a humble background.

el **humo** SUSTANTIVO
smoke ◇ *El humo de la chimenea.* The smoke from the chimney.
- **darse* humos** to brag (*coloquial*)
- **echar humo** to smoke
- **bajar los humos a alguien** to take someone down a peg or two
- **Estaba que echaba humo.** She was absolutely fuming. (*coloquial*)

el **humor** SUSTANTIVO
mood ◇ *No está de humor para bromas.* He's not in the mood for jokes.
- **estar* de buen humor** to be in a good mood
- **estar* de mal humor** to be in a bad mood
- **Tiene un gran sentido del humor.** He has a good sense of humor.
- **humor negro** black humor

hundirse VERBO
1 to sink ◇ *El barco se hundió durante la tormenta.* The boat sank during the storm.
2 to collapse ◇ *El techo se hundió con el peso.* The ceiling collapsed under the weight.

el **húngaro,** la **húngara** ADJETIVO, SUSTANTIVO
Hungarian

el **húngaro** SUSTANTIVO
Hungarian (*idioma*)

Hungría SUSTANTIVO FEM
Hungary

el **huracán** SUSTANTIVO
hurricane

hurgar* VERBO
to rummage ◇ *La encontré hurgando en los cajones.* I found her rummaging through the drawers. ◇ *Hurgó en sus bolsillos buscando las llaves.* He rummaged in his pockets for the keys.

◆ **hurgarse la nariz** to pick one's nose

huyendo VERBO *ver* **huir**

I

iba VERBO *ver* **ir**

el **iberoamericano,** la **iberoamericana**
ADJETIVO, SUSTANTIVO
Latin American

el **iceberg** SUSTANTIVO (PL los **icebergs**)
iceberg

el **icono** SUSTANTIVO
icon

la **ictericia** SUSTANTIVO
jaundice

la **ida** SUSTANTIVO
- **¿Cuánto cuesta la ida?** How much is a one-way ticket?
- **¿Me da uno de ida y vuelta para Santiago, por favor?** A round-trip ticket to Santiago please.
- **un boleto de ida y vuelta** a round-trip ticket
- **a la ida** on the way there
- **El viaje de ida duró dos horas.** The journey there took two hours.

la **idea** SUSTANTIVO
idea ◇ *¡Qué buena idea!* What a good idea! ◇ *No tengo ni idea.* I haven't the faintest idea.
- **Mi idea era que nos juntáramos en mi casa.** I thought that we could meet at my house.
- **Ya me voy haciendo a la idea.** I'm beginning to get used to the idea.
- **cambiar de idea** to change one's mind ◇ *Cambié de idea.* I've changed my mind.

ideal ADJETIVO
ideal ◇ *Es el lugar ideal para pasar el verano.* It's the ideal place to spend the summer.

el **ideal** SUSTANTIVO
ideal ◇ *los ideales democráticos* democratic ideals ◇ *Mi ideal sería trabajar cuatro horas diarias.* My ideal would be to work four hours a day.

idear VERBO
to devise ◇ *Idearon un nuevo sistema.* They devised a new system.

idéntico ADJETIVO
identical ◇ *Tiene una falda idéntica a la mía.* She has an identical skirt to mine.
- **Es idéntica a su padre.** She's the spitting image of her father. (*coloquial*)

identificar* VERBO
to identify ◇ *Ya identificaron a la víctima.* They've already identified the victim.
- **identificarse con alguien** to identify with somebody

el **idioma** SUSTANTIVO
language ◇ *Habla tres idiomas a la perfección.* He speaks three languages perfectly.

idiota ADJETIVO
stupid ◇ *¡No seas tan idiota!* Don't be so stupid!

el/la **idiota** SUSTANTIVO
idiot

la **idiotez** SUSTANTIVO (PL las **idioteces**)
- **Deja de decir idioteces.** Stop talking nonsense.

el **ídolo** SUSTANTIVO
idol

la **iglesia** SUSTANTIVO
church (PL churches) ◇ *Voy a la iglesia todos los domingos.* I go to church every Sunday.
- **la Iglesia católica** the Catholic Church

ignorante ADJETIVO
ignorant

ignorar VERBO
1 not to know ◇ *Ignoramos su paradero.* We don't know his whereabouts.
2 to ignore ◇ *Es mejor ignorarla.* It's best to ignore her.

igual (1) ADJETIVO
1 equal ◇ *Se dividieron el dinero en partes iguales.* They divided the money into equal shares.
- **X es igual a Y.** X is equal to Y.

2 the same ◇ *Todas las casas son iguales.* All the houses are the same.
- **Es igual a su madre. (1)** (*físicamente*) She looks just like her mother.
- **Es igual a su madre. (2)** (*en la personalidad*) She's just like her mother.
- **Tengo una falda igual que la tuya.** I have a skirt just like yours.
- **ir* iguales** to be even
- **Van quince iguales.** It's fifteen all.
- **Es igual hoy que mañana.** Today or tomorrow, it doesn't matter.
- **Me da igual.** I don't mind.

igual (2) ADVERBIO
1 the same (*de la misma forma*) ◇ *Se visten igual.* They dress the same.
2 maybe (*a lo mejor*) ◇ *Igual no lo saben todavía.* Maybe they don't know yet.
3 anyway (*de todas formas*) ◇ *No hizo nada pero la castigaron igual.* She didn't do anything, but they punished her anyway.

la **igualdad** SUSTANTIVO
equality ◇ *la igualdad racial* racial equality
- **la igualdad de oportunidades** equal opportunity

igualmente ADVERBIO
the same to you ◇ *¡Feliz Navidad! – Gracias, igualmente.* Merry Christmas! – Thanks, the same to you.

ilegal ADJETIVO
illegal

ilegible ADJETIVO
illegible ◇ *Tiene una letra ilegible.* His handwriting is illegible.

ileso ADJETIVO

unhurt ◇ *Salió ileso del accidente.* He escaped unhurt from the accident.

◆ **Todos resultaron ilesos.** No one was hurt.

la **iluminación** SUSTANTIVO

lighting (*de habitación, calle*) ◇ *La iluminación de las calles es muy deficiente.* The street lighting is very poor.

◆ **Se cortó la iluminación del estadio.** The stadium lights went out.

iluminar VERBO

to light ◇ *los faroles que iluminan la calle* the streetlights that light the road ◇ *Unas velas iluminaban la habitación.* The room was lit by candles.

◆ **El flash le iluminó el rostro.** The flash lit up his face.

◆ **Esta lámpara ilumina muy poco.** This lamp gives out very little light.

◆ **Se le iluminó la cara.** His face lit up.

la **ilusión** SUSTANTIVO (PL las **ilusiones**)

1 hope ◇ *Llegó aquí con muchísima ilusión.* He arrived here full of hope. ◇ *No te hagas muchas ilusiones.* Don't build your hopes up.

2 dream ◇ *Mi mayor ilusión es llegar a ser médico.* My greatest dream is to become a doctor.

3 illusion ◇ *una ilusión óptica* an optical illusion

ilusionar VERBO

◆ **Me ilusiona mucho la idea.** I'm really excited about the idea.

◆ **ilusionarse** to build up one's hopes ◇ *No te ilusiones demasiado.* Don't build up your hopes too much.

◆ **ilusionarse con algo** to get really excited about something

la **ilustración** SUSTANTIVO (PL las **ilustraciones**)

illustration

la **imagen** SUSTANTIVO (PL las **imágenes**)

1 image ◇ *Han decidido cambiar de imagen.* They've decided to change their image.

◆ **ser* la viva imagen de alguien** to be the spitting image of somebody (*coloquial*)

2 picture ◇ *Las películas dan una imagen falsa de América.* The movies give a false picture of America.

la **imaginación** SUSTANTIVO (PL las **imaginaciones**)

imagination ◇ *Tiene mucha imaginación.* He has a vivid imagination.

◆ **Esas son imaginaciones tuyas.** You're imagining things.

◆ **Ni se me pasó por la imaginación.** It never even occurred to me.

imaginarse VERBO

to imagine ◇ *No te imaginas lo mal que me sentí.* You can't imagine how bad I felt. ◇ *Me imagino que seguirá en Europa.* I imagine that he's still in Europe.

◆ **Me imagino que sí.** I imagine so.

◆ **Me imagino que no.** I wouldn't think so.

◆ **¿Se enojó mucho? – ¡Imagínate!** Was he very angry? – What do you think!

el **imán** SUSTANTIVO (PL los **imanes**)

magnet

imbécil ADJETIVO

stupid ◇ *¡No seas imbécil!* Don't be stupid!

la **imitación** SUSTANTIVO (PL las **imitaciones**)

1 impression ◇ *Es muy buena haciendo imitaciones.* She's very good at doing impressions.

2 imitation ◇ *Aprendemos a hablar por imitación.* We learn to speak by imitation. ◇ *los diamantes de imitación* imitation diamonds ◇ *Es imitación cuero.* It's imitation leather.

imitar VERBO

to copy ◇ *Imita todo lo que hace su hermano.* He copies everything his brother does.

◆ **imitar a alguien** to do an impression of somebody ◇ *Imita muy bien a la directora.* She does a very good impression of the principal.

◆ **imitar un acento** to imitate an accent

impaciente ADJETIVO

impatient ◇ *Se estaba empezando a poner impaciente.* He was beginning to get impatient. ◇ *Estarás impaciente por saberlo.* You'll be impatient to know.

impar ADJETIVO (FEM **impar**)

odd ◇ *un número impar* an odd number

el **impar** SUSTANTIVO

odd number

imparcial ADJETIVO

impartial

impecable ADJETIVO

impeccable ◇ *Su comportamiento siempre ha sido impecable.* His behavior has always been impeccable.

◆ **Siempre va impecable.** He is always impeccably dressed.

impedir* VERBO

1 to prevent ◇ *Trataron de impedir la huida de los presos.* They tried to prevent the prisoners' escape. ◇ *impedir que alguien haga algo* to prevent somebody from doing something

2 to stop ◇ *A mí nadie me lo va a impedir.* Nobody is going to stop me.

3 to block ◇ *Un camión nos impedía el paso.* A truck was blocking our way.

el **imperdible** SUSTANTIVO

safety pin

el **imperio** SUSTANTIVO

empire

impermeable ADJETIVO

waterproof ◇ *una tela impermeable* waterproof material

el **impermeable** SUSTANTIVO

raincoat

I

impersonal ADJETIVO
impersonal
impertinente ADJETIVO
impertinent
impidiendo VERBO *ver* **impedir**
impido VERBO *ver* **impedir**
imponer* VERBO
to impose ◊ *Le impusieron una multa de 1.000 pesos.* They imposed a 1000-peso fine on him.
◆ **imponerse (1)** to triumph ◊ *El corredor nigeriano se impuso en la segunda carrera.* The Nigerian runner triumphed in the second race.
◆ **imponerse (2)** to assert oneself ◊ *Sabe imponerse.* He knows how to assert himself.
la **importación** SUSTANTIVO (PL las **importaciones**)
import ◊ *una empresa de importación/exportación* an import-export business
◆ **los artículos de importación** imported goods
◆ **Está prohibida su importación.** There's a ban on importing it.
la **importancia** SUSTANTIVO
importance ◊ *un asunto de suma importancia* a matter of great importance
◆ **dar* importancia a algo** to attach importance to something ◊ *Les da demasiada importancia a los detalles.* He attaches too much importance to details.
◆ **darse* importancia** to give oneself airs
◆ **La educación tiene mucha importancia.** Education is very important.
◆ **¡Se me olvidó tu libro! – No tiene importancia.** I've forgotten your book! – It doesn't matter.
◆ **cuestiones sin importancia** unimportant matters
importante ADJETIVO
important
◆ **lo importante** the important thing ◊ *Lo importante es que vengas.* The important thing is that you come.
importar VERBO
1 to import ◊ *Importa especias del Zaire.* He imports spices from Zaire.
2 to matter ◊ *¿Y eso qué importa?* And what does that matter?
◆ **no importa (1)** it doesn't matter ◊ *No importa lo que piensen los demás.* It doesn't matter what other people think.
◆ **no importa (2)** never mind ◊ *No importa, podemos hacerlo mañana.* Never mind, we can do it tomorrow.
◆ **No me importa levantarme temprano.** I don't mind getting up early.
◆ **¿Le importa que fume?** Do you mind if I smoke?
◆ **¿Y a ti qué te importa?** What's it to you?
◆ **Me importan mucho mis estudios.** My studies are very important to me.
◆ **Me importa un bledo.** I couldn't care less.
imposible ADJETIVO
impossible ◊ *Es imposible predecir quién ganará.* It's impossible to predict who will win. ◊ *Es imposible de predecir.* It's impossible to predict. ◊ *El abuelo está imposible hoy.* Grandpa is being impossible today.
◆ **Me es imposible comprenderla.** I can't understand her.
◆ **Es imposible que lo sepan.** They can't possibly know.
el **impostor**, la **impostora** SUSTANTIVO
impostor
imprescindible ADJETIVO
essential
la **impresión** SUSTANTIVO (PL las **impresiones**)
impression ◊ *Le causó muy buena impresión a mis padres.* He made a very good impression on my parents.
◆ **Tengo la impresión de que no va a venir.** I have a feeling that he won't come.
◆ **Me dio mucha impresión verlo tan delgado.** I was shocked to see him looking so thin.
impresionante ADJETIVO
1 impressive (*hazaña*) ◊ *una colección de monedas de lo más impresionante* a most impressive coin collection
2 amazing (*éxito, memoria*) ◊ *una cantidad impresionante de carros* an amazing number of cars
3 striking (*belleza*) ◊ *El parecido es impresionante.* The likeness is striking.
◆ **paisajes de una belleza impresionante** strikingly beautiful landscapes
impresionar VERBO
1 to shock ◊ *Me impresionó mucho su palidez.* I was really shocked at how pale he was.
2 to impress ◊ *Unos poemas me impresionaron más que otros.* Some poems impressed me more than others.
◆ **Impresiona lo rápido que es.** His speed is impressive.
◆ **impresionarse** to be impressed ◊ *Se impresiona con facilidad.* He's easily impressed.
el **impreso** SUSTANTIVO
form ◊ *un impreso de solicitud* an application form
la **impresora** SUSTANTIVO
printer ◊ *una impresora láser* a laser printer
imprevisible ADJETIVO
1 unforeseeable ◊ *acontecimientos imprevisibles* unforeseeable events
2 unpredictable ◊ *Tiene unas reacciones totalmente imprevisibles.* His reactions are completely unpredictable.
imprevisto ADJETIVO

unexpected

el **imprevisto** SUSTANTIVO
- **si no surge algún imprevisto** if nothing unexpected comes up

imprimir* VERBO
to print

improvisar VERBO
to improvise

la **imprudencia** SUSTANTIVO
- **Saltar la tapia fue una imprudencia.** It was unwise to jump over the wall.
- **El accidente fue debido a una imprudencia del conductor.** The accident was caused by reckless driving.

imprudente ADJETIVO
unwise ◇ *Sería imprudente nadar aquí.* It would be unwise to go swimming here.
- **conductores imprudentes** reckless drivers

impuesto VERBO *ver* **imponer**

el **impuesto** SUSTANTIVO
tax (PL taxes)
- **el impuesto sobre la renta** income tax
- **libre de impuestos** duty-free ◇ *Lo compré en la tienda libre de impuestos.* I bought it at the duty-free shop.

impulsar VERBO
to drive ◇ *Está impulsado por un motor eléctrico.* It's driven by an electric motor. ◇ *La ambición la impulsó a mentir.* Ambition drove her to lie.
- **una política destinada a impulsar el comercio** a policy designed to boost trade

el **impulso** SUSTANTIVO
impulse ◇ *Actué por impulso.* I acted on impulse.
- **Mi primer impulso fue salir corriendo.** My first instinct was to run away.
- **Tomó impulso antes de saltar.** He took a run up before jumping.

inaceptable ADJETIVO
unacceptable

inadecuado ADJETIVO
unsuitable

inadvertido ADJETIVO
- **pasar inadvertido** to go unnoticed ◇ *Tu ausencia no pasó inadvertida.* Your absence didn't go unnoticed.

inapropiado ADJETIVO
unsuitable ◇ *Esos zapatos son inapropiados para caminar por el bosque.* Those shoes are unsuitable for walking in the woods.

la **inauguración** SUSTANTIVO (PL las **inauguraciones**)
opening ◇ *Había mucha gente en la inauguración.* There were a lot of people at the opening. ◇ *la ceremonia de inauguración* the opening ceremony

inaugurar VERBO
to open ◇ *Mañana inauguran el nuevo hospital.* The new hospital is being opened tomorrow.

el/la **inca** ADJETIVO, SUSTANTIVO
Inca

la **incapacidad** SUSTANTIVO
inability ◇ *debido a su incapacidad para concentrarse* owing to his inability to concentrate
- **la incapacidad física** physical disability
- **la incapacidad mental** mental disability

incapaz ADJETIVO (PL **incapaces**)
incapable ◇ *Es incapaz de estarse callado.* He is incapable of keeping quiet.
- **Hoy soy incapaz de concentrarme.** I can't concentrate today.

incendiarse VERBO
to catch fire ◇ *Se le incendió el carro.* His car caught fire.

el **incendio** SUSTANTIVO
fire ◇ *Se declaró un incendio en el hotel.* A fire broke out in the hotel.

el **incentivo** SUSTANTIVO
incentive ◇ *No tengo incentivo para estudiar.* I have no incentive to study.

el **incidente** SUSTANTIVO
incident ◇ *La reunión transcurrió sin incidentes.* The meeting passed off without incident.

incierto ADJETIVO
uncertain ◇ *un porvenir incierto* an uncertain future

inclinar VERBO
to tilt ◇ *Inclina un poco más la sombrilla.* Can you tilt the sunshade a bit more?
- **inclinar la cabeza** to nod
- **inclinarse (1)** to bend down ◇ *Se inclinó para besarlo.* She bent down to kiss him.
- **inclinarse (2)** to lean ◇ *inclinarse sobre algo* to lean over something ◇ *inclinarse hacia delante* to lean forward ◇ *inclinarse hacia atrás* to lean back
- **inclinarse (3)** to bow ◇ *inclinarse ante alguien* to bow to somebody

incluido ADJETIVO
included ◇ *El servicio no está incluido en el precio.* Service is not included.

incluir* VERBO
to include ◇ *El precio incluye las comidas.* The price includes meals.
- **El examen no incluye este tema.** This topic doesn't come into the exam.

inclusive ADVERBIO
1 inclusive ◇ *Está abierto de lunes a sábado inclusive.* It's open from Monday to Saturday inclusive.
2 including ◇ *hasta el capítulo diez inclusive* up to and including chapter ten

incluso ADVERBIO
even ◇ *He tenido que estudiar incluso los domingos.* I've even had to study on Sundays.

incluyendo VERBO *ver* **incluir**

I

incómodo ADJETIVO
uncomfortable ◇ *Este asiento es muy incómodo.* This seat is very uncomfortable. ◇ *Se siente muy incómoda cuando está con él.* She feels very uncomfortable with him.

incompetente ADJETIVO
incompetent

incompleto ADJETIVO
incomplete

incomprensible ADJETIVO
incomprehensible

inconsciente ADJETIVO
[1] unconscious ◇ *estar inconsciente* to be unconscious ◇ *Quedó inconsciente con el golpe.* The force of the blow left him unconscious. ◇ *un deseo inconsciente* an unconscious desire
[2] thoughtless ◇ *¡Qué inconsciente eres!* How thoughtless you are!

inconveniente ADJETIVO
inconvenient ◇ *a una hora inconveniente* at an inconvenient time

el **inconveniente** SUSTANTIVO
[1] problem ◇ *Surgió un inconveniente.* A problem has come up.
[2] drawback ◇ *El plan tiene sus inconvenientes.* The plan has its drawbacks.
◆ **No tengo ningún inconveniente.** I have no objection.
◆ **No tengo inconveniente en preguntárselo.** I don't mind asking him.
◆ **¿Tienes algún inconveniente en que le dé tu teléfono?** Do you mind if I give him your telephone number?

incorrecto ADJETIVO
[1] incorrect ◇ *una respuesta incorrecta* an incorrect answer
[2] impolite ◇ *Has estado muy incorrecto.* You were very impolite.

increíble ADJETIVO
incredible

inculto ADJETIVO
ignorant (*persona*)

incurable ADJETIVO
incurable

indeciso ADJETIVO
indecisive ◇ *Es una persona muy indecisa.* She's very indecisive.
◆ **Estoy indecisa, no sé cuál comprar.** I can't make up my mind; I don't know which to buy.

indefenso ADJETIVO
defenseless

la **indemnización** SUSTANTIVO (PL las **indemnizaciones**)
compensation ◇ *Recibieron mil dólares de indemnización.* They received a thousand dollars compensation.
◆ **la indemnización por daños y perjuicios** damages PL

indemnizar* VERBO
to compensate ◇ *El gobierno indemnizará a las víctimas.* The government will compensate the victims.
◆ **Nos tienen que indemnizar.** They have to pay us compensation.

la **independencia** SUSTANTIVO
independence

independiente ADJETIVO
[1] independent ◇ *Es una chica muy independiente.* She's a very independent girl.
[2] self-contained ◇ *Son departamentos independientes.* They are self-contained apartments.

independientemente ADVERBIO
independently ◇ *Los dos motores funcionan independientemente.* The two engines work independently.
◆ **Iremos, independientemente de lo que hayan decidido.** We'll go, regardless of what they have decided.

independizarse* VERBO
to become independent ◇ *Quiero independizarme.* I want to become independent.

la **india** SUSTANTIVO
Indian

India SUSTANTIVO FEM
◆ **La India** India

la **indicación** SUSTANTIVO (PL las **indicaciones**)
sign
◆ **Nos hizo una indicación para que siguiéramos.** He signaled to us to go on.
◆ **indicaciones (1)** instructions ◇ *Hay que seguir las indicaciones del manual.* You'll need to follow the instructions in the manual.
◆ **indicaciones (2)** directions ◇ *Me dio indicaciones de cómo llegar.* He gave me directions for getting there.

indicar* VERBO
[1] to indicate ◇ *El termómetro indicaba treinta grados.* The thermometer indicated thirty degrees. ◇ *Todo indica que...* Everything indicates that...
[2] to tell ◇ *¿Puede indicarme dónde hay una estación de servicio?* Please can you tell where there's a gas station? ◇ *Un guardia me indicó el camino.* A policeman told me the way.
[3] to advise ◇ *El médico me indicó que no fumara.* The doctor advised me not to smoke.

el **índice** SUSTANTIVO
[1] index (PL indexes *o* indices) ◇ *un índice alfabético* an alphabetical index
◆ **el índice de materias** the table of contents
◆ **el índice de natalidad** the birth rate
[2] index finger (*dedo*)

la **indiferencia** SUSTANTIVO
indifference

indiferente ADJETIVO
indifferent ◇ *Parece indiferente al cariño.* She seems indifferent to affection.
◆ **Es indiferente que viva en Miami o Tampa.** It makes no difference whether he lives in Miami or Tampa.
◆ **Me es indiferente hacerlo hoy o mañana.** I don't mind whether I do it today or tomorrow.

indígena ADJETIVO
indigenous ◇ *la población indígena* the indigenous population

el/la **indígena** SUSTANTIVO
native

la **indigestión** SUSTANTIVO
indigestion

indignado ADJETIVO
angry ◇ *Están muy indignados con ella.* They're very angry with her.

indignar VERBO
to infuriate ◇ *Su comportamiento los indignó.* His behavior infuriated them.
◆ **indignarse por algo** to get angry about something
◆ **indignarse con alguien** to be furious with somebody

el **indio** ADJETIVO, SUSTANTIVO
Indian

la **indirecta** SUSTANTIVO
hint ◇ *lanzar una indirecta* to drop a hint

indirecto ADJETIVO
indirect

indispensable ADJETIVO
essential ◇ *Es indispensable saber inglés.* It's essential to know English.
◆ **Llevaba sólo lo indispensable.** He was carrying only the essentials.

individual ADJETIVO
1 individual (*porción, rasgo*) ◇ *Los venden en paquetes individuales.* They're sold in individual packets.
2 single (*cama, cuarto*) ◇ *Quisiera una habitación individual.* I'd like a single room.

el **individual** SUSTANTIVO
singles PL ◇ *la final del individual femenino* the women's singles final

el **individuo** SUSTANTIVO
individual

la **industria** SUSTANTIVO
industry (PL industries) ◇ *la industria pesada* heavy industry ◇ *la industria petrolera* the oil industry

industrial ADJETIVO
industrial

el/la **industrial** SUSTANTIVO
industrialist

ineficiente ADJETIVO
inefficient

inesperado ADJETIVO
unexpected ◇ *una visita inesperada* an unexpected visit

inestable ADJETIVO
1 unsteady (*mueble*)
2 changeable (*tiempo*)

inevitable ADJETIVO
inevitable

inexacto ADJETIVO
inaccurate ◇ *La biografía contiene muchos datos inexactos.* The biography contains a lot of inaccurate details.

inexperto ADJETIVO
inexperienced

inexplicable ADJETIVO
inexplicable

infantil ADJETIVO
1 children's (*parque, ropa*) ◇ *un programa infantil* a children's program
2 childish (*actitud*) ◇ *¡No seas tan infantil!* Don't be so childish!

el **infarto** SUSTANTIVO
heart attack ◇ *Le dio un infarto.* He had a heart attack.

la **infección** SUSTANTIVO (PL las **infecciones**)
infection ◇ *tener una infección* to have an infection ◇ *Tiene una infección de oídos.* He has an ear infection.

infeliz ADJETIVO (PL **infelices**)
unhappy

inferior (FEM **inferior**) ADJETIVO
1 lower ◇ *Tenía el labio inferior hinchado.* His lower lip was swollen. ◇ *Las temperaturas han sido inferiores a lo normal.* Temperatures have been lower than normal.
2 inferior ◇ *de calidad inferior* of inferior quality
◆ **un número inferior a nueve** a number below nine

el **infierno** SUSTANTIVO
hell

el **infinitivo** SUSTANTIVO
infinitive

inflable ADJETIVO
inflatable

la **inflación** SUSTANTIVO
inflation ◇ *Hay que reducir la inflación.* Inflation has to be reduced.

inflamable ADJETIVO
inflammable

inflar VERBO
1 to blow up (*globo*)
2 to inflate (*rueda*)

la **influencia** SUSTANTIVO
influence ◇ *Mi abuelo tuvo una gran influencia en mí.* My grandfather had a great influence on me.

influenciar VERBO
to influence

influir* VERBO
◆ **dos hombres que influyeron en su vida** two men who influenced his life
◆ **Mis padres influyeron mucho en mí.** My parents had a great influence on me. ☞

I

- **El cansancio ha influido en su rendimiento.** Tiredness has affected his work.

la **información** SUSTANTIVO (PL las **informaciones**)
1 information ◇ *Quisiera información sobre los cursos de inglés.* I'd like some information on English courses.
- **una información muy importante** a very important piece of information

2 news SING ◇ *Este canal tiene mucha información deportiva.* There's a lot of sports news on this channel.
3 directory assistance ◇ *Llama a información y pide que te den el número.* Call directory assistance and ask them for the number.
- **Pregunta en información de dónde sale el tren.** Ask at the information desk which platform the train leaves from.

informal ADJETIVO
1 informal ◇ *un ambiente muy informal* a very informal atmosphere
- **Prefiero la ropa informal.** I prefer casual clothes.

2 unreliable ◇ *Es una persona muy informal.* He's a very unreliable person.

informar VERBO
to inform ◇ *Nos informaron que venía con retraso.* They informed us that it was going to be late.
- **Les han informado mal.** You've been misinformed.
- **¿Me podría informar sobre los cursos de inglés?** Could you give me some information about English courses?
- **informarse de algo** to find out about something

la **informática** SUSTANTIVO
computing ◇ *los avances de la informática* advances in computing
- **Quiere estudiar informática.** He wants to study computer science.

el **informe** SUSTANTIVO
report ◇ *Presentó un informe detallado sobre lo ocurrido.* He gave a detailed report about what had happened.
- **según mis informes** according to my information
- **pedir* informes** to ask for references

la **infusión** SUSTANTIVO (PL las **infusiones**)
herbal tea
- **una infusión de manzanilla** a camomile tea

ingeniar VERBO
to devise ◇ *Habían ingeniado un sistema para evadir impuestos.* They had devised a system for evading taxes.
- **ingeniárselas** to manage ◇ *No sé cómo se las ingenió para conseguir el dinero.* I don't know how he managed to get the money.

la **ingeniera** SUSTANTIVO
engineer ◇ *Quiere ser ingeniera.* She wants to be an engineer.

la **ingeniería** SUSTANTIVO
engineering

el **ingeniero** SUSTANTIVO
engineer ◇ *Quiere ser ingeniero.* He wants to be an engineer.
- **un ingeniero agrónomo** an agriculturist

el **ingenio** SUSTANTIVO
1 ingenuity (*talento*)
2 wit (*agudeza*)
- **un ingenio azucarero** a sugar refinery

ingenioso ADJETIVO
1 ingenious ◇ *¡Qué idea más ingeniosa!* What an ingenious idea!
2 witty ◇ *un comentario ingenioso* a witty comment

ingenuo ADJETIVO
naïve

Inglaterra SUSTANTIVO FEM
England

inglés ADJETIVO (FEM **inglesa**, MASC PL **ingleses**)
English ◇ *la comida inglesa* English food

el **inglés** (PL los **ingleses**) SUSTANTIVO
1 Englishman (PL Englishmen) (*persona*)
- **los ingleses** the English

2 English (*idioma*) ◇ *El inglés le resulta difícil.* He finds English difficult.

la **inglesa** SUSTANTIVO
Englishwoman (PL Englishwomen)

el **ingrediente** SUSTANTIVO
ingredient

ingresar VERBO
- **ingresar en un club** to join a club
- **ingresar en el hospital** to go to the hospital
- **Han vuelto a ingresar a mi abuela en el hospital.** They've taken my grandmother to the hospital again.

los **ingresos** SUSTANTIVO
income SING ◇ *Tiene unos ingresos muy bajos.* He has a very low income.

la **inicial** SUSTANTIVO
initial

la **iniciativa** SUSTANTIVO
initiative ◇ *Lo hizo por iniciativa propia.* He did it on his own initiative.

la **injusticia** SUSTANTIVO
injustice ◇ *Lucharon contra las injusticias sociales.* They fought against social injustices.
- **Es una injusticia que lo hayan expulsado.** It was unfair of them to expel him.

injusto ADJETIVO
unfair

inmaduro ADJETIVO
1 immature (*persona*)
2 unripe (*fruta*)

inmediatamente ADVERBIO
immediately

inmediato ADJETIVO
immediate (*instantáneo*)

* Verbs marked with this symbol are irregular. See pages 346–348 for further details.

◆ **inmediato a algo** next to something ◇ *en el edificio inmediato a la embajada* in the building next to the embassy
◆ **de inmediato** immediately

inmenso ADJETIVO
immense
◆ **la inmensa mayoría** the vast majority

la **inmigración** SUSTANTIVO
immigration

el/la **inmigrante** SUSTANTIVO
immigrant

inmoral ADJETIVO
immoral

inmortal ADJETIVO
immortal

inmóvil ADJETIVO
motionless ◇ *Se quedó inmóvil.* He remained motionless.

innecesario ADJETIVO
unnecessary

inocente ADJETIVO
innocent ◇ *Es inocente.* He's innocent.
◆ **El jurado la declaró inocente.** The jury found her not guilty.

inofensivo ADJETIVO
harmless

inolvidable ADJETIVO
unforgettable

inquietante ADJETIVO
worrying

inquieto ADJETIVO
1 worried ◇ *Estaba inquieta porque su hijo no había llegado.* She was worried because her son hadn't come home.
2 restless ◇ *Es un niño muy inquieto y le cuesta dormirse.* He's a very restless boy and finds it hard to get to sleep.

el **inquilino,** la **inquilina** SUSTANTIVO
1 tenant (*de un departamento, una casa*)
2 lodger (*de una habitación*)

insatisfecho ADJETIVO
dissatisfied

inscribirse* VERBO
to enroll ◇ *Se inscribió en un curso de idiomas.* He enrolled in a language course.

la **inscripción** SUSTANTIVO (PL las **inscripciones**)
1 enrollment ◇ *Mañana se cierra la inscripción.* Tomorrow is the last day for enrollment.
2 inscription ◇ *Sobre la puerta hay una inscripción con el año.* Above the door there's an inscription with the year on it.

inscrito VERBO *ver* **inscribirse**

el **insecto** SUSTANTIVO
insect

la **inseguridad** SUSTANTIVO
insecurity ◇ *la inseguridad en el trabajo* job insecurity
◆ **la inseguridad ciudadana** the lack of safety on the streets

inseguro ADJETIVO
1 insecure (*persona*)
2 unsafe (*lugar*)

insensato ADJETIVO
foolish

insensible ADJETIVO
insensitive ◇ *Se han vuelto insensibles al frío.* They have become insensitive to the cold.
◆ **Es insensible al sufrimiento ajeno.** He is blind to the suffering of others.

la **insignia** SUSTANTIVO
1 badge (*distintivo*)
2 flag (*bandera*)

insignificante ADJETIVO
insignificant

insinuar* VERBO
to hint at ◇ *No lo dijo pero lo insinuó.* He didn't say it but he hinted at it.
◆ **¿Insinúas que miento?** Are you insinuating that I'm lying?

I

insípido ADJETIVO
insipid

insistir VERBO
to insist ◇ *insistir en hacer algo* to insist on doing something ◇ *Insiste en que vea a un médico.* He's insisting that I see a doctor.

la **insolación** SUSTANTIVO
sunstroke

insolente ADJETIVO
insolent

insoportable ADJETIVO
unbearable

el **inspector,** la **inspectora** SUSTANTIVO
inspector

las **instalaciones** SUSTANTIVO
facilities ◇ *El hotel tiene unas estupendas instalaciones deportivas.* The hotel has excellent sports facilities.

instalar VERBO
1 to install ◇ *Instaló una alarma en el carro.* He installed an alarm in the car.
2 to set up ◇ *Aquí van a instalar unas oficinas.* They're going to set up offices here.
◆ **instalarse** to settle ◇ *Decidieron instalarse en el centro.* They decided to settle in the town center.

instantáneo ADJETIVO
instantaneous
◆ **el café instantáneo** instant coffee

el **instante** SUSTANTIVO
moment ◇ *por un instante* for a moment
◆ **A cada instante suena el teléfono.** The phone rings all the time.
◆ **al instante** right away

el **instinto** SUSTANTIVO
instinct

la **institución** SUSTANTIVO (PL las **instituciones**)
institution

el **instituto** SUSTANTIVO
institute

las **instrucciones** SUSTANTIVO

☞

instructions

instructivo ADJETIVO
educational

el **instructor,** la **instructora** SUSTANTIVO
instructor ◇ *un instructor de esquí* a ski instructor ◇ *un instructor de autoescuela* a driving instructor

el **instrumento** SUSTANTIVO
instrument

insuficiente ADJETIVO
insufficient ◇ *una cantidad insuficiente de dinero* an insufficient amount of money

la **insulina** SUSTANTIVO
insulin

insultar VERBO
to insult

el **insulto** SUSTANTIVO
insult

el/la **intelectual** ADJETIVO, SUSTANTIVO
intellectual

la **inteligencia** SUSTANTIVO
intelligence

inteligente ADJETIVO
intelligent

la **intención** SUSTANTIVO (PL las **intenciones**)
intention ◇ *No tengo la más mínima intención de hacerlo.* I don't have the slightest intention of doing it.
◆ **tener* intención de hacer algo** to intend to do something ◇ *Tenía intención de descansar un rato.* He intended to rest for a while.
◆ **Lo que cuenta es la intención.** It's the thought that counts.

intencionado ADJETIVO
deliberate ◇ *La patada fue intencionada.* It was a deliberate kick.
◆ **bien intencionado** well-meaning
◆ **mal intencionado** malicious

intensivo ADJETIVO
intensive ◇ *un curso intensivo de inglés* an intensive English course

intenso ADJETIVO
intense

intentar VERBO
to try ◇ *¿Por qué no lo intentas otra vez?* Why don't you try again? ◇ *intentar hacer algo* to try to do something

el **intento** SUSTANTIVO
attempt ◇ *Aprobó al primer intento.* He passed at the first attempt.

el **intercambio** SUSTANTIVO
exchange

el **interés** SUSTANTIVO (PL los **intereses**)
interest ◇ *Tienes que poner más interés en tus estudios.* You must take more of an interest in your studies. ◇ *El banco da un interés del 5%.* The bank gives 5% interest.
◆ **tener* interés en hacer algo** to be keen to do something
◆ **Todo lo hace por interés.** Everything he does is out of self-interest.

interesante ADJETIVO
interesting

interesar VERBO
to interest ◇ *Eso es algo que siempre me ha interesado.* That's something that has always interested me.
◆ **Me interesa mucho la física.** I'm very interested in physics.
◆ **interesarse por algo** to ask about something

el **interfono** SUSTANTIVO
intercom

interior ADJETIVO (FEM **interior**)
1 inside (*bolsillo*)
2 inner (*mundo*)

el **interior** SUSTANTIVO
◆ **El tren se detuvo en el interior del túnel.** The train stopped inside the tunnel.

el/la **interiorista** SUSTANTIVO
interior designer

intermedio ADJETIVO
1 intermediate (*nivel*)
2 medium (*tamaño*)

el **intermedio** SUSTANTIVO
interval

interminable ADJETIVO
endless

intermitente ADJETIVO
1 intermittent (*lluvia*)
2 flashing (*luz*)

el **intermitente** SUSTANTIVO
turn signal

internacional ADJETIVO
international

el **internado** SUSTANTIVO
boarding school

el/la **internauta** SUSTANTIVO
Internet user

el/la **Internet** SUSTANTIVO
Internet ◇ *en Internet* on the Internet

interno ADJETIVO
◆ **estar* interno en un colegio** to be a boarder at a school

el **interno,** la **interna** SUSTANTIVO
1 boarder (*alumno*)
2 intern (*médico*)

la **interpretación** SUSTANTIVO (PL las **interpretaciones**)
interpretation (*de un texto, papel*)
◆ **la interpretación simultánea** simultaneous translation
◆ **Todo fue producto de una mala interpretación.** It was all the result of a misunderstanding.

interpretar VERBO
1 to interpret ◇ *Sabe interpretar los sueños.* He knows how to interpret dreams.
2 to play ◇ *Interpreta el papel de Victoria.* She plays the part of Victoria.

[3] to perform ◇ *Interpretó una pieza de Mozart.* He performed a piece by Mozart.
◆ **No me interpretes mal.** Don't misunderstand me.

el/la **intérprete** SUSTANTIVO
interpreter ◇ *Quiere ser intérprete.* She wants to be an interpreter.

interrogar* VERBO
to question ◇ *Fue interrogado por la policía.* He was questioned by the police.

interrumpir VERBO
[1] to interrupt (*persona*)
[2] to cut short (*vacaciones*)
[3] to block (*tráfico*) ◇ *Estás interrumpiendo el paso.* You're blocking the way.

la **interrupción** SUSTANTIVO (PL las **interrupciones**)
interruption

el **interruptor** SUSTANTIVO
switch (PL switches)

interurbano ADJETIVO
long-distance (*llamada*)

el **intervalo** SUSTANTIVO
interval (*de tiempo, intermedio*)

la **intimidad** SUSTANTIVO
[1] private life ◇ *Protege mucho su intimidad.* He's very protective of his private life.
[2] privacy ◇ *En esta casa no tengo ninguna intimidad.* I have no privacy in this house.
◆ **La boda se celebró en la intimidad.** It was a private wedding.

intimidar VERBO
to intimidate

íntimo ADJETIVO
intimate ◇ *mis secretos íntimos* my intimate secrets
◆ **Es un amigo íntimo.** He's a close friend.

la **introducción** SUSTANTIVO (PL las **introducciones**)
introduction

introducir* VERBO
[1] to insert ◇ *Introdujo la moneda en la ranura.* He inserted the coin in the slot.
[2] to bring in ◇ *Esperan introducir un nuevo sistema de trabajo.* They're hoping to bring in new working methods.
◆ **Han introducido cambios en el horario.** They've made changes to the timetable.

introvertido ADJETIVO
introverted

el **intruso,** la **intrusa** SUSTANTIVO
intruder

la **intuición** SUSTANTIVO
intuition ◇ *la intuición femenina* feminine intuition
◆ **por intuición** intuitively

la **inundación** SUSTANTIVO (PL las **inundaciones**)
flood

inundar VERBO
to flood ◇ *El río inundó el pueblo.* The river flooded the village.
◆ **inundarse** to be flooded ◇ *Se nos inundó el baño.* Our bathroom was flooded.

inútil ADJETIVO
useless ◇ *La oficina está llena de trastos inútiles.* The office is full of useless trash.
◇ *Es inútil tratar de hacerle entender.* It's useless trying to make him understand.
◆ **Es inútil que esperes.** There's no point in your waiting.

el/la **inútil** SUSTANTIVO (PL los/las **inútiles**)
◆ **¡Es un inútil!** He's useless!

invadir VERBO
to invade

la **inválida** SUSTANTIVO
disabled woman (PL disabled women)

inválido ADJETIVO
disabled ◇ *Quedó inválida después del accidente.* She was left disabled following the accident.

el **inválido** SUSTANTIVO
disabled man (PL disabled men)
◆ **los inválidos** the disabled

la **invasión** SUSTANTIVO (PL las **invasiones**)
invasion

inventar VERBO
[1] to invent ◇ *Inventaron un nuevo sistema.* They invented a new system.
[2] to make up ◇ *Inventó toda la historia.* He made up the whole story.

el **invento** SUSTANTIVO
invention

el **inventor,** la **inventora** SUSTANTIVO
inventor

el **invernadero** SUSTANTIVO
greenhouse
◆ **el efecto invernadero** the greenhouse effect

invernar VERBO
to hibernate

inverosímil ADJETIVO
unlikely

la **inversión** SUSTANTIVO (PL las **inversiones**)
investment

inverso ADJETIVO
reverse ◇ *en orden inverso* in reverse order
◆ **a la inversa** the other way around

invertir* VERBO
[1] to invest (*dinero*) ◇ *He invertido mucho dinero en estas acciones.* I've invested a lot of money in these shares.
[2] to spend (*tiempo*) ◇ *Hemos invertido muchas horas en el proyecto.* We've spent a lot of time on this project.
[3] to reverse (*orden*)

la **investigación** SUSTANTIVO (PL las **investigaciones**)
[1] research (*estudio*) ◇ *Está haciendo una investigación sobre el envejecimiento.* He's doing some research into ageing.
[2] investigation (*por la policía*)

I

☞

[3] hearing (*por una comisión*) ◇ *Se hará una investigación pública.* There will be a public hearing.

el **invierno** SUSTANTIVO
winter ◇ *en invierno* in winter ◇ *el invierno pasado* last winter

invisible ADJETIVO
invisible

la **invitación** SUSTANTIVO (PL las **invitaciones**)
invitation

el **invitado,** la **invitada** SUSTANTIVO
guest ◇ *Es el invitado de honor.* He's the guest of honor.

invitar VERBO
to invite ◇ *Me invitó a una fiesta.* He invited me to a party. ◇ *Me gustaría invitarla a cenar.* I'd like to invite her to dinner.
◆ **Te invito a un café.** I'll buy you a coffee.
◆ **Esta vez invito yo.** This time it's on me.

la **inyección** SUSTANTIVO (PL las **inyecciones**)
injection ◇ *ponerle una inyección a alguien* to give someone an injection

inyectar VERBO
◆ **Le tuvieron que inyectar insulina.** They had to give him insulin injections.
◆ **inyectarse algo** to inject oneself with something ◇ *Se había inyectado heroína.* He had injected himself with heroin.

ir* VERBO
[1] to go ◇ *Anoche fuimos al cine.* We went to the movies last night. ◇ *¿A qué colegio vas?* What school do you go to?
◆ **ir de vacaciones** to go on vacation
◆ **ir por** to go and get ◇ *Voy por el paraguas.* I'll go and get the umbrella. ◇ *Fue por el médico.* She has gone to get the doctor.
◆ **Voy a hacerlo mañana.** I'm going to do it tomorrow.
◆ **vamos** let's go ◇ *Vamos a casa.* Let's go home.
◆ **¡Vamos!** Come on! ◇ *¡Vamos! ¡Di algo!* Come on! Say something!
◆ **¡Vamos a ver!** Let's see!
[2] to be ◇ *Iba muy bien vestido.* He was very well dressed. ◇ *Iba con su madre.* He was with his mother. ◇ *como iba diciendo* as I was saying ◇ *Va a ser difícil.* It will be difficult.
[3] to come ◇ *¡Ahora voy!* I'm just coming!
◆ **¿Puedo ir contigo?** Can I come with you?
◆ **ir a pie** to walk
◆ **ir en avión** to fly
◆ **¿Cómo te va?** How are things?
◆ **¿Cómo te va en los estudios?** How are you getting on with your studies?
◆ **¡Que te vaya bien!** Take care of yourself!
◆ **¡Qué va!** What are you talking about!
◆ **¡Vaya! ¿Qué haces tú por aquí?** Well, what a surprise! What are you doing here?
◆ **¡Vaya carro!** What a car!
◆ **irse (1)** to leave ◇ *Acaba de irse.* He has just left.
◆ **irse (2)** to go out ◇ *Se fue la luz.* The lights have gone out.
◆ **¡Vámonos!** Let's go!
◆ **¡Vete!** Go away!
◆ **Vete a hacer las tareas.** Go and do your homework.

Irak SUSTANTIVO MASC
Iraq

Irán SUSTANTIVO MASC
Iran

el/la **iraní** ADJETIVO, SUSTANTIVO (PL los/las **iraníes**)
Iranian

el/la **iraquí** ADJETIVO, SUSTANTIVO (PL los/las **iraquíes**)
Iraqi

Irlanda SUSTANTIVO FEM
Ireland ◇ *Irlanda del Norte* Northern Ireland

irlandés ADJETIVO (FEM **irlandesa,** MASC PL **irlandeses**)
Irish ◇ *un café irlandés* an Irish coffee

el **irlandés** (PL los **irlandeses**) SUSTANTIVO
[1] Irishman (PL Irishmen) (*persona*)
◆ **los irlandeses** the Irish
[2] Irish (*idioma*)

la **irlandesa** SUSTANTIVO
Irishwoman (PL Irishwomen)

irónico ADJETIVO
ironic

irracional ADJETIVO
irrational

irrelevante ADJETIVO
irrelevant

irresistible ADJETIVO
irresistible

irresponsable ADJETIVO
irresponsible

irritante ADJETIVO
irritating

irrompible ADJETIVO
unbreakable

la **isla** SUSTANTIVO
island ◇ *una isla desierta* a desert island
◆ **la Isla de Pascua** Easter Island

el **Islam** SUSTANTIVO
Islam

islámico ADJETIVO
Islamic

islandés ADJETIVO (FEM **islandesa,** MASC PL **islandeses**)
Icelandic

el **islandés,** la **islandesa** SUSTANTIVO (MASC PL los **islandeses**)
Icelander

el **islandés** SUSTANTIVO
Icelandic (*idioma*)

Islandia SUSTANTIVO FEM
Iceland

el **isleño** SUSTANTIVO
islander

* Verbs marked with this symbol are irregular. See pages 346–348 for further details.

Israel SUSTANTIVO MASC
Israel

el/la **israelí** ADJETIVO, SUSTANTIVO (PL los/las **israelíes**)
Israeli

Italia SUSTANTIVO FEM
Italy

el **italiano,** la **italiana** ADJETIVO, SUSTANTIVO
Italian

el **italiano** SUSTANTIVO
Italian (*idioma*)

el **itinerario** SUSTANTIVO
[1] route ◇ *Hicimos el itinerario de costumbre.* We took the usual route.
[2] itinerary (PL itineraries) ◇ *Me gustaría incluir Toronto en el itinerario el año que viene.* I'd like to include Toronto on our itinerary next year.

izar* VERBO
to hoist ◇ *Izaron la bandera.* They hoisted the flag.

la **izquierda** SUSTANTIVO
[1] left hand (*mano*)
- **Escribo con la izquierda.** I write with my left hand.

[2] left ◇ *doblar a la izquierda* to turn left ◇ *La izquierda ganó las elecciones.* The elections were won by the left.
- **ser* de izquierda** to be left-wing ◇ *un partido de izquierda* a left-wing party
- **a la izquierda** on the left ◇ *la segunda calle a la izquierda* the second turning on the left
- **a la izquierda del edificio** to the left of the building
- **manejar por la izquierda** to drive on the left

izquierdo ADJETIVO
left ◇ *Levanta la mano izquierda.* Raise your left hand.
- **Escribo con la mano izquierda.** I write with my left hand.
- **el lado izquierdo** the left side
- **a mano izquierda** on the left-hand side

J

el **jabón** SUSTANTIVO (PL los **jabones**)
soap

el **jacal** SUSTANTIVO Mexico
shack

la **jaiba** SUSTANTIVO
crab

jalar VERBO
1 to pull ◇ *No le jales el pelo.* Don't pull his hair.
2 to take ◇ *Jaló un folleto de la mesa.* He took a leaflet from the table.

jamás ADVERBIO
never ◇ *Jamás he visto nada parecido.* I've never seen anything like it.

el **jamón** SUSTANTIVO (PL los **jamones**)
ham ◇ *un sandwich de jamón* a ham sandwich
◆ **jamón serrano** cured ham
◆ **jamón de York** boiled ham

Japón SUSTANTIVO MASC
Japan

el **japonés,** la **japonesa** ADJETIVO, SUSTANTIVO (MASC PL los **japoneses**)
Japanese

el **japonés** SUSTANTIVO
Japanese (*idioma*)

el **jarabe** SUSTANTIVO
syrup
◆ **jarabe para la tos** cough syrup

el **jardín** SUSTANTIVO (PL los **jardines**)
garden
◆ **el jardín infantil** nursery school
◆ **el jardín de niños** Mexico nursery school

la **jardinera** SUSTANTIVO
1 gardener (*persona*)
2 window box (*maceta*)

la **jardinería** SUSTANTIVO
gardening

el **jardinero** SUSTANTIVO
gardener

la **jarra** SUSTANTIVO
1 pitcher (*de leche*)
2 mug (*de cerveza*)

el **jarrón** SUSTANTIVO (PL los **jarrones**)
vase

la **jaula** SUSTANTIVO
cage

los **jeans** SUSTANTIVO
jeans
◆ **unos jeans** a pair of jeans

el **jefe,** la **jefa** SUSTANTIVO
1 boss (PL bosses) ◇ *Carlos es mi jefe.* Carlos is my boss.
2 head ◇ *El jefe de la empresa renunció.* The head of the company resigned.
◆ **el jefe del departamento** the head of department
◆ **jefe de estado** head of state
◆ **el jefe del grupo guerrillero** the leader of the guerrilla group

el **jerez** SUSTANTIVO
sherry

Jesús EXCLAMACIÓN
Good God! (*por asombro*)

el **jinete** SUSTANTIVO
jockey

la **jirafa** SUSTANTIVO
giraffe

el **jitomate** SUSTANTIVO Mexico
tomato (PL tomatoes)

la **jornada** SUSTANTIVO
◆ **jornada de trabajo** working day
◆ **trabajar jornada completa** to work full-time
◆ **trabajar media jornada** to work part-time

joven ADJETIVO (PL **jóvenes**)
young ◇ *un chico joven* a young boy

el/la **joven** SUSTANTIVO (PL los/las **jóvenes**)
◆ **un joven** a young man
◆ **una joven** a young woman
◆ **los jóvenes** young people

la **joya** SUSTANTIVO
jewel
◆ **Me robaron las joyas.** My jewelry has been stolen.

la **joyera** SUSTANTIVO
jeweler

la **joyería** SUSTANTIVO
jeweler's (*tienda*)

el **joyero** SUSTANTIVO
1 jeweler (*persona*)
2 jewelry box (*estuche*)

la **jubilación** SUSTANTIVO (PL las **jubilaciones**)
1 retirement ◇ *La edad de jubilación es a los 65 años.* The retirement age is 65.
2 pension ◇ *cobrar la jubilación* to get one's pension

jubilado ADJETIVO
retired
◆ **estar* jubilado** to be retired

el **jubilado,** la **jubilada** SUSTANTIVO
pensioner

jubilarse VERBO
to retire

la **judía** SUSTANTIVO
Jew

judío ADJETIVO
Jewish

el **judío** SUSTANTIVO
Jew

el **judo** SUSTANTIVO
judo

juego VERBO *ver* **jugar**

el **juego** SUSTANTIVO
1 game ◇ *un juego de computadora* a computer game
◆ **juegos de cartas** card games

◆ **juegos de mesa** board games
[2] gambling ◇ *Lo perdió todo en el juego.* He lost everything through gambling.
[3] set ◇ *un juego de café* a coffee set
◆ **Las cortinas hacen juego con el sofá.** The curtains go with the sofa.

la **juerga** SUSTANTIVO
◆ **irse* de juerga** to go out on the town

el **jueves** SUSTANTIVO (PL los **jueves**)
En inglés, los días de la semana se escriben con mayúscula.
Thursday ◇ *La vi el jueves.* I saw her on Thursday. ◇ *todos los jueves* every Thursday ◇ *el jueves pasado* last Thursday ◇ *el jueves que viene* next Thursday ◇ *Jugamos los jueves.* We play on Thursdays.

el **juez**, la **jueza** SUSTANTIVO (MASC PL los **jueces**)
judge
◆ **juez de línea** (*en el fútbol*) linesman (PL linesmen)

el **jugador**, la **jugadora** SUSTANTIVO
player

jugar* VERBO
[1] to play ◇ *jugar tenis* to play tennis
◆ **¿Jugamos un partido de dominó?** Shall we have a game of dominoes?
[2] to gamble ◇ *Perdió un dineral jugando en el casino.* He lost a fortune gambling at the casino.
◆ **jugar a la lotería** to do the lottery

el **jugo** SUSTANTIVO
[1] juice (*de frutas*)
[2] gravy (*de carne, como salsa*)

el **juguete** SUSTANTIVO
toy
◆ **un avión de juguete** a toy plane

la **juguetería** SUSTANTIVO
toy shop

el **juicio** SUSTANTIVO
trial ◇ *El juicio empieza mañana.* The trial starts tomorrow.
◆ **llevar a alguien a juicio** to take someone to court

julio SUSTANTIVO MASC
En inglés, los meses se escriben con mayúscula.
July ◇ *en julio* in July ◇ *Nació el 4 de julio.* He was born on July 4th.

la **jungla** SUSTANTIVO
jungle

junio SUSTANTIVO MASC
En inglés, los meses se escriben con mayúscula.
June ◇ *en junio* in June ◇ *Nací el 20 de junio.* I was born on June 20th.

la **junta** SUSTANTIVO
committee (*comité*)
◆ **La junta directiva tiene la última palabra.** The board of management has the final say.

juntar VERBO
[1] to put together ◇ *Vamos a juntar los pupitres.* Let's put the desks together.
[2] to gather together ◇ *Consiguieron juntar a mil personas.* They managed to gather together one thousand people.
◆ **juntarse (1)** to move closer together ◇ *Si se juntan más cabremos todos.* If you move closer together we'll all fit in.
◆ **juntarse (2)** to meet up ◇ *Nos juntamos los domingos para comer.* We meet up for dinner on Sundays.

junto (1) ADJETIVO
[1] close together ◇ *Los muebles están demasiado juntos.* The furniture is too close together.
[2] together ◇ *Cuando estamos juntos apenas hablamos.* We hardly talk when we're together.
◆ **todo junto** all together ◇ *Ponlo todo junto en una sola bolsa.* Put it all together in one bag.

junto (2) ADVERBIO
◆ **junto a** by ◇ *Hay una mesa junto a la ventana.* There's a table by the window.
◆ **junto con** together with
◆ **Mi apellido se escribe todo junto.** My surname is all one word.

el **jurado** SUSTANTIVO
[1] jury (PL juries) (*en un juicio*)
[2] panel (*en un concurso*)

jurar VERBO
to swear

la **justicia** SUSTANTIVO
justice

justificar VERBO
to justify

justo (1) ADJETIVO
[1] fair ◇ *Tuvo un juicio justo.* He had a fair trial.
[2] right ◇ *Este reloj siempre da la hora justa.* This watch always tells the right time. ◇ *Apareció en el momento justo.* He appeared at the right time.
[3] tight ◇ *Estos pantalones me quedan muy justos.* These pants are tight on me.
[4] just enough ◇ *Tengo el dinero justo para el boleto.* I have just enough money for the ticket.

justo (2) ADVERBIO
just ◇ *El supermercado está justo al doblar la esquina.* The supermarket is just around the corner. ◇ *La vi justo cuando entrábamos.* I saw her just as we came in.
◆ **Me dio un puñetazo justo en la nariz.** He punched me right on the nose.

juvenil ADJETIVO
[1] youth (*paro, centro*)
***youth** en este caso va siempre delante del sustantivo.*
[2] junior (*equipo, torneo*)
◆ **la literatura juvenil** children's literature

la **juventud** SUSTANTIVO ☞

J

[1] youth ◇ *Fue soldado en su juventud.* He was a soldier in his youth. ◇ *En mi juventud, no había computadoras.* In my youth, there were no computers. ◇ *la juventud de hoy* the youth of today
[2] youngsters PL ◇ *La juventud viene aquí a divertirse.* Youngsters come here to have fun.

el **juzgado** SUSTANTIVO
court

juzgar* VERBO
to try ◇ *Lo juzgaron por un delito menor.* He was tried on a minor charge.
- **júzguelo usted misma** judge for yourself
- **juzgar mal** to misjudge

* Verbs marked with this symbol are irregular. See pages 346–348 for further details.

K

el **karate** SUSTANTIVO
karate

el **kilo** SUSTANTIVO
kilo ◇ *un kilo de tomates* a kilo of tomatoes

el **kilogramo** SUSTANTIVO
kilogram

> ℹ *En los Estados Unidos el peso a menudo se expresa en libras,* ***pounds****. Un kilogramo equivale a 2,2 libras aproximadamente.*

el **kilómetro** SUSTANTIVO
kilometer

> ℹ *En los Estados Unidos las distancias se expresan en millas,* ***miles****. Un kilómetro equivale a 0,6 millas aproximadamente.*

◇ *Está a tres kilómetros de aquí.* It's three kilometers from here. ◇ *a 90 kilómetros por hora* at 90 kilometers per hour

◆ **¡Caminamos kilómetros y kilómetros!** We walked for miles!

el **kiosco** SUSTANTIVO
newsstand

L

la (1) ARTÍCULO
the ◇ *la pared* the wall

◆ **la del sombrero rojo** the girl in the red hat

◆ **Yo fui la que te desperté.** It was I who woke you up.

El artículo se traduce por el posesivo en inglés cuando se refiere a una parte del cuerpo, a una prenda que se lleva puesta o a algo que se posee.

◆ **Ayer me lavé la pelo.** I washed my hair yesterday.

◆ **Abróchate la camisa.** Button your shirt up.

◆ **Tiene una casa bonita, pero prefiero la de Juan.** He has a lovely house, but I prefer Juan's.

El artículo a veces no se traduce en inglés; por ejemplo cuando se refiere a algo en general, con algunas expresiones de tiempo, o con apellidos.

◆ **No me gusta la fruta.** I don't like fruit.

◆ **Vendrá la semana que viene.** He'll come next week.

◆ **Me encontré con la Sra. Sendra.** I met Mrs. Sendra.

la (2) PRONOMBRE

1 her

Cuando nos referimos a "ella".

◇ *La quiero.* I love her.

◆ **La despidieron.** She has been fired.

2 you

Cuando nos referimos a "usted".

◇ *La acompaño hasta la puerta.* I'll see you out.

3 it

Cuando nos referimos a una cosa.

◇ *No la toques.* Don't touch it.

el **labio** SUSTANTIVO
lip

la **labor** SUSTANTIVO
work ◇ *Mi labor consiste básicamente en regar las plantas.* My work is basically watering the plants.

◆ **las labores domésticas** the housework SING

laborable ADJETIVO

◆ **día laborable** working day

el **laboratorio** SUSTANTIVO
laboratory (PL laboratories)

la **laca** SUSTANTIVO

1 hair spray (*para el pelo*)

2 lacquer (*para los muebles*)

lácteo ADJETIVO

◆ **los productos lácteos** dairy products

la **ladera** SUSTANTIVO
hillside

el **lado** SUSTANTIVO
side ◇ *a los dos lados de la carretera* on both sides of the road

También se traduce por ***-where*** *en palabras compuestas.*

◇ *Hay gente por todos lados.* There are people everywhere. ◇ *Tiene que estar en otro lado.* It must be somewhere else.

◆ **Mi casa está aquí al lado.** My house is right nearby.

◆ **la mesa de al lado** the next table

◆ **al lado de** beside ◇ *La silla que está al lado del armario.* The chair beside the closet.

◆ **Felipe se sentó a mi lado.** Felipe sat beside me.

◆ **por un lado..., por otro lado...** on the one hand..., on the other hand...

ladrar VERBO
to bark ◇ *El perro les ladró.* The dog barked at them.

el **ladrillo** SUSTANTIVO
brick

el **ladrón**, la **ladrona** SUSTANTIVO

1 thief (PL thieves) (*de objetos*) ◇ *Un ladrón me quitó el bolso.* A thief took my bag.

☞

[2] burglar (*de una casa*) ◇ *Los ladrones entraron de noche en la casa.* The burglars broke into the house during the night.
[3] robber (*de un banco*) ◇ *Tres ladrones atracaron el banco.* Three robbers raided the bank.

el **lagarto** SUSTANTIVO
lizard

el **lago** SUSTANTIVO
lake

la **lágrima** SUSTANTIVO
tear

la **laguna** SUSTANTIVO
lake

lamentar VERBO
- **Lamento lo ocurrido.** I am sorry about what happened.
- **lamentarse** to complain ◇ *De nada vale lamentarse.* There's no use complaining.

lamer VERBO
to lick

la **lámina** SUSTANTIVO
[1] sheet (*de metal*)
[2] plate (*ilustración*)

la **lámpara** SUSTANTIVO
lamp

la **lana** SUSTANTIVO
wool
- **una bufanda de lana** a woolen scarf

la **lancha** SUSTANTIVO
motorboat
- **una lancha de salvamento** a lifeboat

la **langosta** SUSTANTIVO
[1] lobster (*de mar*)
[2] locust (*insecto*)

el **langostino** SUSTANTIVO
king-size shrimp

lanzar* VERBO
[1] to throw (*piedra, balón, granada*) ◇ *Lanzó una piedra al río.* He threw a stone into the river.
[2] to launch (*cohete, producto*) ◇ *Lanzaron dos satélites al espacio.* They have launched two satellites into space.
- **lanzarse** to dive ◇ *Los niños se lanzaron a la piscina.* The children dove into the swimming pool.

la **lápida** SUSTANTIVO
gravestone

el **lápiz** SUSTANTIVO (PL los **lápices**)
pencil ◇ *Escribió mi dirección a lápiz.* He wrote my address in pencil.
- **los lápices de colores** crayons
- **un lápiz de labios** a lipstick
- **un lápiz de ojos** eyeliner

largo ADJETIVO
long ◇ *Fue una conferencia muy larga.* It was a very long conference. ◇ *Esta cuerda es demasiado larga.* This piece of string is too long.

el **largo** SUSTANTIVO
length ◇ *Nadé cuatro largos de la piscina.* I swam four lengths of the pool.
- **¿Cuánto mide de largo?** How long is it?
- **Tiene nueve metros de largo.** It's nine meters long.
- **a lo largo del río** along the river
- **a lo largo de la semana** throughout the week
- **Pasó de largo sin saludar.** He passed by without saying hello.

No confundir ***largo*** *con* ***large.***

las (1) ARTÍCULO PL
the ◇ *las paredes* the walls
- **las del estante de arriba** the ones on the top shelf

El artículo se traduce por el posesivo en inglés cuando se refiere a una parte del cuerpo, a una prenda que se lleva puesta o a algo que se posee.

- **Me duelen las piernas.** My legs hurt.
- **Pónganse las bufandas.** Put on your scarves.
- **Estas fotos son bonitas, pero prefiero las de Pedro.** These photos are nice, but I prefer Pedro's.

El artículo plural a veces no se traduce en inglés; por ejemplo cuando se refiere a algo en general o para expresar la hora.

- **No me gustan las arañas.** I don't like spiders.
- **Vino a las seis de la tarde.** He came at six in the evening.

las (2) PRONOMBRE
[1] them
Cuando nos referimos a "ellas".
◇ *Las vi por la calle.* I saw them in the street.
- **Las despidieron.** They've been fired.

[2] you
Cuando nos referimos a "ustedes".
◇ *Las acompañaré hasta la puerta, señoras.* I'll see you out, ladies.

el **láser** SUSTANTIVO
laser

la **lástima** SUSTANTIVO
- **Ella me da lástima.** I feel sorry for her.
- **Es una lástima que no puedas venir.** It's a shame you can't come.
- **¡Qué lástima!** What a shame!

lastimar VERBO
to hurt
- **¡Me estás lastimando!** You're hurting me!
- **lastimarse** to hurt oneself ◇ *¿Te lastimaste?* Did you hurt yourself?

la **lata** SUSTANTIVO
can (*de sardinas, cerveza*)
- **Deja de dar lata.** Stop being a pain.

lateral ADJETIVO
side

side *en este caso va siempre delante del sustantivo.*

◇ *la puerta lateral* the side door

el **latido** SUSTANTIVO
beat

el **látigo** SUSTANTIVO
whip

el **latín** SUSTANTIVO
Latin

Latinoamérica SUSTANTIVO FEM
Latin America

el **latinoamericano,** la **latinoamericana** ADJETIVO, SUSTANTIVO
Latin American

latir VERBO
to beat

el **laurel** SUSTANTIVO
laurel
◆ **una hoja de laurel** a bay leaf

la **lavadora** SUSTANTIVO
washing machine

la **lavandería** SUSTANTIVO
Laundromat®

el **lavaplatos** SUSTANTIVO (PL los **lavaplatos**)
1 dishwasher (*electrodoméstico*)
2 sink *Mexico*

lavar VERBO
to wash ◇ *Lava estos vasos.* Wash these glasses.
◆ **lavar la ropa** to do the washing
◆ **lavarse** to wash ◇ *Me lavo todos los días.* I wash every day.
◆ **Ayer me lavé la pelo.** I washed my hair yesterday.
◆ **Lávate los dientes**. Brush your teeth.

el **lavavajillas** SUSTANTIVO (PL los **lavavajillas**)
1 dishwasher (*lavaplatos*)
2 dishwashing liquid (*detergente*)

el **lazo** SUSTANTIVO
1 bow (*nudo*)
2 ribbon (*cinta*)

le PRONOMBRE
1 him
Cuando nos referimos a "él".
◇ *Le mandé una carta.* I sent him a letter.
◆ **Le abrí la puerta**. I opened the door for him.
2 her
Cuando nos referimos a "ella".
◇ *Le mandé una carta.* I sent her a letter.
◆ **No le hablé de ti.** I didn't speak to her about you.
◆ **Le busqué el libro.** I looked for the book for her.
3 you
Cuando nos referimos a "usted".
◇ *Le presento a la Señora Gutiérrez.* Let me introduce you to Mrs. Gutiérrez.
◆ **Le arreglé la computadora**. I've fixed the computer for you.
Con partes del cuerpo o con prendas que se llevan puestas se usa el adjetivo posesivo.
◇ *Le huelen los pies.* His feet smell. ◇ *Le arrastra la falda.* Her skirt is trailing on the floor.

la **lealtad** SUSTANTIVO
loyalty (PL loyalties)

la **lección** SUSTANTIVO (PL las **lecciones**)
lesson

la **leche** SUSTANTIVO
milk
◆ **la leche descremada** skim milk
◆ **la leche en polvo** powdered milk

la **lechuga** SUSTANTIVO
lettuce

la **lechuza** SUSTANTIVO
owl

el **lector,** la **lectora** SUSTANTIVO
reader ◇ *Varios lectores se quejaron del artículo.* Several readers complained about the article.

el **lector** SUSTANTIVO
◆ **un lector de CD** a CD player

la **lectura** SUSTANTIVO
reading ◇ *Me encanta la lectura.* I love reading.

leer* VERBO
to read

legal ADJETIVO
legal

la **legaña** SUSTANTIVO
◆ **tener* legañas** to have sleep in one's eyes

la **legumbre** SUSTANTIVO
pulse

lejano ADJETIVO
distant ◇ *un sitio muy lejano* a very distant place

la **lejía** SUSTANTIVO
bleach

lejos ADVERBIO
far ◇ *¿Está lejos?* Is it far? ◇ *No está lejos de aquí.* It's not far from here.
◆ **De lejos parecía un avión.** From a distance it looked like a plane.

la **lencería** SUSTANTIVO
lingerie

la **lengua** SUSTANTIVO
1 tongue ◇ *Me mordí la lengua.* I've bitten my tongue.
2 language ◇ *Habla varias lenguas.* He speaks several languages.
◆ **mi lengua materna** my mother tongue

el **lenguado** SUSTANTIVO
sole (*pez*)

el **lenguaje** SUSTANTIVO
language

la **lente** SUSTANTIVO
lens (PL lenses)
◆ **las lentes de contacto** contact lenses

la **lenteja** SUSTANTIVO
lentil

los **lentes** SUSTANTIVO
glasses
◆ **los lentes de sol** sunglasses

lento (1) ADJETIVO
slow ◇ *un proceso lento* a slow progress

lento (2) ADVERBIO
slowly ◇ *Vas un poco lento.* You're going a ☞

L

bit slowly.

la **leña** SUSTANTIVO
firewood

Leo SUSTANTIVO MASC
Leo ◇ *Soy leo.* I'm a Leo.

el **león** SUSTANTIVO (PL los **leones**)
lion

la **leona** SUSTANTIVO
lioness (PL lionesses)

el **leopardo** SUSTANTIVO
leopard

los **leotardos** SUSTANTIVO
leotards

les PRONOMBRE
1 them
Cuando nos referimos a "ellos" o "ellas".
◇ *Les mandé una carta.* I sent them a letter.
◆ **Les abrí la puerta.** I opened the door for them.
◆ **Les di de comer a los gatos.** I gave the cats something to eat.
2 you
Cuando nos referimos a "ustedes".
◇ *Les presento a la Señora Gutiérrez.* Let me introduce you to Mrs. Gutiérrez.
◆ **Les arreglé la computadora.** I've fixed the computer for you.
Con partes del cuerpo o con prendas que se llevan puestas se usa el adjetivo posesivo.
◇ *Les huelen los pies.* Their feet smell.
◇ *Les arrastraban los abrigos.* Their coats were trailing on the floor.

la **lesbiana** SUSTANTIVO
lesbian

la **lesión** SUSTANTIVO (PL las **lesiones**)
injury (PL injuries)

lesionado ADJETIVO
injured ◇ *Está lesionado.* He's injured.

la **letra** SUSTANTIVO
1 letter ◇ *la letra "a"* the letter "a"
2 handwriting ◇ *Tengo muy mala letra.* My handwriting's very poor.
3 lyrics PL ◇ *Él escribe la letra de sus canciones.* He writes the lyrics for his songs.

el **letrero** SUSTANTIVO
sign

levantar VERBO
to lift ◇ *Levanta la tapa.* Lift the lid.
◆ **Levanten la mano si tienen alguna duda.** Raise your hand if you are unclear.
◆ **levantarse** to get up ◇ *Hoy me levanté temprano.* I got up early this morning. ◇ *Me levanté y seguí caminando.* I got up and kept on walking.

leve ADJETIVO
minor ◇ *Sólo tiene heridas leves.* He only has minor injuries. ◇ *Cometió una falta leve.* He committed a minor mistake.

la **ley** SUSTANTIVO (PL las **leyes**)
law ◇ *la ley de la gravedad* the law of gravity

leyendo VERBO *ver* **leer**

liar* VERBO
to tie up (*atar*) ◇ *Lía este paquete con una cuerda.* Tie up this package with some string.

Líbano SUSTANTIVO MASC
Lebanon

el/la **liberal** ADJETIVO, SUSTANTIVO
liberal

liberar VERBO
to free

la **libertad** SUSTANTIVO
freedom ◇ *libertad de expresión* freedom of expression
◆ **No tengo libertad para hacer lo que quiera.** I'm not free to do what I want.
◆ **El rehén está en libertad.** The hostage is free.
◆ **poner* a alguien en libertad** to release somebody

la **libra** SUSTANTIVO
pound (*moneda, unidad de peso*)

> ❶ *En los Estados Unidos el peso a menudo se expresa en libras,* ***pounds****. Un kilogramo equivale a 2,2 libras aproximadamente.*

◆ **libra esterlina** pound sterling

Libra SUSTANTIVO MASC
Libra ◇ *Soy libra.* I'm a Libra.

librarse VERBO
◆ **librarse de (1)** (*evitar*) to get out of ◇ *¡No te creas que te vas a librar de fregar los platos!* Don't think you're going to get out of doing the dishes!
◆ **librarse de (2)** to get rid of ◇ *Logré librarme de mi hermana.* I managed to get rid of my sister.
◆ **Se libró del castigo por pura suerte.** He got away with it by pure good luck.

libre ADJETIVO
free ◇ *¿Está libre este asiento?* Is this seat free? ◇ *El martes estoy libre, así que podemos encontrarnos.* I'm free on Tuesday, so we can meet up.
◆ **los 100 metros libres** the 100 meters freestyle

la **librería** SUSTANTIVO
bookstore (*tienda*)
No confundir ***librería*** *con* ***library****.*

el **librero** SUSTANTIVO Mexico
bookcase

la **libreta** SUSTANTIVO
notebook
◆ **una libreta de ahorros** a bankbook

el **libro** SUSTANTIVO
book
◆ **un libro de bolsillo** a paperback
◆ **un libro de texto** a textbook

la **licencia** SUSTANTIVO
license ◇ *una licencia de armas* a gun license ◇ *una licencia de manejar* Mexico

a driver's license
- **la licencia de obras** planning permission
- **estar* de licencia** to be on leave

el **licenciado,** la **licenciada** SUSTANTIVO
graduate ◇ *un licenciado en historia* a history graduate

la **licenciatura** SUSTANTIVO
degree

el **licor** SUSTANTIVO
liqueur (*bebida dulce*) ◇ *un licor de pera* a pear liqueur
- **Bebimos cerveza y licores.** We drank beer and liquor.

el/la **líder** SUSTANTIVO
leader

la **liebre** SUSTANTIVO
hare

la **liga** SUSTANTIVO
1 league (*en deportes*)
2 garter (*para medias*)
3 rubber band *Mexico*

ligar* VERBO
- **Ayer ligué con una chica.** I scored with a girl yesterday. (*coloquial*)

ligero ADJETIVO
1 light ◇ *Me gusta llevar ropa ligera.* I like to wear light clothing. ◇ *Comimos algo ligero.* We ate something light.
2 slight ◇ *Tengo un ligero dolor de cabeza.* I have a slight headache.
- **Andaba a paso ligero.** He walked quickly.

la **lila** SUSTANTIVO
lilac

la **lima** SUSTANTIVO
1 file (*herramienta*) ◇ *una lima de uñas* a nail file
2 lime (*fruta*)

limitar VERBO
to limit ◇ *Limitaron el tiempo de examen a dos horas.* The exam time was limited to two hours.
- **México limita con América.** Mexico has a border with America.
- **Yo me limité a observar.** I just watched.

el **límite** SUSTANTIVO
1 limit ◇ *el límite de velocidad* the speed limit
- **fecha límite** deadline

2 boundary (PL boundaries) ◇ *Está dentro de los límites de la finca.* It's within the boundaries of the estate.

el **limón** SUSTANTIVO (PL los **limones**)
lemon

la **limonada** SUSTANTIVO
lemonade

la **limosna** SUSTANTIVO
- **pedir* limosna** to beg

el **limpiaparabrisas** SUSTANTIVO (PL los **limpiaparabrisas**)
windshield wiper

limpiar VERBO
1 to clean ◇ *El sábado voy a limpiar la casa.* I'm going to clean the house on Saturday.
2 to wipe (*con la mano, con un trapo*) ◇ *¿Limpiaste la mesa?* Have you wiped the table? ◇ *Límpiate la nariz.* Wipe your nose.

la **limpieza** SUSTANTIVO
cleaning ◇ *Yo hago la limpieza y tú paseas al perro.* I'll do the cleaning and you can walk the dog.
- **limpieza en seco** dry cleaning

limpio ADJETIVO
clean ◇ *El baño está muy limpio.* The bathroom is very clean.
- **Voy a pasar esto a limpio.** I'm going to write this out neat.

lindo ADJETIVO
1 pretty (*bonito*) ◇ *sus lindos ojos* her pretty eyes
2 nice (*agradable*) ◇ *un día muy lindo* a very nice day

la **línea** SUSTANTIVO
line ◇ *Dibujó una línea recta.* He drew a straight line.
- **Vaya en línea recta.** Go straight ahead.
- **una línea aérea** an airline
- **en línea** on-line

el **lino** SUSTANTIVO
linen

la **linterna** SUSTANTIVO
torch (PL torches)

el **lío** SUSTANTIVO
- **En mi mesa hay un lío enorme de papeles.** My desk is in a real muddle with all these papers.
- **hacerse* un lío** to get muddled up ◇ *Se hizo un lío con tantos nombres.* He got muddled up with all the names.
- **Esta ecuación es un lío.** This equation is a real headache.
- **Si sigues así te vas a meter en un lío.** If you carry on like that you'll get yourself into a real mess.

la **liquidación** SUSTANTIVO (PL las **liquidaciones**)
sale (*rebajas*)
- **una liquidación por cierre del negocio** a going-out-of-business sale

el **líquido** ADJETIVO, SUSTANTIVO
liquid

Lisboa SUSTANTIVO FEM
Lisbon

liso ADJETIVO
1 smooth (*superficie*)
2 straight (*pelo*)
3 plain (*tela, color*)

la **lista** SUSTANTIVO
list ◇ *la lista de espera* the waiting list
- **pasar lista** to take attendance
- **la lista de correo** mailing list

listo ADJETIVO
1 clever ◇ *Es una chica muy lista.* She's a ☞

L

very clever girl.
[2] ready ◇ *¿Estás listo?* Are you ready?

la **litera** SUSTANTIVO
[1] bunk bed (*en dormitorio*)
[2] berth (*en barco, tren*)

la **literatura** SUSTANTIVO
literature

el **litro** SUSTANTIVO
liter

> ℹ *En los Estados Unidos el volumen a menudo se expresa en pintas,* ***pints****. Una pinta equivale a 0,5 litros.*

liviano ADJETIVO
light

la **llaga** SUSTANTIVO
sore

la **llama** SUSTANTIVO
flame

la **llamada** SUSTANTIVO
call
◆ **hacer* una llamada telefónica** to make a phone call

llamar VERBO
[1] to call ◇ *Me llamaron mentiroso.* They called me a liar. ◇ *llamar a la policía* to call the police
[2] to ring (*al timbre*)
[3] to knock (*a la puerta*)
◆ **llamar por teléfono a alguien** to call somebody
◆ **¿Cómo te llamas?** What's your name?
◆ **Me llamo Adela.** My name's Adela.

llano ADJETIVO
flat

la **llanta** SUSTANTIVO
[1] wheel rim (*metálica*)
[2] tire (*neumático*)
◆ **llanta de refacción** [*Mexico*] spare tire

la **llave** SUSTANTIVO
[1] key ◇ *las llaves del carro* the car keys
◆ **Echa la llave de la puerta cuando salgas.** Lock the door when you go out.
◆ **una llave inglesa** a wrench
[2] faucet (*de agua*)

el **llavero** SUSTANTIVO
key ring

la **llegada** SUSTANTIVO
[1] arrival (*de tren, avión, viajeros*)
[2] finish (*meta*)

llegar* VERBO
[1] to get to
Cuando se menciona dónde se llega, se suele usar ***get to****.*
◇ *Cuando llegamos a Cuernavaca estaba lloviendo.* When we got to Cuernavaca it was raining.
◆ **¿A qué hora llegaste a casa?** What time did you get home?
[2] to arrive
Cuando no se menciona dónde se llega, se usa ***arrive****.*
◇ *Carmen no ha llegado todavía.* Carmen hasn't arrived yet.
◆ **No llegues tarde.** Don't be late.
[3] to reach (*alcanzar*) ◇ *No llego al estante de arriba.* I can't reach the top shelf.
◆ **El agua me llegaba hasta las rodillas.** The water came up to my knees.
◆ **llegar a ser** to become

llenar VERBO
to fill ◇ *Llena la jarra de agua.* Fill the pitcher with water.

lleno ADJETIVO
full ◇ *Todos los hoteles están llenos.* All the hotels are full. ◇ *El restaurante estaba lleno de gente.* The restaurant was full of people.

llevar VERBO
[1] to take ◇ *¿Llevas los vasos a la cocina?* Can you take the glasses to the kitchen? ◇ *No llevará mucho tiempo.* It won't take long.
[2] to wear ◇ *María llevaba un abrigo muy bonito.* María was wearing a nice coat.
[3] to give a ride (*en carro*) ◇ *Sofía nos llevó a casa.* Sofía gave us a ride home.
[4] to carry ◇ *Yo te llevo la maleta.* I'll carry your case.
◆ **Sólo llevo 50 pesos.** I have only 50 pesos on me.
◆ **¿Cuánto tiempo llevas aquí?** How long have you been here?
◆ **Llevo horas esperando aquí.** I've been waiting here for hours.
◆ **Mi hermana mayor me lleva ocho años.** My big sister is eight years older than me.
◆ **llevarse algo** to take something ◇ *Llévatelo.* Take it with you. ◇ *¿Le gusta? – Sí, me lo llevo.* Do you like it? – Yes, I'll take it!
◆ **Me llevo bien con mi hermano.** I get on well with my brother.
◆ **Nos llevamos muy mal.** We get on very badly.

llorar VERBO
to cry

llover* VERBO
to rain
◆ **llover a cántaros** to pour down

la **llovizna** SUSTANTIVO
drizzle

llueve VERBO *ver* **llover**

la **lluvia** SUSTANTIVO
rain ◇ *bajo la lluvia* in the rain
◆ **la lluvia ácida** acid rain

lluvioso ADJETIVO
rainy

lo (1) ARTÍCULO
◆ **Lo peor fue que no pudimos entrar.** The

worst thing was we couldn't get in.

- **No me gusta lo picante.** I don't like spicy things.
- **Pon en mi habitación lo de Pedro.** Put Pedro's things in my room.
- **Lo mío son las matemáticas.** Math is my thing.
- **Lo de vender la casa no me parece bien.** I don't like this idea of selling the house.
- **Olvida lo de ayer.** Forget what happened yesterday.

*Cuando se hace hincapié en una cualidad, a menudo se usa **how**.*

- **¡No sabes lo aburrido que es!** You don't know how boring he is!
- **lo que (1)** what ◇ *Lo que más me gusta es nadar.* What I like most is swimming.
- **lo que (2)** whatever ◇ *Ponte lo que quieras.* Wear whatever you like.
- **más de lo que** more than ◇ *Cuesta más de lo que crees.* It costs more than you think.

lo (2) PRONOMBRE

[1] him

Cuando nos referimos a "él".

◇ *No lo conozco.* I don't know him.

- **Lo han despedido.** He's been fired.

[2] you

Cuando nos referimos a "usted".

◇ *Yo a usted lo conozco.* I know you.

[3] it

Cuando nos referimos a "una cosa".

◇ *No lo veo.* I can't see it. ◇ *Voy a pensarlo.* I'll think about it.

- **No lo sabía.** I didn't know.
- **No parece lista pero lo es.** She doesn't seem clever but she is.

el **lobo** SUSTANTIVO

wolf (PL wolves)

la **loca** SUSTANTIVO

madwoman (PL madwomen)

local ADJETIVO

local ◇ *un producto local* a local product

el **local** SUSTANTIVO

premises PL ◇ *Lo echaron del local.* They threw him off the premises.

- **Ensayan en un local cerca de aquí.** They rehearse in a place near here.

la **localidad** SUSTANTIVO

[1] town (*población*) ◇ *una localidad al sur de Cuenca* a town south of Cuenca

[2] seat (*asiento*) ◇ *Reserve sus localidades con antelación.* Book your seats in advance.

localizar* VERBO

[1] to reach ◇ *Me puedes localizar en este teléfono.* You can reach me at this number.

[2] to locate ◇ *No han conseguido localizar a las víctimas.* They have been unable to locate the victims.

la **loción** SUSTANTIVO (PL las **lociones**)

lotion

loco ADJETIVO

[1] mad ◇ *volverse loco* to go mad

- **volver* loco a alguien** to drive somebody mad

[2] crazy ◇ *¿Estás loco?* Are you crazy? ◇ *Está loco con su moto nueva.* He's crazy about his new motorbike.

- **Me vuelve loco el marisco.** I'm crazy about seafood.

el **loco** SUSTANTIVO

madman (PL madmen)

la **locura** SUSTANTIVO

madness ◇ *Es una locura ir solo.* It's madness to go on your own.

el **locutor**, la **locutora** SUSTANTIVO

announcer

lógico ADJETIVO

[1] logical ◇ *No es un razonamiento lógico.* It's not logical reasoning.

[2] natural ◇ *Es una reacción lógica.* It's a natural reaction.

- **Es lógico que no quiera venir.** It's only natural he doesn't want to come.

lograr VERBO

[1] to get ◇ *Lograron lo que se proponían.* They got what they wanted.

[2] to manage ◇ *Logré que me concediera una entrevista.* I managed to get an interview with him.

la **lombriz** SUSTANTIVO (PL las **lombrices**)

worm

el **lomo** SUSTANTIVO

[1] back (*de animal*)

[2] loin (*para comer*)

[3] spine (*de un libro*)

la **lona** SUSTANTIVO

canvas (PL canvases)

la **loncha** SUSTANTIVO

slice

Londres SUSTANTIVO MASC

London

la **longitud** SUSTANTIVO

length

- **Tiene tres metros de longitud.** It's three meters long.

el **loro** SUSTANTIVO

parrot

los (1) ARTÍCULO

the ◇ *los barcos* the boats

- **los de las bufandas rojas** the people in the red scarves

El artículo se traduce por el posesivo cuando se refiere a una parte del cuerpo, a una prenda que se lleva puesta o a algo que se posee.

- **Se lavaron los pies en el río.** They washed their feet in the river.
- **Amárrate los zapatos.** Tie your shoelaces.
- **Me gustan sus cuadros, pero prefiero los de Ana.** I like his paintings, but I prefer Ana's.

El artículo a veces no se traduce; por ejemplo cuando se refiere a algo en general o con algunas expresiones de tiempo.

☞

◆ **No me gustan los duraznos.** I don't like peaches.
◆ **Sólo vienen los lunes.** They only come on Mondays.

los (2) PRONOMBRE
[1] them
Cuando nos referimos a "ellos".
◇ *Los vi por la calle.* I saw them in the street.
◆ **Los despideron.** They've been fired.
[2] you
Cuando nos referimos a "ustedes".
◇ *Los acompaño hasta la puerta, señores.* I'll see you to the door, gentlemen.

la **lotería** SUSTANTIVO
lottery (PL lotteries) ◇ *Le tocó la lotería.* He won the lottery.

la **lucha** SUSTANTIVO
fight
◆ **lucha libre** wrestling

luchar VERBO
to fight

lucir* VERBO
to shine ◇ *Lucían las estrellas.* The stars were shining.
◆ **Carlos se lució en el examen.** Carlos performed brilliantly on the exam.

luego (1) ADVERBIO
[1] then (*después*) ◇ *Primero se puso de pie y luego habló.* First he stood up and then he spoke.
[2] later (*más tarde*) ◇ *Mi mujer viene luego.* My wife's coming later.
◆ **desde luego** of course ◇ *¡Desde luego que me gusta!* Of course I like it!
◆ **¡Hasta luego!** See you!
[3] soon *Mexico* ◇ *Vuelvo luego.* I'll be back soon.

luego (2) CONJUNCIÓN
therefore ◇ *Yo pagué, luego tengo derecho a verlo.* I've paid, therefore I have a right to see it.

el **lugar** SUSTANTIVO
place ◇ *Este lugar es muy bonito.* This is a nice place.
◆ **Llegó en último lugar.** He came last.
◆ **en lugar de** instead of
◆ **tener* lugar** to take place

el **lujo** SUSTANTIVO
luxury (PL luxuries)
◆ **un carro de lujo** a luxury car

lujoso ADJETIVO
luxurious

la **luna** SUSTANTIVO
[1] moon (*satélite*)
[2] window pane (*de un escaparate*)
[3] window (*de un carro*)
◆ **la luna de miel** honeymoon

el **lunar** SUSTANTIVO
mole (*en la piel*)
◆ **una corbata de lunares** a spotted necktie

el **lunes** SUSTANTIVO (PL los **lunes**)
En inglés, los días de la semana se escriben con mayúscula.
Monday ◇ *La vi el lunes.* I saw her on Monday. ◇ *todos los lunes* every Monday ◇ *el lunes pasado* last Monday ◇ *el lunes que viene* next Monday ◇ *Jugamos los lunes.* We play on Mondays.

la **lupa** SUSTANTIVO
magnifying glass

el **luto** SUSTANTIVO
◆ **estar* de luto por alguien** to be in mourning for somebody

Luxemburgo SUSTANTIVO MASC
Luxembourg

la **luz** SUSTANTIVO (PL las **luces**)
[1] light ◇ *Prende la luz, por favor.* Turn on the light please.
[2] electricity ◇ *No hay luz en todo el edificio.* There's no electricity in the whole building.
◆ **dar* a luz** to give birth

M

los **macarrones** SUSTANTIVO
macaroni SING ◇ *Los macarrones no engordan.* Macaroni isn't fattening.

la **macedonia** SUSTANTIVO
fruit salad (*de fruta*)

la **maceta** SUSTANTIVO
flowerpot

machacar* VERBO
1 to crush ◇ *Machacó los ajos en el mortero.* He crushed the garlic in the mortar.
2 to thrash ◇ *El equipo visitante los machacó.* The visiting team thrashed them.

el **macho** ADJETIVO, SUSTANTIVO
male ◇ *una rata macho* a male rat

la **madera** SUSTANTIVO
wood ◇ *Está hecho de madera.* It's made of wood.
◆ **un juguete de madera** a wooden toy
◆ **Dame esa madera.** Give me that piece of wood.
◆ **Tiene madera de profesor.** He has the makings of a teacher.

la **madrastra** SUSTANTIVO
stepmother

la **madre** SUSTANTIVO
mother
◆ **¡Madre mía!** Goodness!

Madrid SUSTANTIVO MASC
Madrid

madrileño ADJETIVO
from Madrid ◇ *Soy madrileño.* I'm from Madrid.

la **madrina** SUSTANTIVO
1 godmother (*en bautizo*)
2 matron of honor (PL matrons of honor) (*en boda*)

la **madrugada** SUSTANTIVO
early morning
◆ **levantarse de madrugada (1)** (*temprano*) to get up early
◆ **levantarse de madrugada (2)** (*al amanecer*) to get up at daybreak
◆ **a las cuatro de la madrugada** at four o'clock in the morning

madrugar* VERBO
to get up early

maduro ADJETIVO
1 mature (*persona*)
2 ripe (*fruta*)

el **maestro,** la **maestra** SUSTANTIVO
teacher ◇ *Mi tía es maestra.* My aunt is a teacher.
◆ **un maestro de escuela** a schoolteacher

la **magia** SUSTANTIVO
magic

mágico ADJETIVO
magic ◇ *una varita mágica* a magic wand

el **magisterio** SUSTANTIVO
◆ **Estudia magisterio.** He's training to be a teacher.

magnífico ADJETIVO
splendid

el **mago,** la **maga** SUSTANTIVO
magician
◆ **los Reyes Magos** the Three Wise Men

el **maíz** SUSTANTIVO (PL los **maíces**)
1 corn (*planta*)
2 sweet corn (*desgranado*)
◆ **una mazorca de maíz** a corncob

la **majestad** SUSTANTIVO
◆ **Su Majestad (1)** (*rey*) His Majesty
◆ **Su Majestad (2)** (*reina*) Her Majesty

mal (1) ADJETIVO = **malo**

mal (2) ADVERBIO
1 badly ◇ *Toca la guitarra muy mal.* He plays the guitar very badly. ◇ *un trabajo mal pagado* a badly paid job
◆ **Esta habitación huele mal.** This room smells bad.
◆ **Lo pasé muy mal.** I had a very bad time.
◆ **Me entendió mal.** He misunderstood me.
◆ **hablar mal de alguien** to speak ill of someone
2 wrong ◇ *Escribieron mal mi apellido.* They've spelled my surname wrong. ◇ *Está mal mentir.* It's wrong to tell lies.

el **mal** SUSTANTIVO
evil ◇ *el bien y el mal* good and evil

la **mala** SUSTANTIVO
◆ **la mala de la película** the villain in the movie

malcriado ADJETIVO
badly brought up

maldito ADJETIVO
damned (*coloquial*) ◇ *¡Malditos vecinos!* Damned neighbors!
◆ **¡Malditas las ganas que tengo de verlo!** I really don't feel like seeing him!
◆ **¡Maldita sea!** Damn it!

maleducado ADJETIVO
bad-mannered

el **malentendido** SUSTANTIVO
misunderstanding

el **malestar** SUSTANTIVO
discomfort

la **maleta** SUSTANTIVO
suitcase
◆ **hacer* la maleta** to pack

el **maletero** SUSTANTIVO
1 trunk (*de carro*)
2 porter (*de estación*)

el **maletín** SUSTANTIVO (PL los **maletines**)
briefcase

la **maleza** SUSTANTIVO
weeds PL (*malas hierbas*)

malgastar VERBO
to waste

malhumorado ADJETIVO
bad-tempered (*por naturaleza*)
◆ **Hoy parece malhumorado.** He appears to be ☞

in a bad mood today.

la **malicia** SUSTANTIVO
1 malice (*mala intención*)
2 mischief (*picardía*)

malicioso ADJETIVO
malicious

la **malla** SUSTANTIVO
1 mesh (*tejido*)
2 leotard (*de gimnasia*)
- **mallas (1)** (*con pie*) pantyhose SING
- **mallas (2)** (*hasta el tobillo*) leggings

Mallorca SUSTANTIVO FEM
Majorca

el **malo** SUSTANTIVO
- **el malo de la película** the villain in the movie

malo ADJETIVO
*Use **mal** before a masculine noun.*
1 bad ◇ *un mal día* a bad day ◇ *Este programa es muy malo.* This is a very bad program. ◇ *Soy muy mala para las matemáticas.* I'm very bad at math. ◇ *Esta carne está mala.* This meat is bad.
- **Lo malo es que...** The trouble is that...

2 naughty ◇ *¿Por qué eres tan malo?* Why are you so naughty?
3 ill ◇ *Mi hija está mala.* My daughter is ill. ◇ *Se puso malo después de comer.* He started to feel ill after lunch.

maltratar VERBO
to mistreat ◇ *Maltrata a su perro.* He mistreats his dog.
- **los niños maltratados** abused children

malvado ADJETIVO
evil

la **mama** SUSTANTIVO
1 breast (*pecho*)
2 mom (*coloquial: madre*)

la **mamá** SUSTANTIVO (PL las **mamás**)
mom (*coloquial*) ◇ *tu mamá* your mom ◇ *¡Hola mamá!* Hi Mom!

mamar VERBO
to suckle (*animal*) ◇ *El cordero aún mama.* The lamb is still suckling.
- **El bebé mama cada cuatro horas.** The baby nurses every four hours.
- **dar* de mamar** to breast-feed

el **mamífero** SUSTANTIVO
mammal

el **manantial** SUSTANTIVO
spring (*fuente*)

la **mancha** SUSTANTIVO
stain

manchar VERBO
to stain ◇ *La cerveza no mancha.* Beer doesn't stain.
- **mancharse** to get dirty ◇ *No te manches la camisa.* Don't get your shirt dirty.
- **Me manché el vestido de tinta.** I have ink stains on my dress.

mandar VERBO
1 to order ◇ *El sargento lo mandó barrer el patio.* The sergeant ordered him to sweep the yard.
- **Nos mandó callar.** He told us to be quiet.
- **Aquí mando yo.** I'm the boss here.

2 to send ◇ *Se lo mandaremos por correo.* We'll send it to you by mail. ◇ *Me mandaron a hacer un recado.* They sent me on an errand.
- **mandar llamar a alguien** to send for someone
- **mandar a arreglar algo** to have something repaired
- **¿Mande?** *Mexico* Pardon?
- **El médico me mandó un jarabe.** The doctor gave me a prescription for cough syrup.

la **mandarina** SUSTANTIVO
tangerine

la **mandíbula** SUSTANTIVO
jaw

el **mando** SUSTANTIVO
- **un alto mando** a high-ranking officer
- **Está al mando del proyecto.** He's in charge of the project.
- **el mando a distancia** the remote control
- **los mandos** (*en avión*) the controls

la **manecilla** SUSTANTIVO
hand ◇ *las manecillas del reloj* the hands of the clock

manejable ADJETIVO
1 maneuverable ◇ *un carro muy manejable* a very maneuverable car
2 easy to use ◇ *Este taladro es muy manejable.* This drill is very easy to use.

manejar VERBO
1 to drive (*carro*)
- **un examen de manejar** a driving test

2 to operate (*máquina*)
3 to manage (*casa, negocio*)

la **manera** SUSTANTIVO
way ◇ *Lo hice a mi manera.* I did it my way.
- **de todas maneras** anyway
- **No hay manera de convencerla.** There's nothing anyone can do to convince her.
- **de manera que (1)** so ◇ *No has hecho las tareas, de manera que no hay tele.* You haven't done your homework so there's no TV.
- **de manera que (2)** so that ◇ *Lo hizo de manera que nadie se dio cuenta.* He did it so that nobody noticed.
- **¡De ninguna manera!** Certainly not!

la **manga** SUSTANTIVO
sleeve ◇ *Súbete las mangas.* Roll your sleeves up.
- **de manga corta** short-sleeved
- **de manga larga** long-sleeved

el **mango** SUSTANTIVO (PL mangos *or* mangoes)
1 handle (*asa*)
2 mango (*fruta*)

la **manguera** SUSTANTIVO
hose

el **maní** SUSTANTIVO (PL los **maníes**)
peanut

la **manía** SUSTANTIVO
- **Tiene la manía de repetir todo lo que digo.** He has an irritating habit of repeating everything I say.
- **El profesor me tiene manía.** The teacher has it in for me. (*coloquial*)

maniático ADJETIVO
- **Es muy maniático para comer.** He's very fussy about eating.
- **Es una maniática del orden.** She's obsessed with keeping things neat.

la **manifestación** SUSTANTIVO (PL las **manifestaciones**)
demonstration ◇ *Hicieron una manifestación contra el terrorismo.* They held a demonstration against terrorism.

el/la **manifestante** SUSTANTIVO
demonstrator

manifestarse* VERBO
to demonstrate

la **maniobra** SUSTANTIVO
maneuver ◇ *una maniobra política* a political maneuver
- **hacer* maniobras** to maneuver

manipular VERBO
1 to handle ◇ *La higiene es imprescindible para manipular alimentos.* Hygiene is essential when handling food.
2 to manipulate ◇ *La publicidad manipula a la opinión pública.* Advertising manipulates public opinion.

el/la **maniquí** SUSTANTIVO (PL los/las **maniquíes**)
model (*persona*)

el **maniquí** SUSTANTIVO (PL los **maniquíes**)
dummy (PL dummies) (*de escaparate*)

la **manivela** SUSTANTIVO
crank

la **mano** SUSTANTIVO
hand ◇ *Dame la mano.* Give me your hand.
- **tener* algo a mano** to have something at hand
- **hecho a mano** handmade
- **de segunda mano** secondhand
- **echar una mano** to lend a hand
- **estrechar la mano a alguien** to shake somebody's hand
- **la mano de obra** labor
- **una mano de pintura** a coat of paint

el **manojo** SUSTANTIVO
bunch (PL bunches) ◇ *un manojo de llaves* a bunch of keys

manso ADJETIVO
tame

la **manta** SUSTANTIVO
blanket

la **manteca** SUSTANTIVO
- **manteca de cerdo** lard
- **manteca de cacao** cocoa butter

el **mantel** SUSTANTIVO
tablecloth

mantener* VERBO
1 to keep ◇ *Los mantendremos informados.* We'll keep you informed.
◇ *mantener la calma* to keep calm
2 to support ◇ *Mantiene a su familia.* He supports his family.
- **mantener una conversación** to have a conversation
- **mantenerse** (*económicamente*) to support oneself
- **mantenerse en forma** to keep fit
- **mantenerse en pie** to remain standing

el **mantenimiento** SUSTANTIVO
maintenance ◇ *el encargado de mantenimiento* the person in charge of maintenance
- **ejercicios de mantenimiento** keep-fit exercises

la **mantequilla** SUSTANTIVO
butter

mantuve VERBO *ver* **mantener**

el **manual** ADJETIVO, SUSTANTIVO
manual

el **manubrio** SUSTANTIVO
handlebars PL

el **manuscrito** SUSTANTIVO
manuscript

la **manzana** SUSTANTIVO
1 apple (*fruta*)
2 block (*de edificios*)

el **manzano** SUSTANTIVO
apple tree

la **maña** SUSTANTIVO
- **Tiene mucha maña para hacer arreglos caseros.** She's handy at fixing things around the house.
- **Pedro tiene mañas de solterón.** Pedro is a confirmed bachelor.

la **mañana** SUSTANTIVO
morning ◇ *Llegó a las nueve de la mañana.* He arrived at nine o'clock in the morning.
- **a media mañana** mid-morning

mañana ADVERBIO
tomorrow ◇ *¡Hasta mañana!* See you tomorrow!
- **pasado mañana** the day after tomorrow
- **mañana por la mañana** tomorrow morning
- **mañana por la noche** tomorrow night
- **Por la mañana voy al gimnasio.** In the mornings I go to the gym.

el **mapa** SUSTANTIVO
map ◇ *El pueblo no está en el mapa.* The village isn't on the map. ◇ *un mapa de carreteras* a road map

la **maqueta** SUSTANTIVO
model

el **maquillaje** SUSTANTIVO
makeup

maquillarse VERBO
to put one's makeup on

la **máquina** SUSTANTIVO
machine ◇ *una máquina de coser* a sewing machine ◇ *una máquina expendedora* a vending machine ◇ *una máquina tragamonedas* a slot machine
- **una máquina de afeitar** an electric razor
- **una máquina de cortar pasto** a lawn mower
- **una máquina de escribir** a typewriter
- **escrito a máquina** typed
- **una máquina fotográfica** a camera

el **mar** SUSTANTIVO
sea
- **por mar** by sea

*Note that in certain idiomatic phrases, **mar** is feminine.*
- **en alta mar** on the high seas
- **Lo hizo la mar de bien.** He did it really well.

el **maratón** SUSTANTIVO (PL los **maratones**)
marathon

la **maravilla** SUSTANTIVO
- **¡Qué maravilla de casa!** What a wonderful house!
- **ser* una maravilla** to be wonderful
- **Se llevan de maravilla.** They get on wonderfully well together.

maravilloso ADJETIVO
marvelous

la **marca** SUSTANTIVO
[1] mark ◇ *Había marcas de neumático en la arena.* There were tire marks in the sand.
[2] make (*de máquina, cámara*) ◇ *¿De qué marca es tu carro?* What make is your car?
[3] brand (*de detergente, café*) ◇ *una conocida marca de cigarrillos* a well-known brand of cigarettes
- **la ropa de marca** designer clothes

el **marcador** SUSTANTIVO
[1] scoreboard
[2] bookmark (*informática*)

marcar* VERBO
[1] to mark (*ropa, objetos personales*)
[2] to brand (*ganado*)
[3] to dial (*número de teléfono*)
[4] to score (*gol*)
[5] to set (*en peluquería*)
- **Mi reloj marca las dos.** It's two o'clock according to my watch.
- **marcar algo con una equis** to put an x on something

la **marcha** SUSTANTIVO
[1] departure ◇ *Su marcha los dejó muy tristes.* His departure left them feeling very sad.
[2] gear ◇ *cambiar de marcha* to shift gear
- **a toda marcha** at full speed
- **estar* en marcha (1)** (*motor*) to be running
- **estar* en marcha (2)** (*proyecto*) to be underway
- **dar* marcha atrás** (*en carro*) to back up
- **No te subas nunca a un tren en marcha.** Never get onto a moving train.

marcharse VERBO
to leave

el **marco** SUSTANTIVO
[1] frame (*de fotografía*)
[2] mark (*moneda alemana*)

la **marea** SUSTANTIVO
tide
- **una marea negra** an oil slick

mareado ADJETIVO
- **Estoy mareado. (1)** (*aturdido*) I feel dizzy.
- **Estoy mareado. (2)** (*con náuseas*) I feel sick.

marear VERBO
to make...feel sick ◇ *El olor a alquitrán me marea.* The smell of tar makes me feel sick.
- **marearse (1)** to get dizzy ◇ *Te marearás si das tantas vueltas.* You'll get dizzy going around and around like that.
- **marearse (2)** to get seasick ◇ *¿Te mareas cuando vas en barco?* Do you get seasick when you travel by boat?
- **marearse (3)** to get carsick ◇ *Siempre me mareo en carro.* I always get carsick.
- **¡No me marees!** Stop going on at me!

el **mareo** SUSTANTIVO
[1] sea sickness (*en barco*)
[2] car sickness (*en carro*)
- **Le dio un mareo a causa del calor.** The heat made her feel ill.

el **marfil** SUSTANTIVO
ivory

la **margarina** SUSTANTIVO
margarine

la **margarita** SUSTANTIVO
daisy (PL daisies)

el **margen** SUSTANTIVO (PL los **márgenes**)
margin (*de página*) ◇ *Escribe las notas al margen.* Write your notes in the margin.

el **marido** SUSTANTIVO
husband

el **marinero** SUSTANTIVO
sailor

la **mariposa** SUSTANTIVO
butterfly (PL butterflies)

el **marisco** SUSTANTIVO
shellfish (PL shellfish) ◇ *No me gusta el marisco.* I don't like shellfish.

el **mármol** SUSTANTIVO
marble

marrón (FEM **marrón**, PL **marrones**) ADJETIVO
brown ◇ *un traje marrón* a brown suit

Marruecos SUSTANTIVO MASC
Morocco

el **martes** SUSTANTIVO (PL los **martes**)
En inglés, los días de la semana se escriben con mayúscula.
Tuesday ◇ *La vi el martes.* I saw her on Tuesday. ◇ *todos los martes* every Tuesday

◇ *el martes pasado* last Tuesday ◇ *el martes que viene* next Tuesday ◇ *Jugamos los martes.* We play on Tuesdays.

el **martillo** SUSTANTIVO
hammer

marzo SUSTANTIVO MASC
En inglés, los meses se escriben con mayúscula.
March ◇ *en marzo* in March ◇ *Nací el 17 de marzo.* I was born on March 17th.

más ADVERBIO, ADJETIVO
more ◇ *Ahora salgo más.* I go out more these days.
◆ **Últimamente nos vemos más.** We've been seeing more of each other lately.
◆ **¿Quieres más?** Would you like some more?
◆ **No tengo más dinero.** I don't have any more money.
*La mayoría de los adjetivos y adverbios de una sílaba, o de dos sílabas con terminación en 'y', forman el comparativo añadiendo la terminación **-er**. A veces se produce un cambio ortográfico.*
◇ *barato – más barato* cheap – cheaper
◇ *joven – más joven* young – younger
◇ *largo – más largo* long – longer
◇ *grande – más grande* big – bigger
◇ *contento – más contento* happy – happier
◇ *rápido – más rápido* fast – faster
◇ *temprano – más temprano* early – earlier
◆ **lejos – más lejos** far – further
*El resto de los adjetivos y adverbios forman el comparativo con **more**.*
◇ *hermoso – más hermoso* beautiful – more beautiful ◇ *buen mozo – más buen mozo* handsome – more handsome
*Independientemente del número de sílabas, los adverbios de modo que acaban en **-ly** forman el comparativo con **more**.*
◇ *deprisa – más deprisa* quickly – more quickly
*Para decir **más...que**, se añade **than** a la forma comparativa.*
◇ *Es más grande que el tuyo.* It's bigger than yours. ◇ *Corre más rápido que yo.* He runs faster than I do.
◆ **Trabaja más que yo.** He works harder than I do.
◆ **más de mil libros** more than a thousand books
◆ **No tiene más de dieciséis años.** He isn't more than sixteen.
◆ **más de lo que yo creía** more than I thought
*Siguiendo las mismas normas del comparativo, el superlativo se forma añadiendo **the...-est** o **the most...**.*
◇ *el bolígrafo más barato* the cheapest pen ◇ *el niño más joven* the youngest child ◇ *el carro más grande* the biggest car ◇ *la persona más feliz* the happiest person ◇ *el más inteligente de todos* the most intelligent of all of them
◆ **su película más innovadora** his most innovative movie
◆ **Paco es el que come más.** Paco's the one who eats the most.
◆ **Fue el que más trabajó.** He was the one who worked the hardest.
◆ **el punto más lejano** the furthest point
◆ **¿Qué más?** What else?
◆ **¡Qué perro más sucio!** What a filthy dog!
◆ **Tenemos uno de más.** We have one too many.
◆ **Por más que estudio no paso.** However hard I study I don't pass.
◆ **más o menos** more or less
◆ **2 más 2 son 4** 2 and 2 are 4
◆ **14 más 20 menos 12 es igual a 22** 14 plus 20 minus 12 equals 22

la **masa** SUSTANTIVO
1 dough ◇ *la masa de pan* bread dough
2 mass (PL masses) (*en física*)
◆ **las masas** the masses
◆ **en masa (1)** mass
***mass** en este caso va siempre delante del sustantivo.*
◇ *la producción en masa* mass production
◆ **en masa (2)** en masse ◇ *Fueron en masa a recibir al presidente.* They went en masse to greet the president.

el **masaje** SUSTANTIVO
massage

la **máscara** SUSTANTIVO
mask

masculino ADJETIVO
1 male (*hormona, sexo*) ◇ *el sexo masculino* the male sex
2 men's (*moda, deporte*) ◇ *la ropa masculina* men's clothing
3 masculine (*voz*) ◇ *el pronombre masculino "él"* the masculine pronoun "él"

masticar* VERBO
to chew

matar VERBO
to kill ◇ *El jefe me va a matar.* The boss will kill me.
◆ **matarse** to be killed ◇ *Se mataron en un accidente de carro.* They were killed in a car accident.

el **matasellos** SUSTANTIVO (PL los **matasellos**)
postmark

mate ADJETIVO
matt

el **mate** SUSTANTIVO
1 checkmate (*en ajedrez*)
2 maté (*infusión*)

las **matemáticas** SUSTANTIVO
mathematics SING

la **materia** SUSTANTIVO
1 matter ◇ *materia orgánica* organic matter
2 material ◇ *la materia prima* raw material
3 subject ◇ *Es un experto en la materia.* ☞

M

He's an expert on the subject.
◆ **entrar en materia** to get to the point

el **material** ADJETIVO, SUSTANTIVO
material

materno ADJETIVO
maternal ◇ *mi abuela materna* my maternal grandmother
◆ **mi lengua materna** my mother tongue

el **matiz** SUSTANTIVO (PL los **matices**)
shade (*de color*)

el **matorral** SUSTANTIVO
bushes PL

la **matrícula** SUSTANTIVO
registration (*de colegio, universidad*)
◆ **la matrícula del coche (1)** (*número*) the registration number of the car
◆ **la matrícula del coche (2)** (*placa*) the license plate of the car

matricular VERBO
to register (*coche*)
◆ **matricularse** (*alumno*) to enroll

el **matrimonio** SUSTANTIVO
1 marriage ◇ *El matrimonio se celebró en la iglesia del pueblo.* The marriage took place in the village church.
2 couple ◇ *Eran un matrimonio feliz.* They were a happy couple.

maullar VERBO
to meow

máximo ADJETIVO
maximum ◇ *la velocidad máxima* the maximum speed

el **máximo** SUSTANTIVO
maximum ◇ *un máximo de 3.000 pesos* a maximum of 3000 pesos
◆ **como máximo (1)** at the most ◇ *Te costará 5.000 como máximo.* It'll cost you 5000 at the most.
◆ **como máximo (2)** at the latest ◇ *Llegaré a las diez como máximo.* I'll be there by ten o'clock at the latest.

mayo SUSTANTIVO MASC
En inglés, los meses se escriben con mayúscula.
May ◇ *en mayo* in May ◇ *Nací el 28 de mayo.* I was born on May 28th.

la **mayonesa** SUSTANTIVO
mayonnaise

mayor ADJETIVO, PRONOMBRE (FEM **mayor**)
older ◇ *Paco es mayor que Nacho.* Paco is older than Nacho. ◇ *Es tres años mayor que yo.* He is three years older than me.
◆ **el hermano mayor (1)** (*de dos hermanos*) the older brother
◆ **el hermano mayor (2)** (*de más de dos hermanos*) the oldest brother
◆ **Soy el mayor. (1)** (*de dos*) I'm older.
◆ **Soy el mayor. (2)** (*de más de dos*) I'm the oldest.
◆ **Nuestros hijos ya son mayores.** Our children are grown up now.
◆ **la gente mayor** the elderly

el/la **mayor** SUSTANTIVO
◆ **un mayor de edad** an adult
◆ **los mayores** grown-ups

la **mayoría** SUSTANTIVO
majority (PL majorities)
◆ **Somos mayoría.** We are in the majority.
◆ **La mayoría de los estudiantes son pobres.** Most students are poor.
◆ **la mayoría de nosotros** most of us

la **mayúscula** SUSTANTIVO
capital letter ◇ *Empieza cada frase con una mayúscula.* Start each sentence with a capital letter.
◆ **Escríbelo con mayúsculas.** Write it in capitals.
◆ **una M mayúscula** a capital M

el **mazapán** SUSTANTIVO (PL los **mazapanes**)
marzipan

me PRONOMBRE
1 me ◇ *Me quiere.* He loves me. ◇ *Me regaló una pulsera.* He gave me a bracelet.
◆ **Me lo dio.** He gave it to me.
◆ **¿Me echas esta carta?** Will you mail this letter for me?
2 myself ◇ *No me hice daño.* I didn't hurt myself.
◆ **Me dije a mí mismo.** I said to myself.
Con partes del cuerpo o con prendas que se llevan puestas se usa el adjetivo posesivo.
◇ *Me duelen los pies.* My feet hurt. ◇ *Me puse el abrigo.* I put my coat on.

mear VERBO
to piss (*vulgar*)
◆ **mearse** to wet oneself

la **mecánica** SUSTANTIVO
1 mechanic (*persona*) ◇ *Quiere ser mecánica.* She wants to be a mechanic.
2 mechanics SING (*técnica*)

mecánico ADJETIVO
mechanical

el **mecánico** SUSTANTIVO
mechanic ◇ *Es mecánico.* He's a mechanic.

el **mecanismo** SUSTANTIVO
mechanism

la **mecanografía** SUSTANTIVO
typing

la **mecha** SUSTANTIVO
1 wick (*de vela*)
2 fuse (*de explosivo*)

el **mechero** SUSTANTIVO
cigarette lighter

la **medalla** SUSTANTIVO
medal

la **media** SUSTANTIVO
1 average ◇ *Trabajo una media de seis horas diarias.* I work an average of six hours a day.
2 sock (*calcetín*)

- **medias (1)** (*hasta el muslo*) stockings
- **medias (2)** (*hasta la cintura*) pantyhose
- **a las cuatro y media** at half past four

mediados SUSTANTIVO PL
- **a mediados de** around the middle of

mediano ADJETIVO
medium ◇ *de mediana estatura* of medium height
- **de tamaño mediano** medium-sized
- **el hijo mediano** the middle son

la **medianoche** SUSTANTIVO
midnight ◇ *a medianoche* at midnight

mediante PREPOSICIÓN
- **Izaron las cajas mediante una polea.** They lifted the crates using a pulley.

mediático ADJETIVO
media (*campaña, cultura, estrella*)
***media** en este caso va siempre delante del sustantivo.*

el **medicamento** SUSTANTIVO
medicine

la **medicina** SUSTANTIVO
medicine ◇ *Estudia medicina en la universidad.* He's studying medicine at college. ◇ *¿Te has tomado ya la medicina?* Have you taken your medicine yet?

el **médico**, la **médica** SUSTANTIVO
doctor ◇ *Quiere ser médica.* She wants to be a doctor. ◇ *el médico de cabecera* the family doctor
- **ir* al médico** to go to the doctor's

la **medida** SUSTANTIVO
measure ◇ *medidas de seguridad* security measures ◇ *tomar medidas contra la inflación* to take measures against inflation
- **El sastre le tomó las medidas.** The tailor took his measurements.
- **un traje a la medida** a tailor-made suit
- **a medida que...** as... ◇ *Saludaba a los invitados a medida que iban llegando.* He greeted the guests as they arrived.

medio (1) ADJETIVO
1 half ◇ *medio litro* half a liter ◇ *Nos queda media botella de leche.* We have half a bottle of milk left. ◇ *media hora* half an hour ◇ *una hora y media* an hour and a half
- **Son las ocho y media.** It's half past eight.

2 average ◇ *la temperatura media* the average temperature

medio (2) ADVERBIO
half ◇ *Estaba medio dormido.* He was half asleep. ◇ *una manzana a medio comer* a half-eaten apple

el **medio** SUSTANTIVO
1 middle (*centro*) ◇ *Está en el medio.* It's in the middle.
- **en medio de** in the middle of

2 means SING (*recurso*) ◇ *un medio de transporte* a means of transportation
- **por medio de** by means of
- **medios** means ◇ *por medios pacíficos* by peaceful means
- **los medios de comunicación** the media
- **el medio ambiente** the environment

el **mediodía** SUSTANTIVO
- **al mediodía (1)** (*a las 12 de la mañana*) at midday
- **al mediodía (2)** (*a la hora de comer*) at lunchtime

medir* VERBO
to measure ◇ *¿Has medido la ventana?* Have you measured the window?
- **¿Cuánto mides? – Mido 1.50 m.** How tall are you? – I'm 1.5 m tall.
- **¿Cuánto mide esta habitación? – Mide 3 m por 4.** How big is this room? – It measures 3 m by 4.

el **Mediterráneo** SUSTANTIVO
the Mediterranean

mediterráneo ADJETIVO
Mediterranean

la **medusa** SUSTANTIVO
jellyfish (PL jellyfish)

el **mejicano**, la **mejicana** ADJETIVO, SUSTANTIVO
Mexican

Méjico SUSTANTIVO MASC
Mexico

la **mejilla** SUSTANTIVO
cheek

el **mejillón** SUSTANTIVO (PL los **mejillones**)
mussel

mejor ADJETIVO (FEM **mejor**)
1 better ◇ *Éste es mejor que el otro.* This one is better than the other one.
- **Es el mejor de los dos.** He's the better of the two.

2 best ◇ *mi mejor amiga* my best friend ◇ *el mejor de la clase* the best in the class ◇ *Es el mejor de todos.* He's the best of the lot.

mejor ADVERBIO
1 better ◇ *La conozco mejor que tú.* I know her better than you do.
2 best ◇ *¿Quién lo hace mejor?* Who does it best?
- **a lo mejor** probably
- **Mejor nos vamos.** We had better go.

la **mejora** SUSTANTIVO
improvement

mejorar VERBO
to improve ◇ *El tiempo está mejorando.* The weather is improving. ◇ *Han mejorado el servicio.* They have improved the service.
- **¡Que te mejores!** Get well soon!

la **mejoría** SUSTANTIVO
improvement

la **melena** SUSTANTIVO
1 long hair (*de persona*) ◇ *Lleva una melena rubia.* She has long blond hair.
2 mane (*de león*)

el **mellizo**, la **melliza** ADJETIVO, SUSTANTIVO
twin ◇ *Son mellizos.* They're twins.

el **melocotón** SUSTANTIVO Spain (PL los ☞

M

melocotones)
peach (PL peaches)

la **melodía** SUSTANTIVO
tune ◇ *tararear una melodía* to hum a tune

el **melón** SUSTANTIVO (PL los **melones**)
melon

la **memoria** SUSTANTIVO
memory (PL memories) ◇ *tener mala memoria* to have a bad memory
◆ **aprender algo de memoria** to learn something by heart

memorizar* VERBO
to memorize

mencionar VERBO
to mention

el **mendigo**, la **mendiga** SUSTANTIVO
beggar

menor ADJETIVO, PRONOMBRE (FEM **menor**)
[1] younger ◇ *Es tres años menor que yo.* He's three years younger than me. ◇ *Juanito es menor que Pepe.* Juanito is younger than Pepe.
◆ **el hermano menor (1)** (*de dos hermanos*) the younger brother
◆ **el hermano menor (2)** (*de más de dos hermanos*) the youngest brother
◆ **Yo soy el menor. (1)** (*de dos*) I'm younger.
◆ **Yo soy el menor. (2)** (*de más de dos*) I'm the youngest.
[2] smaller ◇ *una talla menor* a smaller size

el/la **menor** SUSTANTIVO
◆ **un menor de edad** a minor
◆ **los menores** the under-18s

Menorca SUSTANTIVO FEM
Minorca

menos (1) ADVERBIO, ADJETIVO
[1] less ◇ *Mario está menos deprimido.* Mario is less depressed. ◇ *Ahora salgo menos.* I go out less these days.
◆ **Últimamente nos vemos menos.** We've been seeing less of each other recently.
Para formar el comparativo con sustantivos, se utiliza ***less*** *si son incontables y* ***fewer*** *si son contables.*
◇ *menos harina* less flour ◇ *menos gatos* fewer cats ◇ *menos gente* fewer people
◆ **menos...que** less...than ◇ *Me gusta menos que el otro.* I like it less than the other one. ◇ *Lo hizo menos cuidadosamente que ayer.* He did it less carefully than yesterday.
◆ **Trabaja menos que yo.** He doesn't work as hard as I do.
◆ **menos de 50 cajas** fewer than 50 boxes
◆ **Tiene menos de dieciocho años.** He's under eighteen.
[2] least ◇ *el chico menos desobediente de la clase* the least disobedient boy in the class
◆ **Fue el que menos trabajó.** He was the one who worked the least hard.
Para formar el superlativo con sustantivos, se utiliza ***least*** *si son incontables y* ***fewest*** *si son contables.*
◇ *el método que lleva menos tiempo* the method which takes the least time ◇ *el examen con menos errores* the exam paper with the fewest mistakes
◆ **No quiero verlo y menos visitarlo.** I don't want to see him, let alone visit him.
◆ **¡Menos mal!** Thank goodness!
◆ **al menos** at least
◆ **por lo menos** at least
◆ **5 menos 2 son 3** 5 minus 2 is 3

menos (2) PREPOSICIÓN
except
◆ **todos menos él** everyone except him
◆ **a menos que** unless

el **mensaje** SUSTANTIVO
message
◆ **un mensaje de texto** a text message
◆ **el envío de mensajes con foto** picture messaging

el **mensajero**, la **mensajera** SUSTANTIVO
messenger

la **menta** SUSTANTIVO
mint ◇ *un caramelo de menta* a mint candy

la **mentalidad** SUSTANTIVO
mentality (PL mentalities) ◇ *Tiene mentalidad de burócrata.* He has a bureaucratic mentality.
◆ **Tiene una mentalidad muy abierta.** He has a very open mind.

la **mente** SUSTANTIVO
mind ◇ *No me lo puedo quitar de la mente.* I can't get it out of my mind.
◆ **tener* en mente hacer algo** to be thinking of doing something ◇ *Tiene en mente cambiar de empleo.* He's thinking of changing jobs.

mentir* VERBO
to lie ◇ *No me mientas.* Don't lie to me.

la **mentira** SUSTANTIVO
lie ◇ *No digas mentiras.* Don't tell lies.
◆ **Parece mentira que aún no te haya pagado.** It's incredible that he still hasn't paid you.
◆ **una pistola de mentira** a toy pistol

el **mentiroso**, la **mentirosa** SUSTANTIVO
liar

el **menú** SUSTANTIVO (PL los **menús**)
menu (*carta*)
◆ **el menú del día** the set meal

menudo ADJETIVO
slight ◇ *Es una chica muy menuda.* She's a very slight girl.
◆ **¡Menudo lío!** What a mess!
◆ **a menudo** often

el **meñique** SUSTANTIVO
little finger

el **mercado** SUSTANTIVO
market

la **mercancía** SUSTANTIVO
commodity (PL commodities)

la **mercería** SUSTANTIVO
haberdasher's (PL haberdashers')

merecer* VERBO
to deserve ◇ *Mereces que te castiguen.* You deserve to be punished.
◆ **merece la pena** it's worthwhile

merendar* VERBO
to have an afternoon snack

el **merengue** SUSTANTIVO
meringue

la **merienda** SUSTANTIVO
afternoon snack

el **mérito** SUSTANTIVO
merit ◇ *una obra de gran mérito artístico* a work of great artistic merit
◆ **Eso tiene mucho mérito.** That's very commendable.
◆ **El mérito es todo suyo.** The credit is all his.

la **merluza** SUSTANTIVO
hake (PL hake)

la **mermelada** SUSTANTIVO
jelly

mero ADVERBIO *Mexico*
almost ◇ *Por mero me caigo.* I almost fell over.

el **mes** SUSTANTIVO (PL los **meses**)
month ◇ *el mes que viene* next month ◇ *a final de mes* at the end of the month

la **mesa** SUSTANTIVO
table
◆ **poner* la mesa** to set the table
◆ **levantar la mesa** to clear the table

la **mesera** SUSTANTIVO
waitress (PL waitresses)

el **mesero** SUSTANTIVO
waiter

la **meta** SUSTANTIVO
1 aim (*objetivo*)
2 finishing line (*en atletismo*)
3 goal (*en fútbol*)

el **metal** SUSTANTIVO
metal

metálico ADJETIVO
metal
metal *en este caso va siempre delante del sustantivo.*
◇ *un objeto metálico* a metal object
◆ **en metálico** in cash

meter VERBO
to put ◇ *¿Dónde has metido las llaves?* Where have you put the keys?
◆ **meterse** to go into ◇ *Se metió en la cueva.* He went into the cave.
◆ **meterse en política** to go into politics
◆ **No te metas donde no te llaman.** Don't poke your nose in where it doesn't belong.
◆ **meterse con alguien** to pick on somebody

el **método** SUSTANTIVO
method

el **metro** SUSTANTIVO
1 subway ◇ *tomar el metro* to take the subway
2 meter ◇ *Mide tres metros de largo.* It's three meters long.

el **mexicano,** la **mexicana** ADJETIVO, SUSTANTIVO
Mexican

México SUSTANTIVO MASC
Mexico

la **mezcla** SUSTANTIVO
mixture

mezclar VERBO
to mix ◇ *Hay que mezclar el azúcar y la harina.* You need to mix the sugar and the flour.
◆ **mezclarse en algo** to get mixed up in something

mezquino ADJETIVO
mean (*tacaño*)

la **mezquita** SUSTANTIVO
mosque

mi ADJETIVO (PL **mis**)
my ◇ *mis hermanas* my sisters

mí PRONOMBRE
me ◇ *para mí* for me
◆ **Para mí que...** I think that...
◆ **Por mí no hay problema.** There's no problem as far as I'm concerned.

el **microbio** SUSTANTIVO
microbe

el **micrófono** SUSTANTIVO
microphone

el **microondas** SUSTANTIVO (PL los **microondas**)
microwave ◇ *un horno microondas* a microwave oven

el **microscopio** SUSTANTIVO
microscope

midiendo VERBO *ver* **medir**

el **miedo** SUSTANTIVO
fear ◇ *el miedo a la oscuridad* fear of the dark
◆ **tener* miedo** to be afraid ◇ *Le tenía miedo a su padre.* He was afraid of his father. ◇ *Tengo miedo a morir.* I'm afraid of dying. ◇ *Tenemos miedo de que nos ataquen.* We're afraid that they may attack us.
◆ **dar* miedo a** to scare ◇ *Me daba miedo hacerlo.* I was scared of doing it.
◆ **pasarlo de miedo** (*coloquial*) to have a fantastic time

miedoso ADJETIVO
◆ **¡No seas tan miedoso!** Don't be such a coward!
◆ **Mi hijo es muy miedoso.** My son gets frightened very easily.

la **miel** SUSTANTIVO
honey

el/la **miembro** SUSTANTIVO
1 member (*de organización, de familia*)
2 limb (*del cuerpo*)

mientras ADVERBIO, CONJUNCIÓN
while ◇ *Lava tú mientras yo seco.* You wash while I dry. ☞

◆ **Seguiré manejando mientras pueda.** I'll carry on driving for as long as I can.
◆ **mientras que** while
◆ **mientras tanto** meanwhile

el **miércoles** SUSTANTIVO (PL los **miércoles**)
En inglés, los días de la semana se escriben con mayúscula.
Wednesday ◇ *La vi el miércoles.* I saw her on Wednesday. ◇ *todos los miércoles* every Wednesday ◇ *el miércoles pasado* last Wednesday ◇ *el miércoles que viene* next Wednesday ◇ *Jugamos los miércoles.* We play on Wednesdays.

la **mierda** SUSTANTIVO
shit (*vulgar: excremento*)
◆ **Esta película es una mierda.** This movie's a load of crap. (*vulgar*)
◆ **¡Vete a la mierda!** Go to hell! (*coloquial*)

la **miga** SUSTANTIVO
crumb
◆ **hacer* buenas migas** to hit it off (*coloquial*)

mil ADJETIVO, PRONOMBRE
thousand ◇ *miles de personas* thousands of people ◇ *dos mil pesos* two thousand pesos
◆ **miles de veces** hundreds of times

el **milagro** SUSTANTIVO
miracle ◇ *No nos hemos matado de milagro.* It was a miracle we didn't get killed.

la **mili** SUSTANTIVO [Spain]
military service ◇ *hacer la mili* to do one's military service

el **milímetro** SUSTANTIVO
millimeter

el/la **militar** SUSTANTIVO
soldier
◆ **los militares** the military

militar VERBO
◆ **militar en un partido** to be an active member of a party

el **millón** SUSTANTIVO (PL los **millones**)
million ◇ *millones de personas* millions of people
◆ **mil millones** a billion

el **millonario,** la **millonaria** SUSTANTIVO
millionaire

mimado ADJETIVO
spoiled

la **mina** SUSTANTIVO
mine

el **mineral** ADJETIVO, SUSTANTIVO
mineral

el **minero,** la **minera** SUSTANTIVO
miner ◇ *Es minero.* He's a miner.

la **miniatura** SUSTANTIVO
miniature
◆ **una casa en miniatura** a miniature house

el **minidisco** SUSTANTIVO
Minidisc®

la **minifalda** SUSTANTIVO
miniskirt

mínimo ADJETIVO
minimum ◇ *el salario mínimo* the minimum wage
◆ **No tienes ni la más mínima idea.** You haven't the faintest idea.

el **mínimo** SUSTANTIVO
minimum ◇ *un mínimo de 2.000 pesos* a minimum of 2000 pesos
◆ **lo mínimo que puede hacer** the least he can do
◆ **Como mínimo podrías haber llamado.** You could at least have called.

el **ministerio** SUSTANTIVO
ministry (PL ministries)

el **ministro,** la **ministra** SUSTANTIVO
minister

la **minoría** SUSTANTIVO
minority (PL minorities) ◇ *las minorías étnicas* ethnic minorities

minucioso ADJETIVO
thorough

la **minúscula** SUSTANTIVO
small letter

la **minusválida** SUSTANTIVO
disabled woman (PL disabled women)

el **minusválido** SUSTANTIVO
disabled man (PL disabled men)
◆ **los minusválidos** the disabled

el **minuto** SUSTANTIVO
minute ◇ *Espera un minuto.* Wait a minute.

mío ADJETIVO, PRONOMBRE (FEM **mía**)
mine ◇ *Estos caballos son míos.* Those horses are mine. ◇ *¿De quién es esta bufanda? – Es mía.* Whose scarf is this? – It's mine. ◇ *El mío está en el armario.* Mine's in the closet. ◇ *Éste es el mío.* This one's mine.
◆ **un amigo mío** a friend of mine

miope ADJETIVO
nearsighted

la **mirada** SUSTANTIVO
look ◇ *con una mirada de odio* with a look of hatred
◆ **echar una mirada a algo** to have a look at something ◇ *¿Has tenido tiempo de echarle una mirada a mi informe?* Have you had time to have a look at my report?

mirar VERBO
to look ◇ *¡Mira! Un ratón.* Look! A mouse. ◇ *Mira a ver si está ahí.* Look and see if he is there.
◆ **mirar algo** to look at something ◇ *Mira esta foto.* Look at this photo.
◆ **mirar por la ventana** to look out of the window
◆ **mirar algo fijamente** to stare at something
◆ **¡Mira que es tonto!** What an idiot!
◆ **mirarse al espejo** to look at oneself in the mirror
◆ **Se miraron asombrados.** They looked at

each other in amazement.

la **misa** SUSTANTIVO
mass (PL masses) ◇ *la misa del gallo* midnight mass ◇ *ir a misa* to go to mass

la **miseria** SUSTANTIVO
[1] poverty ◇ *estar en la miseria* to be living in poverty
[2] pittance ◇ *Gano una miseria.* I earn a pittance.

la **misión** SUSTANTIVO (PL las **misiones**)
mission

el **misionero,** la **misionera** SUSTANTIVO
missionary (PL missionaries)

mismo (1) ADJETIVO
same ◇ *Nos gustan los mismos libros.* We like the same books. ◇ *Vivo en su misma calle.* I live in the same street as him.
◆ **yo mismo** myself ◇ *Lo hice yo mismo.* I did it myself.

mismo (2) ADVERBIO
◆ **Hoy mismo le escribiré.** I'll write to him today.
◆ **Nos podemos encontrar aquí mismo.** We can meet right here.
◆ **enfrente mismo del colegio** right opposite the school

mismo (3) PRONOMBRE
◆ **lo mismo** the same ◇ *Yo tomaré lo mismo.* I'll have the same.
◆ **Da lo mismo.** It doesn't matter.
◆ **No ha llamado pero lo mismo viene.** He hasn't called but he may well come.

el **misterio** SUSTANTIVO
mystery (PL mysteries)

misterioso ADJETIVO
mysterious

la **mitad** SUSTANTIVO
half (PL halves) ◇ *Se comió la mitad del pastel.* He ate half the cake. ◇ *más de la mitad de los trabajadores* more than half the workers
◆ **La mitad son chicas.** Half of them are girls.
◆ **a mitad de precio** half-price
◆ **a mitad de camino** halfway there
◆ **Corta el pan por la mitad.** Cut the loaf in half.

el **mito** SUSTANTIVO
myth

mixto ADJETIVO
mixed ◇ *una ensalada mixta* a mixed salad

el **mobiliario** SUSTANTIVO
furniture

la **mochila** SUSTANTIVO
backpack

el **moco** SUSTANTIVO
mucus
◆ **Límpiate los mocos.** Wipe your nose.
◆ **tener* mocos** to have a runny nose

la **moda** SUSTANTIVO
fashion
◆ **estar* de moda** to be in fashion
◆ **pasado de moda** old-fashioned

los **modales** SUSTANTIVO
manners ◇ *buenos modales* good manners

el/la **modelo** ADJETIVO, SUSTANTIVO
model ◇ *una niña modelo* a model child
◇ *Quiero ser modelo.* I want to be a model.

moderado ADJETIVO
moderate

modernizar* VERBO
to modernize (*fábrica*)
◆ **modernizarse** (*persona*) to bring up to date

moderno ADJETIVO
modern

la **modestia** SUSTANTIVO
modesty

modesto ADJETIVO
modest

modificar* VERBO
to modify

el **modisto,** la **modista** SUSTANTIVO
dressmaker ◇ *Es modista.* She's a dressmaker.

el **modo** SUSTANTIVO
way ◇ *Le gusta hacerlo todo a su modo.* She likes to do everything her own way.
◆ **de todos modos** anyway
◆ **de modo que (1)** so ◇ *No has hecho los deberes, de modo que no puedes salir.* You haven't done your homework so you can't go out.
◆ **de modo que (2)** so that ◇ *Mueve la tele de modo que todos la podamos ver.* Move the TV so that we can all see it.
◆ **los buenos modos** good manners
◆ **los malos modos** bad manners
◆ **"modo de empleo"** "how to use"

el **moho** SUSTANTIVO
[1] mold (*en pan, fruta*)
[2] rust (*en metal*)

mojar VERBO
to get...wet ◇ *¡No mojes la alfombra!* Don't get the carpet wet! ◇ *Me mojé las mangas.* I got my sleeves wet.
◆ **Moja el pan en la salsa.** Dip the bread into the sauce.

el **molde** SUSTANTIVO
mold

moler* VERBO
to grind (*café, pimienta, carne*)
◆ **Estoy molido.** I'm bushed. (*coloquial*)

molestar VERBO
[1] to bother ◇ *¿Te molesta la radio?* Is the radio bothering you? ◇ *Siento molestarlo.* I'm sorry to bother you.
[2] to disturb ◇ *No me molestes, que estoy trabajando.* Don't disturb me; I'm working.
◆ **molestarse** to get upset ◇ *Se molestó por algo que dije.* She got upset because of something I said.
◆ **molestarse en hacer algo** to bother to do something

la **molestia** SUSTANTIVO ☞

M

◆ **tomarse la molestia de hacer algo** to take the trouble to do something
◆ **"perdonen las molestias"** "we apologize for any inconvenience"
◆ **Aún tengo molestias en el hombro.** My shoulder still bothers me.

molesto ADJETIVO
annoying (*ruido*)
◆ **estar* molesto** (*enojado*) to be annoyed

el **molinillo** SUSTANTIVO
◆ **un molinillo de café** a coffee grinder
◆ **un molinillo de carne** a meat grinder

el **molino** SUSTANTIVO
mill ◇ *un molino de viento* a windmill

el **momento** SUSTANTIVO
moment ◇ *Espera un momento.* Wait a moment. ◇ *en un momento* in a moment
◆ **en este momento** at the moment ◇ *Tenemos mucho trabajo en este momento.* We have a lot of work at the moment.
◆ **de un momento a otro** any moment now ◇ *Llegarán de un momento a otro.* They'll be here any moment now.
◆ **por el momento** for the moment
◆ **Llegó el momento de irnos.** The time came for us to go.

la **momia** SUSTANTIVO
mummy (PL mummies)

el/la **monarca** SUSTANTIVO
monarch

la **monarquía** SUSTANTIVO
monarchy (PL monarchies)

el **monasterio** SUSTANTIVO
monastery (PL monasteries)

la **moneda** SUSTANTIVO
coin ◇ *una moneda de cinco pesos* a five-peso coin
◆ **la moneda extranjera** foreign currency

el **monedero** SUSTANTIVO
coin purse

el **monitor, la monitora** SUSTANTIVO
instructor ◇ *un monitor de esquí* a skiing instructor

el **monitor** SUSTANTIVO
monitor (*pantalla*)

la **monja** SUSTANTIVO
nun

el **monje** SUSTANTIVO
monk

mono ADJETIVO
pretty ◇ *¡Qué departamento tan mono!* What a pretty apartment!
◆ **¡Qué niña tan mona!** What a sweet little girl!

el **mono** SUSTANTIVO
monkey

el **monopatín** SUSTANTIVO (PL los **monopatines**)
skateboard

monótono ADJETIVO
monotonous

el **monstruo** SUSTANTIVO
monster

la **montaña** SUSTANTIVO
mountain ◇ *Todos los años pasamos un mes en la montaña.* We spend a month in the mountains every year.
◆ **la montaña rusa** the roller-coaster

montañoso ADJETIVO
mountainous

montar VERBO
1 to assemble (*máquina, armario*)
2 to set up (*negocio*)
◆ **montar una carpa** to put up a tent
◆ **montar a caballo** to ride a horse
◆ **montar en bici** to ride a bicycle
◆ **montarse** to get on ◇ *Llegó corriendo y se montó en el tren.* He came running up and got on the train.

el **monte** SUSTANTIVO
mountain

el **montón** SUSTANTIVO (PL los **montones**)
pile (*pila*) ◇ *Puso el montón de libros sobre la mesa.* He put the pile of books on the table.
◆ **un montón de...** (*coloquial: muchos*) loads of... ◇ *un montón de gente* loads of people ◇ *un montón de dinero* loads of money

el **monumento** SUSTANTIVO
monument

el **moño** SUSTANTIVO
bun ◇ *Mi abuela siempre lleva moño.* My grandmother always wears her hair in a bun.

la **mora** SUSTANTIVO
1 blackberry (PL blackberries) (*de la zarzamora*)
2 mulberry (PL mulberries) (*del moral*)

morado ADJETIVO
purple ◇ *un vestido morado* a purple dress

moral ADJETIVO
moral

la **moral** SUSTANTIVO
1 morale (*ánimo*)
◆ **levantar la moral a alguien** to cheer somebody up
◆ **estar* bajo de moral** to be down
2 morals PL (*moralidad*) ◇ *No tienen moral.* They have no morals.

la **moraleja** SUSTANTIVO
moral

la **morcilla** SUSTANTIVO
blood sausage

morder* VERBO
to bite
◆ **morderse* las uñas** to bite one's nails

el **mordisco** SUSTANTIVO
bite ◇ *Dame un mordisco de tu manzana.* Let me have a bite of your apple.
◆ **dar* un mordisco** to bite ◇ *Me dio un mordisco.* He bit me.

moreno ADJETIVO
1 dark (*pelo, piel*)

◆ **Es moreno. (1)** (*de pelo moreno*) He has dark hair.
◆ **Es moreno. (2)** (*de tez morena*) He is dark-skinned.
[2] brown (*pan, azúcar*)

morir* VERBO
to die ◇ *Murió de cáncer.* He died of cancer.
◆ **morirse de hambre** to starve ◇ *¡Me muero de hambre!* I'm starving!
◆ **morirse de vergüenza** to die of shame
◆ **Me muero de ganas de ir a nadar.** I'm dying to go for a swim.

la **mortadela** SUSTANTIVO
mortadella

mortal ADJETIVO
[1] fatal (*herida, accidente*)
[2] mortal (*enemigo*)

la **mosca** SUSTANTIVO
fly (PL flies)
◆ **por si las moscas** just in case

el **mosquito** SUSTANTIVO
mosquito (PL mosquitoes)

la **mostaza** SUSTANTIVO
mustard

el **mostrador** SUSTANTIVO
counter (*de tienda*)

mostrar* VERBO
to show ◇ *Nos mostró el camino.* He showed us the way.
◆ **mostrarse amable** to be kind

el **mote** SUSTANTIVO
nickname

el **motivo** SUSTANTIVO
[1] reason ◇ *Dejó el trabajo por motivos personales.* He left the job for personal reasons.
◆ **sin motivo** for no reason
[2] motive ◇ *¿Cuál fue el motivo del crimen?* What was the motive for the crime?

la **moto** SUSTANTIVO
motorbike

el **motociclista**, la **motociclista** SUSTANTIVO
motorcyclist

el **motor** SUSTANTIVO
motor

el/la **motorista** SUSTANTIVO
motorcyclist

mover* VERBO
to move ◇ *Mueve un poco las cajas para que podamos pasar.* Move the boxes a bit so that we can get past.
◆ **moverse** to move ◇ *¡No te muevas!* Don't move!

móvil ADJETIVO
mobile

el **móvil** SUSTANTIVO
[1] cellular phone (*teléfono*)
[2] motive (*de un crimen*)

el **movimiento** SUSTANTIVO
movement

el **MP3** SUSTANTIVO
MP3
◆ **un reproductor de MP3** an MP3 player

la **muchacha** SUSTANTIVO
[1] girl (*chica*)
[2] maid (*criada*)

el **muchacho** SUSTANTIVO
boy

la **muchedumbre** SUSTANTIVO
crowd

mucho (1) ADJETIVO
[1] a lot of
a lot of *se usa en oraciones afirmativas, sobre todo en medio de la oración.*
◇ *Había mucha gente.* There were a lot of people. ◇ *Tiene muchas plantas.* He has a lot of plants.
[2] much (PL many)
much *y* ***many*** *se usan en oraciones negativas e interrogativas. También se usan al principio de oraciones afirmativas.*
◇ *No tenemos mucho tiempo.* We don't have much time. ◇ *¿Conoces a mucha gente?* Do you know many people?
◇ *Muchas personas creen que...* Many people think that...
◆ **no hace mucho tiempo** not long ago
◆ **Hace mucho calor.** It's very hot.
◆ **Tengo mucho frío.** I'm very cold.
◆ **Tengo mucha hambre.** I'm very hungry.
◆ **Tengo mucha sed.** I'm very thirsty.

mucho (2) PRONOMBRE
[1] a lot
a lot *se usa en oraciones afirmativas, sobre todo en medio de la oración.*
◇ *Tengo mucho que hacer.* I have a lot to do.
◇ *¿Cuántos había? – Muchos.* How many were there? – A lot.
much *y* ***many*** *se usan en oraciones negativas e interrogativas. También se usan al principio de oraciones afirmativas.*
[2] much (PL many) ◇ *No tengo mucho que hacer.* I don't have much to do. ◇ *¿Hay manzanas? – Sí pero no muchas.* Are there any apples? – Yes, but not many.
◆ **¿Vinieron muchos?** Did many people come?
◆ **Muchos dicen que...** Many people say that...

mucho (3) ADVERBIO
[1] very much ◇ *Te quiero mucho.* I love you very much. ◇ *No me gusta mucho la carne.* I don't like meat very much.
También se usa ***really*** *con el mismo significado.*
◇ *Me gusta mucho el jazz.* I really like jazz.
[2] a lot ◇ *Come mucho.* He eats a lot.
◆ **mucho más** a lot more
◆ **mucho antes** long before
◆ **No tardes mucho.** Don't be long.
◆ **Como mucho leo un libro al mes.** At most I read one book a month.
◆ **Fue, con mucho, el mejor.** He was by far the best.
◆ **Por mucho que lo quieras no debes mimarlo.** ☞

M

No matter how much you love him, you shouldn't spoil him.

la **mudanza** SUSTANTIVO
move

mudarse VERBO
to move
- **mudarse de casa** to move house

mudo ADJETIVO
dumb
- **quedarse mudo de asombro** to be dumbfounded

el **mueble** SUSTANTIVO
- **un mueble** a piece of furniture
- **los muebles** furniture SING
- **seis muebles** six pieces of furniture

la **muela** SUSTANTIVO
tooth (PL teeth)
- **una muela del juicio** a wisdom tooth

el **muelle** SUSTANTIVO
1 spring (*de colchón*)
2 quay (*de puerto*)

muelo VERBO *ver* **moler**

muerdo VERBO *ver* **morder**

la **muerta** SUSTANTIVO
dead woman (PL dead women)

la **muerte** SUSTANTIVO
death ◇ *Lo condenaron a muerte.* He was sentenced to death.
- **Nos dio un susto de muerte.** He nearly frightened us to death. (*coloquial*)
- **un hotel de mala muerte** a shabby hotel (*coloquial*)

muerto VERBO *ver* **morir**

muerto ADJETIVO
dead
- **Está muerto de cansancio.** He's dead tired. (*coloquial*)

el **muerto** SUSTANTIVO
dead man (PL dead men)
- **los muertos** the dead
- **Hubo tres muertos.** Three people were killed.
- **hacer* el muerto** to float

la **muestra** SUSTANTIVO
1 sample ◇ *una muestra gratuita* a free sample
2 sign ◇ *dar muestras de* to show signs of
3 token ◇ *Me lo regaló como muestra de afecto.* She gave it to me as a token of affection.

muestro VERBO *ver* **mostrar**

muevo VERBO *ver* **mover**

la **mujer** SUSTANTIVO
1 woman (PL women) ◇ *Vino a verte una mujer.* A woman came to see you.
2 wife (PL wives) ◇ *la mujer del médico* the doctor's wife

la **muleta** SUSTANTIVO
crutch (PL crutches) (*para andar*)

ℹ *In bullfighting, the **muleta** is a special stick with a red cloth attached to it that the matador uses.*

la **multa** SUSTANTIVO
fine ◇ *una multa de 500 pesos* a 500-peso fine
- **poner* una multa a alguien** to fine somebody

multiplicar* VERBO
to multiply ◇ *Hay que multiplicarlo por cinco.* You have to multiply it by five.
- **la tabla de multiplicar** the multiplication tables PL

la **multitud** SUSTANTIVO
crowd
- **multitud de** lots of

mundial ADJETIVO
1 world (*política, historia, guerra*)
***world** en este caso va siempre delante del sustantivo.*
2 worldwide (*problema, reconocimiento*)

el **mundial** SUSTANTIVO
world championship

el **mundo** SUSTANTIVO
world
- **todo el mundo** everybody ◇ *Se lo ha dicho a todo el mundo.* He has told everybody.
- **No lo cambiaría por nada del mundo.** I wouldn't change it for anything in the world.

el **municipio** SUSTANTIVO
1 municipality (PL municipalities) (*territorio*)
2 town council (*organismo*)

la **muñeca** SUSTANTIVO
1 wrist (*del brazo*)
2 doll (*juguete*)

el **muñeco** SUSTANTIVO
1 doll (*con forma humana*)
- **un muñeco de peluche** a soft toy

2 figure (*dibujo*)

la **muralla** SUSTANTIVO
city wall

el **murciélago** SUSTANTIVO
bat

el **murmullo** SUSTANTIVO
murmur

la **murmuración** SUSTANTIVO (PL las **murmuraciones**)
gossip SING

el **muro** SUSTANTIVO
wall

el **músculo** SUSTANTIVO
muscle

el **museo** SUSTANTIVO
museum
- **un museo de arte** an art gallery

la **música** SUSTANTIVO
1 music (*arte*) ◇ *la música pop* pop music
2 musician (*persona*)

el **músico** SUSTANTIVO

* Verbs marked with this symbol are irregular. See pages 346–348 for further details.

musician

el **muslo** SUSTANTIVO
thigh

el **musulmán,** la **musulmana** ADJETIVO, SUSTANTIVO (MASC PL los **musulmanes**)
Moslem

mutuo ADJETIVO
mutual ◇ *de mutuo acuerdo* by mutual agreement

muy ADVERBIO
very ◇ *muy bonito* very pretty
- **Eso es muy mexicano.** That's typically Mexican.
- **No me gusta por muy bonita que sea.** No matter how pretty she is, I don't like her.

N

el **nabo** SUSTANTIVO
turnip

nacer* VERBO
to be born ◇ *Nació en 1964.* He was born in 1964.

el **nacimiento** SUSTANTIVO
1 birth (*de persona*)
2 crib (*pesebre*)

la **nación** SUSTANTIVO (PL las **naciones**)
nation
◆ **las Naciones Unidas** the United Nations

nacional ADJETIVO
1 national (*himno, frontera*)
2 home (*mercado*)
***home** en este caso va siempre delante del sustantivo.*
◆ **vuelos nacionales** domestic flights

la **nacionalidad** SUSTANTIVO
nationality (PL nationalities)

el **nacionalismo** SUSTANTIVO
nationalism

el/la **nacionalista** ADJETIVO, SUSTANTIVO
nationalist

nada (1) PRONOMBRE
1 nothing
*Se usa **nothing** cuando el verbo está en la forma afirmativa.*
◇ *¿Qué has comprado? – Nada.* What have you bought? – Nothing. ◇ *No dijo nada.* He said nothing.
2 anything
*Se usa **anything** cuando el verbo está en la forma negativa.*
◇ *No quiero nada.* I don't want anything.
◆ **No dijo nada más.** He didn't say anything else.
◆ **Quiero uno nada más.** I only want one, that's all.
◆ **Prendió la tele nada más llegar.** He turned on the TV as soon as he came in.
◆ **¡Gracias! – De nada.** Thanks! – Don't mention it.
◆ **Se lo advertí, pero como si nada.** I warned him but he paid no attention.
◆ **No sabe nada de español.** He knows no Spanish at all.
◆ **No me dio nada de nada.** He gave me absolutely nothing.

nada (2) ADVERBIO
at all ◇ *Esto no me gusta nada.* I don't like this at all. ◇ *No está nada triste.* He isn't sad at all.

nadar VERBO
to swim
◆ **nadar estilo espalda** to swim backstroke
◆ **nadar de dorso** Mexico to swim backstroke
◆ **nadar estilo pecho** to swim breaststroke
◆ **nadar de pecho** Mexico to swim breaststroke

nadie PRONOMBRE
1 nobody
*Se usa **nobody** cuando el verbo está en la forma afirmativa.*
◇ *Nadie habló.* Nobody spoke. ◇ *No había nadie.* There was nobody there.
2 anybody
*Se usa **anybody** cuando el verbo está en la forma negativa.*
◇ *No quiere ver a nadie.* He doesn't want to see anybody.

el **naipe** SUSTANTIVO
playing card

las **nalgas** SUSTANTIVO
buttocks

la **nana** SUSTANTIVO
lullaby (PL lullabies)

naranja ADJETIVO
orange ◇ *un anorak naranja* an orange raincoat

el **naranja** SUSTANTIVO
orange (*color*)

la **naranja** SUSTANTIVO
orange (*fruta*)

la **nariz** SUSTANTIVO (PL las **narices**)
nose
◆ **No metas las narices en mis asuntos.** Don't poke your nose into my business.
◆ **estar* hasta las narices de algo** to be totally fed up with something

la **narración** SUSTANTIVO (PL las **narraciones**)
story (PL stories)

narrar VERBO
to tell

la **narrativa** SUSTANTIVO
fiction

la **nata** SUSTANTIVO
1 skin (*de la leche*)
2 cream (*crema*) Spain
◆ **la nata montada** whipped cream

la **natación** SUSTANTIVO
swimming

natal ADJETIVO
home
***home** en este caso va siempre delante del sustantivo.*
◇ *su pueblo natal* his home town

las **natillas** SUSTANTIVO
custard SING

nato ADJETIVO
◆ **un actor nato** a born actor

natural ADJETIVO
natural ◇ *con ingredientes naturales* with natural ingredients ◇ *Comes mucho y es natural que estés gordo.* You eat a lot, so it's only natural you're fat.
◆ **Es natural de Cancún.** He's from Cancún.

la **naturaleza** SUSTANTIVO
nature ◇ *Es despistado por naturaleza.* He's absent-minded by nature.

el **naufragio** SUSTANTIVO
shipwreck

las **náuseas** SUSTANTIVO
◆ **tener* náuseas** to feel sick

náutico ADJETIVO
◆ **club náutico** yacht club

la **navaja** SUSTANTIVO
pocketknife (PL pocketknives)
◆ **una navaja de afeitar** a razor

Navarra SUSTANTIVO FEM
Navarre

la **nave** SUSTANTIVO
ship (*barco*)
◆ **una nave espacial** a spaceship

el **navegador** SUSTANTIVO
browser
◆ **un navegador de web** (*informática*) a web browser

navegar* VERBO
to sail
◆ **navegar por Internet** to surf the Net

la **Navidad** SUSTANTIVO
Christmas
◆ **¡Feliz Navidad!** Merry Christmas!

la **neblina** SUSTANTIVO
mist

necesario ADJETIVO
necessary ◇ *No estudié más de lo necesario.* I didn't study any more than necessary.
◆ **Ya tengo el dinero necesario para el pasaje.** Now I have the money I need for the ticket.
◆ **Llamaré al médico si es necesario.** I'll call the doctor if necessary.
◆ **No es necesario que vengas.** You don't have to come.

la **necesidad** SUSTANTIVO
1 need ◇ *No hay necesidad de hacerlo.* There is no need to do it.
2 necessity (PL necessities) (*cosa esencial*) ◇ *Comer bien es una necesidad, no un lujo.* Eating well is a necessity, not a luxury.
◆ **Hizo sus necesidades.** He did his business.

necesitar VERBO
to need ◇ *Necesito mil pesos.* I need a thousand pesos. ◇ *Necesito sacar una buena nota en el examen.* I need to get a good grade on the exam. ◇ *Necesito que me ayudes.* I need you to help me.
◆ **"Se necesita mesero"** "Waiter wanted"

negar* VERBO
1 to deny ◇ *Decían que era el ladrón, pero él lo negaba.* They said that he was the thief, but he denied it.
◆ **negar con la cabeza** to shake one's head
2 to refuse ◇ *Me negaron el permiso para entrar en el bar.* They refused me permission to go into the bar.
◆ **Se negó a pagar la multa.** He refused to pay the fine.

negativo ADJETIVO
negative

el **negativo** SUSTANTIVO
negative (*de foto*)

negociar VERBO
◆ **Su empresa negocia con armas.** His company deals in arms.
◆ **Los dos gobiernos están negociando un acuerdo.** The two governments are negotiating an agreement.

el **negocio** SUSTANTIVO
business (PL businesses) (*empresa*) ◇ *Hemos montado un negocio de videojuegos.* We set up a video game business.
◆ **el mundo de los negocios** the business world

la **negra** SUSTANTIVO
black woman (PL black women) (*persona*)

negro ADJETIVO
black

el **negro** SUSTANTIVO
1 black (*color*)
2 black man (PL black men) (*persona*)
◆ **los negros** Blacks

el **nervio** SUSTANTIVO
nerve
◆ **Me pone los nervios de punta.** He gets on my nerves.

el **nerviosismo** SUSTANTIVO
◆ **Me entra nerviosismo cuando la veo.** I get nervous when I see her.

nervioso ADJETIVO
nervous ◇ *Me pongo muy nervioso en los exámenes.* I get very nervous during exams.
◆ **¡Me pone nervioso!** He gets on my nerves!

el **neumático** SUSTANTIVO
tire

neutral ADJETIVO
neutral

la **nevada** SUSTANTIVO
snowfall

nevar* VERBO
to snow

la **nevera** SUSTANTIVO
refrigerator

ni CONJUNCIÓN
1 or ◇ *No bebe ni fuma.* He doesn't drink or smoke.
2 neither ◇ *Ella no fue, ni yo tampoco.* She didn't go and neither did I.
◆ **ni...ni** neither...nor ◇ *No vinieron ni Carlos ni Sofía.* Neither Carlos nor Sofía came.
◆ **No me gustan ni el bacalao ni el hígado.** I don't like either cod or liver.
◆ **No compré ni uno ni otro.** I didn't buy either of them.
◆ **Ni siquiera me saludó.** He didn't even say hello.

Nicaragua SUSTANTIVO FEM

N ☞

Nicaragua

el/la **nicaragüense** ADJETIVO, SUSTANTIVO
Nicaraguan

la **nicotina** SUSTANTIVO
nicotine

el **nido** SUSTANTIVO
nest

la **niebla** SUSTANTIVO
fog
- **Hay niebla.** It's foggy.

niego VERBO *ver* **negar**

la **nieta** SUSTANTIVO
granddaughter

el **nieto** SUSTANTIVO
grandson
- **los nietos** grandchildren

nieva VERBO *ver* **nevar**

la **nieve** SUSTANTIVO
snow

ningún PRONOMBRE *ver* **ninguno**

ninguno ADJETIVO, PRONOMBRE (FEM **ninguna**)
[1] no
*Se usa **no** cuando el verbo está en la forma afirmativa.*
◇ *No tengo ningún interés en ir.* I have no interest in going.
[2] any
*Se usa **any** cuando el verbo está en la forma negativa.*
◇ *No vimos ninguna serpiente en el río.* We didn't see any snakes in the river.
[3] none ◇ *¿Cuál eliges? – Ninguno.* Which do you want? – None of them. ◇ *No me queda ninguno.* I have none left. ◇ *Ninguno de nosotros va a ir a la fiesta.* None of us are going to the party.
- **No lo encuentro por ningún sitio.** I can't find it anywhere.
- **ninguno de los dos (1)** neither of them ◇ *A ninguna de los dos les gusta el café.* Neither of them likes coffee.
- **ninguno de los dos (2)** either of them ◇ *No me gusta ninguno de los dos.* I don't like either of them.

la **niña** SUSTANTIVO
girl

la **niñera** SUSTANTIVO
nursemaid

la **niñez** SUSTANTIVO
childhood

niño ADJETIVO
young ◇ *Es todavía muy niño.* He's still very young.

el **niño** SUSTANTIVO
boy
- **de niño** as a child
- **los niños** the children

el **nitrógeno** SUSTANTIVO
nitrogen

el **nivel** SUSTANTIVO
[1] level ◇ *el nivel del agua* the water level
[2] standard ◇ *Pretenden aumentar el nivel educativo.* They are trying to raise the standard of education.
- **el nivel de vida** the standard of living

no ADVERBIO
no ◇ *¿Quieres venir? – No.* Do you want to come? – No.
- **¿Te gusta? – No mucho.** Do you like it? – Not really.

En inglés, la mayoría de los verbos necesitan auxiliares para formar la negación.
◇ *No me gusta.* I don't like it. ◇ *María no habla inglés.* María doesn't speak English.
*Los verbos modales y el verbo **to be** no necesitan auxiliar.*
◇ *No puedo venir esta noche.* I can't come tonight. ◇ *No tengo tiempo.* I don't have time. ◇ *No debes preocuparte.* You mustn't worry. ◇ *No hace frío.* It isn't cold.
En inglés no se usa la doble negación.
◇ *No conozco a nadie.* I don't know anyone.
Cuando se usa al final para confirmar, en inglés se usa un verbo auxiliar.
◇ *Esto es tuyo, ¿no?* This is yours, isn't it?
◇ *Fueron al cine, ¿no?* They went to the movie theater, didn't they?
- **¿Puedo salir esta noche? – ¡Que no!** Can I go out tonight? – I said no!
- **los no fumadores** non-smokers

noble ADJETIVO
noble

la **noche** SUSTANTIVO
night ◇ *Pasó la noche sin dormir.* He had a sleepless night.
- **¡Buenas noches! (1)** (*saludo*) Good evening!
- **¡Buenas noches! (2)** (*al acostarse*) Goodnight!
- **esta noche** tonight
- **hoy por la noche** tonight
- **por la noche** at night ◇ *Estudia por la noche.* He studies at night.
- **el sábado por la noche** on Saturday night
- **Era de noche cuando llegamos a casa.** It was nighttime when we got back home.
- **No me gusta manejar de noche.** I don't like driving at night.
- **la noche de Fin de Año** New Year's Eve

la **Nochebuena** SUSTANTIVO
Christmas Eve

> ℹ *En los Estados Unidos no se celebra la cena de **Nochebuena**. La celebración familiar es el día de Navidad.*

la **Nochevieja** SUSTANTIVO *Spain*
New Year's Eve

las **nociones** SUSTANTIVO
- **Tengo nociones de informática.** I know a little about computers.

nocturno ADJETIVO

1 night (*club*)

***night** en este caso va siempre delante del sustantivo.*

2 evening (*clases*)

***evening** en este caso va siempre delante del sustantivo.*

nomás ADVERBIO

just ◇ *Está ahí nomás.* It's just there.

◆ **así nomás** just like that

nombrar VERBO

1 to appoint ◇ *Lo nombraron director del colegio.* He was appointed principal of the school.

2 to mention ◇ *Me nombró en su discurso.* He mentioned me in his speech.

el **nombre** SUSTANTIVO

1 name (*de persona*)

◆ **nombre de pila** first name

◆ **nombre y apellidos** full name

2 noun (*en gramática*)

la **nómina** SUSTANTIVO

pay stub (*hoja de pago*)

◆ **estar* en nómina** to be on the payroll

el **nordeste** SUSTANTIVO

northeast

el **noreste** SUSTANTIVO

northeast

la **noria** SUSTANTIVO *Spain*

Ferris wheel (*atracción*)

la **norma** SUSTANTIVO

rule (*regla*)

normal ADJETIVO

1 normal ◇ *una persona normal* a normal person ◇ *Es normal que quiera divertirse.* It's only normal that he wants to enjoy himself.

2 ordinary ◇ *¿Es buen mozo? – No, normal.* Is he handsome? – No, just ordinary.

normalmente ADVERBIO

normally

el **noroeste** SUSTANTIVO

northwest

el **norte** SUSTANTIVO

north

el **norteamericano**, la **norteamericana** ADJETIVO, SUSTANTIVO

American

Noruega SUSTANTIVO FEM

Norway

el **noruego**, la **noruega** ADJETIVO, SUSTANTIVO

Norwegian

el **noruego** SUSTANTIVO

Norwegian (*idioma*)

nos PRONOMBRE

1 us ◇ *Nos vinieron a ver.* They came to see us. ◇ *Nos dio un consejo.* He gave us some advice.

◆ **Nos lo dio.** He gave it to us.

◆ **Nos tienen que arreglar la computadora.** They have to fix the computer for us.

2 ourselves ◇ *Tenemos que defendernos.* We must defend ourselves.

◆ **Nos levantamos a las ocho.** We got up at eight o'clock.

3 each other ◇ *No nos hablamos desde hace tiempo.* We haven't spoken to each other for a long time.

Con partes del cuerpo o con prendas que se llevan puestas se usa el adjetivo posesivo.

◇ *Nos dolían los pies.* Our feet were hurting.

◇ *Nos pusimos el abrigo.* We put our coats on.

nosotros PRONOMBRE (FEM **nosotras**)

1 we ◇ *Nosotros no somos italianos.* We are not Italian.

2 us ◇ *¿Quién es? – Somos nosotros.* Who is it? – It's us. ◇ *Tu hermano vino con nosotros.* Your brother came with us. ◇ *Llegaron antes que nosotros.* They arrived before us.

◆ **nosotros mismos** ourselves

la **nota** SUSTANTIVO

1 grade ◇ *Saca muy malas notas.* He gets very bad grades.

2 note ◇ *Tomó muchas notas en la conferencia.* He took a lot of notes during the lecture. ◇ *Te dejé una nota encima de la mesa.* I've left you a note on the table.

notar VERBO

1 to notice ◇ *Notó que lo seguían.* He noticed they were following him.

2 to feel ◇ *Con este abrigo no noto el frío.* I don't feel the cold with this coat on.

◆ **Se nota que has estudiado mucho este trimestre.** You can tell that you've studied a lot this term.

el **notario**, la **notaria** SUSTANTIVO

notary (PL notaries)

la **noticia** SUSTANTIVO

news SING ◇ *Tengo una buena noticia que darte.* I have some good news for you.

◆ **Fue una noticia excelente para la economía.** It was an excellent piece of news for the economy.

◆ **Vi las noticias de las seis.** I watched the six o'clock news.

◆ **No tengo noticias de Juan.** I haven't heard from Juan.

*No confundir **noticia** con **notice**.*

notificar* VERBO

to notify

el **novato**, la **novata** SUSTANTIVO

beginner

novecientos ADJETIVO, PRONOMBRE (FEM **novecientas**)

nine hundred

la **novedad** SUSTANTIVO

◆ **Las últimas novedades en moda infantil.** The latest in children's fashions.

◆ **¿Cómo sigue tu hijo? – Sin novedad.** How's your son? – There's no change.

la **novela** SUSTANTIVO

novel

N ☞

♦ **una novela policíaca** a detective story

noveno ADJETIVO, PRONOMBRE (FEM **novena**)
ninth
♦ **Vivo en el noveno.** I live on the tenth floor.

noventa ADJETIVO, PRONOMBRE
ninety
♦ **el noventa aniversario** the ninetieth anniversary

la **novia** SUSTANTIVO
[1] girlfriend (*amiga íntima*)
[2] fiancée (*prometida*)
[3] bride (*en la boda*)

el **noviazgo** SUSTANTIVO
relationship ◇ *Su noviazgo duró muy poco.* Their relationship didn't last very long.

noviembre SUSTANTIVO MASC
En inglés, los meses se escriben con mayúscula.
November ◇ *en noviembre* in November ◇ *Llegará el 30 de noviembre.* He'll arrive on November 30th.

los **novillos** SUSTANTIVO
♦ **hacer* novillos** to play hooky

el **novio** SUSTANTIVO
[1] boyfriend (*amigo íntimo*)
[2] fiancé (*prometido*)
[3] bridegroom (*en boda*)
♦ **los novios** (*en la boda*) the bride and groom

la **nube** SUSTANTIVO
cloud

nublado ADJETIVO
cloudy

nublarse VERBO
to cloud over (*cielo*)

la **nuca** SUSTANTIVO
nape of neck

nuclear ADJETIVO
nuclear
♦ **una central nuclear** a nuclear power station

el **núcleo** SUSTANTIVO
♦ **el núcleo urbano** the city center

el **nudo** SUSTANTIVO
knot
♦ **atar con un nudo** to tie in a knot

la **nuera** SUSTANTIVO
daughter-in-law (PL daughters-in-law)

nuestro ADJETIVO, PRONOMBRE (FEM **nuestra**)
[1] our ◇ *nuestro perro* our dog ◇ *nuestras bicicletas* our bicycles
[2] ours ◇ *¿De quién es esto? – Es nuestro.* Whose is this? – It's ours. ◇ *Esta casa es la nuestra.* This house is ours.
♦ **un amigo nuestro** a friend of ours

nueve ADJETIVO, PRONOMBRE
nine
♦ **Son las nueve.** It's nine o'clock.
♦ **el nueve de marzo** March ninth

nuevo ADJETIVO
new ◇ *Necesito una computadora nueva.* I need a new computer. ◇ *Soy nuevo en el colegio.* I'm new at the school.
♦ **El mecánico me dejó el carro como nuevo.** The mechanic left my car like new.
♦ **Tuve que leer el libro de nuevo.** I had to read the book again.

la **nuez** SUSTANTIVO (PL las **nueces**)
[1] walnut (*del nogal*)
[2] pecan nut [Mexico]
♦ **nuez de Castilla** [Mexico] walnut
♦ **la nuez moscada** nutmeg
[3] Adam's apple (*en el cuello*)

el **número** SUSTANTIVO
[1] number (*cifra*)
[2] size (*de zapato*)
[3] issue (*de publicación*)
♦ **Calle Aribau, sin número.** Aribau Street, no number.
♦ **número de teléfono** telephone number
♦ **montar un número** to make a scene

nunca ADVERBIO
[1] never ◇ *No viene nunca.* He never comes.
♦ **No lo veré nunca más.** I'll never see him again.
[2] ever ◇ *Ninguno de nosotros había esquiado nunca.* Neither of us had ever skied before. ◇ *Casi nunca me escribe.* He hardly ever writes to me.

la **nutria** SUSTANTIVO
otter

el **nylon** SUSTANTIVO
nylon

Ñ

ñango ADJETIVO Mexico
puny

ñandu SUSTANTIVO

> *A **ñandu** is a fast-running flightless bird, similiar to an ostrich. In English, this bird is called a rhea.*

la **ñapa** SUSTANTIVO
for free ◇ *Me dieron una de ñapa.* They gave me an extra one for free.

ñata SUSTANTIVO
nose

el **ñu** SUSTANTIVO
gnu (PL gnus)

O

o CONJUNCIÓN
or ◇ *¿Quieres té o café?* Would you like tea or coffee? ◇ *¿Vas a ayudarme o no?* Are you going to help me or not?
◆ **o...o...** either...or... ◇ *O ha salido o no contesta el teléfono.* Either he's out or he's not answering the phone.
◆ **O te callas o no sigo hablando.** If you're not quiet, I won't go on.

obedecer* VERBO
to obey
◆ **obedecer a alguien** to obey someone

obediente ADJETIVO
obedient

obeso ADJETIVO
obese

el **obispo** SUSTANTIVO
bishop

la **objeción** SUSTANTIVO (PL las **objeciones**)
objection
◆ **No puso ninguna objeción.** He didn't object.

el **objetivo** SUSTANTIVO
objective ◇ *un objetivo militar* a military objective
◆ **Nuestro principal objetivo es ganar las elecciones.** Our main aim is to win the elections.

el **objeto** SUSTANTIVO
object ◇ *un objeto metálico* a metal object
◆ **¿Cuál es el objeto de su visita?** What's the reason for your visit?
◆ **con objeto de hacer algo** in order to do something
◆ **los objetos de valor** valuables

la **obligación** SUSTANTIVO (PL las **obligaciones**)
obligation
◆ **Obedecer a tus padres es tu obligación.** It's your duty to obey your parents.

obligado ADJETIVO
◆ **estar* obligado a hacer algo** to be forced to do something ◇ *Se vieron obligados a vender su casa.* They were forced to sell their house.
◆ **No estás obligado a venir si no quieres.** You don't have to come if you don't want to.

obligar* VERBO
[1] to force ◇ *Me obligaron a venir.* They forced me to come. ◇ *Nadie te obliga a aceptar este empleo.* Nobody's forcing you to accept this job.
[2] to make ◇ *No puedes obligarme a ir.* You can't make me go.

obligatorio ADJETIVO
compulsory

la **obra** SUSTANTIVO
[1] work
◆ **una obra de arte** a work of art
◆ **la obra completa de Neruda** the complete works of Neruda
◆ **una obra de teatro** a play
◆ **una obra maestra** a masterpiece
[2] building site (*edificio en construcción*)
◆ **"obras"** (*en carretera*) "roadworks"

el **obrero**, la **obrera** SUSTANTIVO
worker ◇ *Mi primo es obrero de la construcción.* My cousin is a construction worker.

el **obsequio** SUSTANTIVO
gift ◇ *como obsequio* as a gift

la **observación** SUSTANTIVO (PL las **observaciones**)
[1] observation ◇ *El paciente está en observación.* The patient is under observation.
[2] comment ◇ *hacer una observación* to make a comment

observador ADJETIVO (FEM **observadora**)
observant

observar VERBO
[1] to observe (*mirar*)
[2] to remark (*comentar*)

la **obsesión** SUSTANTIVO (PL las **obsesiones**)
obsession ◇ *su obsesión por la limpieza* his obsession with cleanliness

obsesionar VERBO
◆ **Es un tema que le obsesiona.** He's obsessed by the subject.

el **obstáculo** SUSTANTIVO
obstacle ◇ *Nos puso muchos obstáculos.* He put many obstacles in our way.

obstinado ADJETIVO
obstinate

obstinarse VERBO
to insist ◇ *¿Por qué te obstinas en hacerlo?* Why do you insist on doing it?

obtener* VERBO
to obtain

obvio ADJETIVO
obvious

la **oca** SUSTANTIVO
goose (PL geese)

la **ocasión** SUSTANTIVO (PL las **ocasiones**)
1 opportunity (PL opportunities) ◇ *Ésta es la ocasión que esperábamos.* This is the opportunity we've been waiting for.
2 occasion ◇ *en varias ocasiones* on several occasions
◆ **un libro de ocasión** a secondhand book

ocasionar VERBO
to cause

occidental ADJETIVO
western
◆ **los países occidentales** the West

el **occidente** SUSTANTIVO
◆ **el Occidente** the West

el **océano** SUSTANTIVO
ocean ◇ *el océano Atlántico* the Atlantic Ocean

ochenta ADJETIVO, PRONOMBRE
eighty ◇ *Tiene ochenta años.* He's eighty.
◆ **el ochenta aniversario** the eightieth anniversary

ocho ADJETIVO, PRONOMBRE
eight
◆ **Son las ocho.** It's eight o'clock.
◆ **el ocho de agosto** August eighth

ochocientos ADJETIVO, PRONOMBRE (FEM **ochocientas**)
eight hundred

el **ocio** SUSTANTIVO
◆ **en mis ratos de ocio** in my spare time

octavo ADJETIVO, PRONOMBRE (FEM **octava**)
eighth
◆ **Vivo en el octavo.** I live on the ninth floor.

octubre SUSTANTIVO MASC
En inglés, los meses se escriben con mayúscula.
October ◇ *en octubre* in October ◇ *Llegaré el 3 de octubre.* I'll arrive on October 3rd.

el/la **oculista** SUSTANTIVO
eye specialist ◇ *Es oculista.* He's an eye specialist.

ocultar VERBO
to conceal ◇ *Nos ocultó su edad.* He concealed his age from us.
◆ **No nos ocultes la verdad.** Don't try to hide the truth from us.
◆ **ocultarse** to hide

la **ocupación** SUSTANTIVO (PL las **ocupaciones**)
1 activity (PL activities) ◇ *Tiene muchas ocupaciones.* He's involved in many activities.
2 occupation (*empleo*) ◇ *¿Qué ocupación tiene?* What's his occupation? ◇ *la ocupación de la embajada por parte de los guerrilleros* the occupation of the embassy by the guerrillas

ocupado ADJETIVO
busy ◇ *Estoy muy ocupado.* I'm very busy. ◇ *Si la línea está ocupada vuelva a llamar.* If the line's busy please call back later.
◆ **"ocupado"** "occupied"
◆ **¿Está ocupado este asiento?** Is this seat taken?

ocupar VERBO
1 to occupy ◇ *Los obreros ocuparon la fábrica.* The workers have occupied the factory. ◇ *El edifico ocupa todo el solar.* The building occupies the whole site.
2 to take up ◇ *Ocupa casi todo mi tiempo.* It takes up almost all my time.
◆ **Los espectadores ocuparon sus asientos.** The spectators took their seats.
◆ **ocuparse de algo** to look after something ◇ *Ahora los hijos se ocupan de la empresa.* The sons look after the business now.
◆ **Yo me ocuparé de decírselo.** I'll tell him.

la **ocurrencia** SUSTANTIVO
◆ **Juan tuvo la ocurrencia de decírselo en la cara.** Juan took it into his head to tell her to her face.
◆ **¡Qué ocurrencia!** What a crazy idea!

ocurrir VERBO
to happen ◇ *Lo que ocurrió podría haberse evitado.* What happened could have been avoided.
◆ **¿Qué te ocurre?** What's the matter?
◆ **Se nos ocurrió una idea estupenda.** We had a great idea.

odiar VERBO
to hate ◇ *Odio levantarme pronto.* I hate getting up early.

el **odio** SUSTANTIVO
hate

el **oeste** SUSTANTIVO, ADJETIVO
west ◇ *el oeste del país* the west of the country ◇ *en la costa oeste* on the west coast
◆ **al oeste de la ciudad** west of the city
◆ **Viajábamos hacia el oeste.** We were traveling west.
◆ **una película del oeste** a western movie
◆ **vientos del oeste** westerly winds

ofender VERBO
offend
◆ **ofenderse** to take offense ◇ *Se ofendió cuando le dije lo que pensaba.* He took offense when I told him what I thought.

la **ofensa** SUSTANTIVO
insult

la **oferta** SUSTANTIVO

offer
- **una oferta especial** a special offer
- **estar* de oferta** to be on special offer
- **"ofertas de trabajo"** "job openings"

oficial ADJETIVO
official

el/la **oficial** SUSTANTIVO
officer ◇ *Es oficial de marina.* He's an officer in the navy.

la **oficina** SUSTANTIVO
office
- **la oficina de turismo** the tourist office
- **la oficina de empleo** the employment office
- **la oficina de correos** the post office
- **la oficina de objetos perdidos** lost and found

el/la **oficinista** SUSTANTIVO
clerk

el **oficio** SUSTANTIVO
trade ◇ *Es ingeniero de oficio.* He's an engineer by trade.

ofrecer* VERBO
to offer ◇ *Nos ofrecieron unos cigarrillos.* They offered us some cigarettes.
- **ofrecerse para hacer algo** to offer to do something
- **¿Qué se le ofrece?** What can I get you?

el **ofrecimiento** SUSTANTIVO
offer

el **oído** SUSTANTIVO
1 hearing (*sentido*)
2 ear (*órgano*)
- **tener* oído** to have a good ear *

oír* VERBO
1 to hear ◇ *Oí un ruido.* I heard a noise. ◇ *¿Me oyes bien desde la habitación?* Can you hear me all right from your room?
2 to listen to ◇ *Óyeme bien, no vuelvas a hacerlo.* Now listen to what I'm telling you, don't do it again.
- **oír el radio** to listen to the radio
- **¡Oye!** Hey! (*coloquial*)
- **¡Oiga, por favor!** Excuse me!

el **ojal** SUSTANTIVO
buttonhole

ojalá EXCLAMACIÓN
1 I hope ◇ *¡Ojalá Toni venga hoy!* I hope Toni comes today!
2 if only ◇ *¡Ojalá pudiera!* If only I could!

las **ojeras** SUSTANTIVO
- **tener* ojeras** to have bags under one's eyes

el **ojo** SUSTANTIVO
eye ◇ *Tengo algo en el ojo.* I have something in my eye.
- **ir* con ojo** to keep one's eyes open for trouble
- **costar* un ojo de la cara** to cost an arm and a leg (*coloquial*)
- **¡Ojo! Es muy mentiroso.** Look out! He's an terrible liar.

la **ola** SUSTANTIVO
wave (*de mar*)

oler* VERBO
to smell ◇ *Me gusta oler las flores.* I like smelling the flowers.
- **Huele a tabaco.** It smells of cigarette smoke.
- **oler bien** to smell good ◇ *Esta salsa huele muy bien.* This sauce smells very good.
- **oler mal** to smell awful ◇ *¡Qué mal huelen estos zapatos!* These shoes smell awful!

el **olfato** SUSTANTIVO
sense of smell

las **Olimpiadas** SUSTANTIVO
the Olympics

la **oliva** SUSTANTIVO
olive
- **el aceite de oliva** olive oil

el **olivo** SUSTANTIVO
olive tree

la **olla** SUSTANTIVO
pot
- **una olla a presión** a pressure cooker

el **olor** SUSTANTIVO
smell ◇ *un olor a tabaco* a smell of tobacco
- **¡Qué mal olor!** What a horrible smell!

olvidar VERBO
1 to forget ◇ *No olvides comprar el pan.* Don't forget to buy the bread.
- **olvidarse de hacer algo** to forget to do something ◇ *Me olvidé de decírtelo.* I forgot to tell you.
- **Se me olvidó por completo.** I completely forgot.

2 to leave ◇ *Olvidé las llaves encima de la mesa.* I left the keys on top of the table.

el **olvido** SUSTANTIVO
- **Fue un olvido imperdonable.** It was an unforgivable oversight.

el **ombligo** SUSTANTIVO
navel

omitir VERBO
to leave out ◇ *Omitieron varios nombres de la lista.* They've left several names out of the list.

once ADJETIVO, PRONOMBRE
eleven ◇ *Tengo once años.* I'm eleven.
- **Son las once.** It's eleven o'clock.
- **el once de agosto** August eleventh

la **onda** SUSTANTIVO
wave
- **onda corta** short wave

ondear VERBO
to fly (*bandera*)

ondulado ADJETIVO
wavy ◇ *un chico con el pelo ondulado* a boy with wavy hair

la **ONU** SUSTANTIVO (= *Organización de las Naciones Unidas*)
the UN (= the United Nations)

opaco ADJETIVO
1 opaque (*no transparente*)
2 dull (*sin brillo*)

la **opción** SUSTANTIVO (PL las **opciones**)

☞

option ◇ *No tienes otra opción.* You have no option.

la **ópera** SUSTANTIVO
opera

la **operación** SUSTANTIVO (PL **operaciones**)
operation ◇ *una operación de cataratas* a cataract operation

operar VERBO
to operate on ◇ *Le tienen que operar.* They have to operate on him.
◆ **Me van a operar del corazón.** I'm going to have a heart operation.
◆ **operarse** to have an operation ◇ *Me tengo que operar de la rodilla.* I have to have a knee operation.

opinar VERBO
to think ◇ *¿Y tú qué opinas de la propuesta?* So what do you think about the proposal?

la **opinión** SUSTANTIVO (PL las **opiniones**)
opinion
◆ **en mi opinión** in my opinion

oponerse* VERBO
to oppose ◇ *Se opuso al proyecto.* He opposed the project.
◆ **No me opongo.** I don't object.

la **oportunidad** SUSTANTIVO
chance ◇ *No tuvo la oportunidad de hacerlo.* He didn't have a chance to do it.
◆ **dar* otra oportunidad a alguien** to give someone another chance

oportuno ADJETIVO
◆ **en el momento oportuno** at the right time

la **oposición** SUSTANTIVO (PL las **oposiciones**)
opposition

optar VERBO
◆ **optar por hacer algo** to choose to do something ◇ *Al final, optó por ir.* In the end, she chose to go.
◆ **optar a** to apply for ◇ *Optaba a la plaza de director.* He was applying for the post of principal.

optativo ADJETIVO
optional ◇ *las asignaturas optativas* optional subjects

la **óptica** SUSTANTIVO
optician's ◇ *En la óptica de mi barrio hay una oferta de monturas.* There's a special offer on frames at my local optician's.

el **optimismo** SUSTANTIVO
optimism

optimista ADJETIVO
optimistic

el/la **optimista** SUSTANTIVO
optimist

óptimo ADJETIVO
optimum

opuesto ADJETIVO
1 conflicting (*opinión, punto de vista*)
2 opposite (*extremos, direcciones*)

opuse VERBO *ver* **oponer**

la **oración** SUSTANTIVO (PL las **oraciones**)
1 prayer (*rezo*)
2 sentence (*frase*)

el **orador,** la **oradora** SUSTANTIVO
speaker

oral ADJETIVO
oral
◆ **por vía oral** orally
◆ **un examen oral** an oral test

la **órbita** SUSTANTIVO
1 orbit (*de satélite*)
2 eye socket (*de ojo*)

el **orden** SUSTANTIVO
order
◆ **por orden alfabético** in alphabetical order
◆ **poner* en orden algo** to straighten something up ◇ *Tienes que poner en orden tu habitación.* You need to straighten your room up.
◆ **el orden del día** the agenda

la **orden** SUSTANTIVO (PL las **órdenes**)
order
◆ **¡No me des más ordenes!** Stop bossing me about!

ordenado ADJETIVO
neat ◇ *Siempre tiene la habitación muy ordenada.* He always keep his room very neat.

el **ordenador** SUSTANTIVO Spain
computer

ordenar VERBO
1 to straighten up ◇ *¿Por qué no ordenas tu habitación?* Why don't you straighten your room up?
2 to order ◇ *El policía nos ordenó que saliéramos del edificio.* The policeman ordered us to get out of the building.

ordeñar VERBO
to milk

ordinario ADJETIVO
1 common (*vulgar*) ◇ *Es una mujer muy ordinaria.* She's a very common woman.
2 ordinary (*corriente*) ◇ *los acontecimientos ordinarios* ordinary events
◆ **de ordinario** usually ◇ *De ordinario toma el metro para ir a trabajar.* He usually takes the subway to work.

la **oreja** SUSTANTIVO
ear

orgánico ADJETIVO
organic

el **organismo** SUSTANTIVO
organization ◇ *un organismo internacional* an international organization

la **organización** SUSTANTIVO (PL las **organizaciones**)
organization

organizar* VERBO
to organize
◆ **organizarse** to organize oneself ◇ *Te tienes*

que organizar mejor. You need to organize yourself better.

el **órgano** SUSTANTIVO
organ

el **orgullo** SUSTANTIVO
pride

orgulloso ADJETIVO
proud

la **orientación** SUSTANTIVO (PL las **orientaciones**)
- **tener* sentido de la orientación** to have a good sense of direction
- **la orientación profesional** career advice

el **oriente** SUSTANTIVO
- **el Oriente** the East

el **origen** SUSTANTIVO (PL los **orígenes**)
origin

original ADJETIVO
original

la **originalidad** SUSTANTIVO
originality

la **orilla** SUSTANTIVO
1 shore (*del mar, de un lago*)
2 bank (*de un río*)
- **a orillas de (1)** (*del mar, de un lago*) on the shores of
- **a orillas de (2)** (*de un río*) on the banks of
- **un paseo a la orilla del mar** a walk along the seashore

la **orina** SUSTANTIVO
urine

orinar VERBO
to urinate

el **oro** SUSTANTIVO
gold ◇ *un collar de oro* a gold necklace

la **orquesta** SUSTANTIVO
orchestra
- **una orquesta de jazz** a jazz band

ortodoxo ADJETIVO
orthodox

la **ortografía** SUSTANTIVO
spelling

la **oruga** SUSTANTIVO
caterpillar

os PRONOMBRE *Spain*
1 you ◇ *No os oigo.* I can't hear you.
- **Os lo doy.** I'll give it to you.

2 yourselves ◇ *¿Os habéis hecho daño?* Did you hurt yourselves?
3 each other ◇ *Quiero que os pidáis perdón.* I want you to say sorry to each other.

oscilar VERBO
to range ◇ *Las máximas han oscilado entre los 15 y los 20 grados.* Maximum temperatures have ranged from 15 to 20 degrees.

oscurecer* VERBO
to get dark

la **oscuridad** SUSTANTIVO
darkness
- **Estaban hablando en la oscuridad.** They were talking in the dark.

oscuro ADJETIVO
dark ◇ *una habitación muy oscura* a very dark room
- **azul oscuro** dark blue
- **a oscuras** in darkness

el **oso,** la **osa** SUSTANTIVO
bear
- **un oso de peluche** a teddy bear

la **ostentación** SUSTANTIVO
ostentation
- **hacer* ostentación de algo** to flaunt something

el **ostión** SUSTANTIVO (PL los **ostiones**)
oyster *Mexico*

la **ostra** SUSTANTIVO
oyster

el **otoño** SUSTANTIVO
fall ◇ *en otoño* in fall ◇ *el otoño pasado* last fall

otro ADJETIVO, PRONOMBRE
1 another (*singular*) ◇ *otro carro* another car ◇ *¿Me das otra manzana, por favor?* Can you give me another apple, please?
- **¿Se te perdió el lápiz? – No importa, tengo otro.** Have you lost your pencil? – It doesn't matter, I have another one.
- **¿Hay alguna otra manera de hacerlo?** Is there any other way of doing it?
- **No quiero éste, quiero el otro.** I don't want this one, I want the other one.

2 other (*plural*) ◇ *Tengo otros planes.* I have other plans.
- **Quiero otra cosa.** I want something else.
- **otra vez** again
- **otros tres libros** another three books
- **Que lo haga otro.** Let someone else do it.
- **Están enamorados el uno del otro.** They're in love with each other.

ovalado ADJETIVO
oval

la **oveja** SUSTANTIVO
sheep (PL sheep)

el **ovillo** SUSTANTIVO
ball ◇ *un ovillo de lana* a ball of wool

el **OVNI** SUSTANTIVO (= *objeto volador no identificado*)
UFO (= unidentified flying object)

oxidado ADJETIVO
rusty

oxidarse VERBO
to rust ◇ *Se oxidó la barandilla.* The rail has rusted.

el **oxígeno** SUSTANTIVO
oxygen

oyendo VERBO *ver* **oír**

el/la **oyente** SUSTANTIVO
1 listener (*de programa de radio*)
2 auditor (*en instituto, universidad*)

P

la **paciencia** SUSTANTIVO
patience ◇ *No tengo paciencia.* I have very little patience. ◇ *Perdí la paciencia y le grité.* I lost my patience and I shouted at him.
◆ **¡Ten paciencia!** Be patient!

el/la **paciente** ADJETIVO, SUSTANTIVO
patient

el **Pacífico** SUSTANTIVO
the Pacific

pacífico ADJETIVO
peaceful

el/la **pacifista** ADJETIVO, SUSTANTIVO
pacifist
◆ **el movimiento pacifista** the peace movement

el **pacto** SUSTANTIVO
agreement ◇ *hacer un pacto* to make an agreement

padecer* VERBO
1 to suffer from ◇ *Padece de una enfermedad grave.* He suffers from a serious illness.
◆ **Padece del corazón.** He has heart trouble.
2 to suffer ◇ *El pobrecito ha padecido mucho.* The poor man has suffered a lot.

el **padrastro** SUSTANTIVO
stepfather

el **padre** SUSTANTIVO
father
◆ **Es padre de familia.** He's a family man.
◆ **mis padres** my parents
◆ **rezar* el Padre Nuestro** to say the Lord's Prayer

el **padrino** SUSTANTIVO
godfather
◆ **mis padrinos** my godparents

> ℹ *At a Latin American wedding, the* ***padrino*** *is the person, usually her father, who escorts the bride down the aisle and gives her away.*

la **paella** SUSTANTIVO
paella

la **paga** SUSTANTIVO
pay (*sueldo*)

pagar* VERBO
1 to pay (*facturas, impuestos, deuda*) ◇ *No han pagado el alquiler.* They haven't paid the rent. ◇ *Me pagan muy poco.* I get paid very little.
◆ **Se puede pagar con tarjeta de crédito.** You can pay by credit card.
2 to pay for (*producto, compra*) ◇ *Tengo que pagar las entradas.* I have to pay for the tickets.

la **página** SUSTANTIVO
page ◇ *Está en la página 17.* It's on page 17.
◆ **una página web** a web page
◆ **las páginas amarillas** the yellow pages®

el **pago** SUSTANTIVO
1 payment (*de deuda*)
2 pay (*sueldo*)

el **país** SUSTANTIVO (PL los **países**)
country (PL countries)
◆ **el País Vasco** the Basque Country
◆ **los Países Bajos** the Netherlands

el **paisaje** SUSTANTIVO
1 landscape ◇ *el paisaje de Perú* the Peruvian landscape ◇ *pintar un paisaje* to paint a landscape
2 scenery
Se utiliza ***scenery*** *cuando se habla de la belleza del paisaje.*
◇ *Estaba contemplando el paisaje.* I was looking at the scenery.

la **paja** SUSTANTIVO
1 straw ◇ *un sombrero de paja* a straw hat
2 padding ◇ *El resto del texto es sólo paja.* The rest of the text is just padding.

la **pajarita** SUSTANTIVO
bow tie

el **pájaro** SUSTANTIVO
bird

la **pajita** SUSTANTIVO
drinking straw

la **pala** SUSTANTIVO
1 spade (*para cavar, de niño*)
2 shovel (*para mover tierra, nieve*)
3 paddle (*de ping pong*)
4 blade (*de remo*)

la **palabra** SUSTANTIVO
word ◇ *un título de dos palabras* a two-word title ◇ *Cumplió su palabra.* He was true to his word. ◇ *sin decir palabra* without a word
◆ **No me dirige la palabra.** He doesn't speak to me.

la **palabrota** SUSTANTIVO *Spain*
swearword

el **palacio** SUSTANTIVO
palace

el **paladar** SUSTANTIVO
palate

la **palanca** SUSTANTIVO
lever
◆ **la palanca de cambio** gearshift
◆ **Se consiguió el puesto con palanca.** He got the job through pulling strings.

la **palangana** SUSTANTIVO
sink

el **palco** SUSTANTIVO
box (PL boxes)

Palestina SUSTANTIVO FEM
Palestine

el **palestino,** la **palestina** ADJETIVO, SUSTANTIVO
Palestinian

la **paleta** SUSTANTIVO
1 trowel (*de albañil*)
2 palette (*de pintor*)
◆ **una paleta helada** a Popsicle®

pálido ADJETIVO
pale ◇ *Se puso pálida.* She turned pale.

el **palillo** SUSTANTIVO
1 toothpick (*para los dientes*)
2 chopstick (*para la comida oriental*)

la **paliza** SUSTANTIVO
1 beating ◇ *Los ladrones le dieron una paliza.* The burglars gave him a beating.
2 thrashing ◇ *Si mi padre se entera me va a dar una paliza.* If my father finds out he'll give me a thrashing.
◆ **Sus clases son una paliza.** His classes are a real pain. (*coloquial*)
◆ **¡No me des la paliza!** Don't be such a pain! (*coloquial*)

la **palma** SUSTANTIVO
palm
◆ **dar* palmas** to clap

la **palmera** SUSTANTIVO
palm tree

el **palmo** SUSTANTIVO
◆ **Mide un palmo.** It's several inches long.
◆ **Se conoce el lugar de palmo a palmo.** He knows the place like the back of his hand.

el **palo** SUSTANTIVO
1 stick ◇ *Le pegó con un palo.* He hit him with a stick.
2 club (*de golf*)
3 suit (*de baraja*)
◆ **una cuchara de palo** a wooden spoon

la **paloma** SUSTANTIVO
pigeon ◇ *una paloma mensajera* a carrier pigeon
◆ **la paloma de la paz** the dove of peace

las **palomitas** SUSTANTIVO
◆ **las palomitas de maíz** popcorn SING

palpar VERBO
to feel

la **palpitación** SUSTANTIVO (PL las **palpitaciones**)
palpitation

palpitar VERBO
1 to pound ◇ *El corazón me palpitaba de miedo.* My heart was pounding with fear.
2 to beat ◇ *El corazón del enfermo dejó de palpitar.* The patient's heart stopped beating.

el **pan** SUSTANTIVO
1 bread ◇ *pan con mantequilla* bread and butter ◇ *pan integral* wholewheat bread ◇ *pan de molde* sliced bread ◇ *una barra de pan* a loaf of bread
◆ **pan rallado** breadcrumbs PL
◆ **pan tostado** toast
2 loaf (PL loaves) ◇ *Compré dos panes.* I bought two loaves.

la **pana** SUSTANTIVO
corduroy

la **panadera** SUSTANTIVO
baker ◇ *Es panadera.* She's a baker.

la **panadería** SUSTANTIVO
bakery (PL bakeries)

el **panadero** SUSTANTIVO
baker ◇ *Es panadero.* He's a baker.

Panamá SUSTANTIVO MASC
Panama

el **panameño**, la **panameña** ADJETIVO, SUSTANTIVO
Panamanian

la **pancarta** SUSTANTIVO
banner

el **pancito** SUSTANTIVO
bread roll

el **panda** SUSTANTIVO
panda

la **pandereta** SUSTANTIVO
tambourine

la **pandilla** SUSTANTIVO
gang

el **panfleto** SUSTANTIVO
pamphlet

el **pánico** SUSTANTIVO
panic ◇ *en un momento de pánico* in a moment of panic
◆ **Me entró pánico.** I panicked.
◆ **Les tengo pánico a las arañas.** I'm terrified of spiders.

las **pantaletas** SUSTANTIVO Mexico
panties ◇ *unas pantaletas* a pair of panties

la **pantalla** SUSTANTIVO
1 screen (*de cine, televisión, computadora*)
2 lampshade (*de lámpara*)

los **pantalones** SUSTANTIVO
pants PL
◆ **unos pantalones** a pair of pants
◆ **pantalones cortos** shorts
◆ **pantalones vaqueros** jeans

el **pantano** SUSTANTIVO
bog

la **pantera** SUSTANTIVO
panther

las **pantimedias** SUSTANTIVO Mexico
pantyhose

los **pantis** SUSTANTIVO
pantyhose ◇ *unos pantis* a pair of pantyhose

la **pantorrilla** SUSTANTIVO
calf (PL calves)

los **pants** SUSTANTIVO Mexico
sweatsuit SING

el **pañal** SUSTANTIVO
diaper

el **paño** SUSTANTIVO
cloth
◆ **un paño de cocina** a dishcloth

el **pañuelo** SUSTANTIVO
1 handkerchief (PL handkerchiefs) (*para la nariz*)
2 scarf (PL scarves) (*para la cabeza, el*

P ☞

cuello)

el **papa** SUSTANTIVO
pope
◆ **el Papa** the Pope

la **papa** SUSTANTIVO
potato (PL potatoes)
◆ **un paquete de papas fritas** a bag of potato chips

el **papá** SUSTANTIVO (PL los **papás**)
dad
◆ **mis papás** my mom and dad
◆ **Papá Noel** Santa Claus

el **papalote** SUSTANTIVO *Mexico*
kite ◇ *volar un papalote* to fly a kite

el **papel** SUSTANTIVO
1 paper ◇ *una bolsa de papel* a paper bag
2 piece of paper ◇ *Lo escribí en un papel.* I wrote it on a piece of paper.
◆ **papel de aluminio** tinfoil
◆ **papel higiénico** toilet paper
◆ **papel pintado** wallpaper
3 role ◇ *la actriz que tiene el papel principal* the actress who has the leading role
◆ **Jugó un papel muy importante en las negociaciones.** He played a very important part in the negotiations.
◆ **¿Qué papeles te piden para sacar el pasaporte?** What documents do you need to get a passport?

el **papeleo** SUSTANTIVO
paperwork

la **papelera** SUSTANTIVO
1 wastepaper basket (*en la oficina, en casa*)
2 trash can (*en la calle*)

la **papelería** SUSTANTIVO
stationery store

la **papeleta** SUSTANTIVO
1 transcript (*de examen*)
2 ballot (*de votación*)
3 raffle ticket (*de rifa*)

las **paperas** SUSTANTIVO
mumps ◇ *tener paperas* to have the mumps

la **papilla** SUSTANTIVO
1 baby food (*para bebé*)
2 puree (*para enfermos*)

el **paquete** SUSTANTIVO
1 pack (*de galletas, cigarrillos*)
2 package ◇ *Me mandaron un paquete por correo.* I got a package in the mail.

Paquistán SUSTANTIVO MASC
Pakistan

el/la **paquistaní** ADJETIVO, SUSTANTIVO (PL los **paquistaníes**)
Pakistani

par ADJETIVO (FEM **par**)
◆ **número par** even number

el **par** SUSTANTIVO
1 couple ◇ *un par de horas al día* a couple of hours a day
2 pair ◇ *un par de calcetines* a pair of socks
◆ **Abrió la ventana de par en par.** He opened the window wide.

para PREPOSICIÓN
1 for ◇ *Es para ti.* It's for you. ◇ *Tengo muchos deberes para mañana.* I have a lot of homework to do for tomorrow.
◆ **¿Para qué lo quieres?** What do you want it for?
◆ **¿Para qué sirve?** What's it for?
◆ **para siempre** forever
◆ **Para entonces ya era tarde.** It was already too late by then.
2 to ◇ *Estoy ahorrando para comprarme una moto.* I'm saving up to buy a motorbike. ◇ *Tengo bastante para vivir.* I have enough to live on. ◇ *Son cinco para las ocho.* It's five to eight. ◇ *el vuelo para Caracas* the flight to Caracas
◆ **Entré despacito para no despertarla.** I went in slowly so as not to wake her.
◆ **para que te acuerdes de mí** so that you remember me

la **parabólica** SUSTANTIVO
satellite dish

el **parabrisas** SUSTANTIVO (PL los **parabrisas**)
windshield

el **paracaídas** SUSTANTIVO (PL los **paracaídas**)
parachute

el/la **paracaidista** SUSTANTIVO
1 paratrooper (*soldado*)
2 parachutist (*civil*)

el **parachoques** SUSTANTIVO (PL los **parachoques**)
fender

la **parada** SUSTANTIVO
stop ◇ *Hicimos una parada corta para descansar.* We made a short stop to rest.
◆ **una parada de autobús** a bus stop
◆ **una parada de taxis** a taxi stand

el **paradero** SUSTANTIVO
bus stop

parado ADJETIVO
standing ◇ *Estuve toda la mañana parado.* I was standing all morning.
◆ **No te quedes ahí parado.** Don't just stand there.

el **paraguas** SUSTANTIVO (PL los **paraguas**)
umbrella

Paraguay SUSTANTIVO MASC
Paraguay

el **paraguayo**, la **paraguaya** ADJETIVO, SUSTANTIVO
Paraguayan

el **paraíso** SUSTANTIVO
paradise

el **paralelo** ADJETIVO, SUSTANTIVO
parallel

la **parálisis** SUSTANTIVO (PL las **parálisis**)

paralysis (PL paralyses)
◆ **parálisis cerebral** cerebral palsy

paralítico ADJETIVO
◆ **Está paralítico.** He's paralyzed.

el **parapente** SUSTANTIVO
1 paragliding (*deporte*)
2 paraglider (*aparato*)

parar VERBO
to stop ◇ *Paramos a poner gasolina.* We stopped to get some gas. ◇ *No paró de llover en toda la noche.* It didn't stop raining all night.
◆ **Nos equivocamos de tren y fuimos a parar a Filadelfia.** We got on the wrong train and ended up in Philadelphia.
◆ **pararse (1)** to stop ◇ *El reloj se paró.* The clock has stopped.
◆ **pararse (2)** (*ponerse de pie*) to stand up
◆ **hablar sin parar** to talk nonstop

el **pararrayos** SUSTANTIVO (PL los **pararrayos**)
lightning rod

la **parcela** SUSTANTIVO
plot of land

el **parche** SUSTANTIVO
patch (PL patches)

el **parchís** SUSTANTIVO
Parcheesi®

parcial ADJETIVO
1 partial (*retirada, victoria*) ◇ *un eclipse parcial* a partial eclipse
◆ **a tiempo parcial** part-time
2 biased (*árbitro, juicio*)

el **parcial** SUSTANTIVO
midterm exam

parecer* VERBO
1 to seem ◇ *Parece muy simpática.* She seems very nice. ◇ *Todo parecía indicar que estaba muy interesado.* It all seemed to indicate that he was interested.
◆ **Parece mentira que ya haya pasado tanto tiempo.** I can't believe it has been so long.
2 to look ◇ *Parece más joven.* He looks younger.
◆ **Parece una modelo.** She looks like a model.
◆ **Parece que va a llover.** It looks as if it's going to rain.
3 to think ◇ *¿Qué te pareció la película?* What did you think of the movie? ◇ *Me parece bien que los multen.* I think it's right that they should be fined.
◆ **Me parece que sí.** I think so.
◆ **Me parece que no.** I don't think so.
◆ **si te parece bien** if that's all right with you
◆ **parecerse** to look alike ◇ *María y Ana se parecen mucho.* María and Ana look very much alike.
◆ **parecerse a** to look like ◇ *Te pareces mucho a tu mamá.* You look a lot like your mother.

parecido ADJETIVO
similar ◇ *Las casas son todas parecidas.* The houses are all similar. ◇ *Tu blusa es parecida a la mía.* Your blouse is similar to mine.
◆ **o algo parecido** or something like that

la **pared** SUSTANTIVO
wall

la **pareja** SUSTANTIVO
1 couple (*hombre y mujer*) ◇ *Había varias parejas bailando.* There were several couples dancing.
2 pair ◇ *En este juego hay que formar parejas.* For this game you have to get into pairs.
3 partner (*compañero*) ◇ *Vino con su pareja.* He came with his partner.

parejo ADJETIVO
even (*superficie, color*)

el **paréntesis** SUSTANTIVO (PL los **paréntesis**)
parenthesis (PL parentheses) ◇ *entre paréntesis* in parenthesis

el/la **pariente** SUSTANTIVO
relative ◇ *Es pariente mío.* He's a relative of mine.
No confundir ***pariente*** *con* ***parent.***

París SUSTANTIVO MASC
Paris

el/la **parisiense** ADJETIVO, SUSTANTIVO
Parisian

el **parisino**, la **parisina** ADJETIVO, SUSTANTIVO
Parisian

el **parking** SUSTANTIVO (PL los **parkings**) Spain
parking lot

el **parlamento** SUSTANTIVO
parliament

parlanchín ADJETIVO (FEM **parlanchina**, MASC PL **parlanchines**)
chatty

el **parlante** SUSTANTIVO
loudspeaker

el **paro** SUSTANTIVO
1 strike (*huelga*) ◇ *un paro de tres días* a three-day strike ◇ *Los profesores están en paro.* The teachers are on strike.
2 unemployment (*desempleo*) Spain

parpadear VERBO
to blink

el **párpado** SUSTANTIVO
eyelid

el **parque** SUSTANTIVO
park ◇ *un parque nacional* a national park
◆ **un parque de diversiones** an amusement park
◆ **un parque temático** a theme park
◆ **un parque zoológico** a zoo

el **parquímetro** SUSTANTIVO
parking meter

la **parra** SUSTANTIVO
vine

el **párrafo** SUSTANTIVO
paragraph

la **parrilla** SUSTANTIVO
1 grill
◆ **carne a la parrilla** barbecued meat

P

☞

[2] roof rack (*de carro*)

la **parrillada** SUSTANTIVO
grill

el **párroco** SUSTANTIVO
parish priest

la **parroquia** SUSTANTIVO
parish (PL parishes)

la **parte** SUSTANTIVO
[1] part ◇ *El examen está compuesto de dos partes.* The exam consists of two parts. ◇ *¿De qué parte de Estados Unidos eres?* What part of the United States are you from?
[2] share ◇ *mi parte de la herencia* my share of the inheritance
También se traduce por ***-where*** *en palabras compuestas.*
◇ *Tengo que haberlo dejado en alguna parte.* I must have left it somewhere. ◇ *por todas partes* everywhere
◆ **en parte** partly ◇ *Se debe en parte a su falta de experiencia.* It's partly due to his lack of experience.
◆ **la mayor parte de los mexicanos** most Mexican people
◆ **la parte delantera** the front
◆ **la parte de atrás** the back
◆ **la parte de arriba** the top
◆ **la parte de abajo** the bottom
◆ **por una parte..., por otra...** on the one hand..., on the other hand...
◆ **Llamo de parte de Juan.** I'm calling on behalf of Juan.
◆ **¿De parte de quién?** (*al teléfono*) Who's calling please?
◆ **Estoy de tu parte.** I'm on your side.

participar VERBO
to take part
◆ **participar en un concurso** to take part in a competition

el **participio** SUSTANTIVO
participle

particular ADJETIVO
private ◇ *clases particulares* private classes
◆ **El vestido no tiene nada de particular.** The dress is nothing special.
◆ **en particular** in particular

la **partida** SUSTANTIVO
[1] game ◇ *echar una partida de cartas* to have a game of cards
[2] certificate ◇ *partida de nacimiento* birth certificate

partidario ADJETIVO
◆ **ser* partidario de algo** to be in favor of something

el **partidario**, la **partidaria** SUSTANTIVO
supporter

el **partido** SUSTANTIVO
[1] party (PL parties) (*político*)
[2] game (*de fútbol, tenis*) ◇ *un partido de ajedrez* a game of chess
◆ **Sabe sacarle partido a todo.** He knows how to make the most out of everything.

partir VERBO
[1] to cut (*tarta, sandía*)
[2] to crack (*nuez, almendra*)
[3] to break off (*rama, tableta de chocolate*)
[4] to leave ◇ *La expedición partirá mañana de Lima.* The expedition is to leave from Lima tomorrow.
◆ **a partir de enero** from January ◇ *a partir de ahora* from now on
◆ **partirse** to break ◇ *El remo se partió en dos.* The oar broke in two.
◆ **partirse de risa** to split one's sides laughing

la **partitura** SUSTANTIVO
score

el **parto** SUSTANTIVO
birth
◆ **estar* de parto** to be in labor

la **pasa** SUSTANTIVO
raisin

pasado ADJETIVO
[1] last ◇ *el verano pasado* last summer
[2] after ◇ *Pasado el semáforo verás un cine.* After the traffic lights you'll see a movie theater. ◇ *Volvió pasadas las tres de la mañana.* He returned after three in the morning.
◆ **pasado mañana** the day after tomorrow
◆ **un sombrero pasado de moda** an old-fashioned hat

el **pasado** SUSTANTIVO
past ◇ *en el pasado* in the past

el **pasador** SUSTANTIVO
[1] hair clip (*de pelo*)
[2] tiepin (*de corbata*)

el **pasaje** SUSTANTIVO
[1] ticket (*de barco, avión*)
◆ **un pasaje electrónico** an e-ticket
[2] passage (*de un texto*)

pasajero ADJETIVO
[1] temporary (*dolor, molestia*)
[2] passing (*moda, fase*)

el **pasajero**, la **pasajera** SUSTANTIVO
passenger

el **pasamanos** SUSTANTIVO (PL los **pasamanos**)
banister

el **pasaporte** SUSTANTIVO
passport

pasar VERBO
[1] to pass ◇ *¿Me pasas la sal, por favor?* Can you pass me the salt, please?
◆ **Cuando termines pásasela a Isabel.** When you've finished pass it on to Isabel.
◆ **La foto fue pasando de mano en mano.** The photo was passed around.
◆ **Cuando muera la empresa pasará al hijo.** When he dies, the company will go to his son.
◆ **Un momento, te paso con Pedro.** Just a moment, I'll put you on to Pedro.

* Verbs marked with this symbol are irregular. See pages 346–348 for further details.

2 to go past ◇ *Pasaron varios carros.* A number of cars went past. ◇ *El autobús pasó de largo.* The bus went straight past.
- **¡Pase, por favor!** Please come in.
- **El tiempo pasa deprisa.** Time goes so quickly.
- **Pasaron cinco años.** Five years went by.
- **Ya ha pasado una hora.** It's been an hour already.

3 to spend ◇ *Voy a pasar el fin de semana con ella.* I'm going to spend the weekend with her. ◇ *Me pasé el fin de semana estudiando.* I spent the weekend studying.

4 to happen ◇ *Por suerte no le pasó nada.* Luckily nothing happened to him. ◇ *pase lo que pase* whatever happens
- **¿Qué pasa? (1)** (*¿cuál es el problema?*) What's the matter?
- **¿Qué pasa? (2)** (*¿qué está ocurriendo?*) What's happening?
- **¿Qué le pasa a Juan?** What's the matter with Juan?
- **pasar la aspiradora** to do the vacuuming
- **pasarlo bien** to have a good time
- **pasarlo mal** to have a bad time
- **Hemos pasado mucho frío.** We were very cold.
- **Están pasando hambre.** They are starving.
- **pasar algo a máquina** to type something
- **pasar por (1)** to go though ◇ *Pasamos por un túnel muy largo.* We went through a very long tunnel. ◇ *No creo que el sofá pase por esa puerta.* I don't think the sofa will go through the door. ◇ *pasar por la aduana* to go through customs ◇ *Está pasando por un mal momento.* He's going through a bad patch. ◇ *No pasamos por la ciudad.* We don't go through the city.
- **pasar por (2)** to go past ◇ *Ese autobús pasa por mi colegio.* That bus goes past my school.
- **No puedo pasar sin teléfono.** I can't get by without a telephone.
- **Está bien hacer ejercicio pero no hay que pasarse.** It's OK to exercise but there's no point in overdoing it.
- **Podrían perfectamente pasar por gemelos.** They could easily pass for twins.
- **pasarse de moda** to go out of fashion

el **pasatiempo** SUSTANTIVO
hobby (PL hobbies)

la **Pascua** SUSTANTIVO
Easter (*Semana Santa*)
- **¡Felices Pascuas!** Merry Christmas!

el **pase** SUSTANTIVO
pass (PL passes) ◇ *un pase gratis* a free pass
- **un pase de modelos** a fashion show

pasear VERBO
to walk
- **ir* a pasear** to go for a walk

el **paseo** SUSTANTIVO
walk ◇ *Salimos a dar un paseo.* We went out for a walk.
- **ir* de paseo** to go for a walk
- **un paseo en barco** a boat trip
- **un paseo en bicicleta** a bike ride
- **el paseo marítimo** the promenade

el **pasillo** SUSTANTIVO
1 corridor (*de casa, oficina*)
2 aisle (*de cine, avión*)

la **pasión** SUSTANTIVO (PL las **pasiones**)
passion

pasivo ADJETIVO
passive

pasmado ADJETIVO
amazed ◇ *Cuando me enteré me quedé pasmado.* I was amazed when I found out.

el **paso** SUSTANTIVO
1 step ◇ *Dio un paso hacia atrás.* He took a step backwards. ◇ *paso a paso* step by step
- **He oído pasos.** I heard footsteps.
- **Vive a un paso de aquí.** He lives right near here.
- **A ese paso no terminarán nunca.** At this rate they'll never finish.

2 way ◇ *Cerraron el paso.* They've blocked the way. ◇ *La policía le abría paso.* The police made way for him.
- **"Ceda el paso"** "Yield"
- **"Prohibido el paso"** "No entry"
- **El banco me queda de paso.** The bank is on my way.
- **Están de paso por Buenos Aires.** They're just passing through Buenos Aires.
- **un paso de peatones** a crosswalk

la **pasta** SUSTANTIVO
1 pasta (*macarrones, fideos*)
2 dough (*coloquial: dinero*)
- **pasta de dientes** toothpaste

pastar VERBO
to graze

el **pastel** SUSTANTIVO
cake

la **pastelería** SUSTANTIVO
patisserie

la **pastilla** SUSTANTIVO
1 pill (*medicina*)
- **pastillas para la tos** cough drops

2 bar (*de jabón*)
3 piece (*de chocolate*)

el **pasto** SUSTANTIVO
grass

el **pastor** SUSTANTIVO
shepherd
- **un pastor alemán** a German shepherd
- **un perro pastor** a sheepdog

la **pastora** SUSTANTIVO
shepherdess

la **pata** SUSTANTIVO
leg (*de animal, mueble*) ◇ *las patas de la silla* the chair legs
- **saltar a la pata coja** to hop
- **Encontramos la casa patas arriba.** We found the house in a big mess.

P

◆ **¡Volví a meter la pata!** I've gone and put my foot in it again!
◆ **Me parece que metí la pata en el examen de física.** I think I messed up my physics exam.

la **patada** SUSTANTIVO
◆ **Me dio una patada.** He kicked me.

Patagonia SUSTANTIVO FEM
Patagonia

la **patata** SUSTANTIVO Spain
potato (PL potatoes)

el **paté** SUSTANTIVO (PL los **patés**)
paté

paterno ADJETIVO
paternal

las **patillas** SUSTANTIVO
1 sideburns ◇ *dejarse patillas* to grow sideburns
2 arms (*de anteojos*)

el **patín** SUSTANTIVO (PL los **patines**)
1 roller skate (*con ruedas*)
2 ice skate (*de hielo*)
3 pedal boat (*de playa*)

el **patinaje** SUSTANTIVO
1 roller skating (*sobre ruedas*)
2 ice skating (*sobre hielo*)
◆ **patinaje artístico** figure skating

patinar VERBO
1 to roller-skate (*sobre ruedas*)
2 to ice-skate (*sobre hielo*)
3 to skid (*vehículo*)

la **patineta** SUSTANTIVO Mexico
scooter

el **patinete** SUSTANTIVO
scooter

el **patio** SUSTANTIVO
1 playground (*de colegio*)
2 courtyard (*de convento, edificio de departamentos*)
◆ **el patio de butacas** the orchestra seats PL

el **pato** SUSTANTIVO
duck

patoso ADJETIVO
clumsy

la **patria** SUSTANTIVO
homeland

patriota ADJETIVO
patriotic

el **patrocinador**, la **patrocinadora** SUSTANTIVO
sponsor

patrocinar VERBO
to sponsor

el **patrón** SUSTANTIVO (PL los **patrones**)
1 patron saint (*santo*)
2 boss (PL bosses) (*en trabajo*)

la **patrona** SUSTANTIVO
1 patron saint (*santa*)
2 landlady (PL landladies) (*de pensión*)

la **patrulla** SUSTANTIVO
patrol ◇ *estar de patrulla* to be on patrol

la **pausa** SUSTANTIVO
1 pause (*al hablar, leer*)
2 break (*en medio de programa, reunión*)

el **pavimento** SUSTANTIVO
1 paving (*de calle*)
2 surface (*de carretera*)

el **pavo** SUSTANTIVO
turkey
◆ **un pavo real** a peacock

el **payaso**, la **payasa** SUSTANTIVO
clown
◆ **Deja de hacer el payaso.** Stop clowning around.

la **paz** SUSTANTIVO (PL las **paces**)
peace
◆ **¡Déjame en paz!** Leave me alone!
◆ **Ha hecho las paces con su novio.** She's made up with her boyfriend.

el **PC** ABREVIATURA
PC (PL PCs)

P.D. ABREVIATURA (= *posdata*)
P.S.

el **peaje** SUSTANTIVO
toll

el **peatón** SUSTANTIVO (PL los **peatones**)
pedestrian

la **peca** SUSTANTIVO
freckle

el **pecado** SUSTANTIVO
sin

pecar* VERBO
to sin

el **pecho** SUSTANTIVO
1 chest (*tórax*)
2 breast (*de mujer*)
◆ **dar* el pecho a un niño** to breast-feed a baby
◆ **¡No te lo tomes a pecho! Era una broma.** Don't take it to heart. I was only joking.

la **pechuga** SUSTANTIVO
breast

el **pedal** SUSTANTIVO
pedal ◇ *el pedal del freno* the brake pedal

pedalear VERBO
to pedal

pedante ADJETIVO
pedantic

el **pedazo** SUSTANTIVO
piece ◇ *un pedazo de pan* a piece of bread
◆ **hacer* pedazos (1)** (*jarrón*) to smash
◆ **hacer* pedazos (2)** (*carta*) to tear up

el/la **pediatra** SUSTANTIVO
pediatrician

el **pedido** SUSTANTIVO
order ◇ *hacer un pedido* to place an order

pedir* VERBO
1 to ask for ◇ *Le pedí dinero a mi padre.* I asked my father for some money. ◇ *He pedido hora para el médico.* I've asked for a doctor's appointment.
2 to ask ◇ *¿Te puedo pedir un favor?* Can I

ask you a favor? ◇ *¿Cuánto pide por el carro?* How much is he asking for the car?
◆ **Pedí que me enviaran la información por correo.** I asked them to mail me the information.
[3] to order ◇ *Yo pedí paella.* I ordered paella.
◆ **Le pedí disculpas.** I apologized to him.
◆ **Tuve que pedir dinero prestado.** I had to borrow some money.

el **pedo** SUSTANTIVO
fart (*vulgar*)
◆ **tirarse un pedo** to fart (*vulgar*)

pegajoso ADJETIVO
[1] sticky (*sustancia, calor*)
[2] catchy (*canción*)

el **pegamento** SUSTANTIVO
glue

pegar* VERBO
[1] to hit ◇ *Andrés me pegó.* Andrés hit me. ◇ *La pelota pegó en el árbol.* The ball hit the tree.
[2] to stick ◇ *Lo puedes pegar con pegamento.* You can stick it on with glue. ◇ *Tengo que pegar las fotos en el álbum.* I have to stick the photos in the album.
◆ **Se te va a pegar el arroz.** Be careful or the rice will stick.
[3] to give ◇ *Le pegaron un tremendo empujón.* They gave him a great push. ◇ *Le pegó una bofetada.* He gave him a slap. ◇ *Me pegaste la gripe.* You've given me the flu. ◇ *¡Qué susto me pegaste!* What a fright you gave me!
◆ **Pegó un grito.** He shouted.
◆ **Le pegaron un tiro.** They shot him.
[4] to look right ◇ *Ese jarrón no pega aquí.* This vase doesn't look right here.
◆ **Esta camisa no pega con el traje.** This shirt doesn't look right with the suit.
◆ **El niño se pegó a su madre.** The boy clung to his mother.

la **pegatina** SUSTANTIVO
sticker

el **peinado** SUSTANTIVO
hairstyle

peinar VERBO
[1] to comb (*con peine*) ◇ *Péinate antes de salir.* Comb your hair before you go out.
[2] to brush (*con cepillo*) ◇ *Su madre la estaba peinando.* Her mother was brushing her hair.
◆ **Mañana voy a peinarme.** I'm going to have my hair done tomorrow.

el **peine** SUSTANTIVO
comb

p. ej. ABREVIATURA (= *por ejemplo*)
e.g.

pelar VERBO
[1] to peel (*papas, naranjas*)
[2] to shell (*nueces*)
◆ **Se me está pelando la espalda.** My back is peeling.
◆ **Hace un frío que pela.** It's bitterly cold.

el **peldaño** SUSTANTIVO
[1] step (*de escalera*)
[2] rung (*de escalera de mano*)

la **pelea** SUSTANTIVO
[1] fight (*lucha*) ◇ *Hubo una pelea en la discoteca.* There was a fight at the disco.
[2] argument (*discusión*) ◇ *Tuvo una pelea con su novio.* She had an argument with her boyfriend.

peleado ADJETIVO
◆ **Están peleados.** They've had a quarrel.

pelear VERBO
[1] to fight (*luchar*) ◇ *¡Deja de pelear con tu hermano!* Stop fighting with your brother! ◇ *Dos niños se estaban peleando en el patio.* There were two children fighting in the playground.
[2] to argue (*discutir*) ◇ *Pelean por cualquier tontería.* They argue over the slightest thing.

el **pelícano** SUSTANTIVO
pelican

la **película** SUSTANTIVO
movie ◇ *A las ocho ponen una película.* There's a movie on at eight.
◆ **una película de dibujos animados** a cartoon
◆ **una película del oeste** a western
◆ **una película de suspense** a thriller

el **peligro** SUSTANTIVO
danger ◇ *Está fuera de peligro.* He's out of danger.

peligroso ADJETIVO
dangerous

pelirrojo ADJETIVO
◆ **es pelirrojo** he has red hair

el **pellejo** SUSTANTIVO
skin
◆ **No me gustaría estar en su pellejo.** I wouldn't like to be in his shoes.
◆ **arriesgar el pellejo** to risk one's neck (*coloquial*)

pellizcar* VERBO
to pinch ◇ *Me pellizcó el brazo.* He pinched my arm.

el **pellizco** SUSTANTIVO
pinch ◇ *un pellizco de sal* a pinch of salt

el **pelmazo,** la **pelmaza** SUSTANTIVO
bore (*coloquial*)

el **pelo** SUSTANTIVO
hair ◇ *Tiene el pelo rizado.* He has curly hair.
◆ **No perdí el avión por un pelo.** I just caught the plane by a whisker.
◆ **Se me pusieron los pelos de punta.** It made my hair stand on end.
◆ **Me estás tomando el pelo.** You're pulling my leg.

la **pelota** SUSTANTIVO
ball ◇ *jugar a la pelota* to play ball

la **peluca** SUSTANTIVO

P

☞

wig

peludo ADJETIVO
hairy

la **peluquera** SUSTANTIVO
hairdresser

la **peluquería** SUSTANTIVO
hairdresser's

el **peluquero** SUSTANTIVO
hairdresser

la **pena** SUSTANTIVO
shame ◇ *Es una pena que no puedas venir.* It's a shame you can't come. ◇ *¡Qué pena!* What a shame!
◆ **Me dio tanta pena el pobre animal.** I felt so sorry for the poor animal.
◆ **Me da pena tener que marcharme.** I'm so sad to have to go away.
◆ **No tengas pena.** Don't be embarrassed.
◆ **Vale la pena.** It's worth it.
◆ **No vale la pena gastarse tanto dinero.** It's not worth spending so much money.
◆ **la pena de muerte** the death penalty

el **penalty** SUSTANTIVO (PL los **penaltys**)
penalty (PL penalties) ◇ *pitar penalty* (*fútbol*) to award a penalty

el **pendejo,** la **pendeja** SUSTANTIVO
nerd (*coloquial*)

pendiente ADJETIVO
◆ **Tenemos un par de asuntos pendientes.** We have a couple of matters to sort out.
◆ **Tiene una asignatura pendiente.** He has to take one subject over again.
◆ **Estaban pendientes de ella.** They were watching her intently.

el **pendiente** SUSTANTIVO
earring

la **pendiente** SUSTANTIVO
slope

el **pene** SUSTANTIVO
penis (PL penises)

penetrar VERBO
◆ **penetrar en** to find one's way into ◇ *Ocho hombres armados penetraron en la embajada.* Eight gunmen found their way into the embassy. ◇ *La luz apenas penetra en la cueva.* The light hardly finds its way into the cave.

la **penicilina** SUSTANTIVO
penicillin

la **península** SUSTANTIVO
peninsula
◆ **la Península Ibérica** the Iberian Peninsula

el **penique** SUSTANTIVO
penny (PL pennies)

el **pensamiento** SUSTANTIVO
[1] thought (*mental*)
[2] pansy (PL pansies) (*flor*)

pensar* VERBO
[1] to think ◇ *Piénsalo bien antes de responder.* Think carefully before you answer. ◇ *¿Piensas que vale la pena?* Do you think it's worth it? ◇ *¿Qué piensas de Manolo?* What do you think of Manolo?
◆ **¿Qué piensas del aborto?** What do you think about abortion?
[2] to think about ◇ *Tengo que pensarlo.* I'll have to think about it.
◆ **Sólo piensa en pasarlo bien.** All he thinks about is having a good time.
◆ **Estaba pensando en ir al cine esta tarde.** I was thinking of going to the movies this evening.
◆ **¡Ni pensarlo!** No way! (*coloquial*)
◆ **pensándolo bien...** on second thoughts...
◆ **Piénsatelo.** Think it over.

pensativo ADJETIVO
pensive

la **pensión** SUSTANTIVO (PL las **pensiones**)
[1] pension (*de jubilación, viudedad*)
[2] guest house (*casa de huéspedes*)

el/la **pensionista** SUSTANTIVO
pensioner

penúltimo ADJETIVO
◆ **la penúltima estación** the next to last station

el **penúltimo,** la **penúltima** SUSTANTIVO
◆ **Soy el penúltimo.** I'm next to last.

el **peñón** SUSTANTIVO (PL los **peñones**)
◆ **el Peñón de Gibraltar** the Rock of Gibraltar

el **peón** SUSTANTIVO (PL los **peones**)
[1] laborer (*albañil*)
[2] pawn (*en ajedrez*)

la **peonza** SUSTANTIVO
spinning top

peor ADJETIVO, ADVERBIO (FEM **peor**)
[1] worse (*comparativo*) ◇ *Su caso es peor que el nuestro.* His case is worse than ours. ◇ *Hoy me siento peor.* I feel worse today.
[2] worst (*superlativo*) ◇ *el peor día de mi vida* the worst day of my life ◇ *Sacó la peor nota de toda la clase.* He got the worst grade in the whole class.
◆ **el restaurante donde peor se come** the restaurant with the worst food
◆ **y lo peor es que...** and the worst thing is that...
◆ **Si no viene, peor para ella.** If she doesn't come, too bad for her.

el **pepinillo** SUSTANTIVO
gherkin

el **pepino** SUSTANTIVO
cucumber
◆ **Me importa un pepino lo que piense.** I couldn't care less what he thinks. (*coloquial*)

la **pepita** SUSTANTIVO
[1] seed (*de fruta*)
[2] nugget (*de oro*)

pequeño ADJETIVO
small ◇ *Prefiero los carros pequeños.* I prefer small cars. ◇ *Estos zapatos me quedan pequeños.* These shoes are too small for me.

* Verbs marked with this symbol are irregular. See pages 346–348 for further details.

- **¿Cuál prefieres? – El pequeño.** Which one do you prefer? – The small one.
- **Tuvimos un pequeño problema.** We had a slight problem.

el **pequinés** SUSTANTIVO
Pekinese

la **pera** SUSTANTIVO
pear

percatarse VERBO
- **percatarse de algo** to notice something

la **percha** SUSTANTIVO
1 coat hanger (*en un armario*)
2 coat hook (*en la pared*)

el **perchero** SUSTANTIVO
1 coat hook (*en la pared*)
2 coat rack (*de pie*)

la **percusión** SUSTANTIVO
percussion

perdedor (FEM **perdedora**) ADJETIVO
losing ◇ *la pareja perdedora* the losing pair

el **perdedor**, la **perdedora** SUSTANTIVO
loser ◇ *Eres mal perdedor.* You're a bad loser.

perder* VERBO
1 to lose ◇ *He perdido la cartera.* I've lost my purse. ◇ *Está intentando perder peso.* He's trying to lose weight. ◇ *perder el conocimiento* to lose consciousness ◇ *Perdimos dos a cero.* We lost two to nothing.
- **Se le perdieron las llaves.** He lost his keys.

2 to miss (*autobús, avión*) ◇ *Date prisa o perderás el tren.* Hurry up or you'll miss the train. ◇ *No quiero perder esta oportunidad.* I don't want to miss this opportunity.
- **¡No te lo pierdas!** Don't miss it!
- **¡Me estás haciendo perder el tiempo!** You're wasting my time!
- **Has echado a perder la sorpresa.** You've ruined the surprise.
- **Ana es la que saldrá perdiendo.** Ana is the one who will lose out.
- **Tenía miedo de perderme.** I was afraid of getting lost.

la **perdición** SUSTANTIVO
ruin

la **pérdida** SUSTANTIVO
1 loss (PL losses) (*de calor, peso*)
2 leak (*escape de líquido, gas*)
- **Fue una pérdida de tiempo.** It was a waste of time.

perdido ADJETIVO
1 lost ◇ *la oficina de objetos perdidos* the lost and found office
2 remote ◇ *un pueblecito perdido en la montaña* a remote little village in the mountains
- **Es tonto perdido.** He's a complete idiot.

el **perdigón** SUSTANTIVO (PL los **perdigones**)
pellet

la **perdiz** SUSTANTIVO (PL las **perdices**)
partridge

el **perdón** SUSTANTIVO
- **Le pedí perdón.** I apologized to him.
- **¡Perdón! (1)** (*para disculparse*) Sorry!
- **¡Perdón! (2)** (*para llamar la atención*) Excuse me!

perdonar VERBO
to forgive ◇ *¿Me perdonas?* Do you forgive me? ◇ *No perdona que me haya olvidado de su cumpleaños.* He hasn't forgiven me for forgetting his birthday.
- **¡Perdona! ¿Tienes hora?** Excuse me, do you have the time?
- **¡Perdona! ¿Te he hecho daño?** I'm so sorry. Did I hurt you?

el **peregrino**, la **peregrina** SUSTANTIVO
pilgrim

el **perejil** SUSTANTIVO
parsley

la **pereza** SUSTANTIVO
laziness
- **¡Qué pereza tengo!** I feel so lazy!
- **Me da pereza levantarme.** I can't be bothered to get up.

perezoso ADJETIVO
lazy

perfeccionar VERBO
to improve (*mejorar*) ◇ *Fue a Estados Unidos para perfeccionar el inglés.* He went to the United States to improve his English.

perfectamente ADVERBIO
perfectly

perfecto ADJETIVO
perfect

el **perfil** SUSTANTIVO
profile ◇ *un retrato de perfil* a profile portrait
- **ponerse* de perfil** to stand sideways

el **perfume** SUSTANTIVO
perfume

la **perfumería** SUSTANTIVO
perfume shop

periódico ADJETIVO
periodic

el **periódico** SUSTANTIVO
newspaper

el **periodismo** SUSTANTIVO
journalism

el/la **periodista** SUSTANTIVO
journalist ◇ *Mi tío es periodista.* My uncle is a journalist.

el **periodo** SUSTANTIVO
period ◇ *un periodo de tres meses* a three-month period
- **Tiene el periodo.** She has her period.

el **periquito** SUSTANTIVO
parakeet

perjudicar* VERBO
1 to damage (*salud, reputación*)
2 to be harmful to (*intereses, desarrollo, economía*) ◇ *Esta nueva ley puede*

P

perjudicarnos. This new law could be harmful to our interests.

◆ **El cambio ha perjudicado sus estudios.** The change has had an adverse effect on his studies.

perjudicial ADJETIVO
damaging

◆ **El tabaco es perjudicial para la salud.** Smoking damages your health.

la **perla** SUSTANTIVO
pearl

permanecer* VERBO
to remain

permanente ADJETIVO
permanent

la **permanente** SUSTANTIVO
permanent

◆ **hacerse* la permanente** to have a permanent

el **permiso** SUSTANTIVO
[1] permission ◇ *Tengo que pedirles permiso a mis padres.* I have to ask my parents' permission.
[2] leave ◇ *Pidió cinco días de permiso.* He requested five days' leave. ◇ *Mi hermano está de permiso.* My brother is on leave.
[3] permit (*documento*) ◇ *Necesitas un permiso de trabajo.* You need a work permit.

◆ **un permiso de conducir** a driver's license

◆ **¡Con permiso!** (*para abrirse paso*) Excuse me.

permitir VERBO
to allow ◇ *No nos permiten fumar en la oficina.* We're not allowed to smoke in the office.

◆ **No me lo puedo permitir.** I can't afford it.

◆ **¿Me permite?** May I?

pero CONJUNCIÓN
but ◇ *Me gustaría, pero no puedo.* I'd like to, but I can't.

perpendicular ADJETIVO
at right angles ◇ *una pared perpendicular a otra* one wall at right angles to another

perplejo ADJETIVO
puzzled

la **perra** SUSTANTIVO
dog ◇ *Es una perra muy buena.* She's a very good dog.

◆ **Las perras son más cariñosas.** Bitches are more affectionate.

la **perrera** SUSTANTIVO
kennel

el **perrito** SUSTANTIVO

◆ **un perrito caliente** a hot dog

el **perro** SUSTANTIVO
dog

◆ **un perro callejero** a stray dog

◆ **un perro guardián** a guard dog

◆ **un perro pastor** a sheepdog

◆ **un perro policía** a police dog

◆ **un perro salchicha** a dachshund

el/la **persa** ADJETIVO, SUSTANTIVO
Persian

perseguir* VERBO
[1] to chase (*delincuente*) ◇ *Me persigue la policía.* The police are chasing me.
[2] to persecute (*por ideología, raza*) ◇ *Se siente perseguido por su ideología.* He feels persecuted for his ideology.

la **persiana** SUSTANTIVO
blind

persiguiendo VERBO *ver* **perseguir**

la **persona** SUSTANTIVO
person ◇ *Es una persona encantadora.* He's a charming person.

◆ **en persona** in person

◆ **personas** people PL ◇ *Había unas diez personas en la sala.* There were about ten people in the hall.

el **personaje** SUSTANTIVO
[1] character ◇ *los personajes de la novela* the characters in the novel
[2] figure ◇ *un personaje público* a public figure

personal ADJETIVO
personal

el **personal** SUSTANTIVO
staff

la **personalidad** SUSTANTIVO
personality (PL personalities)

personalmente ADVERBIO
personally

la **perspectiva** SUSTANTIVO
perspective (*espacial*) ◇ *en perspectiva* in perspective

◆ **perspectivas** prospects ◇ *buenas perspectivas económicas* good economic prospects

persuadir VERBO
to persuade ◇ *Me persuadió para que la acompañara.* She persuaded me to go with her.

pertenecer* VERBO

◆ **pertenecer a** to belong to ◇ *Este reloj perteneció a su abuelo.* This watch belonged to his grandfather. ◇ *No pertenezco a ningún partido político.* I don't belong to any political party.

las **pertenencias** SUSTANTIVO
belongings

la **pértiga** SUSTANTIVO
pole

◆ **el salto con pértiga** the pole vault

Perú SUSTANTIVO MASC
Peru

el **peruano**, la **peruana** ADJETIVO, SUSTANTIVO
Peruvian

perverso ADJETIVO
wicked

el **pervertido**, la **pervertida** SUSTANTIVO

pervert

la **pesa** SUSTANTIVO
weight
- **hacer* pesas** to do weight training

la **pesadez** SUSTANTIVO
- **Es una pesadez tener que madrugar.** It's such a pain having to get up early. (*coloquial*)
- **¡Qué pesadez de película!** What a boring movie!

la **pesadilla** SUSTANTIVO
nightmare

pesado ADJETIVO
1 heavy (*paquete, comida*)
2 tiring (*trabajo, viaje*)
3 boring (*película, novela*)
- **¡No seas pesado!** Don't be a pain in the neck! (*coloquial*)

el **pesado**, la **pesada** SUSTANTIVO
- **Mi primo es un pesado.** My cousin is a pain in the neck. (*coloquial*)

el **pésame** SUSTANTIVO
condolences PL ◇ *Fuimos a darle el pésame.* We went to offer our condolences.

pesar VERBO
1 to weigh ◇ *El paquete pesaba dos kilos.* The package weighed two kilos. ◇ *¿Cuánto pesas?* How much do you weigh? ◇ *Tengo que pesarme.* I must weigh myself.
2 to be heavy ◇ *Esta maleta pesa mucho.* This suitcase is very heavy. ◇ *¡No pesa nada!* It's not heavy at all!
- **pesar poco** to be very light
- **Me pesa haberlo hecho.** I regret having done it.
- **a pesar del mal tiempo** in spite of the bad weather
- **a pesar de que la quiero** even though I love her

la **pesca** SUSTANTIVO
fishing ◇ *ir* de pesca* to go fishing

la **pescadería** SUSTANTIVO
fish market

la **pescadilla** SUSTANTIVO
whiting (PL whiting)

el **pescado** SUSTANTIVO
fish (PL fish) ◇ *Quiero comprar pescado.* I want to buy some fish.

el **pescador** SUSTANTIVO
fisherman (PL fishermen) ◇ *Mi tío es pescador.* My uncle is a fisherman.

pescar* VERBO
1 to fish ◇ *Los domingos íbamos a pescar.* On Sundays we used to go fishing.
2 to catch ◇ *Pescamos varias truchas.* We caught several trout. ◇ *Me pescaron fumando.* I got caught smoking.

el **pesero** SUSTANTIVO [Mexico]
minibus (PL minibuses)

la **peseta** SUSTANTIVO
peseta

pesimista ADJETIVO
pessimistic ◇ *una visión pesimista* a pessimistic view
- **No seas pesimista.** Don't be a pessimist.

el/la **pesimista** SUSTANTIVO
pessimist

pésimo ADJETIVO
terrible ◇ *La comida era pésima.* The food was terrible.

el **peso** SUSTANTIVO
1 weight ◇ *ganar peso* to gain weight ◇ *Ha perdido mucho peso.* He's lost a lot of weight.
- **La fruta se vende a peso.** Fruit is sold by weight.

2 scales PL (*en la cocina*)
3 peso (*moneda*)

pesquero ADJETIVO
fishing

***fishing** en este caso va siempre delante del sustantivo.*

◇ *un pueblecito pesquero* a fishing village

la **pestaña** SUSTANTIVO
eyelash (PL eyelashes)

pestañear VERBO
to blink

la **peste** SUSTANTIVO
1 plague (*enfermedad*)
2 stink (*mal olor*) ◇ *¡Qué peste hay aquí!* There's a real stink in here!

el **pesticida** SUSTANTIVO
pesticide

el **pestillo** SUSTANTIVO
1 bolt (*de puerta, ventana*)
2 latch (PL latches) (*de cerradura*)

la **petaca** SUSTANTIVO
hip flask (*botella*)

el **pétalo** SUSTANTIVO
petal

el **petardo** SUSTANTIVO
firecracker

la **petición** SUSTANTIVO (PL las **peticiones**)
1 request (*ruego*) ◇ *Hicieron una petición al gobierno.* They made a request to the government. ◇ *a petición de la pareja* at the couple's request
2 petition (*escrito*) ◇ *firmar una petición* to sign a petition

el **petirrojo** SUSTANTIVO
robin

el **petróleo** SUSTANTIVO
oil

el **petrolero** SUSTANTIVO
oil tanker

el **pez** SUSTANTIVO (PL los **peces**)
fish (PL fish) ◇ *Cogimos tres peces.* We caught three fish.
- **un pez de colores** a goldfish
- **Se sentía como el pez en el agua.** He felt in his element.

la **pezuña** SUSTANTIVO
hoof (PL hooves)

P

el/la **pianista** SUSTANTIVO
pianist ◇ *Soy pianista.* I'm a pianist.

el **piano** SUSTANTIVO
piano
◆ **un piano de cola** a grand piano

piar* VERBO
to chirp

la **picada** SUSTANTIVO
◆ **El avión cayó en picada.** The plane took a nosedive.

picado ADJETIVO
1 bad (*diente*)
2 choppy (*mar*)
◆ **El avión cayó en picado.** Spain The plane took a nosedive.

la **picadura** SUSTANTIVO
1 bite (*de mosquito, serpiente*)
2 sting (*de avispa, abeja*)

picante ADJETIVO
hot (*comida, salsa*)

el **picaporte** SUSTANTIVO
door handle

picar* VERBO
1 to bite (*mosquito, serpiente*) ◇ *Me han picado los mosquitos.* I've been bitten by mosquitoes.
2 to sting (*avispa, abeja*)
3 to chop up (*cebolla, pimiento*) ◇ *Luego picas un poquito de jamón.* Then you chop up a bit of ham.
4 to grind (*carne*)
◆ **La salsa pica bastante.** The sauce is quite hot.
◆ **Saqué algunas cosas para picar.** I put out some things to nibble on.
◆ **Me pica la espalda.** I have an itchy back.
◆ **Me pica la garganta.** My throat tickles.

el **pichi** SUSTANTIVO Spain
jumper

el **picnic** SUSTANTIVO (PL los **picnics**)
picnic

el **pico** SUSTANTIVO
1 beak (*de ave*)
2 peak (*de montaña*)
3 pickax (PL pickaxes) (*herramienta*)
◆ **Eran las tres y pico.** It was after three.
◆ **tres mil pesos y pico** over three thousand pesos
◆ **cuello de pico** V-neck
◆ **la hora pico** the rush hour

picoso ADJETIVO Mexico
hot (*comida*)

pidiendo VERBO *ver* **pedir**

el **pie** SUSTANTIVO
foot (PL feet) ◇ *Fuimos a pie.* We went on foot. ◇ *Al pie de la página hay una explicación.* There's an explanation at the foot of the page.
◆ **Estaba de pie junto a mi cama.** He was standing next to my bed.
◆ **ponerse* de pie** to stand up
◆ **de pies a cabeza** from head to foot

la **piedad** SUSTANTIVO
mercy ◇ *tener piedad de alguien* to have mercy on someone

la **piedra** SUSTANTIVO
stone ◇ *Nos tiraban piedras.* They were throwing stones at us.
◆ **una piedra preciosa** a precious stone
◆ **Cuando me lo dijeron me quedé de piedra.** I was stunned when they told me.

la **piel** SUSTANTIVO
1 skin ◇ *Tengo la piel grasa.* I have oily skin.
2 fur ◇ *un abrigo de pieles* a fur coat
3 leather ◇ *un bolso de piel* a leather bag
4 peel (*de naranja, papa, manzana*)

pienso VERBO *ver* **pensar**

pierdo VERBO *ver* **perder**

la **pierna** SUSTANTIVO
leg
◆ **una pierna de cordero** a leg of lamb

la **pieza** SUSTANTIVO
piece ◇ *una pieza del rompecabezas* a piece of the jigsaw puzzle
◆ **una pieza de recambio** a spare part

el **pijama** SUSTANTIVO
pajamas PL

la **pila** SUSTANTIVO
1 battery (PL batteries) ◇ *Funciona con pilas.* It runs on batteries.
2 pile ◇ *una pila de revistas* a pile of magazines
3 sink (*fregadero*)

el **pilar** SUSTANTIVO
pillar

la **píldora** SUSTANTIVO
pill ◇ *¿Tomas la píldora?* Are you on the pill?

pillar VERBO
to catch ◇ *pillar a un ladrón* to catch a thief ◇ *¡Vaya catarro que has pillado!* That's a nasty cold you've caught. ◇ *Lo pillé fumando.* I caught him smoking.
◆ **Se pilló los dedos en la puerta.** He caught his fingers in the door.

pillo ADJETIVO
1 crafty (*astuto*)
2 naughty (*travieso*)

el/la **piloto** SUSTANTIVO
1 pilot (*de avión*)
2 driver (*de carro*)
◆ **piloto de carreras** race car driver

el **pimentón** SUSTANTIVO
paprika

la **pimienta** SUSTANTIVO
pepper ◇ *pimienta negra* black pepper

el **pimiento** SUSTANTIVO
pepper ◇ *un pimiento morrón* a red pepper

el **pincel** SUSTANTIVO
paintbrush (PL paintbrushes)

pinchar VERBO
[1] to prick ◇ *Me pinché con un alfiler.* I pricked myself with a pin.
[2] to burst ◇ *El clavo pinchó la pelota.* The nail burst the ball.
◆ **Me pincharon en el brazo.** They gave me an injection in the arm.
◆ **Se me pinchó una rueda.** I had a flat tire.
◆ **Los cactus pinchan.** Cactuses are prickly.

el **pinchazo** SUSTANTIVO
[1] puncture ◇ *Tuvieron un pinchazo en la autopista.* They got a puncture on the freeway.
[2] sharp pain (*de dolor*)

el **ping-pong** SUSTANTIVO
ping pong ◇ *jugar ping-pong* to play ping pong

el **pingüino** SUSTANTIVO
penguin

el **pino** SUSTANTIVO
pine tree

la **pinta** SUSTANTIVO
◆ **tener* buena pinta** to look good
◆ **La paella tiene muy buena pinta.** The paella looks delicious.
◆ **Con esos anteojos tienes pinta de maestra.** You look like a teacher with those glasses on.
◆ **irse* de pinta** *Mexico* to play hooky

las **pintadas** SUSTANTIVO *Spain*
graffiti

el **pintalabios** SUSTANTIVO (PL los **pintalabios**) *Spain*
lipstick

pintar VERBO
[1] to paint (*con pintura*) ◇ *Quiero pintar la habitación de azul.* I want to paint the room blue.
[2] to color in (*con lápices de colores*) ◇ *Dibujó un árbol y lo pintó.* He drew a tree and colored it in.
◆ **Nunca me pinto durante el día.** I never wear makeup during the day.
◆ **pintarse los labios** to put on lipstick
◆ **pintarse las uñas** to paint one's nails

el **pintor**, la **pintora** SUSTANTIVO
painter ◇ *Soy pintor.* I'm a painter.

pintoresco ADJETIVO
picturesque

la **pintura** SUSTANTIVO
[1] paint ◇ *Tengo que comprar más pintura.* I have to buy some more paint.
[2] painting ◇ *Me gusta la pintura abstracta.* I like abstract painting. ◇ *Tiene varias pinturas al óleo* He has several oil paintings

la **pinza** SUSTANTIVO
[1] clothespin (*para la ropa*)
[2] bobby pin (*para el pelo*)
[3] pincer (*de cangrejo*)
◆ **unas pinzas** (*para depilar*) a pair of tweezers

la **piña** SUSTANTIVO
[1] pine cone (*de pino*)
[2] pineapple (*fruta tropical*)

la **piñata** SUSTANTIVO

> ℹ *A* ***piñata*** *is a container containing sweets or presents which is hung up at parties and is beaten with sticks until the sweets or presents fall out.*

el **piñón** SUSTANTIVO (PL los **piñones**)
[1] pine nut (*del pino*)
[2] sprocket (*de bicicleta*)

el **piojo** SUSTANTIVO
louse (PL lice)

la **pipa** SUSTANTIVO
pipe ◇ *Fuma en pipa.* He smokes a pipe.

el **pipí** SUSTANTIVO
pee (*coloquial*) ◇ *hacer pipí* to take a pee

la **piragua** SUSTANTIVO
canoe (PL canoes)

el **piragüismo** SUSTANTIVO
canoeing

la **pirámide** SUSTANTIVO
pyramid

pirata ADJETIVO
pirate (*barco, video*)
pirate *en este caso va siempre delante del sustantivo.*

el/la **pirata** SUSTANTIVO
pirate
◆ **un pirata informático** (*informática*) a hacker

piratear VERBO
to hack into a system (*informática*)

los **Pirineos** SUSTANTIVO
the Pyrenees

el **piropo** SUSTANTIVO
compliment ◇ *Se puso colorada con el piropo.* The compliment made her blush.
◆ **echar piropos a alguien** to compliment someone

el **pirulí** SUSTANTIVO (PL los **pirulís**)
lollipop

la **pisada** SUSTANTIVO
[1] footprint (*huella*)
[2] footstep (*sonido*)

el **pisapapeles** SUSTANTIVO (PL los **pisapapeles**)
paperweight

pisar VERBO
[1] to walk on
◆ **¿Se puede pisar el suelo de la cocina?** Can I walk on the kitchen floor?
[2] to step on ◇ *Perdona, te pisé.* Sorry, I stepped on your foot.
◆ **Pisé el acelerador a fondo.** I put my foot down.

la **piscina** SUSTANTIVO
swimming pool

Piscis SUSTANTIVO MASC
Pisces ◇ *Soy piscis.* I'm a Pisces.

el **piso** SUSTANTIVO
[1] floor (*planta, suelo*) ◇ *Su oficina está en* ☞

P

el segundo piso. His office is on the third floor.

Nótese que en los Estados Unidos los pisos se enumeran de una manera distinta. "La planta baja" es "the first floor", "el primer piso" es "the second floor", "el segundo piso" es "the third floor" etc.

◇ *El piso estaba lleno de papeles.* The floor was covered in pieces of paper.

[2] apartment (*departamento*) [Spain]

la **pista** SUSTANTIVO

[1] clue (*dato*) ◇ *¿Te doy una pista?* Shall I give you a clue?

[2] track (*huella*) ◇ *Los cazadores siguen las pistas del animal.* The hunters follow the animal's tracks.

[3] court (*de deportes*) [Spain]

- **la pista de aterrizaje** the runway
- **la pista de baile** the dance floor
- **la pista de carreras** the racetrack
- **la pista de esquí** the ski slope
- **la pista de patinaje** the ice rink

la **pistola** SUSTANTIVO

pistol

pitar VERBO

[1] to blow one's whistle (*con silbato*) ◇ *El policía nos pitó.* The policeman blew his whistle at us.

[2] to blow one's horn (*con claxon*) ◇ *No sé por qué me pita.* I don't know why he's blowing his horn at me.

el **pito** SUSTANTIVO

whistle

- **Me importa un pito.** I don't care a hoot. (*coloquial*)

el **piyama** SUSTANTIVO

pajamas PL

la **pizarra** SUSTANTIVO

[1] chalkboard (*encerado*)

[2] slate (*mineral*)

el **pizarrón** SUSTANTIVO (PL los **pizarrones**)

chalkboard

la **pizca** SUSTANTIVO

pinch ◇ *una pizca de sal* a pinch of salt

la **pizza** SUSTANTIVO

pizza

la **placa** SUSTANTIVO

[1] plaque (*letrero*) ◇ *una placa conmemorativa* a commemorative plaque

[2] badge (*de policía*)

[3] plate (*de una cocina eléctrica*)

- **una placa de matrícula** a license plate

el **placer** SUSTANTIVO

pleasure

la **plaga** SUSTANTIVO

[1] pest ◇ *una plaga que estropea los cultivos* a pest that damages the crops

[2] plague ◇ *las plagas de Egipto* the plagues of Egypt

- **la plaga del terrorismo** the scourge of terrorism

el **plan** SUSTANTIVO

plan ◇ *¿Qué planes tienes para este verano?* What are your plans for the summer?

- **viajar en plan económico** to travel cheap
- **Lo dije en plan de broma.** I said it as a joke.
- **el plan de estudios** the syllabus

la **plancha** SUSTANTIVO

iron (*aparato*)

- **pescado a la plancha** grilled fish

planchar VERBO

[1] to iron ◇ *Tengo que planchar esta camisa.* I have to iron this shirt.

[2] to do the ironing ◇ *¿Quieres que planche?* Do you want me to do the ironing?

el **planeador** SUSTANTIVO

glider

planear VERBO

[1] to plan (*organizar*)

[2] to glide (*avión*)

el **planeta** SUSTANTIVO

planet

la **planificación** SUSTANTIVO

planning

- **planificación familiar** family planning

planificar* VERBO

to plan

plano ADJETIVO

flat (*superficie, zapato*)

el **plano** SUSTANTIVO

[1] street plan (*de la ciudad, el metro*)

[2] plan (*de edificio*)

- **en primer plano** in close-up

la **planta** SUSTANTIVO

[1] plant ◇ *regar las plantas* to water the plants

[2] floor ◇ *El edificio tiene tres plantas.* The building has three floors. ◇ *la planta baja* the first floor

- **la planta del pie** the sole of the foot

plantado ADJETIVO

- **dejar a alguien plantado** to stand someone up

plantar VERBO

to plant

plantear VERBO

to bring up ◇ *Se lo plantearé al jefe.* I'll bring it up with the boss.

- **Incluso me planteé dejar los estudios.** I even thought of giving up my studies.

la **plantilla** SUSTANTIVO

[1] insole (*de zapato*)

[2] staff (*de empresa*) [Spain]

el **plástico** SUSTANTIVO

plastic ◇ *utensilios de plástico* plastic utensils

la **plastilina**® SUSTANTIVO

Plasticine®

la **plata** SUSTANTIVO

1 silver (*metal*)
2 money (*dinero*)

la **plataforma** SUSTANTIVO
platform ◇ *zapatos de plataforma* platform shoes
◆ **una plataforma petrolífera** an oil rig

el **plátano** SUSTANTIVO
banana

platicar* VERBO Mexico
1 to talk (*hablar*) ◇ *Estuve platicando con Manuel.* I was talking to Manuel.
2 to tell (*decir*) ◇ *¿Qué te platicaron?* What did they tell you?

el **platillo** SUSTANTIVO
◆ **un platillo volador** a flying saucer
◆ **los platillos** (*instrumento musical*) the cymbals

el **platino** SUSTANTIVO
platinum

el **plato** SUSTANTIVO
1 plate ◇ *¿Me pasas un plato?* Could you pass me a plate?
2 dish (PL dishes) ◇ *un plato típico de Argentina* a typical Argentinian dish
◆ **el plato del día** the daily special
3 course ◇ *¿Qué hay de segundo plato?* What's the main course?
4 saucer (*para la taza*)

la **playa** SUSTANTIVO
1 beach (PL beaches) ◇ *Los niños jugaban en la playa.* The children were playing on the beach.
2 seaside (*costa*) ◇ *Prefiero la playa a la montaña.* I prefer the seaside to the mountains.

la **playera** SUSTANTIVO
1 canvas shoe (*zapatilla*)
2 T-shirt (*camiseta*) Mexico

la **plaza** SUSTANTIVO
1 square ◇ *la plaza del pueblo* the town square
◆ **la plaza mayor** the main square
◆ **una plaza de toros** a bullring
2 market ◇ *No había pescado en la plaza.* There was no fish at the market.
3 place (*en colegio, sala*) ◇ *Todavía quedan plazas.* There are still some places left.

el **plazo** SUSTANTIVO
1 period ◇ *en un plazo de diez días* within a period of ten days
◆ **El viernes se cumple el plazo.** Friday is the deadline.
2 installment ◇ *pagar a plazos* to pay in installments ◇ *comprar a plazos* to buy in installments
◆ **una solución a corto plazo** a short-term solution

plegable ADJETIVO
folding

plegar* VERBO
to fold

pleno ADJETIVO
◆ **en pleno verano** in the middle of summer
◆ **a plena luz del día** in broad daylight

la **pletina** SUSTANTIVO
tape deck

pliegue VERBO *ver* **plegar**

el **pliegue** SUSTANTIVO
1 fold (*en papel, tela*)
2 pleat (*de falda*)

el **plomero,** la **plomera** SUSTANTIVO
plumber

el **plomo** SUSTANTIVO
lead
◆ **gasolina sin plomo** unleaded gas

la **pluma** SUSTANTIVO
1 feather (*de ave*)
2 pen (*para escribir*)
◆ **una pluma atómica** Mexico a ballpoint pen
◆ **una pluma fuente** a fountain pen

el **plural** ADJETIVO, SUSTANTIVO
plural

la **población** SUSTANTIVO (PL las **poblaciones**)
1 population (*habitantes*)
2 town (*ciudad*)

pobre ADJETIVO
poor ◇ *Somos pobres.* We're poor.
◆ **¡Pobre Pedro!** Poor Pedro!
◆ **los pobres** the poor

la **pobreza** SUSTANTIVO
poverty

poco ADJETIVO, ADVERBIO, PRONOMBRE
not much ◇ *Hay poca leche.* There isn't much milk.
◆ **Tenemos muy poco tiempo.** We have very little time.
◆ **Sus libros son poco conocidos aquí.** His books are not very well known here.
◆ **un poco** a bit ◇ *¿Tienes frío? – Un poco.* Are you cold? – A bit. ◇ *¿Me das un poco?* Can I have a bit? ◇ *He bebido un poco, pero no estoy borracho.* I had a bit to drink, but I'm not drunk.
◆ **Tomé un poco de vino.** I drank a little wine.
◆ **pocos** not many ◇ *Tiene pocos amigos.* He doesn't have many friends.
◆ **unos pocos** a few ◇ *Me llevé unos pocos.* I took a few with me.
◆ **poco a poco** little by little
◆ **poco después** shortly after
◆ **dentro de poco** in a short time
◆ **hace poco** not long ago
◆ **por poco** nearly ◇ *Por poco me caigo.* I nearly fell.
◆ **de a poco** little by little
◆ **¡A poco!** Mexico Really!

la **podadora** SUSTANTIVO Mexico
lawn mower

podar VERBO
to prune

el **poder** SUSTANTIVO
power ◇ *estar en el poder* to be in power

P

poder* VERBO
[1] can
*El verbo **can** no tiene forma de infinitivo ni futuro. La forma del pasado es **could**.*
◇ *Yo puedo ayudarte.* I can help you. ◇ *¡No puede ser!* That can't be true! ◇ *¿Puedo usar tu teléfono?* Can I use your telephone? ◇ *Pudiste haberte hecho daño.* You could have hurt yourself. ◇ *¡Me lo podías haber dicho!* You could have told me! ◇ *Aquí no se puede fumar.* You can't smoke here.
[2] to be able to
*Para formar el futuro se utiliza **to be able to**.*
◇ *Creo que mañana no voy a poder ir.* I don't think I'll be able to come tomorrow.
◆ **¿Se puede?** May I?
◆ **Puede que llegue mañana.** He might arrive tomorrow.
◆ **Puede ser.** It's possible.
◆ **No puedo con tanto trabajo.** I can't cope with so much work.

poderoso ADJETIVO
powerful

el **podólogo,** la **podóloga** SUSTANTIVO
podiatrist

podrido ADJETIVO
rotten

podrirse VERBO = **pudrirse**

el **poema** SUSTANTIVO
poem

la **poesía** SUSTANTIVO
[1] poetry ◇ *Me gusta la poesía.* I like poetry.
[2] poem ◇ *una poesía de Neruda* a poem by Neruda

el/la **poeta** SUSTANTIVO
poet

el **póker** SUSTANTIVO
poker

polaco ADJETIVO
Polish

el **polaco,** la **polaca** SUSTANTIVO
Pole
◆ **los polacos** the Poles

el **polaco** SUSTANTIVO
Polish (*idioma*)

la **polémica** SUSTANTIVO
controversy (PL controversies)

polémico ADJETIVO
controversial

el **polen** SUSTANTIVO
pollen
◆ **alergia al polen** hay fever

el **policía** SUSTANTIVO
policeman (PL policemen) ◇ *Es policía.* He's a policeman.

la **policía** SUSTANTIVO
[1] police ◇ *Llamamos a la policía.* We called the police.
[2] policewoman (PL policewomen) (*mujer policía*) ◇ *Soy policía.* I'm a policewoman.

policíaco ADJETIVO
◆ **una novela policíaca** a detective story

la **polilla** SUSTANTIVO
moth

la **polio** SUSTANTIVO
polio

la **política** SUSTANTIVO
[1] politics SING ◇ *Hablaban de política.* They were talking about politics.
[2] policy (PL policies) ◇ *política exterior* foreign policy
[3] politician (*mujer*) ◇ *Soy política.* I'm a politician.

político ADJETIVO
political

el **político** SUSTANTIVO
politician

el **pollo** SUSTANTIVO
chicken
◆ **pollo asado** roast chicken

el **polluelo** SUSTANTIVO
chick

el **polo** SUSTANTIVO
[1] polo shirt (*camisa*)
[2] Popsicle® (*helado*) [Spain]
◆ **el Polo Norte** the North Pole
◆ **el Polo Sur** the South Pole

Polonia SUSTANTIVO FEM
Poland

el **polvo** SUSTANTIVO
dust
◆ **limpiar el polvo** to dust
◆ **quitar el polvo** to do the dusting
◆ **quitar el polvo a algo** to dust something
◆ **en polvo** powdered ◇ *leche en polvo* powdered milk
◆ **polvos de talco** talcum powder
◆ **Estoy hecho polvo.** I'm bushed. (*coloquial*)

la **pólvora** SUSTANTIVO
gunpowder

la **pomada** SUSTANTIVO
ointment

el **pomelo** SUSTANTIVO
grapefruit (PL grapefruit)

el **pomo** SUSTANTIVO
handle

la **pompa** SUSTANTIVO
[1] bubble (*burbuja*) ◇ *pompas de jabón* soap bubbles
[2] pomp (*ostentación*)

el **pómulo** SUSTANTIVO
cheekbone

la **ponchadura** SUSTANTIVO [Mexico]
puncture ◇ *Tuve una ponchadura en la carretera.* I got a puncture on the highway.

ponchar VERBO [Mexico]
◆ **Se nos ponchó una llanta.** We had a flat tire.

el **ponche** SUSTANTIVO
punch (PL punches)

el **poncho** SUSTANTIVO
poncho

pondrá VERBO *ver* **poner**

poner* VERBO
1 to put (*colocar*) ◇ *¿Dónde pongo mis cosas?* Where shall I put my things?
2 to put on (*prenda*) ◇ *Me puse el abrigo.* I put on my coat. ◇ *Voy a poner la leche.* I'm going to put the milk on. ◇ *¿Pongo música?* Shall I put some music on? ◇ *Pon el radiador.* Put the heater on.
- **No sé que ponerme.** I don't know what to wear.
- **Ponlo más alto.** Turn it up.

3 to set (*deberes, despertador*) ◇ *Puse el despertador para las siete.* I set the alarm for seven o'clock. ◇ *poner la mesa* to set the table
- **La maestra nos puso un examen.** Our teacher gave us an exam.

4 to put in (*instalar*) ◇ *Queremos poner calefacción.* We want to put in central heating.
- **Le pusieron Mónica.** They called her Monica.
- **Cuando se lo dije se puso muy triste.** He was very sad when I told him.
- **Se puso a mi lado en clase.** He sat down beside me in class.
- **ponerse a hacer algo** to start doing something

el **poni** SUSTANTIVO
pony (PL ponies)

pongo VERBO *ver* **poner**

pop ADJETIVO (FEM **pop**, PL **pop**)
pop ◇ *música pop* pop music

el **popote** SUSTANTIVO *Mexico*
straw

popular ADJETIVO
popular

por PREPOSICIÓN
1 for ◇ *Lo hice por mis padres.* I did it for my parents. ◇ *Lo vendió por dos mil pesos.* He sold it for two thousand pesos. ◇ *Me castigaron por mentir.* I was punished for lying.
2 through ◇ *La conozco por mi hermano.* I know her through my brother. ◇ *por la ventana* through the window ◇ *Pasamos por Mérida.* We went through Mérida.
3 by ◇ *Fueron apresados por la policía.* They were captured by the police. ◇ *por correo* by mail ◇ *Me agarró por el brazo.* He grabbed me by the arm.
4 along ◇ *Paseábamos por la playa.* We were walking along the beach.
5 around ◇ *viajar por el mundo* to travel around the world ◇ *Viven por esta zona.* They live around this area.
6 because of ◇ *Tuvo que suspenderse por el mal tiempo.* It had to be canceled because of bad weather.
7 per ◇ *100 millas por hora* 100 miles per hour ◇ *diez pesos por persona* ten pesos per person
- **por aquí cerca** near here
- **por escrito** in writing
- **por la mañana** in the morning
- **por la noche** at night
- **por mí...** as far as I'm concerned...
- **¿Por qué?** Why?

la **porcelana** SUSTANTIVO
porcelain

el **porcentaje** SUSTANTIVO
percentage

el **porche** SUSTANTIVO
porch (PL porches) (*de casa*)

la **porción** SUSTANTIVO (PL las **porciones**)
portion

porno (FEM **porno**, PL **porno**) ADJETIVO
porn
porn *en este caso va siempre delante del sustantivo.*
◇ *una película porno* a porn movie

la **pornografía** SUSTANTIVO
pornography

pornográfico ADJETIVO
pornographic

el **poro** SUSTANTIVO
1 pore (*en la piel*)
2 leek (*vegetal*) *Mexico*

porque CONJUNCIÓN
because ◇ *No fuimos porque llovía.* We didn't go because it was raining.

la **porquería** SUSTANTIVO
- **Este CD es una porquería.** This CD's garbage.

la **porra** SUSTANTIVO
billy club (*de policía*)
- **mandar a alguien a la porra** to tell someone to get lost (*coloquial*)

el **porrazo** SUSTANTIVO
- **Me di un porrazo en la rodilla.** I banged my knee.
- **Daba porrazos en la puerta.** He was banging on the door.

la **portada** SUSTANTIVO
1 front page (*de periódico*)
2 cover (*de revista*)

el **portal** SUSTANTIVO
1 hallway ◇ *Los buzones están en el portal.* The letterboxes are in the hallway.
2 portal (*Internet*)
- **el portal de Belén** the nativity scene

portarse VERBO
- **portarse bien** to behave well
- **portarse mal** to behave badly
- **Se portó muy bien conmigo.** He treated me very well.

portátil ADJETIVO
portable

el **portavoz** SUSTANTIVO (PL los **portavoces**)
spokesman (PL spokesmen)

la **portavoz** SUSTANTIVO (PL las **portavoces**)

P

☞

spokeswoman (PL spokeswomen)

el **portazo** SUSTANTIVO
- **Dio un portazo.** He slammed the door.

la **portera** SUSTANTIVO
1 janitor (*de edificio de departamentos*)
2 goalkeeper (*de equipo*)

la **portería** SUSTANTIVO
goal ◇ *El balón entró en la portería.* The ball went into the goal.

el **portero** SUSTANTIVO
1 janitor (*de edificio de departamentos*)
2 goalkeeper (*de equipo*)
- **un portero automático** a buzzer

el **portorriqueño**, la **portorriqueña** ADJETIVO, SUSTANTIVO
Puerto Rican

Portugal SUSTANTIVO MASC
Portugal

el **portugués**, la **portuguesa** ADJETIVO, SUSTANTIVO (MASC PL los **portugueses**)
Portuguese

el **portugués** SUSTANTIVO
Portuguese (*idioma*)

el **porvenir** SUSTANTIVO
future

posar VERBO
to pose ◇ *Posó para los fotógrafos.* He posed for photographs.
- **posarse** to land ◇ *El pájaro se posó en la rama.* The bird landed on the branch.

la **posdata** SUSTANTIVO
postscript

poseer* VERBO
to possess

la **posguerra** SUSTANTIVO
- **durante la posguerra** during the postwar period
- **los años de posguerra** the years after the war

la **posibilidad** SUSTANTIVO
1 possibility (PL possibilities) ◇ *Es una posibilidad.* It's a possibility.
2 chance ◇ *Tendrás la posibilidad de viajar.* You'll have the chance to travel.
- **Tiene muchas posibilidades de ganar.** He has a good chance of winning.

posible ADJETIVO
possible ◇ *Es posible.* It's possible.
- **hacer* todo lo posible** to do everything possible
- **Es posible que ganen.** They might win.

la **posición** SUSTANTIVO (PL las **posiciones**)
position ◇ *una posición estratégica* a strategic position
- **Está en primera posición.** He's in first place.

positivo ADJETIVO
positive
- **El test dio positivo.** The test was positive.

posponer* VERBO
to postpone

posta ADVERBIO [*Spain*]
- **a posta** on purpose

la **postal** SUSTANTIVO
postcard

el **poste** SUSTANTIVO
1 post (*de valla, portería*)
2 pole (*de teléfono, telégrafo*)

el **poster** SUSTANTIVO (PL los **pósters**)
poster

posterior ADJETIVO (FEM **posterior**)
rear ◇ *los asientos posteriores* the rear seats
- **la parte posterior** the rear

postizo ADJETIVO
false

el **postizo** SUSTANTIVO
hairpiece

el **postre** SUSTANTIVO
dessert ◇ *De postre tomé un helado.* I had ice cream for dessert. ◇ *¿Qué hay de postre?* What's for dessert?

la **postura** SUSTANTIVO
position

potable ADJETIVO
- **agua potable** drinking water

el **potaje** SUSTANTIVO
stew ◇ *potaje de garbanzos* chickpea stew

la **potencia** SUSTANTIVO
power ◇ *la potencia del motor* the power of the engine
- **Es un artista en potencia.** He has the makings of an artist.

potencial ADJETIVO
potential

potente ADJETIVO
powerful

el **potro** SUSTANTIVO
1 colt (*animal*)
2 horse (*para saltar*)

el **pozo** SUSTANTIVO
well

la **práctica** SUSTANTIVO
practice ◇ *No tengo mucha práctica.* I haven't had much practice.
- **en la práctica** in practice
- **poner* algo en práctica** to put something into practice

prácticamente ADVERBIO
practically

practicante ADJETIVO
practicing ◇ *Es una católica practicante.* She is a practicing Catholic.

el/la **practicante** SUSTANTIVO
nurse

practicar* VERBO
to practice (*idioma, profesión, instrumento*) ◇ *Tengo que practicar un poco más.* I need to practice a bit more.
- **No practico ningún deporte.** I don't play any sports.

práctico ADJETIVO

practical ◇ *Es una mujer muy práctica.* She is a very practical woman.

el **prado** SUSTANTIVO
meadow

la **precaución** SUSTANTIVO (PL las **precauciones**)
precaution ◇ *tomar precauciones* to take precautions
◆ **con precaución** with caution

precavido ADJETIVO
◆ **Es muy precavida.** She's always very well-prepared.

el **precinto** SUSTANTIVO
seal

el **precio** SUSTANTIVO
price ◇ *Han subido los precios.* Prices have gone up.
◆ **¿Qué precio tiene?** How much is it?

la **preciosidad** SUSTANTIVO
◆ **La casa es una preciosidad.** The house is beautiful.

precioso ADJETIVO
beautiful ◇ *¡Es precioso!* It's beautiful!

el **precipicio** SUSTANTIVO
precipice

precipitarse VERBO
◆ **No hay que precipitarse.** There's no need to rush into anything.
◆ **Reconozco que me precipité al tomar esa decisión.** I admit I rushed into the decision.

precisamente ADVERBIO
precisely

precisar VERBO
◆ **¿Puedes precisar un poco más?** Can you be a little more specific?
◆ **Precisó que no se trataba de un virus.** He said specifically that it was not a virus.

preciso ADJETIVO
1 precise ◇ *Recibió instrucciones precisas.* He received precise instructions.
◆ **en ese preciso momento** at that very moment
2 accurate ◇ *un reloj muy preciso* a very accurate watch
◆ **si es preciso** if necessary
◆ **No es preciso que vengas.** There's no need for you to come.

precoz ADJETIVO (FEM **precoz**, PL **precoces**)
precocious

predecir* VERBO
to predict

predicar* VERBO
to preach

la **predicción** SUSTANTIVO (PL las **predicciones**)
prediction

predicho VERBO *ver* **predecir**

preescolar ADJETIVO
preschool

***preschool** en este caso va siempre delante del sustantivo.*

prefabricado ADJETIVO
prefabricated

la **preferencia** SUSTANTIVO
1 preference ◇ *No tengo ninguna preferencia.* I have no preference.
2 right of way ◇ *Tienen preferencia los carros que vienen por la derecha.* Cars coming from the right have the right of way.

preferido ADJETIVO
favorite

preferir* VERBO
to prefer ◇ *Prefiero un buen libro a una película.* I prefer a good book to a movie.
◆ **Prefiero ir mañana.** I'd rather go tomorrow.

prefiero VERBO *ver* **preferir**

el **prefijo** SUSTANTIVO
code ◇ *¿Cuál es el prefijo de Guadalajara?* What is the code for Guadalajara?

la **pregunta** SUSTANTIVO
question ◇ *hacer una pregunta* to ask a question

preguntar VERBO
to ask ◇ *Siempre me preguntas lo mismo.* You're always asking me the same question.
◆ **Me preguntó por ti.** He asked about you.
◆ **Me pregunto si estará enterado.** I wonder if he's heard yet.

prehistórico ADJETIVO
prehistoric

el **prejuicio** SUSTANTIVO
prejudice
◆ **Yo no tengo prejuicios.** I'm not prejudiced.

prematuro ADJETIVO
premature

premiar VERBO
1 to award a prize to ◇ *Han premiado su película.* His movie has been awarded a prize.
◆ **el director premiado** the award-winning director
2 to reward ◇ *premiar los esfuerzos de un niño* to reward a child's efforts

el **premio** SUSTANTIVO
1 prize ◇ *llevarse un premio* to get a prize
2 reward ◇ *como premio a tu sacrificio* as a reward for your sacrifice
◆ **el premio gordo** the jackpot

la **prenda** SUSTANTIVO
garment (*de vestir*)

prender VERBO
1 to light (*cerilla, cigarro*)
2 to switch on (*luz, gas, radio*)
◆ **prender fuego a algo** to set fire to something

la **prensa** SUSTANTIVO
press ◇ *una conferencia de prensa* a press conference

la **preocupación** SUSTANTIVO (PL las **preocupaciones**)
worry (PL worries)

preocupado ADJETIVO
worried
◆ **estar* preocupado por algo** to be worried about something

preocupar VERBO
to worry ◇ *No te preocupes.* Don't worry. ◇ *Me preocupa su salud.* I'm worried about his health.
- **preocuparse por algo** to worry about something
- **Si llego un poco tarde se preocupa.** If I arrive a bit late, he gets worried.
- **Yo me preocupo de comprar las entradas.** I'll see to buying the tickets.

preparar VERBO
[1] to prepare ◇ *No he preparado el discurso.* I haven't prepared my speech.
[2] to prepare for ◇ *¿Te has preparado el examen?* Have you prepared for the exam?
[3] to cook (*comida*) ◇ *Mi madre estaba preparando la cena.* My mother was cooking dinner.
- **Me estaba preparando para salir.** I was getting ready to go out.

los **preparativos** SUSTANTIVO
preparations

la **presa** SUSTANTIVO
[1] dam (*de agua*)
[2] prey (*de animal*)
[3] prisoner (*en la cárcel*)

prescindir VERBO
- **prescindir de** to do without ◇ *No puede prescindir de su secretaria.* He can't do without his secretary.

la **presencia** SUSTANTIVO
presence ◇ *en presencia de un sacerdote* in the presence of a priest
- **El puesto requiere buena presencia.** A smart appearance is required for the position.

presenciar VERBO
to witness

el **presentador**, la **presentadora** SUSTANTIVO
[1] host (*de programa*)
[2] newscaster (*de noticias*)

presentar VERBO
[1] to introduce ◇ *Me presentó a sus padres.* He introduced me to his parents.
[2] to hand in ◇ *Mañana tengo que presentar un trabajo.* I have to hand in an essay tomorrow. ◇ *Presentó la dimisión.* He handed in his resignation.
[3] to host ◇ *J. Pérez presenta el programa.* The program is hosted by J. Pérez.
- **presentarse (1)** to turn up ◇ *Se presentó en mi casa a las doce de la noche.* He turned up at my house at twelve o'clock at night.
- **presentarse (2)** to introduce oneself ◇ *Antes de nada, me voy a presentar.* First of all, let me introduce myself.
- **presentarse a un examen** to take an exam

el **presente** ADJETIVO, SUSTANTIVO
present ◇ *Juan no estaba presente en la reunión.* Juan was not present at the meeting.
- **el presente** the present
- **los presentes** those present
- **¡Presente!** Present!

el **presentimiento** SUSTANTIVO
premonition

el **preservativo** SUSTANTIVO
condom

la **presidenta** SUSTANTIVO
[1] president (*de país*)
[2] chairwoman (PL chairwomen) (*de comité, jurado, empresa*)

el **presidente** SUSTANTIVO
[1] president (*de país*)
[2] chairman (PL chairmen) (*de comité, jurado, empresa*)

la **presión** SUSTANTIVO (PL las **presiones**)
pressure
- **la presión sanguínea** blood pressure

presionar VERBO
[1] to put pressure on ◇ *Sus amigos lo están presionando para que se compre otro carro.* His friends are putting pressure on him to buy a new car.
[2] to press (*botón, timbre*)

preso ADJETIVO
- **Estuvo tres años preso.** He was in prison for three years.
- **llevarse a alguien preso** to take someone prisoner

el **preso** SUSTANTIVO
prisoner

prestado ADJETIVO
- **La cinta no es mía, es prestada.** It's not my tape; someone lent it to me.
- **Le pedí prestada la bicicleta.** I asked if I could borrow his bicycle.
- **Me dejó el carro prestado.** He lent me his car.

el **préstamo** SUSTANTIVO
loan ◇ *Pidieron un préstamo al banco.* They asked the bank for a loan.

prestar VERBO
to lend (*dinero, carro*) ◇ *Un amigo me prestó el traje.* A friend lent me the suit.
- **¿Me prestas el lápiz?** Can I borrow your pencil?
- **Tienes que prestar atención.** You must pay attention.
- **Se negó a prestar ayuda.** He refused to help.

el **prestigio** SUSTANTIVO
prestige
- **una marca de prestigio** a prestigious brand

presumido ADJETIVO
vain

presumir VERBO
to show off ◇ *Lleva ropa cara para presumir.* He dresses expensively just to show off.
- **Luis presume de guapo.** Luis thinks he's really handsome.

el **presupuesto** SUSTANTIVO

1 budget ◇ *No puedo salirme del presupuesto.* I can't go over the budget.
2 estimate ◇ *Le pedí un presupuesto al carpintero.* I've asked the carpenter for an estimate.

pretender VERBO
1 to intend ◇ *Pretendo sacarme una buena nota.* I intend to get a good grade.
◆ **¿Qué pretendes decir con eso?** What do you mean by that?
2 to expect ◇ *¡No pretenderás que te pague la comida!* You're not expecting me to pay for your meal, are you?
No confundir ***pretender*** *con* ***to pretend.***

el **pretexto** SUSTANTIVO
excuse ◇ *Era sólo un pretexto.* It was only an excuse.
◆ **Vino con el pretexto de ver al abuelo.** He came in order to see Grandpa, or so he said.

la **prevención** SUSTANTIVO
prevention ◇ *prevención de incendios* fire prevention
◆ **las medidas de prevención** preventive measures

prevenir* VERBO
1 to prevent ◇ *prevenir un accidente* to prevent an accident
2 to warn ◇ *Mi madre ya me había prevenido.* My mother had already warned me.

prever* VERBO
1 to foresee (*anticipar*) ◇ *Nadie había previsto esta tragedia.* Nobody had foreseen this tragedy.
◆ **Han previsto nevadas en el norte.** Snow is forecast for the north.
2 plan (*planear*) ◇ *Prevén terminar el metro para el 2005.* They plan to finish the subway by 2005.

previo ADJETIVO
previous ◇ *No tengo experiencia previa en ese campo.* I have no previous experience in the field.

previsible ADJETIVO
foreseeable

previsto (1) VERBO *ver* **prever**

previsto (2) ADJETIVO
◆ **Tengo previsto volver mañana.** I plan to return tomorrow.
◆ **El avión tiene prevista su llegada a las dos.** The plane is due in at two o'clock.
◆ **Como estaba previsto, ganó él.** As expected, he was the winner.

la **prima** SUSTANTIVO
1 cousin (*pariente*)
2 bonus (PL bonuses) (*pago extra*)

la **primaria** SUSTANTIVO
elementary education

la **primavera** SUSTANTIVO
spring ◇ *en primavera* in spring

primer *ver* **primero**

primero (FEM **primera**) ADJETIVO, PRONOMBRE
first ◇ *el primer día* the first day ◇ *Primer plato: sopa.* First course: soup. ◇ *Primero vamos a comer.* Let's eat first.
◆ **en primera fila** in the front row
◆ **En primer lugar, veamos los datos.** Firstly, let's look at the facts.
◆ **primer ministro** prime minister
◆ **Vivo en el primero.** I live on the second floor.
◆ **Fui la primera en llegar.** I was the first to arrive.
◆ **Juan es el primero de la clase.** Juan is top of the class.
◆ **Lo primero es la salud.** The most important thing is your health.
◆ **El examen será a primeros de mayo.** The exam will be at the beginning of May.

primitivo ADJETIVO
primitive

el **primo** SUSTANTIVO
cousin
◆ **primo segundo** second cousin

la **princesa** SUSTANTIVO
princess (PL princesses)

principal ADJETIVO
main ◇ *el personaje principal* the main character
◆ **Lo principal es estar sano.** The main thing is to stay healthy.

principalmente ADVERBIO
mainly

el **príncipe** SUSTANTIVO
prince

el/la **principiante** SUSTANTIVO
beginner

el **principio** SUSTANTIVO
1 beginning ◇ *El principio del libro es muy interesante.* The beginning of the book is very interesting.
◆ **Al principio parecía fácil.** It seemed easy at first.
◆ **a principios de año** at the beginning of the year
2 principle ◇ *No tiene principios.* He has no principles.
◆ **En principio me parece una buena idea.** On the face of it, it's a good idea.

la **prioridad** SUSTANTIVO
priority (PL priorities)

la **prisa** SUSTANTIVO
rush
◆ **Con las prisas me olvidé el paraguas.** In the rush I forgot my umbrella.
◆ **¡Date prisa!** Hurry up!
◆ **Tengo prisa.** I'm in a hurry.

la **prisión** SUSTANTIVO (PL las **prisiones**)
prison ◇ *Lo condenaron a seis años de prisión.* He was sentenced to six years in prison.

el **prisionero**, la **prisionera** SUSTANTIVO
prisoner

P

los **prismáticos** SUSTANTIVO
binoculars

privado ADJETIVO
private ◊ *un colegio privado* a private school

privarse VERBO
◆ **En vacaciones no me privo de nada.** When I'm on vacation I really spoil myself.

privatizar* VERBO
to privatize

el **privilegio** SUSTANTIVO
privilege

el **pro** SUSTANTIVO
◆ **los pros y contras** the pros and cons

las **probabilidades** SUSTANTIVO
◆ **Tiene muchas probabilidades de ganar.** He has a very good chance of winning.
◆ **No tengo muchas probabilidades de aprobar.** I don't have much chance of passing.

probable ADJETIVO
likely ◊ *Es muy probable.* It's very likely.
◆ **Es probable que llegue tarde.** He'll probably arrive late.

probablemente ADVERBIO
probably

el **probador** SUSTANTIVO
changing room

probar* VERBO
1 to prove ◊ *La policía no pudo probarlo.* The police could not prove it.
2 to taste ◊ *Probé la sopa para ver si le faltaba sal.* I tasted the soup to see if it needed more salt.
3 to try ◊ *Prueba estas fresas a ver si te gustan.* Try these strawberries and see if you like them. ◊ *Pruébalo antes para ver si funciona bien.* Try it first and see if it works properly.
◆ **Me probé un vestido.** I tried on a dress.

la **probeta** SUSTANTIVO
test tube
◆ **un bebé probeta** a test-tube baby

el **problema** SUSTANTIVO
problem ◊ *Tengo que resolver este problema.* I have to solve this problem.
◆ **Este carro nunca me ha dado problemas.** This car has never given me any trouble.
◆ **tener* problemas de estómago** to have stomach trouble

procedente ADJETIVO
◆ **procedente de** from ◊ *el tren procedente de Monterrey* the train from Monterrey

el **procesador** SUSTANTIVO
processor
◆ **un procesador de textos** a word processor

el **procesamiento** SUSTANTIVO
◆ **el procesamiento de textos** word processing

la **procesión** SUSTANTIVO (PL las **procesiones**)
procession

el **proceso** SUSTANTIVO
process (PL processes) ◊ *Será un proceso muy largo.* It will be a long process.
◆ **el proceso de datos** data processing

proclamar VERBO
to proclaim

procurar VERBO
to try
◆ **Procura terminarlo mañana.** Try to finish it tomorrow.

la **producción** SUSTANTIVO (PL las **producciones**)
production
◆ **la producción en serie** mass production

producir* VERBO
1 to produce ◊ *La película fue producida por Juan Pérez.* The movie was produced by Juan Pérez. ◊ *No producimos lo suficiente.* We are not producing enough.
2 to cause ◊ *Puede producir efectos secundarios.* It can cause side effects.
◆ **¿Cómo se produjo el accidente?** How did the accident happen?

productivo ADJETIVO
productive

el **producto** SUSTANTIVO
product ◊ *productos de limpieza* cleaning products ◊ *productos lácteos* dairy products
◆ **los productos del campo** farm produce

el **productor**, la **productora** SUSTANTIVO
producer

la **profesión** SUSTANTIVO (PL las **profesiones**)
profession

el/la **profesional** ADJETIVO, SUSTANTIVO
professional

el **profesor**, la **profesora** SUSTANTIVO
teacher ◊ *Amelia es profesora de inglés.* Amelia is an English teacher.
◆ **mi profesor particular** my private tutor
◆ **un profesor universitario** a university professor

profundamente ADVERBIO
1 deeply (*respirar*)
2 soundly (*dormir*)

la **profundidad** SUSTANTIVO
depth ◊ *la profundidad de la piscina* the depth of the pool ◊ *analizar un texto en profundidad* to analyze a text in depth
◆ **Tiene dos metros de profundidad.** It's two meters deep.

profundo ADJETIVO
deep (*pozo, voz, sueño*)
◆ **una piscina poco profunda** a shallow pool

el **programa** SUSTANTIVO
program (*también informática*) ◊ *un programa de televisión* a television program
◆ **un programa-concurso** a quiz show
◆ **el programa de estudios** the syllabus

la **programación** SUSTANTIVO
1 programs (*de televisión*)

[2] programming (*en informática*)

el **programador,** la **programadora** SUSTANTIVO
programmer ◇ *Balbino es programador.* Balbino is a programmer.

programar VERBO
to programme ◇ *Programé el video para grabar el partido.* I programmed the video to tape the game.

progresar VERBO
to progress

el **progreso** SUSTANTIVO
progress ◇ *progreso tecnológico* technological progress
◆ **Carmen ha hecho muchos progresos este trimestre.** Carmen has made great progress this term.

prohibir* VERBO
to ban ◇ *Le prohibieron la entrada en el edificio.* He was banned from entering the building. ◇ *Han prohibido las armas de fuego.* Firearms have been banned.
◆ **queda terminantemente prohibido** it is strictly forbidden
◆ **Te prohíbo que toques mi computadora.** I won't allow you to touch my computer.
◆ **"prohibido fumar"** "no smoking"

el **prólogo** SUSTANTIVO
prologue

prolongar* VERBO
to extend

el **promedio** SUSTANTIVO
average

la **promesa** SUSTANTIVO
promise

prometer VERBO
to promise ◇ *Prometió llevarnos al cine.* He promised to take us to the movies.
◆ **¡Te lo prometo!** I promise!

el **pronombre** SUSTANTIVO
pronoun

pronosticar* VERBO
to forecast

el **pronóstico** SUSTANTIVO
◆ **el pronóstico del tiempo** the weather forecast

pronto ADVERBIO
soon (*dentro de poco*) ◇ *Los invitados llegarán pronto.* The guests will be here soon.
◆ **lo más pronto posible** as soon as possible
◆ **¡Hasta pronto!** See you soon!
◆ **De pronto, empezó a nevar.** All of a sudden it began to snow.

pronunciar VERBO
to pronounce ◇ *¿Cómo se pronuncia esta palabra?* How do you pronounce that word?

la **propaganda** SUSTANTIVO
[1] advertising ◇ *Las revistas están llenas de propaganda.* Magazines are full of advertising.
◆ **Han hecho mucha propaganda del concierto.** The concert has been well-advertised.
[2] junk mail ◇ *Los buzones están llenos de propaganda.* The mailboxes are full of junk mail.

propagarse* VERBO
to spread

la **propiedad** SUSTANTIVO
property (PL properties)

el **propietario,** la **propietaria** SUSTANTIVO
owner

la **propina** SUSTANTIVO
tip ◇ *¿Vamos a dejar propina?* Shall we leave a tip?
◆ **Siempre doy propina a los meseros.** I always tip waiters.

propio ADJETIVO
[1] own ◇ *Tengo mi propia habitación.* I have my own room.
[2] himself (FEM herself) ◇ *Lo anunció el propio ministro.* It was announced by the minister himself.
[3] typical ◇ *Eso es muy propio de los países mediterráneos.* That's very typical of Mediterranean countries.
◆ **un nombre propio** a proper noun

proponer* VERBO
[1] to suggest ◇ *Nos propuso pagar la cena a medias.* He suggested that we should share the cost of the meal.
◆ **Me propuso un trato.** He made me a proposition.
[2] to nominate ◇ *Propusieron a Manuel para alcalde.* Manuel was nominated for mayor.
◆ **Se ha propuesto adelgazar.** He's decided to lose some weight.

P

la **proporción** SUSTANTIVO (PL las **proporciones**)
proportion

proporcional ADJETIVO
proportional

proporcionar VERBO
to provide ◇ *Ellos me proporcionaron la información.* They provided me with the information.

el **propósito** SUSTANTIVO
purpose ◇ *¿Cuál es el propósito de su visita?* What is the purpose of your visit?
◆ **A propósito, ya tengo las entradas.** By the way, I have the tickets.
◆ **Lo hizo a propósito.** He did it deliberately.

la **propuesta** SUSTANTIVO
proposal

propuesto VERBO *ver* **proponer**

la **prórroga** SUSTANTIVO
[1] extension (*de plazo*)
[2] extra time (*de partido*)

el **prospecto** SUSTANTIVO
leaflet

prosperar VERBO
to do well

próspero ADJETIVO
- **¡Próspero Año Nuevo!** A prosperous New Year!

la **prostituta** SUSTANTIVO
prostitute

el/la **protagonista** SUSTANTIVO
main character ◇ *El protagonista no muere en la película.* The main character doesn't die in the movie.
- **El protagonista es Tom Cruise.** Tom Cruise plays the lead.

la **protección** SUSTANTIVO
protection

protector ADJETIVO (FEM **protectora**)
protective ◇ *una funda protectora* a protective cover

proteger* VERBO
to protect ◇ *El muro lo protegió de las balas.* The wall protected him from the bullets.
- **Nos protegimos de la lluvia en la cabaña.** We sheltered from the rain in the hut.

la **proteína** SUSTANTIVO
protein

la **protesta** SUSTANTIVO
protest ◇ *como protesta por los despidos* as a protest against layoffs

el/la **protestante** ADJETIVO, SUSTANTIVO
Protestant

protestar VERBO
1 to protest ◇ *Protestaron contra la subida de la gasolina.* They protested against the rise in the price of gasoline.
2 to complain ◇ *Cómete las verduras y no protestes.* Eat your vegetables and don't complain.

el **provecho** SUSTANTIVO
- **¡Buen provecho!** Enjoy your meal!
- **Sacó mucho provecho del curso.** He got a lot out of the course.

el **proverbio** SUSTANTIVO
proverb

la **provincia** SUSTANTIVO
province

provisional ADJETIVO
provisional

las **provisiones** SUSTANTIVO
provisions

provisorio ADJETIVO
provisional

provocar* VERBO
1 to provoke ◇ *No quería pegarle pero me provocó.* I didn't mean to hit him but he provoked me.
2 to cause ◇ *La lluvia ha provocado graves inundaciones.* The rain caused serious flooding.
- **El incendio fue provocado.** The fire was started deliberately.

provocativo ADJETIVO
provocative

próximo ADJETIVO
next ◇ *Lo haremos la próxima semana.* We'll do it next week. ◇ *la próxima vez* next time ◇ *la próxima calle a la izquierda* the next street on the left

proyectar VERBO
1 to show (*diapositivas, película*)
2 to cast (*sombra*)
- **la imagen que un país proyecta al extranjero** the image a country projects abroad

el **proyectil** SUSTANTIVO
missile

el **proyecto** SUSTANTIVO
1 plan ◇ *¿Tienes algún proyecto para este verano?* Do you have any plans for the summer?
2 project ◇ *el proyecto en el que estamos trabajando* the project we are working on
- **un proyecto de ley** a bill

el **proyector** SUSTANTIVO
projector

prudente ADJETIVO
wise ◇ *Lo más prudente sería esperar.* It would be wisest to wait.
- **Debería ser más prudente.** He should be more careful.

prueba VERBO *ver* **probar**

la **prueba** SUSTANTIVO
1 test ◇ *El médico me hizo más pruebas.* The doctor did some more tests. ◇ *Mañana tengo una prueba.* I have a test tomorrow.
- **pruebas nucleares** nuclear tests

2 proof ◇ *Eso es la prueba de que lo hizo él.* This is the proof that he did it.
- **El fiscal presentó nuevas pruebas.** The prosecutor presented new evidence.

3 heat ◇ *la prueba de los cien metros valla* the hundred meter hurdles heat
- **a prueba de balas** bulletproof

pruebo VERBO *ver* **probar**

la **psicóloga** SUSTANTIVO
psychologist

la **psicología** SUSTANTIVO
psychology

psicológico ADJETIVO
psychological

el **psicólogo** SUSTANTIVO
psychologist

el/la **psiquiatra** SUSTANTIVO
psychiatrist

psiquiátrico ADJETIVO
psychiatric

ptas. ABREVIATURA (= *pesetas*)
pesetas

la **púa** SUSTANTIVO
1 pick (*para guitarra*)
2 tooth (PL teeth) (*de peine*)

el **pub** SUSTANTIVO (PL los **pubs**)
bar

publicar* VERBO
to publish

la **publicidad** SUSTANTIVO
1 advertising (*de producto*) ◇ *una campaña de publicidad* an advertising campaign
2 publicity (*de suceso, persona*) ◇ *La conferencia tuvo poca publicidad.* The conference received little publicity.

público ADJETIVO
public

el **público** SUSTANTIVO
1 public ◇ *cerrado al público* closed to the public
2 audience (*en teatro, concierto*)
3 spectators PL (*en campo de deporte*)

pude VERBO *ver* **poder**

pudrirse VERBO
to rot

el **pueblo** SUSTANTIVO
1 village (*pequeño*)
2 town (*más grande*)
3 people PL ◇ *El pueblo está a favor de la democracia.* The people are in favor of democracy.

puedo VERBO *ver* **poder**

el **puente** SUSTANTIVO
bridge
◆ **el puente aéreo** the shuttle service
◆ **hacer* puente** to make a long weekend of it

> *In Latin America, when a public holiday falls on a Tuesday or Thursday people often take off Monday or Friday as well to give themselves a long weekend.*

el **puerco** SUSTANTIVO
1 pig (*animal*)
2 pork (*carne*) Mexico

el **puerro** SUSTANTIVO
leek

la **puerta** SUSTANTIVO
1 door
◆ **un carro de cuatro puertas** a four-door car
◆ **Llaman a la puerta.** Somebody's at the door.
◆ **Susana me acompañó a la puerta.** Susana saw me out.
2 gate (*de jardín*)
◆ **la puerta de embarque** boarding gate

el **puerto** SUSTANTIVO
port ◇ *un puerto pesquero* a fishing port
◆ **un puerto deportivo** a marina
◆ **un puerto de montaña** a mountain pass

Puerto Rico SUSTANTIVO MASC
Puerto Rico

el **puertorriqueño**, la **puertorriqueña** ADJETIVO, SUSTANTIVO
Puerto Rican

pues CONJUNCIÓN
1 then ◇ *Tengo sueño.* – *¡Pues vete a la cama!* I'm tired. – Then go to bed!
2 well ◇ *Pues, como te iba contando...* Well, as I was saying... ◇ *¡Pues no lo sabía!* Well, I didn't know!
◆ **¡Pues claro!** Yes, of course!

la **puesta** SUSTANTIVO
◆ **la puesta de sol** sunset
◆ **la puesta en libertad de dos presos** the release of two prisoners

puesto VERBO *ver* **poner**

el **puesto** SUSTANTIVO
1 place ◇ *Acabé la carrera en primer puesto.* I finished in first place.
2 stall ◇ *un puesto de verduras* a vegetable stall
◆ **un puesto de trabajo** a job
◆ **un puesto de socorro** a first aid station
◆ **puesto que** since ◇ *Puesto que no lo querías, se lo di a Diego.* Since you didn't want it, I gave it to Diego.

la **pulga** SUSTANTIVO
flea

la **pulgada** SUSTANTIVO
inch (PL inches)

el **pulgar** SUSTANTIVO
thumb

pulir VERBO
to polish

el **pulmón** SUSTANTIVO (PL los **pulmones**)
lung

el **púlpito** SUSTANTIVO
pulpit

el **pulpo** SUSTANTIVO
octopus (PL octopuses) ◇ *Me gusta el pulpo.* I like octopus.

pulque SUSTANTIVO

> ***Pulque** is a traditional alcoholic drink from Mexico which is thick, slightly sweet and milky and brewed from the juice of the agave plant.*

P

pulsar VERBO
to press

la **pulsera** SUSTANTIVO
bracelet
◆ **un reloj de pulsera** a wrist watch

el **pulso** SUSTANTIVO
pulse ◇ *El doctor le tomó el pulso.* The doctor took his pulse.
◆ **Tengo muy mal pulso.** My hand is very unsteady.
◆ **Echamos un pulso y le gané.** We had an arm-wrestling match and I won.
◆ **Lo levantó a pulso.** He lifted it with his bare hands.

el **pulverizador** SUSTANTIVO
spray

el/la **punk** ADJETIVO, SUSTANTIVO
punk

la **punta** SUSTANTIVO
1 tip (*de dedo, lengua*)

☞

2 point (*de bolígrafo, cuchillo*)
- **Sácale punta al lápiz.** Sharpen your pencil.
- **Vivo en la otra punta del pueblo.** I live at the other end of the town.
- **la hora punta** Spain the rush hour

el **puntapié** SUSTANTIVO (PL los **puntapiés**)
- **Le dio un puntapié a la piedra.** He kicked the stone.

la **puntería** SUSTANTIVO
- **tener* buena puntería** to be a good shot

puntiagudo ADJETIVO
pointed

la **puntilla** SUSTANTIVO
lace edging
- **andar* de puntillas** to tiptoe
- **ponerse* de puntillas** to stand on tiptoe

el **punto** SUSTANTIVO
1 point ◇ *Perdieron por tres puntos.* They lost by three points. ◇ *Ése es un punto importante.* That's an important point. ◇ *desde ese punto de vista* from that point of view
2 stitch (PL stitches) (*en costura, cirugía*)
3 dot (*sobre la "i"*)
4 period (*al final de una frase*)
- **punto y seguido** period, new sentence
- **punto y aparte** period, new paragraph
- **punto y coma** semicolon
- **dos puntos** colon
- **puntos suspensivos** ellipsis
- **Estábamos a punto de salir cuando llamaste.** We were about to go out when you called.
- **Mila estaba a punto de llorar.** Mila was on the verge of tears.
- **Estuve a punto de perder el tren.** I very nearly missed the train.
- **a la una en punto** at one o'clock sharp

la **puntuación** SUSTANTIVO (PL las **puntuaciones**)
1 punctuation ◇ *los signos de puntuación* punctuation marks
2 score ◇ *Recibió una alta puntuación.* He got a high score.

puntual ADJETIVO
1 punctual ◇ *Sé puntual.* Be punctual.
- **Jamás llega puntual.** He never arrives on time.

2 specific ◇ *Sólo trató aspectos puntuales del tema.* He only dealt with specific aspects of the subject.

la **puntualidad** SUSTANTIVO
punctuality

puntuar* VERBO
- **Este trabajo no puntúa para la nota final.** This essay doesn't count towards the final grade.
- **un profesor que puntúa muy bajo** a teacher who gives very low grades

el **puñado** SUSTANTIVO
handful ◇ *un puñado de arena* a handful of sand

el **puñal** SUSTANTIVO
dagger

la **puñalada** SUSTANTIVO
- **Le dieron una puñalada.** He was stabbed.

el **puñetazo** SUSTANTIVO
punch (PL punches) ◇ *un puñetazo en la cara* a punch in the face
- **Le pegó un puñetazo.** He punched him.

el **puño** SUSTANTIVO
1 fist (*mano cerrada*)
2 cuff (*de una camisa*)

el **pupitre** SUSTANTIVO
desk

el **puré** SUSTANTIVO (PL los **purés**)
- **puré de verduras** puréed vegetables
- **puré de papas** mashed potatoes

puro ADJETIVO
pure ◇ *pura lana* pure wool ◇ *por pura casualidad* by pure chance
- **Es la pura verdad.** That's the absolute truth.
- **Son puras mentiras.** It's all lies.

el **puro** SUSTANTIVO
cigar

el **pus** SUSTANTIVO
pus

puse VERBO *ver* **poner**

Q

que (1) CONJUNCIÓN

1 than (*en comparaciones*) ◇ *Es más alto que tú.* He's taller than you.

◆ **Yo que tú, iría.** I'd go if I were you.

2 that (*en oraciones subordinadas*) ◇ *José sabe que estás aquí.* José knows that you're here.

*Es frecuente omitir **that** en el habla normal.*

◇ *Dijo que vendría.* He said he'd come.

◆ **Dile a Rosa que me llame.** Ask Rosa to call me.

Cuando introduce frases exclamativas no se traduce.

◆ **¡Que te mejores!** Get well soon!

◆ **¡Que te vaya bien!** Take care!

que (2) PRONOMBRE

1 which ◇ *la película que ganó el premio* the movie which won the award

Es frecuente omitir el pronombre en el habla normal cuando no funciona como sujeto.

◇ *el sombrero que te compraste* the hat you bought ◇ *el libro del que te hablé* the book I spoke to you about

2 who ◇ *el hombre que vino ayer* the man who came yesterday

Es frecuente omitir el pronombre en el habla normal cuando no funciona como sujeto.

◇ *la chica que conocí* the girl I met

qué ADJETIVO, ADVERBIO, PRONOMBRE

1 what

En preguntas en general.

◇ *¿Qué fecha es hoy?* What's today's date? ◇ *No sabe qué es.* He doesn't know what it is. ◇ *No sé qué hacer.* I don't know what to do.

◆ **¿Qué?** What?

2 which

Cuando se pregunta cuál en concreto.

◇ *¿Qué película quieres ver?* Which movie do you want to see?

◆ **¡Qué asco!** How revolting!

◆ **¡Qué día más bonito!** What a glorious day!

◆ **¿Qué tal?** (*saludo*) How are things?

◆ **¿Qué tal está tu mamá?** How's your mother?

◆ **No lo he hecho. ¿Y qué?** I haven't done it. So what? (*coloquial*)

el **quebrado** SUSTANTIVO

fraction

quebrar* VERBO

to go bankrupt (*un negocio*)

◆ **quebrarse** to break ◇ *Alberto se quebró una pierna.* Alberto broke his leg.

quedar VERBO

1 to be left ◇ *No queda ninguno.* There are none left.

◆ **Me quedan 100 pesos.** I have 100 pesos left.

2 to be ◇ *Eso queda muy lejos de aquí.* That's a long way from here.

3 to suit ◇ *No te queda bien ese vestido.* That dress doesn't suit you.

◆ **quedarse** to stay ◇ *Ve tú, yo me quedo.* You go; I'll stay.

◆ **quedarse atrás** to fall behind

◆ **quedarse sordo** to go deaf

◆ **quedarse con algo** to keep something ◇ *Quédate con el cambio.* Keep the change.

los **quehaceres** SUSTANTIVO

◆ **los quehaceres de la casa** the household chores

la **queja** SUSTANTIVO

complaint

quejarse VERBO

to complain

◆ **quejarse de algo** to complain about something

◆ **quejarse de que...** to complain that... ◇ *Pablo se quejó de que nadie lo escuchaba.* Pablo complained that nobody listened to him.

el **quejido** SUSTANTIVO

1 moan (*de persona*)

2 whine (*de animal*)

quemado ADJETIVO

burned

la **quemadura** SUSTANTIVO

burn

◆ **quemaduras de sol** sunburn SING

quemar VERBO

1 to burn ◇ *Un incendio quemó todo el bosque.* A fire burned the entire forest.

2 to be burning hot ◇ *Esta sopa quema.* This soup's burning hot.

◆ **quemarse** to burn oneself ◇ *Me quemé con una cerilla.* I burned myself with a match.

quepa VERBO *ver* **caber**

querer* VERBO

1 to want ◇ *No quiero ir.* I don't want to go.

◆ **Quiero que vayas.** I want you to go.

◆ **¿Quieres un café?** Would you like some coffee?

2 to love ◇ *Ana quiere mucho a sus hijos.* Ana loves her children dearly.

3 to mean ◇ *No quería hacerte daño.* I didn't mean to hurt you. ◇ *Lo hice sin querer.* I didn't mean to do it.

◆ **querer decir** to mean ◇ *¿Qué quieres decir?* What do you mean?

querido ADJETIVO

dear

querré VERBO *ver* **querer**

el **queso** SUSTANTIVO

cheese

el **quicio** SUSTANTIVO

◆ **sacar* a alguien de quicio** to drive somebody up the wall

la **quiebra** SUSTANTIVO

◆ **ir* a la quiebra** to go bankrupt

quien PRONOMBRE

who ◇ *Fue Juan quien nos lo dijo.* It was ☞

Juan who told us.

Quien generalmente no se traduce cuando no funciona como sujeto.

◇ *Vi al chico con quien sales.* I saw the boy you're dating.

quién PRONOMBRE

who ◇ *¿Quién es ésa?* Who's that? ◇ *¿A quién viste?* Who did you see? ◇ *No sé quién es.* I don't know who he is.

◆ **¿De quién es...?** Whose is...? ◇ *¿De quién es este libro?* Whose is this book?

◆ **¿Quién es? (1)** (*en la puerta*) Who's there?

◆ **¿Quién es? (2)** (*al teléfono*) Who's calling?

quiero VERBO *ver* **querer**

quieto ADJETIVO

still

◆ **¡Estáte quieto!** Keep still!

la **química** SUSTANTIVO

1 chemistry (*ciencia*) ◇ *clase de química* chemistry class

2 chemist (*persona*) ◇ *Es química.* She's a chemist.

el **químico** SUSTANTIVO

chemist ◇ *Es químico.* He's a chemist.

quince ADJETIVO, PRONOMBRE

fifteen

◆ **el quince de enero** January fifteenth

◆ **quince días** two weeks

el **quinceañero,** la **quinceañera** SUSTANTIVO

teenager

la **quincena** SUSTANTIVO

two weeks

quincenal ADJETIVO

every two weeks

la **quiniela** SUSTANTIVO Spain

sports lottery

quinientos ADJETIVO, PRONOMBRE (FEM **quinientas**)

five hundred

quinto ADJETIVO, PRONOMBRE (FEM **quinta**)

fifth

◆ **Vivo en el quinto.** I live on the sixth floor.

el **quiosco** SUSTANTIVO

1 newsstand (*de periódicos*)

2 refreshment stand (*de refrescos*)

3 flower stall (*de flores*)

4 bandstand (*de banda de música*)

el **quirófano** SUSTANTIVO

operating theater

quirúrgico ADJETIVO

surgical

◆ **una intervención quirúrgica** an operation

quise VERBO *ver* **querer**

quisquilloso ADJETIVO

1 fussy ◇ *No soy quisquillosa con la comida.* I'm not fussy about what I eat.

2 touchy ◇ *Está muy quisquilloso últimamente.* He's been very touchy lately.

el **quitaesmalte** SUSTANTIVO

nail polish remover

el **quitamanchas** SUSTANTIVO (PL los **quitamanchas**)

stain remover

la **quitanieves** SUSTANTIVO (PL las **quitanieves**)

snowplow

quitar VERBO

1 to remove ◇ *Tardaron dos días en quitar los escombros.* It took two days to remove the rubble. ◇ *Este producto quita todo tipo de manchas.* This product removes all types of stain.

2 to take away ◇ *Su hermana le quitó la pelota.* His sister took the ball away from him.

◆ **Esto te quitará el dolor.** This will relieve the pain.

◆ **quitarse** to take off ◇ *Juan se quitó la chaqueta.* Juan took his jacket off.

quizá ADVERBIO = **quizás**

quizás ADVERBIO

perhaps

R

el **rábano** SUSTANTIVO
radish (PL radishes)
◆ **¡Me importa un rábano!** I don't give a hoot!
la **rabia** SUSTANTIVO
1 rage ◇ *Lo hizo por rabia.* He did it out of rage.
◆ **Me da mucha rabia.** It's really annoying.
2 rabies SING ◇ *Vacunamos al perro contra la rabia.* We had the dog vaccinated against rabies.
la **rabieta** SUSTANTIVO
tantrum
◆ **agarrarse una rabieta** to throw a tantrum
el **rabo** SUSTANTIVO
tail
la **racha** SUSTANTIVO
◆ **una racha de buen tiempo** a spell of good weather
◆ **una racha de viento** a gust of wind
◆ **pasar una mala racha** to go through a bad patch
racial ADJETIVO
racial
el **racimo** SUSTANTIVO
bunch (PL bunches)
el **racismo** SUSTANTIVO
racism
el/la **racista** ADJETIVO, SUSTANTIVO
racist
el **radar** SUSTANTIVO
radar
◆ **"velocidad controlada por radar"** "Speed checked by radar"
la **radiación** SUSTANTIVO
radiation
la **radiactividad** SUSTANTIVO
radioactivity
radiactivo ADJETIVO
radioactive
el **radiador** SUSTANTIVO
radiator
el **radio** SUSTANTIVO
radio ◇ *Por la mañana escucho el radio.* In the morning I listen to the radio.
◆ **Lo oí por el radio.** I heard it on the radio.
el **radio** SUSTANTIVO
1 radius (PL radii *o* radiuses) (*de círculo*) ◇ *La explosión se oyó en un radio de 50 millas.* The explosion could be heard within a 50-mile radius.
2 radio (*medio de comunicación*)
3 spoke (*de rueda*)
el **radiocasete** SUSTANTIVO
radio cassette player
la **radiografía** SUSTANTIVO
X-ray
◆ **Tengo que hacerme una radiografía.** I have to have an X-ray.
el **radiotaxi** SUSTANTIVO
radio taxi
el **raíl** SUSTANTIVO
rail
la **raíz** SUSTANTIVO (PL las **raíces**)
root
◆ **La planta está echando raíces.** The plant is taking root.
◆ **a raíz de** as a result of
la **raja** SUSTANTIVO
1 crack (*grieta*)
2 tear (*rotura en tela*)
3 slice (*de melón, limón*)
rajarse VERBO
1 to crack (*pared, espejo*)
2 to split (*falda, tapicería*)
rallar VERBO
to grate
el **rally** SUSTANTIVO (PL los **rallys**)
rally (PL rallies)
la **rama** SUSTANTIVO
branch (PL branches)
el **ramo** SUSTANTIVO
bunch (PL bunches) ◇ *un ramo de claveles* a bunch of carnations
◆ **el ramo textil** the textile industry
la **rampa** SUSTANTIVO
ramp
la **rana** SUSTANTIVO
frog
la **ranchera** SUSTANTIVO
1 Mexican folk song (*canción*)
2 station wagon (*automóvil*)
el **rancho** SUSTANTIVO
1 ranch (PL ranches) (*hacienda*)
2 shack (*casucha*)
rancio ADJETIVO
rancid (*mantequilla, queso*)
el **rango** SUSTANTIVO
rank
◆ **políticos de alto rango** high-ranking politicians
la **ranura** SUSTANTIVO
slot ◇ *Introduzca la moneda en la ranura.* Put the coin in the slot.
rapar VERBO
1 to crop (*pelo*)
2 to shave (*cabeza*)
el **rape** SUSTANTIVO
monkfish (PL monkfish) (*pescado*)
rápidamente ADVERBIO
quickly
la **rapidez** SUSTANTIVO
speed
◆ **con rapidez** quickly
rápido (1) ADJETIVO
1 fast (*veloz*) ◇ *un carro muy rápido* a very fast car
2 quick (*de poca duración*) ◇ *Fue una visita muy rápida.* It was a very quick visit.

rápido (2) ADVERBIO
fast ◇ *Manejas demasiado rápido.* You drive too fast.
◆ **Lo hice tan rápido como pude.** I did it as quickly as I could.
◆ **¡Rápido!** Hurry up!

raptar VERBO
to kidnap

el **rapto** SUSTANTIVO
kidnapping

la **raqueta** SUSTANTIVO
1 racket (*de tenis, bádminton*)
2 paddle (*de ping-pong*)

raramente ADVERBIO
rarely

raro ADJETIVO
1 strange (*extraño*) ◇ *Tiene unas costumbres muy raras.* He has some very strange habits.
◆ **¡Qué raro!** How strange!
◆ **Sabe un poco raro.** It tastes a bit funny.
2 rare (*poco frecuente*) ◇ *una especie muy rara* a very rare species
◆ **Es raro que haga tan buen tiempo.** It's unusual to have such good weather.
◆ **rara vez** seldom

el **rascacielos** SUSTANTIVO (PL los **rascacielos**)
skyscraper

rascar* VERBO
1 to scratch (*con las uñas*) ◇ *¿Me rascas la espalda?* Could you scratch my back for me?
2 to scrape Spain (*con cuchillo, espátula*) ◇ *Tuvimos que rascar la pintura de la puerta.* We had to scrape the paint off the door.
◆ **rascarse** to scratch ◇ *No deja de rascarse.* He can't stop scratching.

rasgar* VERBO
to rip

el **rasgo** SUSTANTIVO
feature ◇ *Tiene unos rasgos muy delicados.* He has very fine features.

el **rasguño** SUSTANTIVO
scratch (PL scratches)
◆ **Me hice un rasguño.** I've scratched myself.

el **rastrillo** SUSTANTIVO
1 rake (*herramienta*)
2 razor (*de afeitar*) Mexico

el **rastro** SUSTANTIVO
1 trail (*pista, huellas*) ◇ *seguir el rastro de alguien* to follow somebody's trail
2 trace ◇ *Desaparecieron sin dejar rastro.* They vanished without trace.

la **rasuradora** SUSTANTIVO Mexico
electric shaver

rasurarse VERBO
to shave

la **rata** SUSTANTIVO
rat

el **rato** SUSTANTIVO
while ◇ *después de un rato* after a while
◆ **Estaba aquí hace un rato.** He was here a few minutes ago.
◆ **al poco rato** shortly after
◆ **pasar el rato** to while away the time
◆ **pasar un buen rato** to have a good time
◆ **Pasamos un mal rato.** We had a terrible time.
◆ **en mis ratos libres** in my free time
◆ **Tengo para rato con esta redacción.** I have a way to go yet with this essay.
◆ **Tenemos para rato; el avión tiene retraso.** We'll be here for a while yet; the plane has been delayed.

el **ratón** SUSTANTIVO (PL los **ratones**)
mouse (PL mice) (*también informática*)

la **raya** SUSTANTIVO
1 line ◇ *trazar una raya* to draw a line
◆ **pasarse de la raya** to overstep the mark
2 stripe
◆ **un jersey a rayas** a striped jumper
3 part (*de pelo*) ◇ *Me hago la raya en medio.* I have my part in the middle.
4 crease (*del pantalón*)
5 dash (PL dashes) (*guión largo*)

rayar VERBO
to scratch

el **rayo** SUSTANTIVO
1 lightning ◇ *Cayó un rayo en la torre de la iglesia.* The church tower was struck by lightning.
2 ray ◇ *un rayo de luz* a ray of light ◇ *los rayos del sol* the sun's rays
◆ **los rayos X** X-rays
◆ **los rayos láser** laser beams

la **raza** SUSTANTIVO
1 race ◇ *la raza humana* the human race
2 breed (*de animal*) ◇ *¿De qué raza es tu gato?* What breed is your cat?
◆ **un perro de raza** a pedigree dog
◆ **el Día de la Raza**

> ℹ *El **Día de la Raza** is a holiday celebrated in Latin America, on October 12th to commemorate the anniversary of Columbus' discovery of America.*

la **razón** SUSTANTIVO (PL las **razones**)
reason ◇ *¿Cuál era la razón de su visita?* What was the reason for his visit?
◆ **tener* razón** to be right
◆ **dar* la razón a alguien** to agree that somebody is right
◆ **no tener* razón** to be wrong

razonable ADJETIVO
reasonable

la **reacción** SUSTANTIVO (PL las **reacciones**)
reaction

reaccionar VERBO
to react

el **reactor** SUSTANTIVO
1 jet plane (*avión*)

[2] jet engine (*motor*)
◆ **un reactor nuclear** a nuclear reactor

real ADJETIVO
[1] real ◇ *Esta vez el dolor era real.* This time the pain was real.
◆ **La película está basada en hechos reales.** The movie is based on actual events.
[2] royal ◇ *la familia real* the royal family

la **realidad** SUSTANTIVO
reality (PL realities)
◆ **en la realidad** in real life
◆ **en realidad** actually ◇ *Parece mayor, pero en realidad es más joven que yo.* He looks older, but actually he's younger than I am.
◆ **Mi sueño se hizo realidad.** My dream came true.
◆ **realidad virtual** virtual reality

realista ADJETIVO
realistic

realizar* VERBO
[1] to carry out (*proyecto, encuesta*)
◇ *realizar una investigación* to carry out an investigation
◆ **Has realizado un buen trabajo.** You've done a good job.
[2] to realize (*ilusión, ambición*) ◇ *Nunca realizó su sueño de dar la vuelta al mundo.* He never realized his dream of going round the world.
◆ **realizarse** to come true ◇ *Su sueño nunca llegó a realizarse.* His dream never came true.

realmente ADVERBIO
[1] really ◇ *Fue una época realmente difícil.* It was a really difficult period.
[2] actually ◇ *No creí que realmente ganara.* I didn't think he would actually win.

la **rebaja** SUSTANTIVO
[1] discount ◇ *La blusa tenía una mancha y pedí una rebaja.* There was a mark on the blouse so I asked for a discount.
[2] reduction ◇ *una rebaja del 16 por ciento* a 16 per cent reduction
◆ **las rebajas** the sales ◇ *las rebajas de enero* the January sales
◆ **Todos los grandes almacenes están de rebajas.** There are sales on in all the department stores.

rebajar VERBO
to reduce (*artículo, precio*) ◇ *Han rebajado los abrigos.* Coats have been reduced.
◇ *Cada fin de temporada rebajan los precios.* Prices are reduced at the end of every season.
◆ **rebajarse** to demean oneself ◇ *No quiere rebajarse a pedirme perdón.* He won't demean himself by apologizing to me.

la **rebanada** SUSTANTIVO
slice ◇ *Cortó el pan en rebanadas.* He cut the bread into slices.

el **rebaño** SUSTANTIVO
flock ◇ *un rebaño de ovejas* a flock of sheep

la **rebeca** SUSTANTIVO [Spain]
cardigan

rebelarse VERBO
to rebel ◇ *rebelarse contra alguien* to rebel against somebody

rebelde ADJETIVO
rebellious (*muchacho, carácter*)

el/la **rebelde** SUSTANTIVO
rebel

la **rebelión** SUSTANTIVO (PL las **rebeliones**)
rebellion

rebobinar VERBO
to rewind

rebotar VERBO
to bounce
◆ **La pelota rebotó en el poste.** The ball bounced off the post.

rebozado ADJETIVO
[1] breaded (*empanado*)
[2] battered (*con huevo y harina*)

el **recado** SUSTANTIVO
[1] message ◇ *Dejé recado de que me llamara.* I left a message for him to call me.
[2] errand ◇ *Fui a hacer unos recados.* I went to do some errands.

la **recaída** SUSTANTIVO
relapse ◇ *sufrir una recaída* to have a relapse

recalcar* VERBO
to stress ◇ *Me gustaría recalcar que...* I'd like to stress that...

la **recámara** SUSTANTIVO [Mexico]
bedroom

el **recambio** SUSTANTIVO
[1] spare ◇ *la rueda de recambio* the spare tire
◆ **una pieza de recambio** a spare part
[2] refill (*de bolígrafo, pluma*)

recargar* VERBO
[1] to recharge (*pila*)
[2] to fill up (*encendedor, bolígrafo*)

el **recargo** SUSTANTIVO
◆ **El taxista me cobró un recargo por el equipaje.** The cab driver charged me extra for my luggage.

recaudar VERBO
to collect ◇ *Recaudó dinero para una obra benéfica.* He collected money for a charity.

la **recepción** SUSTANTIVO (PL las **recepciones**)
reception

el/la **recepcionista** SUSTANTIVO
receptionist

el **receptor** SUSTANTIVO
receiver (*de teléfono, radio*)

la **recesión** SUSTANTIVO (PL las **recesiones**)
recession

la **receta** SUSTANTIVO
[1] recipe ◇ *Me dio la receta de los raviolis.* He gave me the recipe for the ravioli.
[2] prescription ◇ *Los antibióticos sólo se venden con receta.* Antibiotics are only available by prescription.

R

☞

No confundir ***receta*** *con* ***receipt.***

recetar VERBO
to prescribe ◇ *Las enfermeras no pueden recetar medicamentos.* Nurses can't prescribe drugs.
◆ **El médico me recetó un jarabe.** The doctor gave me a prescription for cough syrup.

rechazar* VERBO
1 to reject (*sugerencia, idea*) ◇ *El director rechazó mi propuesta.* The manager rejected my proposal.
2 to turn down (*oferta, candidato*) ◇ *Tuve que rechazar su oferta.* I had to turn down his offer.

rechoncho ADJETIVO
stocky

el **recibidor** SUSTANTIVO
entrance hall

recibir VERBO
1 to receive ◇ *No he recibido tu carta.* I haven't received your letter.
◆ **Recibí muchos regalos.** I got a lot of presents.
2 to meet ◇ *Vinieron a recibirnos al aeropuerto.* They came and met us at the airport.
◆ **El director me recibió en su despacho.** The manager saw me in his office.

el **recibo** SUSTANTIVO
1 receipt ◇ *No se admiten devoluciones sin recibo.* No refunds will be given without a receipt.
2 bill ◇ *pagar el recibo del teléfono* to pay the telephone bill

el **reciclaje** SUSTANTIVO
recycling

reciclar VERBO
to recycle

recién ADVERBIO
just ◇ *El comedor está recién pintado.* The dining room has just been painted.
◆ **Recién se fueron.** They've just left.
◆ **los recién casados** the newlyweds
◆ **un recién nacido** a newborn baby
◆ **"recién pintado"** "wet paint"

reciente ADJETIVO
recent
◆ **pan reciente** fresh bread

recientemente ADVERBIO
recently

el **recipiente** SUSTANTIVO
container

el **recital** SUSTANTIVO
recital (*de música*) ◇ *dar un recital de piano* to give a piano recital

recitar VERBO
to recite

la **reclamación** SUSTANTIVO (PL las **reclamaciones**)
complaint ◇ *presentar una reclamación* to make a complaint
◆ **el libro de reclamaciones** the complaints' book

reclamar VERBO
1 to complain (*protestar*) ◇ *Fui a reclamar al director.* I went and complained to the manager.
2 to demand ◇ *Reclaman mejores condiciones de trabajo.* They're demanding better working conditions.

el **reclamo** SUSTANTIVO
complaint (*queja*)

el/la **recluta** SUSTANTIVO
recruit

el **recogedor** SUSTANTIVO
dustpan

recoger* VERBO
1 to pick up (*objeto, persona*) ◇ *Se agachó para recoger la cuchara.* He bent down to pick up the spoon. ◇ *Recogí el papel del suelo.* I picked the paper up off the floor. ◇ *Me recogieron en la estación.* They picked me up at the station.
◆ **recoger fruta** to pick fruit
2 to collect (*recolectar*) ◇ *A las diez recogen la basura.* The garbage gets collected at ten o'clock.
3 to clear up (*ordenar*) ◇ *Recógelo todo antes de marcharte.* Clear up everything before you leave.
◆ **Recogí los platos y los puse en el fregadero.** I cleared away the plates and put them in the sink.
◆ **recoger la mesa** to clear the table

la **recogida** SUSTANTIVO
collection ◇ *la recogida de basura* the garbage collection ◇ *el horario de recogida del correo* the mail collection times
◆ **recogida de equipajes** baggage reclaim

la **recomendación** SUSTANTIVO (PL las **recomendaciones**)
1 recommendation (*sugerencia*) ◇ *Fuimos a ese restaurante por recomendación de un amigo.* We went to that restaurant on the recommendation of a friend.
◆ **una carta de recomendación** a letter of recommendation
2 advice (*consejo*) ◇ *Hago régimen por recomendación del médico.* I'm on a diet on my doctor's advice.

recomendar* VERBO
to recommend

la **recompensa** SUSTANTIVO
reward ◇ *Ofrecen una recompensa de 1.000 pesos.* They're offering a 1000-peso reward.

reconciliarse VERBO
◆ **reconciliarse con alguien** to make it up with somebody ◇ *Riñeron, pero se han vuelto a reconciliar.* They had a row, but they've

made it up again.

reconocer* VERBO

[1] to recognize ◇ *No te reconocí con ese sombrero.* I didn't recognize you in that hat.
[2] to admit ◇ *Reconócelo, ha sido culpa tuya.* Admit it; it was your fault.

el **reconocimiento** SUSTANTIVO

checkup ◇ *hacerse un reconocimiento médico* to have a checkup

la **reconquista** SUSTANTIVO

reconquest

reconstruir* VERBO

to rebuild

el **récord** SUSTANTIVO (PL los **récords**)

record ◇ *Posee el récord mundial de salto alto.* He holds the world record in the high jump.

- **batir el récord** to break the record
- **establecer* un récord** to set a record

recordar* VERBO

[1] to remember ◇ *No recuerdo dónde lo puse.* I can't remember where I put it.
[2] to remind ◇ *Recuérdame que hable con Daniel.* Remind me to speak to Daniel. ◇ *Me recuerda a su padre.* He reminds me of his father.

No confundir ***recordar*** *con* ***to record.***

recorrer VERBO

[1] to travel around ◇ *Recorrimos Brasil en moto.* We travelled around Brazil on a motorbike.
[2] to do ◇ *Ese día recorrimos 100 millas.* We did 100 miles that day.

el **recorrido** SUSTANTIVO

- **¿Qué recorrido hace este autobús?** Which route does this bus take?
- **un recorrido turístico** a tour
- **un tren de largo recorrido** an inter-city train

recortar VERBO

to cut out ◇ *Recorté el artículo para enseñárselo a Pedro.* I cut the article out to show it to Pedro.

- **recortar gastos** to cut costs

el **recorte** SUSTANTIVO

- **recortes de prensa** press cuttings
- **recortes de personal** staff cutbacks

recostarse* VERBO

to lie down ◇ *Se recostó en el sofá.* He lay down on the sofa.

el **recreo** SUSTANTIVO

break ◇ *Tenemos 20 minutos de recreo.* We have a 20-minute break.

- **Salimos al recreo a las 11.** (*en colegio*) We have recess at 11 o'clock.
- **la hora del recreo** playtime

la **recta** SUSTANTIVO

straight line

- **la recta final** (*en carrera*) the home straight

rectangular ADJETIVO

rectangular

el **rectángulo** SUSTANTIVO

rectangle

recto ADJETIVO, ADVERBIO

straight ◇ *una línea recta* a straight line ◇ *Mantén la espalda recta.* Keep your back straight.

- **todo recto** straight ahead ◇ *Siga todo recto.* Go straight ahead.

el **recuadro** SUSTANTIVO

box (PL boxes)

recuerdo VERBO *ver* **recordar**

el **recuerdo** SUSTANTIVO

[1] memory (PL memories) ◇ *Me trae buenos recuerdos.* It brings back happy memories.
[2] souvenir ◇ *una tienda de recuerdos* a souvenir shop

- **un recuerdo de familia** a family heirloom
- **¡Recuerdos a tu mamá!** Give my regards to your mother!
- **Dale recuerdos de mi parte.** Give him my regards.

la **recuperación** SUSTANTIVO (PL las **recuperaciones**)

recovery (*de un enfermo*)

recuperar VERBO

to get back ◇ *Tardé unos minutos en recuperar el aliento.* It took me a few minutes to get my breath back.

- **recuperar fuerzas** to get one's strength back
- **recuperarse de (1)** (*gripe, resfriado*) to get over ◇ *Tardé una semana en recuperarme de la gripe.* It took me a week to get over my flu.
- **recuperarse de (2)** (*operación, infarto*) to recover from ◇ *Se está recuperando de la operación.* He's recovering from the operation.
- **recuperar el tiempo perdido** to make up for lost time

recurrir VERBO

- **recurrir a algo** to resort to something ◇ *Hay que evitar recurrir a la violencia.* We must avoid resorting to violence.
- **recurrir a alguien** to turn to somebody ◇ *¿A quién puedo recurrir?* Who can I turn to?

el **recurso** SUSTANTIVO

- **como último recurso** as a last resort
- **recursos** resources ◇ *recursos naturales* natural resources

la **red** SUSTANTIVO

[1] net ◇ *una red de pesca* a fishing net ◇ *La pelota dio contra la red.* The ball went into the net.
[2] network (*de carreteras, ferrocarriles*) ◇ *una red informática* a computer network

- **la Red** (*Internet*) the Net
- **una red de tiendas** a chain of shops

la **redacción** SUSTANTIVO (PL las **redacciones**)

essay

- **hacer* una redacción sobre algo** to write an essay on something
- **el equipo de redacción** the editorial staff

redactar VERBO
to write ◇ *redactar un artículo de periódico* to write a newspaper article

el **redactor,** la **redactora** SUSTANTIVO
editor ◇ *el redactor deportivo* the sports editor ◇ *la redactora jefe* the editor in chief

la **redada** SUSTANTIVO
raid ◇ *Fue detenido en una redada policial.* He was arrested during a police raid.
◆ **La policía hizo una redada en el club.** The police raided the club.

redondo ADJETIVO
round ◇ *una mesa redonda* a round table
◆ **Todo salió redondo.** Everything worked out perfectly.

la **reducción** SUSTANTIVO (PL las **reducciones**)
reduction

reducir* VERBO
1 to reduce (*producción, condena, fotografía*) ◇ *Reduzca la velocidad.* Reduce speed.
2 to cut (*gastos, impuestos*) ◇ *Van a reducir el personal.* They're going to cut staff.

reembolsar VERBO
to refund

el **reembolso** SUSTANTIVO
refund ◇ *Cancelaron la excursión y nos hicieron un reembolso.* They canceled the trip and gave us a refund.
◆ **enviar* algo contra reembolso** to send something cash on delivery

reemplazar* VERBO
to replace

la **referencia** SUSTANTIVO
reference ◇ *un punto de referencia* a point of reference
◆ **con referencia a** with reference to
◆ **hacer* referencia a** to refer to
◆ **referencias** references ◇ *La niñera traía muy buenas referencias.* The babysitter had very good references.

el **referéndum** SUSTANTIVO (PL los **referéndums**)
referendum (PL referenda *o* referendums)

referente ADJETIVO
◆ **referente a** concerning ◇ *el párrafo referente al uniforme escolar* the paragraph concerning the school uniform

referirse* VERBO
◆ **referirse a** to refer to ◇ *¿Te refieres a mí?* Are you referring to me?
◆ **¿A qué te refieres? (1)** (*¿qué quieres decir?*) What exactly do you mean?
◆ **¿A qué te refieres? (2)** (*más en concreto*) What are you referring to?

la **refinería** SUSTANTIVO
refinery (PL refineries)

refiriendo VERBO *ver* **referir**

reflejar VERBO
to reflect

el **reflejo** SUSTANTIVO
reflection ◇ *el reflejo de la luna en el lago* the reflection of the moon in the lake
◆ **reflejos** reflexes ◇ *Estás bien de reflejos.* You have good reflexes.

la **reflexión** SUSTANTIVO (PL las **reflexiones**)
reflection

reflexionar VERBO
to think ◇ *Hace las cosas sin reflexionar.* He does things without thinking. ◇ *reflexionar sobre algo* to think about something
◆ **Reflexiona bien antes de tomar una decisión.** Think it over carefully before taking a decision.

reflexivo ADJETIVO
reflexive (*verbo*)

la **reforma** SUSTANTIVO
1 reform (*de ley*) ◇ *la reforma educativa* the education reforms PL
2 alteration (*de edificio, casa*) ◇ *Estamos haciendo reformas en el departamento.* We're having alterations made to the apartment.
◆ **"Cerrado por reformas"** "Closed for remodelling"

reformar VERBO
1 to reform (*ley*)
2 to fix up (*edificio, casa*)

el **refrán** SUSTANTIVO (PL los **refranes**)
saying

refrescante ADJETIVO
refreshing

refrescar* VERBO
to get cooler
◆ **refrescarse** to freshen up

el **refresco** SUSTANTIVO
soft drink

el **refrigerador** SUSTANTIVO
refridgerator

el **refugiado,** la **refugiada** SUSTANTIVO
refugee

refugiarse VERBO
1 to shelter (*de la lluvia*) ◇ *Nos refugiamos de la lluvia en un portal.* We sheltered from the rain in a doorway.
2 to take refuge (*de peligro, enemigo*) ◇ *La gente se refugiaba en los sótanos.* People took refuge in the cellars.

el **refugio** SUSTANTIVO
refuge ◇ *un refugio de montaña* a mountain refuge
◆ **Los andinistas buscaron refugio en una cueva.** The climbers sheltered in a cave.
◆ **un refugio antiaéreo** an air-raid shelter

la **regadera** SUSTANTIVO
1 watering can (*para las plantas*)
2 shower (*ducha*) *Mexico*

regalar VERBO
1 to give ◇ *¿Y si le regalamos un libro?* What about giving him a book?

- **Ayer fue mi cumpleaños. – ¿Qué te regalaron?** It was my birthday yesterday. – What did you get?

  [2] to give away (*objeto usado*) ◇ *La tele vieja la vamos a regalar.* We're going to give the old TV away.

el **regaliz** SUSTANTIVO

licorice

el **regalo** SUSTANTIVO

present ◇ *hacer un regalo a alguien* to give somebody a present

- **una tienda de regalos** a gift shop
- **papel de regalo** wrapping paper
- **de regalo** free ◇ *un CD de regalo con la compra de una radiocasete* a free CD when you buy a radio cassette player

regañadientes ADVERBIO

- **a regañadientes** reluctantly

regañar VERBO

to tell off ◇ *La maestra me regañó por llegar tarde.* The teacher told me off for being late.

regar* VERBO

to water

la **regata** SUSTANTIVO

yacht race

regatear VERBO

[1] to haggle ◇ *Regateaban por el precio de la alfombra.* They were haggling over the price of the carpet.

[2] to dodge past (*esquivar*) ◇ *Regateó a varios defensas.* He dodged past several defenders.

el **régimen** SUSTANTIVO (PL los **regímenes**)

[1] diet

- **estar* a régimen** to be on a diet
- **ponerse* a régimen** to go on a diet

[2] regime ◇ *un régimen comunista* a communist regime

el **regimiento** SUSTANTIVO

regiment

la **región** SUSTANTIVO (PL las **regiones**)

region

regional ADJETIVO

regional

registrar VERBO

[1] to search (*inspeccionar*) ◇ *Estuvieron registrando la casa.* They were searching the house. ◇ *Me registraron.* They searched me.

[2] to register (*inscribir*) ◇ *Tienes que registrarte en el consulado.* You have to register at the consulate.

[3] to check in ◇ *Fui a recepción a registrarme.* I went to reception to check in.

- **Me registré en el hotel.** I checked into the hotel.

el **registro** SUSTANTIVO

[1] search (PL searches) (*inspección*)

- **realizar* un registro en un lugar** to carry out a search of a place

[2] register (*libro*)

- **el registro civil** the county clerk's office

la **regla** SUSTANTIVO

[1] rule ◇ *saltarse las reglas* to break the rules

[2] period ◇ *Estoy con la regla.* I'm having my period.

[3] ruler ◇ *Trazó la línea con una regla.* He drew the line with a ruler.

- **por regla general** generally
- **tener* todo en regla** to have everything in order

el **reglamento** SUSTANTIVO

regulations PL ◇ *El reglamento no lo permite.* The regulations don't allow it.

regresar VERBO

[1] to go back (*a donde se estaba*) ◇ *Paco regresó a casa a buscar el paraguas.* Paco went back home to pick up his umbrella.

[2] to come back (*a donde se está*) ◇ *Regresaré sobre las ocho.* I'll come back at about eight.

- **Regresamos tarde.** We got back late.

[3] to give back (*devolver*)

- **regresarse (1)** (*a donde se estaba*) to go back
- **regresarse (2)** (*a donde se está*) to come back

el **regreso** SUSTANTIVO

return

- **a nuestro regreso** on our return
- **de regreso** on the way back ◇ *De regreso paramos a comer en Guanajuato.* On the way back we stopped to have lunch in Guanajuato.

regulable ADJETIVO

adjustable

regular (1) ADJETIVO

regular ◇ *un verbo regular* a regular verb ◇ *a intervalos regulares* at regular intervals

- **La obra estuvo regular.** The play was pretty ordinary.

regular (2) ADVERBIO

- **El examen me fue regular.** My exam didn't go brilliantly.
- **¿Cómo te encuentras? – Regular.** How are you? – Not too bad.

rehacer* VERBO

to redo

el/la **rehén** SUSTANTIVO (PL los/las **rehenes**)

hostage

la **reina** SUSTANTIVO

queen

el **reinado** SUSTANTIVO

reign

el **reino** SUSTANTIVO

kingdom

el **Reino Unido** SUSTANTIVO

the United Kingdom

reír* VERBO

to laugh ◇ *No te rías.* Don't laugh.

- **echarse a reír** to burst out laughing
- **Siempre nos reímos con él.** We always have a good laugh with him.

R ☞

◆ **reírse** to laugh
◆ **reírse de** to laugh at ◇ *¿De qué te ríes?* What are you laughing at?

la **reivindicación** SUSTANTIVO (PL las **reivindicaciones**)
claim ◇ *reivindicaciones salariales* wage claims

la **reja** SUSTANTIVO
grille ◇ *La puerta de la joyería está protegida con una reja.* The door to the jeweler's is protected with a grille.
◆ **estar* entre rejas** to be behind bars

la **relación** SUSTANTIVO (PL las **relaciones**)
1 link ◇ *la relación entre el tabaco y el cáncer* the link between smoking and cancer
2 relationship ◇ *Tenemos una relación de amistad.* We have a friendly relationship.
◆ **las relaciones entre empresarios y trabajadores** the relationship between employers and workers
◆ **con relación a** in relation to
◆ **relaciones públicas** public relations
◆ **relaciones sexuales** sexual relations

relacionar VERBO
to link ◇ *Los expertos relacionan el tabaco con el cáncer.* The experts link smoking with cancer.
◆ **Le gusta relacionarse con niños mayores que él.** He likes mixing with older children.
◆ **No se relaciona mucho con la gente.** He doesn't mix much.

relajado ADJETIVO
1 relaxed (*músculo, cuerpo*) ◇ *¿Estás relajado?* Are you feeling relaxed?
2 laid-back (*despreocupado*) ◇ *Es un tipo muy relajado.* He's a very laid-back guy.

relajante ADJETIVO
relaxing

relajar VERBO
to relax ◇ *Relaja los músculos.* Relax your muscles. ◇ *¡Relájate!* Relax!
◆ **La música clásica me relaja mucho.** I find classical music really relaxing.

el **relámpago** SUSTANTIVO
flash of lightning (PL flashes of lightning) ◇ *Vimos varios relámpagos.* We saw several flashes of lightning.
◆ **No me gustan los relámpagos.** I don't like lightning.

relativamente ADVERBIO
relatively

relativo ADJETIVO
relative ◇ *un pronombre relativo* a relative pronoun ◇ *Eso es muy relativo.* That's all relative.
◆ **en lo relativo a** concerning

el **relevo** SUSTANTIVO
◆ **una carrera de relevos** a relay race
◆ **tomar el relevo a alguien** to take over from somebody

la **religión** SUSTANTIVO (PL las **religiones**)
religion

religioso ADJETIVO
religious

el **rellano** SUSTANTIVO
landing (*de escalera*)

rellenar VERBO
1 to stuff (*tomates, pollo, muñeco*) ◇ *Rellene los pimientos con el arroz.* Stuff the peppers with the rice.
2 to fill in (*agujero*) ◇ *Rellenaron la grieta con cemento.* They filled in the crack with cement.

relleno ADJETIVO
stuffed ◇ *aceitunas rellenas* stuffed olives
◆ **relleno de algo** filled with something

el **reloj** SUSTANTIVO
1 clock (*grande, de pared*) ◇ *El reloj de la cocina está atrasado.* The kitchen clock is slow.
◆ **un reloj despertador** an alarm clock
◆ **un reloj de cuco** a cuckoo clock
◆ **contra reloj** against the clock
2 watch (PL watches) (*de pulsera*) ◇ *Se me paró el reloj.* My watch has stopped.
◆ **un reloj digital** a digital watch
◆ **un reloj sumergible** a waterproof watch
◆ **El horno tiene un reloj automático.** The stove has an automatic timer.
◆ **un reloj de sol** a sundial

la **relojera** SUSTANTIVO
watchmaker

la **relojería** SUSTANTIVO
watchmaker's (PL watchmakers')

el **relojero** SUSTANTIVO
watchmaker

relucir* VERBO
to shine

remar VERBO
1 to paddle (*con pala*)
2 to row (*con remos*)

el **remate** SUSTANTIVO
auction

remediar VERBO
to solve (*problema*) ◇ *Con llorar no vas a remediar nada.* You're not going to solve anything by crying.
◆ **Me eché a reír, no lo pude remediar.** I began to laugh; I couldn't help it.

el **remedio** SUSTANTIVO
remedy (PL remedies) ◇ *un remedio contra la tos* a cough remedy ◇ *un remedio casero* a household remedy
◆ **No tuve más remedio que hacerlo.** I had no choice but to do it.

el **remite** SUSTANTIVO
name and address of sender

el/la **remitente** SUSTANTIVO
sender

el **remo** SUSTANTIVO

[1] oar (*objeto*)
[2] rowing (*deporte*)

remojar VERBO
to soak

el **remojo** SUSTANTIVO
◆ **poner* algo en remojo** to leave something to soak

la **remolacha** SUSTANTIVO
beet

remolcar* VERBO
to tow

el **remolque** SUSTANTIVO
trailer (*vehículo*)

el **remordimiento** SUSTANTIVO
remorse ◇ *No siente remordimientos por lo que ha hecho.* He feels no remorse for what he has done.

remoto ADJETIVO
remote

el **renacuajo** SUSTANTIVO
tadpole

el **rencor** SUSTANTIVO
ill-feeling ◇ *Existe mucho rencor entre ella y su ex marido.* There's a lot of ill-feeling between her and her ex-husband.
◆ **guardar rencor a alguien** to bear a grudge against somebody ◇ *No le guardo rencor.* I don't bear him a grudge.

rencoroso ADJETIVO
◆ **No soy rencoroso.** I don't bear grudges.

rendido ADJETIVO
worn out ◇ *Estaba rendido de tanto andar.* I was worn out after so much walking.

la **rendija** SUSTANTIVO
[1] crack (*grieta*)
[2] gap (*hueco*)

el **rendimiento** SUSTANTIVO
performance (*de máquina, empleado*)

rendir* VERBO
◆ **Este negocio no rinde.** This business doesn't pay.
◆ **El dinero rinde poco en una cuenta corriente.** You don't get much interest on your money in a checking account.
◆ **rendirse (1)** to give up ◇ *No sé la respuesta; me rindo.* I don't know the answer; I give up.
◆ **rendirse (2)** to surrender ◇ *El enemigo se rindió.* The enemy surrendered.

el **renglón** SUSTANTIVO (PL los **renglones**)
line

el **reno** SUSTANTIVO
reindeer (PL reindeer *o* reindeers)

renovable ADJETIVO
renewable

renovar* VERBO
[1] to renew (*contrato, carnet*) ◇ *Tengo que renovar el pasaporte.* I must renew my passport.
[2] to renovate (*edificio, casa*) ◇ *Van a renovar la fachada del edificio.* They're going to renovate the front of the building.
[3] to change (*muebles*) ◇ *Renovaron el mobiliario de la casa.* They've changed the furniture in the house.

la **renta** SUSTANTIVO
[1] income (*ingresos*)
[2] rent (*alquiler*)

rentable ADJETIVO
profitable (*inversión, compañía*) ◇ *No es rentable organizar cursos para tan pocos alumnos.* It isn't profitable to put on courses for so few students.
◆ **una fábrica poco rentable** an uneconomic factory

rentar VERBO Mexico
to rent

reñido ADJETIVO
hard-fought (*partido*)

reñir* VERBO
[1] to tell somebody off (*regañar*) ◇ *No la riñas, la culpa no es suya.* Don't tell her off; it's not her fault.
[2] to quarrel (*discutir*) ◇ *Mi hermana y yo siempre estábamos riñendo.* My sister and I were always quarreling.
[3] to fall out (*enemistarse*) ◇ *Ángeles y Manolo riñieron.* Ángeles and Manolo have fallen out. ◇ *Riño con su novio.* She has fallen out with her boyfriend.

la **reparación** SUSTANTIVO (PL las **reparaciones**)
repair
◆ **"reparaciones en el acto"** "repairs while you wait"

reparar VERBO
to repair

repartir VERBO
[1] to hand out (*propaganda, fotocopias*) ◇ *El profesor repartió los exámenes.* The teacher handed out the test papers.
[2] to share out (*beneficios, trabajo, pastel*) ◇ *Nos repartimos el dinero.* We shared out the money.
[3] to deliver (*periódicos*) ◇ *Repartimos pizzas a domicilio.* We deliver pizzas.
[4] to deal (*barajas*)

el **reparto** SUSTANTIVO
[1] delivery (PL deliveries) (*de mercancías*)
◆ **reparto a domicilio** home delivery service
[2] cast (*de película*) ◇ *un reparto estelar* a star-studded cast

repasar VERBO
[1] to check (*suma, texto*) ◇ *Repasé la carta antes de firmarla.* I checked the letter before signing it.
[2] to review (*lección*)
◆ **repasar para un examen** to review for an exam

el **repaso** SUSTANTIVO
review (*para un examen*)
◆ **Tengo que darles un repaso a los apuntes.** I must review my notes.

el **repelente** SUSTANTIVO
repellent (*para insectos*)

R

el/la **repelente** SUSTANTIVO
know-it-all (*niño, persona*)

repente ADVERBIO
◆ **de repente** suddenly

repentino ADJETIVO
sudden

el **repertorio** SUSTANTIVO
repertoire

la **repetición** SUSTANTIVO (PL las **repeticiones**)
repetition

repetidamente ADVERBIO
repeatedly

repetir* VERBO
1 to repeat (*palabra, experimento*)
◇ *¿Podría repetirlo, por favor?* Could you repeat that, please?
2 to have a second helping ◇ *El arroz está tan bueno que voy a repetir.* The rice is so good that I'm going to have a second helping.

repetitivo ADJETIVO
repetitive

la **repisa** SUSTANTIVO
shelf (PL shelves)
◆ **la repisa de la chimenea** the mantlepiece

repitiendo VERBO *ver* **repetir**

el **repollo** SUSTANTIVO
cabbage

el **reportaje** SUSTANTIVO
1 documentary (PL documentaries) (*en televisión*)
2 article (*en periódico*)

el **reposacabezas** SUSTANTIVO (PL los **reposacabezas**)
headrest

la **reposición** SUSTANTIVO (PL las **reposiciones**)
1 rerun (*en televisión*)
2 revival (*en teatro*)

repostar VERBO
to refuel (*avión*)

la **repostería** SUSTANTIVO
confectionery (*dulces*)

la **representación** SUSTANTIVO (PL las **representaciones**)
performance (*de teatro*)

el/la **representante** SUSTANTIVO
1 representative (*de organización, empresa*)
2 agent (*de artista*)

representar VERBO
1 to represent (*país, organización*) ◇ *La representaba su abogado.* Her lawyer was representing her.
2 to put on (*obra teatral*) ◇ *Los niños van a representar una obra de teatro.* The children are going to put on a play.
3 to play (*papel*) ◇ *Representa el papel de Don Juan.* He's playing the part of Don Juan.
◆ **Tiene cuarenta años pero no los representa.** He's forty but he doesn't look it.

representativo ADJETIVO
representative

el **reprimido**, la **reprimida** ADJETIVO, SUSTANTIVO
◆ **Es una reprimida.** She's repressed.

reprobar* VERBO
to fail ◇ *Lo reprobaron en matemáticas.* He failed math.

reprochar VERBO
◆ **Me reprochó que no la hubiera invitado.** He reproached me for not having invited her.

la **reproducción** SUSTANTIVO (PL las **reproducciones**)
reproduction

reproducirse* VERBO
to reproduce

el **reproductor** SUSTANTIVO
◆ **un reproductor de CD** a CD player

el **reptil** SUSTANTIVO
reptile

la **república** SUSTANTIVO
republic

la **República Dominicana** SUSTANTIVO
the Dominican Republic

el **republicano**, la **republicana** ADJETIVO, SUSTANTIVO
republican

el **repuesto** SUSTANTIVO
spare part (*pieza*)
◆ **de repuesto** spare ◇ *la rueda de repuesto* the spare tire

repugnante ADJETIVO
revolting

la **reputación** SUSTANTIVO (PL las **reputaciones**)
reputation
◆ **tener* buena reputación** to have a good reputation

el **requesón** SUSTANTIVO
cottage cheese

el **requisito** SUSTANTIVO
requirement ◇ *Cumple todos los requisitos para el puesto.* He satisfies all the requirements for the job.

la **resaca** SUSTANTIVO
hangover
◆ **tener* resaca** to have a hangover

resaltar VERBO
1 to stand out ◇ *Lo escribí en mayúsculas para que resaltara.* I wrote it in capitals to make it stand out.
2 to highlight ◇ *El conferenciante resaltó el problema del paro.* The speaker highlighted the problem of unemployment.

resbaladizo ADJETIVO
slippery

resbalar VERBO
to skid (*vehículo*) ◇ *El carro resbaló y casi nos estrellamos.* The car skidded and we almost crashed.
◆ **resbalarse** to slip ◇ *Me resbalé con el hielo de la acera.* I slipped on the icy sidewalk.

resbaloso ADJETIVO
slippery

rescatar VERBO
to rescue

el **rescate** SUSTANTIVO
1 rescue (*salvamento*) ◇ *un equipo de rescate* a rescue team
2 ransom (*dinero*)
◆ **pedir* un rescate por alguien** to hold somebody for ransom

el/la **reserva** SUSTANTIVO
reserve (*jugador*)

la **reserva** SUSTANTIVO
1 reservation ◇ *He hecho una reserva en el Hilton para dos noches.* I've made a reservation at the Hilton for two nights.
◆ **Tengo mis reservas al respecto.** I have reservations about it.
2 reserve ◇ *una reserva natural* a nature reserve ◇ *El país tiene abundantes reservas de trigo.* The country has plentiful reserves of wheat.

reservado ADJETIVO
reserved (*persona*)

reservar VERBO
to reserve (*mesa, entradas*)

resfriado ADJETIVO
◆ **estar* resfriado** to have a cold ◇ *No fui porque estaba muy resfriado.* I didn't go because I had a bad cold.

el **resfriado** SUSTANTIVO
cold
◆ **agarrar un resfriado** to catch a cold

resfriarse* VERBO
to catch a cold

el **resguardo** SUSTANTIVO
1 ticket (*de tintorería, relojería*)
2 sales slip (*recibo de compra*)

la **residencia** SUSTANTIVO
residence ◇ *un permiso de residencia* a residence permit ◇ *La reunión tuvo lugar en la residencia del presidente.* The meeting took place at the president's residence.
◆ **una residencia de ancianos** a home for the elderly
◆ **una residencia de estudiantes** residence hall
◆ **una residencia sanitaria** a hospital

residencial ADJETIVO
residential ◇ *una zona residencial* a residential area

los **residuos** SUSTANTIVO
waste SING ◇ *residuos radiactivos* radioactive waste

la **resistencia** SUSTANTIVO
resistance ◇ *Los manifestantes no ofrecieron resistencia.* The demonstrators didn't offer any resistance.
◆ **resistencia física** stamina

resistente ADJETIVO
tough ◇ *El diamante es una piedra muy resistente.* Diamond is a very tough stone.
◆ **resistente al calor** heat-resistant

resistir VERBO
1 to resist (*tentación*) ◇ *No pude resistir las ganas de decírselo.* I couldn't resist the urge to tell him.
2 to take (*peso, presión*) ◇ *Esta caja no va a resistir tanto peso.* This box won't take so much weight.
3 to stand (*dolor*) ◇ *No puedo resistir este frío.* I can't stand this cold.
◆ **Se resisten a cooperar.** They are refusing to cooperate.

resolver* VERBO
to solve (*problema, caso*)

respaldar VERBO
to back up ◇ *Mis hermanos me respaldaron.* My brothers and sisters backed me up.

el **respaldo** SUSTANTIVO
back (*de asiento*)

respectivamente ADVERBIO
respectively

respecto SUSTANTIVO
◆ **con respecto a** with regard to

respetable ADJETIVO
respectable

respetar VERBO
1 to respect (*persona, opinión*)
2 to obey (*código, norma*) ◇ *No se respetan las normas de seguridad.* The safety regulations aren't being obeyed.

el **respeto** SUSTANTIVO
respect ◇ *el respeto a los animales* respect for animals
◆ **tener* respeto a alguien** to respect somebody
◆ **No le faltes al respeto.** Don't be disrespectful to him.

la **respiración** SUSTANTIVO
breathing ◇ *Tenía la respiración irregular.* His breathing was irregular.
◆ **quedarse sin respiración** to be out of breath
◆ **la respiración boca a boca** the kiss of life ◇ *Le hicieron la respiración boca a boca.* They gave him the kiss of life.
◆ **la respiración artificial** artificial respiration

respirar VERBO
to breathe

responder VERBO
1 to answer (*pregunta*) ◇ *Eso no responde a mi pregunta.* That doesn't answer my question.
2 to reply ◇ *No han respondido a mi carta.* They haven't replied to my letter. ◇ *Respondió que habían salido con unos amigos.* He replied that they had gone out with some friends.
3 to respond (*reaccionar*) ◇ *No responde al tratamiento.* He's not responding to the treatment.

la **responsabilidad** SUSTANTIVO

R

responsibility (PL responsibilities)

responsable ADJETIVO
responsible ◇ *Cada cual es responsable de sus acciones.* Everybody is responsible for their own actions.

el/la **responsable** SUSTANTIVO
- **Tú eres la responsable de lo ocurrido.** You're responsible for what happened.
- **Los responsables serán castigados.** Those responsible will be punished.
- **Juan es el responsable de la cocina.** Juan is in charge of the kitchen.

la **respuesta** SUSTANTIVO
answer

resquebrajarse VERBO
to crack

la **resta** SUSTANTIVO
subtraction

restante ADJETIVO
remaining

restar VERBO
to subtract ◇ *Está aprendiendo a restar.* He's learning to subtract.
- **Tienes que restar 16 de 36.** You have to take 16 away from 36.

la **restauración** SUSTANTIVO (PL las **restauraciones**)
restoration

el **restaurante** SUSTANTIVO
restaurant

restaurar VERBO
to restore

el **resto** SUSTANTIVO
rest ◇ *Yo haré el resto.* I'll do the rest.
- **los restos (1)** (*de comida*) the leftovers
- **los restos (2)** (*de avión, naufragio*) the wreckage SING

restregar* VERBO
to rub ◇ *Cuando tiene sueño se restriega los ojos.* He rubs his eyes when he's sleepy.

la **restricción** SUSTANTIVO (PL las **restricciones**)
restriction

resuelto VERBO *ver* **resolver**

resuelvo VERBO *ver* **resolver**

el **resultado** SUSTANTIVO
[1] result (*de examen, experimento*)
[2] score (*de encuentro deportivo*)
- **dar* resultado** to work ◇ *Nuestro plan no dio resultado.* Our plan didn't work.

resultar VERBO
to turn out ◇ *Al final resultó que él tenía razón.* In the end it turned out that he was right.
- **Me resultó violento decírselo.** I found it embarrassing to tell him.

el **resumen** SUSTANTIVO (PL los **resúmenes**)
summary (PL summaries) ◇ *un resumen de las noticias* a news summary
- **hacer* un resumen de algo** to summarize something
- **en resumen** in short

resumir VERBO
to summarize (*artículo, libro*)
- **Dijo, resumiendo, que el viaje había sido un desastre.** He said, in short, that the trip had been a disaster.

retar VERBO
to challenge (*desafiar*)

retirar VERBO
[1] to take away ◇ *La camarera retiró las copas.* The waitress took the glasses away. ◇ *Le retiraron la licencia de manejar.* He's had his driver's license taken away.
[2] to withdraw ◇ *Fui a retirar dinero de la cuenta.* I went to withdraw some money from my account. ◇ *Se retiraron del torneo.* They withdrew from the tournament.
- **retirarse** to retire ◇ *Mi padre se retira el año que viene.* My father will be retiring next year.

el **reto** SUSTANTIVO
challenge

retorcer* VERBO
to twist ◇ *Me retorció el brazo.* He twisted my arm.
- **retorcerse de risa** to double up with laughter

la **retransmisión** SUSTANTIVO (PL las **retransmisiones**)
broadcast ◇ *una retransmisión en directo* a live broadcast

retransmitir VERBO
to broadcast

retrasado ADJETIVO
[1] behind (*en una actividad*) ◇ *Voy retrasado con este trabajo.* I'm behind with this work.
[2] slow (*reloj*) ◇ *Este reloj va retrasado veinte minutos.* This clock is twenty minutes slow.
- **Tienen un hijo un poco retrasado.** They have a son with learning difficulties.

retrasar VERBO
[1] to postpone (*reunión, viaje*) ◇ *Retrasaron la boda al quince.* They postponed the wedding until the fifteenth.
[2] to delay (*salida*) ◇ *El mal tiempo retrasó nuestro vuelo.* Our flight was delayed due to bad weather.
[3] to put back (*reloj*) ◇ *A las doce hay que retrasar los relojes una hora.* At twelve o'clock the clocks have to be put back one hour.
- **retrasarse** (*persona, tren*) to be late ◇ *El tren de las nueve se retrasó.* The nine o'clock train was late.
- **Tu reloj se retrasa.** Your watch is slow.

el **retraso** SUSTANTIVO
delay ◇ *La niebla causó algunos retrasos.* The fog caused some delays.
- **Perdonen por el retraso.** Sorry I'm late.

- **ir* con retraso** to be running late
- **llegar* con retraso** to be late ◇ *El vuelo llegó con una hora de retraso.* The flight was an hour late.

el **retrato** SUSTANTIVO
portrait (*cuadro*)
- **hacer* un retrato a alguien** to paint somebody's portrait

el **retrete** SUSTANTIVO
bathroom

retroceder VERBO
to go back

el **retrovisor** SUSTANTIVO
rearview mirror

retuerzo VERBO *ver* **retorcer**

el **reúma** SUSTANTIVO
rheumatism

la **reunión** SUSTANTIVO (PL las **reuniones**)
1 meeting (*de trabajo*) ◇ *Mañana tenemos una reunión.* We have a meeting tomorrow.
2 gathering (*social*) ◇ *una reunión familiar* a family gathering

reunir* VERBO
1 to gather together (*personas*) ◇ *La maestra reunió a los niños en el patio.* The teacher gathered the children together in the playground.
2 to satisfy (*requisitos*) ◇ *Paula reúne los requisitos para el puesto.* Paula satisfies all the requirements for the job.
3 to raise (*fondos*) ◇ *Estamos reuniendo dinero para el viaje de fin de curso.* We're raising money for the end-of-year trip.
- **reunirse (1)** to gather ◇ *Miles de personas se reunieron en la plaza.* Thousands of people gathered in the square.
- **reunirse (2)** to get together ◇ *En Navidad nos reunimos toda la familia.* The whole family gets together at Christmas.
- **reunirse (3)** to meet ◇ *El comité se reúne una vez al mes.* The committee meets once a month.

revelar VERBO
1 to develop ◇ *Luis revela sus propias fotos.* Luis develops his own photos.
- **Todavía no hemos revelado las fotos.** We haven't had the photos developed yet.
- **Llevé los carretes a revelar.** I took the films to be developed.

2 to reveal (*secreto*) ◇ *No quería revelar su identidad.* He didn't want to reveal his identity.

reventar* VERBO
to burst (*globo, rueda*)
- **Me revienta tener que ponerme corbata.** I hate having to wear a necktie.

el **revés** SUSTANTIVO (PL los **reveses**)
backhand (*en tenis*)
- **al revés (1)** the other way round ◇ *¿Tres, tres, dos? – No, al revés: dos, dos, tres.* Three, three, two? – No, the other way round: two, two, three.
- **al revés (2)** inside out ◇ *Te pusiste los calcetines al revés.* You've put your socks on inside out.
- **al revés (3)** back to front ◇ *Miré el cuello y vi que llevaba el suéter al revés.* I looked at the collar and realized that I had my sweater on back to front.
- **al revés (4)** upside down ◇ *El dibujo está al revés.* The picture is upside down.

reviento VERBO *ver* **reventar**

revisar VERBO
1 to check ◇ *Un electricista me revisó la instalación.* An electrician checked the wiring for me.
- **Tengo que ir a que me revisen el carro.** I must take my car for servicing.

2 to search (*maleta, bolsillos*)

la **revisión** SUSTANTIVO (PL las **revisiones**)
service ◇ *He llevado el carro a revisión.* I've taken the car for servicing.
- **una revisión médica** a checkup

el **revisor,** la **revisora** SUSTANTIVO
ticket collector

la **revista** SUSTANTIVO
magazine
- **una revista electrónica** a webzine

revoltoso ADJETIVO
naughty

la **revolución** SUSTANTIVO (PL las **revoluciones**)
revolution

el **revolucionario,** la **revolucionaria** SUSTANTIVO
revolutionary (PL revolutionaries)

revolver* VERBO
1 to mess up (*desordenar*) ◇ *Los niños han revuelto la habitación otra vez.* The children have messed the room up again.
- **No revuelvas mis papeles.** Don't mess my papers up.

2 to turn upside down ◇ *Los ladrones revolvieron toda la casa.* The burglars turned the whole house upside down.
3 to rummage in (*fisgar*) ◇ *No me gusta que me revuelvas el bolso.* I don't like you rummaging in my bag.

R

el **revólver** SUSTANTIVO (PL los **revólveres**)
revolver

revuelto (1) VERBO *ver* **revolver**

revuelto (2) ADJETIVO
in a mess (*desordenado*) ◇ *Todo estaba revuelto.* Everything was in a mess.
- **Las fotos están revueltas.** The photos are messed up.
- **El tiempo está muy revuelto.** The weather's very unsettled.
- **Tengo el estómago revuelto.** I have an upset stomach.

el **rey** SUSTANTIVO (PL los **reyes**)
king
- **Los reyes visitaron China.** The king and

☞

queen visited China.

◆ **los Reyes Magos** the Three Wise Men

rezar* VERBO
to pray ◇ *rezar por algo* to pray for something

◆ **rezar el Padre nuestro** to say the Lord's Prayer

la **ría** SUSTANTIVO
estuary (PL estuaries)

el **riachuelo** SUSTANTIVO
stream

la **ribera** SUSTANTIVO
bank (*del río*)

la **rica** SUSTANTIVO
rich woman (PL rich women)

el **rico** SUSTANTIVO
rich man (PL rich men)

◆ **los ricos** the rich

rico ADJETIVO
1 rich (*persona, barrio*) ◇ *Son muy ricos.* They're very rich.
2 delicious (*comida*) ◇ *¡Qué rico!* How delicious!

ridiculizar* VERBO
to ridicule

ridículo ADJETIVO
ridiculous ◇ *¿A que suena ridículo?* Doesn't it sound ridiculous?

◆ **hacer* el ridículo** to make a fool of oneself

◆ **poner* a alguien en ridículo** to make a fool of somebody

el **riel** SUSTANTIVO
rail

las **riendas** SUSTANTIVO
reins

riendo VERBO *ver* **reír**

el **riesgo** SUSTANTIVO
risk

◆ **correr riesgos** to take risks ◇ *No quiero correr ese riesgo.* I'd rather not take that risk.

◆ **Corres el riesgo de que te despidan.** You run the risk of being fired.

◆ **un seguro a todo riesgo** a fully comprehensive insurance policy

la **rifa** SUSTANTIVO
raffle

el **rifle** SUSTANTIVO
rifle

rígido ADJETIVO
1 stiff (*tieso*)
2 strict (*estricto*)

riguroso ADJETIVO
1 strict (*control, dieta, disciplina*)
2 severe (*castigo*)

la **rima** SUSTANTIVO
rhyme

el **rímel** SUSTANTIVO
mascara ◇ *No me he puesto rímel.* I haven't put any mascara on.

el **rincón** SUSTANTIVO (PL los **rincones**)
corner

el **rinoceronte** SUSTANTIVO
rhinoceros (PL rhinoceroses *o* rhinoceros)

la **riña** SUSTANTIVO
1 row (*discusión*)
2 brawl (*pelea*)

riñendo VERBO *ver* **reñir**

el **riñón** SUSTANTIVO (PL los **riñones**)
kidney ◇ *un transplante de riñón* a kidney transplant

◆ **Me duelen los riñones.** I have a pain in my lower back.

la **riñonera** SUSTANTIVO
fanny pack

río VERBO *ver* **reír**

el **río** SUSTANTIVO
river ◇ *el río Jordán* the River Jordan

la **riqueza** SUSTANTIVO
1 wealth (*posesiones*) ◇ *la distribución de la riqueza* the distribution of wealth
2 richness (*abundancia*) ◇ *la riqueza de su lenguaje* the richness of his language

la **risa** SUSTANTIVO
laugh ◇ *una risa contagiosa* an infectious laugh

◆ **Me da risa.** It makes me laugh.

◆ **Daba risa la manera en que lo explicaba.** It was so funny the way he told it.

◆ **¡Qué risa!** What a laugh!

◆ **partirse de risa** to split one's sides laughing

el **ritmo** SUSTANTIVO
1 rhythm ◇ *No tiene sentido del ritmo.* He has no sense of rhythm.

◆ **Daban palmas al ritmo de la música.** They were clapping in time to the music.

2 pace ◇ *el ritmo de vida* the pace of life

el **ritual** SUSTANTIVO
ritual

el/la **rival** ADJETIVO, SUSTANTIVO
rival

la **rivalidad** SUSTANTIVO
rivalry (PL rivalries)

rizado ADJETIVO
curly ◇ *Tiene el pelo rizado.* He has curly hair.

rizar* VERBO
1 to curl (*con rulos, rizador*) ◇ *Me rizo las pestañas.* I curl my eyelashes.
2 to perm (*con permanente*)

◆ **Se ha rizado el pelo.** She has had her hair permed.

el **rizo** SUSTANTIVO
curl

robar VERBO
1 to steal (*objeto, dinero*) ◇ *Me robaron la billetera.* My billfold has been stolen. ◇ *Les robaba dinero a sus compañeros de clase.* He was stealing money from his classmates.
2 to rob (*banco, persona*) ◇ *¡Nos robaron!* We've been robbed!

◆ **Entraron a robar en mi casa.** They broke into my house.

el **roble** SUSTANTIVO
oak

el **robo** SUSTANTIVO
1 theft (*de dinero, objetos*)
2 robbery (PL robberies) (*a una persona, tienda, banco*)
3 burglary (PL burglaries) (*en una casa*)
◆ **¡Estos precios son un robo!** This is a rip-off!

el **robot** SUSTANTIVO (PL los **robots**)
robot
◆ **el robot de cocina** the food processor

robusto ADJETIVO
strong

la **roca** SUSTANTIVO
rock

rociar* VERBO
to spray

el **rocío** SUSTANTIVO
dew

la **rodaja** SUSTANTIVO
slice ◇ *cortar algo en rodajas* to cut something into slices

el **rodaje** SUSTANTIVO
shooting (*de película*)
◆ **El carro está en rodaje.** The car's breaking in.

rodar* VERBO
1 to roll ◇ *La pelota bajó rodando por la cuesta.* The ball rolled down the slope.
2 to shoot ◇ *rodar una película* to shoot a movie

rodear VERBO
to surround ◇ *el bosque que rodea el palacio* the forest that surrounds the palace
◆ **rodeado de** surrounded by

la **rodilla** SUSTANTIVO
knee
◆ **ponerse* de rodillas** to kneel down

el **rodillo** SUSTANTIVO
1 rolling pin (*para amasar*)
2 roller (*para pintar*)

rogar* VERBO
1 to beg ◇ *Me rogó que le perdonara.* He begged me to forgive him.
2 to pray (*rezar*) ◇ *Le rogué a Dios que se curara.* I prayed to God to make him better.
◆ **"Se ruega no fumar"** "Please do not smoke"

el **rojo** ADJETIVO, SUSTANTIVO
red ◇ *Va vestida de rojo.* She's wearing red.
◆ **ponerse* rojo** to go red ◇ *Se puso rojo de vergüenza.* He went red with embarrassment.

el **rollo** SUSTANTIVO
roll (*de película, papel, tela*) ◇ *un rollo de papel higiénico* a roll of toilet paper
◆ **La conferencia fue un rollo.** The lecture was really boring.

Roma SUSTANTIVO FEM
Rome

el **romano**, la **romana** ADJETIVO, SUSTANTIVO
Roman ◇ *los números romanos* Roman numerals
◆ **Es romano.** He's from Rome.
◆ **los romanos (1)** (*de la antigua Roma*) the Romans
◆ **los romanos (2)** (*actualmente*) Romans

el **romántico**, la **romántica** ADJETIVO, SUSTANTIVO
romantic

el **rombo** SUSTANTIVO
rhombus (PL rhombuses *o* rhombi)

el **rompecabezas** SUSTANTIVO (PL los **rompecabezas**)
1 jigsaw (*de piezas*)
2 puzzle (*problema*)

romper* VERBO
1 to break (*ventana, objeto, pierna*) ◇ *Me rompí el brazo.* I broke my arm. ◇ *Se rompió una taza.* A cup has been broken. ◇ *romper una promesa* to break a promise
2 to tear up (*papel*) ◇ *Rompí la foto de mi novia.* I tore up the photo of my girlfriend. ◇ *Rompió la carta a pedazos.* He tore the letter up.
◆ **Se rompió una sábana.** A sheet has been torn.
◆ **Se me rompieron los pantalones.** I've torn my pants.
◆ **romper con alguien** to finish with somebody ◇ *Rompió con el novio.* She has finished with her boyfriend.

el **ron** SUSTANTIVO
rum

roncar* VERBO
to snore

ronco ADJETIVO
hoarse
◆ **quedarse ronco** to get hoarse

la **ronda** SUSTANTIVO
round ◇ *Esta ronda la pago yo.* I'll buy this round of drinks.
◆ **hacer* la ronda** (*guarda, soldado*) to be on patrol

el **ronquido** SUSTANTIVO
snore

ronronear VERBO
to purr

la **ropa** SUSTANTIVO
clothes PL ◇ *Voy a cambiarme de ropa.* I'm going to change my clothes.
◆ **la ropa interior** underwear
◆ **ropa de deporte** sportswear
◆ **la ropa de cama** bed linen
◆ **la ropa lavada** the laundry
◆ **la ropa sucia** the dirty laundry

el **rosa** ADJETIVO, SUSTANTIVO
pink ◇ *Va vestida de rosa.* She's wearing pink.
◆ **Llevaba unos calcetines rosa.** He was wearing pink socks.

la **rosa** SUSTANTIVO

R ☞

rose

rosado ADJETIVO
rosé (*vino*)

el **rosal** SUSTANTIVO
rosebush (PL rosebushes)

el **rostro** SUSTANTIVO
face

roto VERBO *ver* **romper**

roto ADJETIVO
1 broken (*ventana, objeto, brazo*)
2 torn (*papel, tela*)
3 worn out (*zapatos*)

el **roto** SUSTANTIVO
hole (*en prenda*)

la **rotonda** SUSTANTIVO
traffic circle

el **rotulador** SUSTANTIVO
1 felt-tip pen (*para escribir, dibujar*)
2 highlighter pen (*fluorescente*)

el **rótulo** SUSTANTIVO
sign (*letrero*)

rozar* VERBO
to rub against ◇ *El sofá roza la pared.* The sofa is rubbing against the wall. ◇ *Las botas me rozan el tobillo.* My boots are rubbing against my ankle.
◆ **La rocé al pasar.** I brushed past her.

rubio ADJETIVO
fair ◇ *Luis tiene el pelo rubio.* Luis has fair hair. ◇ *Yo soy morena pero mi hermana es rubia.* I'm dark but my sister is fair.
◆ **Es rubia con los ojos azules.** She has fair hair and blue eyes.
Si nos referimos a un rubio tipo nórdico (rubio platino), o bien a un rubio teñido, se usa ***blond*** *(FEM:* ***blonde****) en lugar de* ***fair****.*
◇ *Quiero teñirme el pelo de rubio.* I want to dye my hair blond.

ruborizarse* VERBO
to blush

rudimentario ADJETIVO
basic

la **rueda** SUSTANTIVO
wheel ◇ *la rueda delantera* the front wheel ◇ *la rueda trasera* the back wheel
◆ **Se te pinchó la rueda.** You have a flat tire.
◆ **una rueda de prensa** a press conference

ruedo VERBO *ver* **rodar**

ruego VERBO *ver* **rogar**

el **rugby** SUSTANTIVO
rugby ◇ *jugar al rugby* to play rugby

rugir* VERBO
to roar

el **ruido** SUSTANTIVO
noise ◇ *¿Oíste ese ruido?* Did you hear that noise? ◇ *No hagan tanto ruido.* Don't make so much noise.

ruidoso ADJETIVO
noisy

la **ruina** SUSTANTIVO
◆ **Su socio lo llevó a la ruina.** His business partner ruined him financially.
◆ **las ruinas** (*de edificio, ciudad*) the ruins ◇ *El castillo está en ruinas.* The castle is in ruins.

el **rulo** SUSTANTIVO
roller

la **rumana** SUSTANTIVO
Romanian

Rumania SUSTANTIVO FEM
Romania

el **rumano** ADJETIVO, SUSTANTIVO
Romanian (*persona, idioma*)

la **rumba** SUSTANTIVO
rumba

el **rumor** SUSTANTIVO
1 rumor ◇ *Corre el rumor de que se retira.* There's a rumor going round that he's retiring.
2 murmur ◇ *el rumor de las olas* the murmur of the waves

rural ADJETIVO
rural

la **rusa** SUSTANTIVO
Russian

Rusia SUSTANTIVO FEM
Russia

el **ruso** ADJETIVO, SUSTANTIVO
Russian (*persona, idioma*)

la **ruta** SUSTANTIVO
route

la **rutina** SUSTANTIVO
routine ◇ *la rutina diaria* the daily routine
◆ **un chequeo de rutina** a routine checkup

S

el **sábado** SUSTANTIVO

En inglés, los días de la semana se escriben con mayúscula.

Saturday ◇ *La vi el sábado.* I saw her on Saturday. ◇ *todos los sábados* every Saturday ◇ *el sábado pasado* last Saturday ◇ *el sábado que viene* next Saturday ◇ *Jugamos los sábados.* We play on Saturdays.

la **sábana** SUSTANTIVO

sheet

saber* VERBO

1 to know ◇ *No lo sé.* I don't know. ◇ *Sabe mucho de computadoras.* He knows a lot about computers. ◇ *Lo dudo, pero nunca se sabe.* I doubt it, but you never know. ◇ *¡Y yo que sé!* How should I know?

2 to find out ◇ *En cuanto lo supimos fuimos a ayudarlo.* As soon as we found out, we went to help him.

◆ **No sé nada de ella.** I haven't heard from her.

◆ **que yo sepa** as far as I know

3 can ◇ *No sabe nadar.* She can't swim. ◇ *¿Sabes inglés?* Can you speak English?

4 to taste ◇ *Sabe a pescado.* It tastes of fish.

◆ **saberse** to know ◇ *Se sabe la lista de memoria.* He knows the list off by heart.

sabio ADJETIVO

wise

el **sabor** SUSTANTIVO

1 taste ◇ *Tiene un sabor muy raro.* It has a very strange taste.

2 flavor ◇ *¿De qué sabor lo quieres?* What flavor do you want?

el **sabotaje** SUSTANTIVO

sabotage

sabré VERBO *ver* **saber**

sabroso ADJETIVO

tasty

el **sacacorchos** SUSTANTIVO (PL los **sacacorchos**)

corkscrew

el **sacapuntas** SUSTANTIVO (PL los **sacapuntas**)

pencil sharpener

sacar* VERBO

1 to take out ◇ *Voy a sacar dinero del cajero.* I'm going to take some money out of the machine. ◇ *Se sacó las llaves del bolsillo.* He took the keys out of his pocket. ◇ *sacar la basura* to take the garbage out

◆ **Me sacaron una muela.** I've had a tooth taken out.

◆ **sacar a pasear al perro** to take the dog out for a walk

◆ **sacar a alguien a bailar** to get somebody up for a dance

2 to get ◇ *Yo sacaré las entradas.* I'll get the tickets. ◇ *sacar buenas notas* to get good grades

3 to release ◇ *Han sacado un nuevo disco.* They've released a new record.

◆ **sacar algo adelante** (*proyecto, negocio*) to conclude something

◆ **sacar una foto a alguien** to take a photo of somebody

◆ **sacar la lengua a alguien** to stick one's tongue out at somebody

◆ **sacarse el título de abogado** to qualify as a lawyer

◆ **sacarse las botas** to take off one's boots

la **sacarina** SUSTANTIVO

saccharin

el **sacerdote** SUSTANTIVO

priest

el **saco** SUSTANTIVO

1 sack ◇ *un saco de harina* a sack of flour

◆ **un saco de dormir** a sleeping bag

2 jacket (*chaqueta*)

el **sacrificio** SUSTANTIVO

sacrifice

sacudir VERBO

to shake ◇ *Hay que sacudir la alfombra.* The rug needs shaking. ◇ *Un terremoto sacudió la ciudad.* An earthquake shook the city.

Sagitario SUSTANTIVO MASC

Sagittarius ◇ *Soy sagitario.* I'm a Sagittarius.

sagrado ADJETIVO

1 sacred (*lugar*)

2 holy (*escrituras, altar*)

la **sal** SUSTANTIVO

salt

la **sala** SUSTANTIVO

1 room (*habitación*)

2 ward (*en hospital*)

3 hall (*de conferencias, conciertos*)

◆ **sala de embarque** departure lounge

◆ **sala de espera** waiting room

◆ **sala de estar** living room

◆ **sala de fiestas** nightclub

◆ **sala de juegos recreativos** amusement arcade

◆ **sala de profesores** staff room

salado ADJETIVO

1 salty ◇ *La carne está muy salada.* The meat is very salty.

2 savory ◇ *¿Es dulce o salado?* Is it sweet or savory?

el **salario** SUSTANTIVO

pay

◆ **el salario mínimo** the minimum wage

la **salchicha** SUSTANTIVO

sausage

el **salchichón** SUSTANTIVO (PL los **salchichones**)

spiced salami sausage

la **salchichonería** SUSTANTIVO Mexico

delicatessen

el **saldo** SUSTANTIVO

☞

balance (*de cuenta*)
- **saldos** (*rebajas*) sales

saldré VERBO *ver* **salir**

el **salero** SUSTANTIVO
salt shaker

salgo VERBO *ver* **salir**

la **salida** SUSTANTIVO
1 exit ◇ *salida de emergencia* emergency exit ◇ *salida de incendios* fire exit
- **a la salida del teatro** on the way out of the theater

2 departure ◇ *la terminal de salidas nacionales* the domestic departures terminal
- **El tren de Boston efectuará su salida por el andén número dos.** The Boston train will depart from platform two.

3 start (*de una carrera*)
- **El juez dio la salida a la carrera.** The referee started the race.
- **la salida del sol** sunrise

salir* VERBO
1 to come out ◇ *cuando salimos del cine* when we came out of the movie theater ◇ *Acaba de salir un disco suyo.* A record of his has just come out. ◇ *Nos levantamos antes de que saliera el sol.* We got up before the sun came out.
2 to go out ◇ *¿Vas a salir esta noche?* Are you going out tonight?
- **Salió.** She's out.
- **salir con alguien** to go out with somebody ◇ *Está saliendo con un compañero de clase.* She's going out with one of her classmates.

3 to get out ◇ *¡Sal de ahí ahora mismo!* Get out of here right now!
4 to leave ◇ *El tren sale a las ocho.* The train leaves at eight. ◇ *Quiere salir del país.* She wants to leave the country.
5 to appear ◇ *Su foto salió en todos los periódicos.* Her picture appeared in all the newspapers.
- **Me está saliendo una muela del juicio.** One of my wisdom teeth is coming through.
- **No sé cómo vamos a salir adelante.** I don't know how we're going to go on.
- **salir bien** to work out well ◇ *El plan salió bien.* The plan worked out well.
- **Espero que todo salga bien.** I hope everything works out all right.
- **salirse (1)** (*rebosar*) to boil over ◇ *Se salió la leche.* The milk has boiled over.
- **salirse (2)** (*filtrarse*) to leak ◇ *Se salía el aceite del motor.* Oil was leaking out of the engine.
- **salirse (3)** (*desviarse*) to come off ◇ *Nos salimos de la carretera.* We came off the road.
- **salirse (4)** to come out ◇ *Se salió el enchufe.* The plug has come out.

la **saliva** SUSTANTIVO
saliva

el **salmón** SUSTANTIVO (PL los **salmones**)
salmon (PL salmon)
- **rosa salmón** salmon pink

el **salón** SUSTANTIVO (PL los **salones**)
1 living room (*de una casa*)
- **salón de actos** meeting hall
- **salón de belleza** beauty salon
- **salón de juegos recreativos** amusement arcade

2 classroom (*aula*) Mexico

la **salpicadera** SUSTANTIVO
fender Mexico

el **salpicadero** SUSTANTIVO Spain
dashboard

salpicar* VERBO
to splash

la **salsa** SUSTANTIVO
1 sauce ◇ *salsa de tomate* tomato sauce
2 salsa (*música*)

el **saltamontes** SUSTANTIVO (PL los **saltamontes**)
grasshopper

saltar VERBO
to jump ◇ *El caballo saltó la valla.* The horse jumped over the fence. ◇ *saltar por la ventana* to jump out of the window
- **hacer* saltar algo por los aires** to blow something up
- **saltarse** to skip ◇ *Te saltaste una página.* You've skipped a page.
- **saltarse un semáforo en rojo** to go through a red light

el **salto** SUSTANTIVO
1 jump (*hacia arriba*)
2 dive (*en el agua*)
- **dar* un salto** to jump
- **salto alto** high jump
- **salto largo** long jump
- **salto mortal** somersault
- **salto con garrocha** pole vault
- **salto de trampolín** springboard diving

la **salud** SUSTANTIVO
health

salud EXCLAMACIÓN
1 cheers! (*al brindar*)
2 bless you! (*al estornudar*)

saludable ADJETIVO
healthy

saludar VERBO
1 to say hello ◇ *Entré a saludarla.* I went in to say hello to her.
2 to greet ◇ *Me saludó dándome un beso.* He greeted me with a kiss.
- **Lo saludé desde la otra acera.** I waved to him from the other side of the street.

3 to salute (*en el ejército*)

el **saludo** SUSTANTIVO
1 greeting ◇ *No contestó a mi saludo.* He didn't respond to my greeting.
2 regards PL ◇ *Carolina te manda un saludo.* Carolina sends her regards.

◇ *Saludos cordiales.* Kind regards.
◆ **¡Saludos a Teresa de mi parte!** Say hello to Teresa for me!

salvaje ADJETIVO
wild

el **salvapantalla** SUSTANTIVO (PL los **salvapantalla**)
screensaver

salvar VERBO
to save ◇ *Pocos se salvaron del naufragio.* Few were saved from the shipwreck.

el **salvavidas** SUSTANTIVO (PL los **salvavidas**)
life preserver

salvo PREPOSICIÓN
except ◇ *todos salvo yo* everyone except me
◆ **salvo que** unless
◆ **estar* a salvo** to be safe
◆ **Consiguieron ponerse a salvo.** They managed to reach safety.

San ADJETIVO
Saint ◇ *San Pedro* Saint Peter

la **sandalia** SUSTANTIVO
sandal
◆ **unas sandalias** a pair of sandals

la **sandía** SUSTANTIVO
watermelon

el **sandwich** SUSTANTIVO (PL los **sandwiches**)
1 sandwich (PL sandwiches) (*emparedado*)
2 toasted sandwich (*caliente*)

sangrar VERBO
to bleed ◇ *Me sangra la nariz.* My nose is bleeding.

la **sangre** SUSTANTIVO
blood

la **sangría** SUSTANTIVO
sangria (*bebida*)

la **sanidad** SUSTANTIVO
public health

el **sanitario** SUSTANTIVO
1 bathroom (*baño*) Mexico
2 toilet (*retrete*)

sano ADJETIVO
healthy (*con salud*) ◇ *una dieta sana* a healthy diet
◆ **sano y salvo** safe and sound

*No confundir **sano** con **sane**.*

la **santa** SUSTANTIVO
saint ◇ *Santa Clara* Saint Clara

santo ADJETIVO
holy

el **santo** SUSTANTIVO
1 saint ◇ *Santo Domingo* Saint Dominic
2 name day

> ℹ *Besides birthdays, some Latin Americans also celebrate the feast day of the saint they are named after.*

el **sapo** SUSTANTIVO
toad

el **saque** SUSTANTIVO
service (*en tenis*)
◆ **saque de esquina** corner

el **sarampión** SUSTANTIVO (PL los **sarampiones**)
measles SING

sarcástico ADJETIVO
sarcastic

la **sardina** SUSTANTIVO
sardine

el/la **sargento** SUSTANTIVO
sergeant

el **sarpullido** SUSTANTIVO
rash (PL rashes) ◇ *Le salió un sarpullido en la cara el lunes.* His face broke out in a rash on Monday.

el **sarro** SUSTANTIVO
tartar

la **sarta** SUSTANTIVO
◆ **Nos contó una sarta de mentiras.** He told us a pack of lies.

la **sartén** SUSTANTIVO (PL las **sartenes**)
frying pan

el **sartén** SUSTANTIVO (PL los **sartenes**)
frying pan

el **sastre** SUSTANTIVO
tailor

el **satélite** SUSTANTIVO
satellite ◇ *la televisión vía satélite* satellite television

la **satisfacción** SUSTANTIVO (PL las **satisfacciones**)
satisfaction ◇ *Expresó su satisfacción por la victoria.* She expressed her satisfaction at the victory.
◆ **Recibió la noticia con satisfacción.** He was pleased to hear the news.

satisfacer VERBO
to satisfy

satisfactorio ADJETIVO
satisfactory

satisfecho ADJETIVO
satisfied ◇ *No estoy satisfecho con el resultado del examen.* I'm not satisfied with the result of the exam.

la **sauna** SUSTANTIVO
sauna

el **saxofón** SUSTANTIVO (PL los **saxofones**)
saxophone

sazonar VERBO
to season

se PRONOMBRE

*Cuando **se** funciona como complemento indirecto, junto a otro pronombre, se traduce por **him**, **her**, **them** o **you**, según nos refiramos a "él", "ella", "ellos" o "ellas" y "usted" o "ustedes".*

◇ *Pedro necesitaba la calculadora y se la dejé.* Pedro needed the calculator and I lent it to him. ◇ *No quiero que Rosa lo sepa. No se lo digas.* I don't want Rosa to know. Don't tell her. ◇ *Hablé con mis padres y se lo he expliqué.* I've talked to my parents and ☞

S

explained it to them. ◇ *Aquí tiene las flores. ¿Se las envuelvo, señor?* Here are your flowers. Shall I wrap them for you, sir?

Pero cuando se repite el complemento, no se traduce.

◇ *Dáselo a Enrique.* Give it to Enrique. ◇ *No se lo digas a Susana.* Don't tell Susana. ◇ *¿Se lo preguntaste a tus padres?* Have you asked your parents about it?

*Cuando **se** tiene un valor reflexivo se traduce por **himself, herself, itself, themselves, yourself** o **yourselves** según nos refiramos a "él", "ella", "ellos" o "ellas", "usted" o "ustedes".*

◇ *Marcos se cortó con un vidrio.* Marcos cut himself on a piece of broken glass. ◇ *Margarita se estaba preparando para salir.* Margarita was getting herself ready to go out. ◇ *La calefacción se apaga sola.* The heating turns itself off automatically. ◇ *¿Se lastimó?* Have you hurt yourself?

- **Se está afeitando.** He's shaving.
- **Mi hermana nunca se queja.** My sister never complains.

Con partes del cuerpo o con prendas que se llevan puestas se usa el adjetivo posesivo.

◇ *Pablo se lavó los dientes.* Pablo brushed his teeth. ◇ *Carmen no podía abrocharse el vestido.* Carmen couldn't do up her dress.

*Cuando **se** tiene un valor recíproco se traduce por **each other**.*

◇ *Se dieron un beso.* They gave each other a kiss.

*Cuando **se** tiene un valor impersonal suele traducirse por **it** o **you**.*

◇ *Se cree que el tabaco produce cáncer.* It is believed that smoking causes cancer. ◇ *Es lo que pasa cuando se come tan deprisa.* That's what happens when you eat so fast.

- **"se vende"** "for sale"

sé VERBO *ver* **saber**

sea VERBO *ver* **ser**

el **secador** SUSTANTIVO
hair dryer

la **secadora** SUSTANTIVO
[1] dryer (*de ropa*)
[2] hair dryer (*de pelo*) [Mexico]

secar* VERBO
to dry (*pelo, platos*) ◇ *Voy a secarme el pelo.* I'm going to dry my hair.

- **secarse** to dry ◇ *Sécate con la toalla.* Dry yourself with the towel.
- **¿Se secó ya la ropa?** Is the laundry dry yet?
- **Se secaron las plantas.** The plants have dried up.

la **sección** SUSTANTIVO (PL las **secciones**)
[1] section (*división*) ◇ *la sección de deportes del periódico* the sports section of the newspaper
[2] department (*en grandes almacenes*) ◇ *la sección de perfumería* the perfume department

seco ADJETIVO
[1] dry ◇ *El suelo ya está seco.* The floor is dry now. ◇ *Tiene una tos muy seca.* He has a very dry cough.
[2] dried ◇ *flores secas* dried flowers

el **secretario**, la **secretaria** SUSTANTIVO
secretary (PL secretaries)

- **una secretaria de dirección** a director's secretary

el **secreto** SUSTANTIVO
secret ◇ *Te voy a contar un secreto.* I'm going to tell you a secret.

- **en secreto** in secret

secreto ADJETIVO
secret

la **secta** SUSTANTIVO
sect

el **sector** SUSTANTIVO
sector ◇ *el sector de la minería* the mining sector

la **secuencia** SUSTANTIVO
sequence (*de una película*)

el **secuestrador**, la **secuestradora** SUSTANTIVO
[1] kidnapper (*de persona*)
[2] hijacker (*de avión*)

secuestrar VERBO
[1] to kidnap (*persona*)
[2] to hijack (*avión, carro*)

el **secuestro** SUSTANTIVO
[1] kidnapping (*de persona*)
[2] hijack (*de avión, carro*)

secundario ADJETIVO
secondary

la **sed** SUSTANTIVO
thirst

- **tener* sed** to be thirsty

la **seda** SUSTANTIVO
silk ◇ *una camisa de seda* a silk shirt

el **sedal** SUSTANTIVO
fishing line

el **sedante** SUSTANTIVO
sedative

la **sede** SUSTANTIVO
[1] headquarters PL ◇ *la sede de la ONU en Zagreb* the UN headquarters in Zagreb
[2] venue ◇ *Sydney fue la sede de los Juegos Olímpicos del 2000.* Sydney was the venue for the 2000 Olympics.

sediento ADJETIVO
thirsty

segar* VERBO
[1] to reap (*trigo*)
[2] to mow (*hierba*)

seguido ADJETIVO
in a row ◇ *La he visto tres días seguidos.* I've seen her three days in a row.

- **en seguida** straight away ◇ *En seguida estoy con usted.* I'll be with you straight away.

◆ **En seguida termino.** I'm just about to finish.

◆ **todo seguido** straight on ◇ *Vaya todo seguido hasta la plaza y luego...* Go straight on until the square and then...

seguir* VERBO

[1] to carry on (*acción, movimiento*) ◇ *¡Sigue, por favor!* Carry on, please! ◇ *La computadora seguía funcionando pese al apagón.* The computer carried on working despite the blackout.

*Cuando el verbo **seguir** indica la continuidad de una situación, se traduce muchas veces por el adverbio "still".*

◆ **El ascensor sigue estropeado.** The elevator is still not working.

◆ **Sigo sin comprender.** I still don't understand.

◆ **Sigue lloviendo.** It's still raining.

[2] to follow (*ir detrás*) ◇ *Tú ve primero que yo te sigo.* You go first and I'll follow you.

◆ **seguir adelante** to go ahead ◇ *Los Juegos Olímpicos siguieron adelante a pesar del atentado.* The Olympics went ahead despite the attack.

según PREPOSICIÓN

[1] according to ◇ *Según tú, no habrá problemas de entradas.* According to you, there won't be any problems with the tickets.

[2] depending on ◇ *Iremos o no, según esté el tiempo.* We might go, depending on the weather.

segundo ADJETIVO, PRONOMBRE (FEM **segunda**)

second

◆ **el segundo plato** the second course

◆ **Vive en el segundo.** He lives on the third floor.

el **segundo** SUSTANTIVO

second ◇ *Es un segundo nada más.* It'll only take a second.

seguramente ADVERBIO

probably ◇ *Seguramente llegarán mañana.* They'll probably arrive tomorrow.

◆ **¿Lo va a comprar? – Seguramente.** Are you going to buy it? – Almost certainly.

la **seguridad** SUSTANTIVO

[1] safety (*falta de peligro*) ◇ *Hay que mejorar la seguridad en los trenes.* Safety on trains must be improved.

[2] security (*prevención*) ◇ *Las medidas de seguridad son muy estrictas.* The security measures are very strict.

[3] certainty (PL certainties) (*certeza*) ◇ *con toda seguridad* with complete certainty

◆ **seguridad en uno mismo** self-confidence ◇ *Le falta seguridad en sí mismo.* He lacks self-confidence.

◆ **la seguridad social** Social Security

seguro ADJETIVO

[1] safe ◇ *Este avión es muy seguro.* This plane is very safe. ◇ *Aquí estaremos seguros.* We'll be safe here.

[2] sure ◇ *Estoy segura de que ganaremos.* I'm sure we'll win. ◇ *Está muy seguro de sí mismo.* He's very sure of himself.

[3] certain ◇ *No es seguro que vayan a venir.* It's not certain that they're going to come.

el **seguro** SUSTANTIVO

insurance ◇ *el seguro del carro* car insurance

◆ **seguro de vida** life insurance

seis ADJETIVO, PRONOMBRE

six

◆ **Son las seis.** It's six o'clock.

◆ **el seis de enero** January sixth

seiscientos ADJETIVO, PRONOMBRE (FEM **seiscientas**)

six hundred

la **selección** SUSTANTIVO (PL las **selecciones**)

[1] selection ◇ *una selección de los mejores videos* a selection of the finest videos

[2] team ◇ *la selección nacional* the national team

seleccionar VERBO

to pick ◇ *Lo seleccionaron para jugar en la Ryder Cup.* He was picked to play in the Ryder Cup.

sellar VERBO

[1] to seal (*carta, paquete*)

[2] to stamp (*pasaporte*)

el **sello** SUSTANTIVO

[1] stamp ◇ *Colecciona sellos.* He collects stamps.

[2] seal ◇ *El producto lleva un sello de calidad.* The product bears a seal of quality.

la **selva** SUSTANTIVO

jungle

◆ **la selva tropical** the rainforest

el **semáforo** SUSTANTIVO

traffic lights PL

◆ **un semáforo en rojo** a red light

la **semana** SUSTANTIVO

week ◇ *dentro de una semana* in a week's time ◇ *una vez a la semana* once a week

◆ **entre semana** during the week

◆ **Semana Santa** Holy Week

semanal ADJETIVO

weekly

sembrar* VERBO

[1] to plant (*flor, maíz*)

[2] to sow (*semillas*)

semejante ADJETIVO

[1] similar (*parecido*) ◇ *Tenemos los rasgos muy semejantes.* We have very similar features.

[2] such ◇ *Nunca he dicho semejante cosa.* I've never said such a thing.

el **semicírculo** SUSTANTIVO

semicircle

la **semifinal** SUSTANTIVO

semifinal

la **semilla** SUSTANTIVO

seed

el **senado** SUSTANTIVO
senate

el **senador,** la **senadora** SUSTANTIVO
senator

sencillamente ADVERBIO
simply ◊ *Es sencillamente imposible.* It's simply impossible.

sencillo ADJETIVO
1 simple ◊ *Es muy sencillo.* It's really simple. ◊ *Llevó un vestido sencillo.* She wore a simple dress.
2 modest ◊ *Es muy sencillo en el trato.* He has a very modest manner.

el **sencillo** SUSTANTIVO
1 single (*disco*)
2 small change (*dinero suelto*)

el **senderismo** SUSTANTIVO
hiking

el **sendero** SUSTANTIVO
path

la **sensación** SUSTANTIVO (PL las **sensaciones**)
feeling ◊ *Tengo la sensación de que mienten.* I get the feeling they're lying. ◊ *una sensación de picor* an itchy feeling

sensacional ADJETIVO
sensational

sensato ADJETIVO
sensible ◊ *Lo sensato sería no moverse de aquí.* The sensible thing would be not to move from here.

sensible ADJETIVO
sensitive ◊ *Es un chico muy sensible.* He's a very sensitive boy. ◊ *Tengo los ojos muy sensibles.* My eyes are very sensitive.
No confundir ***sensible*** *con la palabra inglesa* ***sensible.***

sensual ADJETIVO
sensuous

sentado ADJETIVO
◆ **estar* sentado** to be sitting down

sentar* VERBO
1 to suit ◊ *Ese vestido te sienta muy bien.* That dress really suits you.
2 to agree with ◊ *No me sienta bien cenar tanto.* Having so much dinner doesn't agree with me.
◆ **Le sentó mal que no lo invitaras a la boda.** He was put out that you didn't invite him to the wedding.
◆ **sentarse** to sit down ◊ *Por favor, siéntese.* Please sit down.

la **sentencia** SUSTANTIVO
sentence

el **sentido** SUSTANTIVO
1 sense ◊ *No tiene sentido.* It doesn't make sense.
2 meaning (*significado*) ◊ *palabras con doble sentido* words with a double meaning
◆ **sentido común** common sense
◆ **sentido del humor** sense of humor
◆ **una calle de sentido único** a one-way street
◆ **en algún sentido** in some respects
◆ **en cierto sentido** in a certain sense

sentimental ADJETIVO
sentimental

el **sentimiento** SUSTANTIVO
feeling

sentir* VERBO
1 to feel ◊ *Sentí un dolor en la pierna.* I felt a pain in my leg.
◆ **De pronto sentí un poco de frío.** Suddenly I felt a bit cold.
2 to hear ◊ *No la sentí entrar.* I didn't hear her come in.
3 to be sorry ◊ *Lo siento mucho.* I'm very sorry. ◊ *Siento llegar tarde.* I'm sorry I'm late.
◆ **sentirse** to feel ◊ *No me siento nada bien.* I don't feel at all well.

la **seña** SUSTANTIVO
sign ◊ *Les hice una seña.* I made a sign to them. ◊ *Nos comunicábamos por señas.* We communicated by signs.
◆ **señas** (*domicilio*) address SING

la **señal** SUSTANTIVO
1 sign
◆ **señal de tráfico** road sign
◆ **señal indicadora** signpost
◆ **señal de llamada** (*al teléfono*) dial tone
2 signal ◊ *Yo daré la señal.* I'll give the signal.
◆ **Les hice una señal para que se fueran.** I signaled to them to go.
3 deposit *Spain*

señalar VERBO
to mark ◊ *Señálalo con un marcador rojo.* Mark it with a red felt-tip pen.
◆ **señalar con el dedo** to point

señalizar* VERBO
1 to indicate (*con la mano*)
2 to signpost (*camino, carretera*)

el **señor** SUSTANTIVO
1 man (PL men) ◊ *Este señor llegó antes que yo.* This man was before me.
◆ **¿Le ocurre algo, señor?** Is there something the matter?
◆ **¿Qué le pongo, señor?** What would you like, sir?
2 Mr. ◊ *el señor Delgado* Mr. Delgado
3 lord ◊ *un señor feudal* a feudal lord
◆ **Muy señor mío...** Dear Sir...
◆ **el señor alcalde** the mayor

la **señora** SUSTANTIVO
1 lady (PL ladies) ◊ *Deja pasar a esta señora.* Let the lady past.
◆ **¿Le ocurre algo, señora?** Is there something the matter?
◆ **¿Qué le pongo, señora?** What would you like, madam?
2 Mrs. ◊ *la señora Delgado* Mrs. Delgado

* Verbs marked with this symbol are irregular. See pages 346–348 for further details.

*La forma abreviada **Mrs.** se usa en inglés cuando queremos especificar que la mujer está casada, pero cuando no queremos dar importancia a este hecho, se prefiere el uso de **Ms.***

[3] wife ◇ *Vino con su señora.* He came with his wife.

la **señorita** SUSTANTIVO
young lady ◇ *Deja pasar a esta señorita.* Let the young lady pass. ◇ *la señorita Delgado* Miss Delgado

*La forma abreviada **Miss** se usa en inglés cuando queremos especificar que la mujer es soltera, pero cuando no queremos dar importancia a este hecho, se prefiere el uso de **Ms.***

sepa VERBO *ver* **saber**

la **separación** SUSTANTIVO (PL las **separaciones**)
[1] separation (*entre personas, de matrimonio*)
[2] gap (*entre objetos*) ◇ *Había una separación entre el andén y la vía.* There was a large gap between the platform and the rails.

separado ADJETIVO
[1] separate ◇ *Duermen en camas separadas.* They sleep in separate beds.
◆ **por separado** separately
[2] separated ◇ *Está separado de su mujer.* He's separated from his wife.

separar VERBO
to separate
◆ **separarse (1)** (*matrimonio*) to separate
◆ **separarse (2)** (*novios, grupo*) to split up

septiembre SUSTANTIVO MASC

En inglés, los meses se escriben con mayúscula.

September ◇ *en septiembre* in September ◇ *Ella nació el 11 de septiembre.* She was born on September 11th.

séptimo ADJETIVO, PRONOMBRE (FEM **séptima**)
seventh
◆ **Vivo en el séptimo.** I live on the eighth floor.

la **sequía** SUSTANTIVO
drought

ser* VERBO
to be ◇ *Es muy alto.* He's very tall. ◇ *Es médico.* He's a doctor. ◇ *La fiesta va a ser en su casa.* The party's going to be at her house. ◇ *Fue construido en 1960.* It was built in 1960. ◇ *Era de noche.* It was night.
◆ **Soy Lucía.** (*al teléfono*) It's Lucía.
◆ **Son las seis y media.** It's half past six.
◆ **Éramos cinco en el carro.** There were five of us in the car.

*Cuando en español decimos **somos tres, son ocho,** esta estructura se traduce al inglés por **there are** + el número + **of us, of them,** etc.*

◆ **¡Es cierto!** That's right!
◆ **Me es imposible asistir.** It's impossible for me to attend.
◆ **ser de (1)** (*pertenecer a*) to belong to ◇ *Es de Joaquín.* It belongs to Joaquín.
◆ **ser de (2)** (*venir de*) to be from ◇ *¿De dónde eres?* Where are you from?
◆ **ser de (3)** (*estar hecho de*) to be made of ◇ *Es de piedra.* It's made of stone.
◆ **a no ser que...** unless... ◇ *a no ser que salgamos mañana* unless we leave tomorrow
◆ **O sea, que no vienes.** So you're not coming.
◆ **mis hijos, o sea, Juan y Pedro** my children, that is, Juan and Pedro

el **ser** SUSTANTIVO
being
◆ **un ser humano** a human being
◆ **un ser vivo** a living being

la **serie** SUSTANTIVO
series (PL series) ◇ *Tuvimos una serie de reuniones.* We had a series of meetings. ◇ *una serie policíaca* a police series

serio ADJETIVO
serious
◆ **en serio** seriously ◇ *No hablaba en serio.* I wasn't speaking seriously.
◆ **¿Lo dices en serio?** Do you really mean it?

el **sermón** SUSTANTIVO (PL los **sermones**)
sermon

la **serpiente** SUSTANTIVO
snake
◆ **una serpiente de cascabel** a rattlesnake

serrar* VERBO
to saw

el **serrucho** SUSTANTIVO
saw

servicial ADJETIVO
helpful

el **servicio** SUSTANTIVO
[1] service ◇ *el servicio militar* national service ◇ *El servicio no va incluido.* Service is not included.
◆ **Tenemos servicio a domicilio.** We have a home delivery service.
◆ **estar* de servicio** to be on duty
◆ **estar* fuera de servicio (1)** (*máquina*) to be out of service
◆ **estar* fuera de servicio (2)** (*persona*) to be off duty
[2] rest room ◇ *Está en el servicio.* He's in the rest room.
◆ **el servicio de caballeros** the men's room
◆ **el servicio de señoras** the ladies' room
◆ **Al servicio, Costa.** (*en tenis*) Costa to serve.

el **servidor** SUSTANTIVO
server (*informática*)

la **servilleta** SUSTANTIVO
napkin

servir* VERBO
[1] to be useful for ◇ *Estas bolsas sirven para guardar alimentos.* These bags are useful for storing food.
◆ **¿Para qué sirve esto?** What's this for?
◆ **Esta radio aún sirve.** This radio still works.
[2] to serve ◇ *Yo serviré la cena.* I'll serve

S

supper.
◆ **Sírveme un poco más de vino.** Give me a little bit more wine.
◆ **Trabaja sirviendo mesas.** She works as a waitress.
◆ **no servir para nada** to be useless
◆ **¿En qué puedo servirlo?** How can I help you?

sesenta ADJETIVO, PRONOMBRE
sixty ◇ *Tiene sesenta años.* He's sixty.
◆ **el sesenta aniversario** the sixtieth anniversary

la **sesión** SUSTANTIVO (PL las **sesiones**)
[1] session ◇ *una sesión informática* a computing session
[2] showing ◇ *Fuimos a la última sesión del sábado.* We went to the last showing on Saturday night.

la **seta** SUSTANTIVO
mushroom
◆ **seta venenosa** toadstool

setecientos ADJETIVO, PRONOMBRE (FEM **setecientas**)
seven hundred

setenta ADJETIVO, PRONOMBRE
seventy ◇ *Tiene setenta años.* He's seventy.
◆ **el setenta aniversario** the seventieth anniversary

el **seto** SUSTANTIVO
hedge

el **seudónimo** SUSTANTIVO
pseudonym

severo ADJETIVO
[1] strict (*profesor*)
[2] harsh (*críticas, castigo, invierno*)

Sevilla SUSTANTIVO FEM
Seville

el/la **sexista** ADJETIVO, SUSTANTIVO
sexist

el **sexo** SUSTANTIVO
sex (PL sexes)

sexto ADJETIVO, PRONOMBRE (FEM **sexta**)
sixth
◆ **Vivo en el sexto.** I live on the seventh floor.

sexual ADJETIVO
sexual ◇ *acoso sexual* sexual harassment
◆ **educación sexual** sex education

la **sexualidad** SUSTANTIVO
sexuality

si CONJUNCIÓN
[1] if ◇ *Si quieres, te presto el carro.* I'll lend you the car if you like. ◇ *¿Sabes si nos han pagado ya?* Do you know if we've been paid yet?
◆ **¿Y si llueve?** And what if it rains?
◆ **Si me hubiera tocado la lotería...** If only I had won the lottery...
[2] whether ◇ *No sé si ir o no.* I don't know whether to go or not.
◆ **si no (1)** otherwise ◇ *Ponte crema. Si no, te quemarás.* Put some cream on, otherwise you'll get sunburned.
◆ **si no (2)** if...not ◇ *Avísenme si no pueden venir.* Let me know if you can't come.

sí (1) ADVERBIO
yes ◇ *¿Quieres un café? – Sí, gracias.* Do you want a coffee? – Yes, please.
◆ **¿Te gusta? – Sí.** Do you like it? – Yes, I do.
◆ **Creo que sí.** I think so.
◆ **Él no quiere pero yo sí.** He doesn't want to but I do.

sí (2) PRONOMBRE
Cuando tiene un valor reflexivo, ***sí*** *se traduce por* ***himself, herself, itself*** *o* ***themselves****, o por el pronombre* ***yourself*** *o* ***yourselves*** *cuando nos referimos a "usted", "ustedes".*
◇ *Sólo habla de sí mismo.* He only talks about himself. ◇ *Se perjudica a sí misma.* She's harming herself. ◇ *Pregúntese a sí mismo el motivo.* Ask yourself the reason. ◇ *La pregunta en sí no era difícil.* The question itself wasn't difficult. ◇ *Hablaban entre sí.* They were talking among themselves.
◆ **La tierra gira sobre sí misma.** The earth turns on its own axis.
Cuando se usa con valor impersonal se traduce por ***yourself****.*
◇ *Es mejor aprender las cosas por sí mismo.* It's better to learn things by yourself.

Sicilia SUSTANTIVO FEM
Sicily

el **sida** SUSTANTIVO
AIDS

la **sidra** SUSTANTIVO
cider

siego VERBO *ver* **segar**

siembro VERBO *ver* **sembrar**

siempre ADVERBIO
always ◇ *Siempre llega tarde.* She always arrives late.
◆ **como siempre** as usual
◆ **para siempre** forever
◆ **siempre y cuando** provided ◇ *siempre y cuando acepte nuestras condiciones* provided he accepts our conditions

siendo VERBO *ver* **ser**

siento VERBO *ver* **sentir**

la **sierra** SUSTANTIVO
[1] saw (*herramienta*)
[2] mountain range (*cordillera*)
◆ **Tenemos una casa en la sierra.** We have a house in the mountains.

la **siesta** SUSTANTIVO
nap
◆ **echarse la siesta** to take a nap
◆ **la hora de la siesta** siesta time

siete ADJETIVO, PRONOMBRE
seven
◆ **Son las siete.** It's seven o'clock.
◆ **el siete de marzo** March seventh

las **siglas** SUSTANTIVO
abbreviation SING

el **siglo** SUSTANTIVO
century (PL centuries) ◇ *el siglo 21* the 21st century

el **significado** SUSTANTIVO
meaning

significar* VERBO
1 to mean ◇ *¿Qué significa "wild"?* What does "wild" mean? ◇ *No sé lo que significa.* I don't know what it means.
2 to stand for (*con siglas*) ◇ *"B.C." significa "before Christ".* "B.C." stands for "before Christ".

significativo ADJETIVO
significant

el **signo** SUSTANTIVO
sign ◇ *Ese apetito es signo de buena salud.* Such an appetite is a sign of good health.
◆ **¿De qué signo del zodíaco eres?** What sign are you?
◆ **signo de admiración** exclamation point
◆ **signo de interrogación** question mark

siguiendo VERBO *ver* **seguir**

siguiente ADJETIVO
next ◇ *el siguiente vuelo* the next flight ◇ *Al día siguiente visitamos Puebla.* The next day we visited Puebla.
◆ **¡Que pase el siguiente, por favor!** Next please!

la **sílaba** SUSTANTIVO
syllable

silbar VERBO
to whistle

el **silbato** SUSTANTIVO
whistle

el **silbido** SUSTANTIVO
whistle

el **silencio** SUSTANTIVO
silence
◆ **guardar silencio** to keep quiet
◆ **¡Silencio!** Quiet!

silencioso ADJETIVO
silent

la **silla** SUSTANTIVO
chair
◆ **silla de montar** saddle
◆ **silla de paseo** (*de bebé*) stroller
◆ **silla de ruedas** wheelchair

el **sillín** SUSTANTIVO (PL los **sillines**)
saddle

el **sillón** SUSTANTIVO (PL los **sillones**)
armchair

la **silueta** SUSTANTIVO
outline
◆ **Tiene una silueta perfecta.** She has a perfect figure.

el **símbolo** SUSTANTIVO
symbol

simpático ADJETIVO
nice ◇ *Estuvo muy simpática con todos.* She was very nice to everybody. ◇ *Los cubanos son muy simpáticos.* Cubans are very nice people.
◆ **Me cae simpático.** I think he's really nice.
*No confundir **simpático** con **sympathetic**.*

simple ADJETIVO
simple

simplemente ADVERBIO
simply

simultáneo ADJETIVO
simultaneous

sin PREPOSICIÓN
without ◇ *Es peligroso ir en moto sin casco.* It's dangerous to ride a motorcycle without a helmet. ◇ *Salió sin hacer ruido.* She went out without making a noise. ◇ *sin que él se diera cuenta* without him realizing
◆ **Dejé el crucigrama sin terminar.** I left the crossword unfinished.
◆ **Me quedé sin habla.** I was speechless.
◆ **la gente sin hogar** the homeless

sincero ADJETIVO
honest ◇ *Fui sincera con él.* I was honest with him.

el/la **sindicalista** SUSTANTIVO
labor unionist

el **sindicato** SUSTANTIVO
labor union

la **sinfonía** SUSTANTIVO
symphony (PL symphonies)

el **singular** ADJETIVO, SUSTANTIVO
singular
◆ **en singular** in the singular

siniestro ADJETIVO
sinister

sino CONJUNCIÓN
but ◇ *No son americanos sino canadienses.* They're not American, but Canadian.
◆ **No hace sino pedirnos dinero.** All he does is ask us for money.
◆ **No sólo nos ayudó, sino que también nos invitó a cenar.** He didn't just help us; he also bought us dinner.

sintético ADJETIVO
synthetic

sintiendo VERBO *ver* **sentir**

el **síntoma** SUSTANTIVO
symptom

el/la **sinvergüenza** SUSTANTIVO
crook (*canalla*)
◆ **Es una sinvergüenza.** She's shameless.

siquiera ADVERBIO
◆ **ni siquiera** not even ◇ *Ni siquiera me dirigió la palabra.* She didn't even acknowledge me.

la **sirena** SUSTANTIVO
1 siren (*de alarma*)
2 mermaid (*personaje mitológico*)

sirviendo VERBO *ver* **servir**

la **sirvienta** SUSTANTIVO
maid

el **sirviente** SUSTANTIVO
servant

el **sistema** SUSTANTIVO
system

el **sitio** SUSTANTIVO
[1] place ◇ *un sitio tranquilo* a peaceful place
◆ **cambiar algo de sitio** to move something around
◆ **en cualquier sitio** anywhere
◆ **en algún sitio** somewhere
◆ **en ningún sitio** nowhere
[2] room ◇ *Hay sitio de sobra.* There's room to spare.
◆ **Hemos hecho sitio para ti en el carro.** We've made room for you in the car.
◆ **un sitio web** website

la **situación** SUSTANTIVO (PL las **situaciones**)
situation

situado ADJETIVO
◆ **está situado en...** it's situated in...

el **SMS** SUSTANTIVO
text message

el **sobaco** SUSTANTIVO
armpit

el **soborno** SUSTANTIVO
[1] bribery (*delito*)
[2] bribe (*cantidad de dinero*)
◆ **Denunció un intento de soborno.** He reported an attempted bribe.

sobra SUSTANTIVO FEM
◆ **Tenemos comida de sobra.** We have more than enough food.
◆ **Sabes de sobra que yo no he sido.** You know full well that it wasn't me.
◆ **las sobras** (*de comida*) the leftovers

sobrar VERBO
[1] to be left over ◇ *Ha sobrado mucha comida.* There's plenty of food left over.
[2] to be spare ◇ *Esta pieza sobra.* This piece is spare.
◆ **Este ejemplo sobra.** This example is unnecessary.
◆ **Con este dinero sobrará.** This money will be more than enough.

sobre PREPOSICIÓN
[1] on ◇ *Dejó el dinero sobre la mesa.* He left the money on the table.
[2] about ◇ *información sobre vuelos* information about flights
◆ **sobre las seis** [Spain] at about six o'clock
◆ **sobre todo** above all

el **sobre** SUSTANTIVO
envelope

la **sobredosis** SUSTANTIVO (PL las **sobredosis**)
overdose

sobrenatural ADJETIVO
supernatural

el **sobresaliente** SUSTANTIVO
distinction

sobrevivir VERBO
to survive

la **sobrina** SUSTANTIVO
niece

el **sobrino** SUSTANTIVO
nephew
◆ **mis sobrinos (1)** (*varones*) my nephews
◆ **mis sobrinos (2)** (*varones y mujeres*) my nieces and nephews

sobrio ADJETIVO
sober

la **socia** SUSTANTIVO
[1] partner (*en negocio*)
[2] member (*de club, organización*)

social ADJETIVO
social

el **socialismo** SUSTANTIVO
socialism

el/la **socialista** ADJETIVO, SUSTANTIVO
socialist

la **sociedad** SUSTANTIVO
society (PL societies)

el **socio** SUSTANTIVO
[1] partner (*en negocio*)
[2] member (*de club, organización*)

la **sociología** SUSTANTIVO
sociology

el/la **socorrista** SUSTANTIVO
lifeguard

el **socorro** SUSTANTIVO
help
◆ **pedir* socorro** to ask for help
◆ **Acudió en su socorro.** She went to his aid.

socorro EXCLAMACIÓN
help!

la **soda** SUSTANTIVO
soda pop

el **sofá** SUSTANTIVO (PL los **sofás**)
sofa
◆ **un sofá-cama** a sofa bed

sofisticado ADJETIVO
sophisticated

el **software** SUSTANTIVO
software

sois VERBO [Spain] *ver* **ser**

la **soya** SUSTANTIVO
soya

el **sol** SUSTANTIVO
sun
◆ **estar* al sol** to be in the sun
◆ **Hace sol.** It's sunny.
◆ **tomar el sol** to sunbathe
◆ **un día de sol** a sunny day

solamente ADVERBIO
only

el **soldado** SUSTANTIVO
soldier

soleado ADJETIVO
sunny

la **soledad** SUSTANTIVO
loneliness

soler* VERBO
*En presente, **soler** se traduce por el adverbio **usually**.*
◇ *Suele salir a las ocho.* He usually leaves at eight.
*En pasado, **soler** se traduce por la construcción **used to**.*
◇ *Solíamos ir todos los años a la playa.* We used to go to the beach every year.

solicitar VERBO
1 to ask for (*ayuda, información*)
2 to apply for (*empleo, puesto*)

la **solicitud** SUSTANTIVO
1 application (*de trabajo*)
◆ **presentar una solicitud** to submit an application
2 request (*de ayuda, información*)

sólido ADJETIVO
solid

solitario ADJETIVO
solitary

sollozar* VERBO
to sob

solo ADJETIVO
1 alone ◇ *¡Déjame solo!* Leave me alone! ◇ *Me quedé solo.* I was left alone.
◆ **¿Estás solo?** Are you on your own?
◆ **Lo hice solo.** I did it on my own.
2 lonely ◇ *A veces me siento solo.* Sometimes I feel lonely.
3 single (*uso enfático*) ◇ *No hubo una sola queja.* There wasn't a single complaint.
◆ **Había un solo problema.** There was just one problem.
◆ **Habla solo.** He talks to himself.

el **solo** SUSTANTIVO
solo ◇ *un solo de guitarra* a guitar solo

sólo ADVERBIO
only ◇ *Sólo cuesta diez dolares.* It only costs ten dollars. ◇ *Era sólo una idea.* It was only an idea. ◇ *Yo también fumo, sólo que en pipa.* I smoke as well, only a pipe.
◆ **no sólo...sino...** not only...but... ◇ *No sólo es barato sino también de buena calidad.* It's not only cheap, but it's good quality too.

el **solomillo** SUSTANTIVO
sirloin

soltar* VERBO
1 to let go of ◇ *No sueltes la cuerda.* Don't let go of the rope.
◆ **¡Suéltame!** Let me go!
2 to put down ◇ *Soltó la bolsa de la compra en un banco.* She put her shopping bag down on a bench.
3 to release ◇ *Han soltado a los rehenes.* They've released the hostages.
4 to let out (*suspiro, grito*) ◇ *Solté un suspiro de alivio.* I let out a sigh of relief.

la **soltera** SUSTANTIVO
single woman

soltero ADJETIVO
single ◇ *Es soltero.* He's single.

el **soltero** SUSTANTIVO
bachelor

la **solución** SUSTANTIVO (PL las **soluciones**)
1 solution (*de problema*)
2 answer (*de crucigrama, preguntas*)

solucionar VERBO
to solve
◆ **un problema sin solucionar** an unsolved problem

la **sombra** SUSTANTIVO
1 shade ◇ *Prefiero quedarme a la sombra.* I prefer to stay in the shade.
2 shadow ◇ *Sólo vi una sombra.* I only saw a shadow.
◆ **sombra de ojos** eye shadow

el **sombrero** SUSTANTIVO
hat

la **sombrilla** SUSTANTIVO
1 parasol (*de mano*)
2 sunshade (*de playa*)

el **somier** SUSTANTIVO
sprung bed base

el **somnífero** SUSTANTIVO
sleeping pill

el **sonajero** SUSTANTIVO
rattle

sonar* VERBO
1 to sound ◇ *Sonabas un poco triste por teléfono.* You sounded a bit sad on the phone.
◆ **Escríbelo tal y como suena.** Write it down just the way it sounds.
2 to play (*música*) ◇ *Sonaba una canción de Madonna por la radio.* They were playing a Madonna song on the radio.
3 to ring (*timbre, teléfono*)
4 to go off (*despertador*)
◆ **Me suena esa cara.** That face rings a bell.
◆ **sonarse la nariz** to blow one's nose

el **sondeo** SUSTANTIVO
◆ **un sondeo de opinión** an opinion poll

el **sonido** SUSTANTIVO
sound

sonreír* VERBO
to smile ◇ *Me sonrió.* She smiled at me.

la **sonrisa** SUSTANTIVO
smile

sonrojarse VERBO
to blush

soñar* VERBO
to dream ◇ *Ayer soñé con él.* I dreamed about him yesterday.

la **sopa** SUSTANTIVO
soup ◇ *sopa de pescado* fish soup

soplar VERBO
to blow ◇ *¡Sopla con fuerza!* Blow hard! ◇ *Soplaba un viento fuerte.* A strong wind was blowing.
◆ **Le soplaron la respuesta.** They whispered ☞

S

the answer to him.

soportar VERBO
to stand ◇ *No lo soporto.* I can't stand him. ◇ *No soporta que la critiquen.* She can't stand being criticized.
No confundir ***soportar*** *con* ***to support***.

la **soprano** SUSTANTIVO
soprano

sorber VERBO
to sip

sordo ADJETIVO
deaf
◆ **quedarse sordo** to go deaf

sordomudo ADJETIVO
deaf and dumb

sorprendente ADJETIVO
surprising

sorprender VERBO
to surprise ◇ *No me sorprende.* It doesn't surprise me.
◆ **Me sorprendí al verlo allí.** I was surprised to see him there.

la **sorpresa** SUSTANTIVO
surprise ◇ *¡Qué sorpresa!* What a surprise!
◆ **tomar a alguien de sorpresa** to take somebody by surprise

el **sorteo** SUSTANTIVO
draw

la **sortija** SUSTANTIVO
ring

soso ADJETIVO
1 dull (*persona*)
2 bland (*sin sabor*)

sospechar VERBO
to suspect
◆ **Sospechan de él.** They suspect him.

el **sospechoso**, la **sospechosa** SUSTANTIVO
suspect

sospechoso ADJETIVO
suspicious

el **sostén** SUSTANTIVO (PL los **sostenes**)
bra

sostener* VERBO
1 to support ◇ *Está sostenido por cuatro columnas.* It is supported by four columns.
2 to hold ◇ *Sostuvieron la caja entre los dos.* They held the box between the two of them.
◆ **¿Puedes sostener la puerta un momento?** Can you hold the door open for a moment?
◆ **La sombrilla no se sostiene con el viento.** The umbrella won't stay up in the wind.

la **sota** SUSTANTIVO
jack

el **sótano** SUSTANTIVO
1 basement (*habitable*)
2 cellar (*para almacenar cosas*)

soy VERBO *ver* **ser**

el **spot** SUSTANTIVO
◆ **un spot publicitario** a commercial

Sr. ABREVIATURA
Mr.

Sra. ABREVIATURA
Mrs.
La forma abreviada ***Mrs.*** *se usa en inglés cuando queremos especificar que la mujer está casada, pero cuando no queremos dar importancia a este hecho, se prefiere el uso de* ***Ms.***

Sres. ABREVIATURA
Messrs (*hombres*)
◆ **los Sres. de Pérez** Mr. and Mrs. Pérez

Srta. ABREVIATURA
Miss
La forma abreviada ***Miss*** *se usa en inglés cuando queremos especificar que la mujer es soltera, pero cuando no queremos dar importancia a este hecho, se prefiere el uso de* ***Ms.***

su ADJETIVO
1 his (*de él*) ◇ *su máquina de afeitar* his razor ◇ *sus padres* his parents
2 her (*de ella*) ◇ *su falda* her skirt ◇ *sus amigas* her friends
3 its (*de cosa, animal*) ◇ *un oso y su cachorro* a bear and its cub ◇ *el carro y sus accesorios* the car and its fittings
4 their (*de ellos, ellas*) ◇ *su equipo favorito* their favorite team ◇ *sus amigos* their friends
5 your (*de usted, ustedes*) ◇ *Su abrigo, señora.* Your coat, madam. ◇ *No olviden sus paraguas.* Don't forget your umbrellas.

suave ADJETIVO
1 smooth (*piel, superficie*)
2 soft (*pelo*)
3 gentle (*brisa, caricia, voz*)
4 mild (*clima, temperaturas*)

el **suavizante** SUSTANTIVO
1 conditioner (*de pelo*)
2 fabric conditioner (*de ropa*)

la **subasta** SUSTANTIVO
auction

el **subcampeón**, la **subcampeona** SUSTANTIVO (MASC PL los **subcampeones**)
runner-up (PL runners-up)

subdesarrollado ADJETIVO
underdeveloped

el **subdirector**, la **subdirectora** SUSTANTIVO
1 assistant principal (*de colegio*)
2 deputy director (*de organización*)
3 deputy assistant (*de empresa*)

la **subida** SUSTANTIVO
1 rise ◇ *una subida de los precios* a rise in prices
2 ascent ◇ *una subida muy empinada* a very steep ascent

subir VERBO
1 to go up ◇ *Subimos la cuesta.* We went up the hill. ◇ *La gasolina ha vuelto a subir.*

Gasoline has gone up again.
[2] to come up ◇ *Sube, que te voy a enseñar unos CDs.* Come up; I have some CDs to show you.
[3] to climb (*montaña*) ◇ *subir una montaña* to climb a mountain
[4] to take up ◇ *¿Me puedes ayudar a subir las maletas?* Can you help me to take up the suitcases?
[5] to put up ◇ *Los taxistas han subido sus tarifas.* Cab drivers have put their fares up.
[6] to raise ◇ *Sube los brazos.* Raise your arms.
[7] to turn up ◇ *Sube la radio, que no se oye.* Turn the radio up; I can't hear it.
◆ **subirse a (1)** (*carro*) to get into
◆ **subirse a (2)** (*bici, autobús, tren, avión*) to get on
◆ **subirse a un árbol** to climb a tree

súbito ADJETIVO
[1] sudden (*repentino*)
[2] unexpected (*imprevisto*)
◆ **de súbito** suddenly

el **subjuntivo** SUSTANTIVO
subjunctive

el **submarino** SUSTANTIVO
submarine

subrayar VERBO
to underline

el **subsidio** SUSTANTIVO
subsidy (PL subsidies) ◇ *subsidio de paro* unemployment compensation

subterráneo ADJETIVO
underground

subtitulado ADJETIVO
subtitled

los **subtítulos** SUSTANTIVO
subtitles

el **suburbio** SUSTANTIVO
[1] slum area (*barrio pobre*)
[2] suburb (*afueras*)

la **subvención** SUSTANTIVO (PL las **subvenciones**)
subsidy (PL subsidies)

subvencionar VERBO
to subsidize

suceder VERBO
to happen (*ocurrir*) ◇ *¿Les ha sucedido algo?* Has something happened to them?

el **suceso** SUSTANTIVO
[1] event ◇ *los sucesos de la última década* the events of the last decade ◇ *sucesos históricos* historical events
[2] incident ◇ *El suceso ocurrió sobre las tres de la tarde.* The incident happened at around three in the afternoon.
◆ **Acudieron rápidamente al lugar del suceso.** They rushed to the scene.
No confundir ***suceso*** *con* ***success.***

la **suciedad** SUSTANTIVO
dirt

sucio ADJETIVO
dirty ◇ *Tienes las manos sucias.* You have dirty hands.

la **sucursal** SUSTANTIVO
branch (PL branches)

la **sudadera** SUSTANTIVO
sweatshirt

Sudáfrica SUSTANTIVO FEM
South Africa

Sudamérica SUSTANTIVO FEM
South America

el **sudamericano,** la **sudamericana** ADJETIVO, SUSTANTIVO
South American

sudar VERBO
to sweat

el **sudeste** SUSTANTIVO
southeast

el **sudoeste** SUSTANTIVO
southwest

el **sudor** SUSTANTIVO
sweat

sudoroso ADJETIVO
sweaty

la **sueca** SUSTANTIVO
Swede

Suecia SUSTANTIVO FEM
Sweden

sueco ADJETIVO
Swedish

el **sueco** SUSTANTIVO
[1] Swede (*persona*)
[2] Swedish (*idioma*)

la **suegra** SUSTANTIVO
mother-in-law (PL mothers-in-law)

el **suegro** SUSTANTIVO
father-in-law (PL fathers-in-law)

los **suegros** SUSTANTIVO
in-laws

la **suela** SUSTANTIVO
sole (*de zapato*)

el **sueldo** SUSTANTIVO
[1] salary (PL salaries) (*mensual*)
[2] wages PL (*semanal*)

S

el **suelo** SUSTANTIVO
[1] floor (*en casa, edificio*) ◇ *un suelo de mármol* a marble floor
[2] ground (*de la calle, del exterior*)
◆ **Me caí al suelo.** I fell over.

suelo VERBO *ver* **soler**

suelto VERBO *ver* **soltar**

suelto ADJETIVO
loose ◇ *Tiene varias hojas sueltas.* Some of the pages are loose. ◇ *Lleva el pelo suelto.* She wears her hair loose. ◇ *No dejes al perro suelto.* Don't let the dog loose.

el **suelto** SUSTANTIVO
change (*dinero*)

sueno VERBO *ver* **sonar**

sueño VERBO *ver* **soñar**

el **sueño** SUSTANTIVO
[1] dream ◇ *Anoche tuve un mal sueño.* I ☞

had a bad dream last night.

[2] sleep ◇ *un sueño profundo* a deep sleep

◆ **Tengo sueño.** I'm sleepy.

la **suerte** SUSTANTIVO

luck ◇ *No ha tenido mucha suerte.* She hasn't had much luck.

◆ **por suerte** luckily

◆ **Tuvo suerte.** She was lucky.

◆ **¡Qué suerte!** How lucky!

◆ **¡Qué mala suerte!** What bad luck!

el **suéter** SUSTANTIVO

sweater

suficiente ADJETIVO

enough ◇ *No tenía dinero suficiente.* I didn't have enough money.

suficientemente ADVERBIO

sufficiently

sufrir VERBO

[1] to have ◇ *Sufrió un ataque al corazón.* He had a heart attack.

[2] to suffer ◇ *Sufre de artritis.* He suffers from arthritis.

◆ **sufrir un colapso** to collapse

la **sugerencia** SUSTANTIVO

suggestion

◆ **hacer* una sugerencia** to make a suggestion

sugerir* VERBO

to suggest ◇ *Sugirió que saliéramos a tomar una pizza.* She suggested going out for a pizza.

sugiero VERBO *ver* **sugerir**

el **suicidio** SUSTANTIVO

suicide

Suiza SUSTANTIVO FEM

Switzerland

el **suizo,** la **suiza** ADJETIVO, SUSTANTIVO

Swiss

◆ **los suizos** the Swiss

el **sujetador** SUSTANTIVO

bra

sujetar VERBO

[1] to hold ◇ *Sujétame estos libros un momento.* Hold these books for me a moment.

[2] to fasten ◇ *Lo sujetó con un clip.* He fastened it with a paper clip.

◆ **Sujeta al perro, que no se escape.** Hold on to the dog so it doesn't get away.

el **sujeto** SUSTANTIVO

subject

la **suma** SUSTANTIVO

sum ◇ *una suma de dinero* a sum of money

◆ **¿Cuánto es la suma de todos los gastos?** What are the total expenses?

◆ **hacer* una suma** to do an addition problem

sumar VERBO

to add up

suministrar VERBO

to supply

el **suministro** SUSTANTIVO

supply (PL supplies)

supe VERBO *ver* **saber**

súper ADJETIVO

◆ **gasolina súper** high-test gasoline

superar VERBO

[1] to get over (*enfermedad, crisis*)

[2] to beat (*récord*)

[3] to pass (*prueba*)

◆ **Las ventas han superado nuestras expectativas.** Sales have exceeded our expectations.

la **superficie** SUSTANTIVO

[1] surface ◇ *en la superficie terrestre* on the earth's surface

[2] area ◇ *una superficie de 100 metros cuadrados* an area of 100 square meters

superior ADJETIVO (FEM **superior**)

[1] upper (*directamente encima*)

◆ **el labio superior** the upper lip

[2] top (*en lo más alto*) ◇ *el piso superior* the top floor

◆ **superior a** (*mejor que*) superior to

◆ **Su inteligencia es superior a la media.** He has above-average intelligence.

◆ **un curso de inglés de nivel superior** an advanced level English course

el **supermercado** SUSTANTIVO

supermarket

el/la **superviviente** SUSTANTIVO

survivor

el **suplemento** SUSTANTIVO

supplement ◇ *el suplemento dominical* the Sunday supplement

el/la **suplente** SUSTANTIVO

[1] reserve (*jugador, deportista*)

[2] substitute teacher (*profesor*)

[3] stand-in (*médico*)

suplicar* VERBO

to beg

suponer* VERBO

[1] to suppose (*indicando expectación*) ◇ *Supongo que vendrá.* I suppose she'll come.

◆ **Supongo que sí.** I suppose so.

[2] to think (*indicando decepción*) ◇ *Te suponía más alto.* I thought you'd be taller. ◇ *Supusimos que no vendrías.* We didn't think you would be coming.

[3] to involve ◇ *Tener un carro supone más gastos.* Having a car involves more expenses.

el **supositorio** SUSTANTIVO

suppository (PL suppositories)

suprimir VERBO

to delete (*borrar*)

supuesto VERBO *ver* **suponer**

el **supuesto** SUSTANTIVO

◆ **¿Y en el supuesto de que no venga?** And supposing he doesn't come?

◆ **por supuesto** of course

◆ **¡Por supuesto que no!** Of course not!

supuse VERBO *ver* **suponer**

el **sur** SUSTANTIVO, ADJETIVO
south ◇ *el sur del país* the south of the country ◇ *en la costa sur* on the south coast
◆ **vientos del sur** southerly winds

el **suramericano**, la **suramericana** ADJETIVO, SUSTANTIVO
South American

sureño ADJETIVO
southern

el **sureste** SUSTANTIVO
southeast

el **surf** SUSTANTIVO
surfing
◆ **surf a vela** windsurfing
◆ **practicar* el surf** to surf

surgir* VERBO
to come up ◇ *Ha surgido un problema.* A problem has come up.

el **suroeste** SUSTANTIVO
southwest

surtido ADJETIVO
assorted ◇ *pasteles surtidos* assorted cakes
◆ **estar* bien surtido** to have a good selection

el **surtido** SUSTANTIVO
selection

el **surtidor** SUSTANTIVO
gas pump (*de gasolina*)

susceptible ADJETIVO
touchy (*persona*)

la **suscripción** SUSTANTIVO (PL las **suscripciones**)
subscription

suspender VERBO
1 to call off (*definitivamente*) ◇ *Han suspendido la boda.* They've called the wedding off.
2 to postpone (*temporalmente*) ◇ *Ha suspendido su visita hasta la semana que viene.* He's postponed his visit until next week.
◆ **El partido se suspendió a causa de la lluvia.** The game was rained out.
3 to fail *Spain* ◇ *He suspendido las matemáticas.* I've failed math.

el **suspenso** SUSTANTIVO
suspense (*misterio*) ◇ *una película de suspenso* a thriller
◆ **Tengo un suspenso en inglés.** *Spain* I failed English.

suspicaz ADJETIVO (PL **suspicaces**)
suspicious

suspirar VERBO
to sigh

el **suspiro** SUSTANTIVO
sigh

la **sustancia** SUSTANTIVO
substance
◆ **una sustancia química** a chemical

el **sustantivo** SUSTANTIVO
noun

sustituir* VERBO
1 to replace (*para siempre*) ◇ *Lo sustituí como secretario de la asociación.* I replaced him as club secretary.
2 to substitute for (*temporalmente*) ◇ *¿Me puedes sustituir un par de semanas?* Can you substitute for me for a couple of weeks?

el **sustituto**, la **sustituta** SUSTANTIVO
1 replacement (*para siempre*)
2 substitute (*temporal*)
◆ **Soy el sustituto del profesor de inglés.** I'm the substitute for the English teacher.

sustituyendo VERBO *ver* **sustituir**

el **susto** SUSTANTIVO
fright ◇ *¡Qué susto!* What a fright!
◆ **dar* un susto a alguien** to give somebody a fright

susurrar VERBO
to whisper ◇ *Me susurró su nombre al oído.* He whispered his name in my ear.

sutil ADJETIVO
subtle

suyo PRONOMBRE, ADJETIVO (FEM **suya**)
1 his
Cuando nos referimos a "él".
◇ *Todas estas tierras son suyas.* All this land is his. ◇ *¿Es éste su cuarto? – No, el suyo está abajo.* Is this his room? – No, his is downstairs.
◆ **un amigo suyo** a friend of his
2 hers
Cuando nos referimos a "ella".
◇ *Es suyo.* It's hers. ◇ *¿Es éste su abrigo? – No, el suyo es verde.* Is this her coat? – No, hers is green.
◆ **un amigo suyo** a friend of hers
3 theirs
Cuando nos referimos a "ellos" o "ellas".
◇ *Es suyo.* It's theirs. ◇ *¿Es ésta su casa? – No, la suya está más adelante.* Is this their house? – No, theirs is further on.
◆ **un amigo suyo** a friend of theirs
4 yours
Cuando nos referimos a "usted" o "ustedes".
◇ *Todos estos libros son suyos.* All these books are yours. ◇ *¿Es ésta nuestra habitación? – No, la suya está arriba.* Is this our room? – No, yours is upstairs.
◆ **un amigo suyo** a friend of yours

T

el **tabaco** SUSTANTIVO
[1] tobacco
◆ **tabaco negro** dark tobacco
◆ **tabaco rubio** Virginia tobacco
[2] cigarettes PL [Spain]

la **taberna** SUSTANTIVO
bar

el **tabique** SUSTANTIVO
partition

la **tabla** SUSTANTIVO
plank ◇ *El agujero estaba cubierto con tablas.* The hole was covered with planks.
◆ **la tabla de multiplicar** the multiplication table
◆ **una tabla de cocina** a chopping board
◆ **la tabla de planchar** the ironing board
◆ **la tabla de surf** the surfboard
◆ **quedar en tablas** to tie

el **tablero** SUSTANTIVO
board
◆ **el tablero de ajedrez** the chessboard
◆ **el tablero de mandos** the dashboard

la **tableta** SUSTANTIVO
tablet (*medicamento*)

la **tablilla** SUSTANTIVO
bar (*de chocolate*)

el **tablón** SUSTANTIVO (PL los **tablones**)
plank ◇ *los tablones del andamio* the scaffolding planks
◆ **el tablón de anuncios** the bulletin board

el **tabú** SUSTANTIVO (PL los **tabúes**)
taboo

el **taburete** SUSTANTIVO
stool

tacaño ADJETIVO
mean

el **tacaño,** la **tacaña** SUSTANTIVO
skinflint

tachar VERBO
to cross out ◇ *No lo taches, bórralo.* Don't cross it out; erase it.
◆ **La tacharon de mentirosa.** They accused her of being a liar.

el **taco** SUSTANTIVO
[1] screw anchor (*para tornillo*)
[2] stud (*de botas de fútbol*)
[3] cue (*en billar*)
[4] taco (*de tortilla*)
[5] snack (*bocado*) [Mexico]
[6] swearword (*palabrota*) [Spain]

el **tacón** SUSTANTIVO (PL los **tacones**)
heel
◆ **zapatos de tacón** high-heeled shoes

la **táctica** SUSTANTIVO
tactics PL ◇ *El equipo cambió de táctica.* The team changed tactics.

el **tacto** SUSTANTIVO
[1] touch (*sentido*) ◇ *suave al tacto* smooth to the touch
[2] tact (*delicadeza*)
◆ **Lo dijo con mucho tacto.** He said it very tactfully.

la **tajada** SUSTANTIVO
slice (*de melón, sandía*)

tajante ADJETIVO
[1] emphatic (*actitud*)
[2] sharp (*tono*) ◇ *Lo dijo de manera tajante.* He said it sharply.

tal ADJETIVO, PRONOMBRE
such ◇ *En tales casos es mejor consultar con un médico.* In such cases it's better to see a doctor. ◇ *¡En el aeropuerto había tal confusión!* There was such confusion at the airport!
◆ **Lo dejé tal como estaba.** I left it just as it was.
◆ **con tal de que** as long as ◇ *con tal de que regresen antes de las once* as long as you get back before eleven
◆ **¿Qué tal?** How are things?
◆ **¿Qué tal has dormido?** How did you sleep?
◆ **tal vez** perhaps

la **taladradora** SUSTANTIVO
pneumatic drill

taladrar VERBO
to drill

el **taladro** SUSTANTIVO
drill

el **talento** SUSTANTIVO
talent ◇ *Sus hijos tienen talento para la música.* Their children have a talent for music.

la **talla** SUSTANTIVO
size ◇ *¿Tienen esta camisa en la talla cuatro?* Do you have this shirt in a size four?

tallar VERBO
[1] to carve (*madera*)
[2] to sculpt (*piedra, mármol*)
[3] to scrub (*suelo, cazuela*) [Mexico]

los **tallarines** SUSTANTIVO
noodles

el **taller** SUSTANTIVO
[1] garage (*de mecánico*) ◇ *Tengo el carro en el taller.* My car is in the garage.
[2] workshop (*de carpintero, electricista*)
◆ **un taller de teatro** a theater workshop

el **tallo** SUSTANTIVO
stem

el **talón** SUSTANTIVO (PL los **talones**)
[1] heel (*de pie, zapato*)
[2] check (*cheque*) [Spain]

el **talonario** SUSTANTIVO
[1] checkbook (*de cheques*)
[2] book of tickets (*de entradas*)
[3] receipt book (*de recibos*)

el **tamaño** SUSTANTIVO
size

- **¿Qué tamaño tiene?** What size is it?

tambalearse VERBO
1 to wobble (*silla*)
2 to stagger (*persona*)

también ADVERBIO
also ◇ *Canta flamenco y también baila.* He sings flamenco and also dances.
- **Tengo hambre. – Yo también.** I'm hungry. – So am I.
- **Yo estoy de acuerdo. – Nosotros también.** I agree. – So do we.

el **tambor** SUSTANTIVO
drum

el **tamiz** SUSTANTIVO (PL los **tamices**)
sieve

tampoco ADVERBIO
1 either ◇ *Yo tampoco lo compré.* I didn't buy it either.
2 neither ◇ *Yo no la vi. -Yo tampoco.* I didn't see her. -Neither did I. ◇ *Nunca he estado en Nueva York. -Yo tampoco.* I've never been to New York. -Neither have I.

el **tampón** SUSTANTIVO (PL los **tampones**)
tampon

tan ADVERBIO
1 so ◇ *No creía que vendrías tan pronto.* I didn't think you'd come so soon. ◇ *¡No es tan difícil!* It's not so difficult!
- **¡Qué hombre tan amable!** What a kind man!
- **tan...que...** so...that...

A menudo se omite ***that*** *en esta construcción.*

◇ *Habla tan deprisa que no la entiendo.* She talks so fast that I can't understand her.
2 such ◇ *No era una idea tan buena.* It wasn't such a good idea. ◇ *¡Tiene unos amigos tan simpáticos!* He has such nice friends!
- **tan...como** as...as ◇ *No es tan bonita como su mamá.* She's not as pretty as her mother. ◇ *Vine tan pronto como pude.* I came as soon as I could.

el **tanque** SUSTANTIVO
tank

tantear VERBO
to weigh up (*situación*)

tanto ADJETIVO, ADVERBIO, PRONOMBRE (FEM **tanta**)
1 so much (PL so many) ◇ *Ahora no bebo tanta leche.* I don't drink so much milk now. ◇ *Se preocupa tanto que no puede dormir.* He worries so much that he can't sleep. ◇ *¡Tengo tantas cosas que hacer hoy!* I have so many things to do today! ◇ *No necesitamos tantas.* We don't need so many.
- **Vinieron tantos que no cabían en la sala.** So many people came that they couldn't fit into the room.
- **No recibe tantas llamadas como yo.** He doesn't get as many calls as I do.
- **Gano tanto como tú.** I earn as much as you.

2 so often ◇ *Ahora no la veo tanto.* I don't see her so often now.
- **¡No corras tanto!** Don't run so fast!
- **tanto tú como yo** both you and I
- **tanto si viene como si no** whether he comes or not
- **¡Tanto gusto!** How do you do?
- **entre tanto** meanwhile
- **por lo tanto** therefore

el **tanto** SUSTANTIVO
1 goal ◇ *Juárez marcó el segundo tanto.* Juárez scored the second goal.
2 amount ◇ *Me paga un tanto fijo cada semana.* He pays me a fixed amount each week.
- **un tanto por ciento** a percentage
- **Había cuarenta y tantos invitados.** There were forty-odd guests.
- **Manténme al tanto.** Keep me informed.

la **tapa** SUSTANTIVO
1 lid (*de cazuela, caja*)
2 top (*de botella, tarro*)
3 cover (*de revista, libro*)
4 hors d'oeuvre (*con bebida*) ◇ *Pedimos unas tapas en el bar.* We ordered some hors d'oeuvres in the bar.

la **tapadera** SUSTANTIVO
lid

tapar VERBO
to cover ◇ *La tapé con una manta.* I covered her with a blanket.
- **Tapa la olla.** Put the lid on the pan.
- **Me estás tapando el sol.** You're keeping the sun off me.
- **Tápate bien que hace frío.** Wrap up well because it's cold.

el **tapete** SUSTANTIVO
1 embroidered tablecloth (*mantel*)
2 rug (*alfombra*) Mexico

la **tapia** SUSTANTIVO
wall ◇ *la tapia del jardín* the garden wall

la **tapicería** SUSTANTIVO
1 upholstery (*de carro, mueble*)
2 upholsterer's (*taller*)

el **tapiz** SUSTANTIVO (PL los **tapices**)
tapestry (PL tapestries)

tapizar* VERBO
to upholster (*sillón*)

el **tapón** SUSTANTIVO (PL los **tapones**)
1 plug (*de bañera, lavabo*)
2 top (*de botella, dentífrico*) ◇ *tapón de rosca* screw top
3 cork (*de corcho*)

la **taquigrafía** SUSTANTIVO
shorthand

la **taquilla** SUSTANTIVO
1 box office (*de teatro*)
2 ticket office (*de estadio, estación*)
3 locker (*armario*)

tararear VERBO
to hum

tardar VERBO
to be late (*retrasarse*) ◇ *Te espero a las*

T ☞

ocho. No tardes. I'll expect you at eight. Don't be late.

◆ **Tardaron una semana en contestar.** They took a week to reply. ◇ *El arroz tarda media hora en hacerse.* Rice takes half an hour to cook.

◆ **En avión se tarda dos horas.** The plane takes two hours.

la **tarde** SUSTANTIVO

1 afternoon (*antes de anochecer*) ◇ *a las tres de la tarde* at three in the afternoon ◇ *¡Buenas tardes!* Good afternoon! ◇ *por la tarde* in the afternoon ◇ *hoy por la tarde* this afternoon

2 evening (*después de anochecer*) ◇ *a las ocho de la tarde* at eight in the evening ◇ *¡Buenas tardes!* Good evening! ◇ *por la tarde* in the evening ◇ *hoy por la tarde* this evening

tarde ADVERBIO

late ◇ *Se está haciendo tarde.* It's getting late.

◆ **más tarde** later

◆ **tarde o temprano** sooner or later

◆ **Llegaré a las nueve como muy tarde.** I'll arrive at nine at the latest.

la **tarea** SUSTANTIVO

task ◇ *Una de sus tareas es repartir la correspondencia.* One of his tasks is to hand out the mail.

◆ **las tareas domésticas** the chores

◆ **las tareas** (*deberes escolares*) homework

la **tarifa** SUSTANTIVO

1 rate (*eléctrica, bancaria*)

2 fare (*de transportes*)

la **tarima** SUSTANTIVO

platform

la **tarjeta** SUSTANTIVO

card ◇ *Me mandó una tarjeta de Navidad.* He sent me a Christmas card.

◆ **una tarjeta de cajero automático** a cash card

◆ **una tarjeta de crédito** a credit card

◆ **una tarjeta de visita** a visiting card

◆ **una tarjeta telefónica** a phonecard

◆ **una tarjeta de embarque** a boarding pass

el **tarro** SUSTANTIVO

1 jar (*frasco*)

2 mug (*taza*) *Mexico*

la **tarta** SUSTANTIVO

1 cake (*pastel*) ◇ *una tarta de cumpleaños* a birthday cake

2 tart (*de hojaldre*)

tartamudear VERBO

to stammer

tartamudo ADJETIVO

◆ **ser* tartamudo** to stutter

la **tasa** SUSTANTIVO

rate ◇ *la tasa de natalidad* the birth rate

tasar VERBO

to value

la **tasca** SUSTANTIVO

tavern

el **tata** SUSTANTIVO

1 daddy (*padre*)

2 grandpa (*abuelo*)

el **tatuaje** SUSTANTIVO

tattoo (PL tattoos)

tatuar* VERBO

to tattoo

Tauro SUSTANTIVO MASC

Taurus ◇ *Soy tauro.* I'm a Taurus.

el **taxi** SUSTANTIVO

taxi ◇ *tomar un taxi* to take a taxi

el **taxímetro** SUSTANTIVO

taximeter

el/la **taxista** SUSTANTIVO

taxi driver

la **taza** SUSTANTIVO

1 cup ◇ *Tomamos una taza de café.* We had a cup of coffee.

2 cupful (*cantidad*) ◇ *una taza de arroz* a cupful of rice

3 bowl (*de retrete*)

el **tazón** SUSTANTIVO (PL los **tazones**)

bowl

te PRONOMBRE

1 you ◇ *Te quiero.* I love you. ◇ *Te voy a dar un consejo.* I'm going to give you some advice.

◆ **Me gustaría comprártelo.** I'd like to buy it for you.

2 yourself ◇ *¿Te lastimaste?* Have you hurt yourself?

Con partes del cuerpo o con prendas que se llevan puestas se usa el adjetivo posesivo.

◇ *¿Te duelen los pies?* Do your feet hurt?

◇ *Te tienes que poner el abrigo.* You should put your coat on.

el **té** SUSTANTIVO (PL los **tés**)

tea

◆ **Me hice un té.** I made myself a cup of tea.

el **teatro** SUSTANTIVO

theater ◇ *Por la noche fuimos al teatro.* At night we went to the theater.

◆ **una obra de teatro** a play

el **techo** SUSTANTIVO

1 ceiling ◇ *El techo está pintado de blanco.* The ceiling is painted white.

2 roof (*tejado*)

la **tecla** SUSTANTIVO

key

◆ **pulsar una tecla** to press a key

el **teclado** SUSTANTIVO

keyboard (*de computadora, de máquina de escribir*)

teclear VERBO

to type

la **técnica** SUSTANTIVO

1 technique (*método*)

2 technology (PL technologies) (*tecnología*)

* Verbs marked with this symbol are irregular. See pages 346–348 for further details.

3 technician (*persona*) ◇ *Mi hermana es técnica de laboratorio.* My sister is a laboratory technician.

técnico ADJETIVO
technical

el **técnico** SUSTANTIVO
1 technician ◇ *un técnico de laboratorio* a laboratory technician
2 repairman (PL repairmen) ◇ *El técnico me arregló la lavadora.* The repairman fixed my washing machine.

el **tecno** SUSTANTIVO
techno

la **tecnología** SUSTANTIVO
technology (PL technologies)
◆ **tecnología punta** state-of-the-art technology

tecnológico ADJETIVO
technological

la **teja** SUSTANTIVO
tile

el **tejado** SUSTANTIVO
roof

los **tejanos** SUSTANTIVO
jeans

tejer VERBO
1 to weave (*en telar*)
2 to knit (*hacer punto*)

el **tejido** SUSTANTIVO
1 fabric (*tela*)
2 tissue (*corporal*)

tel. ABREVIATURA (= *teléfono*)
tel.

la **tela** SUSTANTIVO
fabric
◆ **tela metálica** wire netting

la **telaraña** SUSTANTIVO
cobweb

la **tele** SUSTANTIVO
TV ◇ *Estábamos viendo la tele.* We were watching TV.

las **telecomunicaciones** SUSTANTIVO
telecommunications

el **telediario** SUSTANTIVO
news SING ◇ *el telediario de las seis* the six o'clock news

teledirigido ADJETIVO
remote-controlled (*carro*)

el **teleférico** SUSTANTIVO
cable car

telefonear VERBO
to call ◇ *Tengo que telefonear a mis padres.* I have to call my parents.

telefónico ADJETIVO
telephone

telephone *en este caso va siempre delante del sustantivo.*

◆ **la guía telefónica** the telephone directory

el/la **telefonista** SUSTANTIVO
telephone operator

el **teléfono** SUSTANTIVO
telephone
◆ **No tengo teléfono.** I don't have a telephone.
◆ **Hablamos por teléfono.** We spoke on the phone.
◆ **Está hablando por teléfono.** He's on the phone.
◆ **colgar* el teléfono a alguien** to hang up the phone on somebody
◆ **un teléfono de tarjeta** a card phone
◆ **un teléfono celular** a cellular phone
◆ **un teléfono con cámara** a camera phone
◆ **un teléfono móvil** Spain a cellular phone

el **telegrama** SUSTANTIVO
telegram

la **telenovela** SUSTANTIVO
soap opera

la **telepatía** SUSTANTIVO
telepathy

la **telerrealidad** SUSTANTIVO
reality TV

el **telescopio** SUSTANTIVO
telescope

el **telesilla** SUSTANTIVO
chairlift

el **telespectador**, la **telespectadora** SUSTANTIVO
viewer

el **telesquí** SUSTANTIVO (PL los **telesquís**)
ski-lift

las **televentas** SUSTANTIVO
telemarketing

televisar VERBO
to televise

la **televisión** SUSTANTIVO (PL las **televisiones**)
television
◆ **Dieron la noticia por la televisión.** They gave the news on the television.
◆ **¿Qué dan en la televisión esta noche?** What's on television tonight?
◆ **la televisión por cable** cable television
◆ **la televisión digital** digital TV

el **televisor** SUSTANTIVO
television set

el **telón** SUSTANTIVO (PL los **telones**)
curtain ◇ *Subió el telón.* The curtain rose.

el **tema** SUSTANTIVO
1 topic (*de conferencia, redacción*) ◇ *El tema de la composición era "La Música".* The topic of the essay was "Music".
2 subject (*asunto*) ◇ *Luego hablaremos de ese tema.* We'll talk about that subject later.
◆ **cambiar de tema** to change the subject
◆ **temas de actualidad** current affairs
◆ **el tema de conversación** the topic of conversation

temblar* VERBO
to tremble ◇ *Me temblaban las manos.* My hands were trembling.
◆ **temblar de miedo** to tremble with fear
◆ **temblar de frío** to shiver

el **temblor de tierra** SUSTANTIVO

☞

T

earthquake

tembloroso ADJETIVO
trembling (*manos, voz*)

temer VERBO
1 to be afraid ◇ *No temas.* Don't be afraid.
2 to be afraid of ◇ *Le teme al profesor.* He's afraid of the teacher. ◇ *Temo ofenderles.* I'm afraid of offending them.

temible ADJETIVO
fearsome

el **temor** SUSTANTIVO
fear ◇ *el temor a la oscuridad* fear of the dark ◇ *por temor a equivocarme* for fear of making a mistake

temperamental ADJETIVO
temperamental

el **temperamento** SUSTANTIVO
temperament

la **temperatura** SUSTANTIVO
temperature ◇ *El médico le tomó la temperatura.* The doctor took his temperature.

la **tempestad** SUSTANTIVO
storm

templado ADJETIVO
1 lukewarm (*agua, comida*)
2 mild (*clima*)

el **templo** SUSTANTIVO
temple

la **temporada** SUSTANTIVO
season ◇ *la temporada de esquí* the ski season ◇ *la temporada alta* the high season ◇ *la temporada baja* the off season

temporal ADJETIVO
temporary

el **temporal** SUSTANTIVO
storm

temporario ADJETIVO
temporary

temprano ADVERBIO
early
- **por la mañana temprano** early in the morning

ten VERBO *ver* **tener**

tenaz ADJETIVO (PL **tenaces**)
tenacious

las **tenazas** SUSTANTIVO
pliers

el **tendedero** SUSTANTIVO
1 clothes line (*con cuerda*)
2 clothes horse (*extensible*)

la **tendencia** SUSTANTIVO
tendency (PL tendencies)
- **Tengo tendencia a engordar.** I tend to put on weight.

tender* VERBO
1 to hang out (*ropa*) ◇ *Marta estaba tendiendo la ropa.* Martha was hanging out the wash.
2 to lay out (*sobre una superficie*) ◇ *Tendí la toalla sobre la arena.* I laid the towel out on the sand.
- **Me tendió la mano.** He stretched out his hand to me.
- **tender a hacer algo** to tend to do something
- **tender una trampa** to set a trap
- **tenderse en el sofá** to lie down on the sofa
- **tender la cama** to make the bed
- **tender la mesa** to set the table

el **tendero,** la **tendera** SUSTANTIVO
storekeeper

tendido ADJETIVO
- **La ropa estaba tendida.** The wash was hanging out.
- **Lo encontré tendido en el suelo.** I found him lying on the floor.

el **tendón** SUSTANTIVO (PL los **tendones**)
tendon

tendrá VERBO *ver* **tener**

el **tenedor** SUSTANTIVO
fork

tener* VERBO
1 to have ◇ *Tengo dos hermanas.* I have two sisters. ◇ *¿Tienes dinero?* Do you have any money? ◇ *Tiene el pelo rubio.* He has blond hair. ◇ *Va a tener un niño.* She's going to have a baby. ◇ *Luis tiene la gripe.* Luis has the flu.
- **¿Cuántos años tienes?** How old are you?
- **Tiene cinco metros de largo.** It's five meters long.
- **Ten cuidado.** Be careful.
- **No tengas miedo.** Don't be afraid.
- **Tenía el pelo mojado.** His hair was wet.

2 to hold ◇ *Tenía el pasaporte en la mano.* He was holding his passport in his hand.
- **tener que hacer algo** to have to do something
- **Tendrías que comer más.** You should eat more.
- **No tienes por qué ir.** There's no reason why you should go.
- **Eso no tiene nada que ver.** That has nothing to do with it.
- **¡Tenga!** Here you are!
- **tenerse en pie** to stand up

tenga VERBO *ver* **tener**

el/la **teniente** SUSTANTIVO
lieutenant

el **tenis** SUSTANTIVO
tennis
- **¿Juegas tenis?** Do you play tennis?
- **tenis de mesa** table tennis

el/la **tenista** SUSTANTIVO
tennis player

el **tenor** SUSTANTIVO
tenor

tensar VERBO
to tighten (*cuerda, cable*)

la **tensión** SUSTANTIVO (PL las **tensiones**)
1 tension ◇ *Hubo mucha tensión durante*

* Verbs marked with this symbol are irregular. See pages 346–348 for further details.

la reunión. There was a lot of tension during the meeting.
[2] blood pressure ◇ *El médico me tomó la tensión.* The doctor took my blood pressure.
◆ **un cable de alta tensión** a high-voltage cable

tenso ADJETIVO
[1] tense (*persona, situación*)
[2] taut (*cuerda*)

la **tentación** SUSTANTIVO (PL las **tentaciones**)
temptation
◆ **caer* en la tentación** to give in to temptation

tentador ADJETIVO (FEM **tentadora**)
tempting

tentar* VERBO
to tempt ◇ *Estuve tentado de marcharme.* I was tempted to leave.
◆ **No me tienta la idea.** The idea isn't very tempting.

la **tentativa** SUSTANTIVO
attempt

el **tentempié** SUSTANTIVO (PL los **tentempiés**)
snack

tenue ADJETIVO
faint (*luz, voz*)

teñir* VERBO
to dye ◇ *Se ha teñido el pelo.* He's dyed his hair.

la **teología** SUSTANTIVO
theology

la **teoría** SUSTANTIVO
theory (PL theories) ◇ *En teoría es fácil.* In theory it's easy.

teórico ADJETIVO
theoretical ◇ *Ése es un caso teórico.* It's a theoretical case.
◆ **un examen teórico** a theory exam

terapéutico ADJETIVO
therapeutic

la **terapia** SUSTANTIVO
therapy (PL therapies)

tercer ADJETIVO *ver* **tercero**

tercero ADJETIVO, PRONOMBRE (FEM **tercera**)
third ◇ *la tercera vez* the third time
◇ *Llegué el tercero.* I arrived third.
◆ **una tercera parte de la población** a third of the population
◆ **Vivo en el tercero.** I live on the fourth floor.
◆ **el Tercer Mundo** the Third World

el **tercio** SUSTANTIVO
third

el **terciopelo** SUSTANTIVO
velvet

terco ADJETIVO
obstinate

tergiversar VERBO
to distort

el **terminal** SUSTANTIVO
terminal (*computadora*)

la **terminal** SUSTANTIVO
terminal (*en aeropuerto*)
◆ **la terminal de trenes** the train station

terminante ADJETIVO
[1] categorical (*respuesta*)
[2] strict (*orden*)

terminantemente ADVERBIO
strictly

terminar VERBO
[1] to finish ◇ *Terminé el libro.* I've finished the book.
◆ **cuando terminó de hablar** when he finished talking
[2] to end (*reunión, película*) ◇ *¿A qué hora termina la clase?* What time does the class end?
◆ **Terminé rendido.** I ended up exhausted.
◆ **Terminaron peleándose.** They ended up fighting.
◆ **Se nos terminó el café.** We've run out of coffee.
◆ **Terminé con Andrés.** I've broken up with Andrés.

el **término** SUSTANTIVO
term ◇ *un término médico* a medical term
◆ **por término medio** on average

la **termita** SUSTANTIVO
termite

el **termo**® SUSTANTIVO
Thermos®

el **termómetro** SUSTANTIVO
thermometer
◆ **Le puse el termómetro.** I took his temperature.

el **termostato** SUSTANTIVO
thermostat

la **ternera** SUSTANTIVO
veal (*carne*)

el **ternero**, la **ternera** SUSTANTIVO
calf (PL calves) (*animal*)

la **ternura** SUSTANTIVO
tenderness
◆ **con ternura** tenderly

el/la **terrateniente** SUSTANTIVO
landowner

la **terraza** SUSTANTIVO
[1] balcony (PL balconies) (*balcón*)
[2] roof terrace (*azotea*)
◆ **Salimos a la terraza del bar a tomar algo.** We went out to the beer garden for a drink.

el **terremoto** SUSTANTIVO
earthquake

el **terreno** SUSTANTIVO
[1] land ◇ *una granja con mucho terreno* a farm with a lot of land
◆ **un terreno** a piece of land ◇ *Compramos un terreno.* We've bought a piece of land.
[2] field ◇ *terrenos plantados de naranjos* fields planted with orange trees ◇ *en el terreno de la informática* in the field of computer science
◆ **el terreno de juego** the playing field
◆ **Lo decidiremos sobre el terreno.** We'll decide as we go along.

T

terrestre ADJETIVO
land (*animal, transporte*)
land *en este caso va siempre delante del sustantivo.*

terrible ADJETIVO
terrible ◇ *Fue una experiencia terrible.* It was a terrible experience.
◆ **Tenía un cansancio terrible.** I was awfully tired.

el/la **terrier** SUSTANTIVO (PL los/las **terriers**)
terrier

el **territorio** SUSTANTIVO
territory (PL territories)

el **terrón** SUSTANTIVO (PL los **terrones**)
lump (*de azúcar*)

el **terror** SUSTANTIVO
terror ◇ *Fuimos víctimas de una campaña de terror.* We were the victims of a terror campaign.
◆ **Les tiene terror a los perros.** He's terrified of dogs.
◆ **una película de terror** a horror movie

el **terrorismo** SUSTANTIVO
terrorism

el/la **terrorista** ADJETIVO, SUSTANTIVO
terrorist
◆ **un terrorista suicida** a suicide bomber

la **tesis** SUSTANTIVO (PL las **tesis**)
thesis (PL theses)

el **tesón** SUSTANTIVO
determination

el **tesorero,** la **tesorera** SUSTANTIVO
treasurer

el **tesoro** SUSTANTIVO
treasure
◆ **Ven aquí, tesoro.** Come here, darling.

el **test** SUSTANTIVO (PL los **tests**)
test ◇ *Nos hicieron un test.* We had a test today.

el **testamento** SUSTANTIVO
will
◆ **hacer* testamento** to make one's will
◆ **el Antiguo Testamento** the Old Testament
◆ **el Nuevo Testamento** the New Testament

testarudo ADJETIVO
stubborn

el/la **testigo** SUSTANTIVO
witness (PL witnesses)
◆ **un Testigo de Jehová** a Jehovah's Witness
◆ **Fui testigo del accidente.** I witnessed the accident.

el **testimonio** SUSTANTIVO
evidence

el **tétanos** SUSTANTIVO
tetanus

la **tetera** SUSTANTIVO
[1] teapot (*para el té*)
[2] kettle (*para hervir agua*) [*Mexico*]
[3] baby's bottle (*para el bebé*) [*Mexico*]

la **tetina** SUSTANTIVO
teat

el **textil** ADJETIVO, SUSTANTIVO
textile

el **texto** SUSTANTIVO
text
◆ **un libro de texto** a textbook

la **textura** SUSTANTIVO
texture

la **tez** SUSTANTIVO
complexion

ti PRONOMBRE
you ◇ *una llamada para ti* a call for you
◆ **Sólo piensas en ti mismo.** You only think of yourself.

la **tía** SUSTANTIVO
[1] aunt (*pariente*) ◇ *mi tía* my aunt
[2] girl (*coloquial: mujer*) [*Spain*]

tibio ADJETIVO
lukewarm

el **tiburón** SUSTANTIVO (PL los **tiburones**)
shark

el **tic** SUSTANTIVO
tic ◇ *un tic nervioso* a nervous tic

el **tictac** SUSTANTIVO
ticktock

tiemblo VERBO *ver* **temblar**

el **tiempo** SUSTANTIVO
[1] time ◇ *No tengo tiempo.* I don't have time. ◇ *¿Qué haces en tu tiempo libre?* What do you do in your spare time? ◇ *Me llevó bastante tiempo.* It took me quite a long time.
◆ **¿Cuánto tiempo hace que vives aquí?** How long have you been living here?
◆ **Hace mucho tiempo que no la veo.** I haven't seen her for a long time.
◆ **¿Qué tiempo tiene el niño?** How old is the baby?
◆ **al mismo tiempo** at the same time
◆ **perder* el tiempo** to waste time
◆ **al poco tiempo** soon after
[2] weather
◆ **¿Qué tiempo hace ahí?** What's the weather like there?
◆ **hizo buen tiempo** the weather was fine
◆ **Hace mal tiempo.** The weather's bad.
[3] half (*en partido*)
◆ **Metieron el gol durante el segundo tiempo.** They scored the goal during the second half.

la **tienda** SUSTANTIVO
[1] store ◇ *una tienda de comestibles* a grocery store ◇ *una tienda de abarrotes* [*Mexico*] a grocery store ◇ *una tienda de discos* a record store
◆ **ir* de tiendas** to go shopping
[2] tent (*de campaña*)
◆ **montar la tienda** to pitch the tent
◆ **desmontar la tienda** to take down the tent

tiendo VERBO *ver* **tender**

tiene VERBO *ver* **tener**

tiento VERBO *ver* **tentar**

tierno ADJETIVO
1 tender (*carne, mirada*)
2 fresh (*pan*)

la **tierra** SUSTANTIVO
1 land ◊ *Trabajan la tierra.* They work the land.
◆ **la Tierra Santa** the Holy Land
◆ **tierra adentro** inland
2 soil (*para macetas, plantas*)
◆ **echar algo por tierra** to ruin something ◊ *Echó por tierra todos nuestros planes.* It ruined all our plans.
◆ **la Tierra** the Earth

tieso ADJETIVO
stiff (*rígido*)
◆ **quedarse tieso de frío** to be frozen stiff

el **tiesto** SUSTANTIVO
flowerpot

el **tigre** SUSTANTIVO
tiger

las **tijeras** SUSTANTIVO
scissors ◊ *Es más fácil cortarlo con las tijeras.* It's easier to cut with scissors.
◆ **¿Tienes unas tijeras?** Do you have a pair of scissors?
◆ **unas tijeras de podar** a pair of hedge clippers

timar VERBO
1 to con (*engañar*)
2 to rip off (*cobrar demasiado*) ◊ *Te timaron con ese carro.* They've ripped you off with that car.

el **timbrazo** SUSTANTIVO
ring

el **timbre** SUSTANTIVO
1 bell (*de puerta, alarma, colegio*) ◊ *Ya sonó el timbre.* The bell has already gone.
◆ **llamar al timbre** to ring the bell
2 stamp (*para cartas*) Mexico

la **timidez** SUSTANTIVO
shyness

tímido ADJETIVO
shy

el **timo** SUSTANTIVO
1 con (*engaño*)
2 rip-off (*pago excesivo*)
◆ **¡Vaya timo!** What a rip-off!

la **tinaja** SUSTANTIVO
large earthenware vat

tiñendo VERBO *ver* **teñir**

la **tinta** SUSTANTIVO
ink ◊ *escrito con tinta* written in ink
◆ **tinta China** Indian ink
◆ **sudar tinta** to sweat blood

el **tinte** SUSTANTIVO
dye (*sustancia*)

el **tintero** SUSTANTIVO
inkwell

el **tinto** SUSTANTIVO
red wine (*vino*)

la **tintorería** SUSTANTIVO
dry cleaner's

el **tío** SUSTANTIVO
1 uncle (*pariente*)
◆ **mis tíos** (*tío y tía*) my uncle and aunt
2 guy (*coloquial: hombre*) Spain

típicamente ADVERBIO
typically

típico ADJETIVO
typical
◆ **Eso es muy típico de ella.** That's very typical of her.

el **tipo** SUSTANTIVO
1 kind ◊ *No me gusta este tipo de fiestas.* I don't like this kind of party.
◆ **todo tipo de...** all sorts of...
2 figure ◊ *Marisa tiene un tipo muy bonito.* Marisa has a lovely figure.
3 guy (*coloquial*) ◊ *un tipo de aspecto sospechoso* a suspicious-looking guy

el **tíquet** SUSTANTIVO (PL los **tíquets**)
1 ticket (*de autobús, tren*)
2 receipt (*recibo de compra*)

la **tira** SUSTANTIVO
strip ◊ *una tira de papel* a strip of paper ◊ *una tira cómica* a comic strip

la **tirada** SUSTANTIVO
1 print run ◊ *La tirada inicial fue de 50.000 ejemplares.* The initial print run was 50,000 copies.
2 circulation ◊ *La revista tiene una tirada semanal de 200.000 ejemplares.* The magazine has a weekly circulation of 200,000 copies.
◆ **de una tirada** in one go

tirado ADJETIVO
1 dirt cheap (*coloquial: barato*)
2 dead easy (*coloquial: fácil*)

el **tirador** SUSTANTIVO
handle (*de cajón, puerta*)

la **tirana** SUSTANTIVO
tyrant

tiránico ADJETIVO
tyrannical

el **tirano** SUSTANTIVO
tyrant

tirante ADJETIVO
1 tight (*cuerda*)
2 tense (*situación, relación*)

el **tirante** SUSTANTIVO
strap (*de vestido*)
◆ **tirantes** (*para pantalones*) suspenders

tirar VERBO
1 to throw ◊ *Tírame la pelota.* Throw me the ball. ◊ *Les tiraban piedras a los soldados.* They were throwing stones at the soldiers. ◊ *Se tiró al suelo.* He threw himself to the ground.
2 to throw away (*desechar*) ◊ *No tires la comida.* Don't throw away the food.
◆ **tirar algo a la basura** to throw something out
◆ **tirar al suelo** to knock over ◊ *La moto la tiró al suelo.* The motorbike knocked her over. ☞

T

- **Tropezó con la maceta y la tiró al suelo.** He tripped on the flowerpot and knocked it to the ground.

[3] to knock down (*derribar*) ◇ *Queremos tirar esta pared.* We want to knock this wall down.

[4] to drop (*bomba*)

- **tirar de algo** to pull something
- **tirar la cadena** (*de wáter*) to pull the chain
- **Vamos tirando.** We're getting by.
- **tirarse al agua** to plunge into the water
- **tirarse de cabeza** to dive in head first
- **tirarse en el sofá** to lie down on the sofa
- **Se tiró toda la mañana estudiando.** He spent the whole morning studying.

tiritar VERBO
to shiver
- **tiritar de frío** to shiver with cold

el **tiro** SUSTANTIVO
shot ◇ *Oímos un tiro.* We heard a shot.
- **Lo mataron de un tiro.** They shot him dead.
- **Me salió el tiro por la culata.** It backfired on me.
- **tiro al blanco** target practice
- **un tiro libre** (*en fútbol*) a free kick

el **tiroteo** SUSTANTIVO
shoot-out

el **títere** SUSTANTIVO
puppet

titubear VERBO
to hesitate (*vacilar*) ◇ *Respondí sin titubear.* I answered without hesitating.

titulado ADJETIVO
qualified ◇ *una enfermera titulada* a qualified nurse

el **titular** SUSTANTIVO
headline (*de periódico*)

el/la **titular** SUSTANTIVO
[1] holder (*de pasaporte*)
[2] owner (*de vivienda*)

titular VERBO
to call ◇ *La novela se titula "Marcianos".* The novel is called "Marcianos".
- **¿Cómo vas a titular el trabajo?** What title are you going to give the essay?

el **título** SUSTANTIVO
[1] title ◇ *Tengo que pensar en un título para el poema.* I have to think of a title for the poem.

[2] qualification (*carrera*) ◇ *Exigen un título académico.* They require an academic qualification.
- **Tiene el título de enfermera.** She's a qualified nurse.

[3] certificate (*diploma*) ◇ *Hay varios títulos colgados en la pared.* There are several certificates hanging on the wall.

la **tiza** SUSTANTIVO
chalk (*material*)
- **una tiza** a piece of chalk

la **tlapalería** SUSTANTIVO *Mexico*
hardware store

la **toalla** SUSTANTIVO
towel ◇ *una toalla de baño* a bath towel

el **tobillo** SUSTANTIVO
ankle ◇ *Me torcí el tobillo.* I've twisted my ankle.

el **tobogán** SUSTANTIVO (PL los **toboganes**)
[1] slide (*en parque, piscina*)
[2] toboggan (*trineo*)

el **tocadiscos** SUSTANTIVO (PL los **tocadiscos**)
record player

el **tocador** SUSTANTIVO
dressing table

tocar* VERBO
[1] to touch ◇ *Si lo tocas te quemarás.* If you touch it you'll burn yourself.

[2] to play (*instrumento, vals*) ◇ *Toca el violín.* He plays the violin.

[3] to ring (*campana, timbre*)

[4] to blow (*bocina*)
- **tocar a la puerta** to knock on the door
- **Te toca lavar los platos.** It's your turn to do the dishes.
- **Le tocó la lotería.** He won the lottery.

el **tocino** SUSTANTIVO
bacon

todavía ADVERBIO
[1] still ◇ *¿Todavía estás en la cama?* Are you still in bed? ◇ *¡Y todavía se queja!* And he still complains!

[2] yet (*en oraciones negativas*) ◇ *Todavía no han llegado.* They haven't arrived yet. ◇ *¿Todavía no has comido?* Haven't you eaten yet? ◇ *Todavía no.* Not yet.

todo ADJETIVO, PRONOMBRE (FEM **toda**)
[1] all ◇ *todos los niños* all the children ◇ *Todos son caros.* They're all expensive. ◇ *el más bonito de todos* the prettiest of all
- **toda la noche** all night
- **todos ustedes** all of you
- **todos los que quieran venir** all those who want to come

[2] every (*cada*) ◇ *todos los días* every day

[3] the whole ◇ *Limpié toda la casa.* I've cleaned the whole house.
- **Ha viajado por todo el mundo.** He has traveled throughout the world.
- **Todo el mundo lo sabe.** Everybody knows.

[4] everything ◇ *Lo sabemos todo.* We know everything. ◇ *todo lo que me dijeron* everything they told me

[5] everybody ◇ *Todos estaban de acuerdo.* Everybody agreed.
- **Vaya todo seguido.** Keep straight on.
- **todo lo contrario** quite the opposite

el **todoterreno** SUSTANTIVO
SUV

el **toldo** SUSTANTIVO
[1] blind (*de ventana*)

[2] awning (*de tienda*)
[3] sunshade (*en la playa*)

tolerante ADJETIVO
tolerant

tolerar VERBO
to tolerate ◇ *No voy a tolerar ese comportamiento.* I won't tolerate that behavior.
◆ **Sus padres le toleran demasiado.** His parents let him get away with too much.

el **tomacorriente** SUSTANTIVO
outlet

tomar VERBO
[1] to take (*tren, foto, decisión*) ◇ *En clase tomamos apuntes.* We take notes in class. ◇ *Se lo ha tomado muy en serio.* He's taken it very seriously. ◇ *Se tomó la molestia de acompañarnos.* He took the trouble to accompany us.
◆ **tomar a alguien de la mano** to take somebody by the hand
◆ **tomarse algo a mal** to take something badly
◆ **Toma, esto es tuyo.** Here, this is yours.
[2] to drink (*bebida, alcohol*) ◇ *¿Qué quieren tomar?* What would you like to drink? ◇ *Se tomó tres tazas de café.* She drank three cups of coffee.
◆ **tomar cariño a alguien** to become fond of somebody
◆ **tomar el pelo a alguien** to pull somebody's leg
◆ **tomar el aire** to get some fresh air
◆ **tomar el sol** to sunbathe
◆ **tomar nota de algo** to note something down

el **tomate** SUSTANTIVO
tomato (PL tomatoes)
◆ **ponerse* como un tomate** to turn as red as a beet

el **tomillo** SUSTANTIVO
thyme

el **tomo** SUSTANTIVO
volume

el **tonel** SUSTANTIVO
barrel

la **tonelada** SUSTANTIVO
ton

la **tónica** SUSTANTIVO
tonic

el **tono** SUSTANTIVO
[1] tone (*de voz*) ◇ *Lo dijo en tono cariñoso.* He said it in an affectionate tone.
◆ **un tono de llamada** a ringtone
[2] shade (*de color*) ◇ *un tono un poco más oscuro* a slightly darker shade

la **tonta** SUSTANTIVO
fool
◆ **hacerse* la tonta** to act dumb

la **tontería** SUSTANTIVO
silly thing (*cosa sin importancia*) ◇ *Se pelearon por una tontería.* They quarreled over something silly.
◆ **tonterías** nonsense ◇ *¡Eso son tonterías!* That's nonsense! ◇ *¡No digas tonterías!* Don't talk nonsense!

tonto ADJETIVO
silly ◇ *¡Qué error más tonto!* What a silly mistake!

el **tonto** SUSTANTIVO
fool
◆ **hacer* el tonto** (*hacer payasadas*) to act the fool
◆ **hacerse* el tonto** to act dumb

toparse VERBO
◆ **toparse con alguien** to bump into somebody

los **topes** SUSTANTIVO
◆ **El autobús iba hasta los topes.** The bus was packed.

el **tópico** SUSTANTIVO
cliché

topless ADJETIVO (FEM + PL **topless**)
topless

el **topo** SUSTANTIVO
mole

el **toque** SUSTANTIVO
◆ **dar* los últimos toques a algo** to put the finishing touches to something
◆ **el toque de queda** the curfew

el **tórax** SUSTANTIVO
thorax

la **torcedura** SUSTANTIVO
◆ **una torcedura de tobillo** a sprained ankle

torcer* VERBO
[1] to twist ◇ *¡Me estás torciendo el brazo!* You're twisting my arm!
◆ **torcerse el tobillo** to sprain one's ankle
[2] to turn (*cambiar de dirección*) ◇ *torcer a la derecha* to turn right ◇ *torcer la esquina* to turn the corner

torcido ADJETIVO
[1] crooked (*nariz, línea*) ◇ *Tiene la boca un poco torcida.* His mouth is a bit crooked.
[2] bent (*doblado*) ◇ *El tronco está torcido.* The trunk is bent.
◆ **Ese cuadro está torcido.** That picture isn't straight.

T

el **toreo** SUSTANTIVO
bullfighting

el **torero**, la **torera** SUSTANTIVO
bullfighter

la **tormenta** SUSTANTIVO
storm
◆ **Hubo tormenta.** There was a storm.
◆ **un día de tormenta** a stormy day

el **torneo** SUSTANTIVO
tournament

el **tornillo** SUSTANTIVO
[1] screw
◆ **A tu hermana le falta un tornillo.** Your sister has a screw loose. (*coloquial*)
[2] bolt (*para tuerca*)

el **toro** SUSTANTIVO
bull

☞

- **los toros** bullfighting
- **ir* a los toros** to go to a bullfight

la **toronja** SUSTANTIVO
grapefruit (PL grapefruit)

torpe ADJETIVO
1 clumsy (*manazas*)
2 dim (*zoquete*)

la **torre** SUSTANTIVO
1 tower (*de castillo, iglesia*) ◇ *la torre de control* the control tower
2 pylon (*de alta tensión*)
3 rook (*en ajedrez*)

la **torta** SUSTANTIVO
1 pie (*de verduras*)
2 filled roll (*de pan*) Mexico

la **tortilla** SUSTANTIVO
1 omelette (*de huevos*)
- **una tortilla de papas** a Spanish omelette

2 tortilla (*de maíz*)

la **tortuga** SUSTANTIVO
1 tortoise (*de tierra*)
2 turtle (*de mar*)

la **tortura** SUSTANTIVO
torture

torturar VERBO
to torture

la **tos** SUSTANTIVO (PL las **toses**)
cough
- **Tengo mucha tos.** I have a bad cough.

toser VERBO
to cough

la **tostada** SUSTANTIVO
1 piece of toast ◇ *¿Quieres una tostada?* Do you want a piece of toast?
- **tostadas** toast ◇ *Tomé café con tostadas.* I had coffee and toast.

2 fried corn tortilla Mexico

tostado ADJETIVO
1 toasted (*pan, avellanas*)
2 roasted (*café*)
3 tanned (*bronceado*)

la **tostadora** SUSTANTIVO
toaster

el **tostador** SUSTANTIVO
toaster

tostar* VERBO
1 to toast (*pan, avellanas*)
2 to roast (*café*)

el **total** ADJETIVO, SUSTANTIVO
total ◇ *Fue un fracaso total.* It was a total failure. ◇ *El total son 230 pesos.* The total is 230 pesos.
- **un cambio total** a complete change
- **En total éramos catorce.** There were fourteen of us altogether.

total ADVERBIO
- **Total, que perdí mi trabajo.** So, in the end, I lost my job.

totalitario ADJETIVO
totalitarian

totalmente ADVERBIO
1 totally ◇ *Mario es totalmente distinto a Luis.* Mario is totally different from Luis.
2 completely ◇ *Estoy totalmente de acuerdo.* I completely agree.
- **¿Estás seguro? -Totalmente.** Are you sure? – Absolutely.

tóxico ADJETIVO
toxic

el **toxicómano,** la **toxicómana** SUSTANTIVO
drug addict

la **toxina** SUSTANTIVO
toxin

tozudo ADJETIVO
obstinate

trabajador ADJETIVO (FEM **trabajadora**)
hardworking ◇ *un chico muy trabajador* a very hardworking boy

el **trabajador,** la **trabajadora** SUSTANTIVO
worker ◇ *trabajadores no cualificados* unskilled workers

trabajar VERBO
to work ◇ *No trabajes tanto.* Don't work so hard.
- **¿En qué trabajas?** What's your job?
- **Trabajo de camarero.** I work as a waiter.
- **trabajar jornada completa** to work full time
- **trabajar media jornada** to work part time

el **trabajo** SUSTANTIVO
1 work ◇ *Tengo mucho trabajo.* I have a lot of work. ◇ *Me puedes llamar al trabajo.* You can call me at work.
- **estar* sin trabajo** to be unemployed
- **trabajo en equipo** teamwork
- **el trabajo de la casa** the housework
- **trabajos manuales** handicrafts

2 job (*empleo*) ◇ *Le han ofrecido un trabajo en el banco.* He's been offered a job in the bank. ◇ *No encuentro trabajo.* I can't find a job.
- **quedarse sin trabajo** to find oneself out of work

3 essay (*escolar*) ◇ *Tengo que entregar dos trabajos mañana.* I have to hand in two essays tomorrow.

el **tractor** SUSTANTIVO
tractor

la **tradición** SUSTANTIVO (PL las **tradiciones**)
tradition

tradicional ADJETIVO
traditional

la **traducción** SUSTANTIVO (PL las **traducciones**)
translation ◇ *Una traducción del italiano al inglés.* A translation from Italian into English.

traducir* VERBO
to translate ◇ *traducir del inglés al francés* to translate from English into French

el **traductor,** la **traductora** SUSTANTIVO
translator

traer* VERBO
[1] to bring ◇ *He traído el paraguas por si acaso.* I've brought the umbrella just in case.
[2] to carry ◇ *El periódico trae un artículo sobre el presidente.* The newspaper carries an article on the president.
[3] to wear ◇ *Traía un vestido nuevo.* She was wearing a new dress.

el/la **traficante** SUSTANTIVO
dealer ◇ *traficantes de armas* arms dealers

el **tráfico** SUSTANTIVO
traffic
◆ **un accidente de tráfico** a road accident
◆ **tráfico de drogas** drug trafficking

tragar* VERBO
to swallow (*comida, pastilla*)
◆ **No la trago.** I can't stand her. (*coloquial*)

la **tragedia** SUSTANTIVO
tragedy (PL tragedies)

trágico ADJETIVO
tragic

el **trago** SUSTANTIVO
drink ◇ *¿Te apetece un trago?* Would you like a drink?
◆ **de un trago** in one gulp

la **traición** SUSTANTIVO (PL las **traiciones**)
[1] betrayal (*engaño*)
[2] treason (*contra el Estado*)

traicionar VERBO
to betray

traicionero ADJETIVO
treacherous

el **traidor**, la **traidora** SUSTANTIVO
traitor

traigo VERBO *ver* **traer**

el **tráiler** SUSTANTIVO (PL los **tráilers**)
[1] trailer (*de vehículo*)
[2] semitrailer (*camión*)

el **traje** SUSTANTIVO
[1] suit (*de hombre*) ◇ *Luis llevaba un traje negro.* Luis was wearing a black suit.
◆ **un traje de chaqueta** a suit
◆ **un traje de buzo** a diving suit
[2] dress (PL dresses) (*vestido de mujer*)
◇ *un traje de noche* an evening dress
◆ **el traje de novia** the bridal gown
◆ **un traje de baño (1)** (*de hombre*) a bathing suit
◆ **un traje de baño (2)** (*de mujer*) a bathing suit

la **trama** SUSTANTIVO
plot (*de obra*)

tramitar VERBO
◆ **Estoy tramitando un préstamo con el banco.** I'm negotiating a loan with the bank.
◆ **Estamos tramitando el divorcio.** We are going through the divorce proceedings.

el **tramo** SUSTANTIVO
[1] section (*de carretera*)
[2] flight (*de escalera*)

la **trampa** SUSTANTIVO
trap ◇ *caer en la trampa* to fall into the trap
◆ **Les tendió una trampa.** He set a trap for them.
◆ **hacer* trampa** to cheat

el **trampolín** SUSTANTIVO (PL los **trampolines**)
[1] diving board (*en piscina*) ◇ *Se tiró desde el trampolín.* He jumped from the diving board.
[2] trampoline (*en gimnasia*)

el **tramposo**, la **tramposa** SUSTANTIVO
cheat

tranquilamente ADVERBIO
calmly ◇ *Háblale tranquilamente.* Speak to him calmly.
◆ **Yo estaba sentado tranquilamente viendo la tele.** I was sitting peacefully watching TV.

la **tranquilidad** SUSTANTIVO
peace and quiet ◇ *Necesito un poco de tranquilidad.* I need a little peace and quiet.
◆ **Respondió con tranquilidad.** He answered calmly.
◆ **Llévatelo a casa y léelo con tranquilidad.** Take it home with you and read it at your leisure.
◆ **¡Qué tranquilidad! ¡Ya se acabaron los exámenes!** What a relief! The exams are over at last!

tranquilizar* VERBO
to calm down ◇ *¡Tranquilízate!* Calm down!
◆ **Las palabras del médico me tranquilizaron.** The doctor's words reassured me.

tranquilo ADJETIVO
[1] calm ◇ *El día del examen estaba bastante tranquilo.* On the day of the exam I was quite calm.
[2] peaceful (*pueblo, lugar*)

el **transatlántico** SUSTANTIVO
ocean liner

el **transbordador** SUSTANTIVO
ferry (PL ferries)
◆ **el transbordador espacial** the space shuttle

el **transbordo** SUSTANTIVO
◆ **Hay que hacer transbordo en Vancouver.** You have to change trains in Vancouver.

transcurrir VERBO
to pass ◇ *Transcurrieron dos años.* Two years passed.

el/la **transeúnte** SUSTANTIVO
passerby (PL passersby)

la **transferencia** SUSTANTIVO
transfer ◇ *transferencia bancaria* bank transfer

la **transformación** SUSTANTIVO (PL las **transformaciones**)
transformation

transformar VERBO
to transform (*lugar, país*) ◇ *La cirugía estética lo ha transformado completamente.* Plastic surgery has completely transformed him.
◆ **Hemos transformado el garaje en sala de estar.** We've converted the garage into a

T

living room.
◆ **El príncipe se transformó en un monstruo.** The prince turned into a monster.

la **transfusión** SUSTANTIVO (PL las **transfusiones**)
◆ **Me hicieron una transfusión de sangre.** They gave me a blood transfusion.

transgénico ADJETIVO
genetically modified

la **transición** SUSTANTIVO
transition

el **transistor** SUSTANTIVO
transistor

transitivo ADJETIVO
transitive

el **tránsito** SUSTANTIVO
traffic
◆ **los pasajeros en tránsito para Moscú** transfer passengers to Moscow

la **transmisión** SUSTANTIVO (PL las **transmisiones**)
broadcast ◇ *una transmisión en directo* a live broadcast

transmitir VERBO
1 to transmit (*señal, sonido*)
2 to broadcast (*programa*)

transparente ADJETIVO
transparent

la **transpiración** SUSTANTIVO
perspiration

transportar VERBO
to carry ◇ *El camión transportaba medicamentos.* The truck was carrying medicines.

el **transporte** SUSTANTIVO
transport
◆ **el transporte público** public transportation

el/la **transportista** SUSTANTIVO
haulage contractor

el **tranvía** SUSTANTIVO
streetcar

el **trapo** SUSTANTIVO
cloth ◇ *Lo limpié con un trapo.* I wiped it with a cloth.
◆ **un trapo de cocina** a dishcloth
◆ **Pásale un trapo al espejo.** Give the mirror a wipe over.
◆ **el trapo del polvo** the dust cloth

la **tráquea** SUSTANTIVO
windpipe

tras PREPOSICIÓN
after ◇ *Salimos corriendo tras ella.* We ran out after her. ◇ *semana tras semana* week after week

trasero ADJETIVO
back ◇ *la rueda trasera de la bici* the back wheel of the bike

el **trasero** SUSTANTIVO
bottom

trasladar VERBO
1 to move (*oficina, tienda*) ◇ *Mañana nos trasladamos al departamento.* We're moving to the apartment tomorrow.
2 to transfer (*empleado, preso*) ◇ *Me quieren trasladar a otra sucursal.* They want to transfer me to another branch.

el **traslado** SUSTANTIVO
move (*mudanza*)
◆ **He pedido traslado a Miami.** I've asked for a transfer to Miami.
◆ **los gastos de traslado de la oficina** the office's relocation expenses

el **trasluz** SUSTANTIVO
◆ **al trasluz** against the light

trasnochar VERBO
to stay up late

traspapelarse VERBO
to get mislaid

traspasar VERBO
1 to go through ◇ *La bala traspasó el sofá.* The bullet went through the sofa.
2 to transfer (*empleado, jugador, dinero*)
3 to sell (*tienda*)

el **traspié** SUSTANTIVO (PL los **traspiés**)
◆ **dar* un traspié** to trip

trasplantar VERBO
to transplant

el **trasplante** SUSTANTIVO
transplant

el **trastero** SUSTANTIVO
storage room

los **trastes** SUSTANTIVO *Mexico*
pots and pans
◆ **lavar los trastes** to do the dishes

el **trasto** SUSTANTIVO
piece of junk ◇ *El carro que se compró es un trasto.* The car he's bought is a piece of junk.
◆ **El desván está lleno de trastos.** The loft is full of junk.

trastornado ADJETIVO
disturbed (*mentalmente*)

el **trastorno** SUSTANTIVO
disruption ◇ *La huelga ha causado muchos trastornos.* The strike has caused a lot of disruption.
◆ **trastornos mentales** mental disorders

el **tratado** SUSTANTIVO
treaty (PL treaties)

el **tratamiento** SUSTANTIVO
treatment
◆ **Está en tratamiento médico.** He's getting medical treatment.
◆ **tratamiento de datos** data processing
◆ **tratamiento de textos** word processing

tratar VERBO
1 to treat ◇ *Su novio la trata muy mal.* Her boyfriend treats her very badly.
2 to deal with ◇ *Trataremos este tema en la reunión.* We'll deal with this subject in the meeting.
◆ **Trato con todo tipo de gente.** I deal with all

sorts of people.
- **tratar de hacer algo** to try to do something
- **¿De qué se trata?** What's it about?
- **La película trata de un adolescente en Nueva York.** The movie is about a teenager in New York.

el **trato** SUSTANTIVO
deal ◇ *hacer un trato* to make a deal
- **¡Trato hecho!** It's a deal!
- **No tengo mucho trato con él.** I don't have much to do with him.
- **recibir malos tratos de alguien** to be treated badly by somebody

el **trauma** SUSTANTIVO
trauma

través PREPOSICIÓN
- **a través de (1)** (*de lado a lado*) across ◇ *Nadó a través del río.* He swam across the river.
- **a través de (2)** (*por medio de*) through ◇ *Se enteraron a través de un amigo.* They found out through a friend.

la **travesía** SUSTANTIVO
crossing (*viaje en barco*)

la **travesura** SUSTANTIVO
prank
- **hacer* travesuras** to get up to mischief

travieso ADJETIVO
naughty

el **trayecto** SUSTANTIVO
1 journey (*viaje*)
2 way (*ruta*)
- **¿Qué trayecto hace el 34?** What way does the number 34 bus go?

trazar* VERBO
1 to draw (*línea, mapa*)
2 to draw up (*plan*)

el **trébol** SUSTANTIVO
clover
- **tréboles** (*en la baraja*) clubs

trece ADJETIVO, PRONOMBRE
thirteen ◇ *Tengo trece años.* I'm thirteen.
- **el trece de enero** January thirteenth

treinta ADJETIVO, PRONOMBRE
thirty ◇ *Tiene treinta años.* He's thirty.
- **el treinta aniversario** the thirtieth anniversary

tremendo ADJETIVO
1 terrible (*dolor, ruido, fracaso*) ◇ *Tenía un tremendo dolor de cabeza.* I had a terrible headache.
- **Hacía un frío tremendo.** It was terribly cold.

2 tremendous (*diferencia, velocidad, éxito*) ◇ *La película tuvo un éxito tremendo.* The movie was a tremendous success.

el **tren** SUSTANTIVO
train
- **viajar en tren** to travel by train
- **Tomé un tren directo.** I took an express train.
- **con este tren de vida** with such a hectic life

la **trenza** SUSTANTIVO
braid
- **Le hice una trenza.** I braided her hair.

la **trepadora** SUSTANTIVO
climber (*planta*)

trepar VERBO
to climb
- **trepar a un árbol** to climb a tree

tres ADJETIVO, PRONOMBRE
three
- **Son las tres.** It's three o'clock.
- **el tres de febrero** February third

trescientos ADJETIVO, PRONOMBRE (FEM **trescientas**)
three hundred

el **tresillo** SUSTANTIVO
three-seat sofa (*sofá*)

el **triángulo** SUSTANTIVO
triangle

la **tribu** SUSTANTIVO
tribe

la **tribuna** SUSTANTIVO
1 platform (*para orador*)
2 stand (*para espectadores*)

el **tribunal** SUSTANTIVO
1 court (*de justicia*)
2 board of examiners (*de examen*)

el **triciclo** SUSTANTIVO
tricycle

tridimensional ADJETIVO
three-dimensional

el **trigo** SUSTANTIVO
wheat

trillar VERBO
to thresh

los **trillizos,** las **trillizas** SUSTANTIVO
triplets

trimestral ADJETIVO
quarterly (*revista*)
- **los exámenes trimestrales** the end-of-term exams

el **trimestre** SUSTANTIVO
term (*escolar*)

trinchar VERBO
to carve

la **trinchera** SUSTANTIVO
trench

el **trineo** SUSTANTIVO
1 sled (*para niños*)
2 dog sled (*tirado por perros*)

la **Trinidad** SUSTANTIVO
the Trinity (*deidad*)

el **trío** SUSTANTIVO
trio

la **tripa** SUSTANTIVO
gut (*intestino*)

el **triple** SUSTANTIVO
- **Esta habitación es el triple de grande.** This room is three times as big.
- **Gastan el triple que nosotros.** They spend three times as much as we do.

triplicar* VERBO

T

to treble

la **tripulación** SUSTANTIVO (PL las **tripulaciones**)
crew

triste ADJETIVO
[1] sad ◇ *Me puse muy triste cuando me enteré de la noticia.* I was very sad when I heard the news.
◆ **El invierno me pone triste.** Winter makes me miserable.
[2] gloomy (*color, paisaje*)

la **tristeza** SUSTANTIVO
sadness

triturar VERBO
[1] to crush (*ajos*)
[2] to grind (*nueces*)

triunfar VERBO
to triumph ◇ *Los socialistas triunfaron en las elecciones.* The socialists triumphed in the elections.
◆ **triunfar en la vida** to succeed in life

el **triunfo** SUSTANTIVO
triumph (*victoria*)

trivial ADJETIVO
trivial

las **trizas** SUSTANTIVO
◆ **hacer* algo trizas** (*documento, tela*) to tear something to shreds

el **trofeo** SUSTANTIVO
trophy (PL trophies)

el **trombón** SUSTANTIVO (PL los **trombones**)
trombone

la **trompa** SUSTANTIVO
[1] trunk (*de elefante*)
[2] horn (*instrumento musical*)

la **trompeta** SUSTANTIVO
trumpet

tronar* VERBO
[1] to thunder ◇ *Ha estado tronando toda la noche.* It has been thundering all night.
[2] to flunk (*en un examen*) [Mexico]

el **tronco** SUSTANTIVO
[1] trunk (*de árbol*)
[2] log (*leño*)
◆ **dormir como un tronco** to sleep like a log

el **trono** SUSTANTIVO
throne

las **tropas** SUSTANTIVO
troops

tropezar* VERBO
to trip ◇ *Tropecé y me caí.* I tripped and fell.
◆ **tropezar con una piedra** to trip on a stone
◆ **tropezar contra un árbol** to bump into a tree
◆ **Me tropecé con Juan en el banco.** I bumped into Juan in the bank.

el **tropezón** SUSTANTIVO (PL los **tropezones**)
trip
◆ **dar* un tropezón** to trip

tropical ADJETIVO
tropical

el **trópico** SUSTANTIVO
tropic

tropiece VERBO *ver* **tropezar**

trotar VERBO
to trot

el **trote** SUSTANTIVO
◆ **El abuelo ya no está para estos trotes.** Grandpa is not up to that sort of thing any more.

trozar* VERBO
to cut into pieces

el **trozo** SUSTANTIVO
piece ◇ *un trozo de madera* a piece of wood ◇ *Dame un trocito sólo.* Just give me a small piece.
◆ **Vi la película a trozos.** I saw bits of the movie.

la **trucha** SUSTANTIVO
trout

el **truco** SUSTANTIVO
trick
◆ **Ya le pillé el truco.** I have the hang of it already.

truena VERBO *ver* **tronar**

el **trueno** SUSTANTIVO
◆ **Oímos un trueno.** We heard a clap of thunder.
◆ **Me despertaron los truenos.** The thunder woke me up.

la **trufa** SUSTANTIVO
truffle

tu ADJETIVO
your ◇ *tu carro* your car ◇ *tus familiares* your relations

tú PRONOMBRE
you ◇ *Cuando tú quieras.* Whenever you like. ◇ *Llegamos antes que tú.* We arrived before you.

la **tuberculosis** SUSTANTIVO
tuberculosis

la **tubería** SUSTANTIVO
pipes PL ◇ *Se reventó la tubería.* The pipes have burst.

el **tubo** SUSTANTIVO
[1] pipe ◇ *el tubo de escape* the exhaust
◆ **el tubo de desagüe** the drainpipe
[2] tube ◇ *un tubo de crema para las manos* a tube of hand cream

la **tuerca** SUSTANTIVO
nut (*de metálico*)

tuerto ADJETIVO
◆ **Es tuerto.** He's blind in one eye.

tuerzo VERBO *ver* **torcer**

el **tuétano** SUSTANTIVO
squash

el **tufo** SUSTANTIVO
stench

el **tulipán** SUSTANTIVO (PL los **tulipanes**)
tulip

la **tumba** SUSTANTIVO
[1] grave (*en la tierra*)
[2] tomb ◇ *una tumba egipcia* an Egyptian

* Verbs marked with this symbol are irregular. See pages 346–348 for further details.

tomb

tumbar VERBO

to knock down ◊ *El perro me tumbó.* The dog knocked me down.

◆ **tumbarse** to lie down ◊ *Me tumbé en el sofá.* I lay down on the sofa.

el **tumbo** SUSTANTIVO

◆ **El borracho iba dando tumbos.** The drunk staggered along.

el **tumor** SUSTANTIVO

tumor

el **túnel** SUSTANTIVO

tunnel

◆ **un túnel de lavado** a car wash

Túnez SUSTANTIVO MASC

1 Tunisia (*país*)

2 Tunis (*ciudad*)

tupido ADJETIVO

1 dense (*bosque, vegetación*)

2 close-woven (*tela*)

3 bushy (*cejas*)

el **turbante** SUSTANTIVO

turban

la **turbina** SUSTANTIVO

turbine

turbio ADJETIVO

cloudy (*agua*)

turbulento ADJETIVO

turbulent

turco ADJETIVO

Turkish

el **turco**, la **turca** SUSTANTIVO

Turk (*persona*)

el **turco** SUSTANTIVO

Turkish (*idioma*)

el **turismo** SUSTANTIVO

1 tourism (*industria*) ◊ *El turismo es importante para nuestra economía.* Tourism is important for our economy.

◆ **turismo rural** tourism in rural areas

◆ **casas de turismo rural** vacation cottages

◆ **la oficina de turismo** the tourist office

2 tourists PL (*turistas*) ◊ *En verano hay mucho turismo.* In summer there are a lot of tourists.

3 car (*carro*)

el/la **turista** SUSTANTIVO

tourist

turístico ADJETIVO

tourist (*lugar, folleto*)

turnarse VERBO

to take turns ◊ *Nos turnamos para lavar los platos.* We take turns doing the dishes.

el **turno** SUSTANTIVO

1 turn ◊ *cuando me tocó el turno* when it was my turn

2 shift ◊ *Hago el turno de la tarde.* I work the afternoon shift.

la **turquesa** ADJETIVO, SUSTANTIVO

turquoise ◊ *un anorak turquesa* a turquoise anorak

Turquía SUSTANTIVO FEM

Turkey

el **turrón** SUSTANTIVO (PL los **turrones**)

> ℹ ***Turrón** is a kind of chewy candy traditionally eaten at Christmas mainly in Spain.*

tutear VERBO

> ℹ *To address somebody using the familiar **tú** form rather than the more formal **usted** form.*

◊ *Se tutean con el jefe.* They address the boss in familiar terms.

el **tutor**, la **tutora** SUSTANTIVO

1 tutor (*profesor*)

2 guardian (*de un menor de edad*)

tuve VERBO *ver* **tener**

tuyo ADJETIVO, PRONOMBRE (FEM **tuya**)

yours ◊ *¿Es tuyo este abrigo?* Is this coat yours? ◊ *La tuya está en el armario.* Yours is in the cupboard. ◊ *mis amigos y los tuyos* my friends and yours

◆ **un amigo tuyo** a friend of yours

T

U

u CONJUNCIÓN
or
*u is used instead of **o** before words starting with **o-** or **ho-**.*
◇ *¿Minutos u horas?* Minutes or hours?

ubicado ADJETIVO
situated

ubicar* VERBO
1 to find (*localizar*) ◇ *No he podido ubicar a la profesora.* I couldn't find the teacher.
◆ **¿Ubicas donde está el gimnasio?** Do you know where the gym is?
2 to put (*colocar*) ◇ *Ubicó a los más altos atrás.* He put the tallest at the back.
3 to recognize (*identificar*) ◇ *Ubiqué a tu hermana por la voz.* I recognized your sister by her voice.
◆ **Creo que lo conozco, pero no lo ubico bien.** I think I know him but I am not sure where from.
◆ **ubicarse** to be situated ◇ *Se ubica a orillas de un lago.* It is situated on the banks of a lake.

Ud. ABREVIATURA **= usted**

Uds. ABREVIATURA **= ustedes**

la **UE** ABREVIATURA (= *Unión Europea*)
EU

uf INTERJECCIÓN
1 phew! (*expresión de cansancio*)
2 ugh! (*expresión de asco*)

la **úlcera** SUSTANTIVO
ulcer

últimamente ADVERBIO
recently

el **ultimátum** SUSTANTIVO (PL los **ultimátums**)
ultimatum (PL ultimatums)

último ADJETIVO
1 last (*en el tiempo*) ◇ *la última vez que hablé con ella* the last time I spoke to her
2 top (*más alto*) ◇ *No llego al último estante.* I can't reach the top shelf.
3 back (*más al fondo*) ◇ *Nos sentamos en la última fila.* We sat in the back row.
◆ **la última moda** the latest fashion
◆ **a última hora** at the last minute ◇ *A última hora decidió acompañarme.* He decided to come with me at the last minute.
◆ **llegar* en último lugar** to arrive last

el **último**, la **última** SUSTANTIVO
the last one
◆ **por último** lastly
◆ **llegar* al último** to arrive last

el/la **ultra** SUSTANTIVO
right-wing extremist

ultrasónico ADJETIVO
ultrasonic

ultravioleta ADJETIVO
ultraviolet

un, una ARTÍCULO
1 a ◇ *una silla* a chair
2 an ◇ *un paraguas* an umbrella
3 some (*en plural*) ◇ *Fui con unos amigos.* I went with some friends.
◆ **Tiene unas uñas muy largas.** He has very long nails.
◆ **Había unas 20 personas.** There were about 20 people.
◆ **Me compré unos zapatos de tacón.** I have bought a pair of high heels.

unánime ADJETIVO
unanimous

undécimo, undécima ADJETIVO, PRONOMBRE
eleventh ◇ *Vivo en el undécimo piso.* I live on the twelfth floor.

únicamente ADVERBIO
only ◇ *Me encargo únicamente de cuidar a los niños.* I'm only in charge of looking after the children.

el **único**, la **única** ADJETIVO, SUSTANTIVO
only ◇ *el único día que tengo libre* the only day I have free
◆ **Soy hija única.** I'm an only child.
◆ **el único que me queda** the only one I have left
◆ **Lo único que no me gusta...** The only thing I don't like...
◆ **una colección de monedas única** a unique coin collection

la **unidad** SUSTANTIVO
1 unit ◇ *una unidad de peso* a unit of weight
◆ **unidad de cuidados intensivos** intensive care unit
◆ **unidad de terapia intensiva** Mexico intensive care unit
2 unity (*armonía*) ◇ *falta de unidad en la familia* lack of family unity

unido ADJETIVO
close (*familia, grupo*) ◇ *una familia muy unida* a very close family

uniforme ADJETIVO
even ◇ *una superficie uniforme* an even surface

el **uniforme** SUSTANTIVO
uniform ◇ *Llevaba el uniforme del colegio.* He was wearing his school uniform.

la **unión** SUSTANTIVO (PL las **uniones**)
union
◆ **la Unión Europea** the European Union

unir VERBO
1 to link ◇ *Este pasaje une los dos edificios.* This passage links the two buildings.
2 to join together ◇ *Unió los dos extremos con una cuerda.* He joined the two ends together with some string.
3 to unite ◇ *Los unió en matrimonio.* He

united them in marriage.

[4] to bring together ◇ *La enfermedad de la madre ha unido a los hijos.* The mother's illness has brought the children together.

◆ **unirse a algo** to join something ◇ *Andrés se unió a la expedición.* Andrés joined the expedition.

◆ **Más adelante los dos caminos se unen.** The two paths join further on.

◆ **Los dos bancos se han unido.** The two banks have merged.

universal ADJETIVO
universal

la **universidad** SUSTANTIVO
university (PL universities) ◇ *Se recibió en la universidad de Harvard.* She graduated from Harvard University.

◆ **El año que viene voy a la universidad.** I'm going to college next year.

universitario ADJETIVO
college

***college** en este caso va siempre delante del sustantivo.*

◇ *estudiantes universitarios* college students

el **universitario,** la **universitaria** SUSTANTIVO
[1] college student (*estudiante*)
[2] graduate (*licenciado*)

el **universo** SUSTANTIVO
universe

uno, una ADJETIVO, PRONOMBRE
one ◇ *Vivo en el número uno.* I live at number one. ◇ *Uno de ellos era mío.* One of them was mine.

◆ **unos pocos** a few
◆ **uno mismo** oneself
◆ **Entraron uno a uno.** They came in one by one.
◆ **unas diez personas** about ten people
◆ **el uno de abril** [Spain] April first
◆ **Es la una.** It's one o'clock.
◆ **Unos querían ir, otros no.** Some of them wanted to go, others didn't.
◆ **Se miraron uno al otro.** They looked at each other.

untar VERBO
◆ **untar algo con algo** to spread something on something ◇ *Primero hay que untar el pan con mantequilla.* First you have to spread the butter on the bread.
◆ **Te untaste las manos de chocolate.** You have chocolate all over your hands.
◆ **unta el molde con aceite** grease the baking dish with oil

la **uña** SUSTANTIVO
[1] nail (*de dedo*)
[2] claw (*de gato*)

el **uranio** SUSTANTIVO
uranium

la **urgencia** SUSTANTIVO
emergency (PL emergencies) (*emergencia*)
◇ *en caso de urgencia* in an emergency
◇ *los servicios de urgencia* the emergency services

◆ **urgencias** (*en hospital*) emergency room
◆ **Tuvimos que ir a urgencias.** We had to go to the emergency room.
◆ **con urgencia** urgently

urgente ADJETIVO
urgent (*mensaje, trabajo*)
◆ **Lo mandé por correo urgente.** I sent it express.

la **urna** SUSTANTIVO
ballot box (*para votar*)

Uruguay SUSTANTIVO MASC
Uruguay

el **uruguayo,** la **uruguaya** ADJETIVO, SUSTANTIVO
Uruguayan

usado ADJETIVO
[1] secondhand (*de segunda mano*) ◇ *una tienda de ropa usada* a secondhand clothes store
[2] worn (*viejo*) ◇ *Estas zapatillas están ya muy usadas.* These slippers are very worn now.

usar VERBO
[1] to use ◇ *Uso una afeitadora eléctrica.* I use an electric razor.
[2] to wear (*perfume, ropa*)
◆ **¿Qué número de zapato usas?** What size shoe do you take?
◆ **La minfalda se usa mucho.** Miniskirts are very popular.

el **uso** SUSTANTIVO
use ◇ *instrucciones de uso* instructions for use

usted PRONOMBRE
you ◇ *Quisiera hablar con usted en privado.* I'd like to speak to you in private.

ustedes PRONOMBRE PL
you ◇ *Quisiera hablar con ustedes en privado.* I'd like to speak to you in private.

usual ADJETIVO
usual

el **usuario,** la **usuaria** SUSTANTIVO
user

el **utensilio** SUSTANTIVO
utensil ◇ *utensilios de cocina* kitchen utensils

el **útero** SUSTANTIVO
uterus

útil ADJETIVO
useful

utilizar* VERBO
to use

la **uva** SUSTANTIVO
grape

V

va VERBO *ver* **ir**

la **vaca** SUSTANTIVO

1 cow (*animal*)

2 beef (*carne*) ◇ *No como carne de vaca.* I don't eat beef.

las **vacaciones** SUSTANTIVO

vacation SING

◆ **las vacaciones de Navidad** the Christmas vacation

◆ **La secretaria está de vacaciones.** The secretary is on vacation.

◆ **En agosto me voy de vacaciones.** I'm going on vacation in August.

vacante ADJETIVO

1 vacant (*puesto*)

2 unoccupied (*departamento, habitación*)

la **vacante** SUSTANTIVO

vacancy (PL vacancies)

vaciar* VERBO

to empty ◇ *Vacié el refrigerador para limpiarla.* I emptied the refrigerator to clean it.

vacilar VERBO

to hesitate ◇ *Vaciló unos instantes antes de responder.* He hesitated for a moment or two before answering.

◆ **sin vacilar** without hesitating

vacío ADJETIVO

empty

el **vacío** SUSTANTIVO

void (*precipicio*) ◇ *Se arrojó al vacío.* He hurled himself into the void.

◆ **envasado al vacío** vacuum-packed

la **vacuna** SUSTANTIVO

vaccine ◇ *la vacuna de la hepatitis* the hepatitis vaccine

◆ **¿Te pusieron la vacuna?** Have they given you the vaccination?

vacunar VERBO

to vaccinate

◆ **Mi abuelo se vacuna contra la gripe todos los años.** My grandfather gets a flu shot every year.

la **vaga** SUSTANTIVO

slacker

la **vagabunda** SUSTANTIVO

vagrant

vagabundo ADJETIVO

stray (*perro*)

el **vagabundo** SUSTANTIVO

vagrant

vagar* VERBO

to wander

la **vagina** SUSTANTIVO

vagina

vago ADJETIVO

1 lazy (*persona*)

2 vague (*recuerdo, explicación*)

el **vago** SUSTANTIVO

slacker

el **vagón** SUSTANTIVO (PL los **vagones**)

passenger car

◆ **vagón cama** Pullman car

◆ **vagón restaurante** dining car

el **vaho** SUSTANTIVO

steam (*vapor*)

la **vainilla** SUSTANTIVO

vanilla ◇ *helado de vainilla* vanilla ice cream

la **vajilla** SUSTANTIVO

dishes PL ◇ *La vajilla está en el lavaplatos.* The dishes are in the dishwasher.

◆ **Me regaló una vajilla de porcelana.** She gave me a set of china.

el **vale** SUSTANTIVO

1 voucher ◇ *un vale-regalo* a gift voucher

◆ **un vale de descuento** a money-back coupon

2 credit note (*de compra*)

el **valenciano,** la **valenciana** ADJETIVO, SUSTANTIVO

Valencian

◆ **Hablan valenciano.** They speak Valencian.

la **valentía** SUSTANTIVO

bravery

◆ **con valentía** bravely

valer* VERBO

1 to cost ◇ *¿Cuánto vale?* How much does it cost?

2 to be worth ◇ *El terreno vale más que la casa.* The land is worth more than the house.

◆ **Este cupón vale por dos entradas.** Each coupon is worth two tickets.

◆ **No vale mirar.** You're not allowed to look.

◆ **¡Eso no vale!** That's not fair!

◆ **¡Eso a mí no me vale!** *Mexico* I couldn't care less about that! (*coloquial*)

◆ **Vale la pena.** It's worth it.

◆ **Vale la pena hacer el esfuerzo.** It's worth the effort.

◆ **No vale la pena.** It's not worth it.

◆ **No vale la pena gastar tanto dinero.** It's not worth spending that much money.

◆ **¿Vale?** *Spain* OK?

◆ **Más vale que te lleves el abrigo.** You'd better take your coat.

◆ **No puede valerse por sí mismo.** He can't look after himself.

válido ADJETIVO

valid

valiente ADJETIVO

brave

la **valija** SUSTANTIVO

◆ **valija diplomática** diplomatic pouch

valioso ADJETIVO

valuable

la **valla** SUSTANTIVO

fence
- **valla publicitaria** billboard
- **los cien metros vallas** the hundred meters hurdles

el **valle** SUSTANTIVO
valley

el **valor** SUSTANTIVO
[1] value ◊ *valor sentimental* sentimental value
- **una pulsera de gran valor** an extremely valuable bracelet

[2] courage (*valentía*) ◊ *armarse de valor* to pluck up courage
- **objetos de valor** valuables
- **valor adquisitivo** purchasing power

valorar VERBO
to value (*joya, amistad*)

el **vals** SUSTANTIVO
waltz
- **bailar un vals** to waltz

la **válvula** SUSTANTIVO
valve

el **vampiro,** la **vampira** SUSTANTIVO
vampire

el **vandalismo** SUSTANTIVO
vandalism

la **vanguardia** SUSTANTIVO
avant-garde
- **de vanguardia** avant-garde

la **vanidad** SUSTANTIVO
vanity

vanidoso ADJETIVO
vain

vano ADJETIVO
vain ◊ *un intento vano* a vain attempt
- **en vano** in vain

el **vapor** SUSTANTIVO
steam
- **plancha de vapor** steam iron
- **al vapor** steamed

vaquero ADJETIVO
denim

***denim** en este caso va siempre delante del sustantivo.*

◊ *una falda vaquera* a denim skirt

el **vaquero** SUSTANTIVO
cowboy
- **una película de vaqueros** a western movie
- **vaqueros** [*Spain*] jeans

variable ADJETIVO
variable (*velocidad, ánimo*)
- **El tiempo es muy variable.** The weather is very changeable.

variado ADJETIVO
varied ◊ *Prefiero un trabajo más variado.* I prefer a more varied job.

variar* VERBO
to vary ◊ *Los precios varían según las tallas.* Prices vary according to size.
- **Decidí ir en tren, para variar.** I decided to go by train for a change.

la **varicela** SUSTANTIVO
chicken pox ◊ *Yo no he tenido la varicela.* I've never had chicken pox.

la **variedad** SUSTANTIVO
variety (PL varieties) ◊ *una nueva variedad de clavel* a new variety of carnation

la **varilla** SUSTANTIVO
rod
- **la varilla del aceite** the dipstick

varios ADJETIVO, PRONOMBRE (FEM **varias**)
several ◊ *Estuve enfermo varios días.* I was ill for several days. ◊ *Le hicimos un regalo entre varios.* Several of us got together to buy him a present.

la **váriz** SUSTANTIVO (PL las **várices**)
varicose vein

varón ADJETIVO (PL **varones**)
male ◊ *los herederos varones* the male heirs

el **varón** SUSTANTIVO (PL los **varones**) ◊ *Tiene dos hembras y un varón.* She has two girls and a boy.
- **Sexo: varón.** Sex: male.

Varsovia SUSTANTIVO FEM
Warsaw

el **vasco,** la **vasca** ADJETIVO, SUSTANTIVO
Basque
- **Hablamos vasco.** We speak Basque.
- **el País Vasco** the Basque Country

la **vasija** SUSTANTIVO
container (*cacharro*) ◊ *una vasija fenicia* a Phoenician container

el **vaso** SUSTANTIVO
glass (PL glasses) ◊ *Bebí un vaso de leche.* I drank a glass of milk.
- **un vaso de plástico** a plastic cup
- **un vaso sanguíneo** a blood vessel

el **váter** SUSTANTIVO
bathroom (*coloquial*)

el **Vaticano** SUSTANTIVO
Vatican

el **vatio** SUSTANTIVO
watt

vaya VERBO *ver* **ir**

Vd. ABREVIATURA = **usted**

Vds. ABREVIATURA = **ustedes**

ve VERBO *ver* **ir, ver**

la **vecina** SUSTANTIVO
[1] neighbor (*de la misma calle*)
[2] inhabitant (*habitante*)

el **vecindario** SUSTANTIVO
neighborhood (*barrio*)

vecino ADJETIVO
neighboring ◊ *las ciudades vecinas* the neighboring towns

el **vecino** SUSTANTIVO
[1] neighbor (*de la misma calle*) ◊ *los vecinos de al lado* the next door neighbors
[2] inhabitant (*habitante*) ◊ *todos los vecinos de Torrevieja* all the inhabitants of Torrevieja

V

la **vegetación** SUSTANTIVO (PL las **vegetaciones**)
vegetation (*de plantas*)
◆ **vegetaciones** (*en la nariz*) adenoids

el **vegetal** ADJETIVO, SUSTANTIVO
vegetable ◇ *aceite vegetal* vegetable oil

el **vegetariano**, la **vegetariana** ADJETIVO, SUSTANTIVO
vegetarian ◇ *Es vegetariano.* He's vegetarian.

el **vehículo** SUSTANTIVO
vehicle

veinte ADJETIVO, PRONOMBRE
twenty ◇ *Tiene veinte años.* He's twenty.
◆ **el veinte de enero** January twentieth
◆ **el siglo veinte** the twentieth century

la **vejez** SUSTANTIVO
old age

la **vejiga** SUSTANTIVO
bladder

la **vela** SUSTANTIVO
1 candle ◇ *Encendimos una vela.* We lit a candle.
2 sail (*de barco*)
3 sailing (*deporte*)
◆ **un barco de vela** a yacht
◆ **Pasé la noche en vela.** I had a sleepless night.
◆ **estar* a dos velas** to be broke (*coloquial*)

velarse VERBO
◆ **Se velaron las fotos.** The photos got exposed by accident.

el **velero** SUSTANTIVO
yacht

el **vello** SUSTANTIVO
1 hair (*en el cuerpo*) ◇ *Tiene mucho vello.* He's very hairy.
2 down (*en la cara*)

el **velo** SUSTANTIVO
veil

la **velocidad** SUSTANTIVO
1 speed ◇ *Pasó una moto a toda velocidad.* A motorbike went past at full speed.
◆ **¿A qué velocidad ibas?** How fast were you going?
2 gear (*marcha*) ◇ *cambiar de velocidad* to shift gear

el **velocímetro** SUSTANTIVO
speedometer

el/la **velocista** SUSTANTIVO
sprinter

el **velódromo** SUSTANTIVO
velodrome

veloz ADJETIVO (PL **veloces**)
swift

ven VERBO *ver* **ir, ver**

la **vena** SUSTANTIVO
vein

vencedor ADJETIVO (FEM **vencedora**)
winning ◇ *el equipo vencedor* the winning team

el **vencedor**, la **vencedora** SUSTANTIVO
winner

vencer* VERBO
1 to defeat (*derrotar*)
2 to overcome (*miedo, obstáculo*)
3 to expire (*expirar*) ◇ *Mi pasaporte se vence mañana.* My passport expires tomorrow.

vencido ADJETIVO
◆ **darse* por vencido** to give up

la **venda** SUSTANTIVO
1 bandage (*para herida, lesión*)
◆ **Me pusieron una venda en el brazo.** They bandaged my arm.
2 blindfold (*para los ojos*)
◆ **poner* una venda en los ojos a alguien** to blindfold someone

vendar VERBO
to bandage ◇ *Me vendaron el codo.* They bandaged my elbow.
◆ **vendar los ojos a alguien** to blindfold someone

el **vendedor** SUSTANTIVO
salesman (PL salesmen)
◆ **vendedor ambulante** peddler
◆ **vendedor de periódicos** newspaper vendor

la **vendedora** SUSTANTIVO
saleswoman (PL saleswomen)

vender VERBO
to sell ◇ *Vendí el carro.* I've sold the car.
◆ **Venden la oficina de arriba.** The office upstairs is for sale.
◆ **"se vende"** "for sale"
◆ **venderse por** to sell for ◇ *El cuadro se vendió por cuatro millones de pesetas.* The painting sold for four million pesetas.

la **vendimia** SUSTANTIVO
grape harvest

vendré VERBO *ver* **venir**

el **veneno** SUSTANTIVO
1 poison (*tóxico*)
2 venom (*de serpiente*)

venenoso ADJETIVO
poisonous

el **venezolano**, la **venezolana** ADJETIVO, SUSTANTIVO
Venezuelan

Venezuela SUSTANTIVO FEM
Venezuela

la **venganza** SUSTANTIVO
revenge

vengarse* VERBO
to take revenge
◆ **vengarse de alguien** to take revenge on someone
◆ **vengarse de algo** to avenge something

vengo VERBO *ver* **venir**

la **venida** SUSTANTIVO
arrival (*llegada*)
◆ **La venida la hicimos en autobús.** We came

by bus on the way here.

venir* VERBO

1 to come ◇ *Vino en taxi.* He came by taxi. ◇ *Vinieron a verme al hospital.* They came to see me in the hospital. ◇ *Viene en varios colores.* It comes in several colors. ◇ *¡Ven aquí!* Come here! ◇ *Enseguida vengo.* I'll be back in a minute.

2 to be ◇ *La noticia venía en el periódico.* The news was in the paper.

- **La casa se está viniendo abajo.** The house is falling apart.
- **Mañana me viene mal.** Tomorrow isn't good for me.
- **¿Te viene bien el sábado?** Is Saturday alright for you?
- **el año que viene** next year

la **venta** SUSTANTIVO

sale

- **estar* en venta** to be for sale

la **ventaja** SUSTANTIVO

advantage ◇ *Tiene la ventaja de que está cerca de casa.* It has the advantage of being close to home.

- **llevar ventaja a alguien** to have an advantage over someone
- **jugar* con ventaja** to be at an advantage

la **ventana** SUSTANTIVO

window

la **ventanilla** SUSTANTIVO

1 window (*de carro, banco*) ◇ *Baja la ventanilla.* Open the window.

2 box office (*en cine, teatro*)

la **ventilación** SUSTANTIVO

ventilation

- **El sótano tiene poca ventilación.** The basement is poorly ventilated.

ventilar VERBO

to air (*habitación, ropa*)

la **ventisca** SUSTANTIVO

1 gale force winds (*viento fuerte*)

2 blizzard (*con nieve*)

ver* VERBO

1 to see ◇ *Te vi en el parque.* I saw you in the park. ◇ *¡Cuánto tiempo sin verte!* I haven't seen you for ages! ◇ *No he visto esa película.* I haven't seen that movie. ◇ *El médico todavía no la ha visto.* The doctor hasn't seen her yet. ◇ *¿Ves? Ya te lo dije.* See? I told you so.

- **Voy a ver si está en su despacho.** I'll see if he's in his office.
- **Quedamos en vernos en la estación.** We arranged to meet at the station.
- **¡Luego nos vemos!** See you later!
- **Eso no tiene nada que ver.** That has nothing to do with it.
- **¡No la puede ver!** He can't stand her!
- **A ver...** Let's see...
- **Se ve que no tiene idea de informática.** It's clear he has no idea about computers.

2 to watch (*televisión*)

veranear VERBO

to spend the summer vacation

◇ *Veraneamos en Cuernavaca.* We spend our summer vacation in Cuernavaca.

el **veraneo** SUSTANTIVO

- **lugar de veraneo** summer resort
- **No pudimos ir de veraneo el año pasado.** We couldn't go on vacation last summer.

el **verano** SUSTANTIVO

summer ◇ *En verano hace mucho calor.* It's very hot in summer. ◇ *las vacaciones de verano* the summer vacation

veras SUSTANTIVO FEM PL

- **de veras** really

veraz ADJETIVO (PL **veraces**)

truthful

la **verbena** SUSTANTIVO

open-air dance (*baile*)

- **la verbena de San Roque** the festival of San Roque

el **verbo** SUSTANTIVO

verb

la **verdad** SUSTANTIVO

truth ◇ *Les dije la verdad.* I told them the truth.

- **¡Es verdad!** It's true!
- **La verdad es que no tengo ganas.** I don't really feel like it.
- **¿De verdad?** Really?
- **De verdad que yo no dije eso.** I didn't say that, honestly.
- **No era un policía de verdad.** He wasn't a real policeman.
- **Es bonito, ¿verdad?** It's pretty, isn't it?
- **No te gusta, ¿verdad?** You don't like it, do you?

verdadero ADJETIVO

real ◇ *Su apellido verdadero es Rodríguez.* His real surname is Rodríguez. ◇ *Es un verdadero caballero.* He's a real gentleman.

el **verde** ADJETIVO, SUSTANTIVO

1 green ◇ *Tiene los ojos verdes.* She has green eyes. ◇ *Estos plátanos están todavía verdes.* These bananas are still green.

2 dirty (*coloquial: obsceno*) ◇ *un chiste verde* a dirty joke

- **los verdes** (*grupo político*) the Green Party

el **verdugo** SUSTANTIVO

1 executioner (*en la guillotina*)

2 hangman (*en la horca*)

la **verdulería** SUSTANTIVO

grocery store

la **verdura** SUSTANTIVO

vegetables PL ◇ *Comemos mucha verdura.* We eat a lot of vegetables.

la **vereda** SUSTANTIVO

path (*camino*)

vergonzoso ADJETIVO

1 shy ◇ *Es muy vergonzosa.* She is very shy.

2 disgraceful ◇ *Es vergonzoso cómo los*

V

trataron. It's disgraceful the way they were treated.

la **vergüenza** SUSTANTIVO
1 embarrassment ◇ *Casi me muero de vergüenza.* I almost died of embarrassment.
2 shame (*decencia*) ◇ *No tienen vergüenza.* They have no shame.
◆ **¡Qué vergüenza!** How embarrassing!
◆ **Le da vergüenza pedírselo.** He's embarrassed to ask her.
◆ **¡Es una vergüenza!** It's disgraceful!

verídico ADJETIVO
true

verificar* VERBO
to check

la **verja** SUSTANTIVO
1 railings PL (*cerca*)
2 gate (*puerta*)

el **vermut** SUSTANTIVO
vermouth

la **verruga** SUSTANTIVO
wart

la **versión** SUSTANTIVO (PL las **versiones**)
version
◆ **una película francesa en versión original** a movie in the original French version

el **verso** SUSTANTIVO
1 line (*línea de poema*)
2 verse (*estilo poético*)

la **vértebra** SUSTANTIVO
vertebra (PL vertebrae)

verter* VERBO
1 to pour ◇ *Vertió un poco de leche en el cazo.* He poured a little milk into the saucepan.
2 to dump (*basura, residuos radiactivos*)

vertical ADJETIVO
vertical
◆ **Ponlo vertical.** Put it upright.

el **vértigo** SUSTANTIVO
vertigo
◆ **Me da vértigo.** It makes me dizzy.

la **Vespa** ® SUSTANTIVO
scooter

vespertino ADJETIVO
evening
evening *en este caso va siempre delante del sustantivo.*
◇ *un diario vespertino* an evening paper

el **vestíbulo** SUSTANTIVO
1 hallway (*de casa*)
2 foyer (*de teatro*)

vestido ADJETIVO
◆ **Iba vestida de negro.** She was dressed in black.
◆ **Yo iba vestido de payaso.** I was dressed as a clown.
◆ **un hombre bien vestido** a well-dressed man

el **vestido** SUSTANTIVO
dress (PL dresses) (*de mujer*)
◆ **el vestido de novia** the bridal gown

el **vestidor** SUSTANTIVO *Mexico*
1 locker room (*en el gimnasio, club*)
2 changing room (*en un tienda*)

vestir* VERBO
to wear (*llevar puesto*) ◇ *Vestía pantalones vaqueros y una camiseta.* He was wearing jeans and a T-shirt.
◆ **vestir a alguien** to dress someone ◇ *Estaba vistiendo a los niños.* I was dressing the children.
◆ **vestir bien** to dress well
◆ **vestirse** to get dressed ◇ *Se está vistiendo.* He's getting dressed.
◆ **Se vistió de princesa.** She dressed up as a princess.
◆ **ropa de vestir** smart clothes PL

el **vestuario** SUSTANTIVO
1 changing room (*en piscina, gimnasio*)
2 wardrobe (*de película, obra teatral*)

el **veterinario,** la **veterinaria** SUSTANTIVO
veterinarian

la **vez** SUSTANTIVO (PL las **veces**)
time ◇ *la próxima vez* next time ◇ *¿Cuántas veces al año?* How many times a year?
◆ **a la vez** at the same time
◆ **a veces** sometimes
◆ **algunas veces** sometimes
◆ **muchas veces** (*con frecuencia*) often
◆ **cada vez más** more and more
◆ **cada vez menos** less and less
◆ **de una vez** once and for all
◆ **de vez en cuando** from time to time
◆ **en vez de** instead of
◆ **¿La has visto alguna vez?** Have you ever seen her?
◆ **otra vez** again
◆ **tal vez** maybe
◆ **una vez** once ◇ *La veo una vez a la semana.* I see her once a week.
◆ **dos veces** twice
◆ **una y otra vez** again and again

vi VERBO *ver* **ver**

la **vía** SUSTANTIVO
1 track (*raíl*)
2 platform (*andén*) ◇ *Nuestro tren sale por la vía dos.* Our train leaves from platform two.
◆ **por vía aérea** by airmail
◆ **Madrid-Berlín vía París** Madrid-Berlin via Paris

viajar VERBO
to travel ◇ *viajar en tren* to travel by train

el **viaje** SUSTANTIVO
1 trip
◆ **¡Buen viaje!** Have a good trip!
◆ **un viaje de negocios** a business trip
2 journey (*trayecto*) ◇ *Es un viaje muy largo.* It's a very long journey.

- **estar* de viaje** to be away
- **salir* de viaje** to go away
- **una agencia de viajes** a travel agency
- **un viaje de novios** a honeymoon

el **viajero,** la **viajera** SUSTANTIVO
passenger

la **víbora** SUSTANTIVO
viper

la **vibración** SUSTANTIVO (PL las **vibraciones**)
vibration

vibrar VERBO
to vibrate

la **vicepresidenta** SUSTANTIVO
1 vice president (*de gobierno*)
2 chairwoman (PL chairwomen) (*de empresa, comité*)

el **vicepresidente** SUSTANTIVO
1 vice president (*de gobierno*)
2 chairman (PL chairmen) (*de empresa, comité*)

viceversa ADVERBIO
vice versa

viciarse VERBO
to deteriorate (*estilo, lenguaje*)
- **viciarse con las drogas** to become addicted to drugs

el **vicio** SUSTANTIVO
vice ◇ *El tabaco es mi único vicio.* Smoking is my only vice.
- **Tengo el vicio de morderme las uñas.** I bite my nails; I know it's a bad habit.

la **víctima** SUSTANTIVO
victim

la **victoria** SUSTANTIVO
victory (PL victories) ◇ *la victoria del partido conservador* the conservative party victory
- **su primera victoria fuera de casa** their first away win

la **vid** SUSTANTIVO
vine

la **vida** SUSTANTIVO
life (PL lives) ◇ *He vivido aquí toda mi vida.* I've lived here all my life. ◇ *Llevan una vida muy tranquila.* They lead a very quiet life. ◇ *¡Esto sí que es vida!* This is the life!
- **la media de vida de un televisor** the average life span of a television set
- **vida nocturna** nightlife
- **estar* con vida** to be alive
- **salir* con vida** to escape alive
- **Se gana la vida haciendo traducciones.** He makes his living doing translations.
- **¡Vida mía!** My darling!

el **video** SUSTANTIVO
video ◇ *Tengo la película en video.* I have the movie on video.
- **cinta de video** videotape

el **vídeo** SUSTANTIVO Spain
video

la **videocámara** SUSTANTIVO
video camera

el **videojuego** SUSTANTIVO
video game

la **videollamada** SUSTANTIVO
video call

el **videoteléfono** SUSTANTIVO
videophone

la **vidriera** SUSTANTIVO
1 stained glass window (*en iglesia*)
2 store window (*escaparate*)
- **ir a mirar vidrieras** to go window-shopping

el **vidrio** SUSTANTIVO
1 glass (*material*) ◇ *botellas de vidrio* glass bottles
- **Me corté el dedo con un vidrio.** I cut my finger on a piece of glass.

2 windowpane (*de ventana*)

la **vieja** SUSTANTIVO
old woman (PL old women) ◇ *Había una viejecita sentada a mi lado.* There was an old woman sitting next to me.

viejo ADJETIVO
old ◇ *un viejo amigo mío* an old friend of mine ◇ *Estos zapatos ya están muy viejos.* These shoes are very old now.
- **hacerse* viejo** to get old

el **viejo** SUSTANTIVO
old man (PL old men)
- **los viejos** the elderly
- **llegar* a viejo** to reach old age

viene VERBO *ver* **venir**

el **viento** SUSTANTIVO
wind
- **Hace mucho viento.** It's very windy.

el **vientre** SUSTANTIVO
stomach
- **hacer* de vientre** to go to the bathroom

el **viernes** SUSTANTIVO (PL los **viernes**)
En inglés, los días de la semana se escriben con mayúscula.
Friday ◇ *La vi el viernes.* I saw her on Friday. ◇ *todos los viernes* every Friday ◇ *el viernes pasado* last Friday ◇ *el viernes que viene* next Friday ◇ *Jugamos los viernes.* We play on Fridays.
- **Viernes Santo** Good Friday

vierta VERBO *ver* **verter**

el/la **vietnamita** ADJETIVO, SUSTANTIVO
Vietnamese
- **los vietnamitas** the Vietnamese

V

la **viga** SUSTANTIVO
1 beam (*de madera*)
2 girder (*de acero*)

la **vigilancia** SUSTANTIVO
1 surveillance ◇ *bajo vigilancia policial* under police surveillance
2 attention (*cuidado*) ◇ *El paciente necesita vigilancia constante.* The patient needs constant attention.
- **patrulla de vigilancia** security patrol

el/la **vigilante** SUSTANTIVO
1 security guard (*en banco, edificio público*) ☞

[2] store detective (*en tienda*)
- **vigilante jurado** security guard
- **vigilante nocturno** night watchman (PL night watchmen)

vigilar VERBO
[1] to guard (*frontera, tienda, cuadro*) ◇ *Un policía vigilaba al preso.* A policeman was guarding the prisoner.
[2] to watch (*persona*) ◇ *Nos vigilan.* They're watching us.
[3] to keep an eye on (*cuidar*) ◇ *¿Me vigilas la cartera un momento?* Can you keep an eye on my bag for a minute?

VIH ABREVIATURA (= *virus de inmunodeficiencia humana*)
HIV

la **villa** SUSTANTIVO
[1] town (*población*)
[2] villa (*chalé*)

el **villancico** SUSTANTIVO
carol

el **vinagre** SUSTANTIVO
vinegar

el **vínculo** SUSTANTIVO
bond (*lazo*)

vine VERBO *ver* **venir**

viniendo VERBO *ver* **venir**

el **vino** SUSTANTIVO
wine
- **vino blanco** white wine
- **vino tinto** red wine
- **vino de la casa** house wine

la **viña** SUSTANTIVO
vineyard

el **viñedo** SUSTANTIVO
vineyard

la **violación** SUSTANTIVO (PL las **violaciones**)
[1] rape (*de persona*)
[2] violation (*de ley, acuerdo*)

el **violador**, la **violadora** SUSTANTIVO
rapist

violar VERBO
[1] to rape (*persona*)
[2] to violate (*ley, acuerdo*)

la **violencia** SUSTANTIVO
violence

violento ADJETIVO
[1] violent ◇ *La película contiene algunas escenas violentas.* The movie contains some violent scenes.
[2] embarrassing ◇ *Era una situación violenta.* It was an embarrassing situation.
- **Me resulta violento decírselo.** I'm embarrassed to tell him.

el **violeta** ADJETIVO, SUSTANTIVO
purple (*color*) ◇ *unas cortinas violeta* some purple curtains

la **violeta** SUSTANTIVO
violet (*flor*)

el **violín** SUSTANTIVO (PL los **violines**)
violin

el/la **violinista** SUSTANTIVO
violinist

el **violón** SUSTANTIVO (PL los **violones**)
double bass (PL double basses)

el/la **violonchelista** SUSTANTIVO
cellist

el **violonchelo** SUSTANTIVO
cello

virgen ADJETIVO (PL **vírgenes**)
[1] virgin (*persona, selva*)
- **ser* virgen** to be a virgin

[2] blank (*cinta*)

la **virgen** SUSTANTIVO (PL las **vírgenes**)
virgin
- **la Virgen** the Virgin

Virgo SUSTANTIVO MASC
Virgo
- **Soy virgo.** I'm a Virgo.

viril ADJETIVO
virile

la **virilidad** SUSTANTIVO
virility

la **virtud** SUSTANTIVO
virtue

la **viruela** SUSTANTIVO
smallpox ◇ *Tiene la viruela.* He has smallpox.

el **virus** SUSTANTIVO (PL los **virus**)
virus (PL viruses) (*también informática*)

la **visa** SUSTANTIVO
visa

el **visado** SUSTANTIVO *Spain*
visa

la **visera** SUSTANTIVO
[1] peak (*en gorra*)
[2] visor (*transparente*)

la **visibilidad** SUSTANTIVO
visibility ◇ *Había muy poca visibilidad.* Visibility was very poor.

visible ADJETIVO
visible

el **visillo** SUSTANTIVO
net curtain

la **visión** SUSTANTIVO (PL las **visiones**)
[1] vision ◇ *la visión nocturna* night vision
[2] view (*enfoque*) ◇ *una visión pesimista de la vida* a pessimistic view of life
- **Tú estás viendo visiones.** You're seeing things.

la **visita** SUSTANTIVO
[1] visit
- **hacer* una visita a alguien** to visit someone

[2] visitor (*visitante*) ◇ *Tienes visita.* You have visitors.
- **horario de visita** visiting hours PL
- **tarjeta de visita** business card

el/la **visitante** SUSTANTIVO
visitor

visitar VERBO

to visit ◇ *5.000 personas han visitado ya la exposición.* 5000 people have already visited the exhibition.

el **viso** SUSTANTIVO
slip (*prenda*)
◆ **visos** signs ◇ *La situación no tiene visos de mejorar.* The situation shows no signs of improving.
◆ **esta tela hace visos** this is a two-tone material

el **visón** SUSTANTIVO (PL los **visones**)
mink
◆ **un abrigo de visón** a mink coat

la **víspera** SUSTANTIVO
the day before ◇ *la víspera de la boda* the day before the wedding
◆ **la víspera de Navidad** Christmas Eve

la **vista** SUSTANTIVO
1 sight (*sentido*)
2 view (*panorama*) ◇ *una habitación con vistas al mar* a room with a sea view
◆ **a primera vista** at first glance
◆ **alzar la vista** to look up
◆ **bajar la vista** to look down
◆ **perder* la vista** to lose one's sight
◆ **volver* la vista** to look back
◆ **conocer* a alguien de vista** to know someone by sight
◆ **hacer* la vista gorda** to turn a blind eye
◆ **¡Hasta la vista!** See you!

el **vistazo** SUSTANTIVO
◆ **echar un vistazo a algo** to have a look at something

vistiendo VERBO *ver* **vestir**

visto (1) VERBO *ver* **ver**

visto (2) ADJETIVO
◆ **Está visto que...** It's clear that...
◆ **Hurgarse la nariz está mal visto.** Picking your nose is frowned upon.
◆ **por lo visto** apparently
◆ **dar* el visto bueno a algo** to give something one's approval

vistoso ADJETIVO
showy

vital ADJETIVO
vital

la **vitalidad** SUSTANTIVO
vitality

la **vitamina** SUSTANTIVO
vitamin

vitorear VERBO
to cheer

la **vitrina** SUSTANTIVO
1 glass cabinet (*en casa*)
2 store window (*escaparate*)
◆ **ir a mirar vitrinas** to go window-shopping

viuda ADJETIVO
◆ **Es viuda.** She's a widow.
◆ **quedarse viuda** to be widowed

la **viuda** SUSTANTIVO
widow

viudo ADJETIVO
◆ **Es viudo.** He's a widower.
◆ **Se quedó viudo a los 50 años.** He was widowed at 50.

el **viudo** SUSTANTIVO
widower

vivaracho ADJETIVO
lively (*persona*)

los **víveres** SUSTANTIVO
provisions PL

el **vivero** SUSTANTIVO
nursery (PL nurseries) (*de plantas*)

la **vivienda** SUSTANTIVO
1 house (*casa*)
2 apartment (*departamento*)
3 housing (*alojamiento*) ◇ *la escasez de la vivienda* the housing shortage

vivir VERBO
1 to live ◇ *¿Dónde vives?* Where do you live?
2 to be alive ◇ *¿Todavía vive?* Is he still alive?
◆ **vivir de algo** to live on something ◇ *Viven de su pensión.* They live on his pension.
◆ **¡Viva!** Hurray!

vivo ADJETIVO
1 alive (*con vida*) ◇ *Estaba vivo.* He was alive.
2 bright (*color, ojos*)
◆ **en vivo** live ◇ *una retransmisión en vivo* a live broadcast

el **vocabulario** SUSTANTIVO
vocabulary

la **vocación** SUSTANTIVO (PL las **vocaciones**)
vocation

la **vocal** SUSTANTIVO
vowel

el **vodka** SUSTANTIVO
vodka

el **volante** SUSTANTIVO
1 steering wheel (*de carro*)
2 shuttlecock (*de bádminton*)
3 referral note (*para médico*)
◆ **volantes** flounce SING (*de vestido, colcha*)

volar* VERBO
1 to fly ◇ *El helicóptero volaba muy bajo.* The helicopter was flying very low. ◇ *Se me pasó la semana volando.* The week just flew by.
2 to blow up ◇ *Volaron el puente.* They blew up the bridge.
◆ **Tuvimos que ir volando al hospital.** We had to rush to the hospital.

el **volcán** SUSTANTIVO (PL los **volcanes**)
volcano (PL volcanoes)

volcar* VERBO
1 to knock over (*tumbar*) ◇ *El perro volcó el cubo de la basura.* The dog knocked the garbage can over.
2 to capsize (*barco*)
3 to overturn (*carro*)

V

el **voleibol** SUSTANTIVO
volleyball

el **voltaje** SUSTANTIVO
voltage

la **voltereta** SUSTANTIVO
1 forward roll (*sobre el suelo*)
◆ **dar* una voltereta** to do a forward roll
2 somersault (*en el aire*)

el **voltio** SUSTANTIVO
volt

el **volumen** SUSTANTIVO (PL los **volúmenes**)
volume
◆ **bajar el volumen** to turn the volume down
◆ **subir el volumen** to turn the volume up

la **voluntad** SUSTANTIVO
1 will (*deseo*) ◇ *Lo hizo contra mi voluntad.* He did it against my will.
2 willpower (*fuerza de voluntad*) ◇ *Le cuesta, pero tiene mucha voluntad.* It's difficult for him, but he has a lot of willpower.

la **voluntaria** SUSTANTIVO
volunteer

voluntario ADJETIVO
voluntary
◆ **ofrecerse* voluntario para algo** to volunteer for something

el **voluntario** SUSTANTIVO
volunteer

volver* VERBO
1 to come back (*a donde se está*)
2 to go back (*a donde se estaba*)
3 to turn (*colcha, cabeza, esquina*) ◇ *Me volvió la espalda.* He turned away from me.
◆ **Me volví para ver quién era.** I turned around to see who it was.
4 to become (*convertirse*)
◆ **Se ha vuelto muy cariñoso.** He's become very affectionate.
◆ **volver a hacer algo** to do something again
◆ **volver en sí** to come round

vomitar VERBO
to vomit ◇ *Ha vomitado dos veces.* He's vomited twice.
◆ **Vomitó todo lo que había comido.** He threw up everything he'd eaten.

vosotros PRONOMBRE PL (FEM **vosotras**) *Spain*
you ◇ *Vosotros vendréis conmigo.* You'll come with me.
◆ **Hacedlo vosotros mismos.** Do it yourselves.

la **votación** SUSTANTIVO (PL las **votaciones**)
◆ **Hicimos una votación.** We took a vote.
◆ **Salió elegida por votación.** She was voted in.

votar VERBO
to vote ◇ *Voté por Alcántara.* I voted for Alcántara.
◆ **Votaron a los socialistas.** They voted for the Socialists.

voy VERBO *ver* **ir**

la **voz** SUSTANTIVO (PL las **voces**)
voice ◇ *No tengo buena voz.* I don't have a very good voice.
◆ **hablar en voz alta** to speak loudly
◆ **dar* voces** to shout

vuelco VERBO *ver* **volcar**

el **vuelco** SUSTANTIVO
◆ **dar* un vuelco (1)** (*carro*) to overturn
◆ **dar* un vuelco (2)** (*barco*) to capsize
◆ **Me dio un vuelco el corazón.** My heart missed a beat.

vuelo VERBO *ver* **volar**

el **vuelo** SUSTANTIVO
flight
◆ **vuelo chárter** charter flight
◆ **vuelo regular** scheduled flight
◆ **Las gaviotas levantaron el vuelo.** The seagulls flew away.

la **vuelta** SUSTANTIVO
1 return (*regreso*) ◇ *un pasaje de ida y vuelta* a round-trip ticket
2 lap (*en circuito*) ◇ *Di tres vueltas a la pista.* I did three laps of the track.
◆ **a vuelta de correo** by return mail
◆ **Vive a la vuelta de la esquina.** He lives around the corner.
◆ **El carro dio la vuelta.** The car turned around.
◆ **Dimos una vuelta de campana.** We overturned completely.
◆ **dar* la vuelta a la página** to turn the page
◆ **dar* la vuelta al mundo** to go round the world
◆ **No le des más vueltas a lo que dijo.** Stop worrying about what he said.
◆ **dar* una vuelta (1)** (*a pie*) to go for a walk
◆ **dar* una vuelta (2)** (*en carro*) to go for a drive
◆ **dar* media vuelta** to turn around
◆ **estar* de vuelta** to be back
◆ **vuelta ciclista** bicycle race

vuelto VERBO *ver* **volver**

el **vuelto** SUSTANTIVO
change

vuelvo VERBO *ver* **volver**

vuestro ADJETIVO, PRONOMBRE (FEM **vuestra**) *Spain*
1 your ◇ *Vuestra Majestad* Your Majesty
2 yours ◇ *¿Son vuestros?* Are they yours?

vulgar ADJETIVO
vulgar (*no refinado*)

W

el **walkie-talkie** SUSTANTIVO (PL los **walkie-talkies**)
walkie-talkie

el **walkman**® (PL los **walkmans**) SUSTANTIVO
Walkman®

el **wáter** SUSTANTIVO
bathroom (*coloquial*)

la **web** SUSTANTIVO
1 website (*página*)
2 (World Wide) Web (*red*)

el **western** SUSTANTIVO (PL los **westerns**)
western

el **whisky** SUSTANTIVO (PL los **whiskys**)
whiskey

el **windsurf** SUSTANTIVO
1 windsurfing (*deporte*)
2 windsurf (*tabla*)

X

xenófobo ADJETIVO
xenophobic

el **xilófono** SUSTANTIVO
xylophone

Y

y CONJUNCIÓN
and ◇ *Andrés y su novia.* Andrés and his girlfriend.
◆ **Yo quiero una ensalada. ¿Y tú?** I'd like a salad. What about you?
◆ **¡Y yo!** Me too!
◆ **¿Y qué?** So what?
◆ **Son las tres y cinco.** It's five minutes past three.

ya ADVERBIO
already ◇ *Ya se fue.* They've already left. ◇ *¿Ya terminaste?* Have you finished already?
◆ **ya no** any more ◇ *Ya no salimos juntos.* We're not going out any more.
◆ **Estos zapatos ya me quedan chicos.** These shoes are too small for me now.
◆ **ya que** since
◆ **Ya lo sé.** I know.
◆ **Ya veremos.** We'll see.
◆ **Llena el formulario y ya está.** Fill out the form and that's it.
◆ **¡Ya voy!** I'm coming!

el **yacimiento** SUSTANTIVO
site (*arqueológico*)
◆ **un yacimiento petrolífero** an oilfield

el/la **yanqui** ADJETIVO, SUSTANTIVO (MASC PL los **yanquis**)
Yankee (*coloquial*)

el **yate** SUSTANTIVO
1 pleasure cruiser (*con motor*)
2 yacht (*de vela*)

la **yedra** SUSTANTIVO
ivy

la **yegua** SUSTANTIVO
mare

la **yema** SUSTANTIVO
1 yolk (*de huevo*)
2 fingertip (*del dedo*)

yendo VERBO *ver* **ir**

el **yerno** SUSTANTIVO
son-in-law (PL sons-in-law)

el **yeso** SUSTANTIVO
plaster

yo PRONOMBRE
1 I ◇ *Carlos y yo no fuimos.* Carlos and I didn't go.
2 me ◇ *¿Quién ha visto la película? – Ana y yo.* Who's seen the movie? – Ana and me. ◇ *Es más alta que yo.* She's taller than me. ◇ *Soy yo, María.* It's me, María.
◆ **¡Yo también!** Me too!
◆ **yo mismo** myself ◇ *Lo hice yo misma.* I did it myself.
◆ **yo que tú** if I were you

el **yoga** SUSTANTIVO
yoga

el **yogur** SUSTANTIVO
yoghurt

el **yudo** SUSTANTIVO
judo

Yugoslavia SUSTANTIVO FEM
Yugoslavia ◇ *en la antigua Yugoslavia* in the former Yugoslavia

Z

el **zafiro** SUSTANTIVO
sapphire

zambullirse* VERBO
to dive underwater (*sumergirse*)

zamparse VERBO
to wolf down (*coloquial*) ◇ *Se zampó todo un paquete de galletas.* He wolfed down a whole packet of cookies.

la **zanahoria** SUSTANTIVO
carrot

la **zancadilla** SUSTANTIVO
◆ **poner* la zancadilla a alguien** to trip someone up

el **zancudo** SUSTANTIVO
mosquito (PL mosquitos)

la **zanja** SUSTANTIVO
ditch (PL ditches)

zanjar VERBO
to settle (*deuda, diferencias*)

la **zapatera** SUSTANTIVO
shoemaker

la **zapatería** SUSTANTIVO
1 shoe store (*tienda*)
2 shoe repair shop (*para reparaciones*)

el **zapatero** SUSTANTIVO
shoemaker

la **zapatilla** SUSTANTIVO
slipper (*pantufla*)
◆ **zapatillas de ballet** ballet shoes
◆ **zapatillas de deporte** training shoes

el **zapato** SUSTANTIVO
shoe
◆ **zapatos de tacón** high-heeled shoes
◆ **zapatos planos** flat shoes
◆ **zapatos de piso** *Mexico* flat shoes

la **zarpa** SUSTANTIVO
paw

zarpar VERBO
to set sail

la **zarza** SUSTANTIVO
bramble

la **zarzamora** SUSTANTIVO
blackberry bush

el **zigzag** SUSTANTIVO
zigzag
◆ **una carretera en zigzag** a winding road

Zimbabue SUSTANTIVO MASC
Zimbabwe

el **zinc** SUSTANTIVO
zinc

el **zíper** SUSTANTIVO (PL los **zípers**)
zipper

el **zócalo** SUSTANTIVO
1 baseboard (*rodapié*)
2 public square *Mexico*

el **zodíaco** SUSTANTIVO
zodiac ◇ *los signos del zodíaco* the signs of the zodiac

la **zona** SUSTANTIVO
area ◇ *Viven en una zona muy tranquila.* They live in a very quiet area.
◆ **Fue declarada zona neutral.** It was declared a neutral zone.
◆ **zona verde** green belt
◆ **zona industrial** industrial park

el **zoo** SUSTANTIVO
zoo

la **zoóloga** SUSTANTIVO
zoologist

la **zoología** SUSTANTIVO
zoology

el **zoológico** SUSTANTIVO
zoo

el **zoólogo** SUSTANTIVO
zoologist

el **zoom** SUSTANTIVO (PL los **zooms**)
zoom lens (PL zoom lenses)

zoquete ADJETIVO
dim (*coloquial*)

el/la **zoquete** SUSTANTIVO
blockhead (*coloquial*)

el **zorro** SUSTANTIVO
fox (PL foxes) ◇ *piel de zorro* fox fur

el **zueco** SUSTANTIVO
clog

zumbar VERBO
to buzz (*abeja, oídos*) ◇ *Me zumban los oídos.* My ears are buzzing.
◆ **salir* zumbando** to whizz off (*coloquial*)

el **zumo** SUSTANTIVO *Spain*
juice

zurcir* VERBO
to darn

zurdo ADJETIVO
1 left-handed (*de la mano*)
2 left-footed (*del pie*)

zurrar VERBO
to thrash

* Verbs marked with this symbol are irregular. See pages 346–348 for further details.

SPANISH IN ACTION — INGLÉS ACTIVO

GAMES

The wordgames on the following pages have been designed to give you practice in using your dictionary. Make sure you read the "Dictionary Skills" section at the front of this book before you start. Don't worry, there are answers at the end of the word-games in case you get really stuck!

JUEGOS

Los pasatiempos de las páginas siguientes están pensados para ayudarte a manejar el diccionario de una forma práctica. Para ello, y antes de empezar, te conviene leer la sección "Cómo usar este diccionario" que está al principio, aunque es mejor que intentes resolverlos sin mirar la solución y si te quedas atascado puedes mirar al final de la sección.

WORDGAME 1

► ANTONYMS ◄

Complete the crossword by supplying ANTONYMS (i.e. opposites) in Spanish of the words below. Use your dictionary to help.

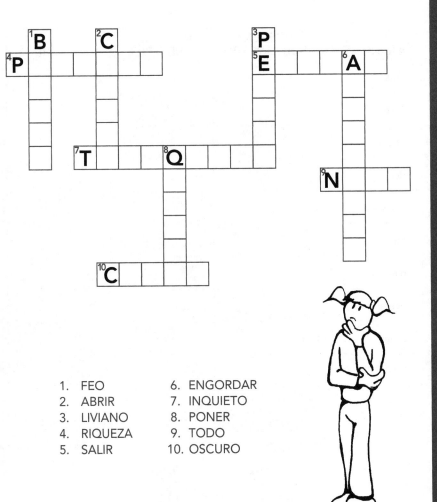

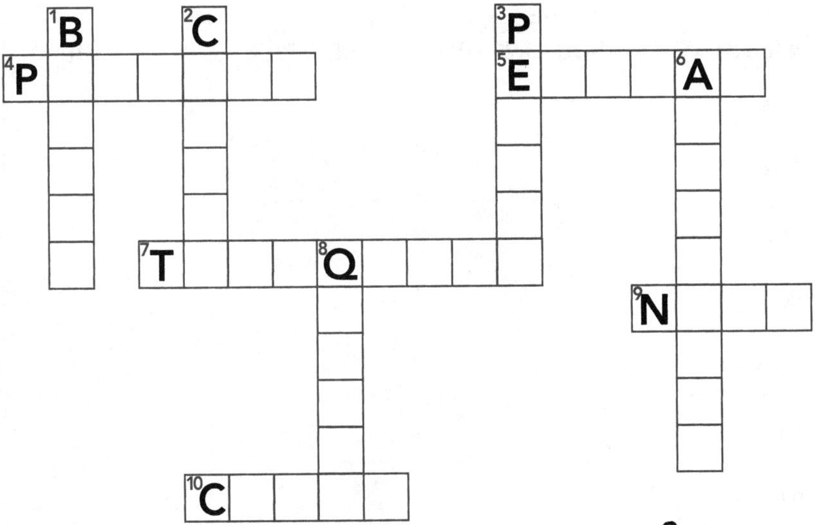

1. FEO
2. ABRIR
3. LIVIANO
4. RIQUEZA
5. SALIR
6. ENGORDAR
7. INQUIETO
8. PONER
9. TODO
10. OSCURO

WORDGAME 2

▶ VERB TENSES ◀

Use your dictionary to help you fill in the blanks in the table below.

INFINITIVE	PRESENT SUBJUNCTIVE	PRETERITE	FUTURE
tener		yo	
hacer			yo
poder			yo
decir		yo	
agradecer	yo		
saber			yo
reír	yo		
querer		yo	
caber	yo		
ir	yo		
salir			yo
ser		yo	

WORDGAME 3

Here is a list of Spanish words for things you will find in the kitchen. Unfortunately, they have all been jumbled up. Try to work out what each word is and put the word in the boxes on the right. You will see that there are seven shaded boxes below. With the seven letters in the shaded boxes make up another Spanish word for an object you can find in the kitchen.

1. **azta** — **¿Quieres una ______ de café?**

2. **fgreirdraeor** — **¡Mete la mantequilla en el ______ !**

3. **asme** — **¡La comida está en la ______!**

4. **locearca** — **Su madre está calentando la leche en el ______.**

5. **roegcanldo** — **¡No saques el helado del ______ todavía!**

6. **uclclohi** — **¿Dónde pusiste el ______ del queso?**

7. **tolpa** — **¿Me pasas un ______ ?**

The word you are looking for is:

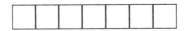

JUEGO 4

► ARTÍCULOS DEL DICCIONARIO ◄

Completa este crucigrama con las traducciones en inglés de la lista de palabras españolas. Hay un pequeño inconveniente: todas estas palabras tienen más de un significado en inglés y sólo una de las traducciones encaja en las casillas del crucigrama. Por lo tanto tienes que fijarte en todos los distintos significados y elegir el que encaje en las casillas.

(Recuerda que si tienes que insertar un verbo en infinitivo, no es necesario que escribas 'to', como en 'to go', que sería sólo 'go'.)

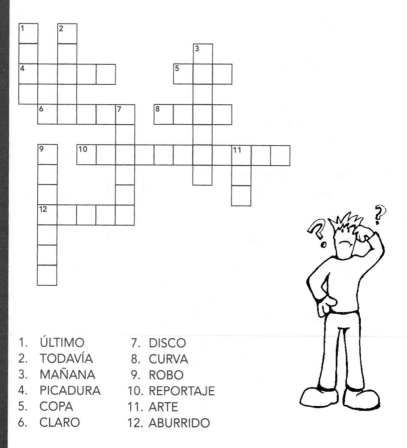

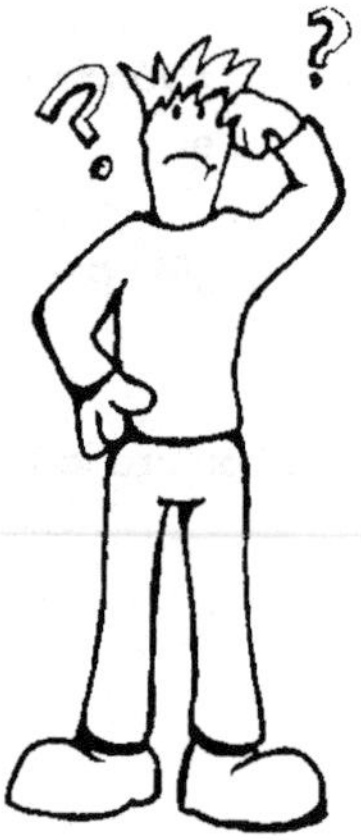

1. ÚLTIMO
2. TODAVÍA
3. MAÑANA
4. PICADURA
5. COPA
6. CLARO
7. DISCO
8. CURVA
9. ROBO
10. REPORTAJE
11. ARTE
12. ABURRIDO

JUEGO 5

▶ PARTES DE LA ORACIÓN ◀

Indica con una cruz la función gramatical que tienen las palabras señaladas en cada una de las siguientes oraciones.

ORACIÓN	SUST	ADJ	ADV	VERBO
1. Are you going to wash your car?				
2. Hand me the hammer, please.				
3. Your dress is not very clean.				
4. Shall we go for a drive?				
5. We arrived just in time.				
6. The garage serviced my car last week.				
7. My foot is very sore.				
8. Are we having stew for dinner?				
9. They live in California.				
10. He switched off the light.				

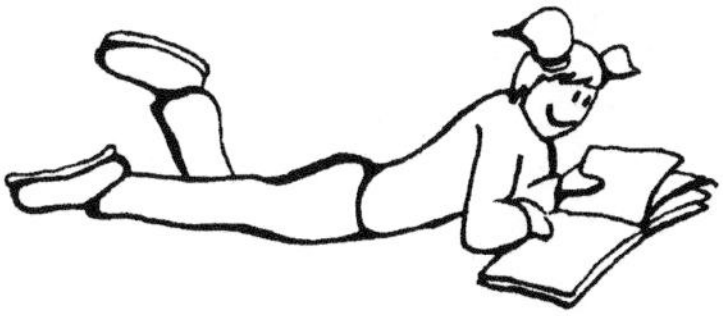

JUEGO 6

▶ TABLERO DE DAMAS ◀

En las siguientes casillas las letras de diez palabras inglesas han sido sustituidas por números. Cada dígito representa siempre la misma letra.

Intenta descifrar el código para encontrar las diez palabras. Puedes recurrir a tu diccionario si necesitas ayuda.

Aquí tienes una pista: Todas las palabras están relacionadas con EL TRANSPORTE.

1.	1 A	2 I	3 R	4	5	6	7	8		
2.	9	10	11							
3.	12	3	1	2	7					
4.	13	14	15	8	3	16	3	1	17	12
5.	16	14	1	16	13					
6.	9	2	16	18	16	5	8			
7.	16	1	3							
8.	12	3	1	2	5	8	3			
9.	11	10	9	19	1	18				
10.	17	8	3	3	18					

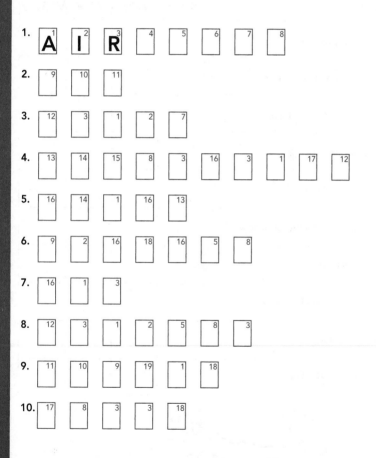

WORDGAME 1

1. bonito
2. cerrar
3. pesado
4. pobreza
5. entrar
6. adelgazar
7. tranquilo
8. quitar
9. nada
10. claro

WORDGAME 2

tuve	ría
haré	quise
podré	quepa
dije	vaya
agradezca	saldré
sabré	fui

WORDGAME 3

1. taza
2. refrigerador
3. mesa
4. cacerola
5. congelador
6. cuchillo
7. plato

Missing word –
ARMARIO

JUEGO 4

1. last
2. still
3. morning
4. sting
5. top
6. clear
7. record
8. bend
9. robbery
10. documentary
11. art
12. bored

JUEGO 5

1. Verbo
2. Verbo
3. Adjetivo
4. Sustantivo
5. Adverbio
6. Verbo
7. Adjetivo
8. Sustantivo
9. Verbo
10. Sustantivo

JUEGO 6

1. airplane
2. bus
3. train
4. hovercraft
5. coach
6. bicycle
7. car
8. trailer
9. subway
10. ferry

CORRESPONDENCE

▶ LETTER

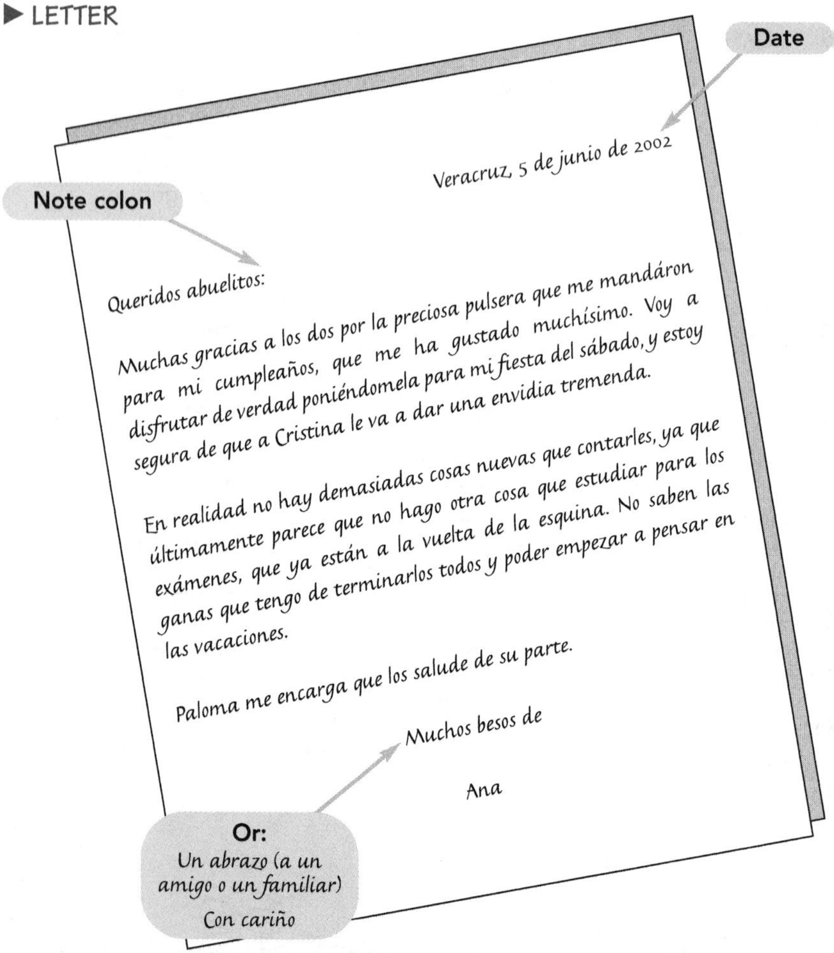

Veracruz, 5 de junio de 2002

Queridos abuelitos:

Muchas gracias a los dos por la preciosa pulsera que me mandáron para mi cumpleaños, que me ha gustado muchísimo. Voy a disfrutar de verdad poniéndomela para mi fiesta del sábado, y estoy segura de que a Cristina le va a dar una envidia tremenda.

En realidad no hay demasiadas cosas nuevas que contarles, ya que últimamente parece que no hago otra cosa que estudiar para los exámenes, que ya están a la vuelta de la esquina. No saben las ganas que tengo de terminarlos todos y poder empezar a pensar en las vacaciones.

Paloma me encarga que los salude de su parte.

Muchos besos de

Ana

STARTING A PERSONAL LETTER

Gracias por tu carta.	*Thank you for your letter.*
Me alegró mucho tener noticias tuyas.	*It was lovely to hear from you.*
Perdona que no te haya escrito antes.	*I'm sorry I didn't write earlier.*

ENDING A PERSONAL LETTER

¡Escríbeme pronto!	*Write soon!*
Dale un beso a Vanesa de mi parte.	*Give my love to Vanesa.*
Samuel te manda saludos.	*Samuel sends his best wishes.*

CORRESPONDENCIA

▶ LA CARTA PERSONAL

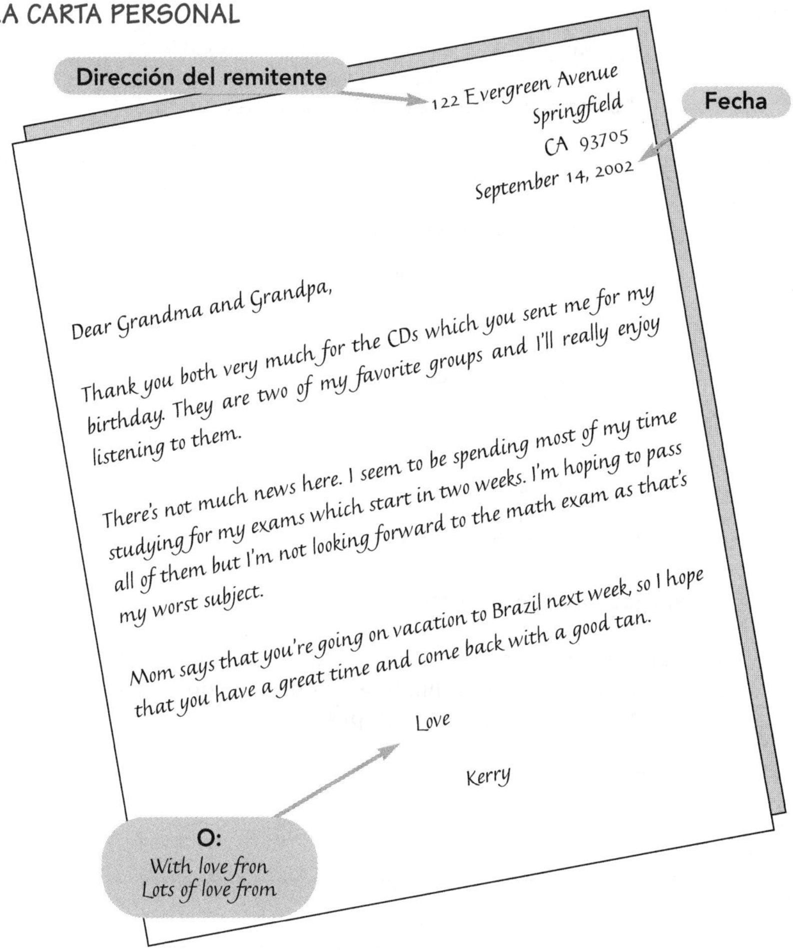

122 Evergreen Avenue
Springfield
CA 93705
September 14, 2002

Dear Grandma and Grandpa,

Thank you both very much for the CDs which you sent me for my birthday. They are two of my favorite groups and I'll really enjoy listening to them.

There's not much news here. I seem to be spending most of my time studying for my exams which start in two weeks. I'm hoping to pass all of them but I'm not looking forward to the math exam as that's my worst subject.

Mom says that you're going on vacation to Brazil next week, so I hope that you have a great time and come back with a good tan.

Love

Kerry

EL SALUDO EN UNA CARTA PERSONAL

Thank you for your letter.	*Gracias por tu carta.*
It was lovely to hear from you.	*Me alegró mucho tener noticias tuyas.*
I'm sorry I didn't write earlier.	*Perdona que no te haya escrito antes.*

LA DESPEDIDA EN UNA CARTA PERSONAL

Write soon!	*¡Escríbeme pronto!*
Give my love to Vanessa.	*Dale un beso a Vanessa de mi parte.*
Samuel sends his best wishes.	*Samuel te manda saludos.*

CORRESPONDENCE

▶ EMAIL

To give your email address to someone in Spanish, say:
"belen punto huertas arroba globanet punto es"

Nuevo Message

a:	belen.huertas@globanet.es
de:	teresa@onemo.es
asunto:	concierto
cc:	pedro@infotec.es
bcc:	

Archivo adjunto   Enviar

Hola, ¿qué tal el fin de semana?

Me sobran dos entradas para el concierto de mañana, de unos amigos que no pueden venir. Si te interesa, o conoces a alguien que quiera ir, avísame en cuanto puedas.

Saludos

Nuevo mensaje	New message
A	To
De	From
Asunto	Subject
cc	cc
Copia oculta	bcc
Archivo adjunto	Attachment
Enviar	Send

CORRESPONDENCIA

▶ CORREO ELECTRÓNICO

En inglés, la dirección electrónica se pronuncia así: **"gemma at n t net dot co dot u k"**
New Message
To:
gemma@ntnet.co.uk
From:
gordon@onemo.net
Subject:
concert next week
cc:
jeremy@blt.com
bcc:
Attachment
Send
Hi guys
I've just bought the new album by Dropzone, and it's great! I've got two spare tickets to a concert they're giving in Chicago next Wednesday evening, so I hope you can both make it.
See you soon!

New message	Nuevo mensaje
To	A
From	De
Subject	Asunto
cc	cc
bcc	Copia oculta
Attachment	Archivo adjunto
Send	Enviar

▶ WHEN YOUR NUMBER ANSWERS / ▶ CUANDO OTROS CONTESTAN

- **Hello! Could I speak to Susana, please?** – Hola, ¿está Susana?
- **Would you ask him/her to call me back, please?** – Le puede decir que me llame, por favor?
- **I'll call back in half an hour.** – La vuelvo a llamar dentro de media hora.

▶ ANSWERING THE TELEPHONE / ▶ PARA CONTESTAR AL TELÉFONO

- **Hello! It's Marcos speaking.** – ¿Aló? Habla Marcos.
- **Speaking.** – Sí, con él/ella habla.
- **Who's speaking?** – ¿Con quién hablo?

▶ WHEN THE SWITCHBOARD ANSWERS / ▶ HABLA EL TELEFONISTA

- **Who shall I say is calling?** – ¿De parte de quién?
- **I'm putting you through.** – Le comunico.
- **Please hold.** – No cuelgue.
- **Would you like to leave a message?** – ¿Quiere dejar un mensaje?

▶ DIFFICULTIES / ▶ DIFICULTADES

- **I can't get through.** – No hay línea.
- **I'm sorry, I've got the wrong number.** – Perdone, me equivoqué de número.
- **This is a very bad line.** – Se oye muy mal.
- **Their phone is out of order.** – No les funciona el teléfono.

NUMBERS — LOS NÚMEROS

1	one	1	uno
2	two	2	dos
3	three	3	tres
4	four	4	cuatro
5	five	5	cinco
6	six	6	seis
7	seven	7	siete
8	eight	8	ocho
9	nine	9	nueve
10	ten	10	diez
11	eleven	11	once
12	twelve	12	doce
13	thirteen	13	trece
14	fourteen	14	catorce
15	fifteen	15	quince
16	sixteen	16	dieciséis
17	seventeen	17	diecisiete
18	eighteen	18	dieciocho
19	nineteen	19	diecinueve
20	twenty	20	veinte
21	twenty-one	21	veintiuno
30	thirty	30	treinta
31	thirty-one	31	treinta y uno
40	forty	40	cuarenta
41	forty-one	41	cuarenta y uno
50	fifty	50	cincuenta
60	sixty	60	sesenta
70	seventy	70	setenta
80	eighty	80	ochenta
90	ninety	90	noventa
100	a hundred	100	cien
101	a hundred and one	101	ciento uno
200	two hundred	200	doscientos
201	two hundred and one	201	doscientos uno
1000	a thousand	1000	mil
1001	a thousand and one	1001	mil uno
,000,000	a million	1,000,000	un millón

EXAMPLES

n page nineteen
n chapter seven
n a scale of one to fifteen

▶ EJEMPLOS

en la página diecinueve
en el capítulo siete
en una escala del uno al quince

NUMBERS — LOS NÚMEROS

1st	first	1°	primero
2nd	second	2°	segundo
3rd	third	3°	tercero
4th	fourth	4°	cuarto
5th	fifth	5°	quinto
6th	sixth	6°	sexto
7th	seventh	7°	séptimo
8th	eighth	8°	octavo
9th	ninth	9°	noveno
10th	tenth	10°	décimo
11th	eleventh	11°	decimoprimero
12th	twelfth	12°	decimosegundo
13th	thirteenth	13°	decimotercero
14th	fourteenth	14°	decimocuarto
15th	fifteenth	15°	decimoquinto
16th	sixteenth	16°	decimosexto
17th	seventeenth	17°	decimoséptimo
18th	eighteenth	18°	decimoctavo
19th	nineteenth	19°	decimonoveno
20th	twentieth	20°	vigésimo
21st	twenty-first	21°	vigésimo primero
30th	thirtieth	30°	trigésimo
100th	hundredth	100°	centésimo
101st	hundred-and-first	101°	centésimo primero
1000th	thousandth	1000°	milésimo

▶FRACTIONS *etc.* — ▶ LAS FRACCIONES *etc.*

1/2	a half	1/2	un medio
1/3	a third	1/3	un tercio
1/4	a quarter	1/4	un cuarto
1/5	a fifth	1/5	un quinto
0.5	(nought) point five	0,5	cero coma cinco
3.4	three point four	3,4	tres coma cuatro
6.89	six point eight nine	6,89	seis coma ochenta y nueve
10%	ten per cent	10%	diez por ciento
100%	a hundred per cent	100%	cien por ciento

▶ EXAMPLES — ▶ EJEMPLOS

he lives on the fifth floor	vive en el quinto piso
he came in third	llegó tercero
a quarter of the cake	un cuarto del pastel

▶ DAYS OF THE WEEK / ▶ DÍAS DE LA SEMANA

Monday	lunes
Tuesday	martes
Wednesday	miércoles
Thursday	jueves
Friday	viernes
Saturday	sábado
Sunday	domingo
When?	**¿Cuándo?**
on Monday	el lunes
on Mondays	los lunes
every Monday	todos los lunes
last Tuesday	el martes pasado
next Friday	el próximo viernes
a week on Saturday	el sábado de la semana que viene
two weeks on Saturday	el sábado de dentro de dos semanas

▶ MONTHS OF THE YEAR / ▶ MESES DEL AÑO

January	enero
February	febrero
March	marzo
April	abril
May	mayo
June	junio
July	julio
August	agosto
September	septiembre
October	octubre
November	noviembre
December	diciembre
When?	**¿Cuándo?**
in February	en febrero
on December 1st *or* first 2002	el primero de diciembre de 2002
in two thousand and two	en dos mil dos
What day is it?	**¿Qué día es hoy?**
It's ...	**Es ...**
Monday, May 26th *or* Monday, May twenty-sixth	lunes, vientiséis de mayo

What time is it? What's the time?		¿Qué hora es?
It's one o'clock		Es la una
It's ten past one		Es la una y diez
It's quarter past one		Es la una y cuarto
It's half past one		Es la una y media
It's twenty to two		Son veinte para las dos
It's quarter to two		Son un cuarto para las dos
What time?		¿A qué hora?
at midnight		a medianoche
at midday		al mediodía
at one o'clock (in the afternoon)		a la una (de la tarde)
at eleven o'clock (in the evening)		a las once (de la noche)
11:15 *o* eleven fifteen		las 11:15 *or* las once quince
8:45 *o* eight forty-five		las 20:45 *or* las veinte cuarenta y cinco
in twenty minutes ten minutes ago		en veinte minutos hace diez minutos

español ≠ English

actual ≠ *actual*

La situación **actual** del país.	→	The country's **present** situation.
The movie is based on **actual** events.	→	La película está basada en hechos **reales**.

agenda ≠ *agenda*

Perdí mi **agenda**.	→	I lost my **diary**.
on the **agenda**	→	en el **orden del día**

apuntar ≠ *appoint*

Apúntalo o se te olvidará.	→	**Write it down** or you'll forget.
They **appointed** him chairman.	→	Lo **nombraron** presidente.

constipado ≠ *constipated*

Estoy **constipado**.	→	I have **a cold**.
I'm **constipated**.	→	Estoy **estreñido**.

decepción ≠ *deception*

Me he llevado una gran **decepción** con él.	→	I was really **disappointed** in him.
Katie continued to keep up the **deception**.	→	Katie siguió manteniendo el **engaño**.

disgustado ≠ *disgusted*

Está **disgustado** porque no pasó el examen.	→	He's **upset** because he failed the exam.
I was completely **disgusted** at his behavior.	→	Estaba **indignado** con su comportamiento.

embarazada ≠ embarrassed

Estaba **embarazada** de cuatro meses. → She was four months **pregnant.**

I was really **embarrassed.** → Me dio mucha **vergüenza.**

espada ≠ spade

Una **espada** de hierro → An iron **sword**

He dug a hole with his **spade.** → Cavó un hoyo con la **pala.**

éxito ≠ exit

Esa novela será un gran **éxito**. → That novel will be a great **success.**

"**Exit**" (sign) → "**Salida**" (letrero)

fábrica ≠ fabric

Trabaja en una **fábrica**. → He works in a **factory.**

400 meters of **fabric** → 400 metros de **tela**

largo ≠ large

Fue una conferencia muy **larga.** → It was a very **long** conference.

a **large** house → una casa **grande**

librería ≠ library

una **librería** de ocasión → a second-hand **bookstore**

the public **library** → la **biblioteca** pública

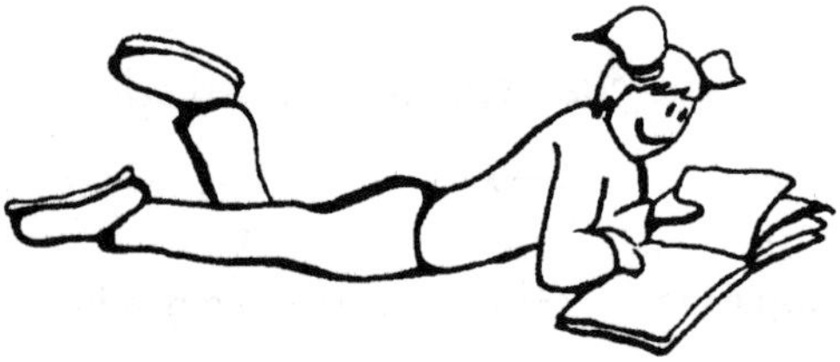

noticia ≠ notice

Tengo una buena **noticia** que darte. ⟶ I've got some good **news** for you.

There's a **notice** on the board about the trip. ⟶ Hay un **aviso** en el tablero sobre el viaje.

pariente ≠ parent

Es **pariente** mío. ⟶ He's a **relative** of mine.

My **parents** are Irish. ⟶ Mis **padres** son irlandeses.

pretender ≠ pretend

Pretendo sacarme una buena nota. ⟶ I **intend** to get a good grade.

He's not really ill, he's just **pretending.** ⟶ No está enfermo, sólo está **fingiendo.**

profesor ≠ professor

Amelia es **profesora** de inglés. ⟶ Amelia is an English **teacher.**

He is a Spanish **professor** at Harvard University. ⟶ Es **catedrático** de español en la Universidad de Harvard.

receta ≠ receipt

Me dio la **receta** de los raviolis. ⟶ He gave me the **recipe** for the ravioli.

Do you have a **receipt** for the dress? ⟶ ¿Tiene el **ticket de compra** del vestido?

recordar ≠ record*

No **recuerdo** dónde lo puse. ⟶ I can't **remember** where I put it.

They've just **recorded** their new album. ⟶ Acaban de **grabar** su nuevo álbum.

sano ≠ sane

una dieta **sana**	⟶	a **healthy** diet
She is as **sane** as you or me.	⟶	Está tan **cuerda** como tú o como yo.

sensible ≠ sensible

Es un chico muy **sensible**.	⟶	He's a very **sensitive** boy.
Be **sensible!**	⟶	¡Sé **sensato**!

simpático ≠ sympathetic

Estuvo muy **simpática** con todos.	⟶	She was very **nice** to everybody.
She is a **sympathetic** listener.	⟶	Es una persona **comprensiva** que sabe escuchar.

soportar ≠ support

No lo **soporto.**	⟶	I can't **stand** him.
My mom has always **supported** me.	⟶	Mi mamá siempre me ha **apoyado.**

suceso ≠ success

Los **sucesos** de la última decada.	⟶	The **events** of the last decade.
He was a great **success** as a writer.	⟶	Tuvo gran **éxito** como escritor.

▶ CONTENTS

SPANISH VERB TABLES

This section contains 16 tables of very important Spanish verbs that you need to learn and 3 pages of other types of irregular verbs.

Spanish verbs fall into two main categories – **regular** and **irregular** – and it is important to learn which verbs fall into which category.

The tables are arranged in the following order:

1. Regular verbs – **hablar**, **comer**, **vivir** and **lavarse**
2. The most basic irregular verbs
3. Other types of irregular verb

At the top of each full-page table you will find the infinitive, the imperative, the past participle, and the gerund. The lower section of the table shows you how to form six tenses of the verb:

PRESENT
IMPERFECT
PRETERITE
PRESENT SUBJUNCTIVE
FUTURE
CONDITIONAL

▶ REGULAR VERBS

There are three groups of regular verbs:

1. "-AR" verbs = verbs that end in -**ar** like **hablar** and **lavarse** on p326 and p329.
2. "-ER" verbs = verbs that end in -**er** like **comer** on p327.
3. "-IR" verbs = verbs that end in -**ir** like **vivir** on p328.

They are called regular verbs because they follow one of three set patterns. When you have learned these patterns, you will be able to form any regular verb.

The subject pronouns like *yo*, *tú*, *él* will appear in parentheses because they are not always necessary in Spanish when **I**, **you**, **he** are in English.

HOW TO FORM A REGULAR VERB

i. a) To form the present, imperfect, preterite, present subjunctive and past subjunctive tenses, take the infinitive minus the last two letters. This is called the **stem** e.g. *hablar* → **habl-**, *comer* → **com-**, and *vivir* → **viv-**.

   b) To form the future or conditional tense, the stem is the whole **infinitive** for all three verb types e.g. *hablar* → **hablar**, *comer* → **comer** and *vivir* → **vivir**.

ii. Next add the appropriate ending. You need to ask yourself three questions:

a) **What sort of** verb am I using (-AR, -ER, -IR)?
b) **Who** is doing the verb? (yo, tú, él *etc*)?
c) **When** are they doing it (in the present, the past or the future)?

Look at the verb tables for **hablar**, **comer** and **vivir**. The verb endings are in color. These endings can be added onto the stem of any regular verb.

▶ THE MOST COMMON IRREGULAR VERBS

Many Spanish verbs are irregular and this means you have to learn them individually. There are full-page tables of the most important irregular verbs such as **tener**, **ser** and **estar** in this section. When you are translating from Spanish and meet an unfamiliar verb form, you may be able to guess from the context that it comes from one of these verbs, and you can use the verb tables to check. Irregular verb parts are listed on the Spanish side of the dictionary, so you could also look there.

HOW TO USE THE VERB TABLES

You will find some useful examples at the top of each verb table, but if you can't find what you need to say or write in Spanish there, use the verb table itself to help you. Imagine that you want to find the Spanish for "he wants". Here's how to do it:

a) Look up **want** on the English-Spanish side of the dictionary to find the Spanish translation
b) Spanish translation = **querer**
c) Turn to the verb tables section of your dictionary and find **querer**
d) When does he want it? He wants it **now**, so look for the heading *PRESENT*
e) Who wants it? **He** does. The Spanish for "he" is **él** so look for **él** under the *PRESENT* heading
f) The Spanish for "he wants" is "**quiere**"

▶ OTHER IRREGULAR VERBS

On pages 346-348 there is an alphabetical list of all irregular verbs, each of which is followed by a number. These numbers refer to the pattern which these verbs follow, and if you look on pages 342-345 you will see these patterns shown in summary form.

▸ hablar

to speak

IMPERATIVE

habla
hablen

EXAMPLE PHRASES

*No **hablo** francés.* I don't speak French
*Ayer **hablé** con tu hermano.* I spoke to your brother yesterday.
*Esta tarde **hablaré** con ella por teléfono.* I'll speak to her on the phone tonight.

PAST PARTICIPLE

hablado

GERUND

hablando

PRESENT

(yo)	hablo
(tú)	hablas
(él)	habla
(nosotros)	hablamos
(vosotros)	habláis
(ellos)	hablan

PRETERITE

(yo)	hablé
(tú)	hablaste
(él)	habló
(nosotros)	hablamos
(vosotros)	hablasteis
(ellos)	hablaron

FUTURE

(yo)	hablaré
(tú)	hablarás
(él)	hablará
(nosotros)	hablaremos
(vosotros)	hablaréis
(ellos)	hablarán

PRESENT SUBJUNCTIVE

(yo)	hable
(tú)	hables
(él)	hable
(nosotros)	hablemos
(vosotros)	habléis
(ellos)	hablen

IMPERFECT

(yo)	hablaba
(tú)	hablabas
(él)	hablaba
(nosotros)	hablábamos
(vosotros)	hablabais
(ellos)	hablaban

CONDITIONAL

(yo)	hablaría
(tú)	hablarías
(él)	hablaría
(nosotros)	hablaríamos
(vosotros)	hablaríais
(ellos)	hablarían

▶ *comer*

to eat

IMPERATIVE

come
coman

EXAMPLE PHRASES

No ***como*** *carne.* I don't eat meat.
Aún no ***hemos comido****.*
We haven't eaten yet.
Ayer ***comimos*** *en un restaurante.*
Yesterday we ate in a restaurant.

PAST PARTICIPLE

comido

GERUND

comiendo

PRESENT

(yo)	como
(tú)	comes
(él)	come
(nosotros)	comemos
(vosotros)	coméis
(ellos)	comen

PRETERITE

(yo)	comí
(tú)	comiste
(él)	comió
(nosotros)	comimos
(vosotros)	comisteis
(ellos)	comieron

FUTURE

(yo)	comeré
(tú)	comerás
(él)	comerá
(nosotros)	comeremos
(vosotros)	comeréis
(ellos)	comerán

PRESENT SUBJUNCTIVE

(yo)	coma
(tú)	comas
(él)	coma
(nosotros)	comamos
(vosotros)	comáis
(ellos)	coman

IMPERFECT

(yo)	comía
(tú)	comías
(él)	comía
(nosotros)	comíamos
(vosotros)	comíais
(ellos)	comían

CONDITIONAL

(yo)	comería
(tú)	comerías
(él)	comería
(nosotros)	comeríamos
(vosotros)	comeríais
(ellos)	comerían

▶ vivir

to live

IMPERATIVE

vive
vivan

EXAMPLE PHRASES

***Vive** en esta calle.* He lives in this street.
*Antes **vivía** en Buenos Aires.*
He used to live in Buenos Aires.
*En verano **viviremos** en el departamento nuevo.*
In the summer we'll be living in the new apartment.

PAST PARTICIPLE

vivido

GERUND

viviendo

PRESENT

(yo)	vivo
(tú)	vives
(él)	vive
(nosotros)	vivimos
(vosotros)	vivís
(ellos)	viven

PRESENT SUBJUNCTIVE

(yo)	viva
(tú)	vivas
(él)	viva
(nosotros)	vivamos
(vosotros)	viváis
(ellos)	vivan

PRETERITE

(yo)	viví
(tú)	viviste
(él)	vivió
(nosotros)	vivimos
(vosotros)	vivisteis
(ellos)	vivieron

IMPERFECT

(yo)	vivía
(tú)	vivías
(él)	vivía
(nosotros)	vivíamos
(vosotros)	vivíais
(ellos)	vivían

FUTURE

(yo)	viviré
(tú)	vivirás
(él)	vivirá
(nosotros)	viviremos
(vosotros)	viviréis
(ellos)	vivirán

CONDITIONAL

(yo)	viviría
(tú)	vivirías
(él)	viviría
(nosotros)	viviríamos
(vosotros)	viviríais
(ellos)	vivirían

▶ lavarse

to wash (oneself)

IMPERATIVE

lávate

lavense

EXAMPLE PHRASES

Se lava *todos los días.*
He washes every day.
Ayer ***me lavé*** *el pelo.*
I washed my hair yesterday.
Nos lavaremos *con agua fría.*
We'll wash in cold water.

PAST PARTICIPLE

lavado

GERUND

lavándose

PRESENT

(yo)	me lavo
(tú)	te lavas
(él)	se lava
(nosotros)	nos lavamos
(vosotros)	os laváis
(ellos)	se lavan

PRESENT SUBJUNCTIVE

(yo)	me lave
(tú)	te laves
(él)	se lave
(nosotros)	nos lavemos
(vosotros)	os lavéis
(ellos)	se laven

PRETERITE

(yo)	me lavé
(tú)	te lavaste
(él)	se lavó
(nosotros)	nos lavamos
(vosotros)	os lavasteis
(ellos)	se lavaron

IMPERFECT

(yo)	me lavaba
(tú)	te lavabas
(él)	se lavaba
(nosotros)	nos lavábamos
(vosotros)	os lavabais
(ellos)	se lavaban

FUTURE

(yo)	me lavaré
(tú)	te lavarás
(él)	se lavará
(nosotros)	nos lavaremos
(vosotros)	os lavaréis
(ellos)	se lavarán

CONDITIONAL

(yo)	me lavaría
(tú)	te lavarías
(él)	se lavaría
(nosotros)	nos lavaríamos
(vosotros)	os lavaríais
(ellos)	se lavarían

▶ dar

to give

IMPERATIVE

da

den

EXAMPLE PHRASES

Mi tía siempre nos ***da*** *dulces.*
My aunt always gives us candy.
Me ***dio*** *un libro.* He gave me a book.
Mañana me ***darán*** *las notas.*
They will give me my grades tomorrow

PAST PARTICIPLE

dado

GERUND

dando

PRESENT

(yo)	doy
(tú)	das
(él)	da
(nosotros)	damos
(vosotros)	dais
(ellos)	dan

PRESENT SUBJUNCTIVE

(yo)	dé
(tú)	des
(él)	dé
(nosotros)	demos
(vosotros)	deis
(ellos)	den

PRETERITE

(yo)	di
(tú)	diste
(él)	dio
(nosotros)	dimos
(vosotros)	disteis
(ellos)	dieron

IMPERFECT

(yo)	daba
(tú)	dabas
(él)	daba
(nosotros)	dábamos
(vosotros)	dabais
(ellos)	daban

FUTURE

(yo)	daré
(tú)	darás
(él)	dará
(nosotros)	daremos
(vosotros)	daréis
(ellos)	darán

CONDITIONAL

(yo)	daría
(tú)	darías
(él)	daría
(nosotros)	daríamos
(vosotros)	daríais
(ellos)	darían

▶ decir

to say

IMPERATIVE

di

digan

EXAMPLE PHRASES

Siempre ***dice*** *lo que piensa.*
He always says what he thinks.
Me ***dijo*** *una mentira.* He told me a lie.
Se lo ***diré*** *a todo el mundo.*
I'll tell everyone about it.

PAST PARTICIPLE

dicho

GERUND

diciendo

PRESENT

(yo)	digo
(tú)	dices
(él)	dice
(nosotros)	decimos
(vosotros)	decís
(ellos)	dicen

PRETERITE

(yo)	dije
(tú)	dijiste
(él)	dijo
(nosotros)	dijimos
(vosotros)	dijisteis
(ellos)	dijeron

FUTURE

(yo)	diré
(tú)	dirás
(él)	dirá
(nosotros)	diremos
(vosotros)	diréis
(ellos)	dirán

PRESENT SUBJUNCTIVE

(yo)	diga
(tú)	digas
(él)	diga
(nosotros)	digamos
(vosotros)	digáis
(ellos)	digan

IMPERFECT

(yo)	decía
(tú)	decías
(él)	decía
(nosotros)	decíamos
(vosotros)	decíais
(ellos)	decían

CONDITIONAL

(yo)	diría
(tú)	dirías
(él)	diría
(nosotros)	diríamos
(vosotros)	diríais
(ellos)	dirían

▶ *estar*

to be

IMPERATIVE

está
estén

EXAMPLE PHRASES

Estoy *enfermo.* I'm ill.
Estaba *muy enojada contigo.* She was very angry with you.
Mañana ***estaré*** *en casa todo el día.* I'll be at home all day tomorrow.

PAST PARTICIPLE

estado

GERUND

estando

PRESENT

(yo)	estoy
(tú)	estás
(él)	está
(nosotros)	estamos
(vosotros)	estáis
(ellos)	están

PRESENT SUBJUNCTIVE

(yo)	esté
(tú)	estés
(él)	esté
(nosotros)	estemos
(vosotros)	estéis
(ellos)	estén

PRETERITE

(yo)	estuve
(tú)	estuviste
(él)	estuvo
(nosotros)	estuvimos
(vosotros)	estuvisteis
(ellos)	estuvieron

IMPERFECT

(yo)	estaba
(tú)	estabas
(él)	estaba
(nosotros)	estábamos
(vosotros)	estabais
(ellos)	estaban

FUTURE

(yo)	estaré
(tú)	estarás
(él)	estará
(nosotros)	estaremos
(vosotros)	estaréis
(ellos)	estarán

CONDITIONAL

(yo)	estaría
(tú)	estarías
(él)	estaría
(nosotros)	estaríamos
(vosotros)	estaríais
(ellos)	estarían

▶ haber

to have (*auxiliary*)

IMPERATIVE

not used

EXAMPLE PHRASES

¿***Hay*** *alguien en la oficina?*
Is there anyone in the office?
Había *mucha gente en la fiesta.*
There were a lot of people at the party.
El domingo ***habrá*** *una manifestación.*
There will be a demonstration on Sunday.

PAST PARTICIPLE

habido

GERUND

habiendo

PRESENT

(yo)	he
(tú)	has
(él)	ha
(nosotros)	hemos
(vosotros)	habéis
(ellos)	han

PRESENT SUBJUNCTIVE

(yo)	haya
(tú)	hayas
(él)	haya
(nosotros)	hayamos
(vosotros)	hayáis
(ellos)	hayan

PRETERITE

(yo)	hube
(tú)	hubiste
(él)	hubo
(nosotros)	hubimos
(vosotros)	hubisteis
(ellos)	hubieron

IMPERFECT

(yo)	había
(tú)	habías
(él)	había
(nosotros)	habíamos
(vosotros)	habíais
(ellos)	habían

FUTURE

(yo)	habré
(tú)	habrás
(él)	habrá
(nosotros)	habremos
(vosotros)	habréis
(ellos)	habrán

CONDITIONAL

(yo)	habría
(tú)	habrías
(él)	habría
(nosotros)	habríamos
(vosotros)	habríais
(ellos)	habrían

▸ hacer

to do, to make

IMPERATIVE

haz
hagan

EXAMPLE PHRASES

¿Qué ***haces****?* What are you doing?
Hice *las camas.*
I made the beds.
Ayer no ***hicimos*** *nada.*
We didn't do anything yesterday.

PAST PARTICIPLE

hecho

GERUND

haciendo

PRESENT

(yo)	hago
(tú)	haces
(él)	hace
(nosotros)	hacemos
(vosotros)	hacéis
(ellos)	hacen

PRETERITE

(yo)	hice
(tú)	hiciste
(él)	hizo
(nosotros)	hicimos
(vosotros)	hicisteis
(ellos)	hicieron

FUTURE

(yo)	haré
(tú)	harás
(él)	hará
(nosotros)	haremos
(vosotros)	haréis
(ellos)	harán

PRESENT SUBJUNCTIVE

(yo)	haga
(tú)	hagas
(él)	haga
(nosotros)	hagamos
(vosotros)	hagáis
(ellos)	hagan

IMPERFECT

(yo)	hacía
(tú)	hacías
(él)	hacía
(nosotros)	hacíamos
(vosotros)	hacíais
(ellos)	hacían

CONDITIONAL

(yo)	haría
(tú)	harías
(él)	haría
(nosotros)	haríamos
(vosotros)	haríais
(ellos)	harían

▶ ir

to go

IMPERATIVE

ve

vayan

EXAMPLE PHRASES

Van *al colegio en autobús.*
They go to school by bus.
Fui *a Chile con mi familia.*
I went to Chile with my family.
*Mañana no **iré** a trabajar.*
I'm not going to work tomorrow.

PAST PARTICIPLE

ido

GERUND

yendo

PRESENT

(yo)	voy
(tú)	vas
(él)	va
(nosotros)	vamos
(vosotros)	vais
(ellos)	van

PRETERITE

(yo)	fui
(tú)	fuiste
(él)	fue
(nosotros)	fuimos
(vosotros)	fuisteis
(ellos)	fueron

FUTURE

(yo)	iré
(tú)	irás
(él)	irá
(nosotros)	iremos
(vosotros)	iréis
(ellos)	irán

PRESENT SUBJUNCTIVE

(yo)	vaya
(tú)	vayas
(él)	vaya
(nosotros)	vayamos
(vosotros)	vayáis
(ellos)	vayan

IMPERFECT

(yo)	iba
(tú)	ibas
(él)	iba
(nosotros)	íbamos
(vosotros)	ibais
(ellos)	iban

CONDITIONAL

(yo)	iría
(tú)	irías
(él)	iría
(nosotros)	iríamos
(vosotros)	iríais
(ellos)	irían

▶ *poner*

to put

IMPERATIVE	*EXAMPLE PHRASES*
pon pongan	*Todos los días* ***pongo*** *la mesa.* I set the table every day. ***Puse*** *el despertador para las cinco.* I set the alarm clock for five o'clock. ***Pondremos*** *la tele después de cenar.* We'll put the TV on after dinner.

PAST PARTICIPLE	*GERUND*
puesto	poniendo

PRESENT

(yo)	pongo
(tú)	pones
(él)	pone
(nosotros)	ponemos
(vosotros)	ponéis
(ellos)	ponen

PRESENT SUBJUNCTIVE

(yo)	ponga
(tú)	pongas
(él)	ponga
(nosotros)	pongamos
(vosotros)	pongáis
(ellos)	pongan

PRETERITE

(yo)	puse
(tú)	pusiste
(él)	puso
(nosotros)	pusimos
(vosotros)	pusisteis
(ellos)	pusieron

IMPERFECT

(yo)	ponía
(tú)	ponías
(él)	ponía
(nosotros)	poníamos
(vosotros)	poníais
(ellos)	ponían

FUTURE

(yo)	pondré
(tú)	pondrás
(él)	pondrá
(nosotros)	pondremos
(vosotros)	pondréis
(ellos)	pondrán

CONDITIONAL

(yo)	pondría
(tú)	pondrías
(él)	pondría
(nosotros)	pondríamos
(vosotros)	pondríais
(ellos)	pondrían

▶ querer

to want

IMPERATIVE

quiere

quieran

EXAMPLE PHRASES

*¿**Quieres** tomar algo?*
Do you want something to drink?
*No **querían** irse a dormir.*
They didn't want to go to sleep.
*¿**Querrás** venir al cine?*
Would you like to come to the movies?

PAST PARTICIPLE

querido

GERUND

queriendo

PRESENT

(yo)	quiero
(tú)	quieres
(él)	quiere
(nosotros)	queremos
(vosotros)	queréis
(ellos)	quieren

PRETERITE

(yo)	quise
(tú)	quisiste
(él)	quiso
(nosotros)	quisimos
(vosotros)	quisisteis
(ellos)	quisieron

FUTURE

(yo)	querré
(tú)	querrás
(él)	querrá
(nosotros)	querremos
(vosotros)	querréis
(ellos)	querrán

PRESENT SUBJUNCTIVE

(yo)	quiera
(tú)	quieras
(él)	quiera
(nosotros)	queramos
(vosotros)	queráis
(ellos)	quieran

IMPERFECT

(yo)	quería
(tú)	querías
(él)	quería
(nosotros)	queríamos
(vosotros)	queríais
(ellos)	querían

CONDITIONAL

(yo)	querría
(tú)	querrías
(él)	querría
(nosotros)	querríamos
(vosotros)	querríais
(ellos)	querrían

▶ saber

to know

IMPERATIVE

sabe
sepan

EXAMPLE PHRASES

No lo ***sé****.* I don't know.
No ***sabía*** *nada.* I didn't know anything.
El martes ***sabremos*** *los resultados.* We'll know the results on Tuesday.

PAST PARTICIPLE

sabido

GERUND

sabiendo

PRESENT

(yo)	sé
(tú)	sabes
(él)	sabe
(nosotros)	sabemos
(vosotros)	sabéis
(ellos)	saben

PRETERITE

(yo)	supe
(tú)	supiste
(él)	supo
(nosotros)	supimos
(vosotros)	supisteis
(ellos)	supieron

FUTURE

(yo)	sabré
(tú)	sabrás
(él)	sabrá
(nosotros)	sabremos
(vosotros)	sabréis
(ellos)	sabrán

PRESENT SUBJUNCTIVE

(yo)	sepa
(tú)	sepas
(él)	sepa
(nosotros)	sepamos
(vosotros)	sepáis
(ellos)	sepan

IMPERFECT

(yo)	sabía
(tú)	sabías
(él)	sabía
(nosotros)	sabíamos
(vosotros)	sabíais
(ellos)	sabían

CONDITIONAL

(yo)	sabría
(tú)	sabrías
(él)	sabría
(nosotros)	sabríamos
(vosotros)	sabríais
(ellos)	sabrían

▶ *ser*

to be

IMPERATIVE

sé
sean

EXAMPLE PHRASES

***Es** inglesa.* She's English.
*La película **era** malísima.*
The movie was awful.
***Seremos** más de cuarenta en la fiesta.*
There will be more than forty of us at the party.

PAST PARTICIPLE

sido

GERUND

siendo

PRESENT

(yo)	soy
(tú)	eres
(él)	es
(nosotros)	somos
(vosotros)	sois
(ellos)	son

PRETERITE

(yo)	fui
(tú)	fuiste
(él)	fue
(nosotros)	fuimos
(vosotros)	fuisteis
(ellos)	fueron

FUTURE

(yo)	seré
(tú)	serás
(él)	será
(nosotros)	seremos
(vosotros)	seréis
(ellos)	serán

PRESENT SUBJUNCTIVE

(yo)	sea
(tú)	seas
(él)	sea
(nosotros)	seamos
(vosotros)	seáis
(ellos)	sean

IMPERFECT

(yo)	era
(tú)	eras
(él)	era
(nosotros)	éramos
(vosotros)	erais
(ellos)	eran

CONDITIONAL

(yo)	sería
(tú)	serías
(él)	sería
(nosotros)	seríamos
(vosotros)	seríais
(ellos)	serían

▶ tener

to have

IMPERATIVE

ten
tengan

EXAMPLE PHRASES

¿***Tienes*** *hambre?* Are you hungry?
El niño ***tenía*** *diez años.*
The boy was ten years old.
Mañana ***tendremos*** *mucho trabajo.*
We'll have a lot of work tomorrow.

PAST PARTICIPLE

tenido

GERUND

teniendo

PRESENT

(yo)	tengo
(tú)	tienes
(él)	tiene
(nosotros)	tenemos
(vosotros)	tenéis
(ellos)	tienen

PRETERITE

(yo)	tuve
(tú)	tuviste
(él)	tuvo
(nosotros)	tuvimos
(vosotros)	tuvisteis
(ellos)	tuvieron

FUTURE

(yo)	tendré
(tú)	tendrás
(él)	tendrá
(nosotros)	tendremos
(vosotros)	tendréis
(ellos)	tendrán

PRESENT SUBJUNCTIVE

(yo)	tenga
(tú)	tengas
(él)	tenga
(nosotros)	tengamos
(vosotros)	tengáis
(ellos)	tengan

IMPERFECT

(yo)	tenía
(tú)	tenías
(él)	tenía
(nosotros)	teníamos
(vosotros)	teníais
(ellos)	tenían

CONDITIONAL

(yo)	tendría
(tú)	tendrías
(él)	tendría
(nosotros)	tendríamos
(vosotros)	tendríais
(ellos)	tendrían

▶ venir

to come

IMPERATIVE

ven

vengan

EXAMPLE PHRASES

*¿De dónde **vienes**?*
Where do you come from?
***Vino** en tren.* He came by train.
*Mi padre **vendrá** a las cuatro.*
My father is coming at four.

PAST PARTICIPLE

venido

GERUND

viniendo

PRESENT

(yo)	vengo
(tú)	vienes
(él)	viene
(nosotros)	venimos
(vosotros)	venís
(ellos)	vienen

PRETERITE

(yo)	vine
(tú)	viniste
(él)	vino
(nosotros)	vinimos
(vosotros)	vinisteis
(ellos)	vinieron

FUTURE

(yo)	vendré
(tú)	vendrás
(él)	vendrá
(nosotros)	vendremos
(vosotros)	vendréis
(ellos)	vendrán

PRESENT SUBJUNCTIVE

(yo)	venga
(tú)	vengas
(él)	venga
(nosotros)	vengamos
(vosotros)	vengáis
(ellos)	vengan

IMPERFECT

(yo)	venía
(tú)	venías
(él)	venía
(nosotros)	veníamos
(vosotros)	veníais
(ellos)	venían

CONDITIONAL

(yo)	vendría
(tú)	vendrías
(él)	vendría
(nosotros)	vendríamos
(vosotros)	vendríais
(ellos)	vendrían

SPANISH IRREGULAR VERB FORMS

The following list is a summary of the main forms of other irregular verbs that you are likely to come across.

1 marcar

PRETERITE	marqué, marcaste, marcó, marcamos, marcasteis, marcaron
PRESENT SUBJUNCTIVE	marque, marques, marque marquemos, marquéis, marquen

2 pagar

PRETERITE	pagué, pagaste, pagó, pagamos, pagasteis, pagaron
PRESENT SUBJUNCTIVE	pague, pagues, pague, paguemos, paguéis, paguen

3 abrazar

PRETERITE	abracé, abrazaste, abrazó, abrazamos, abrazasteis, abrazaron
PRESENT SUBJUNCTIVE	abrace, abraces, abrace, abracemos, abracéis, abracen

4 empezar

PRESENT	empiezo, empiezas, empieza, empezamos, empezáis, empiezan
PRETERITE	empecé, empezaste, empezó, empezamos, empezasteis, empezaron
PRESENT SUBJUNCTIVE	empiece, empieces, empiece, empecemos, empecéis, empiecen

5 encontrar

PRESENT	encuentro, encuentras, encuentra, encontramos, encontráis, encuentran
PRESENT SUBJUNCTIVE	encuentre, encuentres, encuentre, encontremos, encontréis, encuentren

6 pensar

PRESENT	pienso, piensas, piensa, pensamos, pensáis, piensan
PRESENT SUBJUNCTIVE	piense, pienses, piense, pensemos, penséis, piensen

7 negar

PRESENT	niego, niegas, niega, negamos, negáis niegan
PRETERITE	negué, negaste, negó, negamos, negasteis, negaron
PRESENT SUBJUNCTIVE	niegue, niegues, niegue, neguemos, neguéis, nieguen

8 colgar

PRESENT	cuelgo, cuelgas, cuelga, colgamos, colgáis, cuelgan
PRETERITE	colgué, colgaste, colgó, colgamos, colgasteis, colgaron
PRESENT SUBJUNCTIVE	cuelgue, cuelgues, cuelgue, colguemos, colguéis, cuelguen

9 almorzar

PRESENT	almuerzo, almuerzas, almuerza, almorzamos, almorzáis, almuerzan
PRETERITE	almorcé, almorzaste, almorzó, almorzamos, almorzasteis, almorzaron
PRESENT SUBJUNCTIVE	almuerce, almuerces, almuerce, almorcemos, almorcéis, almuercen

10 continuar

PRESENT	continúo, continúas, continúa, continuamos, continuáis, continúan
PRESENT SUBJUNCTIVE	continúe, continúes, continúe, continuemos, continuéis, continúen

11 jugar

PRESENT	juego, juegas, juega, jugamos, jugáis, juegan
PRETERITE	jugué, jugaste, jugó, jugamos, jugasteis, jugaron
PRESENT SUBJUNCTIVE	juegue, juegues, juegue, juguemos, juguéis, jueguen

12 enviar

PRESENT	envío, envías, envía, enviamos, enviáis, envían
PRESENT SUBJUNCTIVE	envíe, envíes, envíe, enviemos, enviéis, envíen

13 andar

PRETERITE	anduve, anduviste, anduvo, anduvimos, anduvisteis, anduvieron

14 vencer

PRESENT	venzo, vences, vence, vencemos, vencéis, vencen
PRESENT SUBJUNCTIVE	venza, venzas, venza, venzamos, venzáis, venzan

15 *conocer*

PRESENT	conozco, conoces, conoce, conocemos, conocéis, conocen
PRESENT SUBJUNCTIVE	conozca, conozcas, conozca, conozcamos, conozcáis, conozcan

16 *coger*

PRESENT	cojo, coges, coge, cogemos, cogéis, cogen
PRESENT SUBJUNCTIVE	coja, cojas, coja, cojamos, cojáis, cojan

17 *entender*

PRESENT	entiendo, entiendes, entiende, entendemos, entendéis, entienden
PRESENT SUBJUNCTIVE	entienda, entiendas, entienda, entendamos, entendáis, entiendan

18 *mover*

PRESENT	muevo, mueves, mueve, movemos, movéis, mueven
PRESENT SUBJUNCTIVE	mueva, muevas, mueva, movamos, mováis, muevan

19 *torcer*

PRESENT	tuerzo, tuerces, tuerce, torcemos, torcéis, tuercen
PRESENT SUBJUNCTIVE	tuerza, tuerzas, tuerza, torzamos, torzáis, tuerzan

20 *volver*

PRESENT	vuelvo, vuelves, vuelve, volvemos, volvéis, vuelven
PAST PARTICIPLE	vuelto
PRESENT SUBJUNCTIVE	vuelva, vuelvas, vuelva, volvamos, volváis, vuelvan

21 *oler*

PRESENT	huelo, hueles, huele, olemos, oléis, huelen
PRESENT SUBJUNCTIVE	huela, huelas, huela, olamos, oláis, huelan

22 *creer*

PRESENT	creí, creíste, creyó, creímos, creísteis, creyeron
PAST PARTICIPLE	creído
GERUND	creyendo

23 *caber*

PRESENT	quepo, cabes, cabe, cabemos, cabéis, caben
PRETERITE	cupe, cupiste, cupo, cupimos, cupisteis, cupieron
FUTURE	cabré, cabrás, cabrá, cabremos, cabréis, cabrán
PRESENT SUBJUNCTIVE	quepa, quepas, quepa, quepamos, quepáis, quepan

24 *caer*

PRESENT	caigo, caes, cae, caemos, caéis, caen
PAST PARTICIPLE	caído
PRETERITE	caí, caíste, cayó, caímos, caísteis, cayeron
PRESENT SUBJUNCTIVE	caiga, caigas, caiga, caigamos, caigáis, caigan
GERUND	cayendo

25 *poder*

PRESENT	puedo, puedes, puede, podemos, podéis, pueden
PRETERITE	pude, pudiste, pudo, pudimos, pudisteis, pudieron
FUTURE	podré, podrás, podrá, podremos, podréis, podrán
PRESENT SUBJUNCTIVE	pueda, puedas, pueda, podamos, podáis, puedan

26 *traer*

PRESENT	traigo, traes, trae, traemos, traéis, traen
PAST PARTICIPLE	traído
PRETERITE	traje, trajiste, trajo, trajimos, trajisteis, trajeron
PRESENT SUBJUNCTIVE	traiga, traigas, traiga, traigamos, traigáis, traigan
GERUND	trayendo

27 *valer*

PRESENT	valgo, vales, vale, valemos, valéis, valen
FUTURE	valdré, valdrás, valdrá, valdremos, valdréis, valdrán
PRESENT SUBJUNCTIVE	valga, valgas, valga, valgamos, valgáis, valgan

[28] *ver*

PRESENT	veo, ves, ve, vemos, veis, ven
PAST PARTICIPLE	visto
PRETERITE	vi, viste, vio, vimos, visteis, vieron
PRESENT SUBJUNCTIVE	vea, veas, vea, veamos, veáis, vean
GERUND	viendo

[29] *romper*

PAST PARTICIPLE	roto

[30] *extinguir*

PRESENT	extingo, extingues, extingue, extinguimos, extinguís, extinguen
PRESENT SUBJUNCTIVE	extinga, extingas, extinga, extingamos, extingáis, extingan

[31] *producir*

PRESENT	produzco, produces, produce, producimos, producís, producen
PRETERITE	produje, produjiste, produjo, produjimos, produjisteis, produjeron
PRESENT SUBJUNCTIVE	produzca, produzcas, produzca, produzcamos, produzcáis, produzcan

[32] *dirigir*

PRESENT	dirijo, diriges, dirige, dirigimos, dirigís, dirigen
PRESENT SUBJUNCTIVE	dirija, dirijas, dirija, dirijamos, dirijáis, dirijan

[33] *corregir*

PRESENT	corrijo, corriges, corrige, corregimos, corregís, corrigen
PRETERITE	corregí, corregiste, corrigió, corregimos, corregisteis, corrigieron
PRESENT SUBJUNCTIVE	corrija, corrijas, corrija, corrijamos, corrijáis, corrijan

[34] *sentir*

PRESENT	siento, sientes, siente, sentimos, sentís, sienten
PRETERITE	sentí, sentiste, sintió, sentimos, sentisteis, sintieron
PRESENT SUBJUNCTIVE	sienta, sientas, sienta, sintamos, sintáis, sientan
GERUND	sintiendo

[35] *adquirir*

PRESENT	adquiero, adquieres, adquiere, adquirimos, adquirís, adquieren
PRESENT SUBJUNCTIVE	adquiera, adquieras, adquiera, adquiramos, adquiráis, adquieran

[36] *pedir*

PRESENT	pido, pides, pide, pedimos, pedís, piden
PRETERITE	pedí, pediste, pidió, pedimos, pedisteis, pidieron
PRESENT SUBJUNCTIVE	pida, pidas, pida, pidamos, pidáis, pidan

[37] *dormir*

PRESENT	duermo, duermes, duerme, dormimos, dormís, duermen
PRETERITE	dormí, dormiste, durmió, dormimos, dormisteis, durmieron
PRESENT SUBJUNCTIVE	duerma, duermas, duerma, durmamos, durmáis, duerman
GERUND	durmiendo

[38] *reír*

PRESENT	río, ríes, ríe, reímos, reís, ríen
PAST PARTICIPLE	reído
PRETERITE	reí, reíste, rió, reímos, reísteis, rieron
FUTURE	reiré, reirás, reirá, reiremos, reiréis, reirán
PRESENT SUBJUNCTIVE	ría, rías, ría, riamos, riáis, rían
GERUND	riendo

[39] *construir*

PRESENT	construyo, construyes, construye, construimos, construís, construyen
PAST PARTICIPLE	construido
PRETERITE	construí, construiste, construyó, construimos, construisteis, construyeron
PRESENT SUBJUNCTIVE	construya, construyas, construya, construyamos, construyáis, construyan
GERUND	construyendo

[40] *prohibir*

PRESENT	prohíbo, prohíbes, prohíbe, prohibimos, prohibís, prohíben
PRESENT SUBJUNCTIVE	prohíba, prohíbas, prohíba, prohibamos, prohibáis, prohíban

41 oír

PRESENT	oigo, oyes, oye, oímos, oís, oyen
PAST PARTICIPLE	oído
PRETERITE	oí, oíste, oyó, oímos, oísteis, oyeron
PRESENT SUBJUNCTIVE	oiga, oigas, oiga, oigamos, oigáis, oigan
GERUND	oyendo

42 salir

PRESENT	salgo, sales, sale, salimos, salís, salen
PRETERITE	salí, saliste, salió, salimos, salisteis, salieron
FUTURE	saldré, saldrás, saldrá, saldremos, saldréis, saldrán
PRESENT SUBJUNCTIVE	salga, salgas, salga, salgamos, salgáis, salgan

43 seguir

PRESENT	sigo, sigues, sigue, seguimos, seguís, siguen
PRETERITE	seguí, seguiste, siguió, seguimos, seguisteis, siguieron
PRESENT SUBJUNCTIVE	siga, sigas, siga, sigamos, sigáis, sigan
GERUND	siguiendo

44 abrir

PAST PARTICIPLE	abierto

45 escribir

PAST PARTICIPLE	escrito

46 freír

PRESENT	frío, fríes, fríe, freímos, freís, fríen
PAST PARTICIPLE	frito
PRETERITE	freí, freíste, frió, freímos, freísteis, frieron
FUTURE	freiré, freirás, freirá, freiremos, freiréis, freirán
PRESENT SUBJUNCTIVE	fría, frías, fría, friamos, friáis, frían
GERUND	friendo

47 morir

PRESENT	muero, mueres, muere, morimos, morís, mueren
PAST PARTICIPLE	muerto
PRETERITE	morí, moriste, murió, morimos, moristeis, murieron
PRESENT SUBJUNCTIVE	muera, mueras, muera, muramos, muráis, mueran
GERUND	muriendo

48 reunir

PRESENT	reúno, reúnes, reúne, reunimos, reunís, reúnen
PRESENT SUBJUNCTIVE	reúna, reúnas, reúna, reunamos, reunáis, reúnan

49 reñir

PRESENT	riño, riñes, riñe, reñimos, reñís, riñen
PRETERITE	reñí, reñiste, riñó, reñimos, reñisteis, riñeron
PRESENT SUBJUNCTIVE	riña, riñas, riña, riñamos, riñáis, riñan
GERUND	riñendo

50 gruñir

PRETERITE	gruñí, gruñiste, gruñó, gruñimos, gruñisteis, gruñeron
GERUND	gruñendo

51 lucir

PRESENT	luzco, luces, luce, lucimos, lucís, lucen
PRESENT SUBJUNCTIVE	luzca, luzcas, luzca, luzcamos, luzcáis, luzcan

52 imprimir

PAST PARTICIPLE	impreso

NB

averiguar, amortiguar: like **hablar** except **u** of the stem is written **ü** before **e**: 1st person preterite **averigüe**, and all the present subjunctive **averigüe, averigües, averigüe, averigüemos, averigüéis, averigüen**

zurcir, fruncir: like **vivir** except stem consonant **c** is written **z** before **a** and **o**: 1st person present **zurzo**, 1st/3rd person subjunctive **zurza**

OTHER IRREGULAR VERBS

The numbers on this list refer to model numbers shown on pages 342-345. Verbs described as FULL PAGE are treated in detail on pages 326-341.

abastecer	15
abrazar	3
abrigar	2
abrir	44
abstenerse	see TENER
acentuarse	10
acercar	1
acertar	6
acoger	16
acordar	5
acostarse	5
actuar	10
acurrucarse	1
adelgazar	3
adquirir	35
advertir	34
agradecer	15
ahogarse	2
ahorcar	1
alargar	2
alcanzar	3
aliarse	12
almorzar	9
alzar	3
amanecer	15
amargar	2
amenazar	3
amortiguar	see NB
ampliar	12
analizar	3
andar	13
anochecer	15
apagar	2
aparcar	1
aparecer	15
apetecer	15
aplazar	3
aplicar	1
apostar	5
apretar	6
aprobar	5
arrancar	1
arrepentirse	34
arriesgarse	2
arrugarse	2
ascender	17
atacar	1
atardecer	15
atender	17
aterrizar	3
atracar	1
atraer	26
atravesar	6
autorizar	3
avanzar	3
aventar	6
avergonzar	3+5
averiarse	12
averiguar	See NB
barnizar	3
bendecir	see DECIR
bostezar	3
brincar	1
buscar	1
caber	23
caducar	1
caer	24
cagar	2
calcar	1
calentar	6
calificar	1
cargar	2
cascar	1
castigar	2
cazar	3
cerrar	6
checar	1
chirriar	12
chocar	1
clasificar	1
cocer	19
coger	16
colgar	8
colocar	1
colonizar	3
compenzar	17
compadecer	15
competir	36
complacer	15
complicar	1
componer	see PONER
comprobar	5
comunicar	1
concertar	6
conducir	31
confesar	6
confiar	12
conmover	18
conocer	15
conseguir	43
consentir	34
consolar	5
construir	39
contar	5
contener	see TENER
continuar	10
contradecir	see DECIR
contraer	26
contribuir	39
convencer	14
convenir	see VENIR
convertir	34
convocar	1
corregir	33
costar	5
crecer	15
creer	22
criar	12
criticar	1
cruzar	3
cubrir	44
dar	FULL PAGE
decir	FULL PAGE
dedicar	1
deducir	31
defender	17
demostrar	5
derretir	36
desafiar	12
desahogarse	2
desaparecer	15
descalzarse	3
descargar	2
descender	17
descolgar	8
descomponerse	see PONER
desconcertar	6
desconfiar	12
descontar	5
describir	45
descubrir	44
desembarcar	1
desembocar	1
desempacar	1
desenroscar	1
desenvolver	20
deshacer	see HACER
deslizarse	3
desobedecer	15
despedir	36
despegar	2
desperezarse	3
despertar	6
desplegar	7
destacar	1
desteñir	49
destrozar	3
destruir	39
desviar	12
detener	see TENER
devolver	20
dialogar	2
digerir	34

LA CONJUGACIÓN INGLESA

▶ ÍNDICE

LA CONJUGACIÓN INGLESA

Las tablas de verbos que siguen a esta breve introducción del verbo en inglé muestran la conjugación de un modelo de verbo regular (**to work**), de los verbo irregulares o auxiliares **to do**, **to have** y **to be** y del auxiliar modal **can**.

En la parte superior de cada modelo aparecen las formas básicas de infinitivo gerundio y participio, así como algunos ejemplos del uso de cada verbo, demá de la forma de pretérito perfecto y el futuro simple y continuo, de cuy conjugación se puede deducir el resto de las formas correspondientes a cada un de las personas verbales.

Al final de esta sección encontraremos las formas afirmativas del PRESENTE del PASADO y del PARTICIPIO de los verbos irregulares.

▶ VERBOS REGULARES E IRREGULARES – PRESENTE SIMPLE

La forma del PRESENTE SIMPLE AFIRMATIVO de la mayoría de los verbos ingle ses es la misma que la de infinitivo para todas las personas verbales, salvo par la tercera persona del singular, que añade normalmente una **-s**:

to say – I say, he say**s**
to speak – I speak, he speak**s**

Pero si un verbo acaba en **s**, **-sh**, **-ch**, o en **x**, se le añade **-es**.

Y si un verbo acaba en CONSONATE + **-y**, se cambia la **y** por **i** y se le añade **-es**

to pass – he pass**es**
to try – he tr**ies**

La negación se forma con **don't** o **do not** delante del INFINITIVO sin *to* par todas las personas, excepto para la tercera persona singular, que utiliza **doesn'** o **does not**, también con el INFINITIVO sin *to*:

to say – I **don't** *o* **do not** say, he **doesn't** *o* **does not** say, etc.
to try – I **don't** *o* **do not** try, he **doesn't** *o* **does not** try, etc.

La interrogación se forma con **do** y el INFINITIVO sin *to* para todas las personas excepto para la tercera persona del singular, que utiliza **does** con el INFINITIVO sin *to*:

to speak – **do** you speak English? **does** he speak English? etc.

▶ PASADO SIMPLE

En inglés, el PASADO SIMPLE AFIRMATIVO de los verbos regulares se suel formar, para todas las personas, añadiendo la terminación **-ed** a la forma d INFINITIVO:

to scream – I scream**ed**, he scream**ed**, etc.

Si un verbo acaba en **-e**, se añada solamente **-d**:

to love – we love**d**, etc.

Si un verbo acaba en una sola VOCAL+CONSONANTE y además consta de una sola sílaba o acaba en sílaba tónica, la consonante se duplica antes de añadir **-ed**:

to shop – they shop**ped**, etc **PERO** to shout – they shout**ed**, etc.
to sob – she sob**bed**, etc **PERO** to seem – it seem**ed**, etc.
to refer – they refer**red**, etc **PERO** to fear – they fear**ed**, etc.

Si un verbo acaba en una sola vocal + -l, no cambia:

to peel – they peel**ed**, etc.

La terminación CONSONANTE + -y se transforma en **-ied**:

to cry – she cr**ied**, etc.
to worry – we worr**ied**, etc.

En el caso de los verbos irregulares ver la lista de las páginas 359–361 en la que se dan las tres formas de cada verbo. La segunda forma es la del PASADO AFIRMATIVO, que sirve para todas las personas.

to swim, **swam**, swum – he **swam**, they **swam**, etc.

Las formas irregulares también aparecen en las entradas correspondientes a verbos en la parte inglés-español del diccionario.

Para la forma negativa se emplea, para todas las personas, **didn't** o **did not** seguido del INFINITIVO sin *to*, tanto si el verbo es regular como irregular:

to say – I **didn't** o **did not** say, etc.
to go – I **didn't** o **did not** go, etc.

Para la forma interrogativa se emplea **did** seguido del INFINITIVO sin *to* con todas las personas tanto si el verbo es regular como irregular:

to scream – **did** she scream? etc.
to swim – **did** they swim? etc.

▶ OTROS TIEMPOS, VERBOS AUXILIARES

Hay otros tiempos verbales que se forman con los verbos auxiliares como **have**, **will** y **be**, que normalmente se contraen en inglés hablado.

El PRETÉRITO PERFECTO se forma con la forma conjugada del verbo **to have** (ver el modelo de la página 356), seguida del PARTICIPIO del verbo principal:

to work

AFIRMATIVO:	I**'ve** *o* I **have** work**ed**, he**'s** *o* he **has** work**ed**, etc.
NEGATIVO:	I **haven't** *o* I **have not** work**ed**, he **hasn't** *o* he **has not** work**ed**, etc.
INTERROGATIVO:	**have** you work**ed**? **has** he work**ed**? etc.

to swim

AFIRMATIVO:	I**'ve** *o* I **have swum**, he**'s** *o* he **has swum**, etc.
NEGATIVO:	I **haven't** *o* I **have not swum**, he **hasn't** *o* he **has not swum**, etc.
INTERROGATIVO:	**have** you **swum**? **has** he **swum**? etc.

Hay que tener en cuenta que los PARTICIPIOS de los verbos regulares acaban en **-ed** y se corresponden con las formas del PASADO SIMPLE. Ver el PARTICIPIO de los verbos irregulares en la tercera columna de las listas de las páginas 359–361.

Para formar el FUTURO, hay que usar el VERBO AUXILIAR **will** delante de la forma de INFINITIVO sin *to* del verbo que queremos conjugar:

to work

AFIRMATIVO: I'**ll** *o* I **will** work, they'**ll** *o* they **will** work, etc.
NEGATIVO: I **won't** *o* I **will not** work, he **won't** *o* he **will not** work, etc.
INTERROGATIVO: **will** you work? **will** he work? etc.

Para formar los tiempos CONTINUOS, se utiliza la forma conjugada del verbo **to be** (habitualmente contraída) seguida del GERUNDIO:

to work

PRESENTE AFIRMATIVO: I'**m** *o* I **am** work**ing**, he'**s** *o* he **is** work**ing**, etc.
PRESENTE NEGATIVO: I'**m not** *o* I **am not** work**ing**, he'**s not** *o* he **is not** work**ing**, etc.
PRESENTE INTERROGATIVO: **are** you work**ing**? **is** he work**ing**? etc.

PASADO AFIRMATIVO: I **was** work**ing**, you **were** work**ing**, etc.
PASADO NEGATIVO: I **wasn't** *o* I **was not** work**ing**, he **wasn't** *o* he **was not** work**ing**, etc.
PASADO INTERROGATIVO: **were** you work**ing**? **was** he work**ing**? etc.

Tal como se ha visto anteriormente, la forma negativa de los AUXILIARES y del verbo **to be** se forma colocando **not** o su forma contraída entre el AUXILIAR y el verbo PRINCIPAL. La forma INTERROGATIVA se forma invirtiendo el orden del AUXILIAR y el SUJETO.

▶ FORMACIÓN DEL GERUNDIO

En inglés, el GERUNDIO de todos los verbos, tanto si son regulares como si no, se forma habitualmente añadiendo la terminación **-ing** a la forma de INFINITIVO:

to scream – scream**ing**

Si el verbo acaba en una sola **-e**, ésta desaparece al añadir **-ing**:

to love – lov**ing**

Si el verbo acaba en una sola VOCAL+CONSONANTE y consta de una sola sílaba o acaba en sílaba tónica, la consonante final se duplica antes de añadir **-ing**:

to shop – shop**ping** **PERO** to shout – shout**ing**
to sob – sob**bing** **PERO** to seem – seem**ing**
to refer – refer**ring** **PERO** to fear – fear**ing**

Si un verbo acaba en una sola VOCAL+-l, no cambia:

to feel – feel**ing**

▶ USO DE LAS FORMAS SIMPLES Y CONTINUAS

En general, las formas continuas se utilizan para describir una acción que transcurre o transcurría en un momento concreto:

Don't distract him, he **is preparing** for his exam.
This time tomorrow, she **will be traveling** down south.
When he came into the room, I **was watching** TV.

Las formas continuas también sirven para mostrar que una acción todavía no ha terminado o que se trata de una situación temporal:

The doorbell rang while I **was having** a shower.
I **am working** with Steve and Will at the moment.

Las formas simples se utilizan para referirse a acciones habituales y a hechos ocurridos en un momento concreto, en el caso del pasado:

I **visited** my grandmother regularly.
I **get up** at seven every morning.
He **cut** his knee when he fell.

Comparar las oraciones siguientes fijándose en el uso de las formas verbales simples y continuas:

I **was speaking** to my friend when the phone rang.
I **spoke** to my friend and then called my mother.

John **reads** the paper at the breakfast table every morning.
John **is** just **reading** the paper.

▶ to work

trabajar

GERUNDIO

working

EJEMPLOS

She **works** *in a bookstore.*
Trabaja en una tienda.
Don't **work** *so hard.*
No trabajes tanto.
He **worked** *hard last month.*
Trabajó mucho el mes pasado.

PARTICIPIO

worked

PRETÉRITO PERFECTO

have/has worked

FUTURO

will work

FUTURO CONTINUO

will be working

PRESENTE SIMPLE

I	work
you	work
he	works
we	work
you	work
they	work

PRESENTE CONTINUO

I	am working
you	are working
he	is working
we	are working
you	are working
they	are working

PASADO SIMPLE

I	worked
you	worked
he	worked
we	worked
you	worked
they	worked

PASADO CONTINUO

I	was working
you	were working
he	was working
we	were working
you	were working
they	were working

▶ to do

hacer

GERUNDIO

doing

EJEMPLOS

What shall we **do** *now?*
¿Ahora qué hacemos?
Where **did** *you go on vacation?*
¿Dónde te fuiste de vacaciones?
*He***'s doing** *his homework.*
Está haciendo las tareas.

PARTICIPIO

done

PRETÉRITO PERFECTO

have/has done

FUTURO SIMPLE

will do

FUTURO CONTINUO

will be doing

PRESENTE SIMPLE

I	do
you	do
he	does
we	do
you	do
they	do

PASADO SIMPLE

I	did
you	did
he	did
we	did
you	did
they	did

PRESENTE CONTINUO

I	am doing
you	are doing
he	is doing
we	are doing
you	are doing
they	are doing

PASADO CONTINUO

I	was doing
you	were doing
he	was doing
we	were doing
you	were doing
they	were doing

▶ to have

tener

GERUNDIO	*EJEMPLOS*
having	*She* **has** *brown hair.* Tiene el pelo castaño. *I* **had** *two eggs for breakfast.* Me comí dos huevos para el desayuno. *We'***re having** *a party tonight.* Esta noche vamos a tener una fiesta.

PARTICIPIO	*PRETÉRITO PERFECTO*
had	have/has had

FUTURO SIMPLE	*FUTURO CONTINUO*
will have	will be having

PRESENTE SIMPLE

I	have
you	have
he	has
we	have
you	have
they	have

PRESENTE CONTINUO

I	am having
you	are having
he	is having
we	are having
you	are having
they	are having

PASADO SIMPLE

I	had
you	had
he	had
we	had
you	had
they	had

PASADO CONTINUO

I	was having
you	were having
he	was having
we	were having
you	were having
they	were having

▶ to be

ser

GERUNDIO

being

EJEMPLOS

How **are** *you?* ¿Cómo estás?
She **is** *thirteen years old.* Tiene trece años.
*It'***s** *cold today*. Hace frío hoy.
*I'***m** *hungry*. Tengo hambre.

PARTICIPIO

been

PRETÉRITO PERFECTO

have/has been

FUTURO SIMPLE

will be

FUTURO CONTINUO

will be being

PRESENTE SIMPLE

I	am
you	are
he	is
we	are
you	are
they	are

PASADO SIMPLE

I	was
you	were
he	was
we	were
you	were
they	were

PRESENTE CONTINUO

I	am being
you	are being
he	is being
we	are being
you	are being
they	are being

PASADO CONTINUO

I	was being
you	were being
he	was being
we	were being
you	were being
they	were being

▶ can

poder, saber

EJEMPLOS

She **can** *swim well.* Sabe nadar bien.
I **can***'t speak French.* No sé hablar francés.
We **could***n't get tickets.* No pudimos conseguir entradas.

PRESENTE SIMPLE		*CONDICIONAL/PASADO SIMPLE*	
I	can	I	could
you	can	you	could
he	can	he	could
we	can	we	could
you	can	you	could
they	can	they	could

VERBOS IRREGULARES EN INGLÉS

PRESENTE	PRETÉRITO	PARTICIPIO DE PASADO
awake	awoke	awoken
be (am, is, are; being)	was, were	been
bear	bore	born(e)
beat	beat	beaten
become	became	become
begin	began	begun
bend	bent	bent
bet	bet, betted	bet, betted
bite	bit	bitten
bleed	bled	bled
blow	blew	blown
break	broke	broken
breed	bred	bred
bring	brought	brought
build	built	built
burst	burst	burst
buy	bought	bought
can	could	(been able)
catch	caught	caught
choose	chose	chosen
come	came	come
cost	cost	cost
creep	crept	crept
cut	cut	cut
deal	dealt	dealt
dig	dug	dug
do (does)	did	done
draw	drew	drawn
drink	drank	drunk
drive	drove	driven
eat	ate	eaten
fall	fell	fallen
feed	fed	fed
feel	felt	felt
fight	fought	fought
find	found	found
fling	flung	flung
fly	flew	flown
forbid	forbad(e)	forbidden
forget	forgot	forgotten
forgive	forgave	forgiven
freeze	froze	frozen
get	got	gotten
give	gave	given

PRESENTE	PRETÉRITO	PARTICIPIO DE PASADO
go (goes)	went	gone
grind	ground	ground
grow	grew	grown
hang	hung	hung
hang (*execute*)	hanged	hanged
have	had	had
hear	heard	heard
hide	hid	hidden
hit	hit	hit
hold	held	held
hurt	hurt	hurt
keep	kept	kept
kneel	kneeled, knelt	knelt, kneeled
know	knew	known
lay	laid	laid
lead	led	led
leap	leaped, leapt	leapt, leaped
leave	left	left
lend	lent	lent
let	let	let
lie (lying)	lay	lain
light	lit, lighted	lit, lighted
lose	lost	lost
make	made	made
may	might	—
mean	meant	meant
meet	met	met
mistake	mistook	mistaken
mow	mowed	mown, mowed
must	(had to)	(had to)
pay	paid	paid
put	put	put
quit	quit, quitted	quit, quitted
read	read	read
rid	rid	rid
ride	rode	ridden
ring	rang	rung
rise	rose	risen
run	ran	run
say	said	said
see	saw	seen
sell	sold	sold
send	sent	sent
set	set	set
sew	sewed	sewn
shake	shook	shaken
shine	shone	shone

PRESENTE	PRETÉRITO	PARTICIPIO DE PASADO
shoot	shot	shot
show	showed	shown
shrink	shrank	shrunk
shut	shut	shut
sing	sang	sung
sink	sank	sunk
sit	sat	sat
sleep	slept	slept
slide	slid	slid
speak	spoke	spoken
speed	sped, speeded	sped, speeded
spend	spent	spent
spit	spat	spat
spread	spread	spread
stand	stood	stood
steal	stole	stolen
stick	stuck	stuck
sting	stung	stung
stink	stank	stunk
strike	struck	struck
swear	swore	sworn
sweep	swept	swept
swim	swam	swum
swing	swung	swung
take	took	taken
teach	taught	taught
tear	tore	torn
tell	told	told
think	thought	thought
throw	threw	thrown
tread	trod	trodden
wake	woke, waked	woken, waked
wear	wore	worn
weep	wept	wept
win	won	won
wind	wound	wound
write	wrote	written

A

a [eɪ,ə] INDEFINITE ARTICLE

*Use **un** for masculine nouns, **una** for feminine nouns.*

1 un MASC ◇ *a book* un libro

2 una FEM ◇ *an apple* una manzana

*Sometimes **a** is not translated, particularly if referring to professions.*

◇ *He's a butcher.* Es carnicero. ◇ *I don't have a car.* No tengo carro. ◇ *a year ago* hace un año

◆ **a hundred dollars** cien dólares

◆ **once a week** una vez a la semana

◆ **70 miles an hour** 70 millas por hora

◆ **30 cents a kilo** 30 centavos el kilo

to **abandon** [ə'bændən] VERB

abandonar

abbey ['æbi] NOUN

la abadía

abbreviation [əbri:vi'eɪʃən] NOUN

la abreviatura

ability [ə'bɪləti] NOUN (PL **abilities**)

la capacidad

◆ **to have the ability to do something** tener* la capacidad de hacer algo

able ['eɪbəl] ADJECTIVE

◆ **to be able to do something** poder* hacer algo ◇ *Will you be able to come on Saturday?* ¿Puedes venir el sábado?

to **abolish** [ə'bɑ:lɪʃ] VERB

abolir*

abortion [ə'bɔ:rʃən] NOUN

el aborto

◆ **to have an abortion** abortar

about [ə'baut] PREPOSITION, ADVERB

1 sobre ◇ *a book about New England* un libro sobre Nueva Inglaterra ◇ *I don't know anything about it.* No sé nada sobre eso.

◆ **I'm phoning you about tomorrow's meeting.** Te llamo por lo de la reunión de mañana.

◆ **What's it about?** ¿De qué trata?

2 unos (FEM unas) (*approximately*) ◇ *It takes about 10 hours.* Se tarda unas 10 horas.

◆ **at about 11 o'clock** sobre las 11

◆ **It costs about $50.** Cuesta alrededor de 50 dólares.

◆ **What about me?** ¿Y yo?

◆ **to be about to do something** estar* a punto de hacer algo ◇ *I was about to go out.* Estaba a punto de salir.

◆ **How about going to the movies?** ¿Qué tal si vamos al cine?

above [ə'bʌv] PREPOSITION, ADVERB

*When something is located above something, use **encima de**. When there is movement involved, use **por encima de**.*

1 encima de ◇ *There was a picture above the fireplace.* Había un cuadro encima de la chimenea.

2 por encima de ◇ *He put his hands above his head.* Puso las manos por encima de la cabeza.

◆ **the apartment above** el departamento de arriba

◆ **above all** sobre todo

3 más de (*more than*) ◇ *above 40 degrees* más de 40 grados

abroad [ə'brɑ:d] ADVERB

◆ **to go abroad** ir* al extranjero

◆ **to live abroad** vivir en el extranjero

abrupt [ə'brʌpt] ADJECTIVE

1 brusco ◇ *He was a bit abrupt with me.* Fue un poco brusco conmigo.

2 repentino ◇ *His abrupt departure aroused suspicion.* Su repentina partida levantó sospechas.

abruptly [ə'brʌptli] ADVERB

de repente ◇ *He got up abruptly.* Se levantó de repente.

absence ['æbsəns] NOUN

1 la ausencia (*of people*)

2 la falta (*of things*)

◆ **absence from school** la falta de asistencia a clase

absent ['æbsənt] ADJECTIVE

ausente

absent-minded ['æbsənt'maɪndɪd] ADJECTIVE

distraído

absolutely [æbsə'lu:tli] ADVERB

totalmente ◇ *I absolutely refuse to do it.* Me niego totalmente a hacerlo.

◆ **Jill is absolutely right.** Jill tiene toda la razón.

◆ **It's absolutely delicious!** ¡Está riquísimo!

◆ **They did absolutely nothing to help him.** No hicieron absolutamente nada para ayudarle.

◆ **Do you think it's a good idea? – Absolutely!** ¿Te parece una buena idea? – ¡Desde luego!

absorbed [əb'zɔ:rbd] ADJECTIVE

◆ **to be absorbed in something** estar* absorto en algo

absorbent cotton [əb'zɔ:rbent'kɑ:tn] NOUN

el algodón (PL los algodones)

absurd [əb'sɜ:rd] ADJECTIVE

absurdo

abuse [ə'bju:s] NOUN

see also **abuse** VERB

el abuso (*of power*)

◆ **to shout abuse at somebody** insultar a alguien

to **abuse** [ə'bju:z] VERB

see also **abuse** NOUN

maltratar ◇ *abused children* niños maltratados

abusive [ə'bju:sɪv] ADJECTIVE

◆ **He became abusive.** Se puso a insultar.

academic [ækə'dɛmɪk] ADJECTIVE

académico ◇ *the academic year* el año académico

academy [ə'kædəmi] NOUN (PL **academies**)

la academia ◇ *a military academy* una

☞

academia militar
◆ **an academy of music** un conservatorio

to **accelerate** [æk'sɛləreɪt] VERB
acelerar

accelerator [æk'sɛləreɪtər] NOUN
el acelerador

accent ['æksɛnt] NOUN
el acento ◇ *He has a Spanish accent.* Tiene acento español.

to **accept** [æk'sɛpt] VERB
aceptar ◇ *She accepted the offer.* Aceptó la oferta.
◆ **to accept responsibility for something** asumir la responsabilidad de algo
◆ **This vending machine accepts all coins.** Esta máquina expendedora admite todo tipo de monedas.

acceptable [æk'sɛptəbəl] ADJECTIVE
aceptable

access ['æksɛs] NOUN
el acceso ◇ *He has access to confidential information.* Tiene acceso a información reservada.
◆ **Her ex-husband has access to the children.** Su ex marido puede ver a los niños.

accessible [æk'sɛsəbəl] ADJECTIVE
accesible

accessory [æk'sɛsəri] NOUN (PL **accessories**)
el accesorio ◇ *fashion accessories* los accesorios en la moda

accident ['æksɪdənt] NOUN
el accidente ◇ *to have an accident* sufrir un accidente
◆ **by accident (1)** por casualidad ◇ *They made the discovery by accident.* Lo descubrieron por casualidad.
◆ **by accident (2)** sin querer* ◇ *The burglar killed him by accident.* El ladrón lo mató sin querer.

accidental [æksɪ'dɛntl] ADJECTIVE
◆ **I didn't do it deliberately; it was accidental.** No lo hice adrede, fue sin querer*.
◆ **accidental death** la muerte por accidente

to **accommodate** [ə'kɑːmədeɪt] VERB
alojar

accommodations [əkɑːmə'deɪʃənz] PL NOUN
el alojamiento SING

to **accompany** [ə'kʌmpəni] VERB (**accompanied, accompanied**)
acompañar

accord [ə'kɔːrd] NOUN
◆ **of his own accord** por su cuenta

accordingly [ə'kɔːrdɪŋli] ADVERB
en consecuencia (*consequently*)

according to [ə'kɔːrdɪŋˌtuː] PREPOSITION
según ◇ *According to him, everyone had gone.* Según él, todos se habían ido.

account [ə'kaunt] NOUN
[1] la cuenta ◇ *a bank account* una cuenta bancaria
[2] la factura (*invoice*)
◆ **to do the accounts** llevar la contabilidad
[3] el informe ◇ *He gave a detailed account of what happened.* Dio un informe detallado de lo ocurrido.
◆ **to take something into account** tener* algo en cuenta
◆ **by all accounts** a decir* de todos
◆ **on account of** a causa de ◇ *We couldn't go out on account of the bad weather.* No pudimos salir a causa del mal tiempo.

to **account for** [ə'kauntˌfɔːr] VERB
explicar* ◇ *If she was ill, that would account for her poor results.* Si estuviera enferma, se explicarían sus malos resultados.

accountable [ə'kauntəbəl] ADJECTIVE
◆ **to be accountable to someone** responder ante alguien

accountancy [ə'kauntənsi] NOUN
la contabilidad

accountant [ə'kauntənt] NOUN
el contador
la contadora
◇ *She's an accountant.* Es contadora.

accuracy ['ækjurəsi] NOUN
la exactitud

accurate ['ækjurɪt] ADJECTIVE
exacto

accurately ['ækjurɪtli] ADVERB
con exactitud

accusation [ækju'zeɪʃən] NOUN
la acusación (PL las acusaciones)

to **accuse** [ə'kjuːz] VERB
◆ **to accuse somebody of something** acusar a alguien de algo ◇ *The police are accusing her of murder.* La policía la acusa de asesinato.

ace [eɪs] NOUN
el as ◇ *the ace of hearts* el as de corazones

ache [eɪk] NOUN
see also **ache** VERB
el dolor ◇ *stomachache* dolor de estómago

to **ache** [eɪk] VERB
see also **ache** NOUN
◆ **My leg is aching.** Me duele la pierna.

to **achieve** [ə'tʃiːv] VERB
conseguir*

achievement [ə'tʃiːvmənt] NOUN
el logro ◇ *That was quite an achievement.* Aquello fue todo un logro.

acid ['æsɪd] NOUN
el ácido

acid rain ['æsɪd'reɪn] NOUN
la lluvia ácida

acne ['ækni] NOUN
el acné

to **acquit** [ə'kwɪt] VERB
absolver*

acre ['eɪkər] NOUN
el acre

Equivale a 4.047 metros cuadrados.

acrobat ['ækrəbæt] NOUN
el/la acróbata

across [ə'krɑːs] PREPOSITION, ADVERB
[1] al otro lado de ◇ *He lives across the river.* Vive al otro lado del río.
[2] a través de ◇ *an expedition across the Sahara* una expedición a través del Sahara
◆ **the store across the road** la tienda en la acera de enfrente
◆ **to run across the road** cruzar* la calle corriendo
◆ **across from** frente a ◇ *He sat down across from her.* Se sentó frente a ella.

ACT [akt] NOUN

> ℹ **ACT** *es la abreviatura de* **American College Testing** *que es una prueba de aptitud estándar, a nivel nacional, y que por lo general hacen los estudiantes que desean entrar a la universidad por primera vez.*

act [ækt] NOUN
see also **act** VERB
el acto ◇ *in the first act* en el primer acto
◆ **It was all an act.** Era todo un cuento.
◆ **an act of Congress** una ley aprobada por el Congreso

to **act** [ækt] VERB
see also **act** NOUN
actuar* ◇ *The police acted quickly.* La policía actuó con rapidez. ◇ *He acts really well.* Actúa muy bien.
◆ **She's acting the part of Juliet.** Interpreta el papel de Julieta.
◆ **She acts as his interpreter.** Ella le hace de intérprete.

to **act up** [ækt'ʌp] VERB
◆ **The engine is acting up again.** El motor está haciendo de las suyas otra vez.

action ['ækʃən] NOUN
la acción (PL las acciones) ◇ *The movie was full of action.* Era una película con mucha acción.
◆ **to take action against** tomar medidas contra

active ['æktɪv] ADJECTIVE
activo ◇ *He's a very active person.* Es una persona muy activa.
◆ **an active volcano** un volcán en actividad

activity [æk'tɪvəti] NOUN (PL **activities**)
la actividad ◇ *outdoor activities* actividades al aire libre

actor ['æktər] NOUN
el actor

actress ['æktrɪs] NOUN (PL **actresses**)
la actriz (PL las actrices)

actual ['æktʃuəl] ADJECTIVE
real ◇ *The movie is based on actual events.* La película está basada en hechos reales.
Be careful not to translate ***actual*** *by the Spanish word* ***actual****.*

actually ['æktʃuəli] ADVERB
[1] realmente ◇ *Did it actually happen?* ¿Ocurrió realmente?
◆ **You only pay for the electricity you actually use.** Sólo pagas la electricidad que consumes.
[2] de hecho ◇ *I was so bored I actually fell asleep!* ¡Me aburría tanto que de hecho me quedé dormido!
◆ **Fiona's awful, isn't she? – Actually, I quite like her.** Fiona es una antipática, ¿verdad? – Pues a mí me cae bien.
◆ **Actually, I don't know him at all.** La verdad es que no lo conozco nada.

acupuncture ['ækjupʌŋktʃər] NOUN
la acupuntura

AD [eɪ'diː] ABBREVIATION (= *Anno Domini*)
d.C. (= después de Cristo) ◇ *in 800 AD* en el año 800 d.C.

ad ['æd] NOUN
el anuncio

to **adapt** [ə'dæpt] VERB
adaptar ◇ *His novel was adapted for television.* Su novela fue adaptada para la televisión.
◆ **to adapt to something** adaptarse a algo ◇ *He adapted to his new school very quickly.* Se adaptó a su nuevo colegio muy rápidamente.

adaptor [ə'dæptər] NOUN
[1] el ladrón (PL los ladrones) (*for several plugs*)
[2] el adaptador (*for different types of plugs*)

to **add** [æd] VERB
añadir ◇ *Add more flour to the dough.* Añada más harina a la masa.

to **add up** [æd'ʌp] VERB
sumar ◇ *Add up the figures.* Suma las cifras.

addict ['ædɪkt] NOUN
el adicto
la adicta
◆ **a drug addict** un drogadicto ◇ *She's a drug addict.* Es drogadicta.
◆ **Martin's a soccer addict.** Martin es un fanático del fútbol.

addicted [ə'dɪktɪd] ADJECTIVE
◆ **to be addicted to drugs** ser* drogadicto
◆ **She's addicted to heroin.** Es heroinómana.
◆ **She's addicted to soaps.** Es una apasionada de las telenovelas.

addition [ə'dɪʃən] NOUN
◆ **in addition** además ◇ *He bought a new car and, in addition, a motorbike.* Se compró un carro nuevo y además una moto.
◆ **in addition to** además de ◇ *In addition to the price of the CD, there's a charge for postage.* Además del precio del CD, hay un recargo por los gastos de envío.

address ['ædrɛs] NOUN (PL **addresses**)
la dirección (PL las direcciones)

adjective ['ædʒɪktɪv] NOUN
el adjetivo

to **adjust** [ə'dʒʌst] VERB
1 regular (*temperature, height*) ◇ *You can adjust the height of the chair.* Se puede regular la altura de la silla.
2 ajustar (*mechanism*) ◇ *It can be easily adjusted using a screwdriver.* Se ajusta fácilmente con un destornillador.
◆ **to adjust to something** adaptarse a algo ◇ *He adjusted to his new school very quickly.* Se adaptó a su nuevo colegio muy rápidamente.

adjustable [ə'dʒʌstəbəl] ADJECTIVE
regulable

administration [ædmɪnɪ'streɪʃən] NOUN
la administración (PL las administraciones)

admiral ['ædmərəl] NOUN
el almirante

to **admire** [æd'maɪər] VERB
admirar

admission [æd'mɪʃən] NOUN
la entrada ◇ *"admission free"* "entrada gratuita"

to **admit** [æd'mɪt] VERB
reconocer* ◇ *I must admit that I've never heard of him.* Tengo que reconocer que nunca he oído hablar de él. ◇ *He admitted that he'd done it.* Reconoció que lo había hecho.

adolescent [ædl'ɛsənt] NOUN
el/la adolescente

to **adopt** [ə'dɑ:pt] VERB
adoptar

adopted [ə'dɑ:ptɪd] ADJECTIVE
adoptivo

adoption [ə'dɑ:pʃən] NOUN
la adopción (PL las adopciones)

to **adore** [ə'dɔ:r] VERB
adorar

adult [ə'dʌlt] NOUN
el adulto
la adulta
◆ **adult education** la educación de adultos

to **advance** [əd'væns] VERB
see also **advance** NOUN
avanzar* ◇ *The troops are advancing.* Las tropas avanzan. ◇ *Technology has advanced a lot.* La tecnología ha avanzado mucho.

advance [əd'væns] NOUN
see also **advance** VERB
◆ **in advance** con antelación ◇ *They bought the tickets a month in advance.* Compraron los billetes con un mes de antelación.

advance booking [əd'væns'bukɪŋ] NOUN
◆ **Advance booking is essential.** Es indispensable reservar con antelación.

advanced [əd'vænst] ADJECTIVE
avanzado

advantage [əd'væntɪdʒ] NOUN
la ventaja ◇ *Going to college has many advantages.* Ir a la universidad tiene muchas ventajas.
◆ **to take advantage of something** aprovechar algo ◇ *He took advantage of his day off to have a rest.* Aprovechó su día libre para descansar.
◆ **to take advantage of somebody** aprovecharse de alguien ◇ *The company was taking advantage of its employees.* La compañía se aprovechaba de sus empleados.

adventure [əd'vɛntʃər] NOUN
la aventura

adverb ['ædvɜ:rb] NOUN
el adverbio

to **advertise** ['ædvərtaɪz] VERB
anunciar ◇ *Jobs are advertised in the papers.* Las ofertas de empleo se anuncian en los periódicos.

advertisement [ædvər'taɪzmənt] NOUN
el anuncio

advertising ['ædvərtaɪzɪŋ] NOUN
la publicidad

advice [əd'vaɪs] NOUN
el consejo ◇ *to ask for advice* pedir* consejo ◇ *I'd like to ask your advice.* Quería pedirte consejo.
◆ **to give somebody advice** aconsejar a alguien
◆ **a piece of advice** un consejo ◇ *He gave me a good piece of advice.* Me dio un buen consejo.

to **advise** [əd'vaɪz] VERB
aconsejar ◇ *He advised me to wait.* Me aconsejó que esperara. ◇ *He advised me not to go there.* Me aconsejó que no fuera.
***aconsejar que** has to be followed by a verb in the subjunctive.*

aerobics [ɛ'roubɪks] NOUN
aerobic MASC
aerobics MASC *Mexico*
◇ *I do aerobics.* Hago aerobic.

aerosol ['ɛrəsɑ:l] NOUN
el aerosol

affair [ə'fɛər] NOUN
1 la aventura ◇ *to have an affair with somebody* tener* una aventura con alguien
2 el asunto ◇ *The government has mishandled the affair.* El gobierno ha llevado mal el asunto.

to **affect** [ə'fɛkt] VERB
afectar

affectionate [ə'fɛkʃənɪt] ADJECTIVE
cariñoso

to **afford** [ə'fɔ:rd] VERB
permitirse ◇ *I can't afford a new pair of jeans.* No puedo permitirme comprar unos bluyines nuevos.
◆ **We can't afford to go on vacation.** No podemos permitirnos el lujo de ir de vacaciones.

A

afraid [ə'freɪd] ADJECTIVE
- **to be afraid of something** tener* miedo a algo ◇ *I'm afraid of spiders.* Tengo miedo a las arañas.
- **I'm afraid I can't come.** Me temo que no puedo ir.
- **I'm afraid so.** Me temo que sí.
- **I'm afraid not.** Me temo que no.

Africa ['æfrɪkə] NOUN
África FEM

African ['æfrɪkən] ADJECTIVE
see also **African** NOUN
africano

African ['æfrɪkən] NOUN
see also **African** ADJECTIVE
el africano
la africana

African-American ['æfrɪkənə'mɛrɪkən] ADJECTIVE
see also **African-American** NOUN
afroamericano

African-American ['æfrɪkənə'mɛrɪkən] NOUN
see also **African-American** ADJECTIVE
el afroamericano
la afroamericana

after ['æftər] PREPOSITION, CONJUNCTION, ADVERB
1 después de ◇ *after the game* después del partido ◇ *After watching the television I went to bed.* Después de ver la televisión me fui a la cama. ◇ *After I had a rest I went for a walk.* Después de descansar me fui a dar un paseo.
2 después de que
When there's a change of subject in an ***after*** *clause, use* ***después de que*** *with a verb in an appropriate tense instead of* ***después de*** *+ infinitive.*
◇ *I met her after she had left the company.* La conocí después de que dejó la empresa.
después de que *has to be followed by a verb in the subjunctive when referring to an event in the future.*
◇ *I'll help you after we finish this.* Te ayudaré después de que terminemos esto. ◇ *She said she'd phone after her mother went out.* Dijo que me llamaría después de que se fuera su mamá.
- **after dinner** después de cenar
- **He ran after me.** Me persiguió.
- **after all** después de todo
- **soon after** poco después
- **It's ten after six.** Son las seis y diez.

afternoon ['æftər'nu:n] NOUN
la tarde ◇ *in the afternoon* en la tarde ◇ *three o'clock in the afternoon* las tres de la tarde ◇ *on Saturday afternoon* el sábado en la tarde

aftershave ['æftərʃeɪv] NOUN
la loción para después de afeitarse
la loción para después de rasurarse *Mexico*

afterward ['æftərwərd] ADVERB
después ◇ *She left not long afterward.* Se fue poco después.

again [ə'gɛn] ADVERB
otra vez ◇ *They're friends again.* Ya son amigos otra vez. ◇ *I'd like to hear it again.* Me gustaría escucharlo otra vez.
In Spanish you often use the verb ***volver* a*** *and an infinitive to talk about doing something* ***again.***
◇ *I'd like to hear it again.* Me gustaría volver a escucharlo. ◇ *I won't tell you again!* ¡No te lo vuelvo a repetir!
- **Can you tell me again?** ¿Me lo puedes repetir?
- **not...again** no...más ◇ *I won't go there again.* No voy más por allí.
- **Do it again!** ¡Hazlo otra vez!
- **again and again** una y otra vez

against [ə'gɛnst] PREPOSITION
1 contra ◇ *He leaned against the wall.* Se apoyó contra la pared.
2 en contra de ◇ *I'm against nuclear testing.* Estoy en contra de las pruebas nucleares.

age [eɪdʒ] NOUN
la edad ◇ *an age limit* un límite de edad
- **children under age 10** niños menores de 10 años
- **at the age of 16** a los 16 años
- **I haven't been to the movies for ages.** Hace siglos que no voy al cine.

agenda [ə'dʒɛndə] NOUN
el orden del día
Be careful not to translate ***agenda*** *by the Spanish word* ***agenda.***

agent ['eɪdʒənt] NOUN
el/la agente ◇ *a real estate agent* un agente inmobiliario
- **She's a travel agent.** Es empleada de una agencia de viajes.

aggressive [ə'grɛsɪv] ADJECTIVE
agresivo

ago [ə'gou] ADVERB
- **two days ago** hace dos días
- **not long ago** no hace mucho
- **How long ago did it happen?** ¿Cuánto hace que ocurrió?

agony ['ægəni] NOUN (PL **agonies**)
- **to be in agony** sufrir mucho dolor
- **It was agony!** ¡Fue un suplicio!

to **agree** [ə'gri:] VERB
estar* de acuerdo ◇ *I don't agree!* ¡No estoy de acuerdo! ◇ *I agree with Carol.* Estoy de acuerdo con Carol.
- **to agree to do something (1)** (*when someone requests*) aceptar hacer algo ◇ *He agreed to go with her.* Aceptó acompañarla.
- **to agree to do something (2)** (*arrange*) acordar* hacer algo ◇ *They agreed to meet again next week.* Acordaron volver a reunirse la semana próxima.
- **to agree that...** reconocer* que... ◇ *I agree* ☞

it's difficult. Reconozco que es difícil.
◆ **Garlic doesn't agree with me.** El ajo no me cae bien.

agreed [ə'gri:d] ADJECTIVE
acordado ◇ *at the agreed price* al precio acordado

agreement [ə'gri:mənt] NOUN
el acuerdo
◆ **to be in agreement** estar* de acuerdo

agricultural [ægrɪ'kʌltʃərəl] ADJECTIVE
agrícola

agriculture ['ægrɪkʌltʃər] NOUN
la agricultura

ahead [ə'hɛd] ADVERB
delante ◇ *She looked straight ahead.* Miró hacia delante.
◆ **ahead of time** con antelación
◆ **to plan ahead** hacer* planes con antelación
◆ **The Mexicans are five points ahead.** Los mexicanos llevan cinco puntos de ventaja.
◆ **Go ahead! Help yourself!** ¡Vamos! ¡Sírvete!

aid [eɪd] NOUN
la ayuda
◆ **in aid of children** a beneficio de la infancia

AIDS [eɪdz] NOUN
el sida

to **aim** [eɪm] VERB
see also **aim** NOUN
◆ **to aim at** apuntar a ◇ *He aimed a gun at me.* Me apuntó con una pistola.
◆ **The movie is aimed at children.** La película está dirigida a los niños.
◆ **to aim to do something** pretender hacer algo

aim [eɪm] NOUN
see also **aim** VERB
el propósito

air [ɛər] NOUN
el aire ◇ *to get some fresh air* tomar un poco el aire
◆ **by air** en avión

air bag ['ɛr,bæg] NOUN
la bolsa de aire

air-conditioned ['ɛrkən'dɪʃənd] ADJECTIVE
con aire acondicionado

air-conditioning ['ɛrkən'dɪʃənɪŋ] NOUN
el aire acondicionado

air force ['ɛr,fɔ:rs] NOUN
la fuerza aérea

airline ['ɛr,laɪn] NOUN
la línea aérea

airmail ['ɛr,meɪl] NOUN
◆ **by airmail** por correo aéreo

air mattress ['ɛr,mætrɪs] NOUN (PL **air mattresses**)
el colchón inflable (PL los colchones inflables)

airplane ['ɛr,pleɪn] NOUN
el avión (PL los aviones)

airport ['ɛr,pɔ:rt] NOUN
el aeropuerto

aisle [aɪl] NOUN
el pasillo (*in a plane, theater*)

alarm [ə'lɑ:rm] NOUN
la alarma
◆ **a fire alarm** una alarma contra incendios

alarm clock [ə'lɑ:rm,klɑ:k] NOUN
el despertador

album ['ælbəm] NOUN
el álbum

alcohol ['ælkəhɑ:l] NOUN
el alcohol

alcoholic [ælkə'hɑ:lɪk] NOUN
see also **alcoholic** ADJECTIVE
el alcohólico
la alcohólica

alcoholic [ælkə'hɑ:lɪk] ADJECTIVE
see also **alcoholic** NOUN
alcohólico ◇ *alcoholic drinks* bebidas alcohólicas

alert [ə'lɜ:rt] ADJECTIVE
1 despierto ◇ *He's a very alert baby.* Es un bebé muy despierto.
2 atento ◇ *We must stay alert.* Hay que estar atentos.

Algeria [æl'dʒɪriə] NOUN
Argelia FEM

alike [ə'laɪk] ADVERB
◆ **to look alike** parecerse* ◇ *The two sisters look alike.* Las dos hermanas se parecen.

alive [ə'laɪv] ADJECTIVE
vivo

all [ɑ:l] ADJECTIVE, PRONOUN, ADVERB
todo ◇ *That's all I can remember.* Eso es todo lo que recuerdo. ◇ *I ate all of it.* Me lo comí todo. ◇ *all day* todo el día ◇ *all the apples* todas las manzanas
◆ **All of us went.** Fuimos todos.
◆ **all alone** completamente solo
◆ **not at all** en absoluto ◇ *I'm not at all tired.* No estoy en absoluto cansado.
◆ **She talks all the time.** No para de hablar.
◆ **The score is five all.** Van empatados a cinco.

allergic [ə'lɜ:rdʒɪk] ADJECTIVE
alérgico ◇ *to be allergic to something* ser* alérgico a algo

alley ['æli] NOUN
la callejón (PL los callejones)

to **allow** [ə'lau] VERB
◆ **to allow somebody to do something** dejar a alguien hacer algo ◇ *His mother allowed him to go out.* Su mamá lo dejó salir. ◇ *He's not allowed to go out at night.* No lo dejan salir por la noche.
◆ **Smoking is not allowed in the office.** Está prohibido fumar en la oficina.

allowance [ə'lauəns] NOUN
el dinero de bolsillo ◇ *How much allowance do you get?* ¿Cuanto dinero de bolsillo te dan?

all right [ɑ:l'raɪt] ADVERB, ADJECTIVE

bien ◇ *Everything turned out all right.* Todo salió bien. ◇ *Are you all right?* ¿Estás bien?
◆ **Is that all right with you?** ¿Te parece bien?
◆ **The movie was all right.** La película no estuvo mal.
◆ **We'll talk about it later. – All right.** Lo hablamos después. – Bueno.

almond [ˈɑːmənd] NOUN
la almendra

almost [ˈɑːlmoust] ADVERB
casi ◇ *I've almost finished.* Ya casi he terminado.

alone [əˈloun] ADJECTIVE, ADVERB
solo ◇ *She lives alone.* Vive sola.
◆ **to leave somebody alone** dejar en paz a alguien ◇ *Leave her alone!* ¡Déjala en paz!
◆ **to leave something alone** no tocar* algo ◇ *Leave my things alone!* ¡No toques mis cosas!

along [əˈlɑːŋ] PREPOSITION, ADVERB
por ◇ *Chris was walking along the beach.* Chris paseaba por la playa.
◆ **all along (1)** a lo largo de ◇ *There were bars all along the street.* Había bares a lo largo de toda la calle.
◆ **all along (2)** desde el principio ◇ *He was lying to me all along.* Me había mentido desde el principio.

aloud [əˈlaud] ADVERB
en voz alta

alphabet [ˈælfəbɛt] NOUN
el alfabeto

already [ɑːlˈrɛdi] ADVERB
ya ◇ *Liz had already gone.* Liz ya se había ido.

also [ˈɑːlsou] ADVERB
también

altar [ˈɑːltər] NOUN
el altar

to **alter** [ˈɑːltər] VERB
cambiar

alternate [ˈɑːltərnət] ADJECTIVE
◆ **on alternate days** en días alternos

alternative [ɑːlˈtɜːrnətɪv] NOUN
see also **alternative** ADJECTIVE
la alternativa ◇ *You have no alternative.* No tienes otra alternativa.
◆ **Fruit is a healthy alternative to chocolate.** La fruta es una opción más sana que el chocolate.
◆ **There are several alternatives.** Hay varias posibilidades.

alternative [ɑːlˈtɜːrnətɪv] ADJECTIVE
see also **alternative** NOUN
otro ◇ *They made alternative plans.* Hicieron otros planes.
◆ **an alternative solution** otra solución
◆ **alternative medicine** la medicina alternativa

alternatively [ɑːlˈtɜːrnətɪvli] ADVERB
◆ **Alternatively, we could just stay at home.** Si no, podemos simplemente quedarnos en casa.

although [ɑːlˈðou] CONJUNCTION
aunque ◇ *Although she was tired, she stayed up late.* Aunque estaba cansada, se quedó levantada hasta tarde.

altogether [ɑːltəˈgɛðər] ADVERB
1 en total (*in total*) ◇ *You owe me 20 dollars altogether.* En total me debes 20 dólares.
2 del todo (*completely*) ◇ *I'm not altogether happy with your work.* No estoy del todo satisfecho con tu trabajo.

aluminum [əˈluːmɪnəm] NOUN
el aluminio
◆ **aluminum foil** el papel de aluminio

always [ˈɑːlweɪz] ADVERB
siempre ◇ *He's always moaning.* Siempre está quejándose.

am [æm] VERB *see* **be**

a.m. [eɪˈɛm] ABBREVIATION
de la mañana ◇ *at 4 a.m.* a las 4 de la mañana

amateur [ˈæmətər] NOUN
el/la amateur (PL los/las amateurs)

amazed [əˈmeɪzd] ADJECTIVE
asombrado ◇ *I was amazed that I managed to do it.* Estaba asombrado de haberlo conseguido.

amazing [əˈmeɪzɪŋ] ADJECTIVE
1 asombroso ◇ *That's amazing news!* ¡Es una noticia asombrosa!
2 extraordinario ◇ *Vivian is an amazing cook.* Vivian es una cocinera extraordinaria.

ambassador [æmˈbæsədər] NOUN
el embajador
la embajadora

ambition [æmˈbɪʃən] NOUN
la ambición (PL las ambiciones)

ambitious [æmˈbɪʃəs] ADJECTIVE
ambicioso

ambulance [ˈæmbjuləns] NOUN
la ambulancia

amenities [əˈmɛnətiz] PL NOUN
◆ **The hotel has very good amenities.** El hotel tiene excelentes servicios e instalaciones.
◆ **The town has many amenities.** La ciudad ofrece una gran variedad de servicios.

America [əˈmɛrɪkə] NOUN
1 los Estados Unidos MASC PL (*United States*)
2 América FEM (*continent*)

American [əˈmɛrɪkən] ADJECTIVE
see also **American** NOUN
norteamericano

American [əˈmɛrɪkən] NOUN
see also **American** ADJECTIVE
el norteamericano
la norteamericana
◇ *the Americans* los norteamericanos

among [əˈmʌŋ] PREPOSITION
entre

amount [əˈmaunt] NOUN
la cantidad ◇ *a huge amount of rice* una

☞

cantidad enorme de arroz
◆ **a large amount of money** una gran suma de dinero

amp [æmp] NOUN
1 el amplificador (*amplifier*)
2 el amperio (*ampere*)

amplifier ['æmplɪfaɪər] NOUN
el amplificador

to **amuse** [ə'mju:z] VERB
1 divertir* ◇ *The thought seemed to amuse him.* La idea parecía divertirlo.
2 entretener* ◇ *He was very amused by the story.* El cuento lo entretuvo mucho.

amusement park [ə'mju:zmənt,pɑ:rk] NOUN
el parque de diversiones

an [æn] INDEFINITE ARTICLE *see* **a**

analysis [ə'næləsɪs] NOUN (PL **analyses**)
el análisis (PL los análisis)

to **analyze** ['ænəlaɪz] VERB
analizar*

ancestor ['ænsɛstər] NOUN
el antepasado
la antepasada

anchor ['æŋkər] NOUN
el ancla FEM
Although it's a feminine noun, remember that you use ***el*** *and* ***un*** *with* ***ancla.***

ancient ['eɪnʃənt] ADJECTIVE
antiguo ◇ *ancient Greece* la antigua Grecia
◆ **an ancient monument** un monumento histórico

and [ænd] CONJUNCTION
y ◇ *Mary and Jane.* Mary y Jane.
Use ***e*** *to translate* ***and*** *before words beginning with "i" or "hi" but not "hie".*
◇ *Miguel and Ignacio.* Miguel e Ignacio.
and *is not translated when linking numbers.*
◇ *two hundred and fifty* doscientos cincuenta
◆ **Please try and come!** ¡Trata de venir!
◆ **He talked and talked.** No paraba de hablar.
◆ **better and better** cada vez mejor

Andes ['ændi:z] NOUN
◆ **the Andes** los Andes

angel ['eɪndʒəl] NOUN
el ángel

anger ['æŋgər] NOUN
el enojo

angle ['æŋgəl] NOUN
el ángulo

angler ['æŋglər] NOUN
el pescador
la pescadora

angling ['æŋglɪŋ] NOUN
◆ **His hobby is angling.** Su hobby es la pesca.

angry ['æŋgri] ADJECTIVE
enojado ◇ *to be angry with somebody* estar* enojado con alguien ◇ *Your father looks very angry.* Tu papá parece estar muy enojado.
◆ **to get angry** enojarse

animal ['ænɪməl] NOUN
el animal

ankle ['æŋkəl] NOUN
el tobillo ◇ *I've twisted my ankle.* Me torcí el tobillo.

anniversary [ænɪ'vɜ:rsəri] NOUN (PL **anniversaries**)
el aniversario ◇ *wedding anniversary* aniversario de bodas

to **announce** [ə'nauns] VERB
anunciar

announcement [ə'naunsmənt] NOUN
el anuncio

to **annoy** [ə'nɔɪ] VERB
molestar ◇ *Make a note of the things that annoy you.* Haz una lista de las cosas que te molestan.
◆ **He's really annoying me.** Me está molestando de verdad.
◆ **to be annoyed with somebody** estar* molesto con alguien
◆ **to get annoyed** enojarse ◇ *Don't get annoyed!* ¡No te enojes!

annoying [ə'nɔɪɪŋ] ADJECTIVE
molesto ◇ *the most annoying problem* el problema más molesto
◆ **I find it very annoying.** Me molesta mucho.

annual ['ænjuəl] ADJECTIVE
anual

anorak ['ænəræk] NOUN
el anorak (PL los anoraks)

another [ə'nʌðər] ADJECTIVE, PRONOUN
otro ◇ *Do you have another skirt?* ¿Tienes otra falda?
◆ **Another two miles.** Dos millas más.

to **answer** ['ænsər] VERB
see also **answer** NOUN
contestar ◇ *Can you answer my question?* ¿Puedes contestar a mi pregunta? ◇ *to answer the phone* contestar al teléfono
◆ **to answer the door** abrir* la puerta ◇ *Can you answer the door, please?* ¿Puedes ir a abrir la puerta?

answer ['ænsər] NOUN
see also **answer** VERB
1 la respuesta (*to question*)
2 la solución (PL las soluciones) (*to problem*)

answering machine ['ænsərɪŋmə'ʃi:n] NOUN
el contestador automático

ant [ænt] NOUN
la hormiga

Antarctic [ænt'ɑ:rktɪk] NOUN
◆ **the Antarctic** la región antártica

antenna [æn'tɛnə] NOUN
la antena

anthem ['ænθəm] NOUN
◆ **the national anthem** el himno nacional

antibiotic [,æntibaɪ'ɑ:tɪk] NOUN

el antibiótico

antidepressant [ˌæntidɪ'prɛsənt] NOUN
el antidepresivo

antique [æn'tiːk] NOUN
la antigüedad

antique store [æn'tiːkˌstɔːr] NOUN
la tienda de antigüedades

antiseptic [æntɪ'sɛptɪk] NOUN
el antiséptico

any ['ɛni] ADJECTIVE, ADVERB
see also **any** PRONOUN
In questions and negative sentences ***any*** *is usually not translated.*
◇ *Do you have any change?* ¿Tienes cambio? ◇ *Are there any beans left?* ¿Quedan frijoles? ◇ *He doesn't have any friends.* No tiene amigos.
Use ***algún/alguna*** *+ singular noun in questions and* ***ningún/ninguna*** *+ singular noun in negatives where* ***any*** *is used with plural nouns and the number of items is important.*
◇ *Do you speak any foreign languages?* ¿Hablas algún idioma extranjero? ◇ *I don't have any books by Borges.* No tengo ningún libro de Borges.
Use ***cualquier*** *in affirmative sentences.*
◇ *Any teacher will tell you.* Cualquier profesor te lo dirá.
◆ **Come any time you like.** Ven cuando quieras.
◆ **Would you like any more coffee?** ¿Quieres más café?
◆ **I don't love him any more.** Ya no lo quiero.

any ['ɛni] PRONOUN
see also **any** ADJECTIVE, ADVERB
1 alguno (FEM alguna) (*in questions*) ◇ *I need an envelope. Do you have any left?* Necesito un sobre. ¿Te queda alguno?
Only use ***alguno/alguna*** *if* ***any*** *refers to a countable noun. Otherwise don't translate it.*
◇ *I would like some soup. Do we have any?* Tengo ganas de tomar sopa. ¿Tenemos?
2 ninguno (FEM ninguna) (*in negatives*) ◇ *I don't like any of them.* No me gusta ninguno.
Only use ***ninguno/ninguna*** *if* ***any*** *refers to a countable noun. Otherwise don't translate it.*
◇ *Did you buy the milk? – No, there wasn't any.* ¿Compraste la leche? – No, no había.

anybody ['ɛniˌbɑːdi] PRONOUN
1 alguien
Use ***alguien*** *in questions.*
◇ *Does anybody have a pencil?* ¿Tiene alguien un lápiz?
2 nadie
Use ***nadie*** *in negative sentences.*
◇ *I can't see anybody.* No veo a nadie.
3 cualquiera
Use ***cualquiera*** *in affirmative sentences.*
◇ *Anybody can learn to swim.* Cualquiera puede aprender a nadar.

anyhow ['ɛniˌhaʊ] ADVERB
de todas maneras ◇ *He doesn't want to go out and anyhow he's not allowed.* No quiere salir y de todas maneras no lo dejan.

anyone ['ɛniˌwʌn] PRONOUN
1 alguien
Use ***alguien*** *in questions.*
◇ *Does anyone have a pencil?* ¿Tiene alguien un lápiz?
2 nadie
Use ***nadie*** *in negative sentences.*
◇ *I can't see anyone.* No veo a nadie.
3 cualquiera
Use ***cualquiera*** *in affirmative sentences.*
◇ *Anyone can learn to swim.* Cualquiera puede aprender a nadar.

anything ['ɛniˌθɪŋ] PRONOUN
1 algo
Use ***algo*** *in questions.*
◇ *Do you need anything?* ¿Necesitas algo?
◇ *Would you like anything to eat?* ¿Quieres algo de comer?
2 nada
Use ***nada*** *in negative sentences.*
◇ *I can't hear anything.* No oigo nada.
3 cualquier cosa
Use ***cualquier cosa*** *in affirmative sentences.*
◇ *Anything could happen.* Puede pasar cualquier cosa.

anyway ['ɛniˌweɪ] ADVERB
de todas maneras ◇ *He doesn't want to go out and anyway he's not allowed.* No quiere salir y de todas maneras no lo dejan.

anywhere ['ɛniˌwɛr] ADVERB
1 en algún lugar
Use ***en*** *or* ***a algún lugar*** *in questions.*
◇ *Have you seen my coat anywhere?* ¿Has visto mi abrigo en algún lugar? ◇ *Are we going anywhere?* ¿Vamos a algún lugar?
2 en ningún lugar
Use ***en*** *or* ***a ningún lugar*** *in negative sentences.*
◇ *I can't find it anywhere.* No lo encuentro en ningún lugar. ◇ *I can't go anywhere.* No puedo ir a ningún lugar.
3 en cualquier lugar
Use ***en cualquier lugar*** *in affirmative sentences.*
◇ *You can buy them almost anywhere.* Se pueden comprar casi en cualquier lugar.
◆ **You can sit anywhere you like.** Siéntate donde quieras.

apart [ə'pɑːrt] ADVERB
◆ **The two towns are 10 miles apart.** Los dos pueblos están a 10 millas el uno del otro.
◆ **It was the first time we had been apart.** Era la primera vez que estábamos separados.
◆ **apart from** aparte de ◇ *Apart from that, everything's fine.* Aparte de eso, todo va bien.

apartment [ə'pɑːrtmənt] NOUN
el departamento ◇ *an apartment building* un edificio de departamentos

to **apologize** [ə'pɑːlədʒaɪz] VERB

☞

disculparse ◇ *He apologized for being late.* Se disculpó por llegar tarde.
◆ **I apologize!** ¡Lo siento!

apology [ə'pɑːlədʒi] NOUN (PL **apologies**)
la disculpa ◇ *I owe you an apology.* Te debo una disculpa.

apostrophe [ə'pɑːstrəfi] NOUN
el apóstrofo

apparatus [æpə'reɪtəs] NOUN (PL **apparatus** *or* **apparatuses**)
los aparatos

apparent [ə'pɛrənt] ADJECTIVE
1 aparente ◇ *for no apparent reason* sin razón aparente
2 claro ◇ *It was apparent that he disliked me.* Estaba claro que no le caigo bien.

apparently [ə'pɛrəntli] ADVERB
por lo visto
◆ **Apparently he was abroad when it happened.** Por lo visto estaba en el extranjero cuando ocurrió.

to **appeal** [ə'piːl] VERB
see also **appeal** NOUN
1 hacer* un llamamiento ◇ *They appealed for help.* Hicieron un llamamiento de ayuda.
2 atraer* ◇ *Texas doesn't appeal to me.* Texas no me atrae.

appeal [ə'piːl] NOUN
see also **appeal** VERB
el llamamiento ◇ *They have launched an appeal for unity.* Han hecho un llamamiento a la unidad.

to **appear** [ə'pɪər] VERB
1 aparecer* ◇ *The sun appeared through the clouds.* El sol apareció por entre las nubes.
◆ **to appear on TV** salir* en la tele
2 parecer* ◇ *She appeared to be asleep.* Parecía estar dormida.

appearance [ə'pɪrəns] NOUN
el aspecto ◇ *She takes great care over her appearance.* Cuida mucho su aspecto.
◆ **to make an appearance** aparecer*

appendicitis [əpɛndɪ'saɪtɪs] NOUN
la apendicitis

appetite ['æpɪtaɪt] NOUN
el apetito
◆ **to have a good appetite** tener buen apetito

appetizer ['æpɪtaɪzər] NOUN
el primer plato (*first course*)

to **applaud** [ə'plɑːd] VERB
aplaudir

applause [ə'plɑːz] NOUN
los aplausos MASC PL

apple ['æpəl] NOUN
la manzana ◇ *apple pie* el pay de manzana
◆ **an apple tree** un manzano

applicant ['æplɪkənt] NOUN
el candidato
la candidata

application [æplɪ'keɪʃən] NOUN
◆ **an application form** una solicitud
◆ **a job application** una solicitud de empleo

application form [æplɪ'keɪʃən,fɔːrm] NOUN
la solicitud

to **apply** [ə'plaɪ] VERB (**applied, applied**)
◆ **to apply for a job** solicitar un empleo
◆ **to apply to** afectar a ◇ *This rule doesn't apply to us.* Esta norma no nos afecta.

to **appoint** [ə'pɔɪnt] VERB
nombrar ◇ *They appointed him chairman.* Lo nombraron presidente.
Be careful not to translate ***to appoint*** *by* ***apuntar.***

appointment [ə'pɔɪntmənt] NOUN
la cita ◇ *to make an appointment with someone* concertar* una cita con alguien
◆ **I have a dental appointment.** Tengo hora con el dentista.

to **appreciate** [ə'priːʃieɪt] VERB
agradecer* ◇ *I really appreciate your help.* Agradezco de veras tu ayuda. ◇ *I appreciate the gesture.* Agradezco el detalle.

apprentice [ə'prɛntɪs] NOUN
el aprendiz (PL los aprendices)
la aprendiza

to **approach** [ə'proutʃ] VERB
1 acercarse* a ◇ *He approached the house.* Se acercó a la casa.
2 abordar ◇ *to approach a problem* abordar un problema

appropriate [ə'proupriɪt] ADJECTIVE
apropiado ◇ *That dress isn't very appropriate for an interview.* Ese vestido no es muy apropiado para una entrevista.
◆ **Check the appropriate box.** Marque la casilla que corresponda.

approval [ə'pruːvəl] NOUN
la aprobación

to **approve** [ə'pruːv] VERB
◆ **I don't approve of his choice.** No me parece bien su elección.
◆ **They didn't approve of his girlfriend.** No veían con buenos ojos a su novia.

approximate [ə'prɑːksɪmɪt] ADJECTIVE
aproximado

apricot ['æprɪkɑːt] NOUN
el albaricoque
el chabacano Mexico

April ['eɪprəl] NOUN
abril MASC ◇ *in April* en abril ◇ *on April 4th* el 4 de abril
◆ **April Fool's Day** el día de los Santos Inocentes

ℹ *In Spanish-speaking countries on* **el día de los Santos Inocentes**, *December 28th, people play practical jokes in the same way as they do on* **April Fool's Day**.

apron ['eɪprən] NOUN
el delantal
Aquarius [ə'kwɛriəs] NOUN
el Acuario (*sign*) ◇ *I'm an Aquarius.* Soy acuario.
◆ **an Aquarius** un/una acuario
Arab ['ærəb] ADJECTIVE
see also **Arab** NOUN
árabe
Arab ['ærəb] NOUN
see also **Arab** ADJECTIVE
el/la árabe ◇ *the Arabs* los árabes
Arabic ['ærəbɪk] ADJECTIVE
árabe
arch [ɑːrtʃ] NOUN (PL **arches**)
el arco
archaeologist [ɑːrki'ɑːlədʒɪst] NOUN
el arqueólogo
la arqueóloga
◇ *He's an archaeologist.* Es arqueólogo.
archaeology [ɑːrki'ɑːlədʒi] NOUN
la arqueología
archbishop [ɑːrtʃ'bɪʃəp] NOUN
el arzobispo
archeologist [ɑːrki'ɑːlədʒɪst] NOUN
el arqueólogo
la arqueóloga
archeology [ɑːrki'ɑːlədʒi] NOUN
la arqueología
architect ['ɑːrkɪtɛkt] NOUN
el arquitecto
la arquitecta
◇ *She's an architect.* Es arquitecta.
architecture ['ɑːrkɪtɛktʃər] NOUN
la arquitectura
Arctic ['ɑːrktɪk] NOUN
◆ **the Arctic** el Ártico
are [ɑːr] VERB *see* **be**
area ['ɛriə] NOUN
1 la zona ◇ *a mountainous area of Chile* una zona montañosa de Chile
2 la superficie ◇ *The field has an area of 1500 m2.* El terreno tiene una superficie de 1500 m2.
3 el área FEM (*in soccer*)
*Although it's a feminine noun, remember that you use **el** and **un** with **área**.*
area code ['ɛriəˌkoud] NOUN
el código (*for telephone*) ◇ *What is the area code for New York?* ¿Cuál es el código de Nueva York?
Argentina [ɑːrdʒən'tiːnə] NOUN
Argentina FEM
Argentinian [ɑːrdʒən'tɪniən] ADJECTIVE
see also **Argentinian** NOUN
argentino
Argentinian [ɑːrdʒən'tɪniən] NOUN
see also **Argentinian** ADJECTIVE
el argentino
la argentina
to **argue** ['ɑːrgjuː] VERB
discutir ◇ *They never stop arguing.* Siempre están discutiendo.
argument ['ɑːrgjəmənt] NOUN
la discusión (PL las discusiones)
◆ **to have an argument** discutir
Aries ['ɛriz] NOUN
el Aries (*sign*) ◇ *I'm an Aries.* Soy aries.
◆ **an Aries** un/una aries
arm [ɑːrm] NOUN
el brazo ◇ *I burned my arm.* Me quemé el brazo.
armchair ['ɑːrmˌtʃɛr] NOUN
el sillón (PL los sillones)
armor ['ɑːrmər] NOUN
la armadura
army ['ɑːrmi] NOUN (PL **armies**)
el ejército
around [ə'raund] PREPOSITION, ADVERB
1 alrededor de ◇ *She wore a scarf around her neck.* Llevaba una bufanda alrededor del cuello.
◆ **She ignored the people around her.** Ignoró a la gente que estaba a su alrededor.
◆ **Shall we meet at around 8 o'clock?** ¿Quedamos alrededor de las 8?
◆ **It's just around the corner.** Está a la vuelta de la esquina.
◆ **to go around to somebody's house** ir* a la casa de alguien
◆ **to have a look around** echar un vistazo ◇ *We had a look around the record section yesterday.* Echamos un vistazo a la sección de discos ayer.
◆ **to go around a museum** visitar un museo
2 por ◇ *I've been walking around the town.* He estado paseando por la ciudad.
◆ **We walked around for a while.** Paseamos por ahí durante un rato.
◆ **around here** por aquí cerca ◇ *He lives around here.* Vive aquí cerca. ◇ *Is there a drugstore around here?* ¿Hay alguna farmacia por aquí?
◆ **all around** por todos lados ◇ *There were vineyards all around.* Había viñedos por todos lados.
◆ **around about** alrededor de ◇ *It costs around about $100.* Cuesta alrededor de 100 dólares.
to **arrange** [ə'reɪndʒ] VERB
organizar* ◇ *to arrange a party* organizar una fiesta
◆ **to arrange to do something** quedar en hacer algo ◇ *They arranged to go out together on Friday.* Quedaron en salir juntos el viernes.
arrangement [ə'reɪndʒmənt] NOUN
◆ **to make an arrangement to do something** quedar en hacer* algo
◆ **a flower arrangement** un arreglo floral
◆ **arrangements** los preparativos ◇ *Pamela is in charge of the travel arrangements.* Pamela se encarga de los preparativos para el viaje.

☞

◆ **They made arrangements to go out on Friday night.** Hicieron planes para salir* el viernes por la noche.

to **arrest** [ə'rɛst] VERB
see also **arrest** NOUN
detener*

arrest [ə'rɛst] NOUN
see also **arrest** VERB
la detención (PL las detenciones)
◆ **You're under arrest!** ¡Queda detenido!

arrival [ə'raɪvəl] NOUN
la llegada ◇ *The airplane's arrival has been delayed.* Se ha retrasado la llegada del avión.

to **arrive** [ə'raɪv] VERB
llegar* ◇ *I arrived at 5 o'clock.* Llegué a las 5.

arrow ['ærou] NOUN
la flecha

art [ɑːrt] NOUN
el arte
◆ **works of art** las obras de arte
◆ **art school** la escuela de Bellas Artes
◆ **the arts** las bellas artes

artery ['ɑːrtəri] NOUN (PL **arteries**)
la arteria

art gallery ['ɑːrt,gæləri] NOUN (PL **art galleries**)
1 el museo (*state-owned*)
2 la galería de arte (*private*)

article ['ɑːrtɪkəl] NOUN
el artículo

artificial [ɑːrtɪ'fɪʃəl] ADJECTIVE
artificial

artist ['ɑːrtɪst] NOUN
el/la artista ◇ *She's an artist.* Es artista.

artistic [ɑːr'tɪstɪk] ADJECTIVE
artístico

as [æz] CONJUNCTION, ADVERB
1 cuando ◇ *He came in as I was leaving.* Entró cuando yo me iba.
2 mientras ◇ *All the jury's eyes were on him as he continued.* Todo el jurado lo observaba mientras él proseguía.
3 como ◇ *As it's Sunday, you can sleep in.* Como es domingo, puedes quedarte en la cama hasta tarde.
4 de ◇ *He works as a waiter in the vacations.* En las vacaciones trabaja de camarero.
◆ **as...as** tan...como ◇ *Peter is as tall as Michael.* Peter es tan alto como Michael.
◆ **as much...as** tanto...como ◇ *I don't have as much energy as you.* No tengo tanta energía como tú. ◇ *Her coat cost twice as much as mine.* Su abrigo costó el doble que el mío.
◆ **as soon as possible** cuanto antes
◆ **as from tomorrow** a partir de mañana
◆ **as if** como si
***como si** has to be followed by a verb in the subjunctive.*
◇ *She acted as if she hadn't seen me.* Hizo como si no me hubiese visto.
◆ **as though** como si ◇ *She acted as though she hadn't seen me.* Hizo como si no me hubiese visto.

asap [,eɪeseɪ'piː] ABBREVIATION (= *as soon as possible*)
cuanto antes

ashamed [ə'ʃeɪmd] ADJECTIVE
◆ **to be ashamed** estar* avergonzado ◇ *I'm ashamed of myself for shouting at you.* Estoy avergonzado de gritarte.
◆ **You should be ashamed of yourself!** ¡Debería darte vergüenza!

ashtray ['æʃ,treɪ] NOUN
el cenicero

Asia ['eɪʒə] NOUN
Ásia FEM

Asian ['eɪʒən] ADJECTIVE
see also **Asian** NOUN
asiático

Asian ['eɪʒən] NOUN
see also **Asian** ADJECTIVE
el asiático
la asiática

to **ask** [æsk] VERB
1 preguntar ◇ *"Have you finished?" she asked.* "¿Has terminado?" preguntó.
◆ **to ask somebody something** preguntar algo a alguien
◆ **to ask about something** preguntar por algo ◇ *I asked about train times to Phoenix.* Pregunté por el horario de trenes a Phoenix.
◆ **to ask somebody a question** hacer* una pregunta a alguien
2 pedir* ◇ *She asked him to do the shopping.* Le pidió que hiciera la compra.
***pedir que** has to be followed by a verb in the subjunctive.*
◆ **to ask for something** pedir algo ◇ *He asked for a cup of tea.* Pidió una taza de té.
◆ **Peter asked her out.** Peter le pidió que saliera con él.
3 invitar ◇ *Have you asked Matthew to the party?* ¿Invitaste a Matthew a la fiesta?

asleep [ə'sliːp] ADJECTIVE
◆ **to be asleep** estar* dormido
◆ **to fall asleep** quedarse dormido

asparagus [ə'spærəgəs] NOUN
los espárragos

aspect ['æspɛkt] NOUN
el aspecto

aspirin ['æsprɪn] NOUN
la aspirina

asset ['æsɛt] NOUN
la ventaja ◇ *Her experience will be an asset to the firm.* Su experiencia supondrá una ventaja para la empresa.

assignment [ə'saɪnmənt] NOUN
la tarea (*at school*)

assistance [ə'sɪstəns] NOUN

la ayuda

assistant [ə'sɪstənt] NOUN
1 el dependiente
la dependienta
(*in store*)
2 el/la ayudante (*helper*)

association [əsousi'eɪʃən] NOUN
la asociación (PL las asociaciones)

assortment [ə'sɔːrtmənt] NOUN
el surtido

to **assume** [ə'suːm] VERB
suponer* ◇ *I assume she won't be coming.* Supongo que no vendrá.

to **assure** [ə'ʃuər] VERB
asegurar ◇ *He assured me he was coming.* Me aseguró que venía.

asthma ['æzmə] NOUN
el asma FEM
*Although it's a feminine noun, remember that you use **el** with **asma**.*
◇ *He has asthma.* Tiene asma.

to **astonish** [ə'stɑːnɪʃ] VERB
pasmar

astrology [ə'strɑːlədʒi] NOUN
la astrología

astronaut ['æstrənɑːt] NOUN
el/la astronauta

astronomy [əs'trɑːnəmi] NOUN
la astronomía

at [æt] PREPOSITION
1 en ◇ *at home* en la casa ◇ *at school* en la escuela ◇ *at the office* en la oficina ◇ *at work* en el trabajo
2 a ◇ *at 50 km/h* a 50 km/h
◆ **two at a time** de dos en dos
◆ **at 4 o'clock** a las 4
◆ **at night** en la noche
◆ **at Christmas** en Navidad

ate [eɪt] VERB *see* **eat**

Athens ['æθɪnz] NOUN
Atenas FEM

athlete ['æθliːt] NOUN
el/la atleta

athletic [æθ'lɛtɪk] ADJECTIVE
atlético

athletics [æθ'lɛtɪks] NOUN
el atletismo ◇ *I enjoy watching the athletics on television.* Me gusta ver el atletismo en la televisión.

Atlantic [æt'læntɪk] NOUN
el Atlántico

atlas ['ætləs] NOUN (PL **atlases**)
el atlas (PL los atlas)

ATM [ˌeɪtiː'ɛm] NOUN (= *automatic teller machine*)
el cajero automático
◆ **ATM card** la tarjeta de cajero automático

atmosphere ['ætməsfɪr] NOUN
la atmósfera

atom ['ætəm] NOUN
el átomo

atomic [ə'tɑːmɪk] ADJECTIVE
atómico

to **attach** [ə'tætʃ] VERB
amarrar ◇ *They attached a rope to the car.* Amarraron una cuerda al carro.
◆ **Please find attached a check for 50 dollars.** Se adjunta cheque de 50 dólares.

attached [ə'tætʃt] ADJECTIVE
◆ **to be attached to somebody** tener* cariño a alguien

attachment NOUN
el documento adjunto (*to email*)

to **attack** [ə'tæk] VERB
see also **attack** NOUN
atacar*

attack [ə'tæk] NOUN
see also **attack** VERB
el ataque
◆ **to be under attack** ser* atacado

attempt [ə'tɛmpt] NOUN
see also **attempt** VERB
el intento

to **attempt** [ə'tɛmpt] VERB
see also **attempt** NOUN
◆ **to attempt to do something** intentar hacer algo ◇ *I attempted to write a song.* Intenté escribir una canción.

to **attend** [ə'tɛnd] VERB
asistir a ◇ *to attend a meeting* asistir a una reunión

attention [ə'tɛnʃən] NOUN
la atención (PL las atenciones)
◆ **to pay attention to** prestar atención a ◇ *He didn't pay attention to what I was saying.* No prestó atención a lo que estaba diciendo.
◆ **Don't pay any attention to him!** ¡No le hagas caso!

attic ['ætɪk] NOUN
el desván (PL los desvanes)

attitude ['ætɪtuːd] NOUN
la actitud

attorney [ə'tɜːrni] NOUN
el abogado
la abogada

to **attract** [ə'trækt] VERB
atraer* ◇ *The Grand Canyon attract lots of tourists.* El Gran cañón del Colorado atrae a muchos turistas.

attraction [ə'trækʃən] NOUN
la atracción (PL las atracciones) ◇ *a tourist attraction* una atracción turística

attractive [ə'træktɪv] ADJECTIVE
atractivo

auction ['ɑːkʃən] NOUN
la subasta

audience ['ɑːdiəns] NOUN
el público

audition [ɑː'dɪʃən] NOUN
la audición (PL las audiciones)

August ['ɑːgəst] NOUN
agosto MASC ◇ *in August* en agosto ◇ *on* ☞

August 13th el 13 de agosto

aunt [ænt] NOUN
la tía
◆ **my aunt and uncle** mis tíos

au pair ['ou'pɛər] NOUN
el/la au pair (PL los/las au pairs)

Australia [ɑ:'streɪljə] NOUN
Australia FEM

Australian [ɑ:'streɪljən] ADJECTIVE
see also **Australian** NOUN
australiano

Australian [ɑ:'streɪljən] NOUN
see also **Australian** ADJECTIVE
el australiano
la australiana
◇ *the Australians* los australianos

Austria ['ɑ:striə] NOUN
Austria FEM

Austrian ['ɑ:striən] ADJECTIVE
see also **Austrian** NOUN
austríaco

Austrian ['ɑ:striən] NOUN
see also **Austrian** ADJECTIVE
el austríaco
la austríaca
◇ *the Austrians* los austríacos

author ['ɑ:θər] NOUN
el autor
la autora
◇ *he's the author of the book* es el autor del libro
◆ **a famous author** un escritor famoso

auto ['ɑ:tou] NOUN
el carro
◆ **auto show** el salón del automóvil

autobiography [ɑ:təbaɪ'ɑ:grəfi] NOUN (PL **autobiographies**)
la autobiografía

autograph ['ɑ:təgræf] NOUN
el autógrafo

automatic [ɑ:tə'mætɪk] ADJECTIVE
automático

automatically [ɑ:tə'mætɪkli] ADVERB
automáticamente

automobile [ˌɑ:təmə'bi:l] NOUN
el carro

autumn ['ɑ:təm] NOUN
el otoño ◇ *in autumn* en el otoño

availability [əveɪlə'bɪləti] NOUN
la disponibilidad

available [ə'veɪləbəl] ADJECTIVE
disponible ◇ *According to the available information, it can't be done.* De acuerdo con la información disponible, no se puede hacer.
◆ **Free brochures are available on request.** Disponemos de folletos gratuitos para quien los solicite.
◆ **Is Mr. Cooke available today?** ¿Está libre el señor Cooke hoy?

avalanche ['ævəlæntʃ] NOUN
el alud

avenue ['ævənju:] NOUN
la avenida

average ['ævərɪdʒ] NOUN
see also **average** ADJECTIVE
la media ◇ *on average* de media

average ['ævərɪdʒ] ADJECTIVE
see also **average** NOUN
medio ◇ *the average price* el precio medio

avocado [ævə'kɑ:dou] NOUN
el aguacate

to **avoid** [ə'vɔɪd] VERB
evitar ◇ *Avoid going out on your own at night.* Evite salir solo por la noche. ◇ *Are you trying to avoid me?* ¿Me estás evitando?

awake [ə'weɪk] ADJECTIVE
◆ **to be awake** estar* despierto
◆ **I was only half awake.** Estaba medio dormido.

award [ə'wɔ:rd] NOUN
el premio ◇ *the award for the best actor* el premio al mejor actor
◆ **an award winner** un premiado

away [ə'weɪ] ADJECTIVE, ADVERB
◆ **It's two miles away.** Está a dos millas de distancia.
◆ **The coast is two hours away by car.** La costa está a dos horas en carro.
◆ **The vacation was two weeks away.** Faltaban dos semanas para las vacaciones.
◆ **to be away** estar* fuera ◇ *Jason was away on a business trip.* Jason estaba fuera en viaje de negocios. ◇ *He'll be away for a week.* Va a estar fuera una semana.
◆ **Go away!** ¡Vete!
◆ **away from** lejos de ◇ *Ross is away from family and friends.* Ross está lejos de la familia y los amigos.
◆ **It's 30 km away from town.** Está a 30 km de la ciudad.
◆ **Keep away from the fire.** No te acerques al fuego.

***away** se emplea a veces para recalcar la continuidad o reiteración de la acción del verbo.*

◇ *He was still working away in the library.* Seguía trabajando sin parar en la biblioteca.

away match [ə'weɪˌmætʃ] NOUN (PL **away matches**)
◆ **It is their last away match.** Es el último partido que juegan fuera.

awful ['ɑ:fəl] ADJECTIVE
horrible ◇ *The weather is awful.* Hace un tiempo horrible.
◆ **I feel awful.** Me siento fatal.
◆ **We met and I thought he was awful.** Nos conocimos y me cayó muy mal.
◆ **I have an awful lot of work.** Tengo un montón de trabajo.
◆ **How awful!** ¡Qué horror!

awfully ['ɑ:fəli] ADVERB
- **I'm awfully sorry.** Lo siento muchísimo.
- **She works awfully hard.** Trabaja durísimo.

awkward ['ɑ:kwərd] ADJECTIVE

[1] incómodo ◇ *It was awkward to carry.* Era incómodo de llevar. ◇ *an awkward situation* una situación incómoda
- **Mike's being awkward about letting me have the car.** Mike no hace más que ponerme inconvenientes para prestarme el carro.
- **It's a bit awkward for me to come and see you today.** Me viene un poco mal pasar a verte hoy.

[2] torpe ◇ *an awkward gesture* un gesto torpe

ax [æks] (PL **axes**) NOUN

el hacha FEM

*Although it's a feminine noun, remember that you use **el** and **un** with **hacha**.*

B

BA [biːˈeɪ] ABBREVIATION (= *Bachelor of Arts*)
la licenciatura en Letras
- **a BA in French** una licenciatura en Filología Francesa
- **She has a BA in History.** Es licenciada en Historia.

baby [ˈbeɪbi] NOUN (PL **babies**)
el/la bebé (PL los/las bebés)

baby carriage [ˈbeɪbiˌkærɪdʒ] NOUN
el cochecito de niño

to **babysit** [ˈbeɪbiˌsɪt] VERB (**babysat, babysat**)
cuidar niños

babysitter [ˈbeɪbiˌsɪtər] NOUN
el/la baby sitter (PL los/las baby sitters)

babysitting [ˈbeɪbiˌsɪtɪŋ] NOUN
- **I don't like babysitting.** No me gusta cuidar niños.

bachelor [ˈbætʃələr] NOUN
el soltero

back [bæk] NOUN
see also **back** ADJECTIVE, ADVERB, VERB
[1] la espalda (*of person*) ◇ *He has a bad back.* Tiene problemas de espalda.
[2] el lomo (*of animal*)
- **the back of a chair** el respaldo de una silla
- **on the back of the check** al dorso del cheque
- **at the back of the house** en la parte de atrás de la casa
- **in the back of the car** en la parte trasera del carro
- **at the back of the class** al fondo de la clase

back [bæk] ADJECTIVE, ADVERB
see also **back** NOUN, VERB
trasero ◇ *the back seat* el asiento trasero
- **the back door** la puerta de atrás
- **He's not back yet.** Todavía no ha vuelto.
- **to get back** volver* ◇ *What time did you get back?* ¿A qué hora volviste? ◇ *We went there by bus and walked back.* Fuimos allí en bus y volvimos a pie.
- **to call somebody back** volver* a llamar a alguien ◇ *I'll call back later.* Volveré a llamar más tarde.

to **back** [bæk] VERB
see also **back** NOUN, ADJECTIVE, ADVERB
respaldar ◇ *The union is backing his claim for compensation.* El sindicato respalda su demanda de compensación.
- **to back a horse** apostar* por un caballo
- **She backed into the parking space.** Estacionó dando marcha atrás.

to **back out** [bækˈaut] VERB
echarse para atrás ◇ *They promised to help us and then backed out.* Prometieron ayudarnos y luego se echaron para atrás.

to **back up** [bækˈʌp] VERB
[1] dar* marcha atrás
meter reversa [*Mexico*]
(*car*)
◇ *He backed up without looking.* Dio marcha atrás sin mirar. [*Mexico:*] Metió reversa sin mirar.
[2] respaldar ◇ *She complained, and her colleagues backed her up.* Presentó una queja y sus colegas la respaldaron.

backache [ˈbækˌeɪk] NOUN
el dolor de espalda ◇ *to have backache* tener* dolor de espalda

backbone [ˈbækˌboun] NOUN
la columna vertebral

to **backfire** [ˈbækˌfaɪər] VERB
tener* el efecto contrario (*go wrong*)

background [ˈbækˌgraund] NOUN
el fondo (*of picture*) ◇ *a house in the background* una casa en el fondo
- **background noise** ruido de fondo
- **his family background** su historial familiar

backhand [ˈbækˌhænd] NOUN
el revés (PL los reveses)

backing [ˈbækɪŋ] NOUN
el apoyo ◇ *They promised their backing.* Prometieron su apoyo.

backpack [ˈbækˌpæk] NOUN
la mochila

backpacker [ˈbækˌpækər] NOUN
el mochilero
la mochilera

backside [ˈbækˌsaɪd] NOUN
el trasero

backstroke [ˈbækˌstrouk] NOUN
el estilo espalda
el estilo de dorso [*Mexico*]
- **to do the backstroke** nadar de espaldas, [*Mexico:*] nadar de dorso

backup [ˈbækˌʌp] NOUN
el apoyo ◇ *We have extensive computer backup.* Tenemos amplio apoyo informático.
- **They have a generator as an emergency backup.** Tienen un generador de reserva para emergencias.
- **a backup file** una copia de seguridad

backward [ˈbækwərd] ADVERB
hacia atrás ◇ *to take a step backward* dar* un paso hacia atrás
- **to fall backward** caerse* de espaldas

backyard [ˌbækˈjɑːrd] NOUN
el patio trasero

bacon [ˈbeɪkən] NOUN
el tocino ◇ *bacon and eggs* los huevos fritos con tocino

bad [bæd] ADJECTIVE
[1] malo ◇ *You bad boy!* ¡Malo!
*Use **mal** before a masculine singular noun.*
◇ *bad weather* mal tiempo
- **to be in a bad mood** estar* de mal humor
- **to be bad at something** ser* malo para algo

* Verbs marked with this symbol are irregular. See pages 346–348 for further details.

B

◇ *I'm really bad at math.* Soy muy malo para las matemáticas.
◆ **to go bad** (*food, milk*) echarse a perder
◆ **I feel bad about it.** (*guilty*) Me siento un poco culpable.
◆ **How are you? – Not bad.** ¿Cómo estás? – Bien
◆ **That's not bad at all.** No está nada mal.
◆ **bad language** las malas palabras
[2] grave (*serious*) ◇ *a bad accident* un accidente grave

badge [bædʒ] NOUN
[1] la chapa (*metal, plastic*)
[2] la insignia (*cloth*)

badly ['bædli] ADVERB
mal ◇ *badly paid* mal pagado
◆ **badly wounded** gravemente herido
◆ **He badly needs a rest.** Le hace muchísima falta un descanso.

badminton ['bæd,mɪntən] NOUN
el bádminton ◇ *to play badminton* jugar* bádminton

bad-tempered ['bæd'tɛmpərd] ADJECTIVE
◆ **to be bad-tempered (1)** (*by nature*) tener* mal genio ◇ *He's a really bad-tempered person.* Es una persona con muy mal genio.
◆ **to be bad-tempered (2)** (*temporarily*) estar* de mal humor ◇ *He was really bad-tempered yesterday.* Ayer estaba de muy mal humor.

to **baffle** ['bæfəl] VERB
desconcertar*

bag [bæg] NOUN
la bolsa

baggage ['bægɪdʒ] NOUN
el equipaje

baggage claim ['bægɪdʒ,kleɪm] NOUN
la recogida de equipajes

baggy ['bægi] ADJECTIVE
ancho (*pants*)

bagpipes ['bæg,paɪps] PL NOUN
la gaita SING

to **bake** [beɪk] VERB
◆ **to bake bread** hacer* pan
◆ **She loves to bake.** Le gusta cocinar al horno.

baked beans [beɪkt'bi:nz] PL NOUN
los frijoles en salsa de tomate

baker ['beɪkər] NOUN
el panadero
la panadera
◇ *He's a baker.* Es panadero.

bakery ['beɪkəri] NOUN (PL **bakeries**)
la panadería ◇ *at the bakery* en la panadería

balance ['bæləns] NOUN
see also **balance** VERB
el equilibrio ◇ *to lose one's balance* perder* el equilibrio

to **balance** ['bæləns] VERB
see also **balance** NOUN
mantener* el equilibrio ◇ *I balanced on the window ledge.* Mantenía el equilibrio en el alféizar de la ventana.
◆ **She balanced on one leg.** Se mantenía en equilibrio en un pie.
◆ **The boxes were carefully balanced.** Las cajas estaban cuidadosamente contrapesadas.

balanced ['bælənst] ADJECTIVE
equilibrado

balcony ['bælkəni] NOUN (PL **balconies**)
el balcón (PL los balcones)

bald [bɑ:ld] ADJECTIVE
calvo

ball [bɑ:l] NOUN
la pelota (*for soccer, tennis, basketball*) ◇ *a golf ball* una pelota de golf

ballerina ['bælə'ri:nə] NOUN
la bailarina

ballet [bæ'leɪ] NOUN
el ballet (PL los ballets) ◇ *We went to a ballet.* Fuimos a ver un ballet. ◇ *ballet lessons* las clases de ballet

ballet shoes [bæ'leɪ,ʃu:z] PL NOUN
las zapatillas de ballet

balloon [bə'lu:n] NOUN
el globo
◆ **a hot-air balloon** un globo aerostático

ballpoint pen ['bɑ:lpɔɪnt'pɛn] NOUN
el bolígrafo
la pluma atómica Mexico

ballroom dancing ['bɑ:lru:m'dænsɪŋ] NOUN
el baile de salón

ban [bæn] NOUN
see also **ban** VERB
la prohibición (PL las prohibiciones)

to **ban** [bæn] VERB
see also **ban** NOUN
prohibir*

banana [bə'nænə] NOUN
el plátano ◇ *a banana peel* una cáscara de plátano

band [bænd] NOUN
[1] el grupo (*pop, rock*)
[2] la banda (*military*)
[3] la orquesta (*at a dance*)

bandage ['bændɪdʒ] NOUN
see also **bandage** VERB
la venda

to **bandage** ['bændɪdʒ] VERB
see also **bandage** NOUN
vendar ◇ *The nurse bandaged his arm.* La enfermera le vendó el brazo.

Band-Aid® ['bænd,eɪd] NOUN
la curita

bandit ['bændɪt] NOUN
el bandido

bang [bæŋ] NOUN
see also **bang** VERB
[1] el estallido (*noise*) ◇ *I heard a loud bang.* Oí un fuerte estallido.
[2] el golpe (*blow*) ◇ *a bang on the head* un golpe en la cabeza

to **bang** [bæŋ] VERB

☞

see also **bang** NOUN
golpear ◇ *I banged my head.* Me golpeé la cabeza.
◆ **to bang on the door** aporrear la puerta
◆ **to bang the door** dar* un portazo

bangs [bæŋz] PL NOUN
el flequillo SING ◇ *She has bangs.* Lleva flequillo.

bank [bæŋk] NOUN
1 el banco (*financial*)
2 la orilla (*of river, lake*)

to **bank on** ['bæŋk,ɑːn] VERB
contar* con ◇ *I was banking on your coming today.* Contaba con que vendrías hoy.
◆ **I wouldn't bank on it.** Yo no me confiaría demasiado.

bank account ['bæŋkə'kaunt] NOUN
la cuenta bancaria

banker ['bæŋkər] NOUN
el banquero
la banquera
◇ *He's a banker.* Es banquero.

banknote ['bæŋk,nout] NOUN
el billete de banco

baptism ['bæptɪzəm] NOUN
el bautizo

Baptist ['bæptɪst] NOUN
el/la baptista

to **baptize** ['bæptaɪz] VERB
bautizar*

bar [bɑːr] NOUN
1 el bar (*pub*)
2 la barra (*counter*)
◆ **a bar of chocolate (1)** (*large*) una barra de chocolate, Mexico: una tablilla de chocolate
◆ **a bar of chocolate (2)** (*small*) una chocolatina
◆ **a bar of soap** una pastilla de jabón

barbaric [bɑːr'bɛrɪk] ADJECTIVE
bárbaro

barbecue ['bɑːrbɪkjuː] NOUN
el asado ◇ *to have a barbecue* hacer* un asado

barber ['bɑːrbər] NOUN
el barbero ◇ *He's a barber.* Es barbero.
◆ **at the barber shop** en la barbería

bare [bɛər] ADJECTIVE
desnudo

barefoot ['bɛr,fut] ADJECTIVE, ADVERB
descalzo ◇ *The children go around barefoot.* Los niños van descalzos.

barely ['bɛrli] ADVERB
apenas ◇ *I could barely hear what she was saying.* Apenas oía lo que estaba diciendo.

bargain ['bɑːrgɪn] NOUN
la ganga ◇ *It was a bargain!* ¡Era una ganga!

barge [bɑːrdʒ] NOUN
la barcaza

to **bark** [bɑːrk] VERB
ladrar

barn [bɑːrn] NOUN
el granero

barrel ['bɛrəl] NOUN
1 el barril (*container*)
2 el cañón (PL los cañones) (*of gun*)

barrier ['bɛriər] NOUN
la barrera

bartender ['bɑːrtɛndər] NOUN
el mesero
la mesera
◇ *He's a bartender.* Es mesero.

base [beɪs] NOUN
la base

baseball ['beɪs,bɑːl] NOUN
el béisbol
el beisbol Mexico
◇ *to play baseball* jugar* béisbol, Mexico: jugar* beisbol
◆ **a baseball cap** una gorra de béisbol, Mexico: una gorra de beisbol

based [beɪst] ADJECTIVE
◆ **based on** basado en

basement ['beɪsmənt] NOUN
el sótano ◇ *a basement apartment* un departamento en el sótano

to **bash** [bæʃ] VERB
see also **bash** NOUN
golpear con fuerza

bash [bæʃ] NOUN
see also **bash** VERB
◆ **I'll have a bash at it.** Lo intentaré.

basic ['beɪsɪk] ADJECTIVE
básico ◇ *It's a basic model.* Es un modelo básico.
◆ **The accommodations were pretty basic.** El alojamiento tenía sólo lo imprescindible.

basically ['beɪsɪkli] ADVERB
básicamente ◇ *They are basically the same thing.* Son básicamente lo mismo.
◆ **Basically, I just don't like him.** Simplemente, no me gusta.

basics ['beɪsɪks] PL NOUN
los principios básicos

basil ['beɪsəl] NOUN
la albahaca

basin ['beɪsən] NOUN
el lavamanos (PL los lavamanos) (*washbowl*)

basis ['beɪsɪs] NOUN
la base ◇ *on the basis of what you've said* en base a lo que has dicho
◆ **on a daily basis** diariamente
◆ **on a regular basis** regularmente

basket ['bæskɪt] NOUN
la canasta ◇ *to score a basket* meter una canasta (*in basketball*)

basketball ['bæskɪt,bɑːl] NOUN
el básquetbol
el basquetbol Mexico
◇ *to play basketball* jugar* básquetbol, Mexico: jugar* basquetbol

bass [beɪs] NOUN (PL **basses**)
el bajo (*voice*)
◆ **a bass guitar** un bajo
◆ **a double bass** un contrabajo
bass drum [beɪs'drʌm] NOUN
el bombo
bassoon [bə'suːn] NOUN
el fagot (PL los fagots)
bat [bæt] NOUN
1 el bate (*for baseball*)
2 el murciélago (*animal*)
bath [bæθ] NOUN
1 el baño ◇ *a hot bath* un baño caliente
◆ **to have a bath** bañarse
2 la tina (*bathtub*)
to **bathe** [beɪð] VERB
bañarse
bathing cap ['beɪðɪŋˌkæp] NOUN
el gorro de baño
bathing suit ['beɪðɪŋˌsuːt] NOUN
el traje de baño
bathrobe ['bæθroub] NOUN
el albornoz (PL los albornoces)
bathroom ['bæθˌruːm] NOUN
el baño
◆ **to go to the bathroom** ir* al servicio
bath towel ['bæθˌtauəl] NOUN
la toalla de baño
bathtub ['bæθˌtʌb] NOUN
la tina
batter ['bætər] NOUN
1 la masa para rebozar
2 el bateador
la bateadora
(*in baseball*)
battery ['bætəri] NOUN (PL **batteries**)
1 la pila (*for flashlight, toy*)
2 la batería (*for car*)
battle ['bætl] NOUN
la batalla ◇ *the Battle of Gettysburg* la batalla de Gettysburg
◆ **It was a battle, but we managed in the end.** Fue muy difícil, pero al final lo conseguimos.
battleship ['bætlʃɪp] NOUN
el acorazado
bay [beɪ] NOUN
la bahía
BC [biː'siː] ABBREVIATION (= *before Christ*)
a.C. (= antes de Cristo)
to **be** [biː] VERB (**is, was, been**)
*There are two basic verbs to translate **be** into Spanish: **estar** and **ser**. **estar** is used to form continuous tenses; to talk about where something is; and with adjectives describing a temporary state. It is also used with past participles used adjectivally even if these describe a permanent state.*
1 estar* ◇ *What are you doing?* ¿Qué estás haciendo? ◇ *Phoenix is in Arizona.* Phoenix está en Arizona. ◇ *I've never been to Alaska.* No he estado nunca en Alaska. ◇ *I'm very happy.* Estoy muy contento. ◇ *The window is broken.* La ventana está rota. ◇ *Is he hurt?* ¿Está herido? ◇ *He's dead.* Está muerto.
◆ **You're late.** Llegas tarde.
***ser** is used to talk about the time and date; with adjectives describing permanent or inherent states such as nationality and color; with nouns to say what somebody or something is; and to form the passive.*
2 ser* ◇ *It's four o'clock.* Son las cuatro. ◇ *It's October 28th today.* Hoy es 28 de octubre. ◇ *She's English.* Es inglesa. ◇ *He's a doctor.* Es médico. ◇ *Washington is the capital of America.* Washington es la capital de America. ◇ *He's very tall.* Es muy alto. ◇ *The house was destroyed by an earthquake.* La casa fue destruida por un terremoto.
Passive constructions are not as common in Spanish as in English. Either the active or a reflexive construction are preferred.
◇ *He was killed by a terrorist.* Lo mató un terrorista. ◇ *These cars are produced in Spain.* Estos carros se fabrican en España.
*When referring to the weather, use **hacer**.*
◆ **It's a nice day, isn't it?** Hace buen día, ¿verdad?
◆ **It's cold.** Hace frío.
◆ **It's too hot.** Hace demasiado calor.
*With certain adjectives, such as **cold, hot, hungry**, and **thirsty**, use **tener*** with a noun.*
◆ **I'm cold.** Tengo frío.
◆ **I'm hungry.** Tengo hambre.
*When saying how old somebody is, use **tener**.*
◆ **I'm fourteen.** Tengo catorce años.
◆ **How old are you?** ¿Cuántos años tienes?
beach [biːtʃ] NOUN (PL **beaches**)
la playa
bead [biːd] NOUN
la cuenta
beak [biːk] NOUN
el pico
beam [biːm] NOUN
el rayo (*of light*)
beans [biːnz] PL NOUN
los frijoles
◆ **green beans** las habichuelas, *Mexico:* los ejotes
bean sprouts ['biːnˌsprauts] PL NOUN
los brotes de soya
bear [bɛər] NOUN
see also **bear** VERB
el oso
to **bear** [bɛər] VERB (**bore, borne**)
see also **bear** NOUN
aguantar ◇ *I can't bear it!* ¡No lo aguanto!
to **bear with** ['bɛərˌwɪð] VERB
◆ **If you would bear with me for a moment...** Tenga la bondad de esperar un momento...
beard [bɪərd] NOUN
la barba ◇ *He has a beard.* Lleva barba. ◇ *a* ☞

man with a beard un hombre con barba

bearded ['bɪərdɪd] ADJECTIVE
con barba

beat [bi:t] NOUN
see also **beat** VERB
el ritmo

to **beat** [bi:t] VERB (**beat, beaten**)
see also **beat** NOUN
1 ganar ◇ *We beat them three to nothing.* Les ganamos tres a cero.
2 golpear (*surface*)
3 tocar* (*drum*)
4 batir (*eggs, cream*)
◆ **Beat it!** ¡Lárgate! (*informal*)

to **beat up** [bi:t'ʌp] VERB
dar* una paliza a

beautiful ['bju:tɪful] ADJECTIVE
precioso

beauty ['bju:ti] NOUN (PL **beauties**)
la belleza

beauty spot ['bju:ti,spɑ:t] NOUN
el lugar pintoresco (*place*)

became [bɪ'keɪm] VERB *see* **become**

because [bɪ'kɑ:z] CONJUNCTION
porque
◆ **because of** debido a

to **become** [bɪ'kʌm] VERB (**became, become**)
llegar* a ser

bed [bɛd] NOUN
la cama
◆ **to go to bed** acostarse*
◆ **to go to bed with somebody** acostarse con alguien

bedclothes ['bɛd,klouz] PL NOUN
la ropa de cama SING

bedding ['bɛdɪŋ] NOUN
la ropa de cama

bedroom ['bɛd,ru:m] NOUN
el dormitorio
la recámara *Mexico*
◆ **a three-bedroom house** una casa de tres dormitorios, *Mexico:* una casa de tres recámaras

bedspread ['bɛd,sprɛd] NOUN
la colcha

bedtime ['bɛd,taɪm] NOUN
◆ **Ten o'clock is my usual bedtime.** Normalmente me voy a la cama a las diez.
◆ **Bedtime!** ¡A la cama!

bee [bi:] NOUN
la abeja

beef [bi:f] NOUN
la carne de vaca
la carne de res *Mexico*
◆ **roast beef** el rosbif

beefburger ['bi:f,bɜ:rgər] NOUN
la hamburguesa

been [bɪn] VERB *see* **be**

beeper ['bi:pər] NOUN
el busca

Although ***busca*** *ends in* ***-a****, it is actually a masculine noun.*

beer [bɪər] NOUN
la cerveza

beet [bi:t] NOUN
la remolacha
la betabel *Mexico*

beetle ['bi:tl] NOUN
el escarabajo

before [bɪ'fɔ:r] PREPOSITION, CONJUNCTION, ADVERB
1 antes de ◇ *before Tuesday* antes del martes ◇ *Before opening the packet, read the instructions.* Antes de abrir el paquete, lea las instrucciones. ◇ *I'll phone before I leave.* Llamaré antes de salir.
2 antes de que

antes de que *has to be followed by a verb in the subjunctive.*

◇ *I'll call her before she leaves.* La llamaré antes de que se vaya.
◆ **I've seen this movie before.** Esta película ya la he visto.
◆ **the week before** la semana anterior

beforehand [bɪ'fɔ:r,hænd] ADVERB
con antelación

to **beg** [bɛg] VERB
1 mendigar* (*for money, food*)
2 suplicar*

suplicar que *has to be followed by a verb in the subjunctive.*

◇ *He begged me to stop.* Me suplicó que parara.

began [bɪ'gæn] VERB *see* **begin**

beggar ['bɛgər] NOUN
el mendigo
la mendiga

to **begin** [bɪ'gɪn] VERB (**began, begun**)
empezar*
◆ **to begin doing something** empezar a hacer algo

beginner [bɪ'gɪnər] NOUN
el/la principiante
◆ **beginner's slope** la pista para principiantes

beginning [bɪ'gɪnɪŋ] NOUN
el comienzo
◆ **in the beginning** al principio

begun [bɪ'gʌn] VERB *see* **begin**

behalf [bɪ'hæf] NOUN
◆ **on behalf of somebody** de parte de alguien

to **behave** [bɪ'heɪv] VERB
comportarse ◇ *He behaved like an idiot.* Se comportó como un idiota.
◆ **to behave oneself** portarse bien ◇ *Did the children behave themselves?* ¿Se portaron bien los niños?
◆ **Behave!** ¡Compórtate!

behavior [bɪ'heɪvjər] NOUN
el comportamiento

behind [bɪ'haɪnd] PREPOSITION, ADVERB
see also **behind** NOUN

* Verbs marked with this symbol are irregular. See pages 346–348 for further details.

detrás de ◇ *behind the television* detrás de la televisión
◆ **to be behind** (*late*) ir* atrasado ◇ *I'm behind with my work.* Voy atrasado con mi trabajo.

behind [bɪ'haɪnd] NOUN
see also **behind** PREPOSITION, ADVERB
el trasero

beige [beɪʒ] ADJECTIVE
beige MASC, FEM, PL

Belgian ['bɛldʒən] ADJECTIVE
see also **Belgian** NOUN
belga ◇ *He's Belgian.* Es belga.

Belgian ['bɛldʒən] NOUN
see also **Belgian** ADJECTIVE
el/la belga ◇ *the Belgians* los belgas

Belgium ['bɛldʒəm] NOUN
Bélgica FEM

to **believe** [bɪ'li:v] VERB
creer* ◇ *I don't believe you.* No te creo.
◆ **I don't believe it!** ¡No me lo creo!
◆ **to believe in something** creer* en algo ◇ *Do you believe in ghosts?* ¿Crees en los fantasmas?

bell [bɛl] NOUN
1 el timbre (*of door, in school*) ◇ *The bell rings at half past three.* El timbre suena a las tres y media.
2 la campana (*of church*) ◇ *the church bell* la campana de la iglesia
3 el cascabel (*of toy, on animal*) ◇ *Our cat has a bell on its collar.* Nuestro gato lleva un cascabel en el collar.

bellboy ['bɛl,bɔɪ] NOUN
el botones

bellhop ['bɛl,hɑ:p] NOUN
el botones

belly ['bɛli] NOUN (PL **bellies**)
la barriga

to **belong** [bɪ'lɑ:ŋ] VERB
◆ **to belong to somebody** pertenecer* a alguien ◇ *This ring belonged to my grandmother.* Este anillo pertenecía a mi abuela.
◆ **Who does it belong to?** ¿De quién es?
◆ **That belongs to me.** Eso es mío.
◆ **Do you belong to any clubs?** ¿Eres miembro de algún club?
◆ **Where does this belong?** ¿Dónde va esto?

belongings [bɪ'lɑ:ŋɪŋz] PL NOUN
◆ **I collected my belongings and left.** Recogí mis cosas y me fui.
◆ **personal belongings** los efectos personales

below [bɪ'lou] PREPOSITION, ADVERB
1 debajo de ◇ *the apartment directly below ours* el departamento que está justo debajo del nuestro
2 abajo ◇ *seen from below* visto desde abajo ◇ *on the floor below* en el piso de abajo
◆ **ten degrees below freezing** diez grados bajo cero

belt [bɛlt] NOUN
el cinturón (PL los cinturones)

beltway ['bɛlt,weɪ] NOUN
la carretera de circunvalación
el libramiento *Mexico*

bench [bɛntʃ] NOUN (PL **benches**)
el banco

bend [bɛnd] NOUN
see also **bend** VERB
la curva

to **bend** [bɛnd] VERB (**bent, bent**)
see also **bend** NOUN
1 doblar ◇ *I can't bend my arm.* No puedo doblar el brazo.
2 torcerse* ◇ *It bends easily.* Se tuerce fácilmente.

to **bend down** [bɛnd'daun] VERB
agacharse

to **bend over** [bɛnd'ouvər] VERB
inclinarse

beneath [bɪ'ni:θ] PREPOSITION
bajo

benefit ['bɛnɪfɪt] NOUN
see also **benefit** VERB
el beneficio
◆ **unemployment benefit** el subsidio de desempleo

to **benefit** ['bɛnɪfɪt] VERB
see also **benefit** NOUN
beneficiar ◇ *This will benefit us all.* Esto nos beneficiará a todos. ◇ *He'll benefit from the change.* Se beneficiará con el cambio.

bent [bɛnt] VERB *see* **bend**

bent [bɛnt] ADJECTIVE
torcido ◇ *a bent fork* un tenedor torcido
◆ **to be bent on doing something** estar* empeñado en hacer algo

beret [bə'reɪ] NOUN
la boina

berm [bɜ:rm] NOUN
el arcén

berserk [bər'sɜ:rk] ADJECTIVE
◆ **to go berserk** ponerse* hecho una fiera

berth [bɜ:rθ] NOUN
la litera (*bunk*)

beside [bɪ'saɪd] PREPOSITION
al lado de ◇ *beside the television* al lado de la televisión
◆ **He was beside himself.** Estaba fuera de sí.
◆ **That's beside the point.** Eso no viene al caso.

besides [bɪ'saɪdz] ADVERB
además ◇ *Besides, it's too expensive.* Además, es demasiado caro.
◆ **...and much more besides.** ...y mucho más todavía.

best [bɛst] ADJECTIVE, ADVERB
mejor ◇ *He's the best player on the team.* Es el mejor jugador del equipo. ◇ *Janet's the best at math.* Janet es la mejor en matemáticas. ◇ *Emma sings best.* Emma es la que canta mejor.

☞

◆ **That's the best I can do.** No puedo hacer más.
◆ **to do one's best** hacer* todo lo posible ◇ *It's not perfect, but I did my best.* No es perfecto, pero he hecho todo lo posible.
◆ **You'll just have to make the best of it.** Tendrás que arreglártelas con lo que hay.

best man [bɛst'mæn] NOUN
el padrino de boda

bet [bɛt] NOUN
see also **bet** VERB
la apuesta

to **bet** [bɛt] VERB (**bet, bet**)
see also **bet** NOUN
apostar* ◇ *I bet you he won't come.* Te apuesto a que no viene.

to **betray** [bɪ'treɪ] VERB
traicionar

better ['bɛtər] ADJECTIVE, ADVERB
mejor ◇ *This one's better than that one.* Éste es mejor que aquél. ◇ *Are you feeling better now?* ¿Te sientes mejor ahora?
◆ **That's better!** ¡Así está mejor!
◆ **better still** mejor todavía
◆ **to get better (1)** mejorar (*improve*) ◇ *I hope the weather gets better soon.* Espero que el tiempo mejore pronto.
◆ **to get better (2)** mejorarse (*from illness*) ◇ *I hope you get better soon.* Espero que te mejores pronto.
◆ **You'd better do it straight away.** Más vale hacerlo enseguida.
◆ **I'd better go home.** Tengo que irme a la casa.

between [bɪ'twiːn] PREPOSITION
entre ◇ *between 15 and 20 minutes* entre 15 y 20 minutos

to **beware** [bɪ'wɛər] VERB
◆ **Beware of the dog!** ¡Cuidado con el perro!

bewildered [bɪ'wɪldərd] ADJECTIVE
desconcertado

beyond [bɪ'ɑːnd] PREPOSITION, ADVERB
al otro lado de ◇ *There is a lake beyond the mountains.* Hay un lago al otro lado de las montañas.
◆ **We have no plans beyond the year 2002.** No tenemos planes para después del año 2002.
◆ **the wheat fields and the mountains beyond** los campos de trigo y las montañas al fondo
◆ **it's beyond me** no lo entiendo
◆ **beyond belief** increíble
◆ **beyond repair** irreparable

biased ['baɪəst] ADJECTIVE
parcial

Bible ['baɪbəl] NOUN
la Biblia

bicycle ['baɪsɪkəl] NOUN
la bicicleta
◆ **a bicycle ride** un paseo en bicicleta

bifocals ['baɪˌfoukəlz] PL NOUN
los lentes bifocales

big [bɪg] ADJECTIVE
grande ◇ *a big house* una casa grande ◇ *a big car* un carro grande
*Use **gran** before a singular noun.*
◇ *it's a big business* es un gran negocio
◆ **my big brother** mi hermano mayor
◆ **He's a big guy.** Es un tipo grandote.
◆ **Big deal!** ¡Vaya cosa!
◆ **the Big Apple** la Gran Manzana

bigheaded ['bɪg'hɛdɪd] ADJECTIVE
◆ **to be bigheaded** ser* engreído

bike [baɪk] NOUN
1 la bici (*bicycle*) ◇ *by bike* en bici
2 la moto (*motorbike*)
*Although **moto** ends in **-o**, it is actually a feminine noun.*

bikeway ['baɪkˌweɪ] NOUN
el carril para bicicletas

bikini [bɪ'kiːni] NOUN
el/la bikini

bilingual [baɪ'lɪŋgwəl] ADJECTIVE
bilingüe

bill [bɪl] NOUN
1 el billete ◇ *a five-dollar bill* un billete de cinco dólares
2 la cuenta (*for gas, electricity, telephone*) ◇ *the gas bill* la cuenta del gas

billfold ['bɪlˌfould] NOUN
la cartera

billion ['bɪljən] NOUN
los mil millones ◇ *two billion dollars* dos mil millones de dólares

bin [bɪn] NOUN
1 la panera (*for bread*)
2 la carbonera (*for coal*)
3 la papelera (*for paper*)
4 el cubo de la basura
el bote de la basura *Mexico*
(*in kitchen*)

bingo ['bɪŋgou] NOUN
el bingo

binoculars [bə'nɑːkjələrz] PL NOUN
los prismáticos
◆ **a pair of binoculars** unos prismáticos

biochemistry [baɪou'kɛmɪstri] NOUN
la bioquímica

biography [baɪ'ɑːgrəfi] NOUN (PL **biographies**)
la biografía

biology [baɪ'ɑːlədʒi] NOUN
la biología

bird [bɜːrd] NOUN
el pájaro

bird-watching ['bɜːrdˌwɑːtʃɪŋ] NOUN
◆ **He likes to go bird-watching on Sundays.** Los domingos le gusta ir a mirar pájaros.

birth [bɜːrθ] NOUN
el nacimiento ◇ *date of birth* la fecha de nacimiento

birth certificate ['bɜːrθsərˌtɪfɪkɪt] NOUN
el certificado de nacimiento
el acta de nacimiento *Mexico*

birth control [ˈbɜːrθkənˌtroul] NOUN
el control de natalidad

birthday [ˈbɜːrθˌdeɪ] NOUN
el cumpleaños (PL los cumpleaños) ◇ *a birthday cake* un pastel de cumpleaños ◇ *a birthday party* una fiesta de cumpleaños ◇ *When's your birthday?* ¿Cuándo es tu cumpleaños?

birthday card NOUN
la tarjeta de cumpleaños

biscuit [ˈbɪskɪt] NOUN
el bollo
el bolillo *Mexico*

bishop [ˈbɪʃəp] NOUN
el obispo

bit [bɪt] VERB *see* **bite**

bit [bɪt] NOUN
el trozo ◇ *Would you like another bit?* ¿Quieres otro trozo?
◆ **a bit** un poco ◇ *He's a bit mad.* Está un poco loco. ◇ *Wait a bit!* ¡Espera un poco!
◆ **a bit of (1)** un trozo de ◇ *a bit of cake* un trozo de pastel
◆ **a bit of (2)** un poco de ◇ *a bit of music* un poco de música
◆ **It's a bit of a nuisance.** Es un poco fastidioso.
◆ **to fall to bits** caerse* a pedazos
◆ **to take something to bits** desarmar algo
◆ **bit by bit** poco a poco

bitch [bɪtʃ] NOUN (PL **bitches**)
la perra (*female dog*)

to **bite** [baɪt] VERB (**bit, bitten**)
see also **bite** NOUN
1 morder* (*person, dog*) ◇ *My dog's never bitten anyone.* Mi perro nunca ha mordido a nadie.
2 picar* (*insect*) ◇ *I got bitten by mosquitoes.* Me picaron los mosquitos.
◆ **to bite one's nails** morderse* las uñas

bite [baɪt] NOUN
see also **bite** VERB
1 la picadura (*insect bite*)
2 el mordisco (*animal bite*)
◆ **to have a bite to eat** comer alguna cosa

bitter [ˈbɪtər] ADJECTIVE
1 amargo ◇ *It tastes bitter.* Sabe amargo.
2 glacial ◇ *It's bitter today.* Hoy hace un frío glacial.

black [blæk] ADJECTIVE
negro ◇ *a black jacket* una chaqueta negra ◇ *She's Black.* Es negra.
◆ **black and white** blanco y negro

blackberry [ˈblækˌbɛri] NOUN (PL **blackberries**)
la mora

blackbird [ˈblækˌbɜːrd] NOUN
el mirlo

black coffee [blækˈkɑːfi] NOUN
el café negro

blackcurrant [ˈblækˌkɜːrənt] NOUN
la grosella negra

blackmail [ˈblækˌmeɪl] NOUN
see also **blackmail** VERB
el chantaje

to **blackmail** [ˈblækˌmeɪl] VERB
see also **blackmail** NOUN
chantajear

blackout [ˈblækˌaut] NOUN
el apagón (PL los apagones) (*power outage*)
◆ **to have a blackout** (*faint*) sufrir un desvanecimiento

blacksmith [ˈblækˌsmɪθ] NOUN
el herrero ◇ *He's a blacksmith.* Es herrero.

blacktop [ˈblæktɑːp] NOUN
el asfalto
el chapopote *Mexico*
(*on road*)

blade [bleɪd] NOUN
la hoja

to **blame** [bleɪm] VERB
echar la culpa a ◇ *Don't blame me!* ¡No me eches la culpa a mí!
◆ **He blamed it on my sister.** Le echó la culpa a mi hermana.

blank [blæŋk] ADJECTIVE
see also **blank** NOUN
1 en blanco (*sheet of paper*)
2 virgen (PL vírgenes) (*cassette*)
◆ **My mind went blank.** Me quedé en blanco.

blank [blæŋk] NOUN
see also **blank** ADJECTIVE
el espacio en blanco ◇ *Fill in the blanks.* Llene los espacios en blanco.

blank check [blæŋkˈtʃɛk] NOUN
el cheque en blanco

blanket [ˈblæŋkɪt] NOUN
la cobija

blast [blæst] NOUN
◆ **a bomb blast** una explosión

blatant [ˈbleɪtnt] ADJECTIVE
descarado

blaze [bleɪz] NOUN
el incendio

blazer [ˈbleɪzər] NOUN
el blazer (PL los blazers)

bleach [bliːtʃ] NOUN (PL **bleaches**)
la lejía
el blanqueador *Mexico*

bleached hair [ˈbliːtʃtˈhɛər] NOUN
el cabello decolorado

bleachers [ˈbliːtʃərz] PL NOUN
las gradas (*in stadium*)

bleak [bliːk] ADJECTIVE
poco prometedor ◇ *The future looks bleak.* Se presenta un futuro poco prometedor.

to **bleed** [bliːd] VERB (**bled, bled**)
sangrar
◆ **to bleed to death** morir* desangrado
◆ **My nose is bleeding.** Me sangra la nariz.

bleeper [ˈbliːpər] NOUN
el busca
el bip *Mexico*
Although **busca** *ends in* **-a**, *it is actually a* ☞

masculine noun.

blender ['blɛndər] NOUN
la licuadora

to **bless** [blɛs] VERB
bendecir*
◆ **Bless you!** ¡Salud! (*after sneezing*)

blew [blu:] VERB *see* **blow**

blind [blaɪnd] ADJECTIVE
see also **blind** NOUN
ciego

blind [blaɪnd] NOUN
see also **blind** ADJECTIVE
la persiana (*for window*)

blindfold ['blaɪnd,fould] NOUN
see also **blindfold** VERB
la venda

to **blindfold** ['blaɪnd,fould] VERB
see also **blindfold** NOUN
◆ **to blindfold somebody** vendar los ojos a alguien

to **blink** [blɪŋk] VERB
parpadear

bliss [blɪs] NOUN
◆ **It was bliss!** ¡Era la gloria!

blister ['blɪstər] NOUN
la ampolla

blizzard ['blɪzərd] NOUN
la ventisca de nieve

blob [blɑ:b] NOUN
la gota ◇ *a blob of glue* una gota de pegamento

block [blɑ:k] NOUN
see also **block** VERB
el bloque ◇ *He lives on our block.* Vive en nuestro bloque.

to **block** [blɑ:k] VERB
see also **block** NOUN
bloquear

blockage ['blɑ:kɪdʒ] NOUN
la obstrucción (PL las obstrucciones)

blond(e) [blɑ:nd] ADJECTIVE
rubio ◇ *She has blonde hair.* Tiene el pelo rubio.

blood [blʌd] NOUN
la sangre

blood pressure ['blʌd,prɛʃər] NOUN
la presión sanguínea ◇ *to have high blood pressure* tener* la presión alta

blood sports ['blʌd,spɔ:rts] PL NOUN
los deportes sangrientos

blood test ['blʌd,tɛst] NOUN
el análisis de sangre (PL los análisis de sangre)

blouse [blaus] NOUN
la blusa

blow [blou] NOUN
see also **blow** VERB
el golpe

to **blow** [blou] VERB (**blew, blown**)
see also **blow** NOUN
soplar ◇ *A cold wind was blowing.* Soplaba un viento frío. ◇ *He blew on his fingers.* Se sopló los dedos.
◆ **They were one-all when the whistle blew.** Iban uno a uno cuando sonó el pito.
◆ **to blow one's nose** sonarse* la nariz

to **blow out** [blou'aut] VERB
apagar* ◇ *Blow out the candles!* ¡Apaga las velas!

to **blow up** [blou'ʌp] VERB
1 volar* ◇ *They blew up a plane.* Volaron un avión.
2 inflar ◇ *We've blown up the balloons.* Inflamos los globos.
3 saltar por los aires ◇ *The house blew up.* La casa saltó por los aires.

blow-dry ['blou,draɪ] NOUN
el secado con secador de mano
◆ **Cut and blow-dry.** Corte y secado a mano.

blue [blu:] ADJECTIVE
azul ◇ *a blue dress* un vestido azul
◆ **out of the blue** en el momento menos pensado

blues [blu:z] PL NOUN
el blues (PL los blues) (*music*)

to **bluff** [blʌf] VERB
see also **bluff** NOUN
hacer* un bluff
blofear *Mexico*

bluff [blʌf] NOUN
see also **bluff** VERB
el bluff
el blof *Mexico*

blunder ['blʌndər] NOUN
la metida de pata

blunt [blʌnt] ADJECTIVE
1 directo (*person*)
2 desafilado (*knife*)

to **blush** [blʌʃ] VERB
ruborizarse*

board [bɔ:rd] NOUN
1 la tabla (*plank*)
2 el pizarrón (PL los pizarrones) (*chalkboard*)
3 el tablero de anuncios (*bulletin board*)
4 el trampolín (PL los trampolines) (*for diving*)
5 el tablero (*for games*)
◆ **a chopping board** una tabla de picar
◆ **on board** a bordo

boarder ['bɔ:rdər] NOUN
el interno
la interna

board game ['bɔ:rd,geɪm] NOUN
el juego de mesa

boarding pass ['bɔ:rdɪŋ,pæs] NOUN (PL **boarding passes**)
la tarjeta de embarque

boarding school ['bɔ:rdɪŋ,sku:l] NOUN
el internado

to **boast** [boust] VERB
alardear
◆ **to boast about something** alardear de algo
◆ **Stop boasting!** ¡Deja ya de presumir!

boat [bout] NOUN
el barco

bobby pin ['bɑ:bi,pɪn] NOUN
la horquilla

body ['bɑ:di] NOUN (PL **bodies**)
1 el cuerpo ◇ *the human body* el cuerpo humano
2 el cadáver (*corpse*)

bodybuilding ['bɑ:di,bɪldɪŋ] NOUN
el culturismo

bodyguard ['bɑ:dii,gɑ:rd] NOUN
el/la guardaespaldas (PL los/las guardaespaldas) ◇ *He's a bodyguard.* Es guardaespaldas.

bog [bɑ:g] NOUN
la ciénaga (*marsh*)

boil [bɔɪl] NOUN
see also **boil** VERB
el furúnculo

to **boil** [bɔɪl] VERB
see also **boil** NOUN
hervir* ◇ *to boil some water* hervir* un poco de agua ◇ *The water is boiling.* El agua está hirviendo.
◆ **to boil an egg** cocer* un huevo

to **boil over** [bɔɪl'ouvər] VERB
salirse*

boiled [bɔɪld] ADJECTIVE
hervido
◆ **a boiled egg** un huevo pasado por agua, *Mexico*: un huevo tibio

boiling ['bɔɪlɪŋ] ADJECTIVE
◆ **It's boiling in here!** ¡Aquí adentro se asa uno!
◆ **a boiling hot day** un día asfixiante de calor

bolt [boult] NOUN
1 el cerrojo (*on door, window*)
2 el perno (*type of screw*)

bomb [bɑ:m] NOUN
see also **bomb** VERB
la bomba

to **bomb** [bɑ:m] VERB
see also **bomb** NOUN
bombardear

bomber ['bɑ:mər] NOUN
el bombardero (*plane*)

bombing ['bɑ:mɪŋ] NOUN
el bombardeo

bond [bɑ:nd] NOUN
el vínculo ◇ *the bond between mother and child* el vínculo entre la madre y el hijo

bone [boun] NOUN
1 el hueso (*of human, animal*)
2 la espina (*of fish*)
◆ **bone marrow** la médula

bone dry ['boun'draɪ] ADJECTIVE
completamente seco

bonfire ['bɑ:n,faɪər] NOUN
la fogata

bonus ['bounəs] NOUN (PL **bonuses**)
1 la bonificación (*extra payment*)
2 la ventaja (*added advantage*)

book [buk] NOUN
see also **book** VERB
el libro

to **book** [buk] VERB
see also **book** NOUN
reservar ◇ *to book a flight* reservar un vuelo

bookcase ['buk,keɪs] NOUN
la biblioteca
el librero *Mexico*

booklet ['buklɪt] NOUN
el folleto

bookmark ['buk,mɑ:rk] NOUN
el marcador (*book, computer*)

bookshelf ['buk,ʃɛlf] NOUN (PL **bookshelves**)
el estante para libros

bookstore ['buk,stɔ:r] NOUN
la librería

boom box ['bu:m,bɑ:ks] NOUN (PL **boom boxes**)
el radiocasete portátil

to **boost** [bu:st] VERB
◆ **The win boosted the team's morale.** La victoria levantó la moral del equipo.
◆ **They're trying to boost the economy.** Intentan dar un empuje a la economía.

boot [bu:t] NOUN
1 la bota (*fashion boots*)
2 el borceguí (PL los borceguíes) (*for hiking*)

bootblack ['bu:t,blæk] NOUN
el bolero
la bolera *Mexico*

booth [bu:θ] NOUN
la cabina

booze [bu:z] NOUN (*informal*)
la bebida

border ['bɔ:rdər] NOUN
la frontera

bore [bɔ:r] VERB *see* **bear**

bored [bɔ:rd] ADJECTIVE
aburrido ◇ *to be bored* estar* aburrido
◆ **to get bored** aburrirse*

boredom ['bɔ:rdəm] NOUN
el aburrimiento

boring ['bɔ:rɪŋ] ADJECTIVE
aburrido ◇ *It's boring.* Es aburrido.

born [bɔ:rn] ADJECTIVE
◆ **to be born** nacer* ◇ *I was born in 1982.* Nací en 1982.

borne [bɔ:rn] VERB *see* **bear**

to **borrow** ['bɔ:rou] VERB
pedir* prestado
◆ **to borrow something from somebody** pedir* algo prestado a alguien ◇ *I borrowed some money from a friend.* Le pedí dinero prestado a un amigo.
◆ **Can I borrow your eraser?** ¿Me prestas la goma?

Bosnia ['bɑ:zniə] NOUN
la Bosnia

Bosnian ['bɑ:zniən] ADJECTIVE
bosnio

boss [bɑ:s] NOUN (PL **bosses**)
el jefe
la jefa

to **boss around** [bɑ:sə'raund] VERB
◆ **to boss somebody around** mandonear a alguien

bossy ['bɑ:si] ADJECTIVE
mandón (MASC PL mandones, FEM mandona)

both [bouθ] ADJECTIVE, PRONOUN, ADVERB
los dos ◇ *We both went.* Fuimos los dos. ◇ *Both of your answers are wrong.* Tus respuestas están las dos mal. ◇ *Both of them play the piano.* Los dos tocan el piano.
◆ **Both Emma and Jane went.** Fueron Emma y Jane.
◆ **He has houses in both Mexico and in Spain.** Tiene casas tanto en México como en España.

to **bother** ['bɑ:ðər] VERB
see also **bother** NOUN
1 preocupar (*worry*) ◇ *What's bothering you?* ¿Qué es lo que te preocupa?
2 molestar (*disturb*) ◇ *I'm sorry to bother you.* Siento molestarlo.
◆ **Don't bother!** ¡No te preocupes!
◆ **to bother to do something** tomarse la molestia de hacer algo ◇ *He didn't bother to tell me about it.* Ni se tomó la molestia de decírmelo.

bother ['bɑ:ðər] NOUN
see also **bother** VERB
la molestia ◇ *no bother* no es ninguna molestia

bottle ['bɑ:tl] NOUN
la botella

bottle-opener ['bɑ:tl,oupənər] NOUN
el destapador

bottom ['bɑ:təm] NOUN
see also **bottom** ADJECTIVE
1 el fondo (*of container, bag, sea*)
◆ **at the bottom of the page** al final de la página
◆ **He was always bottom of the class.** Siempre era el último de la clase.
2 el trasero (*buttocks*)

bottom ['bɑ:təm] ADJECTIVE
see also **bottom** NOUN
de abajo ◇ *the bottom shelf* el estante de abajo

bought [bɑ:t] VERB *see* **buy**

bouillon cube [bul'jɑ:n,kju:b] NOUN
el cubito de caldo

to **bounce** [bauns] VERB
rebotar

bouncer ['baunsər] NOUN
el gorila (*informal*)
Although ***gorila*** *ends in* ***-a,*** *it is actually a masculine noun in this case.*

bound [baund] ADJECTIVE
◆ **He's bound to fail.** Seguro que no pasa.
◆ **She's bound to come.** Es seguro que vendrá.

boundary ['baundri] NOUN (PL **boundaries**)
el límite

bow [bou] NOUN
see also **bow** VERB
1 el lazo (*knot*) ◇ *to tie a bow* hacer* un lazo
2 el arco ◇ *a bow and arrow* un arco y flecha

to **bow** [bau] VERB
see also **bow** NOUN
hacer* una reverencia
hacer* una caravana *Mexico*

bowels ['bauəlz] PL NOUN
los intestinos

bowl [boul] NOUN
see also **bowl** VERB
1 el tazón (PL los tazones) (*for soup, cereals*)
2 el bol (*for cooking, mixing food*)

to **bowl** [boul] VERB
see also **bowl** NOUN
lanzar* la pelota

bowler ['boulər] NOUN
el lanzador
la lanzadora

bowling ['boulɪŋ] NOUN
los bolos
◆ **to go bowling** jugar* a los bolos
◆ **a bowling alley** una bolera

bow tie [,bou'taɪ] NOUN
la corbata de moño

box [bɑ:ks] NOUN (PL **boxes**)
1 la caja ◇ *a box of matches* una caja de fósforos, *Mexico:* una caja de cerillos
◆ **a cardboard box** una caja de cartón
2 la casilla (*on form*)

boxer ['bɑ:ksər] NOUN
el boxeador

boxer shorts ['bɑ:ksər,ʃɔ:rts] PL NOUN
los bóxers
◆ **a pair of boxer shorts** unos bóxers

boxing ['bɑ:ksɪŋ] NOUN
el boxeo

box lunch ['bɑ:ks'lʌntʃ] NOUN (PL **box lunches**)
◆ **I take a box lunch to school.** Me llevo la comida al colegio.

boy [bɔɪ] NOUN
1 el muchacho (*young man*) ◇ *a boy of fifteen* un muchacho de quince años
2 el niño (*child*) ◇ *a boy of seven* un niño de siete años
◆ **She has two boys and a girl.** Tiene dos niños y una niña.
◆ **a baby boy** un niño

boyfriend ['bɔɪ,frɛnd] NOUN
el novio ◇ *Do you have a boyfriend?* ¿Tienes novio?

boy scout [bɔɪskaut] NOUN
el boy scout (PL los boy scouts)

bra [brɑː] NOUN
el sostén (PL los sostenes)
el brasier Mexico

bracelet ['breɪslɪt] NOUN
la pulsera

braces ['breɪsis] PL NOUN
los frenillos
los frenos Mexico
(*on teeth*)
◇ *Richard wears braces.* Richard usa frenillos. Mexico: Richard usa frenos.

braid [breɪd] NOUN
la trenza ◇ *She wears her hair in a braid.* Lleva trenzas.

brain [breɪn] NOUN
el cerebro

brainy ['breɪni] ADJECTIVE
inteligente

brake [breɪk] NOUN
see also **brake** VERB
el freno

to **brake** [breɪk] VERB
see also **brake** NOUN
frenar

branch [bræntʃ] NOUN (PL **branches**)
1 la rama (*of tree*)
2 la sucursal (*of bank*)

brand [brænd] NOUN
la marca ◇ *a well-known brand of coffee* una marca de café muy conocida

brand name ['brænd,neɪm] NOUN
la marca

brand-new ['brænd'nuː] ADJECTIVE
flamante

brandy ['brændi] NOUN (PL **brandies**)
el coñac (PL los coñacs)

brass [bræs] NOUN
el latón (*metal*)
◆ **the brass section** los bronces

brass band ['bræs'bænd] NOUN
la banda de música

brat [bræt] NOUN
el mocoso
la mocosa
◇ *He's a spoiled brat.* Es un mocoso consentido.

brave [breɪv] ADJECTIVE
valiente

Brazil [brə'zɪl] NOUN
el Brasil

bread [brɛd] NOUN
el pan
◆ **bread and butter** el pan con mantequilla

break [breɪk] NOUN
see also **break** VERB
la pausa (*rest*) ◇ *to take a break* hacer* una pausa
◆ **the Christmas break** las vacaciones de Navidad
◆ **Give me a break!** ¡Déjame en paz!

to **break** [breɪk] VERB (**broke, broken**)
see also **break** NOUN
1 romper* ◇ *Careful, you'll break something!* ¡Cuidado, que vas a romper algo!
◆ **I broke my leg.** Me rompí la pierna.
2 romperse* ◇ *Careful, it'll break!* ¡Ten cuidado, que se va a romper!
◆ **to break a promise** faltar a una promesa
◆ **to break a record** batir un récord

to **break down** [breɪk'daun] VERB
descomponerse*
◆ **the car broke down** el carro se descompuso

to **break in** [breɪk'ɪn] VERB
◆ **The thief broke in through a window.** El ladrón se metió por una ventana.

to **break into** [breɪk'ɪntuː] VERB
entrar a ◇ *Thieves broke into the house.* Los ladrones entraron a la casa.

to **break off** [breɪk'ɑːf] VERB
desprenderse (*come free*)

to **break out** [breɪk'aut] VERB
1 estallar (*war*)
2 desencadenarse (*fire, fighting*)
3 escaparse (*prisoner*)
◆ **He broke out in a rash.** Le salió un sarpullido.

to **break up** [breɪk'ʌp] VERB
1 disolver* ◇ *Police broke up the demonstration.* La policía disolvió la demostración.
2 dispersarse (*crowd*)
3 fracasar (*marriage*) ◇ *More and more marriages break up.* Cada día fracasan más matrimonios.
4 romper* (*two lovers*) ◇ *Richard and Marie have broken up.* Richard y Marie rompieron.
◆ **to break up a fight** poner* fin a una pelea

breakdown ['breɪk,daun] NOUN
1 la crisis nerviosa (PL las crisis nerviosas)
◇ *He had a breakdown because of the stress.* Sufrió una crisis nerviosa debida al estrés.
2 la avería
la descompostura Mexico
(*in vehicle*)
◇ *to have a breakdown* tener* una avería, Mexico: tener* una descompostura

breakfast ['brɛkfəst] NOUN
el desayuno
◆ **to have breakfast** desayunar

break-in ['breɪkɪn] NOUN
◆ **There have been a lot of break-ins in my area.** Han entrado a robar en muchas casas de mi barrio.

breast [brɛst] NOUN
el pecho
◆ **chicken breast** la pechuga de pollo

to **breast-feed** ['brɛst,fiːd] VERB (**breast-fed, breast-fed**)
amamantar

breaststroke [ˈbrɛstˌstrouk] NOUN
el estilo pecho

breath [brɛθ] NOUN
el aliento ◇ *He has bad breath.* Tiene mal aliento.
◆ **I'm out of breath.** Estoy sin aliento.
◆ **to get one's breath back** recobrar el aliento

to **breathe** [bri:ð] VERB
respirar

to **breathe in** [bri:ðˈɪn] VERB
aspirar

to **breathe out** [bri:ðˈaut] VERB
espirar

to **breed** [bri:d] VERB (**bred, bred**)
see also **breed** NOUN
reproducirse* (*reproduce*)
◆ **to breed dogs** criar* perros

breed [bri:d] NOUN
see also **breed** VERB
la raza

breeze [bri:z] NOUN
la brisa

brewery [ˈbru:əri] NOUN (PL **breweries**)
la cervecería
la cervecera *Mexico*

bribe [braɪb] NOUN
see also **bribe** VERB
el soborno

to **bribe** [braɪb] VERB
see also **bribe** NOUN
sobornar

brick [brɪk] NOUN
el ladrillo

bricklayer [ˈbrɪkˌleɪər] NOUN
el albañil ◇ *he's a bricklayer* es albañil

bride [braɪd] NOUN
la novia
◆ **the bride and groom** los novios

bridegroom [ˈbraɪdˌgru:m] NOUN
el novio

bridesmaid [ˈbraɪdzˌmeɪd] NOUN
la dama de honor

bridge [brɪdʒ] NOUN
1 el puente ◇ *a suspension bridge* un puente colgante
2 el bridge (*card game*) ◇ *to play bridge* jugar* bridge

brief [bri:f] ADJECTIVE
breve

briefcase [ˈbri:fˌkeɪs] NOUN
el maletín (PL los maletines)

briefly [ˈbri:fli] ADVERB
brevemente

briefs [bri:fs] PL NOUN
los calzoncillos
◆ **a pair of briefs** unos calzoncillos

bright [braɪt] ADJECTIVE
1 vivo ◇ *a bright color* un color vivo ◇ *bright red* rojo vivo
2 brillante (*light*)
3 listo ◇ *He's not very bright.* No es muy listo.

to **bring** [brɪŋ] VERB (**brought, brought**)
traer* ◇ *Bring warm clothes.* Trae ropa de abrigo. ◇ *Can I bring a friend?* ¿Puedo traer a un amigo?

to **bring about** [ˈbrɪŋəˈbaut] VERB
provocar*

to **bring back** [brɪŋˈbæk] VERB
devolver* (*book*)
◆ **That song brings back memories.** Esa canción me trae recuerdos.

to **bring forward** [brɪŋˈfɔ:rwərd] VERB
adelantar ◇ *The meeting was brought forward.* La reunión se adelantó.

to **bring up** [brɪŋˈʌp] VERB
criar* ◇ *She brought up five children on her own.* Crió a cinco hijos ella sola.

Britain [ˈbrɪtn] NOUN
la Gran Bretaña

British [ˈbrɪtɪʃ] ADJECTIVE
británico ◇ *the British* los británicos ◇ *She's British.* Es británica.
◆ **the British Isles** las Islas Británicas

broad [brɑ:d] ADJECTIVE
ancho
◆ **in broad daylight** a plena luz del día

broadband NOUN
la banda ancha

broadcast [ˈbrɑ:dˌkæst] NOUN
see also **broadcast** VERB
la transmisión (PL las transmisiones)

to **broadcast** [ˈbrɑ:dˌkæst] VERB (**broadcast, broadcast**)
see also **broadcast** NOUN
transmitir ◇ *The interview was broadcast all over the world.* La entrevista se transmitió a todo el mundo.
◆ **to broadcast live** transmitir en directo

broad-minded [ˈbrɑ:dˈmaɪndɪd] ADJECTIVE
◆ **He's very broad-minded.** Tiene una mentalidad muy abierta.

broccoli [ˈbrɑ:kəli] NOUN
el brócoli

brochure [brouˈʃuər] NOUN
el folleto

to **broil** [brɔɪl] VERB
1 hacer* al grill (*in an oven*)
2 asar a la parrilla (*barbecue*)

broiler [brɔɪlər] NOUN
la parrilla (*grill*)

broke [brouk] VERB *see* **break**

broke [brouk] ADJECTIVE
◆ **to be broke** no tener* un centavo, *Mexico:* estar* brujo (*informal*)

broken [ˈbroukən] VERB *see* **break**

broken [ˈbroukən] ADJECTIVE
roto ◇ *It's broken.* Está roto. ◇ *He has a broken arm.* Tiene un brazo roto.

bronchitis [brɑ:ŋˈkaɪtɪs] NOUN

* Verbs marked with this symbol are irregular. See pages 346–348 for further details.

la bronquitis
bronze [brɑːnz] NOUN
el bronce ◇ *the bronze medal* la medalla de bronce
brooch [broutʃ] NOUN (PL **brooches**)
el broche
broom [bruːm] NOUN
la escoba
brother [ˈbrʌðər] NOUN
el hermano
brother-in-law [ˈbrʌðərɪnlɑː] NOUN (PL **brothers-in-law**)
el cuñado
brought [brɑːt] VERB *see* **bring**
brown [braun] ADJECTIVE
1 marrón (FEM marrón, PL marrones)
café *Mexico*
(*clothes*)
2 castaño (*hair, eyes*)
3 bronceado (*tanned*)
◆ **brown bread** el pan integral
Brownie [ˈbraunɪ] NOUN
la guía

> ℹ *Un miembro joven de las* **Girl Scouts** *– la versión femenina de los* **Boy Scouts**.

brownie [ˈbrauni] NOUN
el pastelillo de chocolate y nueces (*cookie*)
to **browse** [brauz] VERB
echar una ojeada a (*on Internet*)
browser [ˈbrauzər] NOUN
el navegador
bruise [bruːz] NOUN
el moretón (PL los moretones)
brush [brʌʃ] NOUN (PL **brushes**)
see also **brush** VERB
1 el cepillo (*for hair, teeth*)
2 el pincel (*paintbrush*)
to **brush** [brʌʃ] VERB
see also **brush** NOUN
cepillar
◆ **to brush one's hair** cepillarse el pelo
◆ **to brush one's teeth** cepillarse los dientes
◇ *I brush my teeth every night.* Me cepillo los dientes todas las noches.
Brussels [ˈbrʌsəlz] NOUN
la Bruselas
Brussels sprouts [ˈbrʌsəlzˈsprauts] PL NOUN
las coles de Bruselas
brutal [ˈbruːtl] ADJECTIVE
brutal
BS [biːˈɛs] ABBREVIATION (= *Bachelor of Science*)
la licenciatura en Ciencias
◆ **a BS in Mathematics** una licenciatura en Matemáticas
◆ **She has a BS in Chemistry.** Es licenciada en Química.
bubble [ˈbʌbəl] NOUN
1 la pompa (*of soap*)
2 la burbuja (*of air, gas*)
bubble bath [ˈbʌbəlˌbæθ] NOUN
el baño de espuma
bubble gum [ˈbʌbəlˌgʌm] NOUN
el chicle
bucket [ˈbʌkɪt] NOUN
el balde
la cubeta *Mexico*
buckle [ˈbʌkəl] NOUN
la hebilla (*on belt, watch, shoe*)
Buddhism [ˈbuːdɪzəm] NOUN
el budismo
Buddhist [ˈbuːdɪst] ADJECTIVE
budista
buddy [ˈbʌdi] NOUN (PL **buddies**)
el amigo
la amiga
el/la cuate *Mexico*
◇ *He always goes on vacation with his buddies.* Siempre va de vacaciones con sus amigos.
budget [ˈbʌdʒɪt] NOUN
see also **budget** VERB
el presupuesto
to **budget** [ˈbʌdʒɪt] VERB
see also **budget** NOUN
◆ **I'm learning how to budget.** Estoy aprendiendo a administrar el dinero.
◆ **They budgeted $10 million for advertising.** Asignaron 10 millones de dólares para la publicidad.
buffet [bəˈfeɪ] NOUN
el buffet
bug [bʌg] NOUN
1 el insecto (*insect*)
2 el virus (PL los virus) (*illness, in computer*)
◇ *There's a bug going round.* Hay un virus en el ambiente.
◆ **a stomach bug** una gastroenteritis
bugged [bʌgd] ADJECTIVE
◆ **The phone was bugged.** El teléfono estaba intervenido.
to **build** [bɪld] VERB (**built, built**)
construir* ◇ *They're going to build houses here.* Van a construir viviendas aquí.
to **build up** [bɪldˈʌp] VERB
1 acumular ◇ *He has built up a huge collection of butterflies.* Ha ido acumulando una gran colección de mariposas.
2 acumularse ◇ *Our debts are building up.* Nuestras deudas se están acumulando.
builder [ˈbɪldər] NOUN
1 el/la contratista (*contractor*)
2 el albañil (*worker*)
building [ˈbɪldɪŋ] NOUN
el edificio
built [bɪlt] VERB *see* **build**
bulb [bʌlb] NOUN
1 la bombilla
el foco *Mexico*
2 el bulbo (*of flower*)
bull [bul] NOUN

el toro

bullet ['bulɪt] NOUN
la bala

bulletin board ['bulətn,bɔːrd] NOUN
el tablero de noticias

bullfighting ['bul,faɪtɪŋ] NOUN
◆ **Do you like bullfighting?** ¿Te gustan los toros?

bullring ['bul,rɪŋ] NOUN
la plaza de toros

bully ['buli] NOUN (PL **bullies**)
see also **bully** VERB
el matón (PL los matones) ◇ *He's a big bully.* Es un matón.

to **bully** ['buli] VERB (**bullied, bullied**)
see also **bully** NOUN
intimidar

bump [bʌmp] NOUN
see also **bump** VERB
1 el chichón (PL los chichones) (*on head*)
2 el bulto (*on surface*)
3 el bache (*on road*)
4 el golpe (*minor accident*) ◇ *We had a bump.* Nos dimos un golpe.

to **bump** [bʌmp] VERB
see also **bump** NOUN
◆ **I bumped my head on the wall.** Me di en la cabeza contra la pared.

to **bump into** [bʌmp'ɪntuː] VERB
1 tropezarse* con ◇ *I bumped into Paul yesterday.* Me tropecé con Paul ayer.
2 darse* contra ◇ *We bumped into a tree.* Nos dimos contra un árbol.

bumpy ['bʌmpi] ADJECTIVE
lleno de baches (*road*)

bun [bʌn] NOUN
el bollo
el bolillo Mexico
(*bread*)

bunch [bʌntʃ] NOUN (PL **bunches**)
◆ **a bunch of flowers** un ramo de flores
◆ **a bunch of grapes** un racimo de uvas
◆ **a bunch of keys** un manojo de llaves

bunches ['bʌntʃəz] PL NOUN
las coletas

bungalow ['bʌŋgəlou] NOUN
el bungalow

bunk [bʌŋk] NOUN
la litera

burger ['bɜːrgər] NOUN
la hamburguesa

burglar ['bɜːrglər] NOUN
el ladrón (PL los ladrones)
la ladrona

to **burglarize** ['bɜːrgləraɪz] VERB
entrar a robar a ◇ *Her house was burglarized.* Le entraron a robar a su casa.

burglary ['bɜːrgləri] NOUN (PL **burglaries**)
el robo (*con violación de domicilio*)

burn [bɜːrn] NOUN
see also **burn** VERB
la quemadura

to **burn** [bɜːrn] VERB
see also **burn** NOUN
quemar (*trash, documents*) ◇ *I burned the trash.* Quemé la basura.
◆ **I burned the cake.** Se me quemó el pastel.
◆ **to burn oneself** quemarse
◆ **I've burned my hand.** Me quemé la mano.

to **burn down** [bɜːrn'daun] VERB
quedar reducido a cenizas ◇ *The factory burned down.* La fábrica quedó reducida a cenizas.

to **burst** [bɜːrst] VERB (**burst, burst**)
reventarse* ◇ *The balloon burst.* El globo se reventó.
◆ **to burst a balloon** reventar* un globo
◆ **to burst out laughing** echarse a reír
◆ **to burst into tears** ponerse* a llorar
◆ **to burst into flames** incendiarse

to **bury** ['bɛri] VERB (**buried, buried**)
enterrar*

bus [bʌs] NOUN (PL **buses**)
el bus
el camión (PL los camiones) Mexico
◇ *by bus* en bus
◆ **the school bus** el bus escolar, Mexico: el camión escolar
◆ **a bus ticket** un boleto de bus, Mexico: un boleto de camión
◆ **a bus trip** una excursión en autobús

bush [buʃ] NOUN (PL **bushes**)
el arbusto

business ['bɪznɪs] NOUN (PL **businesses**)
1 el negocio (*firm*) ◇ *He has his own business.* Tiene su propio negocio.
2 los negocios ◇ *He's away on business.* Está en un viaje de negocios.
◆ **a business trip** un viaje de negocios
◆ **It's none of my business.** No es asunto mío.

businessman ['bɪznɪsmən] NOUN (PL **businessmen**)
el hombre de negocios

businesswoman ['bɪznɪs,wumən] NOUN (PL **businesswomen**)
la mujer de negocios

bus pass ['bʌs,pæːs] NOUN (PL **bus passes**)
el pase

bus station ['bʌs,steɪʃən] NOUN
la terminal de buses
la terminal de camiones Mexico

bus stop ['bʌs,stɑːp] NOUN
el paradero de buses
el paradero de camiones Mexico

bust [bʌst] NOUN
el busto

busy ['bɪzi] ADJECTIVE
1 ocupado (*person, telephone line*) ◇ *She's a very busy woman.* Es una mujer muy ocupada.

[2] ajetreado (*day, week*) ◇ *It's been a very busy day.* Ha sido un día muy ajetreado.
[3] concurrido (*street, store*)

busy signal ['bɪzi,sɪgnəl] NOUN
la señal de ocupado

but [bʌt] PREPOSITION, CONJUNCTION
[1] pero ◇ *I'd like to come, but I'm busy.* Me gustaría venir, pero tengo trabajo.
[2] sino
*Use **sino** when you want to correct a previous negative statement.*
◇ *He's not English but French.* No es inglés sino francés.
[3] menos ◇ *They won all but two of their games.* Ganaron todos los partidos menos dos.
◆ **the next but last** el penúltimo

butcher ['butʃər] NOUN
el carnicero
la carnicera
◆ **He's a butcher.** Es carnicero.
◆ **at the butcher's** en la carnicería

butt [bʌt] NOUN
el trasero (*informal*)

butter ['bʌtər] NOUN
la mantequilla

butterfly ['bʌtər,flaɪ] NOUN (PL **butterflies**)
la mariposa (*insect, swimming*) ◇ *Her favorite stroke is the butterfly.* El estilo mariposa es su favorito.

buttocks ['bʌtəks] PL NOUN
las nalgas

button ['bʌtn] NOUN
[1] el botón (PL los botones)
[2] la chapa (*metal, plastic*)

to **buy** [baɪ] VERB (**bought, bought**)
see also **buy** NOUN
comprar ◇ *He bought me an ice cream cone.* Me compró un helado.
◆ **to buy something from somebody** comprar algo a alguien ◇ *I bought a watch from him.* Le compré un reloj.

buy [baɪ] NOUN
see also **buy** VERB
◆ **It was a good buy.** Fue una buena compra.

buzzer ['bʌzər] NOUN
el portero automático (*entry phone*)

by [baɪ] PREPOSITION
[1] por ◇ *The thieves were caught by the police.* Los ladrones fueron capturados por la policía.
[2] de ◇ *a painting by Picasso* un cuadro de Picasso
[3] en ◇ *by car* en carro ◇ *by train* en tren ◇ *by bus* en bus, *Mexico:* en camión
[4] junto a ◇ *Where's the bank? – It's by the post office.* ¿Dónde está el banco? – Está junto al correo.
[5] para ◇ *We have to be there by four o'clock.* Tenemos que estar allí antes de las cuatro.
◆ **by the time...** cuando ◇ *By the time I got there it was too late.* Cuando llegué allí ya era demasiado tarde. ◇ *It'll be ready by the time you get back.* Estará listo para cuando regreses.
◆ **That's fine by me.** Por mí no hay problema.
◆ **all by himself** él solo
◆ **I did it all by myself.** Lo hice yo solo.
◆ **by the way** a propósito

bye [baɪ] EXCLAMATION
¡adiós!

bypass ['baɪ,pæs] NOUN (PL **bypasses**)
la carretera de circunvalación
el libramiento *Mexico*
(*road*)

C

cab [kæb] NOUN
el taxi ◇ *I'll go by cab.* Iré en taxi.
cabbage ['kæbɪdʒ] NOUN
el repollo
la col [Mexico]
cabin ['kæbɪn] NOUN
[1] el camarote (*on ship*)
[2] la cabina (*on airplane*)
cabinet ['kæbɪnɪt] NOUN
◆ **a bathroom cabinet** un armario de cuarto de baño
◆ **a liquor cabinet** un mueble-bar
cable ['keɪbəl] NOUN
el cable
cable car ['keɪbəl,kɑːr] NOUN
el teleférico
cable television ['keɪbəl'tɛlɪvɪʒən] NOUN
la televisión por cable
cadet [kə'dɛt] NOUN
el/la cadete ◇ *a police cadet* un cadete de policía
café [kæ'feɪ] NOUN
el café
cage [keɪdʒ] NOUN
la jaula
cake [keɪk] NOUN
el pastel
to **calculate** ['kælkjuleɪt] VERB
calcular
calculation [kælkju'leɪʃən] NOUN
el cálculo
calculator ['kælkjuleɪtər] NOUN
la calculadora
calendar ['kæləndər] NOUN
el calendario
calf [kæf] NOUN (PL **calves**)
[1] el ternero (*of cow*)
[2] la pantorrilla (*of leg*)
call [kɑːl] NOUN
[*see also* **call** VERB]
la llamada ◇ *Thanks for your call.* Gracias por su llamada. ◇ *a phone call* una llamada telefónica ◇ *to give somebody a call* llamar a alguien por teléfono
◆ **to be on call** (*doctor*) estar* de guardia
to **call** [kɑːl] VERB
[*see also* **call** NOUN]
llamar ◇ *We called the police.* Llamamos a la policía. ◇ *I'll tell him you called.* Le diré que llamaste.
◆ **to call somebody** llamar a alguien
◆ **to call up** llamar por teléfono
◆ **to call collect** llamar a cobro revertido, [Mexico:] llamar por cobrar
◆ **to be called** llamarse ◇ *He's called Fluffy.* Se llama Fluffy. ◇ *What's she called?* ¿Cómo se llama?
to **call back** [kɑːl'bæk] VERB
volver* a llamar ◇ *I'll call back later.* Volveré a llamar más tarde.
◆ **Can I call you back?** ¿Puedo llamarte más tarde?
to **call for** ['kɑːlfɔːr] VERB
[1] pasar a recoger ◇ *Shall I call for you at seven thirty?* ¿Paso a recogerte a las siete y media?
[2] requerir* ◇ *This job calls for strong nerves.* Este trabajo requiere nervios de acero.
◆ **This calls for a drink!** ¡Esto hay que celebrarlo!
to **call off** [kɑːl'ɑːf] VERB
suspender ◇ *The game was called off.* El partido se suspendió.
calm [kɑːm] ADJECTIVE
tranquilo
to **calm down** [kɑːm'daun] VERB
calmarse ◇ *Calm down!* ¡Cálmate!
calorie ['kæləri] NOUN
la caloría
calves [kævz] PL NOUN *see* **calf**
camcorder ['kæm,kɔːrdər] NOUN
la videocámara
came [keɪm] VERB *see* **come**
camel ['kæməl] NOUN
el camello
camera ['kæmərə] NOUN
la cámara
cameraman ['kæmərə,mæn] NOUN (PL **cameramen**)
el cameráman (PL los camerámans)
camera phone NOUN
el teléfono con cámara
to **camp** [kæmp] VERB
[*see also* **camp** NOUN]
acampar
camp [kæmp] NOUN
[*see also* **camp** VERB]
el campamento ◇ *a summer camp* un campamento de verano
◆ **a refugee camp** un campo de refugiados
campaign [kæm'peɪn] NOUN
[*see also* **campaign** VERB]
la campaña
to **campaign** [kæm'peɪn] VERB
[*see also* **campaign** NOUN]
hacer* campaña ◇ *They are campaigning for a change in the law.* Están haciendo campaña a favor de un cambio legislativo.
camp cot ['kæmp,kɑːt] NOUN
la cama plegable
camper ['kæmpər] NOUN
[1] el/la campista
[2] el cámper (*vehicle*)
camping ['kæmpɪŋ] NOUN
◆ **to go camping** ir* de camping

campsite ['kæmp,saɪt] NOUN
el camping (PL los campings)

campus ['kæmpəs] NOUN (PL **campuses**)
el campus (PL los campus)

can [kæn] NOUN
see also **can** VERB
la lata ◇ *a can of peas* una lata de guisantes ◇ *a can of beer* una lata de cerveza
◆ **a can of gas** un bidón de gasolina

can [kæn] VERB (**could**)
see also **can** NOUN
1 poder* (*be able to, be allowed to*) ◇ *Can I use your phone?* ¿Puedo usar el teléfono? ◇ *I can't do that.* No puedo hacer eso. ◇ *I'll do it as soon as I can.* Lo haré tan pronto como pueda. ◇ *That can't be true!* ¡No puede ser cierto! ◇ *You could take a cab.* Podrías tomar un taxi. ◇ *He couldn't concentrate because of the noise.* No se podía concentrar a causa del ruido.
2 saber* (*know how to*) ◇ *I can swim.* Sé nadar. ◇ *He can't drive.* No sabe manejar.
***can** is sometimes not translated.*
◇ *I can't hear you.* No te oigo. ◇ *I can't remember.* No me acuerdo. ◇ *Can you speak French?* ¿Hablas francés?
◆ **You could be right.** Es posible que tengas razón.

Canada ['kænədə] NOUN
el Canadá

Canadian [kə'neɪdiən] ADJECTIVE
see also **Canadian** NOUN
canadiense

Canadian [kə'neɪdiən] NOUN
see also **Canadian** ADJECTIVE
el/la canadiense

canal [kə'næl] NOUN
el canal

Canaries [kə'nɛriz] NOUN
◆ **the Canaries** las Canarias

canary [kə'nɛri] NOUN (PL **canaries**)
el canario
◆ **the Canary Islands** las islas Canarias

to **cancel** ['kænsəl] VERB
cancelar ◇ *I had to cancel my appointment.* Tuve que cancelar la cita. ◇ *Our flight was canceled.* Cancelaron nuestro vuelo.

cancellation [kænsə'leɪʃən] NOUN
la cancelación (PL las cancelaciones)

cancer ['kænsər] NOUN
el cáncer ◇ *He has cancer.* Tiene cáncer.

Cancer ['kænsər] NOUN
el Cáncer (*sign*) ◇ *I'm a Cancer.* Soy cáncer.
◆ **a Cancer** un/una cáncer

candidate ['kændɪdeɪt] NOUN
el candidato
la candidata

candle ['kændl] NOUN
1 la vela
2 el cirio (*in church*)
la veladora *Mexico*

candy ['kændi] NOUN (PL **candies**)
los dulces ◇ *I love candy.* Me encantan los dulces.
◆ **a piece of candy** un dulce

canker sore ['kæŋkər,sɔːr] NOUN
la llaga en la boca

cannabis ['kænəbɪs] NOUN
el canabis

canned [kænd] ADJECTIVE
en lata MASC, FEM, PL (*food*) ◇ *canned peaches* duraznos en lata
◆ **canned products** productos enlatados

cannot ['kænɑːt] VERB = **can not**

canoe [kə'nuː] NOUN
la canoa

canoeing [kə'nuːɪŋ] NOUN
el piragüismo ◇ *to go canoeing* ir* a hacer piragüismo ◇ *We went canoeing in Chile.* Fuimos a hacer piragüismo en Chile.

can opener ['kæn,oupənər] NOUN
el abrelatas (PL los abrelatas)

can't [kænt] VERB = **can not**

canteen [kæn'tiːn] NOUN
1 la cantina (*place*)
2 la cantimplora (*container*)

canvas ['kænvəs] NOUN (PL **canvases**)
la lona

cap [kæp] NOUN
1 el tapón (PL los tapones) (*of bottle, tube*)
2 la gorra (*hat*)

capable ['keɪpəbəl] ADJECTIVE
capaz
◆ **to be capable of doing something** ser* capaz de hacer algo ◇ *She's capable of doing much more.* Es capaz de hacer mucho más.

capacity [kə'pæsɪti] NOUN (PL **capacities**)
la capacidad ◇ *The tank has a four-liter capacity.* El depósito tiene una capacidad de cuatro litros. ◇ *He has a capacity for hard work.* Tiene mucha capacidad de trabajo.

capital ['kæpɪtl] NOUN
1 la capital ◇ *Buenos Aires is the capital of Argentina.* Buenos Aires es la capital de Argentina.
2 la mayúscula (*letter*) ◇ *in capitals* en mayúsculas

capitalism ['kæpɪtlɪzəm] NOUN
el capitalismo

capital punishment ['kæpɪtl'pʌnɪʃmənt] NOUN
la pena de muerte

Capitol ['kæpɪtl] NOUN
el Capitolio
◆ **Capitol Hill** el Congreso de los Estados Unidos

Capricorn ['kæprɪkɔːrn] NOUN
el Capricornio (*sign*) ◇ *I'm a Capricorn.* Soy capricornio.
◆ **a Capricorn** un/una capricornio

to **capsize** ['kæpsaɪz] VERB ☞

volcarse

captain ['kæptɪn] NOUN
el capitán (PL los capitanes)
la capitana

caption ['kæpʃən] NOUN
el pie de foto

to **capture** ['kæptʃər] VERB
capturar

car [kɑ:r] NOUN
1 el carro
◆ **to go by car** ir* en carro ◇ *We went by car.* Fuimos en carro.
◆ **a car crash** un choque de carros
2 el vagón (PL los vagones)
el carro Mexico
(*of train*)

caramel ['kærəməl] NOUN
el caramelo ◇ *a box of caramels* una caja de caramelos

carbonated ['kɑ:rbəneɪtɪd] ADJECTIVE
con gas (*water*)
◆ **a carbonated drink** una bebida gaseosa

card [kɑ:rd] NOUN
1 la tarjeta ◇ *I got lots of cards and presents on my birthday.* Recibí muchas tarjetas y regalos para mi cumpleaños.
2 la carta ◇ *a card game* un juego de cartas

cardboard ['kɑ:rd,bɔ:rd] NOUN
el cartón ◇ *a cardboard box* una caja de cartón

cardigan ['kɑ:rdɪgən] NOUN
la chaqueta de punto

care [kɛər] NOUN
see also **care** VERB
el cuidado ◇ *with care* con cuidado
◆ **to take care of** cuidar a ◇ *I take care of the children on Saturdays.* Yo cuido a los niños los sábados.
◆ **Take care! (1)** (*be careful!*) ¡Ten cuidado!
◆ **Take care! (2)** (*look after yourself!*) ¡Cuídate!

to **care** [kɛər] VERB
see also **care** NOUN
◆ **to care about** preocuparse por ◇ *a company that cares about the environment* una empresa que se preocupa por el medio ambiente ◇ *They don't care about their image.* No se preocupan por su imagen.
◆ **I don't care!** ¡No me importa!
◆ **Who cares?** ¿Y a quién le importa?

to **care for** ['kɛər,fɔ:r] VERB
1 sentir* cariño por ◇ *He wanted me to know he still cared for me.* Quería que supiera que todavía sentía cariño por mí.
2 cuidar ◇ *They employed a nurse to care for her.* Emplearon a una enfermera para cuidarla.

career [kə'rɪər] NOUN
la carrera

careful ['kɛrfəl] ADJECTIVE
◆ **Be careful!** ¡Ten cuidado!

carefully ['kɛrfəli] ADVERB
con cuidado (*cautiously*) ◇ *Drive carefully!* ¡Maneja con cuidado!
◆ **Think carefully!** ¡Piénsalo bien!
◆ **She carefully avoided talking about it.** Tuvo mucho cuidado de no hablar del tema.

careless ['kɛrlɪs] ADJECTIVE
1 poco cuidado (*work*)
◆ **a careless mistake** un error por descuido
2 poco cuidadoso (*person*) ◇ *She's very careless.* Es muy poco cuidadosa.
◆ **a careless driver** un chofer imprudente

caretaker ['kɛr,teɪkər] NOUN
el/la conserje

cargo ['kɑ:rgou] NOUN (PL **cargoes**)
el cargamento

Caribbean [kɛrɪ'bi:ən] ADJECTIVE
see also **Caribbean** NOUN
caribeño

Caribbean [kɛrɪ'bi:ən] NOUN
see also **Caribbean** ADJECTIVE
◆ **We're going to the Caribbean.** Vamos al Caribe.
◆ **the Caribbean** (*sea*) el mar Caribe

caring ['kɛrɪŋ] ADJECTIVE
bondadoso
◆ **the caring professions** las profesiones de vocación social

carnation [kɑ:r'neɪʃən] NOUN
el clavel

carnival ['kɑ:rnɪvəl] NOUN
el parque de atracciones

carol ['kɛrəl] NOUN
◆ **a Christmas carol** un villancico

carpenter ['kɑ:rpɪntər] NOUN
el carpintero
la carpintera
◇ *He's a carpenter.* Es carpintero.

carpet ['kɑ:rpɪt] NOUN
1 la alfombra (*wall to wall*)
2 la alfombra
el tapete Mexico
(*rug*)
◇ *a Persian carpet* una alfombra persa, Mexico: un tapete persa

car phone ['kɑ:r,foun] NOUN
el teléfono de carro

car rental ['kɑ:r,rɛntl] NOUN
el alquiler de carros

carriage ['kɛrɪdʒ] NOUN
el carruaje
el carro Mexico
(*horse-drawn*)

carrot ['kɛrət] NOUN
la zanahoria

to **carry** ['kɛri] VERB (**carried, carried**)
1 llevar ◇ *I'll carry your bag.* Te llevo la bolsa.
2 transportar ◇ *a plane carrying 100 passengers* un avión que transporta 100

pasajeros

to **carry on** [kɛri'ɑ:n] VERB
seguir* ◇ *She carried on talking.* Siguió hablando.
◆ **Carry on!** ¡Sigue! ◇ *Am I boring you? – No, carry on!* ¿Te estoy aburriendo? – ¡No, sigue!

to **carry out** [kɛri'aut] VERB
1 cumplir (*orders*)
2 llevar a cabo (*threat, task, instructions*)

cart [kɑ:rt] NOUN
el carro

carton ['kɑ:rtn] NOUN
el cartón (PL los cartones) (*of milk, fruit juice*)

cartoon [kɑ:r'tu:n] NOUN
1 los dibujos animados (*on TV*)
2 el chiste (*in newspaper*)
◆ **a strip cartoon** una tira cómica

cartridge ['kɑ:rtrɪdʒ] NOUN
el cartucho

to **carve** [kɑ:rv] VERB
trinchar ◇ *Dad carved the roast.* Papá trinchó el asado.
◆ **a carved oak chair** una silla de roble tallado

case [keɪs] NOUN
1 la maleta ◇ *I've packed my case.* Hice mi maleta.
2 el caso ◇ *in some cases* en algunos casos ◇ *The police are investigating the case.* La policía está investigando el caso.
◆ **in case it rains** por si llueve
◆ **just in case** por si acaso ◇ *Take some money with you, just in case.* Llévate algo de dinero por si acaso.

cash [kæʃ] NOUN
see also **cash** VERB
el dinero ◇ *I'm a bit short of cash.* Ando un poco escaso de dinero.
◆ **in cash** en efectivo ◇ *$200 in cash* 200 dólares en efectivo
◆ **to pay cash** pagar* al contado

to **cash** [kæʃ] VERB
see also **cash** NOUN
◆ **to cash a check** cobrar un cheque

cashew nut ['kæʃu:ˌnʌt] NOUN
el anacardo

cashier [kæ'ʃɪər] NOUN
el cajero
la cajera

cashmere ['kæʒmɪr] NOUN
la cachemira ◇ *a cashmere sweater* un suéter de cachemira

cash register ['kæʃˌrɛdʒɪstər] NOUN
la caja registradora

casino [kə'si:nou] NOUN (PL **casinos**)
el casino

casserole ['kæsəroul] NOUN
el guiso ◇ *to make a casserole* hacer* un guiso
◆ **a casserole dish** una cazuela

cassette [kə'sɛt] NOUN
el casete
◆ **a cassette player** un pasacintas
◆ **a cassette recorder** una grabadora de casetes

cast [kæst] NOUN
el reparto ◇ *The cast of the movie includes many famous actors.* El reparto de la película incluye a muchos actores famosos.
◆ **After the play, we met the cast.** Cuando terminó la obra conversamos con los actores.

castle ['kæsəl] NOUN
el castillo

casual ['kæʒu:əl] ADJECTIVE
1 informal ◇ *I prefer casual clothes.* Prefiero la ropa informal.
2 despreocupado ◇ *a casual attitude* una actitud despreocupada
3 eventual ◇ *It's just a casual job.* Es sólo un trabajo eventual.
◆ **a casual remark** un comentario hecho de pasada

casually ['kæʒu:əli] ADVERB
◆ **to dress casually** vestir* informal

casualty ['kæʒu:əlti] NOUN (PL **casualties**)
la víctima ◇ *The casualties include a young boy.* Entre las víctimas se encuentra un niño.

cat [kæt] NOUN
el gato
la gata

catalog ['kætəlɑ:g] NOUN
el catálogo

catalytic converter [kætl'ɪtɪkkən'vɜ:rtər] NOUN
el catalizador

catastrophe [kə'tæstrəfi] NOUN
la catástrofe

to **catch** [kætʃ] VERB (**caught, caught**)
1 agarrar ◇ *They caught the thief.* Agarraron al ladrón. ◇ *He caught her arm.* La agarró del brazo.
◆ **My cat catches birds.** Mi gato caza pájaros.
2 tomar (*train, plane*) ◇ *We caught the last train.* Tomamos el último tren.
◆ **to catch a cold** resfriarse*
◆ **I didn't catch his name.** No me enteré de su nombre.
◆ **He caught her stealing.** La pilló robando.
◆ **If they catch you smoking you'll be in trouble.** Si te pillan fumando estás fregado.

to **catch up** [kætʃʌp] VERB
1 ponerse* al día ◇ *I have to catch up on my work.* Tengo que ponerme al día con el trabajo.
2 alcanzar* ◇ *She caught up with me.* Me alcanzó.

catching ['kætʃɪŋ] ADJECTIVE
contagioso ◇ *Don't worry, it's not catching!* ¡No te preocupes, no es contagioso!

catering ['keɪtərɪŋ] NOUN
◆ **The hotel did all the catering for the wedding.** El hotel se encargó de organizar el ☞

C

banquete de bodas.

cathedral [kə'θi:drəl] NOUN
la catedral

Catholic ['kæθəlɪk] ADJECTIVE
see also **Catholic** NOUN
católico

Catholic ['kæθəlɪk] NOUN
see also **Catholic** ADJECTIVE
el católico
la católica
◇ *I'm a Catholic.* Soy católico.

cattle ['kætl] PL NOUN
el ganado SING

caught [ka:t] VERB *see* **catch**

cauliflower ['ka:lɪflauər] NOUN
la coliflor

cause [ka:z] NOUN
see also **cause** VERB
la causa

to **cause** [ka:z] VERB
see also **cause** NOUN
causar

cautious ['ka:ʃəs] ADJECTIVE
prudente

cautiously ['ka:ʃəsli] ADVERB
con cautela

cave [keɪv] NOUN
la cueva

caviar ['kævia:r] NOUN
el caviar

CCTV [ˌsi:si:ti:'vi:] NOUN (= *closed-circuit television*)
el circuito cerrado de televisión

CD [si:'di:] NOUN
el CD (PL los CDs)

CD player [si:'di:ˌpleɪər] NOUN
el reproductor de CD

CD-ROM [ˌsi:di:'ra:m] NOUN
el CD-ROM

ceasefire ['si:s'faɪər] NOUN
el cese del fuego

ceiling ['si:lɪŋ] NOUN
el techo

to **celebrate** ['sɛləbreɪt] VERB
celebrar

celebrity [sə'lɛbrɪti] NOUN (PL **celebrities**)
la celebridad

celery ['sɛləri] NOUN
el apio

cell [sɛl] NOUN
1 la celda ◇ *Prisoners spend many hours in their cells.* Los prisioneros pasan muchas horas en sus celdas.
2 la célula (*in biology*)

cellar ['sɛlər] NOUN
el sótano
◆ **a wine cellar** una bodega

cello ['tʃɛlou] NOUN (PL **cellos**)
el violonchelo

cellular phone ['sɛljələr'foun] NOUN
el teléfono portátil

cement [sə'mɛnt] NOUN
el cemento

cemetery ['sɛmɪtɛri] NOUN (PL **cemeteries**)
el cementerio

cent [sɛnt] NOUN
el centavo

centennial [sɛn'tɛniəl] NOUN
el centenario

center ['sɛntər] NOUN
el centro

centigrade ['sɛntɪgreɪd] ADJECTIVE
centígrado ◇ *20 degrees centigrade* 20 grados centígrados

centimeter ['sɛntɪmi:tər] NOUN
el centímetro

central ['sɛntrəl] ADJECTIVE
central

central heating ['sɛntrəl'hi:tɪŋ] NOUN
la calefacción central

century ['sɛntʃəri] NOUN (PL **centuries**)
el siglo ◇ *the twentieth century* el siglo veinte

cereal ['sɪriəl] NOUN
los cereales ◇ *I have cereal for breakfast.* Desayuno cereales.

ceremony ['sɛrɪmouni] NOUN (PL **ceremonies**)
la ceremonia

certain ['sɜ:rtn] ADJECTIVE
1 cierto (*particular*) ◇ *a certain person* cierta persona
2 seguro (*definite*) ◇ *I am certain he's not coming.* Estoy seguro de que no viene.
◆ **for certain** con certeza
◆ **to make certain** cerciorarse ◇ *I made certain the door was locked.* Me cercioré de que la puerta estaba cerrada con llave.

certainly ['sɜ:rtnli] ADVERB
por supuesto ◇ *I shall certainly be there.* Por supuesto que estaré allí. ◇ *Certainly not!* ¡Por supuesto que no!
◆ **So it was a surprise? – It certainly was!** ¿Así que fue una sorpresa? – ¡Ya lo creo!

certificate [sər'tɪfɪkɪt] NOUN
el certificado

chain [tʃeɪn] NOUN
la cadena ◇ *a gold chain* una cadena de oro

chair [tʃɛər] NOUN
1 la silla ◇ *a table and four chairs* una mesa y cuatro sillas
2 el sillón (PL los sillones) (*armchair*)

chairlift ['tʃɛrˌlɪft] NOUN
el telesilla

*Although **telesilla** ends in **-a**, it is actually a masculine noun.*

chairman ['tʃɛrmən] NOUN (PL **chairmen**)
el presidente

chairperson ['tʃɛrpɜ:rsən] NOUN
el presidente

la presidenta

chairwoman [ˈtʃɛrmwumәm] NOUN (PL **chairwomen**)
la presidenta

chalet [ʃæˈleɪ] NOUN
el chalet (PL los chalets)

chalk [tʃɑːk] NOUN
la tiza
◆ **a piece of chalk** una tiza

chalkboard [ˈtʃɑːkˌbɔːrd] NOUN
el pizarrón (PL los pizarrones)

challenge [ˈtʃælɪndʒ] NOUN
see also **challenge** VERB
el reto

to **challenge** [ˈtʃælɪndʒ] VERB
see also **challenge** NOUN
retar ◇ *She challenged me to a race.* Me retó a echar una carrera.

challenging [ˈtʃælɪndʒɪŋ] ADJECTIVE
estimulante ◇ *a challenging job* un trabajo estimulante

chambermaid [ˈtʃeɪmbәrˌmeɪd] NOUN
la camarera

champagne [ʃæmˈpeɪn] NOUN
el champán

champion [ˈtʃæmpiәn] NOUN
el campeón (PL los campeones)
la campeona

championship [ˈtʃæmpiәnʃɪp] NOUN
el campeonato

chance [tʃæns] NOUN
1 la posibilidad ◇ *The team's chances of winning are very good.* El equipo tiene muchas posibilidades de ganar.
2 la oportunidad ◇ *I had the chance of working in Brazil.* Tuve la oportunidad de trabajar en Brasil.
◆ **I'll write when I get the chance.** Te escribiré cuando tenga un momento.
◆ **by chance** por casualidad
◆ **No chance!** ¡Ni en broma!
◆ **to take a chance** arriesgarse* ◇ *I'm taking no chances!* ¡No me quiero arriesgar!

to **change** [tʃeɪndʒ] VERB
see also **change** NOUN
1 cambiar ◇ *The town has changed a lot.* La ciudad ha cambiado mucho. ◇ *I'd like to change $50.* Quisiera cambiar 50 dólares. ◇ *I'd like to change this sweater, it's too small.* Me gustaría cambiar este suéter, es demasiado pequeño.
2 cambiar de ◇ *He wants to change his job.* Quiere cambiar de trabajo. ◇ *I'm going to change my shoes.* Voy a cambiarme de zapatos.
◆ **to get changed** cambiarse
◆ **to change one's mind** cambiar de idea

change [tʃeɪndʒ] NOUN
see also **change** VERB
1 el cambio ◇ *There's been a change of plan.* Ha habido un cambio de planes.
◆ **a change of clothes** una muda
◆ **for a change** para variar
2 el sencillo
la feria *Mexico*
◇ *I don't have any change.* No tengo sencillo. *Mexico:* No tengo feria.
◆ **Can you give me change for a dollar?** ¿Me puede cambiar un dólar?
◆ **There's your change.** Aquí tiene el cambio.

changeable [ˈtʃeɪndʒәbәl] ADJECTIVE
variable

changing room [ˈtʃeɪndʒɪŋˌruːm] NOUN
el probador
el vestidor *Mexico*
(*in store*)

channel [ˈtʃænl] NOUN
el canal (*TV*)
◆ **the English Channel** el Canal de la Mancha

chaos [ˈkeɪɑːs] NOUN
el caos

chap [tʃæp] NOUN
el tipo (*informal*)

chapel [ˈtʃæpәl] NOUN
la capilla

chapter [ˈtʃæptәr] NOUN
el capítulo

character [ˈkɛrɪktәr] NOUN
1 el carácter (PL los caracteres) ◇ *Can you give me some idea of his character?* ¿Puede describirme un poco su carácter?
2 el personaje
el carácter *Mexico*
(*in movie, book*)
◇ *She's quite a character.* Es todo un personaje.

characteristic [kɛrɪktәˈrɪstɪk] NOUN
la característica

charcoal [ˈtʃɑːrkoul] NOUN
1 el carbón vegetal (*for barbecue*)
2 el carboncillo (*for drawing*)

charge [tʃɑːrdʒ] NOUN
see also **charge** VERB
◆ **Is there a charge for delivery?** ¿Cobran por el envío?
◆ **an extra charge** un suplemento
◆ **free of charge** gratuito
◆ **to be in charge** ser* el responsable ◇ *She was in charge of the group.* Ella era la responsable del grupo.

to **charge** [tʃɑːrdʒ] VERB
see also **charge** NOUN
1 cobrar ◇ *How much did he charge you?* ¿Cuánto te cobró?
2 acusar (*with crime*) ◇ *The police have charged him with murder.* La policía lo acusó de asesinato.

charity [ˈtʃɛrɪti] NOUN (PL **charities**)
la organización benéfica (PL las organizaciones benéficas) (*organization*)
◇ *He gave the money to charity.* Donó el dinero a una organización benéfica. ☞

C

◆ **to collect for charity** recaudar dinero para obras de caridad

charm [tʃɑːrm] NOUN
el encanto

charming [ˈtʃɑːrmɪŋ] ADJECTIVE
encantador (FEM encantadora)

chart [tʃɑːrt] NOUN
el gráfico ◇ *The chart shows the rise of unemployment.* El gráfico muestra el aumento del desempleo.
◆ **the charts** la lista de éxitos ◇ *His record has been in the charts for 10 weeks.* Su disco ha estado en la lista de éxitos durante 10 semanas.

charter flight [ˈtʃɑːrtərˌflaɪt] NOUN
el vuelo chárter

to **chase** [tʃeɪs] VERB
see also **chase** NOUN
1 perseguir* ◇ *The policeman chased the thief along the road.* El policía persiguió al ladrón a lo largo de la calle.
2 ir* detrás de ◇ *He's always chasing the girls.* Siempre anda detrás de las chicas.

chase [tʃeɪs] NOUN
see also **chase** VERB
la persecución (PL las persecuciones) ◇ *a car chase* una persecución en carro

chat [tʃæt] NOUN
la charla
la plática *Mexico*
◆ **to have a chat** charlar, *Mexico:* platicar*

to **chat up** [tʃætˈʌp] VERB
tratar de ligar con ◇ *Jake was chatting up one of the girls.* Jake estaba tratando de ligar con una de las chicas.

cheap [tʃiːp] ADJECTIVE
1 barato ◇ *a cheap T-shirt* una camiseta barata ◇ *It's cheaper by train.* Es más barato en tren.
◆ **a cheap flight** un vuelo económico
2 tacaño ◇ *He's too cheap to buy presents.* Es demasiado tacaño para comprar regalos.

to **cheat** [tʃiːt] VERB
see also **cheat** NOUN
1 hacer* trampa (*at cards*) ◇ *You're cheating!* ¡Estás haciendo trampa!
2 copiar (*in exam*)

cheat [tʃiːt] NOUN
see also **cheat** VERB
el tramposo
la tramposa

check [tʃɛk] NOUN
see also **check** VERB
1 el control ◇ *a security check* un control de seguridad
2 el cheque ◇ *to write a check* extender* un cheque ◇ *to pay by check* pagar* con cheque
3 la cuenta
la nota *Mexico*
(*in restaurant*)
◇ *Can we have the check, please?* ¿Nos trae la cuenta, por favor?, *Mexico:* ¿Nos trae la nota, por favor?
4 la señal
la palomita *Mexico*

to **check** [tʃɛk] VERB
see also **check** NOUN
1 comprobar* ◇ *Could you check the oil, please?* ¿Podría comprobar el aceite, por favor?
◆ **to check with somebody** preguntarle a alguien ◇ *I'll check with the driver what time the bus leaves.* Le preguntaré al chofer a qué hora sale el autobús.
2 marcar* con una señal
marcar* con una palomita *Mexico*
◇ *Check the appropriate box.* Marque con una señal la casilla correspondiente. *Mexico:* Marque con una palomita la casilla correspondiente.

to **check in** [tʃɛkˈɪn] VERB
1 registrarse (*in hotel*)
2 chequear el equipaje
registrarse *Mexico*
(*at airport*)

to **check off** [tʃɛkˈɑːf] VERB
marcar* con una señal
marcar* con una palomita *Mexico*
(*on form, list*)
◇ *The teacher checked off their names on the attendance sheet.* El profesor marcó con una señal los nombres de la lista.

to **check out** [tʃɛkˈaut] VERB
dejar el hotel

checkbook [ˈtʃɛkˌbuk] NOUN
la chequera

checked [tʃɛkt] ADJECTIVE
a cuadros MASC, FEM, PL

checkerboard [ˈtʃɛkərˌbɔːrd] NOUN
el tablero de damas

checkers [ˈtʃɛkərz] PL NOUN
las damas ◇ *to play checkers* jugar* a las damas

check-in [ˈtʃɛkɪn] NOUN (PL **check-ins**)
el chequeo del equipaje
el registro del equipaje *Mexico*

checking account [ˈtʃɛkɪŋəˌkaunt] NOUN
la cuenta corriente

checkout [ˈtʃɛkˌaut] NOUN
la caja

checkroom [ˈtʃɛkˌruːm] NOUN
la consigna

checkup [ˈtʃɛkʌp] NOUN
el reconocimiento médico

cheek [tʃiːk] NOUN
la mejilla ◇ *He kissed her on the cheek.* La besó en la mejilla.

cheer [tʃɪər] NOUN
see also **cheer** VERB

◆ **Three cheers for the winner!** ¡Viva el ganador!
◆ **Cheers!** (*when drinking*) ¡Salud!

to **cheer** [tʃɪər] VERB
see also **cheer** NOUN
vitorear
◆ **to cheer somebody up** levantar el ánimo a alguien ◇ *I was trying to cheer him up.* Estaba intentando levantarle el ánimo.
◆ **Cheer up!** ¡Anímate!

cheerful ['tʃɪrfəl] ADJECTIVE
alegre

cheerio [tʃɪri'ou] EXCLAMATION
¡hasta luego!

cheerleader ['tʃɪrˌliːdər] NOUN
el animador
la animadora

cheerleading ['tʃɪrˌliːdɪŋ] NOUN

> ℹ *El* **cheerleading** *es un deporte en los centros de educación secundaria y las universidades que tiene por fin crear una actitud positiva hacia los espectáculos deportivos. Se practica por un grupo formado por integrantes de ambos sexos que avivan rítmicamente a un equipo durante un partido, para así despertar el entusiasmo, por el mismo equipo, entre los espectadores.*

cheese [tʃiːz] NOUN
el queso

chef [ʃɛf] NOUN
el/la chef (PL los/las chefs)

chemical ['kɛmɪkəl] NOUN
la sustancia química

chemist ['kɛmɪst] NOUN
el químico
la química
(*scientist*)

chemistry ['kɛmɪstri] NOUN
la química ◇ *the chemistry lab* el laboratorio de química

cherry ['tʃɛri] NOUN (PL **cherries**)
la cereza

chess [tʃɛs] NOUN
el ajedrez ◇ *He likes playing chess.* Le gusta jugar ajedrez.

chessboard ['tʃɛsˌbɔːrd] NOUN
el tablero de ajedrez

chest [tʃɛst] NOUN
el pecho ◇ *I have a pain in my chest.* Tengo un dolor en el pecho.

chestnut ['tʃɛsˌnʌt] NOUN
la castaña

chest of drawers ['tʃɛstəv'drɔːrz] NOUN
la cómoda

to **chew** [tʃuː] VERB
masticar*

chewing gum ['tʃuːɪŋˌgʌm] NOUN
el chicle
◆ **a piece of chewing gum** un chicle

Chicano [tʃɪ'kaːnou] ADJECTIVE
see also **Chicano** NOUN
chicano

Chicano [tʃɪ'kaːnou] NOUN
see also **Chicano** ADJECTIVE
el chicano
la chicana

chick [tʃɪk] NOUN
el pollito ◇ *a hen and her chicks* una gallina y sus pollitos

chicken ['tʃɪkɪn] NOUN
1 la gallina (*animal*)
2 el pollo (*food*)

chickenpox ['tʃɪkɪnˌpaːks] NOUN
la varicela ◇ *I have chickenpox.* Tengo la varicela.

chickpeas ['tʃɪkˌpiːz] PL NOUN
los garbanzos

chief [tʃiːf] NOUN
see also **chief** ADJECTIVE
el jefe
la jefa
◇ *the chief of security* el jefe de seguridad

chief [tʃiːf] ADJECTIVE
see also **chief** NOUN
principal ◇ *His chief reason for resigning was the low pay.* El motivo principal de su renuncia fue el sueldo bajo.

child [tʃaɪld] NOUN (PL **children**)
1 el niño
la niña
◇ *a child of six* un niño de seis años
2 el hijo
la hija
◇ *Susan is our oldest child.* Susan es nuestra hija mayor. ◇ *They have three children.* Tienen tres hijos.

child care provider ['tʃaɪldkɛrprə'vaɪdər] NOUN
la cuidadora de niños

childish ['tʃaɪldɪʃ] ADJECTIVE
infantil

children ['tʃɪldrən] PL NOUN *see* **child**

Chile ['tʃɪli] NOUN
Chile MASC

chili ['tʃɪli] NOUN
el chile
◆ **chili con carne** el chile con carne

to **chill** [tʃɪl] VERB
see also **chill** NOUN
poner* a enfriar (*drink, food*)
◆ **Serve chilled.** Sírvase bien frío.

chill [tʃɪl] NOUN
see also **chill** VERB
◆ **to catch a chill** resfriarse*

chilly ['tʃɪli] ADJECTIVE
frío

chimney ['tʃɪmni] NOUN
la chimenea

chin [tʃɪn] NOUN

☞

la barbilla
◆ **Keep your chin up!** ¡No pierdas el ánimo!

china ['tʃaɪnə] NOUN
la porcelana ◇ *a china plate* un plato de porcelana

China ['tʃaɪnə] NOUN
China FEM

Chinese [tʃaɪ'ni:z] ADJECTIVE
see also **Chinese** NOUN
chino
◆ **a Chinese man** un chino
◆ **a Chinese woman** una china

Chinese [tʃaɪ'ni:z] NOUN
see also **Chinese** ADJECTIVE
el chino (*language*)
◆ **the Chinese** los chinos

chip [tʃɪp] NOUN
1 el chip (PL los chips) (*in computer*)
2 la papa frita de bolsa ◇ *a bag of chips* una bolsa de papas fritas de bolsa

chiropodist [kɪ'rɑ:pədɪst] NOUN
el pedicuro
la pedicura
◇ *She's a chiropodist.* Es pedicura.

chives [tʃaɪvz] PL NOUN
los cebollinos

chocolate ['tʃɑ:klɪt] NOUN
1 el chocolate ◇ *a chocolate cake* un pastel de chocolate ◇ *a cup of hot chocolate* una taza de chocolate
2 el bombón (PL los bombones) ◇ *a box of chocolates* una caja de chocolates

choice [tʃɔɪs] NOUN
la elección (PL las elecciones)
◆ **I had no choice.** No tenía otro remedio.

choir ['kwaɪər] NOUN
el coro

to **choke** [tʃouk] VERB
atragantarse (*on food*)

to **choose** [tʃu:z] VERB (**chose, chosen**)
elegir*

to **chop** [tʃɑ:p] VERB
see also **chop** NOUN
1 picar* (*onion, herbs*)
2 cortar en trozos pequeños (*meat*)

chop [tʃɑ:p] NOUN
see also **chop** VERB
la chuleta ◇ *a pork chop* una chuleta de cerdo, *Mexico:* una chuleta de puerco

chopsticks ['tʃɑ:p,stɪks] PL NOUN
los palillos

chose, chosen [tʃouz,'tʃouzən] VERB *see* **choose**

Christ [kraɪst] NOUN
Cristo MASC

christening ['krɪsnɪŋ] NOUN
el bautizo

Christian ['krɪstʃən] NOUN
see also **Christian** ADJECTIVE
el cristiano
la cristiana

Christian ['krɪstʃən] ADJECTIVE
see also **Christian** NOUN
cristiano

Christian name ['krɪstʃən,neɪm] NOUN
el nombre de pila

Christmas ['krɪsməs] NOUN
la Navidad ◇ *Merry Christmas!* ¡Feliz Navidad!
◆ **Christmas Day** el día de Navidad
◆ **on Christmas Day** el día de Navidad
◆ **Christmas Eve** la Nochebuena
◆ **a Christmas tree** un árbol de Navidad
◆ **Christmas dinner** la cena de Nochebuena

> ℹ *For Latin Americans,* **la cena de Nochebuena** *takes place on Christmas Eve unlike* **Christmas dinner** *in the States, which is usually eaten on Christmas Day.*

◆ **a Christmas present** un regalo de Navidad
◆ **Christmas card** la tarjeta de Navidad
◆ **at Christmas** en Navidad

to **chuck out** ['tʃʌk'aut] VERB
tirar (*throw away*) ◇ *You'll need to chuck out some of these books.* Tendrás que tirar alguno de estos libros.

chunk [tʃʌŋk] NOUN
el pedazo ◇ *Cut the meat into chunks.* Cortar la carne en pedazos.

church [tʃɜ:rtʃ] NOUN (PL **churches**)
la iglesia

cider ['saɪdər] NOUN
la sidra

cigar [sɪ'gɑ:r] NOUN
el puro

cigarette [sɪgə'rɛt] NOUN
el cigarrillo

cigarette lighter [sɪgə'rɛt,laɪtər] NOUN
el encendedor

cinema ['sɪnəmə] NOUN
el cine (*film making*)

cinnamon ['sɪnəmən] NOUN
la canela

circle ['sɜ:rkəl] NOUN
el círculo

circular ['sɜ:rkjələr] ADJECTIVE
circular

circulation [sɜ:rkjə'leɪʃən] NOUN
1 la circulación ◇ *She has poor circulation.* Tiene mala circulación.
2 la tirada ◇ *The newspaper has a circulation of around 8000.* El periódico tiene una tirada de unos 8.000 ejemplares.

circumstances ['sɜ:rkəmstænsɪz] PL NOUN
las circunstancias ◇ *in the circumstances* dadas las circunstancias
◆ **under no circumstances** bajo ningún concepto

circus ['sɜːrkəs] NOUN (PL **circuses**)
el circo

citizen ['sɪtɪzən] NOUN
el ciudadano
la ciudadana

city ['sɪti] NOUN (PL **cities**)
la ciudad ◇ *the city center* el centro de la ciudad

civilization [sɪvɪlɪ'zeɪʃən] NOUN
la civilización (PL las civilizaciones)

civil servant [ˌsɪvɪl'sɜːrvənt] NOUN
el funcionario
la funcionaria
el/la burócrata *Mexico*
◇ *He's a civil servant.* Es funcionario.
Mexico: Es burócrata.

civil war [ˌsɪvɪl'wɔːr] NOUN
la guerra civil

to **claim** [kleɪm] VERB
see also **claim** NOUN
1 asegurar ◇ *He claims he found the money.* Asegura haber encontrado el dinero.
2 reclamar ◇ *He's claiming compensation from the company.* Reclama una indemnización por parte de la empresa.
3 cobrar ◇ *She's claiming unemployment benefits.* Cobra subsidio de desempleo.

claim [kleɪm] NOUN
see also **claim** VERB
1 la reclamación (PL las reclamaciones) (*on insurance policy*)
◆ **to make a claim** reclamar al seguro
2 la afirmación (PL las afirmaciones) ◇ *The manufacturer's claims are obviously untrue.* Las afirmaciones del fabricante son obviamente falsas.

to **clap** [klæp] VERB
aplaudir
◆ **to clap one's hands** dar* palmadas

clarinet [klɛrɪ'nɛt] NOUN
el clarinete

to **clash** [klæʃ] VERB
1 desentonar (*colors*) ◇ *Red clashes with orange.* El rojo desentona con el naranja.
2 coincidir (*events*) ◇ *The party clashes with the meeting.* La fiesta coincide con la reunión.

clasp [klæsp] NOUN
el cierre (*of necklace, handbag*)

class [klæs] NOUN (PL **classes**)
la clase ◇ *We're in the same class.* Estamos en la misma clase. ◇ *I go to dancing classes.* Voy a clases de baile.

classic ['klæsɪk] ADJECTIVE
see also **classic** NOUN
clásico ◇ *a classic example* un ejemplo clásico

classic ['klæsɪk] NOUN
see also **classic** ADJECTIVE
el clásico

classical ['klæsɪkəl] ADJECTIVE
clásico ◇ *classical music* la música clásica

classmate ['klæsˌmeɪt] NOUN
el compañero de clase
la compañera de clase

classroom ['klæsˌruːm] NOUN
la clase
el salón de clases *Mexico*

clause [klɑːz] NOUN
1 la cláusula (*in legal document*)
2 la oración (PL las oraciones) (*in grammar*)

claw [klɑː] NOUN
1 la garra (*of lion, eagle*)
2 la uña (*of cat, parrot*)
3 la pinza (*of crab, lobster*)

clean [kliːn] ADJECTIVE
see also **clean** VERB
limpio

to **clean** [kliːn] VERB
see also **clean** ADJECTIVE
limpiar
◆ **I clean my teeth after every meal.** Me lavo los dientes después de cada comida.

cleaner ['kliːnər] NOUN
1 el hombre de la limpieza
la mujer de la limpieza
(*person*)
2 el producto de limpieza (*substance*)

cleaner's ['kliːnərz] NOUN
la tintorería ◇ *He took his coat to the cleaner's.* Llevó el abrigo a la tintorería.

cleaning lady ['kliːnɪŋ'leɪdi] NOUN (PL **cleaning ladies**)
la mujer de la limpieza

cleansing lotion ['klɛnzɪŋ'louʃən] NOUN
la loción limpiadora (PL las lociones limpiadoras)

clear [klɪər] ADJECTIVE
see also **clear** VERB
1 claro ◇ *a clear explanation* una explicación clara ◇ *It's clear you don't believe me.* Está claro que no me crees.
◆ **Have I made myself clear?** ¿Me explico?
2 despejado ◇ *Wait till the road is clear.* Espera hasta que la carretera esté despejada. ◇ *a clear day* un día despejado
3 transparente ◇ *It comes in a clear plastic bottle.* Viene en una botella de plástico transparente.

to **clear** [klɪər] VERB
see also **clear** ADJECTIVE
1 despejar ◇ *They are clearing the road.* Están despejando la carretera.
2 dispersarse (*fog, mist*)
◆ **She was cleared of murder.** La absolvieron del cargo de asesinato.
◆ **to clear the table** levantar la mesa

to **clear out** [klɪər'aut] VERB
largarse* ◇ *Clear out and leave me alone!* ¡Lárgate y déjame en paz!

to **clear up** [klɪər'ʌp] VERB ☞

1 ordenar ◇ *Who's going to clear all this up?* ¿Quién va a ordenar todo esto?
2 resolver* ◇ *I'm sure we can clear up this problem right away.* Estoy seguro de que podemos resolver este problema enseguida.
◆ **I think it's going to clear up.** (*weather*) Creo que va a despejar.

clearly ['klırli] ADVERB
claramente ◇ *to speak clearly* hablar claramente
◆ **Clearly this project will cost money.** Evidentemente este proyecto costará dinero.

cleat [kli:t] NOUN
el taco (*on sports shoes*)

clementine ['klɛməntaın] NOUN
la clementina

to **clench** [klɛntʃ] VERB
apretar* ◇ *She clenched her fists.* Apretó los puños.

clerk [klɜ:rk] NOUN
el empleado
la empleada
◇ *She's a clerk.* Es empleada.

clever ['klɛvər] ADJECTIVE
1 listo ◇ *She's very clever.* Es muy lista.
2 ingenioso ◇ *a clever system* un sistema ingenioso
◆ **What a clever idea!** ¡Qué idea más genial!

to **click** [klık] VERB
hacer* clic (*computer*)
◆ **to click on the mouse** hacer* clic con el ratón
◆ **to click on an icon** hacer* clic en un icono

client ['klaıənt] NOUN
el cliente
la clienta

cliff [klıf] NOUN
el acantilado

climate ['klaımıt] NOUN
el clima
Although ***clima*** *ends in* ***-a****, it is actually a masculine noun.*

to **climb** [klaım] VERB
1 escalar ◇ *Her ambition is to climb Mount Everest.* Su ambición es escalar el Monte Everest.
2 trepar a ◇ *They climbed a tree.* Treparon a un árbol.
◆ **to climb the stairs** subir las escaleras

climber ['klaımər] NOUN
el escalador
la escaladora

climbing ['klaımıŋ] NOUN
el andinismo
◆ **to go climbing** hacer* andinismo ◇ *We're going climbing in the Rockies.* Vamos a hacer andinismo en Las Rocosas.

clinic ['klınık] NOUN
la clínica (*private hospital*)

clip [klıp] NOUN
1 el pasador
el broche [Mexico]
(*for hair*)
2 la secuencia ◇ *some clips from Brad Pitt's latest movie* unas secuencias de la última película de Brad Pitt

clippers ['klıpərz] PL NOUN
◆ **nail clippers** el cortaúñas (PL los cortaúñas)

cloakroom ['klouk,ru:m] NOUN
el guardarropa (*for coats*)
Although ***guardarropa*** *ends in* ***-a****, it is actually a masculine noun.*

clock [klɑ:k] NOUN
el reloj
◆ **an alarm clock** un despertador
◆ **a clock radio** un radio-despertador

clockwork ['klɑ:k,wɜ:rk] NOUN
◆ **to go like clockwork** ir* sobre ruedas

clone [kloun] NOUN
[*see also* **clone** VERB]
el clon

to **clone** [kloun] VERB
[*see also* **clone** NOUN]
clonar ◇ *to clone a sheep* clonar una oveja
◆ **a cloned sheep** una oveja clónica

close [klous] ADJECTIVE, ADVERB
[*see also* **close** VERB]
1 cerca ◇ *The stores are very close.* Las tiendas están muy cerca. ◇ *The hotel is close to the station.* El hotel está cerca de la estación.
◆ **Come closer.** Acércate más.
◆ **She was close to tears.** Estaba a punto de llorar.
2 cercano ◇ *We have only invited close relations.* Sólo hemos invitado a parientes cercanos.
3 íntimo ◇ *She's a close friend of mine.* Es amiga íntima mía.
◆ **I'm very close to my sister.** Estoy muy unida a mi hermana.
4 reñido ◇ *It was a very close contest.* Fue un concurso muy reñido.
◆ **It's close this afternoon.** Hace bochorno esta tarde. (*of weather*)

to **close** [klouz] VERB
[*see also* **close** ADJECTIVE, ADVERB]
1 cerrar* ◇ *The stores close at eight thirty.* Las tiendas cierran a las ocho y media. ◇ *Please close the door.* Cierra la puerta, por favor.
2 cerrarse* ◇ *The doors close automatically.* Las puertas se cierran automáticamente.

closed [klouzd] ADJECTIVE
cerrado

closely ['klousli] ADVERB
de cerca (*look, examine*)
◆ **This will be a closely fought race.** Será una carrera muy reñida.

closet ['klɑ:zıt] NOUN

el armario

cloth [klɑːθ] NOUN
la tela ◇ *I would like five meters of this cloth.* Quisiera cinco metros de esta tela.
◆ **a cloth** un trapo ◇ *Wipe it with a damp cloth.* Límpialo con un trapo húmedo.

clothes [klouz] PL NOUN
la ropa SING
◆ **clothes line** la cuerda de tender
◆ **clothespin** la pinza para tender la ropa
◆ **clothes dryer** la secadora

cloud [klaud] NOUN
la nube

cloudy ['klaudi] ADJECTIVE
nublado

clove [klouv] NOUN
◆ **a clove of garlic** un diente de ajo

clown [klaun] NOUN
el payaso

club [klʌb] NOUN
1 el club ◇ *a golf club* un club de golf ◇ *the youth club* el club juvenil
2 la discoteca ◇ *We had dinner and went on to a club.* Cenamos y fuimos a una discoteca.
◆ **clubs** (*at cards*) los tréboles ◇ *the ace of clubs* el as de tréboles

clue [kluː] NOUN
la pista ◇ *an important clue* una pista clave
◆ **I don't have a clue.** No tengo ni idea.

clumsy ['klʌmzi] ADJECTIVE
torpe

clutch [klʌtʃ] NOUN
see also **clutch** VERB
el embrague
el clotch *Mexico*
(*of car*)

to **clutch** [klʌtʃ] VERB
see also **clutch** NOUN
agarrar ◇ *She clutched my arm and begged me not to go.* Me agarró el brazo y me suplicó que no me marchara.

coach [koutʃ] NOUN
el entrenador
la entrenadora
(*trainer*)
◆ **the soccer coach** el entrenador de fútbol

coal [koul] NOUN
el carbón
◆ **a coal mine** una mina de carbón
◆ **a coal miner** un minero del carbón

coarse [kɔːrs] ADJECTIVE
1 basto ◇ *The bag was made of coarse black cloth.* La bolsa estaba hecha de una tela basta de color negro.
2 grueso ◇ *The sand is very coarse on that beach.* La arena es muy gruesa en esa playa.

coast [koust] NOUN
la costa ◇ *It's on the west coast of Mexico.* Está en la costa oeste de México.

coastguard ['koust,gɑːrd] NOUN
el guardacostas (PL los guardacostas)

coat [kout] NOUN
el abrigo ◇ *a woolen coat* un abrigo de lana
◆ **a coat of paint** una mano de pintura

coat hanger ['kout,hæŋər] NOUN
la percha
el gancho *Mexico*

cobweb ['kɑːbwɛb] NOUN
la telaraña

cocaine [kou'keɪn] NOUN
la cocaína

cocoa ['koukou] NOUN
la cocoa
◆ **a cup of cocoa** una taza de chocolate

coconut ['koukənʌt] NOUN
el coco

cod [kɑːd] NOUN
el bacalao

code [koud] NOUN
la clave ◇ *It's written in code.* Está escrito en clave.

coeducational [,kouɛdʒə'keɪʃənəl] ADJECTIVE
mixto

coffee ['kɑːfi] NOUN
el café (PL los cafés) ◇ *a cup of coffee* una taza de café
◆ **A cup of coffee, please.** Un café, por favor.
◆ **a coffee with milk** un café con leche
◆ **a black coffee** un café negro
◆ **a coffee bean** un grano de café

coffeepot ['kɑːfi,pɑːt] NOUN
la cafetera

coffee table ['kɑːfi,teɪbəl] NOUN
la mesa de centro

coffin ['kɑːfɪn] NOUN
el ataúd

coin [kɔɪn] NOUN
la moneda ◇ *Do you have a coin for the parking meter?* ¿Tienes una moneda para el parquímetro? ◇ *a five-peso coin* una moneda de cinco pesos

coincidence [kou'ɪnsɪdəns] NOUN
la coincidencia

Coke® [kouk] NOUN
la Coca-Cola®

colander ['kɑːləndər] NOUN
el colador

cold [kould] ADJECTIVE
see also **cold** NOUN
frío ◇ *The water is cold.* El agua está fría. ◇ *It's cold.* Hace frío. ◇ *Are you cold?* ¿Tienes frío?

cold [kould] NOUN
see also **cold** ADJECTIVE
1 el frío ◇ *I can't stand the cold.* No soporto el frío.
2 el resfriado (*illness*)
◆ **to catch a cold** resfriarse*
◆ **to have a cold** estar* resfriado

cold sore ['kould,sɔːr] NOUN
el fuego

coleslaw ['koulslɑ:] NOUN

> *Ensalada de col, zanahoria, cebolla y mayonesa.*

to **collapse** [kə'læps] VERB
1 venirse* abajo
◆ **The bridge collapsed during the storm.** El puente se vino abajo en medio de la tormenta.
2 sufrir un colapso ◇ *He collapsed while playing tennis.* Sufrió un colapso mientras jugaba tenis.

collar ['kɑ:lər] NOUN
1 el cuello (*of coat, shirt*)
2 el collar (*for animal*)

collarbone ['kɑ:lər,boun] NOUN
la clavícula

colleague ['kɑ:li:g] NOUN
el/la colega

to **collect** [kə'lɛkt] VERB
1 recoger* ◇ *The teacher collected the exercise books.* El maestro recogió los cuadernos. ◇ *Jo collects them from school.* Jo los recoge del colegio.
2 coleccionar ◇ *He collects autographs.* Colecciona autógrafos.
3 hacer* una colecta ◇ *I'm collecting for UNICEF.* Estoy haciendo una colecta para la UNICEF.
◆ **to call collect** llamar a cobro revertido

collect call [kə'lɛkt'kɑ:l] NOUN
la llamada a cobro revertido
la llamada por cobrar *Mexico*

collection [kə'lɛkʃən] NOUN
1 la colección (PL las colecciones) ◇ *my CD collection* mi colección de CDs
2 la colecta ◇ *a collection for charity* una colecta para obras de caridad

collector [kə'lɛktər] NOUN
el/la coleccionista

college ['kɑ:lɪdʒ] NOUN
la universidad (*university*) ◇ *She's at college.* Está en la universidad.

to **collide** [kə'laɪd] VERB
chocar*

collision [kə'lɪʒən] NOUN
el choque

colon ['koulən] NOUN
dos puntos (*punctuation mark*)

colonel ['kɜ:rnl] NOUN
el/la coronel

color ['kʌlər] NOUN
el color ◇ *What color is your car?* ¿De qué color es tu carro?
◆ **a color TV** una televisión en colores

colorful ['kʌlərfəl] ADJECTIVE
de colores muy vistosos

coloring ['kʌlərɪŋ] NOUN
el colorante (*for food*)

comb [koum] NOUN
see also **comb** VERB
el peine

to **comb** [koum] VERB
see also **comb** NOUN
◆ **You haven't combed your hair.** No te has peinado.

combination [kɑ:mbɪ'neɪʃən] NOUN
la combinación (PL las combinaciones)

to **combine** [kəm'baɪn] VERB
1 combinar ◇ *The movie combines humor with suspense.* La película combina el humor con el suspenso.
2 compaginar ◇ *It's difficult to combine a career with a family.* Es difícil compaginar la profesión con la vida familiar.

to **come** [kʌm] VERB (**came, come**)
1 venir* ◇ *Helen came with me.* Helen vino conmigo. ◇ *Come home.* Ven a la casa. ◇ *Come and see us soon.* Ven a vernos pronto.
◆ **Where do you come from?** ¿De dónde eres?
2 llegar* ◇ *They came late.* Llegaron tarde. ◇ *The letter came this morning.* La carta llegó esta mañana.
◆ **I'm coming!** ¡Ya voy!

to **come across (1)** ['kʌmə'krɑ:s] VERB
encontrarse* ◇ *I came across a dress that I hadn't worn for years.* Me encontré un vestido que hacía años que no me ponía.

to **come across (2)** ['kʌmə'krɑ:s] VERB
◆ **She comes across as a nice girl.** Da la impresión de ser una chica simpática.

to **come back** [kʌm'bæk] VERB
volver* ◇ *My brother is coming back tomorrow.* Mi hermano vuelve mañana.

to **come down** [kʌm'daun] VERB
bajar

to **come in** [kʌm'ɪn] VERB
entrar ◇ *Come in!* ¡Entra!

to **come on** [kʌm'ɑ:n] VERB
◆ **Come on! (1)** (*expressing encouragement, urging haste*) ¡Vamos!, *Mexico:* ¡Órale!
◆ **Come on! (2)** (*expressing disbelief*) ¡Anda ya!

to **come out** [kʌm'aut] VERB
salir* ◇ *We came out of the movies at 10.* Salimos del cine a las 10. ◇ *Her book comes out in May.* Su libro sale en mayo. ◇ *I don't think this stain will come out.* No creo que esta mancha vaya a salir.
◆ **None of my photos came out.** No salió ninguna de mis fotos.

to **come round** [kʌm'raund] VERB
volver* en sí (*after faint, operation*) ◇ *He came round after about 10 minutes.* Volvió en sí después de unos 10 minutos.

to **come up** [kʌm'ʌp] VERB
1 subir ◇ *Come up here!* ¡Sube aquí!
2 surgir* ◇ *Something's come up so I'll be*

* Verbs marked with this symbol are irregular. See pages 346–348 for further details.

late home. Surgió algo, así es que llegaré tarde a casa.
- **to come up to somebody** acercarse* a alguien ◇ *She came up to me and kissed me.* Se me acercó y me besó.

comedian [kə'mi:diən] NOUN
el cómico
la cómica

comedy ['kɑ:mɪdi] NOUN (PL **comedies**)
la comedia

comfortable ['kʌmfərtəbəl] ADJECTIVE
1 cómodo ◇ *comfortable shoes* zapatos cómodos ◇ *Make yourself comfortable!* ¡Ponte cómodo!
2 confortable (*house, room*) ◇ *Their house is small but comfortable.* Su casa es pequeña pero confortable.

comforter ['kʌmfərtər] NOUN
el edredón (PL los edredones)

comic book ['kɑ:mɪk,buk] NOUN
el cómic (PL los cómics)

comic strip ['kɑ:mɪk,strɪp] NOUN
la tira cómica

coming ['kʌmɪŋ] ADJECTIVE
próximo ◇ *In the coming weeks, we will all have to work hard.* En las próximas semanas todos tendremos que trabajar duro.

comma ['kɑ:mə] NOUN
la coma

command [kə'mænd] NOUN
la orden (PL las órdenes)

comment ['kɑ:mɛnt] NOUN
see also **comment** VERB
el comentario ◇ *He made no comment.* No hizo ningún comentario.
- **No comment!** ¡Sin comentarios!

to **comment** ['kɑ:mɛnt] VERB
see also **comment** NOUN
hacer* comentarios ◇ *The police have not commented on these rumors.* La policía no ha hecho comentarios sobre estos rumores.

commentary ['kɑ:mənteri] NOUN (PL **commentaries**)
la crónica

commentator ['kɑ:mənteɪtər] NOUN
el/la comentarista

commercial [kə'mɜ:rʃəl] NOUN
see also **commercial** ADJECTIVE
el comercial

commercial [kə'mɜ:rʃəl] ADJECTIVE
see also **commercial** NOUN
comercial

commission [kə'mɪʃən] NOUN
la comisión (PL las comisiones) ◇ *The bank charges 1% commission.* El banco cobra un 1% de comisión. ◇ *to work on commission* trabajar a comisión

to **commit** [kə'mɪt] VERB
- **to commit a crime** cometer un delito
- **to commit suicide** suicidarse
- **I don't want to commit myself.** No quiero comprometerme.

committee [kə'mɪti] NOUN
el comité

common ['kɑ:mən] ADJECTIVE
común (PL comunes) ◇ *"Smith" is a very common surname.* "Smith" es un apellido muy común.
- **in common** en común ◇ *We have a lot in common.* Tenemos mucho en común.

common sense ['kɑ:mən'sɛns] NOUN
el sentido común

to **communicate** [kə'mju:nɪkeɪt] VERB
comunicar*

communication [kəmju:nɪ'keɪʃən] NOUN
la comunicación (PL las comunicaciones)

communion [kə'mju:njən] NOUN
la comunión (PL las comuniones)

communism ['kɑ:mjənɪzəm] NOUN
el comunismo

communist ['kɑ:mjənɪst] NOUN
see also **communist** ADJECTIVE
el/la comunista

communist ['kɑ:mjənɪst] ADJECTIVE
see also **communist** NOUN
comunista

community [kə'mju:nɪti] NOUN (PL **communities**)
la comunidad
- **the local community** el vecindario
- **community service**

> ℹ *El* **community service** *es un trabajo comunitario prestado en lugar de cumplir una pena de prisión.*

community college [kə'mju:nɪti'kɑ:lidʒ] NOUN

> ℹ *El* **community college** *es un establecimiento docente de educación terciaria donde se realizan cursos de dos años.*

to **commute** [kə'mju:t] VERB
- **She commutes between Los Angeles and Santa Monica.** Para ir al trabajo se desplaza diariamente de Los Ángeles a Santa Mónica.

compact disk ['kɑ:mpækt'dɪsk] NOUN
el disco compacto
- **compact disk player** el reproductor de CDs

companion [kəm'pænjən] NOUN
el compañero
la compañera

company ['kʌmpəni] NOUN (PL **companies**)
1 la empresa ◇ *He works for a big company.* Trabaja para una empresa grande.
2 la compañía ◇ *an insurance company* una compañía de seguros ◇ *a theater company* una compañía de teatro
- **to keep somebody company** hacerle* compañía a alguien

C

comparatively [kəm'pɛrətɪvli] ADVERB
relativamente

to **compare** [kəm'pɛər] VERB
comparar ◇ *They compared his work to that of Borges.* Compararon su obra a la de Borges. ◇ *People always compare him with his brother.* La gente siempre lo compara con su hermano.
◆ **compared with** en comparación a ◇ *Santa Monica is small compared with Los Angeles.* Santa Mónica es pequeño en comparación con Los Angeles.

comparison [kəm'pɛrɪsən] NOUN
la comparación (PL las comparaciones)

compartment [kəm'pɑ:rtmənt] NOUN
el compartimento

compass ['kʌmpəs] NOUN (PL **compasses**)
la brújula

compensation [kɑ:mpən'seɪʃən] NOUN
la indemnización ◇ *They got $2000 in compensation.* Recibieron 2.000 dólares de indemnización.

to **compete** [kəm'pi:t] VERB
◆ **to compete in** competir* en ◇ *I'm competing in the marathon.* Compito en la maratón.
◆ **to compete for something** competir* por algo ◇ *There are 50 students competing for 6 places.* Hay 50 estudiantes compitiendo por 6 puestos.

competent ['kɑ:mpɪtənt] ADJECTIVE
competente

competition [kɑ:mpɪ'tɪʃən] NOUN
1 el concurso ◇ *a singing competition* un concurso de canto
2 la competencia ◇ *Competition in the computer sector is fierce.* La competencia en el sector de la informática es muy intensa.

competitive [kəm'pɛtɪtɪv] ADJECTIVE
competitivo

competitor [kəm'pɛtɪtər] NOUN
el/la concursante (*contestant*)

to **complain** [kəm'pleɪn] VERB
1 reclamar ◇ *We're going to complain to the manager.* Vamos a reclamar al director.
2 quejarse ◇ *She's always complaining about her husband.* Siempre se está quejando de su marido.

complaint [kəm'pleɪnt] NOUN
la queja

complete [kəm'pli:t] ADJECTIVE
completo

completely [kəm'pli:tli] ADVERB
completamente

complexion [kəm'plɛkʃən] NOUN
el cutis (PL los cutis)

complicated ['kɑ:mplɪkeɪtɪd] ADJECTIVE
complicado

compliment ['kɑ:mplɪmənt] NOUN
see also **compliment** VERB
el cumplido
◆ **to pay somebody a compliment** hacerle* un cumplido a alguien

to **compliment** ['kɑ:mplɪmɛnt] VERB
see also **compliment** NOUN
felicitar ◇ *They complimented me on my Spanish.* Me felicitaron por mi español.

complimentary [kɑ:mplɪ'mɛntəri] ADJECTIVE
◆ **complimentary ticket** entrada de regalo

to **compose** [kəm'pouz] VERB
componer* (*music*)
◆ **to be composed of** componerse* de

composer [kəm'pouzər] NOUN
el compositor
la compositora

comprehension [ˌkɑ:mprɪ'henʃən] NOUN
el ejercicio de comprensión (*school exercise*)

compromise ['kɑ:mprəmaɪz] NOUN
see also **compromise** VERB
el arreglo ◇ *We reached a compromise.* Llegamos a un arreglo.

to **compromise** ['kɑ:mprəmaɪz] VERB
see also **compromise** NOUN
llegar* a un acuerdo

compulsory [kəm'pʌlsəri] ADJECTIVE
obligatorio

computer [kəm'pju:tər] NOUN
la computadora

computer game [kəm'pju:tərˌgeɪm] NOUN
el juego de computadora

computer programmer
[kəm'pju:tər'prougræmər] NOUN
el programador
la programadora

computer science [kəm'pju:tər'saɪəns] NOUN
la informática

computing [kəm'pju:tɪŋ] NOUN
la informática

to **concentrate** ['kɑ:nsəntreɪt] VERB
concentrarse ◇ *I couldn't concentrate.* No me podía concentrar. ◇ *I was concentrating on my homework.* Me estaba concentrando en las tareas.

concentration [kɑ:nsən'treɪʃən] NOUN
la concentración

concerned [kən'sɜ:rnd] ADJECTIVE
preocupado ◇ *His mother is concerned about him.* La mamá está preocupada por él.
◆ **as far as the new project is concerned...** en lo que respecta al nuevo proyecto...
◆ **As far as I'm concerned, you can come any time you like.** Por mí, puedes venir cuando quieras.
◆ **It's a stressful situation for everyone concerned.** Es una situación estresante para todos los involucrados.

concert ['kɑ:nsərt] NOUN
el concierto

concrete ['kɑ:ŋkri:t] NOUN
el concreto

to **condemn** [kən'dɛm] VERB
condenar
condition [kən'dɪʃən] NOUN
la condición (PL las condiciones) ◇ *I'll do it, on one condition.* Lo haré, con una condición.
◆ **in good condition** en buen estado
conditional [kən'dɪʃənl] NOUN
el condicional
conditioner [kən'dɪʃənər] NOUN
el enjuague (*for hair*)
condom ['kɑːndəm] NOUN
el condón (PL los condones)
to **conduct** [kən'dʌkt] VERB
dirigir* (*orchestra*)
conductor [kən'dʌktər] NOUN
1 el revisor
la revisora
(*on train*)
2 el director de orquesta
la directora de orquesta
(*of orchestra*)
cone [koun] NOUN
1 el cucurucho ◇ *an ice cream cone* un cucurucho
2 el cono (*geometric shape*)
◆ **a traffic cone** un cono para señalizar el tráfico
confectioners' sugar [kən'fɛkʃənərz'ʃugər] NOUN
el azúcar glas
conference ['kɑːnfərəns] NOUN
la conferencia
to **confess** [kən'fɛs] VERB
confesar* ◇ *He confessed to the murder.* Confesó haber cometido el asesinato.
confession [kən'fɛʃən] NOUN
la confesión (PL las confesiones)
confidence ['kɑːnfɪdəns] NOUN
1 la confianza ◇ *I have a lot of confidence in him.* Tengo mucha confianza en él.
2 la confianza en sí mismo ◇ *She lacks confidence.* Le falta confianza en sí misma.
◆ **I told you that story in confidence.** Te conté esa historia de manera confidencial.
confident ['kɑːnfɪdənt] ADJECTIVE
1 seguro (*sure of something*) ◇ *I'm confident everything will be okay.* Estoy seguro de que todo saldrá bien.
2 seguro de sí mismo (*self-assured*) ◇ *She seems quite confident.* Parece muy segura de sí misma.
confidential [kɑːnfɪ'dɛnʃəl] ADJECTIVE
confidencial ◇ *"confidential"* "confidencial" (*on envelope*)
to **confirm** [kən'fɜːrm] VERB
confirmar
confirmation [kɑːnfər'meɪʃən] NOUN
la confirmación (PL las confirmaciones)
conflict ['kɑːnflɪkt] NOUN
el conflicto
to **confuse** [kən'fjuːz] VERB
confundir
confused [kən'fjuːzd] ADJECTIVE
confundido (*person*)
confusing [kən'fjuːzɪŋ] ADJECTIVE
poco claro ◇ *The traffic signs are confusing.* Las señales de tráfico están poco claras.
confusion [kən'fjuːʒən] NOUN
la confusión
to **congratulate** [kən'grætʃəleɪt] VERB
felicitar ◇ *My friends congratulated me on passing my test.* Mis amigos me felicitaron por aprobar el examen.
congratulations [kəngrætʃə'leɪʃənz] PL NOUN
las felicitaciones ◇ *Congratulations on your new job!* ¡Felicitaciones por tu nuevo empleo!
Congress ['kɑːŋgris] NOUN
el congreso
conjunction [kən'dʒʌŋkʃən] NOUN
la conjunción (PL las conjunciones)
conjurer ['kɑːndʒərər] NOUN
el prestidigitador
la prestidigitadora
connection [kə'nɛkʃən] NOUN
la conexión (PL las conexiones) ◇ *There's no connection between the two events.* No hay ninguna conexión entre los dos sucesos. ◇ *We missed our connection.* Perdimos la conexión.
◆ **There's a loose connection.** Hay un contacto suelto.
to **conquer** ['kɑːŋkər] VERB
1 conquistar (*country*)
2 vencer* (*enemy, fear*)
conscience ['kɑːnʃəns] NOUN
la conciencia
◆ **to have a guilty conscience** tener* remordimientos de conciencia
conscious ['kɑːnʃəs] ADJECTIVE
consciente ◇ *He was still conscious when the doctor arrived.* Estaba todavía consciente cuando llegó el médico. ◇ *She was conscious of Max looking at her.* Era consciente de que Max la miraba. *Mexico*: Estaba consciente de que Max la miraba.
◆ **He made a conscious decision to tell nobody.** Tomó la firme decisión de no decírselo a nadie.
consciousness ['kɑːnʃəsnɪs] NOUN
el conocimiento ◇ *I lost consciousness.* Perdí el conocimiento.
consequence ['kɑːnsɪkwəns] NOUN
la consecuencia
consequently ['kɑːnsɪkwɛntli] ADVERB
por consiguiente
conservation [kɑːnsər'veɪʃən] NOUN
la conservación
◆ **energy conservation** la conservación de la energía
conservative [kən'sɜːrvətɪv] ADJECTIVE
conservador (FEM conservadora)

conservatory [kən'sɜːrvətɔːri] NOUN (PL **conservatories**)
el invernadero

to **consider** [kən'sɪdər] VERB
1 considerar ◇ *He considers it a waste of time.* Lo considera una pérdida de tiempo.
2 pensar* en ◇ *We considered canceling our vacaction.* Pensamos en cancelar nuestras vacaciones.

considerate [kən'sɪdərɪt] ADJECTIVE
considerado

considering [kən'sɪdərɪŋ] PREPOSITION
1 teniendo en cuenta ◇ *Considering we were there for a month, we did not spend too much money.* Teniendo en cuenta que estuvimos allí durante un mes no gastamos mucho dinero.
2 después de todo ◇ *I got a good grade, considering.* Saqué buena nota, después de todo.

to **consist** [kən'sɪst] VERB
◆ **to consist of** consistir en

consonant ['kɑːnsənənt] NOUN
la consonante

constant ['kɑːnstənt] ADJECTIVE
constante

constantly ['kɑːnstəntli] ADVERB
constantemente

constipated ['kɑːnstɪpeɪtɪd] ADJECTIVE
estreñido ◇ *I'm constipated.* Estoy estreñido.
*Be careful not to translate **constipated** by **constipado**.*

to **construct** [kən'strʌkt] VERB
construir*

construction [kən'strʌkʃən] NOUN
la construcción (PL las construcciones)

to **consult** [kən'sʌlt] VERB
consultar

consumer [kən'suːmər] NOUN
el consumidor
la consumidora

contact ['kɑːntækt] NOUN
see also **contact** VERB
el contacto ◇ *I'm in contact with her.* Estoy en contacto con ella.

to **contact** ['kɑːntækt] VERB
see also **contact** NOUN
ponerse* en contacto con ◇ *Where can we contact you?* ¿Dónde podemos ponernos en contacto contigo?

contact lenses ['kɑːntækt,lɛnzɪz] PL NOUN
los lentes de contacto

to **contain** [kən'teɪn] VERB
contener*

container [kən'teɪnər] NOUN
el recipiente

contempt [kən'tɛmpt] NOUN
el desprecio

contents ['kɑːntɛnts] PL NOUN
el contenido SING

contest ['kɑːntɛst] NOUN
la competencia ◇ *a fishing contest* una competencia de pesca
◆ **a beauty contest** un concurso de belleza

contestant [kən'tɛstənt] NOUN
el/la concursante

context ['kɑːntɛkst] NOUN
el contexto

continent ['kɑːntɪnənt] NOUN
el continente
◆ **the Continent** el continente europeo

continental breakfast ['kɑːntɪnɛntl'brɛkfəst] NOUN
el desayuno continental

to **continue** [kən'tɪnju] VERB
continuar* ◇ *She continued talking to her friend.* Continuó hablando con su amiga. ◇ *We continued working after lunch.* Continuamos trabajando después de la comida.

continuing education [kən'tɪnjuɪŋɛdʒə'keɪʃən] NOUN

ℹ *Son cursos de formación no universitaria que se ofrecen después de la etapa de educación obligatoria.*

continuous [kən'tɪnjuəs] ADJECTIVE
continuo
◆ **continuous assessment** la evaluación continua

contraceptive [kɑːntrə'sɛptɪv] NOUN
el anticonceptivo

contract ['kɑːntrækt] NOUN
el contrato

to **contradict** [kɑːntrə'dɪkt] VERB
contradecir*

contrary ['kɑːntrɛri] NOUN
◆ **on the contrary** al contrario

contrast ['kɑːntræst] NOUN
el contraste

to **contribute** [kən'trɪbjuːt] VERB
◆ **to contribute to** contribuir* a ◇ *Everyone contributed to the success of the play.* Todos contribuyeron al éxito de la obra. ◇ *She contributed $10 to the collection.* Contribuyó 10 dólares a la colecta.

contribution [kɑːntrɪ'bjuːʃən] NOUN
la contribución (PL las contribuciones)

control [kən'troul] NOUN
see also **control** VERB
el control
◆ **to lose control** perder* el control (*of vehicle*)
◆ **the controls** los mandos (*of machine*)
◆ **He always seems to be in control.** Parece que siempre está en control de la situación.
◆ **She can't keep control of the class.** No sabe controlar a la clase.
◆ **out of control** fuera de control ◇ *That boy is*

out of control. Ese muchacho está fuera de control.

to **control** [kən'troul] VERB
see also **control** NOUN
controlar ◇ *He can't control the class.* No sabe controlar a la clase. ◇ *I couldn't control the horse.* No pude controlar al caballo. ◇ *Please control yourself, everyone's looking at us.* Por favor contrólate, todos nos están mirando.

controversial [kɑːntrə'vɜːrʃəl] ADJECTIVE
polémico ◇ *Euthanasia is a controversial subject.* La eutanasia es un tema polémico.

convenient [kən'viːnjənt] ADJECTIVE
bien situado (*place*) ◇ *The hotel is convenient for the airport.* El hotel está bien situado con respecto al aeropuerto.
◆ **It's not a convenient time for me.** A esa hora no me viene bien.
◆ **Would Monday be convenient for you?** ¿Te vendría bien el lunes?

conventional [kən'vɛnʃənl] ADJECTIVE
convencional

conversation [kɑːnvər'seɪʃən] NOUN
la conversación (PL las conversaciones) ◇ *We had a long conversation.* Tuvimos una larga conversación.

to **convert** [kən'vɜːrt] VERB
convertir* ◇ *We've converted the loft into a bedroom.* Hemos convertido el desván en un dormitorio.

to **convict** [kən'vɪkt] VERB
see also **convict** NOUN
declarar culpable ◇ *He was convicted of the murder.* Fue declarado culpable del asesinato.

convict ['kɑːnvɪkt] NOUN
see also **convict** VERB
el presidiario
la presidiaria

to **convince** [kən'vɪns] VERB
convencer*
◆ **I'm not convinced.** No me convence.

to **cook** [kuk] VERB
see also **cook** NOUN
1 cocinar ◇ *I can't cook.* No sé cocinar.
◆ **The chicken isn't cooked.** El pollo no está hecho.
2 preparar ◇ *She's cooking lunch.* Está preparando el almuerzo.

cook [kuk] NOUN
see also **cook** VERB
el cocinero
la cocinera
◇ *She is a cook in a hotel.* Es cocinera en un hotel. ◇ *Maria's an excellent cook.* María es una cocinera excelente.

cookbook ['kuk,buk] NOUN
el libro de cocina

cookery ['kukəri] NOUN
la cocina (*gastronomía*)

cookie ['kuki] NOUN
la galleta

cooking ['kukɪŋ] NOUN
la cocina (*gastronomía*) ◇ *French cooking* la cocina francesa
◆ **I like cooking.** Me gusta cocinar.

cool [kuːl] ADJECTIVE
fresco ◇ *a cool place* un lugar fresco
◆ **to stay cool** mantenerse* en calma (*keep calm*) ◇ *He stayed cool throughout the crisis.* Se mantuvo en calma durante toda la crisis.

cooperation [kouɑːpə'reɪʃən] NOUN
la cooperación

cop [kɑːp] NOUN
el/la poli
el/la tira *Mexico*
(*informal*)

to **cope** [koup] VERB
arreglárselas ◇ *It was hard, but we coped.* Fue difícil, pero nos las arreglamos.
◆ **She has a lot of problems to cope with.** Tiene muchos problemas a los que hacer frente.

copper ['kɑːpər] NOUN
1 el cobre ◇ *a copper bracelet* un brazalete de cobre
2 el/la poli
el/la tira *Mexico*
(*informal: policeman*)

copy ['kɑːpi] NOUN (PL **copies**)
see also **copy** VERB
1 la copia (*of letter, document*)
2 el ejemplar (*of book*)

to **copy** ['kɑːpi] VERB (**copied**, **copied**)
see also **copy** NOUN
copiar

core [kɔːr] NOUN
el corazón (PL los corazones) (*of fruit*)

cork [kɔːrk] NOUN
el corcho

corkscrew ['kɔːrk,skruː] NOUN
el sacacorchos (PL los sacacorchos)

corn [kɔːrn] NOUN
1 el maíz (*maize*)
2 el maíz tierno
el elote *Mexico*
(*sweet corn*)
◆ **corn on the cob** la mazorca de maíz, *Mexico*: el elote

corner ['kɔːrnər] NOUN
1 la esquina ◇ *the store on the corner* la tienda de la esquina ◇ *He lives just round the corner.* Vive a la vuelta de la esquina.
2 el rincón (PL los rincones) ◇ *in a corner of the room* en un rincón de la habitación
3 el saque de esquina (*in soccer*)

cornet [kɔːr'nɛt] NOUN
1 la corneta (*instrument*)
2 el cucurucho (*ice cream*)

cornflakes ['kɔːrn,fleɪks] PL NOUN
los copos de maíz

cornstarch ['kɔːrn,stɑːrtʃ] NOUN

☞

la maizena®

corporal [ˈkɔːrpərəl] NOUN
el cabo

corporal punishment [ˈkɔːrpərəlˈpʌnɪʃmənt] NOUN
el castigo corporal

corpse [kɔːrps] NOUN
el cadáver

correct [kəˈrɛkt] ADJECTIVE
see also **correct** VERB
correcto ◇ *That's correct!* ¡Correcto! ◇ *the correct answer* la respuesta correcta
◆ **You're absolutely correct.** Tienes toda la razón.

to **correct** [kəˈrɛkt] VERB
see also **correct** ADJECTIVE
corregir*

correction [kəˈrɛkʃən] NOUN
la corrección (PL las correcciones)

correctly [kəˈrɛktli] ADVERB
correctamente

correspondent [kɔːrɪsˈpɑːndənt] NOUN
el/la corresponsal

corridor [ˈkɔːrɪdər] NOUN
el pasillo

corruption [kəˈrʌpʃən] NOUN
la corrupción

cosmetics [kɑːzˈmɛtɪks] PL NOUN
los cosméticos

to **cost** [kɑːst] VERB (**cost, cost**)
see also **cost** NOUN
costar* ◇ *The meal cost $20.* La comida costó 20 dólares. ◇ *How much does it cost?* ¿Cuánto cuesta?

cost [kɑːst] NOUN
see also **cost** VERB
el costo ◇ *the cost of living* el costo de vida
◆ **at all costs** a toda costa

costume [ˈkɑːstuːm] NOUN
el traje
◆ **a costume ball** un baile de disfraces

cot [kɑːt] NOUN
la cama plegable

cottage [ˈkɑːtɪdʒ] NOUN
el chalet (PL los chalets)

cottage cheese [ˈkɑːtɪdʒˌtʃiːz] NOUN
el requesón

cotton [ˈkɑːtn] NOUN
el algodón ◇ *a cotton shirt* una camisa de algodón

cotton candy [ˈkɑːtnˈkændi] NOUN
el algodón de azúcar

couch [kautʃ] NOUN (PL **couches**)
el sofá (PL los sofás)

to **cough** [kɑːf] VERB
see also **cough** NOUN
toser

cough [kɑːf] NOUN
see also **cough** VERB
la tos ◇ *I have a cough.* Tengo tos.
◆ **cough syrup** el jarabe para la tos

could [kud] VERB *see* **can**

council [ˈkaunsəl] NOUN
el ayuntamiento (*in town*) ◇ *He's on the council.* Es concejal del ayuntamiento.

councilor [ˈkaunslər] NOUN
el concejal
la concejala

to **count** [kaunt] VERB
contar*

to **count on** [ˈkauntˌɑːn] VERB
contar* con ◇ *You can count on me.* Puedes contar conmigo.

counter [ˈkauntər] NOUN
1 el mostrador (*in store*)
2 la ventanilla (*in bank, post office*)
3 la ficha (*in game*)

country [ˈkʌntri] NOUN (PL **countries**)
1 el país ◇ *the border between the two countries* la frontera entre los dos países
2 el campo ◇ *I live in the country.* Vivo en el campo.

countryside [ˈkʌntriˌsaɪd] NOUN
el campo

county [ˈkaunti] NOUN (PL **counties**)
el condado

couple [ˈkʌpəl] NOUN
1 la pareja ◇ *the couple who live next door* la pareja que vive al lado
2 el par ◇ *a couple of hours* un par de horas

coupon [ˈkuːpɑːn] NOUN
el cupón

courage [ˈkʌrɪdʒ] NOUN
el valor

courier [ˈkuriər] NOUN
1 el/la guía (*for tourists*)
2 el servicio de mensajero (*delivery service*) ◇ *They sent it by courier.* Lo enviaron por servicio de mensajero.

course [kɔːrs] NOUN
1 el curso ◇ *a Spanish course* un curso de español ◇ *to take a course* hacer* un curso
2 el plato ◇ *the main course* el segundo plato ◇ *the first course* el primer plato
3 el campo ◇ *a golf course* un campo de golf
◆ **of course** por supuesto ◇ *Do you love me? – Of course I do!* ¿Me quieres? – ¡Por supuesto que te quiero!

court [kɔːrt] NOUN
el tribunal (*of law*)
◆ **a tennis court** una cancha de tenis

courtyard [ˈkɔːrtˌjɑːrd] NOUN
el patio

cousin [ˈkʌzən] NOUN
el primo
la prima

cover [ˈkʌvər] NOUN
see also **cover** VERB

1 la tapa (*of book*)
2 la funda (*of pillow*)

to **cover** [ˈkʌvər] VERB
see also **cover** NOUN
cubrir* ◇ *My face was covered with mosquito bites.* Tenía la cara cubierta de picaduras de mosquito. ◇ *Our insurance didn't cover it.* Nuestro seguro no lo cubría.

to **cover up** [ˌkʌvərˈʌp] VERB
ocultar ◇ *The government tried to cover up the details of the accident.* El gobierno trató de ocultar los detalles del accidente.

cow [kau] NOUN
la vaca

coward [ˈkauərd] NOUN
el/la cobarde

cowardly [ˈkauərdli] ADJECTIVE
cobarde

cowboy [ˈkauˌbɔɪ] NOUN
el vaquero

cozy [ˈkouzi] ADJECTIVE
acogedor (FEM acogedora) ◇ *a cozy room* una habitación acogedora

crab [kræb] NOUN
el cangrejo

crack [kræk] NOUN
see also **crack** VERB
1 la grieta (*in wall*)
2 la raja (*in cup, window*)
3 el crack (*drug*)
◆ **He opened the door a crack.** Abrió la puerta un poquito.
◆ **I'll have a crack at it.** Lo intentaré.

to **crack** [kræk] VERB
see also **crack** NOUN
cascar* (*nut, egg*)
◆ **He cracked his head on the sidewalk.** Se dio con la cabeza en la acera.
◆ **to crack a joke** contar* un chiste

to **crack down on** [krækˈdaunˌɑːn] VERB
tomar medidas severas contra ◇ *The police are cracking down on theft.* La policía está tomando medidas severas contra el robo.

cracked [krækt] ADJECTIVE
1 rajado (*cup, window*)
2 agrietado (*wall*)

cracker [ˈkrækər] NOUN
la galleta salada (*biscuit*)

cradle [ˈkreɪdl] NOUN
la cuna

craft [kræft] NOUN
la artesanía ◇ *a craft shop* una tienda de artesanías

craftsman [ˈkræftsmən] NOUN (PL **craftsmen**)
el artesano

to **cram** [kræm] VERB
◆ **We crammed our stuff into the trunk.** Apretamos nuestras cosas dentro del maletero.
◆ **She crammed her bag with books.** Abarrotó su bolso de libros.
◆ **to cram for an exam** matarse estudiando a última hora para un examen (*informal*)

cranberry [ˈkrænbɛri] NOUN (PL **cranberries**)
el arándano

crane [kreɪn] NOUN
la grúa (*machine*)

to **crash** [kræʃ] VERB
see also **crash** NOUN
chocar* ◇ *The two cars crashed.* Los dos carros chocaron.
◆ **to crash into something** chocar con algo
◆ **He crashed his car.** Tuvo un accidente con el carro.
◆ **The plane crashed.** El avión se estrelló.

crash [kræʃ] NOUN (PL **crashes**)
see also **crash** VERB
el accidente
el choque
◆ **a crash helmet** un casco protector
◆ **a crash course** un curso intensivo

to **crawl** [krɑːl] VERB
see also **crawl** NOUN
gatear (*baby*)

crawl [krɑːl] NOUN
see also **crawl** VERB
el crol
◆ **to do the crawl** nadar estilo crol

crazy [ˈkreɪzi] ADJECTIVE
loco ◇ *He's crazy about soccer.* Está loco por el fútbol.
◆ **She's crazy about horses.** Le encantan los caballos.

cream [kriːm] ADJECTIVE
see also **cream** NOUN
de color crema MASC, FEM, PL ◇ *a cream silk blouse* una blusa de seda de color crema

cream [kriːm] NOUN
see also **cream** ADJECTIVE
1 la crema de leche
◆ **strawberries and cream** fresas con crema
◆ **cream cheese** el queso cremoso
2 la crema (*for skin*)

crease [kriːs] NOUN
1 la arruga (*in clothes, paper*)
2 la raya (*in pants*)

creased [kriːst] ADJECTIVE
arrugado

to **create** [kriːˈeɪt] VERB
crear

creation [kriːˈeɪʃən] NOUN
la creación (PL las creaciones)

creative [kriːˈeɪtɪv] ADJECTIVE
creativo

creature [ˈkriːtʃər] NOUN
la criatura

credit [ˈkrɛdɪt] NOUN
el crédito ◇ *on credit* a crédito
◆ **He's a credit to his family.** Es un orgullo para su familia.

credit card [ˈkrɛdɪtˌkɑːrd] NOUN
la tarjeta de crédito

C

to **creep** [kriːp] VERB (**crept**, **crept**)
avanzar* sigilosamente
◆ **to creep up on somebody** acercarse* sigilosamente a alguien
◆ **to creep out of somewhere** salir* sigilosamente de alguna parte

crept [krɛpt] VERB *see* **creep**

cress [krɛs] NOUN
el berro

crew [kruː] NOUN
la tripulación (PL las tripulaciones) (*of plane, boat*)
◆ **a film crew** un equipo de rodaje

crew cut [ˈkruːˌkʌt] NOUN
el pelo cortado al rape

crib [krɪb] NOUN
la cuna

cricket [ˈkrɪkɪt] NOUN
1 el grillo (*insect*)
2 el críquet ◇ *I play cricket.* Juego críquet.

crime [kraɪm] NOUN
1 el delito (*offense*) ◇ *He committed a crime.* Cometió un delito. ◇ *the scene of the crime* el lugar del delito
2 el crimen (PL los crímenes) (*very serious*) ◇ *a crime against humanity* un crimen contra la humanidad
3 la delincuencia (*activity*) ◇ *Crime is rising.* La delincuencia va en aumento.

criminal [ˈkrɪmɪnl] NOUN
see also **criminal** ADJECTIVE
el/la delincuente

criminal [ˈkrɪmɪnl] ADJECTIVE
see also **criminal** NOUN
◆ **It's a criminal offense.** Constituye un delito.
◆ **to have a criminal record** tener* antecedentes penales

crippled [ˈkrɪpəld] ADJECTIVE
◆ **He was crippled in an accident.** Quedó lisiado en un accidente.
◆ **He was crippled with arthritis.** La artritis lo tenía paralizado.

crisis [ˈkraɪsɪs] NOUN (PL **crises**)
la crisis (PL las crisis)

crisp [krɪsp] ADJECTIVE
crujiente (*food*)

criterion [kraɪˈtɪriən] NOUN (PL **criteria**)
el criterio ◇ *the selection criteria* los criterios de selección
◆ **Only one candidate met all the criteria.** Sólo uno de los candidatos cumplía todos los requisitos.

critic [ˈkrɪtɪk] NOUN
el crítico
la crítica

critical [ˈkrɪtɪkəl] ADJECTIVE
crítico

criticism [ˈkrɪtɪsɪzəm] NOUN
la crítica

to **criticize** [ˈkrɪtɪsaɪz] VERB
criticar*

Croatia [krouˈeɪʃə] NOUN
Croacia FEM

to **crochet** [krouˈʃeɪ] VERB
tejer a crochet ◇ *She enjoys crocheting.* Le gusta tejer a crochet.

crocodile [ˈkrɑːkədaɪl] NOUN
el cocodrilo

crook [kruk] NOUN
el/la sinvergüenza

crop [krɑːp] NOUN
la cosecha ◇ *a good crop of apples* una buena cosecha de manzanas

cross [krɑːs] NOUN (PL **crosses**)
see also **cross** ADJECTIVE, VERB
la cruz (PL las cruces)

cross [krɑːs] ADJECTIVE
see also **cross** NOUN, VERB
enojado ◇ *He was cross about something.* Estaba enojado por algo.

to **cross** [krɑːs] VERB
see also **cross** NOUN, ADJECTIVE
cruzar* (*road, river*)

to **cross out** [krɑːsˈaut] VERB
tachar

cross-country [ˈkrɑːsˈkʌntri] ADJECTIVE
◆ **a cross-country race** un cross
◆ **cross-country skiing** el esquí de fondo

crossing [ˈkrɑːsɪŋ] NOUN
la travesía ◇ *a 10-hour crossing* una travesía de 10 horas

crossroads [ˈkrɑːsˌroudz] NOUN
el cruce

crosswalk [ˈkrɑːsˌwɔːk] NOUN
el paso de peatones (*for pedestrians*)

crossword [ˈkrɑːsˌwɜːrd] NOUN
el crucigrama
Although ***crucigrama*** *ends in* ***-a****, it is actually a masculine noun.*

to **crouch down** [krautʃˈdaun] VERB
agacharse

crow [krou] NOUN
el cuervo

crowd [kraud] NOUN
1 la muchedumbre
2 el público (*at sports game*)

crowded [ˈkraudɪd] ADJECTIVE
abarrotado de gente

crown [kraun] NOUN
la corona

crucifix [ˈkruːsɪfɪks] NOUN (PL **crucifixes**)
el crucifijo

crude [kruːd] ADJECTIVE
vulgar ◇ *crude language* lenguaje vulgar
◆ **crude oil** el petróleo crudo

cruel [ˈkruːəl] ADJECTIVE
cruel

cruise [kruːz] NOUN
el crucero

crumb [krʌm] NOUN
la miga

to **crush** [krʌʃ] VERB
1 aplastar (*box, fingers*)
2 machacar* ◇ *Crush two cloves of garlic.* Machacar dos dientes de ajo.

crutch [krʌtʃ] NOUN (PL **crutches**)
la muleta

cry [kraɪ] NOUN (PL **cries**)
see also **cry** VERB
el grito ◇ *He gave a cry of pain.* Dio un grito de dolor.
◆ **She had a good cry.** Se dio una buena llorada.

to **cry** [kraɪ] VERB (**cried, cried**)
see also **cry** NOUN
1 llorar ◇ *The baby's crying.* El bebé está llorando.
2 gritar ◇ *"You're wrong", he cried.* "No es cierto", gritó.

crystal ['krɪstl] NOUN
el cristal

cub [kʌb] NOUN
el cachorro (*animal*)
◆ **cub scout** el lobato

cube [kju:b] NOUN
1 el cubo (*geometric shape*)
2 el dado ◇ *Cut the meat into cubes.* Cortar la carne en dados.
3 el terrón (PL los terrones) (*of sugar*)

cubic ['kju:bɪk] ADJECTIVE
◆ **a cubic meter** un metro cúbico

cucumber ['kju:kʌmbər] NOUN
el pepino

to **cuddle** ['kʌdl] VERB
abrazar*
apapachar *Mexico*

cue [kju:] NOUN
el taco (*for pool*)

culottes ['ku:lɑ:ts] PL NOUN
la falda pantalón (PL las faldas pantalón)

culture ['kʌltʃər] NOUN
la cultura

cunning ['kʌnɪŋ] ADJECTIVE
1 astuto (*person*)
2 ingenioso ◇ *a cunning plan* un plan ingenioso

cup [kʌp] NOUN
1 la taza ◇ *a china cup* una taza de porcelana ◇ *a cup of coffee* una taza de café
2 la copa (*trophy*)

cupboard ['kʌbərd] NOUN
el armario

curb [k3:rb] NOUN
el bordillo
el borde de la banqueta *Mexico*

to **cure** [kjuər] VERB
see also **cure** NOUN
curar

cure [kjuər] NOUN
see also **cure** VERB
la cura ◇ *There is no simple cure for the common cold.* No hay una cura sencilla para el resfriado común.

curious ['kjuriəs] ADJECTIVE
curioso
◆ **to be curious about something** sentir* curiosidad por algo

curl [k3:rl] NOUN
el rizo
el chino *Mexico*

curly ['k3:rli] ADJECTIVE
rizado
chino *Mexico*

currant ['k3:rənt] NOUN
la pasa

currency ['k3:rənsi] NOUN (PL **currencies**)
la moneda ◇ *foreign currency* la moneda extranjera

current ['k3:rənt] NOUN
see also **current** ADJECTIVE
la corriente ◇ *The current is very strong.* La corriente es muy fuerte.

current ['k3:rənt] ADJECTIVE
see also **current** NOUN
1 actual ◇ *the current situation* la situación actual
2 presente ◇ *the current financial year* el presente año financiero

current affairs ['k3:rəntə'fɛərz] PL NOUN
los temas de actualidad

curriculum [kə'rɪkjuləm] NOUN (PL **curricula**)
el plan de estudios

curry ['k3:ri] NOUN (PL **curries**)
el curry (PL los curries)

curse [k3:rs] NOUN
la maldición (PL las maldiciones)

curtain ['k3:rtn] NOUN
la cortina

cushion ['kuʃən] NOUN
el cojín (PL los cojines)

custard ['kʌstərd] NOUN
las natillas

custody ['kʌstədi] NOUN
la custodia ◇ *The mother has custody of the children.* La madre tiene la custodia de los hijos.
◆ **to be remanded in custody** estar* detenido

custom ['kʌstəm] NOUN
la costumbre ◇ *It's an old custom.* Es una vieja costumbre.

customer ['kʌstəmər] NOUN
el cliente
la clienta

customs ['kʌstəmz] PL NOUN
la aduana SING
◆ **to go through customs** pasar por la aduana

customs officer ['kʌstəmz'ɑ:fɪsər] NOUN
el/la oficial de aduanas

cut [kʌt] NOUN
see also **cut** VERB
1 el corte ◇ *He has a cut on his forehead.* ☞

C

Tiene un corte en la frente.
[2] la reducción (PL las reducciones) (*in price, spending*)

to **cut** [kʌt] VERB (**cut, cut**)
see also **cut** NOUN
[1] cortar ◇ *I'll cut some bread.* Voy a cortar pan. ◇ *I cut my foot on a piece of glass.* Me corté el pie con un vidrio.
◆ **to cut oneself** cortarse
[2] reducir* (*price, spending*)

to **cut down (1)** [kʌt'daun] VERB
cortar (*tree*)

to **cut down (2)** [kʌt'daun] VERB
◆ **I'm cutting down on coffee and cigarettes.** Estoy tratando de tomar menos café y fumar menos.

to **cut off** [kʌt'ɑːf] VERB
cortar ◇ *The electricity has been cut off.* Cortaron la electricidad.
◆ **We've been cut off.** Se cortó la comunicación.

to **cut up** [kʌt'ʌp] VERB
picar* (*vegetables, meat*)

cutback ['kʌtbæk] NOUN
el recorte ◇ *There have been large cutbacks in public services.* Ha habido grandes recortes en los servicios públicos.

cute [kjuːt] ADJECTIVE
lindo (*baby, pet*) ◇ *Isn't he cute!* ¡Qué lindo es!

CV [siː'viː] NOUN
el currículum vitae (PL los currículums vitae)

to **cycle** ['saɪkəl] VERB
see also **cycle** NOUN
ir* en bicicleta ◇ *I cycle to school.* Voy al colegio en bicicleta.

cycle ['saɪkəl] NOUN
see also **cycle** VERB
la bicicleta

cycling ['saɪklɪŋ] NOUN
el ciclismo
◆ **The roads round here are ideal for cycling.** Las carreteras de por aquí son ideales para ir en bicicleta.

cyclist ['saɪklɪst] NOUN
el/la ciclista

cylinder ['sɪlɪndər] NOUN
el cilindro

Cyprus ['saɪprəs] NOUN
Chipre FEM

Czech [tʃɛk] NOUN
see also **Czech** ADJECTIVE
[1] el checo
la checa
(*person*)
◇ *the Czechs* los checos
[2] el checo (*language*)

Czech [tʃɛk] ADJECTIVE
see also **Czech** NOUN
checo
◆ **the Czech Republic** la República Checa

D

dad [dæd] NOUN
el papá ◇ *my dad* mi papá ◇ *I'll ask Dad.* Se lo preguntaré a papá.

daddy ['dædi] NOUN (PL **daddies**)
papi

daffodil ['dæfədɪl] NOUN
el narciso

daft [dæft] ADJECTIVE
estúpido

daily ['deɪli] ADJECTIVE, ADVERB
1 diario ◇ *daily life* la vida diaria ◇ *It's part of my daily routine.* Forma parte de mi rutina diaria.
◆ **a daily paper** un periódico
2 todos los días ◇ *The library is open daily.* La biblioteca abre todos los días.

dairy ['dɛri] NOUN (PL **dairies**)
la lechería

dairy products ['dɛri,prɑːdʌkts] PL NOUN
los productos lácteos

daisy ['deɪzi] NOUN (PL **daisies**)
la margarita

dam [dæm] NOUN
la presa

damage ['dæmɪdʒ] NOUN
see also **damage** VERB
los daños ◇ *The storm did a lot of damage.* La tormenta provocó muchos daños.

to **damage** ['dæmɪdʒ] VERB
see also **damage** NOUN
dañar

damn [dæm] NOUN
see also **damn** ADJECTIVE
◆ **I don't give a damn!** ¡Me importa un rábano! (*informal*)
◆ **Damn!** ¡Maldita sea! (*informal*)

damn [dæm] ADJECTIVE
see also **damn** NOUN
◆ **It's a damn nuisance!** ¡Es una verdadera lata! (*informal*)

damp [dæmp] ADJECTIVE
húmedo

dance [dæns] NOUN
see also **dance** VERB
el baile

to **dance** [dæns] VERB
see also **dance** NOUN
bailar

dancer ['dænsər] NOUN
1 el bailador
la bailadora
◆ **He is not a very good dancer.** No baila muy bien.
2 el bailarín (PL los bailarines)
la bailarina
(*professional*)

dancing ['dænsɪŋ] NOUN
◆ **to go dancing** ir* a bailar

dandruff ['dændrəf] NOUN
la caspa

Dane [deɪn] NOUN
el danés (PL los daneses)
la danesa
◆ **the Danes** los daneses

danger ['deɪndʒər] NOUN
el peligro
◆ **in danger** en peligro
◆ **We were in danger of missing the plane.** Corríamos el riesgo de perder el avión.

dangerous ['deɪndʒərəs] ADJECTIVE
peligroso

Danish ['deɪnɪʃ] ADJECTIVE
see also **Danish** NOUN
danés (FEM danesa)
◆ **Danish pastry** bollo de masa de hojaldre con pasas, manzana o crema

Danish ['deɪnɪʃ] NOUN
see also **Danish** ADJECTIVE
el danés (*language*)

to **dare** [dɛər] VERB
atreverse ◇ *I didn't dare to tell my parents.* No me atrevía a decírselo a mis padres.
◆ **I dare say it'll be okay.** Yo diría que va a salir bien.
◆ **Don't you dare!** ¡Ni se te ocurra!
◆ **I dare you!** ¡A que no te atreves!

daring ['dɛrɪŋ] ADJECTIVE
atrevido

dark [dɑːrk] ADJECTIVE
see also **dark** NOUN
oscuro ◇ *a dark green sweater* un suéter verde oscuro ◇ *It's dark in here.* Está oscuro aquí adentro. ◇ *She has dark hair.* Tiene el pelo oscuro.
◆ **He has dark skin.** Tiene la piel morena.
◆ **It's getting dark.** Está oscureciendo.
◆ **dark chocolate** chocolate amargo

dark [dɑːrk] NOUN
see also **dark** ADJECTIVE
la oscuridad ◇ *I'm afraid of the dark.* Me da miedo la oscuridad.
◆ **after dark** después del anochecer

darkness ['dɑːrknɪs] NOUN
la oscuridad ◇ *in the darkness* en la oscuridad
◆ **The room was in darkness.** La habitación estaba a oscuras.

darling ['dɑːrlɪŋ] NOUN
cariño ◇ *Thank you, darling.* Gracias, cariño.

dart [dɑːrt] NOUN
el dardo ◇ *to play darts* jugar* a los dardos

to **dash** [dæʃ] VERB
see also **dash** NOUN
ir* corriendo ◇ *Everyone dashed to the window.* Todos fueron corriendo a la ventana.
◆ **I need to dash!** ¡Tengo que salir corriendo!

dash [dæʃ] NOUN (PL **dashes**)
see also **dash** VERB
1 el chorrito ◇ *a dash of vinegar* un chorrito de vinagre
2 la raya (*punctuation mark*)

dashboard ['dæʃˌbɔːrd] NOUN
el tablero de mandos

data ['deɪtə] PL NOUN
los datos

database ['deɪtəˌbeɪs] NOUN
la base de datos

date [deɪt] NOUN
1 la fecha ◇ *my date of birth* mi fecha de nacimiento
◆ **What's the date today?** ¿A cuántos estamos hoy?
◆ **He has a date with his girlfriend.** Tiene una cita con su novia.
◆ **out of date (1)** (*document*) caducado ◇ *My passport is out of date.* Tengo el pasaporte vencido.
◆ **out of date (2)** (*technology, idea*) anticuado
2 el dátil (*fruit*)

daughter ['dɑːtər] NOUN
la hija

daughter-in-law ['dɑːtərɪnˌlɑː] NOUN (PL **daughters-in-law**)
la nuera

dawn [dɑːn] NOUN
el amanecer ◇ *at dawn* al amanecer

day [deɪ] NOUN
el día
*Although **día** ends in **-a**, it is actually a masculine noun.*
◇ *during the day* por el día ◇ *It's a lovely day.* Hace un día precioso. ◇ *every day* todos los días
◆ **the day after tomorrow** pasado mañana
◆ **the day before yesterday** anteayer
◆ **a day off** un día libre

daycare center ['deɪkɛr'sɛntər] NOUN
la guardería

dead [dɛd] ADJECTIVE
see also **dead** ADVERB
muerto ◇ *He was dead.* Estaba muerto.
◆ **He was shot dead.** Lo mataron de un tiro.

dead [dɛd] ADVERB
see also **dead** ADJECTIVE
◆ **You're dead right!** ¡Tienes toda la razón!
◆ **It was dead easy.** Fue facilísimo.
◆ **dead center** justo en el centro
◆ **dead on time** a la hora exacta

dead end [dɛd'ɛnd] NOUN
el callejón sin salida

deadline ['dɛdˌlaɪn] NOUN
◆ **October is the deadline for applications.** El plazo para presentar las solicitudes se acaba en octubre.
◆ **We're going to miss the deadline.** No vamos a poder cumplir con el plazo.

deaf [dɛf] ADJECTIVE
sordo

deafening ['dɛfnɪŋ] ADJECTIVE
ensordecedor (FEM ensordecedora)

deal [diːl] NOUN
see also **deal** VERB
el trato ◇ *It's a good deal.* Es un buen trato. ◇ *He made a deal with the kidnappers.* Hizo un trato con los secuestradores.
◆ **It's a deal!** ¡Trato hecho!
◆ **Big deal!** ¡Vaya cosa!
◆ **It's no big deal.** No es gran cosa.
◆ **a great deal** mucho ◇ *a great deal of money* mucho dinero

to **deal** [diːl] VERB (**dealt, dealt**)
see also **deal** NOUN
dar* cartas ◇ *It's your turn to deal.* Te toca dar cartas.

to **deal with** ['diːlˌwɪð] VERB
ocuparse de ◇ *He promised to deal with it immediately.* Prometió ocuparse de ello enseguida.

dealer ['diːlər] NOUN
◆ **a drug dealer** un traficante de drogas
◆ **an antique dealer** un anticuario

dealt [dɛlt] VERB *see* **deal**

dear [dɪər] ADJECTIVE
1 querido ◇ *Dear Paul* Querido Paul
◆ **Dear Mrs Smith** Estimada señora Smith
◆ **Dear Sir** Muy señor mío
◆ **Dear Madam** Estimada señora
◆ **Dear Sir/Madam** (*in a circular*) Estimados Sres.
◆ **Oh dear! I've spilled my coffee.** ¡Ay! Derramé el café.
2 caro (*expensive*) ◇ *These shoes are too dear.* Estos zapatos son demasiado caros.

death [dɛθ] NOUN
la muerte ◇ *after his death* después de su muerte
◆ **I was bored to death.** Estaba más aburrido que una ostra.

debate [dɪ'beɪt] NOUN
see also **debate** VERB
el debate

to **debate** [dɪ'beɪt] VERB
see also **debate** NOUN
discutir

debit card ['dɛbɪtˌkɑːrd] NOUN
la tarjeta de cobro automático

debt [dɛt] NOUN
la deuda ◇ *heavy debts* grandes deudas
◆ **to be in debt** estar* endeudado

decade ['dɛkeɪd] NOUN
la década

decaffeinated [dɪ'kæfɪneɪtɪd] ADJECTIVE
descafeinado

decay [dɪ'keɪ] NOUN
◆ **tooth decay** la caries

to **deceive** [dɪ'siːv] VERB

engañar

December [dɪ'sɛmbər] NOUN
diciembre MASC
- **in December** en diciembre
- **on December 22nd** el 22 de diciembre

decent ['di:sənt] ADJECTIVE
decente

deception [dɪ'sɛpʃən] NOUN
el engaño ◇ *Katie continued to keep up the deception.* Katie siguió manteniendo el engaño.
*Be careful not to translate **deception** by **decepción**.*

to **decide** [dɪ'saɪd] VERB
1 decidir ◇ *I decided to write to her.* Decidí escribirle. ◇ *I decided not to go.* Decidí no ir.
2 decidirse ◇ *Haven't you decided yet?* ¿Todavía no te has decidido?

to **decide on** [dɪ'saɪd,ɑ:n] VERB
decidirse por

decimal ['dɛsəməl] ADJECTIVE
decimal ◇ *the decimal system* el sistema decimal
*Although **sistema** ends in **-a**, it is actually a masculine noun.*
- **decimal point** la coma decimal

decision [dɪ'sɪʒən] NOUN
la decisión (PL las decisiones)
- **to make a decision** tomar una decisión

decisive [dɪ'saɪsɪv] ADJECTIVE
decidido (*person*)

deck [dɛk] NOUN
1 la cubierta (*of ship*)
- **on deck** en cubierta

2 el piso (*of bus*)
- **a deck of cards** una baraja

deckchair ['dɛk,tʃɛər] NOUN
la silla de playa

to **declare** [dɪ'klɛər] VERB
declarar

to **decline** [dɪ'klaɪn] VERB
disminuir* ◇ *The birth rate has declined by five per cent.* La tasa de natalidad ha disminuido un cinco por ciento.

to **decorate** ['dɛkəreɪt] VERB
1 decorar ◇ *I decorated the cake with candy.* Decoré el pastel con caramelos.
2 pintar (*paint*)
3 empapelar (*wallpaper*)

decrease [dɪ'kri:s] NOUN
see also **decrease** VERB
la disminución (PL las disminuciones)
◇ *There has been a decrease in the number of unemployed people.* Ha habido una disminución del número de desempleados.

to **decrease** [dɪ'kri:s] VERB
see also **decrease** NOUN
disminuir*

dedicated ['dɛdɪkeɪtɪd] ADJECTIVE
- **a very dedicated teacher** un maestro totalmente entregado a su trabajo
- **dedicated followers of classical music** devotos seguidores de la música clásica

to **deduct** [dɪ'dʌkt] VERB
descontar*

deep [di:p] ADJECTIVE
1 profundo
- **a hole four meters deep** un agujero de cuatro metros de profundidad
- **How deep is the lake?** ¿Qué profundidad tiene el lago?

2 espeso ◇ *a deep layer of snow* una capa espesa de nieve
3 grave ◇ *He has a deep voice.* Tiene la voz grave.
- **to take a deep breath** respirar hondo
- **to be deep in debt** estar* hasta el cuello de deudas

deeply ['di:pli] ADVERB
profundamente ◇ *deeply grateful* profundamente agradecido

deer [dɪər] NOUN (PL **deer**)
el ciervo

defeat [dɪ'fi:t] NOUN
see also **defeat** VERB
la derrota

to **defeat** [dɪ'fi:t] VERB
see also **defeat** NOUN
derrotar

defect ['di:fɛkt] NOUN
el defecto

to **defend** [dɪ'fɛnd] VERB
defender*

defender [dɪ'fɛndər] NOUN
1 el defensor
la defensora
(*of person, ideas*)
2 el/la defensa (*in sports*)

defense ['di:fɛns] NOUN
la defensa

to **define** [dɪ'faɪn] VERB
definir

definite ['dɛfənɪt] ADJECTIVE
1 concreto ◇ *I don't have any definite plans.* No tengo planes concretos.
2 definitivo ◇ *It's too soon to give a definite answer.* Es pronto aún para dar una respuesta definitiva.
3 seguro ◇ *Maybe we'll go to Spain, but it's not definite.* Quizá vayamos a España, pero no es seguro.
- **He was definite about it.** Fue rotundo acerca de esto.

4 claro ◇ *It's a definite improvement.* Es una clara mejoría.

definitely ['dɛfənɪtli] ADVERB
sin duda ◇ *He's definitely the best player.* Es sin duda el mejor jugador.
- **He's the best player. – Definitely!** Es el mejor jugador. – ¡Desde luego!
- **Are you going out with him? – Definitely not!** ¿Vas a salir con él? – ¡En absoluto!

D

definition [dɛfəˈnɪʃən] NOUN
la definición (PL las definiciones)

degree [dɪˈgriː] NOUN
1 el grado ◇ *a temperature of 30 degrees* una temperatura de 30 grados
2 la licenciatura ◇ *a degree in English* una licenciatura en filología inglesa
◆ **She has a degree in English.** Es licenciada en filología inglesa.

to **delay** [dɪˈleɪ] VERB
see also **delay** NOUN
retrasar ◇ *We decided to delay our departure.* Decidimos retrasar la salida.
◆ **Don't delay!** ¡No te demores!
◆ **to be delayed** retrasarse ◇ *Our flight was delayed.* Nuestro vuelo se retrasó.

delay [dɪˈleɪ] NOUN
see also **delay** VERB
el retraso ◇ *The tests have caused some delay.* Las pruebas han ocasionado algún retraso.
◆ **without delay** enseguida

to **delete** [dɪˈliːt] VERB
suprimir

deliberate [dɪˈlɪbərɪt] ADJECTIVE
intencionado

deliberately [dɪˈlɪbərɪtli] ADVERB
a propósito

delicate [ˈdɛlɪkɪt] ADJECTIVE
delicado

delicatessen [dɛlɪkəˈtɛsən] NOUN
la charcutería
la salchichonería *Mexico*

ℹ *En un* **delicatessen** *se venden productos de charcutería, mantequería, etc., de alta calidad.*

delicious [dɪˈlɪʃəs] ADJECTIVE
delicioso

delight [dɪˈlaɪt] NOUN
el placer

delighted [dɪˈlaɪtɪd] ADJECTIVE
encantado ◇ *He'll be delighted to see you.* Estará encantado de verte.

delightful [dɪˈlaɪtfəl] ADJECTIVE
encantador (FEM encantadora)

to **deliver** [dɪˈlɪvər] VERB
1 repartir ◇ *I deliver newspapers.* Reparto periódicos.
2 entregar* ◇ *The package was delivered in the morning.* Entregaron el paquete por la mañana.
◆ **Doctor Hamilton delivered the twins.** El Doctor Hamilton asistió en el parto de los gemelos.

delivery [dɪˈlɪvəri] NOUN (PL **deliveries**)
1 la entrega ◇ *Allow 28 days for delivery.* La entrega se realizará en un plazo de 28 días.
2 el parto (*of baby*)

to **demand** [dɪˈmænd] VERB
see also **demand** NOUN
exigir* ◇ *I demand an explanation.* Exijo una explicación.

demand [dɪˈmænd] NOUN
see also **demand** VERB
1 la petición (PL las peticiones) (*firm request*) ◇ *His demand for compensation was rejected.* Rechazaron su petición de indemnización.
2 la reivindicación (PL las reivindicaciones) (*of trade union*) ◇ *They met to discuss the union's demands.* Se reunieron para discutir las reivindicaciones del sindicato.
3 la demanda ◇ *Demand for coal is down.* Ha bajado la demanda de carbón.

demanding [dɪˈmændɪŋ] ADJECTIVE
◆ **It's a very demanding job.** Es un trabajo que exige mucho.
◆ **a demanding child** un niño exigente

demo [ˈdɛmou] NOUN (PL **demos**)
la manifestación (PL las manifestaciones)

democracy [dɪˈmɑːkrəsi] NOUN (PL **democracies**)
la democracia

Democrat [ˈdeməkræt] NOUN
el/la demócrata

democratic [dɛməˈkrætɪk] ADJECTIVE
democrático

Democratic Party [ˈdɛməkrætɪkˈpɑːrti] NOUN
el Partido Demócrata

to **demolish** [dɪˈmɑːlɪʃ] VERB
derribar

to **demonstrate** [ˈdɛmənstreɪt] VERB
1 demostrar* ◇ *You have to demonstrate that you are reliable.* Tienes que demostrar que se puede confiar en ti.
◆ **She demonstrated the technique.** Hizo una demostración de la técnica.
2 manifestarse* ◇ *They demonstrated outside the court.* Se manifestaron a las puertas del tribunal.

demonstration [dɛmənˈstreɪʃən] NOUN
1 la demostración (PL las demostraciones) (*of method, product*)
2 la manifestación (PL las manifestaciones) (*protest*)

demonstrator [ˈdɛmənstreɪtər] NOUN
el/la manifestante

denial [dɪˈnaɪəl] NOUN
◆ **an official denial** un desmentido oficial

denim [ˈdɛnɪm] NOUN
◆ **a denim jacket** una saco de tela de jeans

denims [ˈdɛnɪmz] PL NOUN
los vaqueros

Denmark [ˈdɛnmɑːrk] NOUN
Dinamarca FEM

dense [dɛns] ADJECTIVE
1 denso (*smoke, fog*)
2 espeso (*vegetation*)

◆ **He's so dense!** ¡Es tan corto de entendederas! (*informal*)

dent [dɛnt] NOUN
see also **dent** VERB
la abolladura

to **dent** [dɛnt] VERB
see also **dent** NOUN
abollar

dental ['dɛntl] ADJECTIVE
dental ◇ *dental treatment* el tratamiento dental
◆ **a dental appointment** una cita con el dentista
◆ **dental floss** la seda dental

dentist ['dɛntɪst] NOUN
el/la dentista ◇ *Catherine is a dentist.* Catherine es dentista. ◇ *at the dentist's* en el dentista
◆ **dentist's office** el consultorio dental

to **deny** [dɪ'naɪ] VERB (**denied, denied**)
negar* ◇ *She denied everything.* Lo negó todo.

deodorant [diː'oudərənt] NOUN
el desodorante

to **depart** [dɪ'pɑːrt] VERB
1 partir* (*person*) ◇ *He departed at three o'clock precisely.* Partió a las tres en punto.
2 salir* ◇ *Trains depart for the airport every half hour.* Los trenes salen para el aeropuerto cada media hora.

department [dɪ'pɑːrtmənt] NOUN
1 la sección (PL las secciones) ◇ *the toy department* la sección de juguetes
2 el departamento ◇ *the English department* el departamento de inglés

department store [dɪ'pɑːrtmənt,stɔːr] NOUN
los grandes almacenes
la tienda de departamentos *Mexico*

departure [dɪ'pɑːrtʃər] NOUN
la salida ◇ *The departure of this flight has been delayed.* Han atrasado la salida de este vuelo.
◆ **His sudden departure worried us.** Su marcha repentina nos dejó preocupados.

departure lounge [dɪ'pɑːrtʃər,laundʒ] NOUN
la sala de embarque

to **depend** [dɪ'pɛnd] VERB
◆ **to depend on** depender de ◇ *The price depends on the quality.* El precio depende de la calidad.
◆ **You can depend on him.** Puedes contar con él.
◆ **depending on** según
***según** has to be followed by a verb in the subjunctive.*
◇ *depending on the weather* según el tiempo que haga
◆ **It depends.** Depende.

to **deport** [dɪ'pɔːrt] VERB
deportar

deposit [dɪ'pɑːzɪt] NOUN
1 el depósito (*on hired goods*) ◇ *You get the deposit back when you return the bike.* Al devolver la bici te devuelven el depósito.
2 la señal (*advance payment*) ◇ *You have to pay a deposit when you book.* Se paga una señal al hacer una reservación.
3 la entrega inicial
el enganche *Mexico*
(*in house buying*)

depressed [dɪ'prɛst] ADJECTIVE
deprimido ◇ *I'm feeling depressed.* Estoy deprimido.

depressing [dɪ'prɛsɪŋ] ADJECTIVE
deprimente

depth [dɛpθ] NOUN
la profundidad ◇ *14 feet in depth* 14 pies de profundidad
◆ **to deal with a subject in depth** tratar un tema a fondo

to **descend** [dɪ'sɛnd] VERB
descender* ◇ *They descended the mountain slowly.* Descendieron lentamente de la montaña.

to **describe** [dɪ'skraɪb] VERB
describir*

description [dɪ'skrɪpʃən] NOUN
la descripción (PL las descripciones)

desert ['dɛzərt] NOUN
el desierto

desert island [,dɛzərt'aɪlənd] NOUN
la isla desierta

to **deserve** [dɪ'zɜːrv] VERB
merecer*

design [dɪ'zaɪn] NOUN
see also **design** VERB
1 el diseño ◇ *The design of the plane makes it safer.* El diseño del avión lo hace más seguro. ◇ *a design fault* una falla en el diseño
2 el motivo ◇ *a geometric design* un motivo geométrico
◆ **fashion design** diseño de modas

to **design** [dɪ'zaɪn] VERB
see also **design** NOUN
1 diseñar ◇ *She designed the dress herself.* Ella misma diseñó el vestido.
2 elaborar ◇ *We will design an exercise plan specially for you.* Elaboraremos un programa de ejercicios especial para ti.

designer [dɪ'zaɪnər] NOUN
el/la modista (*of clothes*)
◆ **designer clothes** la ropa de diseño

desire [dɪ'zaɪər] NOUN
see also **desire** VERB
el deseo

to **desire** [dɪ'zaɪər] VERB
see also **desire** NOUN
desear

desk [dɛsk] NOUN
1 el escritorio (*in office*)
2 el pupitre (*for pupil*)
3 el mostrador (*in hotel, at airport*)

D

desk clerk ['dɛsk,klɜːrk] NOUN
el/la recepcionista

despair [dɪ'spɛər] NOUN
la desesperación ◇ *a feeling of despair* un sentimiento de desesperación
◆ **to be in despair** estar* desesperado

desperate ['dɛspərɪt] ADJECTIVE
desesperado ◇ *a desperate situation* una situación desesperada
◆ **I was starting to get desperate.** Estaba empezando a desesperarme.

desperately ['dɛspərɪtli] ADVERB
1 tremendamente ◇ *We're desperately worried.* Estamos tremendamente preocupados.
2 desesperadamente ◇ *He was desperately trying to persuade her.* Intentaba desesperadamente convencerla.

to **despise** [dɪ'spaɪz] VERB
despreciar

despite [dɪ'spaɪt] PREPOSITION
a pesar de

dessert [dɪ'zɜːrt] NOUN
el postre ◇ *for dessert* de postre ◇ *What's for dessert?* ¿Qué hay de postre?

destination [dɛstɪ'neɪʃən] NOUN
el destino

to **destroy** [dɪ'strɔɪ] VERB
destruir*

destruction [dɪ'strʌkʃən] NOUN
la destrucción

detail ['diːteɪl] NOUN
el detalle ◇ *I can't remember the details.* No recuerdo los detalles.
◆ **in detail** detalladamente

detailed ['diːteɪld] ADJECTIVE
detallado

detective [dɪ'tɛktɪv] NOUN
el/la detective ◇ *He's a detective.* Es detective. ◇ *a private detective* un detective privado
◆ **a detective story** una novela policíaca

detention [dɪ'tɛnʃən] NOUN
◆ **to get a detention** quedarse castigado después de clase

detergent [dɪ'tɜːrdʒənt] NOUN
el detergente

determined [dɪ'tɜːrmɪnd] ADJECTIVE
decidido ◇ *She's determined to succeed.* Está decidida a triunfar.

detour ['diːtur] NOUN
el desvío (*for traffic*)

devaluation [dɪvælju'eɪʃən] NOUN
la devaluación (PL las devaluaciones)

devastated ['dɛvəsteɪtɪd] ADJECTIVE
deshecho ◇ *I was devastated when they told me.* Cuando me lo dijeron me quedé deshecho.

devastating ['dɛvəsteɪtɪŋ] ADJECTIVE
devastador (FEM devastadora) (*flood, storm*) ◇ *Unemployment has a devastating effect on people.* El desempleo tiene efectos devastadores en la gente.
◆ **She received some devastating news.** Recibió unas noticias desoladoras.

to **develop** [dɪ'vɛləp] VERB
1 desarrollar (*idea, quality*) ◇ *I developed his original idea.* Yo desarrollé su idea original.
2 desarrollarse ◇ *Girls develop faster than boys.* Las chicas se desarrollan más rápido que los chicos.
3 revelar ◇ *to get a roll of film developed* revelar un rollo de fotos
◆ **to develop into** convertirse* en ◇ *The argument developed into a fight.* La discusión se convirtió en una pelea.

developing [dɪ'vɛləpɪŋ] ADJECTIVE
◆ **a developing country** un país en vías de desarrollo

development [dɪ'vɛləpmənt] NOUN
el desarrollo ◇ *Economic development in Pakistan.* El desarrollo económico de Pakistán.
◆ **the latest developments** los últimos acontecimientos

device [dɪ'vaɪs] NOUN
el dispositivo

devil ['dɛvəl] NOUN
el diablo

to **devise** [dɪ'vaɪz] VERB
idear

devoted [dɪ'voutɪd] ADJECTIVE
leal (*friend*)
◆ **a devoted wife** una abnegada esposa
◆ **He's completely devoted to her.** Está totalmente entregado a ella.

diabetes [daɪə'biːtɪs] NOUN
la diabetes

diabetic [daɪə'bɛtɪk] ADJECTIVE
diabético ◇ *I'm diabetic.* Soy diabético.
◆ **diabetic chocolate** el chocolate para diabéticos

diagonal [daɪ'ægənəl] ADJECTIVE
diagonal

diagram ['daɪəgræm] NOUN
el diagrama

*Although **diagrama** ends in **-a**, it is actually a masculine noun.*

to **dial** ['daɪəl] VERB
marcar*

dialogue ['daɪəlɑːg] NOUN
el diálogo

dial tone ['daɪəl,toun] NOUN
el tono de marcar

diamond ['daɪmənd] NOUN
el diamante ◇ *a diamond ring* un anillo de diamantes
◆ **diamonds** (*at cards*) los diamantes ◇ *the ace of diamonds* el as de diamantes

diaper ['daɪpər] NOUN
el pañal

diarrhea [daɪə'riːə] NOUN
la diarrea ◇ *to have diarrhea* tener* diarrea

diary ['daɪəri] NOUN (PL **diaries**)
1 la agenda ◇ *I have her phone number in my diary.* Tengo su número de teléfono en la agenda.
2 el diario ◇ *I keep a diary.* Estoy escribiendo un diario.

dice [daɪs] NOUN (PL **dice**)
el dado

dictation [dɪk'teɪʃən] NOUN
el dictado

dictator ['dɪkteɪtər] NOUN
el dictador
la dictadora

dictionary ['dɪkʃənɛri] NOUN (PL **dictionaries**)
el diccionario

did [dɪd] VERB *see* **do**

didn't ['dɪdnt] = **did not**

to **die** [daɪ] VERB
morir* ◇ *He died last year.* Murió el año pasado. ◇ *She's dying.* Se está muriendo.
◆ **to be dying to do something** morirse* de ganas de hacer algo

to **die down** [daɪ'daun] VERB
amainar ◇ *The wind is dying down.* El viento está amainando.

diesel ['diːzəl] NOUN
1 el diesel (*fuel*)
2 el motor diesel (*engine*)

diet ['daɪət] NOUN
see also **diet** VERB
1 la dieta ◇ *a healthy diet* una dieta sana
2 el régimen (PL los regímenes) ◇ *I'm on a diet.* Estoy a régimen.
◆ **a diet Coke®** una Coca-Cola light®

to **diet** ['daɪət] VERB
see also **diet** NOUN
hacer* régimen ◇ *I've been dieting for two months.* Llevo dos meses haciendo régimen.

difference ['dɪfrəns] NOUN
la diferencia ◇ *There's not much difference in age between us.* No hay mucha diferencia de edad entre nosotros.
◆ **Good weather makes all the difference.** Con buen tiempo la cosa cambia mucho.
◆ **It makes no difference.** Da lo mismo.

different ['dɪfrənt] ADJECTIVE
distinto

difficult ['dɪfɪkʌlt] ADJECTIVE
difícil ◇ *It was difficult to choose.* Era difícil escoger. ◇ *It was a difficult decision to make.* Era una decisión difícil de tomar.

difficulty ['dɪfɪkʌlti] NOUN (PL **difficulties**)
la dificultad ◇ *What's the difficulty?* ¿Cuál es la dificultad?
◆ **to have difficulty doing something** tener* dificultades para hacer algo

to **dig** [dɪg] VERB (**dug, dug**)
1 cavar ◇ *They're digging a hole in the road.* Están cavando un hoyo en la calle. ◇ *Dad is out digging the garden.* Papá está fuera cavando en el jardín.
2 escarbar ◇ *The dog dug a hole in the sand.* El perro escarbó un hoyo en la arena.

to **dig up** [dɪg'ʌp] VERB
1 arrancar* ◇ *The cat dug up my plants.* El gato me arrancó las plantas.
2 desenterrar* ◇ *The police have dug up a body.* La policía desenterró un cadáver.

digestion [dɪ'dʒɛstʃən] NOUN
la digestión

digital camera NOUN
la cámara digital

digital television ['dɪdʒɪtl'tɛlɪvɪʒən] NOUN
la televisión digital (PL las televisiones digitales)

digital watch ['dɪdʒɪtl'wɑːtʃ] NOUN (PL **digital watches**)
el reloj digital (PL los relojes digitales)

dim [dɪm] ADJECTIVE
1 tenue (*light*)
2 lerdo (*person*)

dimension [dɪ'mɛnʃən] NOUN
la dimensión (PL las dimensiones)

to **diminish** [dɪ'mɪnɪʃ] VERB
disminuir*

din [dɪn] NOUN
1 el estruendo (*of traffic, machinery*)
2 el alboroto (*of crowd, voices*)

diner ['daɪnər] NOUN
el restaurante barato

dinghy ['dɪŋi] NOUN (PL **dinghies**)
◆ **a rubber dinghy** una lancha neumática
◆ **a sailing dinghy** una embarcación de vela ligera

dining car ['daɪnɪŋˌkɑːr] NOUN
el vagón restaurante (PL los vagones restaurante)

dining room ['daɪnɪŋˌruːm] NOUN
el comedor

dinner ['dɪnər] NOUN
1 el almuerzo (*at midday*)
2 la cena (*in the evening*)
◆ **The children have dinner at school.** Los niños almuerzan en la escuela.

dinner party ['dɪnərˌpɑːrti] NOUN (PL **dinner parties**)
la cena

dinnertime ['dɪnərˌtaɪm] NOUN
1 la hora del almuerzo (*at midday*)
2 la hora de la cena (*in the evening*)

dinosaur ['daɪnəsɔːr] NOUN
el dinosaurio

dip [dɪp] NOUN
see also **dip** VERB
la salsa ◇ *a spicy dip* una salsa picante
◆ **to go for a dip** ir* a darse un chapuzón

to **dip** [dɪp] VERB

D ☞

see also **dip** NOUN
mojar ◇ *He dipped the bread in his coffee.* Mojó el pan en el café.

diploma [dɪ'ploumə] NOUN
el diploma

Although ***diploma*** *ends in* ***-a****, it is actually a masculine noun.*

diplomat ['dɪpləmæt] NOUN
el diplomático
la diplomática

diplomatic [dɪplə'mætɪk] ADJECTIVE
diplomático

direct [dɪ'rɛkt] ADJECTIVE, ADVERB
see also **direct** VERB
directo ◇ *the most direct route* el camino más directo
◆ **You can fly to Caracas direct from Miami.** Hay vuelos directos a Caracas desde Miami.

to **direct** [dɪ'rɛkt] VERB
see also **direct** ADJECTIVE, ADVERB
dirigir*

direction [dɪ'rɛkʃən] NOUN
la dirección (PL las direcciones) ◇ *We're going in the wrong direction.* Vamos en la dirección equivocada.
◆ **to ask somebody for directions** preguntar el camino a alguien

director [dɪ'rɛktər] NOUN
1 el director
la directora
2 el director de orquesta
la directora de orquesta
(*of orchestra*)

directory [dɪ'rɛktəri] NOUN (PL **directories**)
1 la guía telefónica
el directorio Mexico
(*telephone*)
◆ **directory assistance** información telefónica
2 el directorio (*in computing*)

dirt [dɜːrt] NOUN
la suciedad

dirty ['dɜːrti] ADJECTIVE
sucio ◇ *It's dirty.* Está sucio.
◆ **to get dirty** ensuciarse
◆ **to get something dirty** ensuciarse algo ◇ *He got his hands dirty.* Se ensució las manos.
◆ **a dirty joke** un chiste verde, Mexico: un chiste colorado

disabled [dɪs'eɪbəld] ADJECTIVE, NOUN
minusválido
◆ **the disabled** los minusválidos

disadvantage [dɪsəd'væntɪdʒ] NOUN
la desventaja
◆ **to be at a disadvantage** estar* en desventaja

disadvantaged [dɪsəd'væntɪdʒd] ADJECTIVE
desfavorecido (*person*)

to **disagree** [dɪsə'griː] VERB
◆ **We always disagree.** Nunca estamos de acuerdo.
◆ **He disagrees with me.** No está de acuerdo conmigo.

disagreement [dɪsə'griːmənt] NOUN
el desacuerdo

to **disappear** [dɪsə'pɪər] VERB
desaparecer*

disappearance [dɪsə'pɪrəns] NOUN
la desaparición (PL las desapariciones)

disappointed [dɪsə'pɔɪntɪd] ADJECTIVE
decepcionado ◇ *I'm disappointed.* Estoy decepcionado.

disappointing [dɪsə'pɔɪntɪŋ] ADJECTIVE
decepcionante ◇ *It's disappointing.* Es decepcionante.

disappointment [dɪsə'pɔɪntmənt] NOUN
la decepción (PL las decepciones)

disaster [dɪ'zæstər] NOUN
el desastre

disastrous [dɪ'zæstrəs] ADJECTIVE
desastroso

disc [dɪsk] NOUN
el disco

discipline ['dɪsɪplɪn] NOUN
la disciplina

disco ['dɪskou] NOUN (PL **discos**)
la discoteca (*place*)
◆ **disco music** la música disco

to **disconnect** [dɪskə'nɛkt] VERB
desconectar (*appliance*)
◆ **to disconnect the water supply** cortar el agua

discount ['dɪskaunt] NOUN
el descuento ◇ *a 20% discount* un descuento del 20 por ciento

to **discourage** [dɪ'skɜːrɪdʒ] VERB
desanimar
◆ **to get discouraged** desanimarse

to **discover** [dɪ'skʌvər] VERB
descubrir*

discrimination [dɪskrɪmɪ'neɪʃən] NOUN
la discriminación ◇ *racial discrimination* la discriminación racial

to **discuss** [dɪ'skʌs] VERB
1 discutir ◇ *I'll discuss it with my parents.* Lo discutiré con mis padres.
2 hablar de (*topic*) ◇ *We discussed the topic at length.* Hablamos del tema largo y tendido.

discussion [dɪ'skʌʃən] NOUN
la discusión (PL las discusiones)

disease [dɪ'ziːz] NOUN
la enfermedad

disgraceful [dɪs'greɪsfəl] ADJECTIVE
vergonzoso

disguise [dɪs'gaɪz] NOUN
el disfraz (PL los disfraces)
◆ **in disguise** disfrazado

disguised [dɪs'gaɪzd] ADJECTIVE
◆ **He was disguised as a policeman.** Iba disfrazado de policía.

disgusted [dɪs'gʌstɪd] ADJECTIVE

indignado ◇ *I was completely disgusted.* Estaba totalmente indignado.
*Be careful not to translate **disgusted** by **disgustado**.*

disgusting [dɪs'gʌstɪŋ] ADJECTIVE
[1] asqueroso (*food, smell*) ◇ *It looks disgusting.* Tiene un aspecto asqueroso.
[2] indignante (*disgraceful*) ◇ *That's disgusting!* ¡Es indignante!

dish [dɪʃ] NOUN (PL **dishes**)
el plato ◇ *a china dish* un plato de porcelana ◇ *a vegetarian dish* un plato vegetariano
◆ **to do the dishes** lavar los platos
◆ **a satellite dish** una antena parabólica

dishonest [dɪs'ɑːnɪst] ADJECTIVE
poco honrado

dish soap ['dɪʃˌsoup] NOUN
el lavavajillas (PL los lavavajillas)

dish towel ['dɪʃˌtauəl] NOUN
el paño de cocina

dishwasher ['dɪʃˌwɑːʃər] NOUN
el lavaplatos (PL los lavaplatos)

dishwashing detergent ['dɪʃˌwɑːʃɪŋdɪ'tɜːrdʒənt] NOUN
el lavavajillas (PL los lavavajillas)

disinfectant [dɪsɪn'fɛktənt] NOUN
el desinfectante

disk [dɪsk] NOUN
el disco
◆ **the hard disk drive** el disco duro

diskette [dɪs'kɛt] NOUN
el disquete

disk jockey ['dɪskˌdʒɑːki] NOUN
el/la disc jockey (PL los/las disc jockeys) ◇ *he's a disk jockey* es discjokey

to **dislike** [dɪs'laɪk] VERB
see also **dislike** NOUN
◆ **I dislike it.** No me gusta.

dislike [dɪs'laɪk] NOUN
see also **dislike** VERB
◆ **to take a dislike to somebody** tomarle antipatía a alguien
◆ **my likes and dislikes** lo que me gusta y lo que no

to **dismiss** [dɪs'mɪs] VERB
despedir* (*employee*)

dismissal [dɪs'mɪsəl] NOUN
el despido

disobedient [dɪsə'biːdiənt] ADJECTIVE
desobediente

display [dɪ'spleɪ] NOUN
see also **display** VERB
◆ **The assistant took the watch out of the display.** El dependiente sacó el reloj de la vitrina.
◆ **There was a lovely display of fruit in the window.** Había un estupendo surtido de fruta en el vidriera.
◆ **to be on display** estar* expuesto
◆ **a fireworks display** fuegos artificiales

to **display** [dɪ'spleɪ] VERB
see also **display** NOUN
[1] mostrar* ◇ *She proudly displayed her medal.* Mostró con orgullo su medalla.
[2] exponer* (*in store window*)

disposable [dɪ'spouzəbəl] ADJECTIVE
desechable ◇ *a disposable cup* un vaso desechable

to **disqualify** [dɪs'kwɑːlɪfaɪ] VERB (**disqualified, disqualified**)
descalificar*
◆ **to be disqualified** ser* descalificado ◇ *They were disqualified from the competition.* Fueron descalificados del campeonato.
◆ **He was disqualified from driving.** Le retiraron la licencia de manejar.

to **disrupt** [dɪs'rʌpt] VERB
interrumpir ◇ *The meeting was disrupted by protesters.* La reunión fue interrumpida por unos manifestantes.
◆ **Train services are being disrupted by the strike.** El servicio ferroviario se está viendo alterado por la huelga.

dissatisfied [dɪs'sætɪsfaɪd] ADJECTIVE
insatisfecho ◇ *We were dissatisfied with the service.* Estábamos insatisfechos con el servicio.

to **dissolve** [dɪ'zɑːlv] VERB
disolver*

distance ['dɪstəns] NOUN
la distancia ◇ *a distance of ten miles* una distancia de diez millas
◆ **It's within walking distance.** Se puede ir andando.
◆ **in the distance** a lo lejos

distant ['dɪstənt] ADJECTIVE
lejano ◇ *in the distant future* en un futuro lejano

distinction [dɪ'stɪŋkʃən] NOUN
[1] la distinción (PL las distinciones) ◇ *to make a distinction between two things* hacer* una distinción entre dos cosas
[2] la matrícula de honor ◇ *I graduated with distinction in Spanish.* Me gradué con matrícula de honor en lengua española.

distinctive [dɪ'stɪŋktɪv] ADJECTIVE
característico

to **distract** [dɪ'strækt] VERB
distraer*

to **distribute** [dɪ'strɪbjuːt] VERB
distribuir*

district ['dɪstrɪkt] NOUN
[1] el barrio (*of town*)
[2] la región (PL las regiones) (*of country*)

to **disturb** [dɪs'tɜːrb] VERB
molestar ◇ *I'm sorry to disturb you.* Siento molestarte.

ditch [dɪtʃ] NOUN (PL **ditches**)
see also **ditch** VERB
la zanja

to **ditch** [dɪtʃ] VERB
see also **ditch** NOUN

D

☞

plantar ◇ *She's just ditched her boyfriend.* Acaba de plantar al novio.

dive [daɪv] NOUN
see also **dive** VERB
1 el salto de cabeza (*into water*)
2 el buceo (*under water*)

to **dive** [daɪv] VERB (**dived** *or* **dove**)
see also **dive** NOUN
1 tirarse de cabeza (*into water*)
2 bucear (*under water*)

diver ['daɪvər] NOUN
el/la buzo

to **divide** [dɪ'vaɪd] VERB
1 dividir ◇ *Divide the pastry in half.* Divide la masa en dos.
◆ **12 divided by 3 is 4.** 12 dividido entre 3 es 4.
2 dividirse ◇ *We divided into two groups.* Nos dividimos en dos grupos.

diving ['daɪvɪŋ] NOUN
1 el buceo ◇ *diving equipment* equipo de buceo
2 el salto de trampolín ◇ *a diving competition* una competencia de saltos de trampolín

diving board ['daɪvɪŋˌbɔːrd] NOUN
el trampolín (PL los trampolines)

division [dɪ'vɪʒən] NOUN
la división (PL las divisiones)

divorce [dɪ'vɔːrs] NOUN
el divorcio

divorced [dɪ'vɔːrst] ADJECTIVE
divorciado ◇ *My parents are divorced.* Mis padres están divorciados.
◆ **to get divorced** divorciarse

dizzy ['dɪzi] ADJECTIVE
◆ **I feel dizzy.** Estoy mareado.

DJ ['diːˌdʒeɪ] NOUN
el/la disc jockey (PL los/las disc jockeys)
◇ *he's a DJ* es disc jockey

to **do** [duː] VERB (**does, did, done**)
1 hacer* ◇ *What are you doing this evening?* ¿Qué vas a hacer esta noche?
◇ *She did it by herself.* Lo hizo ella sola. ◇ *I'll do my best.* Haré todo lo que pueda.
◆ **I want to do physics in college.** Quiero estudiar física en la universidad.
◆ **What does your father do?** ¿A qué se dedica tu padre?
2 ir* ◇ *She's doing well at school.* Va bien en el colegio.
◆ **How are you doing?** ¿Qué tal estás?
◆ **How do you do?** Mucho gusto.
3 servir* ◇ *It's not very good, but it'll do.* No es muy bueno, pero servirá.
◆ **Will $10 do?** ¿Estará bien con 10 dólares?
◆ **That'll do, thanks.** Así está bien, gracias.
__Do__ is not translated when used to form questions.
◇ *Do you speak English?* ¿Hablas inglés?
◇ *Do you like reading?* ¿Te gusta leer?
◇ *Where does he live?* ¿Dónde vive?
◇ *Where did you go on vacation?* ¿Dónde te fuiste de vacaciones?
Use __no__ in negative sentences for __don't__.
◇ *I don't understand.* No entiendo. ◇ *You didn't tell me anything.* No me dijiste nada.
◇ *He didn't come.* No vino. ◇ *Why didn't you come?* ¿Por qué no viniste?
__Do__ is not translated when it is used in place of another verb.
◇ *I hate math. – So do I.* Odio las matemáticas. – Yo también. ◇ *I didn't like the movie. – Neither did I.* No me gustó la película. – A mí tampoco. ◇ *Do you speak English? – Yes, I do.* ¿Hablas inglés? – Sí.
◇ *Do you like horses? – No, I don't.* ¿Te gustan los caballos? – No.
Use __¿no?__ or __¿verdad?__ to check information.
◇ *You go swimming on Fridays, don't you?* Los viernes vas a nadar, ¿no? ◇ *It doesn't matter, does it?* No importa, ¿verdad?

to **do up** [duː'ʌp] VERB
1 atarse (*shoes*)
2 abrocharse (*shirt, cardigan, coat*) ◇ *Do your coat up.* Abróchate el abrigo. ◇ *Do up the buttons on your shirt!* ¡Abróchate los botones de la camisa!

to **do with** ['duːwɪð] VERB
◆ **I could do with a vacation.** Me vendrían bien unas vacaciones.

to **do without** ['duːwɪð'aut] VERB
pasar sin ◇ *I can't do without my computer.* Yo no puedo pasar sin la computadora.

dock [dɑːk] NOUN
el muelle

doctor ['dɑːktər] NOUN
el médico
la médica
◇ *He's a doctor.* Es médico. ◇ *at the doctor's* en el médico
◆ **doctor's office** el consultorio médico (*room*)

document ['dɑːkjəmənt] NOUN
el documento

documentary [dɑːkjə'mɛntəri] NOUN (PL **documentaries**)
el documental

to **dodge** [dɑːdʒ] VERB
esquivar (*attacker, blow*)

does [dʌz] VERB *see* **do**

doesn't ['dʌzənt] = **does not**

dog [dɑːg] NOUN
el perro ◇ *Do you have a dog?* ¿Tienes perro?

doghouse ['dɑːgˌhaus] NOUN
la caseta del perro (*in garden*)

do-it-yourself ['duːətʃər'sɛlf] NOUN
el bricolaje

doll [dɑːl] NOUN
la muñeca

dollar ['dɑːlər] NOUN

el dólar ◇ *20 dollars* 20 dólares

dolphin ['dɑːlfɪn] NOUN
el delfín (PL los delfines)

domestic [də'mɛstɪk] ADJECTIVE
doméstico ◇ *the domestic chores* las tareas domésticas
◆ **a domestic flight** un vuelo nacional

dominoes ['dɑːmɪnouz] PL NOUN
◆ **to have a game of dominoes** jugar* una partida de dominó

to **donate** ['douneɪt] VERB
donar

done [dʌn] VERB *see* **do**

done [dʌn] ADJECTIVE
listo ◇ *Is the pasta done?* ¿Está lista la pasta?
◆ **How do you like your steak? – Well done.** ¿Cómo quieres el filete? – Bien cocido.

donkey ['dɑːŋki] NOUN
el burro

donor ['dounər] NOUN
el/la donante

don't [dount] = **do not**

door [dɔːr] NOUN
la puerta

doorbell ['dɔːrˌbɛl] NOUN
el timbre

doorman ['dɔːrˌmæn] NOUN (PL **doormen**)
el portero
la portera

doorstep ['dɔːrˌstɛp] NOUN
el peldaño de la puerta
◆ **on my doorstep** en mi puerta

dormitory ['dɔːrmɪtɔːri] NOUN (PL **dormitories**)
1 el dormitorio (*bedroom*)
2 la residencia (*at college*)

dose [dous] NOUN
la dosis (PL las dosis)

dot [dɑːt] NOUN
el punto
◆ **on the dot** en punto ◇ *He arrived at nine on the dot.* Llegó a las nueve en punto.

to **double** ['dʌbəl] VERB
see also **double** ADJECTIVE, ADVERB
1 doblar ◇ *They doubled their prices.* Doblaron los precios.
2 duplicarse ◇ *The number of attacks has doubled.* El número de agresiones se ha duplicado.

double ['dʌbəl] ADJECTIVE, ADVERB
see also **double** VERB
doble ◇ *a double helping* una porción doble ◇ *to cost double* costar* el doble
◆ **double bed** la cama de matrimonio
◆ **a double room** una habitación doble

double bass ['dʌbəl'beɪs] NOUN (PL **double basses**)
el contrabajo

to **double-click** ['dʌblˌklɪk] VERB
hacer* doble clic

doubles ['dʌbəlz] PL NOUN
dobles MASC PL (*in tennis*) ◇ *to play mixed doubles* jugar* un partido de dobles mixtos

doubt [daut] NOUN
see also **doubt** VERB
la duda ◇ *I have my doubts.* Tengo mis dudas.
◆ **no doubt** sin duda ◇ *as you no doubt know* como sin duda sabrá

to **doubt** [daut] VERB
see also **doubt** NOUN
dudar ◇ *I doubt it.* Lo dudo.
*Use the subjunctive after **dudar que**.*
◇ *I doubt that he'll agree.* Dudo que vaya a estar de acuerdo.

doubtful ['dautfəl] ADJECTIVE
dudoso ◇ *It's doubtful.* Es dudoso.
◆ **to be doubtful about doing something** no estar* seguro de hacer algo
◆ **I'm doubtful about going by myself.** Tengo mis dudas acerca de ir solo.
◆ **You sound doubtful.** No pareces muy convencido.

dough [dou] NOUN
la masa

doughnut ['dounʌt] NOUN
el buñuelo
la dona *Mexico*
◇ *a jelly doughnut* un buñuelo de mermelada, *Mexico:* una dona de mermelada

dove [douv] VERB *see* **dive**

down [daun] ADJECTIVE, ADVERB, PREPOSITION
1 abajo ◇ *His office is down on the first floor.* Su despacho está abajo en la planta baja. ◇ *It's down there.* Está allí abajo.
2 al suelo ◇ *He threw down his racket.* Tiró la raqueta al suelo.
◆ **They live just down the road.** Viven más adelante en esta calle.
◆ **to feel down** estar* desanimado
◆ **my brother is down with the flu** Mi hermano tiene gripe. *Mexico:* Mi hermano tiene gripa.
◆ **The computer is down.** La computadora no funciona.

to **download** ['daunloud] VERB
bajar ◇ *to download a file* bajar un fichero

downpour ['daunˌpɔːr] NOUN
el chaparrón (PL los chaparrones)

downstairs ['daun'stɛərz] ADVERB, ADJECTIVE
1 abajo ◇ *The bathroom is downstairs.* El baño está abajo.
◆ **to go downstairs** bajar
2 de abajo ◇ *the downstairs bathroom* el baño de abajo ◇ *the neighbors downstairs* los vecinos de abajo

downtown ['daun'taun] ADVERB
al centro
◆ **I live downtown.** Vivo en el centro.

to **doze** [douz] VERB
dormitar

to **doze off** [douz'ɑːf] VERB

☞

quedarse dormido

dozen ['dʌzən] NOUN
la docena ◇ *a dozen eggs* una docena de huevos ◇ *two dozen* dos docenas
◆ **I've told you that dozens of times.** Te lo he dicho cientos de veces.

drab [dræb] ADJECTIVE
sin gracia (*clothes*)

draft [dræft] NOUN
la corriente de aire ◇ *There's a draft from the window.* Entra corriente por la ventana.
◆ **draft beer** la cerveza de barril

to **drag** [dræg] VERB
see also **drag** NOUN
arrastrar (*thing, person*)

drag [dræg] NOUN
see also **drag** VERB
◆ **It's a real drag!** ¡Es una verdadera lata! (*informal*)

dragon ['drægən] NOUN
el dragón (PL los dragones)

drain [dreɪn] NOUN
see also **drain** VERB
1 el desagüe (*of house*)
2 la alcantarilla (*in street*)

to **drain** [dreɪn] VERB
see also **drain** NOUN
escurrir (*vegetables, pasta*)

drainboard ['dreɪn,bɔːrd] NOUN
el escurridero

drainpipe ['dreɪn,paɪp] NOUN
el tubo de desagüe

drama ['drɑːmə] NOUN
1 el drama
*Although **drama** ends in **-a**, it is actually a masculine noun.*
◇ *a TV drama* un drama para televisión
2 el teatro ◇ *Greek drama* el teatro griego ◇ *Drama is my favorite subject.* Mi asignatura favorita es teatro.
◆ **drama school** la escuela de arte dramático

dramatic [drə'mætɪk] ADJECTIVE
espectacular ◇ *a dramatic improvement* una espectacular mejoría
◆ **dramatic news** noticias sensacionales

drank [dræŋk] VERB *see* **drink**

drapes [dreɪps] PL NOUN
las cortinas

drastic ['dræstɪk] ADJECTIVE
drástico ◇ *to take drastic action* tomar medidas drásticas

to **draw** [drɑː] VERB (**drew, drawn**)
dibujar (*a scene, a person*)
◆ **to draw a picture** hacer* un dibujo
◆ **to draw a picture of somebody** hacer* un retrato de alguien
◆ **to draw a line** trazar* una línea
◆ **to draw the drapes (1)** (*open*) descorrer las cortinas
◆ **to draw the drapes (2)** (*close*) correr las cortinas

to **draw on** ['drɑː,ɑːn] VERB
recurrir a ◇ *He drew on his own experience to write the book.* Recurrió a su propia experiencia para escribir el libro.

to **draw up** [drɑː'ʌp] VERB
pararse ◇ *The car drew up in front of the house.* El carro se paró delante de la casa.

drawback ['drɑː,bæk] NOUN
el inconveniente

drawer [drɔːr] NOUN
el cajón (PL los cajones)

drawing ['drɑːɪŋ] NOUN
el dibujo ◇ *He's good at drawing.* Es bueno para el dibujo.

drawn [drɑːn] VERB *see* **draw**

dreadful ['drɛdfəl] ADJECTIVE
1 terrible ◇ *a dreadful mistake* un error terrible
2 horrible ◇ *The weather was dreadful.* Hizo un tiempo horrible.
◆ **You look dreadful.** Tienes muy mal aspecto.
◆ **I feel dreadful about not having phoned.** Me siento muy mal por no haber llamado.

to **dream** [driːm] VERB
see also **dream** NOUN
soñar* ◇ *Do you dream every night?* ¿Sueñas todas las noches?
◆ **She dreamed about her baby.** Soñó con su bebé.

dream [driːm] NOUN
see also **dream** VERB
el sueño

to **drench** [drɛntʃ] VERB
◆ **I got drenched.** Me empapé.

dress [drɛs] NOUN (PL **dresses**)
see also **dress** VERB
el vestido

to **dress** [drɛs] VERB
see also **dress** NOUN
vestirse* ◇ *I got up, dressed, and went downstairs.* Me levanté, me vestí y bajé.
◆ **to dress somebody** vestir* a alguien
◆ **to get dressed** vestirse*

to **dress up** [drɛs'ʌp] VERB
disfrazarse* ◇ *I dressed up as a ghost.* Me disfracé de fantasma.

dressed [drɛst] ADJECTIVE
vestido ◇ *I'm not dressed yet.* Aún no estoy vestido. ◇ *How was she dressed?* ¿Cómo iba vestida? ◇ *She was dressed in white.* Iba vestida de blanco.
◆ **She was dressed in a green sweater and jeans.** Llevaba un suéter verde y jeans.

dresser ['drɛsər] NOUN
el aparador (*furniture*)

dressing ['drɛsɪŋ] NOUN
el aliño (*for salad*)

dressing gown ['drɛsɪŋ,gaun] NOUN
la bata

dressing table ['drɛsɪŋˌteɪbəl] NOUN
el tocador

drew [druː] VERB *see* **draw**

dried [draɪd] ADJECTIVE
seco
◆ **dried milk** la leche en polvo
◆ **dried fruits** las frutas pasas

drier ['draɪər] = **dryer**

drift [drɪft] NOUN
see also **drift** VERB
◆ **a snow drift** el ventisquero

to **drift** [drɪft] VERB
see also **drift** NOUN
1 ir* a la deriva (*boat*)
2 amontonarse (*snow*)

drill [drɪl] NOUN
see also **drill** VERB
la taladradora

to **drill** [drɪl] VERB
see also **drill** NOUN
taladrar
◆ **He drilled a hole in the wall.** Hizo un agujero en la pared.

to **drink** [drɪŋk] VERB (**drank, drunk**)
see also **drink** NOUN
beber ◇ *She drank three cups of tea.* Se bebió tres tazas de té.
◆ **What would you like to drink?** ¿Qué quieres tomar?

drink [drɪŋk] NOUN
see also **drink** VERB
1 la bebida ◇ *a cold drink* una bebida fría
2 la copa (*alcoholic*) ◇ *They've gone out for a drink.* Salieron a tomar una copa.
◆ **to have a drink** tomar algo
◆ **Would you like a drink?** ¿Quieres tomar algo?

drinking water ['drɪŋkɪŋ'wɑːtər] NOUN
el agua potable FEM
*Although it's a feminine noun, remember that you use **el** with **agua**.*

drive [draɪv] NOUN
see also **drive** VERB
1 el paseo en carro ◇ *to go for a drive* ir* a dar un paseo en carro
◆ **We have a long drive tomorrow.** Mañana nos espera un largo viaje en carro.
2 el camino de entrada a la casa ◇ *He parked his car in the drive.* Estacionó el carro en el camino de entrada a la casa.
◆ **disk drive** la unidad de disco

to **drive** [draɪv] VERB (**drove, driven**)
see also **drive** NOUN
1 manejar (*a car*) ◇ *Can you drive?* ¿Sabes manejar?
2 ir* en carro (*go by car*) ◇ *We never drive into the town center.* Nunca vamos en carro al centro.
3 llevar en carro (*transport*) ◇ *My mother drives me to school.* Mi mamá me lleva al colegio en el carro.
◆ **to drive somebody home** llevar a alguien a su casa en carro
◆ **to drive somebody mad** volver* loco a alguien ◇ *He drives her mad.* La vuelve loca.

drive-in ['draɪvˌɪn] NOUN
el drive in
*Un **drive-in** es un restaurante donde se sirve a los clientes en su propio carro.*

driver ['draɪvər] NOUN el/la chofer ◇ *He's a bus driver.* Es chofer de bus. *Mexico:* Es chofer de camión.
◆ **She's an excellent driver.** Maneja muy bien.

driver's license ['draɪvərzˌlaɪsəns] NOUN
la licencia de manejar

driving instructor ['draɪvɪŋɪn'strʌktər] NOUN
el instructor de autoescuela
la instructora de autoescuela
◇ *He's a driving instructor.* Es instructor de autoescuela.

driving lesson ['draɪvɪŋˌlɛsən] NOUN
la clase de manejar

driving test ['draɪvɪŋˌtɛst] NOUN
◆ **to take one's driving test** hacer* el examen de manejar
◆ **She's just passed her driving test.** Acaba de pasar el examen de manejar.

drizzle ['drɪzəl] NOUN
la llovizna

drop [drɑːp] NOUN
see also **drop** VERB
1 la gota (*of liquid*) ◇ *Would you like some milk? – Just a drop.* ¿Quieres leche? – Una gota no más.
2 la bajada ◇ *a drop in temperature* una bajada de las temperaturas

to **drop** [drɑːp] VERB
see also **drop** NOUN
1 bajar ◇ *The temperature will drop tonight.* La temperatura bajará esta noche.
2 soltar* ◇ *The cat dropped the mouse at my feet.* El gato soltó al ratón junto a mis pies.
◆ **I dropped the glass.** Se me cayó el vaso.
3 dejar ◇ *Could you drop me at the station?* ¿Me puedes dejar en la estación?
◆ **I'm going to drop chemistry.** No voy a seguir estudiando química.

drought [draut] NOUN
la sequía

drove [drouv] VERB *see* **drive**

to **drown** [draun] VERB
ahogarse* ◇ *A boy drowned here yesterday.* Un chico se ahogó ayer aquí.

drug [drʌg] NOUN
1 el medicamento ◇ *They need food and drugs.* Necesitan comida y medicamentos.
2 la droga ◇ *hard drugs* drogas duras
◇ *soft drugs* drogas blandas
◆ **to take drugs** drogarse*
◆ **a drug addict** un drogadicto (FEM una drogadicta)
◆ **a drug pusher** un camello, *Mexico:* un ☞

D

conecte (*informal*)
◆ **a drug smuggler** un narcotraficante
druggist ['drʌgɪst] NOUN
el farmacéutico
la farmacéutica
(*dispenser*)
drugstore ['drʌg,stɔːr] NOUN

> ℹ *Tienda donde se venden artículos muy variados como medicinas, prensa, cosméticos y comida rápida.*

drum [drʌm] NOUN
el tambor ◇ *an African drum* un tambor africano
◆ **a drum kit** una batería
◆ **to play the drums** tocar* la batería
drummer ['drʌmər] NOUN
el/la batería (*in group etc*)
drunk [drʌŋk] VERB *see* **drink**
drunk [drʌŋk] ADJECTIVE
see also **drunk** NOUN
borracho ◇ *He was drunk.* Estaba borracho.
◆ **to get drunk** emborracharse
drunk [drʌŋk] NOUN
see also **drunk** ADJECTIVE
el borracho
la borracha
dry [draɪ] ADJECTIVE
see also **dry** VERB
seco ◇ *The paint isn't dry yet.* Aún no está seca la pintura. ◇ *It's been exceptionally dry this spring.* Esta primavera ha sido extraordinariamente seca.
◆ **a long dry period** un largo periodo sin lluvia
to **dry** [draɪ] VERB (**dried, dried**)
see also **dry** ADJECTIVE
1 secar* ◇ *to dry the dishes* secar los platos ◇ *There's nowhere to dry clothes here.* Aquí no hay un sitio para poner a secar la ropa.
2 secarse* ◇ *The laundry will dry quickly in the sun.* La ropa lavada se secará rápido al sol.
◆ **to dry one's hair** secarse* el pelo
dry cleaner's ['draɪ'kliːnərz] NOUN
la tintorería
dryer ['draɪər] NOUN
la secadora
◆ **a hair dryer** un secador, *Mexico:* una secadora de mano
dubbed [dʌbd] ADJECTIVE
doblado ◇ *The movie was dubbed into Spanish.* La película estaba doblada al español.
dubious ['duːbiəs] ADJECTIVE
◆ **My parents were a bit dubious about it.** Mis padres tenían sus dudas sobre eso.
duck [dʌk] NOUN
el pato
dude [duːd] NOUN
el tipo (*informal*)
due [duː] ADJECTIVE, ADVERB
◆ **He's due to arrive tomorrow.** Debe llegar mañana.
◆ **The plane is due in half an hour.** El avión llegará en media hora.
◆ **When is the baby due?** ¿Para cuándo nacerá el niño?
◆ **due to** debido a ◇ *The trip was canceled due to bad weather.* El viaje se suspendió debido al mal tiempo.
dug [dʌg] VERB *see* **dig**
dull [dʌl] ADJECTIVE
1 soso ◇ *He's nice, but a bit dull.* Es simpático, pero un poco soso.
2 gris ◇ *It's always dull and wet.* El tiempo está siempre gris y lluvioso.
dumb [dʌm] ADJECTIVE
1 mudo
◆ **She's deaf and dumb.** Es sordomuda.
2 bobo ◇ *Don't be so dumb!* ¡No seas bobo!
◆ **That was a really dumb thing I did!** ¡Lo que hice fue una verdadera bobada!
dump [dʌmp] NOUN
see also **dump** VERB
◆ **It's a real dump!** ¡Es una auténtica pocilga!
◆ **a garbage dump** un vertedero, *Mexico:* un tiradero
to **dump** [dʌmp] VERB
see also **dump** NOUN
verter* (*waste*) ◇ *"No dumping."* "Prohibido verter basuras."
Dumpster® ['dʌmpstər] NOUN
el contenedor de basuras
dungarees [dʌŋgə'riːz] PL NOUN
1 el overol (*for work*)
2 los jeans (*jeans*)
dungeon ['dʌndʒən] NOUN
la mazmorra
duplex ['duːplɛks] NOUN (PL **duplexes**)

> ℹ *Una casa para dos familias formada por dos viviendas adosadas.*

duration [du'reɪʃən] NOUN
la duración ◇ *Courses are of two years' duration.* Los cursos tienen una duración de dos años.
◆ **for the duration of the trial** durante todo el juicio
during ['durɪŋ] PREPOSITION
durante
dusk [dʌsk] NOUN
el anochecer
◆ **at dusk** al anochecer
dust [dʌst] NOUN
see also **dust** VERB
el polvo

to **dust** [dʌst] VERB
see also **dust** NOUN
limpiar el polvo de
sacudir Mexico
◇ *I dusted the shelves.* Limpié el polvo de las estanterías. Mexico: Sacudí los estantes.

dusty ['dʌsti] ADJECTIVE
polvoriento

Dutch [dʌtʃ] ADJECTIVE
see also **Dutch** NOUN
holandés (FEM holandesa) ◇ *She's Dutch.* Es holandesa.

Dutch [dʌtʃ] NOUN
see also **Dutch** ADJECTIVE
el holandés (*language*)
◆ **the Dutch** los holandeses

Dutchman ['dʌtʃmən] NOUN (PL **Dutchmen**)
el holandés

Dutchwoman ['dʌtʃˌwumən] NOUN (PL **Dutchwomen**)
la holandesa

duty ['du:ti] NOUN (PL **duties**)
el deber ◇ *It was his duty to tell the police.* Su deber era decírselo a la policía.
◆ **to be on duty (1)** (*policeman*) estar* de servicio
◆ **to be on duty (2)** (*doctor, nurse*) estar* de guardia

duty-free ['du:tiˌfri:] ADJECTIVE
libre de impuestos

DVD [ˌdi:vi:'di:] NOUN
el DVD

dwarf [dwɔ:rf] NOUN (PL **dwarves** *o* **dwarfs**)
el enano
la enana

dying ['daɪɪŋ] VERB *see* **die**

dynamic [daɪ'næmɪk] ADJECTIVE
dinámico

dyslexia [dɪs'lɛksiə] NOUN
la dislexia

D

E

each [iːtʃ] ADJECTIVE, PRONOUN
1 cada (FEM cada) ◊ *each day* cada día
◆ **Each house has its own garden.** Todas las casas tienen su propio jardín.
2 cada uno (FEM cada una) ◊ *They have 10 points each.* Tienen 10 puntos cada uno. ◊ *The plates cost $5 each.* Los platos cuestan 5 dólares cada uno. ◊ *He gave each of us $10.* Nos dio 10 dólares a cada uno.
Use a reflexive verb to translate ***each other.***
◊ *They hate each other.* Se odian. ◊ *We write to each other.* Nos escribimos. ◊ *They don't know each other.* No se conocen.

eager [ˈiːgər] ADJECTIVE
◆ **He was eager to tell us about his experiences.** Estaba impaciente por contarnos sus experiencias.

eagle [ˈiːgəl] NOUN
el águila FEM
Although it's a feminine noun, remember that you use ***el*** *and* ***un*** *with* ***águila.***

ear [ɪər] NOUN
la oreja

earache [ˈɪreɪk] NOUN
◆ **to have an earache** tener* dolor de oídos

earlier [ˈɜːrliər] ADVERB
1 antes ◊ *I saw him earlier.* Lo vi antes.
2 más temprano (*in the morning*) ◊ *I ought to get up earlier.* Debería levantarme más temprano.

early [ˈɜːrli] ADVERB, ADJECTIVE
1 temprano ◊ *I have to get up early.* Tengo que levantarme temprano.
◆ **to have an early night** irse* a la cama temprano
2 temprano (*ahead of time*) ◊ *I came early to avoid the heavy traffic.* Vine temprano para evitar el tráfico pesado.

to **earn** [ɜːrn] VERB
ganar ◊ *She earns $5 an hour.* Gana 5 dólares a la hora.

earnings [ˈɜːrnɪŋz] PL NOUN
los ingresos ◊ *Average earnings rose two percent last year.* Los ingresos promedios aumentaron un dos por ciento el año pasado.

earring [ˈɪrɪŋ] NOUN
el pendiente
el arete Mexico

earth [ɜːrθ] NOUN
la tierra
◆ **What on earth are you doing here?** ¿Qué diablos haces aquí?

earthquake [ˈɜːrθkweɪk] NOUN
el terremoto

easily [ˈiːzɪli] ADVERB
fácilmente

east [iːst] ADJECTIVE, ADVERB
see also **east** NOUN
hacia el este ◊ *We were traveling east.* Viajábamos hacia el este.
◆ **an east wind** un viento del este
◆ **the east coast** la costa oriental
◆ **east of** al este de ◊ *It's east of San Juan.* Está al este de San Juan.

east [iːst] NOUN
see also **east** ADJECTIVE, ADVERB
el este (*direction, region*) ◊ *in the east of the country* al este del país

Easter [ˈiːstər] NOUN
la Pascua
◆ **Easter egg** el huevo de Pascua
◆ **the Easter vacation** las vacaciones de Semana Santa

eastern [ˈiːstərn] ADJECTIVE
oriental ◊ *the eastern part of the island* la parte oriental de la isla
◆ **Eastern Europe** la Europa del Este

easy [ˈiːzi] ADJECTIVE
fácil
◆ **Take it easy!** ¡Calma!

easy chair [ˈiːziˌtʃɛr] NOUN
el sillón (PL los sillones)

easygoing [ˈiːziˌgoʊɪŋ] ADJECTIVE
◆ **to be easygoing** ser* una persona de trato fácil ◊ *She's very easygoing and gets on well with everybody.* Es una persona de trato fácil y se lleva bien con todos.

to **eat** [iːt] VERB (**ate, eaten**)
comer ◊ *Would you like something to eat?* ¿Quieres comer algo?

EC [iːˈsiː] NOUN (= *European Community*)
la CE (= la Comunidad Europea)

eccentric [ɪkˈsɛntrɪk] ADJECTIVE
excéntrico

echo [ˈɛkoʊ] NOUN (PL **echoes**)
el eco

ecology [ɪˈkɑːlədʒi] NOUN
la ecología

economic [ˌiːkəˈnɑːmɪk] ADJECTIVE
1 económico (*growth, development, policy*)
2 rentable (*profitable*)

economical [ˌiːkəˈnɑːmɪkəl] ADJECTIVE
económico ◊ *My car is very economical to run.* Mi carro me sale muy económico.

economics [ˌiːkəˈnɑːmɪks] NOUN
la economía ◊ *the economics of the third world countries* la economía de los países tercermundistas ◊ *He's studying economics at the university.* Estudia economía en la universidad.

to **economize** [ɪˈkɑːnəmaɪz] VERB
economizar*
◆ **to economize on something** economizar en algo

economy [ɪˈkɑːnəmi] NOUN (PL **economies**)
la economía

* Verbs marked with this symbol are irregular. See pages 346–348 for further details.

ecstasy ['ɛkstəsi] NOUN
el éxtasis ◊ *to be in ecstasy* estar* en éxtasis
eczema [ɪg'ziːmə] NOUN
el eczema
Although ***eczema*** *ends in* ***-a****, it is actually a masculine noun.*
◊ *She has eczema.* Tiene eczema.
edge [ɛdʒ] NOUN
1 el borde ◊ *on the edge of the desk* en el borde del escritorio
◆ **They live on the edge of the town.** Viven en los límites de la ciudad.
2 la orilla (*of lake*)
◆ **to be on the edge of tears** estar* a punto de llorar
edgy ['ɛdʒi] ADJECTIVE
nervioso
Edinburgh ['ɛdɪnbərə] NOUN
Edimburgo MASC
editor ['ɛdɪtər] NOUN
1 el director
la directora
(*of newspaper, magazine*)
2 el redactor
la redactora
◊ *the sports editor* el redactor de la sección de deportes
educated ['ɛdʒəkeɪtɪd] ADJECTIVE
culto
education [ˌɛdʒə'keɪʃən] NOUN
1 la educación ◊ *There should be more investment in education.* Debería invertirse más dinero en educación.
2 la enseñanza (*teaching*) ◊ *She works in education.* Trabaja en la enseñanza.
educational [ˌɛdʒə'keɪʃənl] ADJECTIVE
1 educativo (*toy*)
2 instructivo (*experience, movie*)
effect [ɪ'fɛkt] NOUN
el efecto ◊ *special effects* los efectos especiales
effective [ɪ'fɛktɪv] ADJECTIVE
eficaz (PL eficaces)
efficient [ɪ'fɪʃənt] ADJECTIVE
1 eficiente ◊ *His secretary is very efficient.* Su secretaria es muy eficiente.
2 eficaz (PL eficaces) ◊ *It's a very efficient system.* Es un sistema muy eficaz.
effort ['ɛfərt] NOUN
el esfuerzo
◆ **to make an effort to do something** esforzarse* en hacer algo
e.g. [iː'dʒiː] ABBREVIATION
p.ej. (= por ejemplo)
egg [ɛg] NOUN
el huevo ◊ *a hard-boiled egg* un huevo duro ◊ *a soft-boiled egg* un huevo pasado por agua, *Mexico:* un huevo tibio ◊ *a fried egg* un huevo frito, *Mexico:* un huevo estrellado ◊ *scrambled eggs* los huevos revueltos
eggcup ['ɛgˌkʌp] NOUN
la huevera
eggplant ['ɛgˌplænt] NOUN
la berenjena
Egypt ['iːdʒɪpt] NOUN
Egipto MASC
eight [eɪt] NUMERAL
ocho ◊ *She's eight.* Tiene ocho años.
eighteen [eɪ'tiːn] NUMERAL
dieciocho ◊ *She's eighteen.* Tiene dieciocho años.
eighteenth [eɪ'tiːnθ] ADJECTIVE
decimoctavo
◆ **the eighteenth floor** el piso dieciocho
◆ **August eighteenth** el dieciocho de agosto
eighth [eɪθ] ADJECTIVE
octavo ◊ *the eighth floor* el octavo piso
◆ **August eighth** el ocho de agosto
eighty ['eɪti] NUMERAL
ochenta ◊ *He's eighty.* Tiene ochenta años.
Eire ['ɛrə] NOUN
Eire MASC
either ['iːðər] ADJECTIVE, CONJUNCTION, PRONOUN, ADVERB
tampoco ◊ *I don't like milk, and I don't like eggs either.* No me gusta la leche, y tampoco me gustan los huevos. ◊ *I've never been to Spain. – I haven't either.* No he estado nunca en España. – Ni yo tampoco.
◆ **either...or...** o...o... ◊ *You can have either ice cream or yogurt.* Puedes tomar o helado o yogur.
◆ **either of them** uno u otro
◆ **I don't like either of them.** No me gusta ninguno de los dos.
◆ **Choose either of them.** Elige cualquiera de los dos.
◆ **on either side of the road** a ambos lados de la carretera
elastic [ɪ'læstɪk] NOUN
el elástico
elastic band [ɪˌlæstɪk'bænd] NOUN
la goma elástica
la liga *Mexico*
elbow ['ɛlbou] NOUN
el codo
elder ['ɛldər] ADJECTIVE
mayor ◊ *my elder sister* mi hermana mayor
elderly ['ɛldərli] ADJECTIVE
anciano
◆ **an elderly man** un anciano
◆ **the elderly** los ancianos
eldest ['ɛldɪst] ADJECTIVE, NOUN
mayor ◊ *my eldest sister* mi hermana mayor ◊ *He's the eldest.* Él es el mayor.
to **elect** [ɪ'lɛkt] VERB
elegir*
election [ɪ'lɛkʃən] NOUN
la elección (PL las elecciones)
elective [ɪ'lɛktɪv] NOUN
la asignatura optativa (*at school*) ◊ *I'm*

E

doing geology as my elective. Tengo geología como asignatura optativa.

electric [ɪ'lɛktrɪk] ADJECTIVE
eléctrico ◇ *an electric fire* una estufa eléctrica ◇ *an electric guitar* una guitarra eléctrica ◇ *an electric blanket* una cobija eléctrica

electrical [ɪ'lɛktrɪkəl] ADJECTIVE
eléctrico ◇ *electrical engineering* la ingeniería eléctrica
◆ **an electrical engineer** un ingeniero electrónico

electrician [ɪlɛk'trɪʃən] NOUN
el/la electricista ◇ *He's an electrician.* Es electricista.

electricity [ɪlɛk'trɪsəti] NOUN
la electricidad

electronic [ɪlɛk'trɑːnɪk] ADJECTIVE
electrónico

electronics [ɪlɛk'trɑːnɪks] NOUN
la electrónica

elegant ['ɛlɪgənt] ADJECTIVE
elegante

elementary school [ɛlɪ'mɛntəri,skuːl] NOUN
la escuela primaria

elephant ['ɛlɪfənt] NOUN
el elefante

elevator ['ɛlɪveɪtər] NOUN
el ascensor
el elevador *Mexico*
◇ *The elevator isn't working.* El ascensor no funciona. *Mexico:* El elevador no funciona.

eleven [ɪ'lɛvən] NUMERAL
once ◇ *She's eleven.* Tiene once años.

eleventh [ɪ'lɛvənθ] ADJECTIVE
undécimo
◆ **the eleventh floor** el piso once
◆ **August eleventh** el once de agosto

else [ɛls] ADVERB
◆ **somebody else** otra persona
◆ **nobody else** nadie más
◆ **something else** otra cosa
◆ **nothing else** nada más
◆ **somewhere else** en algún otro lugar
◆ **Did you look anywhere else?** ¿Miraste en otro lugar?
◆ **I would be happy anywhere else.** Estaría contento en cualquier otro lugar.
◆ **I didn't look anywhere else.** No miré en ningún otro lugar.
◆ **Would you like anything else?** ¿Desea alguna otra cosa?
◆ **I don't want anything else.** No quiero nada más.
◆ **Arrive on time or else!** ¡Llega a tiempo o si no...!

email ['iːmeɪl] NOUN
see also **email** VERB
el correo electrónico

to **email** ['iːmeɪl] VERB
see also **email** NOUN
◆ **to email somebody** enviar* un mensaje a alguien por correo electrónico
◆ **I'll email you the details.** Te mandaré la información por correo electrónico.

email address ['iːmeɪlə,drɛs] NOUN (PL **email addresses**)
la dirección de correo electrónico ◇ *my email address is jones at collins dot uk* mi dirección de correo electrónico es jones arroba collins punto uk

embarrassed [ɪm'bɛrəst] ADJECTIVE
◆ **I was really embarrassed.** Me dio mucha vergüenza. *Mexico:* Me dio mucha pena.
Be careful not to translate ***embarrassed*** *by* ***embarazada.***

embarrassing [ɪm'bɛrəsɪŋ] ADJECTIVE
embarazoso (*mistake, situation*)
◆ **It was so embarrassing.** Fue una situación muy violenta.
◆ **How embarrassing!** ¡Qué vergüenza!, *Mexico:* ¡Qué pena!

embassy ['ɛmbəsi] NOUN (PL **embassies**)
la embajada

to **embroider** [ɪm'brɔɪdər] VERB
bordar

embroidery [ɪm'brɔɪdəri] NOUN
el bordado
◆ **I do embroidery in the afternoon.** Bordo por las tardes.

emcee ['ɛm'siː] NOUN
el presentador
la presentadora
(*informal*)

emergency [ɪ'mɜːrdʒənsi] NOUN (PL **emergencies**)
la emergencia ◇ *This is an emergency!* ¡Es una emergencia!
◆ **in an emergency** en caso de emergencia
◆ **an emergency exit** una salida de emergencia
◆ **an emergency landing** un aterrizaje forzoso
◆ **the emergency services** los servicios de urgencia
◆ **emergency room** urgencias FEM PL ◇ *He was taken to the emergency room after the accident.* Lo llevaron a urgencias después del accidente.

to **emigrate** ['ɛmɪgreɪt] VERB
emigrar

emotion [ɪ'moʊʃən] NOUN
la emoción (PL las emociones)

emotional [ɪ'moʊʃənl] ADJECTIVE
emotivo ◇ *She's very emotional.* Es una persona muy emotiva.
◆ **He got very emotional at the farewell party.** Se emocionó mucho en la fiesta de despedida.

emperor ['ɛmpərər] NOUN
el emperador

to **emphasize** ['ɛmfəsaɪz] VERB

recalcar* ◇ *He emphasized the importance of the issue.* Recalcó la importancia de la cuestión.
◆ **to emphasize that...** subrayar que...

empire ['ɛmpaɪər] NOUN
el imperio

to **employ** [ɪm'plɔɪ] VERB
emplear ◇ *The factory employs 600 people.* La fábrica emplea a 600 trabajadores.
◆ **Thousands of people are employed in tourism.** Miles de personas trabajan en el sector de turismo.

employee [ɪm,plɔɪ'i:] NOUN
el empleado
la empleada

employer [ɪm'plɔɪər] NOUN
el empleador
la empleadora

employment [ɪm'plɔɪmənt] NOUN
el empleo

empty ['ɛmpti] ADJECTIVE
see also **empty** VERB
vacío

to **empty** ['ɛmpti] VERB (**emptied, emptied**)
see also **empty** ADJECTIVE
vaciar*
◆ **to empty something out** vaciar algo

to **encourage** [ɪn'kɜ:rɪdʒ] VERB
animar ◇ *to encourage somebody to do something* animar a alguien a hacer algo

encouragement [ɪn'kɜ:rɪdʒmənt] NOUN
el estímulo

encyclopedia [ɛnsaɪklə'pi:diə] NOUN
la enciclopedia

end [ɛnd] NOUN
see also **end** VERB
1 el final ◇ *the end of the movie* el final de la película ◇ *the end of the vacation* el final de las vacaciones
◆ **in the end** al final ◇ *In the end I decided to stay at home.* Al final decidí quedarme en casa. ◇ *It turned out all right in the end.* Al final resultó bien.
2 el extremo ◇ *at the other end of the table* al otro extremo de la mesa
◆ **at the end of the street** al final de la calle
◆ **for hours on end** durante horas enteras

to **end** [ɛnd] VERB
see also **end** NOUN
terminar ◇ *What time does the movie end?* ¿A qué hora termina la película?
◆ **to end up doing something** terminar haciendo algo ◇ *I ended up walking home.* Terminé yendo a mi casa andando.

ending ['ɛndɪŋ] NOUN
el final ◇ *a happy ending* un final feliz

endless ['ɛndlɪs] ADJECTIVE
interminable ◇ *The journey seemed endless.* El viaje parecía interminable.

enemy ['ɛnəmi] NOUN (PL **enemies**)
el enemigo
la enemiga

energetic [ɛnər'dʒɛtɪk] ADJECTIVE
activo ◇ *She's very energetic.* Es muy activa.

energy ['ɛnərdʒi] NOUN
la energía

engaged [ɪn'geɪdʒd] ADJECTIVE
comprometido ◇ *Brian and Mary are engaged.* Brian y Mary están comprometidos.
◆ **to get engaged** comprometerse

engagement [ɪn'geɪdʒmənt] NOUN
compromiso ◇ *They announced their engagement yesterday.* Anunciaron su compromiso ayer.
◆ **The engagement lasted 10 months.** El noviazgo duró 10 meses.
◆ **engagement ring** anillo de compromiso

engine ['ɛndʒɪn] NOUN
1 el motor (*of vehicle*)
2 la locomotora (*of train*)

engineer [ɛndʒə'nɪər] NOUN
1 el ingeniero
la ingeniera
◇ *He's an engineer.* Es ingeniero.
2 el/la maquinista (*on railroads*)

engineering [ɛndʒə'nɪrɪŋ] NOUN
la ingeniería

England ['ɪŋglənd] NOUN
Inglaterra FEM

English ['ɪŋglɪʃ] ADJECTIVE
see also **English** NOUN
inglés (MASC PL ingleses, FEM inglesa)

English ['ɪŋglɪʃ] NOUN
see also **English** ADJECTIVE
el inglés (*language*) ◇ *the English teacher* el profesor de inglés
◆ **the English** (*people*) los ingleses

Englishman ['ɪŋglɪʃmən] NOUN (PL **Englishmen**)
el inglés (PL los ingleses)

Englishwoman ['ɪŋglɪʃ,wumən] NOUN (PL **Englishwomen**)
la inglesa

to **enjoy** [ɪn'dʒɔɪ] VERB
◆ **Did you enjoy the movie?** ¿Te gustó la película?
◆ **to enjoy oneself** divertirse* ◇ *Did you enjoy yourselves at the party?* ¿Se divirtieron en la fiesta?

enjoyable [ɪn'dʒɔɪəbəl] ADJECTIVE
agradable

enlargement [ɪn'lɑ:rdʒmənt] NOUN
la ampliación (PL las ampliaciones) (*of photo*)

enormous [ɪ'nɔ:rməs] ADJECTIVE
enorme

enough [ɪ'nʌf] ADJECTIVE, PRONOUN, ADVERB
bastante ◇ *I didn't have enough money.* No tenía bastante dinero. ◇ *Do you have enough?* ¿Tienes bastante?
◆ **big enough** suficientemente grande

E

- **I've had enough!** ¡Ya estoy harto!
- **That's enough!** ¡Ya basta!

to **enquire** [ɪn'kwaɪər] VERB
- **to enquire about something** informarse acerca de algo

enquiry [ɪn'kwaɪəri] NOUN (PL **enquiries**)
la investigación (PL las investigaciones) (*official investigation*)

to **enter** ['ɛntər] VERB
entrar a ◇ *He entered the room and sat down.* Entró a la habitación y se sentó.
- **to enter a competition** presentarse a un concurso

to **entertain** [ˌɛntər'teɪn] VERB
recibir (*guests*)

entertainer [ˌɛntər'teɪnər] NOUN
el animador
la animadora

entertaining [ˌɛntər'teɪnɪŋ] ADJECTIVE
entretenido (*book, movie*)

enthusiasm [ɪn'θuːzɪæzəm] NOUN
el entusiasmo

enthusiast [ɪn'θuːzɪæst] NOUN
el/la entusiasta ◇ *She's a jazz enthusiast.* Es una entusiasta del jazz.

enthusiastic [ɪnθuːzɪ'æstɪk] ADJECTIVE
entusiasta (*response, welcome*)
- **She didn't seem very enthusiastic about your idea.** No pareció muy entusiasmada con tu idea.

entire [ɪn'taɪər] ADJECTIVE
entero ◇ *the entire world* el mundo entero

entirely [ɪn'taɪərli] ADVERB
completamente ◇ *an entirely new approach* un enfoque completamente nuevo
- **I agree entirely.** Estoy totalmente de acuerdo.

entrance ['ɛntrəns] NOUN
la entrada
- **an entrance exam** un examen de admisión
- **entrance fee** la cuota de entrada

entry ['ɛntri] NOUN (PL **entries**)
la entrada
- **"no entry" (1)** (*on door*) "prohibido el paso"
- **"no entry" (2)** (*on road sign*) "dirección prohibida"
- **an entry form** un formulario de inscripción, *Mexico:* una forma de inscripción

envelope ['ɛnvəloup] NOUN
el sobre

envious ['ɛnviəs] ADJECTIVE
envidioso

environment [ɪn'vaɪərənmənt] NOUN
el entorno (*surroundings*) ◇ *She adjusted to the changes in her environment.* Se adaptó a los cambios de su nuevo entorno.
- **the environment** el medio ambiente ◇ *We are fighting pollution to protect the environment.* Estamos combatiendo la contaminación para proteger el medio ambiente.

environmental [ɪnˌvaɪərən'mɛntl] ADJECTIVE
medioambiental ◇ *environmental pollution* contaminación ambiental
- **environmental groups** grupos ecologistas

environmentally-friendly [ɪn'vaɪərənmɛntəli'frɛndli] ADJECTIVE
ecológico

envy ['ɛnvi] NOUN
see also **envy** VERB
la envidia

to **envy** ['ɛnvi] VERB (**envied, envied**)
see also **envy** NOUN
envidiar

epileptic [ɛpɪ'lɛptɪk] NOUN
el epiléptico
la epiléptica

episode ['ɛpɪsoud] NOUN
el episodio

equal ['iːkwəl] ADJECTIVE
igual ◇ *The cake was divided into 12 equal parts.* El pastel se dividió en 12 partes iguales.
- **Women demand equal rights at work.** Las mujeres exigen igualdad de derechos en el trabajo.

equality [iː'kwɑːlɪti] NOUN
la igualdad

to **equalize** ['iːkwəlaɪz] VERB
empatar (*in sport*)

equator [ɪ'kweɪtər] NOUN
el ecuador

equipment [ɪ'kwɪpmənt] NOUN
el equipo ◇ *skiing equipment* el equipo de esquí

equipped [ɪ'kwɪpt] ADJECTIVE
equipado ◇ *This trailer is equipped for four people.* Este trailer está equipado para cuatro personas.
- **equipped with** provisto de ◇ *All rooms are equipped with phones, computers and fax machines.* Todas las habitaciones están provistas de teléfonos, computadoras y fax.
- **He was well equipped for the job.** Estaba bien preparado para el puesto.

equivalent [ɪ'kwɪvələnt] ADJECTIVE
see also **equivalent** NOUN
equivalente
- **to be equivalent to something** equivaler* a algo

equivalent [ɪ'kwɪvələnt] NOUN
see also **equivalent** ADJECTIVE
el equivalente

ER [iː'ɑːr] NOUN (= *emergency room*)
la sala de urgencias

eraser [ɪ'reɪsər] NOUN
la goma de borrar

error ['ɛrər] NOUN
el error

escalator ['ɛskəleɪtər] NOUN

la escalera mecánica

escape [ɪs'keɪp] NOUN
see also **escape** VERB
la fuga (*from prison*)
- **We had a narrow escape.** Nos salvamos por muy poco.

to **escape** [ɪs'keɪp] VERB
see also **escape** NOUN
escaparse ◊ *A lion has escaped.* Se escapó un león.
- **The passengers escaped unhurt.** Los pasajeros salieron ilesos.
- **to escape from prison** fugarse* de la cárcel

escort ['ɛskɔ:rt] NOUN
la escolta ◊ *a police escort* una escolta policial

Eskimo ['ɛskɪmou] NOUN (PL **Eskimos**)
el/la esquimal

especially [ɪ'spɛʃəli] ADVERB
especialmente ◊ *It's very hot there, especially in the summer.* Allí hace mucho calor, especialmente en verano. ◊ *Do you like opera? – Not especially.* ¿Te gusta la ópera? – No especialmente.

essay ['ɛseɪ] NOUN
la redacción (PL las redacciones) ◊ *a history essay* una redacción de historia

essential [ɪ'sɛnʃəl] ADJECTIVE
esencial ◊ *It's essential to bring warm clothes.* Es esencial traer ropa de abrigo.

estate [ɪs'teɪt] NOUN
la finca ◊ *He has a large estate in the country.* Tiene una finca grande en el campo.

to **estimate** ['ɛstɪmeɪt] VERB
calcular ◊ *They estimated it would take three weeks.* Calcularon que llevaría tres semanas.

etc. [ɛt'setrə] ABBREVIATION (= *et cetera*)
etc.

Ethiopia [i:θi'oupiə] NOUN
Etiopía FEM

ethnic ['ɛθnɪk] ADJECTIVE
1 étnico ◊ *an ethnic minority* una minoría étnica
- **ethnic cleansing** la limpieza étnica

2 exótico (*restaurant, food*)

e-ticket NOUN
el boleto electrónico

EU [i:'ju:] NOUN (= *European Union*)
la UE (= la Unión Europea)

euro ['jurou] NOUN (PL **euros**)
el euro

Europe ['jurəp] NOUN
Europa FEM

European [jurə'pi:ən] ADJECTIVE
see also **European** NOUN
europeo

European [jurə'pi:ən] NOUN
see also **European** ADJECTIVE
el europeo
la europea

to **evacuate** [ɪ'vækjueɪt] VERB
evacuar*

eve [i:v] NOUN
- **Christmas Eve** la Nochebuena
- **New Year's Eve** la Nochevieja

even ['i:vən] ADVERB
see also **even** ADJECTIVE
incluso ◊ *I like all animals, even snakes.* Me gustan todos los animales, incluso las serpientes.
- **not even** ni siquiera ◊ *He didn't even say hello.* Ni siquiera saludó.
- **even if** aunque

Use the subjunctive after ***aunque*** *when translating* ***even if.***

◊ *I'd never do that, even if you asked me.* Nunca haría eso, aunque me lo pidieras.
- **even though** aunque ◊ *He never has any money, even though his parents are quite rich.* Nunca tiene dinero aunque sus padres son bastante ricos.
- **even more** aún más ◊ *I liked Cuenca even more than Quito.* Me gustó Cuenca aún más que Quito.

even ['i:vən] ADJECTIVE
see also **even** ADVERB
uniforme ◊ *an even layer of snow* una capa uniforme de nieve
- **an even surface** una superficie lisa
- **an even number** un número par
- **to get even with somebody** ajustar cuentas con alguien

evening ['i:vnɪŋ] NOUN
1 la tarde (*before dark*)
2 la noche (*after dark*) ◊ *in the evening* en la tarde/noche
- **Good evening!** ¡Buenas tardes/noches!
- **evening class** la clase nocturna

event [ɪ'vɛnt] NOUN
1 el acontecimiento ◊ *It was one of the most important events in his life.* Fue uno de los acontecimientos más importantes de su vida.
- **a sporting event** un acontecimiento deportivo

2 la prueba ◊ *She took part in two events at the last Olympic Games.* Participó en dos pruebas en los últimos Juegos Olímpicos.
- **in the event of** en caso de ◊ *in the event of an accident* en caso de accidente

eventful [ɪ'vɛntful] ADJECTIVE
lleno de incidentes (*race, journey*)

eventually [ɪ'vɛntʃuəli] ADVERB
finalmente

ever ['ɛvər] ADVERB
- **Have you ever been to Portugal?** ¿Has estado alguna vez en Portugal?
- **Have you ever seen her?** ¿La has visto alguna vez?
- **the best I've ever seen** el mejor que he visto
- **I haven't ever done that.** Jamás he hecho eso.

E

◆ **It will become ever more complex.** Se irá haciendo cada vez más complicado.
◆ **for the first time ever** por primera vez
◆ **ever since** desde que ◇ *ever since I met him* desde que lo conozco
◆ **ever since then** desde entonces

every ['ɛvri] ADJECTIVE
cada (FEM cada) ◇ *every pupil* cada alumno ◇ *every time* cada vez
◆ **every day** todos los días
◆ **every now and then** de vez en cuando

everybody ['ɛvri,baːdi] PRONOUN
todo el mundo ◇ *Everybody makes mistakes.* Todo el mundo se equivoca.
◆ **Everybody had a good time.** Todos lo pasaron bien.

everyone ['ɛvriwʌn] PRONOUN
todo el mundo ◇ *Everyone makes mistakes.* Todo el mundo se equivoca.
◆ **Everyone had a good time.** Todos lo pasaron bien.

everything ['ɛvriθɪŋ] PRONOUN
todo ◇ *You've thought of everything!* ¡Has pensado en todo! ◇ *Money isn't everything.* El dinero no lo es todo.

everywhere ['ɛvriwɛr] ADVERB
en todas partes ◇ *I looked everywhere, but I couldn't find it.* Miré en todas partes, pero no lo encontré.
◆ **I see him everywhere I go.** Lo veo dondequiera que vaya.

***dondequiera** has to be followed by a verb in the subjunctive.*

evil ['iːvəl] ADJECTIVE
1 malvado (*person*)
2 maligno (*plan, spirit*)

ex- [ɛks] PREFIX
ex- ◇ *his ex-wife* su ex-esposa

exact [ɪg'zækt] ADJECTIVE
exacto

exactly [ɪg'zæktli] ADVERB
exactamente ◇ *exactly the same* exactamente igual
◆ **It's exactly 10 o'clock.** Son las 10 en punto.

to **exaggerate** [ɪg'zædʒəreɪt] VERB
exagerar

exaggeration [ɪg,zædʒə'reɪʃən] NOUN
la exageración (PL las exageraciones)

exam [ɪg'zæm] NOUN
el examen (PL los exámenes) ◇ *a French exam* un examen de francés ◇ *the exam results* los resultados de los exámenes

examination [ɪgzæmə'neɪʃən] NOUN
el examen (PL los exámenes)

to **examine** [ɪg'zæmɪn] VERB
examinar ◇ *He examined her passport.* Le examinó el pasaporte. ◇ *The doctor examined him.* El médico lo examinó.

examiner [ɪg'zæmɪnər] NOUN
el examinador
la examinadora

example [ɪg'zæmpəl] NOUN
el ejemplo ◇ *for example* por ejemplo

excavator ['ɛkskəveɪtər] NOUN
la excavadora

excellent ['ɛksələnt] ADJECTIVE
excelente

except [ɪk'sɛpt] PREPOSITION
excepto ◇ *everyone except me* todos excepto yo
◆ **except for** excepto
◆ **except that** salvo que ◇ *The weather was great, except that it was a bit cold.* El tiempo estuvo estupendo, salvo que hizo un poco de frío.

***salvo que** may be followed by a verb in subjunctive.*

exception [ɪk'sɛpʃən] NOUN
la excepción (PL las excepciones) ◇ *to make an exception* hacer* una excepción

exceptional [ɪk'sɛpʃənl] ADJECTIVE
excepcional

excess baggage ['ɛksɛs'bægɪdʒ] NOUN
el exceso de equipaje

to **exchange** [ɪks'tʃeɪndʒ] VERB
see also **exchange** NOUN
cambiar ◇ *I exchanged the book for a CD.* Cambié el libro por un CD.

exchange [ɪks'tʃeɪndʒ] NOUN
see also **exchange** VERB
el intercambio ◇ *I'd like to do an exchange with a Spanish student.* Me gustaría hacer un intercambio con un estudiante español.
◆ **in exchange for** a cambio de

exchange rate [ɪks'tʃeɪndʒ,reɪt] NOUN
la tasa de cambio

excited [ɪk'saɪtɪd] ADJECTIVE
entusiasmado

exciting [ɪk'saɪtɪŋ] ADJECTIVE
emocionante

exclamation point [,ɛksklə'meɪʃən,pɔɪnt] NOUN
el signo de admiración (PL los signos de admiración)

excuse [ɪks'kjuːs] NOUN
see also **excuse** VERB
la excusa

to **excuse** [ɪks'kjuːz] VERB
see also **excuse** NOUN
◆ **Excuse me! (1)** (*to attract attention, apologize*) ¡Perdón!
◆ **Excuse me! (2)** (*when you want to get past*) ¡Con permiso!

to **execute** ['ɛksɪkjuːt] VERB
ejecutar

execution [,ɛksɪ'kjuːʃən] NOUN
la ejecución (PL las ejecuciones)

executive [ɪg'zɛkjətɪv] NOUN
el ejecutivo
la ejecutiva

◇ *He's an executive.* Es ejecutivo.

exercise ['ɛksərsaɪz] NOUN
el ejercicio ◇ *page ten, exercise three* página diez, ejercicio tres ◇ *to take some exercise* hacer* un poco de ejercicio
◆ **an exercise bike** una bicicleta estática

exhaust [ɪg'zɑːst] NOUN
1 el tubo de escape (*pipe*)
2 los gases del tubo de escape (*fumes*)

exhausted [ɪg'zɑːstɪd] ADJECTIVE
agotado

exhaust fumes [ɪg'zɑːstfjuːmz] PL NOUN
los gases del tubo de escape

exhaust pipe [ɪg'zɑːst,paɪp] NOUN
el tubo de escape

exhibition [ɛksɪ'bɪʃən] NOUN
la exposición (PL las exposiciones)

to **exist** [ɪg'zɪst] VERB
existir

exit ['ɛgzɪt] NOUN
la salida

Be careful not to translate ***exit*** *by* ***éxito.***

exorbitant [ɪg'zɔːrbɪtənt] ADJECTIVE
exorbitante

exotic [ɪg'zɑːtɪk] ADJECTIVE
exótico

to **expect** [ɪks'pɛkt] VERB
1 esperar ◇ *I'm expecting him for dinner.* Lo espero para cenar. ◇ *She's expecting a baby.* Está esperando un bebé. ◇ *I didn't expect that from him.* No me esperaba eso de él.
2 imaginarse ◇ *I expect he'll be late.* Me imagino que llegará tarde.
◆ **I expect so.** Me imagino que sí.

expedition [ɛkspə'dɪʃən] NOUN
la expedición (PL las expediciones)

to **expel** [ɪks'pɛl] VERB
◆ **to get expelled** ser* expulsado (*from school*)

expenses [ɪks'pɛnsɪz] PL NOUN
los gastos

expensive [ɪks'pɛnsɪv] ADJECTIVE
caro

experience [ɪks'pɪriəns] NOUN
la experiencia

experienced [ɪks'pɪriənst] ADJECTIVE
◆ **an experienced teacher** un maestro con experiencia
◆ **She's very experienced in looking after children.** Tiene mucha experiencia en cuidar niños.

experiment [ɪks'pɛrɪmənt] NOUN
el experimento

expert ['ɛkspɜːrt] NOUN
see also **expert** ADJECTIVE
el experto
la experta
◇ *He's a computer expert.* Es un experto en computación.

expert ['ɛkspɜːrt] ADJECTIVE
see also **expert** NOUN
experto ◇ *He's an expert cook.* Es un experto cocinero.

expiration date [ɛkspə'reɪʃən,deɪt] NOUN
la fecha de caducidad

to **expire** [ɪks'paɪər] VERB
caducar* ◇ *My passport has expired.* Mi pasaporte ha caducado.

to **explain** [ɪks'pleɪn] VERB
explicar*

explanation [ɛksplə'neɪʃən] NOUN
la explicación (PL las explicaciones)

to **explode** [ɪks'ploud] VERB
estallar

to **exploit** [ɪks'plɔɪt] VERB
explotar

exploitation [,ɛksplɔɪ'teɪʃən] NOUN
la explotación

to **explore** [ɪks'plɔːr] VERB
explorar (*place*)

explorer [ɪks'plɔːrər] NOUN
el explorador
la exploradora

explosion [ɪks'plouʒən] NOUN
la explosión (PL las explosiones)

explosive [ɪks'plousɪv] ADJECTIVE
see also **explosive** NOUN
explosivo

explosive [ɪks'plousɪv] NOUN
see also **explosive** ADJECTIVE
el explosivo

to **express** [ɪks'prɛs] VERB
expresar
◆ **to express oneself** expresarse ◇ *It's not easy to express oneself in a foreign language.* No es fácil expresarse en un idioma extranjero.

expression [ɪks'prɛʃən] NOUN
la expresión (PL las expresiones) ◇ *It's an English expression.* Es una expresión inglesa.

expressway [ɪks'prɛsweɪ] NOUN
la autopista

extension [ɪks'tɛnʃən] NOUN
1 la ampliación (PL las ampliaciones) (*of building*)
2 la extensión (PL las extensiones) (*telephone*) ◇ *Extension 3137, please.* Con la extensión tres uno tres siete, por favor.

extensive [ɪks'tɛnsɪv] ADJECTIVE
1 extenso ◇ *The hotel is situated in extensive grounds.* El hotel está situado en medio de extensos jardines.
2 amplio ◇ *My brother has an extensive knowledge of this subject.* Mi hermano tiene amplio conocimiento sobre esta materia.
◆ **extensive damage** daños de consideración

extent [ɪks'tɛnt] NOUN
◆ **to some extent** hasta cierto punto

exterior [ɛks'tɪriər] ADJECTIVE
exterior

extinct [ɪks'tɪŋkt] ADJECTIVE

E

extinto ◇ *to be extinct* estar* extinto ◇ *Dinosaurs are extinct.* Los dinosaurios están extintos.
◆ **to become extinct** extinguirse*

extinguisher [ɪks'tɪŋgwɪʃər] NOUN
el extinguidor

extortionate [ɪks'tɔːrʃənɪt] ADJECTIVE
exorbitante

extra ['ɛkstrə] ADJECTIVE, ADVERB
◆ **He gave me an extra hour.** Me dio una hora más.
◆ **to pay extra** pagar* un suplemento
◆ **Breakfast is extra.** El desayuno no está incluido.
◆ **Be extra careful!** ¡Ten muchísimo cuidado!

extraordinary [ɪks'trɔːrdn,ɛri] ADJECTIVE
extraordinario

extravagant [ɪks'trævəgənt] ADJECTIVE
derrochador (FEM derrochadora) (*person*)

extreme [ɪks'triːm] ADJECTIVE
extremo
◆ **with extreme caution** con sumo cuidado

extremely [ɪks'triːmli] ADVERB
sumamente

extremist [ɪks'triːmɪst] NOUN
el/la extremista

eye [aɪ] NOUN
el ojo ◇ *I have green eyes.* Tengo los ojos verdes.
◆ **to keep an eye on something** vigilar algo

eyebrow ['aɪbrau] NOUN
la ceja

eyelash ['aɪlæʃ] NOUN (PL **eyelashes**)
la pestaña

eyelid ['aɪlɪd] NOUN
el párpado

eyeliner ['aɪ,laɪnər] NOUN
el delineador

eye shadow ['aɪ,ʃædou] NOUN
la sombra de ojos

eyesight ['aɪsaɪt] NOUN
la vista ◇ *to have good eyesight* tener* buena vista

F

fabric ['fæbrɪk] NOUN
la tela
*Be careful not to translate **fabric** by **fábrica**.*
fabulous ['fæbjələs] ADJECTIVE
fabuloso
face [feɪs] NOUN
see also **face** VERB
1 la cara ◇ *He was red in the face.* Tenía la cara colorada. ◇ *the north face of the mountain* la cara norte de la montaña
2 la esfera (*of clock*)
◆ **on the face of it** a primera vista
◆ **in the face of these difficulties** en vista de estas dificultades
◆ **face to face** cara a cara
to **face** [feɪs] VERB
see also **face** NOUN
1 estar* frente a ◇ *They stood facing each other.* Estaban de pie el uno frente al otro.
◆ **The garden faces south.** El jardín da al sur.
2 enfrentarse a ◇ *They face serious problems.* Se enfrentan a graves problemas.
◆ **Let's face it, we're lost.** Tenemos que admitirlo, estamos perdidos.
to **face up to** [feɪs'ʌptuː] VERB
afrontar ◇ *He refuses to face up to his responsibilities.* Se niega a afrontar sus responsabilidades.
facilities [fə'sɪlɪtiz] PL NOUN
las instalaciones ◇ *This school has excellent facilities.* Esta escuela tiene unas instalaciones magníficas.
◆ **The youth hostel has cooking facilities.** El albergue juvenil dispone de cocina.
fact [fækt] NOUN
◆ **the fact that...** el hecho de que...
*Use the subjunctive after **el hecho de que**.*
◇ *The fact that you are very busy is of no interest to me.* El hecho de que estés muy ocupado no me interesa.
◆ **facts and figures** datos y cifras
◆ **in fact** de hecho
factory ['fæktəri] NOUN (PL **factories**)
la fábrica
faculty ['fækəlti] NOUN (PL **faculties**)
el profesorado (*teaching staff*)
to **fade** [feɪd] VERB
1 desteñirse* ◇ *My jeans have faded.* Se me han desteñido los jeans.
2 apagarse* ◇ *The light was fading fast.* La luz se apagaba con rapidez. ◇ *The noise gradually faded.* El ruido se fue apagando.
to **fail** [feɪl] VERB
see also **fail** NOUN
1 ser* reprobado
reprobar *Mexico*
◇ *He failed his driving test.* Fue reprobado en el examen de manejar. *Mexico*: Reprobó el examen de manejar.
2 fallar ◇ *The truck's brakes failed.* Al camión le fallaron los frenos.
3 fracasar ◇ *The plan failed.* El plan fracasó.
◆ **to fail to do something** no lograr hacer algo ◇ *They failed to reach the quarter finals.* No lograron llegar a los cuartos de final.
◆ **The bomb failed to explode.** La bomba no llegó a estallar.
fail [feɪl] NOUN
see also **fail** VERB
el reprobado ◇ *D is a pass, E is a fail.* D es un aprobado, E es un reprobado.
◆ **without fail** sin falta
failure ['feɪljər] NOUN
1 el fracaso ◇ *The attempt was a complete failure.* El intento fue un completo fracaso.
2 la falla ◇ *a mechanical failure* una falla mecánica
◆ **I feel like a failure.** Me siento un fracasado.
faint [feɪnt] ADJECTIVE
see also **faint** VERB
débil ◇ *His voice was very faint.* Tenía la voz muy débil.
◆ **to feel faint** sentirse* mareado
to **faint** [feɪnt] VERB
see also **faint** ADJECTIVE
desmayarse
fair [fɛr] ADJECTIVE
see also **fair** NOUN
1 justo ◇ *That's not fair.* Eso no es justo.
◆ **I paid more than my fair share.** Pagué más de lo que me correspondía.
2 rubio
güero *Mexico*
◇ *He has fair hair.* Tiene el pelo rubio. *Mexico*: Tiene [el] pelo güero.
3 blanco ◇ *people with fair skin* la gente con la piel blanca
4 considerable ◇ *That's a fair distance.* Esa es una distancia considerable.
◆ **I have a fair chance of winning.** Tengo bastantes posibilidades de ganar.
5 bueno (*weather*) ◇ *The weather was fair.* El tiempo era bueno.
*Use **buen** before a masculine singular noun.*
fair [fɛr] NOUN
see also **fair** ADJECTIVE
la feria (*market*) ◇ *a book fair* una feria del libro
◆ **a trade fair** una exposición industrial
fair-haired ['fɛr,hɛrd] ADJECTIVE
rubio
güero *Mexico*
fairly ['fɛrli] ADVERB
1 equitativamente ◇ *The cake was divided fairly.* La tarta se repartió equitativamente.
2 bastante ◇ *My car is fairly new.* Mi coche es bastante nuevo. ◇ *The weather was fairly good.* El tiempo estuvo bastante bueno.
fairy ['fɛri] NOUN (PL **fairies**)

la hada

fairy tale [ˈfɛriˌteɪl] NOUN
el cuento de hadas

faith [feɪθ] NOUN
1 la confianza ◇ *People have lost faith in the government.* La gente ha perdido la confianza en el gobierno.
2 la fe ◇ *the Catholic faith* la fe católica

faithful [ˈfeɪθful] ADJECTIVE
fiel

faithfully [ˈfeɪθfəli] ADVERB
◆ **Yours faithfully...** (*in letter*) Lo saluda atentamente...

fake [feɪk] NOUN
see also **fake** ADJECTIVE
la falsificación (PL las falsificaciones) ◇ *The painting was a fake.* El cuadro era una falsificación.

fake [feɪk] ADJECTIVE
see also **fake** NOUN
falso ◇ *a fake $20 bill* un billete de 20 dólares falso
◆ **a fake fur coat** un abrigo de piel sintética

fall [fɑːl] NOUN
see also **fall** VERB
1 el otoño (*autumn*) ◇ *in fall* en el otoño
2 la caída ◇ *She had a nasty fall.* Tuvo una mala caída.
◆ **a fall of snow** una nevada
◆ **Niagara Falls** las cataratas del Niágara

to **fall** [fɑːl] VERB (**fell, fallen**)
see also **fall** NOUN
1 caer* ◇ *Bombs fell on the town.* Las bombas caían sobre la ciudad.
When the action of falling is not deliberate, use ***caerse.***
◇ *He tripped and fell.* Tropezó y se cayó.
◇ *The book fell off the shelf.* El libro se cayó del estante.
◆ **to fall in love with someone** enamorarse de alguien
2 bajar ◇ *Prices are falling.* Están bajando los precios.

to **fall apart** [ˈfɑːləˈpɑːrt] VERB
romperse* ◇ *The book fell apart when he opened it.* El libro se rompió cuando lo abrió.

to **fall down** [ˈfɑːlˈdaun] VERB
caerse* ◇ *She's fallen down.* Se cayó.
◇ *The house is slowly falling down.* La casa se está cayendo poco a poco.

to **fall for** [ˈfɑːlˌfɔːr] VERB
1 tragarse* ◇ *They fell for it!* ¡Se lo tragaron!
2 enamorarse de ◇ *She fell for him immediately.* Se enamoró de él en el acto.

to **fall out** [ˈfɑːlˈaut] VERB
pelarse ◇ *Sarah has fallen out with her boyfriend.* Sarah se peleó con el novio.

to **fall through** [ˈfɑːlˈθruː] VERB
fracasar ◇ *Our plans have fallen through.* Nuestros planes han fracasado.

false [fɑːls] ADJECTIVE
falso ◇ *a false alarm* una falsa alarma
◆ **false teeth** la dentadura postiza

fame [feɪm] NOUN
la fama

familiar [fəˈmɪljər] ADJECTIVE
familiar ◇ *The name sounded familiar to me.* El nombre me sonaba familiar.
◆ **a familiar face** un rostro conocido
◆ **to be familiar with something** conocer* bien algo ◇ *I'm familiar with his work.* Conozco bien su obra.

family [ˈfæmɪli] NOUN (PL **families**)
la familia ◇ *the Cooke family* la familia Cooke

famine [ˈfæmɪn] NOUN
la hambruna

famous [ˈfeɪməs] ADJECTIVE
famoso

fan [fæn] NOUN
1 el/la hincha ◇ *the team's fans* los hinchas del equipo
2 el/la fan (PL los/las fans) ◇ *the Will Smith fan club* el club de fans de Will Smith
◆ **I'm one of his greatest fans.** Soy uno de sus mayores admiradores.
3 el aficionado
la aficionada
◇ *a rap music fan* un aficionado al rap
4 el abanico ◇ *a silk fan* un abanico de seda
◆ **an electric fan** un ventilador

fanatic [fəˈnætɪk] NOUN
el fanático
la fanática

fancy dress [ˌfænsiˈdrɛs] NOUN
el disfraz (PL los disfraces)

fanny pack [ˈfæniˌpæk] NOUN
la riñonera

fantastic [fænˈtæstɪk] ADJECTIVE
fantástico

far [fɑːr] ADJECTIVE, ADVERB
lejos ◇ *Is it far?* ¿Está lejos? ◇ *It's not far from San Diego.* No está lejos de San Diego.
◆ **How far is it to Madrid?** ¿A qué distancia está Madrid?
◆ **It's far from easy.** No es nada fácil.
◆ **How far have you gotten?** ¿Hasta dónde has llegado?
◆ **at the far end of the swimming pool** al otro extremo de la piscina
◆ **far better** mucho mejor
◆ **as far as I know** por lo que yo sé
◆ **so far** hasta ahora

fare [fɛr] NOUN
la tarifa ◇ *Train fares are very high in this country.* Las tarifas de tren son muy altas en este país. ◇ *The air fare was very reasonable.* La tarifa del vuelo fue bastante razonable.

- **He didn't have the bus fare, so he had to walk.** No tenía dinero para el bus, así que tuvo que ir andando.
- **full fare** el precio del pasaje completo
- **Children pay half fare on the train.** Los niños pagan la mitad en el tren.

Far East [ˈfɑːrˈiːst] NOUN
- **the Far East** el Extremo Oriente

farm [fɑːrm] NOUN
la granja

farmer [ˈfɑːrmər] NOUN
el granjero
la granjera
◇ *He's a farmer.* Es granjero.

farmhouse [ˈfɑːrmhaus] NOUN
la casa de granjero

farming [ˈfɑːrmɪŋ] NOUN
la agricultura ◇ *organic farming* agricultura biológica
- **dairy farming** la ganadería (*especializada en la producción de leche*)

fascinating [ˈfæsɪneɪtɪŋ] ADJECTIVE
fascinante

fashion [ˈfæʃən] NOUN
la moda
- **to be in fashion** estar* de moda
- **to go out of fashion** pasar de moda

fashionable [ˈfæʃənəbəl] ADJECTIVE
de moda MASC, FEM, PL ◇ *That color is very fashionable.* Ese color está muy de moda.
- **Jane wears fashionable clothes.** Jane viste a la moda.

fast [fæst] ADJECTIVE, ADVERB
rápido ◇ *a fast car* un carro rápido ◇ *They work very fast.* Trabajan muy rápido.
- **That clock is fast.** Ese reloj va adelantado.
- **He's fast asleep.** Está profundamente dormido.

fat [fæt] ADJECTIVE
see also **fat** NOUN
gordo ◇ *She thinks she's too fat.* Piensa que es demasiado gorda.

fat [fæt] NOUN
see also **fat** ADJECTIVE
1 la grasa (*on meat, in food*) ◇ *It's very high in fat.* Es muy rico en grasas.
2 la manteca (*used for cooking*)

fatal [ˈfeɪtl] ADJECTIVE
1 mortal ◇ *a fatal accident* un accidente mortal
2 fatal ◇ *a fatal mistake* un error fatal

father [ˈfɑːðər] NOUN
el padre
- **my father and mother** mis padres

father-in-law [ˈfɑːðərɪnlɑː] NOUN (PL **fathers-in-law**)
el suegro

faucet [ˈfɑːsɪt] NOUN
la llave ◇ *the hot water faucet* la llave de agua caliente

fault [fɑːlt] NOUN
1 la culpa ◇ *It wasn't my fault.* No fue culpa mía.
2 el defecto ◇ *He has his faults, but I still like him.* Tiene sus defectos, pero aun así me gusta.
- **a mechanical fault** una falla mecánica

faulty [ˈfɑːlti] ADJECTIVE
defectuoso

fava bean [ˈfɑːvəˌbiːn] NOUN
el haba FEM
*Although it's a feminine noun, remember that you use **el** and **un** with **haba**.*

favor [ˈfeɪvər] NOUN
el favor ◇ *Could you do me a favor?* ¿Me harías un favor?
- **to be in favor of something** estar* a favor de algo

favorite [ˈfeɪvrɪt] ADJECTIVE
see also **favorite** NOUN
favorito ◇ *Blue's my favorite color.* El azul es mi color favorito.

favorite [ˈfeɪvrɪt] NOUN
see also **favorite** ADJECTIVE
el favorito
la favorita
◇ *The Miami Dolphins are the favorites to win the Super Bowl.* Los Miami Dolphins son los favoritos para ganar la SuperCopa.

fawn [fɑːn] ADJECTIVE
beige MASC, FEM, PL (*color*)

fawn [fɑːn] NOUN
el cervato (*young deer*)

fax [fæks] NOUN (PL **faxes**)
see also **fax** VERB
el fax (PL los faxes)

to **fax** [fæks] VERB
see also **fax** NOUN
mandar por fax ◇ *I'll fax you the details.* Te mandaré la información por fax.

fear [fɪər] NOUN
see also **fear** VERB
el miedo

to **fear** [fɪər] VERB
see also **fear** NOUN
temer ◇ *You have nothing to fear.* No tienes nada que temer.

feather [ˈfɛðər] NOUN
la pluma

feature [ˈfiːtʃər] NOUN
la característica ◇ *an important feature* una característica importante

February [ˈfɛbruɛri] NOUN
febrero MASC ◇ *in February* en febrero ◇ *on February 18th* el 18 de febrero

fed [fɛd] VERB *see* **feed**

fed up [fɛdˈʌp] ADJECTIVE
- **to be fed up with something** estar* harto de algo

to **feed** [fiːd] VERB (**fed, fed**)
dar* de comer a ◇ *Have you fed the cat?* ¿Le diste de comer al gato? ◇ *He worked hard to* ☞

F

feed his family. Trabajaba mucho para dar de comer a su familia.

to **feel** [fi:l] VERB (**felt, felt**)

1 sentir* ◇ *I didn't feel much pain.* No sentí mucho dolor.

2 sentirse* ◇ *I don't feel well.* No me siento bien. ◇ *I felt lonely.* Me sentía solo.

◆ **I was feeling hungry.** Tenía hambre.

◆ **I was feeling cold, so I went inside.** Tenía frío, así que entré.

3 tocar* ◇ *The doctor felt his forehead.* El médico le tocó la frente.

◆ **to feel like doing something** tener* ganas de hacer algo ◇ *I don't feel like going out tonight.* No tengo ganas de salir esta noche.

◆ **Do you feel like an ice cream cone?** ¿Tienes ganas de tomar un helado?, *Mexico*: ¿Apeteces un helado?

feeling ['fi:lɪŋ] NOUN

1 la sensación (PL las sensaciones) ◇ *a burning feeling* una sensación de escozor

2 el sentimiento ◇ *He was afraid of hurting my feelings.* Tenía miedo de herir mis sentimientos.

◆ **What are your feelings about it?** ¿Tú qué opinas de ello?

feet [fi:t] PL NOUN *see* **foot**

fell [fɛl] VERB *see* **fall**

fellow ['fɛlou] ADJECTIVE

◆ **fellow students** los compañeros de clase

◆ **fellow workers** los compañeros de trabajo

felt [fɛlt] VERB *see* **feel**

felt-tip pen ['fɛlttɪp'pɛn] NOUN

el rotulador

female ['fi:meɪl] ADJECTIVE

see also **female** NOUN

1 hembra MASC, FEM, PL ◇ *a female bat* un murciélago hembra

2 femenino ◇ *the female sex* el sexo femenino

female ['fi:meɪl] NOUN

see also **female** ADJECTIVE

la hembra (*animal*)

feminine ['fɛmɪnɪn] ADJECTIVE

femenino

feminist ['fɛmɪnɪst] NOUN

el/la feminista

fence [fɛns] NOUN

la valla

la barda *Mexico*

fender ['fɛndər] NOUN

el parachoques (PL los parachoques)

fern [fɜ:rn] NOUN

el helecho

ferocious [fə'rouʃəs] ADJECTIVE

feroz (PL feroces)

ferry ['fɛri] NOUN (PL **ferries**)

el ferry (PL los ferrys)

fertile ['fɜ:rtl] ADJECTIVE

fértil

fertilizer ['fɜ:rtlaɪzər] NOUN

el abono

festival ['fɛstɪvəl] NOUN

el festival ◇ *a jazz festival* un festival de jazz

to **fetch** [fɛtʃ] VERB

1 ir* a buscar ◇ *Fetch the dictionary.* Ve a buscar el diccionario.

◆ **to fetch something for someone** traer* algo a alguien ◇ *Fetch me a glass of water.* Tráeme un vaso de agua.

2 venderse por ◇ *His painting fetched $5000.* Su cuadro se vendió por 5.000 dólares.

fever ['fi:vər] NOUN

la fiebre

◆ **fever blister** un fuego

few [fju:] ADJECTIVE, PRONOUN

1 pocos ◇ *He has few friends.* Tiene pocos amigos.

◆ **a few** unos ◇ *She was silent for a few seconds.* Se quedó callada unos segundos.

2 algunos ◇ *a few of them* algunos de ellos

◆ **quite a few people** bastante gente

fewer ['fju:ər] ADJECTIVE

menos ◇ *There were fewer people than yesterday.* Había menos gente que ayer.

fiancé [ˌfi:ɑ:n'seɪ] NOUN

el novio (*prometido*)

fiancée [ˌfi:ɑ:n'seɪ] NOUN

la novia (*prometida*)

fiction ['fɪkʃən] NOUN

la narrativa (*novels*)

field [fi:ld] NOUN

1 el campo ◇ *a field of wheat* un campo de trigo

2 la cancha (*in soccer, baseball*)

◆ **He's an expert in his field.** Es un experto en su campo.

◆ **field hockey** el hockey sobre hierba

field goal ['fi:ldˌgoul] NOUN

1 el gol de campo (*in football*)

2 la canasta de dos puntos (*in basketball*)

fierce [fɪərs] ADJECTIVE

1 feroz (PL feroces)

◆ **a fierce dog** un perro bravo

2 encarnizado ◇ *There's fierce competition between the companies.* Existe una encarnizada competencia entre las empresas.

3 violento ◇ *a fierce attack* un violento ataque

fifteen ['fɪfti:n] NUMERAL

quince ◇ *I'm fifteen.* Tengo quince años.

fifteenth ['fɪfti:nθ] ADJECTIVE

decimoquinto

◆ **the fifteenth floor** el piso catorce

◆ **August fifteenth** el quince de agosto

fifth [fɪfθ] ADJECTIVE

quinto ◇ *the fifth floor* el cuarto piso

◆ **August fifth** el cinco de agosto

fifty [ˈfɪfti] NUMERAL
cincuenta ◇ *He's fifty.* Tiene cincuenta años.

fifty-fifty [ˈfɪftiˈfɪfti] ADJECTIVE, ADVERB
a medias ◇ *They split the prize money fifty-fifty.* Se repartieron a medias el dinero del premio.
◆ **a fifty-fifty chance** un cincuenta por ciento de posibilidades

fight [faɪt] NOUN
see also **fight** VERB
1 la pelea ◇ *There was a fight in the bar.* Hubo una pelea en el bar.
◆ **She had a fight with her best friend.** Se peleó con su mejor amiga.
2 la lucha ◇ *the fight against cancer* la lucha contra el cáncer

to **fight** [faɪt] VERB (**fought, fought**)
see also **fight** NOUN
1 pelearse ◇ *The fans started fighting.* Los hinchas empezaron a pelearse.
2 luchar ◇ *She has fought against racism all her life.* Ha luchado toda su vida contra el racismo. ◇ *The demonstrators fought with the police.* Los manifestantes lucharon con la policía.
◆ **The doctors tried to fight the disease.** Los médicos intentaron combatir la enfermedad.

to **fight back** [faɪtˈbæk] VERB
defenderse*

fighting [ˈfaɪtɪŋ] NOUN
1 la pelea ◇ *Fighting broke out outside the pub.* Se desató una pelea afuera del bar.
2 los combates ◇ *Many people have died in the fighting.* Ha muerto mucha gente en los combates.

figure [ˈfɪgjər] NOUN
1 la cifra ◇ *Can you give me the exact figures?* ¿Me puedes dar las cifras exactas?
2 la silueta ◇ *Helen saw the figure of a man on the bridge.* Helen vio la silueta de un hombre en el puente.
◆ **She has a good figure.** Tiene buen tipo.
◆ **I have to watch my figure.** Tengo que mantener la línea.
3 la figura ◇ *She's an important political figure.* Es una importante figura política.

to **figure out** [ˌfɪgjərˈaut] VERB
1 calcular ◇ *I'll try to figure out how much it'll cost.* Intentaré calcular lo que va a costar.
2 llegar* a comprender ◇ *I couldn't figure out what it meant.* No llegué a comprender lo que significaba.

file [faɪl] NOUN
see also **file** VERB
1 el expediente ◇ *There was stuff in that file that was private.* Había cosas privadas en ese expediente.
◆ **The police have a file on him.** Está fichado por la policía.
2 la carpeta ◇ *She put the photocopy into her file.* Metió la fotocopia en su carpeta.
3 la lima ◇ *a nail file* una lima de uñas
4 el fichero (*on computer*)

to **file** [faɪl] VERB
see also **file** NOUN
1 archivar ◇ *You have to file all these documents.* Tienes que archivar todos estos documentos.
2 limarse ◇ *She was filing her nails.* Se estaba limando las uñas.

to **fill** [fɪl] VERB
llenar ◇ *She filled the glass with water.* Llenó el vaso de agua.

to **fill in** [fɪlˈɪn] VERB
llenar ◇ *He filled the hole in with soil.* Llenó el agujero de tierra.

to **fill out** [fɪlˈaut] VERB
rellenar ◇ *Can you fill out this form, please?* Rellene este impreso, por favor.

to **fill up** [fɪlˈʌp] VERB
llenar ◇ *He filled the cup up to the brim.* Llenó la taza hasta el borde.
◆ **Fill it up, please.** (*at gas station*) Lleno, por favor.

film [fɪlm] NOUN
1 el carrete ◇ *I need a 36 exposure film.* Quería un carrete de 36.
2 la película (*movie*)

filthy [ˈfɪlθi] ADJECTIVE
mugriento

final [ˈfaɪnl] ADJECTIVE
see also **final** NOUN
1 último ◇ *a final attempt* un último intento
2 definitivo ◇ *a final decision* una decisión definitiva
◆ **I'm not going and that's final.** He dicho que no voy y se acabó.

final [ˈfaɪnl] NOUN
see also **final** ADJECTIVE
la final ◇ *Boris Becker is in the final.* Boris Becker ha llegado a la final.

finally [ˈfaɪnəli] ADVERB
1 por último ◇ *Finally, I would like to say thank you to all of you.* Por último me gustaría darles las gracias a todos.
2 al final ◇ *They finally decided to leave on Saturday.* Al final decidieron salir el sábado.

to **find** [faɪnd] VERB (**found, found**)
encontrar* ◇ *I can't find the exit.* No encuentro la salida.

to **find out** [faɪndˈaut] VERB
enterarse de ◇ *I found out what happened.* Me enteré de lo que ocurrió.
◆ **to find out about** enterarse de ◇ *Try to find out about the cost of a hotel.* Intenta enterarte de lo que costaría un hotel. ◇ *Find out as much as possible about the town.* Entérate de todo lo que puedas sobre la ciudad.

fine [faɪn] ADJECTIVE, ADVERB
see also **fine** NOUN
1 estupendo ◇ *He's a fine musician.* Es un ☞

F

músico estupendo.

◆ **How are you? – I'm fine.** ¿Qué tal estás? – Bien.

◆ **I feel fine.** Me siento bien.

◆ **It'll be ready tomorrow. – That's fine, thanks.** Mañana estará listo. – Muy bien, gracias.

◆ **The weather is fine today.** Hoy hace muy buen tiempo.

[2] fino ◇ *She has very fine hair.* Tiene el pelo muy fino.

fine [faɪn] NOUN
see also **fine** ADJECTIVE, ADVERB
la multa ◇ *I got a fine for driving through a red light.* Me pusieron una multa por saltarme un semáforo en rojo.

finger ['fɪŋgər] NOUN
el dedo

◆ **my little finger** el meñique ◇ *I hurt my little finger.* Me lastimé el meñique.

fingernail ['fɪŋgər,neɪl] NOUN
la uña

finish ['fɪnɪʃ] NOUN
see also **finish** VERB
[1] el fin ◇ *from start to finish* de principio a fin
[2] la llegada ◇ *We saw the finish of the Boston Marathon.* Vimos la llegada del maratón de Boston.

to **finish** ['fɪnɪʃ] VERB
see also **finish** NOUN
terminar ◇ *I've finished!* ¡Ya terminé! ◇ *to finish doing something* terminar de hacer algo ◇ *Have you finished eating?* ¿Terminaste de comer?

Finland ['fɪnlənd] NOUN
Finlandia FEM

Finn [fɪn] NOUN
el finlandés (PL los finlandeses)
la finlandesa
◇ *the Finns* los finlandeses

Finnish ['fɪnɪʃ] ADJECTIVE
see also **Finnish** NOUN
finlandés (MASC PL finlandeses, FEM finlandesa)

Finnish ['fɪnɪʃ] NOUN
see also **Finnish** ADJECTIVE
el finlandés (*language*)

fir [fɜːr] NOUN
el abeto

fire ['faɪər] NOUN
see also **fire** VERB
[1] el fuego (*flames*) ◇ *The fire spread quickly.* El fuego se extendió rápidamente.
[2] el incendio (*blaze*) ◇ *The house was destroyed by a fire.* La casa fue destruida por un incendio.
[3] la hoguera ◇ *He made a fire to warm himself up.* Encendió una hoguera para calentarse.
[4] la estufa ◇ *an electric fire* una estufa eléctrica

◆ **to be on fire** estar* ardiendo

to **fire** ['faɪər] VERB
see also **fire** NOUN
disparar ◇ *She fired at him.* Le disparó.

◆ **to fire a gun** disparar

◆ **to fire somebody** despedir* a alguien ◇ *He was fired from his job.* Lo despidieron del trabajo.

fire alarm ['faɪərə'lɑːrm] NOUN
la alarma contra incendios

fire department ['faɪərdɪ,pɑːrtmənt] NOUN
el cuerpo de bomberos

fire escape ['faɪərɪskeɪp] NOUN
la escalera de incendios

fire extinguisher ['faɪərɪk,stɪŋgwɪʃər] NOUN
el extinguidor

firefighter ['faɪər,faɪtər] NOUN
el bombero
la bombera
◇ *She is a firefighter.* Es bombera.

fireman ['faɪərmən] NOUN (PL **firemen**)
el bombero

fireplace ['faɪər,pleɪs] NOUN
la chimenea

fire station ['faɪər,steɪʃən] NOUN
la estación de bomberos

fire truck ['faɪər,trʌk] NOUN
el carro de bomberos

firewoman ['faɪər,wumən] NOUN (PL **firewomen**)
la bombera

fireworks ['faɪər,wɜːrks] PL NOUN
los fuegos artificiales

firm [fɜːrm] ADJECTIVE
see also **firm** NOUN
[1] firme ◇ *to be firm with somebody* mostrarse* firme con alguien
[2] duro ◇ *a firm mattress* un colchón duro

firm [fɜːrm] NOUN
see also **firm** ADJECTIVE
la empresa

first [fɜːrst] ADJECTIVE, NOUN, ADVERB
[1] primero ◇ *for the first time* por primera vez

Use ***primer*** *before a masculine singular noun.*

◇ *my first job* mi primer trabajo ◇ *Rachel came first in the race.* Rachel llegó primera en la carrera. ◇ *She was the first to arrive.* Fue la primera en llegar.

◆ **September first** el primero de septiembre

◆ **at first** al principio

[2] antes ◇ *I want to get a job, but first I have to pass my exams.* Quiero conseguir un trabajo, pero antes tengo que aprobar los exámenes.

◆ **first of all** ante todo

◆ **the first lady** la primera dama

first aid [fɜːrst'eɪd] NOUN
los primeros auxilios

◆ **a first aid kit** un botiquín

first-class [ˈfɜːrstˈklæs] ADJECTIVE
1 de primera clase MASC, FEM, PL ◇ *a first-class ticket* un pasaje de primera clase
2 de primera MASC, FEM, PL ◇ *a first-class meal* una comida de primera
◆ **a first-class stamp** una estampilla para correo urgente, Mexico: un timbre para correo urgente

> ℹ *In Latin America there is no first-class or second-class postage. If you want your mail to arrive fast, you must have it sent express –* **urgente** *– from a post office.*

firstly [ˈfɜːrstli] ADVERB
en primer lugar

first name [ˈfɜːrstˈneɪm] NOUN
el nombre de pila

fish [fɪʃ] NOUN (PL **fish**)
see also **fish** VERB
1 el pez (PL los peces) ◇ *I caught three fish.* Pesqué tres peces.
2 el pescado (*food*) ◇ *I don't like fish.* No me gusta el pescado.
◆ **fish store** la pescadería

to **fish** [fɪʃ] VERB
see also **fish** NOUN
pescar*
◆ **to go fishing** ir* a pescar

fisherman [ˈfɪʃərmən] NOUN (PL **fishermen**)
el pescador ◇ *He's a fisherman.* Es pescador.

fishing [ˈfɪʃɪŋ] NOUN
la pesca ◇ *I enjoy fishing.* Me gusta la pesca.
◆ **a fishing boat** un barco pesquero
◆ **fishing rod** la caña de pescar

fishing tackle [ˈfɪʃɪŋˌtækəl] NOUN
los aparejos de pesca

fish market [ˈfɪʃˌmɑːrkɪt] NOUN
la pescadería

fish sticks [ˈfɪʃˌstɪks] PL NOUN
los palitos de pescado

fist [fɪst] NOUN
el puño

fit [fɪt] ADJECTIVE
see also **fit** VERB, NOUN
en forma ◇ *He felt relaxed and fit after his vacation.* Se sentía relajado y en forma tras las vacaciones.
◆ **Will he be fit to play next Saturday?** ¿Estará en condiciones de jugar el próximo sábado?

fit [fɪt] NOUN
see also **fit** ADJECTIVE, VERB
◆ **to have a fit (1)** sufrir un ataque de epilepsia (*epileptic*)
◆ **to have a fit (2)** (*be angry*) ponerse* hecho una furia ◇ *She will have a fit when she sees the carpet!* ¡Se va a poner hecha una furia cuando vea la alfombra!

to **fit** [fɪt] VERB
see also **fit** ADJECTIVE, NOUN
1 caber* (*go into a space*) ◇ *It's small enough to fit into your pocket.* Es lo bastante pequeño como para caber en el bolsillo.
2 encajar ◇ *Make sure the cork fits well into the bottle.* Asegúrese de que el corcho encaje bien en la botella.
3 instalar (*install*) ◇ *He fitted an alarm in his car.* Instaló una alarma en el carro.
4 poner* (*attach*) ◇ *She fitted a plug to the hair dryer.* Le puso un enchufe al secador.
◆ **to fit somebody** quedar bien a alguien ◇ *These pants don't fit me.* Estos pantalones no me quedan bien.
◆ **Does it fit?** ¿Te queda bien?

to **fit in** [fɪtˈɪn] VERB
1 encajar ◇ *That story doesn't fit in with what he told us.* Esa historia no encaja con lo que él nos contó.
2 adaptarse ◇ *She fitted in well at her new school.* Se adaptó bien al nuevo colegio.

fitted carpet [fɪtɪdˈkɑːrpɪt] NOUN
la alfombra (*de pared a pared*)

five [faɪv] NUMERAL
cinco ◇ *He's five.* Tiene cinco años.

to **fix** [fɪks] VERB
1 arreglar ◇ *Can you fix my bike?* ¿Me puedes arreglar la bici?
2 fijar ◇ *Let's fix a date for the party.* Fijemos una fecha para la fiesta.

fixed [fɪkst] ADJECTIVE
fijo ◇ *at a fixed time* a una hora fija ◇ *My parents have very fixed ideas.* Mis papás son de ideas fijas.

fizzy [ˈfɪzi] ADJECTIVE
gaseoso

flabby [ˈflæbi] ADJECTIVE
fofo

flag [flæg] NOUN
la bandera

flame [fleɪm] NOUN
la llama
la flama Mexico

flamingo [fləˈmɪŋgou] NOUN (PL **flamingos** *or* **flamingoes**)
el flamenco (*pájaro*)

flan [flɑːn] NOUN
la tarta (*dessert*)

flannel [ˈflænəl] NOUN
la franela (*fabric*)

to **flap** [flæp] VERB
◆ **The bird flapped its wings.** El pájaro batió las alas.

flash [flæʃ] NOUN (PL **flashes**)
see also **flash** VERB
el flash (*of camera*)
◆ **a flash of lightning** un relámpago
◆ **in a flash** en un abrir y cerrar de ojos

to **flash** [flæʃ] VERB
see also **flash** NOUN
◆ **A truck driver flashed his lights at him.** Un ☞

F

camionero le hizo una señal con las luces.

flashlight ['flæʃlaɪt] NOUN
la linterna (*electric*)

flask [flæsk] NOUN
el termo (*vacuum flask*)

flat [flæt] NOUN
see also **flat** ADJECTIVE
el pinchazo
la ponchadura Mexico
◇ *After I got back on the road, I developed a flat.* Al volver a la carretera, tuve un pinchazo. Mexico: Al volver a la carretera, tuve una ponchadura.

flat [flæt] ADJECTIVE
see also **flat** NOUN
plano ◇ *a flat surface* una superficie plana
◆ **flat shoes** zapatos bajos, Mexico: zapatos de piso
◆ **I have a flat tire.** Tengo una rueda desinflada.

flattered ['flætərd] ADJECTIVE
halagado

flatware ['flætwɛr] NOUN
la cubertería

flavor ['fleɪvər] NOUN
el sabor (PL los sabores) ◇ *a very strong flavor* un sabor muy fuerte ◇ *Which flavor of ice cream would you like?* ¿De qué sabor quieres el helado?

flavoring ['fleɪvərɪŋ] NOUN
el condimento

flew [flu:] VERB *see* **fly**

flexible ['flɛksəbəl] ADJECTIVE
flexible ◇ *flexible working hours* un horario de trabajo flexible

to **flick** [flɪk] VERB
◆ **She flicked the switch to turn the light on.** Le dio al interruptor para encender la luz.

to **flicker** ['flɪkər] VERB
parpadear (*light*)

flight [flaɪt] NOUN
el vuelo ◇ *What time is the flight to Paris?* ¿A qué hora es el vuelo para París?
◆ **a flight of stairs** un tramo de escaleras

flight attendant ['flaɪtə'tɛndənt] NOUN
el/la auxiliar de vuelo

to **fling** [flɪŋ] VERB (**flung, flung**)
arrojar
aventar Mexico
(*stone, ball*)
◇ *He flung the dictionary onto the floor.* Arrojó el diccionario al suelo.

to **float** [flout] VERB
flotar

flock [flɑ:k] NOUN
◆ **a flock of sheep** un rebaño de ovejas
◆ **a flock of birds** una bandada de pájaros

flood [flʌd] NOUN
see also **flood** VERB
la inundación (PL las inundaciones) ◇ *The rain has caused many floods.* La lluvia ha provocado muchas inundaciones.
◆ **He received a flood of letters.** Recibió un aluvión de cartas.

to **flood** [flʌd] VERB
see also **flood** NOUN
inundar ◇ *The river has flooded the village.* El río ha inundado el pueblo.

flooding ['flʌdɪŋ] NOUN
la inundación

floor [flɔ:r] NOUN
1 el suelo ◇ *a tiled floor* un suelo embaldosado
◆ **the dance floor** la pista de baile
2 la planta ◇ *the first floor* la planta baja ◇ *on the first floor* en la planta baja
Note that floors are numbered differently in Latin America. The first floor is called 'la planta baja', the second floor is 'el primer piso', the third floor is 'el segundo piso' etc.

flop [flɑ:p] NOUN
el fracaso ◇ *The movie was a flop.* La película fue un fracaso.

floppy disk ['flɑ:pi'dɪsk] NOUN
el disquete

florist ['flɑ:rɪst] NOUN
el/la florista

flour ['flauər] NOUN
la harina

to **flow** [flou] VERB
fluir* ◇ *The river flows through the valley.* El río fluye por el valle. ◇ *Traffic is now flowing normally.* El tráfico ya fluye con normalidad.
◆ **Water was flowing from the pipe.** El agua brotaba de la cañería.

flower ['flauər] NOUN
see also **flower** VERB
la flor

to **flower** ['flauər] VERB
see also **flower** NOUN
florecer*

flower pot ['flauər,pɑ:t] NOUN
la maceta

flown [floun] VERB *see* **fly**

flu [flu:] NOUN
la gripe
la gripa Mexico
◇ *I have the flu.* Tengo gripe. Mexico: Tengo gripa.

fluent ['flu:ənt] ADJECTIVE
◆ **He speaks fluent Spanish.** Habla español con fluidez.

flung [flʌŋ] VERB *see* **fling**

to **flush** [flʌʃ] VERB
◆ **to flush the toilet** tirar de la cadena

flute [flu:t] NOUN
la flauta

fly [flaɪ] NOUN (PL **flies**)
see also **fly** VERB
la mosca

to **fly** [flaɪ] VERB (**flew, flown**)

see also **fly** NOUN
volar* ◇ *He flew from Houston to Lima.* Voló de Houston a Lima.
◆ **The bird flew away.** El pájaro salió volando.

foal [foul] NOUN
el potro

focus ['foukəs] NOUN (PL **foci**)
see also **focus** VERB
el centro ◇ *He was the focus of attention.* Era el centro de atención.
◆ **to be out of focus** estar* desenfocado

to **focus** ['foukəs] VERB
see also **focus** NOUN
enfocar* ◇ *Try to focus the binoculars.* Intenta enfocar los prismáticos.
◆ **to focus on something (1)** enfocar* algo (*with camera, telescope*) ◇ *The cameraman focused on the bird.* El cámara enfocó al pájaro.
◆ **to focus on something (2)** centrarse en algo (*concentrate on*)

fog [fɑːg] NOUN
la niebla

foggy ['fɑːgi] ADJECTIVE
◆ **It's foggy.** Hay niebla.
◆ **a foggy day** un día de niebla

fold [fould] NOUN
see also **fold** VERB
el pliegue

to **fold** [fould] VERB
see also **fold** NOUN
doblar ◇ *He folded the newspaper in half.* Dobló el periódico por la mitad.
◆ **to fold one's arms** cruzarse* de brazos

to **fold up** [fould'ʌp] VERB
plegar* ◇ *She folded the chair up and walked off.* Plegó la silla y se marchó.

folder ['fouldər] NOUN
la carpeta

folding ['fouldɪŋ] ADJECTIVE
plegable (*bed, chair*)

to **follow** ['fɑːlou] VERB
seguir* ◇ *You go first and I'll follow.* Ve tú primero y yo te sigo. ◇ *He followed my advice.* Siguió mi consejo.

following ['fɑːlouɪŋ] ADJECTIVE
siguiente ◇ *the following day* al día siguiente

fond [fɑːnd] ADJECTIVE
◆ **to be fond of somebody** tener* cariño a alguien ◇ *I'm very fond of her.* Le tengo mucho cariño.

food [fuːd] NOUN
la comida ◇ *cat food* comida para gatos ◇ *We need to buy some food.* Hay que comprar comida.

food processor ['fuːd,prɑːsesər] NOUN
el robot de cocina (PL los robots de cocina)

fool [fuːl] NOUN
el/la idiota
el tonto
la tonta

foot [fut] NOUN (PL **feet**)
1 el pie (*of person*) ◇ *My feet are aching.* Me duelen los pies.
◆ **on foot** a pie

> ℹ *In Latin America measurements are in meters and centimeters rather than feet and inches. A foot is about 30 centimeters.*

◇ *Dave is six feet tall.* Dave mide un metro ochenta.
2 la pata (*of animal*)

football ['futbɑːl] NOUN
1 el fútbol americano
el futbol americano Mexico
◇ *I like playing football.* Me gusta jugar fútbol americano. Mexico: Me gusta jugar futbol americano.
2 el balón (PL los balones) ◇ *Paul threw the football over the fence.* Paul lanzó el balón por encima de la valla.

football player ['futbɑːl'pleɪər] NOUN
el jugador de fútbol americano
la jugadora de fútbol americano
el jugador de futbol americano
la jugadora de futbol americano Mexico

footpath ['fut,pæθ] NOUN
el sendero

footprint ['fut,prɪnt] NOUN
la pisada ◇ *He saw some footprints in the sand.* Vio algunas pisadas en la arena.

footstep ['fut,stɛp] NOUN
el paso ◇ *I can hear footsteps on the stairs.* Oigo pasos en la escalera.

for [fɔːr] PREPOSITION
*There are three basic ways of translating **for** into Spanish: **para, por** and **durante**. Check the boxes at the beginning of each translation to find the meaning or example you need. If you can't find it look at the phrases at the end of the entry.*
1 para
***para** is used to indicate destination, employment, intention and purpose.*
◇ *a present for me* un regalo para mí ◇ *the train for Washington* el tren para Washington ◇ *He works for the government.* Trabaja para el gobierno. ◇ *What for?* ¿Para qué? ◇ *What's it for?* ¿Para qué es?
2 por
***por** is used to indicate reason or cause. Use it also when talking about amounts of money.*
◇ *for fear of being criticized* por temor a ser criticado ◇ *Colorado is famous for its university.* Colorado es famoso por su universidad. ◇ *I'll do it for you.* Lo haré por ti. ◇ *I'm sorry for Steve, but it's his own fault.* Lo siento por Steve, pero es culpa suya. ◇ *I sold it for $5.* Lo vendí por 5 dólares. ◇ *What did he do that for?* ¿Para qué hizo eso?

F

[3] durante

*When referring to periods of time, use **durante** to refer to the future and completed actions in the past. Note that it can often be omitted, as in the next two examples.*

◇ *She will be away for a month.* Estará fuera (durante) un mes. ◇ *He worked in Spain for two years.* Trabajó (durante) dos años en España.

*Use **hace...que** and the present to describe actions and states that started in the past and are still going on. Alternatively use the present and **desde hace**. Another option is **llevar** and an **-ando/-iendo** form.*

◇ *He has been learning French for two years.* Hace dos años que estudia francés. ◇ *She's been learning German for four years.* Lleva cuatro años estudiando alemán. ◇ *I haven't seen her for two years.* No la veo desde hace dos años.

*See how the tenses change when talking about something that **had** happened or **had been** happening **for** a time.*

◇ *He had been learning French for two years.* Hacía dos años que estudiaba francés. ◇ *I hadn't seen her for two years.* No la veía desde hacía dos años. ◇ *She had been learning German for four years.* Llevaba cuatro años estudiando alemán.

- **There are road repairs for three miles.** Hay obras por tres millas.
- **What's the English for "león"?** ¿Cómo se dice "león" en inglés?
- **It's time for supper.** Es la hora de cenar.
- **Can you do it for tomorrow?** ¿Puedes hacerlo para mañana?
- **Are you for or against the idea?** ¿Estás a favor o en contra de la idea?

to **forbid** [fər'bɪd] VERB (**forbade, forbidden**)
prohibir* ◇ *to forbid somebody to do something* prohibir a alguien que haga algo

force [fɔːrs] NOUN
see also **force** VERB
la fuerza ◇ *the force of the explosion* la fuerza de la explosión ◇ *UN forces* las fuerzas de la ONU

- **in force** (*law, rules*) en vigor

to **force** [fɔːrs] VERB
see also **force** NOUN
obligar* ◇ *They forced him to open the safe.* Lo obligaron a abrir la caja fuerte.

forecast ['fɔːrkæst] NOUN

- **the weather forecast** el pronóstico del tiempo

foreground ['fɔːr,graund] NOUN
el primer plano ◇ *in the foreground* en primer plano

forehead ['fɔːrəd] NOUN
la frente

foreign ['fɑːrɪn] ADJECTIVE
[1] extranjero ◇ *a foreign language* una lengua extranjera
[2] exterior ◇ *US foreign policy* la política exterior estadounidense

foreigner ['fɑːrɪnər] NOUN
el extranjero
la extranjera

to **foresee** [fɔːr'siː] VERB (**foresaw, foreseen**)
prever*

forest ['fɑːrɪst] NOUN
el bosque

forever [fə'rɛvər] ADVERB
[1] para siempre ◇ *He's gone forever.* Se ha ido para siempre.
[2] siempre ◇ *She's forever complaining.* Siempre se está quejando.

forgave [fər'geɪv] VERB *see* **forgive**

to **forge** [fɔːrdʒ] VERB
falsificar* ◇ *She forged his signature.* Falsificó su firma.

to **forget** [fər'gɛt] VERB (**forgot, forgotten**)
olvidar ◇ *I've forgotten his name.* Olvidé su nombre.

- **to forget to do something** olvidarse de hacer algo ◇ *I forgot to close the window.* Me olvidé de cerrar la ventana.
- **I'm sorry, I had completely forgotten!** ¡Lo siento, se me había olvidado por completo!
- **Don't forget your passport!** ¡No te olvides del pasaporte!
- **Forget it!** ¡No importa!

to **forgive** [fər'gɪv] VERB (**forgave, forgiven**)
perdonar ◇ *I forgive you.* Te perdono.

- **to forgive somebody for doing something** perdonar a alguien por haber hecho algo

forgot, forgotten [fər'gɑːt,fər'gɑːtn] VERB *see* **forget**

fork [fɔːrk] NOUN
[1] el tenedor (*for eating*)
[2] la horca ◇ *He was piling up hay with a fork.* Apilaba heno con una horca.
[3] la bifurcación (PL las bifurcaciones) (*in road*)

form [fɔːrm] NOUN
[1] el formulario
la forma *Mexico*

- **to fill out a form** llenar un formulario, *Mexico*: llenar una forma

[2] la forma ◇ *I'm against hunting in any form.* Estoy en contra de cualquier forma de caza.

- **in top form** en plena forma

formal ['fɔːrməl] ADJECTIVE
[1] oficial ◇ *a formal visit* una visita oficial

- **a formal dinner** una cena de gala
- **formal clothes** la ropa de etiqueta

[2] formal ◇ *In English, "residence" is a formal term.* En inglés, "residence" es un término formal.

- **He has no formal education.** No tiene formación académica.

former [ˈfɔːrmər] ADJECTIVE
antiguo
*Put **antiguo** before the noun when translating **former**.*
◇ *a former pupil* un antiguo alumno

formerly [ˈfɔːrmərli] ADVERB
antiguamente

fort [fɔːrt] NOUN
el fuerte

forth [fɔːrθ] ADVERB
◆ **to go back and forth** ir* de acá para allá
◆ **and so forth** y demás

fortunate [ˈfɔːrtʃənɪt] ADJECTIVE
◆ **He was extremely fortunate to survive.** Tuvo la gran suerte de salir vivo.
◆ **It's fortunate that I remembered the map.** Menos mal que me acordé de traer el mapa.

fortunately [ˈfɔːrtʃənɪtli] ADVERB
afortunadamente

fortune [ˈfɔːrtʃən] NOUN
la fortuna ◇ *He made his fortune in car sales.* Consiguió su fortuna con la venta de carros.
◆ **Kate earns a fortune!** ¡Kate gana un dineral!
◆ **to tell somebody's fortune** decir* la buenaventura a alguien

forty [ˈfɔːrti] NUMERAL
cuarenta ◇ *He's forty.* Tiene cuarenta años.

forward [ˈfɔːrwərd] ADVERB
see also **forward** VERB
hacia delante ◇ *to look forward* mirar hacia delante
◆ **to move forward** avanzar*

to **forward** [ˈfɔːrwərd] VERB
see also **forward** ADVERB
remitir (*letter*)

to **foster** [ˈfɑːstər] VERB
acoger* ◇ *She has fostered more than fifteen children.* Ha acogido a más de quince niños.

foster child [ˈfɑːstərˌtʃaɪld] NOUN (PL **foster children**)
el niño acogido en una familia

fought [fɑːt] VERB *see* **fight**

foul [faul] ADJECTIVE
see also **foul** NOUN
1 horrible ◇ *The weather was foul.* El tiempo era horrible.
2 asqueroso ◇ *It smells foul.* Huele asqueroso.
◆ **Brenda is in a foul mood.** Brenda está de muy mal humor.

foul [faul] NOUN
see also **foul** ADJECTIVE
la falta (*in sports*)

found [faund] VERB *see* **find**

to **found** [faund] VERB
fundar

foundations [faunˈdeɪʃənz] PL NOUN
los cimientos

fountain [ˈfauntən] NOUN
la fuente

fountain pen [ˈfauntənˌpɛn] NOUN
la pluma estilográfica

four [fɔːr] NUMERAL
cuatro ◇ *She's four.* Tiene cuatro años.

fourteen [ˈfɔːrtiːn] NUMERAL
catorce ◇ *I'm fourteen.* Tengo catorce años.

fourteenth [ˈfɔːrtiːnθ] ADJECTIVE
decimocuarto
◆ **the fourteenth floor** el piso trece
◆ **July fourteenth** el catorce de julio

fourth [fɔːrθ] ADJECTIVE
cuarto ◇ *the fourth floor* el piso tercero
◆ **July fourth** el cuatro de julio

F

fox [fɑːks] NOUN (PL **foxes**)
el zorro

fragile [ˈfrædʒəl] ADJECTIVE
frágil

fragrance [ˈfreɪgrəns] NOUN
el perfume

frame [freɪm] NOUN
el marco ◇ *a silver frame* un marco de plata
◆ **glasses with plastic frames** anteojos con montura de plástico

France [fræns] NOUN
Francia FEM

frantic [ˈfræntɪk] ADJECTIVE
frenético ◇ *There was frantic activity backstage on the opening night.* Había una actividad frenética entre bastidores la noche del estreno. ◇ *I was going frantic.* Me estaba poniendo frenético.
◆ **to be frantic with worry** estar* muerto de preocupación

fraud [frɑːd] NOUN
1 el fraude ◇ *He was jailed for fraud.* Lo encarcelaron por fraude.
2 el impostor
la impostora
◇ *You're a fraud!* ¡Eres un impostor!

freckles [ˈfrɛkəlz] PL NOUN
las pecas

free [friː] ADJECTIVE
see also **free** VERB
1 gratuito ◇ *a free brochure* un folleto gratuito
◆ **You can get it for free.** Se puede conseguir gratis.
2 libre ◇ *Is this seat free?* ¿Está libre este asiento? ◇ *Are you free after school?* ¿Estás libre después de clase?

to **free** [friː] VERB
see also **free** ADJECTIVE
liberar

freedom [ˈfriːdəm] NOUN
la libertad

freeway [ˈfriːweɪ] NOUN
la autopista ◇ *I had an accident on the freeway.* Tuve un accidente en la autopista.

to **freeze** [friːz] VERB (**froze**, **frozen**)
1 congelar ◇ *She froze the rest of the raspberries.* Congeló el resto de las

☞

frambuesas.
[2] helarse* ◇ *The water had frozen.* El agua se había helado.

freezer ['fri:zər] NOUN
el congelador

freezing ['fri:zɪŋ] ADJECTIVE
◆ **It's freezing!** ¡Hace un frío que pela! (*informal*)
◆ **I'm freezing!** ¡Me estoy congelando!
◆ **three degrees below freezing** tres grados bajo cero

freight [freɪt] NOUN
las mercancías (*goods*)
◆ **a freight train** un tren de carga

French [frɛntʃ] ADJECTIVE
see also **French** NOUN
francés (MASC PL franceses, FEM francesa)

French [frɛntʃ] NOUN
see also **French** ADJECTIVE
el francés (*language*) ◇ *the French teacher* el profesor de francés
◆ **the French** los franceses

French bread ['frɛntʃˌbrɛd] NOUN
la barra de pan

French doors [frɛntʃ'dɔ:rs] PL NOUN
la puerta ventana

french fries ['frɛntʃˌfraɪz] PL NOUN
las papas fritas

French horn [frɛntʃ'hɔ:rn] NOUN
la trompa de llaves

Frenchman ['frɛntʃmən] NOUN (PL **Frenchmen**)
el francés (PL los franceses)

Frenchwoman ['frɛntʃˌwumən] NOUN (PL **Frenchwomen**)
la francesa

frequent ['fri:kwənt] ADJECTIVE
frecuente

fresh [frɛʃ] ADJECTIVE
fresco ◇ *I always buy fresh fish.* Siempre compro pescado fresco.
◆ **I need some fresh air.** Necesito tomar aire.

to **freshen up** [ˌfrɛʃən'ʌp] VERB
refrescarse*

freshman [frɛʃmən] (PL **freshmen**) NOUN
el/la estudiante de primer año (*at college*)

to **fret** [frɛt] VERB
preocuparse

Friday ['fraɪdi] NOUN
el viernes (PL los viernes) ◇ *I saw her on Friday.* La vi el viernes. ◇ *every Friday* todos los viernes ◇ *last Friday* el viernes pasado ◇ *next Friday* el viernes que viene ◇ *on Fridays* los viernes

fridge [frɪdʒ] NOUN
el refrigerador

fried [fraɪd] ADJECTIVE
frito ◇ *a fried egg* un huevo frito, *Mexico*: un huevo estrellado

friend [frɛnd] NOUN
el amigo
la amiga
◇ *my friends* mis amigos

friendly ['frɛndli] ADJECTIVE
simpático ◇ *She's really friendly.* Es muy simpática.
◆ **New Orleans is a friendly city.** Nueva Orleans es una ciudad agradable.
◆ **a friendly game** un partido amistoso

friendship ['frɛndʃɪp] NOUN
la amistad

fright [fraɪt] NOUN
el susto ◇ *She gave us a fright.* Nos dio un susto. ◇ *to get a fright* llevarse un susto

to **frighten** ['fraɪtn] VERB
asustar ◇ *She was trying to frighten him.* Intentaba asustarlo.
◆ **Horror movies frighten him.** Le dan miedo las películas de terror.

frightened ['fraɪtnd] ADJECTIVE
◆ **to be frightened** tener* miedo ◇ *I'm frightened!* ¡Tengo miedo!
◆ **Anna's frightened of spiders.** A Anna le dan miedo las arañas.

frightening ['fraɪtnɪŋ] ADJECTIVE
aterrador (FEM aterradora)

Frisbee® ['frɪzbi] NOUN
el Frisbee®

fro [frou] ADVERB
◆ **to go to and fro** ir* de acá para allá

frog [frɑ:g] NOUN
la rana

from [frʌm] PREPOSITION
[1] de ◇ *Where do you come from?* ¿De dónde eres? ◇ *a letter from my sister* una carta de mi hermana ◇ *The hotel is one kilometer from the beach.* El hotel está a un kilómetro de la playa. ◇ *The price was reduced from $10 to $5.* Rebajaron el precio de 10 a 5 dólares.
[2] desde ◇ *Breakfast is available from 6 a.m.* Se puede desayunar desde las 6 de la mañana. ◇ *I can't see anything from here.* Desde aquí no veo nada.

In the following phrases ***de*** *and* ***desde*** *are interchangeable. Use* ***a*** *to translate* ***to*** *if you have chosen* ***de*** *and* ***hasta*** *if you have opted for* ***desde****.*

◆ **He flew from New York to Buenos Aires.** Voló de Nueva York a Buenos Aires.
◆ **from one o'clock to three** desde la una hasta las tres
◆ **She works from nine to five.** Trabaja de nueve a cinco.
◆ **from...onwards** a partir de... ◇ *We'll be at home from seven o'clock onwards.* Estaremos en la casa a partir de las siete.

front [frʌnt] NOUN
see also **front** ADJECTIVE
la parte delantera ◇ *The switch is at the front*

of the vacuum cleaner. El interruptor está en la parte delantera de la aspiradora.
- **the front of the dress** el delantero del vestido
- **the front of the house** la fachada de la casa
- **I was sitting in the front.** (*of car*) Yo iba sentado adelante.
- **at the front of the train** al principio del tren
- **in front** adelante ◇ *the car in front* el carro de adelante
- **in front of** delante de ◇ *Irene sits in front of me in class.* Irene se sienta delante de mí en clase.

front [frʌnt] ADJECTIVE
see also **front** NOUN
1 primero ◇ *the front row* la primera fila
Use **primer** *before a masculine singular noun.*
2 delantero ◇ *the front seats of the car* los asientos delanteros del coche
- **the front door** la puerta principal
- **front desk** la recepción (*of hotel, hospital etc*)

frontier [frʌnˈtɪər] NOUN
la frontera

frost [frɑːst] NOUN
la helada ◇ *There was a frost last night.* Anoche cayó una helada.

frosting [ˈfrɑːstɪŋ] NOUN
el glaseado (*on cake*)

frosty [ˈfrɑːsti] ADJECTIVE
- **It's frosty today.** Hoy ha helado.

to **frown** [fraun] VERB
fruncir* el ceño

froze, frozen [frouz, ˈfrouzən] VERB *see* **freeze**

frozen [ˈfrouzən] ADJECTIVE
congelado

fruit [fruːt] NOUN
la fruta
- **fruit juice** el jugo de fruta
- **fruit salad** la macedonia de frutas

frustrated [ˈfrʌstreɪtɪd] ADJECTIVE
frustrado

to **fry** [fraɪ] VERB (**fried, fried**)
freír*

frying pan [ˈfraɪɪŋˌpæn] NOUN
el sartén (PL los sartenes)

fuel [ˈfjuəl] NOUN
el combustible ◇ *We've run out of fuel.* Nos quedamos sin combustible.

to **fulfill** [fulˈfɪl] VERB
realizar* ◇ *He fulfilled his dream to visit China.* Realizó su sueño de viajar a China.
- **to fulfill a promise** cumplir una promesa

full [ful] ADJECTIVE
1 lleno ◇ *The tank is full.* El depósito está lleno. ◇ *I'm full.* Estoy lleno. ◇ *There was a full moon.* Había luna llena.
2 completo ◇ *He asked for full information on the job.* Solicitó información completa sobre el trabajo. ◇ *My full name is Dolores García Soto.* Mi nombre completo es Dolores García Soto.
- **full board** la pensión completa
- **at full speed** a toda velocidad

full-time [ˈfulˈtaɪm] ADJECTIVE, ADVERB
- **She has a full-time job.** Tiene un trabajo a tiempo completo.
- **She works full-time.** Trabaja a tiempo completo.

fully [ˈfuli] ADVERB
completamente ◇ *He hasn't fully recovered from his illness.* No se ha recuperado completamente de su enfermedad.

fumes [fjuːmz] PL NOUN
los gases ◇ *exhaust fumes* los gases del tubo de escape

fun [fʌn] ADJECTIVE
see also **fun** NOUN
divertido ◇ *She's a fun person.* Es una persona divertida.

fun [fʌn] NOUN
see also **fun** ADJECTIVE
- **to have fun** divertirse*
- **It's fun!** ¡Es divertido!
- **Have fun!** ¡Que te diviertas!
- **for fun** por gusto
- **to make fun of somebody** reírse* de alguien

funds [fʌndz] PL NOUN
los fondos ◇ *to raise funds* recaudar fondos

funeral [ˈfjuːnərəl] NOUN
el funeral

funny [ˈfʌni] ADJECTIVE
1 gracioso ◇ *a funny joke* un chiste gracioso
2 raro ◇ *There's something funny about him.* Hay algo raro en él.

fur [fɜːr] NOUN
1 la piel
- **a fur coat** un abrigo de pieles

2 el pelaje ◇ *the cat's fur* el pelaje del gato

furious [ˈfjuriəs] ADJECTIVE
furioso

furniture [ˈfɜːrnɪtʃər] NOUN
los muebles
- **a piece of furniture** un mueble

further [ˈfɜːrðər] ADVERB, ADJECTIVE
1 más lejos ◇ *Santa Fe is further from here than Dallas.* Santa Fe está más lejos de aquí que Dallas.
- **I can't walk any further.** No puedo caminar más.
- **How much further is it?** ¿Cuánto queda todavía?

2 más ◇ *Please write to us if you need any further information.* No dude en escribirnos si necesita más información.

fuse [fjuːz] NOUN
el fusible ◇ *The fuse has blown.* Se fundió el fusible.

fuss [fʌs] NOUN
el alboroto ◇ *What's all the fuss about?* ¿A qué viene tanto alboroto?
- **He's always making a fuss about nothing.**

Siempre arma un escándalo por cualquier cosa.

fussy ['fʌsi] ADJECTIVE
quisquilloso ◇ *She is very fussy about her food.* Es muy quisquillosa con la comida.

future ['fju:tʃər] NOUN
el futuro ◇ *What are your plans for the future?* ¿Qué planes tienes para el futuro?
◆ **in future** de ahora en adelante ◇ *Be more careful in future.* De ahora en adelante ten más cuidado.

G

to **gain** [geɪn] VERB
ganar ◇ *What do you hope to gain from this?* ¿Qué esperas ganar con esto?
- **to gain speed** adquirir* velocidad
- **to gain weight** engordar

gallery ['gæləri] NOUN (PL **galleries**)
1 el museo de arte (*state-owned*)
2 una galería de arte (*private*)

to **gamble** ['gæmbəl] VERB
jugar* ◇ *He gambled $100 at the casino.* Jugó 100 dólares en el casino.

gambler ['gæmblər] NOUN
el jugador
la jugadora

gambling ['gæmblɪŋ] NOUN
el juego (*de azar*)

game [geɪm] NOUN
1 el juego ◇ *The children were playing a game.* Los niños jugaban un juego.
2 el partido ◇ *a game of soccer* un partido de fútbol
- **a game of cards** una partida de cartas
- **the Olympic games** las Olimpiadas

gang [gæŋ] NOUN
1 la banda (*of thieves, troublemakers*)
2 la pandilla (*of friends*)

gangster ['gæŋstər] NOUN
el gángster (PL los gángsters)

gap [gæp] NOUN
1 el hueco ◇ *There's a gap in the hedge.* Hay un hueco en el seto.
2 el intervalo ◇ *a gap of four years* un intervalo de cuatro años

garage [gə'rɑːʒ] NOUN
1 el garaje (*for keeping the car*)
2 el taller (*for car repairs*)

garbage ['gɑːrbɪdʒ] NOUN
la basura ◇ *They sell a lot of garbage at the market.* Venden mucha basura en el mercado.
- **garbage can** el cubo de la basura, *Mexico*: el bote de la basura
- **garbage dump** el basural
- **That's garbage!** ¡Eso son tonterías!
- **That magazine is garbage!** ¡Esa revista es una porquería! (*informal*)

garbage collector ['gɑːrbɪdʒkə'lɛktər] NOUN
el basurero

garbageman ['gɑːrbɪdʒˌmæn] NOUN (PL **garbagemen**)
el basurero

garden ['gɑːrdn] NOUN
el jardín (PL los jardines)

gardener ['gɑːrdnər] NOUN
el jardinero
la jardinera
◇ *He's a gardener.* Es jardinero.

gardening ['gɑːrdnɪŋ] NOUN
la jardinería ◇ *Margaret loves gardening.* A Margaret le encanta la jardinería.

gardens ['gɑːrdnz] PL NOUN
el parque

garlic ['gɑːrlɪk] NOUN
el ajo

garment ['gɑːrmənt] NOUN
la prenda de vestir

gas [gæs] NOUN
1 el gas
- **a gas cooker** una cocina de gas, *Mexico*: una estufa de gas
- **a gas cylinder** una bombona de gas, *Mexico*: un tanque de gas
- **a gas fire** una estufa de gas
- **a gas leak** un escape de gas

2 la gasolina (*for car*)

gasoline ['gæsəliːn] NOUN
la gasolina
- **unleaded gasoline** gasolina sin plomo
- **high-test gasoline** gasolina súper

gas pedal ['gæsˌpɛdl] NOUN
el acelerador

gas station ['gæsˌsteɪʃən] NOUN
la gasolinera

gas tank ['gæsˌtæŋk] NOUN
el depósito de gasolina

gate [geɪt] NOUN
1 la puerta (*made of wood*)
2 la verja (*made of metal*)
- **Please go to gate seven.** Diríjanse a la puerta siete.

gateau [gæ'tou] NOUN (PL **gateaux**)
el pastel

to **gather** ['gæðər] VERB
1 reunirse* ◇ *We gathered around the fireplace.* Nos reunimos en torno a la chimenea.
2 reunir* ◇ *We gathered enough firewood to last the night.* Reunimos leña suficiente para toda la noche. ◇ *to gather information* reunir información
- **to gather speed** adquirir* velocidad ◇ *The train gathered speed.* El tren adquirió velocidad.

gave [geɪv] VERB *see* **give**

gay [geɪ] ADJECTIVE
gay

to **gaze** [geɪz] VERB
- **to gaze at** mirar fijamente ◇ *He was gazing at her.* La miraba fijamente.

gear [gɪər] NOUN
1 la marcha ◇ *to shift gear* cambiar de marcha ◇ *He left the car in gear.* Dejó el carro con una marcha metida.
- **in first gear** en primera

2 el equipo ◇ *camping gear* el equipo de camping
- **sports gear** la ropa de deporte

gearshift ['gɪərʃɪft] NOUN

la palanca de cambio
la palanca de velocidades [Mexico]

GED ['dʒi:i:'di:] NOUN (= *General Equivalency Diploma*)

> ℹ *El* **GED** *es un diploma otorgado a aquellos alumnos que han terminado la enseñanza secundaria con la cantidad de créditos y el trabajo escolar que se exigen en el sistema educativo de los Estados Unidos. Es necesario para poder optar a un gran número de empleos.*

geese [gi:s] PL NOUN *see* **goose**

gel [dʒɛl] NOUN
el gel
◆ **hair gel** el fijador

gem [dʒɛm] NOUN
la gema

Gemini ['dʒɛmɪnaɪ] NOUN
el Géminis (*sign*) ◇ *I'm a Gemini.* Soy géminis.
◆ **a Gemini** un/una géminis

gender ['dʒɛndər] NOUN
el género (*of noun*)

general ['dʒɛnərəl] NOUN
[*see also* **general** ADJECTIVE]
el general

general ['dʒɛnərəl] ADJECTIVE
[*see also* **general** NOUN]
general
◆ **in general** en general

general election ['dʒɛnərəlɪ'lɛkʃən] NOUN
las elecciones generales

general knowledge ['dʒɛnərəl'nɑ:lɪdʒ] NOUN
la cultura general

generally ['dʒɛnərəli] ADVERB
generalmente ◇ *I generally go shopping on Saturdays.* Generalmente voy de compras los sábados.

generation [dʒɛnə'reɪʃən] NOUN
la generación (PL las generaciones) ◇ *the younger generation* la nueva generación

generator ['dʒɛnəreɪtər] NOUN
el generador

generous ['dʒɛnərəs] ADJECTIVE
generoso ◇ *That's very generous of you.* Es muy generoso de tu parte.

Geneva [dʒɪ'ni:və] NOUN
Ginebra FEM

genius ['dʒi:niəs] NOUN (PL **geniuses**)
el genio ◇ *She's a genius.* Es un genio.

gentle ['dʒɛntl] ADJECTIVE
[1] dulce (*person, voice*)
[2] suave (*wind, touch*)

gentleman ['dʒɛntlmən] NOUN (PL **gentlemen**)
el caballero

gently ['dʒɛntli] ADVERB
[1] dulcemente (*say, smile*)
[2] suavemente (*touch*)

genuine ['dʒɛnjuɪn] ADJECTIVE
[1] auténtico ◇ *These are genuine diamonds.* Estos son diamantes auténticos.
[2] sincero ◇ *She's a very genuine person.* Es una persona muy sincera.

geography [dʒi'ɑ:grəfi] NOUN
la geografía

gerbil NOUN
el gerbo

germ [dʒɜ:rm] NOUN
el microbio

German ['dʒɜ:rmən] ADJECTIVE
[*see also* **German** NOUN]
alemán (MASC PL alemanes, FEM alemana)

German ['dʒɜ:rmən] NOUN
[*see also* **German** ADJECTIVE]
[1] el alemán (PL los alemanes)
la alemana
(*person*)
◇ *the Germans* los alemanes
[2] el alemán (*language*) ◇ *our German teacher* nuestro profesor de alemán

German measles ['dʒɜ:rmən'mi:zəlz] NOUN
la rubéola ◇ *to have German measles* tener* rubéola

Germany ['dʒɜ:rməni] NOUN
Alemania FEM

gesture ['dʒɛstʃər] NOUN
el gesto

to **get** [gɛt] (**got, gotten**) VERB

There are several ways of translating ***get****. Scan the examples to find one that is similar to what you want to say.*

[1] recibir (*have, receive*) ◇ *I got a letter from him.* Recibí una carta de él.
◆ **I got lots of presents.** Me hicieron muchos regalos.
[2] conseguir* (*obtain*) ◇ *He had trouble getting a hotel room.* Tuvo dificultades para conseguir una habitación de hotel.
◆ **to get something for somebody** conseguir algo a alguien ◇ *The librarian got the book for me.* El bibliotecario me consiguió el libro.
◆ **Jackie got good test results.** Jackie sacó buenas notas en los exámenes.
[3] ir* a buscar (*fetch*) ◇ *Quick, get help!* ¡Rápido, ve a buscar ayuda!
[4] agarrar (*catch, take*) ◇ *They have gotten the thief.* Agarraron al ladrón. ◇ *I'm getting the bus into town.* Voy a tomar un taxi al centro.
[5] entender* (*understand*) ◇ *I don't get the joke.* No entiendo el chiste.
[6] llegar* (*arrive*) ◇ *He should get here soon.* Debería llegar pronto. ◇ *How do you get to the movies?* ¿Cómo se llega al cine?
◆ **to get angry** enfadarse, enojarse
◆ **to get tired** cansarse

For other phrases with ***get*** *and an adjective, such as "to get old, to get drunk", you should* *look under the word **old, drunk**, etc.*

- **to get something done** mandar hacer algo ◇ *I'm getting my car fixed.* Mandé arreglar el coche.
- **I got my hair cut.** Me corté el pelo.
- **I'll get it! (1)** (*telephone*) ¡Yo contesto!
- **I'll get it! (2)** (*door*) ¡Ya voy yo!, ¡Yo abro!

to **get around to** [gɛtə'raundtu:] VERB
encontrar* tiempo para ◇ *I'll get around to it eventually.* Ya encontraré tiempo para hacerlo.

to **get away** [gɛtə'weɪ] VERB
escapar ◇ *One of the burglars got away.* Uno de los ladrones escapó.

to **get away with** [gɛtə'weɪwɪð] VERB
- **You'll never get away with it.** Esto no te lo van a consentir.

to **get back** [gɛt'bæk] VERB
1 volver* ◇ *What time did you get back?* ¿A qué hora volviste?
2 recuperar ◇ *He got his money back.* Recuperó su dinero.

to **get down** [gɛt'daun] VERB
bajar ◇ *Get down from there!* ¡Bájate de ahí!

to **get in** [gɛt'ɪn] VERB
llegar* ◇ *What time did you get in last night?* ¿A qué hora llegaste anoche?

to **get into** [gɛt'ɪntu:] VERB
entrar a ◇ *How did you get into the house?* ¿Cómo entraste a la casa?
- **Sharon got into the car.** Sharon subió al coche.
- **Get into bed!** ¡Métete en la cama!

to **get off** [gɛt'ɑ:f] VERB
1 bajarse de ◇ *Isobel got off the train.* Isobel se bajó del tren.
2 salir* ◇ *He managed to get off early from work yesterday.* Logró salir temprano del trabajo ayer.

to **get on** [gɛt'ɑ:n] VERB
1 subirse a ◇ *Phyllis got on the train.* Phyllis se subió al tren.
2 llevarse bien ◇ *We got on really well.* Nos llevábamos muy bien. ◇ *He doesn't get on with his parents.* No se lleva bien con sus padres.
- **How are you getting on?** ¿Cómo te va?

to **get out** [gɛt'aut] VERB
1 salir* ◇ *Get out!* ¡Sal!
- **She got out of the car.** Se bajó del carro.

2 sacar* ◇ *She got the map out.* Sacó el mapa.

to **get over** [gɛt'ouvər] VERB
1 recuperarse de ◇ *It took her a long time to get over the illness.* Tardó mucho tiempo en recuperarse de la enfermedad.
2 superar ◇ *He managed to get over the problem.* Logró superar el problema.

to **get together** [ˌgɛttə'gɛðər] VERB
reunirse* ◇ *Could we get together this evening?* ¿Podemos reunirnos esta tarde?

to **get up** [gɛt'ʌp] VERB
levantarse ◇ *What time do you get up?* ¿A qué hora te levantas?

ghost [goust] NOUN
el fantasma
*Although **fantasma** ends in **-a**, it is actually a masculine noun.*

giant ['dʒaɪənt] ADJECTIVE
see also **giant** NOUN
enorme

giant ['dʒaɪənt] NOUN
see also **giant** ADJECTIVE
el gigante
la giganta

gift [gɪft] NOUN
el regalo
- **to have a gift for something** tener* dotes para algo ◇ *Johnny has a gift for painting.* Johnny tiene dotes para la pintura.

gift certificate ['gɪftsərˌtɪfɪkɪt] NOUN
el vale-regalo

gifted ['gɪftɪd] ADJECTIVE
talentoso ◇ *Janice is a gifted dancer.* Janice es una bailarina talentosa. ◇ *He's one of this country's most gifted artists.* Es uno de los artistas más talentosos de este país.

gift shop ['gɪftʃɑ:p] NOUN
la tienda de regalos

gigantic [dʒaɪ'gæntɪk] ADJECTIVE
gigantesco

to **giggle** ['gɪgəl] VERB
soltar* una risita tonta

gin [dʒɪn] NOUN
la ginebra

ginger ['dʒɪndʒər] NOUN
see also **ginger** ADJECTIVE
el jengibre

ginger ['dʒɪndʒər] ADJECTIVE
see also **ginger** NOUN
- **a ginger cat** un gato de color melado

gipsy ['dʒɪpsi] NOUN (PL **gipsies**)
el gitano
la gitana

giraffe [dʒə'ræf] NOUN
la jirafa

girl [gɜ:rl] NOUN
1 la niña (*young*) ◇ *a five-year old girl* una niña de cinco años ◇ *They have a girl and two boys.* Tienen una niña y dos niños.
2 la chica (*older*) ◇ *a sixteen-year old girl* una chica de dieciséis años

girlfriend ['gɜ:rlfrɛnd] NOUN
1 la novia ◇ *Paul's girlfriend is called Janice.* La novia de Paul se llama Janice.
2 la amiga ◇ *She often went out with her girlfriends.* Solía salir con sus amigas.

girl scout ['gɜ:rlskaut] NOUN
la girl scout (PL las girl scouts)

to **give** [gɪv] VERB (**gave, given**)
dar*
- **to give something to somebody** dar algo a ☞

alguien ◇ *He gave me $10.* Me dio 10 dólares.
- **to give somebody a present** hacer* un regalo a alguien

to **give away** [gɪvəˈweɪ] VERB
regalar
- **She gave away all her money.** Regaló todo su dinero.

to **give back** [gɪvˈbæk] VERB
devolver* ◇ *I gave the book back to him.* Le devolví el libro.

to **give in** [gɪvˈɪn] VERB
rendirse* ◇ *I give in!* ¡Me rindo!

to **give out** [gɪvˈaut] VERB
repartir ◇ *He gave out the exam papers.* Repartió las hojas de examen.

to **give up** [gɪvˈʌp] VERB
darse* por vencido ◇ *I couldn't do it, so I gave up.* No podía hacerlo, así que me di por vencido.
- **to give oneself up** entregarse* ◇ *She gave herself up.* Se entregó.
- **to give up doing something** dejar de hacer algo ◇ *He gave up smoking.* Dejó de fumar.

glad [glæd] ADJECTIVE
contento ◇ *She's glad she's done it.* Está contenta de haberlo hecho.
- **I'm glad you're here.** Me alegro de que estés aquí.

***alegrarse de que** has to be followed by a verb in the subjunctive.*

glamorous [ˈglæmərəs] ADJECTIVE
atractivo

to **glance** [glæns] VERB
see also **glance** NOUN
- **to glance at something** echar una mirada a algo ◇ *Peter glanced at his watch.* Peter echó una mirada al reloj.

glance [glæns] NOUN
see also **glance** VERB
la mirada ◇ *We exchanged a glance.* Intercambiamos una mirada.
- **at first glance** a primera vista

to **glare** [glɛər] VERB
- **to glare at somebody** lanzar* una mirada de odio a alguien ◇ *She glared at him.* Le lanzó una mirada de odio.

glaring [ˈglɛərɪŋ] ADJECTIVE
- **a glaring mistake** un error patente

glass [glæs] NOUN (PL **glasses**)
1 el vaso (*without stem*) ◇ *a glass of milk* un vaso de leche
2 la copa (*with stem*) ◇ *a glass of champagne* una copa de champán
3 el vidrio (*substance*) ◇ *a glass door* una puerta de vidrio

glasses [ˈglæsɪz] PL NOUN
los anteojos

to **gleam** [gliːm] VERB
brillar ◇ *Her eyes gleamed with excitement.* Los ojos le brillaban de emoción.

glider [ˈglaɪdər] NOUN
el planeador

to **glitter** [ˈglɪtər] VERB
relucir*

global [ˈgloubəl] ADJECTIVE
mundial ◇ *on a global scale* a escala mundial
- **a global view** una visión global

global warming [ˈgloubəlˈwɔːrmɪŋ] NOUN
el calentamiento del planeta

globe [gloub] NOUN
el globo terráqueo

gloomy [ˈgluːmi] ADJECTIVE
oscuro ◇ *He lives in a small gloomy apartment.* Vive en un departamento pequeño y oscuro.
- **She's been feeling very gloomy recently.** Últimamente está muy desanimada.

glorious [ˈglɔːriəs] ADJECTIVE
espléndido

glove [glʌv] NOUN
el guante

glove compartment [ˈglʌvkəm,pɑːrtmənt] NOUN
la guantera

to **glow** [glou] VERB
brillar ◇ *He bought a watch which glows in the dark.* Se compró un reloj que brilla en la oscuridad.

glue [gluː] NOUN
see also **glue** VERB
el pegamento

to **glue** [gluː] VERB
see also **glue** NOUN
pegar*
- **to glue something together** pegar algo

go [gou] NOUN
see also **go** VERB
- **to have a go at doing something** probar* a hacer algo ◇ *He had a go at making a cake.* Probó a hacer una tarta.
- **It's your go.** Te toca a ti.

to **go** [gou] VERB (**went, gone**)
see also **go** NOUN
1 ir* ◇ *Where are you going?* ¿Adónde vas? ◇ *I'm going to the movies tonight.* Voy al cine esta noche.
2 irse* (*leave, go away*) ◇ *Where's Judy? – She's gone.* ¿Dónde está Judy? – Se fue. ◇ *I'm going now.* Yo me voy ya.
3 funcionar (*work*) ◇ *My car won't go.* El carro no funciona.
- **to go home** irse* a la casa ◇ *We went home.* Nos fuimos a la casa.
- **to go into** entrar a ◇ *She went into the kitchen.* Entró a la cocina.
- **to go for a walk** ir a dar un paseo
- **How did the exam go?** ¿Cómo te fue en el examen?

- **I'm going to do it tomorrow.** Lo voy a hacer mañana.
- **It's going to be difficult.** Va a ser difícil.

to **go after** [gou'æftər] VERB
perseguir* ◇ *Quick, go after them!* ¡Rápido, persíguelos!

to **go ahead** [gouə'hɛd] VERB
seguir* adelante ◇ *We'll go ahead with your suggestion.* Seguiremos adelante con su propuesta.

to **go around** ['gouə'raund] VERB
1 visitar ◇ *We want to go around the museum today.* Hoy queremos visitar el museo.
- **I love going around the shops.** Me encanta ir de tiendas.
- **to go around to somebody's house** ir* a la casa de alguien ◇ *We're all going around to Linda's house tonight.* Esta noche vamos todos a la casa de Linda.

2 correr ◇ *There's a rumor going around that they're getting married.* Corre el rumor de que se van a casar.
- **There's a bug going around.** Hay un virus por ahí rondando.
- **Is there enough food to go around?** ¿Hay comida suficiente para todos?

to **go away** [gouə'weɪ] VERB
irse* ◇ *Go away!* ¡Vete!

to **go back** [gou'bæk] VERB
volver* ◇ *We went back to the same place.* Volvimos al mismo sitio. ◇ *He went back home.* Volvió a casa.

to **go by** [gou'baɪ] VERB
pasar ◇ *Two policemen went by.* Pasaron dos policías.

to **go down** [gou'daun] VERB
1 bajar ◇ *He went down the stairs.* Bajó las escaleras. ◇ *The price of computers has gone down.* Ha bajado el precio de las computadoras.
2 desinflarse ◇ *My air mattress has gone down.* Mi colchoneta se ha desinflado.

to **go for** ['goufɔːr] VERB
atacar* ◇ *Suddenly the dog went for me.* De pronto el perro me atacó.
- **Go for it!** ¡Adelante!
- **I don't go for it much.** No me gusta mucho.

to **go in** [gou'ɪn] VERB
entrar ◇ *He knocked on the door and went in.* Llamó a la puerta y entró.

to **go off** [gou'ɑːf] VERB
1 irse* ◇ *They went off after lunch.* Se fueron después de comer.
2 estallar ◇ *The bomb went off at 10 o'clock.* La bomba estalló a las 10.
- **The gun went off by accident.** El arma se disparó accidentalmente.

3 sonar* ◇ *My alarm goes off at seven.* Mi despertador suena a las siete.
4 apagarse* ◇ *All the lights went off.* Se apagaron todas las luces.
- **I've gone off that idea.** Ya no me gusta la idea.

to **go on** [gou'ɑːn] VERB
1 pasar ◇ *What's going on?* ¿Qué pasa?
2 seguir*
- **to go on doing** seguir* haciendo ◇ *He went on reading.* Siguió leyendo.

3 durar ◇ *The concert went on until 11 o'clock at night.* El concierto duró hasta las 11 de la noche.
- **Go on!** ¡Vamos! ◇ *Go on, tell me what the problem is!* ¡Vamos, dime cuál es el problema!

to **go out** [gou'aut] VERB
1 salir* ◇ *Are you going out tonight?* ¿Vas a salir esta noche? ◇ *I went out with Steven last night.* Anoche salí con Steven. ◇ *They went out for a meal.* Salieron a comer.
- **Are you going out with him?** ¿Estás saliendo con él?

2 apagarse* ◇ *Suddenly the lights went out.* De pronto se apagaron las luces.

G

to **go past** [gou'pæst] VERB
- **to go past something** pasar por delante de algo ◇ *He went past the store.* Pasó por delante de la tienda.

to **go through** [gou'θruː] VERB
1 atravesar* ◇ *We went through Philadelphia to get to Washington.* Atravesamos Filadelfia para llegar a Washington.
2 pasar por ◇ *I know what you're going through.* Sé por lo que estás pasando.
3 repasar ◇ *They went through the plan again.* Repasaron de nuevo el plan.
4 registrar
esculcar* *Mexico*
◇ *Someone had gone through her things.* Alguien había registrado sus cosas.
Mexico: Alguien había esculcado sus cosas.

to **go up** [gou'ʌp] VERB
subir ◇ *She went up the stairs.* Subió las escaleras. ◇ *The price has gone up.* El precio ha subido.
- **to go up in flames** arder en llamas

to **go with** [gou'wɪð] VERB
quedar bien con ◇ *Does this blouse go with that skirt?* ¿Queda bien esta blusa con esta falda?

goal [goul] NOUN
1 el gol ◇ *He scored the first goal.* Él metió el primer gol.
2 el objetivo ◇ *His goal is to become the world champion.* Su objetivo es ser campeón del mundo.

goalie ['gouli] NOUN
el arquero
la arquera

goat [gout] NOUN
la cabra
- **goat cheese** el queso de cabra

god [gɑːd] NOUN

☞

el dios ◇ *I believe in God.* Creo en Dios.
◆ **the Greek gods** los dioses griegos

goddaughter ['gɑːd,dɑːtər] NOUN
la ahijada

godfather ['gɑːd,fɑːðər] NOUN
el padrino

godmother ['gɑːd,mʌðər] NOUN
la madrina

godson ['gɑːd,sʌn] NOUN
el ahijado

goggles ['gɑːgəlz] PL NOUN
los anteojos protectores

gold [gould] NOUN
el oro ◇ *a gold necklace* un collar de oro ◇ *the gold medal* la medalla de oro

goldfish ['gouldfɪʃ] NOUN (PL **goldfish**)
el pez de colores (PL los peces de colores)

gold-plated ['gould'pleɪtɪd] ADJECTIVE
chapado en oro

golf [gɑːlf] NOUN
el golf
◆ **a golf club (1)** (*stick*) un palo de golf
◆ **a golf club (2)** (*place*) un club de golf
◆ **a golf course** una cancha de golf

gone [gɑːn] VERB *see* **go**

good [gud] ADJECTIVE
1 bueno
*Use **buen** before a masculine singular noun.*
◇ *It's a very good movie.* Es una película muy buena. ◇ *a good day* un buen día ◇ *Be good!* ¡Sé bueno! ◇ *The soup is very good here.* Aquí la sopa es muy buena.
2 amable (*kind*) ◇ *That's very good of you.* Es muy amable de tu parte.
◆ **They were very good to me.** Se portaron muy bien conmigo.
◆ **Have a good journey!** ¡Buen viaje!
◆ **Good!** ¡Bien!
◆ **Good morning!** ¡Buenos días!
◆ **Good afternoon!** ¡Buenas tardes!
◆ **Good evening!** ¡Buenas noches!
◆ **Good night!** ¡Buenas noches!
◆ **I'm feeling really good today.** Hoy me siento realmente bien.
◆ **to be good for somebody** hacer* bien a alguien ◇ *Vegetables are good for you.* La verdura te hace bien.
◆ **Jane's very good at math.** Jane tiene mucha facilidad para las matemáticas.
◆ **for good** definitivamente ◇ *One day he left for good.* Un día se marchó definitivamente.
◆ **It's no good complaining.** De nada sirve quejarse.

goodbye [gud'baɪ] EXCLAMATION
¡adiós!

Good Friday [gud'fraɪdi] NOUN
el Viernes Santo

good-looking ['gud'lukɪŋ] ADJECTIVE
buenmozo

good-natured ['gud'neɪtʃərd] ADJECTIVE
bueno
*Use **buen** before a masculine singular noun.*

goods ['gudz] PL NOUN
los productos ◇ *They sell a wide range of goods.* Venden una amplia gama de productos.

goose [guːs] NOUN (PL **geese**)
el ganso

gorgeous ['gɔːrdʒəs] ADJECTIVE
1 buenmozísimo ◇ *She's gorgeous!* ¡Es buenmozísima!
2 estupendo ◇ *The weather was gorgeous.* El tiempo estuvo estupendo.

gorilla [gə'rɪlə] NOUN
el gorila
*Although **gorila** ends in **-a**, it is actually a masculine noun.*

gospel ['gɑːspəl] NOUN
el evangelio

gossip ['gɑːsɪp] NOUN
see also **gossip** VERB
1 el chismorreo ◇ *Tell me the gossip!* ¡Cuéntame el chismorreo!
2 el chismoso
la chismosa
◇ *What a gossip!* ¡Qué chismoso!

to **gossip** ['gɑːsɪp] VERB
see also **gossip** NOUN
chismorrear ◇ *They were always gossiping.* Siempre estaban chismorreando.

got [gɑːt] VERB
◆ **to have got** tener* (*own*) ◇ *How many have you got?* ¿Cuántos tienes?
◆ **to have got to do something** tener que hacer algo ◇ *I've got to tell him.* Tengo que decírselo. ◇ *He has got to stop soon.* Tiene que parar pronto.

government ['gʌvərnmənt] NOUN
el gobierno

GP ['dʒiː'piː] NOUN (= *General Practitioner*)
el médico de cabecera
la médica de cabecera

to **grab** [græb] VERB
agarrar ◇ *He grabbed my arm.* Me agarró el brazo.

graceful ['greɪsfəl] ADJECTIVE
elegante

grade [greɪd] NOUN
la nota ◇ *He got good grades on his tests.* Sacó buenas notas en los exámenes.
◆ **She's in the first grade.** Está haciendo el primer año de primaria.

grade crossing ['greɪd,krɑːsɪŋ] NOUN
el paso a nivel
el crucero *Mexico*

grade school ['greɪd,skuːl] NOUN
la escuela primaria

gradual ['grædʒuəl] ADJECTIVE
gradual

gradually ['grædʒuəli] ADVERB

gradualmente
graduate ['grædʒuɪt] NOUN
see also **graduate** VERB
1 el egresado
la egresada
(*from college*)
2 el/la bachiller (*from high school*)
to **graduate** ['grædʒueɪt] VERB
see also **graduate** NOUN
1 recibirse (*from college, university*)
2 recibirse de bachiller (*from high school*)
graffiti [grə'fi:ti] PL NOUN
los graffiti
grain [greɪn] NOUN
1 los cereales PL ◇ *She only eats grain and beans.* Sólo come cereales y frijoles.
2 el grano ◇ *a grain of rice* un grano de arroz
3 el trigo (*corn*)
gram [græm] NOUN
el gramo
grammar ['græmər] NOUN
la gramática ◇ *a grammar exercise* un ejercicio de gramática
grammar school ['græmər,sku:l] NOUN
la escuela de enseñanza primaria
grammatical [grə'mætɪkəl] ADJECTIVE
gramatical
grand [grænd] ADJECTIVE
grandioso ◇ *Her house is very grand.* Su casa es grandiosa.
◆ **the Grand Canyon** el Gran Cañón del Colorado
grandchildren ['grænd,tʃɪldrən] PL NOUN
los nietos
granddad ['grændæd] NOUN
el abuelo
granddaughter ['græn,dɑ:tər] NOUN
la nieta
grandfather ['grænd,fɑ:ðər] NOUN
el abuelo
grandma ['grænmɑ:] NOUN
la abuela
grandmother ['grænd,mʌðər] NOUN
la abuela
grandpa ['grænpɑ:] NOUN
el abuelo
grandparents ['grænd,pɛrənts] PL NOUN
los abuelos
grandson ['grænd,sʌn] NOUN
el nieto
granny ['græni] NOUN (PL **grannies**)
la abuelita
grant [grænt] NOUN
1 la beca (*for study*)
2 la subvención (PL las subvenciones) (*for industry, organization*)
grape [greɪp] NOUN
la uva
grapefruit ['greɪpfru:t] NOUN
la toronja
graph [græf] NOUN
el gráfico
to **grasp** [græsp] VERB
agarrar
grass [græs] NOUN
1 la hierba ◇ *The grass is long.* La hierba está alta.
2 el césped (*lawn*) ◇ *"Keep off the grass"* "Prohibido pisar el césped" ◇ *to cut the grass* cortar el césped
grasshopper ['græs,hɑ:pər] NOUN
el saltamontes (PL los saltamontes)
to **grate** [greɪt] VERB
rallar ◇ *grated cheese* el queso rallado
grateful ['greɪtfəl] ADJECTIVE
agradecido
grave [greɪv] NOUN
la tumba
gravel ['grævəl] NOUN
la grava
graveyard ['greɪvjɑ:rd] NOUN
el cementerio
gravy ['greɪvi] NOUN
el jugo de carne
gray [greɪ] ADJECTIVE
gris ◇ *They wore gray suits.* Llevaban trajes grises.
◆ **He's going gray.** Le están saliendo canas.
◆ **gray hair** las canas
gray-haired [greɪ'hɛərd] ADJECTIVE
canoso
grease [gri:s] NOUN
1 la grasa (*in hair, on skin*)
2 el aceite (*for cars, machines*)
greasy ['gri:si] ADJECTIVE
1 grasiento ◇ *The food was very greasy.* La comida estaba muy grasienta.
2 graso ◇ *He has greasy hair.* Tiene el pelo graso.
great [greɪt] ADJECTIVE
1 estupendo ◇ *That's great!* ¡Estupendo!
2 grande
*Use **gran** before a singular noun.*
◇ *a great oak tree* un gran roble ◇ *a greatest hits album* un disco de grandes éxitos
Great Britain [greɪt'brɪtn] NOUN
Gran Bretaña FEM
great-grandfather [greɪt'grænd,fɑ:ðər] NOUN
el bisabuelo
great-grandmother [greɪt'grændmʌðər] NOUN
la bisabuela
Greece [gri:s] NOUN
Grecia FEM
greedy ['gri:di] ADJECTIVE
1 glotón (MASC PL glotones, FEM glotona)
◇ *Don't be greedy; you've already had three doughnuts.* No seas glotón, ya te has comido tres rosquillas.
2 codicioso ◇ *She is greedy and selfish.* Es codiciosa y egoísta.

G

Greek [gri:k] ADJECTIVE
see also **Greek** NOUN
griego

Greek [gri:k] NOUN
see also **Greek** ADJECTIVE
1 el griego
la griega
(*person*)
◇ *the Greeks* los griegos
2 el griego (*language*) ◇ *our Greek teacher* nuestro profesor de griego

green [gri:n] ADJECTIVE
see also **green** NOUN
verde ◇ *a green car* un carro verde ◇ *a green light* un semáforo en verde (*at traffic lights*)
◆ **the Green Party** el Partido Verde

green [gri:n] NOUN
see also **green** ADJECTIVE
el verde ◇ *a dark green* un verde oscuro
◆ **greens** (*vegetables*) la verdura

greenhouse ['gri:nhaus] NOUN
el invernadero
◆ **the greenhouse effect** el efecto invernadero

to **greet** [gri:t] VERB
saludar ◇ *He greeted me with a kiss.* Me saludó con un beso.

greeting card ['gri:tɪŋ,kɑ:rd] NOUN
la tarjeta de felicitación

greetings ['gri:tɪŋz] PL NOUN
◆ **Greetings from Lima!** ¡Saludos desde Lima!
◆ **Season's Greetings** Felices Fiestas

grew [gru:] VERB *see* **grow**

grid [grɪd] NOUN
1 la cuadrícula (*in road, on map*)
2 la red (*of electricity*)

grief [gri:f] NOUN
el dolor

grill [grɪl] NOUN
see also **grill** VERB
1 la parrilla (*for barbecue, in diner*)
2 el grill (*of stove*)

to **grill** [grɪl] VERB
see also **grill** NOUN
asar a la parrilla (*barbecue*)

grim [grɪm] ADJECTIVE
deprimente ◇ *The outskirts of the city are very grim.* Las afueras de la ciudad son muy deprimentes.

to **grin** [grɪn] VERB
see also **grin** NOUN
sonreír* ampliamente ◇ *Brad grinned at me.* Brad me sonrió ampliamente.

grin [grɪn] NOUN
see also **grin** VERB
la sonrisa amplia

to **grind** [graɪnd] VERB (**ground, ground**)
moler* (*coffee, pepper, meat*)

to **grip** [grɪp] VERB
agarrar

gripping ['grɪpɪŋ] ADJECTIVE
emocionante

grit [grɪt] NOUN
la gravilla

to **groan** [groun] VERB
see also **groan** NOUN
gemir* ◇ *He groaned with pain.* Gimió de dolor.

groan [groun] NOUN
see also **groan** VERB
el gemido

grocer ['grousər] NOUN
el tendero
la tendera
el abarrotero
la abarrotera Mexico

groceries ['grousəriz] PL NOUN
los comestibles
los abarrotes Mexico
◆ **I'll get some groceries.** Traeré algunas provisiones.

grocery store ['grousəri,stɔ:r] NOUN
la tienda de comestibles
la tienda de abarrotes Mexico

groom [gru:m] NOUN
el novio ◇ *the groom and his best man* el novio y su padrino de boda

to **grope** [group] VERB
◆ **to grope for something** buscar* algo a tientas ◇ *He groped for the light switch.* Buscó a tientas el interruptor.

gross [grous] ADJECTIVE
1 horrible (*revolting*)
◆ **That's gross!** ¡Qué asco!
2 bruto ◇ *gross income* ingresos brutos

grossly ['grousli] ADVERB
enormemente ◇ *It's grossly unfair.* Es enormemente injusto.

ground [graund] NOUN
see also **ground** VERB
1 el suelo ◇ *The ground is wet.* El suelo está húmedo.
2 la cancha ◇ *the city's baseball grounds* la cancha de béisbol de la ciudad
3 el motivo ◇ *We have grounds for complaint.* Tenemos motivos para quejarnos.
◆ **on the ground** en el suelo ◇ *We sat on the ground.* Nos sentamos en el suelo.

ground [graund] VERB *see* **grind**
see also **ground** NOUN

ground beef [graund'bi:f] NOUN
la carne molida

ground coffee [graund'kɑ:fi] NOUN
el café molido

ground floor [graund'flɔ:r] NOUN
la planta baja

group [gru:p] NOUN
el grupo

to **grow** [grou] VERB (**grew, grown**)

1 crecer* ◊ *Haven't you grown!* ¡Cómo has crecido!
2 aumentar ◊ *The number of unemployed has grown.* Ha aumentado el número de desempleados.
3 cultivar ◊ *He grew vegetables in his garden.* Cultivaba hortalizas en su jardín.
◆ **He's grown out of his jacket.** La chaqueta le queda chica.
◆ **to grow a beard** dejarse la barba ◊ *I'm growing a beard.* Me estoy dejando la barba.
◆ **He grew a mustache.** Se dejó el bigote.

to **grow up** [grou'ʌp] VERB
criarse* ◊ *I grew up in Chicago.* Me crié en Chicago.
◆ **Oh, grow up!** ¡No seas infantil!

to **growl** [graul] VERB
gruñir*

grown [groun] VERB *see* **grow**

growth [grouθ] NOUN
el crecimiento ◊ *economic growth* crecimiento económico

grub [grʌb] NOUN
la comida

grudge [grʌdʒ] NOUN ◊ *to bear a grudge against somebody* guardar rencor a alguien ◊ *He's always had a grudge against me.* Siempre me ha guardado rencor.

gruesome ['gru:səm] ADJECTIVE
horroroso

guarantee [gɛrən'ti:] NOUN
see also **guarantee** VERB
la garantía ◊ *a five-year guarantee* una garantía de cinco años ◊ *It's still under guarantee.* Todavía tiene garantía.

to **guarantee** [gɛrən'ti:] VERB
see also **guarantee** NOUN
garantizar* ◊ *I can't guarantee he'll come.* No puedo garantizar que venga.

to **guard** [ga:rd] VERB
see also **guard** NOUN
vigilar ◊ *The police were guarding the entrance.* La policía vigilaba la entrada.

guard [ga:rd] NOUN
see also **guard** VERB
el/la guardia (*person*) ◊ *a security guard* una guardia de seguridad

guard dog ['ga:rd,da:g] NOUN
el perro guardián

to **guess** [gɛs] VERB
see also **guess** NOUN
adivinar ◊ *Can you guess what it is?* A ver si adivinas qué es.
◆ **to guess wrong** equivocarse*
◆ **Guess what!** ¿Sabes qué?

guess [gɛs] NOUN (PL **guesses**)
see also **guess** VERB
la suposición (PL las suposiciones) ◊ *It's just a guess.* Sólo es una suposición.
◆ **Take a guess!** ¡Adivina!

guest [gɛst] NOUN
1 el invitado
la invitada
◊ *We have guests staying with us.* Tenemos invitados en casa.
2 el/la huésped (*in hotel*)

guesthouse ['gɛst,haus] NOUN
la pensión (PL las pensiones)

guide [gaɪd] NOUN
1 la guía ◊ *We bought a guide to Caracas.* Compramos una guía de Caracas.
2 el/la guía ◊ *The guide showed us around the castle.* El guía nos enseñó el castillo.

guidebook ['gaɪd,buk] NOUN
la guía

guide dog ['gaɪd,da:g] NOUN
el perro lazarillo

guilty ['gɪlti] ADJECTIVE
culpable ◊ *She was found guilty.* Fue declarada culpable. ◊ *He felt guilty.* Se sentía culpable.
◆ **He has a guilty conscience.** Tiene remordimientos de conciencia.

guinea pig ['gɪni,pɪg] NOUN
el cobayo ◊ *She has a guinea pig.* Tiene un cobayo.

guitar [gɪ'ta:r] NOUN
la guitarra

gum [gʌm] NOUN
el chicle (*chewing gum*)
◆ **a piece of gum** un chicle
◆ **gums** (*in mouth*) las encías

gun [gʌn] NOUN
1 la pistola (*small*)
2 el fusil (*rifle*)

gunpoint ['gʌnpɔɪnt] NOUN
◆ **at gunpoint** a punta de pistola

gust [gʌst] NOUN
◆ **a gust of wind** una ráfaga de viento

guts [gʌts] PL NOUN
◆ **He certainly has guts.** Desde luego tiene agallas.
◆ **I hate his guts.** Lo odio con toda mi alma.

guy [gaɪ] NOUN
el tipo (*informal*) ◊ *Who's that guy?* ¿Quién es ese tipo? ◊ *He's a nice guy.* Es un tipo simpático.

gym [dʒɪm] NOUN
el gimnasio ◊ *I go to the gym every day.* Voy al gimnasio todos los días.
◆ **I have a gym class on Tuesday.** Tengo la clase de gimnasia los martes.

gymnast ['dʒɪmnɪst] NOUN
el/la gimnasta

gymnastics [dʒɪm'næstɪks] NOUN
la gimnasia

gym shoes ['dʒɪm,ʃu:z] PL NOUN
las zapatillas de deporte

gypsy ['dʒɪpsi] NOUN (PL **gypsies**)
el gitano
la gitana

G

H

habit ['hæbɪt] NOUN
la costumbre
had [hæd] VERB *see* **have**
haddock ['hædək] NOUN (PL **haddock**)
el abadejo
hadn't ['hædnt] = **had not**
hail [heɪl] NOUN
see also **hail** VERB
el granizo
to **hail** [heɪl] VERB
see also **hail** NOUN
granizar*
hair [hɛər] NOUN
el pelo ◇ *She has long hair.* Tiene el pelo largo. ◇ *I'm allergic to cat hair.* Soy alérgico al pelo de los gatos.
◆ **to have one's hair cut** cortarse el pelo
◆ **gray hair** las canas
◆ **to brush one's hair** cepillarse el pelo
◆ **to wash one's hair** lavarse el pelo
hairbrush ['hɛrˌbrʌʃ] NOUN (PL **hairbrushes**)
el cepillo (*para el pelo*)
haircut ['hɛrˌkʌt] NOUN
el corte de pelo ◇ *You need a haircut.* Necesitas un corte de pelo.
◆ **to get a haircut** cortarse el pelo
hairdresser ['hɛrˌdrɛsər] NOUN
el peluquero
la peluquera
◇ *He's a hairdresser.* Es peluquero.
◆ **at the hairdresser's** en la peluquería
hair dryer ['hɛrˌdraɪər] NOUN
el secador de pelo
la secadora de pelo *Mexico*
hair gel ['hɛrˌdʒɛl] NOUN
el fijador
hairspray ['hɛrˌspreɪ] NOUN
la laca (*para el pelo*)
hairstyle ['hɛrˌstaɪl] NOUN
el peinado
hairy ['hɛri] ADJECTIVE
peludo ◇ *He's very hairy.* Es muy peludo.
◆ **He has hairy legs.** Tiene mucho pelo en las piernas.
half [hæf] NOUN (PL **halves**)
see also **half** ADJECTIVE
la mitad ◇ *half of the cake* la mitad del pastel
◆ **to cut something in half** cortar algo por la mitad
◆ **two and a half** dos y medio
◆ **half a chicken** medio pollo
◆ **half a pound** media libra
◆ **half an hour** media hora
◆ **half past ten** las diez y media
half [hæf] ADJECTIVE, ADVERB
see also **half** NOUN
medio ◇ *a half dozen eggs* una media docena de huevos
*When you use **medio** before an adjective, it does not change*
◇ *She was half asleep.* Estaba medio dormida. ◇ *They were half drunk.* Estaban medio borrachos.
half price ['hæf'praɪs] ADJECTIVE, ADVERB
a mitad de precio (*ticket etc*) ◇ *I bought it at half price.* Lo compré a mitad de precio.
half-time ['hæfˌtaɪm] NOUN
el medio tiempo (*del partido*)
halfway ['hæf'weɪ] ADVERB
1 a medio camino ◇ *Memphis is halfway between Dallas and Atlanta.* Memphis está a medio camino entre Dallas y Atlanta.
2 a la mitad ◇ *halfway through the movie* a la mitad de la película
hall [hɑːl] NOUN
1 el pasillo (*passage*)
2 la sala ◇ *a lecture hall* una sala de conferencias
◆ **a concert hall** un auditorio
◆ **a sports hall** un gimnasio
◆ **town hall** el salón de actos municipal
◆ **city hall** el ayuntamiento, *Mexico:* la presidencia municipal
Halloween [ˌhælou'iːn] NOUN
la víspera de Todos los Santos

> ℹ *La tradición dice que* **Halloween**, *la noche del 31 de octubre, es la noche de las brujas. Los niños, disfrazados de fantasmas y portando faroles hechos con calabazas vacías, van de casa en casa pidiendo golosinas o un aguinaldo.*

hallway ['hɑːlweɪ] NOUN
el pasillo
halt [hɑːlt] NOUN
◆ **to come to a halt** pararse
halves [hævz] PL NOUN *see* **half**
ham [hæm] NOUN
el jamón (PL los jamones)
hamburger ['hæmˌbɜːrgər] NOUN
la hamburguesa
hammer ['hæmər] NOUN
el martillo
hamster ['hæmstər] NOUN
el hámster
hand [hænd] NOUN
see also **hand** VERB
1 la mano (*of person*)
*Although **mano** ends in **-o** it is actually a feminine noun.*
2 la manecilla (*of clock*)
◆ **to give someone a hand** echar una mano a alguien ◇ *Can you give me a hand?* ¿Me echas una mano?
◆ **on the one hand..., on the other hand...** por

* Verbs marked with this symbol are irregular. See pages 346–348 for further details.

un lado..., por otro...

to **hand** [hænd] VERB
see also **hand** NOUN
pasar ◇ *He handed me the book.* Me pasó el libro.

to **hand in** [hænd'ɪn] VERB
entregar* ◇ *Martin handed in his exam paper.* Martin entregó su examen.

to **hand out** [hænd'aut] VERB
repartir ◇ *The teacher handed out the books.* El profesor repartió los libros.

to **hand over** [hænd'ouvər] VERB
entregar* ◇ *She handed the keys over to me.* Me entregó las llaves.

handbag ['hænd,bæg] NOUN
la cartera
la bolsa Mexico

handball ['hænd,bɑːl] NOUN
el handball

handbook ['hænd,buk] NOUN
el manual

handcuffs ['hænd,kʌfs] PL NOUN
las esposas

handkerchief ['hæŋkərtʃɪf] NOUN
el pañuelo

handle ['hændl] NOUN
see also **handle** VERB
1 el picaporte (*of door*)
2 el asa (*of cup, briefcase*)
Although it's a feminine noun, remember that you use ***el*** *and* ***un*** *with* ***asa.***
3 el mango (*of knife, saucepan*)

to **handle** ['hændl] VERB
see also **handle** NOUN
1 encargarse* de ◇ *Kathy handled the travel arrangements.* Kathy se encargó de organizar el viaje.
2 manejar ◇ *It was a difficult situation, but he handled it well.* Era una situación difícil, pero él supo manejarla bien.
3 tratar ◇ *She's good at handling children.* Sabe tratar a los niños.
◆ **"handle with care"** "frágil"

handlebars ['hændl,bɑːrz] PL NOUN
el manubrio

handmade ['hænd'meɪd] ADJECTIVE
hecho a mano (FEM hecha a mano)

handsome ['hænsəm] ADJECTIVE
buen mozo
guapo Mexico
◇ *My father is very handsome.* Mi papá es muy buen mozo. Mexico: Mi padre es muy guapo.

handwriting ['hænd,raɪtɪŋ] NOUN
la letra ◇ *His handwriting is terrible.* Tiene una letra horrible.

handy ['hændi] ADJECTIVE
1 práctico ◇ *This knife is very handy.* Este cuchillo es muy práctico.
2 a mano ◇ *Do you have a pen handy?* ¿Tienes un bolígrafo a mano?

to **hang** [hæŋ] VERB (**hung, hung**)
1 colgar* ◇ *Mike hung the painting on the wall.* Mike colgó el cuadro en la pared.
◇ *There was a light hanging from the ceiling.* Una lámpara colgaba del techo.
2 ahorcar*
Se usa ***hanged*** *para el pasado y participio pasado de este sentido de* ***to hang***
◇ *In the past criminals were hanged.* Antiguamente se ahorcaba a los criminales.

to **hang around** [hæŋə'raund] VERB
pasar el rato ◇ *On Saturdays we hang around the park.* Los sábados pasamos el rato en el parque.

to **hang on** [hæŋ'ɑːn] VERB
esperar ◇ *Hang on a minute please.* Espera un momento, por favor.

to **hang up** [hæŋ'ʌp] VERB
colgar* (*clothes, phone*) ◇ *Don't hang up!* ¡No cuelgues! ◇ *He hung up on me.* Me colgó.

hanger ['hæŋər] NOUN
el gancho (*for clothes*)

hang-gliding ['hæŋ,glaɪdɪŋ] NOUN
el ala delta
Although it's a feminine noun, remember that you use ***el*** *and* ***un*** *with* ***ala.***
◇ *to go hang-gliding* hacer* ala delta

hangover ['hæŋ,ouvər] NOUN
la resaca
la cruda Mexico
◇ *I woke up with a hangover.* Me desperté con resaca. Mexico: Me desperté con la cruda.

to **happen** ['hæpən] VERB
pasar ◇ *What happened?* ¿Qué pasó?
◆ **As it happens, I do know him.** Da la casualidad de que lo conozco.
◆ **Do you happen to know if she's at home?** ¿Por casualidad sabes si está en casa?

happily ['hæpəli] ADVERB
1 alegremente ◇ *"Don't worry!", he said happily.* "¡No te preocupes!" dijo alegremente.
2 felizmente ◇ *He's happily married.* Está felizmente casado.
◆ **And they lived happily ever after.** Y vivieron felices y comieron perdices.
3 afortunadamente ◇ *Happily, everything went well.* Afortunadamente todo salió bien.

happiness ['hæpinɪs] NOUN
la felicidad

happy ['hæpi] ADJECTIVE
feliz (PL felices) ◇ *Janet looks happy.* Janet se ve feliz.
◆ **to be happy with something** estar* contento con algo ◇ *I'm very happy with your work.* Estoy muy contento con tu trabajo.
◆ **Happy birthday!** ¡Feliz cumpleaños!
◆ **a happy ending** un final feliz

harbor ['hɑːrbər] NOUN
el puerto

hard [hɑːrd] ADJECTIVE, ADVERB
[1] duro ◇ *This cheese is very hard.* Este queso está muy duro. ◇ *to work hard* trabajar duro
[2] difícil ◇ *The exam was very hard.* El examen fue muy difícil.

hard disk ['hɑːrd,dɪsk] NOUN
el disco duro

hardly ['hɑːrdli] ADVERB
apenas ◇ *I hardly know you.* Apenas te conozco.
◆ **I have hardly any money.** Casi no tengo dinero.
◆ **hardly ever** casi nunca
◆ **hardly anything** casi nada

hard up [hɑːrd'ʌp] ADJECTIVE
◆ **to be hard up** estar* pelado, *Mexico:* estar* sin lana (*informal*)

hardware store ['hɑːrdwɛr,stɔːr] NOUN
la ferretería
la tlapalería *Mexico*

hare [hɛər] NOUN
la liebre

to **harm** [hɑːrm] VERB
◆ **to harm somebody** hacer* daño a alguien ◇ *I didn't mean to harm you.* No quería hacerte daño.
◆ **to harm something** dañar algo ◇ *Chemicals harm the environment.* Los productos químicos dañan el medio ambiente.

harmful ['hɑːrmfəl] ADJECTIVE
perjudicial ◇ *harmful to the environment* perjudicial para el medio ambiente

harmless ['hɑːrmlɪs] ADJECTIVE
inofensivo

harsh [hɑːrʃ] ADJECTIVE
[1] severo ◇ *He deserves a harsh punishment for what he did.* Merece un castigo severo por lo que ha hecho.
[2] áspero ◇ *She has a very harsh voice.* Tiene una voz muy áspera.

has [hæz] VERB *see* **have**

hasn't ['hæznt] = **has not**

hat [hæt] NOUN
el sombrero

to **hate** [heɪt] VERB
odiar

hatred ['heɪtrɪd] NOUN
el odio

haunted ['hɑːntɪd] ADJECTIVE
◆ **a haunted house** una casa embrujada

to **have** [hæv] VERB (**had, had**)
Use the verb ***haber*** *to form the perfect tenses.*
[1] haber* ◇ *Have you seen that movie?* ¿Has visto esa película? ◇ *He hasn't gone yet.* No se ha ido todavía. ◇ *If you had called me I would have come round.* Si me hubieras llamado habría venido.
If you are using ***have*** *in question tags to confirm a statement use* ***¿no?*** *or* ***¿verdad?.***
◇ *You've never been there, have you?* No has estado nunca allí, ¿verdad? ◇ *They've arrived, haven't they?* Ya llegaron, ¿no?
Have *is not translated when giving simple negative or positive answers to questions.*
◇ *Have you read that book? – Yes, I have.* ¿Has leído ese libro? – Sí. ◇ *Has he told you? – No, he hasn't.* ¿Te lo ha dicho? – No.
[2] tener* ◇ *I have a terrible cold.* Tengo un resfriado horrible. ◇ *She had a baby last year.* Tuvo un niño el año pasado. ◇ *Do you have any brothers or sisters?* ¿Tienes hermanos?
◆ **to have to do something** tener que hacer algo
[3] tomar ◇ *I'll have a cup of coffee.* Tomaré un café. ◇ *Shall we have a drink?* ¿Tomemos algo?
◆ **to have a shower** ducharse
◆ **to have one's hair cut** cortarse el pelo

haven't ['hævənt] = **have not**

hay [heɪ] NOUN
el heno

hay fever ['heɪ,fiːvər] NOUN
la fiebre de heno

hazelnut ['heɪzəl,nʌt] NOUN
la avellana

he [hiː] PRONOUN
él
he *generally isn't translated unless it is emphatic.*
◇ *He is very tall.* Es muy alto.
Use ***él*** *for emphasis.*
◇ *He did it but she didn't.* Él lo hizo, pero ella no.

head [hɛd] NOUN
see also **head** VERB
[1] la cabeza ◇ *Mind your head!* ¡Cuidado con la cabeza! ◇ *The wine went to my head.* El vino se me subió a la cabeza. ◇ *He lost his head and started screaming.* Perdió la cabeza y empezó a gritar.
[2] el jefe
la jefa
(*leader*)
◇ *a head of state* un jefe de Estado
◆ **I don't have a head for figures.** No tengo cabeza para los números.
◆ **Heads or tails? – Heads.** ¿Cara o cruz? – Cara. *Mexico:* ¿Águila o sol? – Águila.

to **head** [hɛd] VERB
see also **head** NOUN
◆ **to head for** dirigirse* a ◇ *They headed for the church.* Se dirigieron a la iglesia.

headache ['hɛdeɪk] NOUN
el dolor de cabeza ◇ *I have a headache.* Tengo dolor de cabeza.

headlight ['hɛd,laɪt] NOUN
el faro (*de carro*)

headline ['hɛd,laɪn] NOUN
el titular

headphones ['hɛd,founz] PL NOUN
los auriculares

headquarters ['hɛd,kwɔ:rtərz] PL NOUN
el cuartel general (*of army*)
◆ **The bank's headquarters are in Quito.** La oficina central del banco está en Quito.

to **heal** [hi:l] VERB
curar

health [hɛlθ] NOUN
la salud ◇ *She's in good health.* Tiene buena salud.

healthy ['hɛlθi] ADJECTIVE
sano ◇ *She's very healthy.* Es muy sana. ◇ *a healthy diet* una dieta sana

heap [hi:p] NOUN
el montón (PL los montones)

to **hear** [hɪər] VERB (**heard, heard**)
oír* ◇ *We heard the dog bark.* Oímos ladrar al perro. ◇ *She can't hear very well.* No oye bien.
◆ **I heard she was ill.** Me dijeron que estaba enferma.
◆ **to hear about something** enterarse de algo ◇ *I've heard about your new job.* Me he enterado de que tienes un nuevo trabajo. ◇ *Did you hear the good news?* ¿Te enteraste de la buena noticia?
◆ **to hear from somebody** tener* noticias de alguien ◇ *I haven't heard from him recently.* Últimamente no he tenido noticias de él.

heart [hɑ:rt] NOUN
el corazón (PL los corazones)
◆ **hearts** (*at cards*) los corazones ◇ *the ace of hearts* el as de corazones
◆ **to learn something by heart** aprenderse algo de memoria

heart attack ['hɑ:rtə,tæk] NOUN
el infarto

heartbroken ['hɑ:rt,broukən] ADJECTIVE
◆ **to be heartbroken** tener* el corazón partido

heat [hi:t] NOUN
see also **heat** VERB
el calor

to **heat** [hi:t] VERB
see also **heat** NOUN
calentar* ◇ *Heat gently for five minutes.* Caliente a fuego lento durante cinco minutos.

to **heat up** [hi:t'ʌp] VERB
1 calentar* ◇ *He heated the soup up.* Calentó la sopa.
2 calentarse* (*water, oven*) ◇ *The water is heating up.* El agua se está calentando.

heater ['hi:tər] NOUN
el calentador ◇ *a water heater* un calentador de agua
◆ **an electric heater** una estufa eléctrica
◆ **Could you put on the heater?** ¿Puedes poner la calefacción? (*in car*)

heather ['hɛðər] NOUN
el brezo

heating ['hi:tɪŋ] NOUN
la calefacción

heaven ['hɛvən] NOUN
el cielo
◆ **to go to heaven** ir* al cielo

heavily ['hɛvəli] ADVERB
◆ **It rained heavily during the night.** Llovió con fuerza por la noche.
◆ **He's a heavily built man.** Es un hombre corpulento.
◆ **He drinks heavily.** Toma demasiado.

heavy ['hɛvi] ADJECTIVE
pesado ◇ *a heavy load* una carga pesada
◆ **This bag is very heavy.** Esta bolsa pesa mucho.
◆ **heavy rain** fuerte lluvia
◆ **He's a heavy drinker.** Es un bebedor empedernido.

he'd [hi:d] = **he would, he had**

hedge [hɛdʒ] NOUN
el seto

hedgehog ['hɛdʒ,hɑ:g] NOUN
el erizo

heel [hi:l] NOUN
1 el tacón (PL los tacones) (*of shoe*) ◇ *high-heel shoes* los zapatos de tacón alto
2 el talón (PL los talones) (*of foot*)

height [haɪt] NOUN
1 la estatura (*of person*)
2 la altura (*of object, mountain*)

heir [ɛər] NOUN
el heredero

heiress ['ɛrəs] NOUN (PL **heiresses**)
la heredera

held [hɛld] VERB *see* **hold**

helicopter ['hɛlɪkɑ:ptər] NOUN
el helicóptero

hell [hɛl] NOUN
el infierno
◆ **Hell!** ¡Maldita sea!

he'll [hi:l] = **he will, he shall**

hello [hə'lou] EXCLAMATION
1 ¡hola! (*when you see somebody*)
2 ¡sí!
¡bueno! Mexico
(*on the phone*)

helmet ['hɛlmɪt] NOUN
el casco

to **help** [hɛlp] VERB
see also **help** NOUN
ayudar ◇ *Can you help me?* ¿Puedes ayudarme?
◆ **Help!** ¡Socorro!
◆ **Help yourself!** ¡Sírvete!
◆ **I couldn't help laughing.** No pude evitar reírme.

help [hɛlp] NOUN
see also **help** VERB
la ayuda ◇ *Do you need any help?*

H

☞

¿Necesitas ayuda?

helpful ['hɛlpfəl] ADJECTIVE
útil ◇ *He gave me some helpful advice.* Me dio algunos consejos útiles.
◆ **You've been very helpful!** ¡Muchas gracias por su ayuda!

hen [hɛn] NOUN
la gallina

her [hɜːr] ADJECTIVE
see also **her** PRONOUN
su (PL sus) ◇ *her father* su papá ◇ *her house* su casa ◇ *her two best friends* sus dos mejores amigos ◇ *her sisters* sus hermanas
***her** is usually translated by the definite article **el/los** or **la/las** when it's clear from the sentence who the possessor is or when referring to clothing or parts of the body.*
◇ *They stole her car.* Le robaron el coche.
◇ *She took off her coat.* Se quitó el abrigo.
◇ *She's washing her hair.* Se está lavando el pelo.

her [hɜːr] PRONOUN
see also **her** ADJECTIVE
1 la
*Use **la** when **her** is the direct object of the verb in the sentence.*
◇ *I saw her.* La vi. ◇ *Look at her!* ¡Mírala!
2 le
*Use **le** when **her** means **to her**.*
◇ *I gave her a book.* Le di un libro. ◇ *You have to tell her the truth.* Tienes que decirle la verdad.
3 se
*Use **se** not **le** when **her** is used in combination with a direct-object pronoun.*
◇ *Give it to her.* Dáselo.
4 ella
*Use **ella** after prepositions, in comparisons, and with the verb **to be**.*
◇ *I'm going with her.* Voy con ella. ◇ *I'm older than her.* Soy mayor que ella. ◇ *It must be her.* Debe de ser ella.
◆ **She was carrying it on her.** Lo llevaba consigo.

herb [ɜːrb] NOUN
la hierba (*medicinal o aromática*)

here [hɪər] ADVERB
aquí ◇ *I live here.* Vivo aquí. ◇ *Here he is!* ¡Aquí está! ◇ *Here are the books.* Aquí están los libros.
◆ **Here's your coffee.** Aquí tienes el café.
◆ **Do you have my pencil? – Here you are.** ¿Tienes mi lápiz? – Aquí tienes.
◆ **Here are the papers you asked for.** Aquí tienes los papeles que pediste.

hero ['hɪrou] NOUN (PL **heroes**)
el héroe

heroin ['hɛrouən] NOUN
la heroína
◆ **a heroin addict** un heroinómano

heroine ['hɛrouən] NOUN
la heroína

hers [hɜːrz] PRONOUN
1 el suyo MASC (PL los suyos) ◇ *Is this her coat? – No, hers is black.* ¿Es éste su abrigo? – No, el suyo es negro. ◇ *We had dinner with my parents and hers.* Cenamos con mis padres y los suyos.
2 la suya FEM (PL las suyas) ◇ *Is this her scarf? – No, hers is red.* ¿Es ésta su bufanda? – No, la suya es roja. ◇ *We met my sisters and hers.* Nos encontramos con mis hermanas y las suyas.
3 suyo MASC (PL suyos) ◇ *Is that car hers?* ¿Es suyo ese carro?
4 suya FEM (PL suyas) ◇ *Is that wallet hers?* ¿Es suya esa cartera?
◆ **Isobel is a friend of hers.** Isobel es amiga suya.
*Use **de ella** instead of **suyo** if you want to avoid confusion with "his", "theirs", etc.*
◇ *Whose is this? – It's hers.* ¿De quién es esto? – Es de ella.

herself [hɜːr'sɛlf] PRONOUN
1 se (*reflexive*) ◇ *She hurt herself.* Se hizo daño.
2 sí misma (*after preposition*) ◇ *She talked mainly about herself.* Habló principalmente de sí misma.
3 ella misma (*for emphasis*) ◇ *She did it herself.* Lo hizo ella misma.
◆ **by herself** (*alone*) sola ◇ *She came by herself.* Vino sola.

he's [hiːz] = **he is, he has**

to **hesitate** ['hɛzɪteɪt] VERB
dudar ◇ *Don't hesitate to ask.* No dudes en preguntar.

heterosexual [ˌhɛtərou'sɛkʃuəl] ADJECTIVE
heterosexual

hi [haɪ] EXCLAMATION
¡hola!

hiccup ['hɪkʌp] NOUN
el hipo ◇ *The baby has hiccups.* El bebé tiene hipo.

to **hide** [haɪd] VERB (**hid, hidden**)
1 esconder ◇ *Paula hid the present.* Paula escondió el regalo.
2 esconderse ◇ *He hid behind a bush.* Se escondió detrás de un arbusto.

hide-and-seek ['haɪdn'siːk] NOUN
◆ **to play hide-and-seek** jugar* a las escondidas

hideous ['hɪdiəs] ADJECTIVE
horroroso

hi-fi ['haɪfaɪ] NOUN
el equipo de alta fidelidad

high [haɪ] ADJECTIVE, ADVERB
1 alto ◇ *The gate is too high.* La verja es demasiado alta. ◇ *Prices are higher in Germany.* Los precios están más altos en

Alemania. ◇ *It's very high in fat.* Tiene un alto contenido en grasas. ◇ *The plane flew high over the mountains.* El avión volaba alto sobre las montañas.

◆ **How high is the wall?** ¿Cómo es de alto el muro?

◆ **The wall is two meters high.** El muro tiene dos metros de altura.

[2] agudo ◇ *She has a very high voice.* Tiene la voz muy aguda.

◆ **at high speed** a gran velocidad

◆ **to be high** (*on drugs*) estar* volado, *Mexico:* estar* pedo (*informal*)

◆ **to get high** (*on drugs*) ponerse* volado, *Mexico:* ponerse* pedo (*informal*)

higher education [ˈhaɪərɛdʒəˈkeɪʃən] NOUN
la enseñanza superior

high jump [ˈhaɪˌdʒʌmp] NOUN
el salto alto

highlight [ˈhaɪlaɪt] NOUN
see also **highlight** VERB
el punto culminante ◇ *the highlight of the evening* el punto culminante de la velada

to **highlight** [ˈhaɪlaɪt] VERB
see also **highlight** NOUN
poner* de relieve

highlighter [ˈhaɪˌlaɪtər] NOUN
el marcador

high rise [ˈhaɪˌraɪz] NOUN
el edificio de muchos pisos

high-rise [ˈhaɪraɪz] ADJECTIVE
◆ **high-rise building** edificio de muchos pisos

high school [ˈhaɪˌskuːl] NOUN
el colegio secundario
◆ **high school diploma** el bachillerato

highway [ˈhaɪweɪ] NOUN
la carretera (*main road*)

to **hijack** [ˈhaɪdʒæk] VERB
secuestrar

hijacker [ˈhaɪˌdʒækər] NOUN
el secuestrador
la secuestradora

hike [haɪk] NOUN
la caminata (*por el campo*)

hiking [ˈhaɪkɪŋ] NOUN
◆ **to go hiking** ir* de excursión al campo

hilarious [hɪˈlɛriəs] ADJECTIVE
graciosísimo

hill [hɪl] NOUN
[1] la colina ◇ *a house at the top of a hill* una casa en lo alto de una colina
[2] la cuesta (*slope*) ◇ *I climbed the hill up to the office.* Subí la cuesta hasta la oficina.

him [hɪm] PRONOUN
[1] lo
Use ***lo*** *when* ***him*** *is the direct object of the verb in the sentence.*
◇ *I saw him.* Lo vi. ◇ *Look at him!* ¡Míralo!
[2] le
Use ***le*** *when* ***him*** *means* ***to him.***
◇ *I gave him a book.* Le di un libro. ◇ *You have to tell him the truth.* Tienes que decirle la verdad.
[3] se
Use ***se*** *not* ***le*** *when* ***him*** *is used in combination with a direct-object pronoun.*
◇ *Give it to him.* Dáselo.
[4] él
Use ***él*** *after prepositions, in comparisons and with the verb* ***to be.***
◇ *I'm going with him.* Voy con él. ◇ *I'm older than him.* Soy mayor que él. ◇ *It must be him.* Debe de ser él.
◆ **He was carrying it on him.** Lo llevaba consigo.

himself [hɪmˈsɛlf] PRONOUN
[1] se (*reflexive*) ◇ *He hurt himself.* Se hizo daño.
[2] sí mismo (*after preposition*) ◇ *He talked mainly about himself.* Habló principalmente de sí mismo.
[3] él mismo (*for emphasis*) ◇ *He did it himself.* Lo hizo él mismo.
◆ **by himself** (*alone*) solo ◇ *He came by himself.* Vino solo.

Hindu [ˈhɪnduː] ADJECTIVE
hindú (PL hindúes)

hint [hɪnt] NOUN
see also **hint** VERB
la indirecta
◆ **to drop a hint** soltar* una indirecta
◆ **to take a hint** captar una indirecta

to **hint** [hɪnt] VERB
see also **hint** NOUN
insinuar* ◇ *He hinted that I had a good chance of getting the job.* Insinuó que tenía muchas posibilidades de conseguir el trabajo.

hip [hɪp] NOUN
la cadera ◇ *She put her hands on her hips.* Se puso las manos en las caderas.

hippie [ˈhɪpi] NOUN
el/la hippy (PL los hippies)

hippo [ˈhɪpou] NOUN
el hipopótamo

to **hire** [ˈhaɪər] VERB
contratar ◇ *They hired a lawyer.* Contrataron a un abogado.

his [hɪz] ADJECTIVE
see also **his** PRONOUN
su (PL sus) ◇ *his father* su padre ◇ *his house* su casa ◇ *his two best friends* sus dos mejores amigos ◇ *his sisters* sus hermanas
his *is usually translated by the definite article* ***el/los*** *or* ***la/las*** *when it's clear from the sentence who the possessor is or when referring to clothing or parts of the body.*
◇ *They stole his car.* Le robaron el carro.
◇ *He took off his coat.* Se sacó el abrigo.
◇ *He's washing his car.* Está lavando el carro.

his [hɪz] PRONOUN
see also **his** ADJECTIVE

☞

H

1 el suyo MASC (PL los suyos) ◇ *Is this his coat? – No, his is black.* ¿Es éste su abrigo? – No, el suyo es negro. ◇ *We had dinner with my parents and his.* Cenamos con mis padres y los suyos.
2 la suya FEM (PL las suyas) ◇ *Is this his scarf? – No, his is red.* ¿Es ésta su bufanda? – No, la suya es roja. ◇ *We met my sisters and his.* Nos encontramos con mis hermanas y las suyas.
3 suyo MASC (PL suyos) ◇ *Is that car his?* ¿Es suyo ese carro?
4 suya FEM (PL suyas) ◇ *Is that wallet his?* ¿Es suya esa cartera?
◆ **Isobel is a friend of his.** Isobel es amiga suya.
*Use **de él** instead of **suyo** if you want to avoid confusion with "hers", "theirs", etc.*
◇ *Whose is this? – It's his.* ¿De quién es esto? – Es de él.

Hispanic [hɪ'spænɪk] ADJECTIVE
see also **Hispanic** NOUN
hispano ◇ *the Hispanic community* la comunidad hispana

Hispanic [hɪ'spænɪk] NOUN
see also **Hispanic** ADJECTIVE
el hispano
la hispana

history ['hɪstəri] NOUN
la historia

to **hit** [hɪt] VERB (**hit**, **hit**)
see also **hit** NOUN
1 pegar* ◇ *He hit the ball.* Le pegó a la pelota. ◇ *Andrew hit him.* Andrew le pegó.
2 chocar* con ◇ *The car hit a road sign.* El carro chocó con una señal de tráfico.
◆ **He was hit by a car.** Lo atropelló un carro.
◆ **to hit the target** dar* en el blanco
◆ **to hit it off with somebody** hacer* buenas migas con alguien

hit [hɪt] NOUN
see also **hit** VERB
el éxito ◇ *Eminem's latest hit.* El último éxito de Eminem. ◇ *The movie was a massive hit.* La película fue un éxito enorme.

hitch [hɪtʃ] NOUN (PL **hitches**)
el contratiempo ◇ *There's been a slight hitch.* Ha habido un pequeño contratiempo.

to **hitchhike** ['hɪtʃ,haɪk] VERB
hacer* autoestop
ir* de aventón *Mexico*

hitchhiker ['hɪtʃ,haɪkər] NOUN
el/la autoestopista

hitchhiking ['hɪtʃ,haɪkɪŋ] NOUN
el autoestop

hit man ['hɪt,mæn] NOUN (PL **hit men**)
el asesino a sueldo

HIV [,eɪtʃaɪ'viː] NOUN (= *human immunodeficiency virus*)
el VIH

HIV-positive [,eɪtʃaɪviː'pɑːzɪtɪv] ADJECTIVE
seropositivo

hobby ['hɑːbi] NOUN (PL **hobbies**)
el hobby (PL los hobbies)

hockey ['hɑːki] NOUN
el hockey sobre hielo. ◇ *I like playing hockey.* Me gusta jugar hockey sobre hielo.

to **hold** [hould] VERB (**held**, **held**)
1 tener* ◇ *He was holding her in his arms.* La tenía entre sus brazos.
2 sujetar ◇ *Hold the ladder.* Sujeta la escalera.
3 contener* ◇ *This bottle holds one liter.* Esta botella contiene un litro.
◆ **to hold a meeting** celebrar una reunión
◆ **Hold the line!** (*on telephone*) ¡No cuelgue!
◆ **Hold it!** ¡Espera!
◆ **to get hold of something** hacerse* con algo

to **hold on** [hould'ɑːn] VERB
1 agarrar (*keep hold*) ◇ *The cliff was slippery but he managed to hold on.* El acantilado era resbaloso, pero logró agarrarse.
◆ **to hold on to something** agarrarse a algo
2 esperar (*wait*) ◇ *Hold on, I'm coming!* ¡Espera que ya voy!
◆ **Hold on!** (*on telephone*) ¡No cuelgue!

to **hold up** [hould'ʌp] VERB
1 levantar ◇ *Peter held up his hand.* Peter levantó la mano.
2 retrasar ◇ *We were held up by the traffic.* Nos retrasamos por culpa del tráfico.
3 atracar* ◇ *to hold up a bank* atracar un banco
◆ **I was held up at the office.** Me entretuvieron en la oficina.

holdup ['hould ʌp] NOUN
1 el atraco ◇ *A bank clerk was injured in the holdup.* Un empleado del banco resultó herido en el atraco.
2 el retraso ◇ *No-one explained the reason for the holdup.* Nadie explicó el motivo del retraso.
3 el embotellamiento ◇ *a holdup on the freeway* un embotellamiento en la autopista

hole [houl] NOUN
1 el agujero (*in general*) ◇ *a hole in the wall* un agujero en la pared
2 el hoyo (*in the ground, in golf*) ◇ *to dig a hole* cavar un hoyo

holiday ['hɑːlɪdeɪ] NOUN
el día feriado ◇ *Next Monday is a holiday.* El lunes que viene es día feriado.

Holland ['hɑːlənd] NOUN
Holanda FEM

hollow ['hɑːlou] ADJECTIVE
hueco

holly ['hɑːli] NOUN
el acebo

holy ['houli] ADJECTIVE
1 santo ◇ *the Holy Spirit* el Espíritu Santo

2 sagrado ◇ *a holy place* un lugar sagrado

home [houm] NOUN
see also **home** ADVERB
la casa ◇ *at home* en la casa
◆ **Make yourself at home.** Estás en tu casa.
◆ **an old people's home** una residencia de ancianos
◆ **home run** el jonrón (PL los jonrones) (*in baseball*)

home [houm] ADVERB
see also **home** NOUN
1 en la casa ◇ *I'll be home at five o'clock.* Estaré en la casa a las cinco.
2 a la casa ◇ *to get home* llegar* a la casa

home address [houmə'drɛs] NOUN (PL **home addresses**)
el domicilio

homecoming ['houm'kʌmɪŋ] NOUN

> ℹ *El* **homecoming** *tiene lugar todos los años, en el otoño, en los centros de educación secundaria y en las universidades, cuando los antiguos alumnos regresan para participar en celebraciones especiales, acontecimientos sociales y asistir a la* **homecoming parade**. *Un organismo estudiantil elige una* **homecoming queen** *y su acompañante es el* **homecoming king**.

home game ['houm,geɪm] NOUN
el partido en casa

homeless ['houmlɪs] ADJECTIVE, NOUN
sin hogar
◆ **the homeless** los sin techo

homeopathy [houmi'ɑːpəθi] NOUN
la homeopatía

home page ['houm,peɪdʒ] NOUN
la página principal

homesick ['houmsɪk] ADJECTIVE
◆ **I'm homesick.** Extraño a mi familia.

homework ['houmwɜːrk] NOUN
los deberes ◇ *Have you done your homework?* ¿Has hecho los deberes? ◇ *my geography homework* mis deberes de geografía

homicide ['hɑːmɪsaɪd] NOUN
el homicidio

homosexual [houmə'sɛkʃuəl] ADJECTIVE
homosexual

honest ['ɑːnɪst] ADJECTIVE
1 honrado ◇ *She's a very honest person.* Es una persona muy honrada.
2 sincero ◇ *Tell me your honest opinion.* Dame tu opinión sincera.
◆ **To be honest, I don't like the idea.** La verdad es que no me gusta la idea.

honestly ['ɑːnɪstli] ADVERB
francamente ◇ *I honestly don't know.* Francamente no lo sé.

honesty ['ɑːnɪsti] NOUN
la honradez

honey ['hʌni] NOUN
la miel

honeymoon ['hʌni,muːn] NOUN
la luna de miel
◆ **to go on honeymoon** irse* de luna de miel

honor ['ɑːnər] NOUN
el honor

hood [hud] NOUN
1 la capucha (*on coat*)
2 el capó
el capote *Mexico*
(*of car*)

hook [huk] NOUN
1 el gancho ◇ *The jacket hung from a hook.* La chaqueta estaba colgada de un gancho.
◇ *He hung the painting on the hook.* Colgó el cuadro del gancho.
2 el anzuelo ◇ *He felt a fish pull at his hook.* Notó que un pez tiraba del anzuelo.
◆ **to take the phone off the hook** descolgar* el teléfono

H

hooky ['huki] NOUN
◆ **to play hooky** hacer* novillos

hooligan ['huːlɪgən] NOUN
el vándalo
la vándala
el porro
la porra *Mexico*

hooray [hu'reɪ] EXCLAMATION
¡hurra!

to **hop** [hɑːp] VERB
1 brincar* (*animal*)
2 ir* a la pata coja
brincar* de cojito *Mexico*
(*person*)

to **hope** [houp] VERB
see also **hope** NOUN
esperar
Use the subjunctive after ***esperar que***.
◇ *I hope he comes.* Espero que venga.
◆ **I hope so.** Espero que sí.
◆ **I hope not.** Espero que no.

hope [houp] NOUN
see also **hope** VERB
la esperanza
◆ **to give up hope** perder* la esperanza

hopeful ['houpfəl] ADJECTIVE
prometedor (FEM prometedora) ◇ *The prospects look hopeful.* Las perspectivas parecen prometedoras.
◆ **He's hopeful of winning.** Tiene esperanzas de ganar.
◆ **How did the interview go? – I'm hopeful.** ¿Cómo fue la entrevista? – Tengo esperanzas.
◆ **We're hopeful everything will go okay.** Confiamos en que todo irá bien.

hopefully ['houpfəli] ADVERB
◆ **Hopefully, he'll make it in time.** Esperemos que llegue a tiempo.
Use the subjunctive after ***esperar que***.

hopeless ['houplɪs] ADJECTIVE
◆ **She's hopeless at math.** Es una negada para las matemáticas.

horizon [hə'raɪzən] NOUN
el horizonte

horizontal [hɔːrɪ'zɑːntl] ADJECTIVE
horizontal

horn [hɔːrn] NOUN
1 el claxon ◇ *He sounded the horn.* Tocó el claxon.
2 la trompa ◇ *He plays the horn.* Toca la trompa.
3 el cuerno ◇ *a bull's horns* los cuernos de un toro

horoscope ['hɔːrəskoup] NOUN
el horóscopo

horrible ['hɔːrɪbəl] ADJECTIVE
horrible ◇ *What a horrible dress!* ¡Qué vestido tan horrible!

to **horrify** ['hɔːrɪfaɪ] VERB
horrorizar*

horror ['hɔːrər] NOUN
el horror ◇ *To my horror I discovered I was locked out.* Descubrí con horror que me quedé afuera sin llaves.

horror movie ['hɔːrər,muːvi] NOUN
la película de terror

horse [hɔːrs] NOUN
el caballo

horse racing ['hɔːrs,reɪsɪŋ] NOUN
las carreras de caballos

horseshoe ['hɔːrsʃuː] NOUN
la herradura

hose [houz] NOUN
la manguera

hosepipe ['houz,paɪp] NOUN
la manguera

hospital ['hɑːspɪtl] NOUN
el hospital ◇ *to go into hospital* ingresar en el hospital

hospitality [hɑːspɪ'tælɪti] NOUN
la hospitalidad

host [houst] NOUN
see also **host** VERB
1 el anfitrión (PL los anfitriones)
la anfitriona
2 el presentador
la presentadora
(*on television, radio*)

to **host** [houst] VERB
see also **host** NOUN
presentar ◇ *He agreed to host the show.* Aceptó presentar el espectáculo.

hostage ['hɑːstɪdʒ] NOUN
el rehén (PL los rehenes)
◆ **to take somebody hostage** tomar como rehén a alguien

hostile ['hɑːstəl] ADJECTIVE
hostil

hot [hɑːt] ADJECTIVE
1 caliente ◇ *a hot bath* un baño caliente
2 caluroso ◇ *a hot country* un país caluroso

When you are talking about a person being hot, you use ***tener* calor.***

◇ *I'm hot.* Tengo calor.

When you talk about the weather being hot, you use ***hacer* calor.***

◇ *It's hot today.* Hoy hace calor.
3 picante ◇ *Mexican food is too hot.* La comida mejicana es demasiado picante.

hot dog ['hɑːt,dɑːg] NOUN
el perrito caliente

hotel [hou'tɛl] NOUN
el hotel

hour ['auər] NOUN
la hora ◇ *She always takes hours to get ready.* Siempre demora horas en arreglarse.
◆ **a quarter of an hour** un cuarto de hora
◆ **two and a half hours** dos horas y media
◆ **half an hour** media hora

hourly ['auərli] ADJECTIVE, ADVERB
◆ **There are hourly buses.** Hay autobuses cada hora.
◆ **She is paid an hourly wage.** Le pagan por horas.

house [haus] NOUN
la casa ◇ *at his house* en su casa
◆ **the House of Representatives** la Cámara de Representantes

housewife ['haus,waɪf] NOUN (PL **housewives**)
el ama de casa (PL las amas de casa)

Although it's a feminine noun, remember that you use ***el*** *and* ***un*** *with* ***ama.***

◇ *She's a housewife.* Es ama de casa.

housework ['haus,wɜːrk] NOUN
las tareas de la casa

housing project ['hauzɪŋ,prɑːdʒekt] NOUN
el complejo de viviendas subsidiadas

hovercraft ['hʌvər,kræft] NOUN
el aerodeslizador

how [hau] ADVERB
1 cómo ◇ *How are you?* ¿Cómo estás?
2 qué ◇ *How strange!* ¡Qué raro!
◆ **He told them how happy he was.** Les dijo lo feliz que era.
◆ **How many?** ¿Cuántos?
◆ **How much?** ¿Cuánto? ◇ *How much is it?* ¿Cuánto es? ◇ *How much sugar do you want?* ¿Cuánto azúcar quieres?
◆ **How old are you?** ¿Cuántos años tienes?
◆ **How far is it to San Diego?** ¿Qué distancia hay de aquí a San Diego?
◆ **How long have you been here?** ¿Cuánto tiempo llevas aquí?
◆ **How long does it take?** ¿Cuánto se tarda?

Remember the accents on question and exclamation words ***cómo, qué*** *and* ***cuánto.***

however [hau'ɛvər] CONJUNCTION
sin embargo ◇ *This, however, isn't true.*

Esto, sin embargo, no es cierto.

to **howl** [haul] VERB
aullar* ◇ *The dog howled all night.* El perro estuvo aullando toda la noche. ◇ *He howled with pain.* Aullaba de dolor.

HTML [ˌeɪtʃtiːɛmˈɛl] NOUN
el HTML

to **hug** [hʌg] VERB
see also **hug** NOUN
abrazar* ◇ *They hugged each other.* Se abrazaron.

hug [hʌg] NOUN
see also **hug** VERB
el abrazo ◇ *to give somebody a hug* dar* un abrazo a alguien

huge [hjuːdʒ] ADJECTIVE
enorme

to **hum** [hʌm] VERB
tararear

human [ˈhjuːmən] ADJECTIVE
humano ◇ *the human body* el cuerpo humano

human being [ˌhjuːmənˈbiːɪŋ] NOUN
el ser humano

humble [ˈhʌmbəl] ADJECTIVE
humilde

humor [ˈhjuːmər] NOUN
el humor
◆ **to have a sense of humor** tener* sentido del humor

hundred [ˈhʌndrəd] NUMERAL
*Use **cien** before nouns or before another number that is being multiplied by a hundred.*
◆ **a hundred** cien ◇ *a hundred people* cien personas ◇ *a hundred thousand* cien mil
*Use **ciento** before a number that is not multiplied but simply added to a hundred.*
◇ *a hundred and one* ciento uno
*When **hundred** follows another number, use the compound forms, which must agreee with the noun.*
◇ *three hundred* trescientos ◇ *five hundred people* quinientas personas ◇ *five hundred and one* quinientos uno
◆ **hundreds of people** cientos de personas

hung [hʌŋ] VERB *see* **hang**

Hungary [ˈhʌŋgəri] NOUN
Hungría FEM

hunger [ˈhʌŋgər] NOUN
el hambre FEM
*Although it's a feminine noun, remember that you use **el** and **un** with **hambre**.*

hungry [ˈhʌŋgri] ADJECTIVE
◆ **to be hungry** tener* hambre ◇ *I'm very hungry.* Tengo mucha hambre.

to **hunt** [hʌnt] VERB
1 cazar* ◇ *They hunt deer.* Cazan ciervos.
◆ **to go hunting** ir* de caza
2 buscar* ◇ *The police are hunting the killer.* La policía está buscando al asesino.
◆ **to hunt for something** buscar* algo ◇ *I've hunted everywhere for that book.* He buscado ese libro por todas partes.

hunting [ˈhʌntɪŋ] NOUN
la caza ◇ *deer-hunting* la caza del ciervo

hurricane [ˈhɜːrɪkeɪn] NOUN
el huracán (PL los huracanes)

to **hurry** [ˈhɜːri] VERB (**hurried, hurried**)
see also **hurry** NOUN
apurarse ◇ *Hurry up!* ¡Apúrate!
◆ **Julia hurried back home.** Julia se apuró en volver a la casa.

hurry [ˈhɜːri] NOUN
see also **hurry** VERB
◆ **to be in a hurry** tener* apuro
◆ **to do something in a hurry** hacer* algo apurado
◆ **There's no hurry.** No hay apuro.

to **hurt** [hɜːrt] VERB (**hurt, hurt**)
see also **hurt** ADJECTIVE
1 hacer* daño a ◇ *You're hurting me!* ¡Me haces daño! ◇ *Have you hurt yourself?* ¿Te hiciste daño?
2 doler* ◇ *My leg hurts.* Me duele la pierna.
◆ **Hey! That hurts!** ¡Oye! ¡Que me haces daño!
3 herir* ◇ *His remarks really hurt me.* Sus comentarios me hirieron mucho.

hurt [hɜːrt] ADJECTIVE
see also **hurt** VERB
herido ◇ *Is he badly hurt?* ¿Está herido de gravedad? ◇ *Luckily, nobody got hurt.* Por suerte, nadie resultó herido.
◆ **I was hurt by what he said.** Me hirió lo que dijo.

husband [ˈhʌzbənd] NOUN
el marido

hut [hʌt] NOUN
la cabaña

hymn [hɪm] NOUN
el himno (*religioso*)

hyphen [ˈhaɪfən] NOUN
el guión (PL los guiones)

H

I

I [aɪ] PRONOUN
yo ◇ *Ann and I.* Ann y yo.
I generally isn't translated unless it is emphatic.
◇ *I speak Spanish.* Hablo español.
*Use **yo** for emphasis.*
◇ *He was frightened but I wasn't.* Él estaba asustado, pero yo no.

ice [aɪs] NOUN
el hielo

iceberg ['aɪsbɜːrg] NOUN
el iceberg (PL los icebergs)

icebox ['aɪsbɑːks] NOUN (PL **iceboxes**)
el regfrigerador

ice cream ['aɪsˌkriːm] NOUN
el helado ◇ *vanilla ice cream* el helado de vainilla

ice cube ['aɪsˌkjuːb] NOUN
el cubito de hielo

ice hockey ['aɪsˌhɑːki] NOUN
el hockey sobre hielo ◇ *I like playing ice hockey.* Me gusta jugar hockey sobre hielo.

Iceland ['aɪslənd] NOUN
Islandia FEM

ice-skating ['aɪsˌskeɪtɪŋ] NOUN
el patinaje sobre hielo
◆ **Yesterday we went ice-skating.** Ayer fuimos a patinar sobre hielo.

icing ['aɪsɪŋ] NOUN
el glaseado (*on cake*)

icon ['aɪkɑːn] NOUN
el icono

icy ['aɪsi] ADJECTIVE
helado ◇ *an icy wind* un viento helado
◇ *The roads are icy.* Las carreteras están heladas.

I'd [aɪd] = **I had, I would**

ID card [aɪ'diːˌkɑːrd] NOUN
el carnet de identidad

idea [aɪ'diːə] NOUN
la idea ◇ *Good idea!* ¡Buena idea!

ideal [aɪ'diːəl] ADJECTIVE
ideal

identical [aɪ'dɛntɪkəl] ADJECTIVE
idéntico

identification [aɪdɛntɪfɪ'keɪʃən] NOUN
la identificación (PL las identificaciones)

to **identify** [aɪ'dɛntɪfaɪ] VERB (**identified, identified**)
identificar*

idiom ['ɪdiəm] NOUN
el modismo

idiot ['ɪdiət] NOUN
el/la idiota

idiotic [ɪdɪ'ɑːtɪk] ADJECTIVE
idiota

idle ['aɪdl] ADJECTIVE
◆ **It's just idle gossip.** No es más que chismorreo.
◆ **I asked out of idle curiosity.** Lo pregunté por pura curiosidad.
◆ **to be idle** (*worker*) estar* sin trabajo
◆ **The plant has been idle during the strike.** La fábrica ha estado parada durante la huelga.

i.e. [aɪ'iː] ABBREVIATION
es decir

if [ɪf] CONJUNCTION
si ◇ *You can go if you like.* Puedes ir si quieres. ◇ *He asked me if I had eaten.* Me preguntó si había comido. ◇ *If it's fine we'll go swimming.* Si hace buen tiempo, iremos a nadar.
*Use **si** with a past subjunctive to translate **if** followed by a past tense when talking about conditions.*
◇ *If you studied harder you would pass your exams.* Si estudiaras más aprobarías los exámenes.
◆ **if only** ojalá
***ojalá** has to be followed by a verb in the subjunctive.*
◇ *If only I had more money!* ¡Ojalá tuviera más dinero!
◆ **if not** si no ◇ *Are you coming? If not, I'll go with Mark.* ¿Vienes? Si no, iré con Mark.
◆ **if so** si es así ◇ *Are you coming? If so, I'll wait.* ¿Vienes? Si es así te espero.
◆ **If I were you I would go to Cuba.** Yo que tú iría a Cuba.

ignorant ['ɪgnərənt] ADJECTIVE
ignorante

to **ignore** [ɪg'nɔːr] VERB
◆ **to ignore something** hacer* caso omiso de algo ◇ *She ignored my advice.* Hizo caso omiso de mi consejo.
◆ **to ignore somebody** ignorar a alguien
◇ *She saw me, but she ignored me.* Me vió, pero me ignoró completamente.
◆ **Just ignore him!** ¡No le hagas caso!

ill [ɪl] ADJECTIVE
enfermo ◇ *She was taken ill.* Se enfermó.

I'll [aɪl] = **I will**

illegal [ɪ'liːgəl] ADJECTIVE
ilegal

illegal immigrant [ɪ'liːgəl'ɪmɪgrənt] NOUN
el/la inmigrante ilegal

illegible [ɪ'lɛdʒɪbəl] ADJECTIVE
ilegible

illness ['ɪlnɪs] NOUN (PL **illnesses**)
la enfermedad

illusion [ɪ'luːʒən] NOUN
la ilusión (PL las ilusiones) ◇ *an optical illusion* una ilusión óptica
◆ **He was under the illusion that he would win.** Se creía que iba a ganar.

illustration [ɪlə'streɪʃən] NOUN

la ilustración (PL las ilustraciones)

I'm [aɪm] = **I am**

image [ˈɪmɪdʒ] NOUN
la imagen (PL las imágenes) ◇ *The company has changed its image.* La empresa ha cambiado de imagen.

imagination [ɪmædʒɪˈneɪʃən] NOUN
la imaginación (PL las imaginaciones) ◇ *She lets her imagination run away with her.* Se deja llevar por su imaginación. ◇ *It's only your imagination.* Son imaginaciones tuyas.

to **imagine** [ɪˈmædʒɪn] VERB
imaginarse ◇ *You can imagine how I felt!* ¡Imagínate cómo me sentí! ◇ *Is he angry? – I imagine so!* ¿Está enfadado? – ¡Me imagino que sí!

to **imitate** [ˈɪmɪteɪt] VERB
imitar

imitation [ɪmɪˈteɪʃən] NOUN
la imitación (PL las imitaciones)
◆ **imitation leather** el cuero de imitación

immediate [ɪˈmiːdiət] ADJECTIVE
inmediato ◇ *We need an immediate answer.* Necesitamos una respuesta inmediata.

immediately [ɪˈmiːdiətli] ADVERB
inmediatamente

immigrant [ˈɪmɪgrənt] NOUN
el/la inmigrante

immigration [ɪmɪˈgreɪʃən] NOUN
la inmigración (PL las inmigraciones)

immoral [ɪˈmɔːrəl] ADJECTIVE
inmoral

immune [ɪˈmjuːn] ADJECTIVE
◆ **to be immune to something** ser* inmune a algo ◇ *She is immune to measles.* Es inmune al sarampión.

impartial [ɪmˈpɑːrʃəl] ADJECTIVE
imparcial

impatience [ɪmˈpeɪʃəns] NOUN
la impaciencia

impatient [ɪmˈpeɪʃənt] ADJECTIVE
impaciente
◆ **to get impatient** impacientarse ◇ *People are getting impatient.* La gente se está impacientando.

impatiently [ɪmˈpeɪʃəntli] ADVERB
con impaciencia

impersonal [ɪmˈpɜːrsənl] ADJECTIVE
impersonal

to **implement** [ˈɪmplɪmɛnt] VERB
implementar ◇ *It'll take a few months to implement the plan.* Se tardarán unos cuantos meses en implementar el plan.

to **imply** [ɪmˈplaɪ] VERB
insinuar* ◇ *Are you implying I did it on purpose?* ¿Insinúas que lo hice adrede?

importance [ɪmˈpɔːrtns] NOUN
la importancia

important [ɪmˈpɔːrtnt] ADJECTIVE
importante

impossible [ɪmˈpɑːsɪbəl] ADJECTIVE
imposible

to **impress** [ɪmˈprɛs] VERB
impresionar ◇ *She's trying to impress you.* Está tratando de impresionarte.

impressed [ɪmˈprɛst] ADJECTIVE
impresionado ◇ *I'm very impressed!* ¡Estoy impresionado!

impression [ɪmˈprɛʃən] NOUN
la impresión (PL las impresiones) ◇ *I was under the impression that you were going out.* Tenía la impresión de que ibas a salir.

impressive [ɪmˈprɛsɪv] ADJECTIVE
impresionante

to **improve** [ɪmˈpruːv] VERB
mejorar ◇ *They have improved the service.* Han mejorado el servicio. ◇ *The weather is improving.* El tiempo está mejorando.

improvement [ɪmˈpruːvmənt] NOUN
[1] la mejora (*in situation, design*)
◆ **There's been an improvement in his French.** Su francés ha mejorado.
[2] la mejoría (*in health*)

I

in [ɪn] PREPOSITION, ADVERB
*There are several ways of translating **in**. Scan the examples to find one that is similar to what you want to say. For other expressions with **in**, see the verbs **go**, **come**, **get**, **give**, etc.*
[1] en ◇ *in the house* en la casa ◇ *in my bag* en mi bolsa ◇ *in the country* en el campo ◇ *in town* en la ciudad ◇ *in Mexico* en México ◇ *in school* en el colegio ◇ *in the hospital* en el hospital ◇ *in Miami* en Miami ◇ *in spring* en primavera ◇ *in May* en Mayo ◇ *in 1996* en mil novecientos noventa y seis ◇ *I did it in three hours.* Lo hice en tres horas. ◇ *in French* en francés ◇ *in a loud voice* en voz alta ◇ *in good condition* en buen estado ◇ *I have a test in the morning.* Tengo un examen en la mañana. ◇ *I always feel sleepy in the afternoon.* Siempre tengo sueño en la tarde.
[2] de ◇ *the best pupil in the class* el mejor alumno de la clase ◇ *at two o'clock in the afternoon* a las dos de la tarde ◇ *at six in the morning* a las seis de la mañana ◇ *the boy in the blue shirt* el muchacho de la camisa azul
[3] dentro de ◇ *I'll see you in three weeks.* Te veré dentro de tres semanas. ◇ *I'll be back in one hour.* Volveré dentro de una hora.
◆ **in the sun** al sol
◆ **in the rain** bajo la lluvia
◆ **It was written in pencil.** Estaba escrito a lápiz.
◆ **in here** aquí adentro ◇ *It's hot in here.* Aquí adentro hace calor.
◆ **one person in ten** una persona de cada diez
◆ **to be in** (*at home, work*) estar* ◇ *He wasn't in.* No estaba.
◆ **in writing** por escrito

inaccurate [ɪnˈækjurət] ADJECTIVE
inexacto

incentive [ɪnˈsɛntɪv] NOUN
el incentivo ◇ *There's no incentive to work.* ☞

No hay incentivo para trabajar.

inch [ɪntʃ] NOUN (PL **inches**)
la pulgada ◇ *six inches* seis pulgadas (*= 15 centímetros*)

incident [ˈɪnsɪdənt] NOUN
el incidente

inclined [ɪnˈklaɪnd] ADJECTIVE
◆ **to be inclined to do something** tener* tendencia a hacer algo ◇ *He's inclined to arrive late.* Tiene tendencia a llegar tarde.

to **include** [ɪnˈkluːd] VERB
incluir* ◇ *Service is not included.* El servicio no está incluido.

including [ɪnˈkluːdɪŋ] PREPOSITION
◆ **It will be two hundred dollars, including tax.** Son doscientos dólares con impuesto incluido.

inclusive [ɪnˈkluːsɪv] ADJECTIVE
◆ **The inclusive price is two hundred dollars.** Son doscientos dólares con todo incluido.

income [ˈɪnkʌm] NOUN
los ingresos ◇ *his main source of income* su principal fuente de ingresos

income tax [ˈɪnkʌmˌtæks] NOUN
el impuesto sobre la renta

incompetent [ɪnˈkaːmpɪtnt] ADJECTIVE
incompetente

incomplete [ɪnkəmˈpliːt] ADJECTIVE
incompleto

inconvenience [ɪnkənˈviːnjəns] NOUN
las molestias PL ◇ *I don't want to cause any inconvenience.* No quiero causar molestias.

inconvenient [ɪnkənˈviːnjənt] ADJECTIVE
◆ **It's a bit inconvenient at the moment.** Me viene un poco mal en este momento.

incorrect [ɪnkəˈrɛkt] ADJECTIVE
incorrecto

increase [ˈɪnkriːs] NOUN
see also **increase** VERB
el aumento ◇ *an increase in road accidents* un aumento de accidentes de tránsito

to **increase** [ɪnˈkriːs] VERB
see also **increase** NOUN
aumentar ◇ *Traffic on the highways has increased.* El tránsito en las autopistas ha aumentado. ◇ *They have increased his salary.* Le aumentaron el sueldo.
◆ **to increase in size** aumentar de tamaño

incredible [ɪnˈkrɛdɪbəl] ADJECTIVE
increíble

indecisive [ɪndɪˈsaɪsɪv] ADJECTIVE
indeciso (*person*)

indeed [ɪnˈdiːd] ADVERB
realmente ◇ *It's very hard indeed.* Es realmente difícil.
◆ **Know what I mean? – Indeed I do.** ¿Me comprendes? – Por supuesto que sí.
◆ **Thank you very much indeed!** ¡Muchísimas gracias!

independence [ɪndɪˈpɛndəns] NOUN
la independencia
◆ **Independence Day** el Día de la Independencia

> ℹ *El 4 de julio,* **Independence Day** *es la fiesta nacional más importante en los Estados Unidos y se conmemora el aniversario de la Declaración de Independencia en 1776.*

independent [ɪndɪˈpɛndənt] ADJECTIVE
independiente

index [ˈɪndɛks] NOUN (PL **indexes**)
el índice alfabético (*in book*)

index finger [ˈɪndɛksˌfɪŋgər] NOUN
el dedo índice

India [ˈɪndiə] NOUN
la India

Indian [ˈɪndiən] ADJECTIVE
see also **Indian** NOUN
1 indio (*of India*)
2 indígena (*of America*)

Indian [ˈɪndiən] NOUN
see also **Indian** ADJECTIVE
1 el indio
la india
(*from India*)
◇ *the Indians* los indios
2 el/la indígena (*Native American*)

to **indicate** [ˈɪndɪkeɪt] VERB
indicar* ◇ *The report indicates that changes are needed.* El informe indica que se necesitan cambios.

indigestion [ɪndɪˈdʒɛstʃən] NOUN
la indigestión (PL las indigestiones) ◇ *I have indigestion.* Tengo indigestión.

individual [ɪndɪˈvɪdʒuəl] ADJECTIVE
see also **individual** NOUN
individual

individual [ɪndɪˈvɪdʒuəl] NOUN
see also **individual** ADJECTIVE
el individuo

indoor [ˈɪndɔːr] ADJECTIVE
◆ **an indoor swimming pool** una piscina cubierta, Mexico: una alberca techada

indoors [ɪnˈdɔːrz] ADVERB
adentro ◇ *They're indoors.* Están adentro.
◆ **We'd better go indoors.** Es mejor que entremos.

industrial [ɪnˈdʌstriəl] ADJECTIVE
industrial

industrial park [ɪnˈdʌstriəlˌpaːrk] NOUN
la zona industrial

industry [ˈɪndəstri] NOUN (PL **industries**)
la industria ◇ *the oil industry* la industria petrolífera ◇ *I'd like to work in industry.* Me gustaría trabajar en la industria.
◆ **the tourist industry** el turismo

inefficient [ɪnɪˈfɪʃənt] ADJECTIVE
ineficiente

inevitable [ɪnˈɛvɪtəbəl] ADJECTIVE

inevitable

inexpensive [ɪnɪk'spɛnsɪv] ADJECTIVE
económico

inexperienced [ɪnɪk'spɪriənst] ADJECTIVE
inexperto

infection [ɪn'fɛkʃən] NOUN
la infección (PL las infecciones) ◇ *an ear infection* una infección de oído

infectious [ɪn'fɛkʃəs] ADJECTIVE
contagioso

infinitive [ɪn'fɪnɪtɪv] NOUN
el infinitivo

infirmary [ɪn'fɜːrməri] NOUN (PL **infirmaries**)
el hospital

inflatable [ɪn'fleɪtəbəl] ADJECTIVE
inflable (*mattress, dinghy*)

inflation [ɪn'fleɪʃən] NOUN
la inflación (las inflaciones)

influence ['ɪnfluəns] NOUN
see also **influence** VERB
la influencia ◇ *He's a bad influence on her.* Ejerce mala influencia sobre ella.

to **influence** ['ɪnfluəns] VERB
see also **influence** NOUN
influir* en

influenza [ɪnflu'ɛnzə] NOUN
la gripe
la gripa *Mexico*
◇ *to have influenza* tener* gripe, *Mexico*: tener* gripa

to **inform** [ɪn'fɔːrm] VERB
informar ◇ *Nobody informed me of the change of plan.* Nadie me informó del cambio de planes.

informal [ɪn'fɔːrməl] ADJECTIVE
- **informal language** el lenguaje coloquial
- **an informal visit** una visita informal
- **"informal dress"** "no se requiere traje de etiqueta"

information [ɪnfər'meɪʃən] NOUN
1 la información (PL las informaciones) ◇ *I need some information about trains to Wisconsin.* Necesito información sobre los trenes a Wisconsin.
- **a piece of information** un dato

2 información telefónica (*informal*) ◇ *You have to dial 411 to get information.* Marca el 411 para comunicarte con información telefónica.

information office [ɪnfər'meɪʃənˌɑːfɪs] NOUN
la oficina de información

infuriating [ɪn'fjurieɪtɪŋ] ADJECTIVE
exasperante

ingredient [ɪn'griːdiənt] NOUN
el ingrediente

inhabitant [ɪn'hæbɪtnt] NOUN
el/la habitante

to **inherit** [ɪn'hɛrɪt] VERB
heredar ◇ *She inherited her father's house.* Heredó la casa de su padre.

initials [ɪ'nɪʃlz] PL NOUN
las iniciales ◇ *Her initials are C.D.T.* Sus iniciales son C.D.T.

initiative [ɪ'nɪʃətɪv] NOUN
la iniciativa

to **inject** [ɪn'dʒɛkt] VERB
inyectar ◇ *They injected me with antibiotics.* Me inyectaron antibióticos.

injection [ɪn'dʒɛkʃən] NOUN
la inyección (PL las inyecciones) ◇ *The doctor gave me an injection.* El médico me puso una inyección.

to **injure** ['ɪndʒər] VERB
herir* ◇ *He injured his leg.* Se hirió la pierna.

injured ['ɪndʒərd] ADJECTIVE
herido

injury ['ɪndʒəri] NOUN (PL **injuries**)
la lesión (PL las lesiones)

injustice [ɪn'dʒʌstɪs] NOUN
la injusticia

ink [ɪŋk] NOUN
la tinta

in-laws ['ɪnlɑːz] PL NOUN
los suegros

inn [ɪn] NOUN
la hostería

inner ['ɪnər] ADJECTIVE
interior
- **the inner city** los núcleos urbanos deprimidos

inner tube ['ɪnərˌtuːb] NOUN
la cámara de aire

innocent ['ɪnəsənt] ADJECTIVE
inocente

inquest ['ɪnkwɛst] NOUN
la investigación judicial (PL las investigaciones judiciales)

to **inquire** [ɪn'kwaɪər] VERB
- **to inquire about something** informarse acerca de algo

inquiry ['ɪŋkwəri] NOUN (PL **inquiries**)
la investigación (PL las investigaciones) (*official investigation*)

inquisitive [ɪn'kwɪzɪtɪv] ADJECTIVE
curioso

insane [ɪn'seɪn] ADJECTIVE
loco

inscription [ɪn'skrɪpʃən] NOUN
la inscripción (PL las inscripciones)

insect ['ɪnsɛkt] NOUN
el insecto

insect repellent ['ɪnsɛktrɪˌpɛlənt] NOUN
la loción anti-insectos (PL las lociones anti-insectos)

insensitive [ɪn'sɛnsɪtɪv] ADJECTIVE
insensible

to **insert** [ɪn'sɜːrt] VERB
introducir* ◇ *I inserted the coin into the slot.* Introduje la moneda en la ranura.

inside [ɪn'saɪd] NOUN
see also **inside** ADVERB, PREPOSITION
el interior

I

inside [ɪn'saɪd] ADVERB, PREPOSITION
see also **inside** NOUN
adentro ◇ *inside the house* adentro de la casa ◇ *He opened the envelope and read what was inside.* Abrió el sobre y leyó lo que había adentro.
◆ **Come inside!** ¡Entra!
◆ **Let's go inside, it's starting to rain.** Entremos, está empezando a llover.
◆ **inside out** al revés ◇ *He put his sweater on inside out.* Se puso el jersey al revés.

insincere [ɪnsɪn'sɪər] ADJECTIVE
falso

to **insist** [ɪn'sɪst] VERB
insistir ◇ *I didn't want to, but he insisted.* Yo no quería, pero él insistió. ◇ *He insisted he was innocent.* Insistía en que era inocente.
◆ **to insist on doing something** insistir en hacer algo ◇ *She insisted on paying.* Insistió en pagar.

inspector [ɪn'spɛktər] NOUN
1 el inspector
la inspectora
2 el perito tasador
la perita tasadora
(*of buildings*)

to **install** [ɪn'stɑːl] VERB
instalar

installment [ɪn'stɑːlmənt] NOUN
1 el plazo (*of payment*) ◇ *to pay in installments* pagar* a plazos
2 el episodio (*of TV, radio serial*)
3 el fascículo (*of publication*)

instance ['ɪnstəns] NOUN
◆ **for instance** por ejemplo

instant ['ɪnstənt] ADJECTIVE
see also **instant** NOUN
inmediato ◇ *It was an instant success.* Fue un éxito inmediato.
◆ **instant coffee** el café instantáneo
◆ **instant messaging** la mensajería instantánea

instant ['ɪnstənt] NOUN
see also **instant** ADJECTIVE
el instante

instantly ['ɪnstəntli] ADVERB
al instante

instead [ɪn'stɛd] PREPOSITION, ADVERB
◆ **instead of** en lugar de ◇ *We played tennis instead of going swimming.* Jugamos al tenis en lugar de ir a nadar. ◇ *She went instead of Peter.* En lugar de ir Peter, fue ella.
◆ **The gym was closed, so we played tennis instead.** El gimnasio estaba cerrado, así que jugamos al tenis.

instinct ['ɪnstɪŋkt] NOUN
el instinto

institute ['ɪnstɪtuːt] NOUN
el instituto

institution [ɪnstɪ'tuːʃən] NOUN
la institución (PL las instituciones)

to **instruct** [ɪn'strʌkt] VERB
◆ **to instruct somebody to do something** ordenar a alguien que haga algo
ordenar que *has to be followed by a verb in the subjunctive.*
◇ *She instructed us to wait outside.* Nos ordenó que esperáramos afuera.

instructions [ɪn'strʌkʃənz] PL NOUN
las instrucciones

instructor [ɪn'strʌktər] NOUN
el instructor
la instructora
◇ *skiing instructor* el instructor de esquí
◇ *driving instructor* el instructor de autoescuela, *Mexico:* el instructor de la escuela de manejo

instrument ['ɪnstrumənt] NOUN
el instrumento ◇ *Do you play an instrument?* ¿Tocas algún instrumento?

insufficient [ɪnsə'fɪʃənt] ADJECTIVE
insuficiente

insulin ['ɪnsəlɪn] NOUN
la insulina

insult ['ɪnsʌlt] NOUN
see also **insult** VERB
el insulto

to **insult** [ɪn'sʌlt] VERB
see also **insult** NOUN
insultar

insurance [ɪn'ʃurəns] NOUN
el seguro ◇ *his car insurance* su seguro de automóvil
◆ **an insurance policy** una póliza de seguros

intelligent [ɪn'tɛlɪdʒənt] ADJECTIVE
inteligente

to **intend** [ɪn'tɛnd] VERB
◆ **to intend to do something** tener* la intención de hacer algo ◇ *I intend to study languages at college.* Tengo la intención de estudiar idiomas en la universidad.

intense [ɪn'tɛns] ADJECTIVE
intenso

intensive [ɪn'tɛnsɪv] ADJECTIVE
intensivo

intention [ɪn'tɛnʃən] NOUN
la intención (PL las intenciones)

intercom ['ɪntərkɑːm] NOUN
el portero eléctrico

interest ['ɪntrɪst] NOUN
see also **interest** VERB
1 el interés (PL los intereses) ◇ *to show an interest in something* mostrar* interés en algo
2 la afición (PL las aficiones) ◇ *My main interest is music.* Mi mayor afición es la música.
◆ **It's in your own interest to study hard.** Te conviene estudiar mucho.

to **interest** ['ɪntrɪst] VERB

see also **interest** NOUN
interesar ◇ *It doesn't interest me.* No me interesa.
◆ **to be interested in something** estar* interesado en algo ◇ *I'm very interested in what you're telling me.* Estoy muy interesado en lo que me dices.
◆ **Are you interested in politics?** ¿Te interesa la política?

interesting [ˈɪntrɪstɪŋ] ADJECTIVE
interesante

interior [ɪnˈtɪriər] NOUN
el interior

interior designer [ɪnˈtɪriərdɪˈzaɪnər] NOUN
el diseñador de interiores
la diseñadora de interiores

intermediate [ɪntərˈmiːdiət] ADJECTIVE
intermedio

intermission [ɪntərˈmɪʃən] NOUN
el intermedio (*in performance, movie, game*)

internal [ɪnˈtɜːrnl] ADJECTIVE
interno

international [ɪntərˈnæʃənl] ADJECTIVE
internacional

Internet [ˈɪntərnɛt] NOUN
el/la Internet ◇ *on the Internet* en Internet

Internet café [ˈɪntərnɛtkæˈfeɪ] NOUN
el cibercafé

Internet user [ˈɪntərnɛtˌjuːzər] NOUN
el/la internauta

to **interpret** [ɪnˈtɜːrprɪt] VERB
hacer* de intérprete ◇ *Steve couldn't speak Spanish so his friend interpreted.* Steve no hablaba español, así que su amigo hizo de intérprete.

interpreter [ɪnˈtɜːrprɪtər] NOUN
el/la intérprete

to **interrupt** [ɪntəˈrʌpt] VERB
interrumpir

interruption [ɪntəˈrʌpʃən] NOUN
la interrupción (PL las interrupciones)

intersection [ˈɪntərsekʃən] NOUN
el cruce (*of roads*)

interval [ˈɪntərvəl] NOUN
el descanso (*in sport*)

interview [ˈɪntərvjuː] NOUN
see also **interview** VERB
la entrevista

to **interview** [ˈɪntərvjuː] VERB
see also **interview** NOUN
entrevistar ◇ *I was interviewed on the radio.* Me entrevistaron en el radio.

interviewer [ˈɪntərvjuːər] NOUN
el entrevistador
la entrevistadora

intimate [ˈɪntɪmət] ADJECTIVE
íntimo

into [ˈɪntu] PREPOSITION
1 a ◇ *I'm going into town.* Voy a la ciudad. ◇ *Translate it into Spanish.* Tradúcelo al español. ◇ *He got into the car.* Se subió al carro.
2 en ◇ *to get into bed* meterse en la cama ◇ *I poured the milk into a cup.* Vertí la leche en una taza. ◇ *They divided into two groups.* Se dividieron en dos grupos.
◆ **to walk into a lamppost** tropezar* con un farol

intranet [ˈɪntrənɛt] NOUN
la intranet

to **introduce** [ɪntrəˈduːs] VERB
presentar ◇ *He introduced me to his parents.* Me presentó a sus padres.

introduction [ɪntrəˈdʌkʃən] NOUN
la introducción (PL las introducciones) (*in book*)

intruder [ɪnˈtruːdər] NOUN
el intruso
la intrusa

intuition [ɪntuˈɪʃən] NOUN
la intuición (PL las intuiciones)

to **invade** [ɪnˈveɪd] VERB
invadir

invalid [ˈɪnvəlɪd] NOUN
el inválido
la inválida

to **invent** [ɪnˈvɛnt] VERB
inventar

invention [ɪnˈvɛnʃən] NOUN
el invento

inventor [ɪnˈvɛntər] NOUN
el inventor
la inventora

investigation [ɪnvɛstɪˈgeɪʃən] NOUN
la investigación (PL las investigaciones)

investment [ɪnˈvɛstmənt] NOUN
la inversión (PL las inversiones)

invisible [ɪnˈvɪzɪbəl] ADJECTIVE
invisible

invitation [ɪnvɪˈteɪʃən] NOUN
la invitación (PL las invitaciones)

to **invite** [ɪnˈvaɪt] VERB
invitar ◇ *Michael is not invited.* Michael no está invitado. ◇ *You're invited to a party at Claire's house.* Estás invitado a una fiesta en la casa de Claire.

to **involve** [ɪnˈvɑːlv] VERB
suponer* ◇ *It involves a lot of work.* Supone mucho trabajo.
◆ **He wasn't involved in the robbery.** No estuvo implicado en el robo.
◆ **She was involved in politics.** Estaba metida en política.
◆ **to be involved with somebody** tener* una relación con alguien ◇ *She was involved with a married man.* Tenía una relación con un hombre casado.
◆ **I don't want to get involved in the argument.** No quiero meterme en la discusión.

IQ [aɪˈkjuː] NOUN (= *intelligence quotient*)
el CI (= el coeficiente intelectual)

Iran [ɪˈrɑːn] NOUN ☞

Irán MASC

Iraq [ɪ'rɑːk] NOUN
Iraq MASC

Ireland ['aɪərlənd] NOUN
Irlanda FEM

Irish ['aɪrɪʃ] NOUN
see also **Irish** ADJECTIVE
el irlandés (*language*)
◆ **the Irish** (*people*) los irlandeses

Irish ['aɪrɪʃ] ADJECTIVE
see also **Irish** NOUN
irlandés (MASC PL irlandeses, FEM irlandesa)

Irishman ['aɪrɪʃmən] NOUN (PL **Irishmen**)
el irlandés (PL los irlandeses)

Irishwoman ['aɪrɪʃˌwʊmən] NOUN (PL **Irishwomen**)
la irlandesa

iron ['aɪərn] NOUN
see also **iron** VERB
1 la plancha (*for clothes*)
2 el hierro (*metal*)

to **iron** ['aɪərn] VERB
see also **iron** NOUN
planchar ◇ *I hate ironing.* Odio planchar.

ironic [aɪ'rɑːnɪk] ADJECTIVE
irónico

ironing ['aɪərnɪŋ] NOUN
◆ **to do the ironing** planchar

ironing board ['aɪərnɪŋˌbɔːrd] NOUN
la tabla de planchar
el burro *Mexico*

irrelevant [ɪ'rɛləvənt] ADJECTIVE
irrelevante ◇ *That's irrelevant.* Eso es irrelevante.

irresponsible [ɪrɪ'spɑːnsɪbəl] ADJECTIVE
irresponsable ◇ *That was irresponsible of him.* Eso fue irresponsable por su parte.

irritating ['ɪrɪteɪtɪŋ] ADJECTIVE
irritante

is [ɪz] VERB *see* **be**

Islam [ɪs'lɑːm] NOUN
el Islam

Islamic [ɪs'lɑːmɪk] ADJECTIVE
islámico ◇ *Islamic law* la ley islámica

island ['aɪlənd] NOUN
la isla

isle [aɪl] NOUN
la isla
◆ **Grand Isle** La Isla Grande

isn't ['ɪzənt] = **is not**

isolated ['aɪsəleɪtɪd] ADJECTIVE
aislado

ISP [ˌaɪes'piː] NOUN (= *Internet Service Provider*)
el proveedor de servicios de internet

Israel ['ɪzriəl] NOUN
Israel MASC

issue ['ɪʃuː] NOUN
see also **issue** VERB
1 el tema
Although ***tema*** *ends in* ***-a****, it is actually a masculine noun.*
◇ *a controversial issue* un tema polémico
2 el número (*magazine*) ◇ *a back issue* un número atrasado

to **issue** ['ɪʃuː] VERB
see also **issue** NOUN
1 hacer* público ◇ *The minister issued a statement yesterday.* El ministro hizo pública una declaración ayer.
2 proporcionar (*equipment, supplies*)

it [ɪt] PRONOUN
When ***it*** *is the subject of a sentence it is practically never translated.*
◇ *Where's my book? – It's on the table.* ¿Dónde está mi libro? – Está sobre la mesa. ◇ *It's raining.* Está lloviendo. ◇ *It's six o'clock.* Son las seis. ◇ *It's Friday tomorrow.* Mañana es viernes. ◇ *It's expensive.* Es caro. ◇ *Who is it? – It's me.* ¿Quién es? – Soy yo.
When ***it*** *is the direct object of the verb in a sentence, use* ***lo*** *if it stands for a masculine noun or* ***la*** *if it stands for a feminine noun.*
◇ *There's a banana left. Do you want it?* Queda un plátano. ¿Lo quieres? ◇ *I doubt it.* Lo dudo. ◇ *It's a good movie. Have you seen it?* Es una buena película. ¿La has visto?
Use ***le*** *when* ***it*** *is the indirect object of the verb in the sentence.*
◇ *Give it another coat of paint.* Dale otra mano de pintura.
For general concepts use the word ***ello****.*
◇ *I spoke to him about it.* Hablé con él sobre ello. ◇ *I'm against it.* Estoy en contra de ello.

Italian [ɪ'tæljən] ADJECTIVE
see also **Italian** NOUN
italiano

Italian [ɪ'tæljən] NOUN
see also **Italian** ADJECTIVE
1 el italiano
la italiana
(*person*)
◇ *the Italians* los italianos
2 el italiano (*language*)

italics [ɪ'tælɪks] PL NOUN
la cursiva ◇ *in italics* en cursiva

Italy ['ɪtəli] NOUN
Italia FEM

to **itch** [ɪtʃ] VERB
picar* ◇ *It itches.* Me pica. ◇ *My head is itching.* Me pica la cabeza.

it'd ['ɪtəd] = **it had, it would**

item ['aɪtəm] NOUN
1 la pieza ◇ *a collector's item* una pieza de colección
2 el artículo ◇ *The first item he bought was an alarm clock.* El primer artículo que compró fue un despertador.

3 la partida ◊ *He checked the items on his bill.* Comprobó las partidas de su factura.
4 el punto ◊ *The next item on the agenda is...* El siguiente punto del orden del día es...
◆ **an item of news** una noticia

itinerary [aɪˈtɪnərɛri] NOUN (PL **itineraries**)
el itinerario

it'll [ˈɪtl] = **it will**

its [ɪts] ADJECTIVE
su (PL sus) ◊ *Everything in its place.* Cada cosa en su sitio. ◊ *It has its advantages.* Tiene sus ventajas.
***Its** is usually translated by the definite article **el/los** or **la/las** when it's clear from the sentence who the possessor is or when referring to clothing or parts of the body.*
◊ *The dog is losing its hair.* El perro está perdiendo el pelo. ◊ *The bird was in its cage.* El pájaro estaba en la jaula.

it's [ɪts] = **it is, it has**

itself [ɪtˈsɛlf] PRONOUN
se (*reflexive*) ◊ *The heating switches itself off.* La calefacción se apaga sola. ◊ *The dog scratched itself.* El perro se rascó.
◆ **The lesson itself was easy but the homework was very difficult.** La clase en sí fue fácil, pero las tareas eran difíciles.

I've [aɪv] = **I have**

J

jack [dʒæk] NOUN
1 el gato ◇ *The jack is in the trunk.* El gato está en el maletero.
2 la jota (*in ordinary pack of cards*)
3 la sota (*in Spanish pack of cards*)

jacket ['dʒækɪt] NOUN
la chaqueta

jackpot ['dʒæk,pɑːt] NOUN
el gordo ◇ *to hit the jackpot* sacarse* el gordo

jail [dʒeɪl] NOUN
see also **jail** VERB
la cárcel ◇ *to go to jail* ir* a la cárcel

to **jail** [dʒeɪl] VERB
see also **jail** NOUN
◆ **He was jailed for ten years.** Lo condenaron a diez años de cárcel.

jam [dʒæm] NOUN
◆ **a traffic jam** un embotellamiento

jammed [dʒæmd] ADJECTIVE
atascado
atorado *Mexico*
◇ *The window is jammed.* La ventana está atascada. *Mexico:* La ventana está atorada.

jam-packed ['dʒæm'pækt] ADJECTIVE
atestado ◇ *The room was jam-packed.* La habitación estaba atestada.

janitor ['dʒænɪtər] NOUN
el/la conserje
◆ **school janitor** el/la bedel

January ['dʒænjuɛri] NOUN
enero MASC ◇ *in January* en enero ◇ *the January sales* las rebajas de enero

Japan [dʒə'pæn] NOUN
el Japón

Japanese [dʒæpə'niːz] ADJECTIVE
see also **Japanese** NOUN
japonés (MASC PL japoneses, FEM japonesa)

Japanese [dʒæpə'niːz] NOUN (PL **Japanese**)
see also **Japanese** ADJECTIVE
1 el japonés
la japonesa
(*person*)
◇ *the Japanese* los japoneses
2 el japonés (*language*)

jar [dʒɑːr] NOUN
el tarro ◇ *a jar of honey* un tarro de miel

jaundice ['dʒɑːndɪs] NOUN
la ictericia ◇ *He has jaundice.* Tiene icotericia.

javelin ['dʒævlɪn] NOUN
la jabalina

jaw [dʒɑː] NOUN
la mandíbula

jazz [dʒæz] NOUN
el jazz

jealous ['dʒɛləs] ADJECTIVE
celoso ◇ *to be jealous* estar* celoso

jeans [dʒiːnz] PL NOUN
los jeans ◇ *a pair of jeans* unos jeans

Jehovah's Witness [dʒɪ'houvəz'wɪtnɪs] NOUN
(PL **Jehovah's Witnesses**)
el/la testigo de Jehová ◇ *She's a Jehovah's Witness.* Es testigo de Jehová.

Jell-O® ['dʒɛlou] NOUN
la gelatina

jelly ['dʒɛli] NOUN (PL **jellies**)
la mermelada ◇ *strawberry jelly* la mermelada de fresas

jellyfish ['dʒɛli,fɪʃ] NOUN (PL **jellyfish**)
la medusa
la aguamala *Mexico*

jersey ['dʒɜːrzi] NOUN
el suéter

Jesus ['dʒiːzəs] NOUN
Jesús MASC

jet [dʒɛt] NOUN
el reactor

jet lag ['dʒɛt,læg] NOUN
◆ **to be suffering from jet lag** tener* jet lag

jetty ['dʒɛti] NOUN (PL **jetties**)
el embarcadero

Jew [dʒuː] NOUN
el judío
la judía

jewel ['dʒuːəl] NOUN
la joya

jeweler ['dʒuːələr] NOUN
el joyero
la joyera
◇ *She's a jeweler.* Es joyera.

jewelry ['dʒuːəlri] NOUN
las joyas

jewelry store ['dʒuːəlri,stɔːr] NOUN
la joyería

Jewish ['dʒuːɪʃ] ADJECTIVE
judío

jigsaw ['dʒɪg,sɑː] NOUN
el rompecabezas (PL los rompecabezas)

job [dʒɑːb] NOUN
el trabajo ◇ *a part-time job* un trabajo de media jornada
◆ **You've done a good job.** Lo has hecho muy bien.

jobless ['dʒɑːblɪs] ADJECTIVE
desempleado

jock [dʒɑːk] NOUN
(*informal*)
el deportista

jockey ['dʒɑːki] NOUN
el/la jockey (PL los/las jockeys)

to **jog** [dʒɑːg] VERB
hacer* jogging

jogging ['dʒɑːgɪŋ] NOUN
el jogging ◇ *to go jogging* hacer* jogging

john [dʒɑːn] NOUN

el wáter (*informal*)

to **join** [dʒɔɪn] VERB
hacerse* socio de ◇ *I'm going to join the ski club.* Voy a hacerme socio del club de esquí.
◆ **I'll join you later if I can.** Yo iré luego si puedo.
◆ **Do you mind if I join you?** ¿Les importa que los acompañe?

to **join in** [dʒɔɪn'ɪn] VERB
◆ **He doesn't join in with what we do.** No participa en lo que hacemos.
◆ **She started singing, and the audience joined in.** Empezó a cantar, y el público se unió a ella.

joiner ['dʒɔɪnər] NOUN
el carpintero
la carpintera
◇ *He's a joiner.* Es carpintero.

joint [dʒɔɪnt] NOUN
1 la articulación (PL las articulaciones) ◇ *I have pains in my joints.* Me duelen las articulaciones.
◆ **We had a joint of lamb for lunch.** Comimos asado de cordero.
2 el porro
el toque *Mexico*
(*informal: drugs*)

joke [dʒouk] NOUN
see also **joke** VERB
1 la broma ◇ *Don't get upset; it was only a joke.* No te enojes, era sólo una broma.
◆ **to play a joke on somebody** hacerle* una broma a alguien
2 el chiste
◆ **to tell a joke** contar* un chiste

to **joke** [dʒouk] VERB
see also **joke** NOUN
bromear
◆ **You must be joking!** ¡Estás bromeando!

jolly ['dʒɑːli] ADJECTIVE
alegre

Jordan ['dʒɔːrdn] NOUN
Jordania FEM

to **jot down** [dʒɑːt'daun] VERB
apuntar

journalism ['dʒɜːrnəlɪzəm] NOUN
el periodismo

journalist ['dʒɜːrnəlɪst] NOUN
el/la periodista ◇ *I'm a journalist.* Soy periodista.

journey ['dʒɜːrni] NOUN
el viaje ◇ *to go on a journey* hacer* un viaje
◆ **The journey to school takes about an hour.** Se tarda una hora en ir al colegio.

joy [dʒɔɪ] NOUN
la alegría

joystick ['dʒɔɪˌstɪk] NOUN
el mando (*for computer games*)

judge [dʒʌdʒ] NOUN
see also **judge** VERB
el/la juez (PL los/las jueces)

to **judge** [dʒʌdʒ] VERB
see also **judge** NOUN
juzgar*

judo ['dʒuːdou] NOUN
el judo

jug [dʒʌg] NOUN
la jarra

juggler ['dʒʌglər] NOUN
el/la malabarista

juice [dʒuːs] NOUN
el jugo ◇ *orange juice* el jugo de naranja

July [dʒu'laɪ] NOUN
julio MASC ◇ *in July* en julio

to **jump** [dʒʌmp] VERB
saltar ◇ *They jumped over the wall.* Saltaron el muro. ◇ *He jumped out of the window.* Saltó por la ventana.
◆ **You made me jump!** ¡Qué susto me diste!

jumper ['dʒʌmpər] NOUN
el jumper (PL los jumpers)

June [dʒuːn] NOUN
junio MASC ◇ *in June* en junio

jungle ['dʒʌŋgəl] NOUN
la selva

junior ['dʒuːnjər] NOUN
1 joven (*younger person*) ◇ *He is three years my junior.* Es tres años más joven que yo.
2 el/la estudiante de penúltimo año (*at college, high school*)

junior high school ['dʒuːnjər'haɪˌskuːl] NOUN
el colegio de enseñanza secundaria

junk [dʒʌŋk] NOUN
los trastos viejos ◇ *The attic is full of junk.* El desván está lleno de trastos viejos.
◆ **to eat junk food** comer alimento chatarra
◆ **junk store** la tienda de viejo

jury ['dʒurɪ] NOUN (PL **juries**)
el jurado

just [dʒʌst] ADVERB
1 justo ◇ *just in time* justo a tiempo ◇ *just after Christmas* justo después de Navidad ◇ *We had just enough money.* Teníamos el dinero justo.
◆ **He has just arrived.** Acaba de llegar.
◆ **I did it just now.** Lo acabo de hacer.
◆ **She's rather busy just now.** Ahora mismo está bastante ocupada.
◆ **I'm just coming!** ¡Ya voy!
◆ **just here** aquí mismo
2 sólo ◇ *It's just a suggestion.* Es sólo una sugerencia.
◆ **I just thought that you would like it.** Yo pensé que te gustaría.
◆ **Just a minute!** ¡Un momento!
◆ **just about** casi ◇ *It's just about finished.* Está casi terminado.

justice ['dʒʌstɪs] NOUN
la justicia

to **justify** ['dʒʌstɪfaɪ] VERB (**justified, justified**)
justificar*

K

kangaroo [kæŋgə'ru:] NOUN
el canguro

karate [kə'rɑ:ti] NOUN
el karate ◇ *My favorite sport is karate.* Mi deporte favorito es el karate.

kebab [kə'bɑ:b] NOUN
la brocheta

keen [ki:n] ADJECTIVE
entusiasta ◇ *He's a keen supporter.* Es un hincha entusiasta.
- ◆ **He doesn't seem very keen.** No parece muy entusiasmado.
- ◆ **She's a keen student.** Es una alumna aplicada.
- ◆ **I'm not very keen on math.** No me gustan mucho las matemáticas.
- ◆ **He's keen on her.** Ella le gusta.
- ◆ **to be keen on doing something** tener* ganas de hacer algo ◇ *I'm not very keen on going.* No tengo muchas ganas de ir.

to **keep** [ki:p] VERB (**kept, kept**)
1 quedarse con ◇ *You can keep the watch.* Puedes quedarte con el reloj. ◇ *You can keep it.* Puedes quedarte con él.
2 mantenerse* (*remain*) ◇ *to keep fit* mantenerse en forma
- ◆ **Keep still!** ¡Estáte quieto!
- ◆ **Keep quiet!** ¡Cállate!

3 seguir* ◇ *Keep straight on.* Siga derecho.
- ◆ **I keep forgetting my keys.** Siempre me olvido las llaves.
- ◆ **"keep out"** "prohibida la entrada"
- ◆ **"keep off the grass"** "prohibido pisar el césped"

to **keep on** [ki:p'ɑ:n] VERB
continuar* ◇ *He kept on reading.* Continuó leyendo.
- ◆ **The car keeps on breaking down.** El carro no deja de descomponerse.

to **keep up** [ki:p'ʌp] VERB
- ◆ **Matthew walks so fast I can't keep up.** Matthew camina tan rápido que no puedo seguirle el ritmo.

kennel ['kɛnl] NOUN
- ◆ **a kennel** una residencia canina

kept [kɛpt] VERB *see* **keep**

kerosene ['kɛrəsi:n] NOUN
la parafina

ketchup ['kɛtʃəp] NOUN
la salsa de tomate
el catsup *Mexico*

kettle ['kɛtl] NOUN
el hervidor

key [ki:] NOUN
la llave

keyboard ['ki:,bɔ:rd] NOUN
el teclado

key ring ['ki:,rɪŋ] NOUN
el llavero

kick [kɪk] NOUN
see also **kick** VERB
la patada

to **kick** [kɪk] VERB
see also **kick** NOUN
- ◆ **to kick somebody** dar* una patada a alguien ◇ *He kicked me.* Me dio una patada.
- ◆ **He kicked the ball hard.** Le dio un puntapié fuerte al balón.
- ◆ **to kick off** hacer* el saque inicial (*in football*)

kickoff ['kɪk,ɑ:f] NOUN
el saque inicial
- ◆ **The kickoff is at 10 o'clock.** El partido empieza a las diez.

kid [kɪd] NOUN (*informal*)
see also **kid** VERB
el chiquillo
la chiquilla
el escuincle
la escuincla *Mexico*
- ◆ **they have three kids** tienen tres hijos

to **kid** [kɪd] VERB
see also **kid** NOUN
bromear ◇ *I'm not kidding; it's snowing.* No estoy bromeando, está nevando.
- ◆ **I'm just kidding.** Es una broma.

to **kidnap** ['kɪdnæp] VERB
secuestrar

kidney ['kɪdni] NOUN
el riñón (PL los riñones) ◇ *He has kidney trouble.* Tiene problemas de riñón.

kidney beans ['kɪdni,bi:nz] PL NOUN
los frijoles

to **kill** [kɪl] VERB
matar ◇ *She killed her husband.* Mató a su marido.
- ◆ **to be killed** morir* ◇ *He was killed in a car accident.* Murió en un accidente automovilístico.
- ◆ **to kill oneself** suicidarse ◇ *He killed himself.* Se suicidó.

killer ['kɪlər] NOUN
1 el asesino
la asesina
(*murderer*)
◇ *The police are searching for the killer.* La policía está buscando al asesino.
2 el asesino a sueldo
la asesina a sueldo
(*hired killer*)
- ◆ **Meningitis can be a killer.** La meningitis puede ser mortal.

kilo ['ki:lou] NOUN (PL **kilos**)
el kilo ◇ *at $5 a kilo* a 5 dólares el kilo

kilometer [kɪ'lɑ:mɪtər] NOUN
el kilómetro

kilt [kɪlt] NOUN
la falda escocesa

kind [kaɪnd] ADJECTIVE
see also **kind** NOUN
amable ◇ *to be kind to somebody* ser* amable con alguien
◆ **Thank you for being so kind.** Gracias por su amabilidad.

kind [kaɪnd] NOUN
see also **kind** ADJECTIVE
el tipo ◇ *It's a kind of sausage.* Es un tipo de salchicha.

kindergarten ['kɪndərgɑːrtn] NOUN
el jardín de infancia (PL los jardines de infancia)
el jardín de niños (PL los jardines de niños) *Mexico*

kindly ['kaɪndli] ADVERB
amablemente

kindness ['kaɪndnɪs] NOUN
la amabilidad

king [kɪŋ] NOUN
el rey
◆ **the King and Queen** los reyes

kingdom ['kɪŋdəm] NOUN
el reino

kiosk ['kiːɑːsk] NOUN
el quiosco (*stall*)

kipper ['kɪpər] NOUN
el arenque ahumado

kiss [kɪs] NOUN (PL **kisses**)
see also **kiss** VERB
el beso

to **kiss** [kɪs] VERB
see also **kiss** NOUN
1 besar ◇ *He kissed her passionately.* La besó apasionadamente.
2 besarse ◇ *They kissed.* Se besaron.

kit [kɪt] NOUN
el equipo ◇ *I've forgotten my gym kit.* Se me olvidó el equipo de gimnasia.
◆ **a tool kit** un juego de herramientas
◆ **a sewing kit** un costurero
◆ **a first-aid kit** un botiquín
◆ **a tire repair kit** un juego para reparar llantas pinchadas, *Mexico*: un juego para reparar llantas ponchadas
◆ **a drum kit** una batería

kitchen ['kɪtʃɪn] NOUN
la cocina
◆ **the kitchen cupboards** los armarios de cocina
◆ **a kitchen knife** un cuchillo de cocina

kite [kaɪt] NOUN
la cometa
el papalote *Mexico*

kitten ['kɪtn] NOUN
el gatito
la gatita

knee [niː] NOUN
la rodilla ◇ *to be on one's knees* estar* de rodillas

to **kneel** [niːl] VERB (**knelt** *o* **kneeled**, **knelt** *o* **kneeled**)
arrodillarse

to **kneel down** [niːl'daun] VERB
arrodillarse

knew [nuː] VERB *see* **know**

knife [naɪf] NOUN (PL **knives**)
el cuchillo
◆ **a kitchen knife** un cuchillo de cocina
◆ **a hunting knife** un cuchillo de caza
◆ **a penknife** una navaja

to **knit** [nɪt] VERB
tejer ◇ *I like knitting.* Me gusta tejer. ◇ *She is knitting a sweater.* Está tejiendo un suéter.

knives [naɪvz] PL NOUN *see* **knife**

knob [nɑːb] NOUN
1 el botón (*on radio, TV*)
2 la perilla
el botón *Mexico*
(*on door*)

to **knock** [nɑːk] VERB
see also **knock** NOUN
llamar ◇ *Someone's knocking at the door.* Alguien llama a la puerta.
◆ **to knock somebody down** atropellar a alguien ◇ *She was knocked down by a car.* La atropelló un carro.
◆ **to knock somebody out (1)** (*defeat*) eliminar a alguien ◇ *They were knocked out early in the tournament.* Fueron eliminados a poco de iniciarse el torneo.
◆ **to knock somebody out (2)** (*stun*) dejar sin sentido a alguien ◇ *They knocked out the watchman.* Dejaron al vigilante sin sentido.

knock [nɑːk] NOUN
see also **knock** VERB
el golpe

knockout ['nɑːkˌaut] NOUN
el nocaut (*boxing*) ◇ *to win by a knockout* ganar por nocaut
◆ **She's a real knockout.** Es una belleza.

knot [nɑːt] NOUN
el nudo ◇ *to tie a knot in something* hacer* un nudo en algo

to **know** [nou] VERB (**knew**, **known**)
Use ***saber*** *for knowing facts,* ***conocer*** *for knowing people and places.*
1 saber* ◇ *Yes, I know.* Sí, ya lo sé. ◇ *I don't know.* No sé. ◇ *I don't know any German.* No sé nada de alemán.
◆ **to know that** saber* que ◇ *I didn't know that your dad was a policeman.* No sabía que tu padre era policía.
2 conocer* ◇ *I know her.* La conozco. ◇ *I know Paris well.* Conozco bien París.
◆ **to know about something (1)** (*be aware of*) estar* enterado de algo ◇ *Do you know about the meeting this afternoon?* ¿Estás enterado de la reunión de esta tarde?
◆ **to know about something (2)** (*be knowledgeable about*) saber* de algo ◇ *He*

☞

knows a lot about cars. Sabe mucho de carros. ◇ *I don't know much about computers.* No sé mucho de computadoras.

◆ **to get to know somebody** llegar* a conocer a alguien

◆ **How should I know?** ¿Y yo qué sé?

◆ **You never know!** ¡Nunca se sabe!

know-how ['nou,hau] NOUN
la pericia

know-it-all ['nouɪt,ɑ:l] NOUN
el/la sabelotodo ◇ *He's such a know-it-all!* ¡Es un sabelotodo!

knowledge ['nɑ:lɪdʒ] NOUN
el conocimiento ◇ *scientific knowledge* el conocimiento científico

◆ **my knowledge of French** mis conocimientos de francés

knowledgeable ['nɑ:lɪdʒəbəl] ADJECTIVE

◆ **to be knowledgeable about something** saber* mucho de algo

known [noun] VERB *see* **know**

Koran [kə'rɑ:n] NOUN
el Corán

Korea [kə'ri:ə] NOUN
Corea FEM

kosher ['kouʃər] ADJECTIVE
kosher

L

lab [læb] NOUN
el laboratorio ◇ *a lab technician* un técnico de laboratorio

label [ˈleɪbəl] NOUN
la etiqueta

labor [ˈleɪbər] NOUN
◆ **to be in labor** estar* de parto
◆ **the labor market** el mercado de trabajo
◆ **Labor Day** el Día de los Trabajadores

laboratory [ˈlæbrətɔːri] NOUN (PL **laboratories**)
el laboratorio

laborer [ˈleɪbərər] NOUN
el peón (PL los peones)
◆ **farm laborer** el jornalero

labor union [ˈleɪbərˌjuːnjən] NOUN
el sindicato

lace [leɪs] NOUN
1 el cordón (PL los cordones)
la agujeta *Mexico*
(*of shoe*)
2 el encaje ◇ *a lace collar* un cuello de encaje

lack [læk] NOUN
la falta ◇ *He got the job, despite his lack of experience.* Consiguió el empleo, a pesar de su falta de experiencia.

lacquer [ˈlækər] NOUN
la laca

lad [læd] NOUN
el muchacho

ladder [ˈlædər] NOUN
la escalera
el burro *Mexico*
(*de mano*)

lady [ˈleɪdi] NOUN (PL **ladies**)
la señora
◆ **Ladies and gentlemen...** Damas y caballeros...
◆ **ladies' room** los servicios de señoras
◆ **a young lady** una señorita

ladybug [ˈleɪdiˌbʌg] NOUN
la mariquita

to **lag behind** [ˈlægbɪˈhaɪnd] VERB
quedarse atrás

lager [ˈlɑːgər] NOUN
la cerveza rubia

laid [leɪd] VERB *see* **lay**

laid-back [leɪdˈbæk] ADJECTIVE
relajado (*informal*)

lain [leɪn] VERB *see* **lie**

lake [leɪk] NOUN
el lago ◇ *Lake Michigan* el Lago Michigan

lamb [læm] NOUN
el cordero ◇ *a lamb chop* una chuleta de cordero

lame [leɪm] ADJECTIVE
cojo ◇ *to be lame* estar* cojo ◇ *The accident left her lame.* Se quedó coja después del accidente.
◆ **My pony is lame.** Mi pony cojea.

lamp [læmp] NOUN
la lámpara

lamppost [ˈlæmpˌpoust] NOUN
el farol

lampshade [ˈlæmpʃeɪd] NOUN
la pantalla

land [lænd] NOUN
see also **land** VERB
la tierra ◇ *We have a lot of land.* Tenemos mucha tierra. ◇ *to work on the land* trabajar la tierra
◆ **a piece of land** un terreno

to **land** [lænd] VERB
see also **land** NOUN
aterrizar* ◇ *The plane landed at five o'clock.* El avión aterrizó a las cinco.

landing [ˈlændɪŋ] NOUN
1 el aterrizaje (*of plane*)
2 el rellano (*of staircase*)

landlady [ˈlændˌleɪdi] NOUN (PL **landladies**)
la casera (*of rented property*)

landlord [ˈlændˌlɔːrd] NOUN
el casero (*of rented property*)

landmark [ˈlændmɑːrk] NOUN
el punto de referencia ◇ *The Empire State Building is one of New York's landmarks.* El Empire State es uno de los puntos de referencia de Nueva York.

landowner [ˈlændˌounər] NOUN
el/la terrateniente

landscape [ˈlændˌskeɪp] NOUN
el paisaje

lane [leɪn] NOUN
1 el camino ◇ *a country lane* un camino rural
2 el carril ◇ *a two-lane highway* una carretera de dos carriles ◇ *a four-lane highway* una autopista de cuatro carriles

language [ˈlæŋgwɪdʒ] NOUN
el idioma
*Although **idioma** ends in **-a**, it is actually a masculine noun.*
◇ *Greek is a difficult language.* El griego es un idioma difícil.
◆ **to use bad language** decir* palabrotas

language lab [ˈlæŋgwɪdʒˌlæb] NOUN
el laboratorio de idiomas

lap [læp] NOUN
la vuelta ◇ *I ran 10 laps.* Corrí 10 vueltas.
◆ **Andrew was sitting on his mother's lap.** Andrew estaba sentado en las rodillas de su madre.

laptop [ˈlæpˌtɑːp] NOUN
la computadora portátil

large [lɑːrdʒ] ADJECTIVE
grande ◇ *a large house* una casa grande ◇ *a large dog* un perro grande
*Use **gran** before a singular noun.*

◇ *a large number of people* un gran número de personas

largely ['lɑ:rdʒli] ADVERB
en gran parte

laser ['leɪzər] NOUN
el láser

last [læst] ADJECTIVE, ADVERB
see also **last** VERB
1 pasado ◇ *last Friday* el viernes pasado
2 último ◇ *the last time* la última vez
3 por última vez ◇ *I lost my wallet. – When did you last see it?* Se me perdió la billetera. – ¿Cuándo la viste por última vez?
4 en último lugar ◇ *the team which finished last* el equipo que quedó en último lugar
◆ **He arrived last.** Llegó el último.
◆ **last night** anoche ◇ *I got home at midnight last night.* Anoche llegué a la casa a medianoche. ◇ *I couldn't sleep last night.* Anoche no pude dormir.
◆ **at last** por fin

to **last** [læst] VERB
see also **last** ADJECTIVE, ADVERB
durar ◇ *The concert lasts two hours.* El concierto dura dos horas.

lastly ['læstli] ADVERB
por último

late [leɪt] ADJECTIVE, ADVERB
tarde ◇ *Hurry up or you'll be late!* ¡Date prisa o llegarás tarde! ◇ *I'm often late for school.* A menudo llego tarde al colegio. ◇ *I went to bed late.* Me fui a la cama tarde. ◇ *to arrive late* llegar* tarde
◆ **The flight will be one hour late.** El vuelo llegará con una hora de retraso.
◆ **in the late afternoon** al final de la tarde
◆ **in late May** a finales de mayo
◆ **the late Mr. Philips** el difunto Sr. Philips

lately ['leɪtli] ADVERB
últimamente ◇ *I haven't seen him lately.* No lo he visto últimamente.

later ['leɪtər] ADVERB
más tarde ◇ *I'll do it later.* Lo haré más tarde.
◆ **See you later!** ¡Hasta luego!

latest ['leɪtɪst] ADJECTIVE
último ◇ *their latest CD* su último CD
◆ **at the latest** como muy tarde ◇ *by 10 o'clock at the latest* a las 10 como muy tarde

Latin ['lætn] NOUN
el latín ◇ *I study Latin.* Estudio latín.

Latin America ['lætnə'mɛrɪkə] NOUN
América Latina FEM

Latin American ['lætnə'mɛrɪkən] ADJECTIVE
see also **Latin American** NOUN
latinoamericano

Latin American ['lætnə'mɛrɪkən] NOUN
see also **Latin American** ADJECTIVE
el latinoamericano
la latinoamericana

laugh [læf] NOUN
see also **laugh** VERB
la risa
◆ **It was a good laugh.** Fue muy divertido.

to **laugh** [læf] VERB
see also **laugh** NOUN
reírse*
◆ **to laugh at something** reírse de algo ◇ *He laughed at my accent.* Se rió de mi acento.
◆ **to laugh at somebody** reírse de alguien ◇ *They laughed at her.* Se rieron de ella.

to **launch** [lɑ:ntʃ] VERB
lanzar* (*product, rocket*)

Laundromat® ['lɑ:ndrəmæt] NOUN
la lavandería automática

laundry ['lɑ:ndri] NOUN
la ropa para lavar
◆ **She does my laundry.** Me lava la ropa.
◆ **laundry detergent** el detergente

lavatory ['lævətɔ:ri] NOUN (PL **lavatories**)
el baño

lavender ['lævəndər] NOUN
la lavanda

law [lɑ:] NOUN
1 la ley ◇ *strict laws* leyes severas
◆ **It's against the law.** Es ilegal.
2 el derecho ◇ *My sister is studying law.* Mi hermana estudia derecho.

lawn [lɑ:n] NOUN
el pasto

lawnmower ['lɑ:n,mouər] NOUN
la máquina de cortar el pasto

law school ['lɑ:,sku:l] NOUN
la facultad de derecho

lawyer ['lɑ:jər] NOUN
el abogado
la abogada
◇ *My mother's a lawyer.* Mi madre es abogada.

to **lay** [leɪ] VERB (**laid, laid**)
poner* ◇ *She laid the baby in his crib.* Puso al bebé en la cuna.

to **lay off** [leɪ'ɑ:f] VERB
despedir* ◇ *My father's been laid off.* Despidieron a mi padre.

to **lay on** [leɪ'ɑ:n] VERB
1 proporcionar (*provide*) ◇ *They laid on extra buses.* Proporcionaron más autobuses.
2 preparar (*prepare*) ◇ *They laid on a special meal.* Prepararon una comida especial.

layer ['leɪər] NOUN
la capa

lazy ['leɪzi] ADJECTIVE
perezoso

lead (1) [lɛd] NOUN
el plomo (*metal*) ◇ *a lead pipe* una cañería de plomo

lead (2) [li:d] NOUN

see also **lead** VERB
la cabeza (*in competition, game*) ◇ *to be in the lead* ir* en cabeza

to **lead** [li:d] VERB (**led, led**)
see also **lead (2)** NOUN
llevar ◇ *the street that leads to the station* la calle que lleva a la estación ◇ *It could lead to a civil war.* Podría llevar a una guerra civil.
◆ **to lead the way** ir* adelante

to **lead away** ['li:də'weɪ] VERB
llevarse ◇ *The police led the man away.* La policía se llevó al hombre.

leaded gasoline ['lɛdɪd'gæsəli:n] NOUN
la gasolina con plomo

leader ['li:dər] NOUN
el/la líder

lead singer ['li:d'sɪŋər] NOUN
el/la cantante principal

leaf [li:f] NOUN (PL **leaves**)
la hoja

leaflet ['li:flɪt] NOUN
el folleto

league [li:g] NOUN
la liga ◇ *They are at the top of the league.* Están a la cabeza de la liga.

leak [li:k] NOUN
see also **leak** VERB
1 el escape ◇ *a gas leak* un escape de gas ◇ *a leak in the pipe* un escape en la cañería
2 la gotera ◇ *a leak in the roof* una gotera en el techo

to **leak** [li:k] VERB
see also **leak** NOUN
1 tener* un agujero (*bucket, pipe*)
2 tener* goteras (*roof*)
3 salirse* (*water, gas*)

to **lean** [li:n] VERB
apoyar ◇ *to lean something against the wall* apoyar algo contra la pared
◆ **to lean on something** apoyarse en algo ◇ *He leaned on the table.* Se apoyó en la mesa.
◆ **to be leaning against something** estar* apoyado contra algo ◇ *The ladder was leaning against the wall.* La escalera estaba apoyada contra la pared.

to **lean forward** [li:n'fɔ:rwərd] VERB
inclinarse hacia adelante

to **lean out** [li:n'aut] VERB
asomarse ◇ *She leaned out of the window.* Se asomó a la ventana.

to **lean over** [li:n'ouvər] VERB
inclinarse ◇ *Don't lean over too far.* No te inclines demasiado.

to **leap** [li:p] VERB (**leapt** *or* **leaped, leapt** *or* **leaped**)
saltar
◆ **He leapt out of his chair when his team scored.** Saltó de la silla cuando su equipo marcó.

leap year ['li:pjɪər] NOUN
el año bisiesto

to **learn** [lɜ:rn] VERB
aprender ◇ *I'm learning to ski.* Estoy aprendiendo a esquiar.

learner ['lɜ:rnər] NOUN
◆ **She's a quick learner.** Aprende con mucha rapidez.
◆ **Spanish learners** los estudiantes de español

leash [li:ʃ] NOUN
la correa ◇ *Dogs must be kept on a leash.* Los perros deben llevarse sujetos con una correa.

least [li:st] ADJECTIVE, PRONOUN, ADVERB
1 menor ◇ *the city with the least crime* la ciudad con el menor índice criminal
2 menos ◇ *Go for the ones with least fat.* Escoge los que tengan menos grasa. ◇ *the least expensive hotel* el hotel menos caro ◇ *It takes the least time.* Es lo que menos tiempo lleva. ◇ *It's the least I can do.* Es lo menos que puedo hacer. ◇ *Math is the subject I like the least.* Las matemáticas es la asignatura que menos me gusta. ◇ *That's the least of my worries.* Eso es lo que menos me preocupa. ◇ *James is the least likely to win of all the candidates.* James es el candidato con menos posibilidades de ganar.
◆ **at least** por lo menos ◇ *It'll cost at least $200.* Costará por lo menos 200 dólares.
◆ **There was a lot of damage but at least nobody was hurt.** Hubo muchos daños pero al menos nadie resultó herido.
◆ **It's very unfair; at least that's my opinion.** Es muy injusto, al menos eso pienso yo.

leather ['lɛðər] NOUN
el cuero ◇ *a black leather jacket* una chaqueta de cuero negra

leave [li:v] NOUN
see also **leave** VERB
el permiso (*from job, army*) ◇ *My brother is on leave for a week.* Mi hermano está de permiso durante una semana.

to **leave** [li:v] VERB (**left, left**)
see also **leave** NOUN
1 dejar ◇ *Don't leave your camera in the car.* No dejes la cámara en el carro.
2 salir* ◇ *The train leaves at eight.* El tren sale a las ocho.
3 salir* de ◇ *We leave Miami at six o'clock.* Salimos de Miami a las seis.
4 irse* ◇ *They left yesterday.* Se fueron ayer. ◇ *She left home when she was sixteen.* Se fue de la casa a los dieciséis años.
◆ **to leave somebody alone** dejar a alguien en paz ◇ *Leave me alone!* ¡Déjame en paz!

to **leave behind** ['li:vbɪ'haɪnd] VERB
dejar ◇ *I left my umbrella behind in the store.* Dejé el paraguas en la tienda.

to **leave out** [li:v'aut] VERB
excluir* ◇ *Not knowing the language I felt really left out.* Al no saber el idioma me sentía muy excluido.

leaves [li:vz] PL NOUN *see* **leaf**

L

Lebanon [ˈlɛbənɑːn] NOUN
el Líbano

lecture [ˈlɛktʃər] NOUN
see also **lecture** VERB
1 la clase (*at college*)
2 la conferencia (*public*)

to **lecture** [ˈlɛktʃər] VERB
see also **lecture** NOUN
1 dar* clases ◇ *She lectures at Princeton.* Da clases en Princeton.
2 sermonear ◇ *He's always lecturing us.* Siempre nos está sermoneando.

led [lɛd] VERB *see* **lead**

leek [liːk] NOUN
el puerro

left [lɛft] VERB *see* **leave**

left [lɛft] ADJECTIVE, ADVERB
see also **left** NOUN
1 izquierdo ◇ *my left hand* mi mano izquierda
2 a la izquierda ◇ *Turn left at the traffic lights.* Doble a la izquierda al llegar al semáforo.
◆ **I don't have any money left.** No me queda nada de dinero.
◆ **Is there any ice cream left?** ¿Queda algo de helado?

left [lɛft] NOUN
see also **left** ADJECTIVE
la izquierda ◇ *on the left* a la izquierda

left-hand [ˈlɛftˈhænd] ADJECTIVE
◆ **the left-hand side** la izquierda ◇ *It's on the left-hand side.* Está a la izquierda.

left-handed [ˈlɛftˈhændɪd] ADJECTIVE
zurdo

leg [lɛg] NOUN
la pierna ◇ *She broke her leg.* Se rompió la pierna.
◆ **a chicken leg** una pata de pollo
◆ **a leg of lamb** una pierna de cordero

legal [ˈliːgəl] ADJECTIVE
legal

leggings [ˈlɛgɪŋz] PL NOUN
las mallas

leisure [ˈliːʒər] NOUN
el tiempo libre ◇ *What do you do in your leisure time?* ¿Qué haces en tu tiempo libre?

lemon [ˈlɛmən] NOUN
el limón (PL los limones)

lemonade [lɛməˈneɪd] NOUN
la limonada

to **lend** [lɛnd] VERB (**lent, lent**)
prestar ◇ *I can lend you some money.* Te puedo prestar algo de dinero.

length [lɛŋθ] NOUN
la longitud
◆ **It's about a meter in length.** Mide aproximadamente un metro de largo.

lens [lɛnz] NOUN (PL **lenses**)
1 el lente de contacto (*contact lens*)
2 el cristal (*of spectacles*)
3 el objetivo (*of camera*)

Lent [lɛnt] NOUN
la Cuaresma

lent [lɛnt] VERB *see* **lend**

lentil [ˈlɛntɪl] NOUN
la lenteja

Leo [ˈliːou] NOUN
el Leo (*sign*) ◇ *I'm a Leo.* Soy leo.
◆ **a Leo** un/una leo

leotard [ˈliːətɑːrd] NOUN
la malla

lesbian [ˈlɛzbiən] NOUN
la lesbiana

less [lɛs] ADJECTIVE, PRONOUN, ADVERB
menos ◇ *A bit less, please.* Un poco menos, por favor. ◇ *It's less than a kilometer from here.* Está a menos de un kilómetro de aquí. ◇ *less than half* menos de la mitad ◇ *I have less than you.* Tengo menos que tú. ◇ *It cost less than we thought.* Costó menos de lo que pensábamos.
◆ **less and less** cada vez menos

lesson [ˈlɛsən] NOUN
1 la clase ◇ *an English lesson* una clase de inglés ◇ *The lessons last forty minutes.* Las clases duran cuarenta minutos.
2 la lección (PL las lecciones) (*in textbook*)

to **let** [lɛt] VERB (**let, let**)
dejar
◆ **to let somebody do something** dejar a alguien hacer algo ◇ *Let me have a look.* Déjame ver.
◆ **Let me go!** ¡Suéltame!
◆ **to let somebody know something** informar a alguien de algo ◇ *We must let him know that we are coming to stay.* Tenemos que informarle que venimos a quedarnos.
◆ **When can you come to dinner? – I'll let you know.** ¿Cuándo puedes venir a cenar? – Ya te lo diré.
◆ **to let in** dejar entrar ◇ *They wouldn't let me in because I was under 18.* No me dejaron entrar porque tenía menos de 18 años.

*To make suggestions using **let's**, you can ask questions using **por qué no**.*
◇ *Let's go to the movies!* ¿Por qué no vamos al cine?
◆ **Let's take a break! – Yes, let's.** Vamos a descansar un poco. – ¡Buena idea!

to **let down** [lɛtˈdaun] VERB
defraudar ◇ *I won't let you down.* No te defraudaré.

letter [ˈlɛtər] NOUN
1 la carta ◇ *She wrote me a long letter.* Me escribió una carta larga.
2 la letra ◇ *A is the first letter of the alphabet.* La "a" es la primera letra del alfabeto.

lettuce [ˈlɛtɪs] NOUN

la lechuga

leukemia [luːˈkiːmiə] NOUN
la leucemia ◇ *He suffers from leukemia.* Tiene leucemia.

level [ˈlɛvəl] ADJECTIVE
see also **level** NOUN
llano ◇ *a level surface* una superficie plana

level [ˈlɛvəl] NOUN
see also **level** ADJECTIVE
el nivel ◇ *The level of the river is rising.* El nivel del río está subiendo.

lever [ˈlɛvər] NOUN
la palanca

liable [ˈlaɪəbəl] ADJECTIVE
◆ **He's liable to panic.** Tiene tendencia a dejarse llevar por el pánico.

liar [ˈlaɪər] NOUN
el mentiroso
la mentirosa

liberal [ˈlɪbərəl] ADJECTIVE
liberal (*view, system*)

liberation [lɪbəˈreɪʃən] NOUN
la liberación

Libra [ˈliːbrə] NOUN
la Libra (*sign*) ◇ *I'm a Libra.* Soy libra.
◆ **a Libra** un/una libra

librarian [laɪˈbrɛriən] NOUN
el bibliotecario
la bibliotecaria
◇ *I'm a librarian.* Soy bibliotecaria.

library [ˈlaɪbrɛri] NOUN (PL **libraries**)
la biblioteca
*Be careful not to translate **library** by **librería**.*

Libya [ˈlɪbiə] NOUN
Libia FEM

license [ˈlaɪsəns] NOUN
el permiso
◆ **a driver's license** un carnet de conducir, *Mexico:* una licencia para manejar

license number [ˈlaɪsənsˈnʌmbər] NOUN
el número de placa

license plate [ˈlaɪsənsˌpleɪt] NOUN
la placa

to **lick** [lɪk] VERB
lamer

lid [lɪd] NOUN
la tapa

lie [laɪ] NOUN
see also **lie** VERB
la mentira
◆ **to tell a lie** mentir*

to **lie** [laɪ] VERB
see also **lie** NOUN
1 mentir* ◇ *I know she's lying.* Sé que está mintiendo. ◇ *You lied to me!* ¡Me mentiste!
2 tenderse
*Se usa **lay** para el pasado y **lain** para el participio pasado de este sentido de **lie**.*
◇ *I lay on the floor.* Me tendí en el suelo.
◆ **He was lying on the sofa.** Estaba tendido en el sofá.

to **lie down** [laɪˈdaun] VERB
acostarse* ◇ *Why not go and lie down for a bit?* ¿Por qué no vas a acostarte un rato?
◆ **to be lying down** estar* tendido

lieutenant [luːˈtɛnənt] NOUN
el/la teniente

life [laɪf] NOUN (PL **lives**)
la vida

lifebelt [ˈlaɪfˌbɛlt] NOUN
el salvavidas (PL los salvavidas)

lifeboat [ˈlaɪfˌbout] NOUN
el bote salvavidas (PL los botes salvavidas)

lifeguard [ˈlaɪfˌgɑːrd] NOUN
el/la socorrista

life jacket [ˈlaɪfˌdʒækɪt] NOUN
el chaleco salvavidas (PL los chalecos salvavidas)

life preserver [ˈlaɪfprɪˈzɜːrvər] NOUN
el salvavidas (PL los salvavidas)

lifesaving [ˈlaɪfˌseɪvɪŋ] NOUN
el socorrismo ◇ *I've done a course in lifesaving.* Hice un curso de socorrismo.

life-style [ˈlaɪfˌstaɪl] NOUN
el estilo de vida

to **lift** [lɪft] VERB
see also **lift** NOUN
levantar ◇ *It's too heavy; I can't lift it.* Pesa mucho, no lo puedo levantar.

lift [lɪft] NOUN
see also **lift** VERB
◆ **He gave me a lift to the movies.** Me acercó al cine en carro. *Mexico:* Me dio aventón al cine.
◆ **Would you like a lift?** ¿Quieres que te lleve en carro?, *Mexico:* ¿Quieres que dé aventón?

light [laɪt] ADJECTIVE
see also **light** NOUN, VERB
1 liviano (*not heavy*) ◇ *a light jacket* un saco liviano ◇ *a light meal* una comida liviana
2 claro (*color*) ◇ *a light blue sweater* un suéter azul claro

light [laɪt] NOUN
see also **light** ADJECTIVE, VERB
la luz (PL las luces) ◇ *He switched on the light.* Prendió la luz. ◇ *He switched off the light.* Apagó la luz.
◆ **the traffic lights** el semáforo
◆ **Do you have a light?** ¿Tienes fuego?

to **light** [laɪt] VERB (**lit, lit**)
see also **light** ADJECTIVE, NOUN
prender

light bulb [ˈlaɪtˌbʌlb] NOUN
la bombilla
el foco *Mexico*

lighter [ˈlaɪtər] NOUN
el encendedor

lighthouse [ˈlaɪtˌhaus] NOUN
el faro

lightning [ˈlaɪtnɪŋ] NOUN
el relámpago ◇ *thunder and lightning* ☞

L

truenos y relámpagos ◇ *a flash of lightning* un relámpago

to **like** [laɪk] VERB

see also **like** PREPOSITION

*The most common translation for **to like** when talking about things and activities is **gustar**. Remember that the construction is the opposite of English, with the thing you like being the subject of the sentence.*

◇ *I don't like mustard.* No me gusta la mostaza. ◇ *Do you like apples?* ¿Te gustan las manzanas? ◇ *I like riding.* Me gusta andar a caballo.

◆ **I like him.** Me cae bien.

◆ **I'd like...** quería... ◇ *I'd like this blouse in size 10, please.* Quería esta blusa en la talla 10, por favor.

◆ **I'd like an orange juice, please.** Un jugo de naranja, por favor.

◆ **I'd like to...** Me gustaría... ◇ *I'd like to go to China.* Me gustaría ir a China.

*To ask someone if they would like something, or like to do something, use **querer**.*

◇ *Would you like some coffee?* ¿Quieres café? ◇ *Would you like to go for a walk?* ¿Quieres ir a dar un paseo?

◆ **...if you like** ...si quieres

like [laɪk] PREPOSITION

see also **like** VERB

como ◇ *a city like Paris* una ciudad como París

*When asking questions, use **cómo** instead of **como**.*

◇ *What was his house like?* ¿Cómo era su casa?

◆ **What's the weather like?** ¿Qué tiempo hace?

◆ **It's a bit like salmon.** Se parece un poco al salmón.

◆ **It's fine like that.** Así está bien.

◆ **Do it like this.** Hazlo así.

◆ **something like that** algo así

likely ['laɪkli] ADJECTIVE

probable ◇ *That's not very likely.* Es poco probable.

***es probable que** has to be followed by a verb in the subjunctive.*

◇ *She's likely to come.* Es probable que venga. ◇ *She's not likely to come.* Es probable que no venga.

lime [laɪm] NOUN

la lima

el limón verde Mexico

(*fruit*)

limit ['lɪmɪt] NOUN

el límite ◇ *the speed limit* el límite de velocidad

limousine ['lɪməziːn] NOUN

la limusina

to **limp** [lɪmp] VERB

cojear

line [laɪn] NOUN

1 la línea ◇ *a straight line* una línea recta ◇ *He wrote a few lines.* Escribió unas cuantas líneas. ◇ *to draw a line* trazar* una línea

2 la cola ◇ *a line of people* una cola de gente ◇ *People were standing in a line outside the movie theater.* La gente hacía cola afuera del cine.

◆ **railroad line** la vía férrea

◆ **Hold the line, please.** No cuelgue, por favor.

◆ **It's a very bad line.** Se oye muy mal.

to **line up** [laɪn'ʌp] VERB

1 hacer* cola ◇ *We had to line up for tickets.* Tuvimos que hacer cola para comprar las entradas.

2 poner* en fila (*stand in line*)

linen ['lɪnɪn] NOUN

el lino ◇ *a linen jacket* una chaqueta de lino

liner ['laɪnər] NOUN

el transatlántico

link [lɪŋk] NOUN

see also **link** VERB

la relación (PL las relaciones) ◇ *the link between smoking and cancer* la relación entre fumar y el cáncer

◆ **cultural links** los lazos culturales

to **link** [lɪŋk] VERB

see also **link** NOUN

1 asociar (*facts*)

2 conectar (*towns, terminals*)

linoleum [lɪ'nouliəm] NOUN

el linóleo

lion ['laɪən] NOUN

el león (PL los leones)

lioness ['laɪənɪs] NOUN (PL **lionesses**)

la leona

lip [lɪp] NOUN

el labio

lip balm ['lɪpˌbɑːm] NOUN

la crema protectora para los labios

to **lip-read** ['lɪpˌriːd] VERB (**lip-read, lip-read**)

leer* los labios

lipstick ['lɪpstɪk] NOUN

el lápiz de labios (PL los lápices de labios)

liqueur [lɪ'kɜːr] NOUN

el licor

liquid ['lɪkwɪd] NOUN

el líquido

liquor ['lɪkər] NOUN

el alcohol

liquor store ['lɪkərˌstɔːr] NOUN

la tienda de vinos y licores

Lisbon ['lɪzbən] NOUN

Lisboa FEM

list [lɪst] NOUN

see also **list** VERB

la lista

to **list** [lɪst] VERB

see also **list** NOUN

1 hacer* una lista de (*in writing*)
2 enumerar (*verbally*)

to **listen** ['lɪsən] VERB
escuchar ◇ *Listen to this!* ¡Escucha esto! ◇ *Listen to me!* ¡Escúchame!

listener ['lɪsnər] NOUN
el/la oyente

lit [lɪt] VERB *see* **light**

liter ['li:tər] NOUN
el litro

literally ['lɪtərəli] ADVERB
literalmente ◇ *It was literally impossible to find a seat.* Era literalmente imposible encontrar un asiento. ◇ *to translate literally* traducir* literalmente

literature ['lɪtərətʃər] NOUN
la literatura

litter ['lɪtər] NOUN
la basura

little ['lɪtl] ADJECTIVE, PRONOUN
pequeño ◇ *a little girl* una niña pequeña
◆ **a little** un poco ◇ *How much would you like? – Just a little.* ¿Cuánto quiere? – Sólo un poco.
◆ **very little** muy poco ◇ *We have very little time.* Tenemos muy poco tiempo.
◆ **little by little** poco a poco

live [laɪv] ADJECTIVE
see also **live** VERB
vivo ◇ *I'm against tests on live animals.* Estoy en contra de los experimentos en animales vivos.
◆ **a live broadcast** una transmisión en directo
◆ **a live concert** un concierto en vivo

to **live** [lɪv] VERB
see also **live** ADJECTIVE
vivir ◇ *I live with my grandmother.* Vivo con mi abuela. ◇ *Where do you live?* ¿Dónde vives? ◇ *I live in Tampa.* Vivo en Tampa.

to **live together** ['lɪvtə'gɛðər] VERB
vivir juntos

lively ['laɪvli] ADJECTIVE
◆ **She has a lively personality.** Tiene un carácter muy alegre.

liver ['lɪvər] NOUN
el hígado

lives [laɪvz] PL NOUN *see* **life**

living ['lɪvɪŋ] NOUN
◆ **to make a living** ganarse la vida
◆ **What does she do for a living?** ¿A qué se dedica?

living room ['lɪvɪŋˌru:m] NOUN
la sala de estar

lizard ['lɪzərd] NOUN
1 la lagartija (*small*)
2 el lagarto (*big*)

load [loud] NOUN
see also **load** VERB
◆ **loads of** un montón de (*informal*) ◇ *They have loads of money.* Tienen un montón de dinero.
◆ **You're talking a load of garbage!** (*informal*) ¡Lo que dices es una estupidez!

to **load** [loud] VERB
see also **load** NOUN
cargar* ◇ *a cart loaded with luggage* un carrito cargado de equipaje

loaf [louf] NOUN (PL **loaves**)
el pan
◆ **a loaf of bread** un pan

loan [loun] NOUN
see also **loan** VERB
el préstamo

to **loan** [loun] VERB
see also **loan** NOUN
prestar

to **loathe** [louð] VERB
detestar ◇ *I loathe her.* La detesto.

loaves [louvz] PL NOUN *see* **loaf**

lobster ['lɑ:bstər] NOUN
la langosta

local ['loukəl] ADJECTIVE
local ◇ *the local paper* el periódico local
◆ **a local call** una llamada local

loch [lɑ:x] NOUN
el lago

lock [lɑ:k] NOUN
see also **lock** VERB
la cerradura

to **lock** [lɑ:k] VERB
see also **lock** NOUN
cerrar* con llave ◇ *Make sure you lock your door.* No te olvides de cerrar tu puerta con llave.

to **lock out** [lɑ:k'aut] VERB
◆ **The door slammed and I was locked out.** La puerta se cerró de golpe y me quedé afuera sin llaves.

locker ['lɑ:kər] NOUN
el lóker (PL los lókers) ◇ *baggage lockers* los lókers de consigna
◆ **locker room** el vestuario, *Mexico*: el vestidor

locket ['lɑ:kɪt] NOUN
el relicario

lodger ['lɑ:dʒər] NOUN
el inquilino
la inquilina

loft [lɑ:ft] NOUN
el desván (PL los desvanes)

log [lɑ:g] NOUN
el leño

logical ['lɑ:dʒɪkəl] ADJECTIVE
lógico

to **log in** [lɑ:g'ɪn] VERB
entrar en el sistema

to **log off** [lɑ:g'ɑ:f] VERB
salir* del sistema

to **log on** [lɑ:g'ɑ:n] VERB
entrar en el sistema
◆ **to log on to the Net** conectarse a la Red

to **log out** [lɑ:g'aut] VERB
salir* del sistema

L

lollipop ['lɑːlipɑːp] NOUN
el pirulí (PL los pirulís)

loneliness ['lounlinɪs] NOUN
la soledad

lonely ['lounli] ADJECTIVE
solo ◇ *I sometimes feel lonely.* A veces me siento solo.
◆ **a lonely cottage** una casita aislada

lonesome ['lounsəm] ADJECTIVE
solo (*person*)

long [lɑːŋ] ADJECTIVE, ADVERB
see also **long** VERB
largo ◇ *She has long hair.* Tiene el pelo largo. ◇ *The room is six meters long.* La habitación tiene seis metros de largo.
◆ **a long time** mucho tiempo ◇ *It takes a long time.* Lleva mucho tiempo. ◇ *I've been waiting a long time.* Llevo esperando mucho tiempo.
◆ **How long?** (*time*) ¿Cuánto tiempo? ◇ *How long have you been here?* ¿Cuánto tiempo llevas aquí? ◇ *How long will it take?* ¿Cuánto tiempo llevará?
◆ **How long is the flight?** ¿Cuánto dura el vuelo?
◆ **as long as** siempre que
***siempre que** has to be followed by a verb in the subjunctive.*
◇ *I'll come as long as it's not too expensive.* Iré siempre que no sea demasiado caro.

to **long** [lɑːŋ] VERB
see also **long** ADJECTIVE
◆ **to long to do something** estar* deseando hacer algo

long-distance [lɑːŋ'dɪstəns] ADJECTIVE
◆ **a long-distance call** una llamada de larga distancia

longer ['lɑːŋgər] ADVERB
see also **long** ADJECTIVE
◆ **They're no longer going out together.** Ya no salen juntos.
◆ **I can't stand it any longer.** Ya no lo aguanto más.

long jump ['lɑːŋˌdʒʌmp] NOUN
el salto de longitud

look [luk] NOUN
see also **look** VERB
◆ **Take a look at this!** ¡Échale una ojeada a esto!
◆ **I don't like the look of it.** No me gusta nada.

to **look** [luk] VERB
see also **look** NOUN
1 mirar ◇ *Look!* ¡Mira!
◆ **to look at something** mirar algo ◇ *Look at the picture.* Mira la foto.
◆ **Look out!** ¡Cuidado!
2 parecer* ◇ *She looks surprised.* Parece sorprendida.
◆ **That cake looks nice.** Ese pastel tiene buena pinta.
◆ **to look like somebody** parecerse* a alguien ◇ *He looks like his brother.* Se parece a su hermano.
◆ **What does she look like?** ¿Cómo es físicamente?

to **look after** [luk'æftər] VERB
cuidar ◇ *I look after my little sister.* Cuido a mi hermana pequeña.

to **look around** [lukə'raund] VERB
1 volverse* ◇ *I called him and he looked around.* Lo llamé y se volvió.
2 mirar ◇ *I'm just looking around.* Sólo estoy mirando.
◆ **to look around an exhibition** visitar una exposición
◆ **I like looking around the stores.** Me gusta ir a ver tiendas.

to **look for** ['lukˌfɔːr] VERB
buscar* ◇ *I'm looking for my passport.* Estoy buscando mi pasaporte.

to **look forward to** [luk'fɔːrwərdˌtuː] VERB
tener* muchas ganas de ◇ *to look forward to doing something* tener muchas ganas de hacer algo ◇ *I'm looking forward to meeting you.* Tengo muchas ganas de conocerte.
◆ **I'm really looking forward to the vacations.** Estoy deseando que lleguen las vacaciones.
◆ **Looking forward to hearing from you...** A la espera de sus noticias...

to **look up** [luk'ʌp] VERB
buscar* ◇ *If you don't know a word, look it up in the dictionary.* Si no conoces una palabra, búscala en el diccionario.

loose [luːs] ADJECTIVE
holgado ◇ *a loose shirt* una camisa holgada
◆ **a loose screw** un tornillo flojo
◆ **loose change** dinero suelto, *Mexico:* feria

lord [lɔːrd] NOUN
el señor (*feudal*)
◆ **the Lord** el Señor (*God*)
◆ **Good Lord!** ¡Dios mío!

to **lose** [luːz] VERB (**lost, lost**)
perder* ◇ *I've lost my purse.* Perdí la cartera.
◆ **to get lost** perderse* ◇ *I was afraid of getting lost.* Tenía miedo de perderme.
◆ **I'm trying to lose weight.** Estoy tratando de adelgazar.

loss [lɑːs] NOUN (PL **losses**)
la pérdida

lost [lɑːst] VERB *see* **lose**

lost [lɑːst] ADJECTIVE
perdido

lost-and-found ['lɑːstən'faund] NOUN
la oficina de objetos perdidos

lot [lɑːt] NOUN
◆ **a lot** mucho ◇ *She talks a lot.* Habla mucho. ◇ *Do you like tennis? – Not a lot.* ¿Te gusta el tenis? – No mucho.
◆ **a lot of** mucho ◇ *I drink a lot of coffee.* Tomo mucho café. ◇ *We saw a lot of interesting*

things. Vimos muchas cosas interesantes. ◇ *He has lots of friends.* Tiene muchos amigos. ◇ *She has lots of self-confidence.* Tiene mucha confianza en sí misma.

lottery ['lɑːtəri] NOUN (PL **lotteries**)
la lotería ◇ *to win the lottery* ganar la lotería

loud [laud] ADJECTIVE
fuerte ◇ *The television is too loud.* La televisión está muy fuerte.

loudly ['laudli] ADVERB
fuerte

loudspeaker ['laud,spiːkər] NOUN
el altoparlante

lounge [laundʒ] NOUN
la sala de estar

lousy ['lauzi] ADJECTIVE
asqueroso (*informal*) ◇ *It was a lousy meal.* Fue una comida asquerosa.
◆ **I feel lousy.** Me siento pésimo.

love [lʌv] NOUN
see also **love** VERB
el amor
◆ **to be in love** estar* enamorado ◇ *She's in love with Paul.* Está enamorada de Paul.
◆ **to make love** hacer* el amor
◆ **Give Gloria my love.** Cariños a Gloria.
◆ **Love, Rosemary.** Cariños, Rosemary.

to **love** [lʌv] VERB
see also **love** NOUN
querer* ◇ *Everybody loves her.* Todos la quieren. ◇ *I love you.* Te quiero.
◆ **I love chocolate.** Me encanta el chocolate.
◆ **Would you like to come? – Yes, I'd love to.** ¿Te gustaría venir? – Sí, me encantaría.

lovely ['lʌvli] ADJECTIVE
encantador (FEM encantadora) (*person*) ◇ *She's a lovely person.* Es una persona encantadora.

lover ['lʌvər] NOUN
el/la amante

low [lou] ADJECTIVE, ADVERB
bajo ◇ *low prices* los bajos precios ◇ *That plane is flying very low.* Ese avión vuela muy bajo.

to **lower** ['louər] VERB
see also **lower** ADJECTIVE
bajar ◇ *He was so tall that the dentist had to lower the chair.* Era tan alto que el dentista tuvo que bajar la silla.

lower ['louər] ADJECTIVE
see also **lower** VERB
inferior

low-fat ['lou'fæt] ADJECTIVE
1 de bajo contenido graso (*margarine, cheese etc*)
2 descremado (*milk, yoghurt*)

loyalty ['lɔıəlti] NOUN (PL **loyalties**)
la lealtad

luck [lʌk] NOUN
la suerte ◇ *She hasn't had much luck.* No ha tenido mucha suerte.
◆ **Bad luck!** ¡Mala suerte!
◆ **Good luck!** ¡Suerte!

luckily ['lʌkıli] ADVERB
afortunadamente

lucky ['lʌki] ADJECTIVE
afortunado ◇ *I consider myself lucky.* Me considero afortunado.
◆ **to be lucky** tener* suerte (*fortunate*) ◇ *He's lucky, he has a job.* Tiene suerte de tener trabajo.
◆ **That was lucky!** ¡Qué suerte!
◆ **a lucky horseshoe** una herradura de la suerte

luggage ['lʌgıdʒ] NOUN
el equipaje

luggage rack ['lʌgıdʒ,ræk] NOUN
la baca

lukewarm ['luːk'wɔːrm] ADJECTIVE
tibio

lump [lʌmp] NOUN
1 el trozo ◇ *a lump of butter* un trozo de mantequilla
2 el chichón (PL los chichones) (*swelling*) ◇ *He has a lump on his forehead.* Tiene un chichón en la frente.

lunatic ['luːnətık] NOUN
el loco
la loca
◆ **He's an absolute lunatic.** Está loco perdido.

lunch [lʌntʃ] NOUN (PL **lunches**)
el almuerzo
la comida *Mexico*
◆ **to have lunch** almorzar*, *Mexico*: comer ◇ *We have lunch at half past twelve.* Almorzamos a las doce y media. *Mexico*: Comemos a las doce y media.

lung [lʌŋ] NOUN
el pulmón (PL los pulmones) ◇ *lung cancer* el cáncer de pulmón

luscious ['lʌʃəs] ADJECTIVE
exquisito

lush [lʌʃ] ADJECTIVE
exuberante

lust [lʌst] NOUN
la lujuria

luxurious [lʌg'ʒuriəs] ADJECTIVE
lujoso

luxury ['lʌgʒəri] NOUN (PL **luxuries**)
el lujo ◇ *It was luxury!* ¡Era un lujo!
◆ **a luxury hotel** un hotel de lujo

lying ['laııŋ] VERB *see* **lie**

lyrics ['lırıks] PL NOUN
la letra

M

macaroni [mækə'rouni] NOUN
los macarrones
machine [mə'ʃi:n] NOUN
la máquina ◇ *It's a complicated machine.* Es una máquina complicada.
◆ **I put my clothes in the washing machine.** Puse mi ropa en la lavadora.
machine gun [mə'ʃi:n,gʌn] NOUN
la ametralladora
machinery [mə'ʃi:nəri] NOUN
la maquinaria
mackerel ['mækərəl] NOUN (PL **mackerel**)
la caballa
mad [mæd] ADJECTIVE
1 furioso ◇ *She'll be mad when she finds out.* Se pondrá furiosa cuando se entere.
2 loco ◇ *You're mad!* ¡Estás loco! ◇ *Have you gone mad?* ¿Te has vuelto loco? ◇ *He is absolutely mad about her.* Está completamente loco por ella.
madam ['mædəm] NOUN
la señora ◇ *How may I help you, Madam?* ¿Qué desea la señora?
made [meɪd] VERB *see* **make**
madly ['mædli] ADVERB
◆ **They're madly in love.** Están locamente enamorados.
madman ['mædmən] NOUN (PL **madmen**)
el loco
madness ['mædnɪs] NOUN
la locura ◇ *It's absolute madness.* Es una locura.
magazine [mægə'zi:n] NOUN
la revista
maggot ['mægət] NOUN
el gusano
magic ['mædʒɪk] NOUN
see also **magic** ADJECTIVE
la magia ◇ *My hobby is magic.* Mi hobby es la magia.
magic ['mædʒɪk] ADJECTIVE
see also **magic** NOUN
mágico ◇ *a magic wand* una varita mágica
◆ **It was magic!** ¡Fue fantástico! (*fantastic*)
magician [mə'dʒɪʃən] NOUN
el mago
la maga
◇ *There was a magician at the party.* Había un mago en la fiesta.
magnet ['mægnɪt] NOUN
el imán (PL los imanes)
magnificent [mæg'nɪfɪsənt] ADJECTIVE
espléndido ◇ *a magnificent view* una vista espléndida
◆ **It was a magnificent effort on their part.** Fue un esfuerzo extraordinario por su parte.
magnifying glass ['mægnɪfaɪŋ'glæs] NOUN (PL **magnifying glasses**)
la lupa
maid [meɪd] NOUN
1 la sirvienta (*servant*)
2 la camarera (*in hotel*)
◆ **an old maid** una solterona (*spinster*)
maiden name ['meɪdn'neɪm] NOUN
el apellido de soltera

> ℹ *When women marry in Latin America they don't usually take the name of their husband but keep their own instead. If the couple have children they take both their father's and mother's surnames.*

mail [meɪl] NOUN
see also **mail** VERB
1 el correo ◇ *Has the mail arrived yet?* ¿Llegó ya el correo?
◆ **by mail** por correo
◆ **Is there any mail for me?** ¿Tengo alguna carta?
2 la correspondencia (*letters*) ◇ *We receive a lot of mail.* Recibimos mucha correspondencia.
to **mail** [meɪl] VERB
see also **mail** NOUN
mandar por correo ◇ *You could mail it.* Puedes mandarlo por correo.
◆ **I have some cards to mail.** Tengo que mandar algunas postales.
◆ **Would you mail this letter for me?** ¿Me echas esta carta al correo?
mailbox ['meɪl,bɑ:ks] NOUN (PL **mailboxes**)
el buzón (PL los buzones)
mailing list ['meɪlɪŋ,lɪst] NOUN
la lista de direcciones
mailman ['meɪl,mæn] NOUN (PL **mailmen**)
el cartero ◇ *He's a mailman.* Es cartero.
main [meɪn] ADJECTIVE
principal ◇ *the main suspect* el principal sospechoso
◆ **The main thing is to get it finished.** Lo principal es terminarlo.
mainly ['meɪnli] ADVERB
principalmente
main road ['meɪn'roud] NOUN
la carretera principal
to **maintain** [meɪn'teɪn] VERB
mantener* ◇ *Teachers try hard to maintain standards.* Los maestros se esfuerzan por mantener el nivel educativo. ◇ *Old houses are expensive to maintain.* Las casas viejas son costosas de mantener.
maintenance ['meɪntənəns] NOUN
1 el mantenimiento ◇ *car maintenance* el mantenimiento del carro
2 la pensión alimenticia ◇ *$30 a week in maintenance* 30 dólares a la semana por

concepto de pensión alimenticia

maize [meɪz] NOUN
el maíz

majesty ['mædʒɪsti] NOUN (PL **majesties**)
la majestad
- **Your Majesty** su Majestad

major ['meɪdʒər] ADJECTIVE
see also **major** NOUN, VERB
muy importante ◇ *a major factor* un factor muy importante
- **Drugs are a major problem.** La droga es un grave problema.
- **in C major** en do mayor

major ['meɪdʒər] NOUN
see also **major** VERB, ADJECTIVE
la asignatura principal (*subject*)
- **He's a Spanish major.** Estudia español como asignatura principal.

major ['meɪdʒər] VERB
see also **major** NOUN, ADJECTIVE
- **to major in something** especializarse en algo (*at college*)

majority [mə'dʒɑːrɪti] NOUN (PL **majorities**)
la mayoría

make [meɪk] NOUN
see also **make** VERB
la marca ◇ *What make is it?* ¿De qué marca es?

to **make** [meɪk] VERB (**made, made**)
see also **make** NOUN
1 hacer* ◇ *I'm going to make a cake.* Voy a hacer un pastel. ◇ *I'd like to make a phone call.* Quisiera hacer una llamada. ◇ *I make my bed every morning.* Me hago la cama cada mañana. ◇ *It's well made.* Está bien hecho.
- **She's making lunch.** Está preparando el almuerzo.
- **Two and two make four.** Dos y dos son cuatro.

2 fabricar* ◇ *"made in Spain"* "fabricado en España"
3 ganar ◇ *He makes a lot of money.* Gana mucho dinero.
- **to make somebody do something** hacer* a alguien hacer algo ◇ *My mother makes me eat vegetables.* Mi madre me hace comer verduras.
- **You'll have to make do with a cheaper car.** Tendrás que conformarte con un carro más barato.
- **What time do you make it?** ¿Qué hora tienes?

to **make out** [meɪk'aut] VERB
1 descifrar ◇ *I can't make out the address on the label.* No consigo descifrar la dirección que viene en la etiqueta.
2 comprender ◇ *I can't make her out at all.* No la comprendo en absoluto.
3 dar* a entender ◇ *They're making out it was my fault.* Están dando a entender que fue culpa mía.
- **to make a check out to somebody** hacer* un cheque a favor de alguien
- **to make out with somebody** besuquearse y toquetearse con alguien, *Mexico:* fajar con algn (*informal*)

to **make up** [meɪk'ʌp] VERB
1 componer* ◇ *Women make up 30 per cent of the police force.* Las mujeres componen el 30 por ciento del cuerpo de policía.
2 inventarse ◇ *He made up the whole story.* Se inventó toda la historia.
3 hacer* las paces ◇ *They had a quarrel, but soon made up.* Riñeron, pero poco después hicieron las paces.
4 maquillarse ◇ *She spends hours making herself up.* Pasa horas maquillándose.

maker ['meɪkər] NOUN
el/la fabricante ◇ *Spain's biggest car maker.* El mayor fabricante de automóviles de España.

makeup ['meɪkʌp] NOUN
el maquillaje
- **She put on her makeup.** Se maquilló.

male [meɪl] ADJECTIVE
see also **male** NOUN
1 macho (*animal, plant*) ◇ *a male kitten* un gatito macho
2 varón (PL varones) (*person*) ◇ *Sex: Male* Sexo: Varón
- **Most football players are male.** La mayoría de los futbolistas son hombres.
- **a male nurse** un enfermero
- **a male chauvinist** un machista

male [meɪl] NOUN
see also **male** ADJECTIVE
el macho (*animal*)

mall [mɑːl] NOUN
el centro comercial

mammoth ['mæməθ] NOUN
see also **mammoth** ADJECTIVE
el mamut (PL los mamuts)

mammoth ['mæməθ] ADJECTIVE
see also **mammoth** NOUN
colosal (*project, building*)
- **a mammoth task** una obra de titanes

man [mæn] NOUN (PL **men**)
el hombre

to **manage** ['mænɪdʒ] VERB
1 arreglárselas ◇ *We don't have much money, but we manage.* No tenemos mucho dinero, pero nos las arreglamos.
2 dirigir* ◇ *She manages a big store.* Dirige una tienda grande. ◇ *He manages our soccer team.* Dirige nuestro equipo de fútbol.
- **to manage to do something** conseguir* hacer algo ◇ *Luckily I managed to pass the exam.* Por suerte, conseguí pasar el examen.
- **Can you manage a bit more?** ¿Te pongo un poco más? (*food*)
- **Can you manage with that suitcase?** ¿Puedes con la maleta?

manageable ['mænɪdʒəbəl] ADJECTIVE
factible (*task, goal*)
management ['mænɪdʒmənt] NOUN
la dirección ◇ *He's responsible for the management of the project.* Es responsable de la dirección del proyecto. ◇ *management and workers* la dirección y los trabajadores
manager ['mænɪdʒər] NOUN
1 el director
la directora
(*of company, department, performer*)
◇ *I complained to the manager.* Fui a reclamar al director.
2 el/la gerente (*of restaurant, store*)
3 el entrenador
la entrenadora
(*of team*)
◇ *the manager of the Red Sox* el entrenador de los Red Sox
manageress [mænɪdʒə'rɛs] NOUN (PL **manageresses**)
la gerente (*of restaurant, store*)
mandarin orange ['mændərɪn'ɑ:rɪndʒ] NOUN
la mandarina
mango ['mæŋgou] NOUN (PL **mangos** *or* **mangoes**)
el mango
maniac ['meɪnɪæk] NOUN
el maníaco
la maníaca
◆ **He drives like a maniac.** Maneja como un loco.
to **manipulate** [mə'nɪpjəleɪt] VERB
manipular
mankind ['mækaɪnd] NOUN
el género humano
man-made ['mæn'meɪd] ADJECTIVE
sintético (*fiber*)
manner ['mænər] NOUN
la manera ◇ *She was behaving in an odd manner.* Se comportaba de una manera extraña.
◆ **He has a confident manner.** Se muestra seguro de sí mismo.
manners ['mænərz] PL NOUN
los modales ◇ *Her manners are appalling.* Tiene muy malos modales.
◆ **good manners** la buena educación
◆ **It's bad manners to talk with your mouth full.** Es de mala educación hablar con la boca llena.
manpower ['mæn,pauər] NOUN
la mano de obra
Although ***mano*** *ends in* ***-o, mano de obra*** *is actually a feminine noun.*
mansion ['mænʃən] NOUN
la mansión (PL las mansiones)
mantelpiece ['mæntl,pi:s] NOUN
la repisa de la chimenea
manual ['mænjuəl] NOUN
el manual
to **manufacture** [mænju'fæktʃər] VERB
fabricar*
manufacturer [mænju'fæktʃərər] NOUN
el/la fabricante
manure [mə'nuər] NOUN
el estiércol
manuscript ['mænjuskrɪpt] NOUN
el manuscrito
many ['mɛni] ADJECTIVE, PRONOUN
muchos (FEM muchas) ◇ *He doesn't have many friends.* No tiene muchos amigos.
◆ **Were there many people at the concert? – Not many.** ¿Había mucha gente en el concierto? – No mucha.
◆ **very many** muchos (FEM muchas) ◇ *I don't have very many CDs.* No tengo muchos CDs.
◆ **How many?** ¿cuántos? (FEM ¿cuántas?) ◇ *How many hours a week do you work?* ¿Cuántas horas trabajas a la semana?
◆ **too many** demasiados (FEM demasiadas) ◇ *Sixteen people? That's too many.* ¿Dieciséis personas? Son demasiadas.
◆ **so many** tantos (FEM tantas) ◇ *He told so many lies!* ¡Dijo tantas mentiras!
map [mæp] NOUN
1 el mapa (*of country, region*)
Although ***mapa*** *ends in* ***-a****, it is actually a masculine noun.*
2 el plano (*of town, city*)
marathon ['mærəθɑ:n] NOUN
el maratón (los maratones)
marble ['mɑ:rbəl] NOUN
el mármol ◇ *a marble statue* una estatua de mármol
◆ **a marble** una canica
March [mɑ:rtʃ] NOUN
marzo MASC ◇ *in March* en marzo ◇ *on March 9th* el 9 de marzo
to **march** [mɑ:rtʃ] VERB
see also **march** NOUN
desfilar ◇ *The troops marched past the king.* Las tropas desfilaron delante del Rey.
march [mɑ:rtʃ] NOUN (PL **marches**)
see also **march** VERB
la marcha ◇ *a peace march* una marcha por la paz
mare [mɛər] NOUN
la yegua
margarine ['mɑ:rdʒərən] NOUN
la margarina
margin ['mɑ:rdʒɪn] NOUN
el margen (PL los márgenes) ◇ *She wrote a note in the margin.* Escribió una nota al margen.
marijuana [mærɪ'wɑ:nə] NOUN
la marihuana
marital status ['mærɪtl'steɪtəs] NOUN
el estado civil
mark [mɑ:rk] NOUN

* Verbs marked with this symbol are irregular. See pages 346–348 for further details.

see also **mark** VERB
1 la mancha ◇ *There were red marks all over his back.* Tenía manchas rojas por toda la espalda. ◇ *You have a mark on your shirt.* Tienes una mancha en la camisa.
2 el marco (*German currency*) ◇ *30 million marks* 30 millones de marcos

to **mark** [mɑːrk] VERB
see also **mark** NOUN
1 corregir* ◇ *The teacher hasn't marked my homework yet.* El maestro no me ha corregido los deberes todavía.
2 señalar ◇ *Mark its position on the map.* Señala su posición en el mapa.

market [ˈmɑːrkɪt] NOUN
el mercado

marketing [ˈmɑːrkɪtɪŋ] NOUN
el márketing

marmalade [ˈmɑːrməleɪd] NOUN
la mermelada de naranja

maroon [məˈruːn] ADJECTIVE
granate MASC, FEM, PL

marriage [ˈmɛrɪdʒ] NOUN
el matrimonio

married [ˈmɛrid] ADJECTIVE
casado ◇ *They are not married.* No están casados.
◆ **a married couple** un matrimonio
◆ **to get married** casarse

to **marry** [ˈmɛri] VERB (**married, married**)
1 casarse ◇ *They married in June.* Se casaron en junio.
2 casarse con ◇ *He wants to marry her.* Quiere casarse con ella.
◆ **to get married** casarse ◇ *My brother's getting married in March.* Mi hermano se casa en marzo.

marvelous [ˈmɑːrvələs] ADJECTIVE
estupendo ◇ *The weather was marvelous.* Hacía un tiempo estupendo. ◇ *That's a marvelous idea!* ¡Es una idea estupenda!

marzipan [ˈmɑːrzɪpæn] NOUN
el mazapán

mascara [mæˈskærə] NOUN
el rímel

masculine [ˈmæskjulɪn] ADJECTIVE
masculino

mashed potatoes [ˌmæʃtpəˈteɪtouz] PL NOUN
el puré de papas

mask [mæsk] NOUN
la máscara

masked [mæskt] ADJECTIVE
encapuchado (*terrorist, attacker*)

mass [mæs] NOUN (PL **masses**)
1 el montón (PL los montones) ◇ *a mass of books and papers* un montón de libros y papeles
2 la misa ◇ *We go to mass on Sunday.* Vamos a misa los domingos.
◆ **the mass media** los medios de comunicación de masas

massage [məˈsɑːʒ] NOUN
el masaje

massive [ˈmæsɪv] ADJECTIVE
enorme

master [ˈmæstər] NOUN
see also **master** VERB
1 el dueño (*of house*)
2 el amo (*of servant*)
3 el maestro (*at school*)

to **master** [ˈmæstər] VERB
see also **master** NOUN
dominar ◇ *Students need to master a second language.* Los estudiantes tienen que dominar un segundo idioma.

masterpiece [ˈmæstərˌpiːs] NOUN
la obra maestra (PL las obras maestras)

mat [mæt] NOUN
el felpudo (*doormat*)
◆ **a table mat** un mantel individual

match [mætʃ] NOUN (PL **matches**)
see also **match** VERB
1 el partido ◇ *a tennis match* un partido de tenis
2 el fósforo
el cerillo *Mexico*
◇ *a box of matches* una caja de fósforos, *Mexico*: una caja de cerillos

to **match** [mætʃ] VERB
see also **match** NOUN
1 hacer* juego con ◇ *The jacket matches the pants.* La chaqueta hace juego con los pantalones.
2 hacer* juego ◇ *These colors don't match.* Estos colores no hacen juego.

matching [ˈmætʃɪŋ] ADJECTIVE
haciendo juego ◇ *My bedroom has matching wallpaper and curtains.* Mi habitación tiene el papel y las cortinas haciendo juego.

material [məˈtɪriəl] NOUN
1 la tela ◇ *The curtains are made of a thin material.* Las cortinas están hechas de una tela fina.
2 el material ◇ *I'm collecting material for my project.* Estoy recogiendo material para mi proyecto.

math [mæθ] NOUN
las matemáticas

mathematics [mæθəˈmætɪks] NOUN
las matemáticas

matter [ˈmætər] NOUN
see also **matter** VERB
el asunto ◇ *It's a matter of life and death.* Es un asunto de vida o muerte.
◆ **What's the matter?** ¿Qué pasa?
◆ **as a matter of fact** de hecho

to **matter** [ˈmætər] VERB
see also **matter** NOUN
importar ◇ *I can't give you the money today. – It doesn't matter.* No te puedo dar el dinero hoy. – No importa.

- **Shall I phone today or tomorrow? – Whenever. It doesn't matter.** ¿Telefoneo hoy o mañana? – Cuando quieras, da igual.
- **It matters a lot to me.** Significa mucho para mí.

mattress ['mætrɪs] NOUN (PL **mattresses**)
el colchón (PL los colchones)

mature [mə'tjuər] ADJECTIVE
maduro

maximum ['mæksɪməm] NOUN
see also **maximum** ADJECTIVE
el máximo ◇ *a maximum of two years in prison* un máximo de dos años de cárcel

maximum ['mæksɪməm] ADJECTIVE
see also **maximum** NOUN
máximo ◇ *The maximum speed is 100 mph.* La velocidad máxima permitida es 100 mph.

May [meɪ] NOUN
mayo MASC ◇ *in May* en mayo ◇ *on May 7th* el 7 de mayo
- **May Day** el primero de Mayo

may [meɪ] VERB
poder* ◇ *The police may come and catch us here.* La policía puede venir y pillarnos aquí. ◇ *May I smoke?* ¿Puedo fumar?

***Puede que** has to be followed by a verb in the subjunctive.*

◇ *I may go.* Puede que vaya. ◇ *It may rain.* Puede que llueva.

***A lo mejor** can also be used but it is a more colloquial alternative.*

◇ *Are you going to the party? – I don't know, I may.* ¿Vas a ir a la fiesta? – No sé, a lo mejor.

maybe ['meɪbiː] ADVERB
a lo mejor ◇ *Maybe she's at home.* A lo mejor está en casa. ◇ *Maybe he'll change his mind.* A lo mejor cambia de idea.

mayonnaise ['meɪəneɪz] NOUN
la mayonesa

mayor ['meɪər] NOUN
el alcalde
la alcaldesa

maze [meɪz] NOUN
el laberinto

me [miː] PRONOUN

*Use **me** to translate **me** when it is the direct object of the verb in the sentence, or when it means **to me**.*

me ◇ *Look at me!* ¡Mírame! ◇ *Could you lend me your pencil?* ¿Me prestas tu lápiz?

*Use **yo** after the verb **to be** and in comparisons.*

◇ *It's me.* Soy yo. ◇ *He's older than me.* Es mayor que yo.

*Use **mí** after prepositions.*

◇ *without me* sin mí

*Remember that **with me** translates as **conmigo**.*

◇ *He was with me.* Estaba conmigo.

meal [miːl] NOUN
la comida
- **Enjoy your meal!** ¡Que aproveche!

mealtime ['miːl,taɪm] NOUN
- **at mealtimes** a las horas de comer

to **mean** [miːn] VERB (**meant, meant**)
see also **mean** ADJECTIVE
1 significar* ◇ *What does "alcalde" mean?* ¿Qué significa "alcalde"? ◇ *I don't know what it means.* No sé lo que significa.
2 querer* decir ◇ *That's not what I meant.* Eso no es lo que quería decir.
3 referirse* a ◇ *Which one did he mean?* ¿A cuál se refería? ◇ *Do you mean me?* ¿Te refieres a mí?
- **to mean to do something** querer* hacer algo ◇ *I didn't mean to hurt you.* No quería hacerte daño.
- **Do you really mean it?** ¿Lo dices en serio?
- **He means what he says.** Habla en serio.

mean [miːn] ADJECTIVE
see also **mean** VERB
mezquino ◇ *You're being mean to me.* Estás siendo mezquino conmigo.
- **That's a really mean thing to say!** ¡Parece mentira que digas eso!

meaning ['miːnɪŋ] NOUN
el significado

means [miːnz] NOUN
el medio ◇ *a means of transport* un medio de transporte ◇ *He'll do it by any possible means.* Lo hará por todos los medios.
- **by means of** por medio de
- **Can I come in? – By all means!** ¿Puedo entrar? – ¡Claro que sí!

meant [mɛnt] VERB *see* **mean**

meanwhile ['miːn,waɪl] ADVERB
mientras tanto

measles ['miːzəlz] NOUN
el sarampión ◇ *I have measles.* Tengo sarampión.

to **measure** ['mɛʒər] VERB
medir*

measurement ['mɛʒərmənt] NOUN
la medida ◇ *What are the measurements of the room?* ¿Cuáles son las medidas de la habitación? ◇ *Are you sure the measurements are correct?* ¿Estás seguro de que las medidas son correctas?
- **What's your waist measurement?** ¿Cuánto mides de cintura?

meat [miːt] NOUN
la carne

Mecca ['mɛkə] NOUN
La Meca

mechanic [mɪ'kænɪk] NOUN
el mecánico
la mecánica
◇ *He's a mechanic.* Es mecánico.

mechanical [mɪ'kænɪkəl] ADJECTIVE
mecánico

medal ['mɛdl] NOUN
la medalla

media ['mi:diə] PL NOUN
◆ **the media** los medios de comunicación

median strip ['mi:diən'strɪp] NOUN
la mediana
el bandejón central *Mexico*

Medicaid ['mɛdɪkeɪd] NOUN

> ℹ *Programa estatal de asistencia médica para personas de bajos ingresos.*

medical ['mɛdɪkəl] ADJECTIVE
médico ◇ *medical treatment* el tratamiento médico ◇ *He had a medical checkup last week.* Se hizo un chequeo médico la semana pasada.
◆ **medical insurance** el seguro médico
◆ **to have medical problems** tener* problemas de salud
◆ **She's a medical student.** Es una estudiante de medicina.

Medicare ['mɛdɪkɛr] NOUN

> ℹ *Programa estatal de asistencia médica para ancianos y minusválidos.*

medicine ['mɛdɪsɪn] NOUN
1 la medicina (*science*) ◇ *I want to study medicine.* Quiero estudiar medicina.
◆ **alternative medicine** la medicina alternativa
2 el medicamento (*medication*) ◇ *I need some medicine.* Necesito un medicamento.

Mediterranean [mɛdɪtə'reɪniən] ADJECTIVE
see also **Mediterranean** NOUN
mediterráneo

Mediterranean [mɛdɪtə'reɪniən] NOUN
see also **Mediterranean** ADJECTIVE
◆ **the Mediterranean** el Mediterráneo

medium ['mi:diəm] ADJECTIVE
mediano ◇ *a man of medium height* un hombre de estatura mediana

medium-sized ['mi:diəm'saɪzd] ADJECTIVE
◆ **a medium-sized town** una ciudad de tamaño mediano

to **meet** [mi:t] VERB (**met, met**)
1 encontrarse* con (*by chance*) ◇ *I met Paul in town.* Me encontré con Paul en el centro.
◆ **We met by chance in the supermarket.** Nos encontramos por casualidad en el supermercado.
2 reunirse* (*by arrangement*) ◇ *The committee met at two o'clock.* El comité se reunió a las dos.
◆ **Where shall we meet?** ¿Dónde nos encontramos?
◆ **I'm going to meet my friends at the movie theater.** Me voy a encontrar con mis amigos en el cine.
◆ **I'll meet you at the station.** Te voy a buscar a la estación.
3 conocer* (*get to know*) ◇ *He met Tim at a party.* Conoció a Tim en una fiesta.
◆ **Have you met her before?** ¿La conoces?

meeting ['mi:tɪŋ] NOUN
1 el encuentro (*socially*) ◇ *their first meeting* su primer encuentro
2 la reunión (PL las reuniones) (*for work*) ◇ *a business meeting* una reunión de trabajo

mega ['mɛgə] ADJECTIVE
◆ **He's mega rich.** Es super rico. (*informal*)

melody ['mɛlədi] NOUN (PL **melodies**)
la melodía

melon ['mɛlən] NOUN
el melón (PL los melones)

to **melt** [mɛlt] VERB
1 derretir* ◇ *Melt some butter in a saucepan.* Derrita un poco de mantequilla en una sartén.
2 derretirse* ◇ *The snow is melting.* La nieve se está derritiendo.

member ['mɛmbər] NOUN
el/la miembro
◆ **"members only"** "reservado para los socios"
◆ **a Member of Congress** un diputado (FEM una diputada)

membership ['mɛmbərʃɪp] NOUN
la afiliación (PL las afiliaciones)
◆ **I'm going to apply for membership in the club.** Voy a solicitar el ingreso al club.

membership card ['mɛmbərʃɪp'kɑ:rd] NOUN
el carnet de socio (PL los carnets de socio)

memento [mə'mɛntou] NOUN (PL **mementos** *or* **mementoes**)
el recuerdo

memorial [mɪ'mɔ:riəl] NOUN
◆ **a war memorial** un monumento a los caídos

to **memorize** ['mɛməraɪz] VERB
memorizar*

memory ['mɛməri] NOUN (PL **memories**)
1 la memoria (*also for computer*) ◇ *I have a terrible memory.* Tengo una memoria espantosa.
2 el recuerdo ◇ *happy memories* los recuerdos felices

men [mɛn] PL NOUN *see* **man**

to **mend** [mɛnd] VERB
arreglar

meningitis [mɛnɪn'dʒaɪtɪs] NOUN
la meningitis ◇ *Her daughter has meningitis.* Su hija tiene meningitis.

men's room ['mɛnz,ru:m] NOUN
el baño de caballeros

mental ['mɛntl] ADJECTIVE
mental ◇ *mental illness* la enfermedad mental
◆ **mental hospital** el hospital psiquiátrico

to **mention** ['mɛnʃən] VERB
mencionar ◇ *He didn't mention it to me.* No me lo mencionó.
◆ **I mentioned she might come later.** Dije que a ☞

M

lo mejor vendría más tarde.
◆ **Thank you! – Don't mention it!** ¡Gracias! – ¡No hay de qué!

menu ['mɛnjuː] NOUN
el menú (PL los menús) ◇ *Could I have the menu please?* ¿Me trae el menú por favor?

merchant ['mɜːrtʃənt] NOUN
el/la comerciante
◆ **a wine merchant** un vinatero

mercy ['mɜːrsi] NOUN
la compasión

mere [mɪər] ADJECTIVE
◆ **a mere five percent** sólo un cinco por ciento
◆ **It's a mere formality.** No es más que una formalidad.

meringue [mə'ræŋ] NOUN
el merengue

merry ['mɛri] ADJECTIVE
◆ **Merry Christmas!** ¡Feliz Navidad!

merry-go-round ['mɛrigou,raund] NOUN
el carrusel

mess [mɛs] NOUN
el desorden
◆ **My hair is a mess, it needs cutting.** Tengo el pelo hecho un desastre; tengo que cortármelo.
◆ **I'll be in a mess if I fail the exam.** Voy a tener problemas si no paso el examen.

to **mess around** ['mɛsə'raund] VERB
◆ **I didn't do much at the weekend, just messed around with some friends.** No hice mucho el fin de semana; estuve pasando el rato con unos amigos.
◆ **Stop messing around with my computer!** ¡Deja de toquetear mi computadora!

to **mess up** [mɛs'ʌp] VERB
estropear ◇ *You've messed up my cassettes!* ¡Me estropeaste los casetes!
◆ **I messed up my chemistry exam.** Metí la pata en el examen de química.

message ['mɛsɪdʒ] NOUN
el mensaje ◇ *a secret message* un mensaje secreto
◆ **Would you like to leave him a message?** ¿Quiere dejarle un recado?

messenger ['mɛsɪndʒər] NOUN
el mensajero
la mensajera

messy ['mɛsi] ADJECTIVE
desordenado ◇ *Your room is really messy.* Tu habitación está muy desordenada.
◇ *She's so messy!* ¡Es más desordenada!
◆ **a really messy job** un trabajo muy sucio
◆ **Her writing is very messy.** Tiene muy mala letra.

met [mɛt] VERB *see* **meet**

metal ['mɛtl] NOUN
el metal

meter ['miːtər] NOUN
1 el contador (*for gas, electricity*)
2 el taxímetro (*for taxi*)
3 el parquímetro (*parking meter*)
4 el metro (*unit of measurement*)

method ['mɛθəd] NOUN
el método

Methodist ['mɛθədɪst] ADJECTIVE
see also **Methodist** NOUN
metodista

Methodist ['mɛθədɪst] NOUN
see also **Methodist** ADJECTIVE
el/la metodista ◇ *He's a Methodist.* Es metodista.

metric ['mɛtrɪk] ADJECTIVE
métrico

Mexico ['mɛksɪkou] NOUN
México MASC

to **miaow** [miː'au] VERB
maullar*

mice [maɪs] PL NOUN *see* **mouse**

microchip ['maɪkroutʃɪp] NOUN
el microchip (PL los microchips)

microphone ['maɪkrəfoun] NOUN
el micrófono

microscope ['maɪkrəskoup] NOUN
el microscopio

microwave ['maɪkrəweɪv] NOUN
el microondas (PL los microondas)

mid [mɪd] ADJECTIVE
◆ **in mid May** a mediados de mayo
◆ **He's in his mid twenties.** Tiene unos veinticinco años.

midday [mɪd'deɪ] NOUN
el mediodía ◇ *at midday* al mediodía
*Although **mediodía** ends in **-a**, it is actually a masculine noun.*

middle ['mɪdl] NOUN
see also **middle** ADJECTIVE
el medio ◇ *The car was in the middle of the road.* El carro estaba en medio de la carretera.
◆ **in the middle of May** a mediados de mayo
◆ **I woke up in the middle of the morning.** Me desperté a media mañana.
◆ **She was in the middle of her exams.** Estaba en plenos exámenes.

middle ['mɪdl] ADJECTIVE
see also **middle** NOUN
del medio MASC, FEM, PL ◇ *the middle seat* el asiento del medio

middle-aged ['mɪdl'eɪdʒd] ADJECTIVE
de mediana edad MASC, FEM, PL

Middle Ages ['mɪdl'eɪdʒɪz] PL NOUN
◆ **the Middle Ages** la Edad Media

middle class ['mɪdl'klæs] ADJECTIVE
de clase media MASC, FEM, PL

Middle East ['mɪdl'iːst] NOUN
◆ **the Middle East** el Oriente Medio

middle name ['mɪdl'neɪm] NOUN
el segundo nombre

midge [mɪdʒ] NOUN

el mosquito

midnight ['mɪdnaɪt] NOUN
la medianoche ◇ *at midnight* a medianoche

midwife ['mɪdwaɪf] NOUN (PL **midwives**)
la comadrona ◇ *She's a midwife.* Es comadrona.

might [maɪt] VERB
poder* ◇ *The teacher might come at any moment.* El profesor podría venir en cualquier momento.

***Puede que** has to be followed by a verb in the subjunctive.*

◇ *He might come later.* Puede que venga más tarde. ◇ *She might not have understood.* Puede que no haya entendido.

***A lo mejor** can also be used but it is a more colloquial alternative.*

◇ *We might go to Chile next year.* A lo mejor vamos a Chile el año que viene.

migraine ['maɪgreɪn] NOUN
la jaqueca ◇ *I have a migraine.* Tengo jaqueca.

mike [maɪk] NOUN
el micro

mild [maɪld] ADJECTIVE
suave ◇ *a mild flavor* un sabor suave ◇ *The winters are quite mild.* Los inviernos son bastante suaves. ◇ *mild soap* el jabón suave

mile [maɪl] NOUN
la milla

> *In Latin America distances are expressed in kilometers. A mile is about 1.6 kilometers.*

◇ *It's five miles from here.* Está a unas cinco millas de aquí. ◇ *at 50 miles per hour* a 50 millas por hora

◆ **We walked for miles!** ¡Caminamos kilómetros y kilómetros!

military ['mɪlɪtɛri] ADJECTIVE
militar

milk [mɪlk] NOUN
see also **milk** VERB
la leche

◆ **one percent milk** la leche entera
◆ **two percent milk** la leche descremada

to **milk** [mɪlk] VERB
see also **milk** NOUN
ordeñar

milk chocolate [mɪlk'tʃɑ:klɪt] NOUN
el chocolate con leche

milkman ['mɪlk,mæn] NOUN (PL **milkmen**)
el lechero

milk shake ['mɪlk,ʃeɪk] NOUN
la leche malteada

mill [mɪl] NOUN
el molino (*for grain*)

millennium [mə'lɛniəm] NOUN (PL **millenniums** *or* **millennia**)
el milenio

millimeter ['mɪlɪmi:tər] NOUN
el milímetro

million ['mɪljən] NOUN
el millón (PL los millones) ◇ *two million dollars* dos millones de dólares

millionaire [mɪljə'nɛər] NOUN
el millonario
la millonaria

to **mimic** ['mɪmɪk] VERB (**mimicked, mimicked**)
imitar

to **mind** [maɪnd] VERB
see also **mind** NOUN
importar (*matter*) ◇ *Do you mind if I open the window? – No, I don't mind.* ¿Le importa que abra la ventana? – No, no me importa.

◆ **I don't mind the noise.** No me molesta el ruido.
◆ **Never mind! (1)** (*don't worry*) ¡No te preocupes!
◆ **Never mind! (2)** (*it's not important*) ¡No importa!
◆ **mind your manners** no seas mal educado

mind [maɪnd] NOUN
see also **mind** VERB
la mente ◇ *What do you have in mind?* ¿Qué tienes en mente?

◆ **I haven't made up my mind yet.** No me he decidido todavía.
◆ **He's changed his mind.** Ha cambiado de idea.
◆ **Are you out of your mind?** ¿Estás loco?

mine [maɪn] PRONOUN
see also **mine** NOUN
1 el mío MASC (PL los míos) ◇ *Is this your coat? – No, mine is black.* ¿Es éste tu abrigo? – No, el mío es negro. ◇ *I've invited your parents and mine.* He invitado a tus padres y a los míos.
2 la mía FEM (PL las mías) ◇ *Is this your scarf? – No, mine is red.* ¿Es ésta tu bufanda? – No, la mía es roja. ◇ *We had dinner with her sisters and mine.* Cenamos con sus hermanas y las mías.
3 mío MASC (PL míos) ◇ *That car is mine.* Ese carro es mío.
4 mía FEM (PL mías) ◇ *Sorry, that beer is mine.* Disculpa, esa cerveza es mía.

◆ **Isabel is a friend of mine.** Isabel es amiga mía.

mine [maɪn] NOUN
see also **mine** PRONOUN
la mina ◇ *a coal mine* una mina de carbón ◇ *a land mine* una mina

miner ['maɪnər] NOUN
el minero
la minera
◇ *My father was a miner.* Mi padre era minero.

mineral water ['mɪnərəl,wɑ:tər] NOUN
el agua mineral FEM

*Although it's a feminine noun, remember that you use **el** and **un** with **agua mineral**.*

miniature ['mɪniətʃər] ADJECTIVE ☞

M

en miniatura
minibus ['mɪnibʌs] NOUN (PL **minibuses**)
el microbús (PL los microbuses)
el pesero Mexico
Minidisc ['mɪnidɪsk]® NOUN
el minidisco
minimum ['mɪnɪməm] NOUN
see also **minimum** ADJECTIVE
el mínimo
minimum ['mɪnɪməm] ADJECTIVE
see also **minimum** NOUN
mínimo ◇ *The firm offered a minimum wage of 200 cents an hour.* La empresa ofreció un salario mínimo de 200 centavos la hora.
miniskirt ['mɪni,skɜːrt] NOUN
la minifalda
minister ['mɪnɪstər] NOUN
el pastor
la pastora
(*of church*)
ministry ['mɪnɪstri] NOUN (PL **ministries**)
1 el sacerdocio (*religious*)
2 el ministerio
la secretaría Mexico
(*in politics*)
minor ['maɪnər] ADJECTIVE
secundario ◇ *a minor problem* un problema secundario
◆ **a minor operation** una operación de poca importancia
◆ **in D minor** en re menor
minority [maɪ'nɑːrɪti] NOUN (PL **minorities**)
la minoría
mint [mɪnt] NOUN
1 el caramelo de menta (*candy*)
2 la menta (*plant*) ◇ *mint jelly* salsa de menta
minus ['maɪnəs] PREPOSITION
menos ◇ *sixteen minus three* dieciséis menos tres ◇ *I got a B minus in French.* Me pusieron menos B en francés.
◆ **minus two degrees** dos grados bajo cero
minute ['mɪnɪt] NOUN
see also **minute** ADJECTIVE
el minuto ◇ *Wait a minute!* ¡Espera un minuto!
minute [maɪ'nuːt] ADJECTIVE
see also **minute** NOUN
minúsculo ◇ *Her apartment is minute.* Su apartamento es minúsculo.
miracle ['mɪrəkəl] NOUN
el milagro
mirror ['mɪrər] NOUN
1 el espejo ◇ *She looked at herself in the mirror.* Se miró en el espejo.
2 el retrovisor ◇ *She got in the car and adjusted the rearview mirror.* Entró en el carro y ajustó el retrovisor.
to **misbehave** [mɪsbɪ'heɪv] VERB
portarse mal
mischief ['mɪstʃɪf] NOUN
◆ **She's always up to mischief.** Siempre está haciendo travesuras.
◆ **full of mischief** travieso
mischievous ['mɪstʃɪvəs] ADJECTIVE
travieso
miser ['maɪzər] NOUN
el avaro
la avara
miserable ['mɪzərəbəl] ADJECTIVE
infeliz (PL infelices) ◇ *a miserable life* una vida infeliz
◆ **I'm feeling miserable.** Me siento deprimido.
◆ **miserable weather** un tiempo deprimente
misfortune [mɪs'fɔːrtʃən] NOUN
la desgracia
mishap ['mɪshæp] NOUN
el contratiempo ◇ *without mishap* sin contratiempos
to **misjudge** [mɪs'dʒʌdʒ] VERB
juzgar* mal ◇ *I may have misjudged him.* A lo mejor lo juzgué mal.
◆ **The driver misjudged the bend.** El conductor no calculó bien la curva.
to **mislay** [mɪs'leɪ] VERB (**mislaid, mislaid**)
◆ **I've mislaid my glasses.** No sé dónde puse las anteojos.
misleading [mɪs'liːdɪŋ] ADJECTIVE
engañoso
misprint ['mɪsprɪnt] NOUN
el error de imprenta
Miss [mɪs] NOUN
1 señorita FEM ◇ *Miss Peters wants to see you.* La señorita Peters quiere verte.
2 Srta. (*in address*)
to **miss** [mɪs] VERB
perder* ◇ *Hurry or you'll miss the bus.* Date prisa o perderás el autobús.
◆ **It's too good an opportunity to miss.** Es una oportunidad demasiado buena para dejarla pasar.
◆ **He missed the target.** No dio en el blanco.
◆ **I miss my family.** Echo de menos a mi familia.
◆ **You've missed a page.** Te saltaste una página.
missing ['mɪsɪŋ] ADJECTIVE
perdido ◇ *the missing link* el eslabón perdido
◆ **to be missing** faltar ◇ *Two members of the group are missing.* Faltan dos miembros del grupo.
◆ **a missing person** una persona desaparecida
missionary ['mɪʃənɛri] NOUN (PL **missionaries**)
el misionero
la misionera
mist [mɪst] NOUN
la neblina
mistake [mɪ'steɪk] NOUN
see also **mistake** VERB

el error ◇ *There must be some mistake.* Debe de haber algún error.
- **a spelling mistake** una falta de ortografía
- **to make a mistake (1)** (*in speaking*) cometer un error ◇ *He makes a lot of mistakes when he speaks English.* Comete muchos errores cuando habla inglés.
- **to make a mistake (2)** (*get mixed up*) equivocarse* ◇ *I'm sorry, I made a mistake.* Lo siento, me equivoqué.
- **by mistake** por error

to **mistake** [mɪ'steɪk] VERB (**mistook, mistaken**)
see also **mistake** NOUN
confundir ◇ *He mistook me for my sister.* Me confundió con mi hermana.

mistaken [mɪ'steɪkən] ADJECTIVE
- **to be mistaken** estar* equivocado ◇ *If you think I'm going to pay, you're mistaken.* Estás equivocado si piensas que voy a pagar.

mistletoe ['mɪsltou] NOUN
el muérdago

mistook [mɪ'stuk] VERB *see* **mistake**

mistress ['mɪstrɪs] NOUN (PL **mistresses**)
la amante ◇ *He has a mistress.* Tiene una amante.

to **mistrust** [mɪs'trʌst] VERB
desconfiar* de

misty ['mɪsti] ADJECTIVE
neblinoso ◇ *a misty morning* una mañana neblinosa

to **misunderstand** [mɪsʌndər'stænd] VERB (**misunderstood, misunderstood**)
entender* mal ◇ *Sorry, I misunderstood you.* Lo siento, te entendí mal.

misunderstanding [ˌmɪsʌndər'stændɪŋ] NOUN
el malentendido

misunderstood [mɪsʌndər'stud] VERB *see* **misunderstand**

mix [mɪks] NOUN (PL **mixes**)
see also **mix** VERB
la mezcla ◇ *The movie is a mix of science fiction and comedy.* La película es una mezcla de ciencia ficción y comedia.
- **a cake mix** un preparado para pastel

to **mix** [mɪks] VERB
see also **mix** NOUN
mezclar ◇ *Mix the flour with the sugar.* Mezcle la harina con el azúcar. ◇ *He's mixing business with pleasure.* Está mezclando los negocios con el placer.
- **I like mixing with all sorts of people.** Me gusta tratar con todo tipo de gente.
- **He doesn't mix much.** No se relaciona mucho.

to **mix up** [mɪks'ʌp] VERB
confundir ◇ *He mixed up their names.* Confundió sus nombres. ◇ *The travel agent mixed up the reservations.* La agencia de viajes confundió las reservas.
- **I'm getting mixed up.** Me estoy confundiendo.

mixed [mɪkst] ADJECTIVE
mixto ◇ *a mixed salad* una ensalada mixta
- **I have mixed feelings about it.** No sé qué pensar de ello.

mixer ['mɪksər] NOUN
la batidora (*for food*)

mixture ['mɪkstʃər] NOUN
la mezcla

mix-up ['mɪksʌp] NOUN
la confusión (PL las confusiones)

to **moan** [moun] VERB
quejarse ◇ *She's always moaning about something.* Siempre se está quejando de algo.

mobile home ['moubəl'houm] NOUN
el trailer

mobile phone ['moubəl'foun] NOUN
el teléfono celular

to **mock** [mɑːk] VERB
see also **mock** ADJECTIVE
ridiculizar*

mock [mɑːk] ADJECTIVE
see also **mock** VERB
- **a mock exam** un examen de práctica

model ['mɑːdl] NOUN
see also **model** ADJECTIVE
1. el modelo ◇ *His car is the latest model.* Su carro es el último modelo.
2. la maqueta ◇ *a model of the castle* una maqueta del castillo
3. el/la modelo ◇ *She's a famous model.* Es una modelo famosa.

model ['mɑːdl] ADJECTIVE
see also **model** NOUN
- **a model railway** una vía férrea en miniatura
- **a model plane** una maqueta de avión
- **He's a model pupil.** Es un alumno modelo.

modem ['moudəm] NOUN
el módem (PL los módems)

moderate ['mɑːdərɪt] ADJECTIVE
moderado ◇ *His views are quite moderate.* Tiene opiniones bastante moderadas.
- **I do a moderate amount of exercise.** Hago un poco de ejercicio.

modern ['mɑːdərn] ADJECTIVE
moderno

to **modernize** ['mɑːdərnaɪz] VERB
modernizar*

modest ['mɑːdɪst] ADJECTIVE
modesto

to **modify** ['mɑːdɪfaɪ] VERB (**modified, modified**)
modificar*

moist [mɔɪst] ADJECTIVE
húmedo ◇ *Sow the seeds in moist compost.* Plantar las semillas en abono húmedo.

moisture ['mɔɪstʃər] NOUN
la humedad

moisturizer ['mɔɪstʃəraɪzər] NOUN
la crema hidratante

moldy ['mouldi] ADJECTIVE

M

mohoso

mole [moul] NOUN
1 el lunar ◇ *I have a mole on my back.* Tengo un lunar en la espalda.
2 el topo (*animal*)

mom [mɑːm] NOUN
mamá FEM ◇ *I'll ask Mom.* Le preguntaré a mamá. ◇ *my mom* mi mamá

moment ['moumənt] NOUN
el momento ◇ *Just a moment!* ¡Un momento! ◇ *at the moment* en este momento ◇ *any moment now* de un momento a otro

mommy ['mɑːmi] NOUN (PL **mommies**)
la mamá ◇ *Mommy says I can go.* Mamá dice que puedo ir.

monarch ['mɑːnərk] NOUN
el/la monarca

monarchy ['mɑːnərki] NOUN (PL **monarchies**)
la monarquía

monastery ['mɑːnəstɛri] NOUN (PL **monasteries**)
el monasterio

Monday ['mʌndi] NOUN
el lunes (PL los lunes) ◇ *I saw her on Monday.* La vi el lunes. ◇ *every Monday* todos los lunes ◇ *last Monday* el lunes pasado ◇ *next Monday* el lunes que viene ◇ *on Mondays* los lunes

money ['mʌni] NOUN
el dinero ◇ *I need to change some money.* Tengo que cambiar dinero. ◇ *to make money* ganar dinero

mongrel ['mʌŋgrəl] NOUN
el perro mestizo
◆ **My dog's a mongrel.** Mi perro es mestizo.

monitor ['mɑːnɪtər] NOUN
el monitor (*on computer*)

monk [mʌŋk] NOUN
el monje

monkey ['mʌŋki] NOUN
el mono
la mona

monster ['mɑːnstər] NOUN
el monstruo

month [mʌnθ] NOUN
el mes ◇ *this month* este mes ◇ *next month* el mes que viene ◇ *last month* el mes pasado ◇ *at the end of the month* a fin de mes

monthly ['mʌnθli] ADJECTIVE
mensual

monument ['mɑːnjəmənt] NOUN
el monumento

mood [muːd] NOUN
el humor ◇ *to be in a good mood* estar* de buen humor ◇ *to be in a bad mood* estar* de mal humor

moody ['muːdi] ADJECTIVE
malhumorado (*in a bad mood*)
◆ **to be moody** tener* un humor cambiante (*temperamental*)

moon [muːn] NOUN
la luna ◇ *There's a full moon tonight.* Esta noche hay luna llena.

moor [muər] NOUN
see also **moor** VERB
el páramo

to **moor** [muər] VERB
see also **moor** NOUN
amarrar

mop [mɑːp] NOUN
el trapeador

moped ['moupɛd] NOUN
el ciclomotor

moral ['mɔːrəl] NOUN
la moraleja ◇ *the moral of the story is...* la moraleja de la historia es...
◆ **morals** la moral

morale [mə'ræl] NOUN
la moral ◇ *Morale was at an all-time low.* La moral estaba más baja que nunca.

more [mɔːr] ADJECTIVE, PRONOUN, ADVERB
más ◇ *It costs a lot more.* Cuesta mucho más. ◇ *There isn't any more.* Ya no hay más. ◇ *A bit more?* ¿Un poco más? ◇ *Is there any more?* ¿Hay más? ◇ *It'll take a few more days.* Llevará unos cuantos días más.
◆ **more than** más que
Use ***más que*** *when comparing two things or people and* ***más de*** *when talking about quantities.*
◇ *He's more intelligent than me.* Es más inteligente que yo. ◇ *I spent more than $10.* Yo gasté más de 10 dólares. ◇ *more than 20 people* más de 20 personas
◆ **more or less** más o menos
◆ **more than ever** más que nunca
◆ **more and more** cada vez más

moreover [mɔːr'ouvər] ADVERB
además

morning ['mɔːrnɪŋ] NOUN
la mañana ◇ *in the morning* por la mañana ◇ *at seven o'clock in the morning* a las siete de la mañana ◇ *on Saturday morning* el sábado por la mañana ◇ *tomorrow morning* mañana por la mañana
◆ **the morning papers** los periódicos de la mañana

Morocco [mə'rɑːkou] NOUN
Marruecos MASC

mortgage ['mɔːrgɪdʒ] NOUN
la hipoteca

Moscow ['mɑːskau] NOUN
Moscú MASC

Moslem ['mɑːzləm] NOUN
el musulmán (PL los musulmanes)
la musulmana
◇ *He's a Moslem.* Es musulmán.

mosque [mɑːsk] NOUN

la mezquita

mosquito [məˈski:tou] NOUN (PL **mosquitoes**)
el mosquito
- **a mosquito bite** una picadura de mosquito

most [moust] ADJECTIVE, PRONOUN, ADVERB
más ◇ *the thing she feared most* lo que más temía ◇ *He's the one who talks the most.* Es el que más habla. ◇ *the most expensive restaurant* el restaurante más caro ◇ *He won the most votes.* Fue el que sacó más votos.
- **most of** la mayor parte de ◇ *most of the time* la mayor parte del tiempo ◇ *I did most of the work alone.* Hice la mayor parte del trabajo solo.
- **most of them** la mayoría ◇ *Most of them have cars.* La mayoría tienen carros. ◇ *Most people go out on Friday nights.* La mayoría de la gente sale los viernes por la noche.
- **at the most** como mucho ◇ *two hours at the most* dos horas como mucho
- **to make the most of something** aprovechar algo al máximo ◇ *He made the most of his vacation.* Aprovechó sus vacaciones al máximo.

mostly [ˈmoustli] ADVERB
- **The teachers are mostly quite nice.** La mayoría de los profesores son bastante simpáticos.

motel [mouˈtɛl] NOUN
el motel

moth [mɑ:θ] NOUN
1 la mariposa nocturna
2 la polilla (*clothes moth*)

mother [ˈmʌðər] NOUN
la madre
- **my mother and father** mis padres
- **mother tongue** la lengua materna

mother-in-law [ˈmʌðərɪn,lɑ:] NOUN (PL **mothers-in-law**)
la suegra

Mother's Day [ˈmʌðərz,deɪ] NOUN
el Día de la Madre

motionless [ˈmouʃənlɪs] ADJECTIVE
inmóvil

motivated [ˈmoutɪveɪtɪd] ADJECTIVE
- **He is highly motivated.** Está muy motivado.

motivation [moutɪˈveɪʃən] NOUN
la motivación (PL las motivaciones)

motive [ˈmoutɪv] NOUN
1 el motivo ◇ *the motive for the killing* el motivo del homicidio
2 la intención (PL las intenciones) ◇ *for the best of motives* con la mejor de las intenciones

motor [ˈmoutər] NOUN
el motor

motorbike [ˈmoutər,baɪk] NOUN
la moto

Although ***moto*** *ends in* ***-o****, it is actually a feminine noun.*

motorboat [ˈmoutər,bout] NOUN
la lancha motora

motorcycle [ˈmoutər,saɪkəl] NOUN
la motocicleta

motorcyclist [ˈmoutər,saɪklɪst] NOUN
el/la motociclista

motorist [ˈmoutərɪst] NOUN
el conductor
la conductora

motor racing [ˈmoutər,reɪsɪŋ] NOUN
las carreras de carros

mountain [ˈmauntən] NOUN
la montaña ◇ *in the mountains* en la montaña
- **a mountain bike** una bicicleta de montaña
- **the Rocky Mountains** las Montañas Rocosas

mountaineer [mauntəˈnɪər] NOUN
el/la montañista

mountaineering [mauntəˈnɪrɪŋ] NOUN
el montañismo ◇ *I go mountaineering.* Hago montañismo.

mountainous [ˈmauntənəs] ADJECTIVE
montañoso

mouse [maus] NOUN (PL **mice**)
el ratón (PL los ratones) (*also for computer*)

mouse pad [ˈmaus,pæd] NOUN
la alfombrilla del ratón

mousse [mu:s] NOUN
1 la mousse ◇ *chocolate mousse* la mousse de chocolate
2 la espuma (*for hair*)

mouth [mauθ] NOUN
la boca

mouthful [ˈmauθful] NOUN
1 el bocado (*of food*)
2 el trago (*of drink*)

mouth organ [ˈmauθ,ɔ:rgən] NOUN
la armónica

mouthwash [ˈmauθ,wɑ:ʃ] NOUN
el enjuague bucal

move [mu:v] NOUN
see also **move** VERB
1 el paso ◇ *That was a good move!* ¡Ese fue un paso bien dado!
- **It's your move.** Te toca jugar.
2 la mudanza ◇ *our move from Omaha to Minneapolis* nuestra mudanza de Omaha a Minneapolis
- **Get a move on!** ¡Date prisa!

to **move** [mu:v] VERB
see also **move** NOUN
1 moverse* ◇ *Don't move!* ¡No te muevas!
2 mover* ◇ *He can't move his arm.* No puede mover el brazo.
- **Could you move your stuff please?** ¿Podrías quitar tus cosas de aquí, por favor?
3 avanzar* ◇ *The car was moving very slowly.* El carro avanzaba muy lentamente.
4 conmover* ◇ *I was very moved by the movie.* La película me conmovió mucho.

☞

◆ **to move house** mudarse de casa ◇ *We're moving in July.* Nos mudamos en julio.

to **move forward** [muːvˈfɔːrwərd] VERB
avanzar*

to **move in** [muːvˈɪn] VERB
◆ **When are the new tenants moving in?** ¿Cuándo vienen los nuevos inquilinos?

to **move over** [muːvˈouvər] VERB
correrse ◇ *Could you move over a bit, please?* ¿Te podrías correr un poco, por favor?

movement [ˈmuːvmənt] NOUN
el movimiento

movie [ˈmuːvi] NOUN
la película
◆ **the movies** el cine
◆ **the movie industry** la industria cinematográfica

moviegoer [ˈmuːvɪˌgouər] NOUN
el aficionado al cine
la aficionada al cine

movie star [ˈmuːviˌstɑːr] NOUN
la estrella de cine

movie theater [ˈmuːvɪˌθɪətər] NOUN
el cine

moving [ˈmuːvɪŋ] ADJECTIVE
1 en movimiento ◇ *a moving bus* un autobús en movimiento
2 conmovedor (FEM conmovedora) ◇ *a moving story* una historia conmovedora
◆ **a moving van** un camión de mudanzas

to **mow** [mou] VERB (**mowed, mowed** *or* **mown**)
cortar ◇ *I sometimes mow the lawn.* A veces corto el pasto.

mower [ˈmouər] NOUN
la máquina de cortar el pasto

mown [moun] VERB *see* **mow**

MP3 NOUN
el MP3
◆ **an MP3 player** un reproductor de MP3

Mr. [ˈmɪstər] ABBREVIATION
1 señor MASC ◇ *Mr. Jones wants to see you.* El señor Jones quiere verte.
2 Sr. (*in address*)

Mrs. [ˈmɪsɪz] ABBREVIATION
1 señora FEM ◇ *Mrs. Philips wants to see you.* La señora Philips quiere verte.
2 Sra. (*in address*)

Ms. [mɪz] ABBREVIATION
1 señora FEM ◇ *Ms. Brown wants to see you.* La señora Brown quiere verte.
2 Sra. (*in address*)

> ℹ *There isn't a direct equivalent of* **Ms.** *in Spanish. If you are writing to a woman and don't know whether she is married, use* **Señora**.

much [mʌtʃ] ADJECTIVE, PRONOUN, ADVERB
mucho ◇ *I feel much better now.* Ahora me siento mucho mejor. ◇ *I don't have much money.* No tengo mucho dinero. ◇ *Do you have a lot of luggage? – No, not much.* ¿Tienes mucho equipaje? – No, no mucho.
◆ **very much** mucho ◇ *I enjoyed myself very much.* Me divertí mucho.
◆ **Thank you very much.** Muchas gracias.
◆ **How much?** ¿cuánto? ◇ *How much time do you have?* ¿Cuánto tiempo tienes? ◇ *How much is it?* ¿Cuánto es?
◆ **too much** demasiado ◇ *That's too much!* ¡Eso es demasiado! ◇ *They give us too much homework.* Nos mandan demasiadas tareas.
◆ **so much** tanto ◇ *I didn't think it would cost so much.* No pensé que costaría tanto. ◇ *I've never seen so much rain.* Nunca había visto tanta lluvia.
◆ **What's on TV? – Not much.** ¿Qué dan en la tele? – Nada especial.

mud [mʌd] NOUN
el barro

muddle [ˈmʌdl] NOUN
◆ **to be in a muddle** estar* todo revuelto ◇ *The photos are in a muddle.* Las fotos están todas revueltas.

to **muddle up** [ˌmʌdlˈʌp] VERB
confundir ◇ *He gets muddled up between my sister and me.* Me confunde con mi hermana.
◆ **to get muddled up** hacerse* un lío (*informal*) ◇ *I'm getting muddled up.* Me estoy haciendo un lío.

muddy [ˈmʌdi] ADJECTIVE
lleno de barro

muesli [ˈmjuːzli] NOUN
el muesli

muffin [ˈmʌfɪn] NOUN
especie de pan dulce

muffler [ˈmʌflər] NOUN
1 el silenciador
el mofe [*Mexico*]
(*on car exhaust*)
2 la bufanda (*scarf*)

mug [mʌg] NOUN
[*see also* **mug** VERB]
la taza alta ◇ *Do you want a cup or a mug?* ¿Quieres una taza normal o una taza alta?
◆ **a beer mug** una jarra de cerveza, [*Mexico*:] un tarro de cerveza

to **mug** [mʌg] VERB
[*see also* **mug** NOUN]
atracar* ◇ *He was mugged in the city center.* Lo atracaron en el centro de la ciudad.

mugger [ˈmʌgər] NOUN
el atracador
la atracadora

mugging [ˈmʌgɪŋ] NOUN
el atraco

muggy [ˈmʌgi] ADJECTIVE

◆ **It's muggy today.** Hoy hace bochorno.

multi-level parking garage ['mʌltilevəl'pɑːrkɪŋgəˌrɑːʒ] NOUN
el estacionamiento de varios niveles

multiple choice test ['mʌltɪpəl'tʃɔɪsˌtest] NOUN
el examen tipo test

multiple sclerosis ['mʌltɪpəlsklə'rousɪs] NOUN
la esclerosis múltiple ◇ *She has multiple sclerosis.* Tiene esclerosis múltiple.

multiplication [mʌltɪplɪ'keɪʃən] NOUN
la multiplicación (PL las multiplicaciones)

to **multiply** ['mʌltɪplaɪ] VERB (**multiplied, multiplied**)
multiplicar* ◇ *to multiply six by three* multiplicar seis por tres

mummy ['mʌmi] NOUN (PL **mummies**)
la momia (*Egyptian*)

mumps [mʌmps] NOUN
las paperas ◇ *My brother has the mumps.* Mi hermano tiene paperas.

murder ['mɜːrdər] NOUN
see also **murder** VERB
el asesinato

to **murder** ['mɜːrdər] VERB
see also **murder** NOUN
asesinar ◇ *He was murdered.* Fue asesinado.

murderer ['mɜːrdərər] NOUN
el asesino
la asesina

muscle ['mʌsəl] NOUN
el músculo

muscular ['mʌskjələr] ADJECTIVE
musculoso

museum [mjuː'ziːəm] NOUN
el museo

mushroom ['mʌʃruːm] NOUN
el champiñón (PL los champiñones)

music ['mjuːzɪk] NOUN
la música

musical ['mjuːzɪkəl] ADJECTIVE
see also **musical** NOUN
musical

◆ **I'm not musical.** No tengo aptitudes para la música.

musical ['mjuːzɪkəl] NOUN
see also **musical** ADJECTIVE
el musical

musician [mjuː'zɪʃən] NOUN
el músico
la música
◇ *He's a musician.* Es músico.

Muslim ['mʌzləm] NOUN
el musulmán (PL los musulmanes)
la musulmana
◇ *She's a Muslim.* Es musulmana.

mussel ['mʌsəl] NOUN
el mejillón (PL los mejillones)

must [mʌst] VERB
[1] tener* que (*it's necessary*) ◇ *I must do it.* Tengo que hacerlo. ◇ *I really must go now.* De verdad que me tengo que ir ya. ◇ *You must come again next year.* Tienes que volver el año que viene.

◆ **You mustn't forget to send her a card.** No se te vaya a olvidar de mandarle una tarjeta.
[2] deber* de (*I suppose*) ◇ *There must be some problem.* Debe de haber algún problema. ◇ *You must be tired.* Debes de estar cansada.

mustache ['mʌstæʃ] NOUN
el bigote ◇ *He has a mustache.* Tiene bigote.

mustard ['mʌstərd] NOUN
la mostaza

mustn't ['mʌsənt] VERB = **must not**

to **mutter** ['mʌtər] VERB
mascullar

mutton ['mʌtn] NOUN
la carne de cordero

mutual ['mjuːtʃuəl] ADJECTIVE
mutuo ◇ *The feeling was mutual.* El sentimiento era mutuo.

◆ **a mutual friend** un amigo común

my [maɪ] ADJECTIVE
mi (PL mis) ◇ *my father* mi padre ◇ *my house* mi casa ◇ *my two best friends* mis dos mejores amigos ◇ *my sisters* mis hermanas

***My** is usually translated by the definite article **el/los** or **la/las** when it's clear from the sentence who the possessor is or when referring to clothing or parts of the body.*

◇ *They stole my car.* Me robaron el carro. ◇ *I took off my coat.* Me saqué el abrigo. ◇ *I'm washing my hair.* Me estoy lavando el pelo.

myself [maɪ'sɛlf] PRONOUN
[1] me (*reflexive*) ◇ *I've hurt myself.* Me hice daño.
[2] mí mismo (FEM mí misma) (*after preposition*) ◇ *I talked mainly about myself.* Hablé principalmente de mí mismo.

◆ **a beginner like myself** un principiante como yo
[3] yo mismo (FEM yo misma) (*for emphasis*) ◇ *I made it myself.* Lo hice yo misma.

◆ **by myself** solo (FEM sola) ◇ *I don't like traveling by myself.* No me gusta viajar solo.

mysterious [mɪ'stɪriəs] ADJECTIVE
misterioso

mystery ['mɪstəri] NOUN (PL **mysteries**)
el misterio

◆ **a murder mystery** una novela policíaca

myth [mɪθ] NOUN
el mito ◇ *a Greek myth* un mito griego ◇ *That's a myth.* Eso es un mito. (*untrue story*)

mythology [mɪ'θɑːlədʒi] NOUN
la mitología

N

to **nag** [næg] VERB
dar* la lata ◇ *She's always nagging me.* Siempre me está dando la lata.

nail [neɪl] NOUN
1 la uña ◇ *She bites her nails.* Se come las unas.
2 el clavo (*made of metal*)

nailbrush ['neɪl,brʌʃ] NOUN (PL **nailbrushes**)
el cepillo de uñas

nailfile ['neɪl,faɪl] NOUN
la lima para las uñas

nail polish ['neɪl,pɑːlɪʃ] NOUN (PL **nail polishes**)
el esmalte de uñas
◆ **nail polish remover** el quitaesmaltes

nail scissors ['neɪl,sɪzərz] PL NOUN
las tijeras para las uñas

naked ['neɪkɪd] ADJECTIVE
desnudo

name [neɪm] NOUN
el nombre
◆ **What's your name?** ¿Cómo te llamas?

nanny ['næni] NOUN (PL **nannies**)
la niñera (*nursemaid*)

nap [næp] NOUN
la siesta ◇ *She likes to have a nap in the afternoon.* Le gusta echarse una siesta por la tarde.

napkin ['næpkɪn] NOUN
la servilleta

narrow ['nɛrou] ADJECTIVE
estrecho

narrow-minded ['nɛrou'maɪndɪd] ADJECTIVE
estrecho de miras

nasty ['næsti] ADJECTIVE
1 malo
*Use **mal** before a masculine singular noun.*
◇ *Don't be nasty.* No seas malo. ◇ *What nasty weather!* ¡Qué tiempo más malo!
2 desagradable ◇ *a nasty smell* un olor desagradable
◆ **He gave me a nasty look.** Me miró de mala manera.

nation ['neɪʃən] NOUN
la nación (PL las naciones)

national ['næʃənl] ADJECTIVE
nacional

national anthem ['næʃənl'ænθəm] NOUN
el himno nacional

national holiday ['næʃənl'hɑːlɪdeɪ] NOUN
el día festivo

nationalism ['næʃnəlɪzəm] NOUN
el nacionalismo

nationalist ['næʃnəlɪst] NOUN
el/la nacionalista

nationality [næʃə'nælɪti] NOUN (PL **nationalities**)
la nacionalidad

national park ['næʃənl'pɑːrk] NOUN
el parque nacional

native ['neɪtɪv] ADJECTIVE
natal ◇ *my native country* mi país natal
◆ **his native language** su lengua materna

Native American ['neɪtɪvə'mɛrɪkən] NOUN
el indio americano
la india americana

natural ['nætʃərəl] ADJECTIVE
natural ◇ *Helping him seemed the natural thing to do.* Ayudarlo parecía lo más natural.

naturalist ['nætʃərəlɪst] NOUN
el/la naturalista

naturally ['nætʃərəli] ADVERB
naturalmente ◇ *Naturally, we were very disappointed.* Naturalmente, estábamos muy decepcionados.

nature ['neɪtʃər] NOUN
la naturaleza ◇ *the wonders of nature* las maravillas de la naturaleza
◆ **It's not in his nature to behave like that.** Comportarse así no es propio de él.

naughty ['nɑːti] ADJECTIVE
travieso ◇ *Naughty girl!* ¡Qué traviesa!

navy ['neɪvi] NOUN (PL **navies**)
see also **navy** ADJECTIVE
la armada ◇ *He's in the navy.* Está en la armada.

navy ['neɪvi] ADJECTIVE
see also **navy** NOUN
azul marino MASC, FEM, PL

navy blue ['neɪvi'bluː] ADJECTIVE
azul marino MASC, FEM, PL ◇ *a navy blue skirt* una falda azul marino

near [nɪər] ADJECTIVE
see also **near** PREPOSITION, ADVERB
1 cerca ◇ *It's fairly near.* Está bastante cerca. ◇ *My house is near enough to walk.* Mi casa está muy cerca, se puede ir andando.
2 cercano ◇ *Where's the nearest service station?* ¿Dónde está la gasolinera más cercana?
◆ **in the near future** en un futuro cercano

near [nɪər] PREPOSITION, ADVERB
see also **near** ADJECTIVE
1 cerca ◇ *Is there a bank near here?* ¿Hay algún banco por aquí cerca?
2 cerca de ◇ *I live near Liverpool.* Vivo cerca de Liverpool.
◆ **near to** cerca de ◇ *It's very near to the school.* Está muy cerca del colegio.

nearby [nɪr'baɪ] ADJECTIVE
see also **nearby** ADVERB
cercano ◇ *a nearby village* un pueblo cercano

nearby [nɪr'baɪ] ADVERB
see also **nearby** ADJECTIVE
cerca ◇ *There's a supermarket nearby.* Hay un supermercado cerca.

nearly ['nɪrli] ADVERB
casi ◇ *Dinner's nearly ready.* La cena está casi lista. ◇ *I'm nearly fifteen.* Tengo casi quince años.
◆ **I nearly missed the train.** Por poco pierdo el tren.

nearsighted ['nɪr'saɪtɪd] ADJECTIVE
miope

neat [ni:t] ADJECTIVE
ordenado ◇ *My roommate is not very neat.* Mi compañero de cuarto no es muy ordenado.
◆ **He always looks very neat.** Siempre está muy pulcro.

neatly ['ni:tlɪi] ADVERB
◆ **neatly folded** cuidadosamente doblado
◆ **neatly dressed** bien vestido

necessarily [nɛsɪ'sɛrɪli] ADVERB
◆ **not necessarily** no necesariamente

necessary ['nɛsɪsɛri] ADJECTIVE
necesario

necessity [nɪ'sɛsɪti] NOUN (PL **necessities**)
la necesidad ◇ *A car is a necessity, not a luxury.* Un carro es una necesidad, no un lujo.

neck [nɛk] NOUN
el cuello ◇ *a V-neck sweater* un suéter de cuello en pico
◆ **She had a stiff neck.** Tenía tortícolis.
◆ **the back of your neck** la nuca

necklace ['nɛklɪs] NOUN
el collar

necktie ['nɛktaɪ] NOUN
la corbata

to **need** [ni:d] VERB
see also **need** NOUN
necesitar ◇ *I need a bigger size.* Necesito una talla más grande. ◇ *I need to change some money.* Necesito cambiar dinero.
◆ **You don't need to go.** No tienes por qué ir.

need [ni:d] NOUN
see also **need** VERB
◆ **There's no need to make reservations.** No hace falta hacer reservación.
hace falta que *has to be followed by a verb in the subjunctive.*
◇ *There's no need for you to do that.* No hace falta que hagas eso.

needle ['ni:dl] NOUN
la aguja

needlework ['ni:dl,wɜ:rk] NOUN
la costura

negative ['nɛgətɪv] NOUN
see also **negative** ADJECTIVE
el negativo (*photo*)

negative ['nɛgətɪv] ADJECTIVE
see also **negative** NOUN
negativo ◇ *He has a very negative attitude.* Tiene una actitud muy negativa.

neglected [nɪ'glɛktɪd] ADJECTIVE
abandonado ◇ *The garden is neglected.* El jardín está abandonado.

to **negotiate** [nɪ'goʊʃieɪt] VERB
negociar

negotiations [nɪgoʊʃi'eɪʃənz] PL NOUN
las negociaciones

neighbor ['neɪbər] NOUN
el vecino
la vecina

neighborhood ['neɪbərhud] NOUN
el barrio

neither ['ni:ðər] ADJECTIVE, CONJUNCTION, PRONOUN
1 ninguno de los dos (FEM ninguna de las dos) ◇ *Carrots or potatoes? – Neither, thanks.* ¿Zanahorias o papas? – Ninguna de las dos, gracias. ◇ *Neither of them is coming.* No viene ninguno de los dos. ◇ *Neither woman looked happy.* Ninguna de las dos parecía contenta.
2 tampoco ◇ *I don't like him. – Neither do I!* No me cae bien. – ¡A mí tampoco! ◇ *I've never been to Spain. – Neither have we.* No he estado nunca en España. – Nosotros tampoco.
◆ **neither...nor...** ni...ni... ◇ *Neither Sarah nor Tamsin is coming to the party.* Ni Sarah ni Tamsin vienen a la fiesta.

neon ['ni:ɑ:n] NOUN
el neón ◇ *a neon light* una lámpara de neón

nephew ['nɛfju:] NOUN
el sobrino

nerve [nɜ:rv] NOUN
el nervio ◇ *That noise really gets on my nerves.* Ese ruido me pone los nervios de punta.
◆ **He has some nerve!** ¡Qué descaro tiene!
◆ **I wouldn't have the nerve to do that!** ¡Yo no me atrevería a hacer eso!

nerve-wracking ['nɜ:rv,rækɪŋ] ADJECTIVE
angustioso

nervous ['nɜ:rvəs] ADJECTIVE
nervioso ◇ *I bite my nails when I'm nervous.* Cuando estoy nervioso me como las uñas. ◇ *I'm a bit nervous about the exams.* Estoy un poco nervioso por los exámenes.

nest [nɛst] NOUN
el nido

net [nɛt] NOUN
la red ◇ *a fishing net* una red de pesca

Net [nɛt] NOUN
la Red
◆ **to surf the Net** navegar* por la Red

Netherlands ['nɛðərləndz] PL NOUN
◆ **the Netherlands** los Países Bajos

network ['nɛtwɜ:rk] NOUN
la red

neurotic [nu'rɑ:tɪk] ADJECTIVE
neurótico

never ['nɛvər] ADVERB
nunca ◇ *Have you ever been to Argentina? – No, never.* ¿Has estado alguna vez en Argentina? – No, nunca. ◇ *Never leave*

N

valuables in your car. No dejen nunca objetos de valor en el carro.
*When **nunca** comes before the verb in Spanish it is not necessary to use **no** as well.*
◇ *I never believed him.* Yo nunca le creí.
- **Never again!** ¡Nunca más!
- **Never, ever do that again!** ¡No vuelvas a hacer eso nunca jamás!
- **Never mind.** No importa.

new [nuː] ADJECTIVE
nuevo ◇ *her new boyfriend* su nuevo novio

newborn [ˈnuːˌbɔːrn] ADJECTIVE
- **a newborn baby** un bebé recién nacido

newcomer [ˈnuːˌkʌmər] NOUN
- **They were newcomers to the area.** Eran nuevos en la zona.

news [nuːz] NOUN
1 las noticias ◇ *good news* buenas noticias ◇ *I watch the news every evening.* Veo las noticias todas las noches.
- **It was nice to have your news.** Me dio alegría saber de ti.

2 la noticia ◇ *That's wonderful news!* ¡Qué buena noticia!
- **an interesting piece of news** una noticia interesante

newscaster [ˈnuːzˌkæstər] NOUN
1 el presentador
la presentadora
(*on television*)
2 el locutor
la locutora
(*on radio*)

newsdealer [ˈnuːzˌdiːlər] NOUN
el vendedor de periódicos
la vendedora de periódicos

newspaper [ˈnuːzˌpeɪpər] NOUN
el periódico

New Year [ˈnuːˈjɪər] NOUN
el Año Nuevo ◇ *to celebrate New Year* celebrar el Año Nuevo
- **Happy New Year!** ¡Feliz Año Nuevo!
- **New Year's Day** el día de Año Nuevo
- **New Year's Eve** la noche de Fin de Año
- **a New Year's Eve party** una fiesta de Fin de Año

New Zealand [nuːˈziːlənd] NOUN
Nueva Zelandia FEM

New Zealander [nuːˈziːləndər] NOUN
el neozelandés (PL los neozelandeses)
la neozelandesa

next [nɛkst] ADJECTIVE, ADVERB, PREPOSITION
1 próximo ◇ *next Saturday* el próximo sábado ◇ *the next time I see you* la próxima vez que te vea
2 siguiente ◇ *Next please!* ¡El siguiente, por favor! ◇ *The next day we visited León.* Al día siguiente visitamos León.
3 luego ◇ *What did you do next?* ¿Qué hiciste luego?
- **next to** al lado de ◇ *next to the bank* al lado del banco
- **next door** al lado ◇ *They live next door.* Viven al lado.
- **the next-door neighbors** los vecinos de al lado
- **the next room** la habitación de al lado

nice [naɪs] ADJECTIVE
1 simpático (*friendly*) ◇ *Your parents are very nice.* Tus padres son muy simpáticos.
2 amable (*kind*) ◇ *She was always very nice to me.* Siempre fue muy amable conmigo. ◇ *It was very nice of you to remember my birthday.* Fue muy amable de tu parte que te acordaras de mi cumpleaños.
3 bonito (*pretty*) ◇ *That's a nice dress!* ¡Qué vestido más bonito! ◇ *Acapulco is a nice town.* Acapulco es una ciudad bonita.
4 precioso (*beautiful*) ◇ *They have a very nice house.* Tienen una casa preciosa.
5 bueno (*good*)
*Use **buen** before a masculine singular noun.*
◇ *nice weather* buen tiempo ◇ *It's a nice day.* Hace buen día. ◇ *a nice cup of coffee* una buena taza de café
- **What a nice surprise!** ¡Qué sorpresa tan agradable!
- **Have a nice time!** ¡Que te diviertas!

nickname [ˈnɪkˌneɪm] NOUN
el apodo

niece [niːs] NOUN
la sobrina

night [naɪt] NOUN
la noche ◇ *I want a single room for two nights.* Quiero una habitación individual por dos noches.
- **at night** por la noche
- **Good night!** ¡Buenas noches!
- **last night** anoche ◇ *We went to a party last night.* Anoche fuimos a una fiesta.

nightclub [ˈnaɪtˌklʌb] NOUN
el club nocturno (PL los clubes or clubs nocturnos)

nightgown [ˈnaɪtˌgaun] NOUN
el camisón (PL los camisones)

nightie [ˈnaɪti] NOUN
el camisón (PL los camisones)

nightlife [ˈnaɪtˌlaɪf] NOUN
la vida nocturna ◇ *There's plenty of nightlife in Acapulco.* Hay mucha vida nocturna en Acapulco.

nightmare [ˈnaɪtmɛr] NOUN
la pesadilla ◇ *to have nightmares* tener* pesadillas ◇ *The whole trip was a nightmare.* El viaje entero fue una pesadilla.

night shift [ˈnaɪtˌʃɪft] NOUN
el turno de noche

nil [nɪl] NOUN
el cero

nine [naɪn] NUMERAL

* Verbs marked with this symbol are irregular. See pages 346–348 for further details.

nueve ◇ *She's nine.* Tiene nueve años.

nineteen [naɪn'tiːn] NUMERAL
diecinueve ◇ *She's nineteen.* Tiene diecinueve años.

nineteenth [naɪn'tiːnθ] ADJECTIVE
decimonoveno
- **the nineteenth floor** el piso diecinueve
- **March nineteenth** el diecinueve de marzo

ninety ['naɪnti] NUMERAL
noventa ◇ *He's ninety.* Tiene noventa años.

ninth [naɪnθ] ADJECTIVE
noveno ◇ *on the ninth floor* en el noveno piso
- **August ninth** el noveno de agosto

no [nou] ADVERB, ADJECTIVE
no ◇ *Are you coming? – No.* ¿Vienes? – No. ◇ *Would you like some more? – No thank you.* ¿Quieres un poco más? – No, gracias. ◇ *There's no hot water.* No hay agua caliente.
- **I have no idea.** No tengo ni idea.
- **I have no questions.** No tengo ninguna pregunta.
- **No way!** ¡Ni hablar!
- **"no smoking"** "prohibido fumar"

nobody ['noubaːdi] PRONOUN
nadie ◇ *Who's going with you? – Nobody.* ¿Quién va contigo? – Nadie. ◇ *There was nobody in the office.* No había nadie en la oficina.
- **I have nobody to play with.** No tengo a nadie con quien jugar.

*When **nobody** goes before a verb in English it can be translated by either **nadie...** or **no...nadie**.*

◇ *Nobody likes him.* No le cae bien a nadie. ◇ *Nobody saw me.* Nadie me vio.

to **nod** [naːd] VERB
[1] asentir* con la cabeza (*in agreement*)
[2] saludar con la cabeza (*as greeting*)

noise [nɔɪz] NOUN
el ruido
- **to make a noise** hacer* ruido

noisy ['nɔɪzi] ADJECTIVE
ruidoso ◇ *the noisiest city in the world* la ciudad más ruidosa del mundo
- **It's very noisy here.** Hay mucho ruido aquí.

to **nominate** ['naːmɪneɪt] VERB
nombrar ◇ *She was nominated for the post.* La nombraron para el cargo.
- **He was nominated for an Oscar.** Lo nominaron para un Oscar.

none [nʌn] PRONOUN

*When **none** refers to something you can count, such as sisters or friends, Spanish uses **ninguno** with a singular verb. When it refers to something you cannot count, such as wine, Spanish uses **nada**.*

[1] ninguno (FEM ninguna) ◇ *How many sisters do you have? – None.* ¿Cuántas hermanas tienes? – Ninguna. ◇ *None of my friends wanted to come.* Ninguno de mis amigos quiso venir. ◇ *There are none left.* No queda ninguno.
[2] nada ◇ *There's none left.* No queda nada.

nonsense ['naːnsɛns] NOUN
las tonterías PL ◇ *She talks a lot of nonsense.* Dice muchas tonterías. ◇ *Nonsense!* ¡Tonterías!

nonsmoker ['naːn'smoukər] NOUN
el no fumador
la no fumadora
- **He's a nonsmoker.** No fuma.

nonsmoking ['naːn'smoukɪŋ] ADJECTIVE
- **a nonsmoking area** un área reservada para no fumadores

*Although it's a feminine noun, remember that you use **el** and **un** with **área**.*

- **a nonsmoking car** un vagón para no fumadores

nonstop ['naːn'staːp] ADJECTIVE, ADVERB
[1] directo ◇ *a nonstop flight* un vuelo directo
- **We flew nonstop.** Tomamos un vuelo directo.

[2] sin parar ◇ *He talks nonstop.* Habla sin parar.

noodles ['nuːdlz] PL NOUN
los fideos

noon [nuːn] NOUN
las doce del mediodía
- **at noon** a las doce del mediodía

no one ['nouwʌn] PRONOUN
nadie ◇ *Who's going with you? – No one.* ¿Quién va contigo? – Nadie. ◇ *There was no one in the office.* No había nadie en la oficina.
- **I have no one to play with.** No tengo a nadie con quien jugar.

*When **no one** goes before a verb in English it can be translated by either **nadie...** or **no...nadie**.*

◇ *No one likes him.* No le cae bien a nadie. ◇ *No one saw me.* Nadie me vio.

nor [nɔːr] CONJUNCTION
tampoco ◇ *I didn't like the movie. – Nor did I.* No me gustó la película. – A mí tampoco. ◇ *We haven't seen him. – Nor have we.* No lo hemos visto. – Nosotros tampoco.
- **neither...nor** ni...ni ◇ *neither the movie theater nor the swimming pool* ni el cine ni la piscina

normal ['nɔːrməl] ADJECTIVE
normal

normally ['nɔːrməli] ADVERB
[1] normalmente (*usually*) ◇ *I normally arrive at nine o'clock.* Normalmente llego a las nueve.
[2] con normalidad (*as normal*) ◇ *In spite of the strike, airports are working normally.* A pesar de la huelga, los aeropuertos funcionan con normalidad.

north [nɔːrθ] NOUN
see also **north** ADJECTIVE, ADVERB

N ☞

el norte ◇ *in the north of Mexico* en el norte de México

north [nɔːrθ] ADJECTIVE, ADVERB
see also **north** NOUN
1 el norte de ◇ *North Boston* el norte de Boston
2 hacia el norte ◇ *We were traveling north.* Viajábamos hacia el norte.
◆ **north of** al norte de ◇ *It's north of Denver.* Está al norte de Denver.
◆ **the north coast** la costa septentrional

North America [ˈnɔːrθəˈmɛrɪkə] NOUN
América del Norte FEM

northbound [ˈnɔːrθˌbaund] ADJECTIVE
◆ **Northbound traffic is moving very slowly.** El tráfico que se dirige hacia el norte avanza muy despacio.

northeast [nɔːrθˈiːst] NOUN
el noreste
◆ **in the northeast** al noreste

northern [ˈnɔːrðərn] ADJECTIVE
del norte ◇ *Northern Europe* Europa del Norte
◆ **the northern part of the island** la zona norte de la isla

Northern Ireland [ˈnɔːrðərnˈaɪərlənd] NOUN
Irlanda del Norte FEM

North Pole [ˈnɔːrθˈpoul] NOUN
◆ **the North Pole** el Polo Norte

North Sea [ˈnɔːrθˈsiː] NOUN
◆ **the North Sea** el Mar del Norte

northwest [nɔːrθˈwɛst] NOUN
el noroeste
◆ **in the northwest** al noroeste

Norway [ˈnɔːrweɪ] NOUN
Noruega FEM

Norwegian [nɔːrˈwiːdʒən] ADJECTIVE
see also **Norwegian** NOUN
noruego

Norwegian [nɔːrˈwiːdʒən] NOUN
see also **Norwegian** ADJECTIVE
1 el noruego
la noruega
(*person*)
◇ *the Norwegians* los noruegos
2 el noruego (*language*)

nose [nouz] NOUN
la nariz (PL las narices)

nosebleed [ˈnouzˌbliːd] NOUN
◆ **I often get nosebleeds.** Me sangra la nariz a menudo.

nosy [ˈnouzi] ADJECTIVE
fisgón (FEM fisgona) (*informal*)

not [nɑːt] ADVERB
no ◇ *I'm not sure.* No estoy seguro. ◇ *Are you coming or not?* ¿Vienes o no? ◇ *Did you like it? – Not really.* ¿Te gustó? – No mucho.
◆ **Thank you very much. – Not at all.** Muchas gracias. – De nada.
◆ **not yet** todavía no ◇ *They haven't arrived yet.* Todavía no han llegado.

note [nout] NOUN
la nota ◇ *I'll drop her a note.* Le dejaré una nota.
◆ **Remember to take notes.** Acuérdate de tomar apuntes.
◆ **to make a note of something** tomar nota de algo

to **note down** [noutˈdaun] VERB
anotar

notebook [ˈnoutˌbuk] NOUN
el cuaderno

notepad [ˈnoutˌpæd] NOUN
el bloc de notas (PL los blocs de notas)

notepaper [ˈnoutˌpeɪpər] NOUN
el papel de cartas

nothing [ˈnʌθɪŋ] NOUN
nada ◇ *What's wrong? – Nothing.* ¿Qué pasa? – Nada. ◇ *What are you doing tonight? – Nothing special.* ¿Qué haces esta noche? – Nada especial. ◇ *He does nothing at all.* No hace nada.
◆ **He does nothing but sleep.** No hace nada más que dormir.
◆ **There's nothing to do.** No hay nada que hacer.

*When **nothing** goes before a verb in English it can be translated by either **nada...** or **no...nada.***

◇ *Nothing frightens him.* Nada lo asusta.
◇ *Nothing will happen.* No pasará nada.
◆ **We won one to nothing.** Ganamos uno a cero.

notice [ˈnoutɪs] NOUN
see also **notice** VERB
1 el letrero (*physical object*) ◇ *There was a notice outside the house.* Había un letrero fuera de la casa.
2 el aviso (*information*) ◇ *There's a notice on the board about the trip.* Hay un aviso en el tablón sobre el viaje.
◆ **a warning notice** un aviso
◆ **He was transferred without notice.** Lo trasladaron sin previo aviso.
◆ **until further notice** hasta nuevo aviso
◆ **Don't take any notice of him!** ¡No le hagas caso!

*Be careful not to translate **notice** by **noticia**.*

to **notice** [ˈnoutɪs] VERB
see also **notice** NOUN
◆ **to notice something** darse* cuenta de algo
◇ *Don't worry. He won't notice the mistake.* No te preocupes. No se dará cuenta del error.

nought [nɑːt] NOUN
cero MASC

noun [naun] NOUN
el nombre

novel [ˈnɑːvəl] NOUN
la novela

novelist [ˈnɑːvəlɪst] NOUN

el/la novelista

November [nou'vɛmbər] NOUN
noviembre MASC ◇ *in November* en noviembre ◇ *on November 7th* el 7 de noviembre

now [nau] ADVERB
ahora ◇ *What are you doing now?* ¿Qué haces ahora?
◆ **just now** en este momento ◇ *I'm rather busy just now.* En este momento estoy muy ocupado.
◆ **I did it just now.** Lo acabo de hacer.
◆ **It should be ready by now.** Ya debería estar listo.
◆ **from now on** de ahora en adelante
◆ **now and then** de vez en cuando

nowhere ['nouwɛr] ADVERB
a ninguna parte ◇ *Where are you going for your vacations? – Nowhere.* ¿Adónde vas de vacaciones? – A ninguna parte.
◆ **nowhere else** a ninguna otra parte ◇ *You can go to the stores but nowhere else.* Puedes ir a las tiendas pero a ninguna otra parte.
◆ **The children were nowhere to be seen.** No se podía ver a los niños por ninguna parte.
◆ **There was nowhere to play.** No se podía jugar en ninguna parte.

nuclear ['nu:kliər] ADJECTIVE
nuclear ◇ *nuclear power* la energía nuclear

nude [nu:d] NOUN
see also **nude** ADJECTIVE
◆ **in the nude** desnudo

nude [nu:d] ADJECTIVE
see also **nude** NOUN
desnudo

nudist ['nu:dɪst] NOUN
el/la nudista

nuisance ['nu:səns] NOUN
fastidio ◇ *It's a nuisance having to clean the car.* Es un fastidio tener que limpiar el carro.
◆ **Sorry to be a nuisance.** Siento molestarle.
◆ **You're a nuisance!** ¡Eres un pesado!

numb [nʌm] ADJECTIVE
entumecido ◇ *numb with cold* entumecido de frío

number ['nʌmbər] NOUN
el número ◇ *I can't read the second number.* No puedo leer el segundo número. ◇ *They live at number five.* Viven en el número cinco. ◇ *You have the wrong number.* Se ha equivocado de número.
◆ **a large number of people** un gran número de gente
◆ **What's your number?** (*telephone*) ¿Cuál es tu teléfono?

nun [nʌn] NOUN
la monja

nurse [nɜ:rs] NOUN
el enfermero
la enfermera
◆ **She's a nurse.** Es enfermera.

nursery ['nɜ:rsəri] NOUN (PL **nurseries**)
1 la guardería infantil (*for children*)
2 el vivero (*for plants*)

nursery school ['nɜ:rsəri,sku:l] NOUN
el jardín infantil (PL los jardines infantiles)
el jardín de niños (PL los jardines de niños) *Mexico*

nut [nʌt] NOUN
1 la almendra (*almond*)
2 el maní (PL los maníes)
el cacahuate *Mexico*
(*peanut*)
3 la avellana (*hazelnut*)
4 la nuez (PL las nueces) (*walnut*)
◆ **I don't like nuts.** No me gustan los frutos secos.
5 la tuerca (*made of metal*)

nutmeg ['nʌtmɛg] NOUN
la nuez moscada

nutritious [nu:'trɪʃəs] ADJECTIVE
nutritivo

nuts [nʌts] ADJECTIVE
◆ **He's nuts.** Está chiflado. (*informal*)

nylon ['naɪlɑ:n] NOUN
nylon
◆ **nylons** las medias de nylon

N

O

oak [ouk] NOUN
el roble ◇ *an oak barrel* un barril de roble
oar [ɔːr] NOUN
el remo
oatmeal ['outmiːl] NOUN
la avena cocida
oats [outs] PL NOUN
la avena
obedient [ou'biːdiənt] ADJECTIVE
obediente
to **obey** [ou'beɪ] VERB
obedecer*
◆ **to obey the rules** (*in game*) atenerse a las reglas del juego
object ['ɑːbdʒɪkt] NOUN
el objeto
objection [əb'dʒɛkʃən] NOUN
la objeción (PL las objeciones) ◇ *There were no objections to the plan.* No hubo objeciones al plan.
objective [əb'dʒɛktɪv] NOUN
see also **objective** ADJECTIVE
el objetivo
objective [əb'dʒɛktɪv] ADJECTIVE
see also **objective** NOUN
objetivo
oblong ['ɑːblɑːŋ] ADJECTIVE
rectangular
oboe ['oubou] NOUN
el oboe
obscene [əb'siːn] ADJECTIVE
obsceno
observant [əb'zɜːrvənt] ADJECTIVE
observador (FEM observadora)
to **observe** [əb'zɜːrv] VERB
observar
obsessed [əb'sɛst] ADJECTIVE
obsesionado ◇ *He's obsessed with video games.* Está obsesionado con los videojuegos.
obsession [əb'sɛʃən] NOUN
la obsesión (PL las obsesiones) ◇ *Art is an obsession of mine.* El arte es una obsesión mía.
obsolete [ɑːbsə'liːt] ADJECTIVE
obsoleto
obstacle ['ɑːbstəkəl] NOUN
el obstáculo
obstinate ['ɑːbstənɪt] ADJECTIVE
terco
to **obstruct** [əb'strʌkt] VERB
bloquear ◇ *A truck was obstructing the traffic.* Un camión bloqueaba el tráfico.
to **obtain** [əb'teɪn] VERB
obtener*
obvious ['ɑːbviəs] ADJECTIVE
obvio
obviously ['ɑːbviəsli] ADVERB
claro ◇ *Do you want to pass the exam? – Obviously!* ¿Quieres aprobar el examen? – ¡Claro! ◇ *It was obviously impossible.* Estaba claro que era imposible.
◆ **Obviously not!** ¡Claro que no!
occasion [ə'keɪʒən] NOUN
la ocasión (PL las ocasiones) ◇ *a special occasion* una ocasión especial
◆ **on several occasions** en varias ocasiones
occasionally [ə'keɪʒənlɪ] ADVERB
de vez en cuando
occupation [ɑːkjə'peɪʃən] NOUN
el empleo
to **occupy** ['ɑːkjəpaɪ] VERB (**occupied, occupied**)
ocupar ◇ *The bathroom was occupied.* El baño estaba ocupado.
to **occur** [ə'kɜːr] VERB
ocurrir ◇ *The accident occurred yesterday.* El accidente ocurrió ayer.
◆ **It suddenly occurred to me that...** De repente se me ocurrió que...
ocean ['ouʃən] NOUN
el océano
o'clock [ə'klɑːk] ADVERB
◆ **at four o'clock** a las cuatro
◆ **It's one o'clock.** Es la una.
◆ **It's five o'clock.** Son las cinco.
October [ɑːk'toubər] NOUN
octubre MASC ◇ *in October* en octubre ◇ *on October 12th* el 12 de octubre
octopus ['ɑːktəpəs] NOUN (PL **octopuses**)
el pulpo
odd [ɑːd] ADJECTIVE
1 raro ◇ *That's odd!* ¡Qué raro!
2 impar ◇ *an odd number* un número impar
◆ **odd socks** calcetines desparejados
of [ʌv] PREPOSITION
de ◇ *a boy of 10* un niño de 10 años ◇ *a pound of oranges* una libra de naranjas ◇ *It's made of wood.* Es de madera. ◇ *a glass of wine* un vaso de vino
de* + *el* changes to *del
◇ *the wheels of the car* las ruedas del carro
◆ **There were three of us.** Éramos tres.
◆ **a friend of mine** un amigo mío
◆ **That's very kind of you.** Es muy amable de su parte.
off [ɑːf] ADJECTIVE, ADVERB, PREPOSITION
*For other expressions with **off**, see the verbs **get**, **take**, **turn**, etc.*
1 apagado (*heater, light, TV*) ◇ *All the lights are off.* Todas las luces están apagadas.
2 cerrado (*faucet, gas*) ◇ *Are you sure the faucet is off?* ¿Seguro que la llave está cerrada?
◆ **a day off** un día libre ◇ *She took a day off*

work to go to the wedding. Se tomó un día libre para ir a la boda.

◆ **I have tomorrow off.** Mañana tengo el día libre.

◆ **She's off school today.** Hoy no ha ido al colegio.

◆ **I must be off now.** Me tengo que ir ahora.

◆ **I'm off.** Me voy.

◆ **The game is off.** El partido se ha suspendido.

◆ **in the off season** en temporada baja

offense [ə'fɛns] NOUN
el delito (*crime*)

offensive [ə'fɛnsɪv] ADJECTIVE
ofensivo

offer ['ɑːfər] NOUN
see also **offer** VERB
1 la oferta (*of money, job*)
2 el ofrecimiento (*of help*)

◆ **There was a special offer on tapes.** Las cintas estaban de oferta.

to **offer** ['ɑːfər] VERB
see also **offer** NOUN
ofrecer* ◇ *He offered me a cigarette.* Me ofreció un cigarrillo.

◆ **He offered to help me.** Se ofreció a ayudarme.

office ['ɑːfɪs] NOUN
la oficina

◆ **during office hours** en horas de oficina

officer ['ɑːfɪsər] NOUN
el/la oficial (*in the army*)

◆ **police officer** el/la agente de policía

official [ə'fɪʃəl] ADJECTIVE
oficial

off-peak ['ɑːf'piːk] ADJECTIVE

◆ **off-peak calls** llamadas de tarifa reducida

offside ['ɑːf'saɪd] ADJECTIVE
fuera de juego

often ['ɑːfən] ADVERB
a menudo ◇ *It often rains.* Llueve a menudo.

◆ **How often do you go to the gym?** ¿Cada cuánto vas al gimnasio?

oil [ɔɪl] NOUN
see also **oil** VERB
1 el aceite (*for lubrication, cooking*)
2 el petróleo (*crude oil*)

◆ **an oil painting** una pintura al óleo

to **oil** [ɔɪl] VERB
see also **oil** NOUN
engrasar

oil rig ['ɔɪl,rɪg] NOUN
la plataforma petrolífera

oil slick ['ɔɪl,slɪk] NOUN
la marea negra

oil well ['ɔɪl,wɛl] NOUN
el pozo de petróleo

ointment ['ɔɪntmənt] NOUN
la pomada

okay ['ou'keɪ] EXCLAMATION, ADVERB
1 de acuerdo (*more formally*) ◇ *Your appointment is at six o'clock. – Okay.* Su cita es a las seis. – De acuerdo.
2 okay (*less formally*) ◇ *I'll meet you at six o'clock, okay?* Te veré a las seis, ¿okay?

◆ **Are you okay?** ¿Estás bien?

◆ **I'll do it tomorrow, if that's okay with you.** Lo haré mañana, si te parece bien.

◆ **The movie was okay.** La película no estuvo mal.

old [ould] ADJECTIVE
1 viejo ◇ *an old house* una casa vieja ◇ *an old man* un viejo
When talking about people it is more polite to use ***anciano*** *instead of* ***viejo.***
◇ *old people* los ancianos
2 antiguo (*former*) ◇ *my old English teacher* mi antiguo profesor de inglés

◆ **How old are you?** ¿Cuántos años tienes?

◆ **How old is the baby?** ¿Cuánto tiempo tiene el bebé?

◆ **a twenty-year-old woman** una mujer de veinte años

◆ **He's ten years old.** Tiene diez años.

◆ **older** mayor ◇ *my older brother* mi hermano mayor ◇ *my older sister* mi hermana mayor ◇ *Rachel is two years older than me.* Rachel es dos años mayor que yo.

◆ **I'm the oldest in the family.** Soy el mayor de la familia.

old-fashioned ['ould'fæʃənd] ADJECTIVE
anticuado ◇ *My parents are rather old-fashioned.* Mis padres son bastante anticuados.

olive ['ɑːlɪv] NOUN
la aceituna

olive oil ['ɑːlɪv,ɔɪl] NOUN
el aceite de oliva

olive tree ['ɑːlɪv,triː] NOUN
el olivo

Olympic [ou'lɪmpɪk] ADJECTIVE
olímpico

◆ **the Olympics** las Olimpiadas

omelette ['ɑːmlɪt] NOUN
la omelette
la tortilla a la francesa *Mexico*

on [ɑːn] PREPOSITION, ADVERB
see also **on** ADJECTIVE
There are several ways of translating ***on.*** *Scan the examples to find one that is similar to what you want to say. For other expressions with* ***on,*** *see the verbs* ***go, put, turn,*** *etc.*
1 en ◇ *on an island* en una isla ◇ *on the wall* en la pared ◇ *It's on channel four.* Lo dan en el canal cuatro. ◇ *on TV* en la tele ◇ *on the 1st floor* en la planta baja ◇ *I go to school on my bicycle.* Voy al colegio en bicicleta. ◇ *We went on the train.* Fuimos en tren.
2 sobre (*on top of, about*) ◇ *on the table* sobre la mesa ◇ *a book on Ghandi* un libro sobre Ghandi
With days and dates, the definite article – ***el,*** ☞

O

los – is used in Spanish instead of a preposition.
◇ *on Friday* el viernes ◇ *on Fridays* los viernes ◇ *on June 20th* el 20 de junio
- **on the left** a la izquierda
- **on vacation** de vacaciones
- **It's about 10 minutes on foot.** Está a unos 10 minutos andando.
- **She was on antibiotics for a week.** Estuvo una semana tomando antibióticos.
- **The coffee is on the house.** Al café invita la casa.
- **What is he on about?** ¿De qué está hablando?

on [ɑːn] ADJECTIVE
see also **on** PREPOSITION, ADVERB
1 prendido (*heater, light, TV*) ◇ *I think I left the light on.* Me parece que dejé la luz prendida.
2 abierto (*faucet, gas*) ◇ *Turn the faucet on.* Deja la llave abierta. ◇ *Who left the gas on?* ¿Quién dejó el gas abierto?
3 en marcha ◇ *Is the dishwasher on?* ¿Está en marcha el lavavajillas?
- **What's on at the movies?** ¿Qué dan en el cine?
- **Is the party still on?** ¿Todavía se va a hacer la fiesta?
- **I have a lot on this weekend.** Tengo mucho que hacer este fin de semana.

once [wʌns] ADVERB
una vez ◇ *once a week* una vez a la semana ◇ *once more* una vez más ◇ *I've been to Bolivia once before.* Ya he estado una vez en Bolivia.
- **Once upon a time...** Érase una vez...
- **once in a while** de vez en cuando
- **once and for all** de una vez por todas
- **at once** enseguida

one [wʌn] NUMERAL, PRONOUN
uno (FEM una)
*Use **un** before a masculine noun.*
◇ *I have one brother and one sister.* Tengo un hermano y una hermana. ◇ *I need a smaller one.* Necesito uno más pequeño.
- **one by one** uno a uno
- **One never knows.** Nunca se sabe.
- **one another** unos a otros ◇ *They all looked at one another.* Se miraron todos unos a otros.

oneself [wʌn'sɛlf] PRONOUN
1 se (*reflexive*) ◇ *to hurt oneself* hacerse* daño ◇ *to wash oneself* lavarse
2 uno mismo (FEM una misma) (*after preposition, for emphasis*) ◇ *It's quicker to do it oneself.* Es más rápido si lo hace uno mismo.

one-way ['wʌn,weɪ] ADJECTIVE
- **a one-way street** una calle de sentido único
- **a one-way ticket (1)** un boleto de ida (*for train*)
- **a one-way ticket (2)** un pasaje de ida (*for plane, boat*)

onion ['ʌnjən] NOUN
la cebolla

on-line ['ɑːn,laɪn] ADJECTIVE
en línea

only ['ounli] ADVERB
see also **only** ADJECTIVE, CONJUNCTION
sólo ◇ *How much was it? – Only $10.* ¿Cuánto valía? – Sólo 10 dólares. ◇ *We only want to stay for one night.* Sólo queremos quedarnos una noche. ◇ *It's only a game!* ¡Es sólo un juego!

only ['ounli] ADJECTIVE
see also **only** ADVERB, CONJUNCTION
único ◇ *She's an only child.* Es hija única. ◇ *Monday is the only day I'm free.* El lunes es el único día que tengo libre.

only ['ounli] CONJUNCTION
see also **only** ADJECTIVE, ADVERB
pero ◇ *I'd like the same sweater, only in black.* Quería el mismo suéter, pero en negro.

onward ['ɑːnwərd] ADVERB
en adelante ◇ *from July onward* de julio en adelante

open ['oupən] ADJECTIVE
see also **open** VERB
abierto ◇ *The store is open on Sunday mornings.* La tienda está abierta los domingos por la mañana.
- **Are you open tomorrow?** ¿Abre mañana?
- **in the open air** al aire libre

to **open** ['oupən] VERB
see also **open** ADJECTIVE
1 abrir* ◇ *What time do the stores open?* ¿A qué hora abren las tiendas? ◇ *Can I open the window?* ¿Puedo abrir la ventana?
2 abrirse* ◇ *The door opens automatically.* La puerta se abre automáticamente.

opening hours ['oupənɪŋ'auərz] PL NOUN
el horario de apertura

opera ['ɑːpərə] NOUN
la ópera

to **operate** ['ɑːpəreɪt] VERB
operar (*machine*)
- **to operate on someone** operar a alguien

operation [ɑːpə'reɪʃən] NOUN
la operación (PL las operaciones)
- **I've never had an operation.** Nunca me han operado.

operator ['ɑːpəreɪtər] NOUN
el operador
la operadora

opinion [ə'pɪnjən] NOUN
la opinión (PL las opiniones) ◇ *in my opinion* en mi opinión
- **What's your opinion?** ¿Tú qué opinas?

opinion poll [ə'pɪnjən,poul] NOUN

el sondeo de opinión

opponent [ə'pounənt] NOUN
el adversario
la adversaria

opportunity [ɑːpər'tuːnɪti] NOUN (PL **opportunities**)
la oportunidad ◇ *I've never had the opportunity to go to Spain.* No he tenido nunca la oportunidad de ir a España.

opposed [ə'pouzd] ADJECTIVE
◆ **to be opposed to something** oponerse* a algo ◇ *I've always been opposed to violence.* Siempre me he opuesto a la violencia.

opposing [ə'pouzɪŋ] ADJECTIVE
contrario ◇ *the opposing team* el equipo contrario

opposite ['ɑːpəzɪt] ADJECTIVE, ADVERB, PREPOSITION
1 contrario ◇ *It's in the opposite direction.* Está en dirección contraria.
2 opuesto ◇ *the opposite sex* el sexo opuesto
3 enfrente ◇ *They live opposite.* Viven enfrente.
4 frente a ◇ *the girl sitting opposite me* la chica sentada frente a mí

opposition [ɑːpə'zɪʃən] NOUN
la oposición ◇ *There is a lot of opposition to the new law.* Hay una fuerte oposición a la nueva ley.

optician [ɑːp'tɪʃən] NOUN
el óptico
la óptica
◆ **He's gone to the optician's.** Ha ido a la óptica.

optimist ['ɑːptəmɪst] NOUN
el/la optimista

optimistic [ɑːptə'mɪstɪk] ADJECTIVE
optimista

option ['ɑːpʃən] NOUN
la opción (PL las opciones) ◇ *I have no option.* No tengo otra opción.

optional ['ɑːpʃənl] ADJECTIVE
1 optativo (*subject*) ◇ *Biology was optional at my school.* La biología era optativa en mi colegio.
2 opcional (*feature*) ◇ *Fog lights are available as optional extras.* Los faros antiniebla son opcionales.

or [ɔːr] CONJUNCTION
1 o ◇ *Would you like tea or coffee?* ¿Quieres té o café?
*Use **u** before words beginning with "o" or "ho".*
◇ *six or eight* seis u ocho ◇ *men or women* mujeres u hombres
◆ **Hurry up or you'll miss the train.** Date prisa, que vas a perder el tren.
2 ni ◇ *I don't eat meat or fish.* No como carne ni pescado. ◇ *She can't dance or sing.* No sabe bailar ni cantar.

oral ['ɔːrəl] ADJECTIVE
see also **oral** NOUN
oral ◇ *an oral test* un examen oral

oral ['ɔːrəl] NOUN
see also **oral** ADJECTIVE
el examen oral (PL los exámenes orales)
◇ *I've got my Spanish oral soon.* Tengo el examen oral de español pronto.

orange ['ɑːrɪndʒ] NOUN
see also **orange** ADJECTIVE
la naranja
◆ **orange juice** el jugo de naranja

orange ['ɑːrɪndʒ] ADJECTIVE
see also **orange** NOUN
naranja MASC, FEM, PL

orchard ['ɔːrtʃərd] NOUN
el huerto

orchestra ['ɔːrkɪstrə] NOUN
1 la orquesta
2 la platea (*seating*)

order ['ɔːrdər] NOUN
see also **order** VERB
1 el orden (*arrangement*) ◇ *in alphabetical order* por orden alfabético
2 la orden (PL las órdenes) (*command*) ◇ *to obey an order* obedecer* una orden
◆ **The waiter took our order.** El mesero tomó nota de lo que íbamos a pedir.
◆ **in order to** para ◇ *He does it in order to earn money.* Lo hace para ganar dinero.
◆ **"out of order"** "averiado"

to **order** ['ɔːrdər] VERB
see also **order** NOUN
pedir* ◇ *We ordered steak and fries.* Pedimos un filete con papas fritas. ◇ *Are you ready to order?* ¿Han decidido qué van a pedir?

to **order around** ['ɔːrdərə'raund] VERB
dar* órdenes a ◇ *She was fed up with being ordered around.* Estaba harta de que le dieran órdenes.

ordinary ['ɔːrdnɛri] ADJECTIVE
normal y corriente ◇ *He's an ordinary man.* Es un hombre normal y corriente. ◇ *an ordinary day* un día normal y corriente

organ ['ɔːrgən] NOUN
el órgano (*instrument*)

organic [ɔːr'gænɪk] ADJECTIVE
biológico (*fruit, vegetables*)

organization [ɔːrgənɪ'zeɪʃən] NOUN
la organización (PL las organizaciones)

to **organize** ['ɔːrgənaɪz] VERB
organizar*

origin ['ɔːrɪdʒɪn] NOUN
el origen (PL los orígenes)

original [ə'rɪdʒɪnl] ADJECTIVE
original

originally [ə'rɪdʒɪnli] ADVERB
al principio

ornament ['ɔːrnəmənt] NOUN
el adorno

orphan ['ɔːrfən] NOUN
el huérfano
la huérfana

ostrich ['ɑːstrɪtʃ] NOUN (PL **ostriches**)
el avestruz (PL los avestruces)

other ['ʌðər] ADJECTIVE, PRONOUN
otro (FEM otra) ◇ *Do you have these jeans in other colors?* ¿Tienen estos jeans en otros colores? ◇ *on the other side of the street* al otro lado de la calle
◆ **the other one** el otro (FEM la otra) ◇ *This one? – No, the other one.* ¿Éste? – No, el otro.
◆ **the others** los demás (FEM las demás) ◇ *The others are going but I'm not.* Los demás van, pero yo no.

otherwise ['ʌðərwaɪz] ADVERB, CONJUNCTION
1 si no (*if not*) ◇ *Note down the number, otherwise you'll forget it.* Apúnta el número, si no se te olvidará.
2 por lo demás (*in other ways*) ◇ *I'm tired, but otherwise I'm fine.* Estoy cansado, pero por lo demás estoy bien.

ought [ɑːt] VERB
*To translate **ought to** use the conditional tense of **deber**.*
◇ *I ought to phone my parents.* Debería llamar a mis padres. ◇ *You ought not to do that.* No deberías hacer eso. ◇ *He ought to win.* Debería ganar.
*For **ought to have** use the conditional tense of **deber** plus **haber** or the imperfect of **deber**.*
◇ *You ought to have warned me.* Me deberías haber avisado. ◇ *He ought to have known.* Debía haberlo sabido.

ounce [auns] NOUN
la onza

ⓘ *In Latin America measurements are in grams and kilograms. One ounce is about 28 grams.*

our [auər] ADJECTIVE
nuestro ◇ *our house* nuestra casa ◇ *Our neighbors are very nice.* Nuestros vecinos son muy simpáticos.
***Our** is usually translated by the definite article **el/los** or **la/las** when it's clear from the sentence who the possessor is or when referring to clothing or parts of the body.*
◇ *We took off our coats.* Nos quitamos el abrigo. ◇ *They stole our car.* Nos robaron el carro.

ours [auərz] PRONOUN
1 el nuestro MASC (PL los nuestros) ◇ *Your car is much bigger than ours.* El carro de ustedes es mucho más grande que el nuestro. ◇ *Our teachers are strict. – Ours are too.* Nuestros profesores son estrictos. – Los nuestros también.
2 la nuestra FEM (PL las nuestras) ◇ *Your house is very different from ours.* La casa de ustedes es muy distinta de la nuestra.
3 nuestro MASC (PL nuestros) ◇ *Is this ours?* ¿Esto es nuestro? ◇ *a friend of ours* un amigo nuestro
4 nuestra FEM (PL nuestras) ◇ *Sorry, that table is ours.* Disculpen, esa mesa es nuestra. ◇ *Isabel is a close friend of ours.* Isabel es muy amiga nuestra.

ourselves [auər'sɛlvz] PRONOUN
1 nos (*reflexive*) ◇ *We really enjoyed ourselves.* Nos divertimos mucho.
2 nosotros mismos (FEM nosotras mismas) (*after preposition, for emphasis*) ◇ *Let's not talk about ourselves any more.* No hablemos más de nosotros mismos. ◇ *We built our garage ourselves.* Nos construimos el garaje nosotros mismos.
◆ **by ourselves** solos (FEM solas) ◇ *We prefer to be by ourselves.* Preferimos estar solos.

out [aut] PREPOSITION, ADVERB
see also **out** ADJECTIVE
*There are several ways of translating **out**. Scan the examples to find one that is similar to what you want to say. For other expressions with **out**, see the verbs **go**, **put**, **turn** etc.*
fuera ◇ *It's cold out.* Fuera hace frío. ◇ *It's dark out there.* Está oscuro ahí fuera.
◆ **She's out.** Salió.
◆ **She's out for the afternoon.** No estará en toda la tarde.
◆ **to go out** salir* ◇ *I'm going out tonight.* Voy a salir esta noche.
◆ **to go out with somebody** salir* con alguien ◇ *I've been going out with him for two months.* Llevo dos meses saliendo con él.
◆ **a night out with my friends** una noche por ahí con mis amigos
◆ **to be out sick** estar* ausente por enfermedad
◆ **"way out"** "salida"
◆ **out of town** fuera de la ciudad ◇ *He lives out of town.* Vive fuera de la ciudad.
◆ **three miles out of town** a tres millas de la ciudad
◆ **to take something out of your pocket** sacar* algo del bolsillo
◆ **out of curiosity** por curiosidad
◆ **We're out of milk.** Se nos acabó la leche.
◆ **in nine cases out of ten** en nueve de cada diez casos

out [aut] ADJECTIVE
see also **out** PREPOSITION, ADVERB
1 apagado (*lights, fire*) ◇ *All the lights are out.* Todas las luces están apagadas.
2 eliminado (*eliminated*) ◇ *Our team are out of the tournament.* Nuestro equipo queda eliminado del torneo.
◆ **The movie is now out on video.** La película ya salió en video.

outbreak ['aut͵breɪk] NOUN
1 el brote ◇ *a salmonella outbreak* un

brote de salmonelosis
[2] el comienzo ◇ *the outbreak of war* el comienzo de la guerra

outcome ['autkʌm] NOUN
el resultado

outdoor [aut'dɔːr] ADJECTIVE
al aire libre ◇ *an outdoor swimming pool* una piscina al aire libre, [*Mexico*:] una alberca descubierta

outdoors [aut'dɔːrz] ADVERB
al aire libre

outfit ['autfɪt] NOUN
el traje ◇ *a cowboy outfit* un traje de vaquero

outgoing ['aut,gouɪŋ] ADJECTIVE
extrovertido

outing ['autɪŋ] NOUN
la excursión (PL las excursiones) ◇ *to go on an outing* ir* de excursión

outlet ['autlet] NOUN
el tomacorriente

outline ['autlaɪn] NOUN
[1] el esquema (*summary*)
*Although **esquema** ends in **-a**, it is actually a masculine noun.*
◇ *This is an outline of the plan.* Aquí tienen un esquema del plan.
[2] el contorno (*shape*) ◇ *We could see the outline of the mountain.* Veíamos el contorno de la montaña.

outlook ['autluk] NOUN
[1] la actitud (*attitude*)
[2] las perspectivas (*prospects*)

outrageous [aut'reɪdʒəs] ADJECTIVE
[1] escandaloso (*behavior*)
[2] exorbitante (*price*)
[3] extravagante (*clothes*)

outset ['aut,sɛt] NOUN
◆ **at the outset** al principio

outside [aut'saɪd] NOUN, ADJECTIVE
[*see also* **outside** PREPOSITION, ADVERB]
[1] el exterior ◇ *the outside of the house* el exterior de la casa
[2] exterior ◇ *the outside walls* las paredes exteriores

outside [aut'saɪd] PREPOSITION, ADVERB
[*see also* **outside** NOUN, ADJECTIVE]
[1] fuera ◇ *It's very cold outside.* Hace mucho frío fuera.
[2] fuera de ◇ *outside the school* fuera del colegio ◇ *outside school hours* fuera del horario escolar

outsize ['aut,saɪz] ADJECTIVE
◆ **outsize clothes** ropa de tallas muy grandes

outskirts ['aut,skɜːrts] PL NOUN
las afueras ◇ *on the outskirts of town* en las afueras de la ciudad

outstanding [aut'stændɪŋ] ADJECTIVE
excepcional

oval ['ouvəl] ADJECTIVE
ovalado
◆ **the Oval Office** el Despacho Oval

oven ['ʌvən] NOUN
el horno

over ['ouvər] ADJECTIVE, ADVERB, PREPOSITION
*When something is located over something, use **encima de**. When there is movement over something, use **por encima de**.*
[1] encima de ◇ *There's a mirror over the sink.* Encima del lavamanos hay un espejo.
[2] por encima de ◇ *The ball went over the wall.* La pelota pasó por encima de la pared.
◆ **a bridge over the Hudson** un puente sobre el Hudson
[3] más de ◇ *It weighs over 20 pounds.* Pesa más de 20 libras.
◆ **The temperature was over 30 degrees.** La temperatura superaba los 30 grados.
[4] durante ◇ *over the vacations* durante las vacaciones ◇ *over Christmas* durante las Navidades
[5] terminado ◇ *I'll be happy when the exams are over.* Estaré feliz cuando se hayan terminado los exámenes.
◆ **over here** aquí
◆ **It's over there.** Está por allí.
◆ **all over Canada** en todo Canadá
◆ **I spilled coffee over my shirt.** Me manché la camisa de café.

overall ['ouvər'ɑːl] ADJECTIVE
[*see also* **overall** ADVERB]
general ◇ *What was your overall impression?* ¿Cuál fue tu impresión general?

overall ['ouvər'ɑːl] ADVERB
[*see also* **overall** ADJECTIVE]
en general ◇ *Overall, we played very well.* En general jugamos muy bien.

overalls ['ouvərɑːlz] PL NOUN
el overol (*for work*)

overcast ['ouvər,kæst] ADJECTIVE
cubierto ◇ *The sky was overcast.* El cielo estaba cubierto.

to **overcharge** [,ouvər'tʃɑːrdʒ] VERB
cobrar de más ◇ *They overcharged us for the meal.* Nos cobraron de más por la comida.

overcoat ['ouvər,kout] NOUN
el abrigo

overdone [,ouvər'dʌn] ADJECTIVE
[1] recocido (*vegetables*)
[2] demasiado hecho (*steak*)

overdose ['ouvər,dous] NOUN
la sobredosis (PL las sobredosis)

overdraft ['ouvər,dræft] NOUN
el descubierto

to **overestimate** ['ouvər'ɛstɪmeɪt] VERB
sobreestimar ◇ *We overestimated how long it would take.* Sobreestimamos el tiempo que se tardaría.

overhead projector ['ouvərhɛdprə'dʒɛktər] NOUN
el retroproyector

O

to **overlook** [ˌouvərˈluk] VERB
1 tener* vistas a ◇ *The hotel overlooked the beach.* El hotel tenía vistas a la playa.
2 pasar por alto ◇ *He had overlooked one important problem.* Había pasado por alto un problema importante.

overseas [ˌouvərˈsiːz] ADVERB
en el extranjero (*live, work*) ◇ *I'd like to work overseas.* Me gustaría trabajar en el extranjero.

oversight [ˈouvərˌsaɪt] NOUN
el descuido

to **oversleep** [ˌouvərˈsliːp] VERB (**overslept, overslept**)
quedarse dormido ◇ *I overslept this morning.* Me quedé dormido esta mañana.

overtime [ˈouvərˌtaɪm] NOUN
1 las horas extras ◇ *to work overtime* trabajar* horas extras
2 el tiempo suplementario (*in various sports*)

overweight [ˌouvərˈweɪt] ADJECTIVE
◆ **to be overweight** estar* demasiado gordo (*person*)
◆ **the suitcase is a kilo overweight** la maleta tiene un exceso de peso de un kilo

to **owe** [ou] VERB
deber ◇ *How much do I owe you?* ¿Cuánto te debo?

owing to [ˈouɪŋtuː] PREPOSITION
debido a ◇ *owing to bad weather* debido al mal tiempo

owl [aul] NOUN
el búho

own [oun] ADJECTIVE, PRONOUN
see also **own** VERB
propio ◇ *This is my own recipe.* Ésta es mi propia receta. ◇ *I wish I had a room of my own.* Me gustaría tener mi propia habitación.
◆ **on his own** él solo ◇ *on her own* ella sola ◇ *on our own* nosotros solos

to **own** [oun] VERB
see also **own** ADJECTIVE
tener*

to **own up** [ounˈʌp] VERB
confesarse* culpable
◆ **to own up to something** confesar* algo

owner [ˈounər] NOUN
el proprietario
la propietaria

oxygen [ˈɑːksɪdʒən] NOUN
el oxígeno

oyster [ˈɔɪstər] NOUN
la ostra
el ostión (PL los ostiones) Mexico

ozone [ˈouzoun] NOUN
el ozono ◇ *ozone layer* la capa de ozono

P

PA ['piː'eɪ] NOUN
- **the PA system** (*public address*) la megafonía

pace [peɪs] NOUN
el ritmo ◇ *the frantic pace of life in New York* el frenético ritmo de vida de Nueva York

Pacific [pə'sɪfɪk] NOUN
- **the Pacific** el Pacífico

pacifier ['pæsɪfaɪər] NOUN
el chupete (*for baby*)

to **pack** [pæk] VERB
see also **pack** NOUN
hacer* las maletas ◇ *I'll help you pack.* Te ayudaré a hacer las maletas.
- **I've already packed my case.** Ya hice mi maleta.
- **Pack it in!** ¡Para, ya!, *Mexico*: ¡Ya, párele!

pack [pæk] NOUN
see also **pack** VERB
el paquete ◇ *a pack of cigarettes* un paquete de cigarrillos

package ['pækɪdʒ] NOUN
el paquete
- **a package tour** unas vacaciones organizadas

packed [pækt] ADJECTIVE
abarrotado ◇ *The movie theater was packed.* El cine estaba abarrotado.

packet ['pækɪt] NOUN
el paquete
- **a packet of chips** un paquete de papas fritas

pad [pæd] NOUN
el bloc

to **paddle** ['pædl] VERB
see also **paddle** NOUN
1 chapotear (*swim*)
2 remar ◇ *to paddle a canoe* remar en canoa

paddle ['pædl] NOUN
see also **paddle** VERB
la pala (*en ping-pong*)
- **to go for a paddle** mojarse los pies

padlock ['pædlɑːk] NOUN
el candado

page [peɪdʒ] NOUN
see also **page** VERB
la página ◇ *on page 13* en la página 13

to **page** [peɪdʒ] VERB
see also **page** NOUN
- **to page somebody** llamar a alguien por el busca, *Mexico*: llamar a alguien por el bip

pager ['peɪdʒər] NOUN
el busca
*Although **busca** ends in **-a**, it is actually a masculine noun.*
el bip *Mexico*

paid [peɪd] VERB *see* **pay**

paid [peɪd] ADJECTIVE
1 remunerado ◇ *to do paid work* realizar* trabajo remunerado
2 pagado ◇ *three weeks' paid vacation* tres semanas de vacaciones pagadas

pail [peɪl] NOUN
el balde
la cubeta *Mexico*
- **garbage pail** el cubo de la basura, *Mexico*: el bote de la basura

pain [peɪn] NOUN
el dolor ◇ *a terrible pain* un dolor tremendo
- **I have a pain in my stomach.** Me duele el estómago.
- **She's in a lot of pain.** Tiene muchos dolores.
- **He's a real pain.** Es un auténtico pelmazo. (*informal*)

painful ['peɪnfəl] ADJECTIVE
__doloroso__ is used when talking about what causes pain, and __dolorido__ for the person or thing that feels pain.
1 doloroso ◇ *a painful injury* una herida dolorosa
2 dolorido ◇ *Her feet were swollen and painful.* Tenía los pies hinchados y doloridos.
- **Is it painful?** ¿Duele?

painkiller ['peɪnˌkɪlər] NOUN
el analgésico

paint [peɪnt] NOUN
see also **paint** VERB
la pintura

to **paint** [peɪnt] VERB
see also **paint** NOUN
pintar ◇ *to paint something green* pintar algo de verde

paintbrush ['peɪntˌbrʌʃ] NOUN (PL **paintbrushes**)
1 el pincel (*for an artist*)
2 la brocha (*for decorating*)

painter ['peɪntər] NOUN
el pintor
la pintora
◇ *The painters made a real mess of the windows.* Los pintores dejaron las ventanas hechas un desastre.

painting ['peɪntɪŋ] NOUN
1 el cuadro ◇ *a painting by Picasso* un cuadro de Picasso
2 la pintura ◇ *My hobby is painting.* Mi hobby es la pintura.

pair [pɛər] NOUN
el par ◇ *a pair of shoes* un par de zapatos
- **a pair of scissors** unas tijeras
- **a pair of pants** unos pantalones
- **in pairs** por parejas

pajamas [pə'dʒɑːməz] PL NOUN
el pijama
*Although **pijama** ends in **-a**, it is actually a masculine noun.*
◇ *my pajamas* mi pijama
- **a pair of pajamas** un pijama

Pakistan ['pækɪstæn] NOUN
Paquistán MASC

Pakistani [pækɪ'stæni] ADJECTIVE
see also **Pakistani** NOUN
paquistaní (PL paquistaníes)

Pakistani [pækɪ'stæni] NOUN
see also **Pakistani** ADJECTIVE
el/la paquistaní (PL los paquistaníes)

pal [pæl] NOUN
el/la compinche
el/la cuate *Mexico*

palace ['pæləs] NOUN
el palacio

pale [peɪl] ADJECTIVE
1 pálido ◇ *She still looks very pale.* Está todavía muy pálida.
◆ **to turn pale** ponerse* pálido
2 claro ◇ *pale green* verde claro
◆ **pale pink** rosa pálido
◆ **pale blue** azul celeste

Palestine ['pælɪstaɪn] NOUN
Palestina FEM

Palestinian [pælɪs'tɪniən] ADJECTIVE
see also **Palestinian** NOUN
palestino

Palestinian [pælɪs'tɪniən] NOUN
see also **Palestinian** ADJECTIVE
el palestino
la palestina

palm [pɑːm] NOUN
la palma ◇ *the palm of your hand* la palma de la mano
◆ **a palm tree** una palmera

pamphlet ['pæmflɪt] NOUN
el folleto

pan [pæn] NOUN
1 la cacerola (*saucepan*)
2 el/la sartén (PL los/las sartenes) (*frying pan*)
3 el molde para el horno (*baking pan*)

pancake ['pænkeɪk] NOUN
la crepe
la crepa *Mexico*

panic ['pænɪk] NOUN
see also **panic** VERB
el pánico ◇ *The shouting caused quite a panic.* El griterío provocó el pánico.

to **panic** ['pænɪk] VERB
see also **panic** NOUN
◆ **He panicked as soon as he saw the blood.** Le entró pánico en cuanto vio la sangre.
◆ **Don't panic!** ¡Tranquilo!

panther ['pænθər] NOUN
la pantera

panties ['pæntiz] PL NOUN
los calzones
las pantaletas *Mexico*

pantry ['pæntri] NOUN (PL **pantries**)
la despensa

pants [pænts] PL NOUN
los pantalones (*slacks*) ◇ *a pair of pants* unos pantalones

pantyhose ['pænti,houz] PL NOUN
los pantis
las pantimedias *Mexico*

paper ['peɪpər] NOUN
1 el papel ◇ *a paper bag* una bolsa de papel
◆ **a piece of paper** un papel
◆ **an exam paper** un examen
2 el periódico ◇ *I saw an advertisement in the paper.* Vi un anuncio en el periódico.

paperback ['peɪpər,bæk] NOUN
el libro de bolsillo

paperboy ['peɪpər,bɔɪ] NOUN
el repartidor de periódicos

paper clip ['peɪpər,klɪp] NOUN
el clip (PL los clips)

papergirl ['peɪpər,gɜːrl] NOUN
la repartidora de periódicos

paper route ['peɪpər,ruːt] NOUN
◆ **to do a paper route** repartir los periódicos a domicilio

paperweight ['peɪpər,weɪt] NOUN
el pisapapeles (PL los pisapapeles)

paperwork ['peɪpər,wɜːrk] NOUN
el papeleo ◇ *I have a lot of paperwork to do.* Tengo un montón de papeleo que hacer.

parachute ['pɛrəʃuːt] NOUN
el paracaídas (PL los paracaídas)

parade [pə'reɪd] NOUN
el desfile

paradise ['pɛrədaɪs] NOUN
el paraíso

paraffin wax ['pɛrəfɪn,wæks] NOUN
la parafina

paragraph ['pɛrəgræf] NOUN
el párrafo

parakeet ['pɛrəkiːt] NOUN
el periquito

parallel ['pɛrəlɛl] ADJECTIVE
paralelo

paralyzed ['pɛrəlaɪzd] ADJECTIVE
paralizado

paramedic [,pɛrə'mɛdɪk] NOUN
el auxiliar sanitario
la auxiliar sanitaria

parcel ['pɑːrsəl] NOUN
el paquete

pardon ['pɑːrdn] NOUN
◆ **Pardon?** ¿Cómo?

parentheses [pə'rɛnθəsiːz] PL NOUN
◆ **in parentheses** entre paréntesis

parents ['pɛrənts] PL NOUN
los padres
*Be careful not to translate **parents** by **parientes**.*

Paris ['pɛrɪs] NOUN
París MASC

park [pɑːrk] NOUN
see also **park** VERB
el parque
◆ **a national park** un parque nacional

* Verbs marked with this symbol are irregular. See pages 346–348 for further details.

◆ **a theme park** un parque temático

to **park** [pa:rk] VERB
see also **park** NOUN
estacionar ◇ *Where can I park my car?* ¿Dónde puedo estacionar el carro?
◆ **"no parking"** "Prohibido estacionar"

parking lot ['pa:rkɪŋ,la:t] NOUN
el estacionamiento

parking meter ['pa:rkɪŋ,mi:tər] NOUN
el parquímetro
el estacionómetro Mexico

parking ticket ['pa:rkɪŋ,tɪkɪt] NOUN
la multa por estacionamiento indebido

parliament ['pa:rləmənt] NOUN
el parlamento

parole [pə'roul] NOUN
◆ **on parole** en libertad condicional

parrot ['pɛrət] NOUN
el loro

parsley ['pa:rsli] NOUN
el perejil

part [pa:rt] NOUN
see also **part** VERB
1 la parte ◇ *The first part of the play was boring.* La primera parte de la obra fue aburrida.
2 el papel ◇ *She had a small part in the movie.* Tenía un pequeño papel en la película.
3 la pieza ◇ *spare parts* piezas de repuesto, Mexico: refacciones
◆ **to take part in something** participar en algo ◇ *Thousands of people took part in the demonstration.* Miles de personas participaron en la manifestación.
4 la raya (*in hair*)

to **part** [pa:rt] VERB
see also **part** NOUN
◆ **to part with something** desprenderse de algo ◇ *I hate to part with this lamp.* Odio tener que desprenderme de esta lámpara.

particular [pər'tɪkjələr] ADJECTIVE
1 concreto (*definite*) ◇ *I can't remember that particular movie.* No recuerdo esa película concreta.
2 especial (*special*) ◇ *He showed a particular interest in the subject.* Mostró un interés especial en el tema.
◆ **in particular** en concreto ◇ *Are you looking for anything in particular?* ¿Busca algo en concreto? ◇ *nothing in particular* nada en concreto

particularly [pər'tɪkjələrli] ADVERB
especialmente ◇ *a particularly boring lecture* una clase especialmente aburrida

partly ['pa:rtli] ADVERB
en parte ◇ *It was partly my own fault.* En parte fue culpa mía.

partner ['pa:rtnər] NOUN
1 el socio
la socia
◇ *He's a partner in a law firm.* Es socio de un bufete de abogados.
2 la pareja ◇ *That doesn't mean you don't love your partner.* Eso no significa que no quieras a tu pareja. ◇ *my dancing partner* mi pareja de baile

part-time ['pa:rt'taɪm] ADJECTIVE, ADVERB
a tiempo parcial ◇ *a part-time job* un trabajo a tiempo parcial ◇ *She works part-time.* Trabaja a tiempo parcial.

party ['pa:rti] NOUN (PL **parties**)
1 la fiesta ◇ *a birthday party* una fiesta de cumpleaños
2 el grupo ◇ *a party of tourists* un grupo de turistas

pass [pæs] NOUN (PL **passes**)
see also **pass** VERB
1 el pase (*in football, soccer*) ◇ *a short pass* un pase corto
2 el paso ◇ *The pass was blocked with snow.* El paso estaba cortado por la nieve.
◆ **a bus pass** Un pase para el bus.

to **pass** [pæs] VERB
see also **pass** NOUN
1 pasar ◇ *Could you pass me the salt, please?* ¿Me pasas la sal, por favor? ◇ *The time has passed quickly.* El tiempo ha pasado rápido.
2 adelantar
rebasar Mexico
◇ *We were passed by a huge truck.* Nos adelantó un camión enorme. Mexico: Nos rebasó un camión enorme.
3 pasar por delante de ◇ *I pass his house on my way to school.* Paso por delante de su casa de camino al colegio.
4 aprobar* ◇ *Did you pass?* ¿Aprobaste? ◇ *to pass an exam* aprobar un examen

to **pass out** [pæs'aut] VERB
desmayarse

passage ['pæsɪdʒ] NOUN
1 el pasaje ◇ *Read the passage carefully.* Lea el pasaje con atención.
2 el pasillo ◇ *a narrow passage* un estrecho pasillo

passenger ['pæsɪndʒər'] NOUN
el pasajero
la pasajera

passion ['pæʃən] NOUN
la pasión (PL las pasiones) ◇ *Music is a passion of his.* La música es una de sus pasiones.

passive ['pæsɪv] ADJECTIVE
pasivo
◆ **a passive smoker** un fumador pasivo

Passover ['pæsouvər] NOUN
la Pascua judía

passport ['pæspɔ:rt] NOUN
el pasaporte ◇ *passport control* el control de pasaportes

password ['pæs,wɜ:rd] NOUN
la contraseña

past [pæst] ADJECTIVE, ADVERB, PREPOSITION
see also **past** NOUN
pasado ◇ *This past year has been very difficult.* Este año pasado ha sido muy difícil. ◇ *The school is 100 yards past the traffic lights.* El colegio está a unos 100 yardas pasado el semáforo.
◆ **to go past** pasar ◇ *The bus went past without stopping.* El autobús pasó sin parar.
◆ **It's half past ten.** Son las diez y media.
◆ **It's a quarter past nine.** Son las nueve y cuarto.
◆ **It's ten past eight.** Son las ocho y diez.
◆ **It's past midnight.** Es pasada la medianoche.

past [pæst] NOUN
see also **past** ADJECTIVE, ADVERB, PREPOSITION
el pasado ◇ *I try not to think of the past.* Intento no pensar en el pasado.
◆ **This was common in the past.** Antiguamente esto era normal.

pasta ['pɑːstə] NOUN
la pasta

paste [peɪst] NOUN
el engrudo (*glue*)

pasteurized ['pæstʃəraɪzd] ADJECTIVE
pasteurizado

pastime ['pæstaɪm] NOUN
el pasatiempo

pastry ['peɪstri] NOUN (PL **pastries**)
1 la masa (*dough*)
2 el pastel (*cake*)

patch [pætʃ] NOUN (PL **patches**)
el parche ◇ *a patch of material* un parche de tela
◆ **He has a bald patch.** Tiene una calva incipiente.
◆ **They're going through a rough patch.** Están pasando una mala racha.

patched [pætʃt] ADJECTIVE
◆ **a pair of patched jeans** unos jeans con parches

pâté [pɑː'teɪ] NOUN
el paté

path [pæθ] NOUN
el sendero

pathetic [pə'θɛtɪk] ADJECTIVE
penoso ◇ *That was a pathetic excuse.* Fue una excusa penosa.

patience ['peɪʃəns] NOUN
1 la paciencia ◇ *He doesn't have much patience.* No tiene mucha paciencia.
2 el solitario (*game*)

patient ['peɪʃənt] NOUN
see also **patient** ADJECTIVE
el/la paciente

patient ['peɪʃənt] ADJECTIVE
see also **patient** NOUN
paciente

patio ['pætiou] NOUN
el patio

patriotic [peɪtri'ɑːtɪk] ADJECTIVE
patriótico

patrol [pə'troul] NOUN
la patrulla
◆ **to be on patrol** estar* de patrulla

patrol car [pə'troul,kɑːr] NOUN
el carro patrulla (PL los carros patrulla)

pattern ['pætərn] NOUN
1 el motivo (*design*) ◇ *a geometric pattern* un motivo geométrico
2 el patrón (*for sewing*)

pause [pɑːz] NOUN
la pausa

pavement ['peɪvmənt] NOUN
el pavimento

paw [pɑː] NOUN
la pata

pay [peɪ] NOUN
see also **pay** VERB
el sueldo ◇ *a pay raise* un aumento de sueldo

to **pay** [peɪ] VERB (**paid, paid**)
see also **pay** NOUN
pagar* ◇ *They pay me more on Sundays.* Me pagan más los domingos. ◇ *Can I pay by check?* ¿Puedo pagar con cheque?
◆ **to pay money into an account** depositar dinero en una cuenta
◆ **I'll pay you back tomorrow.** Mañana te devuelvo el dinero.
◆ **to pay for something** pagar* algo ◇ *I paid for my ticket.* Pagué el pasaje.
◆ **I paid $50 for it.** Me costó 50 dólares.
◆ **Does your checking account pay interest?** ¿Le rinde intereses su cuenta corriente?
◆ **to pay somebody a visit** ir* a ver a alguien
◆ **Paul paid us a visit last night.** Paul vino a vernos anoche.

payable ['peɪəbəl] ADJECTIVE
◆ **Who's the check payable to?** ¿A nombre de quién extiendo el cheque?

payment ['peɪmənt] NOUN
el pago ◇ *mortgage payments* los pagos de la hipoteca

pay phone ['peɪ,foun] NOUN
el teléfono público

PC ['piː'siː] NOUN (= *personal computer*)
el PC

PE [piː'iː] NOUN (= *physical education*)
la educación física ◇ *We have PE twice a week.* Tenemos educación física dos veces a la semana.

pea [piː] NOUN
la arveja
el chícharo *Mexico*

peace [piːs] NOUN
la paz
◆ **peace talks** conversaciones de paz
◆ **a peace treaty** un tratado de paz

peaceful ['piːsful] ADJECTIVE

1 pacífico (*nonviolent*) ◇ *a peaceful protest* una manifestación pacífica
2 apacible (*restful*) ◇ *a peaceful afternoon* una tarde apacible

peach [piːtʃ] NOUN (PL **peaches**)
el durazno

peacock [ˈpiːkɑːk] NOUN
el pavo real

peak [piːk] NOUN
1 la cumbre ◇ *the snow-covered peaks* las cumbres nevadas
2 el apogeo ◇ *She's at the peak of her career.* Está en el apogeo de su carrera profesional.
◆ **in peak season** en temporada alta

peak hours [ˈpiːkˈauərz] PL NOUN
la tarifa máxima (*on telephone*) ◇ *A cellular call during peak hours now costs about 37 cents.* Una llamada por el celular a las horas de tarifa máxima cuesta alrededor de 37 centavos

peanut [ˈpiːnʌt] NOUN
el maní (PL los maníes)
el cacahuate *Mexico*

peanut butter [ˈpiːnʌtˌbʌtər] NOUN
la mantequilla de maní
la mantequilla de cacahuate *Mexico*

pear [pɛər] NOUN
la pera

pearl [pɜːrl] NOUN
la perla

pebble [ˈpɛbəl] NOUN
el guijarro

peckish [ˈpɛkɪʃ] ADJECTIVE
◆ **to feel a bit peckish** tener* un poquito de hambre

peculiar [pɪˈkjuːljər] ADJECTIVE
raro ◇ *He's a peculiar person.* Es una persona rara. ◇ *It tastes peculiar.* Sabe raro.

pedal [ˈpɛdl] NOUN
el pedal

pedestrian [pɪˈdɛstriən] NOUN
el peatón (PL los peatones)

pedestrian mall [pɪˈdɛstriənˈmɑːl] NOUN
la zona peatonal

pedestrian zone [pɪˈdɛstriənˌzoun] NOUN
la zona peatonal

pedigree [ˈpɛdɪgriː] ADJECTIVE
de raza ◇ *a pedigree dog* un perro de raza
◆ **a pedigree labrador** un labrador de pura raza

pee [piː] NOUN
◆ **to take a pee** hacer* pis

peek [piːk] NOUN
◆ **to have a peek at something** echar una ojeada a algo ◇ *I had a peek at your dress and it's lovely.* Le eché una ojeada a tu vestido y es muy bonito.

peel [piːl] NOUN
see also **peel** VERB
1 la cáscara (*of fruit*)
2 la piel (*of potato*)

to **peel** [piːl] VERB
see also **peel** NOUN
pelar ◇ *Shall I peel the potatoes?* ¿Pelo las papas?
◆ **My nose is peeling.** Se me está pelando la nariz.

peg [pɛg] NOUN
1 el gancho (*for coats*)
2 la estaca (*tent peg*)

Pekinese [piːkɪˈniːz] NOUN (PL **Pekinese**)
el pequinés (PL los pequineses)

pellet [ˈpɛlɪt] NOUN
el perdigón (PL los perdigones) (*for gun*)

pelvis [ˈpɛlvɪs] NOUN (PL **pelvises**)
la pelvis (PL las pelvis)

pen [pɛn] NOUN
1 el bolígrafo
la pluma atómica *Mexico*
(*ballpoint pen*)
2 la pluma (*fountain pen*)
3 el marcador (*felt-tip pen*)

penalty [ˈpɛnlti] NOUN (PL **penalties**)
1 la pena ◇ *The penalty for this offense is life imprisonment.* La pena por este delito es cadena perpetua.
◆ **the death penalty** la pena de muerte
2 el penalty (PL los penaltys) (*in football, soccer*)
◆ **a penalty shoot-out** una tanda de penaltys (*in soccer*)

pencil [ˈpɛnsəl] NOUN
el lápiz (PL los lápices)
◆ **to write in pencil** escribir* a lápiz

pencil case [ˈpɛnsəlˌkeɪs] NOUN
el estuche

pencil sharpener [ˈpɛnsəlˌʃɑːrpənər] NOUN
el sacapuntas (PL los sacapuntas)

penguin [ˈpɛŋgwɪn] NOUN
el pingüino

penicillin [pɛnɪˈsɪlɪn] NOUN
la penicilina

penis [ˈpiːnɪs] NOUN (PL **penises**)
el pene

penitentiary [pɛnɪˈtɛnʃəri] NOUN (PL **penitentiaries**)
la cárcel

penknife [ˈpɛnˌnaɪf] NOUN (PL **penknives**)
la navaja

penny [ˈpɛni] NOUN (PL **pennies**)
el penique

pen pal [ˈpɛnˌpæl] NOUN
el amigo por correspondencia
la amiga por correspondencia

pension [ˈpɛnʃən] NOUN
la pensión (PL las pensiones)

pensioner [ˈpɛnʃənər] NOUN
el/la pensionista

Pentagon [ˈpɛntəgɑːn] NOUN
el Pentágono

pentathlon [pɛnˈtæθlən] NOUN
el pentatlón

P

people ['pi:pəl] PL NOUN
[1] la gente ◇ *The people were nice.* La gente era simpática. ◇ *a lot of people* mucha gente
[2] las personas ◇ *six people* seis personas ◇ *several people* varias personas
◆ **People say that...** Dicen que...
◆ **How many people are there in your family?** ¿Cuántos son en tu familia?
◆ **Mexican people** los mexicanos

pepper ['pɛpər] NOUN
[1] la pimienta ◇ *Pass the pepper, please.* ¿Me pasas la pimienta?
[2] el pimiento ◇ *a green pepper* un pimiento verde

peppermint ['pɛpərmɪnt] NOUN
el caramelo de menta
◆ **peppermint chewing gum** el chicle de menta

pepper shaker ['pɛpər,ʃeɪkər] NOUN
el pimentero

per [pɜ:r] PREPOSITION
por ◇ *per person* por persona ◇ *30 miles per hour* 30 millas por hora
◆ **per day** al día
◆ **per week** a la semana

percent [pər'sɛnt] ADVERB
por ciento ◇ *50 percent* 50 por ciento

percentage [pər'sɛntɪdʒ] NOUN
el porcentaje

percolator ['pɜ:rkəleɪtər] NOUN
la cafetera de filtro

percussion [pər'kʌʃən] NOUN
la percusión ◇ *I play percussion.* Toco la percusión.

perfect ['pɜ:rfɪkt] ADJECTIVE
perfecto ◇ *Dave speaks perfect Spanish.* Dave habla un español perfecto.

perfectly ['pɜ:rfɪktli] ADVERB
◆ **You know perfectly well what happened.** Sabes perfectamente lo que ocurrió.
◆ **a perfectly normal child** un niño completamente normal

to **perform** [pər'fɔ:rm] VERB
representar (*a play*) ◇ *to perform a play* representar una obra
◆ **The team performed brilliantly.** El equipo tuvo una brillante actuación.

performance [pər'fɔ:rməns] NOUN
[1] el espectáculo ◇ *The performance lasts two hours.* El espectáculo dura dos horas.
[2] la interpretación (PL las interpretaciones) ◇ *his performance as Hamlet* su interpretación de Hamlet

perfume ['pɜ:rfju:m] NOUN
el perfume

perhaps [pər'hæps] ADVERB
quizás ◇ *Perhaps they were tired.* Quizás estaban cansados.
Use the present subjunctive after ***quizás*** *to refer to the future.*
◇ *Perhaps he'll come tomorrow.* Quizás venga mañana.
◆ **perhaps not** quizás no

period ['pɪriəd] NOUN
[1] el periodo ◇ *for a limited period* por un periodo limitado
[2] la clase ◇ *Each period lasts forty minutes.* Cada clase dura cuarenta minutos.
[3] la época ◇ *the Victorian period* la época victoriana
[4] la regla ◇ *I'm having my period.* Estoy con la regla.
[5] el punto (*signo de puntuación*)

permanent ['pɜ:rmənənt] ADJECTIVE
see also **permanent** NOUN
[1] permanente ◇ *a permanent state of tension* un estado permanente de tensión
[2] fijo ◇ *a permanent job* un trabajo fijo

permanent ['pɜ:rmənənt] NOUN
see also **permanent** ADJECTIVE
la permanente
el permanente *Mexico*
(*hairstyle*)

permission [pər'mɪʃən] NOUN
el permiso ◇ *Could I have permission to leave early?* ¿Tengo permiso para salir antes?

permit ['pɜ:rmɪt] NOUN
el permiso ◇ *a work permit* un permiso de trabajo

Persian ['pɜ:rʒən] ADJECTIVE
◆ **a Persian cat** un gato persa

persistent [pər'sɪstənt] ADJECTIVE
persistente

person ['pɜ:rsən] NOUN
la persona ◇ *She's a very nice person.* Es muy buena persona.
◆ **in person** en persona

personal ['pɜ:rsənl] ADJECTIVE
personal ◇ *Those letters are personal.* Son cartas personales.
◆ **He's a personal friend of mine.** Es amigo íntimo mío.

personality [pɜ:rsə'nælɪti] NOUN (PL **personalities**)
la personalidad

personally ['pɜ:rsənli] ADVERB
personalmente ◇ *Personally, I don't agree.* Yo personalmente no estoy de acuerdo.
◆ **I don't know him personally.** No lo conozco en persona.
◆ **Don't take it personally.** No te lo tomes como algo personal.

personals ['pɜ:rsənəlz] PL NOUN
la sección de anuncios personales

personal secretary ['pɜ:rsənl'sɛkrətɛri] NOUN
el secretario de dirección
la secretaria de dirección
◇ *She's a personal secretary to the head of the company.* Es secretaria de la dirección.

personnel [pɜːrsəˈnɛl] NOUN
el personal

perspiration [pɜːrspɪˈreɪʃən] NOUN
la transpiración

to **persuade** [pərˈsweɪd] VERB
convencer*
Use the subjunctive after ***convencer de que*** *when translating "to persuade somebody to do something".*
◇ *to persuade somebody to do something* convencer a alguien de que haga algo ◇ *She persuaded me to go with her.* Me convenció de que fuera con ella.

Peru [pəˈruː] NOUN
Perú MASC

Peruvian [pəˈruːviən] ADJECTIVE
see also **Peruvian** NOUN
peruano

Peruvian [pəˈruːviən] NOUN
see also **Peruvian** ADJECTIVE
el peruano
la peruana

pessimist [ˈpɛsɪmɪst] NOUN
el/la pesimista

pessimistic [pɛsɪˈmɪstɪk] ADJECTIVE
pesimista ◇ *Don't be so pessimistic!* ¡No seas tan pesimista! ◇ *a pessimistic forecast* un pronóstico pesimista

pest [pɛst] NOUN
el pesado
la pesada
◇ *He's a real pest!* ¡Es un pesado!

to **pester** [ˈpɛstər] VERB
dar* la lata a ◇ *He's always pestering me.* Siempre me está dando la lata.

pet [pɛt] NOUN
el animal doméstico
- **Do you have a pet?** ¿Tienen algún animal en casa?
- **She's the teacher's pet.** Es la favorita del profesor.

petition [pəˈtɪʃən] NOUN
la petición (PL las peticiones)

petrified [ˈpɛtrəfaɪd] ADJECTIVE
- **She's petrified of spiders.** Las arañas le dan terror.

phantom [ˈfæntəm] NOUN
el fantasma
Although ***fantasma*** *ends in* ***-a****, it is actually a masculine noun.*

pharmacist [ˈfɑːrməsist] NOUN
el farmacéutico
la farmacéutica

pharmacy [ˈfɑːrməsi] NOUN (PL **pharmacies**)
la farmacia ◇ *You get it from the pharmacy.* Se compra en la farmacia.

pheasant [ˈfɛzənt] NOUN
el faisán (PL los faisanes)

philosophy [fɪˈlɑːsəfi] NOUN (PL **philosophies**)
la filosofía

phobia [ˈfoubiə] NOUN
la fobia

phone [foun] NOUN
see also **phone** VERB
el teléfono
- **by phone** por teléfono
- **to be on the phone** (*talking*) estar* hablando por teléfono ◇ *She's on the phone at the moment.* Ahora mismo está hablando por teléfono.
- **Can I use the phone, please?** ¿Puedo hacer una llamada?

to **phone** [foun] VERB
see also **phone** NOUN
llamar ◇ *I'll phone you tomorrow.* Mañana te llamo. ◇ *Could you phone me a taxi, please?* ¿Me puedes llamar a un taxi, por favor?

phone bill [ˈfoun,bɪl] NOUN
la cuenta del teléfono

phone book [ˈfoun,buk] NOUN
la guía telefónica
el directorio *Mexico*

phone booth [ˈfoun,buːθ] NOUN
la cabina telefónica

phone call [ˈfoun,kɑːl] NOUN
la llamada de teléfono
- **There's a phone call for you.** Tienes una llamada.
- **to make a phone call** hacer* una llamada

phonecard [ˈfoun,kɑːrd] NOUN
la tarjeta telefónica

phone number [ˈfoun,nʌmbər] NOUN
el número de teléfono

photo [ˈfoutou] NOUN
la foto
Although ***foto*** *ends in* ***-o****, it is actually a feminine noun.*
- **to take a photo** tomar una foto ◇ *I took a photo of the bride and groom.* Les tomé una foto a los novios.

photocopier [ˈfoutou,kɑːpiər] NOUN
la fotocopiadora

photocopy [ˈfoutou,kɑːpi] NOUN (PL **photocopies**)
see also **photocopy** VERB
la fotocopia

to **photocopy** [ˈfoutou,kɑːpi] VERB (**photocopied, photocopied**)
see also **photocopy** NOUN
fotocopiar

photograph [ˈfoutəgræf] NOUN
see also **photograph** VERB
la fotografía
- **to take a photograph** tomar una fotografía ◇ *I took a photograph of the bride and groom.* Les tomé una fotografía a los novios.

to **photograph** [ˈfoutəgræf] VERB
see also **photograph** NOUN
fotografiar*

photographer [fəˈtɑːgrəfər] NOUN
el fotógrafo

P ☞

la fotógrafa
◇ *She's a photographer.* Es fotógrafa.

photography [fə'tɑːgrəfi] NOUN
la fotografía ◇ *My hobby is photography.* Mi hobby es la fotografía.

phrase [freɪz] NOUN
la frase

phrase book ['freɪz,buk] NOUN
el manual de conversación

physical ['fɪzɪkəl] ADJECTIVE
see also **physical** NOUN
físico

physical ['fɪzɪkəl] NOUN
see also **physical** ADJECTIVE
el examen médico

physicist ['fɪzɪsɪst] NOUN
el físico
la física
◇ *a nuclear physicist* un físico nuclear

physics ['fɪzɪks] NOUN
la física ◇ *She teaches physics.* Enseña física.

physiotherapist [,fɪziou'θɛrəpɪst] NOUN
el/la fisioterapeuta

physiotherapy [,fɪziou'θɛrəpi] NOUN
la fisioterapia

pianist ['piːənɪst] NOUN
el/la pianista

piano [pi'ænou] NOUN
el piano ◇ *I play the piano.* Toco el piano.

pick [pɪk] NOUN
see also **pick** VERB
◆ **Take your pick!** ¡Elige el que quieras!
Replace ***el que*** *with* ***la que, los que*** *or* ***las que*** *as appropriate to agree with the thing or things you can take your pick of.*

to **pick** [pɪk] VERB
see also **pick** NOUN
1 elegir* (*choose*) ◇ *I picked the biggest piece.* Elegí el trozo más grande.
2 seleccionar (*for team*) ◇ *I've been picked for the team.* Me han seleccionado para el equipo.
3 recoger* (*fruit, flowers*)
◆ **to pick on somebody** meterse con alguien
◇ *She's always picking on me.* Siempre se está metiendo conmigo.

to **pick out** [pɪk'aut] VERB
escoger* ◇ *I like them all – it's difficult to pick one out.* Todos me gustan, es difícil escoger uno.

to **pick up** [pɪk'ʌp] VERB
1 recoger* ◇ *We'll come to the airport to pick you up.* Iremos a recogerte al aeropuerto. ◇ *Could you help me pick up the toys?* ¿Me ayudas a recoger los juguetes?
2 aprender ◇ *I picked up some Spanish during my vacation.* Aprendí un poco de español en las vacaciones.

pickpocket ['pɪk,pɑːkɪt] NOUN
el/la carterista

picnic ['pɪknɪk] NOUN
el picnic (PL los picnics)
◆ **to have a picnic** irse* de picnic

picture ['pɪktʃər] NOUN
1 la ilustración (PL las ilustraciones)
◇ *Children's books have lots of pictures.* Los libros para niños tienen muchas ilustraciones.
2 la foto
Although ***foto*** *ends in* ***-o****, it is actually a feminine noun.*
◇ *My picture was in the paper.* Mi foto salió en el periódico.
3 el cuadro (*painting*) ◇ *a picture by Picasso* un cuadro de Picasso
◆ **a picture of his wife** un retrato de su mujer
4 el dibujo (*drawing*)
◆ **to draw a picture of something** dibujar algo
◆ **to paint a picture of something** pintar algo

picture message NOUN
el mensaje con foto

picture messaging NOUN
el envío de mensajes con foto

picturesque [pɪktʃə'rɛsk] ADJECTIVE
pintoresco

pie [paɪ] NOUN
la tarta (*dessert*) ◇ *an apple pie* una tarta de manzana

piece [piːs] NOUN
1 el trozo ◇ *a piece of cake* un trozo de pastel
◆ **A small piece, please.** Un trocito, por favor.
2 pieza (*part*) ◇ *a 500-piece jigsaw* un rompecabezas de 500 piezas ◇ *piece by piece* pieza por pieza
3 pedazo (*of something larger*) ◇ *A piece of plaster fell from the roof.* Un pedazo de yeso se cayó del tejado.
◆ **a piece of furniture** un mueble
◆ **a piece of advice** un consejo
◆ **a 50-cents piece** una moneda de 50 centavos

pier [pɪər] NOUN
el muelle

pierced [pɪərst] ADJECTIVE
◆ **I have pierced ears.** Tengo agujeros hechos en las orejas.

pig [pɪg] NOUN
el cerdo

pigeon ['pɪdʒən] NOUN
la paloma

piggyback ['pɪgi,bæk] ADJECTIVE
◆ **to give somebody a piggyback ride** llevar a alguien a cuestas

piggy bank ['pɪgi,bæŋk] NOUN
la alcancía

pigtail ['pɪg,teɪl] NOUN
la trenza

pile [paɪl] NOUN
1 el montón (PL los montones) (*untidy*

heap) ◇ *a pile of dirty laundry* un montón de ropa sucia

2 la pila *(neat stack)*

◆ **Put your books in a pile on my desk.** Apilen los cuadernos en mi mesa.

piles [paɪlz] PL NOUN
las almorranas

pileup ['paɪlʌp] NOUN
el accidente en cadena
la carambola *Mexico*

pill [pɪl] NOUN
la píldora

◆ **to be on the pill** tomar la píldora

pillar ['pɪlər] NOUN
el pilar

pillow ['pɪlou] NOUN
la almohada

pilot ['paɪlət] NOUN
el/la piloto ◇ *He's a pilot.* Es piloto.

pimple ['pɪmpəl] NOUN
el grano

pin [pɪn] NOUN
el alfiler

◆ **pins and needles** el hormigueo ◇ *I have pins and needles.* Tengo hormigueo.

PIN [pɪn] NOUN (= *personal identification number*)
el número de identificación personal

pinafore ['pɪnəfɔːr] NOUN
el delantal

pinball ['pɪn,bɑːl] NOUN
el flipper

◆ **They're playing pinball.** Están jugando flipper.

to **pinch** [pɪntʃ] VERB

1 pellizcar* ◇ *He pinched me!* ¡Me pellizcó!

2 birlar* *(informal)* ◇ *Who pinched my pencil?* ¿Quién me birló el lápiz?

pine [paɪn] NOUN
el pino ◇ *a pine table* una mesa de pino

pineapple ['paɪnæpəl] NOUN
la piña

pink [pɪŋk] ADJECTIVE
rosa MASC, FEM, PL

pint [paɪnt] NOUN
la pinta

> ℹ *In Latin America measurements are in liters and centiliters. A pint is about 0.5 liters.*

pipe [paɪp] NOUN

1 el tubo ◇ *a gas pipe* un tubo de gas

◆ **The pipes froze.** Se heló la tubería.

2 la pipa ◇ *He smokes a pipe.* Fuma en pipa.

pirate ['paɪrət] NOUN
el/la pirata

pirated ['paɪrətɪd] ADJECTIVE
pirata MASC, FEM, PL ◇ *a pirated video* un video pirata

Pisces ['paɪsiːz] NOUN
el Piscis *(sign)* ◇ *I'm a Pisces.* Soy piscis.

◆ **a Pisces** un/una piscis

pissed [pɪst] ADJECTIVE
cabreado *(annoyed)* ◇ *to be pissed at somebody* estar cabreado con alguien

pistol ['pɪstl] NOUN
la pistola

pit [pɪt] NOUN
el hueso *(in fruit)*

pitch [pɪtʃ] NOUN (PL **pitches**)
see also **pitch** VERB
el lanzamiento *(in baseball)* ◇ *He threw the first pitch in the World series.* Efectuó el primer lanzamiento de las series mundiales.

to **pitch** [pɪtʃ] VERB
see also **pitch** NOUN

1 montar ◇ *We pitched our tent near the beach.* Montamos la tienda cerca de la playa.

2 tirar *(in baseball)*

pitcher ['pɪtʃər] NOUN
la jarra

pity ['pɪti] NOUN
see also **pity** VERB
la compasión ◇ *They showed no pity.* No demostraron ninguna compasión.

◆ **What a pity!** ¡Qué pena!

to **pity** ['pɪti] VERB (**pitied**)
see also **pity** NOUN
compadecer* ◇ *I don't hate him; I pity him.* No lo odio, lo compadezco.

pizza ['piːtsə] NOUN
la pizza

place [pleɪs] NOUN
see also **place** VERB

1 el lugar ◇ *It's a quiet place.* Es un lugar tranquilo.

2 la plaza ◇ *Book your place for the trip now.* Reserve ya su plaza para el viaje. ◇ *a place at college* una plaza en la universidad

3 el puesto *(in sports)* ◇ *America won third place in the games.* Estados Unidos consiguió el tercer puesto en los juegos.

◆ **a parking place** un lugar para estacionar

◆ **to change places** cambiarse de lugar

◆ **to take place** tener* lugar ◇ *Elections will take place on November 25th.* Las elecciones tendrán lugar el 25 de noviembre.

◆ **at your place** en tu casa ◇ *Shall we meet at your place?* ¿Nos vemos en tu casa?

◆ **Do you want to come round to my place?** ¿Quieres venir a mi casa?

to **place** [pleɪs] VERB
see also **place** NOUN
colocar* ◇ *He placed his hand on hers.* Colocó su mano sobre la de ella.

plain [pleɪn] ADJECTIVE, ADVERB
see also **plain** NOUN

1 liso *(not patterned)* ◇ *a plain tie* una corbata lisa

2 sencillo *(not fancy)* ◇ *a plain white blouse* una blusa blanca sencilla

P ☞

◆ **It was plain to see.** Era obvio.

plain [pleɪn] NOUN
see also **plain** ADJECTIVE, ADVERB
la llanura

plan [plæn] NOUN
see also **plan** VERB
1 el plan ◇ *What are your plans for the vacation?* ¿Qué planes tienes para las vacaciones?
◆ **to make plans** hacer* planes
◆ **Everything went according to plan.** Todo salió según lo previsto.
2 el plano ◇ *a plan of the campsite* un plano del camping
◆ **my essay plan** el esquema de mi trabajo

to **plan** [plæn] VERB
see also **plan** NOUN
1 planear (*make plans for*) ◇ *We're planning a trip to France.* Estamos planeando hacer un viaje a Francia.
2 planificar* (*schedule*) ◇ *Plan your revision carefully.* Tienes que planificar bien el repaso.
◆ **to plan to do something** tener* la intención de hacer algo ◇ *I'm planning to get a job during the vacation.* Tengo la intención de encontrar un trabajo durante las vacaciones.

plane [pleɪn] NOUN
el avión (PL los aviones) ◇ *by plane* en avión

planet ['plænɪt] NOUN
el planeta
Although ***planeta*** *ends in* ***-a****, it is actually a masculine noun.*

planning ['plænɪŋ] NOUN
◆ **The trip needs careful planning.** Hay que planear bien el viaje.
◆ **family planning** la planificación familiar

plant [plænt] NOUN
see also **plant** VERB
la planta ◇ *I water my plants every week.* Riego las plantas todas las semanas.
◆ **a chemical plant** una planta química

to **plant** [plænt] VERB
see also **plant** NOUN
plantar ◇ *We planted fruit trees and vegetables.* Plantamos árboles frutales y hortalizas.

plaque [plæk] NOUN
1 la placa conmemorativa (*to famous person, event*)
2 el sarro (*on teeth*)

plaster cast ['plæstər'kæst] NOUN
el yeso
◆ **Her leg's in a plaster cast.** Tiene la pierna enyesada.

plastic ['plæstɪk] NOUN
see also **plastic** ADJECTIVE
el plástico ◇ *It's made of plastic.* Es de plástico.

plastic ['plæstɪk] ADJECTIVE
see also **plastic** NOUN
de plástico ◇ *a plastic bowl* un tazón de plástico

plastic bag ['plæstɪk'bæg] NOUN
la bolsa de plástico

plastic wrap ['plæstɪk'ræp] NOUN
el envoltorio de plástico transparente

plate [pleɪt] NOUN
el plato

platform ['plætfɔːrm] NOUN
1 el andén (PL los andenes) (*at train station*)
2 el estrado (*for speaker, performer*)

play [pleɪ] NOUN
see also **play** VERB
la obra de teatro
◆ **a play by Shakespeare** una obra de Shakespeare
◆ **to put on a play** montar una obra

to **play** [pleɪ] VERB
see also **play** NOUN
1 jugar* ◇ *He's playing with his friends.* Está jugando con sus amigos. ◇ *Can you play pool?* ¿Sabes jugar billar?
2 jugar* contra ◇ *Ireland will play Argentina next month.* Irlanda juega contra Argentina el mes que viene.
3 tocar* ◇ *I play the guitar.* Toco la guitarra. ◇ *What sort of music do they play?* ¿Qué clase de música tocan?
4 poner* ◇ *She's always playing that record.* Siempre está poniendo ese disco.
5 hacer* de ◇ *I would love to play Cleopatra.* Me encantaría hacer de Cleopatra.

to **play down** [pleɪ'daun] VERB
quitar importancia a ◇ *He tried to play down his illness.* Trató de quitarle importancia a su enfermedad.

player ['pleɪər] NOUN
1 el jugador
la jugadora
◇ *a game for four players* un juego para cuatro jugadores
◆ **a soccer player** un futbolista
2 el músico
la música
(*musician*)
◆ **a piano player** un pianista
◆ **a saxophone player** un saxofonista

playful ['pleɪfəl] ADJECTIVE
juguetón (FEM juguetona)

playground ['pleɪˌgraund] NOUN
1 el patio de recreo (*at school*)
2 los columpios (*in park*)

playgroup ['pleɪˌgruːp] NOUN
el jardín infantil (PL los jardines infantiles)
el jardín de niños (PL los jardines de niños)
Mexico

playing card ['pleɪɪŋˌkɑːrd] NOUN
el naipe

playing field ['pleɪɪŋ,fi:ld] NOUN
la cancha de deportes

playtime ['pleɪ,taɪm] NOUN
el recreo

playwright ['pleɪraɪt] NOUN
el dramaturgo
la dramaturga

pleasant ['plɛzənt] ADJECTIVE
agradable ◇ *We had a very pleasant evening.* Pasamos una tarde muy agradable.

please [pli:z] EXCLAMATION
por favor ◇ *Two coffees, please.* Dos cafés, por favor.
***por favor** is not as common as **please** and can be omitted in many cases. Spanish speakers may show their politeness by their intonation, or by using **usted**.*
◆ **Can we have the check, please?** ¿Nos puede traer la cuenta?
◆ **Please come in.** Pase.
◆ **Would you please be quiet?** ¿Quieres hacer el favor de callarte?

pleased [pli:zd] ADJECTIVE
◆ **My mother's not going to be very pleased.** A mi madre no le va a hacer mucha gracia.
◆ **It's beautiful. She'll be very pleased with it.** Es precioso. Le va a gustar mucho.
◆ **Pleased to meet you!** ¡Encantado!

pleasure ['plɛʒər] NOUN
el placer ◇ *I read for pleasure.* Leo por placer.

plenty ['plɛnti] PRONOUN
◆ **Fifteen minutes is plenty.** Quince minutos es más que suficiente.
◆ **I have plenty.** Tengo de sobra.
◆ **That's plenty, thanks.** Así está bien, gracias.
◆ **I have plenty to do.** Tengo un montón de cosas que hacer.
◆ **plenty of (1)** (*lots of*) mucho ◇ *He has plenty of energy.* Tiene mucha energía.
◆ **plenty of (2)** (*more than enough*) de sobra ◇ *We have plenty of time.* Tenemos tiempo de sobra.

pliers ['plaɪərz] NOUN
los alicates

plot [plɑ:t] NOUN
see also **plot** VERB
1 el argumento (*of story, play*)
2 el complot (PL los complots) (*conspiracy*) ◇ *a plot against the president* un complot contra el presidente
3 el huerto (*for vegetables*)

to **plot** [plɑ:t] VERB
see also **plot** NOUN
conspirar

plow [plau] NOUN
see also **plow** VERB
el arado

to **plow** [plau] VERB
see also **plow** NOUN
arar

plug [plʌg] NOUN
1 el enchufe (*electrical*)
2 el tapón (PL los tapones) (*for sink*)

to **plug in** [plʌg'ɪn] VERB
enchufar ◇ *Is the iron plugged in?* ¿Está enchufada la plancha?

plum [plʌm] NOUN
la ciruela

plumber ['plʌmər] NOUN
el plomero
la plomera
◇ *She's a plumber.* Es plomera.

plump [plʌmp] ADJECTIVE
rechoncho

to **plunge** [plʌndʒ] VERB
zambullirse* ◇ *He plunged into the water.* Se zambulló en el agua.

plural ['plurəl] NOUN
el plural

plus [plʌs] PREPOSITION, ADJECTIVE
más ◇ *four plus three equals seven* cuatro más tres son siete
◆ **three children plus a dog** tres niños y un perro
◆ **I got a B plus.** Saqué entre A y B.

p.m. [pi:'ɛm] ABBREVIATION
◆ **at 2 p.m.** a las dos de la tarde
◆ **at 9 p.m.** a las nueve de la noche
*Use **de la tarde** if it's light and **de la noche** if it's dark.*

pneumonia [nu'mounjə] NOUN
la pulmonía

to **poach** [poutʃ] VERB
◆ **a poached egg** un huevo escalfado

pocket ['pɑ:kɪt] NOUN
el bolsillo ◇ *He had his hands in his pockets.* Tenía las manos en los bolsillos.

pocket billiards ['pɑ:kɪt'bɪljərdz] PL NOUN
el billar SING

pocketbook ['pɑ:kɪtbuk] NOUN
la cartera
la bolsa *Mexico*

pocket calculator ['pɑ:kɪt'kælkjəleɪtər] NOUN
la calculadora de bolsillo

pocket money ['pɑ:kɪt,mʌni] NOUN
el dinero para gastos personales

podiatrist [pə'daɪətrɪst] NOUN
el pedicuro
la pedicura
◇ *He's a podiatrist.* Es pedicuro.

poem ['pouəm] NOUN
el poema
*Although **poema** ends in **-a**, it is actually a masculine noun.*

poet ['pouɪt] NOUN
el poeta
la poetisa

poetry ['pouɪtri] NOUN
la poesía

point [pɔɪnt] NOUN
see also **point** VERB

P

1 el punto ◇ *a point on the horizon* un punto en el horizonte ◇ *They scored five points.* Sacaron cinco puntos.
2 el momento ◇ *At that point, we decided to leave.* En aquel momento decidimos marcharnos.
3 la punta ◇ *a pencil with a sharp point* un lápiz con la punta afilada
4 el comentario ◇ *He made some interesting points.* Hizo algunos comentarios de interés.
- **They were on the point of finding it.** Estaban a punto de encontrarlo.
- **Sorry, I don't get the point.** Perdona, pero no lo entiendo.
- **a point of view** un punto de vista
- **That's a good point!** ¡Tiene razón!
- **That's not the point.** Eso no tiene nada que ver.
- **There's no point.** No tiene sentido. ◇ *There's no point in waiting.* No tiene sentido esperar.
- **What's the point?** ¿Para qué? ◇ *What's the point of leaving so early?* ¿Para qué salir tan pronto?
- **Punctuality isn't my strong point.** La puntualidad no es mi fuerte.
- **two point five (2.5)** dos coma cinco (2,5)

to **point** [pɔɪnt] VERB
see also **point** NOUN
señalar con el dedo ◇ *Don't point!* ¡No señales con el dedo!
- **to point at somebody** señalar a alguien con el dedo ◇ *She pointed at Anne.* Señaló a Anne con el dedo.
- **to point a gun at somebody** apuntar a alguien con una pistola

to **point out** [pɔɪnt'aut] VERB
1 señalar ◇ *The guide pointed out the White House to us.* El guía nos señaló la Casa Blanca.
2 indicar* ◇ *I should point out that...* Me gustaría indicar que...

pointless ['pɔɪntlɪs] ADJECTIVE
inútil ◇ *It's pointless arguing.* Es inútil discutir.

poison ['pɔɪzən] NOUN
see also **poison** VERB
el veneno

to **poison** ['pɔɪzən] VERB
see also **poison** NOUN
envenenar

poisonous ['pɔɪzənəs] ADJECTIVE
1 venenoso (*animal, plant*)
2 tóxico (*chemical*) ◇ *poisonous gases* gases tóxicos

to **poke** [pouk] VERB
- **He poked me in the eye.** Me metió un dedo en el ojo.

poker ['poukər] NOUN
el póker ◇ *I play poker.* Juego póker.

Poland ['poulənd] NOUN
Polonia FEM

polar bear ['poulər,bɛər] NOUN
el oso polar

Pole [poul] NOUN
el polaco
la polaca
(*person*)

pole [poul] NOUN
el poste ◇ *a telephone pole* un poste de teléfonos
- **a tent pole** un mástil de tienda
- **a ski pole** un bastón de esquí
- **the North Pole** el Polo Norte
- **the South Pole** el Polo Sur

pole beans ['poul,bi:nz] PL NOUN
las habichuelas trepadoras

pole vault ['poul,vɑ:lt] NOUN
- **the pole vault** el salto con garrocha

police [pə'li:s] PL NOUN
la policía ◇ *We called the police.* Llamamos a la policía.

police car [pə'li:s,kɑ:r] NOUN
el carro de policía

policeman [pə'li:smən] NOUN (PL **policemen**)
el policía

police officer [pə'li:s,ɑ:fɪsər] NOUN
el/la policía

police station [pə'li:s,steɪʃən] NOUN
la comisaría

policewoman [pə'li:s,wumən] NOUN (PL **policewomen**)
la mujer policía

polio ['pouliou] NOUN
la polio
*Although **polio** ends in **-o**, it is actually a feminine noun.*

Polish ['poulɪʃ] ADJECTIVE
see also **Polish** NOUN
polaco

Polish ['poulɪʃ] NOUN
see also **Polish** ADJECTIVE
el polaco (*language*)

polish ['pɑ:lɪʃ] NOUN (PL **polishes**)
see also **polish** VERB
1 el betún (*for shoes*)
2 la cera (*for furniture*)

to **polish** ['pɑ:lɪʃ] VERB
see also **polish** NOUN
limpiar (*metal, glass*)
- **to polish one's shoes** lustrar los zapatos
- **to polish the furniture** sacar* brillo a los muebles

polite [pə'laɪt] ADJECTIVE
educado ◇ *a polite child* un niño educado
- **It's not polite to point.** Es de mala educación señalar con el dedo.

politeness [pə'laɪtnɪs] NOUN
la cortesía

political [pə'lɪtɪkəl] ADJECTIVE

político

politician [pɑːlɪ'tɪʃən] NOUN
el político
la política

politics ['pɑːlɪtɪks] NOUN
la política ◇ *I'm not interested in politics.* No me interesa la política.

poll [poul] NOUN
el sondeo de opinión

pollen ['pɑːlən] NOUN
el polen

to **pollute** [pə'luːt] VERB
contaminar

pollution [pə'luːʃən] NOUN
la contaminación

polo shirt ['poulouˌʃɜːrt] NOUN
el polo

pond [pɑːnd] NOUN
1 la laguna (*natural*)
2 el estanque (*artificial*)

pony ['pouni] NOUN (PL **ponies**)
el poni

ponytail ['pouniˌteɪl] NOUN
la coleta ◇ *He has a ponytail.* Lleva coleta. ◇ *She has her hair in ponytails.* Lleva coletas.

poodle ['puːdl] NOUN
el perro faldero

pool [puːl] NOUN
1 el estanque (*pond*)
2 la piscina
la alberca Mexico
(*swimming pool*)
3 el billar (*game*)
◆ **a pool table** una mesa de billar
◆ **typing pool** el servicio de mecanografía

pooped [puːpt] ADJECTIVE (*informal*)
reventado (*tired*)

poor [puər] ADJECTIVE
1 pobre
***pobre** goes after the noun when it means that someone does not have very much money. It goes before the noun when you want to show that you feel sorry for someone.*
◇ *a poor family* una familia pobre ◇ *Poor David, he's very unlucky!* ¡Pobre David, tiene muy mala suerte!
◆ **the poor** los pobres
2 malo
*Use **mal** before a masculine singular noun.*
◇ *He's a poor actor.* Es un mal actor. ◇ *a poor grade* una mala nota

poorly ['purli] ADJECTIVE
◆ **She's feeling a bit poorly.** No se siente muy bien.

pop [pɑːp] ADJECTIVE
see also **pop** NOUN
pop MASC, FEM, PL ◇ *pop music* la música pop ◇ *a pop star* una estrella pop
◆ **a pop group** un grupo de música pop

pop [pɑːp] NOUN
see also **pop** ADJECTIVE
1 papá MASC (*dad*)
2 el refresco (*carbonated drink*)

to **pop in** [pɑːp'ɪn] VERB
entrar un momento

to **pop out** [pɑːp'aut] VERB
salir* un momento

popcorn ['pɑːpkɔːrn] NOUN
las palomitas de maíz
los esquites Mexico

Pope [poup] NOUN
◆ **the Pope** el Papa
*Although **Papa** ends in **-a**, it is actually a masculine noun.*

poppy ['pɑːpi] NOUN (PL **poppies**)
la amapola

Popsicle ® ['pɑːpsɪkəl] NOUN
la paleta helada

popular ['pɑːpjələr] ADJECTIVE
popular ◇ *Baseball is the most popular game in this country.* El béisbol es el deporte más popular de este país.
◆ **She's a very popular girl.** Es una chica que cae bien a todo el mundo.
◆ **This is a very popular style.** Este estilo está muy de moda.

population [pɑːpjə'leɪʃən] NOUN
la población (PL las poblaciones)

porch [pɔːrtʃ] NOUN (PL **porches**)
el porche

pork [pɔːrk] NOUN
la carne de cerdo
la carne de puerco Mexico
◆ **a pork chop** una chuleta de cerdo, Mexico: una chuleta de puerco

porn [pɔːrn] NOUN
see also **porn** ADJECTIVE
el porno

porn [pɔːrn] ADJECTIVE
see also **porn** NOUN
porno MASC, FEM, PL ◇ *a porn movie* una película porno

pornographic [pɔːrnə'græfɪk] ADJECTIVE
pornográfico ◇ *a pornographic magazine* una revista pornográfica

pornography [pɔːr'nɑːgrəfi] NOUN
la pornografía

porridge ['pɔːrɪdʒ] NOUN
la avena cocida

port [pɔːrt] NOUN
el puerto ◇ *a fishing port* un puerto pesquero

portable ['pɔːrtəbəl] ADJECTIVE
portátil ◇ *a portable TV* un televisor portátil

porter ['pɔːrtər] NOUN
1 el mozo de equipajes
la moza de equipajes
(*at train station, hotel*)
2 el mozo de los coches-cama
la moza de los coches-cama
(*on train*)

P

portion ['pɔːrʃən] NOUN
la porción (PL las porciones) ◇ *a large portion of fries* una porción grande de papas fritas ◇ *a small portion of your salary* una pequeña porción de tu salario

portrait ['pɔːrtrɪt] NOUN
el retrato

Portugal ['pɔːrtʃəgəl] NOUN
Portugal MASC

Portuguese [pɔːrtʃə'giːz] ADJECTIVE
see also **Portuguese** NOUN
portugués (MASC PL portugueses, FEM portuguesa)

Portuguese [pɔːrtʃə'giːz] NOUN
see also **Portuguese** ADJECTIVE
el portugués (*language*)
◆ **the Portuguese** los portugueses

posh [pɑːʃ] ADJECTIVE
elegante ◇ *a posh car* un carro elegante

position [pə'zɪʃən] NOUN
la posición (PL las posiciones) ◇ *an uncomfortable position* una posición incómoda

positive ['pɑːzɪtɪv] ADJECTIVE
1 positivo ◇ *a positive attitude* una actitud positiva
2 seguro (*sure*) ◇ *I'm positive.* Estoy completamente seguro.

to **possess** [pə'zɛs] VERB
poseer* ◇ *She lost everything she possessed.* Perdió todo lo que poseía.

possession [pə'zɛʃən] NOUN
◆ **Do you have all your possessions?** ¿Tienes todas tus pertenencias?

possibility [pɑːsɪ'bɪlɪti] NOUN (PL **possibilities**)
la posibilidad ◇ *There were several possibilities.* Había varias posibilidades.

possible ['pɑːsɪbəl] ADJECTIVE
posible
◆ **as soon as possible** lo antes posible
es posible que *has to be followed by a verb in the subjunctive.*
◆ **It's possible that he's gone away.** Es posible que se haya ido.

possibly ['pɑːsɪbli] ADVERB
tal vez ◇ *Are you coming to the party? – Possibly.* ¿Vas a venir a la fiesta? – Tal vez.
◆ **...if you possibly can.** ...si es que puedes.
◆ **I can't possibly go.** Me es imposible ir.

post [poust] NOUN
el poste ◇ *The ball hit the post.* El pelota dio en el poste.

postage ['poustɪdʒ] NOUN
el franqueo

postcard ['pəust,kɑːrd] NOUN
la postal

poster ['poustər] NOUN
1 el cartel (*public*) ◇ *There are posters all over town.* Hay carteles por toda la ciudad.
2 el póster (PL los pósters) (*personal*) ◇ *I have posters on my bedroom walls.* Tengo pósters en las paredes de mi cuarto.

postmark ['poust,mɑːrk] NOUN
el matasellos (PL los matasellos)

post office ['poust,ɑːfɪs] NOUN
el correo ◇ *Where's the post office, please?* ¿Sabe donde está el correo? ◇ *She works for the post office.* Trabaja en el correo.

to **postpone** [pous'poun] VERB
aplazar* ◇ *The game has been postponed.* El partido ha sido aplazado.

pot [pɑːt] NOUN
1 el tarro ◇ *a pot of jelly* un tarro de mermelada
◆ **a pot of paint** un bote de pintura
2 la tetera (*teapot*)
◆ **a coffee pot** una cafetera
◆ **to smoke pot** fumar maría, *Mexico:* fumar mota (*informal*)
◆ **the pots and pans** las cacerolas, *Mexico:* los trastes

potato [pə'teɪtou] NOUN (PL **potatoes**)
la papa
◆ **mashed potatoes** el puré de papas
◆ **a baked potato** una papa al horno

potato chips [pə'teɪtou,tʃɪpz] PL NOUN
las papas fritas de paquete

potential [pə'tɛnʃəl] NOUN
see also **potential** ADJECTIVE
◆ **He has great potential.** Promete mucho.

potential [pə'tɛnʃəl] ADJECTIVE
see also **potential** NOUN
posible ◇ *a potential problem* un posible problema

pothole ['pɑːt,houl] NOUN
el bache

potted plant ['pɑːtɪd'plænt] NOUN
la planta de interior

pottery ['pɑːtəri] NOUN
la cerámica

pound [paund] NOUN
see also **pound** VERB
1 la libra

> ℹ *In Latin America measurements are in grams and kilograms. One pound is about 450 grams.*

◇ *a pound of carrots* una libra de zanahorias
2 la libra esterlina (*British currency*)

to **pound** [paund] VERB
see also **pound** NOUN
latir con fuerza ◇ *My heart was pounding.* El corazón me latía con fuerza.

to **pour** [pɔːr] VERB
1 echar ◇ *She poured some water into the pan.* Echó un poco de agua en la olla.
2 llover* a cántaros ◇ *It's pouring.* Está lloviendo a cántaros.
◆ **in the pouring rain** bajo una lluvia torrencial

poverty ['pɑːvərti] NOUN
la pobreza
powder ['paudər] NOUN
el polvo
- **a fine white powder** un polvillo blanco

power ['pauər] NOUN
1 la corriente (*electrical*) ◇ *The power is off.* Se fue la corriente.
2 la energía ◇ *nuclear power* la energía nuclear ◇ *solar power* la energía solar
3 el poder ◇ *They were in power for 18 years.* Estuvieron 18 años en el poder.
powerful ['pauərfəl] ADJECTIVE
1 poderoso (*person, organization*) ◇ *the most powerful country in the world* el país más poderoso del mundo
2 potente (*machine, substance*) ◇ *a powerful computer system* un sistema informático potente
power outage ['pauər,autɪdʒ] NOUN
el apagón (PL los apagones)
power station ['pauər,steɪʃən] NOUN
la central eléctrica
practical ['præktɪkəl] ADJECTIVE
práctico ◇ *a practical suggestion* un consejo práctico ◇ *She's very practical.* Es muy práctica.
practically ['præktɪkli] ADVERB
prácticamente ◇ *It's practically impossible.* Es prácticamente imposible.
practice ['præktɪs] NOUN
see also **practice** VERB
1 la práctica ◇ *You'll get better with practice.* Mejorarás con la práctica.
- **in practice** en la práctica
- **It's normal practice in our school.** Es lo normal en nuestro colegio.

2 el entrenamiento ◇ *field hockey practice* entrenamiento de hockey
- **I'm out of practice.** Estoy desentrenado.
- **I have to do my piano practice.** Tengo que hacer los ejercicios de piano.
- **a medical practice** una consulta médica

to **practice** ['præktɪs] VERB
see also **practice** NOUN
1 practicar* ◇ *I ought to practice more.* Debería practicar más. ◇ *I practice the flute every evening.* Practico flauta todas las tardes. ◇ *I practiced my Spanish when we were on vacation.* Practiqué el español cuando estuvimos de vacaciones.
2 entrenarse (*train*) ◇ *The team practices on Thursdays.* El equipo entrena los jueves.
practicing ['præktɪsɪŋ] ADJECTIVE
practicante ◇ *She's a practicing Catholic.* Es católica practicante.
to **praise** [preɪz] VERB
elogiar ◇ *Everyone praises her cooking.* Todo el mundo elogia cómo cocina.
to **pray** [preɪ] VERB
rezar* ◇ *to pray for something* rezar por algo
prayer [prɛər] NOUN
la oración (PL las oraciones)
precaution [prɪ'kɑːʃən] NOUN
la precaución (PL las precauciones)
- **to take precautions** tomar precauciones

preceding [prɪ'siːdɪŋ] ADJECTIVE
anterior
precinct ['priːsɪŋkt] NOUN
- **a police precinct** un distrito policial

precious ['prɛʃəs] ADJECTIVE
precioso ◇ *a precious stone* una piedra preciosa
precise [prɪ'saɪs] ADJECTIVE
preciso ◇ *at that precise moment* en aquel preciso instante
- **to be precise** para ser exacto

precisely [prɪ'saɪsli] ADVERB
precisamente ◇ *That is precisely what it's meant for.* Para eso precisamente está hecho.
- **Precisely!** ¡Exactamente!
- **at 10 a.m. precisely** a las diez en punto de la mañana

to **predict** [prɪ'dɪkt] VERB
predecir*
predictable [prɪ'dɪktəbəl] ADJECTIVE
previsible
to **prefer** [prɪ'fɜːr] VERB
preferir* ◇ *Which would you prefer?* ¿Tú cuál prefieres? ◇ *I prefer chemistry to math.* Prefiero la química a las matemáticas.
preference ['prɛfrəns] NOUN
la preferencia
pregnant ['prɛgnənt] ADJECTIVE
embarazada ◇ *She's six months pregnant.* Está embarazada de seis meses.
prehistoric ['priːhɪs'tɔːrɪk] ADJECTIVE
prehistórico
prejudice ['prɛdʒudɪs] NOUN
el prejuicio ◇ *That's just a prejudice.* Eso no es más que un prejuicio.
- **There's a lot of racial prejudice.** Hay muchos prejuicios raciales.

prejudiced ['prɛdʒudɪst] ADJECTIVE
- **to be prejudiced against somebody** tener* prejuicios contra alguien

premature [priːmə'tuər] ADJECTIVE
prematuro ◇ *a premature baby* un bebé prematuro
premises ['prɛmɪsɪz] PL NOUN
el local ◇ *They're moving to new premises.* Se cambian de local.
premonition [prɛmə'nɪʃən] NOUN
el presentimiento
preoccupied [priː'ɑːkjəpaɪd] ADJECTIVE
preocupado
preparations [prɛpə'reɪʃənz] PL NOUN
los preparativos ◇ *Preparations are being made for the president's visit.* Se están realizando los preparativos para la visita del presidente.

to **prepare** [prɪ'pɛər] VERB
preparar ◇ *He was preparing dinner.* Estaba preparando la cena.
◆ **to prepare for something** hacer* los preparativos para algo ◇ *We're preparing for our vacation.* Estamos haciendo los preparativos para las vacaciones.

prepared [prɪ'pɛərd] ADJECTIVE
◆ **to be prepared to do something** estar* dispuesto a hacer algo ◇ *I'm prepared to help you.* Estoy dispuesto a ayudarte.

prep school ['prɛpˌskuːl] NOUN
el colegio privado (*de enseñanza secundaria*)

Presbyterian [prɛzbɪ'tɪriən] ADJECTIVE
see also **Presbyterian** NOUN
presbiteriano

Presbyterian [prɛzbɪ'tɪriən] NOUN
see also **Presbyterian** ADJECTIVE
el presbiteriano
la presbiteriana

pre-school ['priːskuːl] NOUN
el jardín infantil (PL los jardines infantiles)
el jardín de niños (PL los jardines de niños)
Mexico

to **prescribe** [prɪ'skraɪb] VERB
recetar ◇ *The doctor prescribed a course of antibiotics for me.* El doctor me recetó antibióticos.

prescription [prɪ'skrɪpʃən] NOUN
la receta ◇ *a prescription for penicillin* una receta de penicilina
◆ **by prescription** con receta médica

presence ['prɛzəns] NOUN
la presencia
◆ **presence of mind** presencia de ánimo

present ['prɛzənt] ADJECTIVE
see also **present** NOUN, VERB
1 presente ◇ *He wasn't present at the meeting.* No estuvo presente en la reunión.
2 actual ◇ *the present situation* la situación actual
◆ **the present tense** el presente

present ['prɛzənt] NOUN
see also **present** ADJECTIVE, VERB
1 el regalo
◆ **to give somebody a present** hacer* un regalo a alguien ◇ *He gave me a lovely present.* Me hizo un regalo precioso.
2 el presente ◇ *to live in the present* vivir el presente
◆ **at present** actualmente
◆ **for the present** por el momento
◆ **up to the present** hasta el momento presente

to **present** [prɪ'zɛnt] VERB
see also **present** ADJECTIVE, NOUN
◆ **to present somebody with something** entregar* algo a alguien ◇ *The mayor presented the winner with a medal.* El alcalde le entregó una medalla al vencedor.

presenter [prɪ'zɛntər] NOUN
el presentador
la presentadora
(*on television*)

presently ['prɛzntli] ADVERB
1 enseguida ◇ *You'll feel better presently.* Enseguida te sentirás mejor.
2 actualmente ◇ *They're presently on tour.* Actualmente están de gira.

preserve [prɪ'zɜːrv] NOUN
◆ **strawberry preserve** la mermelada de fresas

president ['prɛzɪdənt] NOUN
el presidente
la presidenta

press [prɛs] NOUN
see also **press** VERB
la prensa ◇ *The story appeared in the press last week.* La historia salió en la prensa la semana pasada.

to **press** [prɛs] VERB
see also **press** NOUN
apretar* ◇ *Don't press too hard!* ¡No aprietes muy fuerte!
◆ **He pressed the accelerator.** Pisó el acelerador.

press conference ['prɛsˌkɑːnfərəns] NOUN
la rueda de prensa

pressed [prɛst] ADJECTIVE
◆ **We are pressed for time.** Andamos mal de tiempo.

pressure ['prɛʃər] NOUN
see also **pressure** VERB
la presión (PL las presiones)
◆ **a pressure group** un grupo de presión
◆ **to be under pressure** estar* presionado ◇ *She was under pressure from the management.* Estaba presionada por la dirección.
◆ **He's been under a lot of pressure recently.** Últimamente ha estado muy agobiado.

to **pressure** ['prɛʃər] VERB
see also **pressure** NOUN
◆ **to pressure somebody to do something** presionar a alguien para que haga algo ◇ *My parents are pressuring me to stay on at school.* Mis padres me están presionando para que siga estudiando.

prestige [prɛs'tiːʒ] NOUN
el prestigio

prestigious [prɛ'stiːdʒəs] ADJECTIVE
prestigioso

presumably [prɪ'zuːməbli] ADVERB
◆ **Presumably, she already knows what's happened.** Supongo que ya sabe lo que ha pasado.

to **presume** [prɪ'zuːm] VERB
suponer* ◇ *I presume so.* Supongo que sí. ◇ *I presume he'll come.* Supongo que vendrá.

to **pretend** [prɪ'tɛnd] VERB

- **to pretend to do something** fingir* hacer algo
- **to pretend to be asleep** hacerse* el dormido

*Be careful not to translate **to pretend** by **pretender**.*

pretty ['prɪti] ADJECTIVE, ADVERB
1 bonito ◇ *She wore a pretty dress.* Llevaba un vestido bonito. ◇ *She's very pretty.* Es muy bonita.
2 bastante ◇ *The movie was pretty bad.* La película era bastante mala.

- **The weather was pretty awful.** Hacía un tiempo horroroso.
- **It's pretty much the same.** Es más o menos lo mismo.

to **prevent** [prɪ'vɛnt] VERB
evitar ◇ *Every effort had been made to prevent the accident.* Se había hecho todo lo posible para evitar el accidente.

***evitar que** has to be followed by a verb in the subjunctive.*

◇ *to prevent something happening* evitar que pase algo ◇ *I want to prevent this happening again.* Quiero evitar que esto se repita.

***impedir a alguien que** has to be followed by a verb in the subjunctive.*

◇ *to prevent somebody from doing something* impedir* a alguien que haga algo ◇ *My only idea was to prevent him from speaking.* Mi única idea era impedirle que hablara.

preview ['pri:vju:] NOUN
el preestreno (*of movie*)

previous ['pri:viəs] ADJECTIVE
anterior ◇ *the previous night* la noche anterior

- **He has no previous experience.** No tiene experiencia previa.

previously ['pri:viəsli] ADVERB
antes

prey [preɪ] NOUN
la presa

- **a bird of prey** un ave rapaz

price [praɪs] NOUN
el precio ◇ *What is the price of this painting?* ¿Qué precio tiene este cuadro?

- **to go up in price** subir de precio
- **to come down in price** bajar de precio

price list ['praɪs,lɪst] NOUN
la lista de precios

to **prick** [prɪk] VERB
pinchar
picar* Mexico
◇ *I've pricked my finger.* Me pinché el dedo.
Mexico: Me piqué el dedo

pride [praɪd] NOUN
el orgullo

priest [pri:st] NOUN
el sacerdote

primary election ['praɪmɛriɪ'lɛkʃən] NOUN
la elección primaria

prime minister ['praɪm'mɪnɪstər] NOUN
el primer ministro
la primera ministra

prime time ['praɪm,taɪm] NOUN
el horario de máxima audiencia (*on television*)

primitive ['prɪmɪtɪv] ADJECTIVE
primitivo

prince [prɪns] NOUN
el príncipe

- **Prince Charming** el príncipe azul

princess ['prɪnsɛs] NOUN (PL **princesses**)
la princesa ◇ *Princess Grace.* La princesa Grace.

principal ['prɪnsɪpəl] ADJECTIVE
see also **principal** NOUN
principal

principal ['prɪnsɪpəl] NOUN
see also **principal** ADJECTIVE
el director
la directora
(*in school*)

principle ['prɪnsɪpəl] NOUN
el principio ◇ *the basic principles of physics* los principios básicos de física

- **in principle** en principio
- **on principle** por principio

print [prɪnt] NOUN
1 la foto

*Although **foto** ends in **-o**, it is actually a feminine noun.*

◇ *color prints* fotos a color
2 la letra ◇ *in small print* en letra pequeña
3 la huella ◇ *The policeman took his prints.* El policía le tomó las huellas.
4 el grabado ◇ *a framed print* un grabado enmarcado

printer ['prɪntər] NOUN
la impresora

printout ['prɪnt,aut] NOUN
la copia impresa

priority [praɪ'ɑ:rɪti] NOUN (PL **priorities**)
la prioridad ◇ *My family takes priority over my work.* Mi familia tiene prioridad sobre mi trabajo.

prison ['prɪzən] NOUN
la cárcel ◇ *to send somebody to prison for five years* condenar a alguien a cinco años de cárcel

- **in prison** en la cárcel

prisoner ['prɪznər] NOUN
1 el preso
la presa
(*in prison*)
2 el prisionero
la prisionera
(*captive*)

- **to take somebody prisoner** hacer* prisionero a alguien

prison guard ['prɪzən,gɑ:rd] NOUN
el carcelero

P

la carcelera

privacy ['praɪvəsi] NOUN
la privacidad

private ['praɪvɪt] ADJECTIVE
see also **private** NOUN
1 privado ◇ *a private school* un colegio privado
◆ **private life** la vida privada
◆ **private property** la propiedad privada
2 particular (*for one person only*) ◇ *private lessons* clases particulares ◇ *She has a private secretary.* Tiene secretaria particular.
◆ **a private bathroom** un baño individual
◆ **in private** en privado

private ['praɪvɪt] NOUN
see also **private** ADJECTIVE
el soldado raso

to **privatize** ['praɪvətaɪz] VERB
privatizar*

privilege ['prɪvəlɪdʒ] NOUN
el privilegio

prize [praɪz] NOUN
el premio ◇ *to win a prize* ganar un premio

prize-giving ['praɪz,gɪvɪŋ] NOUN
la entrega de premios

prizewinner ['praɪz,wɪnər] NOUN
el premiado
la premiada

pro [prou] NOUN (PL **pros**)
◆ **the pros and cons** los pros y los contras
◆ **a golf pro** un jugador de golf profesional

probable ['prɑ:bəbəl] ADJECTIVE
probable

probably ['prɑ:bəbli] ADVERB
probablemente ◇ *He'll probably come tomorrow.* Probablemente vendrá mañana.

problem ['prɑ:bləm] NOUN
el problema
Although **problema** *ends in* **-a**, *it is actually a masculine noun.*
◇ *the drug problem* el problema de la droga
◆ **No problem! (1)** ¡Por supuesto! ◇ *Can you repair it? – No problem!* ¿Lo puedes arreglar? – ¡Por supuesto!
◆ **No problem! (2)** ¡No importa! ◇ *I'm sorry about that – No problem!* Lo siento – ¡No importa!
◆ **What's the problem?** ¿Qué pasa?

proceeds ['prousi:dz] PL NOUN
la recaudación ◇ *All proceeds will go to charity.* Toda la recaudación se destinará a obras benéficas.

process ['prɑ:sɛs] NOUN (PL **processes**)
el proceso ◇ *the peace process* el proceso de paz
◆ **We're in the process of painting the kitchen.** Ahora mismo estamos pintando la cocina.

procession [prə'sɛʃən] NOUN
la procesión (PL las procesiones)

to **produce** [prə'du:s] VERB
1 producir* (*manufacture, create*)
2 poner* en escena (*on stage*)

producer [prə'du:sər] NOUN
1 el productor
la productora
(*of movie, record, TV program*)
2 el director
la directora
(*of play, show*)

product ['prɑ:dʌkt] NOUN
el producto

production [prə'dʌkʃən] NOUN
1 la producción (PL las producciones)
◇ *They're increasing production of luxury models.* Están aumentando la producción de modelos de lujo.
2 el montaje ◇ *a production of "Hamlet"* un montaje de "Hamlet"

profession [prə'fɛʃən] NOUN
la profesión (PL las profesiones)

professional [prə'fɛʃənl] NOUN
see also **professional** ADJECTIVE
el/la profesional

professional [prə'fɛʃənl] ADJECTIVE
see also **professional** NOUN
profesional ◇ *a professional musician* un músico profesional ◇ *a very professional piece of work* un trabajo muy profesional

professionally [prə'fɛʃnəli] ADVERB
◆ **She sings professionally.** Es cantante profesional.

professor [prə'fɛsər] NOUN
el catedrático
la catedrática

profit ['prɑ:fɪt] NOUN
los beneficios ◇ *to make a profit* sacar* beneficios ◇ *a profit of $10,000* unos beneficios de 10.000 dólares

profitable ['prɑ:fɪtəbəl] ADJECTIVE
rentable

program ['prougræm] NOUN
see also **program** VERB
el programa
Although **programa** *ends in* **-a**, *it is actually a masculine noun.*
◇ *a computer program* un programa informático ◇ *a TV program* un programa de televisión

to **program** ['prougræm] VERB
see also **program** NOUN
programar

programmer ['prougræmər] NOUN
el programador
la programadora
◇ *She's a programmer.* Es programadora.

programming ['prougræmɪŋ] NOUN
la programación

progress ['prɑ:grɛs] NOUN
el progreso ◇ *You're making progress!* ¡Estás haciendo progresos!

to **prohibit** [prou'hɪbɪt] VERB
prohibir* ◇ *Smoking is prohibited.* Está prohibido fumar.

project ['prɑːdʒɛkt] NOUN
1 el proyecto ◇ *an international project* un proyecto internacional
2 el trabajo (*research*) ◇ *I'm doing a project on the greenhouse effect.* Estoy haciendo un trabajo sobre el efecto invernadero.

projector [prə'dʒɛktər] NOUN
el proyector

prom [prɑːm] NOUN

> *En los Estados Unidos un* **prom** *es un baile de gala que se celebra para los alumnos de un centro de educación secundaria. De todos estos bailes el más famoso es el* **senior prom** *al que los alumnos acuden normalmente con su pareja y visten de etiqueta.*

promenade [prɑːmə'neɪd] NOUN
el paseo marítimo
la rambla Mexico

promise ['prɑːmɪs] NOUN
see also **promise** VERB
la promesa ◇ *He made me a promise.* Me hizo una promesa.
- **That's a promise!** ¡Lo prometo!

to **promise** ['prɑːmɪs] VERB
see also **promise** NOUN
prometer ◇ *He didn't do what he promised.* No hizo lo que prometió.
- **She promised to write.** Prometió que escribiría.
- **I'll write, I promise!** ¡Escribiré, lo prometo!

promising ['prɑːmɪsɪŋ] ADJECTIVE
prometedor (FEM prometedora) ◇ *a promising tennis player* un tenista prometedor

to **promote** [prə'mout] VERB
ascender* (*employee, team*) ◇ *She was promoted six months later.* La ascendieron seis meses después.

promotion [prə'mouʃən] NOUN
el ascenso

prompt [prɑːmpt] ADJECTIVE, ADVERB
1 rápido ◇ *a prompt reply* una rápida respuesta
2 puntual ◇ *He's always very prompt.* Siempre es muy puntual.
- **at eight o'clock prompt** a las ocho en punto

promptly ['prɑːmptli] ADVERB
1 puntualmente (*on time*) ◇ *We left promptly at seven.* Nos fuimos puntualmente a las siete.
2 enseguida (*immediately*) ◇ *He sat down and promptly fell asleep.* Se sentó y se quedó dormido enseguida.

pronoun ['prounaun] NOUN
el pronombre

to **pronounce** [prə'nauns] VERB
pronunciar ◇ *How do you pronounce that word?* ¿Cómo se pronuncia esa palabra?

pronunciation [prənʌnsi'eɪʃən] NOUN
la pronunciación (PL las pronunciaciones)

proof [pruːf] NOUN
la prueba
- **I have proof that he did it.** Tengo pruebas de que lo hizo.

proper ['prɑːpər] ADJECTIVE
1 de verdad (*genuine*) ◇ *It's difficult to get a proper job.* Es difícil conseguir un trabajo de verdad.
2 adecuado (*suitable*) ◇ *You have to have the proper equipment.* Tienes que tener el equipo adecuado.
- **If you had come at the proper time...** Si hubieras llegado a tu hora...

properly ['prɑːpərli] ADVERB
correctamente ◇ *You're not doing it properly.* No lo estás haciendo correctamente. ◇ *Dress properly for your interview.* Vaya correctamente vestido a la entrevista.

property ['prɑːpərti] NOUN
la propiedad
- **"private property"** "propiedad privada"
- **stolen property** objetos robados

proportional [prə'pɔːrʃənl] ADJECTIVE
proporcional ◇ *proportional representation* la representación proporcional

proposal [prə'pouzəl] NOUN
la propuesta

to **propose** [prə'pouz] VERB
proponer* ◇ *I propose a new plan.* Propongo un cambio de planes. ◇ *What do you propose to do?* ¿Qué te propones hacer?
***proponer que** has to be followed by a verb in the subjunctive.*
◇ *He proposed that we stay at home.* Propuso que nos quedáramos en casa.
- **to propose to somebody** (*for marriage*) declararse a alguien

to **prosecute** ['prɑːsɪkjuːt] VERB
- **They were prosecuted for murder.** Los procesaron por asesinato.

prospect ['prɑːspɛkt] NOUN
la perspectiva ◇ *His future prospects are good.* Tiene buenas perspectivas de futuro.

prospectus [prə'spɛktəs] (PL **prospectuses**) NOUN
el prospecto

prostitute ['prɑːstɪtuːt] NOUN
la prostituta
- **a male prostitute** un prostituto

to **protect** [prə'tɛkt] VERB
proteger*

protection [prə'tɛkʃən] NOUN
la protección

protein ['proutiːn] NOUN
la proteína

P

protest ['proutɛst] NOUN
see also **protest** VERB
la protesta ◇ *He ignored their protests.* Ignoró sus protestas.
◆ **a protest march** una manifestación de protesta

to **protest** [prə'tɛst] VERB
see also **protest** NOUN
protestar

Protestant ['prɑːtɪstənt] NOUN
see also **Protestant** ADJECTIVE
el/la protestante ◇ *I'm a Protestant.* Soy protestante.

Protestant ['prɑːtɪstənt] ADJECTIVE
see also **Protestant** NOUN
protestante

protester ['proutɛstər] NOUN
el/la manifestante

proud [praud] ADJECTIVE
orgulloso ◇ *Her parents are proud of her.* Sus padres están orgullosos de ella.

to **prove** [pruːv] VERB
probar* ◇ *The police couldn't prove it.* La policía no pudo probarlo.

proverb ['prɑːvərb] NOUN
el proverbio ◇ *a Chinese proverb* un proverbio chino

to **provide** [prə'vaɪd] VERB
proporcionar
◆ **to provide somebody with something** proporcionar algo a alguien ◇ *They provided us with maps.* Nos proporcionaron mapas.

to **provide for** [prə'vaɪd,fɔːr] VERB
mantener* ◇ *He can't provide for his family any more.* Ya no puede mantener a su familia.

provided [prə'vaɪdɪd] CONJUNCTION
siempre que
***siempre que** has to be followed by a verb in the subjunctive.*
◇ *He'll play in the next match provided he's fit.* Jugará el próximo partido siempre que esté en condiciones.

prowler ['praulər] NOUN
el merodeador
la merodeadora

prune [pruːn] NOUN
la ciruela seca

to **pry** [praɪ] VERB
inmiscuirse* ◇ *He's always prying into other people's affairs.* Siempre está inmiscuyéndose en asuntos ajenos.

pseudonym ['suːdnɪm] NOUN
el seudónimo

psychiatrist [saɪ'kaɪətrɪst] NOUN
el/la psiquiatra

psychoanalyst [,saɪkou'ænəlɪst] NOUN
el/la psicoanalista

psychological [saɪkə'lɑːdʒɪkəl] ADJECTIVE
psicológico

psychologist [saɪ'kɑːlədʒɪst] NOUN
el psicólogo
la psicóloga

psychology [saɪ'kɑːlədʒi] NOUN
la psicología

PTA [,piːtiː'eɪ] ABBREVIATION (= *Parent-Teacher Association*)
la Asociación de Padres y Profesores

PTO [,piːtiː'ou] ABBREVIATION (= *please turn over*)
sigue

public ['pʌblɪk] NOUN
see also **public** ADJECTIVE
◆ **the public** el público ◇ *open to the public* abierto al público
◆ **in public** en público

public ['pʌblɪk] ADJECTIVE
see also **public** NOUN
público
◆ **a public holiday** un día feriado
◆ **public opinion** la opinión pública
◆ **the public address system** la megafonía
◆ **to be in the public eye** ser* un personaje público

public defender ['pʌblɪkdɪ'fɛndər] NOUN
el defensor de oficio
la defensora de oficio

publicity [pʌb'lɪsɪti] NOUN
la publicidad

public school ['pʌblɪk,skuːl] NOUN
el colegio público

public transportation ['pʌblɪktrænspər'teɪʃən] NOUN
el transporte público

to **publish** ['pʌblɪʃ] VERB
publicar*

publisher ['pʌblɪʃər] NOUN
1 el editor
la editora
(*person*)
2 la editorial (*company*)

pudding ['pudɪŋ] NOUN
el pudín
◆ **chocolate pudding** el pudín de chocolate

puddle ['pʌdl] NOUN
el charco

puff pastry ['pʌf,peɪstri] NOUN
el hojaldre

to **pull** [pul] VERB
1 tirar (*to make something move*) ◇ *Pull as hard as you can.* Tira con todas tus fuerzas.
2 tirar de (*to tug at something*) ◇ *She pulled my hair.* Me tiró del pelo.
◆ **He pulled the trigger.** Apretó el gatillo.
◆ **I pulled a muscle when I was training.** Me desgarré un músculo mientras entrenaba.
◆ **You're pulling my leg!** ¡Me estás tomando el pelo!
◆ **Pull yourself together!** ¡Tranquilízate!

to **pull down** [pul'daun] VERB

echar abajo ◇ *The old school was pulled down last year.* El año pasado echaron abajo la vieja escuela.

to **pull out** [pul'aut] VERB
1 sacar* (*remove*) ◇ *to pull a tooth out* sacar* una muela
2 hacerse* a un lado (*car*) ◇ *The car pulled out to pass.* El carro se hizo a un lado para que adelantara.
3 retirarse (*from competition*) ◇ *She pulled out of the tournament.* Se retiró del torneo.

to **pull through** [pul'θruː] VERB
recuperarse ◇ *They think he'll pull through.* Creen que se recuperará.

to **pull up** [pul'ʌp] VERB
parar (*car*) ◇ *A black car pulled up beside me.* Un carro negro paró a mi lado.

pull-off ['pulɑːf] NOUN
el área de descanso

*Although it's a feminine noun, remember that you use **el** and **un** with **área**.*

pullover ['pulˌouvər] NOUN
el suéter

pulse [pʌls] NOUN
el pulso ◇ *The nurse took his pulse.* La enfermera le tomó el pulso.

pulses ['pʌlsəz] PL NOUN
las legumbres

pump [pʌmp] NOUN
see also **pump** VERB
1 la bomba ◇ *a bicycle pump* una bomba de bicicleta
- **a gas pump** un surtidor de gasolina

2 el escarpín (*zapato*)

to **pump** [pʌmp] VERB
see also **pump** NOUN
bombear
- **to pump up a tire** inflar una rueda

pumpkin ['pʌmpkɪn] NOUN
la calabaza

punch [pʌntʃ] NOUN (PL **punches**)
see also **punch** VERB
1 el puñetazo (*blow*)
2 el ponche (*drink*)

to **punch** [pʌntʃ] VERB
see also **punch** NOUN
dar* un puñetazo a ◇ *He punched me!* ¡Me dio un puñetazo!

punctual ['pʌŋktʃuəl] ADJECTIVE
puntual

punctuation [pʌŋktʃu'eɪʃən] NOUN
la puntuación

puncture ['pʌŋktʃər] NOUN
el pinchazo
la ponchadura *Mexico*

to **punish** ['pʌnɪʃ] VERB
castigar* ◇ *They were severely punished for their disobedience.* Les castigaron severamente por su desobediencia.
- **to punish somebody for doing something** castigar a alguien por hacer algo

punishment ['pʌnɪʃmənt] NOUN
el castigo

punk [pʌŋk] NOUN
el/la punki
- **a punk rock band** un grupo punk

pupil ['pjuːpəl] NOUN
el alumno
la alumna

puppet ['pʌpɪt] NOUN
el títere

puppy ['pʌpi] NOUN (PL **puppies**)
el cachorro

to **purchase** ['pɜːrtʃɪs] VERB
adquirir*

pure [pjuər] ADJECTIVE
puro ◇ *He's doing pure math.* Estudia matemáticas puras.

purple ['pɜːrpəl] ADJECTIVE
morado

purpose ['pɜːrpəs] NOUN
el objetivo ◇ *What is the purpose of these changes?* ¿Cuál es el objetivo de estos cambios?
- **his purpose in life** su meta en la vida
- **It's being used for military purposes.** Se está usando con fines militares.
- **on purpose** a propósito ◇ *He did it on purpose.* Lo hizo a propósito.

to **purr** [pɜːr] VERB
ronronear

purse [pɜːrs] NOUN
la cartera
la bolsa *Mexico*
(*handbag*)

pursuit [pər'suːt] NOUN
la actividad ◇ *outdoor pursuits* actividades al aire libre

push [puʃ] NOUN (PL **pushes**)
see also **push** VERB
el empujón (PL los empujones)
- **to give somebody a push** dar* un empujón a alguien

to **push** [puʃ] VERB
see also **push** NOUN
empujar ◇ *Don't push!* ¡No empujes!
- **to push a button** pulsar un botón
- **to push drugs** pasar droga
- **I'm pushed for time today.** Hoy ando muy mal de tiempo.
- **Push off!** ¡Lárgate! (*informal*)
- **Don't push your luck!** ¡No tientes a la suerte!

to **push around** [ˌpuʃə'raund] VERB
dar* órdenes a ◇ *He likes pushing people around.* Le gusta dar órdenes a la gente.

to **push on** [puʃɑːn] VERB
seguir* ◇ *There's a lot to do, so I have to push on now.* Hay mucho que hacer, así que ahora tengo que seguir.

to **push through** [puʃθruː] VERB
- **I pushed my way through.** Me abrí camino a empujones.

P

pusher ['puʃər] NOUN
el camello (*of drugs*)

push-up ['puʃ,ʌp] NOUN
◆ **to do push-ups** hacer* flexiones

to **put** [put] VERB (**put, put**)
poner* ◇ *Where shall I put my things?* ¿Dónde pongo mis cosas? ◇ *Don't forget to put your name on the paper.* No te olvides de poner tu nombre en la hoja.
◆ **She's putting the baby to bed.** Está acostando al niño.

to **put across** [,putə'krɑ:s] VERB
comunicar* ◇ *He finds it hard to put his ideas across.* Le cuesta comunicar sus ideas.

to **put aside** [,putə'saɪd] VERB
apartar ◇ *Can you put this aside for me till tomorrow?* ¿Me lo puede apartar hasta mañana?

to **put away** [,putə'weɪ] VERB
1 guardar ◇ *Can you put the dishes away, please?* ¿Puedes guardar los platos?
2 encerrar* (*in prison*) ◇ *I hope they put him away for a long time.* Espero que lo encierren por muchos años.

to **put back** [put'bæk] VERB
1 poner* en su sitio (*in place*) ◇ *Put it back when you've finished with it.* Ponlo en su sitio cuando hayas terminado.
2 aplazar* (*postpone*) ◇ *The meeting has been put back till two o'clock.* La reunión ha sido aplazada hasta las dos.

to **put down** [put'daun] VERB
1 soltar* ◇ *I'll put these bags down for a minute.* Voy a soltar estas bolsas un momento.
2 apuntar (*note*) ◇ *I've put down a few ideas.* He apuntado algunas ideas.
◆ **to have an animal put down** sacrificar* a un animal ◇ *We had to have our dog put down.* Tuvimos que sacrificar a nuestro perro.
◆ **to put the phone down** colgar*

to **put forward** [put'fɔ:rwərd] VERB
adelantar (*clock*)

to **put in** [put'ɪn] VERB
poner* (*install*) ◇ *We're going to get central heating put in.* Vamos a poner calefacción central.
◆ **He has put in a lot of work on this project.** Ha dedicado mucho trabajo a este proyecto.
◆ **I've put in for a new job.** He solicitado otro empleo.

to **put off** [put'ɑ:f] VERB
1 aplazar* (*delay*) ◇ *I keep putting it off.* No hago más que aplazarlo.
2 distraer* (*distract*) ◇ *Stop putting me off!* ¡Deja ya de distraerme!
3 desanimar (*discourage*) ◇ *He's not easily put off.* No es de los que se desaniman fácilmente.

to **put on** [put'ɑ:n] VERB
1 ponerse* (*clothes, lipstick*) ◇ *I put my coat on.* Me puse el abrigo.
2 poner* (*tape, record*) ◇ *Put on some music.* Pon algo de música.
3 prender* (*light, TV*) ◇ *Shall I put the heater on?* ¿Prendo el calentador?
4 representar (*play, show*) ◇ *We're putting on "Bugsy Malone".* Estamos representando "Bugsy Malone".
◆ **I'll put the rice on.** Voy a poner a cocer el arroz.
◆ **to put on weight** engordar ◇ *He has put on a lot of weight.* Ha engordado mucho.
◆ **She's not ill; she's just putting you on.** No está enferma: es puro teatro.

to **put out** [put'aut] VERB
apagar* (*light*) ◇ *Will you please put out the lights when you leave?* ¿Podrías apagar la luz al salir? ◇ *It took them five hours to put out the fire.* Tardaron cinco horas en apagar el incendio.
◆ **He's a bit put out that nobody came.** Le sentó mal que no viniera nadie.

to **put through** [put'θru:] VERB
comunicar* ◇ *Can you put me through to the manager?* ¿Me comunica con el director? ◇ *I'm putting you through.* Lo comunico.

to **put up** [put'ʌp] VERB
1 colgar* (*on wall*) ◇ *The poster's great. I'll put it up on my wall.* El póster es genial. Lo colgaré en la pared.
2 montar ◇ *We put up our tent in a field.* Montamos la tienda en un prado.
3 subir ◇ *They've put up the price.* Subieron el precio.
◆ **My friend will put me up for the night.** Me quedaré a dormir en la casa de mi amigo.
◆ **to put one's hand up** levantar la mano ◇ *If you have any questions, put your hand up.* Quien tenga alguna pregunta que levante la mano.
◆ **to put up with something** aguantar algo ◇ *I'm not going to put up with it any longer.* No pienso aguantarlo más.
◆ **to put something up for sale** poner* algo en venta ◇ *They're going to put their house up for sale.* Van a poner la casa en venta.

puzzle ['pʌzəl] NOUN
el rompecabezas (PL los rompecabezas)

puzzled ['pʌzəld] ADJECTIVE
perplejo ◇ *You look puzzled!* ¡Te has quedado perplejo!

puzzling ['pʌzlɪŋ] ADJECTIVE
desconcertante

pyramid ['pɪrəmɪd] NOUN
la pirámide

Pyrenees [pɪrə'ni:z] PL NOUN
◆ **the Pyrenees** los Pirineos

Q

quaint [kweɪnt] ADJECTIVE
pintoresco (*house, village*)

qualification [kwɑːlɪfɪˈkeɪʃən] NOUN
el título ◇ *He left school without any qualifications.* Dejó la escuela sin obtener ningún título.
◆ **She has all the qualifications for the job.** Reúne todos los requisitos para el puesto.

qualified [ˈkwɑːlɪfaɪd] ADJECTIVE
1 calificado ◇ *a qualified ski instructor* un instructor de esquí calificado
2 titulado ◇ *a qualified teacher* un profesor titulado
◆ **She was well qualified for the position.** Estaba suficientemente capacitada para el puesto.

to **qualify** [ˈkwɑːlɪfaɪ] VERB (**qualified, qualified**)
1 titularse ◇ *She qualified as a teacher last year.* Se tituló de profesora el año pasado.
2 clasificarse* ◇ *Our team didn't qualify for the finals.* Nuestro equipo no se clasificó para la final.

quality [ˈkwɑːlɪti] NOUN (PL **qualities**)
1 la calidad ◇ *a good quality of life* una buena calidad de vida ◇ *high-quality paper* el papel de calidad
2 la cualidad ◇ *She has lots of good qualities.* Tiene un montón de buenas cualidades.

quantity [ˈkwɑːntɪti] NOUN (PL **quantities**)
la cantidad

quarantine [ˈkwɔːrntiːn] NOUN
la cuarentena ◇ *in quarantine* en cuarentena

quarrel [ˈkwɔːrəl] NOUN
see also **quarrel** VERB
la pelea (*discusión*)
◆ **We had a quarrel.** Nos peleamos.

to **quarrel** [ˈkwɔːrəl] VERB
see also **quarrel** NOUN
pelearse (*discutir*)

quarry [ˈkwɔːri] NOUN (PL **quarries**)
la cantera (*for stone*)

quarter [ˈkwɔːrtər] NOUN
1 el cuarto
◆ **three quarters** tres cuartos
◆ **a quarter of an hour** un cuarto de hora
◆ **a quarter after ten** las diez y cuarto
◆ **a quarter to eleven** un cuarto para las once
2 la moneda de cuarto de dólar (*25 cents*)

quarterfinals [ˈkwɔːrtərˈfaɪnəlz] PL NOUN
los cuartos de final

quartet [kwɔːrˈtɛt] NOUN
el cuarteto ◇ *a string quartet* un cuarteto de cuerda

quay [kiː] NOUN
el muelle (*embarcadero*)

queasy [ˈkwiːzi] ADJECTIVE
◆ **I feel queasy.** Tengo náuseas.

queen [kwiːn] NOUN
1 la reina ◇ *Queen Elizabeth* la reina Isabel
2 la dama ◇ *the queen of hearts* la dama de corazones

query [ˈkwɪri] NOUN (PL **queries**)
see also **query** VERB
la pregunta

to **query** [ˈkwɪri] VERB
see also **query** NOUN
poner* en duda ◇ *No one queried my decision.* Nadie puso en duda mi decisión.

question [ˈkwɛstʃən] NOUN
see also **question** VERB
1 la pregunta ◇ *Can I ask a question?* ¿Puedo hacer una pregunta?
2 la cuestión (PL las cuestiones) ◇ *That's a difficult question.* Ésa es una cuestión complicada. ◇ *It's just a question of...* Tan sólo es cuestión de...
◆ **It's out of the question.** Es imposible.

to **question** [ˈkwɛstʃən] VERB
see also **question** NOUN
interrogar* ◇ *He was questioned by the police.* Lo interrogó la policía.
◆ **They questioned the bill.** Pidieron explicaciones sobre la factura.

question mark [ˈkwɛstʃən,mɑːrk] NOUN
el signo de interrogación

questionnaire [kwɛstʃəˈnɛər] NOUN
el cuestionario

quiche [kiːʃ] NOUN
el quiche

quick [kwɪk] ADJECTIVE, ADVERB
rápido ◇ *a quick lunch* un almuerzo rápido ◇ *It's quicker by train.* Se va más rápido en tren.
◆ **She's a quick learner.** Aprende rápido.
◆ **Quick, call the police!** ¡Rápido, llama a la policía!
◆ **Be quick!** ¡Date prisa!

quickly [ˈkwɪkli] ADVERB
rápidamente ◇ *It was all over very quickly.* Se acabó todo muy rápidamente.

quiet [ˈkwaɪət] ADJECTIVE
1 callado ◇ *You're very quiet today.* Estás muy callado hoy. ◇ *She's a very quiet girl.* Es una chica muy callada.
2 silencioso ◇ *The engine is very quiet.* El motor es muy silencioso.
3 tranquilo ◇ *a quiet little town* un pueblecito tranquilo ◇ *a quiet weekend* un fin de semana tranquilo
◆ **Be quiet!** ¡Cállate!
◆ **Quiet!** ¡Silencio!

quietly [ˈkwaɪətli] ADVERB
1 en voz baja ◇ *"She's dead," he said quietly.* "Está muerta," dijo en voz baja.
2 sin hacer ruido ◇ *He quietly opened the door.* Abrió la puerta sin hacer ruido.

quilt [kwɪlt] NOUN

☞

el edredón (PL los edredones)

to **quit** [kwɪt] VERB

1 dejar ◇ *I quit my job last week.* Dejé mi trabajo la semana pasada.

◆ **to quit doing something** dejar de hacer algo ◇ *I quit smoking.* Dejé de fumar.

◆ **Quit stalling!** ¡déjate de rodeos! (*informal*)

2 irse* ◇ *I've decided to quit this city.* He decido irme de esta ciudad.

quite [kwaɪt] ADVERB

1 bastante ◇ *It's quite warm today.* Hoy hace bastante calor. ◇ *It's quite a long way.* Está bastante lejos. ◇ *I quite liked the movie, but it was too long.* La película me gustó bastante, pero fue demasiado larga.

◆ **How was the movie? – Quite good.** ¿Qué tal la película? – No está mal.

2 totalmente ◇ *It's quite different.* Es totalmente distinto. ◇ *I quite agree with you.* Estoy totalmente de acuerdo contigo.

◆ **It's quite clear that this plan won't work.** Está clarísimo que este plan no va a funcionar.

◆ **not quite...** no del todo... ◇ *I'm not quite sure.* No estoy del todo seguro.

◆ **It's not quite the same.** No es exactamente lo mismo.

◆ **quite a...** todo un ◇ *It was quite a shock.* Fue todo un susto. ◇ *That's quite an experience.* Eso es toda una experiencia.

◆ **quite a lot** bastante ◇ *I've been there quite a lot.* He estado allí bastante. ◇ *quite a lot of money* bastante dinero ◇ *It costs quite a lot to go abroad.* Es bastante caro ir al extranjero.

◆ **There were quite a few people there.** Había bastante gente allí.

quiz [kwɪz] NOUN (PL **quizzes**)

el concurso (*de preguntas*) ◇ *a quiz show* un programa concurso

quota [ˈkwoutə] NOUN

el cupo

quotation [kwouˈteɪʃən] NOUN

la cita ◇ *a quotation from Shakespeare* una cita de Shakespeare

quotation marks [kwouˈteɪʃən,mɑːrks] PL NOUN

las comillas

quote [kwout] NOUN

see also **quote** VERB

1 la cita ◇ *a Shakespeare quote* una cita de Shakespeare

2 el presupuesto ◇ *Can you give me a quote for the work?* ¿Puede darme un presupuesto por el trabajo?

◆ **quotes** las comillas ◇ *in quotes* entre comillas

to **quote** [kwout] VERB

see also **quote** NOUN

citar

R

rabbi ['ræbaɪ] NOUN
el rabino
la rabina
rabbit ['ræbɪt] NOUN
el conejo
◆ **rabbit hutch** la conejera
rabies ['reɪbiːz] NOUN
la rabia
◆ **a dog with rabies** un perro rabioso
race [reɪs] NOUN
see also **race** VERB
[1] la carrera
◆ **a bicycle race** una carrera ciclista
[2] la raza
◆ **race relations** las relaciones interraciales
◆ **the human race** el género humano
to **race** [reɪs] VERB
see also **race** NOUN
[1] correr ◇ *We raced to get there on time.* Corrimos para llegar allí a tiempo.
[2] echarle una carrera a ◇ *I'll race you!* ¡Te echo una carrera!
race car ['reɪsˌkɑːr] NOUN
el carro de carreras
race car driver ['reɪsˌkɑːrˌdraɪvər] NOUN
el/la piloto de carreras
racehorse ['reɪsˌhɔːrs] NOUN
el caballo de carreras
racetrack ['reɪsˌtræk] NOUN
[1] el circuito (*for cars*)
[2] el velódromo (*for bicycles*)
[3] el hipódromo (*for horses*)
racial ['reɪʃəl] ADJECTIVE
racial ◇ *racial discrimination* la discriminación racial
racism ['reɪsɪzəm] NOUN
el racismo
racist ['reɪsɪst] ADJECTIVE
see also **racist** NOUN
racista
racist ['reɪsɪst] NOUN
see also **racist** ADJECTIVE
el/la racista ◇ *He's a racist.* Es racista.
rack [ræk] NOUN
el portaequipajes (PL los portaequipajes) (*for luggage*)
racket ['rækɪt] NOUN
[1] la raqueta (*for sport*) ◇ *my tennis racket* mi raqueta de tenis
[2] el jaleo (*informal: noise*) ◇ *They're making a terrible racket.* Están armando muchísimo jaleo.
racquet ['rækɪt] NOUN
la raqueta
radar ['reɪdɑːr] NOUN
el radar
radiation [reɪdɪ'eɪʃən] NOUN
la radiación
radiator ['reɪdɪeɪtər] NOUN
el radiador
radio ['reɪdiou] NOUN (PL **radios**)
el radio
◆ **on the radio** por el radio
◆ **a radio station** una estación de radio
radioactive ['reɪdiou'æktɪv] ADJECTIVE
radiactivo
radio cassette ['reɪdioukə'sɛt] NOUN
el radiocasete
radio-controlled ['reɪdioukən'trould] ADJECTIVE
teledirigido
radish ['rædɪʃ] NOUN (PL **radishes**)
el rábano
raffle ['ræfəl] NOUN
la rifa ◇ *a raffle ticket* una papeleta de rifa
raft [ræft] NOUN
la balsa
rag [ræg] NOUN
el trapo ◇ *a piece of rag* un trapo
◆ **dressed in rags** cubierto de harapos
rage [reɪdʒ] NOUN
rabia ◇ *mad with rage* loco de rabia
◆ **to be in a rage** estar* furioso
◆ **It's all the rage.** Es el último grito.
raid [reɪd] NOUN
see also **raid** VERB
la redada ◇ *a police raid* una redada policial
to **raid** [reɪd] VERB
see also **raid** NOUN
hacer* una redada en ◇ *The police raided a club in SoHo.* La policía hizo una redada en un club del SoHo.
rail [reɪl] NOUN
[1] la barandilla (*on stairs, bridge, balcony*)
[2] el riel (*for curtains*)
◆ **by rail** por ferrocarril
railroad ['reɪlˌroud] NOUN
el ferrocarril
◆ **railroad crossing** el paso a nivel, *Mexico:* el crucero
◆ **railroad line** la línea ferroviaria
◆ **railroad station** la estación de ferrocarril
rain [reɪn] NOUN
see also **rain** VERB
la lluvia ◇ *in the rain* bajo la lluvia ◇ *It looks like rain.* Parece que va a llover.
to **rain** [reɪn] VERB
see also **rain** NOUN
llover* ◇ *It rains a lot here.* Aquí llueve mucho. ◇ *It's raining.* Está lloviendo.
rainbow ['reɪnbou] NOUN
el arco iris (PL los arco iris)
raincoat ['reɪnkout] NOUN
el impermeable
rainfall ['reɪnˌfɑːl] NOUN
las precipitaciones
rainforest ['reɪnˌfɔːrɪst] NOUN
la selva tropical

rainy ['reɪni] ADJECTIVE
lluvioso

raise [reɪz] NOUN
see also **raise** VERB
el aumento (*in salary*)

to **raise** [reɪz] VERB
see also **raise** NOUN
1 levantar ◊ *He raised his hand.* Levantó la mano.
2 mejorar ◊ *They want to raise standards in schools.* Quieren mejorar el nivel escolar.
3 aumentar ◊ *to raise interest rates* aumentar las tasas de interés
◆ **to raise money** recaudar fondos ◊ *The school is raising money for a new gym.* El colegio está recaudando fondos para un gimnasio nuevo.

raisin ['reɪzɪn] NOUN
la pasa

rake [reɪk] NOUN
el rastrillo

rally ['ræli] NOUN (PL **rallies**)
1 la concentración (PL las concentraciones) (*of people*) ◊ *There was a rally in Washington Square.* Hubo una concentración en Washington Square.
2 el rally (PL los rallys) (*sport*) ◊ *a rally driver* un piloto de rally
3 el peloteo (*in tennis*)

to **ram** [ræm] VERB
embestir* contra ◊ *The thieves rammed a police car.* Los ladrones embistieron contra un carro de la policía.

Ramadan NOUN
el Ramadán

ramble ['ræmbəl] NOUN
◆ **to go for a ramble** dar* un paseo

rambler ['ræmblər] NOUN
el/la excursionista

ramp [ræmp] NOUN
la rampa

ran [ræn] VERB *see* **run**

ranch [ræntʃ] NOUN (PL **ranches**)
el rancho

random ['rændəm] ADJECTIVE
◆ **a random selection** una selección hecha al azar
◆ **at random** al azar ◊ *We picked the number at random.* Elegimos el número al azar.

rang [ræŋ] VERB *see* **ring**

range [reɪndʒ] NOUN
see also **range** VERB
la variedad ◊ *There's a wide range of colors.* Hay una gran variedad de colores.
◆ **It's out of my price range.** Está fuera de mis posibilidades.
◆ **a range of mountains** una cadena montañosa

to **range** [reɪndʒ] VERB
see also **range** NOUN
◆ **to range from...to...** oscilar entre...y... ◊ *Temperatures in summer range from 20 to 35 degrees.* En verano las temperaturas oscilan entre los 20 y los 35 grados.
◆ **Tickets range from $2 to $20.** El precio de las entradas va de 2 a 20 dólares.

rank [ræŋk] NOUN
see also **rank** VERB
la categoría (*status*)

to **rank** [ræŋk] VERB
see also **rank** NOUN
◆ **He's ranked third in the United States.** Está clasificado tercero en Estados Unidos.

ransom ['rænsəm] NOUN
el rescate

rap [ræp] NOUN
el rap

rape [reɪp] NOUN
see also **rape** VERB
la violación (PL las violaciones)

to **rape** [reɪp] VERB
see also **rape** NOUN
violar

rapist ['reɪpɪst] NOUN
el violador

rare [rɛər] ADJECTIVE
1 raro (*unusual*)
2 poco cocido
a la inglesa Mexico
(*steak*)

rash [ræʃ] NOUN (PL **rashes**)
see also **rash** ADJECTIVE
el sarpullido ◊ *I have a rash on my chest.* Tengo un sarpullido en el pecho.

rash [ræʃ] ADJECTIVE
see also **rash** NOUN
precipitado

rasher ['ræʃər] NOUN
◆ **a rasher of bacon** una loncha de tocino

raspberry ['ræzbɛri] NOUN (PL **raspberries**)
la frambuesa

rat [ræt] NOUN
la rata

rate [reɪt] NOUN
see also **rate** VERB
1 la tarifa ◊ *There are reduced rates for students.* Hay tarifas reducidas para estudiantes.
2 la tasa ◊ *a high rate of interest* una tasa de interés elevada ◊ *the birth rate* la tasa de natalidad
◆ **the divorce rate** el porcentaje de divorcios

to **rate** [reɪt] VERB
see also **rate** NOUN
considerar ◊ *He was rated the best.* Era considerado el mejor.

rather ['ræðər] ADVERB
bastante ◊ *I was rather disappointed.* Quedé bastante decepcionado.
◆ **$20! That's rather a lot!** ¡20 dólares! ¡Eso es

mucho!

- **rather a lot of** mucho ◇ *I have rather a lot of homework to do.* Tengo muchas tareas que hacer.
- **I'd rather...** Preferiría... ◇ *Would you like a piece of candy? – I'd rather have an apple.* ¿Quieres un dulce? – Preferiría una manzana. ◇ *I'd rather stay in tonight.* Preferiría no salir esta noche.

***preferiría que** has to be followed by a verb in the subjunctive.*

◇ *I'd rather he didn't come to the party.* Preferiría que no viniera a la fiesta.

- **rather than...** en lugar de... ◇ *We decided to camp, rather than stay at a hotel.* Decidimos acampar, en lugar de quedarnos en un hotel.

rattle ['rætl] NOUN
el sonajero
la sonaja | Mexico |

to **rave** [reɪv] VERB ◇ *They raved about the movie.* Pusieron la película por las nubes.

raven ['reɪvən] NOUN
el cuervo

raving ['reɪvɪŋ] ADJECTIVE
- **to be raving mad** estar* loco como una cabra

raw [rɑ:] ADJECTIVE
crudo (*food*)
- **raw material** la materia prima

razor ['reɪzər] NOUN
la máquina de afeitar
la rasuradora | Mexico |
- **razor blade** la hoja de afeitar, | Mexico: | la hoja de rasurar

reach [ri:tʃ] NOUN
| *see also* **reach** VERB |
- **out of reach** fuera del alcance ◇ *Keep medicine out of reach of children.* Guárdense los medicamentos fuera del alcance de los niños.
- **within easy reach of** a poca distancia de ◇ *The hotel is within easy reach of the town center.* El hotel está a poca distancia del centro de la ciudad.

to **reach** [ri:tʃ] VERB
| *see also* **reach** NOUN |
1 llegar* a ◇ *We reached the hotel at seven o'clock.* Llegamos al hotel a las siete. ◇ *We hope to reach the finals.* Esperamos llegar a la final. ◇ *Eventually they reached a decision.* Finalmente llegaron a una decisión.
2 ponerse* en contacto con (*get in touch*) ◇ *How can I reach you?* ¿Cómo puedo ponerme en contacto contigo?

to **react** [ri'ækt] VERB
reaccionar

reaction [ri'ækʃən] NOUN
la reacción (PL las reacciones)

reactor [ri'æktər] NOUN
el reactor
- **a nuclear reactor** un reactor nuclear

to **read** [ri:d] VERB (**read**, **read**)
leer* ◇ *I don't read much.* No leo mucho. ◇ *Read the text out loud.* Lee el texto en voz alta.

to **read out** [ri:d'aut] VERB
leer* (*en voz alta*) ◇ *I was reading it out to the children.* Se lo estaba leyendo a los niños.

reader ['ri:dər] NOUN
el lector
la lectora
(*person*)

reading ['ri:dɪŋ] NOUN
la lectura ◇ *I'll see you in the reading room.* Te veo en la sala de lectura.
- **I like reading.** Me gusta leer.

ready ['rɛdi] ADJECTIVE
preparado ◇ *The meal is ready.* La comida está preparada.
- **She's nearly ready.** Está casi lista.
- **He's always ready to help.** Siempre está dispuesto a ayudar.
- **to get ready** prepararse
- **to get something ready** preparar algo ◇ *He's getting the dinner ready.* Está preparando la cena.

real [ri:əl] ADJECTIVE
1 verdadero ◇ *the real reason* el verdadero motivo ◇ *It was a real nightmare.* Fue una verdadera pesadilla.
- **In real life these things don't happen.** Estas cosas no pasan en la vida real.

2 auténtico ◇ *It's real fur.* Es piel auténtica.

real estate ['ri:lɪs'teɪt] NOUN
los bienes raíces PL

real estate agent ['ri:lɪs'teɪt'eɪdʒənt] NOUN
el agente inmobiliario
la agente inmobiliaria

realistic [ri:ə'lɪstɪk] ADJECTIVE
realista

reality [ri'æləti] NOUN
la realidad

reality TV NOUN
la telerrealidad

to **realize** ['ri:əlaɪz] VERB
- **to realize that...** darse* cuenta de que... ◇ *We realized that something was wrong.* Nos dimos cuenta de que algo iba mal.

really ['ri:əli] ADVERB
de verdad ◇ *I'm learning German. – Really?* Estoy aprendiendo alemán. – ¿De verdad?
- **Do you really think so?** ¿Tú crees?
- **She's really nice.** Es muy simpática.
- **Do you want to go? – Not really.** ¿Quieres ir? – La verdad es que no.

Realtor® ['ri:əltər] NOUN
el agente inmobiliario
la agente inmobiliaria

rear [rɪər] ADJECTIVE
| *see also* **rear** NOUN |
trasero ◇ *the rear wheel* la rueda trasera

rear [rɪər] NOUN

R ☞

see also **rear** ADJECTIVE
la parte trasera ◇ *at the rear of the train* en la parte trasera del tren

reason ['ri:zən] NOUN
la razón (PL las razones) ◇ *There's no reason to think that he's dangerous.* No hay razón para pensar que es peligroso.
◆ **for security reasons** por motivos de seguridad
◆ **That was the main reason I went.** Fui mayormente por eso.

reasonable ['ri:zənəbəl] ADJECTIVE
1 razonable ◇ *Be reasonable!* ¡Sé razonable!
2 bastante aceptable ◇ *He wrote a reasonable essay.* Escribió una redacción bastante aceptable.

reasonably ['ri:zənəbli] ADVERB
bastante ◇ *The team played reasonably well.* El equipo jugó bastante bien.
◆ **reasonably priced accommodations** alojamiento a precios razonables

to **reassure** [ri:ə'ʃuər] VERB
tranquilizar*

reassuring [ri:ə'ʃurɪŋ] ADJECTIVE
tranquilizador

rebel ['rɛbəl] NOUN
el/la rebelde

rebellious [rɪ'bɛljəs] ADJECTIVE
rebelde

receipt [rɪ'si:t] NOUN
el recibo
*Be careful not to translate **receipt** by **receta**.*

to **receive** [rɪ'si:v] VERB
recibir

receiver [rɪ'si:vər] NOUN
el auricular
◆ **to pick up the receiver** descolgar*

recent ['ri:sənt] ADJECTIVE
reciente ◇ *recent scientific discoveries* los recientes descubrimientos científicos
◆ **in recent weeks** en las últimas semanas

recently ['ri:səntli] ADVERB
últimamente ◇ *I haven't seen him recently.* No lo he visto últimamente. ◇ *I've been doing a lot of training recently.* Últimamente he estado entrenando mucho.
◆ **until recently** hasta hace poco

reception [rɪ'sɛpʃən] NOUN
la recepción (PL las recepciones) ◇ *Please leave your key at the reception desk.* Por favor dejen la llave en recepción. ◇ *The reception will be at a big hotel.* La recepción tendrá lugar en un gran hotel.

receptionist [rɪ'sɛpʃənɪst] NOUN
el/la recepcionista ◇ *She's a receptionist in a hospital.* Es recepcionista en un hospital.

recess ['ri:sɛs] NOUN
el recreo (*at school*)

recession [rɪ'sɛʃən] NOUN
la recesión (PL las recesiones)

recipe ['rɛsəpi] NOUN
la receta

to **reckon** ['rɛkən] VERB
creer* ◇ *What do you reckon?* ¿Tú qué crees?

reclining [rɪ'klaɪnɪŋ] ADJECTIVE
◆ **a reclining seat** un asiento reclinable

recognizable ['rɛkəgnaɪzəbəl] ADJECTIVE
reconocible

to **recognize** ['rɛkəgnaɪz] VERB
reconocer*

to **recommend** [rɛkə'mɛnd] VERB
recomendar* ◇ *What do you recommend?* ¿Qué me recomienda?

to **reconsider** [ri:kən'sɪdər] VERB
reconsiderar

record ['rɛkərd] NOUN
see also **record** VERB
1 el disco
2 el récord (PL los récords) ◇ *the world record* el récord mundial
◆ **in record time** en un tiempo récord
◆ **criminal record** los antecedentes penales ◇ *He has a criminal record.* Tiene antecedentes penales.
◆ **There is no record of your reservation.** No tenemos constancia de su reserva.
◆ **records** los archivos ◇ *I'll check in the records.* Miraré en los archivos.

to **record** [rɪ'kɔ:rd] VERB
see also **record** NOUN
grabar ◇ *They've just recorded their new album.* Acaban de grabar su nuevo álbum.
*Be careful not to translate **to record** by **recordar**.*

recorder [rɪ'kɔ:rdər] NOUN
la flauta dulce (*musical instrument*)
◆ **cassette recorder** el cassette
◆ **video recorder** el aparato de video

recording [rɪ'kɔ:rdɪŋ] NOUN
la grabación (PL las grabaciones)

record player ['rɛkərd,pleɪər] NOUN
el tocadiscos (PL los tocadiscos)

to **recover** [rɪ'kʌvər] VERB
recuperarse ◇ *He's recovering from a knee injury.* Se está recuperando de una lesión de rodilla.

recovery [rɪ'kʌvəri] NOUN
la mejora
◆ **Best wishes for a speedy recovery!** ¡Que te mejores pronto!

recreation center [rekri'eɪʃn,sɛntər] NOUN
el centro recreativo

rectangle ['rɛktæŋgəl] NOUN
el rectángulo

rectangular [rɛk'tæŋgjələr] ADJECTIVE
rectangular

to **recycle** [ri:'saɪkəl] VERB
reciclar

recycling [riːˈsaɪklɪŋ] NOUN
el reciclaje

red [rɛd] ADJECTIVE
rojo ◇ *a red rose* una rosa roja ◇ *red meat* la carne roja
◆ **Michael has red hair.** Michael es pelirrojo.
◆ **to go through a red light** saltarse un semáforo en rojo, Mexico: pasarse una luz roja
◆ **red wine** vino tinto

Red Cross [ˈrɛdˈkrɑːs] NOUN
la Cruz Roja

red currant [ˈrɛdˈkʌrənt] NOUN
la grosella

to **redecorate** [riːˈdɛkəreɪt] VERB
1 volver* a pintar (*with paint*)
2 volver* a empapelar (*with wallpaper*)

red-haired [ˈrɛdˈhɛərd] ADJECTIVE
pelirrojo

red-handed [ˈrɛdˈhændɪd] ADJECTIVE
◆ **to catch somebody red-handed** agarrar a alguien con las manos en la masa

redhead [ˈrɛdˌhɛd] NOUN
el pelirrojo
la pelirroja

to **redo** [riːˈduː] VERB (**redid, redone**)
rehacer*

to **reduce** [rɪˈduːs] VERB
reducir* ◇ *at a reduced price* a precio reducido
◆ **"reduce speed"** "disminuya la velocidad"

reduction [rɪˈdʌkʃən] NOUN
la reducción (PL las reducciones)
◆ **a five percent reduction** un descuento del cinco por ciento
◆ **"huge reductions!"** "¡grandes rebajas!"

redundant [rɪˈdʌndənt] ADJECTIVE
superfluo

reed [riːd] NOUN
el junco

reel [riːl] NOUN
1 el carrete (*of fishing line*)
2 el rollo (*of cable*)

to **refer** [rɪˈfɜːr] VERB
◆ **to refer to** referirse* a ◇ *What are you referring to?* ¿A qué te refieres?

referee [rɛfəˈriː] NOUN
el árbitro
la árbitra

reference [ˈrɛfrəns] NOUN
1 la referencia ◇ *He made no reference to the murder.* No hizo referencia al homicidio.
2 las referencias ◇ *Would you please give me a reference?* ¿Me podría facilitar referencias?
◆ **a reference book** un libro de consulta

to **refill** [riːˈfɪl] VERB
volver* a llenar ◇ *He refilled my glass.* Volvió a llenarme el vaso.

refinery [rɪˈfaɪnəri] NOUN (PL **refineries**)
la refinería

to **reflect** [rɪˈflɛkt] VERB
1 reflejar (*image*)
2 reflexionar (*think*)

reflection [rɪˈflɛkʃən] NOUN
el reflejo (*image*)

reflex [ˈriːflɛks] NOUN (PL **reflexes**)
el reflejo

reflexive [rɪˈflɛksɪv] ADJECTIVE
reflexivo ◇ *a reflexive verb* un verbo reflexivo

refresher course [rɪˈfrɛʃərˌkɔːrs] NOUN
el curso de reciclaje

refreshing [rɪˈfrɛʃɪŋ] ADJECTIVE
1 refrescante ◇ *a refreshing drink* una bebida refrescante
2 estimulante ◇ *It was a refreshing change.* Fue un cambio estimulante.

refreshments [rɪˈfrɛʃmənts] PL NOUN
el refrigerio

refrigerator [rɪˈfrɪdʒəreɪtər] NOUN
el refrigerador

to **refuel** [riːˈfjuəl] VERB
repostar ◇ *The plane stops in Boston to refuel.* El avión hace escala en Boston para repostar.

refuge [ˈrɛfjuːdʒ] NOUN
el refugio

refugee [rɛfjuˈdʒiː] NOUN
el refugiado
la refugiada

refund [ˈriːfʌnd] NOUN
see also **refund** VERB
el reembolso

to **refund** [rɪˈfʌnd] VERB
see also **refund** NOUN
reembolsar

refusal [rɪˈfjuːzəl] NOUN
la negativa ◇ *her refusal to accept money* su negativa a aceptar dinero

to **refuse** [rɪˈfjuːz] VERB
see also **refuse** NOUN
negarse* ◇ *He refused to comment.* Se negó a hacer comentarios.

refuse [ˈrɛfjuːs] NOUN
see also **refuse** VERB
la basura
◆ **refuse collection** la recogida de basuras

to **regain** [rɪˈgeɪn] VERB
◆ **to regain consciousness** recobrar el conocimiento

regard [rɪˈgɑːrd] NOUN
see also **regard** VERB
◆ **with regard to** con respecto a
◆ **Give my regards to Alice.** Dale recuerdos a Alice.
◆ **"with kind regards"** "un cordial saludo"

to **regard** [rɪˈgɑːrd] VERB
see also **regard** NOUN
◆ **They regarded it as unfair.** Lo consideraron injusto.
◆ **as regards...** en lo que se refiere a...

R

regarding [rɪ'gɑ:rdɪŋ] PREPOSITION
referente a ◇ *the laws regarding the export of animals* las leyes referentes a la exportación de animales
◆ **Regarding John,...** En lo que respecta a John,....
regardless [rɪ'gɑ:rdlɪs] ADVERB
◆ **to carry on regardless** continuar* como si nada
regiment ['rɛdʒəmənt] NOUN
el regimiento
region ['ri:dʒən] NOUN
la región (PL las regiones)
regional ['ri:dʒənl] ADJECTIVE
regional
register ['rɛdʒɪstər] NOUN
see also **register** VERB
el registro (*in hotel*)
to **register** ['rɛdʒɪstər] VERB
see also **register** NOUN
inscribirse* (*enroll*)
◆ **The car was registered in his wife's name.** El carro estaba matriculado a nombre de su esposa.
registered ['rɛdʒɪstərd] ADJECTIVE
◆ **registered mail** el correo certificado
registration [rɛdʒɪ'streɪʃən] NOUN
la inscripción (*for class, course*)
◇ *Registration starts at 8.30.* La inscripción empieza a las ocho y media.
regret [rɪ'grɛt] NOUN
see also **regret** VERB
◆ **I have no regrets.** No me arrepiento.
to **regret** [rɪ'grɛt] VERB
see also **regret** NOUN
arrepentirse* ◇ *Try it, you won't regret it!* ¡Pruébalo! ¡No te arrepentirás!
◆ **to regret doing something** arrepentirse de haber hecho algo ◇ *I regret saying that.* Me arrepiento de haber dicho eso.
regular ['rɛgjələr] ADJECTIVE
1 regular ◇ *at regular intervals* a intervalos regulares
◆ **to take regular exercise** hacer* ejercicio con regularidad
2 normal ◇ *a regular portion of fries* una porción normal de papas fritas
regularly ['rɛgjələrli] ADVERB
con regularidad
regulations [rɛgjə'leɪʃənz] PL NOUN
el reglamento ◇ *It's against regulations.* Va en contra del reglamento.
◆ **safety regulations** las normas de seguridad
rehearsal [rɪ'h3:rsəl] NOUN
el ensayo
◆ **dress rehearsal** el ensayo general
to **rehearse** [rɪ'h3:rs] VERB
ensayar
reindeer ['reɪndɪr] NOUN
el reno
reins [reɪnz] PL NOUN
las riendas
to **reject** [rɪ'dʒɛkt] VERB
1 rechazar* (*proposal, invitation*)
2 desechar (*idea, advice*)
◆ **I applied but they rejected me.** Presenté una solicitud, pero no me aceptaron.
relapse ['ri:læps] NOUN
la recaída
◆ **to have a relapse** tener* una recaída
related [rɪ'leɪtɪd] ADJECTIVE
◆ **We're related.** Somos parientes.
◆ **Are you related to her?** ¿Eres pariente suyo?
◆ **The two events are not related.** Los dos sucesos no están relacionados.
relation [rɪ'leɪʃən] NOUN
1 el/la pariente ◇ *He's a distant relation.* Es un pariente lejano mío.
2 la relación (PL las relaciones) ◇ *It has no relation to reality.* No guarda ninguna relación con la realidad.
◆ **in relation to** con relación a
relationship [rɪ'leɪʃənʃɪp] NOUN
la relación (PL las relaciones) ◇ *We have a good relationship.* Tenemos una buena relación.
◆ **I'm not in a relationship at the moment.** No tengo relaciones sentimentales con nadie en este momento.
◆ **the relationship between A and B** la relación entre A y B
relative ['rɛlətɪv] NOUN
el/la pariente
relatively ['rɛlətɪvli] ADVERB
relativamente
to **relax** [rɪ'læks] VERB
relajarse ◇ *I relax listening to music.* Me relajo escuchando música.
◆ **Relax! Everything's fine.** ¡Tranquilo! No pasa nada.
relaxation [ri:læk'seɪʃən] NOUN
el esparcimiento
◆ **I don't have much time for relaxation.** No tengo muchos momentos de esparcimiento.
relaxed [rɪ'lækst] ADJECTIVE
relajado
relaxing [rɪ'læksɪŋ] ADJECTIVE
relajante ◇ *Taking a bath is very relaxing.* Darse un baño es muy relajante.
◆ **I find cooking relaxing.** Cocinar me relaja.
relay ['ri:leɪ] NOUN
◆ **a relay race** una carrera de relevos
to **release** [rɪ'li:s] VERB
see also **release** NOUN
1 poner* en libertad (*prisoner*)
2 hacer* público (*report, news*)
3 sacar* a la venta (*record, video*)
release [rɪ'li:s] NOUN
see also **release** VERB
la puesta en libertad ◇ *the release of Nelson*

Mandela la puesta en libertad de Nelson Mandela
◆ **the band's latest release** el último disco del grupo

relegated ['rɛləgeɪtɪd] ADJECTIVE
◆ **to be relegated** descender* de división (*sport*)

relevant ['rɛləvənt] ADJECTIVE
pertinente (*documents*)
◆ **That's not relevant.** Eso no viene al caso.
◆ **to be relevant to something** guardar relación con algo ◇ *Education should be relevant to real life.* La educación debería guardar relación con la vida real.

reliable [rɪ'laɪəbəl] ADJECTIVE
fiable ◇ *a reliable car* un carro fiable ◇ *He's not very reliable.* No es una persona muy fiable.

relief [rɪ'li:f] NOUN
el alivio ◇ *That's a relief!* ¡Es un alivio! ◇ *Much to my relief she made no objection.* Para mi gran alivio, no hizo objeción alguna.

to **relieve** [rɪ'li:v] VERB
aliviar ◇ *This injection will relieve the pain.* Esta inyección le aliviará el dolor.

relieved [rɪ'li:vd] ADJECTIVE
◆ **to be relieved** sentir* un gran alivio ◇ *I was relieved to hear he was better.* Sentí un gran alivio al saber que estaba mejor.

religion [rɪ'lɪdʒən] NOUN
la religión (PL las religiones) ◇ *What religion are you?* ¿De qué religión eres?

religious [rɪ'lɪdʒəs] ADJECTIVE
religioso ◇ *I'm not religious.* No soy religioso.

reluctant [rɪ'lʌktənt] ADJECTIVE
reacio
◆ **to be reluctant to do something** ser* reacio a hacer algo ◇ *They were reluctant to help us.* Eran reacios a ayudarnos.

reluctantly [rɪ'lʌktəntli] ADVERB
de mala gana ◇ *She reluctantly accepted.* Aceptó de mala gana.

to **rely on** [rɪ'laɪˌɑ:n] VERB
confiar* en ◇ *I'm relying on you.* Confío en ti.

to **remain** [rɪ'meɪn] VERB
permanecer* ◇ *to remain silent* permanecer callado

remaining [rɪ'meɪnɪŋ] ADJECTIVE
restante ◇ *the remaining ingredients* los ingredientes restantes

remains [rɪ'meɪnz] PL NOUN
los restos ◇ *the remains of the picnic* los restos del picnic ◇ *human remains* restos humanos ◇ *Roman remains* los restos romanos

remake ['ri:meɪk] NOUN
la nueva versión

remark [rɪ'mɑ:rk] NOUN
el comentario

remarkable [rɪ'mɑ:rkəbəl] ADJECTIVE
extraordinario

remarkably [rɪ'mɑ:rkəbli] ADVERB
extraordinariamente

to **remarry** [ri:'mɛri] VERB (**remarried, remarried**)
volver* a casarse ◇ *She remarried three years ago.* Se volvió a casar hace tres años.

rematch ['ri:mætʃ] NOUN
el partido de vuelta (*return match*)
◆ **There will be a rematch on Friday.** El partido se volverá a jugar el viernes.

remedy ['rɛmədi] NOUN (PL **remedies**)
el remedio ◇ *a good remedy for a sore throat* un buen remedio para el dolor de garganta

to **remember** [rɪ'mɛmbər] VERB
1 acordarse* ◇ *I don't remember.* No me acuerdo.
2 acordarse* de ◇ *I can't remember his name.* No me acuerdo de su nombre. ◇ *I don't remember saying that.* No me acuerdo de haber dicho eso.
In Spanish you often say ***no te olvides*** *–* ***don't forget*** *– instead of* ***remember****.*
◇ *Remember to write your name on the form.* No te olvides de poner tu nombre en el impreso.

to **remind** [rɪ'maɪnd] VERB
recordar* ◇ *The scenery here reminds me of Texas.* Este paisaje me recuerda a Texas.
When talking about reminding someone to do something, ***recordar a alguien que*** *has to be followed by a verb in the subjunctive.*
◇ *Remind me to speak to Daniel.* Recuérdame que hable con Daniel.

remorse [rɪ'mɔ:rs] NOUN
el remordimiento ◇ *He showed no remorse.* No tenía ningún remordimiento.

remote [rɪ'mout] ADJECTIVE
see also **remote** NOUN
remoto ◇ *a remote village* un pueblo remoto

remote [rɪ'mout] NOUN
see also **remote** ADJECTIVE
el mando a distancia ◇ *I can't find the remote.* No encuentro el mando a distancia.

remote control [rɪ'moutkən'troul] NOUN
el mando a distancia

removable [rɪ'mu:vəbəl] ADJECTIVE
separable

removal [rɪ'mu:vəl] NOUN
el traslado (*taking away*)

to **remove** [rɪ'mu:v] VERB
quitar ◇ *Please remove your bag from my seat.* Por favor, quite su bolsa de mi asiento. ◇ *Did you remove the stain?* ¿Quitaste la mancha?

rendezvous ['rɑ:ndeɪvu:] NOUN (PL **rendezvous**)
la cita

to **renew** [rɪ'nu:] VERB

R

renovar* (*passport, license*)

renewable [rɪ'nu:əbəl] ADJECTIVE
renovable

to **renovate** ['rɛnəveɪt] VERB
renovar* ◇ *The building has been renovated.* Han renovado el edificio.

renowned [rɪ'naund] ADJECTIVE
renombrado

rent [rɛnt] NOUN
see also **rent** VERB
el alquiler
◆ **"for rent"** "se alquila"

to **rent** [rɛnt] VERB
see also **rent** NOUN
alquilar
rentar *Mexico*
◇ *We rented a car.* Alquilamos un carro.
Mexico: Rentamos un carro.

rental ['rɛntl] NOUN
el alquiler
la renta *Mexico*
◇ *Car rental is included in the price.* El alquiler del carro está incluido en el precio.
Mexico: La renta del carro está incluido en el precio.

rental car ['rentl,kɑ:r] NOUN
el carro de alquiler

to **reorganize** [ri'ɔ:rgənaɪz] VERB
reorganizar*

rep [rɛp] NOUN (= *representative*)
el/la representante

repaid [ri:'peɪd] VERB *see* **repay**

to **repair** [rɪ'pɛər] VERB
see also **repair** NOUN
arreglar ◇ *Can you repair this for me?* ¿Me puede arreglar esto? ◇ *I got the washing machine repaired.* Me areglaron la lavadora.

repair [rɪ'pɛər] NOUN
see also **repair** VERB
el arreglo

to **repay** [ri:'peɪ] VERB (**repaid, repaid**)
devolver* (*money*)
◆ **I don't know how I can ever repay you.** No sé cómo podré devolverle el favor.

repayment [ri:'peɪmənt] NOUN
el pago

to **repeat** [rɪ'pi:t] VERB
see also **repeat** NOUN
repetir*

repeat [rɪ'pi:t] NOUN
see also **repeat** VERB
la repetición (PL las repeticiones)

repeatedly [rɪ'pi:tɪdli] ADVERB
repetidamente

repellent [rɪ'pɛlənt] NOUN
◆ **insect repellent** la loción anti-insectos (PL las lociones anti-insectos)

repetitive [rɪ'pɛtətɪv] ADJECTIVE
repetitivo

to **replace** [rɪ'pleɪs] VERB
1 sustituir* ◇ *Computers have replaced typewriters.* Las computadoras han sustituido a las máquinas de escribir.
2 cambiar (*batteries*)

replay ['ri:pleɪ] NOUN
see also **replay** VERB
◆ **instant replay** la repetición de la jugada (*football, baseball*)

to **replay** [ri:'pleɪ] VERB
see also **replay** NOUN
volver* a poner (*tape*)

replica ['rɛplɪkə] NOUN
la réplica

reply [rɪ'plaɪ] NOUN (PL **replies**)
see also **reply** VERB
la respuesta

to **reply** [rɪ'plaɪ] VERB (**replied, replied**)
see also **reply** NOUN
responder

report [rɪ'pɔ:rt] NOUN
see also **report** VERB
1 el informe (*of event*)
2 el reportaje (*news report*) ◇ *a report in the paper* un reportaje en el periódico
◆ **I've received good reports about your progress.** He recibido buenos informes acerca de tu progreso.

to **report** [rɪ'pɔ:rt] VERB
see also **report** NOUN
1 dar* parte de ◇ *I reported the theft to the police.* Di parte del robo a la policía.
2 presentarse ◇ *Report to reception when you arrive.* Preséntese en recepción cuando llegue.
◆ **I'll report back as soon as I hear anything.** En cuanto tenga noticias, te lo haré saber.

report card [rɪ'pɔ:rt,kɑ:rd] NOUN
el informe escolar
la boleta de notas *Mexico*

> ℹ *Un* **report card** *es un informe oficial escrito acerca del rendimiento de un estudiante durante cierto periodo o durante un año que acaba de terminar.*

reporter [rɪ'pɔ:rtər] NOUN
el/la periodista

to **represent** [rɛprɪ'zɛnt] VERB
1 representar a (*client, country*)
2 representar (*change, achievement*)

representative [rɛprɪ'zɛntətɪv] ADJECTIVE
representativo

reproduction [ri:prə'dʌkʃən] NOUN
la reproducción (PL las reproducciones)

reptile ['rɛptaɪl] NOUN
el reptil

republic [rɪ'pʌblɪk] NOUN
la república

Republican Party [rɪ'pʌblɪkən'pɑ:rti] NOUN
el Partido Republicano

repulsive [rɪ'pʌlsɪv] ADJECTIVE
repugnante

reputable ['rɛpjətəbəl] ADJECTIVE
acreditado

reputation [rɛpjə'teɪʃən] NOUN
la reputación (PL las reputaciones)

request [rɪ'kwɛst] NOUN
see also **request** VERB
la petición (PL las peticiones)

to **request** [rɪ'kwɛst] VERB
see also **request** NOUN
solicitar

to **require** [rɪ'kwaɪər] VERB
requerir* ◇ *Her job requires a lot of patience.* Su trabajo requiere mucha paciencia.

requirement [rɪ'kwaɪərmənt] NOUN
el requisito ◇ *What are the requirements for the job?* ¿Cuáles son los requisitos para el puesto?
◆ **entry requirements** (*for college*) los requisitos para la admisión

rerun ['riːrʌn] NOUN
la reposición (PL las reposiciones) ◇ *There are too many reruns on TV.* Hay demasiadas reposiciones en la tele.

to **rescue** ['rɛskjuː] VERB
see also **rescue** NOUN
rescatar

rescue ['rɛskjuː] NOUN
see also **rescue** VERB
el rescate ◇ *a rescue operation* una operación de rescate ◇ *a mountain rescue team* un equipo de rescate de montaña
◆ **to come to somebody's rescue** acudir en auxilio de alguien

research [rɪ'sɜːrtʃ] NOUN
la investigación (PL las investigaciones)
◇ *He's doing research.* Realiza trabajos de investigación.
◆ **She's doing some research in the library.** Está investigando en la biblioteca.

resemblance [rɪ'zɛmbləns] NOUN
el parecido

to **resent** [rɪ'zɛnt] VERB
◆ **I resent being dependent on her.** Me molesta tener que depender de ella.

reservation [rɛzər'veɪʃən] NOUN
la reserva ◇ *I have a reservation for two nights.* Tengo una reserva para dos noches.
◇ *I'd like to make a reservation for this evening.* Quisiera hacer una reserva para esta tarde.
◆ **I have reservations about the idea.** Tengo mis reservas al respecto.

reserve [rɪ'zɜːrv] NOUN
see also **reserve** VERB
la reserva (*place*) ◇ *a nature reserve* una reserva natural

to **reserve** [rɪ'zɜːrv] VERB
see also **reserve** NOUN
reservar ◇ *I'd like to reserve a table for tomorrow evening.* Quisiera reservar una mesa para mañana por la noche.

reserved [rɪ'zɜːrvd] ADJECTIVE
reservado ◇ *a reserved seat* un asiento
reservado ◇ *He's quite reserved.* Es bastante reservado.

reservoir ['rɛzərvwɑːr] NOUN
el embalse

residence hall ['rezɪdənsˌhɑːl] NOUN
la residencia universitaria

resident ['rɛzɪdənt] NOUN
el vecino
la vecina
◇ *local residents* los vecinos del lugar

residential [rɛzɪ'dɛnʃəl] ADJECTIVE
residencial ◇ *a residential area* una zona residencial

to **resign** [rɪ'zaɪn] VERB
dimitir

resistance [rɪ'zɪstəns] NOUN
la resistencia

resolution [rɛzə'luːʃən] NOUN
el propósito ◇ *Have you made any New Year's resolutions?* ¿Has hecho algún buen propósito para el Año Nuevo?

resort [rɪ'zɔːrt] NOUN
el centro turístico ◇ *a resort in the Caribbean* un centro turístico en el Caribe
◆ **a ski resort** una estación de esquí
◆ **as a last resort** como último recurso

resource ['riːsɔːrs] NOUN
el recurso

respect [rɪ'spɛkt] NOUN
see also **respect** VERB
el respeto
◆ **in some respects** en algunos aspectos

to **respect** [rɪ'spɛkt] VERB
see also **respect** NOUN
respetar

respectable [rɪ'spɛktəbəl] ADJECTIVE
1 respetable ◇ *a respectable family* una familia respetable
2 aceptable ◇ *My grades were quite respectable.* Mis notas eran bastante aceptables.

respectively [rɪ'spɛktɪvli] ADVERB
respectivamente ◇ *Chile and Argentina came in third and fourth respectively.* Chile y Argentina llegaron en tercero y cuarto lugar respectivamente.

responsibility [rɪspɑːnsə'bɪləti] NOUN (PL **responsibilities**)
la responsabilidad

responsible [rɪ'spɑːnsəbəl] ADJECTIVE
responsable ◇ *You should be more responsible!* ¡Deberías ser más responsable!
◆ **to be responsible for something** ser* responsable de algo ◇ *He's responsible for booking the tickets.* Es responsable de reservar las entradas.

R

◆ **It's a responsible job.** Es un puesto de responsabilidad.

rest [rɛst] NOUN
see also **rest** VERB
1 el descanso ◇ *five minutes' rest* cinco minutos de descanso
◆ **to have a rest** descansar ◇ *We stopped to have a rest.* Nos paramos a descansar.
2 el resto ◇ *I'll do the rest.* Yo haré el resto. ◇ *the rest of the money* el resto del dinero
◆ **the rest of them** los demás ◇ *The rest of them went swimming.* Los demás fueron a nadar.

to **rest** [rɛst] VERB
see also **rest** NOUN
1 descansar ◇ *She's resting in her room.* Está descansando en su habitación. ◇ *He has to rest his knee.* Tiene que descansar la rodilla.
2 apoyar ◇ *I rested my bicycle against the window.* Apoyé la bicicleta en la ventana.

rest area ['rɛst,ɛriə] NOUN
el área de servicios FEM
*Although it's a feminine noun, remember that you use **el** and **un** with **área**.*

restaurant ['rɛstərɑ:nt] NOUN
el restaurante ◇ *We don't often go to restaurants.* No solemos ir a restaurantes.

restful ['rɛstfəl] ADJECTIVE
plácido

restless ['rɛstlɪs] ADJECTIVE
inquieto

restoration [rɛstə'reɪʃən] NOUN
la restauración

to **restore** [rɪ'stɔ:r] VERB
restaurar (*building, painting*)

to **restrict** [rɪ'strɪkt] VERB
limitar

restroom ['rɛst,ru:m] NOUN
el baño

result [rɪ'zʌlt] NOUN
el resultado ◇ *my exam results* los resultados de mis exámenes ◇ *The result was one to nothing.* El resultado fue uno a cero.

resumé ['rɛzumeɪ] NOUN
el currículum vitae

to **retake** [ri:'teɪk] VERB (**retook, retaken**)
volver* a presentarse a ◇ *I'm retaking the exam in December.* Me vuelvo a presentar al examen en diciembre.

to **retire** [rɪ'taɪər] VERB
jubilarse

retired [rɪ'taɪərd] ADJECTIVE
jubilado ◇ *She's retired.* Está jubilada. ◇ *a retired teacher* un maestro jubilado

retirement [rɪ'taɪərmənt] NOUN
◆ **since his retirement** desde que se jubiló

to **retrace** [ri:'treɪs] VERB
◆ **I retraced my steps.** Volví sobre mis pasos.

return [rɪ'tɜ:rn] NOUN
see also **return** VERB
el regreso ◇ *his sudden return home* su repentino regreso a casa
◆ **the return journey** el viaje de vuelta
◆ **in return** a cambio ◇ *She helps me and I help her in return.* Me ayuda y yo la ayudo a cambio.
◆ **in return for** a cambio de
◆ **Many happy returns!** ¡Que cumplas muchos más!

to **return** [rɪ'tɜ:rn] VERB
see also **return** NOUN
1 volver* ◇ *I've just returned from vacation.* Acabo de volver de vacaciones. ◇ *He returned home the following year.* Volvió a casa al año siguiente.
2 devolver* ◇ *She borrows my things and doesn't return them.* Toma prestadas mis cosas y no las devuelve.

reunion [ri:'ju:njən] NOUN
la reunión (PL las reuniones) ◇ *a big family reunion* una gran reunión familiar

to **reuse** [ri:'ju:z] VERB
reutilizar*

to **reveal** [rɪ'vi:l] VERB
revelar

revenge [rɪ'vɛndʒ] NOUN
la venganza ◇ *in revenge* como venganza
◆ **to take revenge** vengarse* ◇ *They planned to take revenge on him.* Planearon vengarse de él.

reverse [rɪ'vɜ:rs] ADJECTIVE
inverso ◇ *in reverse order* en orden inverso
◆ **in reverse gear** en marcha atrás, *Mexico*: en reversa

review [rɪ'vju:] NOUN
see also **review** VERB
1 la revisión (PL las revisiones) (*of policy, salary*)
2 el repaso (*of subject*)

to **review** [rɪ'vju:] VERB
see also **review** NOUN
estudiar para un examen

to **revise** [rɪ'vaɪz] VERB
1 revisar (*text*)
2 corregir (*estimate, figure*)
◆ **I've revised my opinion.** He cambiado de opinión.

revision [rɪ'vɪʒən] NOUN
◆ **This paper needs a lot of revision.** Hay que hacerle muchas correcciones a este trabajo.

to **revive** [rɪ'vaɪv] VERB
resucitar ◇ *The nurses tried to revive him.* Las enfermeras intentaron resucitarlo.

revolting [rɪ'voultɪŋ] ADJECTIVE
repugnante

revolution [rɛvə'lu:ʃən] NOUN
la revolución (PL las revoluciones)

revolutionary [rɛvə'lu:ʃənɛri] ADJECTIVE

revolucionario

revolver [rɪ'vɑːlvər] NOUN
el revólver

reward [rɪ'wɔːrd] NOUN
la recompensa

rewarding [rɪ'wɔːrdɪŋ] ADJECTIVE
gratificante ◇ *a rewarding job* un trabajo gratificante

to **rewind** [riː'waɪnd] VERB (**rewound**, **rewound**)
rebobinar ◇ *to rewind a cassette* rebobinar una cinta

rheumatism ['ruːmətɪzəm] NOUN
el reumatismo ◇ *I have rheumatism.* Tengo reumatismo.

rhinoceros [raɪ'nɑːsərəs] NOUN
el rinoceronte

rhubarb ['ruːbɑːrb] NOUN
el ruibarbo

rhythm ['rɪðəm] NOUN
el ritmo

rib [rɪb] NOUN
la costilla

ribbon ['rɪbən] NOUN
la cinta

rice [raɪs] NOUN
el arroz
◆ **rice pudding** el arroz con leche

rich [rɪtʃ] ADJECTIVE
rico
◆ **the rich people** los ricos

to **rid** [rɪd] VERB
◆ **to get rid of** deshacerse* de ◇ *I want to get rid of some old clothes.* Quiero deshacerme de ropa vieja.

ridden ['rɪdn] VERB *see* **ride**

ride [raɪd] NOUN
see also **ride** VERB
◆ **to go for a ride (1)** (*on horse*) montar a caballo
◆ **to go for a ride (2)** (*on bicycle*) dar* un paseo en bicicleta ◇ *We went for a bicycle ride.* Fuimos a dar un paseo en bicicleta.
◆ **He gave me a ride into town.** Me llevó hasta el centro en carro. *Mexico:* Me dio aventón hasta el centro.
◆ **It's a short bus ride to the town center.** El centro de la ciudad queda cerca en autobús.

to **ride** [raɪd] VERB (**rode**, **ridden**)
see also **ride** NOUN
montar a caballo ◇ *I'm learning to ride.* Estoy aprendiendo a montar a caballo.
◆ **to ride a bicycle** ir* en bicicleta ◇ *Can you ride a bicycle?* ¿Sabes ir en bicicleta?

rider ['raɪdər] NOUN
1 el/la jinete ◇ *She's a good rider.* Ella es muy buena jinete.
2 el/la ciclista (*cyclist*)

ridiculous [rɪ'dɪkjələs] ADJECTIVE
ridículo

riding ['raɪdɪŋ] NOUN
la equitación (*as sport*) ◇ *a riding school* una escuela de equitación
◆ **to go riding** montar a caballo

rifle ['raɪfəl] NOUN
el rifle

rig [rɪg] NOUN
◆ **oil rig** la plataforma petrolífera

right [raɪt] ADJECTIVE, ADVERB
see also **right** NOUN

There are several ways of translating ***right****. Scan the examples to find one that is similar to what you want to say.*

1 correcto ◇ *the right answer* la respuesta correcta
2 adecuado (*place, time*) ◇ *We're on the right train.* Estamos en el tren adecuado. ◇ *It isn't the right size.* Ésta no es la talla adecuada.
◆ **Is this the right road for Ávila?** ¿Vamos bien por aquí para Ávila?
◆ **to be right (1)** (*person*) tener* razón ◇ *You were right!* ¡Tenías razón!
◆ **to be right (2)** (*statement, opinion*) ser* verdad ◇ *That's right!* ¡Es verdad!
◆ **Do you have the right time?** ¿Tienes hora?
3 bien ◇ *It's not right to behave like that.* No está bien comportarse así. ◇ *Am I pronouncing it right?* ¿Lo pronuncio bien?
◆ **I think you did the right thing.** Creo que hiciste bien.
4 derecho (*not left*) ◇ *my right hand* mi mano derecha
5 a la derecha (*turn, look*) ◇ *Turn right at the traffic lights.* Cuando llegues al semáforo dobla a la derecha.
◆ **Right! Let's get started!** ¡Bueno! ¡Empecemos!
◆ **right away** enseguida ◇ *I'll do it right away.* Lo haré enseguida.

right [raɪt] NOUN
see also **right** ADJECTIVE
1 el derecho ◇ *You have no right to do that.* No tienes derecho de hacer eso.
2 la derecha
◆ **on the right** a la derecha ◇ *on the right of Mr. Yates* a la derecha del Sr. Yates
◆ **right of way** la prioridad ◇ *We had right of way.* Teníamos prioridad.

right-hand ['raɪt'hænd] ADJECTIVE
◆ **the right-hand side** la derecha ◇ *It's on the right-hand side.* Está a la derecha.

right-handed ['raɪt'hændɪd] ADJECTIVE
diestro

rim [rɪm] NOUN
la montura ◇ *glasses with metal rims* los anteojos con montura metálica

ring [rɪŋ] NOUN
see also **ring** VERB
1 el anillo ◇ *a gold ring* un anillo de oro
◆ **a wedding ring** una alianza
2 el círculo ◇ *to stand in a ring* formar un círculo
3 el timbrazo (*at door*) ◇ *After three or four* ☞

R

rings the door was opened. Después de tres o cuatro timbrazos la puerta se abrió.
- **There was a ring at the door.** Se oyó el timbre de la puerta.

to **ring** [rɪŋ] VERB (**rang, rung**)
see also **ring** NOUN
1 sonar* ◇ *The phone is ringing.* El teléfono está sonando.
- **to ring the bell** tocar* el timbre

2 llamar ◇ *Your mother rang this morning.* Tu mamá llamó esta mañana.
- **to ring somebody** llamar a alguien

ring binder [ˈrɪŋ,baɪndər] NOUN
la carpeta de anillos

ringtone NOUN
el tono de llamada

rink [rɪŋk] NOUN
1 la pista de hielo (*for ice-skating*)
2 la pista de patinaje (*for roller-skating*)

to **rinse** [rɪns] VERB
enjuagar*

riot [ˈraɪət] NOUN
see also **riot** VERB
el disturbio

to **riot** [ˈraɪət] VERB
see also **riot** NOUN
causar disturbios

to **rip** [rɪp] VERB
rasgar* ◇ *I've ripped my jeans.* Me he rasgado los jeans. ◇ *My shirt is ripped.* Mi camisa está rasgada.

to **rip off** [rɪpˈɑːf] VERB
timar (*informal*) ◇ *The hotel ripped us off.* En el hotel nos timaron.

to **rip up** [rɪpˈʌp] VERB
hacer* pedazos ◇ *He read the note and then ripped it up.* Leyó la nota y la hizo pedazos.

ripe [raɪp] ADJECTIVE
maduro

rip-off [ˈrɪp,ɑːf] NOUN
- **It's a rip-off!** ¡Es un timo! (*informal*)

rise [raɪz] NOUN
see also **rise** VERB
la subida (*in prices, temperature*) ◇ *a sudden rise in temperature* una repentina subida de las temperaturas

to **rise** [raɪz] VERB (**rose, risen**)
see also **rise** NOUN
1 subir (*increase*) ◇ *Prices are rising.* Los precios están subiendo.
2 salir* ◇ *The sun rises early in June.* En junio el sol sale temprano.

riser [ˈraɪzər] NOUN
- **to be an early riser** ser* madrugador

risk [rɪsk] NOUN
see also **risk** VERB
el riesgo
- **to take risks** correr riesgos
- **It's at your own risk.** Es por tu propia cuenta y riesgo.

to **risk** [rɪsk] VERB
see also **risk** NOUN
arriesgarse* ◇ *You risk getting a fine.* Te arriesgas a que te multen. ◇ *I wouldn't risk it if I were you.* Yo en tu lugar no me arriesgaría.

risky [ˈrɪski] ADJECTIVE
arriesgado

rival [ˈraɪvəl] NOUN
see also **rival** ADJECTIVE
el/la rival

rival [ˈraɪvəl] ADJECTIVE
see also **rival** NOUN
1 rival ◇ *a rival gang* una banda rival
2 competidor (FEM competidora) ◇ *a rival company* una empresa competidora

rivalry [ˈraɪvlri] NOUN (PL **rivalries**)
la rivalidad

river [ˈrɪvər] NOUN
el río
- **the river Tagus** el río Tajo

road [roud] NOUN
1 la carretera ◇ *There's a lot of traffic on the roads.* Hay mucho tráfico en las carreteras.
- **a road accident** un accidente de tránsito

2 la calle ◇ *They live across the road.* Viven al otro lado de la calle.

road map [ˈroud,mæp] NOUN
el mapa de carreteras
*Although **mapa** ends in **-a**, it is actually a masculine noun.*

road rage [ˈroud,reɪdʒ] NOUN
la conducta agresiva al volante

road sign [ˈroud,saɪn] NOUN
la señal de tráfico

roast [roust] ADJECTIVE
asado ◇ *roast chicken* pollo asado
- **roast pork** el asado de cerdo, *Mexico*: el asado de puerco
- **roast beef** el rosbif, *Mexico*: la carne de res al horno

roasting [ˈroustɪŋ] ADJECTIVE
- **It's roasting in here!** ¡Aquí hace un calor insoportable!

to **rob** [rɑːb] VERB
- **to rob somebody** robar a alguien ◇ *I've been robbed.* Me robaron.
- **to rob somebody of something** robar algo a alguien ◇ *He was robbed of his wallet.* Le robaron la cartera.
- **to rob a bank** asaltar un banco

robber [ˈrɑːbər] NOUN
el ladrón
la ladrona
- **a bank robber** un asaltante de bancos

robbery [ˈrɑːbəri] NOUN (PL **robberies**)
el robo
- **a bank robbery** un asalto a un banco
- **an armed robbery** un asalto a mano armada

* Verbs marked with this symbol are irregular. See pages 346–348 for further details.

robin ['ra:bɪn] NOUN
el petirrojo
robot ['roubaːt] NOUN
el robot (PL los robots)
rock [raːk] NOUN
see also **rock** VERB
1 la roca ◇ *They tunneled through the rock.* Abrieron un túnel a través de la roca. ◇ *I sat on a rock.* Me senté encima de una roca.
2 la piedra ◇ *The crowd started to throw rocks.* La multitud empezó a lanzar piedras.
3 el rock ◇ *a rock concert* un concierto de rock
◆ **rock and roll** el rock and roll
◆ **a rock candy** un palo de caramelo
to **rock** [raːk] VERB
see also **rock** NOUN
1 mecer ◇ *to rock a baby (in one's arms)* acunar a un bebé
2 sacudir ◇ *The explosion rocked the building.* La explosión sacudió el edificio.
rocket ['raːkɪt] NOUN
el cohete (*spacecraft, firework*)
rocking chair ['raːkɪŋ,tʃɛər] NOUN
la mecedora
rocking horse ['raːkɪŋ,hɔːrs] NOUN
el caballo de balancín
rod [raːd] NOUN
la caña de pescar (*for fishing*)
rode [roud] VERB *see* **ride**
role [roul] NOUN
el papel ◇ *to play a role* hacer* un papel
role play ['roul,pleɪ] NOUN
el juego de roles
roll [roul] NOUN
see also **roll** VERB
1 el rollo ◇ *a roll of toilet paper* un rollo de papel higiénico ◇ *a roll of film* un rollo de fotos
2 el panecito
el bolillo *Mexico*
◇ *a cheese roll* un panecito de queso, *Mexico:* un bolillo de queso
◆ **Roll call is at 8.30.** Pasan lista a las ocho y media.
to **roll** [roul] VERB
see also **roll** NOUN
rodar* (*ball*)
to **roll out** [roul'aut] VERB
extender* (*pastry*)
roller ['roulər] NOUN
el rulo
el chino *Mexico*
(*for hair*)
Rollerblades ® ['roulər,bleɪds] NOUN
los patines en línea
roller coaster ['roulər,koustər] NOUN
la montaña rusa
roller skates ['roulər,skeɪts] PL NOUN
los patines de ruedas
roller-skating ['roulər,skeɪtɪŋ] NOUN
el patinaje sobre ruedas
◆ **to go roller-skating** ir* a patinar (*sobre ruedas*)
rolling pin ['roulɪŋ,pɪn] NOUN
el rodillo
Roman ['roumən] ADJECTIVE, NOUN
romano ◇ *the Roman empire* el imperio romano
◆ **the Romans** los romanos
Roman Catholic ['roumən'kæθəlɪk] NOUN
el católico
la católica
◇ *He's a Roman Catholic.* Es católico.
romance [rou'mæns] NOUN
1 las novelas románticas (*novels*) ◇ *I read a lot of romance.* Leo muchas novelas románticas.
2 el romanticismo ◇ *the romance of Paris* el romanticismo de París
◆ **a holiday romance** un romance de verano
Romania [rou'meɪniə] NOUN
Rumania FEM
Romanian [rou'meɪniən] ADJECTIVE
rumano
romantic [rou'mæntɪk] ADJECTIVE
romántico
roof [ruːf] NOUN
el techo
room [ruːm] NOUN
see also **room** VERB
1 la habitación (PL las habitaciones)
◇ *She's in her room.* Está en su habitación.
◆ **a single room** una habitación individual
◆ **a double room** una habitación doble
2 sala (*in school*) ◇ *the music room* la sala de música
3 el espacio ◇ *There's no room for that box.* No hay espacio para esa caja.
to **room** [ruːm] VERB
see also **room** NOUN
◆ **to room with someone** compartir un departamento con alguien (*at college*)
roommate ['ruːm,meɪt] NOUN
el compañero de cuarto
la compañera de cuarto
rooster ['ruːstər] NOUN
el gallo
root [ruːt] NOUN
la raíz (PL las raíces)
rope [roup] NOUN
la cuerda
rose [rouz] VERB *see* **rise**
rose [rouz] NOUN
la rosa (*flower*)
to **rot** [raːt] VERB
pudrirse* ◇ *As far as I'm concerned he can rot in jail.* Por mí, que se pudra en la cárcel.
◇ *The wood had rotted.* La madera se había podrido.
◆ **Sugar rots your teeth.** El azúcar pica los dientes.

R

rotten ['rɑːtn] ADJECTIVE
podrido ◇ *a rotten apple* una manzana podrida
◆ **rotten weather** un tiempo asqueroso
◆ **That's a rotten thing to do!** ¡Eso es una maldad!
◆ **to feel rotten** sentirse* pésimo

rough [rʌf] ADJECTIVE, ADVERB
1 áspero ◇ *My hands are rough.* Tengo las manos ásperas.
2 violento ◇ *Ice hockey is a rough sport.* El hockey sobre hielo es un deporte violento.
3 peligroso ◇ *It's a rough area.* Es una zona peligrosa.
4 agitado ◇ *The sea was rough.* El mar estaba agitado.
5 aproximado ◇ *I have a rough idea.* Tengo una idea aproximada.

roughly ['rʌfli] ADVERB
aproximadamente ◇ *It weighs roughly 20 pounds.* Pesa aproximadamente 20 libras.

round [raund] ADJECTIVE, ADVERB, PREPOSITION
see also **round** NOUN
1 redondo ◇ *a round table* una mesa redonda
2 alrededor de ◇ *We were sitting round the table.* Estábamos sentados alrededor de la mesa.
◆ **round here** por aquí cerca ◇ *Is there a drugstore round here?* ¿Hay alguna farmacia por aquí cerca?
◆ **all year round** todo el año

round [raund] NOUN
see also **round** ADJECTIVE, ADVERB, PREPOSITION
1 la vuelta (*of tournament*)
2 el round (PL los rounds) (*of boxing match*)
◆ **a round of golf** una vuelta de golf
◆ **a round of drinks** una ronda de bebidas ◇ *He bought them a round of drinks.* Los invitó a una ronda de bebidas.
◆ **I think it's my round.** Creo que me toca pagar.

round trip ['raund'trɪp] NOUN
el viaje de ida y vuelta
el viaje redondo *Mexico*
◆ **a round-trip ticket** un pasaje de ida y vuelta, *Mexico:* un boleto redondo

route [ruːt] NOUN
el itinerario ◇ *We are planning our route.* Estamos planeando el itinerario.
◆ **bus route** el recorrido del autobús

routine [ruː'tiːn] NOUN
la rutina ◇ *my daily routine* mi rutina diaria

row (1) [rau] NOUN
1 el jaleo ◇ *What's that terrible row?* ¿Qué es ese jaleo tan tremendo?
2 la pelea
◆ **to have a row** pelearse ◇ *They've had a row.* Se pelearon.

row (2) [rou] NOUN
see also **row** VERB
1 la hilera ◇ *a row of houses* una hilera de casas
◆ **a row house** una casa adosada
2 la fila (*of people, seats*) ◇ *in the front row* en primera fila
◆ **five times in a row** cinco veces seguidas

to **row** [rou] VERB
see also **row (2)** NOUN
remar

rowboat ['rou,bout] NOUN
la barca de remos

rowing ['rouɪŋ] NOUN
el remo ◇ *My hobby is rowing.* My hobby es el remo.

royal ['rɔɪəl] ADJECTIVE
real ◇ *the royal family* la familia real

to **rub** [rʌb] VERB
1 frotar (*stain*)
2 restregarse*
tallarse *Mexico*
(*part of body*)
◇ *Don't rub your eyes.* No te restriegues los ojos. *Mexico:* No te talles los ojos.

to **rub out** [rʌb'aut] VERB
borrar

rubber ['rʌbər] NOUN
1 la goma ◇ *rubber soles* suelas de goma
◆ **rubber boots** botas de agua
2 el preservativo (*informal*)

rubber band ['rʌbərbænd] NOUN
la goma elástica
la liga de hule *Mexico*

rude [ruːd] ADJECTIVE
grosero ◇ *He was very rude to me.* Fue muy grosero conmigo.
◆ **It's rude to interrupt.** Es de mala educación interrumpir.
◆ **a rude joke** un chiste verde, *Mexico:* un chiste colorado
◆ **a rude word** una palabrota

rug [rʌg] NOUN
la alfombra
el tapete *Mexico*
(*carpet*)

rugby ['rʌgbi] NOUN
el rugby ◇ *He enjoys playing rugby.* Le gusta jugar rugby.

ruin ['ruːɪn] NOUN
see also **ruin** VERB
la ruina ◇ *the ruins of the castle* las ruinas del castillo
◆ **in ruins** en ruinas

to **ruin** ['ruːɪn] VERB
see also **ruin** NOUN
1 estropear ◇ *You'll ruin your shoes.* Te vas a estropear los zapatos. ◇ *It ruined our vacation.* Nos estropeó las vacaciones.
2 arruinar (*financially*)

rule [ruːl] NOUN

see also **rule** VERB

1 la regla ◇ *the rules of grammar* las reglas de la gramática

◆ **as a rule** por regla general

2 la norma ◇ *It's against the rules.* Va en contra de las normas.

to **rule** [ru:l] VERB

see also **rule** NOUN

gobernar*

to **rule out** [ru:l'aut] VERB

descartar (*possibility*)

ruler ['ru:lər] NOUN

la regla

rum [rʌm] NOUN

el ron

rummage sale ['rʌmɪdʒˌseɪl] NOUN

la venta de objetos usados (*con fines benéficos*)

rumor ['ru:mər] NOUN

el rumor ◇ *It's just a rumor.* Es sólo un rumor.

run [rʌn] NOUN

see also **run** VERB

la carrera (*in pantyhose*)

◆ **to go for a run** salir* a correr ◇ *I go for a run every morning.* Salgo a correr todas las mañanas.

◆ **I did a 10-mile run.** Corrí 10 millas.

◆ **The criminals are still on the run.** Los delincuentes siguen fugados.

◆ **in the long run** a la larga

◆ **to score a run** hacer* una carrera (*in baseball*)

to **run** [rʌn] VERB (**ran, run**)

see also **run** NOUN

1 correr

◆ **I ran five miles.** Corrí cinco millas.

◆ **to run a marathon** correr un maratón

2 dirigir* ◇ *He runs a large company.* Dirige una gran empresa.

3 organizar* ◇ *They run music courses during vacation.* Organizan cursos de música en las vacaciones.

4 llevar (*by car*) ◇ *I can run you to the station.* Te puedo llevar a la estación.

◆ **Don't leave the faucet running.** No dejen la llave abierta.

◆ **to run a bath** llenar la bañera

◆ **The buses stop running at midnight.** Los autobuses dejan de funcionar a medianoche.

to **run away** [ˌrʌnə'weɪ] VERB

huir* ◇ *They ran away before the police came.* Huyeron antes de que llegara la policía.

to **run out** [rʌn'aut] VERB

◆ **Time is running out.** Queda poco tiempo.

◆ **to run out of something** quedarse sin algo ◇ *We ran out of money.* Nos quedamos sin dinero.

to **run over** [rʌn'ouvər] VERB

atropellar

◆ **to get run over** ser* atropellado

rung [rʌŋ] VERB *see* **ring**

runner ['rʌnər] NOUN

el corredor

la corredora

runner-up ['rʌnər'ʌp] NOUN (PL **runners-up**)

el subcampeón (PL los subcampeones)

la subcampeona

running ['rʌnɪŋ] NOUN

el jogging

◆ **Running is my favorite sport.** El jogging es mi deporte favorito. ◇ *to go running* hacer* jogging

runway ['rʌnweɪ] NOUN

la pista de aterrizaje

rural ['rurəl] ADJECTIVE

rural

rush [rʌʃ] NOUN

see also **rush** VERB

la prisa ◇ *I'm in a rush.* Tengo prisa. ◇ *There's no rush.* No corre prisa.

◆ **to do something in a rush** hacer* algo deprisa

to **rush** [rʌʃ] VERB

see also **rush** NOUN

1 correr ◇ *Everyone rushed outside.* Todos corrieron hacia afuera.

2 precipitarse ◇ *There's no need to rush.* No hay por qué precipitarse.

rush hour ['rʌʃˌauər] NOUN

la hora pico

rusk [rʌsk] NOUN

la galleta para bebés

Russia ['rʌʃə] NOUN

Rusia FEM

Russian ['rʌʃən] ADJECTIVE

see also **Russian** NOUN

ruso

Russian ['rʌʃən] NOUN

see also **Russian** ADJECTIVE

1 el ruso

la rusa

(*person*)

◇ *the Russians* los rusos

2 el ruso (*language*)

rust [rʌst] NOUN

el óxido

rusty ['rʌsti] ADJECTIVE

oxidado

rutabaga [ˌru:tə'beɪgə] NOUN

el nabo sueco

ruthless ['ru:θlɪs] ADJECTIVE

despiadado

RV [ɑ:r'vi:] NOUN

el cámper

rye [raɪ] NOUN

el centeno

◆ **rye bread** el pan de centeno

R

S

sack [sæk] NOUN
see also **sack** VERB
1 el saco ◇ *a sack of maize* un saco de maíz
2 la bolsa de papel (*at checkout*)
◆ **to give somebody the sack** despedir* a alguien
◆ **He got the sack.** Lo despidieron.

to **sack** [sæk] VERB
see also **sack** NOUN
◆ **to sack somebody** despedir* a alguien ◇ *He was sacked.* Lo despidieron.

sacred ['seɪkrɪd] ADJECTIVE
sagrado ◇ *sacred places* lugares sagrados
◆ **sacred music** música sacra

sacrifice ['sækrɪfaɪs] NOUN
el sacrificio

sad [sæd] ADJECTIVE
triste

saddle ['sædl] NOUN
1 la silla de montar (*for horse*)
2 el sillín (*on bicycle*)

saddlebag ['sædl,bæg] NOUN
1 la cartera (*on bicycle*)
2 la alforja (*for horse*)

sadly ['sædli] ADVERB
1 con tristeza ◇ *"She's gone", he said sadly.* "Se fue" dijo con tristeza.
2 desgraciadamente ◇ *Sadly, it was too late.* Desgraciadamente, ya era demasiado tarde.

safe [seɪf] NOUN
see also **safe** ADJECTIVE
la caja fuerte (PL las cajas fuerte)

safe [seɪf] ADJECTIVE
see also **safe** NOUN
1 seguro ◇ *This car isn't safe.* Este carro no es seguro.
2 a salvo ◇ *You're safe now.* Ya estás a salvo.
◆ **to feel safe** sentirse* protegido
◆ **Is the water safe to drink?** ¿Es agua potable?
◆ **Don't worry, it's perfectly safe.** No te preocupes, no hay ningún peligro.
◆ **safe sex** el sexo sin riesgo

safety ['seɪfti] NOUN
la seguridad
◆ **safety belt** el cinturón de seguridad (PL los cinturones de seguridad)
◆ **safety pin** el imperdible, *Mexico*: el seguro
◆ **Her car passed the safety inspection.** El carro pasó la revisión técnica.

Sagittarius [sædʒɪ'tɛriəs] NOUN
el Sagitario (*sign*) ◇ *I'm a Sagittarius.* Soy sagitario.
◆ **a Sagittarius** un/una sagitario

said [sɛd] VERB *see* **say**

sail [seɪl] NOUN
see also **sail** VERB
la vela
◆ **to set sail** zarpar

to **sail** [seɪl] VERB
see also **sail** NOUN
1 navegar* ◇ *to sail around the world* dar* la vuelta al mundo navegando
2 zarpar ◇ *The boat sails at eight o'clock.* El barco zarpa a las ocho.

sailboat ['seɪl,bout] NOUN
el barco de vela

sailing ['seɪlɪŋ] NOUN
la vela (*sport*)
◆ **to go sailing** hacer* vela
◆ **sailing ship** el velero

sailor ['seɪlər] NOUN
el marinero ◇ *He's a sailor.* Es marinero.

saint [seɪnt] NOUN
el santo
la santa

When used before a man's name, the word ***Santo*** *is shortened to* ***San****, the exceptions being* ***Santo Tomás*** *and* ***Santo Domingo****.*

◇ *Saint John* San Juan

sake [seɪk] NOUN
◆ **for the sake of argument** pongamos por caso
◆ **for the sake of the children** por el bien de los niños
◆ **For goodness sake!** ¡Por el amor de Dios!

salad ['sæləd] NOUN
la ensalada
◆ **salad dressing** el aliño para la ensalada

salami [sə'lɑːmi] NOUN
el salami

salary ['sæləri] NOUN (PL **salaries**)
el sueldo

sale [seɪl] NOUN
1 las rebajas ◇ *There's a sale on at Sears.* En Sears están de rebajas. ◇ *the January sales* las rebajas de enero
2 la venta ◇ *Newspaper sales have fallen.* Ha descendido la venta de periódicos.
◆ **on sale** a la venta
◆ **The house is for sale.** La casa está en venta.
◆ **"for sale"** "se vende"

sales clerk ['seɪlz,klɜːrk] NOUN
el vendedor
la vendedora

salesman ['seɪlzmən] NOUN (PL **salesmen**)
1 el representante (*commercial*) ◇ *an insurance salesman* un representante de seguros
2 el vendedor (*sales clerk*) ◇ *a car salesman* un vendedor de carros

sales rep ['seɪlz,rɛp] NOUN
el/la representante

sales slip ['seɪlz,slɪp] NOUN
el recibo (*for goods bought*)

saleswoman ['seɪlz,wumən] NOUN (PL

saleswomen)
[1] la representante (*commercial*) ◇ *an insurance saleswoman* una representante de seguros
[2] la vendedora (*sales clerk*)

salmon ['sæmən] NOUN (PL **salmons** *or* **salmon**)
el salmón (PL los salmones)

salon [sə'lɑːn] NOUN
el salón (PL los salones) ◇ *hair salon* salón de peluquería ◇ *beauty salon* salón de belleza

salt [sɑːlt] NOUN
la sal

salty ['sɑːlti] ADJECTIVE
salado

to **salute** [sə'luːt] VERB
saludar

Salvation Army [sæl'veɪʃən'ɑːrmi] NOUN
el Ejército de Salvación

same [seɪm] ADJECTIVE
mismo ◇ *the same model* el mismo modelo ◇ *It's not the same.* No es lo mismo.
◆ **They're exactly the same.** Son exactamente iguales.
◆ **The house is still the same.** La casa sigue igual.

sample ['sæmpəl] NOUN
la muestra ◇ *a free sample of perfume* una muestra gratuita de perfume

sand [sænd] NOUN
la arena

sandal ['sændl] NOUN
la sandalia ◇ *a pair of sandals* unas sandalias

sand castle ['sænd,kæsəl] NOUN
el castillo de arena

sandwich ['sændwɪtʃ] NOUN (PL **sandwiches**)
el sandwich (PL los sandwiches)
◆ **submarine sandwich**

> ℹ *Un* **submarine sandwich** *o* **sub** *es un pan largo que tiene la forma de un submarino y que se rellena con jamón u otros fiambres.*

sane [seɪn] ADJECTIVE
cuerdo ◇ *She was as sane as you or me.* Está tan cuerda como tú o como yo.
Be careful not to translate ***sane*** *by* ***sano***.

sang [sæŋ] VERB *see* **sing**

sanitary napkin ['sænɪteri'næpkɪn] NOUN
la toalla higiénica

sank [sæŋk] VERB *see* **sink**

Santa Claus ['sæntə'klɑːz] NOUN
Papá Noel MASC

sarcastic [sɑːr'kæstɪk] ADJECTIVE
sarcástico

sassy ['sæsi] ADJECTIVE
descarado ◇ *Don't be sassy!* ¡No seas descarado!

SAT [,ɛseɪ'tiː] NOUN

> ℹ **SAT** *es la abreviatura de* **Scholastic Aptitude Test** *que es una prueba de aptitud estándar, a nivel nacional, y que por lo general hacen los estudiantes que desean entrar a la universidad por primera vez.*

sat [sæt] VERB *see* **sit**

satchel ['sætʃəl] NOUN
la mochila

satellite ['sætəlaɪt] NOUN
el satélite ◇ *by satellite* vía satélite
◆ **a satellite dish** una antena parabólica
◆ **satellite television** la televisión vía satélite

satisfactory [sætɪs'fæktəri] ADJECTIVE
satisfactorio

satisfied ['sætɪsfaɪd] ADJECTIVE
satisfecho

Saturday ['sætərdi] NOUN
el sábado (PL los sábados) ◇ *I saw her on Saturday.* La vi el sábado. ◇ *every Saturday* todos los sábados ◇ *last Saturday* el sábado pasado ◇ *next Saturday* el sábado que viene ◇ *on Saturdays* los sábados
◆ **I have a Saturday job.** Tengo un trabajo los sábados.

sauce [sɑːs] NOUN
[1] la salsa ◇ *tomato sauce* salsa de tomate
[2] la crema ◇ *chocolate sauce* crema de chocolate

saucepan ['sɑːs,pæn] NOUN
la cacerola

saucer ['sɑːsər] NOUN
el platillo

Saudi Arabia ['saudiə'reɪbiə] NOUN
Arabia Saudí FEM

sauna ['sɑːnə] NOUN
la sauna

sausage ['sɑːsɪdʒ] NOUN
la salchicha

to **save** [seɪv] VERB
[1] ahorrar ◇ *I saved money by staying in youth hostels.* Ahorré dinero yendo a albergues juveniles. ◇ *I've saved $50 already.* Ya llevo ahorrados 50 dólares. ◇ *It saved us time.* Nos ahorró tiempo.
◆ **We went in a taxi to save time.** Para ganar tiempo fuimos en taxi.
[2] salvar ◇ *The drug has saved thousands of lives.* El medicamento ha salvado miles de vidas.
◆ **Luckily, all the passengers were saved.** Afortunadamente, todos los pasajeros se salvaron.
[3] guardar ◇ *I saved the file onto a diskette.* Guardé el archivo en un disquete.

to **save up** [seɪv'ʌp] VERB
ahorrar ◇ *I'm saving up for a new bike.* Estoy ahorrando para una bici nueva.

savings ['seɪvɪŋz] PL NOUN
los ahorros ◇ *She spent all her savings on a* ☞

S

computer. Se gastó todos sus ahorros en una computadora.

savory ['seɪvəri] ADJECTIVE
salado ◇ *Is it sweet or savory?* ¿Es dulce o salado?

saw [sɑː] VERB *see* **see**

saw [sɑː] NOUN
la sierra

sax [sæks] NOUN (PL **saxes**)
el saxo

saxophone ['sæksəfoun] NOUN
el saxofón (PL los saxofones)

to **say** [seɪ] VERB (**said, said**)
decir* ◇ *to say yes* decir que sí ◇ *What did he say?* ¿Qué dijo él?
◆ **Could you say that again?** ¿Podrías repetir eso?
◆ **The clock said four minutes after eleven.** El reloj marcaba las once y cuatro minutos.
◆ **It goes without saying that...** Ni que decir tiene que...

saying ['seɪɪŋ] NOUN
el dicho

scale [skeɪl] NOUN
la escala ◇ *a large-scale map* un mapa a gran escala
◆ **He underestimated the scale of the problem.** Ha subestimado la envergadura del problema.

scales [skeɪlz] PL NOUN
1 la balanza (*in kitchen*)
2 la báscula (*in store*)
◆ **bathroom scales** la báscula de baño

scallion ['skæljən] NOUN
la cebolleta

scampi ['skæmpi] PL NOUN
los camarones rebozados

scandal ['skændl] NOUN
1 el escándalo (*outrage*) ◇ *It caused a scandal.* Causó un escándalo.
2 las habladurías (*gossip*) ◇ *It's just scandal.* No son más que habladurías.

scar [skɑːr] NOUN
la cicatriz (PL las cicatrices)

scarce [skɛərs] ADJECTIVE
escaso ◇ *scarce resources* recursos escasos
◆ **Jobs are scarce.** Escasean los trabajos.

scarcely ['skɛərsli] ADVERB
apenas ◇ *I scarcely knew him.* Apenas lo conocía.

scare [skɛər] NOUN
see also **scare** VERB
el susto ◇ *We got a bit of a scare.* Nos pegamos un susto.
◆ **a bomb scare** una amenaza de bomba

to **scare** [skɛər] VERB
see also **scare** NOUN
asustar ◇ *You scared me!* ¡Me asustaste!

scarecrow ['skɛrkrou] NOUN
el espantapájaros (PL los espantapájaros)

scared ['skɛərd] ADJECTIVE
◆ **to be scared** tener* miedo ◇ *Are you scared of him?* ¿Le tienes miedo?
◆ **I was scared stiff.** Estaba muerto de miedo.

scarf [skɑːrf] NOUN (PL **scarfs** *or* **scarves**)
1 la bufanda (*woolen*)
2 el pañuelo (*light*)

scary ['skɛri] ADJECTIVE
◆ **It was really scary.** Daba verdadero miedo.
◆ **a scary movie** una película de miedo

scene [siːn] NOUN
1 la escena ◇ *love scenes* las escenas de amor ◇ *It was an amazing scene.* Era una escena asombrosa.
2 el lugar ◇ *at the scene of the crime* en el lugar del crimen ◇ *The police were soon on the scene.* La policía no tardó en acudir al lugar de los hechos.
◆ **to make a scene** armar un escándalo

scenery ['siːnəri] NOUN
el paisaje

scent [sɛnt] NOUN
el perfume (*of flowers, perfume*)

schedule ['skɛdʒuːl] NOUN
el programa
Although ***programa*** *ends in* ***-a****, it is actually a masculine noun.*
◇ *a production schedule* un programa de producción
◆ **There's a tight schedule for this project.** Este proyecto tiene un calendario muy justo.
◆ **class schedule** el horario
◆ **a busy schedule** una agenda muy apretada
◆ **on schedule** sin retraso
◆ **to be behind schedule** ir* con retraso

scheduled flight ['skɛdʒuːld'flaɪt] NOUN
el vuelo regular

scheme [skiːm] NOUN
el plan ◇ *a road-widening scheme* un plan de ensanchamiento de calzadas ◇ *a crazy scheme he dreamed up* un plan descabellado que se le ocurrió

scholarship ['skɑːlərʃɪp] NOUN
la beca

school [skuːl] NOUN
1 el colegio (*for children*) ◇ *at school* en el colegio ◇ *to go to school* ir* al colegio
◆ **after school** después de clase
2 la facultad (*at a university*) ◇ *art school* la facultad de bellas artes

schoolbook ['skuːlbuk] NOUN
el libro de texto

schoolboy ['skuːl,bɔɪ] NOUN
el colegial

schoolchildren ['skuːl,tʃɪldrən] PL NOUN
los colegiales

schoolgirl ['skuːl,gɜːrl] NOUN
la colegiala

science ['saɪəns] NOUN
la ciencia

science fiction ['saɪəns'fɪkʃən] NOUN
la ciencia ficción

scientific [saɪən'tɪfɪk] ADJECTIVE
científico

scientist ['saɪəntɪst] NOUN
el científico
la científica

scissors ['sɪzərz] PL NOUN
las tijeras ◇ *a pair of scissors* unas tijeras

to **scoff** [skɑ:f] VERB
mofarse ◇ *My friends scoffed at the idea.* Mis amigos se mofaron de la idea.

scooter ['sku:tər] NOUN
1 la Vespa® (*motorcycle*)
2 el patinete
la patineta Mexico
(*child's toy*)

score [skɔ:r] NOUN
see also **score** VERB
1 la puntuación (PL las puntuaciones) ◇ *the highest score by an NBA player* la puntuación más alta obtenida por un jugador de la NBA
2 el resultado ◇ *The score was three nothing.* El resultado fue de tres a cero.
◆ **What's the score?** ¿Cómo van?

to **score** [skɔ:r] VERB
see also **score** NOUN
1 marcar* ◇ *to score a goal* marcar un gol
◆ **to score a point** anotar un punto
◆ **to score six out of ten** sacar* una puntuación de seis sobre diez, sacar* un puntaje de seis sobre diez
2 llevar el tanteo ◇ *Who's going to score?* ¿Quién va a llevar el tanteo?

Scorpio ['skɔ:rpiou] NOUN
el Escorpión (*sign*) ◇ *I'm a Scorpio.* Soy escorpión.
◆ **a Scorpio** un/una escorpión

Scot [skɑ:t] NOUN
el escocés
la escocesa
(*person*)

Scotch tape® ['skɑ:tʃ'teɪp] NOUN
la cinta Scotch®
la cinta Dúrex® Mexico

Scotland ['skɑ:tlənd] NOUN
Escocia FEM

Scots [skɑ:ts] ADJECTIVE
escocés (FEM escocesa) ◇ *a Scots accent* un acento escocés

Scotsman ['skɑ:tsmən] NOUN (PL **Scotsmen**)
el escocés (PL los escoceses)

Scotswoman ['skɑ:ts,wumən] NOUN (PL **Scotswomen**)
la escocesa

Scottish ['skɑ:tɪʃ] ADJECTIVE
escocés (MASC PL escoceses, FEM escocesa)
◇ *a Scottish accent* un acento escocés

scout [skaut] NOUN
el boy scout (PL los boy scouts)
la girl scout (PL las girl scouts)

scrambled eggs ['skræmbəld'ɛgz] PL NOUN
los huevos revueltos

scrap [skræp] NOUN
see also **scrap** VERB
1 el trocito ◇ *a scrap of paper* un trocito de papel
2 la pelea ◇ *There was a scrap outside the bar.* Hubo una pelea a la salida del bar.
◆ **scrap iron** la chatarra

to **scrap** [skræp] VERB
see also **scrap** NOUN
desechar ◇ *In the end the plan was scrapped.* Al final se desechó el plan.

scrapbook ['skræp,buk] NOUN
el álbum de recortes (PL los álbumes de recortes)

to **scratch** [skrætʃ] VERB
see also **scratch** NOUN
1 rascarse* (*when itchy*) ◇ *Stop scratching!* ¡Deja de rascarte!
2 arañar (*cut*) ◇ *He scratched his arm on the bushes.* Se arañó el brazo con las zarzas.
3 rayar (*scrape*) ◇ *You'll scratch the table with that knife.* Vas a rayar la mesa con ese cuchillo.

scratch [skrætʃ] (PL **scratches**) NOUN
see also **scratch** VERB
el arañazo (*on skin, floor*)
◆ **to start from scratch** partir de cero
◆ **a scratch card** una tarjeta de "raspe y gane"
◆ **scratch paper** el papel de borrador

scream [skri:m] NOUN
see also **scream** VERB
el grito

to **scream** [skri:m] VERB
see also **scream** NOUN
gritar

screen [skri:n] NOUN
la pantalla (*television, cinema, computer*)

screen saver ['skri:n,seɪvər] NOUN
el protector de pantalla

screw [skru:] NOUN
el tornillo

screwdriver ['skru:,draɪvər] NOUN
el destornillador
el desarmador Mexico

to **scribble** ['skrɪbəl] VERB
garabatear

to **scrub** [skrʌb] VERB
fregar*
tallar Mexico

sculpture ['skʌlptʃər] NOUN
la escultura

sea [si:] NOUN
el mar
*The word **mar** is masculine in most cases, but in some set expressions it is feminine.*
◇ *by sea* por mar ◇ *a house by the sea* una casa junto al mar
◆ **The fishermen put to sea.** Los pescadores se ☞

S

hicieron a la mar.

seafood ['si:fu:d] NOUN
los mariscos ◇ *I don't like seafood.* No me gustan los mariscos.
◆ **a seafood restaurant** una marisquería

seagull ['si:gʌl] NOUN
la gaviota

seal [si:l] NOUN
see also **seal** VERB
1 la foca (*animal*)
2 la estampilla
el timbre *Mexico*
(*on letter*)

to **seal** [si:l] VERB
see also **seal** NOUN
sellar

seaman ['si:mən] NOUN (PL **seamen**)
el marinero

to **search** [sɜ:rtʃ] VERB
see also **search** NOUN
1 buscar* ◇ *They're searching for the missing climbers.* Están buscando a los escaladores desaparecidos.
2 registrar ◇ *The police searched him for drugs.* La policía lo registró en busca de drogas.
◆ **They searched the woods for the little girl.** Rastrearon el bosque en busca de la niña.

search [sɜ:rtʃ] NOUN (PL **searches**)
see also **search** VERB
1 la búsqueda ◇ *The search was abandoned.* Se abandonó la búsqueda.
◆ **to go in search of** ir* en busca de
2 el registro ◇ *a search of the building* un registro del edificio

search engine ['sɜ:rtʃˌɛndʒɪn] NOUN
el buscador

search party ['sɜ:rtʃˌpɑ:rti] NOUN (PL **search parties**)
el equipo de búsqueda

seashore ['si:ʃɔ:r] NOUN
la orilla del mar ◇ *on the seashore* a la orilla del mar

seasick ['si:sɪk] ADJECTIVE
◆ **to be seasick** marearse en barco

seaside ['si:saɪd] NOUN
la playa
◆ **a seaside resort** un balneario

season ['si:zən] NOUN
la estación (PL las estaciones) ◇ *What's your favorite season?* ¿Cuál es tu estación preferida?
◆ **out of season** fuera de temporada
◆ **during the vacation season** en la temporada de vacaciones
◆ **a season ticket** un abono

seat [si:t] NOUN
1 el asiento ◇ *I was sitting in the back seat.* Yo iba sentada en el asiento trasero.
◆ **Are there any seats left?** ¿Quedan localidades?
2 el escaño
la silla curul *Mexico*
◇ *to win a seat in the election* conseguir* un escaño en las elecciones, *Mexico*: obtener* una silla curul en las elecciones

seat belt ['si:tˌbɛlt] NOUN
el cinturón de seguridad (PL los cinturones de seguridad)

seaweed ['si:wi:d] NOUN
el alga marina FEM
*Although it's a feminine noun, remember that you use **el** and **un** with **alga**.*

second ['sɛkənd] ADJECTIVE, ADVERB
see also **second** NOUN
segundo ◇ *the second time* la segunda vez
◆ **to come in second** llegar* en segundo lugar
◆ **March second** el dos de marzo

second ['sɛkənd] NOUN
see also **second** ADJECTIVE, ADVERB
el segundo ◇ *It'll only take a second.* Es un segundo nada más.

secondary school ['sɛkəndɛriˌsku:l] NOUN
el colegio de enseñanza secundaria

second-class [sɛkənd'klæs] ADJECTIVE, ADVERB
de segunda clase (*ticket, compartment*)
◆ **to travel second-class** viajar en segunda
◆ **a second-class citizen** un ciudadano de segunda clase
◆ **second-class postage**

> ℹ *En los Estados Unidos, el **second-class postage** es el tipo de franqueo que se usa para enviar periódicos y revistas.*

secondhand ['sɛkənd'hænd] ADJECTIVE
de segunda mano

secondly ['sɛkəndli] ADVERB
en segundo lugar

secret ['si:krɪt] ADJECTIVE
see also **secret** NOUN
secreto ◇ *a secret mission* una misión secreta

secret ['si:krɪt] NOUN
see also **secret** ADJECTIVE
el secreto ◇ *Can you keep a secret?* ¿Sabes guardar un secreto?
◆ **in secret** en secreto

secretary ['sɛkrətɛri] NOUN (PL **secretaries**)
1 el secretario
la secretaria
(*in office*)
2 el ministro
la ministra
el secretario
la secretaria *Mexico*
(*in government*)
◆ **the Secretary of State** el Ministro de Relaciones Exteriores, *Mexico*: el Secretario de Relaciones Exteriores

- **the Secretary of Education** el Ministro de Educación, Mexico: el Secretario de Educación

secretly ['si:krɪtli] ADVERB
en secreto

section ['sɛkʃən] NOUN
la sección (PL las secciones)

security [sɪ'kjurɪti] NOUN
la seguridad ◇ *They are trying to improve airport security.* Intentan mejorar las medidas de seguridad en el aeropuerto. ◇ *They have no job security.* No tienen seguridad en el empleo.

- **security guard** el/la guarda jurado

sedan [sə'dæn] NOUN
el sedán

to **see** [si:] VERB (**saw, seen**)
ver* ◇ *I can't see.* No veo nada. ◇ *I saw him yesterday.* Lo vi ayer.

- **You need to see a doctor.** Tienes que ir a ver a un médico.
- **See you!** ¡Hasta luego!
- **See you soon!** ¡Hasta pronto!

to **see to** ['si:tu:] VERB
encargarse* de ◇ *The shower isn't working. Can you see to it please?* La ducha se descompuso. ¿Podrías encargarte de eso?

seed [si:d] NOUN
la semilla ◇ *sunflower seeds* semillas de girasol

to **seem** [si:m] VERB
parecer* ◇ *She seems tired.* Parece cansada. ◇ *That seems like a good idea.* Me parece una buena idea.

- **The store seemed to be closed.** Parecía que la tienda estaba cerrada.
- **It seems that...** Parece que... ◇ *It seems you have no alternative.* Parece que no tienes otra opción.
- **It seems she's getting married.** Por lo visto se casa.
- **There seems to be a problem.** Parece que hay un problema.

seen [si:n] VERB *see* **see**

seesaw ['si:sɑ:] NOUN
el balancín (PL los balancines)

see-through ['si:θru:] ADJECTIVE
transparente

seldom ['sɛldəm] ADVERB
rara vez

to **select** [sɪ'lɛkt] VERB
seleccionar

selection [sɪ'lɛkʃən] NOUN
1 la selección (PL las selecciones)
2 el surtido ◇ *the widest selection on the market* el más amplio surtido del mercado

self-addressed stamped envelope ['sɛlfədrɛst,stæmpt'ɛnvəloup] NOUN

- **please enclose a self-addressed stamped envelope** adjunte un sobre franqueado con su nombre y dirección

self-assured [,sɛlfə'ʃuərd] ADJECTIVE
seguro de sí mismo (FEM segura de sí misma)

self-centered [sɛlf'sɛntərd] ADJECTIVE
egocéntrico

self-confidence [sɛlf'kɑ:nfɪdəns] NOUN
la confianza en uno mismo ◇ *I lost all my self-confidence.* Perdí toda la confianza en mí mismo.

self-conscious [sɛlf'kɑ:nʃəs] ADJECTIVE
1 cohibido ◇ *She was really self-conscious at first.* Al principio estaba muy cohibida.
2 acomplejado ◇ *She was self-conscious about her height.* Estaba acomplejada por su estatura.

self-contained [,sɛlfkən'teɪnd] ADJECTIVE
independiente

self-control [,sɛlfkən'troul] NOUN
el autocontrol

self-defense [,sɛlfdɪ'fɛns] NOUN
la defensa personal ◇ *self-defense classes* clases de defensa personal

- **She killed him in self-defense.** Lo mató en defensa propia.

self-discipline [sɛlf'dɪsɪplɪn] NOUN
la autodisciplina

self-employed [,sɛlfɪm'plɔɪd] ADJECTIVE
autónomo ◇ *to be self-employed* ser* autónomo

- **the self-employed** los trabajadores autónomos

selfish ['sɛlfɪʃ] ADJECTIVE
egoísta

self-respect [,sɛlfrɪ'spɛkt] NOUN
el amor propio

self-service [sɛlf'sɜ:rvɪs] ADJECTIVE
de autoservicio

to **sell** [sɛl] VERB (**sold, sold**)
vender ◇ *He sold it to me.* Me lo vendió.

to **sell off** [sɛl'ɑ:f] VERB
liquidar

to **sell out** [sɛl'aut] VERB

- **The tickets sold out in three hours.** Las entradas se agotaron en tres horas.

selling price ['sɛlɪŋ,praɪs] NOUN
el precio de venta

semester [sə,mɛstər] NOUN
el semestre ◇ *the fall semester* el segundo semestre

semicircle ['sɛmi,sɜ:rkəl] NOUN
el semicírculo

semicolon ['sɛmi,koulən] NOUN
el punto y coma (PL los punto y coma)

semifinal ['sɛmi,faɪnl] NOUN
la semifinal

Senate ['sɛnɪt] NOUN
el Senado

senator ['sɛnətər] NOUN
el senador
la senadora

to **send** [sɛnd] VERB (**sent, sent**)
mandar ◇ *She sent me a birthday card.* Me ☞

S

mandó una tarjeta de cumpleaños. ◇ *He was sent to Los Angeles.* Lo mandaron a Los Angeles.

to **send back** [sɛnd'bæk] VERB
devolver*

to **send off** [sɛnd'ɑːf] VERB
enviar* por correo ◇ *We sent off your order yesterday.* Le enviamos el pedido por correo ayer.

to **send off for** [sɛnd'ɑːf,fɔːr] VERB
escribir* pidiendo (*free*) ◇ *I've sent off for a brochure.* He escrito pidiendo un folleto.

to **send out** [sɛnd'aut] VERB
enviar*

to **send out for** [sɛnd'aut,fɔːr] VERB
pedir* por teléfono ◇ *Let's send out for a pizza.* Vamos a pedir una pizza por teléfono.

sender ['sɛndər] NOUN
el/la remitente

senior ['siːnjər] ADJECTIVE, NOUN
1 alto ◇ *senior officials in the American government* altos cargos del gobierno americano ◇ *senior management* los altos directivos
◆ **She's five years my senior.** Es cinco años mayor que yo.
2 el/la estudiante del último año (*at school*)

senior citizen ['siːnjər'sɪtɪzən] NOUN
la persona de la tercera edad

senior high school ['siːnjər'haɪ,skuːl] NOUN
el colegio secundario

sensational [sɛn'seɪʃənl] ADJECTIVE
sensacional

sense [sɛns] NOUN
el sentido ◇ *the five senses* los cinco sentidos ◇ *Use your common sense!* ¡Usa el sentido común!
◆ **It makes sense.** Tiene sentido.
◆ **It doesn't make sense.** No tiene sentido.
◆ **a keen sense of smell** un olfato finísimo
◆ **sense of humor** el sentido del humor

senseless ['sɛnslɪs] ADJECTIVE
1 sin sentido ◇ *senseless violence* violencia sin sentido
◆ **It is senseless to protest.** No tiene sentido protestar.
2 inconsciente ◇ *He was lying senseless on the floor.* Yacía inconsciente en el suelo.

sensible ['sɛnsɪbəl] ADJECTIVE
sensato ◇ *Be sensible!* ¡Sé sensato! ◇ *It would be sensible to check first.* Lo más sensato sería comprobarlo antes.
*Be careful not to translate **sensible** by the Spanish word **sensible**.*

sensitive ['sɛnsɪtɪv] ADJECTIVE
sensible

sensuous ['sɛnʃuəs] ADJECTIVE
sensual

sent [sɛnt] VERB *see* **send**

sentence ['sɛntns] NOUN
see also **sentence** VERB
1 la oración (PL las oraciones) ◇ *What does this sentence mean?* ¿Qué significa esta oración?
2 la sentencia ◇ *to pass sentence* dictar sentencia
3 la condena ◇ *a sentence of 10 years* una condena de 10 años
◆ **the death sentence** la pena de muerte
◆ **He got a life sentence.** Fue condenado a cadena perpetua.

to **sentence** ['sɛntns] VERB
see also **sentence** NOUN
◆ **to sentence somebody to life imprisonment** condenar a alguien a cadena perpetua
◆ **to sentence somebody to death** condenar a muerte a alguien

sentimental [sɛntɪ'mɛntl] ADJECTIVE
sentimental

separate ['sɛpərət] ADJECTIVE
see also **separate** VERB
distinto ◇ *Men and women have separate exercise rooms.* Los hombres y las mujeres tienen salas de ejercicios distintas.
◆ **The children have separate rooms.** Los niños tienen cada uno su habitación.
◆ **I wrote it on a separate sheet.** Lo escribí en una hoja aparte.
◆ **on separate occasions** en diversas ocasiones

to **separate** ['sɛpəreɪt] VERB
see also **separate** ADJECTIVE
1 separar ◇ *Police moved in to separate the two groups.* La policía intervino para separar a los dos grupos.
2 separarse ◇ *Her parents separated last year.* Sus padres se separaron el año pasado.

separately ['sɛprətli] ADVERB
por separado

separation [sɛpə'reɪʃən] NOUN
la separación (PL las separaciones)

September [sɛp'tɛmbər] NOUN
septiembre MASC ◇ *in September* en septiembre ◇ *on September 23rd* el 23 de septiembre

sequel ['siːkwəl] NOUN
la continuación (PL las continuaciones)

sequence ['siːkwəns] NOUN
1 la serie ◇ *a sequence of events* una serie de acontecimientos
2 el orden ◇ *in sequence* en orden
3 la secuencia ◇ *the best sequence in the movie* la mejor secuencia de la película

sergeant ['sɑːrdʒənt] NOUN
1 el/la sargento (*army*)
2 el/la oficial de policía (*police*)

serial ['sɪriəl] NOUN
1 el serial (*on TV, radio*)
2 la novela por entregas (*in magazine*)

series ['sɪri:z] NOUN (PL **series**)
la serie

serious ['sɪriəs] ADJECTIVE
1 serio ◇ *You're looking very serious.* Estás muy serio.
◆ **Are you serious?** ¿Lo dices en serio?
2 grave ◇ *a serious illness* una enfermedad grave

seriously ['sɪriəsli] ADVERB
en serio ◇ *No, but seriously...* No, pero ya en serio... ◇ *to take somebody seriously* tomar en serio a alguien
◆ **seriously injured** gravemente herido
◆ **Seriously?** ¿De verdad?

sermon ['sɜ:rmən] NOUN
el sermón (PL los sermones)

servant ['sɜ:rvənt] NOUN
el criado
la criada

to **serve** [sɜ:rv] VERB
see also **serve** NOUN
1 servir* ◇ *Dinner is served.* La cena está servida.
◆ **It's Agassi's turn to serve.** Al servicio Agassi.
◆ **Are you being served?** ¿Lo atienden? (*in restaurant*)
2 cumplir ◇ *to serve a life sentence* cumplir cadena perpetua ◇ *to serve time* cumplir condena
◆ **It serves you right.** Lo tienes bien merecido.

serve [sɜ:rv] NOUN
see also **serve** VERB
el servicio

server ['sɜ:rvər] NOUN
1 el servidor (*computer*)
2 el jugador
la jugadora
(*in tennis*)

to **service** ['sɜ:rvɪs] VERB
see also **service** NOUN
hacer* un servicio a (*car, washing machine*)

service ['sɜ:rvɪs] NOUN
see also **service** VERB
1 el servicio ◇ *Service is included.* El servicio está incluido. ◇ *the postal service* el servicio de correos
◆ **a bus service** una línea de bus
2 el oficio religioso ◇ *a memorial service* un oficio religioso conmemorativo
◆ **the armed services** las fuerzas armadas

service charge ['sɜ:rvɪs,tʃɑ:rdʒ] NOUN
el servicio ◇ *There's no service charge.* El servicio va incluido.

serviceman ['sɜ:rvɪsmən] NOUN (PL **servicemen**)
el militar

service station ['sɜ:rvɪs,steɪʃən] NOUN
la estación de servicio (PL las estaciones de servicio)

servicing ['sɜ:rvɪsɪŋ] NOUN
el servicio ◇ *The car needs a servicing.* Al carro le hace falta un servicio.

session ['sɛʃən] NOUN
la sesión (PL las sesiones)

set [sɛt] NOUN
see also **set** VERB
1 el juego (*of objects, tools*) ◇ *a set of keys* un juego de llaves
◆ **The sofa and chairs are only sold as a set.** El sofá y los sillones no se venden por separado.
◆ **a chess set** un ajedrez
◆ **a train set** un tren eléctrico
2 el conjunto (*of ideas, actions*) ◇ *a set of calculations* un conjunto de cálculos
3 el set (PL los sets) (*in tennis*) ◇ *She was leading 5-1 in the first set.* Iba ganando 5 a 1 en el primer set.

to **set** [sɛt] VERB (**set, set**)
see also **set** NOUN
1 poner* ◇ *I set the alarm for seven o'clock.* Puse el despertador a las siete.
2 establecer* ◇ *The world record was set last year.* El récord mundial se estableció el año pasado.
3 ponerse* ◇ *The sun was setting.* Se estaba poniendo el sol.
◆ **The movie is set in Morocco.** La película se desarrolla en Marruecos.
◆ **to set something on fire** prender fuego a algo
◆ **to set sail** zarpar
◆ **to set the table** poner* la mesa

to **set off** [sɛt'ɑ:f] VERB
salir* ◇ *We set off for Miami at nine o'clock.* Salimos para Miami a las nueve.

to **set out** [sɛt'aut] VERB
salir* ◇ *We set out for Miami at nine o'clock.* Salimos para Miami a las nueve.

settee [sɛ'ti:] NOUN
el sofá

to **settle** ['sɛtl] VERB
1 zanjar ◇ *That should settle the problem.* Esto debería zanjar el problema.
2 pagar* ◇ *I'll settle the bill tomorrow.* Mañana pagaré la cuenta.

to **settle down** [sɛtl'daun] VERB
calmarse

to **settle in** [sɛtl'ɪn] VERB
adaptarse

to **settle on** ['sɛtl'ɑ:n] VERB
decidirse por

seven ['sɛvən] NUMERAL
siete ◇ *She's seven.* Tiene siete años.

seventeen [sɛvən'ti:n] NUMERAL
diecisiete ◇ *He's seventeen.* Tiene diecisiete años.

seventeenth [sevən'ti:nθ] ADJECTIVE
decimoséptimo
◆ **the seventeenth floor** el piso dieciséis
◆ **April seventeenth** el diecisiete de abril

seventh ['sɛvənθ] ADJECTIVE
séptimo ◇ *the seventh floor* el sexto piso ☞

S

◆ **August seventh** el siete de agosto
seventy ['sɛvənti] NUMERAL
setenta ◇ *She's seventy.* Tiene setenta años.
several ['sɛvrəl] ADJECTIVE, PRONOUN
varios ◇ *several times* varias veces
to **sew** [sou] VERB (**sewed, sewn**)
coser
to **sew up** [sou'ʌp] VERB
coser
sewing ['souɪŋ] NOUN
la costura ◇ *I like sewing.* Me gusta la costura.
◆ **sewing machine** la máquina de coser
sewn [soun] VERB *see* **sew**
sex [sɛks] NOUN (PL **sexes**)
el sexo ◇ *the opposite sex* el sexo opuesto
◆ **to have sex with somebody** tener* relaciones sexuales con alguien
◆ **sex education** la educación sexual
sexism ['sɛksɪzəm] NOUN
el sexismo
sexist ['sɛksɪst] ADJECTIVE
sexista
sexual ['sɛkʃuəl] ADJECTIVE
sexual ◇ *sexual discrimination* la discriminación sexual ◇ *sexual harassment* el acoso sexual
sexuality [sɛkʃu'ælɪti] NOUN
la sexualidad
sexy ['sɛksi] ADJECTIVE
sexy (PL sexy)
shabby ['ʃæbi] ADJECTIVE
andrajoso (*person, clothes*)
shade [ʃeɪd] NOUN
1 la sombra ◇ *It was 35 degrees in the shade.* Hacía 35 grados a la sombra.
2 el tono ◇ *a beautiful shade of blue* un tono de azul muy bonito
3 la persiana (*for window*)
shades [ʃeɪdz] PL NOUN
los anteojos de sol
shadow ['ʃædou] NOUN
la sombra
to **shake** [ʃeɪk] VERB (**shook, shaken**)
1 sacudir ◇ *She shook the towel.* Sacudió la toalla.
◆ **"Shake well before use"** "Agítese bien antes de usarse"
2 temblar* ◇ *He was shaking with cold.* Temblaba de frío.
◆ **Donald shook his head.** Donald negó con la cabeza.
◆ **to shake hands with somebody** dar* la mano a alguien ◇ *They shook hands.* Se dieron la mano.
shaken ['ʃeɪkən] ADJECTIVE
afectado ◇ *I was feeling a bit shaken.* Estaba un poco afectado.
shaky ['ʃeɪki] ADJECTIVE
tembloroso (*hand, voice*)
◆ **I was feeling a bit shaky.** Estaba un poco débil.
shall [ʃæl] VERB
◆ **Shall I shut the window?** ¿Cierro la ventana?
◆ **Shall we ask him to come with us?** ¿Le pedimos que venga con nosotros?
pedir que *has to be followed by a verb in the subjunctive.*
shallow ['ʃælou] ADJECTIVE
poco profundo
shambles ['ʃæmbəlz] NOUN
el desastre ◇ *It's a complete shambles.* Es un desastre total.
shame [ʃeɪm] NOUN
la vergüenza ◇ *I'd die of shame!* ¡Me moriría de vergüenza!
◆ **What a shame!** ¡Qué pena!
◆ **It's a shame that...** Es una pena que...
es una pena que *has to be followed by a verb in the subjunctive.*
◇ *It's a shame he isn't here.* Es una pena que no esté aquí.
shampoo [ʃæm'pu:] NOUN
el champú (PL los champús) ◇ *a bottle of shampoo* un bote de champú
shan't [ʃænt] = **shall not**
shape [ʃeɪp] NOUN
la forma ◇ *in the shape of a star* en forma de estrella
◆ **to be in good shape** estar* en buena forma
share [ʃɛər] NOUN
see also **share** VERB
1 la acción (PL las acciones) ◇ *They have shares in many companies.* Tienen acciones en muchas empresas.
2 la parte ◇ *He refused to pay his share of the bill.* Se negó a pagar su parte de la factura.
to **share** [ʃɛər] VERB
see also **share** NOUN
compartir ◇ *to share a room with somebody* compartir habitación con alguien
to **share out** [ʃɛər'aut] VERB
repartir ◇ *They shared the candy out among the children.* Repartieron los caramelos entre los niños.
shark [ʃɑ:rk] NOUN
el tiburón (PL los tiburones)
sharp [ʃɑ:rp] ADJECTIVE, ADVERB
1 afilado ◇ *Be careful, that knife is sharp!* ¡Cuidado con ese cuchillo que está afilado!
2 puntiagudo (*point, spike*)
3 listo (*intelligent*) ◇ *She's very sharp.* Es muy lista.
◆ **at two o'clock sharp** a las dos en punto
to **shave** [ʃeɪv] VERB
afeitarse
rasurarse *Mexico*
◇ *He took a bath and shaved.* Se dio un baño

* Verbs marked with this symbol are irregular. See pages 346–348 for further details.

y se afeitó. Mexico: Se dio un baño y se rasuró.

◆ **to shave one's legs** depilarse las piernas

shaver [ˈʃeɪvər] NOUN

◆ **electric shaver** la máquina de afeitar, Mexico: la rasuradora

shaving cream [ˈʃeɪvɪŋˌkriːm] NOUN
la crema de afeitar
la crema de rasurar Mexico

shaving foam [ˈʃeɪvɪŋˌfoum] NOUN
la espuma de afeitar
la espuma de rasurar Mexico

she [ʃiː] PRONOUN
ella
***she** generally isn't translated unless it's emphatic.*
◇ *She's very nice.* Es muy simpática.
*Use **ella** for emphasis.*
◇ *She did it but he didn't.* Ella lo hizo, pero él no.

shed [ʃɛd] NOUN
el cobertizo

she'd [ʃiːd] = **she had, she would**

sheep [ʃiːp] NOUN (PL **sheep**)
la oveja

sheepdog [ˈʃiːpˌdɑːg] NOUN
el perro pastor (PL los perros pastores)

sheer [ʃɪər] ADJECTIVE
puro ◇ *It's sheer greed.* Es pura codicia.

sheet [ʃiːt] NOUN
la sábana ◇ *to change the sheets* cambiar las sábanas

◆ **a sheet of paper** una hoja de papel

shelf [ʃɛlf] NOUN (PL **shelves**)
1 el estante (*on wall, in store*)
2 la parrilla (*in oven*)

shell [ʃɛl] NOUN
1 la concha (*on beach, snail*)
2 el caparazón (PL los caparazones) (*of tortoise*)
3 la cáscara (*of egg, nut*)
4 el obús (PL los obuses) (*explosive*)

she'll [ʃiːl] = **she will**

shellfish [ˈʃɛlfɪʃ] NOUN (PL **shellfish**)
el marisco

shelter [ˈʃɛltər] NOUN
el refugio ◇ *a bomb shelter* un refugio antiaéreo

◆ **to take shelter** refugiarse

shelves [ʃɛlvz] PL NOUN *see* **shelf**

shepherd [ˈʃɛpərd] NOUN
el pastor

sheriff [ˈʃɛrɪf] NOUN
el sheriff

sherry [ˈʃɛri] NOUN
el jerez

she's [ʃiːz] = **she is, she has**

shield [ʃiːld] NOUN
el escudo

shift [ʃɪft] NOUN
see also **shift** VERB
el turno ◇ *the night shift* el turno de noche
◇ *His shift starts at eight o'clock.* Su turno empieza a las ocho.

◆ **to do shift work** trabajar por turnos

to **shift** [ʃɪft] VERB
see also **shift** NOUN
trasladar ◇ *I couldn't shift the cabinet on my own.* No podía trasladar el armario yo solo.

◆ **to shift gear** cambiar de marcha (*in car*)

shifty [ˈʃɪfti] ADJECTIVE
sospechoso ◇ *He looked shifty.* Tenía una pinta sospechosa.

◆ **He has shifty eyes.** Tiene una mirada furtiva.

shin [ʃɪn] NOUN
la espinilla

to **shine** [ʃaɪn] VERB (**shone, shone**)
brillar ◇ *The sun was shining.* Brillaba el sol.

◆ **They shone a light in his face.** Le enfocaron la cara con una luz.

shiny [ˈʃaɪni] ADJECTIVE
brillante

ship [ʃɪp] NOUN
el barco ◇ *by ship* en barco

◆ **a merchant ship** un buque mercante

shipbuilding [ˈʃɪpˌbɪldɪŋ] NOUN
la construcción naval

shipwreck [ˈʃɪprɛk] NOUN
el naufragio

shipwrecked [ˈʃɪprɛkt] ADJECTIVE

◆ **to be shipwrecked** naufragar*

shipyard [ˈʃɪpjɑːrd] NOUN
el astillero

shirt [ʃɜːrt] NOUN
la camisa

shit [ʃɪt] EXCLAMATION
¡Mierda! (*rude*)

to **shiver** [ˈʃɪvər] VERB
tiritar ◇ *to shiver with cold* tiritar de frío

shock [ʃɑːk] NOUN
see also **shock** VERB
1 la conmoción (PL las conmociones)
◇ *The news came as a shock.* La noticia causó conmoción.
2 el golpe de corriente
el toque Mexico
◇ *I got a shock when I touched the switch.* Me dio un golpe de corriente al tocar el interruptor. Mexico: Me dio un toque al tocar el interruptor.

◆ **an electric shock** una descarga eléctrica

to **shock** [ʃɑːk] VERB
see also **shock** NOUN
1 horrorizar* (*upset*) ◇ *They were shocked by the tragedy.* Quedaron horrorizados por la tragedia.
2 escandalizar* (*scandalize*) ◇ *Nothing shocks me any more.* Ya nada me escandaliza.

shocking [ˈʃɑːkɪŋ] ADJECTIVE
escandaloso ◇ *It's shocking!* ¡Es escandaloso!

shoe [ʃuː] NOUN
el zapato ◇ *a pair of shoes* un par de zapatos
shoelace ['ʃuːleɪs] NOUN
el cordón (PL los cordones)
la agujeta | *Mexico* |
shoe polish ['ʃuːˌpɑːlɪʃ] NOUN
el betún
shoe store ['ʃuːˌstɔːr] NOUN
la zapatería
shone [ʃoun] VERB *see* **shine**
shook [ʃuk] VERB *see* **shake**
to **shoot** [ʃuːt] VERB (**shot, shot**)
1 disparar (*fire a shot*) ◇ *Don't shoot!* ¡No disparen!
◆ **to shoot at somebody** disparar contra alguien
◆ **He shot himself with a revolver.** Se pegó un tiro con un revólver.
◆ **He was shot dead by the police.** La policía lo mató a tiros.
2 fusilar (*execute*) ◇ *He was shot at dawn.* Lo fusilaron al amanecer.
3 rodar* ◇ *The movie was shot in Prague.* La película se rodó en Prague.
4 tirar (*in basketball, soccer*)
shooting ['ʃuːtɪŋ] NOUN
los disparos ◇ *They heard shooting.* Oyeron disparos.
◆ **a drive-by shooting** un tiroteo desde el carro
shop [ʃɑːp] NOUN
la tienda
◆ **a coffee shop** un café
shoplifting ['ʃɑːpˌlɪftɪŋ] NOUN
el hurto en las tiendas
shopping ['ʃɑːpɪŋ] NOUN
la compra ◇ *Can you get the shopping from the car?* ¿Puedes sacar la compra del carro?
◆ **to go shopping (1)** (*for food*) ir* a hacer la compra
◆ **to go shopping (2)** (*for pleasure*) ir* de compras
◆ **I love shopping.** Me encanta ir de compras.
◆ **shopping bag** la bolsa de la compra
◆ **shopping cart** el carrito
◆ **shopping center** el centro comercial
shore [ʃɔːr] NOUN
la orilla ◇ *on the shores of the lake* a orillas del lago
◆ **on shore** en tierra
short [ʃɔːrt] ADJECTIVE
1 corto ◇ *a short skirt* una falda corta ◇ *a short walk* un paseo corto ◇ *It was a great vacation, but too short.* Fueron unas vacaciones estupendas, pero demasiado cortas.
◆ **a short break** un pequeño descanso
◆ **a short time ago** hace poco
2 bajo ◇ *She's quite short.* Es bastante baja.
◆ **to be short of something** andar* escaso de algo
◆ **at short notice** con poco tiempo de antelación
◆ **In short, the answer is no.** En una palabra, la respuesta es no.
shortage ['ʃɔːrtɪdʒ] NOUN
la escasez ◇ *a water shortage* escasez de agua
short cut ['ʃɔːrtˌkʌt] NOUN
el atajo
shorthand ['ʃɔːrtˌhænd] NOUN
la taquigrafía
shortly ['ʃɔːrtli] ADVERB
dentro de poco ◇ *I'll be there shortly.* Estaré allí dentro de poco.
◆ **She arrived shortly after midnight.** Llegó poco después de la medianoche.
shorts [ʃɔːrts] PL NOUN
los pantalones cortos ◇ *a pair of shorts* unos pantalones cortos
shortsighted [ʃɔːrt'saɪtɪd] ADJECTIVE
con poca visión de futuro (*person*)
short story ['ʃɔːrt'stɔːri] NOUN (PL **short stories**)
el cuento
shot [ʃɑːt] VERB *see* **shoot**
shot [ʃɑːt] NOUN
1 el tiro ◇ *to fire a shot* disparar un tiro ◇ *a shot at goal* un tiro al arco
2 la foto
*Although **foto** ends in **-a**, it is actually feminine noun.*
◇ *a shot of the Grand Canyon* una foto del Gran Cañón del Colorado
3 la inyección (PL las inyecciones)
el piquete | *Mexico* |
(*vaccination*)
shotgun ['ʃɑːtgʌn] NOUN
la escopeta
should [ʃud] VERB
*When **should** means "ought to", use the conditional tense of **deber**.*
deber ◇ *You should get more exercise.* Deberías hacer más ejercicio. ◇ *He should be there by now.* Ya debería estar allí. ◇ *That shouldn't be too hard.* Eso no debería ser muy difícil.
tener que* *is also a very common way to translate **should**.*
◇ *I should have told you before.* Tendría que habértelo dicho antes.
*When **should** means "would", use the conditional tense.*
◇ *I should go if I were you.* Yo que tú, iría.
◆ **I should be so lucky!** ¡Ojalá!
shoulder ['ʃouldər] NOUN
1 el hombro ◇ *I looked over my shoulder.* Miré por encima del hombro.
◆ **shoulder bag** la cartera para colgar del hombro, | *Mexico:* | la bolsa para colgar del

hombro
2 el arcén (*of a freeway*)
shouldn't ['ʃudnt] = **should not**
to **shout** [ʃaut] VERB
see also **shout** NOUN
gritar ◇ *Don't shout!* ¡No grites!
shout [ʃaut] NOUN
see also **shout** VERB
el grito
shovel ['ʃʌvəl] NOUN
la pala
show [ʃou] NOUN
see also **show** VERB
1 el espectáculo ◇ *to stage a show* montar un espectáculo
2 el programa
*Although **programa** ends in **-a**, it is actually a masculine noun.*
◇ *a radio show* un programa de radio
◆ **fashion show** el desfile de modelos
to **show** [ʃou] VERB (**showed, shown**)
see also **show** NOUN
1 mostrar*
◆ **to show somebody something** mostrar algo a alguien ◇ *Have I shown you my hat?* ¿Te mostré ya mi sombrero?
2 demostrar* ◇ *She showed great courage.* Demostró gran valentía.
◆ **It shows.** Se nota. ◇ *I've never been riding before. – It shows.* Nunca había montado a caballo antes. – Se nota.
to **show off** [ʃou'ɑ:f] VERB
presumir
to **show up** [ʃou'ʌp] VERB
aparecer* ◇ *He showed up late as usual.* Apareció tarde, como de costumbre.
shower ['ʃauər] NOUN
1 la ducha
◆ **to have a shower** ducharse
2 el chubasco ◇ *scattered showers* chubascos dispersos
showing ['ʃouɪŋ] NOUN
la proyección (PL las proyecciones) (*of a movie*) ◇ *a private showing* una proyección privada
shown [ʃoun] VERB *see* **show**
show-off ['ʃouɑ:f] NOUN
el fanfarrón (PL los fanfarrones)
la fanfarrona
shrank [ʃræŋk] VERB *see* **shrink**
to **shriek** [ʃri:k] VERB
chillar
shrimp [ʃrɪmp] NOUN
el camarón (PL los camarones)
shrimp cocktail ['ʃrɪmp'kɑ:kteɪl] NOUN
el cóctel de camarón
to **shrink** [ʃrɪŋk] VERB (**shrank, shrunk**)
encogerse* (*clothes, fabric*)
to **shrug** [ʃrʌg] VERB
◆ **to shrug one's shoulders** encogerse* de hombros
shrunk [ʃrʌŋk] VERB *see* **shrink**
to **shudder** ['ʃʌdər] VERB
estremecerse*
to **shuffle** ['ʃʌfəl] VERB
◆ **to shuffle the cards** barajar las cartas
to **shut** [ʃʌt] VERB (**shut, shut**)
cerrar* ◇ *What time do you shut?* ¿A qué hora cierran? ◇ *What time do the stores shut?* ¿A qué hora cierran las tiendas?
to **shut down** [ʃʌt'daun] VERB
cerrar* ◇ *The theater shut down last year.* El cine cerró el año pasado.
to **shut off** [ʃʌt'ɑ:f] VERB
apagar* ◇ *Please shut off the lights.* Por favor apaguen las luces.
to **shut up** [ʃʌt'ʌp] VERB
callarse ◇ *Shut up!* ¡Cállate!
shutters ['ʃʌtərz] PL NOUN
las contraventanas
shuttle ['ʃʌtl] NOUN
◆ **space shuttle** el transbordador espacial
◆ **air shuttle** el puente aéreo (*flight*) ◇ *I'll get the air shuttle.* Tomaré el puente aéreo.
shuttlecock ['ʃʌtlkɑ:k] NOUN
el volante
el gallito *Mexico*
(*de bádminton*)
shy [ʃaɪ] ADJECTIVE
tímido
Sicily ['sɪsɪli] NOUN
Sicilia FEM
sick [sɪk] ADJECTIVE
1 enfermo ◇ *She looks after her sick mother.* Cuida de su madre enferma. ◇ *She hasn't come, she's sick.* No ha venido, está enferma.
2 de mal gusto ◇ *That's really sick!* ¡Eso es de muy mal gusto!
◆ **to be sick** devolver*
◆ **to be sick of something** estar* harto de algo ◇ *I'm sick of your jokes.* Estoy harto de tus bromas.
sickening ['sɪkənɪŋ] ADJECTIVE
repugnante
sick leave ['sɪk,li:v] NOUN
el permiso por enfermedad
la licencia por enfermedad *Mexico*
sickness ['sɪknɪs] NOUN
la enfermedad
sick pay ['sɪk,peɪ] NOUN
la prestación por enfermedad (PL las prestaciones por enfermedad)
side [saɪd] NOUN
1 el lado (*of object, building, car*) ◇ *He was driving on the wrong side of the road.* Iba por el lado contrario de la carretera.
◆ **a house on the side of a mountain** una casa en la ladera de una montaña
◆ **We sat side by side.** Nos sentamos uno al lado del otro.
◆ **the side entrance** la entrada lateral

S ☞

[2] el borde (*of pool, bed, road*) ◇ *The car was abandoned at the side of the road.* El carro estaba abandonado al borde de la carretera.
◆ **by the side of the lake** a la orilla del lago
[3] la cara (*of paper, record, tape*) ◇ *Play side A.* Pon la cara A.
[4] el equipo (*team*) ◇ *He's on my side.* Está en mi equipo.
◆ **I'm on your side.** Yo estoy de tu parte.
◆ **to take somebody's side** ponerse* de parte de alguien
◆ **to take sides** tomar partido

sideboard ['saɪdbɔːrd] NOUN
el aparador

side effect ['saɪdɪˌfɛkt] NOUN
el efecto secundario

side street ['saɪdˌstriːt] NOUN
la calle lateral

sidewalk ['saɪdwɑːk] NOUN
la acera
la banqueta [Mexico]

sideways ['saɪdweɪz] ADVERB
◆ **to look sideways** mirar de reojo
◆ **to move sideways** moverse* de lado

sieve [sɪv] NOUN
[1] el colador (*for liquids*)
[2] el cedazo (*for solids*)

sigh [saɪ] NOUN
[*see also* **sigh** VERB]
el suspiro

to **sigh** [saɪ] VERB
[*see also* **sigh** NOUN]
suspirar

sight [saɪt] NOUN
[1] la vista ◇ *I'm losing my sight.* Estoy perdiendo la vista.
◆ **at first sight** a primera vista
◆ **to know somebody by sight** conocer* a alguien de vista
◆ **in sight** a la vista
[2] el espectáculo ◇ *It was an amazing sight.* Era un espectáculo asombroso.
◆ **Keep out of sight!** ¡Que no te vean!
◆ **the sights** las atracciones turísticas
◆ **to see the sights of Philadelphia** hacer* turismo por Filadelfia

sightseeing ['saɪtˌsiːɪŋ] NOUN
◆ **to go sightseeing** hacer* turismo

sign [saɪn] NOUN
[*see also* **sign** VERB]
[1] el letrero ◇ *There was a big sign saying "private".* Había un gran letrero que decía "privado".
[2] la señal ◇ *She made a sign to the waiter.* Le hizo una señal al mesero. ◇ *There's no sign of improvement.* No hay señales de mejoría.
◆ **road sign** la señal de tráfico
◆ **What's your sign?** ¿De qué signo eres?

to **sign** [saɪn] VERB
[*see also* **sign** NOUN]
firmar

to **sign up for** [saɪn'ʌpˌfɔːr] VERB
matricularse en ◇ *I've signed up for a diving course.* Me matriculé en un curso de buceo.
◆ **to sign up for welfare** inscribirse* como desempleado

signal ['sɪgnəl] NOUN
[*see also* **signal** VERB]
la señal

to **signal** ['sɪgnəl] VERB
[*see also* **signal** NOUN]
señalizar* (*when driving*) ◇ *He signaled a right turn and turned into Gran Vía.* Señalizó hacia la derecha y torció a la Gran Vía.
◆ **to signal to somebody** hacer* señas a alguien

signature ['sɪgnətʃər] NOUN
la firma

significance [sɪg'nɪfɪkəns] NOUN
la importancia

significant [sɪg'nɪfɪkənt] ADJECTIVE
significativo

sign language ['saɪnˌlæŋgwɪdʒ] NOUN
el lenguaje por señas

signpost ['saɪnpoust] NOUN
la señal

silence ['saɪləns] NOUN
el silencio

silent ['saɪlənt] ADJECTIVE
[1] silencioso (*place*) ◇ *a silent room* una habitación silenciosa
[2] callado (*person*)
◆ **to be silent (1)** estar* callado ◇ *He was silent during the visit.* Estuvo callado durante la visita.
◆ **to be silent (2)** ser* callado ◇ *He was a serious, silent man.* Era un hombre serio y callado.

silicon chip ['sɪlɪkən'tʃɪp] NOUN
el chip de silicio (PL los chips de silicio)

silk [sɪlk] NOUN
la seda ◇ *a silk scarf* un pañuelo de seda

silky ['sɪlki] ADJECTIVE
sedoso

silly ['sɪli] ADJECTIVE
tonto

silver ['sɪlvər] NOUN
la plata ◇ *a silver medal* una medalla de plata

silverware ['sɪlvərwɛr] NOUN
la vajilla de plata

similar ['sɪmɪlər] ADJECTIVE
parecido
◆ **similar to** parecido a

simple ['sɪmpəl] ADJECTIVE
[1] sencillo ◇ *It's very simple.* Es muy sencillo.
[2] simple ◇ *He's a bit simple.* Es un poco

simple.
simply ['sɪmpli] ADVERB
sencillamente
simultaneous [saɪməl'teɪniəs] ADJECTIVE
simultáneo
sin [sɪn] NOUN
see also **sin** VERB
el pecado
to **sin** [sɪn] VERB
see also **sin** NOUN
pecar*
since [sɪns] PREPOSITION, ADVERB, CONJUNCTION
1 desde ◇ *since Christmas* desde Navidad ◇ *since then* desde entonces
◆ **I haven't seen him since.** Desde entonces no lo he vuelto a ver.
2 desde que ◇ *I haven't seen her since she left.* No la he visto desde que se fue.
◆ **It's a few years since I've seen them.** Hace varios años que no los veo.
3 como ◇ *Since you're tired, let's stay at home.* Como estás cansado podemos quedarnos en casa.
sincere [sɪn'sɪər] ADJECTIVE
sincero
sincerely [sɪn'sɪrli] ADVERB
◆ **Sincerely yours...** Atentamente...
to **sing** [sɪŋ] VERB (**sang, sung**)
cantar
singer ['sɪŋər] NOUN
el/la cantante
singing ['sɪŋɪŋ] NOUN
el canto ◇ *singing lessons* clases de canto
◆ **flamenco singing** el cante flamenco
single ['sɪŋgəl] ADJECTIVE
see also **single** NOUN
1 individual ◇ *a single room* una habitación individual ◇ *a single bed* una cama individual
2 soltero ◇ *a single mother* una madre soltera
3 solo ◇ *She hadn't said a single word.* No había dicho una sola palabra.
◆ **not a single thing** nada de nada
single ['sɪŋgəl] NOUN
see also **single** ADJECTIVE
el single ◇ *a CD single* un single en CD
single parent ['sɪŋgəl'pɛrənt] NOUN
◆ **She's a single parent.** Es madre soltera.
◆ **a single parent family** una familia monoparental
singles ['sɪŋgəlz] PL NOUN
los individuales (*in tennis*) ◇ *the women's singles* los individuales femeninos
singular ['sɪŋgjələr] NOUN
singular ◇ *in the singular* en singular
sinister ['sɪnɪstər] ADJECTIVE
siniestro
sink [sɪŋk] NOUN
see also **sink** VERB
1 el fregadero
el lavaplatos (PL los lavaplatos) *Mexico* (*in the kitchen*)
2 el lavabo (*in the bathroom*)
to **sink** [sɪŋk] VERB (**sank, sunk**)
see also **sink** NOUN
1 hundir ◇ *We sank the enemy's ship.* Hundimos el buque enemigo.
2 hundirse ◇ *The boat was sinking fast.* El barco se hundía rápidamente.
sir [sɜːr] NOUN
el señor ◇ *Yes, sir.* Sí, señor.
siren ['saɪərən] NOUN
la sirena
sister ['sɪstər] NOUN
1 la hermana ◇ *my little sister* mi hermana pequeña
2 la enfermera jefe (*nurse*)
sister-in-law ['sɪstərɪn,lɑː] NOUN (PL **sisters-in-law**)
la cuñada
to **sit** [sɪt] VERB (**sat, sat**)
sentarse* ◇ *He sat in front of the TV.* Se sentó frente a la tele.
◆ **to be sitting** estar* sentado ◇ *He was sitting in front of the TV.* Estaba sentado frente a la tele.
to **sit down** [sɪt'daun] VERB
sentarse* ◇ *He sat down at his desk.* Se sentó en su escritorio.
sitcom ['sɪtkɑːm] NOUN
la telecomedia
site [saɪt] NOUN
1 el lugar ◇ *the site of the accident* el lugar del accidente
2 el camping (PL los campings) (*campsite*)
◆ **building site** la obra
sitting room ['sɪtɪŋ,ruːm] NOUN
la sala de estar (PL las salas de estar)
situated ['sɪtʃueɪtəd] ADJECTIVE
◆ **to be situated...** estar* situado...
situation [sɪtʃu'eɪʃən] NOUN
la situación (PL las situaciones)
six [sɪks] NUMERAL
seis ◇ *He's six.* Tiene seis años.
sixteen [sɪks'tiːn] NUMERAL
dieciséis ◇ *He's sixteen.* Tiene dieciséis años.
sixteenth [sɪks'tiːnθ] ADJECTIVE
decimosexto
◆ **the sixteenth floor** el piso quince
◆ **February sixteenth** el dieciséis de febrero
sixth [sɪksθ] ADJECTIVE
sexto ◇ *the sixth floor* el quinto piso
◆ **April sixth** el seis de abril
sixty ['sɪksti] NUMERAL
sesenta ◇ *She's sixty.* Tiene sesenta años.
size [saɪz] NOUN
1 el tamaño (*of object, place*) ◇ *plates of various sizes* platos de varios tamaños
2 la talla (*of clothing*) ◇ *What size do you take?* ¿Qué talla usas?

3 el número (*of shoes*)
◆ **I take size five.** Calzo un treinta y ocho.

to **skate** [skeɪt] VERB
patinar

skateboard ['skeɪt,bɔːrd] NOUN
el monopatín (PL los monopatines)

skateboarding ['skeɪt,bɔːrdɪŋ] NOUN
◆ **to go skateboarding** andar* en monopatín

skates [skeɪts] PL NOUN
los patines

skating ['skeɪtɪŋ] NOUN
el patinaje
◆ **to go skating** ir* a patinar
◆ **skating rink** la pista de patinaje

skeleton ['skɛlɪtn] NOUN
el esqueleto

sketch [skɛtʃ] NOUN (PL **sketches**)
see also **sketch** VERB
el boceto

to **sketch** [skɛtʃ] VERB
see also **sketch** NOUN
esbozar*

to **ski** [skiː] VERB
see also **ski** NOUN
esquiar*

ski [skiː] NOUN
see also **ski** VERB
el esquí ◇ *a pair of skis* unos esquís
◆ **ski boots** las botas de esquí
◆ **ski lift** el telesilla
Although ***telesilla*** *ends in* ***-a****, it is actually a masculine noun.*
◆ **ski pants** los pantalones de esquí
◆ **ski pole** el bastón de esquí (PL los bastones de esquí)
◆ **ski slope** la pista de esquí
◆ **ski suit** el traje de esquí

to **skid** [skɪd] VERB
patinar

skier ['skiːər] NOUN
el esquiador
la esquiadora

skiing ['skiːɪŋ] NOUN
el esquí ◇ *I love skiing.* Me encanta el esquí.
◆ **to go skiing** ir* a esquiar
◆ **to go on a skiing vacation** irse* de vacaciones a esquiar

skill [skɪl] NOUN
la habilidad ◇ *It requires a lot of skill.* Requiere mucha habilidad.

skilled [skɪld] ADJECTIVE
◆ **a skilled worker** un trabajador calificado

skillful ['skɪlfəl] ADJECTIVE
hábil

skim milk ['skɪm'mɪlk] NOUN
la leche descremada

skimpy ['skɪmpi] ADJECTIVE
1 mínimo (*clothes*)
2 escaso (*meal*)

skin [skɪn] NOUN
la piel
◆ **skin cancer** el cáncer de piel

skinhead ['skɪnhɛd] NOUN
el/la cabeza rapada (PL los/las cabezas rapadas)

skinny ['skɪni] ADJECTIVE
flaco

skintight ['skɪntaɪt] ADJECTIVE
muy ajustado

to **skip** [skɪp] VERB
saltarse ◇ *You should never skip breakfast.* No debes saltarte nunca el desayuno.
◆ **to skip school** hacer* novillos, *Mexico*: irse* de pinta

skirt [skɜːrt] NOUN
la falda

skull [skʌl] NOUN
1 la calavera (*of corpse*)
2 el cráneo (*in anatomy*)

sky [skaɪ] NOUN (PL **skies**)
el cielo

skyscraper ['skaɪskreɪpər] NOUN
el rascacielos (PL los rascacielos)

slack [slæk] ADJECTIVE
1 flojo (*rope*)
2 descuidado (*person*)

to **slam** [slæm] VERB
cerrar* de un portazo ◇ *She slammed the door.* Cerró la puerta de un portazo.
◆ **The door slammed.** La puerta se cerró de un portazo.

slang [slæŋ] NOUN
el argot

slap [slæp] NOUN
see also **slap** VERB
la bofetada

to **slap** [slæp] VERB
see also **slap** NOUN
dar* una bofetada a

slate [sleɪt] NOUN
la teja de pizarra

sled [slɛd] NOUN
el trineo

sledding ['slɛdɪŋ] NOUN
◆ **to go sledding** ir* en trineo

sleep [sliːp] NOUN
see also **sleep** VERB
el sueño ◇ *lack of sleep* falta de sueño
◆ **I need some sleep.** Necesito dormir.
◆ **to go to sleep** dormirse*

to **sleep** [sliːp] VERB (**slept**, **slept**)
see also **sleep** NOUN
dormir* ◇ *I couldn't sleep last night.* Anoche no podía dormir.

to **sleep around** [,sliːpə'raund] VERB
acostarse* con cualquiera

to **sleep in** [sliːp'ɪn] VERB
dormir* hasta tarde

to **sleep together** ['sliːptə,gɛðər] VERB
acostarse* juntos

to **sleep with** ['sli:pˌwɪð] VERB
acostarse* con
sleeping bag ['sli:pɪŋˌbæg] NOUN
el saco de dormir
sleeping car ['sli:pɪŋˌkɑ:r] NOUN
el coche cama (PL los coches cama)
sleeping pill ['sli:pɪŋˌpɪl] NOUN
el somnífero
sleepy ['sli:pi] ADJECTIVE
◆ **to feel sleepy** tener* sueño
◆ **a sleepy little village** un pueblecito tranquilo
sleet [sli:t] NOUN
see also **sleet** VERB
el aguanieve FEM
*Although it's a feminine noun, remember that you use **el** with **aguanieve**.*
to **sleet** [sli:t] VERB
see also **sleet** NOUN
◆ **It's sleeting.** Está cayendo aguanieve.
sleeve [sli:v] NOUN
la manga (*of shirt, coat*)
sleigh [sleɪ] NOUN
el trineo
slept [slɛpt] VERB *see* **sleep**
slice [slaɪs] NOUN
see also **slice** VERB
1 la rebanada (*of bread*)
2 el trozo (*of cake*)
3 la rodaja (*of lemon, pineapple*)
4 la loncha (*of ham, cheese*)
to **slice** [slaɪs] VERB
see also **slice** NOUN
cortar
slick [slɪk] NOUN
see also **slick** ADJECTIVE
◆ **oil slick** la marea negra
slick [slɪk] ADJECTIVE
see also **slick** NOUN
impecable ◇ *a slick performance* una actuación impecable
slide [slaɪd] NOUN
see also **slide** VERB
1 el tobogán (PL los toboganes)
la resbaladilla *Mexico*
(*in playground*)
2 la diapositiva (*photo*)
to **slide** [slaɪd] VERB (**slid, slid**)
see also **slide** NOUN
deslizarse* ◇ *Tears were sliding down his cheeks.* Las lágrimas se deslizaban por sus mejillas.
◆ **She slid the door open.** Corrió la puerta.
slight [slaɪt] ADJECTIVE
ligero ◇ *a slight improvement* una ligera mejoría
◆ **a slight problem** un pequeño problema
slightly ['slaɪtli] ADVERB
ligeramente ◇ *They are slightly more expensive.* Son ligeramente más caros.
slim [slɪm] ADJECTIVE
see also **slim** VERB
delgado
to **slim down** [slɪm'daun] VERB
see also **slim** ADJECTIVE
adelgazar* ◇ *I'm trying to slim down.* Estoy intentando adelgazar.
sling [slɪŋ] NOUN
el cabestrillo ◇ *She had her arm in a sling.* Llevaba el brazo en cabestrillo.
slip [slɪp] NOUN
see also **slip** VERB
1 el desliz (PL los deslices) (*mistake*)
2 la combinación (PL las combinaciones)
el fondo *Mexico*
(*underskirt*)
◆ **a slip of paper** un papelito
◆ **a slip of the tongue** un lapsus
to **slip** [slɪp] VERB
see also **slip** NOUN
resbalar ◇ *He slipped on the ice.* Resbaló en el hielo.
to **slip up** [slɪp'ʌp] VERB
equivocarse*
slipper ['slɪpər] NOUN
la zapatilla
slippery ['slɪpəri] ADJECTIVE
resbaladizo
slipup ['slɪpˌʌp] NOUN
el desliz (PL los deslices)
slope [sloup] NOUN
1 la cuesta (*surface*) ◇ *The street was on a slope.* La calle era en cuesta.
2 la pendiente (*angle*) ◇ *a slope of 10 degrees* una pendiente del 10 por ciento
sloppy ['slɑ:pi] ADJECTIVE
descuidado
slot [slɑ:t] NOUN
la ranura
slot machine ['slɑ:tmə'ʃi:n] NOUN
1 el tragamonedas (PL los tragamonedas) (*for gambling*)
2 la máquina expendedora (*vending machine*)
slow [slou] ADJECTIVE, ADVERB
lento ◇ *He's a bit slow.* Es un poco lento.
◇ *to go slow* ir* lento
◆ **Drive slower!** ¡Maneja más despacio!
◆ **My watch is slow.** Mi reloj se atrasa.
to **slow down** [slou'daun] VERB
reducir* la velocidad ◇ *The car slowed down.* El carro redujo la velocidad.
slowly ['slouli] ADVERB
lentamente
slug [slʌg] NOUN
la babosa
slum [slʌm] NOUN
el barrio bajo
el barrio *Mexico*
slush [slʌʃ] NOUN
la nieve medio derretida
sly [slaɪ] ADJECTIVE
astuto ◇ *She's very sly.* Es muy astuta.

S ☞

◆ **a sly smile** una sonrisa maliciosa

smack [smæk] NOUN
see also **smack** VERB
la cachetada

to **smack** [smæk] VERB
see also **smack** NOUN
dar* una cachetada a

small [smɑːl] ADJECTIVE
pequeño ◇ *two small children* dos niños pequeños
◆ **small change** el dinero suelto, *Mexico:* la feria

smart [smɑːrt] ADJECTIVE
1 elegante ◇ *a smart navy blue suit* un elegante traje azul marino
2 listo ◇ *He thinks he's smarter than Sarah.* Se cree más listo que Sarah.
◆ **Don't get smart with me!** ¡No te las des de listo conmigo!

smash [smæʃ] NOUN (PL **smashes**)
see also **smash** VERB
el choque

to **smash** [smæʃ] VERB
see also **smash** NOUN
1 romper* ◇ *They smashed windows.* Rompieron ventanas.
2 romperse* ◇ *The glass smashed into tiny pieces.* El vaso se hizo añicos.

smell [smɛl] NOUN
see also **smell** VERB
el olor ◇ *a smell of lemon* un olor a limón
◆ **the sense of smell** el olfato

to **smell** [smɛl] VERB
see also **smell** NOUN
oler* ◇ *That dog smells!* ¡Cómo huele ese perro! ◇ *I can't smell anything.* No huelo nada.
◆ **I can smell gas.** Huele a gas.
◆ **to smell of something** oler a algo ◇ *It smells of burning.* Huele a quemado.

smelly ['smɛli] ADJECTIVE
maloliente ◇ *The bar was dirty and smelly.* El bar era sucio y maloliente.
◆ **He has smelly feet.** Le huelen los pies.

smile [smaɪl] NOUN
see also **smile** VERB
la sonrisa

to **smile** [smaɪl] VERB
see also **smile** NOUN
sonreír*

smoke [smouk] NOUN
see also **smoke** VERB
el humo

to **smoke** [smouk] VERB
see also **smoke** NOUN
fumar ◇ *I don't smoke.* No fumo.

smoker ['smoukər] NOUN
el fumador
la fumadora

smoking ['smoukɪŋ] NOUN
◆ **to stop smoking** dejar de fumar
◆ **Smoking is bad for you.** Fumar es malo para la salud.
◆ **"no smoking"** "prohibido fumar"

smooth [smuːð] ADJECTIVE
liso ◇ *a smooth surface* una superficie lisa

smudge [smʌdʒ] NOUN
el borrón (PL los borrones)

smug [smʌg] ADJECTIVE
engreído

to **smuggle** ['smʌgəl] VERB
◆ **to smuggle in** meter de contrabando
◆ **to smuggle out** sacar* de contrabando

smuggler ['smʌglər] NOUN
el/la contrabandista

smuggling ['smʌglɪŋ] NOUN
el contrabando

smutty ['smʌti] ADJECTIVE
◆ **smutty jokes** los chistes verdes, *Mexico:* los chistes colorados

snack [snæk] NOUN
◆ **to have a snack** picar* algo

snack bar ['snækˌbɑːr] NOUN
la cafetería

snail [sneɪl] NOUN
el caracol

snake [sneɪk] NOUN
la serpiente

to **snap** [snæp] VERB
partirse ◇ *The branch snapped.* La rama se partió.
◆ **to snap one's fingers** chasquear los dedos

snap bean ['snæpˌbiːn] NOUN
la habichuela verde
el ejote *Mexico*

snapshot ['snæpˌʃɑːt] NOUN
la foto
Although ***foto*** *ends in* ***-o****, it is actually a feminine noun.*

to **snarl** [snɑːrl] VERB
gruñir*

to **snatch** [snætʃ] VERB
arrebatar
◆ **to snatch something from somebody** arrebatar algo a alguien ◇ *He snatched the keys from my hand.* Me arrebató las llaves de la mano.
◆ **My bag was snatched.** Me robaron el bolso.

to **sneak** [sniːk] VERB
◆ **to sneak in** entrar a hurtadillas
◆ **to sneak out** salir* a hurtadillas
◆ **to sneak up on somebody** acercarse* sigilosamente a alguien

sneakers [sniːkərz] PL NOUN
las zapatillas de deporte

to **sneeze** [sniːz] VERB
estornudar

to **sniff** [snɪf] VERB
1 sorberse la nariz ◇ *Stop sniffing!* ¡Deja de sorberte la nariz!

[2] olfatear ◇ *The dog sniffed my hand.* El perro me olfateó la mano.
◆ **to sniff glue** esnifar pegamento

snob [snɑːb] NOUN
el/la esnob (PL los/las esnobs)

snooze [snuːz] NOUN
la cabezadita (*informal*) ◇ *to have a snooze* echar una cabezadita

to **snore** [snɔːr] VERB
roncar*

snow [snou] NOUN
see also **snow** VERB
la nieve

to **snow** [snou] VERB
see also **snow** NOUN
nevar* ◇ *It's snowing.* Está nevando.

snowball ['snou,bɑːl] NOUN
la bola de nieve

snowflake ['snou,fleɪk] NOUN
el copo de nieve

snowman ['snoumæn] NOUN (PL **snowmen**)
el muñeco de nieve ◇ *to build a snowman* hacer* un muñeco de nieve

so [sou] CONJUNCTION, ADVERB
[1] así que (*therefore*) ◇ *The store was closed, so I went home.* La tienda estaba cerrada, así que me fui a casa. ◇ *So, have you always lived in Boston?* Así que, ¿siempre has vivido en Boston?
◆ **So what?** ¿Y qué?
[2] para que (*so that*)
***para que** has to be followed by a verb in the subjunctive.*
◇ *He took her upstairs so they wouldn't be overheard.* La llevó al piso de arriba para que nadie los oyera.
[3] tan (*very, as*) ◇ *He was talking so fast I couldn't understand.* Hablaba tan rápido que no le entendía. ◇ *He's like his sister but not so clever.* Es como su hermana pero no tan listo.
◆ **It was so heavy!** ¡Pesaba tanto!
◆ **How's your father? – Not so good.** ¿Cómo está tu padre? – No muy bien.
◆ **so much** tanto ◇ *I love you so much.* Te quiero tanto. ◇ *She has so much energy.* Tiene tanta energía.
◆ **so many** tantos ◇ *I have so many things to do today.* Tengo tantas cosas que hacer hoy.
◆ **That's not so.** No es así.
[4] también (*also*)
◆ **so do I** y yo también ◇ *I work a lot. – So do I.* Trabajo mucho. – Y yo también.
◆ **I love horses. – So do I.** Me encantan los caballos. – A mí también.
◆ **so have we** y nosotros también ◇ *I've been waiting for ages! – So have we.* ¡Llevo esperando un siglo! – Y nosotros también.
◆ **I think so.** Creo que sí.
◆ **...or so** ...o así ◇ *at five o'clock or so* a las cinco o así ◇ *ten or so people* diez personas o así

to **soak** [souk] VERB
[1] poner* en remojo ◇ *Soak the chickpeas for two hours.* Ponga los garbanzos en remojo dos horas.
[2] empapar ◇ *Water had soaked his jacket.* El agua le había empapado la chaqueta.

soaked [soukt] ADJECTIVE
◆ **to get soaked** empaparse

soaking ['soukɪŋ] ADJECTIVE
empapado ◇ *By the time we got back we were soaking.* Cuando regresamos estábamos empapados.
◆ **Your shoes are soaking wet.** Tienes los zapatos calados.

soap [soup] NOUN
el jabón (PL los jabones)

soap opera ['soup,ɑːpərə] NOUN
la telenovela

soap powder ['soup,paudər] NOUN
el detergente en polvo

to **sob** [sɑːb] VERB
sollozar*

sober ['soubər] ADJECTIVE
sobrio

to **sober up** [,soubər'ʌp] VERB
◆ **He sobered up.** Se le pasó la borrachera.

soccer ['sɑːkər] NOUN
el fútbol
el futbol Mexico
◇ *to play soccer* jugar* fútbol, Mexico: jugar* futbol

soccer player ['sɑːkər,pleɪər] NOUN
el/la futbolista

social ['souʃəl] ADJECTIVE
social ◇ *social problems* los problemas sociales
◆ **I have a good social life.** Tengo mucha vida social.

socialism ['souʃəlɪzəm] NOUN
el socialismo

socialist ['souʃəlɪst] ADJECTIVE, NOUN
socialista

Social Security ['souʃəlsɪ'kjurəti] NOUN
la seguridad social
◆ **to be on Social Security** cobrar de la seguridad social

social worker ['souʃəl,wɜːrkər] NOUN
el asistente social
la asistenta social
el trabajador social
la trabajadora social Mexico

society [sə'saɪəti] NOUN (PL **societies**)
[1] la sociedad ◇ *a multicultural society* una sociedad pluricultural
[2] la asociación (PL las asociaciones) ◇ *a drama society* una asociación de amigos del teatro

sociology [sousi'ɑːlədʒi] NOUN
la sociología

sock [sɑːk] NOUN
el calcetín (PL los calcetines)

S

soda ['soudə] NOUN
la soda

soda pop ['soudə,pɑ:p] NOUN
el refresco

sofa ['soufə] NOUN
el sofá (PL los sofás)

soft [sɑ:ft] ADJECTIVE
1 suave ◇ *a soft towel* una toalla suave
2 blando ◇ *The mattress is too soft.* El colchón es demasiado blando.
◆ **to be soft on somebody** ser* blando con alguien
◆ **soft cheeses** los quesos blandos
◆ **a soft drink** un refresco
◆ **soft drugs** las drogas blandas
◆ **soft option** la alternativa fácil

software ['sɑ:ftwɛr] NOUN
el software ◇ *a piece of software* un software

soggy ['sɑ:gi] ADJECTIVE
1 revenido (*bread, biscuits*)
2 pasado (*salad*)

soil [sɔɪl] NOUN
la tierra

solar power ['soulər'pauər] NOUN
la energía solar

sold [sould] VERB *see* **sell**

sold out [sould'aut] ADJECTIVE
agotado ◇ *The tickets are all sold out.* Están agotadas todas las entradas.

soldier ['souldʒər] NOUN
el/la soldado

solicitor [sə'lɪsɪtər] NOUN
el representante

> ℹ *En los Estados Unidos, un* **solicitor** *es un funcionario responsable de los asuntos legales de un municipio, ministerio, condado, etc.*

solid ['sɑ:lɪd] ADJECTIVE
sólido ◇ *a solid wall* un muro sólido
◆ **solid gold** oro macizo
◆ **for three solid hours** durante tres horas seguidas

solo ['soulou] NOUN
el solo ◇ *a guitar solo* un solo de guitarra

solution [sə'lu:ʃən] NOUN
la solución (PL las soluciones)

to **solve** [sɑ:lv] VERB
resolver*

some [sʌm] ADJECTIVE, PRONOUN
When ***some*** *refers to something you can't count, it usually isn't translated.*
◇ *Would you like some bread?* ¿Quieres pan? ◇ *Do you have some mineral water?* ¿Tiene agua mineral? ◇ *Would you like some coffee? – No thanks, I have some.* ¿Quiere café? – No gracias, ya tengo.
◆ **I only want some of it.** Sólo quiero un poco.
When ***some*** *refers to something you can count, use* ***alguno****, which is shortened to* ***algún*** *before a masculine singular noun.*
◇ *some day* algún día ◇ *some books* algunos libros ◇ *You have to be careful with mushrooms: some are poisonous.* Cuidado con los hongos: algunos son venenosos.
◆ **I'm going to buy some envelopes. Do you want some too?** Voy a comprar sobres. ¿Quieres que te traiga?
◆ **some day next week** un día de la semana que viene
◆ **Some people say that...** Hay gente que dice que...
◆ **some of them** algunos ◇ *I only sold some of them.* Sólo vendí algunos.

somebody ['sʌmbɑ:di] PRONOUN
alguien ◇ *I need somebody to help me.* Necesito que me ayude alguien.

somehow ['sʌmhau] ADVERB
de alguna manera
◆ **I'll do it somehow.** De alguna manera lo haré.
◆ **Somehow I don't think he believed me.** Por alguna razón me parece que no me creyó.

someone ['sʌmwʌn] PRONOUN
alguien ◇ *I need someone to help me.* Necesito que me ayude alguien.

something ['sʌmθɪŋ] PRONOUN
algo ◇ *something special* algo especial ◇ *Wear something warm.* Ponte algo que abrigue.
◆ **It cost $100, or something like that.** Costó 100 dólares, o algo así.
◆ **His name is Peter or something.** Se llama Peter o algo por el estilo.

sometime ['sʌmtaɪm] ADVERB
algún día ◇ *You must come and see us sometime.* Tienes que venir a vernos algún día.
◆ **sometime last month** un día del mes pasado

sometimes ['sʌmtaɪmz] ADVERB
a veces ◇ *Sometimes I drink beer.* A veces tomo cerveza.

somewhere ['sʌmwɛər] ADVERB
en algún sitio ◇ *I left my keys somewhere.* Dejé las llaves en algún sitio.
◆ **I'd like to go on vacation, somewhere exotic.** Me gustaría irme de vacaciones a algún sitio exótico.

son [sʌn] NOUN
el hijo

song [sɑ:ŋ] NOUN
la canción (PL las canciones)

son-in-law ['sʌnɪn,lɑ:] NOUN (PL **sons-in-law**)
el yerno

soon [su:n] ADVERB
pronto ◇ *very soon* muy pronto
◆ **soon afterward** poco después
◆ **as soon as possible** cuanto antes

sooner ['su:nər] ADVERB

antes ◇ *Can't you come a bit sooner?* ¿No puedes venir un poco antes?
- **sooner or later** tarde o temprano
- **the sooner the better** cuanto antes mejor

soot [sut] NOUN
el hollín

sophomore ['sɑ:fmɔ:r] NOUN
el/la estudiante de segundo año

soppy ['sɑ:pi] ADJECTIVE
sentimentaloide

soprano [sə'prænou] NOUN
la soprano
*Although **soprano** ends in **-o**, it is actually a feminine noun.*

sore [sɔ:r] ADJECTIVE
see also **sore** NOUN
- **It's sore.** Me duele.
- **I have a sore throat.** Me duele la garganta.
- **That's a sore point.** Ése es un tema delicado.

sore [sɔ:r] NOUN
see also **sore** ADJECTIVE
la llaga

sorry ['sɑ:ri] ADJECTIVE
- **I'm sorry.** Lo siento. ◇ *I'm very sorry.* Lo siento mucho. ◇ *I'm sorry, I don't have any change.* Lo siento, no tengo cambio.
- **I'm sorry I'm late.** Siento llegar tarde.
- **Sorry!** ¡Perdón!
- **Sorry?** ¿Cómo?
- **I'm sorry about the noise.** Perdón por el ruido.
- **You'll be sorry!** ¡Te arrepentirás!
- **to feel sorry for somebody** compadecer* a alguien

sort [sɔ:rt] NOUN
el tipo ◇ *What sort of bicycle do you have?* ¿Qué tipo de bicicleta tienes?
- **all sorts of...** todo tipo de...

to **sort out** [sɔ:rt'aut] VERB
1 ordenar ◇ *Sort out all your books.* Ordena todos tus libros.
2 arreglar ◇ *They have sorted out their problems.* Han arreglado sus problemas.

so-so ['sou,sou] ADVERB
así así ◇ *How are you feeling? – So-so.* ¿Cómo te sientes? – Así, así.

soul [soul] NOUN
1 el alma FEM
*Although it's a feminine noun, remember that you use **el** and **un** with **alma**.*
2 el soul ◇ *a soul singer* una cantante de soul

sound [saund] NOUN
see also **sound** VERB, ADJECTIVE, ADVERB
1 el ruido ◇ *Don't make a sound!* ¡No hagas ruido! ◇ *the sound of footsteps* el ruido de pasos
2 el sonido ◇ *at the speed of sound* a la velocidad del sonido
- **Can you turn the sound down?** ¿Puedes bajar el volumen?

to **sound** [saund] VERB
see also **sound** NOUN, ADJECTIVE, ADVERB
sonar* ◇ *That sounds interesting.* Eso suena interesante.
- **It sounds as if she's doing well at school.** Parece que le va bien en el colegio.
- **That sounds like a good idea.** Eso me parece buena idea.

sound [saund] ADJECTIVE, ADVERB
see also **sound** NOUN, VERB
válido ◇ *His reasoning is perfectly sound.* Su argumentación es perfectamente válida.
- **Peter gave me some sound advice.** Peter me dio un buen consejo.
- **sound asleep** profundamente dormido

soundtrack ['saund,træk] NOUN
la banda sonora

soup [su:p] NOUN
la sopa

sour ['sauər] ADJECTIVE
agrio
- **This milk has gone sour.** Esta leche se echó a perder.

south [sauθ] ADJECTIVE, ADVERB
see also **south** NOUN
1 del sur ◇ *a south wind* un viento del sur
- **the south coast** la costa meridional
2 hacia el sur ◇ *We were traveling south.* Viajábamos hacia el sur.
- **south of** al sur de ◇ *It's south of Denver.* Está al sur de Denver.

south [sauθ] NOUN
see also **south** ADJECTIVE
el sur ◇ *the South of France* el sur de Francia

South Africa [sauθ'æfrɪkə] NOUN
Sudáfrica FEM

South America [,sauθə'mɛrɪkə] NOUN
Sudamérica FEM

South American ['sauθə'mɛrɪkən] ADJECTIVE
see also **South American** NOUN
sudamericano

South American ['sauθə'mɛrɪkən] NOUN
see also **South American** ADJECTIVE
el sudamericano
la sudamericana
◇ *South Americans* los sudamericanos

southbound ['sauθbaund] ADJECTIVE
- **Southbound traffic is moving very slowly.** El tráfico que se dirige hacia el sur avanza muy despacio.

southeast [sauθ'i:st] NOUN
el sudeste

southeastern [sauθ'i:stərn] ADJECTIVE
sudeste
- **in southeastern California** al sudeste de California

southern ['sʌðərn] ADJECTIVE
- **the southern hemisphere** el hemisferio sur
- **Southern Florida** el sur de Florida
- **southern cuisine** la cocina sureña

South Pole ['sauθ'poul] NOUN

S

☞

◆ **the South Pole** el Polo Sur

southwest [sauθ'wɛst] NOUN
el sudoeste

southwestern [sauθ'wɛstərn] ADJECTIVE
sudoeste

souvenir [su:və'nɪər] NOUN
el recuerdo ◇ *souvenir shop* la tienda de recuerdos

soy ['sɔɪ] NOUN
la soya

soybean ['sɔɪbi:n] NOUN
la semilla de soja

soy sauce ['sɔɪˌsɑ:s] NOUN
la salsa de soya

space [speɪs] NOUN
el espacio ◇ *There isn't enough space.* No hay espacio suficiente. ◇ *in space* en el espacio
◆ **a parking space** un lugar para estacionar

spacecraft ['speɪsˌkræft] NOUN
la nave espacial

spade [speɪd] NOUN
la pala
◆ **spades** (*at cards*) las picas ◇ *the ace of spades* el as de picas
Be careful not to translate ***spade*** *by* ***espada****.*

Spain [speɪn] NOUN
España FEM

spam NOUN
el correo basura (*junk e-mail*)

Spaniard ['spænjərd] NOUN
el español
la española
(*person*)

spaniel ['spænjəl] NOUN
el perro de aguas

Spanish ['spænɪʃ] ADJECTIVE
see also **Spanish** NOUN
español

Spanish ['spænɪʃ] NOUN
see also **Spanish** ADJECTIVE
el español

> ℹ *The official name for the Spanish language in Spain and Latin America is* **el castellano** *and is also the term many Spanish speakers prefer to use. Despite controversies, both* **español** *and* **castellano** *are perfectly acceptable.*

◇ *Spanish lessons* las clases de español
◆ **the Spanish** los españoles

to **spank** [spæŋk] VERB
zurrar

spare [spɛər] ADJECTIVE
see also **spare** VERB, NOUN
1 de repuesto ◇ *Take a few spare batteries.* Llévate unas pilas de repuesto. ◇ *spare tire* la rueda de repuesto, *Mexico:* la llanta de refacción
2 de sobra ◇ *Do you have a spare pencil?* ¿Tienes un lápiz de sobra?
◆ **spare part** el repuesto, *Mexico:* la refacción (PL las refacciones)
◆ **spare room** el cuarto de los huéspedes
◆ **spare time** el tiempo libre

to **spare** [spɛər] VERB
see also **spare** ADJECTIVE, NOUN
◆ **Can you spare a moment?** ¿Tienes un momento?
◆ **I can't spare the time.** No tengo tiempo.
◆ **They have no money to spare.** No les sobra el dinero.
◆ **We arrived with time to spare.** Llegamos con tiempo de sobra.

spare [spɛər] NOUN
see also **spare** ADJECTIVE, VERB
◆ **I've lost my key. – Do you have a spare?** Perdí la llave. – ¿Tienes una de sobra?

sparkling ['spɑ:rklɪŋ] ADJECTIVE
con gas ◇ *a sparkling drink* una bebida con gas ◇ *sparkling water* agua con gas
◆ **sparkling wine** vino espumoso

sparrow ['spɛrou] NOUN
el gorrión (PL los gorriones)

spat [spæt] VERB *see* **spit**

to **speak** [spi:k] VERB (**spoke, spoken**)
hablar ◇ *Do you speak English?* ¿Hablas inglés? ◇ *Have you spoken to him?* ¿Has hablado con él? ◇ *She spoke to him about it.* Habló de ello con él.
◆ **Could I speak to Alison? – Speaking!** ¿Podría hablar con Alison? – ¡Con ella habla!

to **speak up** [spi:k'ʌp] VERB
hablar más alto ◇ *You'll need to speak up; we can't hear you.* Habla más alto que no te oímos.

speaker ['spi:kər] NOUN
1 el altavoz (PL los altavoces) (*loudspeaker*)
2 el orador
la oradora
(*at conference*)
◆ **French speakers** los hablantes de francés

special ['spɛʃəl] ADJECTIVE
especial

specialist ['spɛʃəlɪst] NOUN
el/la especialista

to **specialize** ['spɛʃəlaɪz] VERB
especializarse* ◇ *She specialized in Russian.* Se especializó en ruso.
◆ **We specialize in skiing equipment.** Estamos especializados en material de esquí.

specially ['spɛʃəli] ADVERB
especialmente ◇ *It can be very cold here, specially in winter.* Llega a hacer mucho frío aquí, especialmente en invierno. ◇ *It's specially designed for teenagers.* Está especialmente pensado para adolescentes.

specialty ['spɛʃəlti] NOUN (PL **specialties**)
la especialidad

species ['spiːʃiːz] NOUN (PL **species**)
la especie

specific [spə'sɪfɪk] ADJECTIVE
1 específico ◇ *certain specific issues* ciertos temas específicos
2 concreto ◇ *Could you be more specific?* ¿Podrías ser más concreto?

specifically [spə'sɪfɪkli] ADVERB
1 específicamente ◇ *It's specifically designed for teenagers.* Está específicamente pensado para adolescentes.
2 concretamente ◇ *in the West, or more specifically in California* en el Oeste, o más concretamente en California
◆ **I specifically said that...** Especifiqué claramente que...

specs, spectacles [spɛks,'spɛktɪkəlz] PL NOUN
los anteojos

spectacular [spɛk'tækjələr] ADJECTIVE
espectacular

spectator [spɛk'teɪtər] NOUN
el espectador
la espectadora

speech [spiːtʃ] NOUN (PL **speeches**)
el discurso ◇ *to make a speech* dar* un discurso

speechless ['spiːtʃlɪs] ADJECTIVE
◆ **I was speechless.** Me quedé sin habla.

speed [spiːd] NOUN
la velocidad ◇ *at top speed* a toda velocidad
◆ **a three-speed bicycle** una bicicleta de tres marchas

to **speed up** [spiːd'ʌp] VERB
acelerar

speedboat ['spiːdˌbout] NOUN
la lancha motora

speeding ['spiːdɪŋ] NOUN
el exceso de velocidad ◇ *He was fined for speeding.* Lo multaron por exceso de velocidad.

speed limit ['spiːdˌlɪmɪt] NOUN
el límite de velocidad ◇ *to break the speed limit* sobrepasar el límite de velocidad

speedometer [spɪ'dɑːmɪtər] NOUN
el velocímetro

to **spell** [spɛl] VERB
see also **spell** NOUN
deletrear ◇ *Can you spell that please?* ¿Me lo deletrea, por favor?
◆ **How do you spell "library"?** ¿Cómo se escribe "library"?
◆ **I can't spell.** Cometo faltas de ortografía.

spell [spɛl] NOUN
see also **spell** VERB
el hechizo ◇ *to be under somebody's spell* estar* bajo el hechizo de alguien
◆ **to cast a spell on somebody** hechizar* a alguien

spelling ['spɛlɪŋ] NOUN
la ortografía ◇ *My spelling is terrible.* Cometo muchas faltas de ortografía.
◆ **a spelling mistake** una falta de ortografía
◆ **spelling bee**

> ℹ *Un* **spelling bee** *es un certamen ideado para evaluar el nivel ortográfico de los alumnos, y en el que se les pide que deletreen palabras difíciles o complicadas. El alumno que logra deletrear correctamente el mayor número de palabras es el ganador.*

to **spend** [spɛnd] VERB (**spent, spent**)
1 gastar ◇ *They spend enormous amounts of money on advertising.* Gastan cantidades enormes de dinero en publicidad.
2 dedicar* ◇ *He spends a lot of time and money on his hobbies.* Dedica mucho tiempo y dinero a sus aficiones.
3 pasar ◇ *He spent a month in France.* Pasó un mes en Francia.

spice [spaɪs] NOUN
la especia

spicy ['spaɪsi] ADJECTIVE
picante

spider ['spaɪdər] NOUN
la araña

to **spill** [spɪl] VERB
◆ **You've spilled coffee on your shirt.** Te cayó café en la camisa.

spinach ['spɪnɪtʃ] NOUN
las espinacas

spin dryer ['spɪnˌdraɪər] NOUN
la centrifugadora

spine [spaɪn] NOUN
la columna vertebral

spinster ['spɪnstər] NOUN
la solterona

spire ['spaɪər] NOUN
la aguja

spirit ['spɪrɪt] NOUN
1 el espíritu ◇ *a youthful spirit* un espíritu joven
2 el valor ◇ *Everyone admired her spirit.* Todos admiraban su valor.
3 el brío ◇ *They played with great spirit.* Jugaron con mucho brío.

spirits ['spɪrɪts] PL NOUN
los licores ◇ *I don't drink spirits.* No bebo licores.
◆ **to be in good spirits** estar* de buen ánimo

spiritual ['spɪrɪtʃəl] ADJECTIVE
espiritual

spit [spɪt] NOUN
see also **spit** VERB
la saliva

to **spit** [spɪt] VERB (**spat, spat**)
see also **spit** NOUN
escupir

to **spit out** [spɪt'aut] VERB
escupir ◇ *I spat it out.* Lo escupí.

spite [spaɪt] NOUN ☞

see also **spite** VERB
- **in spite of** a pesar de
- **out of spite** por despecho

to **spite** [spaɪt] VERB
see also **spite** NOUN
fastidiar ◇ *He just did it to spite me.* Lo hizo sólo para fastidiarme.

spiteful ['spaɪtfəl] ADJECTIVE
1 rencoroso (*person*)
2 malintencionado (*action*)

to **splash** [splæʃ] VERB
see also **splash** NOUN
salpicar* ◇ *Don't splash me!* ¡No me salpiques!
- **He splashed water on his face.** Se echó agua en la cara.

splash [splæʃ] NOUN (PL **splashes**)
see also **splash** VERB
el chapoteo ◇ *I heard a splash.* Oí un chapoteo.
- **a splash of color** una mancha de color

splendid ['splɛndɪd] ADJECTIVE
espléndido

splint [splɪnt] NOUN
la tablilla

splinter ['splɪntər] NOUN
la astilla

to **split** [splɪt] VERB (**split, split**)
1 partir ◇ *He split the wood with an ax.* Partió la madera con un hacha.
2 partirse ◇ *The ship hit a rock and split in two.* El barco chocó con una roca y se partió en dos.
3 dividir ◇ *a decision that will split the party* una decisión que dividirá al partido
- **They decided to split the profits.** Decidieron repartir los beneficios.

to **split up** [splɪt'ʌp] VERB
separarse

to **spoil** [spɔɪl] VERB
1 estropear ◇ *It spoiled our vacation.* Nos estropeó las vacaciones.
2 mimar ◇ *Grandparents like to spoil their grandchildren.* A los abuelos les encanta mimar a los nietos.

spoiled [spɔɪld] ADJECTIVE
1 mimado ◇ *a spoiled child* un niño mimado
2 malo (*food*)
3 cortado (*milk*)

spoilsport ['spɔɪl͵spɔːrt] NOUN
el/la aguafiestas (PL los/las aguafiestas)

spoke [spouk] VERB *see* **speak**

spoke [spouk] NOUN
el radio

spoken ['spoukən] VERB *see* **speak**

spokesman ['spouksmən] NOUN (PL **spokesmen**)
el portavoz (PL los portavoces)

spokeswoman ['spouks͵wumən] NOUN (PL **spokeswomen**)
la portavoz (PL las portavoces)

sponge [spʌndʒ] NOUN
la esponja
- **sponge cake** el bizcocho

sponsor ['spɑːnsər] NOUN
see also **sponsor** VERB
el patrocinador
la patrocinadora

to **sponsor** ['spɑːnsər] VERB
see also **sponsor** NOUN
patrocinar ◇ *The tournament was sponsored by local firms.* El torneo fue patrocinado por empresas locales.

spontaneous [spɑːn'teɪniəs] ADJECTIVE
espontáneo

spooky ['spuːki] ADJECTIVE
- **The house is really spooky at night.** La casa te pone los pelos de punta de noche.

spool [spuːl] NOUN
el carrete

spoon [spuːn] NOUN
la cuchara

spoonful ['spuːnful] NOUN
- **a spoonful** una cucharada

sport [spɔːrt] NOUN
el deporte
- **sport jacket** la chaqueta de sport
- **sports car** el carro sport
- **sports center** el centro recreativo

sportsman ['spɔːrtsmən] NOUN (PL **sportsmen**)
el deportista

sportswear ['spɔːrtswɛr] NOUN
la ropa de deporte

sportswoman ['spɔːrts͵wumən] NOUN (PL **sportswomen**)
la deportista

sporty ['spɔːrti] ADJECTIVE
deportista ◇ *I'm not very sporty.* No soy muy deportista.

spot [spɑːt] NOUN
see also **spot** VERB
1 la mancha ◇ *There's a spot on your shirt.* Tienes una mancha en la camisa.
2 el lunar ◇ *a red dress with white spots* un vestido rojo con lunares blancos
3 el grano ◇ *He's covered in spots.* Está lleno de granos.
4 el lugar ◇ *It's a lovely spot for a picnic.* Es un lugar precioso para un picnic.
- **on the spot (1)** en el acto ◇ *They gave her the job on the spot.* Le dieron el trabajo en el acto.
- **on the spot (2)** ahí mismo ◇ *Luckily they were able to mend the car on the spot.* Afortunadamente consiguieron arreglar el carro ahí mismo.

to **spot** [spɑːt] VERB
see also **spot** NOUN

notar ◇ *I spotted a mistake.* Noté un error.

spotless ['spɑ:tlɪs] ADJECTIVE
inmaculado

spotlight ['spɑ:tlaɪt] NOUN
el foco

spotty ['spɑ:ti] ADJECTIVE
con granos

spouse [spaus] NOUN
el/la cónyuge

to **sprain** [spreɪn] VERB
see also **sprain** NOUN
torcerse* ◇ *She's sprained her ankle.* Se torció el tobillo.

sprain [spreɪn] NOUN
see also **sprain** VERB
la torcedura

spray [spreɪ] NOUN
see also **spray** VERB
el spray (PL los sprays) (*spray can*)

to **spray** [spreɪ] VERB
see also **spray** NOUN
1 rociar* ◇ *She sprayed perfume on my hand.* Me roció perfume en la mano.
2 fumigar* ◇ *to spray against insects* fumigar contra los insectos

spread [sprɛd] NOUN
see also **spread** VERB
◆ **cheese spread** el queso para untar

to **spread** [sprɛd] VERB (**spread, spread**)
see also **spread** NOUN
1 extender* ◇ *She spread a towel on the sand.* Extendió una toalla sobre la arena.
2 untar ◇ *Spread the top of the cake with whipped cream.* Unte la parte superior del pastel con crema batida.
3 propagarse* ◇ *The news spread rapidly.* La noticia se propagó rápidamente.

to **spread out** [sprɛd'aut] VERB
1 dispersarse ◇ *The soldiers spread out across the field.* Los soldados se dispersaron por el campo.
2 desplegar* ◇ *He spread the map out on the table.* Desplegó el mapa sobre la mesa.

spreadsheet ['sprɛdʃi:t] NOUN
la hoja de cálculo

spring [sprɪŋ] NOUN
1 la primavera ◇ *in spring* en primavera
2 el muelle (*metal*)
3 el manantial (*of water*)
◆ **spring break**

> ℹ *El* **spring break** *tiene lugar en la primavera y consiste en una semana de vacaciones para los alumnos de los centros de educación secundaria y las universidades. La mayoría se dirige a algún lugar del sur de los Estados Unidos y ve esta semana como una oportunidad para descansar, ir a fiestas y olvidarse de los estudios y los exámenes.*

spring-cleaning [sprɪŋ'kli:nɪŋ] NOUN
la limpieza general

springtime ['sprɪŋtaɪm] NOUN
la primavera

sprinkler ['sprɪŋklər] NOUN
el aspersor

sprint [sprɪnt] NOUN
see also **sprint** VERB
la carrera de velocidad
◆ **the women's 100 meter sprint** los cien metros planos femeninos

to **sprint** [sprɪnt] VERB
see also **sprint** NOUN
correr a toda velocidad ◇ *She sprinted for the train.* Corrió a toda velocidad para tomar el tren.

sprinter ['sprɪntər] NOUN
el/la velocista

sprouts [sprauts] PL NOUN
◆ **Brussels sprouts** las coles de Bruselas

spy [spaɪ] NOUN (PL **spies**)
el/la espía

spying ['spaɪɪŋ] NOUN
el espionaje

to **spy on** ['spaɪˌɑ:n] VERB
espiar*

to **squabble** ['skwɑ:bəl] VERB
pelear

square [skwɛər] NOUN
see also **square** ADJECTIVE
1 el cuadrado ◇ *a square and a triangle* un cuadrado y un triángulo
2 la plaza ◇ *the town square* la plaza mayor, *Mexico:* el zócalo

square [skwɛər] ADJECTIVE
see also **square** NOUN
cuadrado ◇ *two square yards* dos yardas cuadradas
◆ **The garden is two yards square.** El jardín mide dos por dos.

squash [skwɑ:ʃ] NOUN
see also **squash** VERB
1 el squash (*sport*)
◆ **squash court** la cancha de squash
◆ **squash racket** la raqueta de squash
2 la calabaza alargada (*vegetable*)

to **squash** [skwɑ:ʃ] VERB
see also **squash** NOUN
aplastar ◇ *You're squashing me.* Me estás aplastando.

to **squeak** [skwi:k] VERB
1 chillar (*mouse, child*)
2 chirriar* (*door, wheel*)
3 crujir (*shoes*)

to **squeeze** [skwi:z] VERB
1 exprimir ◇ *Squeeze two large lemons.* Exprima dos limones grandes.
2 apretar* ◇ *She squeezed my hand.* Me apretó la mano.
◆ **The thieves squeezed through a tiny window.** Los ladrones se colaron por una pequeña ventana.

to **squeeze in** [skwi:z'ɪn] VERB
hacer* un hueco a ◇ *I can squeeze you in at two o'clock.* Te puedo hacer un hueco a las dos.

squint [skwɪnt] NOUN
el estrabismo
◆ **He has a squint.** Es estrábico.

squirrel ['skwɜ:rəl] NOUN
la ardilla

to **stab** [stæb] VERB
apuñalar

stable ['steɪbəl] NOUN
see also **stable** ADJECTIVE
la cuadra

stable ['steɪbəl] ADJECTIVE
see also **stable** NOUN
estable ◇ *a stable relationship* una relación estable

stack [stæk] NOUN
la pila ◇ *There were stacks of books on the table.* Había pilas de libros sobre la mesa.
◆ **They have stacks of money.** Tienen cantidad de dinero.

stadium ['steɪdiəm] NOUN (PL **stadiums** *or* **stadia**)
el estadio

staff [stæf] NOUN
1 el personal (*in company*)
2 el profesorado (*in school*)

stage [steɪdʒ] NOUN
1 la etapa ◇ *in stages* por etapas
◆ **at this stage in the negotiations** a estas alturas de las negociaciones
2 el escenario ◇ *The band came on stage late.* El grupo salió tarde al escenario.
◆ **I always wanted to go on the stage.** Siempre quise dedicarme al teatro.

to **stagger** ['stægər] VERB
tambalearse

stain [steɪn] NOUN
see also **stain** VERB
la mancha

to **stain** [steɪn] VERB
see also **stain** NOUN
manchar

stainless steel ['steɪnlɪs'sti:l] NOUN
el acero inoxidable

stain remover ['steɪnrɪ'mu:vər] NOUN
el quitamanchas (PL los quitamanchas)

stair [stɛər] NOUN
el escalón (PL los escalones)

staircase ['stɛrkeɪs] NOUN
la escalera

stairs [stɛərz] PL NOUN
las escaleras

stale [steɪl] ADJECTIVE
◆ **stale bread** el pan duro

stalemate ['steɪlmeɪt] NOUN
el punto muerto ◇ *to reach a stalemate* llegar* a un punto muerto
◆ **The game ended in stalemate.** (*in chess*) La partida terminó en tablas.

stall [stɑ:l] NOUN
el puesto ◇ *He has a market stall in the center of town.* Tiene un puesto en el mercado en el centro.

stamina ['stæmɪnə] NOUN
la resistencia física

stammer ['stæmər] NOUN
el tartamudeo
◆ **He has a stammer.** Es tartamudo.

stamp [stæmp] NOUN
see also **stamp** VERB
la estampilla
el timbre *Mexico*
◇ *My hobby is stamp collecting.* Mi afición es coleccionar estampillas. *Mexico*: Mi afición es coleccionar timbres.

to **stamp** [stæmp] VERB
see also **stamp** NOUN
sellar ◇ *The file was stamped "confidential".* El archivo iba sellado como "confidencial".
◆ **The audience stamped their feet.** El público pateaba.

to **stand** [stænd] VERB (**stood, stood**)
1 estar* de pie ◇ *He was standing by the door.* Estaba de pie junto a la puerta.
◆ **What are you standing there for?** ¿Qué haces ahí de pie?
◆ **They all stood when I came in.** Se pusieron de pie cuando entré.
2 soportar ◇ *I can't stand all this noise.* No soporto todo este ruido.

to **stand for** ['stænd,fɔ:r] VERB
1 significar* ◇ *"US" stands for "United States".* "US" significa "United States".
2 consentir* ◇ *I won't stand for it any more!* ¡No pienso consentirlo más!

to **stand in for** [stænd'ɪnfɔ:r] VERB
sustituir*

to **stand out** [stænd'aut] VERB
destacar*

to **stand up** [stænd'ʌp] VERB
1 ponerse* de pie ◇ *I stood up and walked out.* Me puse de pie y me fui.
2 estar* de pie ◇ *Sabrina has to stand up all day.* Sabrina tiene que estar todo el día de pie.

to **stand up for** [stænd'ʌpfɔ:r] VERB
defender* ◇ *Stand up for your rights!* ¡Defiende tus derechos!

standard ['stændərd] ADJECTIVE
see also **standard** NOUN
normal ◇ *the standard procedure* el procedimiento normal
◆ **standard equipment** el equipamiento de serie

standard ['stændərd] NOUN
see also **standard** ADJECTIVE
el nivel ◇ *The standard is very high.* El nivel

es muy alto.
- **She has high standards.** Es muy exigente.
- **standard of living** el nivel de vida

standby ticket ['stændbaɪ'tɪkɪt] NOUN
el pasaje en lista de espera

standpoint ['stændpɔɪnt] NOUN
el punto de vista

stands [stændz] PL NOUN
la tribuna SING

stank [stæŋk] VERB *see* **stink**

staple ['steɪpəl] NOUN
see also **staple** ADJECTIVE
la grapa

staple ['steɪpəl] ADJECTIVE
see also **staple** NOUN
básico ◇ *their staple food* su alimento básico

stapler ['steɪplər] NOUN
la grapadora

star [stɑːr] NOUN
see also **star** VERB
la estrella ◇ *a TV star* una estrella de televisión
- **the stars** el horóscopo
- **the Stars and Stripes** la bandera de los Estados Unidos

to **star** [stɑːr] VERB
see also **star** NOUN
- **to star in a movie** protagonizar* una película
- **The movie stars Ann May.** La protagonista de la película es Ann May.

to **stare** [stɛər] VERB
mirar fijamente ◇ *Andy stared at him.* Andy lo miraba fijamente.

stark [stɑːrk] ADVERB
- **stark naked** en cueros, *Mexico:* encuerado

start [stɑːrt] NOUN
see also **start** VERB
1 el principio ◇ *at the start of the movie* al principio de la película ◇ *from the start* desde el principio
- **for a start** para empezar
- **Shall we make a start on washing the dishes?** ¿Nos ponemos a lavar los platos?

2 la salida (*of race*)

to **start** [stɑːrt] VERB
see also **start** NOUN
1 empezar* ◇ *What time does it start?* ¿A qué hora empieza?
- **to start doing something** empezar a hacer algo ◇ *I started learning Spanish two years ago.* Empecé a aprender español hace dos años.

2 montar (*business, organization, campaign*) ◇ *He wants to start his own business.* Quiere montar su propio negocio.
3 arrancar* ◇ *He couldn't start the car.* No conseguía arrancar el carro. ◇ *The car wouldn't start.* El carro no arrancaba.

to **start off** [stɑːrt'ɑːf] VERB
ponerse* en camino ◇ *We started off first thing in the morning.* Nos pusimos en camino a primera hora de la mañana.

to **starve** [stɑːrv] VERB
morirse* de hambre ◇ *People are starving.* La gente se muere de hambre.
- **I'm starving!** ¡Me muero de hambre!

state [steɪt] NOUN
see also **state** VERB
el estado ◇ *It's an independent state.* Es un estado independiente. ◇ *She was in a state of depression.* Se encontraba en un estado de depresión.
- **He wasn't in a fit state to drive.** No estaba en condiciones de manejar.
- **Tim was in a real state.** Tim estaba nerviosísimo.
- **the States** Estados Unidos MASC

to **state** [steɪt] VERB
see also **state** NOUN
declarar ◇ *He stated his intention to resign.* Declaró que tenía intención de renunciar.
- **Please state your name and address.** Por favor indique su nombre y dirección.

statement ['steɪtmənt] NOUN
1 la declaración (PL las declaraciones) ◇ *statements by witnesses* las declaraciones de testigos
2 la afirmación (PL las afirmaciones) ◇ *Andrew now disowns the statement he made.* Ahora Andrew desmiente la afirmación que hizo.
- **a bank statement** un extracto de cuenta

station ['steɪʃən] NOUN
la estación (PL las estaciones)
- **train station** la estación de trenes
- **police station** la comisaría
- **radio station** la estación de radio

stationer's ['steɪʃənərz] NOUN
la papelería

station wagon ['steɪʃənˌwægən] NOUN
la camioneta

statue ['stætʃuː] NOUN
la estatua
- **Statue of Liberty** la estatua de la libertad

S

stay [steɪ] NOUN
see also **stay** VERB
la estadía
la estancia *Mexico*
◇ *my stay in Spain* mi estadía en España, *Mexico:* mi estancia en España

to **stay** [steɪ] VERB
see also **stay** NOUN
quedarse ◇ *Stay here!* ¡Quédate aquí! ◇ *I'm going to be staying with friends.* Me voy a quedar en la casa de unos amigos.
- **Where are you staying? In a hotel?** ¿Dónde estás? ¿En un hotel?
- **to stay the night** pasar la noche
- **We stayed in Bolivia for a few days.** Pasamos unos días en Bolivia.

to **stay in** [steɪ'ɪn] VERB
quedarse en casa

to **stay up** [steɪ'ʌp] VERB
quedarse levantado ◇ *We stayed up till midnight.* Nos quedamos levantados hasta las doce.

steady ['stɛdi] ADJECTIVE
1 fijo ◇ *a steady job* un trabajo fijo
◆ **a steady boyfriend** un novio formal
2 firme ◇ *a steady hand* un pulso firme
3 constante ◇ *a steady pace* un ritmo constante

steak [steɪk] NOUN
el filete

to **steal** [sti:l] VERB (**stole, stolen**)
robar

steam [sti:m] NOUN
el vapor ◇ *a steam engine* una máquina de vapor

steel [sti:l] NOUN
el acero

steep [sti:p] ADJECTIVE
empinado

steeple ['sti:pəl] NOUN
la aguja

steering wheel ['stɪrɪŋ,wi:l] NOUN
el volante

step [stɛp] NOUN
see also **step** VERB
1 el paso ◇ *He took a step forward.* Dio un paso adelante.
2 el peldaño ◇ *She tripped over the step.* Tropezó con el peldaño.

to **step** [stɛp] VERB
see also **step** NOUN
dar* un paso ◇ *I tried to step forward.* Traté de dar un paso adelante.
◆ **Step this way, please.** Pase por aquí, por favor.

to **step aside** [stɛpə'saɪd] VERB
hacerse* a un lado

to **step back** [stɛp'bæk] VERB
retroceder

stepbrother ['stɛp,brʌðər] NOUN
el hermanastro

stepdaughter ['stɛp,dɑ:tər] NOUN
la hijastra

stepfather ['stɛp,fɑ:ðər] NOUN
el padrastro

stepladder ['stɛp,lædər] NOUN
la escalera de tijera
el burro *Mexico*

stepmother ['stɛp,mʌðər] NOUN
la madrastra

stepsister ['stɛp,sɪstər] NOUN
la hermanastra

stepson ['stɛp,sʌn] NOUN
el hijastro

stereo ['stɛriou] NOUN (PL **stereos**)
el equipo de música

sterling silver ['stɜ:rlɪŋ'sɪlvər] NOUN
la plata de ley

stew [stu:] NOUN
el estofado

steward ['stu:ərd] NOUN
1 el aeromozo (*on plane*)
2 el camarero (*on ship*)

stewardess ['stu:ərdɪs] NOUN (PL **stewardesses**)
1 la aeromoza (*on plane*)
2 la camarera (*on ship*)

stick [stɪk] NOUN
see also **stick** VERB
el palo

to **stick** [stɪk] VERB (**stuck, stuck**)
see also **stick** NOUN
1 pegar* ◇ *Stick the label on the envelope.* Pegue la etiqueta en el sobre.
2 pegarse* ◇ *The rice stuck to the pan.* El arroz se pegó a la olla.
3 meter ◇ *He picked up the papers and stuck them in his briefcase.* Recogió los papeles y los metió en el maletín.

to **stick out** [stɪk'aut] VERB
sacar* ◇ *The little girl stuck out her tongue.* La niña sacó la lengua.
◆ **I'll try to stick it out.** Voy a tratar de aguantar la mecha.

sticker ['stɪkər] NOUN
el adhesivo

stick insect NOUN
el insecto palo

sticky ['stɪki] ADJECTIVE
1 pegajoso ◇ *to have sticky hands* tener* las manos pegajosas
2 adhesivo ◇ *a sticky label* una etiqueta adhesiva

stiff [stɪf] ADJECTIVE, ADVERB
rígido
◆ **to have a stiff neck** tener* tortícolis
◆ **to feel stiff** estar* agarrotado
◆ **to be bored stiff** estar* aburrido como una ostra
◆ **to be frozen stiff** estar* helado hasta los huesos
◆ **to be scared stiff** estar* muerto de miedo

still [stɪl] ADVERB
see also **still** ADJECTIVE
1 todavía ◇ *I still haven't finished.* No he terminado todavía. ◇ *Are you still in bed?* ¿Todavía estás en la cama?
◆ **Do you still live in Atlanta?** ¿Sigues viviendo en Atlanta?
◆ **better still** mejor aún
2 aun así (*even so*) ◇ *She knows I don't like it, but she still does it.* Sabe que no me gusta, pero aun así lo hace.
3 en fin (*after all*) ◇ *Still, it's the thought that counts.* En fin, la intención es lo que cuenta.

still [stɪl] ADJECTIVE
see also **still** ADVERB

quieto ◇ *He stood still.* Se quedó quieto.
◆ **Keep still!** ¡No te muevas!

sting [stɪŋ] NOUN
see also **sting** VERB
la picadura
el piquete *Mexico*
◇ *a bee sting* una picadura de abeja, *Mexico:* un piquete de abeja

to **sting** [stɪŋ] VERB (**stung, stung**)
see also **sting** NOUN
picar*

stingy ['stɪndʒi] ADJECTIVE
tacaño

to **stink** [stɪŋk] VERB (**stank, stunk**)
see also **stink** NOUN
apestar ◇ *You stink of garlic!* ¡Apestas a ajo!

stink [stɪŋk] NOUN
see also **stink** VERB
el tufo ◇ *the stink of beer* el tufo a cerveza

to **stir** [stɜːr] VERB
agitar

to **stitch** [stɪtʃ] VERB
see also **stitch** NOUN
coser

stitch [stɪtʃ] NOUN (PL **stitches**)
see also **stitch** VERB
1 la puntada (*in sewing*)
2 el punto (*in knitting, in wound*) ◇ *I had five stitches.* Me pusieron cinco puntos.

stock [stɑːk] NOUN
see also **stock** VERB
1 la reserva ◇ *stocks of ammunition* reservas de munición
2 las existencias ◇ *the store's stock* las existencias de la tienda
◆ **Yes, we have your size in stock.** Sí, tenemos su número en existencia.
◆ **out of stock** agotado ◇ *I'm sorry, they're both out of stock.* Lo siento, están los dos agotados.
3 el caldo ◇ *chicken stock* caldo de pollo

to **stock** [stɑːk] VERB
see also **stock** NOUN
vender ◇ *Do you stock camping stoves?* ¿Venden hornillos de camping?

to **stock up** [stɑːk'ʌp] VERB
abastecerse* ◇ *to stock up with something* abastecerse de algo

stocking ['stɑːkɪŋ] NOUN
la media

stole [stoul] VERB *see* **steal**

stolen ['stoulən] VERB *see* **steal**

stomach ['stʌmək] NOUN
el estómago

stomachache ['stʌməkˌeɪk] NOUN
el dolor de estómago
◆ **I have a stomachache.** Me duele el estómago.

stone [stoun] NOUN
1 la piedra ◇ *a stone wall* un muro de piedra
2 el hueso ◇ *a peach stone* un hueso de durazno

stood [stud] VERB *see* **stand**

stool [stuːl] NOUN
el taburete

to **stop** [stɑːp] VERB
see also **stop** NOUN
1 parar ◇ *The train doesn't stop there.* El tren no para allí.
2 pararse ◇ *The music stopped.* Se paró la música.
◆ **This has to stop!** ¡Esto se tiene que acabar!
◆ **I think the rain is going to stop.** Creo que va a dejar de llover.
◆ **to stop doing something** dejar de hacer algo
◇ *to stop smoking* dejar de fumar
3 acabar con ◇ *a campaign to stop whaling* una campaña para acabar con la caza de ballenas
◆ **to stop somebody doing something** impedir* que alguien haga algo
impedir que *has to be followed by a verb in the subjunctive.*
◇ *She would have liked to stop us seeing each other.* Le hubiera gustado impedir que nos siguiéramos viendo.
◆ **Stop!** ¡Alto!

stop [stɑːp] NOUN
see also **stop** VERB
el paradero ◇ *a bus stop* un paradero de bus
◆ **This is my stop.** Yo me bajo aquí.

stopwatch ['stɑːpˌwɑːtʃ] NOUN (PL **stopwatches**)
el cronómetro

store [stɔːr] NOUN
see also **store** VERB
1 la tienda ◇ *a furniture store* una tienda de muebles
2 el almacén (PL los almacenes) ◇ *a grain store* un almacén de grano

to **store** [stɔːr] VERB
see also **store** NOUN
1 guardar ◇ *They store onions in the cellar.* Guardan cebollas en el sótano.
2 almacenar ◇ *to store information* almacenar información

storekeeper ['stɔːrˌkiːpər] NOUN
el/la comerciante

store window ['stɔːr'wɪndou] NOUN
la vitrina
el aparador *Mexico*

storm [stɔːrm] NOUN
la tormenta
◆ **storm window** la doble ventana

stormy ['stɔːrmi] ADJECTIVE
tormentoso

story ['stɔːri] NOUN (PL **stories**)
1 el cuento (*tale*)
2 la historia (*account*)
3 el piso ◇ *a three-story building* un edificio de tres pisos

S

stove [stouv] NOUN
1 la cocina
la estufa *Mexico*
(*in kitchen*)
◇ *a gas stove* una cocina de gas, *Mexico*: una estufa de gas
2 el hornillo de camping (*camping stove*)

straight [streɪt] ADJECTIVE, ADVERB
1 recto ◇ *a straight line* una línea recta
2 liso ◇ *straight hair* pelo liso
3 heterosexual (*not gay*)
◆ **He looked straight at me.** Me miró directamente a los ojos.
◆ **straight away** enseguida
◆ **I'll come straight back.** Vuelvo enseguida.
◆ **Keep straight on.** Siga derecho.

straightforward [streɪt'fɔːrwərd] ADJECTIVE
1 sencillo ◇ *It's very straightforward.* Es muy sencillo.
2 sincero ◇ *She's very straightforward.* Es muy sincera.

strain [streɪn] NOUN
see also **strain** VERB
la tensión (PL las tensiones)
◆ **It was a strain.** Fue muy estresante.

to **strain** [streɪn] VERB
see also **strain** NOUN
◆ **to strain one's eyes** forzar* la vista
◆ **I strained my back.** Me dio un tirón en la espalda.
◆ **to strain a muscle** sufrir un tirón muscular

strained [streɪnd] ADJECTIVE
◆ **a strained muscle** un esguince

stranded ['strændɪd] ADJECTIVE
◆ **We were stranded on the highway.** Nos quedamos botados en la carretera.

strange [streɪndʒ] ADJECTIVE
raro ◇ *That's strange!* ¡Qué raro!
__es raro que__ has to be followed by a verb in the subjunctive.
◇ *It's strange that she doesn't talk to us anymore.* Es raro que ya no nos hable.

stranger ['streɪndʒər] NOUN
el desconocido
la desconocida
No confundir __stranger__ con __extranjero__, que a su vez se traduce como __foreigner__.
◇ *Don't talk to strangers.* No hables con desconocidos.
◆ **I'm a stranger here.** Yo no soy de aquí.

to **strangle** ['stræŋgəl] VERB
estrangular

strap [stræp] NOUN
1 el tirante (*of bra, dress*)
2 la correa (*of watch, camera, suitcase*)
3 el asa FEM (*of bag*)
Although it's a feminine noun, remember that you use __el__ and __un__ with __asa__.

straw [strɑː] NOUN
1 la paja ◇ *a straw hat* un sombrero de paja
2 la pajita
el popote *Mexico*
◇ *He was drinking his lemonade through a straw.* Se tomaba la limonada con una pajita. *Mexico*: Se tomaba la limonada con un popote.
◆ **That's the last straw!** ¡Eso es la gota que colma el vaso!

strawberry ['strɑːbɛri] NOUN (PL **strawberries**)
la fresa

stray [streɪ] ADJECTIVE
extraviado ◇ *a stray cat* un gato extraviado

stream [striːm] NOUN
el riachuelo

street [striːt] NOUN
la calle

streetcar ['striːtkɑːr] NOUN
el tranvía
Although __tranvía__ ends in __-a__, it is actually a masculine noun.

streetlight ['striːtlaɪt] NOUN
el farol

street musician ['striːtmjuˌzɪʃən] NOUN
el músico callejero
la música callejera

street plan ['striːtˌplæn] NOUN
el plano de la ciudad

streetwise ['striːtwaɪz] ADJECTIVE
◆ **to be streetwise** sabérselas* todas
◆ **a streetwise kid** un pillo

strength [strɛŋθ] NOUN
la fuerza ◇ *with all his strength* con todas sus fuerzas

to **stress** [strɛs] VERB
see also **stress** NOUN
recalcar* ◇ *I would like to stress that...* Me gustaría recalcar que...

stress [strɛs] NOUN
see also **stress** VERB
el estrés ◇ *She's under a lot of stress.* Tiene mucho estrés.

to **stretch** [strɛtʃ] VERB
1 estirarse ◇ *The dog woke up and stretched.* El perro se despertó y se estiró.
◇ *My sweater stretched after I washed it.* Mi suéter se estiró al lavarlo.
◆ **I went out to stretch my legs.** Salí a estirar las piernas.
2 tender* ◇ *They stretched a rope between two trees.* Tendieron una cuerda entre dos árboles.

to **stretch out** [strɛtʃ'aut] VERB
tenderse* ◇ *They stretched out on the beach.* Se tendieron en la playa.
◆ **to stretch out one's arms** extender* los brazos

stretcher ['strɛtʃər] NOUN
la camilla

stretchy ['strɛtʃi] ADJECTIVE

elástico

strict [strɪkt] ADJECTIVE
estricto

strike [straɪk] NOUN
see also **strike** VERB
1 la huelga
◆ **to be on strike** estar* en huelga
◆ **to go on strike** hacer* huelga
2 el golpe (*in baseball*)

to **strike** [straɪk] VERB (**struck, struck**)
see also **strike** NOUN
golpear ◇ *She struck him across the mouth.* Lo golpeó en la boca.
◆ **The clock struck three.** El reloj dio las tres.
◆ **to strike a match** encender* un fósforo, *Mexico*: encender* un cerillo

striker [ˈstraɪkər] NOUN
1 el/la huelguista (*person on strike*)
2 el delantero
la delantera
(*in soccer and other games*)

striking [ˈstraɪkɪŋ] ADJECTIVE
1 asombroso ◇ *a striking resemblance* un parecido asombroso
2 en huelga ◇ *striking miners* mineros en huelga

string [strɪŋ] NOUN
el cordel
el mecate *Mexico*
◆ **a piece of string** un cordel, *Mexico*: un mecate

string beans [ˈstrɪŋˌbiːnz] PL NOUN
las habichuelas verdes
los ejotes *Mexico*

to **strip** [strɪp] VERB
see also **strip** NOUN
desnudarse

strip [strɪp] NOUN
see also **strip** VERB
la tira
◆ **strip cartoon** la tira cómica

stripe [straɪp] NOUN
la franja

striped [straɪpt] ADJECTIVE
a rayas ◇ *a striped skirt* una falda a rayas

stripper [ˈstrɪpər] NOUN
el/la artista de striptease

stripy [ˈstraɪpi] ADJECTIVE
a rayas

to **stroke** [strouk] VERB
see also **stroke** NOUN
acariciar

stroke [strouk] NOUN
see also **stroke** VERB
el derrame cerebral ◇ *to have a stroke* sufrir un derrame cerebral
◆ **a stroke of luck** un golpe de suerte

stroll [stroul] NOUN
◆ **to go for a stroll** ir* a dar un paseo

stroller [ˈstroulər] NOUN
la silla de paseo
la carreola *Mexico*

strong [strɑːŋ] ADJECTIVE
fuerte

strongly [ˈstrɑːŋli] ADVERB
◆ **We strongly advise you to...** Te recomendamos encarecidamente que...
◆ **He smelled strongly of tobacco.** Olía mucho a tabaco.
◆ **strongly built** corpulento
◆ **I don't feel strongly about it.** Me da un poco igual.

struck [strʌk] VERB *see* **strike**

to **struggle** [ˈstrʌgəl] VERB
see also **struggle** NOUN
forcejear ◇ *He struggled, but he couldn't escape.* Forcejeó, pero no pudo escapar.
◆ **to struggle to do something (1)** (*fight*) luchar por hacer algo ◇ *He struggled to get custody of his daughter.* Luchó por conseguir la custodia de su hija.
◆ **to struggle to do something (2)** (*have difficulty*) pasar apuros para hacer algo ◇ *They struggle to pay their bills.* Pasan apuros para pagar las cuentas.

struggle [ˈstrʌgəl] NOUN
see also **struggle** VERB
la lucha ◇ *a struggle for survival* una lucha por la sobrevivencia
◆ **It was a struggle.** Nos costó mucho.

stub [stʌb] NOUN
la colilla

stubborn [ˈstʌbərn] ADJECTIVE
terco

to **stub out** [stʌbˈaut] VERB
apagar*

stuck [stʌk] VERB *see* **stick**

stuck [stʌk] ADJECTIVE
atascado ◇ *The lid is stuck.* La tapa está atascada.
◆ **to get stuck** quedarse atascado
◆ **We got stuck in a traffic jam.** Nos metimos en un atasco.

S

stuck-up [stʌkˈʌp] ADJECTIVE
creído (*informal*)

stud [stʌd] NOUN
el pendiente
el arete *Mexico*
(*earring*)

student [ˈstuːdnt] NOUN
el/la estudiante

student driver [ˈstuːdntˈdraɪvər] NOUN
el conductor en prácticas
la conductora en prácticas

studio [ˈstuːdiou] NOUN
el estudio ◇ *a TV studio* un estudio de televisión
◆ **a studio apartment** un estudio

to **study** [ˈstʌdi] VERB (**studied, studied**)
estudiar ◇ *I haven't started studying yet.* Todavía no he empezado a estudiar.

stuff [stʌf] NOUN

☞

las cosas ◇ *Do you have all of your stuff?* ¿Tienes todas tus cosas?
◆ **I need some stuff for hay fever.** Necesito algo para la alergia al polen.
stuffy ['stʌfi] ADJECTIVE
◆ **a stuffy room** una habitación mal ventilada
◆ **It's stuffy in here.** Hay un ambiente muy cargado aquí.
to **stumble** ['stʌmbəl] VERB
tropezar*
stung [stʌŋ] VERB *see* **sting**
stunk [stʌŋk] VERB *see* **stink**
stunned [stʌnd] ADJECTIVE
pasmado ◇ *I was stunned.* Me quedé pasmado.
stunning ['stʌnɪŋ] ADJECTIVE
impresionante
stunt [stʌnt] NOUN
◆ **It's a publicity stunt.** Es un truco publicitario.
stuntman ['stʌntmæn] NOUN (PL **stuntmen**)
el especialista
stupid ['stu:pɪd] ADJECTIVE
estúpido
to **stutter** ['stʌtər] VERB
see also **stutter** NOUN
tartamudear
stutter ['stʌtər] NOUN
see also **stutter** VERB
el tartamudeo
◆ **He has a stutter.** Es tartamudo.
style [staɪl] NOUN
el estilo ◇ *That's not his style.* No es su estilo.
subject ['sʌbdʒɪkt] NOUN
1 el tema
Although **tema** *ends in* **-a**, *it is actually a masculine noun.*
◇ *The subject of my project is the internet.* El tema de mi trabajo es Internet.
2 la asignatura ◇ *What's your favorite subject?* ¿Cuál es tu asignatura preferida?
3 el sujeto ◇ *"I" is the subject in "I love you".* "I" es el sujeto en "I love you".
submarine [ˌsʌbmə'ri:n] NOUN
el submarino
subscription [səb'skrɪpʃən] NOUN
la suscripción (PL las suscripciones) (*to paper, magazine*)
◆ **to take out a subscription to** suscribirse* a
subsequently ['sʌbsɪkwɛntli] ADVERB
posteriormente
to **subsidize** ['sʌbsɪdaɪz] VERB
subvencionar
subsidy ['sʌbsɪdi] NOUN (PL **subsidies**)
la subvención (PL las subvenciones)
substance ['sʌbstəns] NOUN
la sustancia
substitute ['sʌbstɪtu:t] NOUN
see also **substitute** VERB
1 el sustituto
la sustituta
(*replacement*)
2 el/la suplente (*in various sports*) ◇ *I was a substitute in the game last Saturday.* Yo era suplente en el partido del sábado.
to **substitute** ['sʌbstɪtu:t] VERB
see also **substitute** NOUN
sustituir* ◇ *to substitute A for B* sustituir a B por A
substitute teacher ['sʌbstɪtu:t'ti:tʃər] NOUN
el profesor interino
la profesora interina
subtitled ['sʌbˌtaɪtld] ADJECTIVE
subtitulado
subtitles ['sʌbˌtaɪtlz] PL NOUN
los subtítulos ◇ *a Cuban movie with English subtitles* una película cubana con subtítulos en inglés
subtle ['sʌtl] ADJECTIVE
sutil
to **subtract** [səb'trækt] VERB
restar ◇ *to subtract 3 from 5* restar 3 a 5
suburb ['sʌbɜ:rb] NOUN
el barrio residencial ◇ *a Chicago suburb* un barrio residencial de Chicago
◆ **They live in the suburbs.** Viven en las afueras.
suburban [sə'bɜ:rbən] ADJECTIVE
◆ **a suburban train** un tren de cercanías
◆ **a suburban shopping center** un centro comercial de las afueras
subway ['sʌbweɪ] NOUN
el metro (*underground*)
to **succeed** [sək'si:d] VERB
1 tener* éxito ◇ *to succeed in business* tener éxito en los negocios
2 salir* bien ◇ *The plan did not succeed.* El plan no salió bien.
◆ **to succeed in doing something** lograr hacer algo
success [sək'sɛs] NOUN (PL **successes**)
el éxito
Be careful not to translate **success** *by* **suceso.**
successful [sək'sɛsfəl] ADJECTIVE
de éxito ◇ *a successful lawyer* un abogado de éxito
◆ **a successful attempt** un intento fructífero
◆ **to be successful** tener* éxito
◆ **to be successful in doing something** lograr hacer algo
successfully [sək'sɛsfəli] ADVERB
con éxito
successive [sək'sɛsɪv] ADJECTIVE
consecutivo ◇ *He was the winner for a second successive year.* Fue el ganador por segundo año consecutivo.
such [sʌtʃ] ADJECTIVE, ADVERB
1 tan ◇ *such clever people* gente tan inteligente ◇ *such a long journey* un viaje tan largo

[2] tal ◇ *I wouldn't dream of doing such a thing.* No se me ocurriría hacer tal cosa. ◇ *The pain was such that...* El dolor era tal que...

◆ **such a lot** tanto ◇ *such a lot of work* tanto trabajo

◆ **such a long time ago** hace tanto tiempo

◆ **such as** como ◇ *a hot country, such as India...* un país caluroso, como la India...

◆ **as such** propiamente dicho ◇ *She's not an expert as such, but...* No es una experta propiamente dicha, pero...

◆ **There's no such thing.** Eso no existe. ◇ *There's no such thing as the yeti.* El yeti no existe.

such and such ['sʌtʃən,sʌtʃ] ADJECTIVE
tal ◇ *such and such a place* tal lugar

to **suck** [sʌk] VERB
chupar

◆ **to suck one's thumb** chuparse el pulgar

sudden ['sʌdn] ADJECTIVE
repentino ◇ *a sudden change* un cambio repentino

◆ **all of a sudden** de repente

suddenly ['sʌdnli] ADVERB
de repente

suede [sweɪd] NOUN
la ante ◇ *a suede jacket* una chaqueta de ante

to **suffer** ['sʌfər] VERB
sufrir ◇ *She was really suffering.* Sufría de verdad.

◆ **to suffer from something** padecer* de algo ◇ *I suffer from hay fever.* Padezco de alergia al polen.

to **suffocate** ['sʌfəkeɪt] VERB
ahogarse*

sugar ['ʃugər] NOUN
el azúcar

to **suggest** [səg'dʒɛst] VERB
[1] sugerir*
*Use the subjunctive after **sugerir que**.*
◇ *She suggested going out for a pizza.* Sugirió que saliéramos a comer una pizza.
[2] aconsejar
*Use the subjunctive after **aconsejar que**.*
◇ *I suggested they set off early.* Yo les aconsejé que salieran temprano.

◆ **What are you trying to suggest?** ¿Qué insinúas?

suggestion [səg'dʒɛstʃən] NOUN
la sugerencia ◇ *to make a suggestion* hacer* una sugerencia
*Be careful not to translate **suggestion** by **sugestión**.*

suicide ['su:ɪsaɪd] NOUN
el suicidio

◆ **to commit suicide** suicidarse

suicide bomber NOUN
el/la terrorista suicida

suicide bombing NOUN
el atentado suicida

suit [su:t] NOUN
see also **suit** VERB
[1] el traje (*man's*)
[2] el traje de chaqueta (*woman's*)

to **suit** [su:t] VERB
see also **suit** NOUN
[1] venir* bien a ◇ *What time would suit you?* ¿Qué hora te vendría bien?

◆ **That suits me fine.** Eso me viene estupendamente.

◆ **Suit yourself!** ¡Haz lo que te parezca!

[2] quedar bien a ◇ *That dress really suits you.* Ese vestido te queda muy bien.

suitable ['su:təbəl] ADJECTIVE
[1] conveniente ◇ *a suitable time* una hora conveniente
[2] apropiado ◇ *suitable clothing* ropa apropiada

suitcase ['su:tkeɪs] NOUN
la maleta

suite [swi:t] NOUN
la suite ◇ *a suite at the New York Hilton* una suite en el Hilton de Nueva York

◆ **a bedroom suite** un dormitorio completo

◆ **three-piece suite** un juego de sofá y tres sillones

to **sulk** [sʌlk] VERB
estar* de mal humor

sulky ['sʌlki] ADJECTIVE
malhumorado

sum [sʌm] NOUN
la suma ◇ *to do sums* hacer* sumas ◇ *a sum of money* una suma de dinero

to **summarize** ['sʌməraɪz] VERB
resumir

summary ['sʌməri] NOUN (PL **summaries**)
el resumen (PL los resúmenes)

summer ['sʌmər] NOUN
el verano ◇ *summer clothes* ropa de verano ◇ *the summer vacations* las vacaciones de verano ◇ *a summer camp* un campamento de verano

summertime ['sʌmərtaɪm] NOUN
el verano

summit ['sʌmɪt] NOUN
la cumbre ◇ *the NATO summit* la cumbre de la OTAN ◇ *the summit of Mount Everest* la cumbre del Everest

to **sum up** [sʌm'ʌp] VERB
resumir

◆ **To sum up...** Resumiendo...

sun [sʌn] NOUN
el sol ◇ *in the sun* al sol

to **sunbathe** ['sʌnbeɪð] VERB
tomar el sol

sunblock ['sʌnblɑ:k] NOUN
la crema solar de protección total

sunburn ['sʌnbɜ:rn] NOUN
la quemadura

sunburned ['sʌnbɜ:rnd] ADJECTIVE

S

☞

quemado por el sol
◆ **Be careful not to get sunburned!** ¡Cuidado de quemarte con el sol!

Sunday ['sʌndi] NOUN
el domingo (PL los domingos) ◇ *I saw her on Sunday.* La vi el domingo. ◇ *every Sunday* todos los domingos ◇ *last Sunday* el domingo pasado ◇ *next Sunday* el domingo que viene ◇ *on Sundays* los domingos

Sunday school ['sʌndi,sku:l] NOUN
la catequesis

sunflower ['sʌnflauər] NOUN
el girasol

sung [sʌŋ] VERB *see* **sing**

sunglasses ['sʌnglæsɪz] PL NOUN
los anteojos de sol

sunk [sʌŋk] VERB *see* **sink**

sunlight ['sʌnlaɪt] NOUN
la luz del sol

sunny ['sʌni] ADJECTIVE
soleado ◇ *a sunny morning* una mañana soleada
◆ **It's sunny.** Hace sol.
◆ **a sunny day** un día de sol

sunrise ['sʌnraɪz] NOUN
la salida del sol

sunroof ['sʌnru:f] NOUN
el techo corredizo

sunscreen ['sʌnskri:n] NOUN
el protector solar

sunset ['sʌnsɛt] NOUN
la puesta de sol

sunshine ['sʌnʃaɪn] NOUN
el sol ◇ *in the sunshine* al sol

sunstroke ['sʌnstrouk] NOUN
la insolación (PL las insolaciones)

suntan ['sʌntæn] NOUN
el bronceado
◆ **to get a suntan** broncearse
◆ **suntan lotion** la crema bronceadora
◆ **suntan oil** el aceite bronceador

super ['su:pər] ADJECTIVE
estupendo

superb [su:'pɜ:rb] ADJECTIVE
magnífico

supermarket ['su:pər,mɑ:rkɪt] NOUN
el supermercado

supernatural [su:pər'nætʃərəl] ADJECTIVE
sobrenatural

superstitious [su:pər'stɪʃəs] ADJECTIVE
supersticioso

to **supervise** ['su:pərvaɪz] VERB
supervisar

supervisor ['su:pərvaɪzər] NOUN
el supervisor
la supervisora

supper ['sʌpər] NOUN
la cena

supplement ['sʌplɪmənt] NOUN
el suplemento

supplies [sə'plaɪz] PL NOUN
las provisiones
◆ **medical supplies** material médico

to **supply** [sə'plaɪ] VERB (**supplied, supplied**)
see also **supply** NOUN
suministrar
◆ **to supply somebody with something** suministrar algo a alguien ◇ *The center supplied us with all the equipment.* El centro nos suministró todo el material.

supply [sə'plaɪ] NOUN (PL **supplies**)
see also **supply** VERB
el suministro ◇ *the water supply* el suministro de agua
◆ **a supply of paper** una remesa de papel

to **support** [sə'pɔ:rt] VERB
see also **support** NOUN
1 apoyar ◇ *My mother has always supported me.* Mi mamá siempre me ha apoyado.
2 mantener* ◇ *She had to support five children on her own.* Tenía que mantener a cinco niños ella sola.
◆ **What team do you support?** ¿De qué equipo eres?

*Be careful not to translate **to support** by **soportar**.*

support [sə'pɔ:rt] NOUN
see also **support** VERB
el apoyo

supporter [sə'pɔ:rtər] NOUN
1 el/la hincha ◇ *a Red Sox supporter* un hincha del Red Sox
2 el partidario
la partidaria
◇ *a supporter of the Green Party* un partidario del partido verde

to **suppose** [sə'pouz] VERB
suponer* ◇ *I suppose he'll be late.* Supongo que llegará tarde. ◇ *Suppose you win the lottery...* Supón que te toca la lotería...
◆ **I suppose so.** Supongo que sí.
◆ **You're supposed to show your passport.** Tienes que mostrar el pasaporte.
◆ **You're not supposed to smoke in the bathroom.** No está permitido fumar en el baño.
◆ **It's supposed to be the best hotel in the city.** Dicen que es el mejor hotel de la ciudad.

supposing [sə'pouzɪŋ] CONJUNCTION
◆ **Supposing you won the lottery...** Suponiendo que te tocara la lotería...

***suponiendo que** has to be followed by a verb in the subjunctive.*

surcharge ['sɜ:rtʃɑ:rdʒ] NOUN
el recargo

sure [ʃuər] ADJECTIVE
seguro ◇ *Are you sure?* ¿Estás seguro?
◆ **Sure!** ¡Claro!

◆ **to make sure that...** asegurarse de que... ◇ *I'm going to make sure the door is locked.* Voy a asegurarme de que la puerta está cerrada con llave.

surely ['ʃurli] ADVERB
◆ **Surely you don't believe that?** ¿No te creerás eso, no?

surf [sɜːrf] NOUN
see also **surf** VERB
la espuma de las olas

to **surf** [sɜːrf] VERB
see also **surf** NOUN
hacer* surf
◆ **to surf the Net** navegar* por Internet

surface ['sɜːrfɪs] NOUN
la superficie

surfboard ['sɜːrfbɔːrd] NOUN
la tabla de surf

surfing ['sɜːrfɪŋ] NOUN
el surf ◇ *to go surfing* hacer* surf

surgeon ['sɜːrdʒən] NOUN
el cirujano
la cirujana

surgery ['sɜːrdʒəri] NOUN (PL **surgeries**)
1 la cirugía (*treatment*)
2 el quirófano (*operating room*)

surname ['sɜːrneɪm] NOUN
el apellido

surprise [sər'praɪz] NOUN
la sorpresa

surprised [sər'praɪzd] ADJECTIVE
◆ **I was surprised to see him.** Me sorprendió verlo.
◆ **I'm not surprised that...** No me sorprende que...

surprising [sər'praɪzɪŋ] ADJECTIVE
sorprendente

to **surrender** [sə'rɛndər] VERB
rendirse*

to **surround** [sə'raund] VERB
rodear ◇ *surrounded by trees* rodeado de árboles

surroundings [sə'raundɪŋz] PL NOUN
el entorno ◇ *a hotel in beautiful surroundings* un hotel en un hermoso entorno

survey ['sɜːrveɪ] NOUN
la encuesta ◇ *They did a survey of a thousand students.* Hicieron una encuesta a mil estudiantes.

surveyor [sər'veɪər] NOUN
1 el agrimensor
la agrimensora
(*of land*)
2 el perito tasador
la perito tasadora
(*of buildings*)

survivor [sər'vaɪvər] NOUN
el/la superviviente ◇ *There were no survivors.* No hubo supervivientes.

to **suspect** [sə'spɛkt] VERB
see also **suspect** NOUN
sospechar

suspect ['sʌspɛkt] NOUN
see also **suspect** VERB
el sospechoso
la sospechosa

to **suspend** [sə'spɛnd] VERB
1 suspender (*from school*)
2 excluir* (*from team*)

suspenders [sə'spɛndərz] PL NOUN
los tirantes

suspense [sə'spɛns] NOUN
1 la incertidumbre ◇ *The suspense was terrible.* La incertidumbre era terrible.
2 el suspenso ◇ *a movie with lots of suspense* una película llena de suspenso

suspension [sə'spɛnʃən] NOUN
1 la suspensión (*from school*)
2 la exclusión (*from team*)

suspicious [sə'spɪʃəs] ADJECTIVE
1 receloso (*mistrustful*) ◇ *He was suspicious at first.* Al principio estaba receloso.
2 sospechoso (*suspicious-looking*) ◇ *a suspicious person* un individuo sospechoso

SUV NOUN (= *sports utility vehicle*)
el todoterreno (PL los todoterreno)

to **swallow** ['swɑːlou] VERB
tragar*

swam [swæm] VERB *see* **swim**

swan [swɑːn] NOUN
el cisne

to **swap** [swɑːp] VERB
cambiar ◇ *to swap A for B* cambiar A por B
◆ **Do you want to swap?** ¿Quieres que cambiemos?

to **swat** [swɑːt] VERB
aplastar

to **sway** [sweɪ] VERB
balancearse

to **swear** [swɛər] VERB (**swore, sworn**)
1 jurar ◇ *to swear allegiance to* jurar fidelidad a
2 decir* palabrotas ◇ *It's wrong to swear.* No se deben decir palabrotas.

swearword ['swɛrwɜːrd] NOUN
la palabrota

sweat [swɛt] NOUN
see also **sweat** VERB
el sudor

to **sweat** [swɛt] VERB
see also **sweat** NOUN
sudar

sweater ['swɛtər] NOUN
el suéter

sweatsuit ['swɛtsuːt] NOUN
el equipo de deportes
los pants Mexico

sweaty ['swɛti] ADJECTIVE
1 transpirado (*hands, face*)
2 sudado (*clothes*)

S

Swede [swi:d] NOUN
el sueco
la sueca
(*person*)

Sweden ['swi:dn] NOUN
Suecia FEM

Swedish ['swi:dɪʃ] ADJECTIVE, NOUN
sueco

to **sweep** [swi:p] VERB (**swept, swept**)
barrer ◇ *to sweep the floor* barrer el suelo

sweet [swi:t] ADJECTIVE
1 dulce ◇ *a sweet wine* un vino dulce
2 amable ◇ *That was really sweet of you.* Fue muy amable de tu parte.
◆ **sweet and sour pork** el cerdo agridulce

sweet corn ['swi:t,kɔ:rn] NOUN
el maíz dulce
el elote *Mexico*

sweltering ['swɛltərɪŋ] ADJECTIVE
◆ **It was sweltering.** Hacía un calor asfixiante.

swept [swɛpt] VERB *see* **sweep**

to **swerve** [swɜ:rv] VERB
girar bruscamente ◇ *I swerved to avoid the cyclist.* Giré bruscamente para esquivar al ciclista.

swim [swɪm] NOUN
see also **swim** VERB
◆ **to go for a swim** ir* a nadar

to **swim** [swɪm] VERB (**swam, swum**)
see also **swim** NOUN
nadar ◇ *Can you swim?* ¿Sabes nadar?
◆ **She swam across the river.** Cruzó el río a nado.

swimmer ['swɪmər] NOUN
el nadador
la nadadora

swimming ['swɪmɪŋ] NOUN
la natación ◇ *swimming lessons* clases de natación
◆ **Do you like swimming?** ¿Te gusta nadar?
◆ **to go swimming** ir* a nadar
◆ **swimming pool** la piscina, *Mexico*: la alberca
◆ **swimming trunks** el traje de baño

swimsuit ['swɪmsu:t] NOUN
el traje de baño

to **swing** [swɪŋ] VERB (**swung, swung**)
see also **swing** NOUN
1 columpiarse (*on a swing*)
2 balancearse ◇ *Her bag swung as she walked.* El bolso se balanceaba según iba andando.
◆ **He was swinging on a rope.** Se balanceaba colgado de una cuerda.
3 colgar* ◇ *A large key swung from his belt.* Le colgaba una gran llave del cinturón.
4 balancear ◇ *He was swinging his bag back and forth.* Balanceaba la bolsa de un lado al otro.
◆ **Roy swung his legs off the couch.** Con un movimiento rápido, Roy quitó las piernas del sofá.
◆ **The canoe suddenly swung round.** De repente la canoa dio un viraje.

swing [swɪŋ] NOUN
see also **swing** VERB
el columpio

Swiss [swɪs] ADJECTIVE, NOUN
suizo
◆ **the Swiss** los suizos

switch [swɪtʃ] NOUN (PL **switches**)
see also **switch** VERB
el interruptor

to **switch** [swɪtʃ] VERB
see also **switch** NOUN
cambiar de ◇ *We switched partners.* Cambiamos de pareja.

to **switch off** [swɪtʃ'ɑ:f] VERB
apagar* (*TV, machine, engine*)

to **switch on** [swɪtʃ'ɑ:n] VERB
prender (*TV, machine, engine*)

Switzerland ['swɪtsərlənd] NOUN
Suiza FEM

swollen ['swoulən] ADJECTIVE
hinchado ◇ *My ankle is very swollen.* Tengo el tobillo muy hinchado.

sword [sɔ:rd] NOUN
la espada

swore [swɔ:r] VERB *see* **swear**

sworn [swɔ:rn] VERB *see* **swear**

swum [swʌm] VERB *see* **swim**

swung [swʌŋ] VERB *see* **swing**

syllabus ['sɪləbəs] NOUN (PL **syllabuses**)
el programa de estudios
*Although **programa** ends in **-a**, it is actually a masculine noun.*

symbol ['sɪmbəl] NOUN
el símbolo

sympathetic [sɪmpə'θɛtɪk] ADJECTIVE
comprensivo
*No confundir **sympathetic** con **simpático**, que se traduce como **nice**.*

to **sympathize** ['sɪmpəθaɪz] VERB
◆ **to sympathize with somebody (1)** (*feel sorry for*) compadecerse* de alguien
◆ **to sympathize with somebody (2)** (*understand*) comprender a alguien

sympathy ['sɪmpəθi] NOUN
1 la compasión (*sorrow*)
2 la comprensión (*understanding*)

symptom ['sɪmptəm] NOUN
el síntoma
*Although **síntoma** ends in **-a**, it is actually a masculine noun.*

syringe [sə'rɪndʒ] NOUN
la jeringuilla

system ['sɪstəm] NOUN
el sistema
*Although **sistema** ends in **-a**, it is actually a masculine noun.*

T

table ['teɪbəl] NOUN
la mesa
◆ **to set the table** poner* la mesa

tablecloth ['teɪbəl,klɑːθ] NOUN
el mantel

tablespoon ['teɪbəlspuːn] NOUN
la cuchara de servir

tablespoonful ['teɪbəlspuːnful] NOUN
◆ **a tablespoonful of sugar** una cucharada grande de azúcar

tablet ['tæblɪt] NOUN
la pastilla

table tennis ['teɪbəl,tɛnɪs] NOUN
el tenis de mesa ◇ *to play table tennis* jugar* tenis de mesa

tabloid ['tæblɔɪd] NOUN
◆ **the tabloids** la prensa amarilla

tackle ['tækəl] NOUN
see also **tackle** VERB
1 el placaje (*in football*)
2 la entrada (*in soccer*)
◆ **fishing tackle** el equipo de pesca

to **tackle** ['tækəl] VERB
see also **tackle** NOUN
◆ **to tackle somebody (1)** placar* a alguien (*in football*)
◆ **to tackle somebody (2)** entrar a alguien (*in soccer*)
◆ **to tackle a problem** abordar un problema

tact [tækt] NOUN
el tacto

tactful ['tæktfəl] ADJECTIVE
diplomático

tactics ['tæktɪks] PL NOUN
la táctica SING

tactless ['tæktlɪs] ADJECTIVE
poco diplomático ◇ *He's so tactless!* ¡Es tan poco diplomático!
◆ **a tactless remark** un comentario falto de tacto

tadpole ['tædpoul] NOUN
el renacuajo

taffy ['tæfi] NOUN
el caramelo

tag [tæg] NOUN
la etiqueta (*label*)

tail [teɪl] NOUN
1 la cola (*of horse, bird, fish*)
2 el rabo (*of dog, bull, ox*)
◆ **Heads or tails?** ¿Cara o cruz?, *Mexico*: ¿Águila o sol?

tailor ['teɪlər] NOUN
el sastre ◇ *He's a tailor.* Es sastre.

to **take** [teɪk] VERB (**took, taken**)
1 tomar ◇ *Do you take sugar?* ¿Tomas azúcar?
◆ **He took some napkins out of the drawer.** Sacó unas servilletas del cajón.
2 llevar ◇ *He goes to the city every week, but he never takes me.* Va a la ciudad todas las semanas, pero nunca me lleva. ◇ *Don't forget to take your camera.* No te olvides de llevar la cámara.
◆ **It takes about one hour.** Se tarda más o menos una hora.
◆ **It won't take long.** No tardará mucho tiempo.
◆ **That takes a lot of courage.** Hace falta mucho valor para eso.
◆ **It takes a lot of money to do that.** Hace falta mucho dinero para hacer eso.
3 soportar ◇ *He can't take being criticized.* No soporta que lo critiquen. ◇ *I can't take it any longer.* Ya no lo soporto más.
4 tomar ◇ *Have you taken your driving test yet?* ¿Ya tomaste el examen de manejar? ◇ *I decided to take French instead of German.* Decidí tomar francés en vez de alemán.
◆ **to take an exam** presentarse a un examen
5 aceptar ◇ *We take credit cards.* Aceptamos tarjetas de crédito.

to **take after** [teɪk'æftər] VERB
parecerse* a ◇ *She takes after her mother.* Se parece a la mamá.

to **take apart** [teɪkə'pɑːrt] VERB
◆ **to take something apart** desmontar algo

to **take away** [teɪkə'weɪ] VERB
1 llevarse ◇ *They took away all his belongings.* Se llevaron todas sus pertenencias.
2 quitar ◇ *She was afraid her children would be taken away from her.* Tenía miedo de que le quitaran a los niños.

to **take back** [teɪk'bæk] VERB
devolver* ◇ *I took it back to the store.* Lo devolví a la tienda.
◆ **I take it all back!** ¡Retiro lo dicho!

to **take down** [teɪk'daun] VERB
quitar ◇ *She took down the painting.* Quitó el cuadro.

to **take in** [teɪk'ɪn] VERB
1 comprender ◇ *I didn't really take it in.* La verdad es que no lo comprendí.
2 engañar ◇ *They were taken in by his story.* Se dejaron engañar por la historia que les contó.

to **take off** [teɪk'ɑːf] VERB
1 despegar* ◇ *The plane took off 20 minutes late.* El avión despegó con 20 minutos de atraso.
2 quitar ◇ *Take your coat off.* Quítate el abrigo.

to **take out** [teɪk'aut] VERB
sacar* ◇ *He opened his wallet and took out some money.* Abrió la billetera y sacó dinero.
◆ **He took her out to the theater.** La invitó al teatro.
◆ **hot meals to take out** platos calientes para llevar

to **take over** [teɪk'ouvər] VERB

hacerse* cargo de ◇ *He took over the running of the company last year.* Se hizo cargo del control de la empresa el año pasado.

◆ **to take over from somebody (1)** sustituir* a alguien (*replace*)

◆ **to take over from somebody (2)** relevar a alguien (*in shift work*)

takeoff ['teɪk,ɑːf] NOUN
el despegue (*of plane*)

takeout ['teɪk,aut] NOUN
la comida para llevar (*meal*)

talcum powder ['tælkəm'paudər] NOUN
los polvos de talco

tale [teɪl] NOUN
el cuento

talent ['tælənt] NOUN
el talento ◇ *He has a lot of talent.* Tiene mucho talento.

◆ **to have a talent for something** tener* talento para algo

◆ **He has a real talent for languages.** Tiene verdadera facilidad para los idiomas.

talented ['tæləntɪd] ADJECTIVE
de talento ◇ *She's a talented pianist.* Es una pianista de talento.

talk [tɑːk] NOUN
see also **talk** VERB
1 la conversación (PL las conversaciones) ◇ *We had a long talk about her problems.* Tuvimos una larga conversación acerca de sus problemas.

◆ **I had a talk with my mother about it.** Hablé sobre eso con mi mamá.

◆ **to give a talk on something** dar* una charla sobre algo ◇ *She gave a talk on ancient Egypt.* Dio una charla sobre el antiguo Egipto.

2 las habladurías (*gossip*) ◇ *It's just talk.* Son sólo habladurías.

to **talk** [tɑːk] VERB
see also **talk** NOUN
hablar ◇ *What did you talk about?* ¿De qué hablaron?

◆ **to talk to somebody** hablar con alguien

◆ **to talk to oneself** hablar consigo mismo

◆ **to talk something over with somebody** discutir algo con alguien

talkative ['tɑːkətɪv] ADJECTIVE
hablador (FEM habladora)

talk show ['tɑːk,ʃou] NOUN

> ℹ *Un* **talk show** *es un programa de televisión en el que un moderador habla de diversos temas con invitados que han sido seleccionados. Por lo general se emiten durante el día.*

tall [tɑːl] ADJECTIVE
alto

◆ **to be two meters tall** medir* dos metros

tame [teɪm] ADJECTIVE
domesticado (*animal*)

tampon ['tæmpɑːn] NOUN
el tampón (PL los tampones)

tan [tæn] NOUN
el bronceado

◆ **to get a tan** broncearse

tangerine [tændʒə'riːn] NOUN
la tangerina

tank [tæŋk] NOUN
1 el depósito (*for water, gas*)
2 la cisterna (*on truck*)
3 el tanque (*military*)

◆ **a fish tank** un acuario

tanker ['tæŋkər] NOUN
1 el petrolero (*ship*)
2 el camión cisterna (PL los camiones cisterna) (*truck*)

◆ **an oil tanker** un petrolero

tap [tæp] NOUN
1 el golpecito (*gentle knock*) ◇ *I heard a tap on the window.* Oí un golpecito en la ventana.

◆ **There was a tap on the door.** Llamaron a la puerta.

2 la llave (*for water*)

tap dancing ['tæp,dænsɪŋ] NOUN
el claqué ◇ *I do tap dancing.* Bailo claqué.

to **tape** [teɪp] VERB
see also **tape** NOUN
grabar ◇ *Did you tape that movie last night?* ¿Grabaste la película de anoche?

tape [teɪp] NOUN
see also **tape** VERB
1 la cinta (*recording*) ◇ *a tape of Madonna* una cinta de Madonna
2 la cinta adhesiva (*adhesive tape*)

tape deck ['teɪp,dek] NOUN
la pletina

tape measure ['teɪp,mɛʒər] NOUN
la cinta métrica

tape recorder ['teɪprɪ,kɔːrdər] NOUN
la grabadora

target ['tɑːrgɪt] NOUN
1 la diana (*board*)
2 el objetivo (*goal*)

tart [tɑːrt] NOUN
la tarta ◇ *an apple tart* una tarta de manzana

tartan ['tɑːrtn] ADJECTIVE
escocés (MASC PL escoceses, FEM escocesa) ◇ *a tartan scarf* una bufanda escocesa

task [tæsk] NOUN
la tarea

taste [teɪst] NOUN
see also **taste** VERB
1 el sabor ◇ *It has a really strange taste.* Tiene un sabor muy extraño.
2 el gusto ◇ *His joke was in bad taste.* Su broma fue de mal gusto.

◆ **Would you like a taste?** ¿Quiere probarlo?

to **taste** [teɪst] VERB
see also **taste** NOUN
probar* ◇ *Would you like to taste it?* ¿Quiere probarlo?
◆ **to taste of something** saber* a algo ◇ *It tastes of fish.* Sabe a pescado.
◆ **You can taste the garlic in it.** Se le nota el sabor a ajo.

tasteful ['teɪstfəl] ADJECTIVE
de buen gusto MASC, FEM, PL

tasteless ['teɪstlɪs] ADJECTIVE
1 soso (*food*)
2 de mal gusto MASC, FEM, PL (*in bad taste*) ◇ *a tasteless remark* un comentario de mal gusto

tasty ['teɪsti] ADJECTIVE
sabroso

tattoo [tæ'tuː] NOUN
el tatuaje

taught [tɑːt] VERB *see* **teach**

Taurus ['tɔːrəs] NOUN
el Tauro (*sign*) ◇ *I'm a Taurus.* Soy tauro.
◆ **a Taurus** un/una tauro

tax [tæks] NOUN (PL **taxes**)
el impuesto ◇ *income tax* el impuesto sobre la renta
◆ **I pay a lot of tax.** Pago muchos impuestos.

taxi ['tæksi] NOUN
el taxi
◆ **a taxi driver** un/una taxista

taxi stand ['tæksi,stænd] NOUN
la parada de taxis
el sitio *Mexico*

TB [tiː'biː] ABBREVIATION (= *tuberculosis*)
la tuberculosis ◇ *He has TB.* Tiene tuberculosis.

tea [tiː] NOUN
té ◇ *Would you like some tea?* ¿Quieres té?
◆ **a cup of tea** una taza de té

tea bag ['tiː,bæg] NOUN
la bolsita de té

to **teach** [tiːtʃ] VERB (**taught, taught**)
1 enseñar ◇ *My sister taught me to swim.* Mi hermana me enseñó a nadar.
2 dar* clases de (*subject*) ◇ *She teaches physics.* Da clases de física.
◆ **That'll teach you!** ¡Así aprenderás!

teacher ['tiːtʃər] NOUN
1 el profesor
la profesora
(*in secondary school*)
◇ *a math teacher* un profesor de matemáticas ◇ *She's a teacher.* Es profesora.
2 el maestro
la maestra
(*in elementary school*)
◇ *He's an elementary school teacher.* Es maestro.

team [tiːm] NOUN
el equipo ◇ *a soccer team* un equipo de fútbol

teapot ['tiːpɑːt] NOUN
la tetera

tear [tɪər] NOUN
see also **tear** VERB
la lágrima
◆ **She was in tears.** Estaba llorando.

to **tear** [tɛər] VERB (**tore, torn**)
see also **tear** NOUN
1 romper* ◇ *Be careful or you'll tear the page.* Ten cuidado que vas a romper la página.
◆ **He tore his jacket.** Se rasgó la chaqueta.
◆ **Your shirt is torn.** Tu camisa está rota.
2 romperse* ◇ *It won't tear; it's very strong.* No se rompe, es muy resistente.

to **tear up** [tɛər'ʌp] VERB
hacer* pedazos ◇ *He tore up the letter.* Hizo pedazos la carta.

tear gas ['tɪr,gæs] NOUN
el gas lacrimógeno

to **tease** [tiːz] VERB
1 atormentar ◇ *Stop teasing that poor animal!* ¡Deja de atormentar al pobre animal!
2 tomar el pelo a ◇ *He's teasing you.* Te está tomando el pelo.
◆ **I was only teasing.** Lo decía en broma.

teaspoon ['tiːspuːn] NOUN
la cucharita

teaspoonful ['tiːspuːnful] NOUN
◆ **a teaspoonful of sugar** una cucharadita de azúcar

technical ['tɛknɪkəl] ADJECTIVE
técnico
◆ **a technical college** la escuela politécnica

technician [tɛk'nɪʃən] NOUN
el técnico
la técnica

technique [tɛk'niːk] NOUN
la técnica

technological [tɛknə'lɑːdʒɪkəl] ADJECTIVE
tecnológico

technology [tɛk'nɑːlədʒi] NOUN (PL **technologies**)
la tecnología

teddy bear ['tɛdi,bɛər] NOUN
el osito de peluche

teen ['tiːn] NOUN
el/la adolescente
◆ **a teen magazine** una revista para adolescentes

teenage ['tiːneɪdʒ] ADJECTIVE
◆ **She has two teenage daughters.** Tiene dos hijas adolescentes.

teenager ['tiːneɪdʒər] NOUN
el/la adolescente

teens [tiːnz] PL NOUN
◆ **She's in her teens.** Es adolescente.

tee-shirt ['tiːʃɜːrt] NOUN

T

la camiseta

teeth [ti:θ] PL NOUN *see* **tooth**

to **teethe** [ti:ð] VERB

◆ **She's teething.** Le están saliendo los dientes.

teetotaler ['ti:,toutlər] NOUN
el abstemio
la abstemia
(*person*)

telecommunications ['tɛlıkəmju:nı'keıʃənz] PL NOUN
las telecomunicaciones

telemarketing ['tɛlə'mɑ:rkıtıŋ] NOUN
las televentas

telephone ['tɛləfoun] NOUN
el teléfono ◇ *to be on the telephone* estar* hablando por teléfono

◆ **a telephone booth** una cabina telefónica
◆ **a telephone call** una llamada telefónica
◆ **a telephone directory** una guía telefónica, *Mexico:* un directorio
◆ **a telephone number** un número de teléfono

telescope ['tɛlıskoup] NOUN
el telescopio

television ['tɛləvıʒən] NOUN
la televisión ◇ *The game is on television tonight.* Dan el partido por televisión esta noche.

to **tell** [tɛl] VERB (**told, told**)
decir*

◆ **to tell somebody something** decir* algo a alguien ◇ *Did you tell your mother?* ¿Se lo dijiste a tu mamá? ◇ *I told him I was going on vacation.* Le dije que me iba de vacaciones.
◆ **to tell somebody to do something** decir* a alguien que haga algo
*Use the subjunctive after **decir a alguien que** when translating "to tell somebody to do something".*
◇ *He told me to wait a moment.* Me dijo que esperara un momento.
◆ **to tell lies** decir* mentiras
◆ **to tell a story** contar* un cuento
◆ **I can't tell the difference between them.** No puedo distinguirlos.
◆ **You can tell he's not serious.** Se nota que no se lo toma en serio.

to **tell off** [tɛl'ɑ:f] VERB
regañar

teller ['tɛlər] NOUN
el cajero
la cajera

temper ['tɛmpər] NOUN
el genio ◇ *He has a terrible temper.* Tiene muy mal genio.

◆ **to be in a temper** estar* de mal humor
◆ **to lose one's temper** perder* los estribos

temperature ['tɛmpərətʃər] NOUN
la temperatura

◆ **to have a temperature** tener* fiebre

temple ['tɛmpəl] NOUN
1 el templo (*building*)
2 la sien (*on head*)

temporary ['tɛmpərɛri] ADJECTIVE
temporal

to **tempt** [tɛmpt] VERB
tentar* ◇ *I'm very tempted!* ¡Tienta mucho!

◆ **to tempt somebody to do something** tentar* a alguien a hacer algo

temptation [tɛmp'teıʃən] NOUN
la tentación (PL las tentaciones)

tempting ['tɛmptıŋ] ADJECTIVE
tentador (FEM tentadora)

ten [tɛn] NUMERAL
diez ◇ *She's ten.* Tiene diez años.

tenant ['tɛnənt] NOUN
el inquilino
la inquilina

to **tend** [tɛnd] VERB

◆ **to tend to do something** tener* tendencia a hacer algo ◇ *He tends to arrive late.* Tiene tendencia a llegar tarde.

tender ['tɛndər] ADJECTIVE
tierno

tennis ['tɛnıs] NOUN
el tenis ◇ *to play tennis* jugar* tenis

◆ **a tennis ball** una pelota de tenis
◆ **a tennis court** una cancha de tenis
◆ **a tennis racket** una raqueta de tenis

tennis player ['tɛnıs,pleıər] NOUN
el/la tenista ◇ *He's a tennis player.* Es tenista.

tenor ['tɛnər] NOUN
el tenor

tense [tɛns] ADJECTIVE
see also **tense** NOUN
tenso

tense [tɛns] NOUN
see also **tense** ADJECTIVE
el tiempo

◆ **the present tense** el presente
◆ **the future tense** el futuro

tension ['tɛnʃən] NOUN
la tensión (PL las tensiones)

tent [tɛnt] NOUN
la carpa

◆ **a tent peg** una estaca
◆ **a tent pole** un palo de carpa

tenth [tɛnθ] ADJECTIVE
décimo ◇ *the tenth floor* el décimo piso

◆ **August tenth** el diez de agosto

term [tɜ:rm] NOUN
1 el trimestre (*at school*) ◇ *It's nearly the end of term.* Ya casi es final de trimestre.
2 el plazo ◇ *in the long term* a largo plazo

◆ **to come to terms with something** aceptar algo ◇ *He hasn't yet come to terms with his disability.* Todavía no ha aceptado su invalidez.

terminal ['tɜːrmɪnl] ADJECTIVE
see also **terminal** NOUN
terminal (*illness, patient*)

terminal ['tɜːrmɪnl] NOUN
see also **terminal** ADJECTIVE
el terminal
la terminal Mexico
(*of computer*)
- **airport terminal** la terminal del aeropuerto
- **bus terminal** la terminal de autobuses
- **oil terminal** la terminal petrolera

terminally ['tɜːrmɪnəli] ADVERB
- **to be terminally ill** estar* en fase terminal

terrace ['tɛrəs] NOUN
la terraza (*patio*) ◇ *We were sitting on the terrace.* Estábamos sentados en la terraza.

terrible ['tɛrɪbəl] ADJECTIVE
espantoso ◇ *This coffee is terrible.* Este café es espantoso.
- **I feel terrible.** Me siento pésimo.

terrier ['tɛriər] NOUN
el/la terrier (PL los/las terriers)

terrific [tə'rɪfɪk] ADJECTIVE
estupendo (*wonderful*) ◇ *That's terrific!* ¡Estupendo!
- **You look terrific!** ¡Te ves muy bien!

terrified ['tɛrɪfaɪd] ADJECTIVE
aterrorizado ◇ *I was terrified!* ¡Estaba aterrorizado!

terrorism ['tɛrərɪzəm] NOUN
el terrorismo

terrorist ['tɛrərɪst] NOUN
el/la terrorista
- **a terrorist attack** un atentado terrorista

test [tɛst] NOUN
see also **test** VERB
1 la prueba ◇ *a spelling test* una prueba de ortografía ◇ *nuclear tests* pruebas nucleares
2 el análisis (PL los análisis) (*on blood, urine*) ◇ *a blood test* un análisis de sangre
- **an eye test** un examen de la vista

3 el examen de manejar (*driving test*) ◇ *He's just passed his test.* Acaba de pasar el examen de manejar.

to **test** [tɛst] VERB
see also **test** NOUN
probar*
- **to test something out** probar* algo
- **He tested us on the new vocabulary.** Nos hizo una prueba del vocabulario nuevo.
- **She was tested for drugs.** Le hicieron la prueba antidoping.

test tube ['tɛst,tuːb] NOUN
la probeta

tetanus ['tɛtnəs] NOUN
el tétano
- **a tetanus injection** una inyección contra el tétano

text NOUN
see also **text** VERB
el mensaje (*text message*)

to **text** VERB
see also **text** NOUN
enviar un mensaje a ◇ *I'll text you when I get there.* Te envío un mensaje cuando llegue.

textbook ['tɛkst,buk] NOUN
el libro de texto ◇ *a Spanish textbook* un libro de texto de español

textiles ['tɛkstaɪlz] PL NOUN
los tejidos

text message NOUN
el mensaje de texto

text messaging NOUN
el envío de mensajes de texto

than [ðæn] CONJUNCTION
1 que ◇ *She's taller than me.* Es más alta que yo. ◇ *I have more CDs than tapes.* Tengo más CDs que cintas.
2 de ◇ *more than once* en más de una ocasión ◇ *more than 10 years* más de 10 años

to **thank** [θæŋk] VERB
dar* las gracias a ◇ *Don't forget to write and thank them.* Acuérdate de escribirles y darles las gracias.
- **thank you** gracias
- **thank you very much** muchas gracias
- **thank you for helping us** gracias por ayudarnos

thanks [θæŋks] EXCLAMATION
¡Gracias!
- **thanks to** gracias a ◇ *Thanks to him, everything went OK.* Gracias a él, todo salió bien.

Thanksgiving Day [θæŋks'gɪvɪŋ,deɪ] NOUN
el Día de Acción de Gracias

> ℹ *En los Estados Unidos, se celebra* **Thanksgiving Day** *el cuarto jueves de noviembre.*

that [ðæt] ADJECTIVE
see also **that** PRONOUN, CONJUNCTION, ADVERB
1 ese MASC (FEM esa) ◇ *that man* ese hombre ◇ *that road* esa carretera
To refer to something more distant, use ***aquel*** *and* ***aquella****.*
2 aquel MASC (FEM aquella) ◇ *Look at that car over there!* ¡Mira aquel carro! ◇ *THAT road there* aquella carretera
- **that one** ése MASC (FEM ésa) ◇ *This man? – No, that one.* ¿Este hombre? – No, ése. ◇ *Do you like this photo? – No, I prefer that one.* ¿Te gusta esta foto? – No, prefiero ésa.

To refer to something more distant, use ***aquél*** *and* ***aquélla****.*
3 aquél MASC (FEM aquélla) ◇ *That one over there is cheaper.* Aquél es más barato. ◇ *Which woman? – That one over there.* ¿Qué mujer? – Aquélla.

that [ðæt] PRONOUN
see also **that** ADJECTIVE, CONJUNCTION, ADVERB

T

[1] ése MASC (FEM ésa, NEUTER eso)
- **Who's that?** (*Who is that man?*) ¿Quién es ése?
- **Who's that?** (*Who is that woman?*) ¿Quién es ésa?
- **That's impossible.** Eso es imposible.
- **What's that?** ¿Qué es eso?

To refer to something more distant, use ***aquél, aquélla*** *and* ***aquello.***

[2] aquél MASC (FEM aquélla, NEUTER aquello) ◇ *That's my French teacher over there.* Aquél es mi profesor de francés. ◇ *That's my sister over by the window.* Aquélla de la ventana es mi hermana. ◇ *That was a silly thing to do.* Aquello fue una tontería.
- **Is that you?** ¿Eres tú?

[3] que (*in relative clauses*) ◇ *the man that saw us* el hombre que nos vio ◇ *the dog that she bought* el perro que ella compró ◇ *the man that we saw* el hombre que vimos

After a preposition ***que*** *becomes* ***el que, la que, los que, las que*** *to agree with the noun.*

◇ *the man that we spoke to* el hombre con el que hablamos ◇ *the women that she was chatting to* las mujeres con las que estaba hablando

that [ðæt] CONJUNCTION

see also **that** ADJECTIVE, PRONOUN, ADVERB

que ◇ *He thought that Henry was ill.* Creía que Henry estaba enfermo. ◇ *I know that she likes chocolate.* Sé que le gusta el chocolate.

that [ðæt] ADVERB

see also **that** ADJECTIVE, PRONOUN, CONJUNCTION

- **It was that big.** Era así de grande.
- **It's about that high.** Es más o menos así de alto.
- **It's not that difficult.** No es tan difícil.

the [ðə,ði:] DEFINITE ARTICLE

[1] el MASC (PL los) ◇ *the boy* el niño ◇ *the cars* los carros

a + el *changes to* ***al*** *and* ***de + el*** *changes to* ***del.***

◇ *They went to the theater.* Fueron al teatro. ◇ *the soup of the day* la sopa del día

[2] la FEM (PL las) ◇ *the woman* la mujer ◇ *the chairs* las sillas

theater ['θɪətər] NOUN

el teatro

theft [θɛft] NOUN

el robo

their [ðɛər] ADJECTIVE

su (PL sus) ◇ *their father* su padre ◇ *their house* su casa ◇ *their parents* sus padres ◇ *their sisters* sus hermanas

Their *is usually translated by the definite article* ***el/los*** *or* ***la/las*** *when it's clear from the sentence who the possessor is, particularly when referring to clothing or parts of the body.*

◇ *They took off their coats.* Se sacaron los abrigos. ◇ *after washing their hands* después de lavarse las manos ◇ *Someone stole their car.* Alguien les robó el carro.

theirs [ðɛərz] PRONOUN

[1] el suyo MASC (PL los suyos) ◇ *Is this their car? – No, theirs is red.* ¿Es éste su carro? – No, el suyo es rojo. ◇ *my parents and theirs* mis padres y los suyos

[2] la suya FEM (PL las suyas) ◇ *Is this their house? – No, theirs is white.* ¿Es ésta su casa? – No, la suya es blanca. ◇ *my sisters and theirs* mis hermanas y las suyas

Use ***de ellos*** *(masculine) or* ***de ellas*** *(feminine) instead of* ***suyo*** *if you want to be specific about a masculine or feminine group.*

◇ *It's not our dog, it's theirs.* No es nuestro perro, es suyo. ◇ *The suitcase is theirs.* La maleta es suya. ◇ *Whose is this? – It's theirs.* ¿De quién es esto? – Es de ellos.
- **Isobel is a friend of theirs.** Isobel es amiga suya.

them [ðɛm] PRONOUN

[1] los MASC (FEM las)

Use ***los*** *or* ***las*** *when* ***them*** *is the direct object of the verb in the sentence.*

◇ *I didn't know them.* No los conocía. ◇ *Have you seen my slippers? I left them here.* ¿Has visto mis zapatillas? Las dejé aquí. ◇ *Look at them!* ¡Míralos! ◇ *I had to give them to her.* Tuve que dárselos.

[2] les

Use ***les*** *when* ***them*** *means* ***to them.***

◇ *I gave them some brochures.* Les di unos folletos. ◇ *You have to tell them the truth.* Tienes que decirles la verdad.

[3] se

Use ***se*** *not* ***les*** *when* ***them*** *is used in combination with a direct-object pronoun.*

◇ *Give it to them.* Dáselo.

[4] ellos MASC (FEM ellas)

Use ***ellos*** *or* ***ellas*** *after prepositions, in comparisons, and with the verb* ***to be.***

◇ *It's for them.* Es para ellos. ◇ *My sisters didn't go. My mother stayed with them.* Mis hermanas no fueron. Mi mamá se quedó con ellas. ◇ *We are older than them.* Somos mayores que ellos. ◇ *It must be them.* Deben de ser ellos.
- **They were carrying them on them.** Los llevaban consigo.

theme [θi:m] NOUN

el tema

Although ***tema*** *ends in* ***-a,*** *it is actually a masculine noun.*

theme park ['θi:mˌpɑ:rk] NOUN

el parque temático

themselves [ðəm'sɛlvz] PRONOUN

[1] se (*reflexive*) ◇ *Did they hurt themselves?* ¿Se hicieron daño?

[2] sí mismos (FEM sí mismas) (*after preposition*) ◇ *They talked mainly about themselves.* Hablaron sobre todo de sí

mismos.

[3] ellos mismos (FEM ellas mismas) (*for emphasis*) ◇ *They built it themselves.* Lo construyeron ellos mismos.

◆ **by themselves** por sí mismos (FEM por sí mismas) ◇ *The girls did it all by themselves.* Las chicas lo hicieron todo por sí mismas.

then [ðɛn] ADVERB, CONJUNCTION

[1] después (*next*) ◇ *I get dressed. Then I have breakfast.* Me visto. Después desayuno.

[2] pues (*in that case*) ◇ *My ink has run out. – Use a pencil then!* Se me acabó la tinta. – ¡Pues usa un lápiz!

[3] en aquella época (*in those days*) ◇ *There was no electricity then.* En aquella época no había electricidad.

◆ **now and then** de vez en cuando ◇ *Do you play chess? – Now and then.* ¿Juegas ajedrez? – De vez en cuando.

◆ **By then it was too late.** Para entonces ya era demasiado tarde.

therapy ['θɛrəpi] NOUN (PL **therapies**)

la terapia

there [ðɛər] ADVERB

ahí ◇ *Put it there, on the table.* Ponlo ahí, en la mesa.

◆ **over there** allí

◆ **in there** ahí adentro

◆ **on there** ahí encima

◆ **up there** ahí arriba

◆ **down there** ahí abajo

◆ **There he is!** ¡Ahí está!

◆ **there is** hay ◇ *There's a factory near my house.* Hay una fábrica cerca de mi casa.

◆ **there are** hay ◇ *There are 20 children in my class.* Hay 20 niños en mi clase.

◆ **There has been an accident.** Ha habido un accidente.

therefore ['ðɛrfɔːr] ADVERB

por lo tanto

there's ['ðɛrz] = **there is, there has**

thermometer [θər'mɑːmɪtər] NOUN

el termómetro

Thermos® ['θɜːrməs] NOUN

el termo

these [ðiːz] ADJECTIVE

see also **these** PRONOUN

estos MASC (FEM estas) ◇ *these shoes* estos zapatos ◇ *THESE shoes* estos zapatos de aquí ◇ *these houses* estas casas

these [ðiːz] PRONOUN

see also **these** ADJECTIVE

éstos MASC (FEM éstas) ◇ *I want these!* ¡Quiero éstos! ◇ *I'm looking for some sandals. – Can I try these?* Quiero unas sandalias. – ¿Puedo probarme éstas?

they [ðeɪ] PRONOUN

ellos MASC (FEM ellas)

***they** generally isn't translated unless it's emphatic.*

◇ *They're fine, thank you.* Están bien, gracias.

*Use **ellos** or **ellas** as appropriate for emphasis.*

◇ *We went to the movie theater but they didn't.* Nosotros fuimos al cine pero ellos no. ◇ *I spoke to my sisters. THEY agree with me.* Hablé con mis hermanas. Ellas estaban de acuerdo conmigo.

◆ **They say that...** Dicen que... ◇ *They say that the house is haunted.* Dicen que la casa está embrujada.

they'd [ðeɪd] = **they had, they would**

they'll [ðeɪl] = **they will**

they're [ðɛr] = **they are**

they've [ðeɪv] = **they have**

thick [θɪk] ADJECTIVE

[1] grueso (*wall, slice*) ◇ *Give him a thick slice.* Dále una rebanada gruesa.

◆ **The walls are one meter thick.** Las paredes tienen un metro de grosor.

[2] espeso (*soup*) ◇ *My soup turned out too thick.* La sopa me quedó demasiado espesa.

[3] corto de entendederas (*informal: stupid*)

thief [θiːf] NOUN (PL **thieves**)

el ladrón (PL los ladrones)

la ladrona

thigh [θaɪ] NOUN

el muslo

thin [θɪn] ADJECTIVE

[1] fino ◇ *a thin slice* una rebanada fina

[2] delgado ◇ *She's very thin.* Está muy delgada.

thing [θɪŋ] NOUN

la cosa ◇ *beautiful things* cosas bonitas ◇ *Where shall I put my things?* ¿Dónde pongo mis cosas?

◆ **How's things?** ¿Qué tal?

◆ **What's that thing called?** ¿Cómo se llama eso?

◆ **You poor thing!** ¡Pobrecito!

◆ **The best thing would be to leave it.** Lo mejor sería dejarlo.

to **think** [θɪŋk] VERB (**thought, thought**)

[1] pensar* ◇ *What do you think about it?* ¿Qué piensas? ◇ *Think carefully before you reply.* Piénsalo bien antes de responder. ◇ *What are you thinking about?* ¿En qué estás pensando?

◆ **I'll think it over.** Lo pensaré.

[2] creer* ◇ *I think you're wrong.* Creo que estás equivocado.

◆ **I think so.** Creo que sí.

◆ **I don't think so.** Creo que no.

[3] imaginar ◇ *Think what life would be like without cars.* Imagínate cómo sería la vida sin automóviles.

third [θɜːrd] ADJECTIVE, ADVERB

see also **third** NOUN

tercero

*Use **tercer** before a masculine singular noun.*

◇ *the third prize* el tercer premio ◇ *the third time* la tercera vez ◇ *Rachel came third in* ☞

the race. Rachel llegó tercera en la carrera.
◆ **March third** el tres de marzo

third [θɜːrd] NOUN
see also **third** ADJECTIVE, ADVERB
el tercio (*fraction*)
◆ **a third of the population** una tercera parte de la población

thirdly ['θɜːrdli] ADVERB
en tercer lugar

Third World ['θɜːrd'wɜːrld] NOUN
el Tercer Mundo

thirst [θɜːrst] NOUN
la sed

thirsty ['θɜːrsti] ADJECTIVE
◆ **to be thirsty** tener* sed

thirteen [θɜːr'tiːn] NUMERAL
trece ◇ *I'm thirteen.* Tengo trece años.

thirteenth [θɜːr'tiːnθ] ADJECTIVE
decimotercero
◆ **the thirteenth floor** el duodécimo piso
◆ **January thirteenth** el trece de enero

thirty ['θɜːrti] NUMERAL
treinta ◇ *He's thirty.* Tiene treinta años.

this [ðɪs] ADJECTIVE
see also **this** PRONOUN
este MASC (FEM esta) ◇ *this boy* este niño ◇ *this road* esta carretera
◆ **this one** éste MASC (FEM ésta) ◇ *Pass me that book. – This one?* Acércame ese libro. – ¿Éste? ◇ *This is my room and this one's my sister's.* Ésta es mi habitación y ésta es la de mi hermana.

this [ðɪs] PRONOUN
see also **this** ADJECTIVE
éste MASC (FEM ésta, NEUTER esto) ◇ *This is my office and this is the meeting room.* Éste es mi despacho y ésta es la sala de reuniones. ◇ *What's this?* ¿Qué es esto?
◆ **Who is this?** (*on the telephone*) ¿Con quién hablo?
◆ **This is my sister.** (*introduction*) Te presento a mi hermana.
◆ **This is Steve speaking.** (*on the phone*) Habla Steve.

thistle ['θɪsəl] NOUN
el cardo

thorough ['θɜːrou] ADJECTIVE
minucioso ◇ *a thorough check* un control minucioso
◆ **She's very thorough.** Es muy meticulosa.

thoroughly ['θɜːrəli] ADVERB
minuciosamente ◇ *I checked the car thoroughly.* Revisé el carro minuciosamente.
◆ **Mix the ingredients thoroughly.** Mézclense bien los ingredientes.
◆ **I thoroughly enjoyed myself.** Me divertí muchísimo.

those [ðouz] ADJECTIVE
see also **those** PRONOUN
1 esos MASC (FEM esas) ◇ *those shoes* esos zapatos ◇ *those girls* esas chicas
To refer to something more distant, use ***aquellos*** *and* ***aquellas***.
2 aquellos MASC (FEM aquellas) ◇ *THOSE shoes* aquellos zapatos ◇ *those houses over there* aquellas casas

those [ðouz] PRONOUN
see also **those** ADJECTIVE
1 ésos MASC (FEM ésas) ◇ *I want those!* ¡Quiero ésos!
To refer to something more distant, use ***aquéllos***.
2 aquéllos MASC (FEM aquéllas) ◇ *Ask those children. – Those over there?* Pregúntales a esos niños. – ¿A aquéllos?

though [ðou] CONJUNCTION, ADVERB
aunque ◇ *Though she was tired she stayed up late.* Aunque estaba cansada, se quedó levantada hasta muy tarde.
◆ **It's difficult, though, to put into practice.** Pero es difícil llevarlo a la práctica.

thought [θɑːt] VERB *see* **think**

thought [θɑːt] NOUN
la idea ◇ *I've just had a thought.* Se me ocurre una idea.
◆ **He kept his thoughts to himself.** No le dijo a nadie lo que pensaba.
◆ **It was a nice thought, thank you.** Fue muy amable de tu parte, gracias.

thoughtful ['θɑːtfəl] ADJECTIVE
1 pensativo (*deep in thought*) ◇ *You look thoughtful.* Pareces pensativo.
2 considerado (*considerate*) ◇ *She's very thoughtful.* Es muy considerada.

thoughtless ['θɑːtlɪs] ADJECTIVE
desconsiderado ◇ *She's very thoughtless.* Es muy desconsiderada.
◆ **It was thoughtless of her to mention it.** Fue una falta de consideración por su parte mencionarlo.

thousand ['θauzənd] NUMERAL
◆ **a thousand** mil ◇ *a thousand pesos* mil pesos
◆ **two thousand dollars** dos mil dólares
◆ **thousands of people** miles de personas

thread [θrɛd] NOUN
el hilo

threat [θrɛt] NOUN
la amenaza

to **threaten** ['θrɛtn] VERB
amenazar* ◇ *He threatened me.* Me amenazó.
◆ **to threaten to do something** amenazar con hacer algo (*person*)

three [θriː] NUMERAL
tres ◇ *She's three.* Tiene tres años.

three-dimensional ['θriːdɪ'mɛnʃənl] ADJECTIVE
tridimensional

three-piece suit ['θriːpiːs'suːt] NOUN

el traje de tres piezas

threw [θruː] VERB *see* **throw**

thrift store [ˈθrɪftˌstɔːr] NOUN

> *Tiendas de artículos de segunda mano baratos que dedica su recaudación a causas benéficas.*

thrifty [ˈθrɪfti] ADJECTIVE
ahorrativo

thrill [θrɪl] NOUN
la emoción (PL las emociones) ◇ *I remember the thrill of Christmas as a child.* Recuerdo la emoción que sentía de niño en Navidades.
- **It was a great thrill to see my team win.** Fue muy emocionante ver ganar a mi equipo.

thrilled [θrɪld] ADJECTIVE
- **I was thrilled.** Estaba emocionada.

thriller [ˈθrɪlər] NOUN
1 la película de suspenso (*movie*)
2 la novela de suspenso (*novel*)

thrilling [ˈθrɪlɪŋ] ADJECTIVE
emocionante

throat [θrout] NOUN
la garganta ◇ *I have a sore throat.* Me duele la garganta.

to **throb** [θrɑːb] VERB
- **My arm is throbbing.** Tengo un dolor punzante en el brazo.
- **a throbbing pain** un dolor punzante

throne [θroun] NOUN
el trono

through [θruː] ADJECTIVE, ADVERB, PREPOSITION
1 a través de ◇ *to look through a telescope* mirar a través de un telescopio ◇ *I know her through my sister.* La conozco a través de mi hermana.
- **I saw him through the crowd.** Lo vi entre la multitud.
- **The window was dirty and I couldn't see through.** La ventana estaba sucia y no podía ver nada.

2 por ◇ *The thief got in through the kitchen window.* El ladrón entró por la ventana de la cocina. ◇ *to go through Detroit* pasar por Detroit ◇ *to walk through the woods* pasear por el bosque
- **to go through a tunnel** atravesar* un túnel
- **He went straight through to the dining room.** Pasó directamente al comedor.
- **a through train** un tren directo
- **"no through road"** "calle sin salida"
- **all through the night** durante toda la noche
- **from May through September** desde mayo hasta septiembre

throughout [θruːˈaut] PREPOSITION
- **throughout the country** en todo el país
- **throughout the year** durante todo el año

to **throw** [θrou] VERB (**threw, threw**)
tirar ◇ *He threw the ball to me.* Me tiró la pelota.
- **to throw a party** dar* una fiesta
- **That really threw him.** Eso lo desconcertó por completo.

to **throw away** [ˌθrouəˈweɪ] VERB
1 tirar (*trash*)
2 desperdiciar (*chance*)

to **throw out** [θrouˈaut] VERB
1 tirar (*throw away*)
2 echar (*person*) ◇ *I threw him out.* Lo eché.

to **throw up** [θrouˈʌp] VERB
devolver* ◇ *I threw up twice last night.* Anoche devolví dos veces.
- **I feel like I'm going to throw up.** Tengo ganas de devolver.

thug [θʌg] NOUN
el matón (PL los matones)

thumb [θʌm] NOUN
el pulgar

thumbtack [ˈθʌmtæk] NOUN
la tachuela
la chinche *Mexico*

to **thump** [θʌmp] VERB
- **to thump somebody** pegar* un puñetazo a alguien

thunder [ˈθʌndər] NOUN
los truenos

thunderstorm [ˈθʌndərˌstɔːrm] NOUN
la tormenta

thundery [ˈθʌndəri] ADJECTIVE
tormentoso

Thursday [ˈθɜːrzdi] NOUN
el jueves (PL los jueves) ◇ *I saw her on Thursday.* La vi el jueves. ◇ *every Thursday* todos los jueves ◇ *last Thursday* el jueves pasado ◇ *next Thursday* el jueves que viene ◇ *on Thursdays* los jueves

thyme [taɪm] NOUN
el tomillo

tick [tɪk] NOUN
see also **tick** VERB
el tictac ◇ *The clock has a loud tick.* El reloj tiene un tictac muy fuerte.

to **tick** [tɪk] VERB
see also **tick** NOUN
hacer* tictac (*clock*)

to **tick off** [tɪkˈɑːf] VERB
fastidiar (*annoy*) ◇ *It really ticked me off that he was late again.* Realmente me fastidió que otra vez llegara tarde.

ticket [ˈtɪkɪt] NOUN
1 el boleto (*for bus, train, tube*)
2 el pasaje
el boleto *Mexico*
(*for plane*)
3 la entrada (*for theater, concert, museum, movie theater*)
4 el ticket (PL los tickets) (*for baggage, coat, parking*)
- **a parking ticket** (*fine*) una multa por estacionamiento indebido

T

ticket inspector ['tɪkɪtɪn'spɛktər] NOUN
el revisor
la revisora
ticket office ['tɪkɪt,ɑːfɪs] NOUN
la taquilla
to **tickle** ['tɪkəl] VERB
hacer* cosquillas a ◇ *She enjoyed tickling the baby.* Le gustaba hacerle cosquillas al niño.
ticklish ['tɪklɪʃ] ADJECTIVE
◆ **to be ticklish** tener* cosquillas, *Mexico*: ser* cosquilludo
tide [taɪd] NOUN
la marea
◆ **high tide** la marea alta
◆ **low tide** la marea baja
tidy ['taɪdi] ADJECTIVE
see also **tidy** VERB
ordenado ◇ *Your room is very tidy.* Tu habitación está muy ordenada. ◇ *She's very tidy.* Es muy ordenada.
to **tidy** ['taɪdi] VERB (**tidied, tidied**)
see also **tidy** ADJECTIVE
ordenar (*room*)
to **tidy up** [taɪdi'ʌp] VERB
recoger* (*toys*)
◆ **Don't forget to tidy up afterwards.** No se olviden de ordenar las cosas después.
tie [taɪ] NOUN
see also **tie** VERB
1 la corbata (*necktie*)
2 el empate (*in sport*)
to **tie** [taɪ] VERB
see also **tie** NOUN
1 atar
amarrar (*shoelaces, parcel*)
◆ **Tie your shoes!** ¡Átate los zapatos!
◆ **to tie a knot in something** hacer* un nudo en algo
2 empatar ◇ *They tied three all.* Empataron a tres.
to **tie up** [taɪ'ʌp] VERB
1 atar (*person, shoelaces, package*)
2 amarrar (*boat*)
tiger ['taɪgər] NOUN
el tigre
tight [taɪt] ADJECTIVE
1 ajustado (*fitting*) ◇ *tight jeans* jeans ajustados
2 estrecho (*too small*) ◇ *This dress is a bit tight.* Este vestido es un poco estrecho.
to **tighten** ['taɪtn] VERB
1 tensar (*rope*)
2 apretar* (*screw*)
tightly ['taɪtli] ADVERB
◆ **tightly closed** fuertemente cerrado
◆ **She held his hand tightly.** Le agarró la mano con fuerza.
tights [taɪts] PL NOUN
los leotardos (*for sport, ballet*)
tile [taɪl] NOUN
1 la teja (*on roof*)
2 el azulejo (*for wall*)
3 la baldosa (*for floor*)
tiled [taɪld] ADJECTIVE
1 de tejas (*roof*)
2 revestido de azulejos (*wall*)
3 de baldosas (*floor*)
till [tɪl] NOUN
see also **till** PREPOSITION, CONJUNCTION
el cajón (*drawer*)
till [tɪl] PREPOSITION, CONJUNCTION
see also **till** NOUN
1 hasta ◇ *I waited till 10 o'clock.* Esperé hasta las 10.
◆ **till now** hasta ahora
◆ **till then** hasta entonces
◆ **It won't be ready till next week.** No estará listo hasta la semana que viene. *Mexico*: Estará listo hasta la semana que viene.
2 hasta que ◇ *We stayed there till the doctor came.* Nos quedamos allí hasta que vino el médico.
***hasta que** has to be followed by a verb in the subjunctive when referring to an event in the future.*
◇ *Don't go till I arrive.* No te vayas hasta que llegue yo. ◇ *Wait till I come back.* Espera hasta que yo vuelva.
time [taɪm] NOUN
1 la hora ◇ *What time is it?* ¿Qué hora es? ◇ *What time do you get up?* ¿A qué hora te levantas? ◇ *It was two o'clock, Mexican time.* Eran las dos, hora de Mexico.
◆ **on time** a la hora ◇ *He never arrives on time.* Nunca llega a la hora.
2 el tiempo ◇ *I'm sorry, I don't have time.* Lo siento, no tengo tiempo. ◇ *We waited a long time.* Esperamos mucho tiempo. ◇ *Have you lived here for a long time?* ¿Hace mucho tiempo que vives aquí?
◆ **from time to time** de vez en cuando
◆ **in time** a tiempo ◇ *We arrived in time for lunch.* Llegamos a tiempo para el almuerzo.
◆ **just in time** justo a tiempo
◆ **in a week's time** dentro de una semana
3 el momento ◇ *This isn't a good time to ask him.* Éste no es buen momento para preguntarle.
◆ **for the time being** por el momento
◆ **in no time** en un momento ◇ *It was ready in no time.* Estuvo listo en un momento.
◆ **Come and see us any time.** Ven a vernos cuando quieras.
◆ **to have a good time** pasarlo bien ◇ *Did you have a good time?* ¿Lo pasaste bien?
4 la vez (PL las veces) ◇ *this time* esta vez ◇ *How many times?* ¿Cuántas veces?
◆ **at times** a veces
◆ **two at a time** de dos en dos
◆ **two times two is four** dos por dos son cuatro

* Verbs marked with this symbol are irregular. See pages 346–348 for further details.

time bomb ['taɪm,bɑːm] NOUN
la bomba de tiempo

time off [taɪm'ɑːf] NOUN
el tiempo libre

timer ['taɪmər] NOUN
el reloj automático (*of video, oven*)
◆ **an egg timer** reloj de arena

time-share ['taɪm,ʃeər] NOUN
◆ **a time-share apartment** un departamento de tiempo compartido

timetable ['taɪm,teɪbəl] NOUN
1 el horario (*for train, bus, school*)
2 el programa (*schedule of events*)
Although ***programa*** *ends in* ***-a****, it is actually a masculine noun.*

time zone ['taɪm,zoun] NOUN
el huso horario

tin [tɪn] NOUN
1 la lata ◇ *a biscuit tin* una lata de galletas
2 el estaño (*metal*)

tinfoil ['tɪnfɔɪl] NOUN
el papel de aluminio

tinsel ['tɪnsəl] NOUN
el oropel

tinted ['tɪntɪd] ADJECTIVE
ahumado (*glasses, window*)

tiny ['taɪni] ADJECTIVE
minúsculo

tip [tɪp] NOUN
see also **tip** VERB
1 la propina (*money*) ◇ *to leave a tip* dejar propina
2 el consejo (*advice*) ◇ *a useful tip* un consejo práctico
3 la punta (*end*) ◇ *It's on the tip of my tongue.* Lo tengo en la punta de la lengua.

to **tip** [tɪp] VERB
see also **tip** NOUN
dar* una propina a ◇ *Don't forget to tip the waiter.* No te olvides de darle una propina al camarero.

tiptoe ['tɪptou] NOUN
◆ **on tiptoe** de puntillas

tire ['taɪər] NOUN
el neumático
◆ **tire pressure** la presión de los neumáticos

tired ['taɪərd] ADJECTIVE
cansado ◇ *I'm tired.* Estoy cansado.
◆ **to be tired of something** estar* harto de algo

tiring ['taɪərɪŋ] ADJECTIVE
cansado

tissue ['tɪʃuː] NOUN
el Kleenex® (PL los Kleenex)

title ['taɪtl] NOUN
el título (*of novel, movie*)

title role ['taɪtl'roul] NOUN
el papel principal

to [tuː] PREPOSITION
1 a
a *+* ***el*** *changes to* ***al****.*
◇ *to go to school* ir* al colegio ◇ *to go to the doctor's* ir* al médico ◇ *Let's go to Anne's place.* Vamos a la casa de Anne. ◇ *to go to Venezuela* ir* a Venezuela ◇ *I sold it to a friend.* Se lo vendí a un amigo. ◇ *the answer to the question* la respuesta a la pregunta ◇ *the train to Baltimore* el tren a Baltimore
◆ **from...to...** de...a... ◇ *from nine o'clock to half past three* de las nueve a las tres y media
2 de ◇ *It's easy to do.* Es fácil de hacer. ◇ *something to drink* algo de beber ◇ *the key to the front door* la llave de la puerta principal
◆ **It's difficult to say**. Es difícil saberlo.
◆ **It's easy to criticize.** Criticar es muy fácil.
◆ **I've never been to Panama**. Nunca he estado en Panamá.
◆ **ten to nine** diez para las nueve
3 hasta ◇ *to count to ten* contar* hasta diez
4 para (*in order to*) ◇ *I did it to help you.* Lo hice para ayudarte. ◇ *She's too young to go to school.* Es muy pequeña para ir al colegio. ◇ *ready to go* listo para irse ◇ *ready to eat* listo para comer
5 con ◇ *to be kind to somebody* ser* amable con alguien ◇ *They were very kind to me.* Fueron muy amables conmigo.
◆ **Give it to her**! ¡Dáselo!
◆ **That's what he said to me.** Eso fue lo que me dijo.
◆ **I have things to do.** Tengo cosas que hacer.

toad [toud] NOUN
el sapo

toadstool ['toudstuːl] NOUN
el hongo venenoso

toast [toust] NOUN
1 el pan tostado (*bread*)
◆ **a piece of toast** una tostada, *Mexico*: un pan tostado
2 el brindis (PL los brindis) (*speech*)
◆ **to drink a toast to somebody** brindar por alguien

toaster ['toustər] NOUN
la tostadora

tobacco [tə'bækou] NOUN
el tabaco

tobacconist's [tə'bækənɪsts] NOUN
la tabaquería

toboggan [tə'bɑːgən] NOUN
el trineo

tobogganing [tə'bɑːgənɪŋ] NOUN
◆ **to go tobogganing** deslizarse* en trineo

today [tə'deɪ] ADVERB
hoy

toddler ['tɑːdlər] NOUN
el niño pequeño
la niña pequeña
(*que empieza a caminar*)

toe [tou] NOUN
el dedo del pie (PL los dedos de los pies)
◇ *The dog bit my big toe.* El perro me mordió el dedo gordo del pie.

together [tə'gɛðər] ADVERB

T ☞

1 juntos ◇ *Are they still together?* ¿Todavía están juntos?
2 a la vez (*at the same time*) ◇ *Don't all speak together!* ¡No hablen todos a la vez!
◆ **together with** junto con
toilet ['tɔɪlət] NOUN
el inodoro (*bowl*)
toilet paper ['tɔɪlət,peɪpər] NOUN
el papel higiénico
toiletries ['tɔɪlətriz] PL NOUN
los artículos de perfumería
token ['toukən] NOUN
el boleto (*for subway, bus*)
told [tould] VERB *see* **tell**
tolerant ['tɑ:lərənt] ADJECTIVE
tolerante
toll [toul] NOUN
el peaje
la cuota Mexico
(*on bridge, highway*)
tomato [tə'meɪtou] NOUN (PL **tomatoes**)
el tomate ◇ *tomato soup* sopa de tomate
tomboy ['tɑ:m,bɔɪ] NOUN
la marimacho
la machetona Mexico
tomorrow [tə'mɑ:rou] ADVERB
mañana ◇ *tomorrow morning* mañana por la mañana ◇ *tomorrow night* mañana por la noche
◆ **the day after tomorrow** pasado mañana
ton [tʌn] NOUN
la tonelada ◇ *a ton of coal* una tonelada de carbón
◆ **That old bike weighs a ton.** Esa bici vieja pesa una tonelada.
tongue [tʌŋ] NOUN
la lengua
◆ **to say something tongue in cheek** decir* algo en plan de broma
tongue-in-cheek ['tʌŋɪn'tʃi:k] ADJECTIVE
irónico (*remark*)
tonic ['tɑ:nɪk] NOUN
la tónica
◆ **a gin and tonic** un gin-tonic
tonight [tə'naɪt] ADVERB
esta noche ◇ *Are you going out tonight?* ¿Vas a salir esta noche? ◇ *I'll sleep well tonight.* Esta noche dormiré bien.
tonsillitis [tɑ:nsɪ'laɪtɪs] NOUN
la amigdalitis ◇ *She has tonsillitis.* Tiene amigdalitis.
tonsils ['tɑ:nsəlz] PL NOUN
las amígdalas
too [tu:] ADVERB
1 también (*as well*) ◇ *My sister came, too.* Mi hermana también vino.
2 demasiado (*excessively*) ◇ *The water is too hot.* El agua está demasiado caliente. ◇ *We arrived too late.* Llegamos demasiado tarde.
◆ **too much** demasiado ◇ *too much noise* demasiado ruido ◇ *too much butter* demasiada mantequilla ◇ *At Christmas we always eat too much.* En Navidad siempre comemos demasiado. ◇ *$50? – That's too much.* ¿50 dólares? – Eso es demasiado.
◆ **too many** demasiados (FEM demasiadas) ◇ *too many problems* demasiados problemas ◇ *too many chairs* demasiadas sillas
◆ **Too bad!** ¡Qué pena! (*what a pity*)
took [tuk] VERB *see* **take**
tool [tu:l] NOUN
la herramienta
toolbox ['tu:l,bɑ:ks] NOUN (PL **toolboxes**)
la caja de herramientas
tooth [tu:θ] NOUN (PL **teeth**)
el diente
toothache ['tu:θeɪk] NOUN
el dolor de muelas ◇ *These pills are good for toothache.* Estas pastillas son buenas para el dolor de muelas.
◆ **I have a toothache.** Me duele una muela.
toothbrush ['tu:θ,brʌʃ] NOUN (PL **toothbrushes**)
el cepillo de dientes
toothpaste ['tu:θ,peɪst] NOUN
el dentífrico
top [tɑ:p] NOUN
see also **top** ADJECTIVE
1 la parte de arriba ◇ *at the top of the page* en la parte de arriba de la página
2 la cima (*of mountain*)
3 la tapa (*of box, jar*)
4 el tapón (PL los tapones) (*of bottle*)
◆ **a bikini top** la parte de arriba de un bikini
◆ **the top of the table** el tablero de la mesa
◆ **on top of the cupboard** encima del armario
◆ **There's a surcharge on top of that.** Hay un recargo, además.
◆ **from top to bottom** de arriba abajo ◇ *I searched the house from top to bottom.* Busqué en la casa de arriba abajo.
top [tɑ:p] ADJECTIVE
see also **top** NOUN
1 de arriba (*shelf*) ◇ *it's on the top shelf* está en el estante de arriba
◆ **the top layer of skin** la capa superior de la piel
◆ **the top floor** el último piso
2 eminente ◇ *a top surgeon* un eminente cirujano
◆ **a top model** una top model
◆ **a top hotel** un hotel de primera
◆ **He always gets the top grades in our French class.** Siempre saca excelentes notas en la clase de francés.
◆ **at top speed** a máxima velocidad
topic ['tɑ:pɪk] NOUN
el tema
*Although **tema** ends in **-a**, it is actually a*

masculine noun.
◇ *The essay can be on any topic.* La redacción puede ser sobre cualquier tema.

topical ['tɑːpɪkəl] ADJECTIVE
de actualidad MASC, FEM, PL ◇ *a topical issue* un tema de actualidad

topless ['tɑːplɪs] ADJECTIVE
topless MASC, FEM, PL
◆ **to go topless** ir* en topless

top secret ['tɑːp'siːkrɪt] ADJECTIVE
de alto secreto MASC, FEM, PL ◇ *top secret documents* documentos de alto secreto

torch [tɔːrtʃ] NOUN (PL **torches**)
la antorcha (*flaming*)

tore, torn [tɔːr, tɔːrn] VERB *see* **tear**

tortoise ['tɔːrtəs] NOUN
la tortuga

torture ['tɔːrtʃər] NOUN
see also **torture** VERB
la tortura ◇ *It was pure torture.* Fué una tortura.

to **torture** ['tɔːrtʃər] VERB
see also **torture** NOUN
torturar ◇ *Stop torturing that poor animal!* ¡Deja de torturar al pobre animal!

to **toss** [tɑːs] VERB
◆ **to toss pancakes** dar* la vuelta a las crepes en el aire
◆ **Shall we toss for it?** ¿Nos lo jugamos a cara o cruz?, Mexico: ¿Juguémolo a águila o sol?

total ['toutl] ADJECTIVE
see also **total** NOUN
total ◇ *The total cost was very high.* El costo total fue muy alto.
◆ **the total amount** el total

total ['toutl] NOUN
see also **total** ADJECTIVE
el total
◆ **the grand total** la suma total

totally ['toutəli] ADVERB
totalmente

touch [tʌtʃ] NOUN
see also **touch** VERB
◆ **to get in touch with somebody** ponerse* en contacto con alguien
◆ **to keep in touch with somebody** mantenerse* en contacto con alguien
◆ **Keep in touch! (1)** ¡Escribe de vez en cuando! (*write*)
◆ **Keep in touch! (2)** ¡Llama de vez en cuando! (*phone*)
◆ **to lose touch with somebody** perder* contacto con alguien

to **touch** [tʌtʃ] VERB
see also **touch** NOUN
tocar* ◇ *Don't touch that!* ¡No toques eso!

touchdown ['tʌtʃˌdaun] NOUN
1 el aterrizaje (*of plane*)
2 el gol (*in football*)

touched [tʌtʃt] ADJECTIVE
emocionado ◇ *I was really touched.* Estaba muy emocionada.

touching ['tʌtʃɪŋ] ADJECTIVE
conmovedor (FEM conmovedora)

touchline [tʌtʃlaɪn] NOUN
la línea de banda

touchy ['tʌtʃi] ADJECTIVE
susceptible ◇ *She's a bit touchy today.* Hoy está un poco susceptible.

tough [tʌf] ADJECTIVE
1 difícil ◇ *It was tough, but I managed okay.* Fue difícil, pero me las arreglé.
◆ **It's a tough job.** Es un trabajo duro.
2 duro ◇ *The meat is tough.* La carne está dura.
3 resistente ◇ *tough leather gloves* guantes de cuero resistentes
◆ **He thinks he's a tough guy.** Le gusta hacerse el duro.
◆ **Tough luck!** ¡Mala suerte!

tour ['tuər] NOUN
see also **tour** VERB
1 el recorrido turístico ◇ *We went on a tour of the city.* Hicimos un recorrido turístico por la ciudad.
◆ **a package tour** un viaje organizado
◆ **a bus tour** un viaje en autobús
2 la visita (*of building, exhibition*)
3 la gira (*of country, world*) ◇ *to go on tour* ir* de gira

to **tour** ['tuər] VERB
see also **tour** NOUN
◆ **Ricky Martin is touring Europe.** Ricky Martin está haciendo una gira por Europa.

tour guide ['turˌgaɪd] NOUN
el guía turístico
la guía turística

tourism ['turɪzəm] NOUN
el turismo

tourist ['turɪst] NOUN
el/la turista
◆ **tourist information office** la oficina de información y turismo

tournament ['turnəmənt] NOUN
el torneo

tour operator ['turˌɑːpəreɪtər] NOUN
el operador turístico

toward [tɔːrd] PREPOSITION
hacia ◇ *He came toward me.* Vino hacia mí.
◇ *my feelings toward him* mis sentimientos hacia él

towel ['tauəl] NOUN
la toalla

tower ['tauər] NOUN
la torre

town [taun] NOUN
la ciudad ◇ *a town plan* un plano de la ciudad ◇ *the town center* el centro de la ciudad

town hall ['taun'hɑːl] NOUN
el ayuntamiento

tow truck ['touˌtrʌk] NOUN

T ☞

la grúa

toy [tɔɪ] NOUN
el juguete
◆ **a toy shop** una juguetería
◆ **a toy car** un carro de juguete

trace [treɪs] NOUN
see also **trace** VERB
el rastro ◇ *There was no trace of the robbers.* No había rastro de los ladrones.

to **trace** [treɪs] VERB
see also **trace** NOUN
1 trazar* (*draw*)
2 encontrar* (*locate*)

tracing paper ['treɪsɪŋ'peɪpər] NOUN
el papel de calco

track [træk] NOUN
1 el camino (*dirt road*) ◇ *a mountain track* un camino de montaña
2 la vía (*railroad line*) ◇ *A woman fell onto the tracks.* Una mujer se cayó a la vía.
3 la pista (*in sport*) ◇ *two laps of the track* dos vueltas a la pista
4 la canción (PL las canciones) (*song*) ◇ *This is my favorite track.* Ésta es mi canción preferida.
5 la huella (*trail*) ◇ *They followed the tracks for miles.* Siguieron las huellas durante millas.

to **track down** [træk'daun] VERB
encontrar* ◇ *The police never tracked down the killer.* La policía nunca encontró al asesino.

track and field ['trækən'fi:ld] NOUN
el atletismo ◇ *track and field events* las pruebas de atletismo

tractor ['træktər] NOUN
el tractor

trade [treɪd] NOUN
el oficio ◇ *to learn a trade* aprender un oficio

trade union ['treɪd,ju:njən] NOUN
el sindicato

trade unionist ['treɪd,ju:njənɪst] NOUN
el/la sindicalista

tradition [trə'dɪʃən] NOUN
la tradición (PL las tradiciones)

traditional [trə'dɪʃənl] ADJECTIVE
tradicional

traffic ['træfɪk] NOUN
el tráfico ◇ *There was a lot of traffic.* Había mucho tráfico.

traffic circle ['træfɪk,sɜ:rkəl] NOUN
la rotonda

traffic cop ['træfɪk,kɑ:p] NOUN
el/la guardia de tráfico
el/la agente de tránsito *Mexico*
◇ *I'm a traffic cop.* Soy guardia de tráfico. *Mexico*: Soy agente de tránsito.

traffic jam ['træfɪk,dʒæm] NOUN
el atasco

traffic lights ['træfɪk,laɪts] PL NOUN
el semáforo

tragedy ['trædʒɪdi] NOUN (PL **tragedies**)
la tragedia

tragic ['trædʒɪk] ADJECTIVE
trágico

trailer ['treɪlər] NOUN
1 el trailer ◇ *a trailer park* un camping para trailers
2 el remolque (*of truck*)
3 los avances PL (*of movie*)

train [treɪn] NOUN
see also **train** VERB
el tren

to **train** [treɪn] VERB
see also **train** NOUN
entrenar ◇ *to train for a race* entrenar para una carrera
◆ **to train as a teacher** estudiar magisterio
◆ **to train an animal to do something** enseñar a un animal a hacer* algo

trained [treɪnd] ADJECTIVE
calificado ◇ *highly trained workers* los trabajadores altamente calificados
◆ **She's a trained nurse.** Es enfermera diplomada.

trainee [treɪ'ni:] NOUN
el aprendiz (PL los aprendices)
la aprendiza
(*apprentice*)
◇ *He's a trainee plumber.* Es aprendiz de plomero.
◆ **She's a teacher trainee.** Es profesora de prácticas.

trainer ['treɪnər] NOUN
1 el entrenador
la entrenadora
(*sports*)
2 el amaestrador
la amaestradora
(*of animals*)

training ['treɪnɪŋ] NOUN
1 la formación ◇ *a training course* un curso de formación
2 el entrenamiento (*in sport*)
◆ **He strained a muscle in training.** Se hizo un esguince entrenando.

tramp [træmp] NOUN
el vagabundo
la vagabunda

trampoline ['træmpəli:n] NOUN
la cama elástica

tranquilizer ['træŋkwɪlaɪzər] NOUN
el sedante ◇ *She's on tranquilizers.* Está tomando sedantes.

transfer ['trænsfər] NOUN
1 la transferencia ◇ *a bank transfer* una transferencia bancaria
2 la calcomanía (*sticker*)

transfusion [træns'fju:ʒən] NOUN
la transfusión (PL las transfusiones)

transistor [træn'zɪstər] NOUN
el transistor

to **translate** [trænz'leɪt] VERB
traducir* ◇ *to translate something into English* traducir* algo al inglés

translation [trænz'leɪʃən] NOUN
la traducción (PL las traducciones)

translator [trænz'leɪtər] NOUN
el traductor
la traductora
◇ *Anita is a translator.* Anita es traductora.

transparent [træns'pɛrənt] ADJECTIVE
transparente

transplant ['trænsplænt] NOUN
el trasplante ◇ *a heart transplant* un trasplante de corazón

transport ['trænspɔːrt] NOUN
see also **transport** VERB
el transporte

to **transport** [træns'pɔːrt] VERB
see also **transport** NOUN
transportar

transportation [trænspər'teɪʃən] NOUN
el transporte ◇ *public transportation* el transporte público

trap [træp] NOUN
la trampa

trash [træʃ] NOUN
la basura ◇ *When do they collect the trash?* ¿Cuándo recogen la basura? ◇ *The book is trash!* ¡El libro es una basura!
◆ **the trash can** el cubo de la basura, *Mexico*: el bote de la basura

trashy ['træʃi] ADJECTIVE
malísimo ◇ *a trashy movie* una película malísima

traumatic [trə'mætɪk] ADJECTIVE
traumático

travel ['trævəl] NOUN
see also **travel** VERB
◆ **Air travel is relatively cheap.** Viajar en avión es relativamente barato.

to **travel** ['trævəl] VERB
see also **travel** NOUN
viajar ◇ *I prefer to travel by train.* Prefiero viajar en tren.
◆ **I'd like to travel round the world.** Me gustaría dar la vuelta al mundo.
◆ **We traveled over 800 miles.** Viajamos más de 800 millas.
◆ **News travels fast!** ¡Las noticias vuelan!

travel agency ['trævəl,eɪdʒənsi] NOUN (PL **travel agencies**)
la agencia de viajes

travel agent ['trævl,eɪdʒənt] NOUN
◆ **She's a travel agent.** Es empleada de una agencia de viajes.

traveler ['trævlər] NOUN
el viajero
la viajera

traveler's check ['trævlərz,tʃɛk] NOUN
el cheque de viaje (PL los cheques de viaje)

traveling ['trævlɪŋ] NOUN
◆ **I love traveling.** Me encanta viajar.

travel sickness ['trævəl,sɪknɪs] NOUN
el mareo

tray [treɪ] NOUN
la bandeja
la charola *Mexico*

to **tread** [trɛd] VERB (**trod, trodden**)
pisar
◆ **to tread on something** pisar algo ◇ *He trod on her foot.* Le pisó el pie.

treasure ['trɛʒər] NOUN
el tesoro

treat [triːt] NOUN
see also **treat** VERB
◆ **As a birthday treat, I'll take you out to dinner.** Como es tu cumpleaños, te invito a cenar.
◆ **She bought a special treat for the children.** Les compró algo especial a los niños.
◆ **I'm going to give myself a treat.** Me voy a dar un gusto.

to **treat** [triːt] VERB
see also **treat** NOUN
tratar ◇ *The hostages were well treated.* Los rehenes fueron tratados bien.
◆ **She was treated for a minor head wound.** La atendieron por una herida leve en la cabeza.
◆ **to treat somebody to something** invitar a alguien a algo ◇ *I'll treat you!* ¡Te invito yo!

treatment ['triːtmənt] NOUN
1 el tratamiento (*medical*) ◇ *an effective treatment for eczema* un tratamiento efectivo contra el eczema
2 el trato (*of person*) ◇ *We don't want any special treatment.* No queremos ningún trato especial.

to **treble** ['trɛbəl] VERB
triplicarse* ◇ *The cost of living has trebled.* El costo de la vida se ha triplicado.

tree [triː] NOUN
el árbol

to **tremble** ['trɛmbəl] VERB
temblar*

trend [trɛnd] NOUN
1 la tendencia ◇ *There's a trend towards part-time employment.* Existe una tendencia hacia el empleo a tiempo parcial.
2 la moda (*fashion*) ◇ *the latest trend* la última moda

trendy ['trɛndi] ADJECTIVE
moderno

trial ['traɪəl] NOUN
el juicio (*in law*)

triangle ['traɪæŋgəl] NOUN
el triángulo

tribe [traɪb] NOUN
la tribu

trick [trɪk] NOUN
see also **trick** VERB
1 la broma ◇ *to play a trick on somebody* ☞

T

hacer* una broma a alguien
[2] el truco ◇ *It's not easy; there's a trick to it.* No es fácil: tiene un truco.
◆ **Trick or treat!**

> ℹ *Frase amenazante que dicen en tono jocoso los niños que rondan las casas en la noche de Halloween; significa: – ¡danos algo o te hacemos una broma pesada!*

to **trick** [trɪk] VERB
see also **trick** NOUN
◆ **to trick somebody** engañar a alguien

tricky ['trɪki] ADJECTIVE
peliagudo (*problem*)

tricycle ['traɪsɪkəl] NOUN
el triciclo

trifle ['traɪfəl] NOUN
el bizcocho borracho

to **trim** [trɪm] VERB
see also **trim** NOUN
recortar

trim [trɪm] NOUN
see also **trim** VERB
◆ **to have a trim** cortarse las puntas

trip [trɪp] NOUN
see also **trip** VERB
el viaje ◇ *to go on a trip* ir* de viaje ◇ *Have a good trip!* ¡Buen viaje!
◆ **a day trip** una excursión de un día

to **trip** [trɪp] VERB
see also **trip** NOUN
tropezarse* (*stumble*) ◇ *He tripped on the stairs.* Se tropezó en las escaleras.
◆ **to trip up** tropezarse*
◆ **to trip somebody up** hacer* una zancadilla a alguien

triple ['trɪpəl] ADJECTIVE
triple

triplets ['trɪplɪts] PL NOUN
los trillizos (FEM las trillizas)

trivial ['trɪviəl] ADJECTIVE
insignificante

trod, trodden [trɑːd, trɑːdn] VERB *see* **tread**

trolley ['trɑːli] NOUN
el tranvía (*vehicle*)
Although ***tranvía*** *ends in* ***-a****, it is actually a masculine noun.*

trombone [trɑːm'boun] NOUN
el trombón (PL los trombones)

troops [truːps] PL NOUN
las tropas

trophy ['troufi] NOUN (PL **trophies**)
el trofeo

tropical ['trɑːpɪkəl] ADJECTIVE
tropical

to **trot** [trɑːt] VERB
trotar

trouble ['trʌbəl] NOUN
el problema
Although ***problema*** *ends in* ***-a****, it is actually a masculine noun.*
◇ *The trouble is, it's too expensive.* El problema es que es demasiado caro.
◆ **What's the trouble?** ¿Qué pasa?
◆ **to be in trouble** tener* problemas
◆ **stomach trouble** problemas de estómago
◆ **to take a lot of trouble over something** poner* mucho cuidado en algo
◆ **Don't worry, it's no trouble.** No te preocupes, no importa.

troublemaker ['trʌbəl,meɪkər] NOUN
el alborotador
la alborotadora

trout [traut] NOUN (PL **trout**)
la trucha

truant ['truːənt] NOUN
◆ **to play truant** hacer* novillos

truck [trʌk] NOUN
el camión (PL los camiones)

truck driver ['trʌk,draɪvər] NOUN
el camionero
la camionera
◇ *He's a truck driver.* Es camionero.

trucker ['trʌkər] NOUN
el camionero
la camionera

true [truː] ADJECTIVE
verdadero (*love, courage*)
◆ **It's true.** Es verdad.
◆ **to come true** hacerse* realidad ◇ *I hope my dream will come true.* Espero que mi sueño se haga realidad.

trumpet ['trʌmpɪt] NOUN
la trompeta

trunk [trʌŋk] NOUN
[1] el tronco (*of tree*)
[2] la trompa (*of elephant*)
[3] el baúl (*luggage*)
[4] el maletero
la cajuela Mexico
(*of car*)

trunks [trʌŋks] PL NOUN
◆ **swimming trunks** el traje de baño

trust [trʌst] NOUN
see also **trust** VERB
la confianza ◇ *to have trust in somebody* tener* confianza en alguien

to **trust** [trʌst] VERB
see also **trust** NOUN
◆ **Don't you trust me?** ¿No tienes confianza en mí?
◆ **Trust me!** ¡Confía en mí!
◆ **I don't trust him.** No me fío de él.

trusting ['trʌstɪŋ] ADJECTIVE
confiado

truth [truːθ] NOUN
la verdad

truthful ['truːθfəl] ADJECTIVE
[1] sincero (*person*) ◇ *She's a very truthful*

person. Es una persona muy sincera.
[2] verídico (*account*)

try [traɪ] NOUN (PL **tries**)
see also **try** VERB
el intento ◇ *his third try* su tercer intento
◆ **to give something a try** intentar algo
◆ **It's worth a try.** Vale la pena intentarlo.
◆ **Have a try!** ¡Inténtalo!

to **try** [traɪ] VERB (**tried, tried**)
see also **try** NOUN
[1] intentar ◇ *to try to do something* intentar hacer algo
◆ **to try again** volver* a intentar
[2] probar* ◇ *Would you like to try some?* ¿Quieres probar un poco?

to **try on** [traɪ'ɑːn] VERB
probarse* (*clothes*)

to **try out** [traɪ'aut] VERB
probar* (*product, machine*)

T-shirt ['tiːʃɜːrt] NOUN
la camiseta

tube [tuːb] NOUN
el tubo

tuberculosis [tubɜːrkjə'lousɪs] NOUN
la tuberculosis ◇ *He has tuberculosis.* Tiene tuberculosis.

Tuesday ['tuːzdi] NOUN
el martes (PL los martes) ◇ *I saw her on Tuesday.* La vi el martes. ◇ *every Tuesday* todos los martes ◇ *last Tuesday* el martes pasado ◇ *next Tuesday* el martes que viene ◇ *on Tuesdays* los martes

tug-of-war ['tʌgəv'wɔːr] NOUN
el juego del tira y afloja con una cuerda

tuition [tu'ɪʃən] NOUN
[1] las clases ◇ *private tuition* clases particulares
[2] la matrícula ◇ *Have you paid your tuition yet?* ¿Ya pagaste la matrícula?

tulip ['tuːlɪp] NOUN
el tulipán (PL los tulipanes)

tummy ['tʌmi] NOUN (PL **tummies**)
la barriga (*informal*)
◆ **he has a tummy ache** le duele la barriga

tuna ['tuːnə] NOUN (PL **tuna** *or* **tunas**)
el atún (PL los atunes)

tune [tuːn] NOUN
la melodía (*melody*)
◆ **to play in tune** tocar* bien
◆ **to sing out of tune** desafinar

Tunisia [tuː'niːʒə] NOUN
Túnez MASC

tunnel ['tʌnl] NOUN
el túnel

Turk [tɜːrk] NOUN
el turco
la turca
◇ *the Turks* los turcos

turkey ['tɜːrki] NOUN
el pavo
el guajolote *Mexico*

Turkey ['tɜːrki] NOUN
Turquía FEM

Turkish ['tɜːrkɪʃ] ADJECTIVE
see also **Turkish** NOUN
turco

Turkish ['tɜːrkɪʃ] NOUN
see also **Turkish** ADJECTIVE
el turco (*language*)

turn [tɜːrn] NOUN
see also **turn** VERB
la curva (*bend in road*)
◆ **"no left turn"** "prohibido girar a la izquierda"
◆ **to take turns** turnarse
◆ **It's my turn!** ¡Me toca a mí!
◆ **Whose turn is it?** ¿A quién le toca?

to **turn** [tɜːrn] VERB
see also **turn** NOUN
[1] girar ◇ *Turn right at the lights.* Gira a la derecha al llegar al semáforo.
[2] ponerse* (*become*) ◇ *When he's drunk, he turns nasty.* Cuando se emborracha se pone desagradable.
◆ **The weather turned cold.** Empezó a hacer frío.
◆ **to turn into something** convertirse* en algo ◇ *The vacation turned into a nightmare.* Las vacaciones se convirtieron en una pesadilla.

to **turn around** [tɜːrnə'raund] VERB
[1] dar* la vuelta (*car*)
[2] darse* la vuelta (*person*)

to **turn back** [tɜːrn'bæk] VERB
volver* hacia atrás ◇ *We turned back.* Volvimos hacia atrás.

to **turn down** [tɜːrn'daun] VERB
[1] rechazar* ◇ *He turned down the offer.* Rechazó la oferta.
[2] bajar ◇ *Shall I turn the heating down?* ¿Bajo la calefacción?

to **turn off** [tɜːrn'ɑːf] VERB
[1] apagar* (*light, radio*)
[2] cerrar* (*faucet*)
[3] parar (*engine*)

to **turn on** [tɜːrn'ɑːn] VERB
[1] prender* (*light, radio*)
[2] abrir* (*faucet*)
[3] poner* en marcha (*engine*)

to **turn out** [tɜːrn'aut] VERB
resultar ◇ *It turned out to be a mistake.* Resultó ser un error. ◇ *It turned out that she was right.* Resultó que ella tenía razón.

to **turn up** [tɜːrn'ʌp] VERB
[1] aparecer* ◇ *She never turned up.* No apareció. ◇ *The lost dog turned up in the next village.* El perro extraviado apareció en el pueblo vecino.
[2] subir ◇ *Could you turn up the radio?* ¿Puedes subir la radio?

turning ['tɜːrnɪŋ] NOUN
◆ **We took the wrong turning. (1)** (*in the country*) Nos equivocamos de carretera.
◆ **We took the wrong turning. (2)** (*in the city*) Nos equivocamos de bocacalle.

T

turnip ['tɜːrnɪp] NOUN
el nabo
turn signal ['tɜːrn,sɪgnl] NOUN
el intermitente
la direccional Mexico
(*in car*)
turquoise ['tɜːrkwɔɪz] ADJECTIVE
turquesa MASC, FEM, PL
turtle ['tɜːrtl] NOUN
la tortuga
turtleneck ['tɜːrtlnek] NOUN
el suéter de cuello alto
tutor ['tuːtər] NOUN
el profesor particular
la profesora particular
(*private teacher*)
tuxedo [tʌk'siːdou] NOUN
el esmoquin (PL los esmóquines)
TV [tiː'viː] NOUN
la tele
tweezers ['twiːzərz] PL NOUN
las pinzas ◇ *a pair of tweezers* unas pinzas
twelfth [twɛlfθ] ADJECTIVE
duodécimo ◇ *the twelfth floor* el duodécimo piso
◆ **August twelfth** el doce de agosto
twelve [twɛlv] NUMERAL
doce ◇ *She's twelve.* Tiene doce años.
◆ **twelve o'clock** las doce
twentieth ['twɛntiɪθ] ADJECTIVE
vigésimo
◆ **the twentieth floor** el piso veinte
◆ **May twentieth** el veinte de mayo
twenty ['twɛnti] NUMERAL
veinte ◇ *He's twenty.* Tiene veinte años.
twice [twaɪs] ADVERB
dos veces ◇ *He had to repeat it twice.* Tuvo que repetirlo dos veces.
◆ **twice as much** el doble ◇ *He gets twice as much pocket money as me.* Le dan el doble de paga que a mí.
twin [twɪn] NOUN
el mellizo
la melliza
◇ *my twin brother* mi hermano mellizo
◇ *her twin sister* su hermana melliza
◆ **identical twins** gemelos, Mexico: cuates
◆ **twin beds** las camas gemelas
to **twist** [twɪst] VERB
1 torcer*
◆ **He's twisted his ankle.** Se torció el tobillo.
2 tergiversar* ◇ *You're twisting my words.* Estás tergiversando lo que he dicho.
twit [twɪt] NOUN
el/la imbécil (*informal*)
two [tuː] NUMERAL
dos ◇ *She's two.* Tiene dos años.
◆ **The two of them can sing.** Los dos saben cantar.
type [taɪp] NOUN
see also **type** VERB
el tipo ◇ *What type of camera do you have?* ¿Qué tipo de cámara tienes?
to **type** [taɪp] VERB
see also **type** NOUN
escribir* a máquina ◇ *Can you type?* ¿Sabes escribir a máquina? ◇ *to type a letter* escribir* una carta a máquina
typewriter ['taɪp,raɪtər] NOUN
la máquina de escribir
typical ['tɪpɪkəl] ADJECTIVE
típico ◇ *That's just typical!* ¡Típico!

* Verbs marked with this symbol are irregular. See pages 346–348 for further details.

U

UFO [juːɛf'ou] ABBREVIATION (= *unidentified flying object*) (PL **UFOs**)
el OVNI (= el Objeto Volador No Identificado)

ugh [ɜːh] EXCLAMATION
¡puf!

ugly ['ʌgli] ADJECTIVE
feo

UK [juː'keɪ] ABBREVIATION (= *United Kingdom*)
el RU (= el Reino Unido)

ulcer ['ʌlsər] NOUN
la úlcera
◆ **a mouth ulcer** una llaga en la boca

ultimate ['ʌltɪmət] ADJECTIVE
máximo ◇ *the ultimate challenge* el máximo desafío
◆ **the ultimate in luxury** lo último en lujo

ultimately ['ʌltɪmətli] ADVERB
a fin de cuentas ◇ *Ultimately, it's your decision.* A fin de cuentas, es tu decisión.

umbrella [ʌm'brɛlə] NOUN
el paraguas (PL los paraguas)

umpire ['ʌmpaɪər] NOUN
el árbitro
la árbitra

UN [juː'ɛn] ABBREVIATION (= *United Nations*)
la ONU (= la Organización de las Naciones Unidas)

unable [ʌn'eɪbəl] ADJECTIVE
◆ **to be unable to do something** no poder* hacer algo ◇ *Unfortunately, he was unable to come.* Lamentablemente, no ha podido venir.

unacceptable [ʌnɪk'sɛptəbəl] ADJECTIVE
inaceptable

unanimous [juː'nænəməs] ADJECTIVE
unánime

unattended [ʌnə'tɛndɪd] ADJECTIVE
◆ **Please do not leave your luggage unattended.** Por favor, no dejen desatendido su equipaje.

unavoidable [ʌnə'vɔɪdəbəl] ADJECTIVE
inevitable

unaware [ʌnə'wɛər] ADJECTIVE
◆ **I was unaware of the regulations.** Ignoraba el reglamento.
◆ **She was unaware that she was being filmed.** No se había dado cuenta de que la estaban filmando.

unbearable [ʌn'bɛrəbəl] ADJECTIVE
insoportable

unbeatable [ʌn'biːtəbəl] ADJECTIVE
inmejorable (*quality, price*)

unbelievable [ʌnbɪ'liːvəbəl] ADJECTIVE
increíble

unborn [ʌn'bɔːrn] ADJECTIVE
◆ **the unborn child** el feto

unbreakable [ʌn'breɪkəbəl] ADJECTIVE
irrompible

uncanny [ʌn'kæni] ADJECTIVE
extraño ◇ *That's very uncanny!* ¡Es muy extraño!
◆ **an uncanny resemblance** un asombroso parecido

uncertain [ʌn'sɜːrtn] ADJECTIVE
incierto ◇ *The future is uncertain.* El futuro es incierto.
◆ **to be uncertain about something** no estar* seguro de algo
◆ **She was uncertain how to begin.** No sabía muy bien cómo empezar.

uncivilized [ʌn'sɪvɪlaɪzd] ADJECTIVE
poco civilizado (*behavior*)

uncle ['ʌŋkəl] NOUN
el tío
◆ **my uncle and aunt** mis tíos

uncomfortable [ʌn'kʌmfərtəbəl] ADJECTIVE
incómodo

unconscious [ʌn'kɑːnʃəs] ADJECTIVE
inconsciente

unconventional [ʌnkən'vɛnʃənl] ADJECTIVE
poco convencional

under ['ʌndər] PREPOSITION
When something is located under something, use ***debajo de****. When there is movement involved, use* ***por debajo de****.*
1 debajo de ◇ *The cat is under the table.* El gato está debajo de la mesa.
2 por debajo de ◇ *The tunnel goes under the river.* El túnel pasa por debajo del río.
◆ **under there** ahí debajo ◇ *What's under there?* ¿Qué hay ahí debajo?
3 menos de ◇ *under 20 people* menos de 20 personas
◆ **children under 10** niños menores de 10 años

underage [ˌʌndər'eɪdʒ] ADJECTIVE
◆ **He's underage.** Es menor de edad.

undercover [ˌʌndər'kʌvər] ADJECTIVE, ADVERB
secreto ◇ *an undercover agent* un agente secreto ◇ *She was working undercover for the FBI.* Trabajaba como agente secreto para el FBI.

to **underestimate** ['ʌndər'ɛstɪmeɪt] VERB
subestimar ◇ *You shouldn't underestimate her.* No la subestimes.

to **undergo** [ˌʌndər'gou] VERB (**underwent**, **undergone**)
someterse a (*operation*)

underground [ˌʌndər'graund] ADJECTIVE
see also **underground** ADVERB
1 subterráneo ◇ *an underground parking garage* un estacionamiento subterráneo
2 clandestino (*resistance*)

underground [ˌʌndər'graund] ADVERB
see also **underground** ADJECTIVE
bajo tierra ◇ *Moles live underground.* Los topos viven bajo tierra.

to **underline** [ˌʌndər'laɪn] VERB
subrayar

underneath [ˌʌndərˈniːθ] PREPOSITION, ADVERB
*When something is located underneath something, use **debajo de**. When there is movement involved, use **por debajo de**.*
1 debajo de ◇ *underneath the bed* debajo de la cama ◇ *I got out of the car and looked underneath.* Me bajé del carro y miré debajo.
2 por debajo de ◇ *I walked underneath a ladder.* Pasé por debajo de una escalera.

underpaid [ˌʌndərˈpeɪd] ADJECTIVE
mal pagado ◇ *Teachers are underpaid.* Los profesores están mal pagados.

underpants [ˈʌndərˌpænts] PL NOUN
los calzoncillos ◇ *a pair of underpants* unos calzoncillos

underpass [ˈʌndərˌpæs] NOUN (PL **underpasses**)
el paso subterráneo

undershirt [ˈʌndərʃɜːrt] NOUN
la camiseta

underskirt [ˈʌndərskɜːrt] NOUN
las enaguas

to **understand** [ʌndərˈstænd] VERB (**understood, understood**)
entender* ◇ *Do you understand?* ¿Entiendes? ◇ *I don't understand the question.* No entiendo la pregunta.
◆ **Is that understood?** ¿Está claro?

understanding [ʌndərˈstændɪŋ] ADJECTIVE
comprensivo ◇ *She's very understanding.* Es muy comprensiva.

understood [ʌndərˈstud] VERB *see* **understand**

undertaker [ˈʌndərˌteɪkər] NOUN
el empleado de una funeraria
la empleada de una funeraria
◆ **the undertaker's** la funeraria

underwater [ˈʌndərˈwɑːtər] ADJECTIVE, ADVERB
1 subacuático ◇ *underwater photography* fotografía subacuática
2 bajo el agua ◇ *This sequence was filmed underwater.* Esta secuencia se filmó bajo el agua.

underwear [ˈʌndərwɛr] NOUN
la ropa interior

underwent [ʌndərˈwɛnt] VERB *see* **undergo**

to **undo** [ʌnˈduː] VERB (**undid, undone**)
1 desabrochar (*button, blouse*)
2 desatar (*knot, parcel, shoelaces*)
3 abrir* (*zipper*)

to **undress** [ʌnˈdrɛs] VERB
desnudarse (*get undressed*) ◇ *The doctor told me to undress.* El médico me dijo que me desnudase.

uneconomic [ˈʌnɛkəˈnɑːmɪk] ADJECTIVE
◆ **an uneconomic factory** una fábrica poco rentable
◆ **It's uneconomic to put on courses for so few students.** No es rentable organizar cursos para tan pocos alumnos.

unemployed [ʌnɪmˈplɔɪd] ADJECTIVE
desempleado ◇ *He's been unemployed for a year.* Hace un año que está desempleado.
◆ **the unemployed** los desempleados

unemployment [ʌnɪmˈplɔɪmənt] NOUN
el desempleo
◆ **unemployment office** la oficina de empleo

unexpected [ʌnɪksˈpɛktɪd] ADJECTIVE
inesperado

unexpectedly [ʌnɪksˈpɛktɪdli] ADVERB
de improviso

unfair [ʌnˈfɛər] ADJECTIVE
injusto ◇ *This law is unfair to women.* Esta ley es injusta para con las mujeres.

unfamiliar [ʌnfəˈmɪljər] ADJECTIVE
desconocido ◇ *I heard an unfamiliar voice.* Oí una voz desconocida.

unfashionable [ʌnˈfæʃənəbəl] ADJECTIVE
pasado de moda

unfit [ʌnˈfɪt] ADJECTIVE
◆ **I'm unfit at the moment.** En este momento no estoy en forma.

to **unfold** [ʌnˈfould] VERB
desplegar* ◇ *She unfolded the map.* Desplegó el mapa.

unforgettable [ʌnfərˈgɛtəbəl] ADJECTIVE
inolvidable

unfortunately [ʌnˈfɔːrtʃənətli] ADVERB
lamentablemente

unfriendly [ʌnˈfrɛndli] ADJECTIVE
antipático ◇ *The waiters are a bit unfriendly.* Los meseros son un poco antipáticos.

ungrateful [ʌnˈgreɪtfəl] ADJECTIVE
desagradecido

unhappy [ʌnˈhæpi] ADJECTIVE
infeliz (PL infelices) ◇ *He was very unhappy as a child.* De niño fue muy infeliz.
◆ **to look unhappy** parecer* triste

unhealthy [ʌnˈhɛlθi] ADJECTIVE
1 malo para la salud (*food*)
2 con mala salud (*ill*)
3 malsano (*atmosphere*)

uniform [ˈjuːnɪfɔːrm] NOUN
el uniforme
◆ **school uniform** el uniforme de colegio

uninhabited [ʌnɪnˈhæbɪtɪd] ADJECTIVE
1 deshabitado (*house*)
2 despoblado (*island*)

union [ˈjuːnjən] NOUN
el sindicato (*trade union*)

unique [juːˈniːk] ADJECTIVE
único

unit [ˈjuːnɪt] NOUN
la unidad ◇ *a unit of measurement* una unidad de medida
◆ **a kitchen unit** un módulo de cocina

United Kingdom [juːˈnaɪtɪdˈkɪŋdəm] NOUN
el Reino Unido

United Nations [juːˈnaɪtɪdˈneɪʃənz] NOUN
las Naciones Unidas

United States [ju:ˈnaɪtɪdˈsteɪts] PL NOUN
los Estados Unidos

universe [ˈju:nɪvɜ:rs] NOUN
el universo

university [ju:nɪˈvɜ:rsɪti] NOUN (PL **universities**)
la universidad ◇ *Duke University* la Universidad de Duke

unleaded gasoline [ˈʌnlɛdɪdˈgæsəli:n] NOUN
la gasolina sin plomo

unless [ʌnˈlɛs] CONJUNCTION
a no ser que
a no ser que *has to be followed by a verb in the subjunctive.*
◇ *I won't come unless you phone me.* No vendré a no ser que me llames.
◆ **Unless I am mistaken, we're lost.** Si no me equivoco, estamos perdidos.

unlike [ʌnˈlaɪk] PREPOSITION
a diferencia de ◇ *Unlike him, I really enjoy flying.* A diferencia de él, a mí me encanta viajar en avión.

unlikely [ʌnˈlaɪkli] ADJECTIVE
poco probable ◇ *That's possible, but unlikely.* Es posible pero poco probable.
◇ *He's unlikely to come.* Es poco probable que venga.
es poco probable que *has to be followed by a verb in the subjunctive.*

unlisted [ˈʌnˈlɪstɪd] ADJECTIVE
◆ **an unlisted number** un número que no figura en la guía telefónica

to **unload** [ʌnˈloud] VERB
descargar* ◇ *We unloaded the furniture.* Descargamos los muebles.

to **unlock** [ʌnˈlɑ:k] VERB
abrir* ◇ *He unlocked the door of the car.* Abrió la puerta del carro.

unlucky [ʌnˈlʌki] ADJECTIVE
◆ **to be unlucky (1)** (*be unfortunate*) tener* mala suerte ◇ *Did you win? – No, I was unlucky.* ¿Ganaste? – No, tuve mala suerte.
◆ **to be unlucky (2)** (*bring bad luck*) traer* mala suerte ◇ *They say thirteen is an unlucky number.* Dicen que el número trece trae mala suerte.

unmarried [ʌnˈmɛrid] ADJECTIVE
soltero ◇ *an unmarried mother* una madre soltera
◆ **an unmarried couple** una pareja no casada

unnatural [ʌnˈnætʃərəl] ADJECTIVE
poco natural

unnecessary [ʌnˈnɛsəsɛri] ADJECTIVE
innecesario

unofficial [ʌnəˈfɪʃəl] ADJECTIVE
no oficial

to **unpack** [ʌnˈpæk] VERB
deshacer* ◇ *I unpacked my suitcase.* Deshice la maleta. ◇ *I went to my room to unpack. (1)* (*one suitcase*) Fui a mi habitación a deshacer la maleta. ◇ *I went to my room to unpack. (2)* (*more than one suitcase*) Fui a mi habitación a deshacer las maletas.
◆ **I haven't unpacked my clothes yet.** Todavía no he sacado la ropa de la maleta.

unpleasant [ʌnˈplɛzənt] ADJECTIVE
desagradable

to **unplug** [ʌnˈplʌg] VERB
desenchufar

unpopular [ʌnˈpɑ:pjələr] ADJECTIVE
impopular ◇ *It was an unpopular decision.* Fue una decisión impopular.
◆ **She's an unpopular child.** Tiene muy pocos amigos.

unpredictable [ʌnprɪˈdɪktəbəl] ADJECTIVE
imprevisible

unreal [ʌnˈri:əl] ADJECTIVE
increíble ◇ *It was unreal!* ¡Fue increíble!

unrealistic [ˌʌnri:əˈlɪstɪk] ADJECTIVE
poco realista

unreasonable [ʌnˈri:zənəbəl] ADJECTIVE
poco razonable ◇ *I think her attitude is unreasonable.* Creo que su actitud es poco razonable.

unreliable [ˌʌnrɪˈlaɪəbəl] ADJECTIVE
poco fiable ◇ *The car was slow and unreliable.* El carro era lento y poco fiable.
◆ **He's completely unreliable.** No se puede contar con él.

to **unroll** [ʌnˈroul] VERB
desenrollar

unsatisfactory [ˌʌnsætɪsˈfæktəri] ADJECTIVE
insatisfactorio

to **unscrew** [ʌnˈskru:] VERB
1 destornillar (*screw*)
2 desenroscar* (*lid*)

unshaven [ʌnˈʃeɪvən] ADJECTIVE
sin afeitar
sin rasurar *Mexico*

unskilled [ʌnˈskɪld] ADJECTIVE
◆ **an unskilled worker** un trabajador no calificado (FEM una trabajadora no calificada)

unstable [ʌnˈsteɪbəl] ADJECTIVE
inestable

unsteady [ʌnˈstɛdi] ADJECTIVE
1 inestable (*chair*)
2 vacilante (*walk, voice*)
◆ **He was unsteady on his feet.** Caminaba con paso vacilante.

unsuccessful [ˌʌnsəkˈsɛsfəl] ADJECTIVE
fallido (*attempt*)
◆ **to be unsuccessful in doing something** no conseguir* hacer algo
◆ **an unsuccessful artist** un artista sin éxito

unsuitable [ʌnˈsu:təbəl] ADJECTIVE
inapropiado (*clothes, equipment*)

untidy [ʌnˈtaɪdi] ADJECTIVE
1 desordenado (*disorganized*) ◇ *Your bedroom is really untidy.* Tu cuarto está muy desordenado.
2 descuidado (*writing*)
◆ **She always looks so untidy.** Siempre anda ☞

U

tan desaliñada.

to **untie** [ʌn'taɪ] VERB

1 deshacer* (*knot, parcel*)

2 desatar (*shoelace, animal*)

until [ən'tɪl] PREPOSITION, CONJUNCTION

1 hasta ◇ *I waited until 10 o'clock.* Esperé hasta las 10. ◇ *It won't be ready until next week.* No estará listo hasta la semana que viene.

- **until now** hasta ahora ◇ *It's never been a problem until now.* Hasta ahora nunca ha sido un problema.
- **until then** hasta entonces ◇ *Until then I'd never been to Honduras.* Hasta entonces no había estado nunca en Honduras.

2 hasta que ◇ *We stayed there until the doctor came.* Nos quedamos allí hasta que vino el médico.

***hasta que** has to be followed by a verb in the subjunctive when referring to a future event.*

◇ *Don't go until I arrive.* No te vayas hasta que llegue yo. ◇ *Wait until I come back.* Espera hasta que yo vuelva.

unusual [ʌn'juːʒuəl] ADJECTIVE

1 poco común ◇ *an unusual shape* una forma poco común

2 raro

***es raro que** has to be followed by a verb in the subjunctive.*

◇ *It's unusual to get snow at this time of year.* Es raro que nieve en esta época del año.

unwilling [ʌn'wɪlɪŋ] ADJECTIVE

- **He was unwilling to help me.** No estaba dispuesto a ayudarme.

to **unwind** [ʌn'waɪnd] VERB (**unwound**, **unwound**)

relajarse (*relax*)

unwise [ʌn'waɪz] ADJECTIVE

imprudente ◇ *That was unwise of you.* Lo que hiciste fue imprudente.

unwound [ʌn'waund] VERB *see* **unwind**

to **unwrap** [ʌn'ræp] VERB

abrir* ◇ *After the meal we unwrapped the presents.* Después de comer abrimos los regalos.

up [ʌp] PREPOSITION, ADVERB

*For other expressions with **up**, see the verbs **come, put, turn** etc.*

arriba ◇ *up on the hill* arriba de la colina ◇ *up here* aquí arriba ◇ *up there* allí arriba

- **up north** en el norte
- **They live up the road.** Viven en esta calle, un poco más allá.
- **to be up** estar* levantado ◇ *We were up at six.* A las seis estábamos levantados.
- **He's not up yet.** Todavía no se ha levantado.
- **What's up?** ¿Qué hay?
- **What's up with her?** ¿Qué le pasa?
- **to go up** subir ◇ *The bus went up the hill.* El autobús subió la colina.
- **to go up to somebody** acercarse* a alguien ◇ *She came up to me.* Se me acercó.
- **up to** hasta ◇ *to count up to 50* contar* hasta 50 ◇ *up to three hours* hasta tres horas ◇ *up to now* hasta ahora
- **It's up to you.** Depende de ti.

upbringing ['ʌpbrɪŋɪŋ] NOUN

la educación

uphill ['ʌp'hɪl] ADJECTIVE

- **It was an uphill struggle.** Fue una tarea muy difícil.

upper ['ʌpər] ADJECTIVE

superior

upright ['ʌpraɪt] ADJECTIVE

- **to stand upright** tenerse* derecho

upset [ʌp'sɛt] NOUN

see also **upset** ADJECTIVE, VERB

- **I had a stomach upset.** Estaba mal del estómago.
- **The game was a surprising upset for the team.** El partido terminó con una derrota inesperada para el equipo.

upset [ʌp'sɛt] ADJECTIVE

see also **upset** NOUN, VERB

disgustado ◇ *She's still a bit upset.* Todavía está un poco disgustada.

- **Don't get upset.** No te enfades.
- **I had an upset stomach.** Estaba mal del estómago.

to **upset** [ʌp'sɛt] VERB (**upset**, **upset**)

see also **upset** NOUN, ADJECTIVE

- **to upset somebody** disgustar a alguien
- **Don't upset yourself.** No te enfades.

upside down ['ʌpsaɪd'daun] ADVERB

al revés ◇ *The painting was hung upside down.* El cuadro estaba colgado al revés.

upstairs [ʌp'stɛərz] ADVERB

arriba ◇ *Where's your coat? – It's upstairs.* ¿Dónde está tu abrigo? – Está arriba.

- **the people upstairs** los de arriba
- **He went upstairs to bed.** Subió para irse a la cama.

uptight [ʌp'taɪt] ADJECTIVE

tenso ◇ *She's very uptight today.* Está muy tensa hoy.

up-to-date ['ʌptə'deɪt] ADJECTIVE

1 moderno (*car, stereo*)

2 actualizado ◇ *an up-to-date schedule* un horario actualizado

- **to bring somebody up-to-date on something** poner* a alguien al corriente de algo
- **to bring something up-to-date** actualizar algo

upwards ['ʌpwərdz] ADVERB

hacia arriba ◇ *to look upwards* mirar hacia arriba

urgent ['ɜːrdʒənt] ADJECTIVE

urgente

urine ['jurən] NOUN

la orina

US [juːˈɛs] ABBREVIATION (= *United States*)
los EEUU (= los Estados Unidos)

us [ʌs] PRONOUN
1 nos
*Use **nos** to translate **us** when it is the direct object of the verb in the sentence, or when it means **to us**.*
◇ *They helped us.* Nos ayudaron. ◇ *Look at us!* ¡Míranos! ◇ *They gave us some brochures.* Nos dieron unos folletos.
2 nosotros (FEM nosotras)
*Use **nosotros** or **nosotras** after prepositions, in comparisons, and with the verb **to be**.*
◇ *Why don't you come with us?* ¿Por qué no vienes con nosotras? ◇ *They are older than us.* Son mayores que nosotros. ◇ *It's us.* Somos nosotros.

USA [ˌjuːɛsˈeɪ] ABBREVIATION (= *United States of America*)
los EEUU (= los Estados Unidos)

USAF [ˌjuːɛseɪˈɛf] ABBREVIATION (= *United States Air Force*)
la Fuerza Aérea de los EEUU

use [juːs] NOUN
see also **use** VERB
el uso ◇ *"directions for use"* "modo de empleo"
- **It's no use shouting, she's deaf.** Es inútil gritar, es sorda.
- **It's no use; I can't do it.** No hay manera, no puedo hacerlo.
- **to make use of something** usar algo

to **use** [juːz] VERB
see also **use** NOUN
usar ◇ *Can I use your phone?* ¿Puedo usar tu teléfono?
- **I used to go camping as a child.** De pequeño solía ir de acampada.
- **I didn't use to like math, but now I love it.** Antes no me gustaban las matemáticas, pero ahora me encantan.
- **to be used to something** estar* acostumbrado a algo ◇ *He wasn't used to driving on the left.* No estaba acostumbrado a manejar por la izquierda. ◇ *Don't worry, I'm used to it.* No te preocupes, estoy acostumbrado.
- **a used car** un carro de segunda mano

to **use up** [juːzˈʌp] VERB
- **We've used up all the paint.** Hemos usado toda la pintura.

useful [ˈjuːsfəl] ADJECTIVE
útil

useless [ˈjuːslɪs] ADJECTIVE
inútil ◇ *a piece of useless information* una información inútil
- **You're useless!** ¡Eres un inútil!
- **This computer is useless.** Esta computadora no sirve para nada.
- **It's useless asking her.** No sirve de nada preguntarle.

user [ˈjuːzər] NOUN
el usuario
la usuaria

user-friendly [ˈjuːzərˈfrɛndli] ADJECTIVE
fácil de usar

usual [ˈjuːʒuəl] ADJECTIVE
habitual
- **as usual** como de costumbre

usually [ˈjuːʒuəli] ADVERB
normalmente ◇ *I usually get to school at about half past eight.* Normalmente llego al colegio alrededor de las ocho y media.

U-turn [ˈjuːtɜːrn] NOUN
el cambio de sentido
- **to do a U-turn** cambiar de sentido
- **"No U-turns"** "Prohibido cambiar de sentido"

V

vacancy ['veɪkənsi] NOUN (PL **vacancies**)
[1] la vacante (*job*)
[2] la habitación libre (FEM las habitaciones libres) (*in hotel*)
◆ **"no vacancies"** "completo"

vacant ['veɪkənt] ADJECTIVE
libre ◇ *a vacant seat* un asiento libre

vacation [veɪ'keɪʃən] NOUN
las vacaciones
◆ **the summer vacations** las vacaciones de verano
◆ **on vacation** de vacaciones ◇ *to go on vacation* irse* de vacaciones ◇ *to be on vacation* estar* de vacaciones
◆ **He took a vacation day.** Se tomó un día libre.

to **vaccinate** ['væksɪneɪt] VERB
vacunar

to **vacuum** ['vækjuːm] VERB
pasar la aspiradora ◇ *He vacuumed the lounge.* Pasó la aspiradora por el salón.

vacuum cleaner ['vækjuːm,kliːnər] NOUN
la aspiradora

vagina [və'dʒaɪnə] NOUN
la vagina

vague [veɪg] ADJECTIVE
[1] vago ◇ *I only have a vague idea what he means.* Tengo sólo una vaga idea de lo que quiere decir.
[2] distraído ◇ *He's getting a bit vague in his old age.* Se está poniendo un poco distraído en su vejez.

vain [veɪn] ADJECTIVE
vanidoso ◇ *He's so vain!* ¡Es más vanidoso!
◆ **in vain** en vano

valentine ['væləntaɪn] NOUN
el novio
la novia
◆ **be my valentine (1)** (*to a woman*) sé mi enamorada
◆ **be my valentine (2)** (*to a man*) sé mi enamorado
◆ **valentine card** la tarjeta del día de los enamorados

Valentine's Day ['væləntaɪnz,deɪ] NOUN
el día de los enamorados (*el 14 de febrero, día de San Valentín*)

valid ['vælɪd] ADJECTIVE
válido ◇ *a valid passport* un pasaporte válido
◆ **This ticket is valid for three months.** Este boleto tiene una validez de tres meses.

valley ['væli] NOUN
el valle

valuable ['væljəbəl] ADJECTIVE
[1] de valor MASC, FEM, PL ◇ *a valuable painting* un cuadro de valor
[2] valioso ◇ *valuable help* una ayuda valiosa

valuables ['væljəbəlz] PL NOUN
los objetos de valor

value ['væljuː] NOUN
el valor

van [væn] NOUN
la furgoneta
la vagoneta [*Mexico*]

vandal ['vændl] NOUN
el vándalo

vandalism ['vændəlɪzəm] NOUN
el vandalismo

to **vandalize** ['vændəlaɪz] VERB
destrozar*

vanilla [və'nɪlə] NOUN
la vainilla ◇ *a vanilla ice cream* un helado de vainilla

to **vanish** ['vænɪʃ] VERB
desaparecer*
◆ **to vanish into thin air** esfumarse

variable ['vɛriəbəl] ADJECTIVE
variable

varied ['vɛrid] ADJECTIVE
variado

variety [və'raɪəti] NOUN (PL **varieties**)
la variedad

various ['vɛriəs] ADJECTIVE
varios ◇ *We visited various villages in the area.* Visitamos varias aldeas de la zona.

to **vary** ['vɛri] VERB (**varied, varied**)
variar*

vase [veɪs] NOUN
el jarrón (PL los jarrones)

VCR [,viːsiː'ɑːr] NOUN (= *video cassette recorder*)
el video (*aparato*)

VDT [,viːdiː'ti] NOUN (= *visual display terminal*)
el monitor

veal [viːl] NOUN
la carne de ternera

vegan ['viːgən] NOUN
el vegetariano estricto
la vegetariana estricta

vegetable ['vɛdʒtəbəl] NOUN
[1] la verdura (*to be cooked*) ◇ *vegetable soup* sopa de verduras
[2] la hortaliza (*for salads*) ◇ *lettuces, cucumbers and other vegetables* lechugas, pepinos y otras hortalizas

vegetarian [vɛdʒɪ'tɛriən] NOUN
[*see also* **vegetarian** ADJECTIVE]
el vegetariano
la vegetariana
◇ *I'm a vegetarian.* Soy vegetariano.

vegetarian [vɛdʒɪ'tɛriən] ADJECTIVE
[*see also* **vegetarian** NOUN]
◆ **a vegetarian lasagne** una lasaña vegetariana

vehicle ['viːɪkəl] NOUN
vehículo

vein [veɪn] NOUN
la vena

velvet ['vɛlvɪt] NOUN
el terciopelo

vending machine ['vɛndɪŋməʃiːn] NOUN
la máquina expendedora

Venetian blind [vɪ'niːʃən'blaɪnd] NOUN
la persiana veneciana

verb [vɜːrb] NOUN
el verbo

verdict ['vɜːrdɪkt] NOUN
el veredicto

vertical ['vɜːrtɪkəl] ADJECTIVE
vertical

vertigo ['vɜːrtɪgou] NOUN
el vértigo ◇ *I get vertigo.* Tengo vértigo.

very ['vɛri] ADVERB
see also **very** ADJECTIVE
muy ◇ *very tall* muy alto
◆ **It's very cold.** Hace mucho frío.
◆ **not very interesting** no demasiado interesante
◆ **very much** muchísimo
◆ **We were thinking the very same thing.** Estábamos pensando exactamente lo mismo.

very ['vɛri] ADJECTIVE
see also **very** ADVERB
mismo ◇ *in this very house* en esta misma casa
◆ **That's the very book I was talking about.** Ese es justamente el libro del que hablaba.
◆ **The very idea!** ¡Cómo se te ocurre!

vest [vɛst] NOUN
el chaleco

vet [vɛt] NOUN
1 el veterinario
la veterinaria
2 el/la excombatiente (*informal: ex-serviceman/woman*)

veteran ['vɛtərən] NOUN
el/la excombatiente (*ex-serviceman/woman*)

Veterans' Day ['vɛtərənzˌdeɪ] NOUN

ℹ *Domingo el 11 de Noviembre en que se conmemora la firma del armisticio de 1918, y se recuerda a todos aquellos que murieron en las dos guerras mundiales.*

veterinarian [vɛtərə'nɛriən] NOUN
el veterinario
la veterinaria
◇ *She's a veterinarian.* Es veterinaria.

via ['vaɪə] PREPOSITION
1 por ◇ *We drove to Lisbon via Salamanca.* Fuimos a Lisboa por Salamanca.
2 vía ◇ *a flight via Chicago* un vuelo vía Chicago

vicar ['vɪkər] NOUN
el párroco

vice president [vaɪs'prɛzidɛnt] NOUN
el vicepresidente
la vicepresidenta

vice principal [vaɪs'prɪnsɪpəl] NOUN
el subdirector
la subdirectora
(*in school*)

vice versa ['vaɪsə'vɜːrsə] ADVERB
viceversa

vicious ['vɪʃəs] ADJECTIVE
1 brutal ◇ *a vicious attack* una brutal agresión
2 feroz ◇ *a vicious dog* un perro feroz
◆ **He was a vicious man.** Era un hombre despiadado.
◆ **a vicious circle** un círculo vicioso

victim ['vɪktɪm] NOUN
la víctima ◇ *He was the victim of a mugging.* Fue víctima de un atraco.

victory ['vɪktəri] NOUN (PL **victories**)
la victoria

video ['vɪdiou] NOUN (PL **videos**)
el video ◇ *to watch a video* ver* un video
◇ *It's out on video.* Salió en video.
◆ **a video call** una videollamada
◆ **a video camera** una videocámara
◆ **a video game** un videojuego
◆ **a video recorder** un video
◆ **a video store** un videoclub

videocassette ['vɪdioukə'sɛt] NOUN
la cinta de video

videophone NOUN
el videoteléfono

to **videotape** ['vɪdiouˌteɪp] VERB
grabar en video ◇ *They videotaped the whole wedding.* Grabaron en video toda la boda.

view [vjuː] NOUN
1 la vista ◇ *There's an amazing view.* La vista es magnífica.
2 la opinión (PL las opiniones) ◇ *in my view* en mi opinión

viewer ['vjuːər] NOUN
el telespectador
la telespectadora

viewpoint ['vjuːˌpɔɪnt] NOUN
el punto de vista

vile [vaɪl] ADJECTIVE
repugnante

villa ['vɪlə] NOUN
el chalet

village ['vɪlɪdʒ] NOUN
1 el pueblo (*large*)
2 la aldea (*small*)

villain ['vɪlən] NOUN
1 el/la maleante (*criminal*)
2 el malo
la mala
(*in movie*)

vine [vaɪn] NOUN
1 la vid (*trailing*)
2 la parra (*climbing*)

vinegar ['vɪnɪgər] NOUN
el vinagre
vineyard ['vɪnjərd] NOUN
el viñedo
viola [vi'oulə] NOUN
la viola
violence ['vaɪələns] NOUN
la violencia
violent ['vaɪələnt] ADJECTIVE
violento
violin [vaɪə'lɪn] NOUN
el violín (PL los violines)
violinist [vaɪə'lɪnɪst] NOUN
el/la violinista
virgin ['vɜːrdʒɪn] NOUN
la virgen (PL las vírgenes) ◇ *to be a virgin* ser* virgen
Virgo ['vɜːrgou] NOUN
el Virgo (*sign*) ◇ *I'm a Virgo.* Soy virgo.
◆ **a Virgo** un/una virgo
virtual reality ['vɜːrtʃuəlri'ælɪti] NOUN
la realidad virtual
virus ['vaɪrəs] NOUN (PL **viruses**)
el virus (PL los virus)
visa ['viːzə] NOUN
la visa
vise [vaɪs] NOUN
el tornillo de banco (*tool*)
visible ['vɪzəbəl] ADJECTIVE
visible
visit ['vɪzɪt] NOUN
see also **visit** VERB
la visita ◇ *my last visit to my grandmother* la última visita que le hice a mi abuela
◆ **I saw him on my latest visit to Ecuador.** Lo vi la última vez que estuve en Ecuador.
to **visit** ['vɪzɪt] VERB
see also **visit** NOUN
visitar
visitor ['vɪzɪtər] NOUN
1 el/la visitante (*tourist*)
2 la visita (*guest*) ◇ *to have a visitor* tener* visita
visual ['vɪʒuəl] ADJECTIVE
visual
to **visualize** ['vɪʒəlaɪz] VERB
imaginar
vital ['vaɪtl] ADJECTIVE
vital
vitamin ['vaɪtəmɪn] NOUN
la vitamina
vivid ['vɪvɪd] ADJECTIVE
vivo ◇ *vivid colors* colores vivos
◆ **to have a vivid imagination** tener* una imaginación desbordante
vocabulary [vou'kæbjulɛri] NOUN (PL **vocabularies**)
el vocabulario
vocational [vou'keɪʃənl] ADJECTIVE
◆ **a vocational course** un curso de formación profesional
vodka ['vɑːdkə] NOUN
el vodka
*Although **vodka** ends in **-a**, it is actually a masculine noun.*
voice [vɔɪs] NOUN
la voz (PL las voces)
voice mail ['vɔɪs,meɪl] NOUN
el buzón de voz
volcano [vɑːl'keɪnou] NOUN (PL **volcanoes**)
el volcán (PL los volcanes)
volleyball ['vɑːli,bɑːl] NOUN
el vóleibol
el volibol *Mexico*
volt [voult] NOUN
el voltio
voltage ['voultɪdʒ] NOUN
el voltaje
voluntary ['vɑːlәntɛri] ADJECTIVE
voluntario ◇ *to do voluntary work* hacer* trabajo voluntario
volunteer [vɑːlən'tɪər] NOUN
see also **volunteer** VERB
el voluntario
la voluntaria
to **volunteer** [vɑːlən'tɪər] VERB
see also **volunteer** NOUN
◆ **to volunteer to do something** ofrecerse* a hacer algo
to **vomit** ['vɑːmɪt] VERB
vomitar
to **vote** [vout] VERB
see also **vote** NOUN
votar ◇ *Who did you vote for?* ¿Por quién votaste?
vote [vout] NOUN
see also **vote** VERB
el voto
voucher ['vautʃər] NOUN
el vale ◇ *a gift voucher* un vale de regalo
vowel ['vauəl] NOUN
la vocal
vulgar ['vʌlgər] ADJECTIVE
vulgar

W

wafer ['weɪfər] NOUN
el barquillo

wage [weɪdʒ] NOUN
el sueldo ◇ *He collected his wages.* Cobró el sueldo.

waist [weɪst] NOUN
la cintura

to **wait** [weɪt] VERB
esperar ◇ *I'll wait for you.* Te esperaré. ◇ *Wait a minute!* ¡Espera un momento! ◇ *I'm waiting for the train.* Estoy esperando el tren.
- **to keep somebody waiting** hacer* esperar a alguien ◇ *They kept us waiting for hours.* Nos hicieron esperar durante horas.
- **I can't wait to go on vacation.** Me muero de ganas de que lleguen las vacaciones. ◇ *I can't wait to see him again.* Me muero de ganas de verlo otra vez.

to **wait up** [weɪt'ʌp] VERB
esperar levantado ◇ *My mom always waits up till I get in.* Mi mamá siempre espera levantada hasta que llego.

waiter ['weɪtər] NOUN
el mesero

waiting list ['weɪtɪŋˌlɪst] NOUN
la lista de espera

waiting room ['weɪtɪŋˌruːm] NOUN
la sala de espera

waitress ['weɪtrɪs] NOUN (PL **waitresses**)
la mesera

to **wake up** [weɪk'ʌp] VERB (**woke up, woken up**)
despertarse* ◇ *I woke up at six o'clock.* Me desperté a las seis.
- **to wake somebody up** despertar* a alguien ◇ *Please would you wake me up at seven o'clock?* ¿Podría despertarme a las siete, por favor?

to **walk** [wɑːk] VERB
see also **walk** NOUN
1 caminar ◇ *Don't walk so fast!* ¡No camines tan rápido! ◇ *We walked two miles.* Caminamos dos millas.
2 ir* a pie (*go on foot*) ◇ *Are you walking or going by bus?* ¿Vas a ir a pie o en autobús?
3 pasear (*for fun*) ◇ *I like walking through the park.* Me gusta pasear por el parque.
- **to walk the dog** pasear al perro

walk [wɑːk] NOUN
see also **walk** VERB
el paseo
- **to go for a walk** ir* a pasear
- **It's a ten minute walk from here.** Está a 10 minutos de aquí a pie.

walker [wɑːkər] NOUN
el andador ortopédico

walkie-talkie ['wɑːki'tɑːki] NOUN
el walkie-talkie

walking ['wɑːkɪŋ] NOUN
el senderismo ◇ *I did some walking in the mountains last summer.* El verano pasado hice senderismo por las montañas. ◇ *Walking is good for your health.* Caminar es bueno para la salud.

walking stick ['wɑːkɪŋˌstɪk] NOUN
el bastón (PL los bastones)

Walkman® ['wɑːkmən] NOUN (PL **Walkmans**)
el walkman®

wall [wɑːl] NOUN
1 la pared (*of room, building*)
2 el muro
la barda Mexico
(*freestanding*)
3 la muralla (*of castle, city*)
- **Wall Street** Wall Street

wallet ['wɑːlɪt] NOUN
la cartera

wallpaper ['wɑːlˌpeɪpər] NOUN
el papel pintado
el papel tapiz Mexico

wall socket ['wɑːlˌsɑːkɪt] NOUN
el tomacorriente

walnut ['wɑːlnʌt] NOUN
la nuez (PL las nueces)
la nuez de Castilla (PL las nueces de Castilla) Mexico

to **wander around** ['wɑːndərə'raund] VERB
pasear ◇ *I just wandered around for a while.* Estuve paseando un poco.

to **want** [wɑːnt] VERB
querer* ◇ *Do you want some cake?* ¿Quieres un poco de pastel?
- **to want to do something** querer hacer algo ◇ *What do you want to do tomorrow?* ¿Qué quieres hacer mañana?
- **to want somebody to do something** querer que alguien haga algo ◇ *They want us to wait here.* Quieren que esperemos aquí.

***querer que** has to be followed by a verb in the subjunctive.*

war [wɔːr] NOUN
la guerra
- **to be at war** estar* en guerra

ward [wɔːrd] NOUN
la sala (*de un hospital*)

warden ['wɔːrdn] NOUN
el director
la directora
(*governor*)

wardrobe ['wɔːrdroub] NOUN
el vestuario

warehouse ['wɛrˌhaus] NOUN
el almacén (PL los almacenes)
la bodega Mexico

warm [wɔːrm] ADJECTIVE
1 caliente ◇ *warm water* agua caliente
2 caluroso ◇ *a warm day* un día caluroso ◇ *a warm welcome* una calurosa bienvenida ☞

- **warm clothing** ropa de abrigo
- **This sweater is very warm.** Este jersey es muy calentito.
- **He's a very warm person.** Es una persona muy afectuosa.
- **It's warm in here.** Aquí dentro hace calor.
- **I'm too warm.** Tengo demasiado calor.

to **warm up** [wɔːrm'ʌp] VERB
1 hacer* ejercicios de calentamiento (*for sport*)
2 calentar* (*food*)

to **warn** [wɔːrn] VERB
advertir* ◇ *Well, I warned you!* ¡Ya te lo había advertido!
- **to warn somebody to do something** aconsejar a alguien que haga algo

*Use the subjunctive after **aconsejar a alguien que**.*

warning ['wɔːrnɪŋ] NOUN
la advertencia

wart [wɔːrt] NOUN
la verruga

was [wʌz] VERB *see* **be**

wash [wɑːʃ] NOUN
see also **wash** VERB
- **to have a wash** lavarse
- **to give something a wash** lavar algo
- **The car needs a wash.** Al carro le hace falta un lavado.

to **wash** [wɑːʃ] VERB
see also **wash** NOUN
1 lavar ◇ *to wash the car* lavar el carro ◇ *to wash the dishes* lavar los platos
2 lavarse (*have a wash*) ◇ *Every morning I get up, wash and get dressed.* Todas las mañanas me levanto, me lavo y me visto.
- **to wash one's hands** lavarse las manos

washbowl ['wɑːʃ,boul] NOUN
el lavabo

washcloth ['wɑːʃ,klɑːθ] NOUN
la toallita para lavarse

washing ['wɑːʃɪŋ] NOUN
la ropa lavada (*clean laundry*)
- **to do the washing** lavar la ropa
- **Do you have any washing?** ¿Tienes ropa para lavar?

washing detergent ['wɑːʃɪŋdɪ'tɜːrdʒənt] NOUN
el detergente

washing machine ['wɑːʃɪŋməʃiːn] NOUN
la lavadora

washroom ['wɑːʃ,ruːm] NOUN
el baño

wasn't ['wʌzənt] = **was not**

wasp [wɑːsp] NOUN
la avispa

waste [weɪst] NOUN
see also **waste** VERB
1 el desperdicio ◇ *It's such a waste!* ¡Qué desperdicio!
- **It's a waste of time.** Es una pérdida de tiempo.

2 los residuos PL ◇ *nuclear waste* residuos radioactivos

to **waste** [weɪst] VERB
see also **waste** NOUN
desperdiciar (*food, space, opportunity*)
- **to waste time** perder* el tiempo ◇ *There's no time to waste.* No hay tiempo que perder.
- **I don't like wasting money.** No me gusta malgastar el dinero.

wastepaper basket ['weɪstpeɪpər'bæskɪt] NOUN
la papelera

watch [wɑːtʃ] NOUN (PL **watches**)
see also **watch** VERB
el reloj

to **watch** [wɑːtʃ] VERB
see also **watch** NOUN
1 mirar ◇ *Watch your step!* ¡Mira por dónde caminas!
- **Watch me!** ¡Mírame!

2 ver* ◇ *to watch TV* ver la tele
3 vigilar ◇ *The police were watching the house.* La policía vigilaba la casa.

to **watch out** [wɑːtʃ'aut] VERB
tener* cuidado
- **Watch out!** ¡Cuidado!

water ['wɑːtər] NOUN
see also **water** VERB
el agua FEM

*Although it's a feminine noun, remember that you use **el** with **agua**.*

to **water** ['wɑːtər] VERB
see also **water** NOUN
regar* ◇ *He was watering his tulips.* Estaba regando los tulipanes.

waterfall ['wɑːtər,fɑːl] NOUN
la cascada

watering can ['wɑːtərɪŋ,kæn] NOUN
la regadera

watermelon ['wɑːtər,mɛlən] NOUN
la sandía

waterproof ['wɑːtər,pruːf] ADJECTIVE
impermeable
- **a waterproof watch** un reloj sumergible

water-skiing ['wɑːtər,skiːɪŋ] NOUN
el esquí acuático ◇ *to go water-skiing* hacer* esquí acuático

wave [weɪv] NOUN
see also **wave** VERB
la ola

to **wave** [weɪv] VERB
see also **wave** NOUN
- **to wave to somebody (1)** (*say hello*) saludar a alguien con la mano
- **to wave to somebody (2)** (*say goodbye*) hacer* adiós con la mano

wavy ['weɪvi] ADJECTIVE
ondulado ◇ *He has wavy hair.* Tiene el pelo

ondulado.

wax [wæks] NOUN
la cera

way [weɪ] NOUN
1 la manera ◇ *She looked at me in a strange way.* Me miró de manera extraña.
◆ **This book tells you the right way to do it.** Este libro explica cómo hay que hacerlo.
◆ **You're doing it the wrong way.** Lo estás haciendo mal.
◆ **in a way...** en cierto sentido...
◆ **a way of life** un estilo de vida
2 el camino (*route*) ◇ *I don't know the way.* No sé el camino. ◇ *We stopped for lunch on the way.* Paramos a comer en el camino.
◆ **Which way is it?** ¿Por dónde es?
◆ **The supermarket is this way.** El supermercado es por aquí.
◆ **Do you know the way to the hotel?** ¿Sabes cómo llegar al hotel?
◆ **He's on his way.** Está en camino.
◆ **It's a long way.** Está lejos. ◇ *It's a long way from the hotel.* Está lejos del hotel.
◆ **"way in"** "entrada"
◆ **"way out"** "salida"
◆ **by the way...** a propósito...

we [wiː] PRONOUN
nosotros (FEM nosotras)
we generally isn't translated unless it is emphatic.
◇ *We were in a hurry.* Teníamos prisa.
*Use **nosotros** or **nosotras** as appropriate for emphasis.*
◇ *They went but we didn't.* Ellos fueron pero nosotros no.

weak [wiːk] ADJECTIVE
1 débil (*person, government*)
2 poco cargado (*tea, coffee*)

wealthy [ˈwɛlθi] ADJECTIVE
rico

weapon [ˈwɛpən] NOUN
el arma FEM
*Although it's a feminine noun, remember that you use **el** and **un** with **arma**.*

to **wear** [wɛər] VERB (**wore, worn**)
llevar ◇ *She was wearing a hat.* Llevaba un sombrero.
◆ **She was wearing black.** Iba vestida de negro.

weather [ˈwɛðər] NOUN
el tiempo ◇ *What's the weather like?* ¿Qué tiempo hace?

weather forecast [ˈwɛðərˌfɔːrkæst] NOUN
el pronóstico del tiempo

Web [wɛb] NOUN
◆ **the Web** la Web

web browser [ˈwɛbˌbrauzər] NOUN
el navegador de Internet

webmaster [ˈwɛbˌmæstər] NOUN
el administrador de la Web
la administradora de la Web

web page [ˈwɛbˌpeɪdʒ] NOUN
la página web

website [ˈwɛbˌsaɪt] NOUN
el sitio web

webzine [ˈwɛbziːn] NOUN
la revista electrónica

we'd [wiːd] = **we had, we would**

wedding [wɛdɪŋ] NOUN
la boda
◆ **wedding dress** el vestido de novia
◆ **wedding anniversary** el aniversario de boda

Wednesday [ˈwɛnzdi] NOUN
el miércoles (PL los miércoles) ◇ *I saw her on Wednesday.* La vi el miércoles. ◇ *every Wednesday* todos los miércoles ◇ *last Wednesday* el miércoles pasado ◇ *next Wednesday* el miércoles que viene ◇ *on Wednesdays* los miércoles

weed [wiːd] NOUN
la maleza ◇ *The garden is full of weeds.* El jardín está lleno de malezas.

week [wiːk] NOUN
la semana ◇ *in a week's time* dentro de una semana
◆ **a week from Friday** el viernes de la semana que viene
◆ **during the week** durante la semana

weekday [ˈwiːkdeɪ] NOUN
el día entre semana
*Although **día** ends in **-a**, it is actually a masculine noun.*
◆ **On weekdays, I go to the gym.** Los días entre semana, voy al gimnasio.

weekend [ˈwiːkɛnd] NOUN
el fin de semana (FEM los fines de semana)
◆ **next weekend** el próximo fin de semana
◆ **What are you doing on the weekend?** ¿Qué haces este fin de semana?

to **weep** [wiːp] VERB (**wept, wept**)
llorar

to **weigh** [weɪ] VERB
pesar ◇ *How much do you weigh?* ¿Cuánto pesas?
◆ **to weigh oneself** pesarse

weight [weɪt] NOUN
el peso
◆ **to lose weight** adelgazar*
◆ **to put on weight** engordar

weightlifter [ˈweɪtˌlɪftər] NOUN
el levantador de pesas
la levantadora de pesas

weightlifting [ˈweɪtˌlɪftɪŋ] NOUN
el levantamiento de pesas

weird [wɪərd] ADJECTIVE
raro

welcome [ˈwɛlkəm] NOUN
see also **welcome** VERB
la bienvenida ◇ *They gave her a warm welcome.* Le dieron una calurosa bienvenida.
◆ **Welcome!** ¡Bienvenido!

☞

*If you're addressing a woman remember to use the feminine form: **¡Bienvenida!** If you're addressing more than one person use the plural form **¡Bienvenidos!** or **¡Bienvenidas!**.*

◆ **Thank you! – You're welcome!** ¡Gracias! – ¡No hay de qué!

> ℹ *Si le dices* **You're welcome** *a alguien que te ha dado las gracias, estás reconociendo sus agracedimientos de una manera amable.*

to **welcome** ['wɛlkəm] VERB
see also **welcome** NOUN
◆ **to welcome somebody** dar* la bienvenida a alguien
◆ **Thank you! – You're welcome!** ¡Gracias! – ¡De nada!

welfare ['welfeər] NOUN
el subsidio de desempleo
◆ **He's on the welfare.** Está desempleado.
◆ **to go on the welfare** quedarse sin empleo

well [wɛl] ADJECTIVE, ADVERB
see also **well** NOUN
1 bien ◇ *You did that really well.* Lo hiciste realmente bien.
◆ **She's doing really well at school.** Le va muy bien en el colegio.
◆ **to be well** estar* bien ◇ *I'm not very well at the moment.* No estoy muy bien en este momento.
◆ **Get well soon!** ¡Que te mejores!
◆ **Well done!** ¡Muy bien!
2 bueno ◇ *It's enormous! Well, quite big anyway.* ¡Es enorme! Bueno, digamos que bastante grande.
◆ **as well** también ◇ *We worked hard, but we had some fun as well.* Trabajamos mucho, pero también nos divertimos.
◆ **as well as** además de ◇ *We went to Boston as well as San Francisco.* Fuimos a Boston, además de San Francisco.

well [wɛl] NOUN
see also **well** ADJECTIVE, ADVERB
el pozo

we'll [wi:l] = **we will**

well-behaved ['wɛlbɪ'heɪvd] ADJECTIVE
◆ **to be well-behaved** portarse bien

well-dressed ['wɛl'drɛst] ADJECTIVE
bien vestido

well-known ['wɛl'noun] ADJECTIVE
conocido ◇ *a well-known movie star* un conocido actor de cine

well-off ['wɛl'ɑ:f] ADJECTIVE
adinerado

went [wɛnt] VERB *see* **go**

were [wɜ:r] VERB *see* **be**

we're [wɪər] = **we are**

weren't [wɜ:rənt] = **were not**

west [wɛst] NOUN
see also **west** ADJECTIVE, ADVERB
el oeste

west [wɛst] ADJECTIVE, ADVERB
see also **west** NOUN
1 occidental ◇ *the west coast* la costa occidental
◆ **west of** al oeste de ◇ *Colorado is west of Kansas.* Colorado está al oeste de Kansas.
2 hacia el oeste ◇ *We were traveling west.* Viajábamos hacia el oeste.

western ['wɛstərn] NOUN
see also **western** ADJECTIVE
el western

western ['wɛstərn] ADJECTIVE
see also **western** NOUN
occidental ◇ *the western part of the island* la parte occidental de la isla
◆ **Western Europe** Europa Occidental

West Indian ['wɛst'ɪndiən] ADJECTIVE
see also **West Indian** NOUN
antillano
◆ **She's West Indian.** Es antillana.

West Indian ['wɛst'ɪndiən] NOUN
see also **West Indian** ADJECTIVE
el antillano
la antillana

West Indies ['wɛst'ɪndiz] PL NOUN
◆ **the West Indies** las Antillas

wet [wɛt] ADJECTIVE
mojado ◇ *wet clothes* ropa mojada
◆ **to get wet** mojarse
◆ **dripping wet** chorreando
◆ **wet weather** el tiempo lluvioso
◆ **It was wet all week.** Llovió toda la semana.

wetsuit ['wɛtsu:t] NOUN
el traje de buzo

we've [wi:v] = **we have**

whale [weɪl] NOUN
la ballena

what [wɑ:t] ADJECTIVE, PRONOUN
1 qué
*Use **qué** (with an accent) in direct and indirect questions and exclamations.*
◇ *What subjects are you studying?* ¿Qué asignaturas estudias? ◇ *What color is it?* ¿De qué color es? ◇ *What's the matter?* ¿Qué te pasa? ◇ *What's it for?* ¿Para qué es? ◇ *I don't know what to do.* No sé qué hacer. ◇ *What a mess!* ¡Qué desorden!
*Only translate **what is** by **qué es** if asking for a definition or explanation.*
◇ *What is it?* ¿Qué es? ◇ *What's a tractor, Daddy?* ¿Qué es un tractor, papá? ◇ *I asked him what DNA was.* Le pregunté qué era el ADN.
2 cuál (FEM cuál, PL cuáles)
*Translate **what is** by **cuál es** when not asking for a definition or explanation.*
◇ *What's the capital of Uruguay?* ¿Cuál es la capital de Uruguay? ◇ *What's her telephone number?* ¿Cuál es su número de teléfono?

* Verbs marked with this symbol are irregular. See pages 346–348 for further details.

3 lo que
*Use **lo que** (no accent) when **what** isn't a question word.*
◇ *I saw what happened.* Vi lo que pasó. ◇ *I heard what he said.* Oí lo que dijo.
◆ **What? (1)** ¿Cómo? (*What did you say?*)
◆ **What? (2)** ¿Qué? (*shocked*)
◆ **What's your name?** ¿Cómo te llamas?

wheat [wi:t] NOUN
el trigo

wheel [wi:l] NOUN
la rueda
◆ **steering wheel** el volante

wheelchair ['wi:lˌtʃɛr] NOUN
la silla de ruedas

when [wɛn] ADVERB
see also **when** CONJUNCTION
cuándo
*Remember the accent on **cuándo** in direct and indirect questions.*
◇ *When did he go?* ¿Cuándo se fue? ◇ *I asked her when the next train was.* Le pregunté cuándo salía el próximo tren.

when [wɛn] CONJUNCTION
see also **when** ADVERB
cuando ◇ *She was reading when I came in.* Cuando entré ella estaba leyendo.
***cuando** has to be followed by a verb in the subjunctive when referring to an event in the future.*
◇ *Call me when you get there.* Llámame cuando llegues.

where [wɛər] ADVERB
see also **where** CONJUNCTION
dónde
*Remember the accent on **dónde** in direct and indirect questions.*
◇ *Where do you live?* ¿Dónde vives?
◇ *Where are you from?* ¿De dónde eres?
◇ *She asked me where I had bought it.* Me preguntó dónde lo había comprado.
◆ **Where are you going?** ¿Adónde vas?

where [wɛər] CONJUNCTION
see also **where** ADVERB
donde ◇ *a store where you can buy clothes* una tienda donde se puede comprar ropa

whether ['wɛðər] CONJUNCTION
si ◇ *I don't know whether to go or not.* No sé si ir o no.

which [wɪtʃ] ADJECTIVE, PRONOUN
1 cuál (FEM cuál, PL cuáles)
*Remember the accent on **cuál** and **cuáles** in direct and indirect questions.*
◇ *I know his sister. – Which one?* Conozco a su hermana. – ¿A cuál? ◇ *Which would you like?* ¿Cuál quieres? ◇ *Of the five pairs, which were sold?* De los cinco pares, ¿cuáles se vendieron?
2 qué
*Use **qué** (with an accent) before nouns.*
◇ *Which flavor do you want?* ¿Qué sabor quieres?
3 que ◇ *It's an illness which causes nerve damage.* Es una enfermedad que daña los nervios. ◇ *This is the skirt which Daphne gave me.* Ésta es la falda que me dio Daphne. ◇ *Our uniform, which is green, is quite nice.* Nuestro uniforme, que es verde, es bastante bonito.
*After a preposition **que** becomes **el que, la que, los que, las que** to agree with the noun.*
◇ *That's the movie which I was telling you about.* Ésa es la película de la que te hablaba.
4 lo cual ◇ *The stove isn't working, which is a nuisance.* La cocina no funciona, lo cual es un fastidio.

while [waɪl] CONJUNCTION
see also **while** NOUN
1 mientras ◇ *You hold the flashlight while I look inside.* Aguanta la linterna mientras yo miro por dentro.
2 mientras que ◇ *Isobel is very dynamic, while Kay is more laid-back.* Isobel es muy dinámica, mientras que Kay es más tranquila.

while [waɪl] NOUN
see also **while** CONJUNCTION
◆ **a while** un rato ◇ *after a while* después de un rato
◆ **a while ago** hace un momento ◇ *He was here a while ago.* Hace un momento estaba aquí.
◆ **for a while** durante un tiempo ◇ *I lived in Phoenix for a while.* Viví en Phoenix durante un tiempo.
◆ **quite a while** mucho tiempo ◇ *I haven't seen him for quite a while.* Hace mucho tiempo que no lo veo.

whip [wɪp] NOUN
see also **whip** VERB
la fusta (*for horse*)

to **whip** [wɪp] VERB
see also **whip** NOUN
1 fustigar* (*animal*)
2 azotar (*person*)
3 batir (*eggs, cream*)

whipped cream ['wɪptˌkri:m] NOUN
la crema batida

whisk [wɪsk] NOUN
el batidor

whiskers ['wɪskərz] PL NOUN
1 los bigotes (*of animal*)
2 la barba (*of man*)

whiskey ['wɪski] NOUN
el whisky (PL los whiskys)

to **whisper** ['wɪspər] VERB
susurrar

whistle ['wɪsəl] NOUN
see also **whistle** VERB
el silbato ◇ *The referee blew his whistle.* El árbitro tocó el silbato.

to **whistle** ['wɪsəl] VERB
see also **whistle** NOUN
1 pitar (*with a whistle*)

W

☞

2 silbar (*with mouth*)

white [waɪt] ADJECTIVE

blanco ◇ *He has white hair.* Tiene el cabello blanco.

◆ **white wine** el vino blanco

◆ **white bread** el pan blanco

◆ **a white man** un hombre blanco

◆ **white people** los blancos

White House ['waɪt,haus] NOUN

la Casa Blanca

who [hu:] PRONOUN

see also **whom**

1 quién (PL quiénes)

*Remember the accent on **quién** and **quiénes** in direct and indirect questions.*

◇ *Who said that?* ¿Quién dijo eso? ◇ *Who is it?* ¿Quién es? ◇ *We don't know who broke the window.* No sabemos quién rompió la ventana.

2 que ◇ *the people who know us* las personas que nos conocen

*After a preposition **que** becomes **el que, la que, los que, las que** to agree with the noun.*

◇ *the women who she was chatting with* las mujeres con las que estaba hablando

*Note that **a + el que** becomes **al que**.*

◇ *the boy who I gave it to* el chico al que se lo di

whole [houl] ADJECTIVE

see also **whole** NOUN

entero ◇ *the whole class* la clase entera ◇ *two whole days* dos días enteros

◆ **the whole afternoon** toda la tarde

◆ **the whole world** todo el mundo

whole [houl] NOUN

see also **whole** ADJECTIVE

◆ **The whole of the country was affected.** Todo el país se vio afectado.

◆ **on the whole** en general

whole wheat [houl'wi:t] ADJECTIVE

integral

whom [hu:m] PRONOUN

see also **who**

1 quién (PL quiénes)

*Remember the accent on **quién** and **quiénes** in direct and indirect questions.*

◇ *With whom did you go?* ¿Con quién fuiste? ◇ *Whom did you call?* ¿A quién llamaste?

2 quien ◇ *the man whom I saw* el hombre a quien vi ◇ *the woman to whom I spoke* la mujer con quien hablé

whose [hu:z] ADJECTIVE

see also **whose** PRONOUN

1 de quién (PL de quiénes) (*in questions*)

*Remember the accent on **quién** and **quiénes** in direct and indirect questions.*

◇ *Whose books are these?* ¿De quiénes son estos libros? ◇ *Do you know whose jacket this is?* ¿Sabes de quién es esta chaqueta?

2 cuyo (*relative*) ◇ *the girl whose picture was in the paper* la muchacha cuya foto venía en el periódico ◇ *a neighbor whose sons go to that school* un vecino cuyos hijos van a ese colegio

whose [hu:z] PRONOUN

see also **whose** ADJECTIVE

de quién (PL de quiénes)

*Remember the accent on **quién** and **quiénes** in direct and indirect questions.*

◇ *Whose is this?* ¿De quién es esto? ◇ *I know whose they are.* Yo sé de quiénes son.

why [waɪ] ADVERB

por qué

*Remember to write **por qué** as two words with an accent on **qué** when translating **why**.*

◇ *Why did you do that?* ¿Por qué hiciste eso?

◆ **Why not?** ¿Por qué no?

◆ **That's why he did it.** Por eso lo hizo.

wicked ['wɪkɪd] ADJECTIVE

1 malvado (*evil*)

2 sensacional (*really great*)

wide [waɪd] ADJECTIVE, ADVERB

ancho ◇ *a wide road* una carretera ancha ◇ *How wide is the room? – It's five feet wide.* ¿Cuánto tiene de ancho la habitación? – Tiene cinco pies de ancho.

◆ **wide open** abierto de par en par ◇ *The door was wide open.* La puerta estaba abierta de par en par.

◆ **wide awake** completamente despierto

widow ['wɪdou] NOUN

la viuda ◇ *She's a widow.* Es viuda.

widower ['wɪdouər] NOUN

el viudo ◇ *He's a widower.* Es viudo.

width [wɪdθ] NOUN

la anchura

wife [waɪf] NOUN (PL **wives**)

la esposa

wig [wɪg] NOUN

la peluca

wild [waɪld] ADJECTIVE

1 salvaje ◇ *a wild animal* un animal salvaje

2 silvestre ◇ *wild flowers* flores silvestres

3 loco ◇ *She's a bit wild.* Es un poco loca.

wildlife ['waɪld,laɪf] NOUN

la flora y fauna

will [wɪl] NOUN

see also **will** VERB

el testamento (*document*)

will [wɪl] VERB

see also **will** NOUN

***will** can often be translated by the present tense, as in the following examples.*

◇ *Come on, I'll help you.* Vamos, te ayudo. ◇ *We'll talk about it later.* Hablamos luego. ◇ *Will you help me?* ¿Me ayudas?

*Use **voy a, va a**, etc + the infinitive to talk about plans and intentions.*

◇ *What will you do?* ¿Qué vas a hacer? ◇ *We'll be having lunch late.* Vamos a comer tarde.

Use the future tense when guessing what will happen or when making a supposition.

◇ *It won't take long.* No llevará mucho tiempo. ◇ *We'll probably go out later.* Seguramente saldremos luego. ◇ *I'll always love you.* Te querré siempre. ◇ *That will be the mailman.* Será el cartero.

*Use **querer** for "to be willing" in emphatic requests, and invitations.*

◇ *Tom won't help me.* Tom no me quiere ayudar. ◇ *Will you be quiet!* ¿Te quieres callar? ◇ *Will you have some tea?* ¿Quieres tomar un té?

willing [ˈwɪlɪŋ] ADJECTIVE
◆ **to be willing to do something** estar* dispuesto a hacer algo

to **win** [wɪn] VERB (**won, won**)
see also **win** NOUN
ganar ◇ *Did you win?* ¿Ganaste? ◇ *to win a prize* ganar un premio

win [wɪn] NOUN
see also **win** VERB
la victoria

to **wind** [waɪnd] VERB (**wound, wound**)
see also **wind** NOUN
enrollar (*rope, wire*)

wind [wɪnd] NOUN
see also **wind** VERB
el viento
◆ **a wind instrument** un instrumento de viento
◆ **wind power** la energía eólica

windmill [ˈwɪndmɪl] NOUN
el molino de viento

window [ˈwɪndoʊ] NOUN
1 la ventana (*of building*)
◆ **a store window** una vitrina, *Mexico*: un aparador
2 la ventanilla (*in car, train*)
3 el vidrio (*window pane*) ◇ *to break a window* romper* un vidrio

windshield [ˈwɪndʃiːld] NOUN
el parabrisas (PL los parabrisas)

windshield wiper [ˈwɪndʃiːldˈwaɪpər] NOUN
el limpiaparabrisas (PL los limpiaparabrisas)
el limpiador *Mexico*

windy [ˈwɪndi] ADJECTIVE
◆ **a windy day** un día de viento
◆ **Chicago is a very windy city.** En Chicago hace mucho viento.
◆ **It's windy.** Hace viento.

wine [waɪn] NOUN
el vino ◇ *white wine* el vino blanco ◇ *red wine* el vino tinto
◆ **a wine bar** un bar especializado en vinos
◆ **a wine glass** una copa de vino
◆ **the wine list** la carta de vinos

wing [wɪŋ] NOUN
el ala FEM

*Although it's a feminine noun, remember that you use **el** and **un** with **ala**.*

to **wink** [wɪŋk] VERB
◆ **to wink at somebody** guiñar el ojo a alguien

winner [ˈwɪnər] NOUN
el ganador
la ganadora

winning [ˈwɪnɪŋ] ADJECTIVE
vencedor (FEM vencedora) ◇ *the winning team* el equipo vencedor
◆ **the winning goal** el gol de la victoria

winter [ˈwɪntər] NOUN
el invierno

winter sports [ˈwɪntərˈspɔːrts] PL NOUN
los deportes de invierno

to **wipe** [waɪp] VERB
limpiar
◆ **to wipe one's feet** limpiarse los pies (*en el felpudo*)
◆ **to wipe one's nose** limpiarse la nariz
◆ **Did you wipe up that water you spilled?** ¿Recogiste el agua que derramaste?

wire [ˈwaɪər] NOUN
1 el alambre
◆ **copper wire** el hilo de cobre
2 el cable
◆ **the telephone wire** el cable del teléfono

wisdom tooth [ˈwɪzdəmˌtuːθ] NOUN (PL **wisdom teeth**)
la muela del juicio

wise [waɪz] ADJECTIVE
sabio

to **wish** [wɪʃ] VERB
see also **wish** NOUN
◆ **to wish for something** desear algo ◇ *What more could you wish for?* ¿Qué más podrías desear?
◆ **to wish to do something** desear hacer algo ◇ *I wish to make a complaint.* Deseo hacer una reclamación.
◆ **I wish you were here!** ¡Ojalá estuvieras aquí!
◆ **I wish you'd told me!** ¡Me lo podrías haber dicho!
◆ **to wish somebody happy birthday** desear a alguien un feliz cumpleaños

wish [wɪʃ] NOUN (PL **wishes**)
see also **wish** VERB
el deseo ◇ *to make a wish* pedir* un deseo
◆ **"best wishes"** (*on birthday card*) "felicidades"
◆ **"with best wishes, Kathy"** "un abrazo, Kathy"

wit [wɪt] NOUN
el ingenio

with [wɪð,wɪθ] PREPOSITION
1 con ◇ *He walks with a cane.* Camina con un bastón. ◇ *Come with me.* Ven conmigo.
2 de ◇ *a woman with blue eyes* una mujer de ojos azules ◇ *green with envy* muerto de envidia ◇ *to shake with fear* temblar* de miedo ◇ *Fill the jug with water.* Llena la jarra de agua.
◆ **We stayed with friends.** Nos quedamos en la casa de unos amigos.

within [wɪð'ɪn] PREPOSITION
dentro de ◇ *I want it back within three days.* Quiero que me lo devuelvas dentro de tres días.
◆ **The police arrived within minutes.** La policía llegó a los pocos minutos.
◆ **The stores are within easy reach.** Las tiendas están cerca.

without [wɪð'aut] PREPOSITION
sin ◇ *without a coat* sin abrigo ◇ *without speaking* sin hablar

witness ['wɪtnɪs] NOUN (PL **witnesses**)
el/la testigo ◇ *There were no witnesses.* No había testigos.

witty ['wɪti] ADJECTIVE
ingenioso

wives [waɪvz] PL NOUN *see* **wife**

woken up ['woukən'ʌp] VERB *see* **wake up**

woke up [wouk'ʌp] VERB *see* **wake up**

wolf [wulf] NOUN (PL **wolves**)
el lobo

woman ['wumən] NOUN (PL **women**)
la mujer ◇ *a woman doctor* una doctora

women's room ['wɪmənz,ru:m] NOUN
el baño de señoras

won [wʌn] VERB *see* **win**

to **wonder** ['wʌndər] VERB
preguntarse ◇ *I wonder why she said that.* Me pregunto por qué dijo eso.
◆ **I wonder where Caroline is.** ¿Dónde estará Caroline?
◆ **No wonder!** ¡Con razón!

wonderful ['wʌndərful] ADJECTIVE
maravilloso

won't [wount] = **will not**

wood [wud] NOUN
1 la madera ◇ *It's made of wood.* Es de madera.
2 la leña (*for fire*)
3 el bosque ◇ *We went for a walk in the woods.* Fuimos a pasear por el bosque.

wooden ['wudn] ADJECTIVE
de madera ◇ *a wooden chair* una silla de madera

woodwork ['wudwɜ:rk] NOUN
la carpintería

wool [wul] NOUN
la lana ◇ *It's made of wool.* Es de lana.

word [wɜ:rd] NOUN
la palabra
◆ **What's the word for "ship" in Spanish?** ¿Cómo se dice "ship" en español?
◆ **in other words** en otras palabras
◆ **to have a word with somebody** hablar con alguien ◇ *Can I have a word with you?* ¿Puedo hablar contigo?
◆ **the words** la letra (*lyrics*)

word processing ['wɜ:rd'prɑ:sɛsɪŋ] NOUN
el procesamiento de textos

word processor ['wɜ:rd'prɑ:sɛsər] NOUN
el procesador de textos

wore [wɔ:r] VERB *see* **wear**

work [wɜ:rk] NOUN
see also **work** VERB
el trabajo ◇ *She's looking for work.* Está buscando trabajo.
◆ **It's hard work.** Es duro.
◆ **at work** en el trabajo ◇ *He's at work until five o'clock.* Está en el trabajo hasta las cinco.
◆ **He's off work today.** Hoy tiene el día libre.
◆ **to be out of work** estar* sin trabajo

to **work** [wɜ:rk] VERB
see also **work** NOUN
1 trabajar ◇ *She works in a store.* Trabaja en una tienda. ◇ *to work hard* trabajar mucho
2 funcionar ◇ *The heating isn't working.* La calefacción no funciona. ◇ *My plan worked perfectly.* Mi plan funcionó a la perfección.

to **work out** [wɜ:rk'aut] VERB
1 hacer* ejercicio (*exercise*) ◇ *I work out twice a week.* Hago ejercicio dos veces a la semana.
2 salir* (*turn out*) ◇ *I hope it will work out well.* Espero que salga bien.
3 calcular (*calculate*) ◇ *I worked it out in my head.* Lo calculé en mi cabeza.
4 entender* (*understand*) ◇ *I just couldn't work it out.* No lograba entenderlo.
◆ **It works out at $10 each.** Sale a 10 dólares por persona.

worker ['wɜ:rkər] NOUN
el trabajador
la trabajadora
◆ **She's a good worker.** Trabaja bien.

work experience ['wɜ:rkɪk'spɪriəns] NOUN
◆ **I'm going to get some work experience in a factory.** Voy a hacer la práctica en una fábrica.

working-class ['wɜ:rkɪŋ'klæs] ADJECTIVE
de clase obrera ◇ *a working-class family* una familia de clase obrera

workman ['wɜ:rkmən] NOUN (PL **workmen**)
el obrero

works [wɜ:rks] NOUN
la fábrica

worksheet ['wɜ:rk,ʃi:t] NOUN
la hoja de ejercicios

workshop ['wɜ:rk,ʃɑ:p] NOUN
el taller ◇ *a drama workshop* un taller de teatro

workstation ['wɜ:rk,steɪʃən] NOUN
la terminal de trabajo

world [wɜ:rld] NOUN
el mundo
◆ **the world champion** el campeón mundial
◆ **the World Cup** la Copa del Mundo

worm [wɜ:rm] NOUN
el gusano

* Verbs marked with this symbol are irregular. See pages 346–348 for further details.

worn [wɔːrn] VERB *see* **wear**

worn [wɔːrn] ADJECTIVE
gastado ◇ *The carpet is a bit worn.* La alfombra está un poco gastada.
◆ **worn out** agotado ◇ *We were worn out after the long walk.* Estábamos agotados después de andar tanto.

worried ['wɜːrid] ADJECTIVE
preocupado ◇ *to be worried about something* estar* preocupado por algo ◇ *to look worried* parecer* preocupado

to **worry** ['wɜːri] VERB (**worried, worried**)
preocuparse
◆ **Don't worry!** ¡No te preocupes!

worse [wɜːrs] ADJECTIVE, ADVERB
peor ◇ *It was even worse than mine.* Era incluso peor que el mío. ◇ *I'm feeling worse.* Me encuentro peor.

to **worship** ['wɜːrʃɪp] VERB
adorar

worst [wɜːrst] ADJECTIVE
see also **worst** NOUN
peor ◇ *the worst student in the class* el peor alumno de la clase ◇ *my worst enemy* mi peor enemigo
◆ **Math is my worst subject.** Las matemáticas es la asignatura en la que peor me va.

worst [wɜːrst] NOUN
see also **worst** ADJECTIVE
◆ **The worst of it is that...** Lo peor es que...
◆ **at worst** en el peor de los casos
◆ **if worst comes to worst** en el peor de los casos

worth [wɜːrθ] ADJECTIVE
◆ **to be worth** valer* ◇ *It's worth a lot of money.* Vale mucho dinero. ◇ *How much is it worth?* ¿Cuánto vale?
◆ **It's worth it.** Vale la pena.

would [wud] VERB
The conditional is often used to translate ***would*** *+ verb.*
◇ *I said I would do it.* Dije que lo haría. ◇ *If you asked him, he would do it.* Si se lo pidieras, lo haría. ◇ *If you had asked him, he would have done it.* Si se lo hubieras pedido, lo habría hecho.
When ***would you*** *is used to make requests, translate using* ***poder*** *in the present.*
◇ *Would you close the door please?* ¿Puedes cerrar la puerta, por favor?
◆ **I'd like... (1)** Me gustaría... ◇ *I'd like to go to China.* Me gustaría ir a China.
◆ **I'd like... (2)** Quería... ◇ *I'd like three tickets please.* Quería tres entradas.
◆ **Would you like a biscuit?** ¿Quieres una galleta? ◇ *Would you like me to iron your jeans for you?* ¿Quieres que te planche los jeans?
Use the subjunctive after ***querer que***.
◆ **Would you like to go to the movies?** ¿Quieres ir al cine?

wouldn't ['wudnt] = **would not**

wound [waund] VERB *see* **wind**

to **wound** [wuːnd] VERB
see also **wound** NOUN
herir* ◇ *He was wounded in the leg.* Fue herido en la pierna.

wound [wuːnd] NOUN
see also **wound** VERB
la herida

to **wrap** [ræp] VERB
envolver* ◇ *She's wrapping her Christmas presents.* Está envolviendo los regalos de Navidad. ◇ *Can you wrap it for me please?* ¿Me lo puede envolver en papel de regalo, por favor?

to **wrap up** [ræp'ʌp] VERB
1 envolver* (*parcel*)
2 abrigarse* (*put on warm clothes*)

wrapping paper ['ræpɪŋˌpeɪpər] NOUN
el papel de regalo

wreck [rɛk] NOUN
see also **wreck** VERB
el cacharro ◇ *That car is a wreck!* ¡Ese coche es un cacharro!
◆ **After the exams I was a complete wreck.** Después de los exámenes quedé hecho polvo.

to **wreck** [rɛk] VERB
see also **wreck** NOUN
1 destruir* ◇ *The explosion wrecked the whole house.* La explosión destruyó toda la casa.
2 destrozar* (*car*)
3 echar por tierra ◇ *The bad weather wrecked our plans.* El mal tiempo echó por tierra nuestros planes.

wreckage ['rɛkɪdʒ] NOUN
1 los restos (*of vehicle*)
2 las ruinas (*of buildings*)

wrench [rentʃ] NOUN (PL **wrenches**)
la llave inglesa

wrestler ['rɛslər] NOUN
el luchador
la luchadora

wrestling ['rɛslɪŋ] NOUN
la lucha libre

wrinkled ['rɪŋkəld] ADJECTIVE
arrugado

wrist [rɪst] NOUN
la muñeca

to **write** [raɪt] VERB (**wrote, written**)
escribir* ◇ *to write a letter* escribir* una carta

to **write down** [raɪt'daun] VERB
anotar ◇ *I wrote down her address.* Anoté su dirección. ◇ *Can you write it down for me, please?* ¿Me lo puedes anotar, por favor?

writer ['raɪtər] NOUN
el escritor
la escritora

writing ['raɪtɪŋ] NOUN
la letra ◇ *I can't read your writing.* No ☞

entiendo tu letra.

◆ **in writing** por escrito

◆ **writing pad** el bloc

written ['rɪtn] VERB *see* **write**

wrong [rɑːŋ] ADJECTIVE, ADVERB

1 incorrecto ◇ *The information they gave us was wrong.* La información que nos dieron era incorrecta. ◇ *the wrong answer* la respuesta incorrecta

◆ **You have the wrong number.** Se equivocó de número.

2 mal ◇ *I think hunting is wrong.* Opino que está mal cazar. ◇ *You've done it wrong.* Lo hiciste mal.

◆ **to go wrong** (*plan*) salir* mal ◇ *The robbery went wrong and they got caught.* El atraco salió mal y los agarraron.

◆ **to be wrong** estar* equivocado ◇ *You're wrong about that.* En eso estás equivocado.

◆ **What's wrong?** ¿Qué pasa? ◇ *What's wrong with her?* ¿Qué le pasa?

wrote [rout] VERB *see* **write**

X

to **Xerox ®** ['zɪrɑːks] VERB
fotocopiar

Xmas ['ɛksməs] NOUN (= *Christmas*)
la Navidad

to **X-ray** ['ɛksreɪ] VERB
see also **X-ray** NOUN
tomar una radiografía de ◇ *They X-rayed my arm.* Me tomaron una radiografía del brazo.

X ray ['ɛksreɪ] NOUN
see also **X-ray** VERB
la radiografía ◇ *I had an X ray taken.* Me tomaron una radiografía.

Y

yacht [jɑːt] NOUN
el yate

yard [jɑːrd] NOUN
[1] la yarda

> *In Spanish-speaking countries measurements are in meters and centimeters rather than feet and inches. A yard is about 90 centimeters.*

[2] el jardín (PL los jardines)
[3] el patio (*of school, house*)

to **yawn** [jɑːn] VERB
bostezar*

year [jɪər] NOUN
el año ◇ *last year* el año pasado
◆ **to be 15 years old** tener* 15 años
◆ **an eight-year-old child** un niño de ocho años

to **yell** [jɛl] VERB
gritar

yellow [ˈjɛlou] ADJECTIVE
amarillo ◇ *a yellow light* (*when driving*) un semáforo en amarillo, *Mexico:* un semáforo en ámbar

yes [jɛs] ADVERB
sí ◇ *Do you like it? – Yes.* ¿Te gusta? – Sí

yesterday [ˈjɛstərdi] ADVERB
ayer ◇ *yesterday morning* ayer por la mañana ◇ *all day yesterday* todo el día de ayer

yet [jɛt] ADVERB
todavía ◇ *Have you eaten? – Not yet.* ¿Ya comiste? – Todavía no. ◇ *It's not finished yet.* Todavía no está terminado. ◇ *There's no news as yet.* Todavía no se tienen noticias.
◆ **Have you finished yet?** ¿Terminaste ya?

to **yield** [jiːld] VERB
ceder el paso (*in car*)

yoga [ˈjougə] NOUN
el yoga

yoghurt [ˈjougərt] NOUN
el yogur

yolk [jouk] NOUN
la yema

you [juː] PRONOUN
[1] tú (*informal: 1 person*) ◇ *What do YOU think about it?* ¿Y tú qué piensas? ◇ *She's younger than you.* Es más joven que tú.
◆ **You don't understand me.** No me entiendes.
[2] usted (*formal: 1 person*) ◇ *They're younger than you.* Son más jóvenes que usted. ◇ *This is for you.* Esto es para usted.
◆ **How are you?** ¿Cómo está?
[3] ustedes (*2 or more people*) ◇ *You have kids but we don't.* Ustedes tienen hijos pero nosotros no. ◇ *They're younger than you.* Son más jóvenes que ustedes. ◇ *I'd like to speak to you.* Quiero hablar con ustedes.
◆ **How are you?** ¿Qué tal están?
*When **you** means "one" or "people" in general, the impersonal **se** is often used.*
◇ *I doubt it, but you never know.* Lo dudo, pero nunca se sabe.
*When **you** is the object of the sentence, you have to use different forms from the ones above. See translations 4 to 8 below.*
[4] te (*informal: 1 person – direct object*) ◇ *I love you.* Te quiero. ◇ *Shall I give it to you?* ¿Te lo doy?
◆ **This is for you.** Esto es para ti.
◆ **Can I go with you?** ¿Puedo ir contigo?
[5] lo MASC SING
la FEM SING (*formal: 1 person – direct object*)
◇ *May I help you?* ¿Puedo ayudarlo? ◇ *I saw you, Mrs. Jones.* La vi, señora Jones.
[6] los MASC PL
las FEM PL (*2 or more people – direct object*)
◇ *I saw you.* Los vi. ◇ *May I help you?* ¿Puedo ayudarlos?
[7] le (*1 person – indirect object*)
*Change **le** to **se** before another object pronoun.*
◇ *I gave you the keys.* Le di las llaves.
◆ **I gave them to you.** Se las di.
[8] les PL (*2 or more people – indirect object*)
*Change **les** to **se** before another object pronoun.*
◇ *I gave you the keys.* Les di las llaves.
◆ **I gave them to you.** Se las di.

young [jʌŋ] ADJECTIVE
joven (FEM joven, PL jóvenes)
◆ **young people** los jóvenes
◆ **He's younger than me.** Es menor que yo.
◆ **my youngest brother** mi hermano menor

your [jɔːr] ADJECTIVE
*Use **tu** with people your own age or that you know well, and **su/sus** otherwise.*
[1] tu (PL tus) (*informal: 1 person*)
*Remember there's no accent on **tu** meaning "your".*
◇ *your house* tu casa ◇ *your books* tus libros ◇ *your sisters* tus hermanas
[2] de ustedes (*informal: 2 or more people*)
◇ *your dog* el perro de ustedes ◇ *These are your keys.* Éstas son las llaves de ustedes.
[3] su (PL sus) (*formal*)
*Use **su** when talking to **one** person or to a **group** of people.*
◇ *Can I see your passport, sir?* ¿Me muestra su pasaporte, señor? ◇ *your wife* su esposa ◇ *your uncle and aunt* sus tíos
*Use **el, la, los, las** as appropriate with parts of the body and to translate **your** referring to people in general.*
◇ *Have you washed your hair?* ¿Te lavaste el pelo? ◇ *Would you like to wash your hands?*

¿Quieren lavarse las manos?
- **It's bad for your health.** Es malo para la salud.

yours [jɔːrz] PRONOUN

*Use **tuyo/tuya** etc with people your own age or that you know well, and **suyo/suya** etc otherwise.*

1 tuyo (*informal: 1 person*)

*Remember to make **tuyo** agree with the person or thing it describes.*

◇ *That's yours.* Eso es tuyo. ◇ *Is that box yours?* ¿Ésa caja es tuya?

*Add the definite article when **yours** means "your one" or "your ones".*

- **I've lost my pencil. Can I use yours?** Perdí el lápiz. ¿Puedo usar el tuyo?
- **These are my keys and those are yours.** Éstas son mis llaves y ésas son las tuyas.

2 de ustedes (*informal: 2 or more people*) ◇ *That's yours.* Eso es de ustedes.

*Add the definite article when **yours** means "your one" or "your ones".*

- **These are my keys and those are yours.** Éstas son mis llaves y ésas son las de ustedes.

3 suyo (*formal*)

*Use **suyo** in more formal situations with **one** person or a **group** of people, and remember to make it agree with the person or thing it describes.*

◇ *That's yours.* Eso es suyo.

*Add the definite article when **yours** means "your one" or "your ones".*

- **I've lost my pencil. Can I use yours?** Perdí el lápiz. ¿Puedo usar el suyo?
- **These are my keys and those are yours.** Éstas son mis llaves y ésas son las suyas.
- **Sincerely yours... (1)** Lo saluda atentamente... (*to a man*)
- **Sincerely yours... (2)** La saluda atentamente... (*to a woman*)

yourself [jɔːr'sɛlf] PRONOUN

*Use **te, tú mismo** and **ti mismo** when you are talking to someone of your own age or that you know well and **se** and **usted mismo** otherwise.*

1 te (*reflexive*) ◇ *Have you hurt yourself?* ¿Te lastimaste?

2 tú mismo (FEM tú misma) (*for emphasis*) ◇ *Do it yourself!* ¡Hazlo tú mismo!

3 ti mismo (FEM ti misma) (*after a preposition*) ◇ *You did it for yourself.* Lo hiciste para ti mismo.

4 se (*reflexive*) ◇ *Have you hurt yourself?* ¿Se lastimó?

5 usted mismo (FEM usted misma) (*after a preposition, for emphasis*) ◇ *You did it for yourself.* Lo hizo para usted mismo. ◇ *Do it yourself!* ¡Hágalo usted mismo!

yourselves [jɔːr'sɛlvz] PRONOUN

1 se (*reflexive*) ◇ *Did you enjoy yourselves?* ¿Se divirtieron?

2 ustedes mismos (FEM ustedes mismas) (*after a preposition, for emphasis*) ◇ *Did you make it yourselves?* ¿Lo hicieron ustedes mismos?

youth club ['juːθˌklʌb] NOUN

el club juvenil (PL los clubs juveniles)

youth hostel ['juːθˌhɑːstl] NOUN

el albergue juvenil

Yugoslavia [ˌjuːgou'slɑːviə] NOUN

Yugoslavia FEM ◇ *in the former Yugoslavia* en la antigua Yugoslavia

Z

zany ['zeɪnɪ] ADJECTIVE
estrafalario
zebra ['zi:brə] NOUN
la cebra
zero ['zɪrəu] NOUN (PL **zeros** *or* **zeroes**)
el cero
Zimbabwe [zɪm'bɑ:bwɪ] NOUN
Zimbabue MASC
zip code ['zɪpkəud] NOUN
el código postal
zipper ['zɪpər] NOUN
el cierre
el zíper (PL los zípers) *Mexico*
zit [zɪt] NOUN (*informal*)
el grano
zodiac ['zoudɪæk] NOUN
el zodíaco ◇ *the signs of the zodiac* los signos del zodíaco
zone [zoun] NOUN
la zona
zoo [zu:] NOUN
el zoo
zoom lens ['zu:mlɛnz] NOUN (PL **zoom lenses**)
el zoom
zucchini [zu'ki:ni] NOUN (PL **zucchini** *or* **zucchinis**)
el calabacín (PL los calabacines)
la calabacita *Mexico*

Z

zany ['zeɪnɪ] ADJECTIVE
estrafalario

zebra ['zi:brə] NOUN
la cebra

zero ['zɪrəu] NOUN (PL **zeros** *or* **zeroes**)
el cero

Zimbabwe [zɪm'bɑ:bwɪ] NOUN
Zimbabue MASC

zip code ['zɪpkəud] NOUN
el código postal

zipper ['zɪpər] NOUN
el cierre
el zíper (PL los zípers) *Mexico*

zit [zɪt] NOUN (*informal*)
el grano

zodiac ['zoudɪæk] NOUN
el zodíaco ◊ *the signs of the zodiac* los signos del zodíaco

zone [zoun] NOUN
la zona

zoo [zu:] NOUN
el zoo

zoom lens ['zu:mlɛnz] NOUN (PL **zoom lenses**)
el zoom

zucchini [zu'ki:ni] NOUN (PL **zucchini** *or* **zucchinis**)
el calabacín (PL los calabacines)
la calabacita *Mexico*